FROMMERS

COMPREHENSIVE TRAVEL GUIDE

SCANDINAVIA
'91-'92

by Darwin Porter
Assisted by Danforth Prince

Kathie Hanson
218 W Arrowhead Rd
Duluth MN 55803

PRENTICE
HALL
PRESS

NEW YORK • LONDON • TORONTO • SYDNEY • TOKYO • SINGAPORE

FROMMER BOOKS

Published by Prentice Hall Press
A division of Simon & Schuster Inc.
15 Columbus Circle
New York, NY 10023

ISBN 0-13-326992-2
ISSN 0278-1069

Manufactured in the United States of America

FROMMER'S SCANDINAVIA '91–'92

Editor-in-Chief: Marilyn Wood
Senior-Editors: Judith de Rubini, Pamela Marshall, Amit Shah
Editors: Alice Fellows, Paige Hughes, Theodore Stavrou
Assistant Editors: Suzanne Arkin, Peter Katucki, Ellen Zucker
Contributing Editors: Christopher Caines, Irene Park, Lisa Renaud
Managing Editor: Leanne Coupe

CONTENTS

LIST OF MAPS

SCANDINAVIA xiv

DENMARK

NORWAY

SWEDEN

FINLAND

INVITATION TO THE READERS

In researching this book, I have come across many wonderful establishments, the best of which I have included here. I am sure that many of you will also come across wonderful hotels, inns, restaurants, guest houses, shops, and attractions. Please don't keep them to yourself. Share your experiences, especially if you want to comment on places that have been included in this edition that have changed for the worse. You can address your letters to: Darwin Porter, Frommer's Scandinavia, c/o Prentice Hall Press, 15 Columbus Circle, New York, NY 10023.

A DISCLAIMER

Readers are advised that prices fluctuate in the course of time and travel information changes under the impact of the varied and volatile factors that affect the travel industry. Neither the author nor the publisher can be held responsible for the experiences of readers while traveling. Readers are invited to write to the publisher with ideas, comments, and suggestions for future editions.

SAFETY ADVISORY

Whenever you're traveling in an unfamiliar city or country, stay alert. Be aware of your immediate surroundings. Wear a moneybelt and keep a close eye on your possessions. Be particularly careful with cameras, purses, and wallets, all favorite targets of thieves and pickpockets.

ABOUT THIS FROMMER GUIDE

What is a Frommer Guide? It's a comprehensive, easy-to-use guide to the best travel values in all price ranges—from very expensive to budget. The one guidebook to take along with you on any trip.

WHAT THE SYMBOLS MEAN

FROMMER'S FAVORITES—hotels, restaurants, attractions, and entertainments you shouldn't miss

SUPER-SPECIAL VALUES—really exceptional values

FROMMER'S SMART TRAVELER TIPS—hints on how to secure the best value for your money

IN HOTEL AND OTHER LISTINGS

The following symbols refer to the standard amenities available in all rooms:

A/C air conditioning   TEL telephone   TV television
MINIBAR refrigerator stocked with beverages and snacks

The following abbreviations are used for credit cards:

AE American Express   DISC Discover   EU Eurocard
CB Carte Blanche   ER EnRoute   MC MasterCard
DC Diners Club   V VISA

TRIP PLANNING WITH THIS GUIDE

Use the following features:

What Things Cost in . . . to help you plan your daily budget
Calendar of Events . . . to plan for or avoid
Suggested Itineraries . . . for the countries and regions
What's Special About Checklist . . . a summary of each region's highlights—which lets you check off those that appeal most to you
Easy-to-read maps . . . walking tours, city sights, hotel and restaurant locations—all referring to or keyed to the text
Distances and Transportation Information . . . at the beginning of each town section
Fast Facts . . . all the essentials at a glance: currency, emergencies, embassies, and more

OTHER SPECIAL FROMMER FEATURES

Cool for Kids—hotels, restaurants, and attractions
Did You Know?—offbeat, fun facts
Famous People—the countrys' greats
Impressions—what others have said
In Their Footsteps—tracking the lives of famous residents

Arctic Ocean

Norwegian Sea

North Cape

Tromsø

Narvik

Bodø

Kiruna

ARCTIC CIRCLE

Rovaniemi

Luleå

Oulu

FINLAND

Umea

Gulf of Bothnia

Vaasa

Molde

Trondheim

Alesund

NORWAY

Sundsvall

SWEDEN

Tampere

Bergen

Gävle

Turku

HELINSKI

OSLO ★

Karlstad

Uppsala

Gulf of Finland

Stavanger

Skara

STOCKHOLM ★

Atlantic Ocean

U.S.

U.S.S.R.

Gothenburg

Gotland

Baltic Sea

North Sea

Ålborg

Århus

Malmö

DENMARK

Odense

COPENHAGEN ★

U.S.S.R.

SCANDINAVIA AT A GLANCE

PLANNING A TRIP TO SCANDINAVIA

Although Scandinavia, as defined by this book, covers four distinct countries—Denmark, Norway, Sweden, and Finland—there are certain common cultural denominators and practical travel facts that apply to traveling in the region. That is what this chapter is about.

1. INFORMATION, DOCUMENTS & MONEY

SOURCES OF INFORMATION

Contact the following **tourist boards** at least three months in advance for maps, sightseeing information, ferry schedules, etc. In the United States, the Danish, Norwegian, and Swedish Tourist Boards can be reached at the following addresses: 655 Third Avenue, New York, NY 10017 (tel. 212/949-2333); 8929 Wilshire Blvd., Beverly Hills, CA 90211 (tel. 213/854-1549); 150 N. Michigan Ave., Suite 2110, Chicago, IL 60601 (tel. 312/726-1120). The Finnish tourist board can be reached at 655 Third Ave., New York, NY 10017 (tel. 212/949-2333) and at 1900 Ave. of Stars, Los Angeles, CA 90067 (tel. 818/277-5226).

In **Canada** contact the Danish Tourist Board at P. O. Box 115, Station N, Toronto, ON M8V 3S4 (tel. 416/823-9620). For the other three countries call or write the U. S. offices.

In **London** contact The Danish Tourist Board, Sceptre House, 169/173 Regent St., London W1R 8PY (tel. 071/734-2637); the Norwegian Tourist Board, Charles House, 5-11 Lower Regent St., London SW1Y 4LR (tel. 071/839-6255); Swedish Tourist Board, 29-31 Oxford St., London W1R 1RE (tel. 071/437-5816) and Finnish Tourist Board, 66/68 Haymarket, London SW1Y 4RS (tel. 071/839-4048).

For general information always check newspapers and magazines. To find the latest articles published about Scandinavia go to your library and ask for the *Reader's Guide to Periodical Literature,* and look up the city or country of interest.

You may also contact the State Department for background information. Write to the Superintendent of Documents, U. S. Government Printing Office, Washington, DC 20402 (tel. 202/783-3238).

You can also contact a **travel agent,** but make sure that the agent is a member of the American Society of Travel Agents (ASTA), so that you can complain to the Consumer Affairs Department of the Society at P. O. Box 23922, Washington, DC 20006 if you receive poor service.

DOCUMENTS

A valid **passport** is all an American, British, Canadian, Australian, or New Zealand citizen needs to enter Denmark, Norway, Sweden, or Finland. You only need to apply for a visa if you wish to stay more than three months.

Your current domestic **driver's license** is acceptable in Denmark, Norway, Sweden, and Finland—an international drivers' license is not required.

MONEY

Before leaving home it is advisable to secure traveler's checks and a small amount of foreign currency to cover costs on arrival overseas. Also take along about $200 in cash.

TRAVELER'S CHECKS   The following are the major issuers of traveler's checks:

American Express (tel. toll free 800/221-7282 in the U.S. and Canada) is the most widely recognized traveler's check. There's a 1% commission. Checks are free to American Automobile Association (AAA) members.

Bank of America (tel. toll free 800/227-3460 in the U.S., or 415/624-5400, collect, in Canada) also issues checks in U.S. dollars for 1% commission everywhere but California.

Citicorp (tel. toll free 800/645-6556 in the U.S., or 813/623-1709, collect, in Canada) issues checks in U.S. dollars, pounds, or German marks.

MasterCard International (tel. toll free 800/223-9920 in the U.S., or 212/974-5696, collect, in Canada) issues checks in about a dozen currencies.

Barclays Bank (tel. toll free 800/221-2426 in the U.S. and Canada) issues checks in both U.S. and Canadian dollars and British pounds.

Thomas Cook (tel. toll free 800/223-7373 in the U.S., or 212/974-5696, collect, in Canada) issues checks in U.S. or Canadian dollars or British pounds. It's affiliated with MasterCard.

Each agency will refund your checks if they are lost or stolen, provided you can produce sufficient documentation. Carry your documentation in a safe place—never along with your checks. When purchasing checks, ask about refund hotlines; American Express and Bank of America have the most offices worldwide. Purchase checks in several denominations—$20, $50, and $100.

Foreign banks may ask up to 5% to convert your checks into Danish kroner. Remember, also, that you get a better rate if you cash traveler's checks at the bank issuing them: VISA at Barclays, American Express at American Express, and so forth.

CREDIT CARDS   These are useful throughout Scandinavia. American Express, Diners Club, and VISA are widely recognized. If you see a Eurocard or Access sign, it means that the establishment accepts MasterCard. With an American Express or VISA card you can also withdraw currency from cash machines at various locations. Always check with your credit card company about this before leaving home.

2. PACKING TIPS

Pack as light as possible, taking only what you can carry (porters and carts are sometimes hard to find at transit terminals). Also airlines have recently become much stricter about luggage allowances. Checked luggage should not be more than 62 inches (width, plus length, plus height) and should not weigh more than 70 pounds. Carry-on luggage shouldn't be more than 45 inches and must fit under your seat or in the bins above.

Wherever you're traveling in Scandinavia in summer, bring a sweater. Most days are not hot, which is why few hotels have air conditioning, even in Denmark. A raincoat with a removable lining is also useful.

In spring, fall, and winter bring a coat and in winter an extra sweater for those few places that are not as well heated as you might wish.

Take at least two pairs of shoes—if one gets soaked you can use the other. One pair should be sturdy walking shoes.

3. HEALTH & INSURANCE CONSIDERATIONS

HEALTH

You will encounter few health problems traveling in Scandinavia. The water is safe to drink, the milk is pasteurized, and health services of each country excellent. Occasionally the change in diet may cause minor diarrhea so you may want to take some antidiarrhea medicine along. In summer, arrive at buffets early so that your smørrebrod open-face sandwiches made with mayonnaise are fresh.

Carry all your vital medicine in your carry-on luggage and bring enough prescribed medicines to sustain you during your stay. Bring along copies of your prescriptions that are written in the generic form. In Norway and Sweden note that pharmacists by law cannot honor a prescription written outside the country; you will have to see a doctor and have one written if you need more or lose your medicines.

If you need a doctor, your hotel will find one. You can also obtain a list of English-speaking doctors from the International Association for Medical Assistance to Travelers (IAMAT) in the United States at 417 Center St., Lewiston, NY 14092 (tel. 716/754-4883); in Canada at 188 Nicklin Rd., Guelph, ON N1H 7LS (tel. 519/836-0102).

If you suffer from a chronic illness, talk to your doctor before taking the trip. For conditions such as a heart condition, epilepsy, or diabetes, wear a Medic Alert Identification Tag, which will immediately alert any doctor to your condition. It also provides the number of Medic Alert's 24-hour hotline so that a foreign doctor can obtain medical records for you. For a lifetime membership, the cost is $25. Contact the Medic Alert Foundation, P. O. Box 1009, Turlock, CA 95381-1009 (tel. toll free 800/432-5378).

In Denmark foreign visitors can be treated free in cases of sudden illness or the aggravation of a chronic disease, provided they did not come with the intention of getting treatment and provided they cannot be moved and return home. The transport home is the visitors' responsibility.

In Norway, Sweden, and Finland the National Health Plans do not cover U.S. or Canadian visitors. Any medical fees incurred must be paid in cash. (Fees are more reasonable than most western nations.)

VACCINATIONS There are no inoculations needed to enter any Scandinavian country, except for yellow fever, and then only if you're coming from an infected area.

INSURANCE

Before purchasing any additional insurance check your homeowner's, automobile, and medical insurance policies as well as the insurance provided by credit card companies and auto and travel clubs.

Remember, Medicare covers U.S. citizens traveling in Mexico and Canada only.

Also note that to submit any claim you must always have thorough documentation including all receipts, police reports, medical records, etc.

If you are prepaying for your vacation or are taking a charter or any other flight that has severe cancellation penalties look into cancellation insurance.

The following companies provide further information:

Travel Guard International, 1100 Center Point Dr., Stevens Point, WI 54481 (tel. toll free 800/826-1300, 800/634-0644 in Wisconsin), which offers a comprehensive 7-day policy that covers basically everything, including lost luggage.

Access America, Inc. (an affiliate of Blue Cross-Blue Shield), 600 Third Ave., New York, NY 10163 (tel. 212/490-5345, or toll free 800/851-2800), writes coverage for single travelers or families, providing medical, trip-cancellation, and lost-luggage policies.

Health Care Abroad, 243 Church St. NW, Vienna, VA 22180 (tel. 703/255-9800, or toll free 800/237-6616), offers accident and sickness coverage on trips lasting 10 to 90 days, charging $3 per day for $100,000 coverage. Luggage loss and trip cancellation can be added to this policy.

Travel Assistance International, 1133 15th St. NW, Suite 400, Washington, DC 20005 (tel. toll free 800/821-2828), offers travel coverage up to $5,000 for urgent hospital care and medical evacuation back to the United States if necessary. For an additional fee you can be covered for trip cancellation, lost baggage, and accidental death and dismemberment. The fee depends on how long you plan to stay. Fees begin at $40 per person ($60 per family) for a 1- to 8-day trip. You can call a 24-hour "hotline" number (tel. 202/347-7113 in Washington, or toll free 800/368-7878 in the U.S. and Canada) that will put you in touch with agents all over Europe, including Spain.

4. TIPS FOR THE DISABLED, SENIORS, SINGLES & STUDENTS

FOR THE DISABLED

In the United States disabled travelers should start by contacting **Travel Information Service,** Moss Rehabilitation Hospital, 12th Street and Tabor Road, Philadelphia, PA 19141 (tel. 215/456-9600). For $5, you can receive a package containing data on three cities or countries of special interest.

You may also want to subscribe to *The Itinerary,* P.O. Box 2012, Bayonne, NJ 07002-2012 (tel. 201/858-3400), at $10 a year. This bimonthly travel magazine is filled with information for the handicapped.

You can also obtain a free copy of **"Air Transportation of Handicapped Persons,"** published by the U.S. Department of Transportation. Write for Free Advisory Circular No. AC12032, Distribution Unit, U.S. Department of Transportation, Publications Division, M-4332, Washington, DC 20590.

You may also consider joining a tour specifically for the disabled. For names and addresses of such tour operators, contact the **Society for the Advancement of Travel for the Handicapped,** 26 Court St., Brooklyn, NY 11242 (tel. 718/858-5483). Yearly membership dues are $40, or $25 for senior citizens and students. Send a self-addressed envelope. One such tour company is **Whole Person Tours,** P.O. Box 1084, Bayonne, NJ 07002-1084 (tel. 201/858-3400, or toll free 800/462-2237 outside New Jersey).

Also consider the **Federation of the Handicapped,** 211 W. 14th St., New York, NY 10011 (tel. 212/206-4200), which offers summer tours for members who pay a yearly fee of $4.

For the blind, the best source is the **American Foundation for the Blind,** 15 W. 16th St., New York, NY 10011 (tel. toll free 800/232-5463). For the legally blind, it also issues identification cards for $6.

Many Scandinavian countries, such as Denmark and Sweden, have been in the vanguard of providing services for the disabled. In general, trains, airlines, and ferries and department stores and malls are accessible. For information about wheelchair access, ferry and air travel, parking, and other information your best bet is to contact the tourist boards listed above.

In **Denmark** also write to DHF Dansk Handicap Forbund (Danish Handicapped

Association), Kollektivhuset, Hans Knudsens Plads 1A, DK-2100 Kobenhaven O (tel. 31-29-35-55).

In **Norway** for further information write to the Norwegian Association of the Disabled, Box 9217, Vaterland, N-0134 Oslo 1 (tel. 02/17-02-55).

In **Sweden** about 2 million people have some disability and the country is very conscious of their needs. Contact the Swedish Tourist Board for their publication.

In **Finland** information about facilities can be obtained from Rullaten ry, Vartickylantie 9, 00950 Helsinki (tel. 90/322-069) which assists the disabled in travel planning. Further information is also available from Invalidilitto ry (Association of the Disabled), Kumpulantie 1A, 00520 Helsinki (tel. 90/718-466). Area Travel Agency, Kaisaniemenkatu 13A 00100 Helsinki (tel. 90/018-551) specializes in travel for the disabled.

FOR SENIORS

There are a number of organizations that seniors can contact before setting out.

For your initial source of information, write for **"Travel Tips for Senior Citizens"** (publication no. 8970), distributed for $1 by the Superintendent of Documents, U.S. Government Printing Office, Washington, DC 20402 (tel. 202/783-3238). A booklet that is free is called **"101 Tips for the Mature Traveler."** Write or phone Grand Circle Travel, 347 Congress St., Suite 3A, Boston, MA 02210 (tel. 617/350-7500, or toll free 800/221-2610).

A dynamic travel organization for seniors is **Elderhostel,** 80 Boylston St., Boston, MA 02116 (tel. 617/426-7788). Established in 1975, it operates a number of good-value programs throughout Europe. Most courses last around 3 weeks, and include airfare, accommodations in student dormitories or modest inns, all meals, and tuition. Courses involve no homework, are upgraded, and are often liberal arts oriented. They're not luxury vacations, but they are fun and fulfilling. Participants must be 60 years of age or older. However, if two members go as a couple, only one member needs to be of age. Write or call for their free newsletter and a list of upcoming courses and destinations.

SAGA International Holidays is also well known for its all-inclusive tours for seniors. They prefer that you be at least 60 years old. Insurance is included in the net price of all their tours, which encompass dozens of locations in Europe and usually last for an average of 17 nights. Contact SAGA International Holidays, 120 Boylston St., Boston, MA 02116 (tel. toll free 800/343-0273).

In the United States, the best organization to belong to is the **American Association of Retired Persons,** 100 N. Sepulveda Blvd., Washington, DC 20049 (tel. 202/872-4700). Members are offered discounts on car rentals, hotels, and airfares, even sightseeing. Its affiliate, **AARP Travel Service,** 1000 N. Sepulveda Blvd., Suite 1020, El Segundo, CA 90024 (tel. toll free 800/227-7737), offers tours and, for those traveling independently, a list of discounts available on the road.

Information is also available from the **National Council of Senior Citizens,** 925 15th St. NW, Washington, DC 20005 (tel. 202/347-8800). A nonprofit organization, the council charges $12 per person to join (couples pay $16) for which you receive a monthly newsletter, part of which is devoted to travel tips. Discounts on hotel and auto rentals are previewed.

In **Denmark,** Seniors are granted discounts on rail travel and the ferries to Sweden and often for certain attractions and performances, including those at the Royal Theater. You may have to be a member of an organization to receive certain discounts.

In **Norway** seniors over 67 are entitled to 50% off the price of first- or second-class train fares. Ask for the discount at the ticket office.

In **Sweden** on Swedish State Railways visitors over 65 are granted 30% off first- and second-class train travel except on Friday and Sunday. In Stockholm discounts on transportation and concert, theater, and opera tickets are available.

In **Finland,** on Finnair flights, passengers aged 65 or over are entitled to a 50% reduction. Any generally accepted document of identification will suffice for this purpose. The passenger's date of birth has to be inserted in the "Fare Basis" column. The domestic route system is divided into blue, black, and red flights; the blue flights are those in the most demand, but reductions for seniors are not granted on the blue flights.

On Finnish national rails, visitors over 65 may buy a special card for 50 markkaa ($13.65) at any railway station in Finland, which entitles the holder a 50% reduction on rail travel.

FOR SINGLE TRAVELERS

Several organizations help singles save money by finding travel companions. **Jens Jurgen, Travel Companion** has made heroic efforts to match single travelers with like-minded companions. It's now the largest and best-listed company in the United States. Jens Jurgen, the German-born founder, charges $36 to $66 for a 6-month listing in his well-publicized records. New applicants interested in a travel companion fill out a form stating their preferences and needs. They then receive a minilisting of the kinds of potential partners who might be suitable for travel. Companions of the same or opposite sex can be requested. Listings are extensive. For an application and more information, write to Jens Jurgen, Travel Companion, P.O. Box P-833, Amityville, NY 11701.

Singleworld, 401 Theodore Fremd Ave., Rye, NY 10580 (tel. 914/967-3334, or toll free 800/223-6490), is a travel agency that operates tours geared to solo travel. Two basic types of tours are available: either a youth-oriented tour for people under 35 or jaunts for any age. Annual dues are $20.

Since single supplements on tours usually carry a hefty price tag, try to find a travel agency that allows you to share a room. One such company that offers a "guaranteed-share plan" is **Cosmos,** with offices at 9525 Queens Blvd., Rego Park, NY 11374 (tel. toll free 800/221-0090), and at 150 S. Los Robles Ave., Pasadena, CA 91101 (tel. 818/449-0919, or toll free 800/556-5454).

FOR STUDENTS

Bonafide students can avail themselves of a number of discounts in travel. The most wide-ranging travel service for students is **CIEE (Council on International Educational Exchange),** 205 E. 42nd St., New York, NY 10017 (tel. 212/661-1414). This outfit provides details about budget travel, studying abroad, working permits, insurance, but, most important, an International Student Identity Card (ISIC). It also sells a number of helpful publications, including the *Student Travel Catalogue* ($1).

To keep costs low, membership in the **IYHF (International Youth Hostel Federation)** is recommended. Many countries have branch offices, including **AYH (American Youth Hostels),** P.O. Box 37613, Washington, DC 20013-7613 (tel. 202/783-6161). Membership costs $25 annually unless you're under 18 (then only $10).

In **Norway** an ISIC gets you a 35% discount on domestic rail travel. Univers Reisen, Universitetssentret (tel. 45-32-00) sells discounted air and rail tickets to people under 26. It's open Monday through Friday from 9am to 3:30pm (Metro: Blindern).

Students headed for **Finland** can take advantage of low-cost flights to and from Finland arranged by Travela Ltd., Mannerheimintie 5C, 00100 Helsinki (tel. 90/624-101). Youth/student discounts are also granted on Finnish domestic routes.

FOR FAMILIES

For $35 you can get 10 issues of *Family Travel Times,* a newsletter about traveling with children. Subscribers to the newsletter can also call in with travel questions, but only Monday through Friday from 10am to noon eastern standard time (later in the West). Contact **Travel with Your Children (TWYCH),** 80 Eighth Ave., New York, NY 10011 (tel. 212/206-0688).

On Finnair flights, the head of the family pays the full applicable one-way or round-trip adult fare, the spouse pays 75% of the fare, and children 12 to 23 pay 50%. Children 2 to 11 pay 25% of the fare. One infant child under 2 may be carried free.

On the Finnish national rail system, a maximum of two children under 6 travel free with one adult. A 50% reduction is granted for children ages 6 to 16.

Baby-sitters can be found at most hotels, but you should always insist, if possible, that the sitter speak English to avoid traumatic experiences for young children. Nearly all Finnish young people speak English, but many of the foreign workers in hotels don't.

5. ALTERNATIVE/ADVENTURE TRAVEL

HOMESTAYS, HOSPITALITY & HOME EXCHANGES

HOMESTAYS **Servas,** 11 John St., New York, NY 10038 (tel. 212/267-0252), is a nonprofit, nongovernmental, international, interfaith network of travelers and hosts whose goal is to help build world peace, goodwill, and understanding. They do this by providing opportunities for deeper, more personal contacts among people of diverse cultural and political backgrounds. Servas travelers are invited to share living space in a privately owned home with a community feeling, normally staying without charge for visits lasting a maximum of 2 days. Visitors pay a $45 annual fee, fill out an application, and are interviewed for suitability by one of more than 200 Servas interviewers throughout the country. They then receive a Servas directory listing the names and addresses of Servas hosts who will allow (and encourage) visitors in their homes.

PEOPLE TO PEOPLE Operating since 1971, **Friends Overseas** places American visitors to Scandinavia in touch with Scandinavians interested in meeting those with similar interests and backgrounds. Names and addresses are given to each applicant, and letters must be written before visitors depart; Scandinavians may not meet visitors unless they have ample time to plan. For more information, write to Friends Overseas, 68-04 Dartmouth St., Forest Hills, NY 11375. Send a self-addressed, stamped business-size envelope, including your age, occupation or occupational goals, approximate dates of your visit, and who you will be traveling with. Those writing from overseas must include the equivalent of $1.50 (U.S.) in return postage.

For $5, **International Visitors Information Service,** 733 15th St. NW, Suite 300, Washington, DC 20005 (tel. 202/783-6540), will mail anyone a booklet listing opportunities for contact with local residents in foreign countries. For example, if you want to find lodgings with a Swedish family whose members earn their living from the sea, this booklet will tell you how. Checks should be made out to Meridian/IVIS.

HOME EXCHANGE House swapping is the rage with many, and the **Vacation Exchange Club,** 12006 11th Ave., Youngtown, AZ 85363 (tel. 602/972-2186), can arrange such exchanges. You swap your house or apartment temporarily for a residence in Europe. Of course, owners agree on the scheduling and the length of duration of the exchange and also what arrangements are to be made (feeding pets, mowing the lawn, or whatever). The cost for a listing in the club's directory is $25. You can obtain a copy of the listings for $16 if you don't want your address listed.

EDUCATIONAL/STUDY TRIPS

WORK CAMPS Those at least age 18 often like to participate in a work camp in Europe, joining with a brigade of international volunteers. Members of such a group pay their own airfare to reach a country, but once there they are given free room and board in exchange for some socially significant work. Work time is limited to 5 days or 30 hours a week. Programs take place from June through September.

For information, contact the **Council on International Educational Exchange (CIEE)**, 205 E. 42nd St., New York, NY 10017 (tel. 212/661-1414), which offers work-camp programs. Participants in programs in Scandinavia must be 18 years or older. A book about international work camps is distributed free, but you must pay a $125 fee for an application.

IN DENMARK

The **International People's College** (Den Internationale Hojskole), Montebello Allé 1, DK-300, Helsingør (tel. 49-21-33-61), established in 1921 on a 13-acre campus 1 mile south of Helsingør Castle, fosters an environment of global learning. All courses are in English, and cover Danish culture and history, global politics, and world events. Sample courses might include intercultural studies, music, journalism, and weaving. The average student is 26, but many are in their 50s and 60s. Summer courses last between 2 and 3 weeks. The rest of the year, only 16-week courses are available. The cost, including tuition, room, and board, is 2,000 kroner ($336.20) per week, based on double occupancy, with a 200-krone ($33.60) supplement for single occupancy.

The **Danish Cultural Institute** (Det Danske Kultur ainstitute), Kultorvet 2, DK-1175 København K, Denmark (tel. 33-13-54-48), offers summer seminars in English, including Meeting Denmark, Care of the Elderly in Denmark, and Education for Adults. Credit programs are available, but many courses are geared toward professional groups from abroad. An especially interesting course for those with some knowledge of Danish is Danmark, Danskerne, Dansk, which includes language instruction.

Among Danish agents specializing in special-interest travel and professional study tours are: **Benns Rejser,** Nørregade 51, DK-7500 Holstebro (tel. 97-42-68-00); **Ritzau Special Tours,** Østbanegade 37-39, DK-2100 København Ø (tel. 31-26-48-88); and **Robinson Scandinavia,** Carit Etlars Vej 3, DK-1814 Frederiksberg C (tel. 31-31-71-77).

TRACING YOUR NORWEGIAN ROOTS If you are of Norwegian ancestry, information on how to trace your family can be obtained from the Norwegian consulate nearest you. In Norway, contact the **Norwegian Emigration Center,** Bergjelandsgata 30, N-4012 Stavanger (tel. 04/52-07-08), for a catalog of information about Norwegian families who relocated in the United States. In the United States, the **Genealogical Society of the Church of Jesus Christ of Latter Day Saints,** 50 E. North Temple, Salt Lake City, UT 84105, has extensive records of Norwegian families who immigrated to the United States and Canada.

ADVENTURE/WILDERNESS TRIPS

IN NORWAY

BIRDWATCHING Europe's largest bird sanctuaries are located in the Lofoten Islands of northern Norway. All kinds of seabirds can be found, including puffins, cormorants, razor-billed aulks, guillemots, gulls, and eider ducks. The outer islands of Vaeroy and Rost are famous for their giant bird colonies. Other bird sanctuaries are found at Runde Island, 2½ hours from Ålesund, and Fokstumyra, a national park near Dombas.

For more information, contact the following: **Lofoten Tourist Office,** Box 210, N-8301 Svolvaer (tel. 088/71-053); or **Christineborg Touristcenter,** N-6096 Runde (tel. 070/85-950).

WHALE WATCHING In Norway, you can get a glimpse of the 65-foot-long, 88,000-pound heavy sperm whales, the largest toothed whales in the world. You may also come across killer whales, harbor porpoises, mink whales, and white-beaked dolphins. Six-hour whale-watching tours are conducted in the Arctic Ocean where a guiding whale researcher will tell you about the life of the whales.

A tour of the whale center (including lunch) at Andoya is $130. Information and bookings for whale watching can be made through **Passage Tours of Scandinavia,** 3100 Windamar St., Fort Lauderdale, FL 33304 (tei. toll free 800/548-5960). Whale watching in the Lofoten Islands is arranged by **Borton Overseas,** 5516 Lyndale Ave. S., Minneapolis, MN 55419 (tel. toll free 800/843-0602).

IN SWEDEN

The Swedish Tourist Board (see "Sources of Information," above) can provide information about wilderness trips and other activities. Or contact **Sweden Tours West,** Box 244, S-651 06, Karlstad, Sweden (tel. 054/10-21-70).

ADVENTURE TRIPS Sarek, in the far north of Sweden, is Europe's last real wilderness, and here the Swede goes to wander in the mountains, pick mushrooms, gather berries, and fish. Along the mountain chain marking the Swedish-Norwegian border, Swedes have set up some 20 white-water-rafting stations on the Åre River, famous for its Tann Rapids.

Hiking is the most popular pastime. **Svenska Turistföreningen,** Drottninggaten 31, Box 25, S-101 20 Stockholm (tel. 08/790-31-00), operates mountain huts with anywhere from 10 to 30 beds, providing temporary accommodations in the area. The outfit knows the north of Sweden very well, and will advise about marked tracks, rowboats, the best excursions, the problems you are likely to encounter, communications, and transportation. They also sell trail and mountain maps.

A wide variety of adventure trips, including family tours on the Klar River in Sweden's Värmland, ballooning over Stockholm, and skiing in Lapland, even kayaking—led by English-speaking guides—are offered by **Äventyrsresor AB,** Hantverkargatan 38, S-112 21 Stockholm (tel. 08/54-03-75). For information before you leave home, contact **World Wide Nordic,** P.O. Box 185, Hartland, WI 53029 (tel. 414/367-7227).

HORSEBACK RIDING THROUGH THE WILDERNESS There are numerous opportunities for overnight pack trips on horses in such regions as the forests of Värmland or Norrbotten, where reindeer, musk oxen, and other creatures roam. The most popular of the overnight horseback trips starts just north of the city of Karlstad in Värmland. Covered-wagon trips with overnight stopovers are also offered. A typical trip by horse begins in the lakeside village of Torsby and follows a forested trail that ascends a mountain. An average of 4 hours a day is spent on the horse, with meals cooked over an open fire.

In northern Sweden, the two popular starting points are Funäsdalen, close to the Norwegian border, and Ammarnäs, not far from the Arctic Circle and the Midnight Sun. These trips begin in June.

IN FINLAND

OFFBEAT TOURS A 6-day **Gold Panning Camp** in Kiilopää books groups of 6 to 14. The tour includes gold panning and hiking in the area, and the price takes care of a room and meals, a guide, and a sauna, plus the program itself. It all takes place in Lapland at the Kiilopää Fell Resort, 31 miles south of Ivalo. The season runs from July 30 to August 5, and the cost for everything is 1,760 markkaa ($479.95) per person. Information is available from Tunturikeskus Kiilopää, 99800 Ivalo (tel. 9697/87-101).

A 6-day **horse-wagon trip** around central Finland for two to four people can be arranged by Kymen Matkailu, Varuskuntakatu 11, 45100 Kouvola (tel. 951/21-763). The length of the journey is 37 to 56 miles. The price includes accommodation in tents, camp meals, and instruction in horsekeeping. The season lasts from June 1 to August 31, and for 3 days it costs 600 markkaa ($163.60) per person.

In northern Finland, a 1-week **canoeing trip** on Lake Inari is offered by Lapp Treks, Kiianpolku 2, 99870 Inari (tel. 9697/51-375). The price of 2,310 markkaa ($621.95) per person includes 2 nights in a holiday village with sauna facilities (and the rest of the time in a log cabin or tent), full board, canoes and equipment, and transport between Ivalo and the holiday village. Participants must bring their own rain gear, warm clothes, sleeping bag, eating utensils, and toiletry. The season lasts from June 26 to September 30.

For special interest tours in Finland, which might be based on architecture, dairies, forestry, agriculture, or gardening, contact **Kaleva Travel Agency Ltd.,** Mikonkatu 6C, SF-00100 Helsinki (tel. 90/61-811).

6. GETTING THERE

BY PLANE FROM THE U.S.

Before moving on to the specifics of each country, to secure the best-priced ticket you should know about fare structures, seasons, and other general rules of air travel.

First, always shop around by calling all the airlines that fly to your destination.

The cheapest fares prevail in the off-season and midweek. Scandinavia's off season is winter (from about Nov 1 to March 21). Summer (about June through September) is peak season and the most expensive, while shoulder season (spring and fall) is in-between. In any season, midweek fares (Monday through Thursday) are the lowest.

REGULAR & APEX FARES

Regular fares include, in order of increasing expense, economy, business class, and first class. These tickets cost, but they carry no restrictions. In economy you pay for drinks and the seats are not spacious; in business the drinks are free, and the seats are wider; in first class amenities and services are the best.

Currently the most popular discount fare is the **APEX** (Advanced Purchase Excursion) which usually carries restrictions—advance purchase requirements, minimum and/or maximum stays abroad—and cancellation or change of date penalties.

In addition, airlines often introduce special promotional discounted fares. Always check the travel sections of your local newspapers for advertisements about these.

THE SCANDINAVIAN MIDWINTER MINI-FARE SAS is currently offering a special advance purchase winter fare from Newark to Oslo, Stockholm or Copenhagen requiring a stay of 7 to 14 days, travel between November and March. Round-trip price is $468 midweek; $518 weekend. A 50% refund is permitted 21 days in advance; otherwise the ticket is nonrefundable.

TWA matches this offer to Oslo.

BUCKET SHOPS, CHARTERS & OTHER OPTIONS

BUCKET SHOPS More politely referred to as consolidators these purchase large blocks of unsold seats from the airlines and sell them to the public at often dramatic discounts (from 20% to 35% off regular fares). Terms of payment may vary from the last minute to 45 days in advance. Check your local newspaper's travel section for their ads. Here are a couple of recommendations to get you started:

Maharaja Travel, 393 Fifth Ave., New York, NY 10016 (tel. 212/213-2020, or toll free 800/223-6862), offers tickets to 400 destinations worldwide, including Copenhagen, Stockholm, and Oslo.

Access International, 101 W. 31st St., Suite 1104, New York, NY 10001 (tel. 212/333-7280, or toll free 800/827-3633), specializes in discount tickets to the capitals of Europe, including Copenhagen, Stockholm, and Oslo.

CHARTER FLIGHTS Strictly speaking, a charter is a one-time-only flight between two predetermined points, for which the aircraft is reserved months in advance. Before paying for a charter, check the restrictions on your ticket or contract. You may be asked to purchase a tour package and pay far in advance, and you'll pay a stiff penalty (or forfeit the ticket entirely) if you cancel. Some charter ticket sellers offer an insurance policy for a legitimate cancellation (like hospitalization or a death in the family). Be aware that a charter might be canceled if the plane is not full.

One reliable charter-flight operator is **Council Charters,** run by the Council on International Educational Exchange, 205 E. 42nd St., New York, NY 10017 (tel. 212/661-0311, or toll free 800/223-7402). This outfit arranges charter seats on regularly scheduled aircraft. It sells tickets to Copenhagen and Stockholm, but not to Oslo.

STANDBY If you're a spontaneous traveler with no schedule demands and you don't mind hanging around the airport, then a standby fare may be for you. Your departure will depend on whether a seat opens up at the last minute. Not all airlines offer standby seats. Call around to see if any such ticket is offered at the last minute.

GOING AS A COURIER Couriers are hired by overnight air-freight firms hoping to skirt the often-tedious Customs delays that regular cargo faces on the other end. For the service, the courier pays the firm a fee much lower than the cost of the ticket, and sometimes may fly free. Don't worry, the service is legal—you won't be asked to haul in illegal drugs. Also, you don't actually handle the merchandise you're "transporting"; you just carry a document (a shipping invoice) to present to Customs when you arrive.

This cost-cutting technique, sometimes costing as little as $199 round-trip to Copenhagen, is not for everyone—there are lots of restrictions and courier opportunities are hard to come by. You're allowed only one piece of carry-on luggage; your checked-baggage allowance is used by the courier firm to transport its cargo. Also, you fly alone; family or friends must make other arrangements.

Check with **Halbart Express,** 147-05 176th St., Jamaica, NY 11434 (tel. 718/656-8189 daily from 10am to 3pm). Also try **Now Voyager,** 74 Varick St., Suite 307, New York, NY 10013 (tel. 212/431-1616 daily from 11:30am to 6pm). An automatic telephone-answering system announces last-minute specials and the firm's fees for the round-trip. Courier services are also listed in the *Yellow Pages* or in advertisements in newspaper travel sections.

PACKAGE TOURS/CRUISES

For those travelers who feel more secure if everything is prearranged—hotels, transportation, sightseeing excursions, luggage handling, tips, taxes, and even meals, a package tour is the obvious choice, and it may even help save money.

One of the best tour operators to Scandinavia is **Crownline Tours,** 3300 S. Gessner, Suite 100, Houston, TX 77063 (tel. 713/977-6916, or toll free 800/255-9509). Crownline offers land packages, with experienced guides and a wide range of prices.

Scandinavian Travel Service is a specialist in Scandinavian vacations, offering a variety of tours. Bookings are made through **Holiday Tours of America,** 40 E. 49th St., New York, NY 10017 (tel. 212/832-8989, or toll free 800/223-0567), or **Scantours, Inc.,** 1535 Sixth St., Suite 209, Santa Monica, CA 90401 (tel. 213/451-0911, or toll free 800/223-SCAN).

NORWAY The most popular cruises in Norway are those of the fjords. **Winge of Scandinavia,** 3568 Sagunto St., Sant Ynez, CA 93460 (tel. 805/688-3299, or toll free 800/328-1209), offers a 3-day cruise of the beautiful Sognefjord on the 90-foot M/S *Epos*. Overnights are spent in resort hotels en route, and overland excursions and meals are included in the price of 3,300 kroner ($547.45). Children under 12 sharing a room with their parents pay half. Departures are from Bergen every Monday in June, July, and August.

Five-day cruises of the Sognefjord and Nordfjord on the M/S *Nordrise* are offered, with on-board accommodations for 45 passengers. Cabins have private facilities and three meals a day are served on board. Departures from Bergen or Oslo leave from mid-May to the end of September for $750 per passenger. Bookings are made through **Bennett Tours,** 270 Madison Ave., New York, NY 10016 (tel. 212/532-5060, or toll-free 800/221-2420).

In summer, cruise-ship lovers always want to visit the North Cape to see the Midnight Sun. The best tour to take is by **Ocean Cruise Lines,** 1510 SE 17th St., Fort Lauderdale FL 33316 (tel. 305/764-5566, or toll free 800/556-8850). It runs 7 to 14 deluxe cruise tours of Scandinavia and Russia, including the Norwegian fjords and the North Cape, with prices from $1,095 per person.

Norwegian Arctic Trips, Box 700, Route 4, Enfield, NH 03748 (tel. 603/632-7654), specializes in adventure trips in the Norwegian Arctic and Lapland, for small groups who want to experience the land and the culture. For example, it offers a 12-day guided canoe/fishing trip for $1,065 per person. It also features river adventures for the physically handicapped.

SWEDEN   Once in Sweden, the most popular tour is the   ✪ **Göta Canàl Cruise** from Gothenburg to Stockholm (or vice versa), dubbed the "Sweden in a nutshell" tour because it offers a wide overview of the country's geography in one trip. The tour (including all meals) costs from $750 (U.S.), takes 4 days and operates from April to September. You can book through many travel agents, like **Mill Run Tours, Inc.,** 20 E. 49th St., New York, NY 10017 (tel. 212/486-9840, or toll free 800/MILL RUN).

FINLAND   For the best of the North Country's tours (the most unusual of which occur in winter), the vast and beautiful wilderness regions of Finland can provide some of the most memorable expeditions in Europe. Among the many tour options are a **ski-trekking** venture into some of Lapland's wildest country with an experienced guide, or cross-country ski weekends in the country around Kuusamo, where Finland's Olympic teams have trained for years and where the trails are said to be among the best in Europe.

The best tours of Finland are offered by **Finnair** (tel. toll free 800/950-5000), including its most popular, the **Midnight Sun Flight** (Helsinki–Rovaniemi–Helsinki). This tour is offered June 1 to July 15 daily. Any Finnair office around the world can provide information about the tour possibilities for exploring Finland.

Finnair also offers a **reindeer safari,** where teams of sleds (one person and one reindeer per sled) make expeditions into Lapp communities far north of the Arctic Circle. Finally, for travelers who want to sail the Baltic, there's a **summer sailing safari,** where each member sails his or her own boat among a flotilla of other vessels and then meets each evening for communal meals and activities at the islets scattered along the south of Finland.

If you'd like to see as much as possible of the highlights of Finland in the shortest possible time, consider the **Finland Grand Tour,** lasting 10 days and 9 nights. It is offered on certain days June through August. This tour is operated by the **Finland Travel Bureau,** Kaivokatu 10A, PB 319, SF-00101 Helsinki (tel. 90/18-261). Bookings can be made through any travel agent.

AIRLINES AND FARES

DENMARK   Nonstop flights to Copenhagen from the New York area take approximately 7½ hours; from Chicago and Anchorage, about 8½ hours; from Los Angeles, 11 hours; and from Seattle, 9½ hours.

Two airlines have nonstop flights from the U.S. to Copenhagen. **SAS (Scandinavian Airlines System)** (tel. toll free 800/221-2350) has more nonstop flights from more North American cities than any other airline, as well as more flights to and from Denmark from anywhere around the world. It offers nonstop flights to Copenhagen daily in midsummer, and almost every day in winter, from Los Angeles, Seattle, Anchorage, and Chicago. Throughout the year SAS also flies nonstop from the Continental Airlines terminal in Newark, N.J.

SAS's routes to Copenhagen are contested only by **TWA (Trans World Airlines)** (tel. toll free 800/433-7300), which flies to Copenhagen daily from New York's JFK.

In addition, several other international airlines service Copenhagen indirectly from various European cities. For example, **Pan Am** (tel. 212/687-2600) flies five times a week from New York's JFK to Copenhagen, with a stop in Berlin. **British Airways** (tel. toll free 800/247-9297) also operates a convenient connection from New York

FROMMER'S SMART TRAVELER: SCANDINAVIAN AIRFARES

1. Shop all airlines that fly to your destination.
2. Always ask for the lowest fare—not just a discount fare.
3. Keep calling the airline—availability of cheap seats changes daily.
4. Fares to other Scandinavian cities are sometimes included in a transatlantic ticket at no extra charge. This must be specified when ticket is written.
5. For domestic flights in Scandinavia, ask about special passes and family discounts.
6. Try to fly in winter, spring, or fall—fares are lower at this time. Check out SAS's midwinter mini-fares.
7. Ask about the cost-conscious APEX (advance-purchase excursion) fare.
8. Find out if it's cheaper to fly on a weekday.
9. Read the section on bucket shops, charter flights, flying standby and going as a courier.

via Manchester to Copenhagen. **KLM** (tel. 212/759-3600) flies to Copenhagen via Amsterdam, and **Lufthansa** (tel. 718/895-1277) flies to Copenhagen via Düsseldorf. (Note, however, that unless you make all flight arrangements from North America before you go, you might find some of these capital-hopping flights prohibitively expensive.)

The lowest price **APEX** on SAS requires 30-day advance payment, 7- to 21-day minimum stay, travel during midweek, and is nonrefundable. It costs from $608 to $875 round-trip depending on the season.

An SAS **economy-class** ticket cost (at press time) $1,816 round-trip.

NORWAY All transatlantic flights from North America land in Oslo at either Gardermoen Airport or more conveniently at Fornebu Airport **SAS** (tel. toll free 800/221-2350) flies nonstop from Newark to Oslo in about 7½ hours. Most other SAS flights from other North American cities are routed through Copenhagen to Oslo with flying times of 9¼ hours from Chicago, 9½ hours from Anchorage, 10½ hours from Seattle, and 11½ hours from Los Angeles, not including the layover in Copenhagen.

If you fly on other airlines, you'll be routed via their gateway European cities. **British Airways** (tel. toll free 800/247-9297) for example, has dozens of daily flights from many North American cities to London from where you can fly to Oslo.

Pan Am (tel. toll free 800/221-1111) flies to Oslo from Detroit, Miami and Washington, DC, via London and from New York (five times a week) via Berlin and Copenhagen.

TWA (tel. toll free 800/221-2000) flies from New York to Oslo nonstop every Wednesday. **KLM** (tel. toll free 800/777-5553) routes you through Amsterdam; **Lufthansa** (tel. toll free 800/645-3880) via Frankfurt; and **Air France** (tel. toll free 800/237-2747) through Paris.

For these non-direct flights make sure you book ahead in North America; otherwise the cost is prohibitive.

Currently, the SAS nonrefundable Special **APEX** ticket requiring 30-day advance purchase, travel between Monday and Thursday in both directions, and a stay abroad from 7 to 21 days costs from $624 to $917 round-trip depending on the season.

TWA has midwinter weekend fares from New York to Oslo for $427 round-trip requiring advance purchase, a stay of 2 to 4 days, and routing via Brussels, Amsterdam, London or Paris with a transfer to another airline.

An **economy** round-trip fare on SAS from Newark costs $1,832. **Business class** (or Euro class on SAS) costs around $2,104.

SWEDEN   Your best bets are **SAS** (tel. toll free 800/221-2350), with the most frequent service from Newark; **Pan Am** (tel. toll free 800/221-1212), which flies nonstop four times a week to Stockholm from JFK New York; and **American Airlines** (tel. toll free 800/443-7300), which has daily flights to Stockholm from Chicago.

Other airlines fly to gateway European cities connecting to Stockholm. **British Airways** (tel. toll free 800/247-9297) for example, flies from 19 U.S. cities to London Heathrow connecting with the eight flights per day leaving for Stockholm. **Delta** (tel. toll free 800/241-4141) **Northwest** (tel. toll free 800/225-2525), and **TWA** (tel. toll free 800/221-2000) do the same.

Currently, SAS charges $618 to $946 plus tax for a round-trip Super **APEX** ticket depending on the season and day of travel.

American from Chicago charges from $693 to $1,020 depending on season and day of travel. Both airlines require 30-day advance purchase, and a 7- to 21-day stay.

For a less restrictive APEX requiring advance purchase of 21 days and a stay of from 7 days to three months (extendable to one year on Pan Am for $100 additional), both SAS and Pan Am charge from $902 to $1,220, depending on the season and day of travel.

For an **economy** round-trip ticket expect to pay $1,982 from New York; $2,250 from Chicago; add about $300 for business class (Euroclass on SAS); for first-class you pay $4,536 from New York.

FINLAND   Finnair (tel. toll free 800/950-5000) flies to Helsinki from more parts of the world (including North America) than any other airline. It is the only airline that flies nonstop from North America to Finland. From New York Finnair flies nonstop on the 8-hour trip to Helsinki every day throughout the year. From Los Angeles, it flies nonstop on Thursday and Saturday, taking 10½ hours. Canadians usually opt for one of Finnair's two or three weekly flights from Toronto to Helsinki, taking 8 hours 40 minutes.

Other airlines fly to gateway European cities connecting to Helsinki. **British Airways** (tel. toll free 800/247-9297) for example, flies from 19 U.S. cities to London Heathrow connecting with the 13 flights per week leaving for Finland. **SAS** (tel. toll free 800/221-2350) will fly you via Copenhagen from where there are three daily nonstop flights to Helsinki taking about 1½ hours. **TWA** (tel. toll free 800/221-2000) and **Pan Am** (tel. toll free 800/221-1212) fly from New York four days a week to Stockholm where you change planes for Helsinki.

Finnair's cheapest ticket from New York to Helsinki is a **weekend winter fare.** A passenger must stay abroad between 5 and 14 days, pay for a ticket 15 days in advance, and travel on certain days in January or February. Tickets are nonrefundable and cost $398 round-trip.

In midsummer, one of the least expensive year-round tickets to Finland from anywhere in North America is a 7-day advance-purchase excursion **(APEX)** fare which is also nonrefundable. Passengers must stay abroad at least a week. APEX round-trip tickets in low season from New York cost $651 to $704, rising to $961 to $1,014 in high season. From Los Angeles, the round-trip ticket costs between $811 and $865 in low season, rising to $1,218 to $1,272 in high season. Fares from Toronto to Helsinki are roughly the same as they are from the West Coast.

BY TRAIN

TO DENMARK   If you're in Europe, it's easy to get to Denmark by rail. Copenhagen is the main rail hub between Scandinavia and the rest of Europe. For example, the London–Copenhagen train via Ostende or Hoek van Holland leaves four times daily (22 hours). About 10 daily express trains run from Hamburg to Copenhagen (5½ hours). There are also intercity trains on the Merkur route from Karlsrube (Germany) to Cologne to Hamburg to Copenhagen. The Berlin–Ostbahnhof–Copenhagen train (8½ hours) connects with East European trains. Two daily express trains make this run.

TO NORWAY/SWEDEN There are three daily trains from Copenhagen to Oslo, seven from Copenhagen to Stockholm and six from Copenhagen to Gothenburg. All connect to the Danish ferries operating either to Norway via Helsingfor or Hirtshals or to Sweden via Helsingfor or Frederikshaven.

TO FINLAND There is a rail and ferryboat link between London and Helsinki which goes via Oostende (Belgium), Cologne, Hamburg, and Stockholm. If you've taken the ferry from Stockholm and are arriving at Turku, on the west coast of Finland, you can catch one of the seven daily trains that will take you across southern Finland to Helsinki. The trip takes 2¼ hours. Rail connections are also possible from London to Den Hoek (The Netherlands), Bremen, Hamburg, and Stockholm. However, each of these itineraries takes about 50 hours, plus a 2-hour stopover in Stockholm. It's possible to reserve sleepers and couchettes, but do so as far in advance as possible. Helsinki is also linked by rail to the major cities of Finland (see individual city listings for details).

BY BUS

TO SWEDEN If you've got plenty of time and your budget is lean, you can actually go by bus from London's Victoria Station to Stockholm, but it's an epic 48-hour journey. An "express" service is operated by **GDG Continentbus,** 52 Grosvenor Gardens (tel. 071/730-82-35), with a routing from London to Dover, followed by a ferry crossing to Zeebrugge. The trip continues by road through the Netherlands and Germany to the ferry at Travemünde, which goes to Trelleborg in southern Sweden. From here it's a 10-hour journey by road from Malmö to Stockholm. Most travel agents in London will sell you this ticket.

TO FINLAND There are international bus links to Finland, but this is the least convenient mode of transportation. One of the most popular would be a bus connection from Stockholm with a sea crossing to Turku, with continuing service by land to Helsinki.

It's also possible to take coaches from Gothenburg going cross country to Stockholm and to the ferry dock beyond, with land travel resuming after Turku on the same coach all the way to Helsinki.

For information about international bus connections and reservations, contact **Oy Matkahuolto Ab,** Simonkatu 3, 00100 Helsinki (tel. 90/642-744).

BY SHIP/FERRY

TO DENMARK It's also easy to travel by water from several ports to Denmark. Liners carrying both cars and passengers operate between England, Germany, Poland, Norway, and Sweden to Denmark. Check with your travel agent about these Denmark cruises.

From England **Scandinavia Seaways** (tel. toll free 800/533-3755) runs vessels from Harwick, England, to Esbjerg in West Jutland (19 hours). Vessels also run from Newcastle, England, to Esbjerg (20 hours) and Oslo to Copenhagen (16 hours).

From Norway/Sweden The **Bergen Line** (tel. 212/986-2711 or toll free 800/3 BERGEN) operates vessels from Bergen to Hirtshals in North Jutland (18 hours). You can also go from Stavanger, Norway, to Hirtshals (11 hours). You can write to Bergen Line at 505 5th Ave., New York, NY 10017.

Stena Line runs popular sea links from Oslo to Frederikshavn, North Jutland (11½ hours), and from Gothenburg, Sweden, to Frederikshavn (3 hours). For information, schedules, and fares, contact: Norstar Travel, 2171 Monroe Ave., Rochester, NY 14618 (tel. 716/244-5484).

From Germany **GT-Link,** Faergegården, DK-4874 Gedser (tel. 53-87-92-33), runs car-ferries from Travemünde (the point closest to Denmark), to Gedser, southern Denmark (3½ hours).

TO NORWAY **From Denmark** Three major ferries operate from Denmark. The first, from Hirtshals to Kristiansand takes 5 hours on the Stena Line and can be booked in the United States through Norstar Travel, 2171 Monroe Ave., Rochester, NY 14618 (tel. 716/244-5484); the second from Frederikshavn to Oslo takes 11 hours and can be reserved through the Larvik Line, Box 265, Skoyen, N-0212 Oslo 2 (tel. 011/47-2-550501). It departs twice daily year round, and includes a night crossing. The third, Scandinavian Seaways operates daily year round from Copenhagen to Oslo overnight taking 16 hours. For reservations contact DFDS Seaways, 6499 NW Ninth Avenue, Suite 212, Fort Lauderdale, FL 33309 (tel. 305/491-7909 or toll free 800/533-3755).

From Sweden   From Strømstad, Sweden, there is a daily crossing in summer to Sandefjord, Norway, taking 2½ hours. Bookings on this Scandi Line operation can be made through **Scandi Line,** Tollbugt 5, N-3200 Sandefjord (tel. 011/47-34-62285).

From England   The **Bergen Line,** 505 Fifth Ave., New York, NY 10017 (tel. 212/986-2711, or toll free 800/323-7436), operates weekly service year round from Harwich, England, to Hirtshals (Denmark) and Oslo. From May to October, it also runs two to three vessels a week between Newcastle, England, and Stavanger and Bergen on the west coast of Norway.

TO SWEDEN   From Denmark   From Copenhagen, you can go to Malmö, Sweden by **hydrofoil,** called *Flyvebådene.* For information in Copenhagen, call 33-12-80-88. A first-class round-trip ticket from Copenhagen to Malmö costs 352 kroner ($59.20), and a second-class round-trip is 158 kroner ($26.55). This is the easiest and fastest way to go, but the hydrofoil doesn't take cars. Travel time is 45 minutes. Hydrofoils depart from the corner of Havnegade and Nyhavn from a terminal directly on the seafront. Departures are daily every hour on the hour from 6am to 1am. In midsummer, make reservations.

Sweden can also be reached by a conventional **ferry** that transports cars. Ferries leave from Dragør, south of Copenhagen, and arrive at Limhamn, 3 miles south of Malmö. The ferry runs daily from 5:30am to 10pm. There are about 19 to 25 crossings daily. The cost for a round-trip, one-day ticket, a car, driver, and up to five passengers is 355 kroner ($59.70) providing you return the same day. It's 440 kroner ($73.95) for a car and five passengers if you plan to spend a night or more. Walk-on pedestrians pay 30 kroner ($5.05) each way, and children under 16 go for half price. If you are a single driver with no passengers, you pay 375 kroner ($63.05) round-trip. If you have only one passenger, it is to your advantage to declare your passenger as a pedestrian, and pay only 60 kroner ($10.10) round-trip. For more information, call 31-53-15-85 in Copenhagen.

Another possibility for motorists is to leave Copenhagen and drive north to Helsingør, where you can take a conventional ferryboat to Helsingborg, Sweden, departing three times an hour. This route is popular with Swedes and Danes because it's less money and only a 25-minute ride. The round-trip fare for a car and up to five passengers is 380 kroner ($63.90). Pedestrians pay just 28 kroner ($4.70) round-trip. For information, call 49-21-12-55.

For a day trip from Copenhagen to Sweden, drive to Dragør, south of Copenhagen, and take the ferry to Limhamn, Sweden, 3 miles south of Malmö. Once there, visit Malmö and Helsingborg. Return to Denmark on the car-ferry to Helsingør (site of "Hamlet's castle") and drive south back to Copenhagen. Round-trip cost for a car, a driver, and up to four passengers is 315 kroner ($52.95), providing it is just 1 day.

From England   You can also make a "grand crossing"—say, from Harwich, England, to Gothenburg, and in summer only from Newcastle-upon-Tyne. These journeys take 24 hours, with two or three sailings per week. For information, contact **Scandinavian Seaways,** Crown Place, Suite 212, 6499 NW Ninth Ave., Fort Lauderdale, FL 33309 (tel. toll free 800/533-3755).

TO FINLAND   From Sweden   Frequent ferries run between Sweden and Finland, especially between Stockholm and Helsinki. Service is on either the Viking or Silja line. Each company also operates a twice-daily service from Stockholm to Turku on Finland's west coast.

From Germany   The Silja Line also maintains regular passenger service between Travemünde (Germany) and Helsinki. Information about the **Silja Line** is obtained at **Oy Silja Line AB,** Finnjetlinja, PB 144, 00161 Helsinki (tel. 90/18-041). Information on the **Viking Line** is available at Mannerheimintie 14, 00100 Helsinki (tel. 90/12-351).

BY CAR

TO DENMARK You can easily drive to Denmark from Germany. Many drive to Jutland from such cities as Hamburg, Bremerhaven, or Lübeck. Jutland is linked to the central island of Funen by bridge. But from Funen you must take a car-ferry from Nyborg to the island of Zealand, site of Copenhagen. Once in West Zealand you will still have to drive east across the island to Copenhagen.

Car-ferry service to Denmark from the United Kingdom generally leaves passengers at Esbjerg, where they then have to cross from Jutland to Copenhagen. From Germany, it's possible to take a car-ferry from Travemünde, northeast of Lübeck, which deposits you at Gedser in Denmark. From there, connect with the E55, an express highway north to Copenhagen.

TO NORWAY If you're driving from the continent you have to go via Sweden. From Copenhagen take the E47/55 express highway north from Copenhagen to Helsingør, catching the car-ferry to the Swedish city of Helsingborg. From there, E6 will take you into Oslo.

From Stockholm you can drive across Sweden along the E18 to Oslo.

TO SWEDEN The ferry routes from England to Denmark and from Denmark to Sweden are the most traveled, but there are better choices from the continent.

From Germany You can drive to the northern German port of Travemünde and catch the 7½-hour ferry to the Swedish port of Trelleborg, a short drive south of Malmö. This route saves many hours by avoiding transit through Denmark. If you want to visit Denmark before Sweden, you can take the 3-hour car-ferry from Travemünde to Gedser in southern Denmark. From Gedser the E64 and the E4 express highway head north to Copenhagen. After a visit there, you can take a car-ferry from Copenhagen to Malmö.

From Norway From Oslo, the E18 goes east via Karlstad all the way to Stockholm. This is a long but scenic drive. If you're in Denmark, car-ferries run frequently from Copenhagen to the southern Swedish city of Malmö and from Helsingør in North Zealand to Helsingborg on Sweden's west coast. To reach Stockholm from Malmö, take the E6 north along the coast in the direction of Helsingborg. In the Helsingborg area, turn northeast at the junction with the E4 and continue all across southern Sweden until you reach Stockholm. Part of this highway is an express motorway and part only a national highway.

TO FINLAND From anywhere in western Scandinavia the quickest route to Finland is the E3 to Stockholm and the year-round 14- to 16-hour ferry from there to Helsinki.

From Germany From Travemunde year round, there's a high speed car-ferry that takes 22 hours to reach Helsinki.

From Denmark Take the car ferry from Helsingør to Helsingborg in Sweden and then drive to Stockholm and catch the car-ferry to Helsinki or Turku.

7. GETTING AROUND SCANDINAVIA

AIR & RAIL PASSES (SCANDINAVIA & EUROPE)

The best way to get around the whole of Scandinavia is to take advantage of the **air and rail passes** that apply to the whole region, or, if you're traveling extensively in

Europe, to use the special European passes. For additional country-specific information see the planning chapters for each country—chapters 3, 12, 23, and 32.

SAS'S VISIT SCANDINAVIA FARE This is a five-coupon ticket costing $250 that's valid for travel on all SAS flights within and between Denmark, Norway, and Sweden, from July 1 to August 14.

THE SCANDINAVIAN RAIL PASS This allows you to travel the rail systems in Denmark, Norway, Sweden, and Finland (except for Stockholm's local train system). It also allows a 50% discount on the following ferry routes: Copenhagen–Malmö; Copenhagen–Ronne; Ronne–Ystaad; Stockholm–Helsinki; and Stockholm–Helsingfors. It also gives you 50% off on express boats between Bergen, Flåm, and Ardalstangen; and Bergen, Slora, and Maloy, plus round-trip fares on the *Larvik* line.

You pay $179 for first class, $139 for second class for 4 days of travel within a 15-day period; $299 for first class, $229 for second class for 9 days of travel within a 21-day period; and $459 for first class, $319 for second class for 14 days of travel within a one-month period. Reservations and information can be made through **French Rail, Inc.,** 226 Westchester Ave., White Plains, NY 10604 (tel. toll free 800/345-1990). Children between 4 and 11 travel for half price. Fares are subject to change, of course.

EURAILPASS If you're touring extensively in Europe, this is your best bet. It's good for unlimited first-class rail travel in 17 European countries. With one ticket, you travel on special trains, whenever and wherever you please; more than 100,000 rail miles are at your disposal. The cost for 15 days is $340; for 21 days, $440; for 1 month, $550; for 2 months, $750; and for 3 months, $930. Children under 12 pay half price, and children under 4 travel free.

Eurailpass Youthpass and **Eurail Saverpass** are also accepted on all four State Railways. The Youthpass costs $380 for 1 month and $500 for 2 months, and is valid for unlimited second-class travel for those 26 or younger. Saverpass is sold to two, three, or more people traveling together and costs $240 per person for 15 days of unlimited first-class travel.

Eurailpasses are also valid for passage on some ferries. Passes are sold by any travel agent.

8. WHERE TO STAY

SPECIAL SCANDINAVIAN PASSES & DISCOUNTS

THE SCANDINAVIAN BONUS PASS From June 1 to September 1, this secures discounts of 15% to 40% off the rates at more than 100 first-class hotels in Scandinavia. The pass costs $23 to $30 depending on the country of purchase, is valid for two adults and their children for an unlimited number of overnight stays (maximum 3 nights per hotel). Make your reservations in advance and on arrival present the pass and pay the guaranteed reduced rate directly to the hotel. These reduced rates start at about $35 per person including breakfast, service, and VAT. Children up to 15 stay free in their parents' room. In Denmark the pass is honored at Danway Hotels; in Norway at Inter Nor Hotels and others; in Finland at Arctia Hotel Partners, Annankatu 42D, 00100 Helsinki (tel. 90/694-8471).

The pass is sold at many agencies, including Bergen line, 505 Fifth Avenue, Suite 1700, New York, NY 10017-4983 (tel. 212/986-2711); and at Royal World Travel Service, 6500 Eighth Ave., NW, Seattle WA 98117 (tel. 206/789-6144).

THE SCANDIC HOTEL CHEQUE This is valid at more than 90 hotels in Scandinavia and benefits the individual traveler by providing reduced room rates. There are different types of cheque. The Summer Cheque valid from mid-May to

September 7 costs from $34 to $40 (depending on the country) per person per night including breakfast. The Weekend Cheque is valid Friday through Monday from January to mid-May and September 8 to January 1, costing $30 to $35 (depending on the country) per person including room and breakfast.

The **Scandic Junior Cheque** which is available in both summer and weekend types provides an extra bed in the parents' room and breakfast.

Cheques are sold by such representatives as Holiday Tours of America, 40 E. 49th St., New York, NY 10017 (tel. 212/832-0567); and Scantours Inc., 1535 Sixth St., Suite 205, Santa Monica, CA 90401-2533 (tel. 213/451-0911).

THE NORDIC HOTEL CARD   Sold for about $9 (depending on the country), this card grants discounts at 140 hotels in Scandinavia from June 23 to August 6. Prices are per person in a twin with private bath, including breakfast, and range from $34 to $55 with children under 15 staying free in their parents' room if no extra bed is required. It's sold by Kon-Tiki Travel Inc., 8311 Fifth Ave., Brooklyn, NY 11209 (tel. 718/748-7400 or toll free 800/822-5838).

BEST WESTERN HOTEL CHEQUE SCANDINAVIA   From May 15 to September 15, this program offers reduced rates for twin rooms including breakfast at some 130 hotels in Scandinavia. Single room supplements are payable directly to the hotel. Cheques are about $35 each depending on the country and there is a minimum purchase of five per person. The hotels are divided into categories. Basic cheques are accepted at "B" hotels; "A" and "S" hotel categories carry a supplement. Among the many agencies offering these are Passage Tours of Scandinavia (tel. toll free 800/548-5960) and Holiday Tours of America (tel. toll free 800/223-0567).

IN DENMARK

Danish Inn Cheques are valid at 67 Danish inns for rooms with private bath and toilet. For 200 kroner ($33.60) per person, a guest is entitled to an overnight stay in a double room, including breakfast. Children under 6 stay free in a parents' bed.

 FROMMER'S SMART TRAVELER: HOTELS

1. Always ask about midsummer reductions from late June to mid-August.
2. Ask also about weekend discounts, which may include Sunday as well as Friday and Saturday.
3. Remember the price you pay in reasonably priced hotels depends on the plumbing. Rooms with showers are cheaper than rooms with bath; rooms containing a sink with bath down the hall are cheapest.
4. Take advantage of special discounts, like the Scandinavian Bonus Pass, Finncheques, Danish Inn Cheques (see this chapter) etc.
5. At smaller, cheaper hotels that take credit cards, ask if cash will secure a reduction.
6. If you're going to spend a week at the hotel, ask about long-term discounts.
7. Parents should ask if children can stay free in the same room.

QUESTIONS TO ASK IF YOU'RE ON A BUDGET

1. Is there a garage? What's the charge for parking?
2. Is there a surcharge on either local or long-distance telephone calls? (There usually is and it could be as much as 40%. Make your calls from a phone box or from the post office.)
3. Is service included? If it's not, add 15% to the rates.
4. Are all taxes included?

Cheques are sold by **Scandinavian American World Tours, Inc.,** 795 Franklin Ave., Franklin Lakes, NJ 07417 (tel. 201/891-6641).

IN NORWAY

You can obtain large reductions at 225 hotels, pensions (boardinghouses), and mountain lodges all over Norway—from Oslo to the fjord district to the North Cape—by purchasing the **Norway Fjord Pass.** The pass is valid for standard room accommodations (not for deluxe rooms or suites) and costs about $7 (U.S.). Holders of the pass are charged 160 to 350 kroner ($26.55 to $58.05) per night for a room, with breakfast included. You can reserve your room in advance at least 3 days before you plan to arrive, or else just drop in at one of the hotels or pensions offering Fjord Pass accommodation. If that one is full, the staff will help you call another one nearby. At hotels offering such accommodation, the pass is valid from May 1 to September 30.

To arrange for your Norway Fjord Pass, get in touch with **Brekke Travel, Inc.,** 802 N. 43rd St., Grand Forks, ND 58201 (tel. toll free 800/437-5301); **Jason Travel,** Scandinavian Department, 717 Market St., San Francisco, CA 94103 (tel. 415/957-9102); **Kon-Tiki Travel,** 8311 Fifth Ave., Brooklyn, NY 11209 (tel. 718/748-7400); **Nordic America Travel,** Sons of Norway Building, 1455 W. Lake St., Minneapolis, MN 55408 (tel. 612/827-3853, or toll free 800/328-5102); or the **Norwegian Tourist Board,** 655 Third Ave., New York, NY 10017 (tel. 212/949-2333).

Nor Camp is a chain of high-standard campsites, cabin and chalet centers, apartment hotels, and motels. A **Nor Camp Pass** allows you to obtain reductions of 10% to 20%. The pass is sold by participants or by contacting **Nor Camp,** Box 98. N-2636 Over (tel. 062/78-700).

IN SWEDEN

With the Pro Skandinavia Nordic Hotel & Tourist Cheque you get reduced rates at 400 first-class or luxury hotels in Sweden. Cheques can be used from June 1 to August 31 and during weekends (Friday and Saturday) from September 1 to May 31. The price for a double room is one hotel cheque, including a breakfast buffet. No charge is made for children under 12, unless an extra bed is required (that charge is also one cheque). The price of each cheque is $35 (U.S.). Bookings must be made no more than 24 hours before arrival. More information is available from **Haman Scandinavia U.S., Inc.,** 10866 Wilshire Blvd., Suite 1270, Westwood, Los Angeles, CA 90024 (tel. 213/475-7038, or toll free 800/475-7330).

IN FINLAND

Hotel discount vouchers called **Finncheques** cut down considerably on costs at some hotels. Costing 155 markkaa ($42.25) each for 1 night's accommodation, Finncheques are valid from June 1 to August 31. Participating in the program are 160 hotels in 80 localities. Only the first night can be reserved in advance, and reservations at the next hotel are handled free. Finncheques can be used by one person each, but there is no lower limit to the number that can be bought. The single-room supplement is 75 markkaa ($20.45) at first-class hotels. Children aged 4 to 14 can have an extra bed placed in their parents' room for 75 markkaa ($20.45) per night. All supplements and charges for children are paid at the hotel.

Finncheques represent substantial savings, which might be 30% or more off the regular rates, but that varies from hotel to hotel. Two people traveling together would each need a Finncheque, making the cost of a double room 210 markkaa ($57.25) per night. If it is a first-class hotel, then the previously mentioned supplement of 75 markkaa ($20.45) per room must be added on for a double-room total of 285 markkaa ($77.70). Even though the single traveler has to pay a supplement, Finncheques discounts are still substantial as opposed to the regular single rate.

Finncheques are available from accredited Finncheque agents. In the U.S., agents are **Crownline Tours,** 3330 S. Gessner, Suite 100, Houston, TX 77063 (tel. 713/977-6916); **Holiday Tours of America,** 40 E. 49th St., New York, NY 10017 (tel. 212/832-9072, or toll free 800/223-0567); **Cosmos Travel, Inc.,** 12 S. Dixie Hwy., Lake Worth, FL 33460 (tel. 305/685-6870); **Ray K. Jones Travel Service, Inc.,** 1905 NW Market St., Seattle, WA 98107 (tel. 206/783-8300, or toll free 800/782-8300); and **Scantours, Inc.,** 1535 6th St., Suite 209, Santa Monica, CA 90401 (tel. 213/451-0911). For further information, contact the agents listed above or **Vesama Tours Ltd.,** Fredrikinkatu 48A, SF-0100 Helsinki (tel. 90/694-8877).

YOUTH HOSTELS

These are found throughout Scandinavia. The accommodations vary considerably from a renovated old manor farm in Denmark's Odense to a boat in Stockholm harbor.

Most hostels have small bedrooms sleeping four, and, occasionally, private rooms for families. They usually close between 1 and 4 pm and impose a curfew and lights-out after 11 pm. Other rules such as no smoking in the bedrooms may also be imposed.

Mandatory membership costs $25 for adults 18 to 54; $10 for under 18s; $15 for seniors; $35 for families; and $250 for life. In Canada costs are $25 for ages 18 and over ($35 for 2 years); $12 for those under 18; $36 for groups; $42 for families; and $175 for a life membership. For information contact American Youth Hostels, P. O. Box 37613, Washington, DC 20013-7613 (tel. 202/783-6161 and, in Canada, Canadian Hostelling Association, 1600 James Naismith Dr., Suite 608, Gloucester, ON K1B 5N4, Canada (tel. 613/748-5638).

You can also become a member at any youth hostel or at the following headquarters in Scandinavia: Landsforeningen Danmarks Vandrerhjem, Vesterbrogade 39, DK-1620 Kobenhavn (tel. 33-31-36-12) Denmark; Norske Vandrerhjem, Dronningensgate 26, N-0154, Oslo 1, Norway (tel. 02/42-14-10); Svenska Turistforeningen, Vasagatan 48, Stockholm, Sweden (tel. 08/790-31-00); or Finnish Youth Hostel Association, Yrjonkatu 38B, SF-00100 Helsinki, Finland (tel. 90/694-0377).

IN DENMARK   There are 101 youth hostels, and guests of all ages are welcomed for stays of usually not more than 3 days. The hostels charge 50 kroner ($8.40) per night, although nonmembers pay a 20-krone ($3.35) supplement. Children under 2 are free, but families are charged an 8-krone ($1.35) supplement for their own room. Children under 10 usually get half-price discounts. Breakfast is available for around 30 kroner ($5.05). Sleeping bags tend to be prohibited.

IN NORWAY   There are about 800 modern and well-maintained youth hostels and prices range from 60 to 125 kroner ($9.95 to $20.75) a night for a bed. Sheet sleeping sacks may be rented. Reasonably priced meals are served in most of them. Many maintain do-it-yourself kitchen facilities. Membership cards are accepted without formality at all hostels in Norway.

IN SWEDEN   There are about 280 youth hostels, called Vandrarhem. Prices are usually 40 to 70 kronor ($7 to $12.20) for members; nonmembers pay an extra 25 to 30 kronor ($4.35 to $5.25). The hostels in Sweden are usually closed between 10am and 5pm daily.

IN FINLAND   There are about 160 youth hostels, about 50 of which open all year, the rest in summer only. The rates depend on the hostel category and number of beds in a room and range from the least expensive, costing 26 markkaa ($7.10) a night, to the top rating, costing from 150 markkaa ($41).

FARMHOUSES/APARTMENTS

IN DENMARK   The best way to see the heart of Denmark and meet the Danes is to spend a week on one of their farms. Take a pin and stick it anywhere on a map of

Denmark away from the cities and seacoast, and you'll find a thatched and timbered farm, or perhaps a more modernized homestead. All are good bases—any point on the island can easily be reached on a day trip.

Select the part of Denmark you'd like to explore, then write the local tourist office in that area, stating your requirements, the number in your party, the length of your stay, the ages of your children (if any), and whether you want full or half board. A minimum stay of 7 days or more is desirable, but not always mandatory.

For more information about the program, contact the headquarters: **Holidays on a Farm (Bonbegardsferie)**, Peberlik 2, DK-6200 Aabenraa (tel. 74-62-01-91). The program costs 185 kroner ($31.10) per person daily, with half board included; children pay half price. Farms rarely take more than eight paying guests at a time, although some of the more commercial ones can take as many as 40.

If you want greater independence, you can inquire about booking an apartment in the countryside of Denmark at the rate of 1,495 kroner ($251.30) per week. No meals are included, and occupancy is limited to four people.

IN NORWAY   Farmhouses charge about 150 kroner ($24.90) per person daily full board. For more information contact Lille Norge, Box 4, N-1353 Baerums Verk (tel. 02/51-14-27).

IN FINLAND   More than 90 English-speaking Finnish farm families have opened their homes for farm holidays. The farms, including some in Lapland, have one thing in common: an opportunity to meet with Finnish people at home and join in their farming activities, or just relax. You can reach your holiday destination most easily in your own car, but if you travel by train or bus, you can arrange to be met. The prices depend on the category in which a house has been placed. A minimum of 6 days is usually required for a farm holiday.

Bookings can be arranged through **Suomen 4H-liitto**, Uudenmaankatu 24, 00120 Helsinki (tel. 90/642-233). Prices range from 1,162 to 1,407 markkaa ($316.85 to $383.70) per person weekly, including full board.

CAMPING

IN DENMARK   There are a number of pleasant, well-equipped campgrounds near Copenhagen and elsewhere. For information about campsites and facilities, contact the **Dansk Camping Union**, Gammel Kongevej 74D, DK-1850 København V (tel. 31-21-06-00). The cost of official campgrounds is about 35 kroner ($5.90) per person. The Camping Union will sell you a campground handbook for 65 kroner ($10.95). A mandatory camping pass is available at all campgrounds for 25 kroner ($4.20), or you can purchase a family pass for 50 kroner ($8.40).

IN NORWAY   There are more than 970 authorized campsites in Norway, classified, according to standards and amenities, as one-, two-, and three-star camps. Charges vary according to the number of stars, but the charge for pitching a tent is about $9 (U.S.) per night. Cabins rent for $22 to $44 or more per night. Most campers prefer to live in tents and prepare their own meals—without a doubt the cheapest way to go.

Norwegian campsites are comfortable and maintain high standards. Most have rental cabins/chalets, which are becoming increasingly popular. If you want to stay in one of these, make your reservation by telephone early in the afternoon. Camping chalets are usually fitted with four bunk beds with mattresses, chairs, and tables, and are electrically heated, with a hotplate for cooking. Other necessary equipment, such as pillows and blankets, must be provided by the camper. If you need more detailed information on camping, contact the Norwegian Automobile Club, **NAF Turistavdelingen**, Storgata 2, N-0155 Oslo 1 (tel. 02/42-94-00), for its manual. For other data, see Nor Camp Pass, above.

IN SWEDEN   Some 780 sites are available, all approved and classified by the Swedish Tourist Board, which has high standards for such facilities. The best time for a camping holiday is from mid-May to September, but some sites remain open in winter as well.

Pitching a tent costs about 35 kronor ($6.10) per night. A comprehensive book, *Camping Sverige,* is available at most Swedish bookstores.

IN FINLAND There are about 340 campsites with some 5,500 camp cabins and holiday cottages. Most have cooking facilities, kiosks, and canteens where food, cigarettes, and candy are sold. *Camping outside an official campsite is forbidden.* Camp cabins cost 100 to 200 markkaa ($27.25 to $54.55) per day. The price of an overnight stay at a campsite for a car, tent, or trailer, and two adults with or without children, is 23 to 66 markkaa ($6.25 to $18). This includes basic facilities, such as cooking and washing up. Campers with an international camping card (FICC) don't need a national camping card. Information about campsites is available at regional tourist offices. Information is also available from the **Finnish Travel Association,** Camping Department, Mikonkatu 25, PB 776, 00101 Helsinki (tel. 90/170-868).

SPECIAL ACCOMMODATIONS

IN NORWAY Norway offers one of the least expensive vacation bargains in Europe: Ideal for outdoors-loving families or groups, **log-cabin chalets** are available throughout the country, on the side of a mountain or by the sea, in a protected valley or woodland, or by a freshwater lake. Some lie in chalet or cabin colonies; others are set on remote and lofty peaks. At night, by paraffin lamplight or the glow of a log fire, you can enjoy aquavit or an early supper, as many Norwegians do. Some cabins are fully equipped with hot and cold running water, showers, and electricity; others are more primitive. Naturally, the rental price varies according to the amenities, as well as the size (some have as many as three bedrooms, most with tiered bunks). The price range is usually $200 to $480 (U.S.) weekly, the latter price for completely modern accommodations. There are chalets in most parts of the country—in the mountains, near lakes, along the coast, and in the fjord country. For a catalog giving prices, locations, and other data, contact **Den Norske Hytteformidling A/S,** Box 3207 Sagene, N-0405 Oslo 4 (tel. 02/35-67-10).

Originally built to accommodate fishermen along the coastal waters, many **fishermen's huts** or *rorbuer* are rented to visitors. Most of these shanties lie in the Lofoten Islands, but they are also located in other parts of Norway. At water's edge, sea fishing is available, and rowboats are usually available for rent. Rental prices for the huts range from 100 to 420 kroner ($16.60 to $69.70) per night, depending on the quality of the hut. For more information about this offbeat vacation, contact **Borton Overseas,** 5516 Lyndale Ave. S., Minneapolis, MN 55419 (tel. toll free 800/843-0602).

Norway with its fresh air and great outdoors is the perfect place for healthy vacation **spas.** You can begin a new life-style and get pampered at the same time at one of the following spas: **Ullensvang Body Invest,** Hotel Ullensvang, N-5774 Lofthus (tel. 054/61-100), offers spa vacations, as does **Selje AKTIV,** Selje Hotel, N-6740 Selje (tel. 057/56-107).

IN SWEDEN Many campsites also offer **cabins,** complete with bunk beds and kitchen. For families this might be a more preferred method of touring Sweden than pitching a tent. Most cabins with four beds cost 150 to 250 kronor ($26.20 to $43.65) per night, depending on the area. The Swedish Tourist Board will furnish details.

Svenska Turistföreningen, Vasagatan 48, Stockholm (tel. 08/790-31-00), also operates **mountain huts** along hiking trails and in national parks, usually in the north. These huts rent for around 80 kronor ($13.95) per person nightly in summer, 90 kronor ($15.70) in winter. Membership details are available from the STF office above.

IN FINLAND There are more than 200 **holiday villages** in Finland, many in the luxury class. These villages consist of self-contained bungalows by lakes and offer varied leisure activities, such as fishing, rowing, hiking, and swimming. Several are open all year. Some villages have hotels and restaurants for those who don't want to do their own cooking. Prices range from 1,000 to 2,500 markkaa ($272.70 to $681.75) per week in the best villages. The cottages contain two to five beds each.

There are also privately owned **holiday cottages** ranging from fishing huts on the coast to villas on the inland lakes, all fully furnished. Prices range from 750 to 6,000 markkaa ($204.55 to $1,636.20) per week, depending on location, size, and equipment.

For information and reservations, get in touch with regional tourist offices.

CHAPTER 2

GETTING TO KNOW DENMARK

The Danes may live in a small country, but they come on with a big welcome (Americans, Canadians, and their old friends, the British, are enthusiastically greeted—and in English too). Denmark should be an important stopover on even the most superficial whirlwind tour of Europe.

This country of islands is a heavily industrialized nation, known for its products and arts and crafts. However, it does boast a quarter of a million farmers (and eight million pigs).

The late British novelist Evelyn Waugh (*Brideshead Revisited*) called the Danes "the most exhilarating people of Europe." Few Danes would dispute this. And neither would I.

1. GEOGRAPHY, HISTORY & POLITICS

GEOGRAPHY

In spite of its small size, Denmark has more than 4,500 miles of irregular coastline. It is a low-lying country, yet the Danes, with their characteristic good humor, will often tell visitors about their "mountains" (the highest hill on Jutland is around 550 feet).

THE REGIONS Mainland **Jutland** is the largest land area of Denmark, connected with the continent of Europe (Germany). Jutland (sometimes written Jylland) is filled with sand dunes and moors along the west coast. Most of the rest of the land is devoted to agriculture and forestry. Fjords run miles inland on the eastern side of Jutland, the part facing Funen. Aalborg, in North Jutland, is one of the oldest cities of Denmark. Its history as a trading post goes back to the 11th century. Århus, also in Jutland, is the second-largest city of Denmark. It was a bishop's see as early as the 12th century.

The largest island of **Funen** (sometimes written Fyn) has an area of 1,150 square miles. Called the garden of Denmark, it is best known to visitors because its major city, Odense, was the birthplace of Hans Christian Andersen. It has many farms, orchards, and much rolling countryside. Romantic old castles and manor

? **DID YOU KNOW . . . ?**

- Denmark is a nation of nearly 500 islands.
- The reigning queen, Margrethe II, also designs postage stamps and opera and ballet sets.
- Second only to the Bible, the writings of Hans Christian Andersen are the most widely translated literary works in the world.
- Some historians argue that the fairytale writer Andersen was the son not of a poor cobbler, but of King Christian VIII.
- Danes pay the highest taxes on earth and have the highest suicide rate.
- Denmark has the greatest number of female priests per inhabitant.
- Denmark is the only country outside the United States that has a celebration honoring the 4th of July.

houses pepper the southern part of the island. Funen has a number of important ports, including Nyborg in the east. Svendborg is a major port at the southern end of the island.

The island of **Zealand** in the east is the most visited, because it is the home of Copenhagen, the capital of Denmark. Zealand is the largest, the wealthiest, and the most densely populated of the Danish islands. Three islands to the south of Zealand are devoted mainly to agriculture: **Falster, Lolland,** and **Moen.** Roskilde is one of the major cities of Zealand, an old royal city lying some 20 miles west of Copenhagen. Many of the kings of Denmark are buried at its ancient cathedral. Visitors are even more fond of going to Helsingør (Elsinore in English), lying 25 miles north of Copenhagen. The attraction here is what is popularly called "Hamlet's Castle."

DATELINE

- **810** The reign of the first Danish king ends.
- **940–985** Harold Bluetooth brings Christianity to Denmark.
- **1013–42** The crowns of Denmark and England are united.
- **1397** Union of Kalmar unites Denmark, Norway, and Sweden.
- **1471** Sweden bows out. Denmark and Norway are ruled by Christian I (1426–81).
- **1530** Lutheran preachers bring the Reformation to Denmark.
- **1577–1648** Long reign of *(continues)*

HISTORY

The best archeological evidence indicates settlements in what is now Denmark before 10,000 B.C., as nomadic hunters gave way to Stone Age farmers. Agriculture developed further during the Bronze Age (1,600–400 B.C.); these early settlers practiced a pagan religion.

The first recorded Danish king was Godfred, who died in 810. However, he is known to have halted the Frankish conquests of the Holy Roman Emperor Charlemagne. Godfred's successor, Hemming, made a treaty marking the Eider River as the southern border of Denmark. This border held until 1864.

Two famous kings emerged in the 10th century: Gorm (883–940) and his son, Harold Bluetooth (940–985) who both united Denmark establishing its center at Jelling. Harold also established Christianity.

Harold conquered Norway and attempted to conquer England. Harold's son, Sweyn I, succeeded in conquering England in 1013. Under Sweyn's son, Canute II (994–1035), England, Denmark, and part of Sweden were ruled under one crown. After Canute's death, however, the Danish kingdom was reduced to only Denmark. Canute's nephew, Sweyn II, ruled the Danish kingdom, and upon his death his five sons governed Denmark successively.

The Holy Roman Empire was the "overlord" of Denmark until the Danes formed their own independent leadership under Archbishop Eskil (1100–82) and King Waldemar I (1131–82). A strong monarchy was established. During a celebration at Ringsted in 1190, the church and

DATELINE

Christian IV brings prosperity, but ends in losing war with Sweden.

- **1814** Denmark cedes Norway to Sweden.
- **1866** Denmark loses Schleswig-Holstein to Prussia.
- **1915** New constitution gives Denmark universal suffrage.
- **1933** Denmark gains all of Greenland.
- **1940–45** Denmark is invaded and occupied by Nazi Germany.
- **1949** Over some protests, Denmark joins NATO.
- **1953** New constitution provides for a single-chamber parliament.
- **1972** Denmark joins the European Economic Community; Margrethe, daughter of Frederik IX to be Queen of Denmark.

state were united. Archbishop Absalon (1128–1201), a soldier and statesman, is chiefly credited with restoring Danish political and ecclesiastical independence from German influences.

Waldemar II (1170–1241) helped to strengthen the Danish government. His son, Eric IV (1216–50), followed him as king, but argued with his brothers and the church. Eric's brother, Duke Abel of Schleswig, proclaimed himself king and assassinated Eric in 1250. Civil wars ensued, and three of the four successive kings were killed in battle. Eric VI (1274–1319) also carried on wars with Norway and Sweden. This led to decay in Denmark. Between 1332 and 1340 Denmark had no king and was ruled by nobles. Waldemar IV Atterdag (1320–75) became king by signing the peace treaty of Stralsund in 1370.

UNITED SCANDINAVIA The dynasty was left without a male heir after Waldemar IV died in 1375. King Olaf, his grandson, became king. Olaf brought about a union of the crowns of Denmark and Norway, and he was also heir to the throne of Sweden. The union of Denmark with Norway came about because Olaf was the son of Margaret (1353–1412), daughter of Waldemar and wife of Haakon VI Magnusson (1339–80), king of Norway. Margaret actually ruled the country as regent. When both Haakon and Olaf died, she was acknowledged as queen of Norway and Denmark. An ambitious woman, she wanted to rule over Norway, Sweden, and Denmark.

The Union of Kalmar came about in 1397. Margaret had her nephew, Eric of Pomerania (1382–1459), crowned king of all three countries as Eric VII. Margaret, however, continued to rule the country until her death.

Eric VII had no heirs, and he tried to pass the kingdom on to one of his family members in Pomerania. That didn't go over too well with the nobility, and he was dethroned in 1439 (he went to Gotland and became a pirate). The Danish Privy Council elected Christopher of Bavaria (Eric's nephew) in 1418, making him King Christopher III.

Upon Christopher's death, the Swedes wanted autonomy. Sweden elected King Charles VIII in 1471, and Denmark and Norway took a joint king, Christian I (1426–81).

THE 16TH CENTURY Christian II (1481–1559) came to the throne in 1513, but he was not liked. He didn't believe in democracy and he was loathed for letting the mother of his mistress control the finances of the kingdom. He recaptured Sweden in 1520, but was defeated a year later by Gustavus Vasa. Christian was deposed in 1523, and he fled to the Netherlands.

His successor, Frederik I (1471–1533), signed a charter granting many privileges to the nobility. Lutheranism became the national religion. The Reformation took hold in Denmark upon Frederik's death. Conflicts between Lutherans and Catholics erupted in a civil war, which ended in 1536 with the surrender of Copenhagen. The Danish Lutheran church was founded in 1536.

This occurred during the reign of Christian III (1534–59), who tried to make the crown hereditary, but failed. Frederik II, Christian's son, was elected in 1559. Frederik launched a war against Eric XIV of Sweden, during a territorial dispute over provinces in the Baltic. This became the Seven Years' War of the North (1563–70), which the Danes failed to win.

WARS WITH SWEDEN Hostilities continued with Sweden, but the reign of Christian IV (1577–1648) was one of relative prosperity. Christiania (now Oslo) was named after him. However, in the closing years of his reign, Sweden invaded Jutland, defeating the Danes. By the Treaty of Christianopel, Denmark was forced to cede many of its former possessions to Sweden.

Frederik III (1609–70) tried to regain lost territories when Sweden went to war with Poland, but he was defeated by Charles X. Frederik ended up giving Sweden more territories than Denmark had had before the war. Charles X tried to attack Denmark so as to take over the whole country, but this time the Danes won, regaining lost territories. Sweden ended the war upon the death of Charles X in 1660.

The Skaane War (1675–79) was started by Christian V (1646–99), as the Danes attempted to gain more territories, but they lost. Frederik IV (1671–1730), his successor, resumed the war with Sweden in 1699. Named the Great Northern War, it raged from 1699 to 1730.

The 18th century brought much reform to Denmark, and the country took over colonies in the West Indies (now the U.S. Virgin Islands) and Greenland. Agriculture and trade prospered.

THE 19TH CENTURY At the start of the Napoleonic wars, Denmark was neutral. In 1801 England destroyed the Danish fleet in Copenhagen, forcing Denmark to choose Napoleon's side. It was a disaster for Denmark. Napoleon lost the war in 1814, and peace was made at Kiel. Denmark was forced to yield Norway to Sweden and Heligoland to England. The Danes sank into poverty.

The rulers following the Napoleonic wars, Frederik VI and Christian VIII, formed very conservative governments. In 1848 the people demanded a more liberal constitution. Absolute rule was abolished, and a government based on representation was set up by Frederik VII. The Danish constitution was signed on June 5, 1849.

In March 1848 the Schleswig-Holstein revolution began, lasting 2 years. The Danes initially triumphed over Prussia. But in the Treaty of Prague in 1866, Denmark again lost Schleswig-Holstein to Prussia.

A new constitution was drawn up on July 28, 1866, which was more conservative than the 1849 constitution. The conservatives quickly gained power, making reforms and improving the economy.

THE 20TH CENTURY When World War I broke out, Denmark remained neutral. However, the Danes mined their waters for Germany. The Danes joined the rest of Scandinavia in November of 1914 and adopted a uniform trade policy. Unemployment and increased taxes marked the war years. A new constitution was signed on June 5, 1915; the parliament consisted of two chambers, and equal voting rights for both men and women were acknowledged.

Because Germany was defeated in World War I, many people felt that all of Schleswig should be returned to Denmark, but in the end, the country retained only North Schleswig.

A new treaty was made between Iceland and Denmark in 1918. The countries were united under one king, although declared separate sovereign states. Danish armed forces represented Iceland.

Denmark helped to form the League of Nations and officially joined it in 1920. A crisis arose in 1931 over Greenland. As of 1921, Norway had claimed this territory. On April 5, 1933, in the Permanent Court of International Justice, Denmark gained all of Greenland.

In May 1939, Hitler asked Denmark to sign a nonaggression pact. Denmark accepted it; Norway and Sweden did not. The pact promised that Denmark and Germany would not go to war with each other for 10 years. When war broke out in 1939, Denmark declared its neutrality. Ties with Iceland were severed, and Greenland and the Faroe Islands were occupied by the United States and Great Britain, respectively.

In spite of their pact, Nazi forces invaded and occupied Denmark in 1940. In 1943, Hitler sent Gen. Hermann von Hanneken to control the Danes by martial law. Danish resistance continued against the German occupying forces. When Germany surrendered in 1945, British troops occupied Denmark. Denmark joined the United Nations.

After the war, the Liberal party under Knud Kristensen took over the government. In 1947 Kristensen resigned. The leader of the Social Democratic party under Hans Hedtoft ran the new government under King Frederik IX. The economy was sluggish until 1948.

In 1949 Denmark joined NATO. In 1953 the Scandinavian Council was formed, including Denmark, Norway, Sweden, and Iceland; the council lasted until 1961. Also in 1953, Denmark adopted a new constitution, providing for a single-chamber parliament.

In 1972 Denmark became the sole Nordic member of the EEC. That same year, Queen Margrethe, born in 1940 (the year of the Nazi invasion), became Queen of Denmark upon the death of her father, Frederik IX.

POLITICS

Denmark is a constitutional monarchy, and one of the most democratic nations on earth. The king or queen exercises power through the State Council and the Folketing (parliament). Prime ministers and other ministers are appointed by the king or queen, but approved by the parliament. There are dozens of Lower Courts of Justice, two Higher Courts, and a Supreme Court. An *ombudsman,* an independent official, supervises the constitution and investigates complaints made by citizens against government authorities.

2. FAMOUS DANES

Hans Christian Andersen (1805–75) Famous writer of fairy tales, novels, dramas, and travel books. *The Little Mermaid* is probably the most well known.

Jorn Asger (b. 1914) Artist and famous member of the COBRA group (an acronym for Copenhagen, Brussels, Amsterdam) formed after WWII. He studied with Leger in Paris and was later influenced by Edvard Munch.

Tycho Brahe (1546–1601) The astronomer who discovered the constellation Cassopeia was born in Scania, Denmark. He was also the astrologer and almanac maker for the royal family of King Frederik II. A planetarium named after him opened in Copenhagen in 1989.

Niels Bohr (1885–1932) This famous Danish scientist formulated his theory of the structure of the atom, which became the basis of quantum physics. After winning the Nobel Prize in 1922, he established a center for atomic and nuclear research. In the closing years of World War II, he worked with the physicists at Los Alamos to develop the first atomic bomb.

Benjamin Christensen (1879–?) An early Scandinavian film director whose best loved film is *Haxan* (Witchcraft through the Ages—1922) with Christensen playing the Devil.

King Christian IV (1577–1648) The country's most popular king was also a great builder, bringing the Renaissance to Denmark. As a king, he was less successful. Under his reign the Danish Army suffered dreadful losses in the 30 Years' War. "Lucky in love, unlucky in war," he died in his bedroom at Rosenborg Castle in Copenhagen.

Isak Dinesen (1885–1962) The pen name of Baroness Karen Blixen, famous for her autobiographical novel *Out of Africa* and her Gothic tales.

Carl Dreyer (1889–?) Genius of the Danish cinema. His masterpiece is *La Passion de Jeanne d'Arc,* a film consisting almost entirely of closeups. He took the trial of Joan of Arc which lasted 1½ years and condensed it to 2 hours on screen.

Jens Peter Jacobsen (1847–85) Born in Thirsted, Jutland, Jacobsen was an independent and original writer—often cited for being "self-conscious and self-critical." Also a lyrical poet, he is mainly known for *Digte of Udkast,* written near the time of his death from tuberculosis.

Søren Kierkegaard (1813–55) Philosopher and theological writer, a founding father of existentialism. His most important work was *Enten-Eller* (Either-Or).

Carl Nielsen (1865–1931) One of Denmark's great musical figures.

Adam G. Oehlenschlager (1779–1850) Leader of the Romantic Movement in Danish Theater. His best known work was *Aladdin* (1805) which was based on the *Arabian Nights.*

Bertel Thorvaldsen (1768–1844) Perhaps the greatest name in Danish sculpture. Often compared to Italy's Antoni Canova.

3. FOOD & DRINK

FOOD Danish food is the best in Scandinavia—in fact, it's among the best in Europe.

Breakfast Breakfast, to begin with, is usually big and hearty, fitting for a day of sightseeing. It usually consists of homemade breads, Danish cheeses, and often a boiled egg or salami. In most establishments, you may order bacon and eggs, two items with which this country is well stocked. You may prefer, however, simply the continental breakfast of Danish **wienerbrød** (pastry) and coffee. The "Danish" is moist, airy, and rich.

Lunch At lunch, the national institution, the ubiquitous **smørrebrød,** open-face sandwiches, is introduced. Literally, this means "bread and butter," but the Danes stack this sandwich as if it were the Leaning Tower of Pisa—then they throw in a slice of curled cucumber and bits of parsley or perhaps sliced peaches or a mushroom for added color.

Two of these sandwiches can make a more-than-filling lunch. They are seen in the grandest dining salons all the way down to the lowliest pushcart. Many restaurants offer a wide selection; guests inspect a checklist and then mark the ones they want. Some are made with sliced pork (perhaps a prune on top), roast beef with béarnaise sauce and crispy fried bits of onion, or liverpaste adorned with an olive or cucumber slice and a gelatin made from strong beef stock.

FROMMER'S SMART TRAVELER: RESTAURANTS

1. Look for the *dagens ret* (daily special), which is usually reasonable in price and prepared fresh that day.
2. The best bargain meal in Denmark is the *Danmenu* (Danish lunch or dinner): two courses offered at a fixed price.
3. Ask for the *daglig kort* (daily card), which features less expensive dishes than those on the *spisekort* (menu).
4. Look for the lunch-only, cellar restaurants where you get good value with old-world charm.
5. Do as the Danes do and make your own *smørrebrød* (open-face sandwiches).
6. Save restaurants in the Tivoli for dessert and dine outside the amusement park. Tivoli restaurants charge about 30% more.
7. Drink beer with your meal. Wine is very expensive in Denmark.
8. Patronize ethnic restaurants, especially Chinese, as they are usually cheaper.

Smørrebrød is often served as an hors d'oeuvre. The most popular, most tempting, and usually most expensive of these delicacies is prepared with a mound of tiny Danish shrimp, on which a lemon slice and caviar often perch, sometimes fresh dill. The "ugly duckling" of the smørrebrød family: anything with a cold sunny-side-up egg on top of it.

Dinner The Danes keep farmers' hours for dinner: 6:30pm is common, although restaurants remain open much later. Many main-course dishes are commonly known to North Americans, but they are prepared with a distinct flourish in Denmark—dishes such as **lever med løg** (liver and fried onion), **bøf** (beef in a thousand different ways), **lammesteg** (roast lamb), or that old reliable, **flaeskesteg med rødkål** (roast pork with red cabbage).

The country's cooks are really noted for their fresh **fish** dishes. The tiny Danish shrimp (**rejer**) are splendid. Herring and kippers meet with much enthusiasm. Really top-notch fish dishes include plaice (rodspaette), salmon (laks), mackerel (makrel), and boiled cod (kogt torsk).

Danish **cheese** is consumed at any of the three meals a day, then eaten on a premidnight smørrebrød at the Tivoli. Danish bleu is too familiar to need definition. For something softer and milder, try Havarti.

Among Danish specialties most worth sampling: **frikadeller,** the Danish meatballs or rissoles, prepared in numerous different ways. Also try a Danish omelet with a rasher of bacon covered with chopped chives and served in a skillet. A familiar dish is Danish hamburger patties topped with fried onions and coated with a rich brown gravy.

Choice **desserts:** Danish apple Charlotte, best when decorated with whipped cream, dried breadcrumbs, and chopped almonds. Another treat is *rødgrød med fløde*—prepared in numerous ways, but basically a jellied fruit-studded juice, over which the diner pours thick cream.

DRINK As for your drink, **Carlsberg or Tuborg beer** is the national beverage of Denmark. A bottle of pilsner costs about half the price of the stronger, more decoratively labeled export beer. To keep from flattening his bank account, a Dane relies on the low-priced **fadøl** (draft beer). Foreigners on skimpy budgets are advised to do the same.

You may gravitate more to **aquavit** (schnapps to the English), which comes from the city of Aalborg in northern Jutland. The Danes, who usually drink it at mealtime, follow it with a beer chaser. Made from a distilling process using potatoes, aquavit should only be served icy cold.

For those with a daintier taste, the world-famous Danish liqueur, **Cherry Heering,** is a delightful drink, made from cherries as the name implies, and it's for consumption at any time other than during meals.

4. RECOMMENDED BOOKS, FILMS & RECORDINGS

BOOKS

HISTORY & PHILOSOPHY *A Kierkegaard Anthology,* edited by Robert Bretall (Princeton University Press), explores the work of the Copenhagen-born philosopher who developed an almost-pathological sense of involvement in theology. A representative selection of some of his more significant works are included.

Copenhagen, A Historical Guide, by Torben Ejlersen (published by Høst & Søn in Denmark, and available at most bookstores there), an 88-page guide, takes you on a brief tour of the city that began as a ferry landing and became one of the most important capitals of Europe.

Of Danish Ways, written by two Danish-Americans, Ingeborg S. MacHiffic and

Margaret A. Nielsen (Harper & Row, 1984), a delightful account of a land and its people, has a little bit of everything: history, social consciousness, customs, food, handcrafts, art, music, and theater.

The Story of Denmark, by Steward Oakley (published in England), is one of the best accounts of the fascinating Middle Ages in Denmark. Other periods, including modern history, are included.

The Vikings, by Johannes Brondsted (Penguin), is perhaps the best book on the subject, a virtual saga on the men who once terrorized Europe. Customs, social life, religious beliefs, even Viking art are explored in this well-written book which does more than trace the military legacy of these once-mighty people.

BIOGRAPHY & LITERATURE *Andersen's Fairy Tales,* by Hans Christian Andersen (New American Library), and *The Complete Hans Christian Andersen Fairy Tales* (Crown). The most translated writer in the world, Andersen published his first children's stories in 1835—and the rest is history. The most famous children's storywriter of all time, these anthologies include all his most important works such as *The Little Mermaid, The Tinderbox, The Princess and the Pea,* among others.

Danish Literature: A Short Critical Guide, by Paul Borum (Nordic Books), is a well-written review that explores Danish literature from the Middle Ages to the 1970s.

Out of Denmark: Danish Women Writers Today (Nordic Books) covers an almost "forgotten person," the Danish woman writer, explored here in critical essays. It's considered a "must read" for those who think Karen Blixen is the only woman writer the country ever produced.

Out of Africa (Modern Library), *Letters from Africa* (University of Chicago Press), and *Seven Gothic Tales* (Random House) are all by Karen Blixen (Isak Dinesen), who gained renewed fame with the release of the 1985 film *Out of Africa,* with Meryl Streep and Robert Redford. One of the major authors of the 20th century, twice nominated for the Nobel Prize, Blixen's world lives on in these almost-flawless stories. *Seven Gothic Tales* is her masterpiece. Another title by Blixen is *Winter's Tales* (Penguin).

Isak Dinesen, by Judith Thurman (St. Martin's Press), is the definitive biography of the Danish writer who has been called "witch, sybil, lion hunter, coffee planter, aristocrat, and despot, a paradox in herself and a creator of paradoxes." The story chronicles an amazing life from an unhappy childhood in Denmark to marriage to Baron Blixen to immigration to Kenya to her passionate love affair with Denys Finch Hatton.

Isak Dinesen/Karen Blixen: The Work and the Life, by Aage Henriksen (St. Martin's Press). One of Denmark's leading contemporary critics and a friend of the writer explores both the woman's work and the persona she created. Dinesen's powerful personality comes across in the pages.

FILMS

Pelle the Conqueror and *Katinka* have been the best-received Danish films in recent times. They played to acclaim at both festivals and arthouses in Europe and America. *Pelle the Conqueror* won the Oscar as best foreign film in Hollywood.

Heaven and Hell (Himmel og Helvede) was directed by Morten Arnfred. Karina Skands plays Maria, a '60s child who wants to be a violinist but whose parents try to stifle her artistic ambitions.

Baby Doll brings a sinister tone, the story of a young mother on maternity leave at a broken-down farm. It's a bit of a psychological thriller and is very well done, bringing a self-inflicted nightmare to the quiet, tranquil countryside.

Århus by Night, directed by Nils Malmros, disappointed many critics but won some fans. It is a virtual tribute to Truffaut's *Day for Night.* It tells the story of the making of a film in an otherwise drab and provincial town.

The Danes continue to excel in films for children, as exemplified in *Shower of Gold* (Guldregn) directed by Søren Kragh-Jacobsen. Four children in a suburb of Copenhagen discover a box stuffed with banknotes.

RECORDINGS

CLASSICAL In Denmark, the 125th anniversary of its greatest musical genius, **Carl Nielsen** (1865–1931) was commemorated in 1990. The occasion was marked with a fresh release of all his important works. These include his operas *Saul og David* (Saul and David; 1903) and *Maskerade* (1906), along with his symphonies, concertos, and choral and chamber music. Other important works in release include *Fynsk Forar* (The Spring of Funen) and *Taken Letter*.

FOLK Paul Dissing has a gravel-like, unresonant voice, but is one of the most popular recording stars in Danish history. Danes say his humor cannot be translated. Some, but not all, of his music has been accompanied by Benny Andersen. Dissing's most popular album to date is *Ten Songs of Paul Dissing and Benny Andersen*.

Singing alone, playing a guitar, and occasionally backed up by one other guitarist, **Erik Grib** sings modern interpretations of 19th-century Danish folksongs. His 19th-century patriotic and nostalgic odes to Denmark profoundly touch his listeners. His most popular album to date is *To Sonia*.

Lars Lilholt sings nostalgic and richly poetic interpretations of Danish folk songs. His most famous album is *Near Contact*.

Kurt Ravn is better known as a mature actor in stage and cinema, but each of his recording efforts meets with critical approval. Recorded in Danish, his music is whimsical and poetic. His most popular album to date is *The Four Seasons*.

POP/ROCK Hanne Boel has been called Denmark's answer to Tina Turner. Moderately electronic with highly danceable music, her work is about life. Sometimes her music is accompanied by backup singers from West Africa. Her most famous album is *Dark Passion*.

D.A.D. (Disneyland after Dark). This group's music is comic, deliberately rude, and punkish. Their videos are a scream, and their most popular album to date is *No Fuel Left for the Pilgrims*.

Hotel Hunger is considered one of the best groups in Denmark. Oddly, their first success came in America. Now back in Denmark, they prefer not to select a single spokesperson from their ranks. Their electronic music meets with wide approval, as did their best-known album, *This Is Where the Fun Starts*.

TV-2 (Stephan Brandt) is a Danish singer whose most famous slogan translates as "Real Men Don't Want to Hear Nonsense Anymore" (that is, from their ex-wives, present wives, alienated girlfriends, rueful parents, and frustrated bosses). This slogan became one of the most copied in the Danish advertising industry. The lyrics of TV-2 are far more important than the tunes.

PLANNING A TRIP TO DENMARK

This chapter is devoted to the nitty gritty of planning a trip to Denmark—costs, events, itineraries, and detailed practicalities like taxes, tipping, and emergencies. It should be read in conjunction with Chapter 1.

1. CURRENCY & COSTS

CASH/CURRENCY For currency, the Danes use the **krone** (crown), or **kroner** in the plural, which breaks down into 100 **øre.** At press time, 1 krone equals approximately 16½¢ U.S., or 5.95 kroner to the U.S. dollar. Of course, rates are subject to change, and you should check current rates before you go.

Banknotes in circulation include 50, 100, 500, and 1,000 kroner. Still in circulation (but being phased out) are 20-krone banknotes. Coins minted are 25 øre, 50 øre, 1 krone, and 5, 10, and 20 kroner. Still in circulation (but being phased out) are 5- and 10-øre coins.

When converting your currency into Danish kroner, beware of varying exchange rates. In general, banks offer the best rate, but even banks charge a commission for the service, often $2 or $3, depending on the transaction. Your hotel will offer the worst exchange rate.

THE KRONE & THE DOLLAR

The dollar prices given in the Denmark section of this book, and in the table below, are based on an exchange rate of 1 krone = 16.8¢ U.S. Since world currencies fluctuate in value from time to time, these dollar values are given only as a guideline and may not be accurate at the time of your visit.

Kroner	U.S	Kroner	U.S
0.50	.08	50	8.41
1	.17	80	13.45
5	.84	100	16.81
10	1.68	125	21.01
15	2.52	175	29.42
25	4.20	200	33.62
30	5.04	300	50.43

WHAT THINGS COST IN COPENHAGEN | U.S. $

Taxi from the airport to the city center	19.00
Taxi from Central Station to Amalienborg Castle	9.00
Subway from Central Station to the suburbs	4.00
Local telephone call	.17
Double room at the Hotel Angleterre (deluxe)	336.00
Double room, with bath, at the Absalon Hotel (moderate)	176.00
Double room, without bath, at the Hotel du Nord (budget)	85.00
Buffet breakfast for one in a hotel	10.00–22.00
Lunch for one at the Els (moderate)	29.40
Lunch for one at Axelborg Bodega (budget)	12.60
Dinner for one, without wine, at Kommandaten (deluxe)	52.95
Dinner for one, without wine, at Kellesbech-Thalund (moderate)	34.95
Dinner for one, without wine, at Parnas (budget)	16.50
Pint of beer (draft pilsner)	3.20
Coca-Cola	2.35
Cup of coffee	1.80
Roll of Kodacolor film, 36 exposures	4.70
Admission to the Tivoli	4.70
Movie ticket	6.75–8.40
Theater ticket (at the Royal Theater)	25.00–38.00

WHAT THINGS COST IN ODENSE | U.S. $

Average taxi ride	6.00
Local telephone call	.17
Double room at the Hotel H.C. Andersen (deluxe)	167.25
Double room, with bath, at the Windsor Hotel (moderate)	100.85
Double room, with bath, at Missionhotellet Ansgar (budget)	84.00
Buffet breakfast for one in a hotel	8.00
Lunch for one at Den Gamle Kro (moderate)	15.15
Lunch for one at Sortebro Kro (budget)	9.00
Dinner for one, without wine, at Under Lindetraet (deluxe)	45.00
Dinner for one, without wine, at Den Gamle Kro (moderate)	31.95
Dinner for one, without wine, at Sortebro Kro (budget)	20.00
Pint of beer (draft pilsner)	3.00
Coca-Cola	1.60
Cup of coffee	2.25
Roll of Kodacolor film, 36 exposures	9.00
Admission to Funen village	2.50
Movie ticket	6.50

2. WHEN TO GO — CLIMATE, HOLIDAYS & EVENTS

CLIMATE Denmark is mild for a Scandinavian country—New England farmers experience harsher winters. Summer temperatures average between 61° and 77° Fahrenheit. Winter temperatures seldom go below 30° Fahrenheit, thanks to the warming waters of the Gulf Stream. Mid-April to November is a good time to visit.

Denmark's Average Daytime Temperatures & Rainfall

	Jan	Feb	Mar	Apr	May	June	July	Aug	Sept	Oct	Nov	Dec
Temp. (°F)	32	32	35	44	53	60	64	63	57	49	42	37
Rainfall "	1.9	1.5	1.2	1.5	1.7	1.8	2.8	2.6	2.4	2.3	1.9	1.9

HOLIDAYS There may be a slight variation in some of these dates, so check with a local tourist office. Danish public holidays (and dates of those that do not vary) are: January 1 (New Year's Day), Maundy Thursday, Good Friday, Easter Sunday, Easter Monday, May 1 (Labor Day), Common Prayers Day, Ascension Day, Whit Sunday, Whit Monday, June 5 (Constitution Day), December 25 (Christmas Day), and December 26 (Boxing Day).

DENMARK CALENDAR OF EVENTS

JULY

☐ **July 4,** Rebild, near Aalborg. One of the only places outside the United States to honor American Independence Day. For more information, contact the Aalborg Tourist Office, Osterågade 8, DK-9000 Aalborg (tel. 12-60-22).

☐ **Sønderborg Tilting Festival.** Dating back to the Middle Ages, the "tilting at the ring" tradition has only survived in the old town of Sønderborg on the island of Als in southern Jutland. While riding at a gallop, the horseman must use his lance to see how many times out of 24 he can take the ring. Parades, music, and entertainment are included. July 7–10. For more information, contact the Turistbureau, Rådhustorvet 7, DK-6400 Sønderborg (tel. 74-42-35-55).

AUGUST

☐ **Fire Festival Regatta,** Silkeborg. Denmark's oldest and biggest festival, its main features are nightly cruises on the lakes with thousands of candles illuminating the shores. On the last night, there is a fireworks display, the largest and most spectacular in northern Europe. Entertainment is provided by popular Danish artists at a large fun fair. For more information, contact the Turistbureau, Torvet 9, DK-8600 Silkeborg (tel. 86-82-19-11). August 2–4.

SEPTEMBER

☐ **Århus Festival Week.** A wide range of cultural activities, including opera, jazz, classical music, folk music, ballet, and theater are presented. Sporting activities and street parties abound as well. It is the largest cultural festival in Scandinavia. For more information, contact the Århus Tourist Office, Rådhuset, Århus C, DK-8000 Århus (tel. 86-12-16-00). Early September.

COPENHAGEN CALENDAR OF EVENTS

MAY

☐ **Ballet and Opera Festival.** Classical and modern dance and two operatic masterpieces are presented at the Old Stage of the Royal Theater in Copenhagen. For tickets, contact Royal Theater, Box 2185, DK-1017 København K, Denmark. Mid-May to June.

JUNE

☐ **Carnival in Copenhagen.** A great citywide event. There's also a children's carnival. June 2–4.

JULY

☐ **Copenhagen Jazz Festival.** Features international jazz musicians in the streets, squares, and theaters. Pick up a copy of *Copenhagen This Week* to find the venues of various performances. July 6–13.

AUGUST

☐ **Fall Ballet Festival.** The Royal Danish Ballet, acclaimed internationally, returns to its home to perform at the Old Stage of the Royal Theater, just before the tourist season ends. For tickets, contact the Royal Theater, Box 2185, DK-1017 København K, Denmark. Mid-August to September 1.

3. GETTING AROUND

BY PLANE

For those in a hurry, **SAS** (tel. 33-15-52-66 in Copenhagen) operates daily service between Copenhagen and points on Jutland's mainland. It's about 40 minutes to fly from Copenhagen to Aalborg, 35 minutes from Copenhagen to Århus, and 30 minutes from Copenhagen to Odense's Beldringe Airport.

Fares to other Danish cities are sometimes included in a transatlantic ticket at no extra charge, providing the extra cities are specified when the ticket is written.

For air travel in Denmark, **Danair** connects with Maersk Air, SAS, and Cimber Air. (Danair is not to be confused with a British Airline, Dan Air, which services parts of Scotland.) Between these local carriers, all parts of Denmark are accessible, including the distant Faroe Islands. An English-speaking sales representative will answer the phone if you call the sales office in Billund, Jutland (tel. 75-33-22-44).

In addition to flights within Denmark, Danair flies to Britain, the Netherlands, Norway, and Sweden, and offers competitive fares when compared to larger airlines.

BY TRAIN

Each city or town in Denmark is linked to Copenhagen by rail. Lyntog (tel. 33-14-17-01) express trains are fast and efficient.

On any train within Denmark, an adult accompanying a child between 4 and 11 will pay only 50% of the fare.

Senior citizens receive a 33% discount on one-way or round-trip tickets at any time of the day or year. No identification is needed at the time of purchase, although the conductor who checks your ticket might request proof of age if there is any doubt.

For regular passengers, regardless of age, there are reductions for travel to any point in Denmark on Tuesday, Wednesday, Thursday, and Saturday. You can also receive a discount if you plan to return to your point of departure on the same day.

A monthly ticket allowing unlimited rail travel throughout Denmark offers substantial reductions, although such a pass is valid only for first-class travel. Inquire at the Central Station in Copenhagen (tel. 33-14-17-01). A passport-size photo is needed. The cost of the card, called **Danmarks Kort**, is 2,050 kroner ($344.60).

BY BUS

Unless you rent a private car, a bus is sometimes your only link to certain villages. In rural Denmark, buses connect with railway terminals.

Round-trip bus tickets are offered at one-way prices for seniors. These reductions are not available, however, on Saturday, Sunday, and during Christmas and Easter. All trips must be more than 20 miles for this reduction to be granted.

BY CAR

RENTALS Hertz, Avis, and Budget all offer well-serviced, well-maintained fleets within Denmark. Depending on the company, you'll need to reserve a car between 1 day and 3 weeks in advance to guarantee the lowest rates.

Budget builds a certain amount of insurance into its rates that is adequate for most drivers and most accidents. If you have a mishap, however, and didn't purchase additional insurance, you'll be responsible for the first 5,700 kroner ($958.15) of damage on small and medium-sized cars, and even more on the expensive cars. You can waive all financial responsibility by buying an optional insurance policy costing between 80 kroner ($13.45) and 100 kroner ($16.80) per day.

At both Hertz and Avis, all insurance for any potential mishap is automatically built into the rate. While this might give you peace of mind, it's usually more expensive.

Budget (tel. toll free 800/527-0700 in the U.S.) has only 10 rental locations within Denmark compared to 29 for Avis and 30 for Hertz, but at press time they were the cheapest. Budget's two Copenhagen locations are in the main arrival section of the Copenhagen airport (tel. 32-52-39-00) and in the center of Copenhagen at Nyropsgade 6, DK-1602 Copenhagen V (tel. 33-13-39-00).

Hertz (tel. toll-free 800/654-3001 in the U.S.) offers a wide selection of cars. Rates and advance booking are 21 days before your departure from home (not 21 days before the anticipated pickup of the car). With a 21-day advance booking, Hertz charges $329 per week for their smallest car, with tax and insurance premiums included. Hertz's office in central Copenhagen is at Ved Vesterport 3 (tel. 31-12-77-00). Another office is at the Copenhagen airport (tel. 31-50-93-00).

Avis maintains two offices in Copenhagen: one in the arrivals hall of the Copenhagen airport and another at Kampmannsgade 1 (tel. 31-12-77-00 for both offices, or toll free 800/331-2112 in the U.S.). Avis builds all insurance premiums, but not the 22% tax, into its rates. Its smallest car, available only at Copenhagen airport, is

$271 per week, with mileage. A roomier Ford Fiesta rents for $308 per week, with mileage.

A small company based in Harrison, New York, **Kremwell** sometimes offers short-term car-rental rates through European-based car-rental outfits. For information, call toll free 800/678-0678.

DRIVING RULES To drive in Denmark, you must have a valid driver's license from your home country. You need car registration papers, a Green Card indicating insurance coverage, a national identity sticker for your car, and a red warning triangle in case of breakdown. If you're renting a car, the firm will supply these items.

Follow road signs (the markings are of the international variety) and drive on the right, passing on the left. Always stop for pedestrian crossings. Both driver and passengers are required by law to wear seat belts. Left dipping headlights are illegal in Denmark. For the most part, Danes are careful, considerate drivers. For information on good map sources, see "Fast Facts," at the end of this chapter.

Whatever you do, don't drink and drive—you could end up in prison.

BREAKDOWNS/ASSISTANCE In case of a car breakdown, emergency help and towing in Zealand is provided by **Falck** (tel. 33-14-22-22) in Copenhagen. Use the orange emergency phones along the motorways.

BY FERRY

Ferries connect much of Denmark, providing a vital link between major points like Funen and Zealand. During the summer, it's important to book ahead, particularly if you want to take your car aboard. Bookings on any of the state-owned ferries can be made at the **Central Railway Station** in Copenhagen or through any of the local offices.

Reservations are not necessary for short crossings: Tickets are purchased on board and service is frequent.

For a day trip from Copenhagen to Sweden, drive to Dragør, south of Copenhagen, and take the ferry to Limhamn, Sweden, 3 miles south of Malmö. Once there, visit Malmö and Helsingborg. Return to Denmark on the car-ferry to Helsingør (site of "Hamlet's castle") and drive south back to Copenhagen. Round-trip cost for a car, a driver, and up to four passengers is 315 kroner ($52.95), providing it is just 1 day.

For additional information on ferries and getting to Sweden, see Chapter 1.

BY BICYCLE

Almost all Danish towns have bicycle rentals—check with the local tourist offices. Youth hostels are close enough to each other (about 12 miles apart) to make a biking trip possible. For those worried about their endurance, you can rent bicycles with auxiliary motors.

DVL Travel in Copenhagen runs 6 to 10 "ready-made" holiday bicycle excursions. Prices depend on whether you stay at youth hostels or at low-cost inns or hotels. All age groups are accepted (the oldest participant so far has been 78). Tours run from 3 to 9 days, and many offer a choice of full or half board. Contact the **Danish Tourist Board**, 655 Third Ave., New York, NY 10017 (tel. 212/949-2333), for information.

Bicycles can be rented cheaply at train stations in North Zealand and returned at another station. For information on the **Take-the-Train, Rent-a-Bike** route, contact the Tourist Information Office or the train station. The cost is about $5 a day.

SUGGESTED ITINERARIES

IF YOU HAVE 1 WEEK

Days 1–3: Spend your first 3 days in Copenhagen. After spending the first day recovering from the flight, have dinner at the Tivoli (in summer). Spend the morning of the second day taking one of our walking tours (see Chapter 6); then (again if it's summer) spend the afternoon wandering through Tivoli Gardens, listening to the free music. Devote Day 3 to more serious sightseeing, including visits to Christiansborg Palace and the Ny Carlsberg Glyptotek.

Day 4: Leave Copenhagen and head north, stopping over at the modern art museum, Louisiana, before heading to Helsingør, site of Kronberg Castle of Hamlet fame. Either spend the night in Helsingør or return to Copenhagen.

Day 5: Journey to Odense on the island of Funen, birthplace of Hans Christian Andersen. Spend the rest of the day and evening exploring its many attractions. What you didn't get done on Day 5 you can see the next morning.

Day 6: Stop in Roskilde, to see its cathedral and Viking Ship Museum. Return to Copenhagen and spend the night.

Day 7: Try another walking tour, and schedule interior visits to Rosenborg Castle and, if you have time, the National Museum. Return to the Tivoli for a farewell drink.

IF YOU HAVE 2 WEEKS

Day 1: Recover from jet lag and have dinner at the Tivoli (in summer) or at Scala (a restaurant complex across from Tivoli) if it's off-season.

Day 2: In the morning, take our first walking tour (see Chapter 6). Spend the afternoon wandering around Tivoli Gardens.

Day 3: Take another walking tour and visit Christiansborg Palace and Ny Carlsberg Glyptotek.

Day 4: Head north from Copenhagen, visit the modern art museum, Louisiana, and have lunch at Helsingør, site of Kronborg Castle of Hamlet fame. Spend the night in Helsingør.

Day 5: Explore North Zealand, with visits to the royal palace at Fredensborg and the 17th-century Frederiksborg Castle at Hillerød. Spend the night in Helsingør.

Day 6: Return to Copenhagen and take another walking tour. Visit Rosenborg Castle and the National Museum.

Day 7: Still in Copenhagen, explore the other attractions of Zealand, journeying outside the capital to the open-air museum, Frilandmusset. Head to Roskilde for lunch, visiting the cathedral, the Viking Ship Museum, and the Iron Age Village at Lejre.

Day 8: Head south from Copenhagen to explore South Zealand. Visit the old market town of Køge, Vallø Castle, and Selso Slot. Spend the night in a typical inn on Zealand.

Day 9: Head west, crossing mid-Zealand. At Korsør, take a ferry to Nyborg. Visit Nyborg Castle before driving to Odense to explore the city of Hans Christian Andersen. Stop overnight in Odense.

Day 10: Spend time exploring more of Odense. Then visit the Viking ship at Ladby and Egeskov Castle outside Odense.

Day 11: Drive south from Odense to Svendborg. Visit the nearby islands of Thurø and Tåsinge.

Day 12: From Svendborg, board a ferry (make a reservation) and head for the island of Aerø. Spend the night in the capital, Aerøskøbing, or at an island inn.

Day 13: Leave Aerø and return to Svendborg by ferry. Drive north toward Odense along Route 9 until you connect with the E20 west, the highway that will take you into Jutland. In Jutland, take Route 32 at the junction with the E20 to Ribe. Spend the night in Ribe.

Day 14: Leave Ribe in the morning and head for Silkeborg to visit Sky Mountain. Take a ride on a paddle steamer on Silkeborg Lakes. Visit the Silkeborg Museum. From Silkeborg, drive to Århus where you can explore the Old Town. Visit also Århus's Tivoli amusement park. Spend the night.

IF YOU HAVE 3 WEEKS

Days 1–12: Follow the first 12 days of the above itinerary.

Day 13: Leave Aerø in the morning and return by ferry to Svendborg. From Svendborg, take Route 44 west to Fåborg to explore the largely bucolic southwestern corner of the island.

Day 14: From Fåborg, take Route 43 north to Odense and connect with the express highway, E20, heading west to Jutland. Drive to Jelling, the seat of the 10th-century kings of Denmark. Accommodations are limited in Jelling, so stay overnight in Vejle, a short drive southeast of Jelling.

Day 15: From Jelling, take Routes E45 and 32 cross country to Ribe, of stork's-nest fame. Explore its attractions, including the cathedral and the smallest house in Denmark. Spend the night.

Day 16: Drive northwest from Ribe to Esbjerg. Take the 20-minute ferry ride to Fanø, an island of heather-covered moors and windswept sand dunes. Overnight at one of the *kros* (inns) on the island.

Day 17: From Fanø, take the return ferry to Esbjerg and head north along various routes to Silkeborg. Visit Sky Mountain and take a ride on a paddleboat steamer on Silkeborg Lakes. Also visit the Silkeborg Museum. Overnight in Silkeborg.

Day 18: From Silkeborg, drive east to Århus. Explore its many attractions, including Den Gamle By (the Old Town). Overnight in Århus.

Day 19: Leave Århus and drive to Ebeltoft, 32 miles northeast. Continue on to Randers for the night, or for more atmosphere, spend the night at Hvidsten Kro, on the outskirts of Hvidsten, lying between Randers and Mariager.

Day 20: Head north to Aalborg, where you can visit Lindholm Hoje, the largest Scandinavian burial site of the Viking period, the Aalborg Zoo, and yet another Tivoli.

Day 21: After Aalborg, spend the rest of the day exploring North Jutland, heading to either Frederikshavn, Hirtshals, or Skagen for an overnight stop. Skagen is the far northern tip of Jutland. At Frederikshavn you can take a car-ferry to Oslo to begin exploring Norway, or a car-ferry to Gothenburg if you're ready for Sweden.

 DENMARK

American Express Offices in Copenhagen are at Amagertorv 18 (tel. 33-12-23-01), open Monday through Friday from 9am to 5pm (April to October, also on Saturday from 9am to noon).

Business Hours Most **banks** in Denmark are open Monday through Friday from 9:30am to 4pm (on Thursday to 6pm), but outside Copenhagen banking hours vary. **Stores** are generally open Monday through Thursday from 9am to 5:30pm, on Friday from 9am to 7 or 8pm, and on Saturday from noon to 2pm; most are closed Sunday.

Camera/Film Film is so expensive that I suggest you bring what you'll need. Film processing is also expensive, so wait until you're home. There are no special restrictions on taking photographs, except in certain museums (signs are generally posted). When in doubt, ask.

Cigarettes The largest-selling brand is Prince. Cigarettes are available everywhere: Danish cigarettes are 28 kroner ($1.65) a pack; international brands cost 30 kroner ($1.80) per pack.

Customs Nearly all items that can safely be viewed as "personal" are allowed in duty-free. Tobacco is limited: you can bring in either 400 cigarettes or 100 cigars. You can also bring in 1½ liters (a standard bottle) of spirits or 2 liters of strong wine, depending on whether you are coming into Denmark from an EC or non-EC country. There are no restrictions on the import of currency into Denmark. Residents of Denmark can take out of the country only 5,000 kroner, but nonresidents can take a higher amount if they prove that the Danish kroner were brought in with them or obtained by conversion of foreign currency they imported.

Upon leaving Denmark, U.S. citizens who have been outside their home country for 48 hours or more are allowed to take home $400 worth of merchandise duty free—if they have claimed no similar exemption within the past 30 days. If you make purchases in Denmark, keep your receipts.

Dentists For a dentist in Copenhagen, see "Fast Facts" in Chapter 4. If you need emergency dental service outside Copenhagen, ask your hotel or host to phone **Falck** (tel. 53-14-22-22) for information about service in your area.

Doctors Most areas have doctors on duty 24 hours a day on Saturday, Sunday, and holidays; weekday emergency hours are 4pm to 7:30am. Every doctor speaks English.

Driving Rules See "Getting Around," above, in this chapter.

Drug Laws There are severe penalties in Denmark for possession, use, purchase, sale, or manufacturing of drugs. The quantity of the controlled substance is more important than the actual type of substance someone might possess. If you're caught with under 5 grams of hard drugs (heroin, LSD, or amphetamines) or under 50 grams of soft drugs (marijuana), you will usually need to pay a heavy fine and face possible deportation. Possession of anything more than those quantities will probably elicit a prison term of between 3 months and 15 years, depending on the circumstance. Danish police are particularly strict with any cases involving sales of drugs to children, the courts tending to impose maximum prison terms in such cases.

Drugstores They're known as *apoteker* in Danish, and are open Monday through Thursday from 9am to 5:30pm, on Friday from 9am to 7pm, and on Saturday from 9am to 1pm.

Electricity Voltage is generally 220 volts A.C., 50 to 60 cycles, but in many camping sites 110-volt power plugs are also available. Adapters and transformers may be purchased in Denmark. It's always best to check at your hotel desk before using any electrical outlet.

Embassies In Copenhagen, the **U.S. Embassy** is at Dag Hammarsjölds Allé 24, DK-2100 København Ø (tel. 31-42-31-44); the **British Embassy,** at Kastelsvej 36-40, DK-2100 København Ø (tel. 31-26-46-00); the **Canadian Embassy,** at Kristen Berniskowsgade I, DK-1105 København K (tel. 33-12-22-99); and the **Australian Embassy,** at Kristianiagade 21, DK-2100 København (tel. 31-26-22-44).

Emergencies Dial 000 for the **fire department,** the **police,** an **ambulance,** or to report a **sea or air accident.** Emergency calls from public telephone kiosks are free (no coins).

Etiquette *God dag* (good day) is said to everyone. *Tak* means "thanks." You should bring flowers (never white ones) if invited to a private home for dinner. Shaking hands is virtually a ritual when you meet someone and take leave. Both men and women shake hands.

Holidays See "When to Go," above, in this chapter.

Language Danish is the national tongue. English is commonly spoken, especially among young people. You should have few, if any, language barriers. For the best phrase book, purchase a copy of *Danish for Travellers* published by Berlitz.

Laundry For listings of laundries, see the individual city chapters.

Liquor Laws To consume alcohol in Danish bars, restaurants, or cafés, a client must be 18 or older. However, there are no age limits imposed upon children under 18 for either drinking at home or drinking, for example, from a bottle in a public park. Danish police tend to be lenient unless drinkers become raucous or uncontrollable. This policy changes abruptly as soon as the driver of a vehicle is apprehended while intoxicated. It is strictly illegal to drive with a blood/alcohol ratio of 0.8 or more. This could be produced by two drinks. If the ratio is 1.5, motorists will pay a serious fine. If the blood/alcohol ratio is more than 1.5, drivers can lose their license. If the ratio is 2.0 or more, a prison term of at least 14 days might follow. Such a ratio is usually produced by six to seven drinks.

Mail   In general, **post offices** are open Monday through Friday from 9 or 10am to 5 or 6pm and on Saturday from 9am to noon; closed Sunday. It costs 4.75 kroner (80¢) to send a regular letter by air or surface mail to the U.S. or Canada and takes from 5 to 8 days to arrive. The rate for an ordinary postcard by air or surface is 3.75 kroner (60¢). The purchasing of **stamps** depends on the town, the circumstances, and the nearness of the post office. You might find stamps for sale at local gas stations or a butcher shop. All **mailboxes** are painted red and contain an embossed crown and trumpet of the Danish Postal Society. To mail a parcel, you must go to the post office.

Maps   The best map for touring Denmark is part of the series published by Hallwag. It can be purchased at all major bookstores in Copenhagen, including the most centrally located one, **Boghallen**, Rådhuspladsen 37 (tel. 33-11-85-11), in the Town Hall Square.

Newspapers/Magazines   English-language newspapers are sold at all major news kiosks in Copenhagen, but are much harder to come by in the provinces. London papers are flown in for early-morning deliveries, but you may find the *International Herald-Tribune* more interesting. Pick up a copy of the booklet "Copenhagen This Week," printed in English, which contains useful information.

Pets   A dog arriving from a rabies-free country is generally admitted if nothing is found wrong with it. Special permits are required to bring in animals other than dogs or cats. Many Danish hotels allow visitors to bring in their dogs, providing the dog is quiet and safe to be around. Fines can be issued if your dog fouls the pavement. Take the animal to one of the special "dog toilets" found in city parks.

Police   Dial 000 for police assistance.

Radio/TV   There are no English-language radio or TV stations broadcasting from Denmark. Only radios and TVs with satellite reception can receive a cornucopia of signals from countries such as Britain. News programs in English are broadcast Monday through Saturday at 8:30am on Radio Denmark, 93.85 MHz. Radio 1 (on 90.8 MHz VHF) features news and classical music. Channels 2 and 3 (96.5/93.9 MHz) include some entertainment, broadcast lighter news items, and offer light music. Most TV stations transmit from 7:30 to 11:30pm. Most films (many American ones) are shown in their original languages, with Danish subtitles.

Rest Rooms   All big plazas, such as Town Hall Square in Copenhagen, have public lavatories. In small towns and villages, head for the marketplace. Hygienic standards are usually adequate. Sometimes both men and women patronize the same toilets. Otherwise, men's rooms are marked HERRER or H, and women's rooms are marked DAMER or D.

Safety   Whenever you're traveling in an unfamiliar city or country, stay alert. Be aware of your immediate surroundings. Wear a moneybelt and don't sling your camera or purse over your shoulder; wear the strap diagonally across your body. This will minimize the possibility of your becoming a victim of crime. Every society has its criminals, but it's your responsibility to be alert.

Taxes   Denmark imposes a 22% VAT (Value-Added Tax) on goods and services. In Denmark it is known as Moms (pronounced "mumps"). Special tax-free exports are possible, and many stores will mail goods home to you, circumventing Moms. If you want to take your purchases with you, look for shops displaying DANISH TAX-FREE SHOPPING notices. Such shops offer tourists tax refunds for personal export. This refund applies to purchases of 600 kroner ($100.85) and up for U.S. and Canadian visitors. Your tax-free invoice must be stamped by Danish Customs when you leave the country. You can receive your refund at Copenhagen's Kastrup International Airport when you depart. If you depart by land or by sea, you can receive your refund by mail. Requests for refunds are to be sent by mail to Danish Tax-Free Shopping A/S, H. J. Holstvej 5A, DK-2605 Brøndby, Denmark. You will be reimbursed by check, cash, or credit-card credit in the currency you wish.

In order for the refund to apply, the 600 kroner must be spent in one store, but not necessarily at the same time. Some major department stores allow purchases to be made over several days or even weeks, at the end of which receipts will be tallied.

Service and handling fees are deducted from the total, so actual refunds come to about 18%. Information on this program is available from the Danish Tourist Board (see "Information, Documents & Money" in Chapter 1).

A 22% MOMS is included in your hotel and restaurant bills, service charges, and entrance fees, as well as on repair of foreign-registered cars. No refunds are possible on these items.

Telephone, Telex & Fax   Danish phones are fully automatic. Dial the eight-digit number. There are no city area codes. At public telephone booths, use two 50-øre coins or a 1-krone or 5-krone coin only. Don't insert coins until your party answers. You can make more than one call on the same payment if your time hasn't run out. Remember that it can be expensive to telephone from your hotel room. Emergency calls are free. The country code for Denmark is 45. This 2-digit number will precede any call which is intended for Denmark dialed from another country.

Most hotels in Denmark will send a fax or Telex for you and put the charge on your bill.

In Copenhagen, to make phone calls or send faxes or Telexes, go to the Telecommunications Center at the Central Station (tel. 33-14-20-00), open Monday through Friday from 8am to 10pm, on Saturday from 9am to 4pm, and on Sunday from 10am to 5pm.

Time   Denmark operates on Central European time—1 hour ahead of Greenwich mean time and 6 hours ahead of eastern standard time. Daylight saving time is observed from the end of March to the end of September.

Tipping   Tips are expected on very few occasions, and even then you should give only 1 or 2 kroner. Porters charge according to fixed prices, and neither hairdressers/barbers nor movie ushers are usually tipped. Know that hotels, restaurants, and even taxis impose a 15% service charge in the rates they quote; service is "built into" the system. Not only that, but with the 22% MOMS, you'll end up paying an addition 37% for some services.

Only special services should be rewarded separately. Some Danes, in fact, are insulted if you offer them a tip.

INTRODUCING COPENHAGEN

Copenhagen, the capital of Denmark, came from the word *københavn,* meaning "merchants' harbor." It grew in size and importance because of its position on the Øresund, the body of water between Denmark and Sweden, guarding the entrance to the Baltic. From its humble beginnings, Copenhagen has become the largest city in Scandinavia, home to 1½ million people. It is the seat of the oldest kingdom in the world.

Over the centuries, Copenhagen suffered more than its share of disasters. In the 17th century the Swedes repeatedly besieged it and in the 18th century it fell to the plague and two devastating fires. The British attacked twice in the Napoleonic wars in the early 1800s. Its last major disaster was in 1940 when the Nazis overpowered the little country and held it in its grip until 1945 when the British army moved in again, this time as liberators.

Copenhagen is a city with much charm, as reflected in its canals, narrow streets, and old houses. Its most famous resident was Hans Christian Andersen, whose memory still lives on in the city. Copenhagen's other world-renowned former citizen, Søren Kierkegaard, also used to take a morning constitutional in the city, plotting his next essay, all of which in time would make him the father of existentialism.

Copenhagen still retains some of the characteristics of a village. If you forget the suburbs, you can cover most of the central belt on foot, making it a great tourist spot. It's almost as if the city was designed for pedestrians, as reflected by its Strøget (strolling street), the longest and oldest walking street in Europe.

1. ORIENTATION

ARRIVING

BY PLANE When you arrive at **Kastrup Airport** (tel. 31-50-93-33) outside Copenhagen, you can cut costs by taking an SAS coach into the city terminal. The SAS bus fare is 25 kroner ($4.20). A taxi to the city center will cost around 125 kroner ($21). Even cheaper is local bus no. 32, which leaves from the international arrivals terminal every 15 or 20 minutes for the Town Hall Square in central Copenhagen and costs only 12 kroner ($2). The same ticket will allow you to transfer to another city bus route, provided you do so within 1 hour after you purchased your initial ticket at the airport.

BY TRAIN Trains arrive at the **Hoved banegård** (Central Station), in the very center of Copenhagen, near the Tivoli and the Rådhuspladsen. The station operates a

WHAT'S SPECIAL ABOUT COPENHAGEN

Castles & Palaces
☐ Christiansborg Palace, center of political power in Denmark.
☐ Rosenborg Castle, Christian's IV's Renaissance castle housing the treasures of the royal family.
☐ Amalienborg Palace, residence of the Danish royal family since 1794. Watch the changing of the guard.

Museums
☐ Open-air Museum (Frilandsmuseet), old houses on 86 acres that re-create Denmark's past.
☐ Ny Carlsberg Glyptotek, a great art museum of Scandinavia—modern works by the beer people.
☐ National Museum, storehouse of Danish treasures, one of the oldest and largest museums in the world.
☐ Thorvaldsen's Museum, housing Bertel Thorvaldsen's (1770–1884) collection, the biggest in neoclassical sculpture.

Parks/Gardens
☐ The Tivoli Gardens, 20 acres of fun and beauty in the heart of Copenhagen.

Buildings
☐ Round Tower, a 17th-century observatory with panoramic views.
☐ Rådhus (Town Hall), where you can climb up for an impressive view; also Jen Olsen's World Clock.

For the Kids
☐ Danish Toy Museum, toys from all over the world for all ages.
☐ Benneweis Circus, the last grand-style circus of Europe.

Special Events/Festivals
☐ Copenhagen Jazz Festival, the jazz mecca of northern Europe (July 6–15).
☐ Copenhagen Summer Festival, young Danish and foreign singers and musicians performing (July to mid-Aug).

---

room-service desk and a luggage-checking service. You can also exchange money at the Bank Handelsbanken, which is open daily in summer from 7am to 10pm (closes at 9pm in winter). It even has a summer-only free shower at the Interrail Center, open daily from 6am to 11pm.

From the Central Station, you can connect with **S-tog,** the local subway system, with trains departing from platforms within the terminus itself. Ask at the information desk near Tracks 5 and 6 as to which train you should board to reach your destination.

For rail information, call 33-14-17-01.

BY BUS   Buses from Zealand or elsewhere in Denmark also pull into the Central Station (see above for services available there).

BY CAR   If you're driving from Germany, a car-ferry will take you from Travemünde to Gedser in southern Denmark. From Gedser, get on the E55 north, an express highway that will take you to the southern outskirts of Copenhagen. If you're coming from Sweden, and crossing at Helsingborg, you will land on the Danish side at Helsingør. From there take express highway E55 south to the northern outskirts of Copenhagen.

BY FERRY   Most ferryboats land at Havnegade at the end of the south side of Nyhavn, a short walk to the center of Copenhagen. Taxis also wait here for ferry arrivals. Most arrivals are from Malmö, Sweden; ferries from continental Europe usually land in South Zealand.

TOURIST INFORMATION

Denmarks Turistråd, H. C. Andersens Boulevard 22 (tel. 33-11-13-25), is located opposite City Hall. It's open May to September, Monday through Friday from 9am to 6pm, on Saturday from 9am to 2pm and on Sunday from 9am to 1pm; from October to the end of April, Monday through Friday from 9am to 5pm and on Saturday from 9am to noon.

CITY LAYOUT

MAIN ARTERIES & STREETS

The heart of Old Copenhagen is a maze of pedestrian streets, formed by Nørreport Station to the north, Town Hall Square (Rådhuspladsen) to the west, and Kongens Nytorv to the east. One continuous pedestrian route, **Strøget,** the world's longest pedestrian street, goes east from Town Hall Square to Kongens Nytorv, and is made up of five streets: Frederiksberggade, Nygade, Vimmelskaftet, Amagertorv, and Østergade. Strøget is lined with shops, bars, restaurants, and in summer sidewalk cafés. **Pistolstraede** is a maze of galleries, restaurants, and boutiques, all housed in restored 18th-century buildings.

Fiolstraede (Violet Street), a dignified street with antiques shops and bookshops, cuts through the university (Latin Quarter). If you turn into Rosengaarden at the top of Fiolstraede, you will come to **Kultorvet** (Coal Square) just before you reach Nørreport Station. Here you join the third main pedestrian street, **Købmagergade** (Butcher Street), which winds around and finally meets Strøget on Amagertorv.

At the end of Strøget you approach **Kongens Nytorv** (King's Square). This is the site of the Royal Theater and Magasin, the latter the largest department store in Copenhagen. This will put you at the beginning of **Nyhavn,** the former seamen's quarter that has been gentrified into an upmarket area of expensive restaurants, apartments, cafés, and boutiques.

Købmagergade is another major pedestrian boulevard, branching off Strøget. A number of streets are linked to it.

The government of Denmark is centered on the small island of **Slotsholmen,** which is connected to the center by eight different bridges. Several museums, notably Christianborg Castle, are found here.

The center of Copenhagen is **Rådhuspladen** (Town Hall Square). From here it is a short walk to the Tivoli Gardens, the major attraction of Copenhagen, and the Central Station, the main railroad and subway terminus. The wide boulevard, **Vesterbrogade,** passes by Tivoli until it reaches the Central Station. Another major boulevard is named after Denmark's most famous writer, **H. C. Andersens Boulevard,** running along Rådhuspladsen and the Tivoli Gardens.

FINDING AN ADDRESS

All even numbers are on one side of the street, and on the opposite side are the alternating odd numbers. Buildings are listed in numerical order, but will often insert A, B, or C after the street number.

NEIGHBORHOODS IN BRIEF

Tivoli Gardens In the heart of Copenhagen, on the south side of Rådhuspladsen, these amusement gardens were built on the site of former fortifications. A total of 160,000 flowers and 110,000 electric lightbulbs brighten the gardens. Built in 1843, Tivoli contains a collection of restaurants, dance halls, theaters, beer gardens, and lakes.

Strøget This is the longest pedestrians-only street in Europe, beginning at Rådhuspladsen. The most interesting parts are Gemmeltorv and Nytorv, "old" and "new" squares, lying on either side of Strøget. They are the site of fruit and vegetable markets, and stalls selling bric-a-brac and handmade jewelry. The word "Strøget" doesn't appear on any maps. Instead, Strøget encompasses five streets: Frederiksberggade, Nygade, Vimmelskaftet, Amagertorv, and Østergade.

Nyhavn   This is the harbor area, for years the haunt of sailors looking for tattoos and other diversions. Nowadays, it's one of the most elegant sections of the city, site of the deluxe Angleterre Hotel and many prestigious restaurants. The Royal Theater stands on Kongens Nytorv.

Indre By   This is the name given to the Old Town, heart of Copenhagen. Once filled with many monasteries, it is a maze of old streets, alleyways, and squares. If you cross Gammeltorv and Nørregade you will be in the university area, nicknamed the Latin Quarter, as in Paris. The Vor Frue Kireke (Cathedral of Copenhagen) is found here, as is Rudetårnet (Round Tower).

Slotsholmen   This island, site of Christiansborg Palace, was where Bishop Absalon built the first fortress in the city in 1167. Today it is the seat of the Danish parliament and the site of Thorvaldsen's Museum, among others. Slotsholmen is linked to Indre by bridges. You can also visit the Royal Library, the Theater Museum, and the Royal Stables. The 17th-century Børsen (stock exchange) is also here.

Christianshavn   This was the "new town" ordered by master builder Christian IV in the early 1500s. The town was originally constructed to house workers in the shipbuilding industry. Visitors come here today mainly to see the Danish Film Museum on Store Søndervoldstraede, and Vors Frelsers Kirke, on the corner of Prinsessegade and Skt. Annaegade. Visitors can climb the spire of this old church for a panoramic view.

Christiania   Within walking distance of Vor Frelsers Kirke at Christianshavn is this offbeat district, once a barracks for soldiers. Then many young and homeless people moved in without the city's permission proclaiming that Christiania was a "free city." It has been a controversial place ever since. Regrettably, this area, founded on idealism, also became a shelter for criminals. Craftshops and restaurants exist here; merchandise and food are fairly cheap, because the residents refuse to pay Denmark's crippling 22% tax.

Dragør   Except for the Tivoli, this seems to be everybody's favorite part of Copenhagen. It is especially recommended if you have time to see only Copenhagen and not the countryside. Dragør is a fishing village south of the city, with origins in the 16th century. Walk its cobblestone streets and enjoy its 65 old, red-roofed houses, designated national landmarks.

2. GETTING AROUND

Copenhagen is a walker's paradise, neat and compact. Many of the major sightseeing attractions are within a short distance of each other.

BY PUBLIC TRANSPORTATION

A joint zone fare system includes Copenhagen Transport buses and State Railway and S-tog trains in Copenhagen and North Zealand, plus some private railway routes in a

IMPRESSIONS

What strikes me now most as regards Denmark is the charm, beauty, and independence of the women.
—ARNOLD BENNETT, JOURNAL, 1913

The Danes that drench their cares in wine.
—BEN JONSON

25-mile radius of the capital, enabling you to transfer from train to bus and vice versa with the same ticket.

A **grundbillet** (basic ticket) for both buses and trains costs 8 kroner ($1.35). You can buy 10 tickets for 70 kroner ($11.75), allowing nine separate journeys on buses or trains in three fare zones within 1 hour.

DISCOUNT PASSES The **Copenhagen Card** entitles you to free and unlimited travel by bus and rail throughout the metropolitan area (including North Zealand), 25% to 50% discounts on crossings to and from Sweden, and free admission to many sights and museums. The card is available for 1, 2, or 3 days and costs 105 kroner ($17.65), 170 kroner ($28.60), and 215 kroner ($36.15), respectively. Children ages 5 to 11 are given a 50% discount. For more information, contact the Danish Tourist Board at H. C. Andersens Blvd. 22, DK-København V (tel. 33-11-13-25).

Students who have an **International Student Identity Card** can get a number of travel breaks in Copenhagen, including up to a 35% discount on domestic rail travel. A card may be purchased in the U.S. from the **Council on International Educational Exchange** (CIEE), 205 E. 42nd St., New York, NY 10017 (tel. 212/661-1414).

For information about low-cost train, ferry, and plane trips, go to **Dis Rejser** (Students' International Committee), Skindergade 28 (tel. 33-11-00-44), in Copenhagen.

Discount tickets or cards are stamped and punched when they are placed face-up in automatic machines at the front of buses or in yellow machines on railway platforms.

Eurailpasses and Nordturistickets are accepted on the local trains in Copenhagen.

BY BUS Copenhagen's well-maintained buses are the least expensive method of getting around. Most buses leave from Radhuspladsen. A basic ticket allows 1 hour of travel and unlimited transfers within the zone where you started your trip. For **information,** call 31-95-17-01.

BY S-TOG [SUBWAY] The S-tog connects heartland Copenhagen with its suburbs. Tickets work under the same conditions as on the buses (see above). You can transfer from a bus line to an S-train on the same ticket. Eurailpass holders generally ride free. For more **information,** call 33-14-17-01.

BY TAXI

Watch for the FRI (free) sign or green light to hail a taxi. Be sure the taxis are metered. **TAXA** (tel. 31-35-35-35) operates the largest fleet of cabs. Tips are included in the meter price: 14 kroner ($2.35) at the drop of the flag and 7 kroner ($1.20) per kilometer thereafter, Monday through Friday from 6am to 6pm. From 6pm to 6am and all day and night on Saturday and Sunday cost is 9.6 kroner ($1.60) per kilometer. Basic drop-of-the-flag costs remain the same, however. The average ride within the city limits costs 34 to 70 kroner ($5.70 to $11.75). Drivers are often bilingual.

BY CAR

Copenhagen is a walking city. It is best to park your car in a city parking lot and pick it up when you're ready to explore the environs. Most car parks are open from 6 or 8am to 8pm (some until midnight). Many lots close Saturday afternoon and Sunday when stores shut down. The average rate is 12 to 15 kroner ($2 to $2.50) per hour or 40 to 75 kroner ($6.70 to $12.60) per 24 hours. Some centrally located car parks include **Dagmarhus Garager,** H. C. Andersens Blvd. 12 (tel. 33-13-90-06), and **Statoil,** Dronningens Tvaergade 4 (tel. 33-14-90-06).

For information on car rentals, see "Getting Around," in Chapter 3.

BY BICYCLE

For rentals, try **Københavns Cyklebors,** Gothersgade 157 (tel. 33-14-07-17). Rates range from 30 to 50 kroner ($5.05 to $8.40) daily, or 125 to 250 kroner ($21 to

$42.05) weekly. Deposits ranging from 100 to 200 kroner ($16.80 to $33.60) are required. Hours are Monday through Friday from 9am to noon and 1 to 5pm and on Saturday from 9am to 1pm; closed Sunday.

Dan Wheel, Colbjørnsensgade 3 (tel. 31-21-22-27), also rents bikes from its location near the Central Station. It is open Monday through Friday from 9am to 5:30pm and on Saturday and Sunday from 9am to 2pm. Daily rentals cost 30 to 60 kroner ($5.05 to $10.10), requiring a deposit of 200 kroner ($33.60).

FAST COPENHAGEN

Here's some helpful information pertaining only to Copenhagen and its suburbs. For general information about such matters, see "Fast Facts: Denmark," in Chapter 3.

American Express Offices are at Amagertorv 18 (tel. 33-12-23-01), open Monday through Friday from 9am to 5pm (April to October, also on Saturday from 9am to noon).

Area Code The country code for Denmark is 45. There are no city area codes. Each telephone number dialed within Denmark has 8 digits.

Baby-Sitters Try **Students** (tel. 31-22-96-96), open Monday through Thursday from 7 to 9am and 3 to 6pm, and on Saturday from 3 to 5pm. The cost is 25 kroner ($4.20) per hour, plus 25 kroner for the booking fee.

Bookstores One of the best and most centrally located is **Boghallen,** Rådhuspladsen 37 (tel. 33-11-85-11), in the Town Hall Square.

Business Hours Most **banks** are open Monday through Friday from 9:30am to 4pm (on Thursday to 6pm). **Stores** are generally open Monday through Thursday from 9am to 5:30pm, on Friday from 9am to 7 or 8pm, and on Saturday from 9am to 2pm; most are closed Sunday. **Offices** are open Monday through Friday from 9 or 10am to 4 or 5pm.

Car Rentals See "Getting Around," in Chapter 3.

Climate See "When to Go," in Chapter 3.

Currency See "Information, Documents & Money," in Chapter 1.

Currency Exchange Banks are generally your best bet. When banks are closed, you can exchange money at the Central Railway Station kiosk, open daily from 7am to 10pm. The Bank of Tivoli is open May to mid-September, daily from noon to 11pm.

Dentist During regular business hours, ask your hotel to call the nearest English-speaking dentist. For emergency dental treatment, go to **Tandlaegevagten,** Oslo Plads 14, near Østerport Station and the U.S. Embassy. It's open Monday through Friday from 8 to 9:30pm and on Saturday, Sunday, and holidays from 10am to noon and 8 to 9:30pm. Go in person—there's no telephone—and be prepared to pay in cash.

Doctor Dial 0041 for house calls 24 hours a day. The doctor's fee is payable in cash. Every doctor speaks English.

Drugstores An *apoteker* (drugstore) open 24 hours a day in central Copenhagen is **Steno Apotek,** Vesterbrogade 6C (tel. 31-14-82-66).

Embassies & Consulates See "Fast Facts: Denmark" in Chapter 3.

Emergencies Dial **000** to report a fire or to call the police or an ambulance. State your phone number and address. Emergency calls from public telephones are free.

Eyeglasses The largest and oldest optical chain in Denmark is **Synoptik,** Købmagergade 22 (tel. 33-15-05-38), with 80 other branches throughout Denmark. Most glasses can be replaced in 2 or 3 hours. Bifocals can take up to 3 days. They also specialize in soft and hard contact lenses, with hundreds of different types in stock.

Hairdresser Stuhr Coiffeur, Scala, Axeltorv 2 (tel. 33-15-11-44), is located on the second floor of the shopping complex across from the Tivoli. Both men and women are received.

Holidays See "When to Go," in Chapter 3.

Hospitals The emergency room at **Kommunehospitalet,** Øster Farimagsgade 5 (tel. 31-15-85-00), is open 24 hours a day.

Information See "Tourist Information," in "Orientation," in this chapter.

Laundry/Dry Cleaning Self-service laundries are all over Copenhagen—ask at your hotel for the one nearest you. A centrally located one is **Vask-Møntvask,** Holbergsgade 9, near the Royal Palace, open daily from 6am to 10pm. Another is **Møntvask,** Istegade 45, open daily from 7am to 9pm.

Your dry-cleaning needs can be taken care of at **Dry Cleaning,** Vester Farimagsgade 3 (tel. 33-12-45-45), a block from the Central Station. It's open Monday through Saturday from 8am to 6pm.

Libraries The best-stocked one is the **University of Copenhagen Library,** Fiolstraede 1, (tel. 33-13-08-75), near Round Tower, which has a large inventory of English-language publications.

Liquor Laws See "Fast Facts: Denmark" in Chapter 3.

Lost Property General property lost should be reported to the police, at Carl Jacobsensvej 20, Valby, which is open Monday through Friday from 10am to 3pm (on Thursday to 5pm). Report property losses on buses or trains to Lyshøjgårdsvej 80, Valby (tel. 31-46-01-44 for buses, 36-44-20-10 for trains).

Luggage Storage/Lockers Luggage can be stored in rental lockers at the Central Station. Lockers are accessible daily from 5:30am to 1am. Depending on the locker's size, daily rental fees range from 10 to 20 kroner ($1.70 to $3.35).

Newspapers Foreign newspapers, particularly the *International Herald-Tribune,* are available at the Central Railway Station; in front of the Palladium movie theater, on Vesterbrogade; in Strøget; and at newsstands of the big hotels.

Photographic Needs In the Scala shopping and restaurant complex, **Express Photo,** Axeltorv 2 (tel. 33-15-27-80), will develop film in about an hour. It's open on Monday from 10am to 7pm, Tuesday through Thursday from 10am to 6pm, on Friday from 10am to 8pm, and on Saturday from 10am to 2pm.

Police In an emergency, dial 000. For other matters, go to the police station at Nyropsgade 20 (tel. 33-91-14-48).

Post Office For information about the Copenhagen post office, phone 33-14-62-98; otherwise, one cannot phone post offices. The **main post office,** where your general delivery (Poste Restante) letters can be picked up, is at Tietgensgade 39, DK-1704 København V (tel. 33-93-25-10). The post office at the Central Railway Station is open Monday through Friday from 8am to 10pm, on Saturday from 9am to 4pm, and on Sunday from 10am to 5pm.

Radio See "Fast Facts: Denmark" in Chapter 3.

Religious Services St. Ansgar's Roman Catholic Church, Bredgade 64 (tel. 33-13-37-62); the English Church of St. Alban's (Anglo-Episcopalian) on Langelinie (tel. 31-62-77-36); the American Church (Protestant and interdenominational) at the U.S. Embassy, Dag Hammarskjölds Allé 24 (tel. 31-42-31-44); and the synagogue at Krystalgade 12 (tel. 33-12-88-68). The International Church of Copenhagen (affiliated with the American Lutheran church) holds services at the Vartov Church, Farvergade 27 (tel. 31-62-47-85), across from the Town Hall.

Rest Rooms Some public toilets can be found at the Rådhuspladsen (Town Hall Square), the Central Station, and at all terminals. Look for the markings TOILETTER, WC, DAMER (women), or HERRER (men). There is no charge.

Safety Stay alert. Be aware of your immediate surroundings. Wear a moneybelt and don't sling your camera or purse across your shoulder; wear the strap diagonally across your body.

Shoe Repair Go to **Magasin,** Kongens Nytorv 13 (tel. 33-11-44-33), a leading Denmark department store, which has a great shoe-repair franchise in its basement, **Mister Minit.**

Taxes Throughout Denmark, you'll come across MOMS on your bills, a government-imposed value-added tax of 22%. It's included in hotel and restaurant bills, service charges, entrance fees, and in repair of foreign-registered cars. No refunds are given on these items. For more information, see "Savvy Shopping," in Chapter 7.

Taxi   See "Getting Around," in this chapter.

Telegrams/Telex   The main telegraph office is at Købmagergade 37 (tel. 33-32-12-12). To send a telegram by phone, dial 0022. There are Telex booths at the telegraph office, Købmagergade 37.

Telephone   For information on making telephone calls in Copenhagen, see "Fast Facts: Denmark" in Chapter 3. Telephone kiosks with operator assistance can be found at the post office in the Central Railway Station and at the main telegraph office.

Television   See "Fast Facts: Denmark" in Chapter 3.

Tourist Information   The **Danmarks Turistråd** is at H. C. Andersens Blvd. 22 (tel. 33-11-13-25), opposite the Rådhus (city hall). It's open May to September, Monday through Friday from 9am to 6pm, on Saturday from 9am to 2pm, and on Sunday from 9am to 1pm; October to April, Monday through Friday from 9am to 5pm and on Saturday from 9am to noon.

Transit Information   Day or night, phone 31-95-17-01 for bus information or 33-14-17-01 for S-tog (subway) information.

3. NETWORKS & RESOURCES

FOR STUDENTS   The Copenhagen **Youth Information Center** (known as **Use It!**), Rådhusstraede 13, DK-1466 København K (tel. 33-15-65-18), provides information on places to visit, things to do, cheap accommodations and restaurants, and more. It issues reports on bed availability, and will also store your luggage for free. From June 15 to September 15, it is open daily from 9am to 7pm; the rest of the year, daily from 10am to 4pm.

FOR GAY MEN & LESBIANS   The national organization for gay men and lesbians is **Landsforeningen for Bøsser og Lesbiske,** Knabrostraede 3 (tel. 33-13-19-48), with branches in several cities such as Århus, Aalborg, and Odense. It was founded in 1948. Its café is open on Monday and Tuesday from 1pm to 2am, on Wednesday, Thursday, and Sunday from 1pm to 3am, and on Friday and Saturday from 1pm to 5am.

For the latest news and events, call the **National Gay Switchboard** (tel. 33-13-01-12), Friday through Monday from 8pm to midnight.

FOR WOMEN   The **Women's House** (Kvindehuset), at Gothersgade 37 (tel. 33-14-28-04), is a kind of information center, with several publications about the feminist movement. The house also operates the Bog Café open Monday through Friday from 3 to 8pm. Men should not visit, even if accompanied by a woman.

CHAPTER 5

COPENHAGEN ACCOMMODATIONS

1. **NEAR KONGENS NYTORV & NYHAVN**
2. **NEAR RÅDHUSPLADSEN & TIVOLI**
3. **ON HELGOLANDSGADE & COLBJØRNSENSGADE**
4. **NEAR NØRREPORT STATION**
- **FROMMER'S COOL FOR KIDS: HOTELS**

Since Denmark doesn't have one of its own, I have devised a hotel-grading system, based on tariffs charged. If any hotel did not belong in its assigned category, it was not included. For example, any hotel deemed expensive that really wasn't worth it was not recommended. Few hotels had to be cut for this reason as the marketplace has a way of keeping prices in check.

Hotels are labeled "Very Expensive" if charging between $250 and $470 per night for a double room. "Expensive" hotels have doubles for $180 to $235; "Moderate," $135 to $180; and "Inexpensive," $65 to $130. Tax and service charges are included.

Peak season in Denmark is summer, from May to September. It practically coincides with the schedule at the Tivoli. Once the Tivoli closes for the winter, plenty of rooms become available. Make sure to ask about winter discounts.

Nearly all doubles contain a private bath. Find out, though, whether this means a shower or a tub bath. You can undercut these prices by requesting a room without bath in hotels in the "Moderate" or "Inexpensive" categories.

Ask if breakfast is included. It usually is in most places, except many first-class choices.

Any accommodation labeled "Budget" falls into a special category—youth hostel, private home, etc. Budget suggests that the place is not a regular hotel, and offers the lowest possible price for a place to stay. Private homes are the cheapest.

Found throughout Scandinavia, **Mission hotels** service tourists of all faiths who are seeking comfortable, clean rooms in well-run hotels for a fair price. Copenhagen has several, each catering to a middle-class family trade. Although originally founded by the old-fashioned Temperance society, now about half of Denmark's mission hotels are fully licensed.

RESERVATIONS SERVICE

At the Central Railway Station, the tourist office maintains the useful hotel/accommodation-booking service **Vaerelseanvisningen** (tel. 33-12-40-45). The charge for this service, whether you have booked a private home or a luxury hotel, is 13 kroner ($2.20) per person. There is no charge for booking a hostel. A deposit must be paid at the kiosk, which will later be deducted from the room rent. For the room, you will have to pay a deposit of 5 kroner (85¢), 10 kroner ($1.70), 15 kroner ($2.50), or 25 kroner ($4.20). You are also given a city map and bus directions.

The kiosk will not accept reservations in advance. This facility can secure private accommodations only when the hotels in the indicated price range are fully booked. For clients who prefer to book hotel rooms in advance, see the Hotel Booking Service staff at the same kiosk (tel. 33-12-28-80).

The kiosk is open May 1 to the end of August, daily from 9am to midnight; in September, daily from 9am to 10pm; in October, Monday through Saturday from

9am to 5pm; November to March, Monday through Friday from 9am to 5pm and on Saturday from 9am to noon; and in April, Monday through Saturday from 9am to 5pm.

1. NEAR KONGENS NYTORV & NYHAVN

Once the home of sailor joints and tattoo parlors, Nyhavn is now a fast-rising chic section of Copenhagen. The central canal filled with 19th-century boats and the 18th-century facades of the buildings surrounding it give the area its special atmosphere.

VERY EXPENSIVE

HOTEL D'ANGLETERRE, Kongens Nytorv 34, DK-1050 København K. Tel. 33-12-00-95. Fax 33-12-11-18. 120 rms, 10 suites. A/C MINIBAR TV TEL **Bus:** 1, 6, 9.

$ Rates: 1,800–2,100 kroner ($302.60–$353) single; 2,000–2,800 kroner ($336.20–$470.70) double; suite 3,800–6,000 kroner ($638.80–$1,008.60). Breakfast costs 98 kroner ($16.45) extra. AE, DC, MC, V.

At the top of Nyhavn, this Leading Hotels of the World member is the premier choice for Denmark. The hotel was built in 1755 and extensively renovated in the 1980s. Guests have included Hans Christian Andersen and about every other celebrity who's ever visited Denmark. It's a medley of styles: Empire, Louis XVI, and modern. Bedrooms are beautifully furnished with art objects and occasional antiques. Light color schemes, subdued lighting, and modern amenities continue to make this a desirable address.

HOTEL NEPTUN, St. Annae Plads 18-20, DK-1250 København K. Tel. 31-13-89-00. Fax 33-14-12-50. 119 rms, 10 suites. MINIBAR TV TEL **Bus:** 1, 6, 9.

$ Rates (including a buffet breakfast): 790–940 kroner ($132.80–$158) single; 1,050–1,290 kroner ($176.50–$216.85) double; from 3,000 kroner ($504.30) suite. AE, DC, MC, V.

Modernized in 1990, the interior of this hotel, originally built in 1854, resembles an upper-class living room, with English-style furniture, warm colors, paneling, and even a chess table. Some rooms overlook a quiet, covered interior courtyard, where you can have a drink in the summer. Bedrooms are tastefully furnished in modern style and have radios, trouser presses, and hairdryers. The hotel is located a block from the Nyhavn Canal, near many city attractions.

Dining/Entertainment: The evening begins at The Bar, where everyone from rock stars to CEOs meet for a drink. La Brasserie, the hotel's democratically priced restaurant, caters to the "young and beautiful," whereas "The Restaurant" is acclaimed for its French cuisine and vintage wines. Light lunches and snacks are also available.

Services: Valet parking, room service from 7am to midnight, laundry service.

Facilities: In-house video, banquet and meeting facilities.

71 NYHAVN, Nyhavn 71, DK-1051 København K. Tel. 33-11-85-85. Fax 33-93-15-85. 76 rms, 6 suites. MINIBAR TV TEL **Bus:** 1, 6, 9.

$ Rates (including a buffet breakfast): 1,050–1,400 kroner ($176.50–$235.35) single; 1,480–1,880 kroner ($248.80–$316.05) double. AE, DC, MC, V.

Lying along Nyhavn, this hotel incorporated a modern interior into a 200-year-old warehouse whose red-brick walls rise above the wooden hulls of ships anchored in the adjacent canal. One of the few buildings in the area that was spared an 1807 British bombardment, the warehouse lasted until it opened as a hotel in 1971. Leather

DENMARK

Copenhagen

Absalon Hotel **1**
Angleterre **2**
Ascot **3**
Carlton **4**
Copenhagen Admiral **5**
Cosmopole **6**
Dania **7**
Grand Hotel **8**
Ibsens Hotel **9**
Jørgensen **10**
Komfort Hotel **11**
Kong Arthur **12**
Kong Frederik **13**
Missionshotellet Ansgar **14**
Missionshotellet Nebo **15**
Neptun **16**
Nord, Hotel du **17**
Palace Hotel **18**
Park Hotel **19**
Plaza **20**
Saga Hotel **21**
SAS Royal Hotel **22**
SAS Scandanavia **23**
Selandia **24**
71 Nyhavn **25**
Sheraton Copenhagen **26**
Sophie Amalie **27**
Viking **28**
West **29**

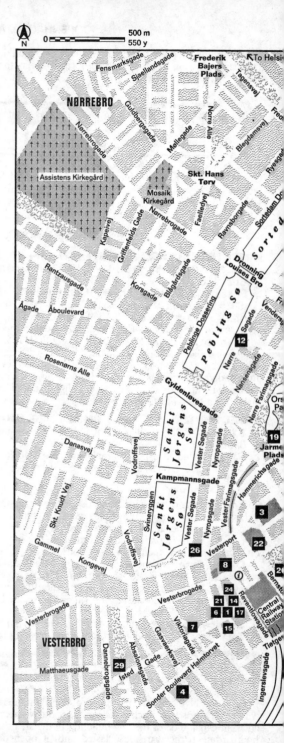

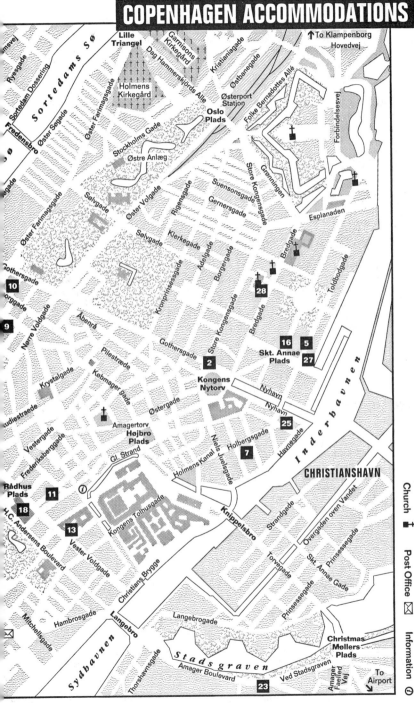

couches, small arched windows, comfortable baths, and carpeting distinguish the bedrooms. Facilities include a small bar area and an elegant restaurant, Pakhuskaelderen, serving French and Danish specialties. Dinner costs 315 kroner ($52.95); buffet lunches go for 168 kroner ($28.25).

MODERATE

COPENHAGEN ADMIRAL HOTEL, Toldbodgade 24-28, DK-1253 København K. Tel. 31-11-82-82. Fax 33-32-55-42. 313 rms, 52 suites (all with bath). TV TEL **Bus:** 1, 9, 10, 28, 41.
$ Rates: 590–765 kroner ($99.20–$128.60) single; 845–990 kroner ($142.05–$166.40) double; from 1,500 kroner ($252.15) suite. Breakfast buffet costs 78 kroner ($13.10) extra. Winter discounts. AE, MC, V.
Only two blocks from Nyhavn Canal, this hotel was a granary built in 1787. Guests navigate between the thick timbers and stone arches of the hotel infrastructure, with partitions creating clean and functional bedrooms. Some rooms have harbor views. A popular luncheon buffet is served with elaborately arranged fish, meat, and Danish cheese dishes.

SOPHIE AMALIE HOTEL, St. Annae Plads 21, DK-1250 København K. Tel. 33-13-34-00. Fax 33-32-55-42. 117 rms, 17 suites (all with bath). A/C TV TEL **Bus:** 1, 9, 10, 28, 41.
$ Rates: 590–825 kroner ($99.20–$138.70) single; 845–940 kroner ($142.05–$158) double; from 1,500 kroner ($252.15) suite. Buffet breakfast costs 78 kroner ($13.10) extra. Winter discounts. AE, MC, V.
Near the ferryboat to Oslo, the hydrofoil to Sweden, and the Nyhavn area, this 1948 hotel has contemporary bedrooms with colorful carpeting and radios. Rooms facing north view Amalienborg Palace, residence of Queen Margrethe II. In the sixth-floor suites, a curved staircase leads from the living room to the bedroom. There's also a nightclub, the Nautilus.

INEXPENSIVE

HOTEL VIKING, Bredgade 65, DK-1260 København K. Tel. 33-12-45-50. Fax 33-12-46-18. 91 rms (26 with bath). TEL **Bus:** 1, 6, 9.
$ Rates (including continental breakfast): 380 kroner ($63.90) single without bath, 480 kroner ($80.70) single with bath; 590 kroner ($99.20) double without bath, 720 kroner ($121.05) double with bath. Winter discounts. MC, V.
A modern hotel only four blocks from the Central Train Station, this hotel is reasonably priced. Bedrooms are comfortable and clean, but a bit worn. Only breakfast is served.

2. NEAR RÅDHUSPLADSEN & TIVOLI

Some of the most expensive hotels in Copenhagen are located here. In the heart of the city, centered around the Rådhuspladsen (Town Hall Square), the Tivoli, and the Central Station, you'll be near all public transportation and many attractions.

VERY EXPENSIVE

KONG FREDERIK, Vester Voldgade 25, DK-1552 København V. Tel. 33-12-59-02. Fax 33-93-59-01. 107 rms. MINIBAR TV TEL **Bus:** 1, 6, 28.
$ Rates: 1,400–1,600 kroner ($235.35–$268.95) single; 1,650–1,850 kroner ($277.35–$311) double. Buffet breakfast costs 95 kroner ($15.95) extra. AE, DC, MC, V.
Lying right off Rådhuspladsen, the renovated Kong Frederik still has the feeling of a private club with its dark paneling and antique-filled lounges. The facade is arched and

balconied. Bedrooms are modern but furnished with traditional pieces of all types. Rooms have hairdryers, separate shower cabinets, and radios. There is elevator service.

Dining/Entertainment: The Queen's Grill, an excellent Danish and international restaurant, has entertained many a king. Meals are also served in a bright courtyard, a special little dining haven. In the cozy Queens Pub, you can order both food and drink (see "Evening Entertainment," in Chapter 7).

Services: Valet parking, same-day dry cleaning, laundry, room service.

PALACE HOTEL, Rådhuspladsen 57, DK-1550 København V. Tel. 33-14-40-50. Fax 33-14-52-79. 155 rms, 4 suites. MINIBAR TV TEL **Bus:** 2, 30, 32, 33, 34, 35.

$ Rates (including buffet breakfast): 1,250–1,450 kroner ($210.15–$243.75) single; 1,450–1,700 kroner ($243.75–$285.75) double; 2,000–2,500 kroner ($336.20–$420.25) suite. AE, DC, MC, V.

Opened in 1910, declared a historical landmark in 1985, this hotel has been visited by Bob Hope, Audrey Hepburn, and Duke Ellington. Modern rooms are attractively furnished in a traditional style, with many amenities, such as trouser presses and hairdryers. The concierge is particularly helpful in arranging for theater tickets, tours, and transportation.

Dining/Entertainment: The Butterfly Bar on the ground floor has a Hollywood atmosphere, and the restaurant, Brasserie on the Square, serves both Danish and international food.

Services: Laundry, concierge.

Facilities: Safe-deposit box in rooms, parking garage, executive meeting rooms.

THE PLAZA, Bernstorffsgade 4, DK-1577 København V. Tel. 33-14-92-62. Fax 33-93-93-62. 77 rms, 6 suites. A/C MINIBAR TV TEL

$ Rates (including buffet breakfast): 1,400–1,800 kroner ($235.35–$302.60) single; 1,600–2,700 kroner ($268.95–$453.85) double; from 5,000 kroner ($840.50) suite. AE, DC, MC, V.

Many consider this the most desirable hotel in Copenhagen for atmosphere and locale (near the Central Rail Station). Mahogany paneling, first-class comfort, and antique furnishings exude a rich, warm feeling. All rooms have an elegant English country home look—traditional, yet with all the modern amenities.

Dining/Entertainment: The evening begins in the elegant Library Bar (see "Evening Entertainment," in Chapter 7), then proceeds to the premier Russian restaurant of Scandinavia, Alexander Nevski (see Chapter 6).

SAS ROYAL HOTEL, Hammerichsgade 1, DK-1611 København V. Tel. 33-14-14-12. Fax 33-14-14-21. 263 rms, 2 suites. A/C MINIBAR TV TEL **Bus:** 14, 16.

$ Rates: 1,840 kroner ($309.30) single; 2,140 kroner ($359.75) double. Breakfast costs 115 kroner ($19.35) extra. Royal Club (including continental breakfast): 2,200 kroner ($369.80) single; 2,400 kroner ($403.45) double; from 5,800 kroner ($975) suite. AE, DC, MC, V.

Long favored by business travelers, this international deluxe hotel in the city center, near the Tivoli and Town Hall Square, is filled with facilities and conveniences. The hotel has sleek modern Danish styling throughout. Rooms have such extra amenities as hairdryers and trouser presses. At the Royal Club on the top floors, guests are pampered for extra money: electronic safes, lounge with complimentary refreshments, speedier check-ins, and free admission to the hotel's facilities such as the dance club and gym.

Dining/Entertainment: The hotel has several restaurants and bars, including its prestigious Summit on the top floor. Others include Café Royal, a lobby bar, the Garden Bar, and the Fellini Nightclub (see "Evening Entertainment," in Chapter 7).

Services: SAS airline check-in, 24-hour room service, 3-hour laundry service, massage, hair stylist, "Office-for-a-Day."

Facilities: Gymnasium, sauna, and solarium.

SAS SCANDINAVIA HOTEL, Amager Blvd. 70, DK-2300 København S.

Tel. 33-11-23-23. Fax 31-57-01-93. 503 rms, 39 suites. A/C MINIBAR TV TEL **Bus:** 5, 30, 32, 33, 35.

$ **Rates:** 1,500 kroner ($252.15) single; 1,700 kroner ($258.75) double. Buffet breakfast costs 115 kroner ($19.35) extra. Royal Club (including continental breakfast): 1,900 kroner ($319.40) single; 2,200 kroner ($369.80) double; penthouse suites from 4,800 kroner ($806.90). AE, DC, MC, V.

A 5-minute walk east of the Tivoli, this international deluxe hotel is rated as the finest and largest modern hotel in the Danish capital, catering primarily to businesspeople. First-class bedrooms are attractive and comfortable, with many amenities such as a video cassette recorder with international movies, trouser press, and hairdryer. Greater comfort is found on the top floors at the Royal Club where guests are given extra privileges like free admission to all hotel facilities.

Dining/Entertainment: The Top of the Town is the only sky restaurant in Copenhagen. You can stop in just for a drink at the Sky Bar—and get the view for free. Others include Restaurant Fleur (less expensive), the Bus Stop bar in the lobby, and the After 8 nightclub with live music Sunday through Thursday until 3am, on Friday and Saturday until 4am.

Services: 24-hour room service, concierge, massages, secretarial assistance, SAS airline check-in, express laundry.

Facilities: Health club with indoor swimming pool, Business Service Center, conference facilities, business club rooms, Danish designer shops.

SHERATON COPENHAGEN HOTEL, Vester Søgade 6 (Box 337), DK-1601 København V. Tel. 33-14-35-35, or toll free 800/325-35-35 in the U.S. Fax 33-32-12-23. 471 rms. A/C MINIBAR TV TEL **Bus:** 29.

$ **Rates** (including continental breakfast): 1,510–2,000 kroner ($253.85–$336.20) single; 1,760–2,200 kroner ($295.85–$369.80) double. AE, DC, MC, V.

Two blocks from the Tivoli Gardens and the major shopping district, this chain hotel makes a good impression in the Danish capital. The hotel, a business executive's favorite, has been massively renovated. The hotel was given a thorough overhaul in safety equipment such as fire alarms and smoke detectors, individual adjustable air conditioners were added, and the sixth floor was made for nonsmokers only. Rooms are bright and modern, and contain many amenities, such as eight international TV channels. The most expensive accommodations are on the top two executive floors.

Dining/Entertainment: The King's Court is the hotel's prestigious restaurant, although meals can also be had at the Felix. The Red Lion Pub is ideal for a drink or nighttime buffet. The King's Court Champagne and Piano Bar provides international entertainment.

Services: 24-hour room service, manicures and pedicures, massages, concierge, laundry service, secretarial services.

Facilities: Parking, health club, shopping arcade, car rental.

EXPENSIVE

GRAND HOTEL, Vesterbrogade 9A. DK-1620 København V. Tel. 31-31-36-00. Fax 31-31-33-50. 140 rms, 2 suites. MINIBAR TV TEL **Bus:** 6, 16, 28, 41.

$ **Rates** (including buffet breakfast): 820–1,020 kroner ($137.85–$171.45) single; 1,200–1,410 kroner ($201.70–$237) double; suites from 2,500 kroner ($420.25). AE, DC, MC, V.

A 1988 renovation brought this landmark near the Central Station a new life. The charm of the old was preserved, but the bedrooms and baths are new, each tastefully furnished and well maintained. Modern amenities such as in-room movies were added. The Grand Bar overflows in summer onto a sidewalk café, and the Grand Restaurant serves Danish freshly prepared specialties.

MODERATE

ASCOT HOTEL, Studiestraede 57, DK-1554 København V. Tel. 33-12-60-00. Fax 33-14-60-40. 115 rms (all with bath). TV TEL **Bus:** 14, 16.

$ Rates (including buffet breakfast): 775 kroner ($130.30) single; 950 kroner ($159.70) double. AE, DC, MC, V. **Parking:** Free.

On a small side street 5 minutes from Town Hall Square, the Ascot is a traditional 19th-century building. Cleverly modernized, it has turned into one of the best small hotels in Copenhagen. The atmosphere is inviting, and bedrooms are sleek and modern, each comfortable and well maintained. Free parking facilities, same-day laundry, and dry cleaning are available. There's also a bar.

KOMFORT HOTEL, Løngangstraede 27, DK-1468 København K. Tel. 31-12-65-70. Fax 33-15-28-99. 201 rms (all with bath). TV TEL **Bus:** 1, 6.

$ Rates (including buffet breakfast): 720 kroner ($121) single; 1,050 kroner ($176.50) double. AE, DC, MC, V.

Close to the Town Hall, this hotel offers clean rooms and good value. Each well-furnished bedroom contains a private shower, radio, and alarm. There's a parking garage on the premises. The popular restaurant, Strikes, offers international meals from 175 kroner ($29.40). Specialties include spareribs, shish kebabs, chicken Kiev, and surf and turf. There is also an English pub, John Bull, on the premises.

KONG ARTHUR, Nørre Søgade 11, DK-1370 København K. Tel. 33-11-12-12. Fax 33-32-61-30. 90 rms (all with bath). MINIBAR TV TEL **Bus:** 5, 7, 16.

$ Rates (including Danish breakfast): 795–875 kroner ($133.65–$147.10) double. Weekend rates available in winter. AE, DC, MC, V. **Parking:** Available.

Originally an orphanage, this hotel sits behind a private courtyard next to the tree-lined Peblinge Lake in a residential part of town. It has been completely renovated into a contemporary hostelry; each of the comfortable carpeted rooms is freshly painted and has an in-home video, safe, and hairdryer. The hotel has a bar and serves only breakfast.

PARK HOTEL, Jarmers Plads 3, DK-1551 København V. Tel. 31-13-30-00. Fax 33-14-30-33. 64 rms (57 with bath). TV TEL **Bus:** 14, 16.

$ Rates: 375 kroner ($63.05) single without bath; 595–725 kroner ($100–$121.85) double without bath, 870–990 kroner ($146.25–$166.40) double with bath. Breakfast costs 75 kroner ($12.60) extra. Winter discounts. AE, DC, MC, V.

The Park Hotel houses my favorite breakfast room in the city. One wall is adorned with the radiator covers from six vintage automobiles while other walls have an airplane propeller from 1916, a collection of antique auto headlights, and lots of machine-age posters and engravings. Bedrooms have tasteful furniture, marble-covered baths, thick carpeting, and lithographs.

INEXPENSIVE

HOTEL CARLTON, Halmtorvet 14, DK-1260 København V. Tel. 31-21-25-51. 60 rms (12 with bath). TEL **Bus:** 10.

$ Rates (including buffet breakfast): 285–345 kroner ($47.90–$58) single without bath, 480 kroner ($80.70) single with bath; 480–660 kroner ($80.70–$110.95) double without bath, 745–765 kroner ($125.25–$128.60) double with bath. Extra bed 210 kroner ($35.35). Winter discounts. AE, DC, MC, V.

This 19th-century hotel, located near Amalienborg Castle, the harbor, and *The Little Mermaid*, has elaborate detail and some grand antiques. Rooms have been modernized and filled with functional Nordic furniture. There are baths on every floor and an all-night bar.

HOTEL DANIA, Istedgade 3, DK-1650 København V. Tel. 31-22-11-00. Fax 31-22-21-99. 60 rms (32 with bath). **Bus:** 6, 16, 28, 41.

$ Rates (including buffet breakfast): 340 kroner ($57.15) single without bath, 510 kroner ($85.75) single with bath; 550 kroner ($92.45) double without bath, 720 kroner ($121.05) double with bath. AE, DC, MC, V.

This comfortable family hotel, near the Central Rail Station, is newly rebuilt. There's a breakfast room, elevator, TV room, large lobby, and rental safety boxes. Many rooms have been modernized. Most have phones, and TVs are available by request. Corridor showers are free.

HOTEL WEST, Dannebrogsgade 8, DK-1661 København V. Tel. 31-24-27-61. 24 rms (10 with bath). **Bus:** 6, 28, 41.
$ Rates: 200 kroner ($33.60) single; 320–370 kroner ($53.80–$62.20) double. Additional bed 90 kroner ($15.15). Winter discounts; 10% discounts on stays of more than 3 nights. No credit cards.

Ⓢ Hotel West takes up two floors of a 1900 corner building about a 10-minute walk from the railway station. There's a public sitting room. Rooms are small, but clean and well maintained. Only a few singles are available; most are twin-bedded and can be used as three-, four-, or five-bedded units. No breakfast is served, but many eating places are nearby including a laundry and supermarket.

MISSIONSHOTELLET NEBO, Istedgade 6, DK-1650 København V. Tel. 31-21-12-17. Fax 31-23-47-73. 96 rms (32 with bath). TV TEL **Bus:** 6, 16, 28, 41.
$ Rates (including breakfast): 330 kroner ($55.45) single without bath, 515 kroner ($86.55) single with bath; 580 kroner ($97.50) double without bath, 785 kroner ($131.95) double with bath. AE, DC, MC, V.
This hotel near the railway station is a quiet retreat, with clean, up-to-date rooms. The lobby is tiny, and a lounge opens onto a side courtyard. Rooms are small, furnished in a Nordic functional style. Bathrooms are on all floors.

3. ON HELGOLANDSGADE & COLBJØRNSENSGADE

Copenhagen's main sleeping street is near the Central Station, where Helgolandsgade runs parallel to Colbjørnsensgade. The many moderately priced accommodations here can be booked through a central office at Helgolandsgade 4 (tel. 31-31-43-44). Colbjørnsensgade, parallel to Helgolandsgade, is the second major sleeping street. From either street, you are within easy walking distance of Rådhuspladsen and the Tivoli.

MODERATE

ABSALON HOTEL, Helgolandsgade 15, DK-1653 København V. Tel. 31-24-22-11. Fax 31-24-22-11. 260 rms (170 with bath). **Bus:** 6, 10, 16, 28, 41.
$ Rates (including an all-you-can-eat buffet breakfast): 450 kroner ($75.65) single without bath, 850 kroner ($142.90) single with bath; 550 kroner ($92.45) double without bath, 1,050 kroner ($176.50) double with bath. Winter discounts. AE, DC, MC, V.

Ⓢ In this district, this has become "the Frommer favorite," known both for its good value and warm reception. The hotel is large—a combination of several buildings joined together. Bedrooms are comfortably modern. Rooms with private baths and showers also have TVs, trouser presses, and hairdryers. There are also laundry facilities. The hotel's basement restaurant, Absalon's Kaelder, is one of the best and most reasonably priced in the area, with meals costing from 160 kroner ($26.90).

HOTEL COSMOPOLE, Colbjørnsensgade 7-11, DK-1652 København V. Tel. 31-21-33-33. Fax 31-31-33-99. 210 rms (all with bath). TV TEL **Bus:** 6, 10, 16, 28, 41.
$ Rates (including breakfast): 730 kroner ($122.70) single; 900 kroner ($151.30) double. Winter discounts. AE, DC, MC, V.
Along with the Hotel Union next door, this hotel is operated by the Copenhagen

Center Hotels chain. It features two reception areas. Rooms have been renovated and furnished in a modern style, with such added amenities as clock radios and hairdryers. There's also a 90-seat restaurant, La Cave, offering French cuisine at moderate prices.

HOTEL SELANDIA, Helgolandsgade 12, DK-1653 København V. Tel. 31-31-46-10. Fax 31-31-46-10. 81 rms (47 with bath). TV TEL **Bus:** 6, 10, 16, 28, 41.

$ Rates (including breakfast): 390 kroner ($65.55) single without bath, 550–650 kroner ($92.45–$109.25) single with bath; 540 kroner ($90.75) double without bath, 850 kroner ($142.90) double with bath. AE, DC, MC, V.

The 1928 Hotel Selandia is a centrally located, immaculate family hotel. Furnishings are sleek and modern. All rooms have radios. Buffet-style breakfast is served in an attractive room. Laundry facilities are available, and baby-sitting can be arranged.

MISSIONSHOTELLET ANSGAR, Colbjørnsensgade 29, DK-1652 København V. Tel. 31-21-21-96. Fax 31-21-61-91. 87 rms (44 with bath). TEL **Bus:** 6, 10, 16, 28, 41.

$ Rates (including breakfast): 375 kroner ($63.05) single without bath; 580 kroner ($97.50) double without bath, 810 kroner ($136.15) double with bath. Children under 3 free; extra bed (for children under 12) 195 kroner ($32.80). AE, DC, MC, V.

Comfortable and cozy, all rooms are decorated with modern Danish furniture. There are showers and baths on each floor (no charge for use). A dozen large rooms that can accommodate up to six are perfect for families, and are available at negotiable rates. There is often free 24-hour parking outside the hotel. Guests arriving at Kastrup Airport can take the SAS bus to the Air Terminal at the Central Station, walk through the station, and be inside the hotel in less than 4 minutes.

INEXPENSIVE

SAGA HOTEL, Colbjørnsensgade 18-20, DK-1652 København V. Tel. 31-24-99-67. Fax 31-24-60-33. 76 rms (15 with bath). **Bus:** 6, 10, 16, 28, 41.

$ Rates (including buffet breakfast): 260–370 kroner ($43.70–$62.20) single without bath, 420–570 ($60.60–$95.80) single with bath; 380–500 kroner ($63.90–$84.05) double without bath, 640–780 kroner ($107.60–$131.10) double with bath. Extra bed 150–180 kroner ($25.20–$30.25). Winter discounts. No credit cards.

This is the safest bet for a family among the hotels on this sometimes-troublesome street. The comfortable rooms are on the upper floors of this nonelevator building. Five units have a TV. Laundry facilities are available.

4. NEAR NØRREPORT STATION

INEXPENSIVE

IBSENS HOTEL, Vendersgade 23, DK-1363 København K. Tel. 31-13-19-13. Fax 33-13-19-16. 49 rms (6 with bath). TV TEL **Bus:** 14, 16, 5, 7E.

$ Rates (including buffet breakfast): 350 kroner ($58.85) single without bath; 500 kroner ($84.05) double without bath, 600–800 kroner ($100.85–$134.50) double with shower. Extra bed 150 kroner ($25.20). No credit cards.

Preferred by budget-conscious travelers and families, this hotel, built in 1906, offers clean, comfortable, and well-maintained bedrooms traditionally furnished. Most rooms are doubles and triples, and each has hot and cold water. Showers and toilets are on every corridor. Only breakfast is served, but many restaurants and cafés are nearby. The hotel lies near Nørreport Station and the Botanical Gardens.

A GAY HOTEL

HOTEL JØRGENSEN, Rømersgade 11, DK-1362 København K. Tel. 33-13-81-86. 12 doubles with shower, 12 dormitory rooms. TV **Bus:** 14, 16.

$ Rates (including continental breakfast): 300–475 kroner ($50.45–$79.85) single; 400–575 kroner ($67.25–$96.65) double; 65 kroner ($10.95) per person in dormitory rooms. Breakfast costs 30 kroner ($5.05) extra. AE, DC, MC, V.

This white stucco hotel, lying on a busy boulevard in central Copenhagen, has an obvious allure for gay men and lesbians, but also welcomes straight people. The staff is most helpful. Prices are reasonable. Bedrooms are conventional and well organized. The dormitory rooms are segregated according to men and women—six each. The hotel also runs the popular Café Adagio in its basement.

 FROMMER'S COOL FOR KIDS

HOTELS

Kong Arthur *(see p. 61)* Once a home for Danish orphans, this is a safe haven near tree-lined Peblinge Lake in a residential Section.

Hotel Carlton *(see p. 61)* One of the best bets for families on a budget. Plenty of extra beds for children and within walking distance to the *The Little Mermaid.*

Hotel Dania *(see p. 61)* A comfortable family hotel, this establishment welcomes children and lies a short distance from the Tivoli.

Missionshotellet Ansgar *(see p. 63)* Children under 3 stay free, and extra beds are available for kids under 12. Twelve large rooms can accommodate up to six family members in each.

CHAPTER 6

COPENHAGEN DINING

1. **NEAR KONGENS NYTORV & NYHAVN**
2. **NEAR RÅDHUSPLADSEN & TIVOLI**
3. **NEAR ROSENBORG SLOT**
4. **AT GRÅBRØDRE TORV**
5. **NEAR KULTORVET**
6. **NEAR CHRISTIANSBORG**
7. **IN TIVOLI**
8. **ON THE OUTSKIRTS**
9. **SPECIALTY DINING**
* **FROMMER'S COOL FOR KIDS: RESTAURANTS**

I t is estimated that there are more than 2,000 cafés, snack bars, and restaurants in Copenhagen. Most of these restaurants are either in the Tivoli or centered around the Rådhuspladsen (Town Hall Square), the Central Station, or in Nyhavn. Others lie in the center of the shopping district, in streets branching off from the Strøget.

You pay for the privilege of dining in the Tivoli; prices are always higher. Reservations are not usually important, but it's best to call in advance. Nearly everyone answering phones in restaurants speaks English.

A 15% service charge is almost always added. Therefore leave only a few extra coins if service has been good. In restaurants rated "Expensive," you'll spend at least $30 not counting drinks, which are lethal in price because they are so heavily taxed. In restaurants in the moderate range, count on spending from $20 to $30 per person without drinks, and in restaurants considered inexpensive, figure about $15 to $20.

1. NEAR KONGENS NYTORV & NYHAVN

VERY EXPENSIVE

KOMMANDANTEN, Ny Adelgade 7. Tel. 33-12-09-90.
Cuisine: INTERNATIONAL. **Reservations:** Required. **Bus:** 1, 6.
$ **Prices:** Fixed-price menus 315–450 kroner ($52.95–$75.65); appetizers 70–110 kroner ($11.75–$18.50); main dishes 175–210 kroner ($29.40–$35.30). AE, DC, MC, V.
Open: Lunch Mon–Fri noon–2:30pm; dinner Mon–Sat 5:30pm–1am.

Built in 1698, the former residence of the military commander of Copenhagen, this restaurant is the epitome of Danish chic and charm. Have an apéritif in the charming bar before going upstairs to one of the beautiful rooms, painted in a cobalt blue.

The finest seasonal ingredients are used, and the menu changes every 2 weeks. You

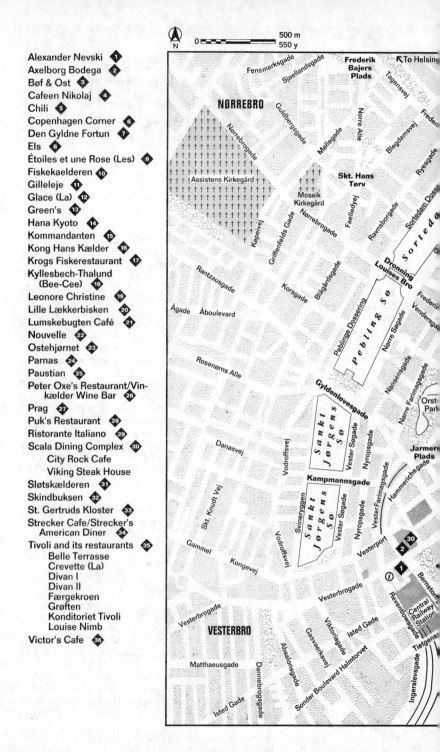

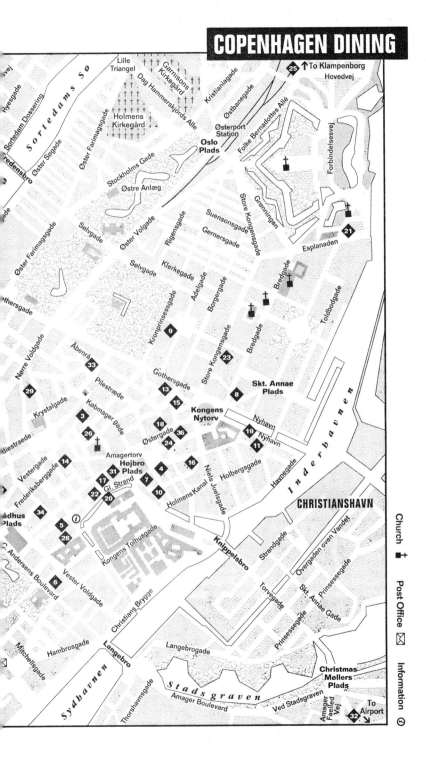

COPENHAGEN DINING

might be offered the grilled catch of the day, breast of duck with port wine sauce, grilled turbot with a spinach sauce, or a gratinée of shellfish. The service is perhaps the best in Copenhagen. Before leaving, look at the valuable Andy Warhol original of Queen Margrethe II in the downstairs dining room.

KONG HANS KAELDER, Vingårdsstraede 6. Tel. 33-11-68-68.
 Cuisine: FRENCH. **Reservations:** Required. **Bus:** 1, 6, 9.
$ **Prices:** Fixed-price menu 650 kroner ($109.25); appetizers 105–145 kroner ($17.65–$24.35); main dishes 220–275 kroner ($37–$46.25). AE, DC, MC, V
 Open: Dinner only, Mon–Sat 6–10pm. **Closed:** July 2–Aug 2.

⭐ This vaulted Gothic cellar, once owned by King Hans (1455–1513), may be the best restaurant in Denmark. It is certainly one of the most expensive. Located on "the oldest corner of Copenhagen," it has been carefully restored and is now a Relais Gourmands. Hans Christian Andersen lived above it and even wrote some of his finest stories here.

Alsace-born Daniel Letz, a leading chef of Scandinavia, creates dishes that one critic claimed "to have been prepared by Matisse or Picasso." The menu changes, but try the breast of duck with figs and lime, quails in a pot-au-feu, or tournedos in a foie gras sauce. Or order filet of lamb with coriander or filet of turbot in an eggplant-and-saffron sauce. For dessert, the plum ice cream with Armagnac is delectably smooth.

EXPENSIVE

LEONORE CHRISTINE, Nyhavn 9. Tel. 33-13-50-40.
 Cuisine: DANISH/FRENCH. **Reservations:** Required. **Bus:** 1, 6, 9.
$ **Prices:** Appetizers 75–95 kroner ($12.60–$15.95); main dishes 178–210 kroner ($29.90–$35.30); three-course fixed-price lunch 188 kroner ($31.60). AE, DC, MC, V.
 Open: Lunch Mon–Sat noon–3pm; dinner Mon–Sat 6–10pm.
It is generally conceded that this restaurant, on the sunny (south) side of the canal, is the best restaurant at Nyhavn. In a 1681 building, the decor is elegant. You can sample Danish veal filet with salsify, guinea fowl with wild cranberries, oven-baked fjord salmon with oysters, and grilled redfish with squash. Service is good and the wine list is extensive.

MODERATE

CAFE LUMSKEBUGTEN, Esplanaden 21. Tel. 33-15-60-29.
 Cuisine: DANISH. **Reservations:** Recommended. **Bus:** 1, 6, 9.
$ **Prices:** Fixed-price meal 385 kroner ($64.70) at dinner, 185 kroner ($31.10) at lunch; appetizers 85–180 kroner ($14.30–$30.25) at dinner, 48 kroner ($8.05) at lunch; main dishes 86–180 kroner ($14.45–$30.25) at dinner, 95–180 kroner ($15.95–$30.25) at lunch. AE, DC, MC, V.
 Open: Lunch daily 11am–4pm; dinner daily 6–10:30pm.
Established in 1854 by Karen Marguerita Krog, this restaurant at the end of the Esplanden was a haven for sailors, serving hash, homemade beer, and schnapps. As Krog's legend grew, aristocrats, artists, and members of the Danish royal family joined the diners. Even today the honorary beef hash is still served.

Two glistening white dining rooms are outfitted with antique ships' models, oil paintings, and pinewood floors. The food is excellent, as is the service. Try the tartare of salmon with herbs, fishcakes (more a flan than a cake), fried herring, baked codfish, or sugar-marinated salmon with mustard-cream sauce.

RESTAURANT ELS, Store Strandstraede 3. Tel. 33-14-13-41.
 Cuisine: DANISH/FRENCH. **Reservations:** Recommended. **Bus:** 1, 6.
$ **Prices:** Three-course dinner 214 kroner ($29.40); two-course lunch 175 kroner ($29.40); main dishes 138 kroner ($23.20) at dinner, 128 kroner ($21.50) at lunch. AE, DC, MC, V.
 Open: Lunch daily noon–3pm; dinner daily 5:30pm–1am.

Just off Kongens Nytorv, this restaurant preserves its original 1863 decor. Several 19th-century murals thought to be the work of Danish classical artist Constantin Hansen (1804–1880) are displayed. Hans Christian Andersen was a regular here.

Meals are priced on a daily changing fixed-price basis, but a selection of Danish open-face sandwiches are offered at lunch for those wanting a lighter meal. The cuisine at night is French, accompanied by excellent wines. Food is based on what is fresh at the market.

RESTAURANT GILLELEJE, Nyhavn 10. Tel. 33-12-58-58.

Cuisine: DANISH/INTERNATIONAL. **Reservations:** Recommended. **Bus:** 9, 10.

$ Prices: Appetizers 60–85 kroner ($10.10–$14.30); main dishes 148–245 kroner ($24.85–$41.20); fixed-price lunch 124 kroner ($20.85). AE, DC, MC, V.

Open: Lunch Mon–Sat 11:30am–3pm; dinner Mon–Sat 5–11pm.

The nautical decor is appealing but diners come for the elaborate rijsttafel (rice table), offering flavored rice and an endless procession of meats, fish, spices, garnishes, and sauces. Other specialties include whisky steak flambé with grilled tomatoes, fish soup, and Danish herring platter. Desserts like papaya and passion-fruit sorbets are available.

VICTOR'S CAFE, Ny Østergade 8. Tel. 33-13-36-13.

Cuisine: DANISH/FRENCH. **Reservations:** Recommended. **Bus:** 1, 6, 9.

$ Prices: Fixed-priced meal 195–245 kroner ($32.80–$41.20) at dinner, 120 kroner ($20.15) at lunch; appetizers 55–75 kroner ($9.25–$12.60); main dishes 125–150 kroner ($21–$25.20). AE, DC, MC, V.

Open: Lunch daily 11:30am–3pm; dinner daily 6–11pm.

This is the Danish version of Paris's famous La Coupole. Decorated in a sophisticated bistro style, it has a café at one end and a restaurant at the other. The art-oriented crowd can sit at the curved, illuminated bar or at one of the tables. The popular Victor Plate, costing 95 kroner ($15.95) at lunch, offers three food items. You can also choose from a selection of open-face sandwiches in the 35- to 60-kroner ($5.90 to $10.10) range. Look for the daily specials posted on the blackboard. Try breast of wild duckling with plums and celery, ragout of fish with red peppers, or baked salmon with chervil sauce and artichoke hearts. The fish menu changes daily.

INEXPENSIVE

RESTAURANT PARNAS, Lille Kongensgade 16. Tel. 33-11-49-10.

Cuisine: DANISH. **Reservations:** Required. **Bus:** 1, 6, 28, 29.

$ Prices: Appetizers 36–59 kroner ($6.05–$9.90); main dishes 52–145 kroner ($8.75–$24.35). AE, DC, MC, V.

Open: Mon–Thurs 5pm–3am, Sat 6pm–5am.

Opposite the city's largest department store, Magasin, this is a late-night refuge decorated like a warm, rustic, old-fashioned Danish *kro* (inn). Begin with three different kinds of herring or marinated salmon, following with fried sliced pork with parsley sauce, several different preparations of sole and salmon, or the house specialty, a Parnas Gryde combining grilled sirloin with bacon, marrow, and mushrooms, with béarnaise sauce on the side. This platter has been on the menu since the restaurant opened in the 1930s. After midnight a limited menu is available. Live music begins at 8:30pm.

2. NEAR RÅDSHUSPLADSEN & TIVOLI

EXPENSIVE

ALEXANDER NEVSKI, in the Plaza Hotel, Bernstorffsgade 4. Tel. 33-14-92-62.

Cuisine: RUSSIAN. **Reservations:** Required. **Bus:** 1, 6.

$ Prices: Appetizers 22–68 kroner ($3.70–$11.45); main dishes 118–168 kroner ($19.85–$28.25). AE, DC, MC, V.
Open: Lunch Mon–Sat 11:30am–3:30pm; dinner Mon–Sat 4:30–11:30pm.

The only Russian restaurant in Denmark, it's named after the Prince of Novgorod, a Russian national hero of the 1200s. After a drink in the Library Bar (see "Evening Entertainment," in Chapter 7), proceed into the tsarist-style restaurant. An impressive range of caviar and more than 20 different vodkas are available.

Some dishes are Russian classics; others are rediscovered recipes. Most food preparation is visible through an opening in the kitchen. Order steaks skewered on fencing swords, marinated in brandy, and then flambéed at your table. Try blinis with caviar, sautéed fresh fish with a pomegranate and pumpkin compote, or beef Stroganoff for two. The sauté of guinea fowl with Jerusalem artichokes is another specialty. Finish with tea from a samovar, after ordering the rum baba with cranberry icing and a vanilla sauce.

MODERATE

COPENHAGEN CORNER, H. C. Andersens Blvd. 18. Tel. 33-91-07-07.
   Cuisine: SCANDINAVIAN. **Reservations:** Recommended. **Bus:** 1, 6, 8.
$ Prices: Two-course meals 118–230 kroner ($19.85–$38.65); three-course meals 310 kroner ($52.10); appetizers 45–115 kroner ($7.55–$19.35); main dishes 75–190 kroner ($12.60–$31.95). AE, DC, MC, V.
   Open: Daily 11am–midnight.

Opening onto Rådhuspladsen, around the corner from the Tivoli, this restaurant is decorated like a greenhouse. The decor is modern Scandinavian, with two large oil paintings by Danish masters P. S. Croyer and Michael Ancher. The menu is extensive, with some 80 dishes, including several different preparations of Norwegian salmon, or butter-fried plaice with parsley sauce and brown butter. Meat dishes include Danish duckling in its own juice, with sautéed red cabbage and fried apples. Try also the roast filet of reindeer with cloudberries glazed in acacia honey.

HANA KYOTO, Vimmelskaftet 39, Strøgarkaden. Tel. 33-32-22-96.
   Cuisine: SUSHI. **Reservations:** Recommended. **Bus:** 1, 6, 28.
$ Prices: Fixed-price meals 160–220 kroner ($26.90–$37) at dinner, 65–100 kroner ($10.95–$16.80) at lunch; sushi 15–50 kroner ($2.50–$8.40) per piece of raw fish before it is cut. AE, DC, MC, V.
   Open: Lunch Mon–Fri noon–3pm; dinner Mon–Fri 5–10pm.

This is the only sushi bar in Copenhagen. Located on the Strøget, it's decorated in typical Japanese simplicity. It imports fresh fish and shellfish from Japan, Britain, Iceland, Greenland, Norway, and the Mediterranean. (The chef will cook the fish upon request.) Tuna, salmon, and eel are the most popular raw fish that Danes order. The chef does not serve typical Japanese dishes such as sukiyaki. A fixed-price dinner includes soup, appetizers, a main-course selection of raw fish, and tea.

RESTAURANT PRAG, Amagerbrogade 37. Tel. 31-54-44-44.
   Cuisine: DANISH. **Reservations:** Recommended. **Bus:** 2, 9.
$ Prices: Fixed-price menus 148–245 kroner ($24.85–$41.20); menu gastronomique 395 kroner ($66.40); appetizers 48–89 kroner ($8.05–$14.95); main dishes 128–188 kroner ($21.50–$31.60). AE, DC, MC, V.
   Open: Lunch Mon–Fri 11:30am–3pm; dinner Mon–Sat 5–10pm.

Near the SAS Scandinavia Hotel, east of Tivoli, this famous Copenhagen restaurant has never been better. Established in 1910 as the Café Sønderborg, it has a new lease on life under two talented brother chefs, Jan and Jorgen Michelsen. It fills the entire block, incorporating an English-style library, and is like a warmly accommodating Danish *kro* (inn), with dark-wood trim, white stucco walls, and impeccable service.

As much attention is paid to the way a dish looks as to the way it tastes. Try the warm leek terrine with a mushroom salad, sautéed fish of the day, lobster bisque with cognac, or filet of veal with a red wine sauce and stuffed onions. The wild breast of duck with spinach is also excellent. For dessert, have prunes marinated in Chartreuse with vanilla ice cream.

VIKING STEAK HOUSE, Scala, Axeltorv 2. Tel. 33-15-37-99.

Cuisine: BEEF. **Reservations:** Not required. **Bus:** 1, 6, 8.

$ Prices: Appetizers 42–98 kroner ($7.05–$16.45); main dishes 88–198 kroner ($14.80–$33.30); three-course lunch 68 kroner ($11.45); children's lunch menu 28 kroner ($4.70). AE, DC, MC, V.

Open: Daily 11am–midnight.

The most expensive dish is lobster from a live tank at the front, but most come to sample the Danish beef steaks, priced according to weight. In this second-floor dining room in the Scala complex across from the Tivoli you check off the kind of steak you want on a card return it to the waitress. While your steak is cooking, help yourself to the salad bar.

INEXPENSIVE

CHILI, Vandkunsten 1. Tel. 33-91-19-18.

Cuisine: MEXICAN. **Reservations:** Recommended. **Bus:** 5, 14, 16, 28, 41.

$ Prices: Appetizers 19–41 kroner ($3.20–$6.90); main dishes 34–68 kroner ($5.70–$11.45). No credit cards.

Open: Mon–Wed 11am–11pm, Thurs–Sat 11am–midnight, Sun 1–9pm.

A short walk from Rådhuspladsen, Chili is the latest reincarnation of the famous old Tokanten, a landmark eating house. It's decorated in the colors of the American Southwest, warm reds, greens, and blues. Many kinds of hamburgers are available, plus a Tex-Mex salad and chili con carne. Service is fast, and clients come and go quickly.

CITY ROCK CAFE, Scala, Axeltorv 2. Tel. 33-15-45-40.

Cuisine: AMERICAN. **Reservations:** Not required. **Bus:** 1, 6, 8.

$ Prices: Appetizers 35–52 kroner ($5.90–$8.75); sandwiches 51–60 kroner ($8.55–$10.10).

Open: Daily 11am–2am.

This is one of the busiest café/bars at Scala. Rock 'n' roll music from the '60s to the '90s is played against a backdrop of banquettes made from the rear end of a 1959 Cadillac and an antique Harley Davidson motorcycle spotlit and displayed as pop art. Kids feast on such fare as a Malibu salad with rice, ham, and olives, or Pacific sandwiches (tuna and cucumber), and of course, hamburgers.

GREEN'S RESTAURANT, Grønnegade 12-14. Tel. 33-15-16-90.

Cuisine: VEGETARIAN. **Reservations:** Recommended. **Bus:** 7, 17, 43.

$ Prices: Salad bar 59 kroner ($9.90); appetizers 42–70 kroner ($7.05–$11.75); main dishes 75–129 kroner ($12.60–$21.70). MC, V.

Open: Mon–Sat 11:30am–10pm.

This popular vegetarian restaurant lies in a commercial neighborhood, off Pistolstraede, at the edge of a pedestrians-only courtyard. It has a cobblestone-covered outdoor terrace for summer dining. You can order onion quiche, vegetarian pizzas, pita-bread sandwiches, a daily soup, fresh-squeezed juice, and a vegetarian dish of the day. Many make a meal just from the salad bar. At lunchtime it is buffet style and at night there's full service.

PUK'S RESTAURANT, Vandkunsten 8. Tel. 33-11-14-17.

Cuisine: DANISH. **Reservations:** Required (summer and Dec only). **Bus:** 28, 29, 41.

$ Prices: Fixed-price menu 98 kroner ($16.45); appetizers 38–62 kroner ($6.40–$10.40); main dishes 26–165 kroner ($4.35–$27.75). AE, DC, MC, V.

Open: Daily 10:30am–5am (kitchen closes at 4am Mon–Sat, at 2am Sun).

Puk's lies in the basement of what was once a 1750 brewery. Take the outside stairs down; the street-level pub is different from Puk's. Smørrebrød is presented more as platters of food than as sandwiches. Typical Danish dishes, such as herring and ham, are served. Many revelers stop here for a snack in the early morning.

BUDGET

AXELBORG BODEGA, Axeltorv 1. Tel. 33-11-06-38.
   Cuisine: DANISH. **Reservations:** Recommended. **Bus:** 1, 6.
$ **Prices:** Appetizers 22–50 kroner ($3.70–$8.40); main dishes 60–110 kroner ($10.10–$18.50); two-course Danmenu at lunch 75 kroner ($12.60). AE, DC, MC, V.
   Open: Daily 11:30am–9:30pm (bar open 10am–2am).

Across from the Circus and near Scala and Tivoli, this well-established 1912 Danish café has outdoor tables. Order the *dagens ret* (daily special). Typical Danish dishes are featured, including frikadeller (meatball) and pork chops. A wide selection of smørrebrød is also always available, costing from 33 kroner ($5.55).

STRECKERS CAFE/STRECKERS AMERICAN DINER, Frederiksberg-gade 3. Tel. 33-13-73-74.
   Cuisine: AMERICAN/DANISH. **Reservations:** Not required. **Bus:** 5.
$ **Prices:** Café pastries 8–25 kroner ($1.35–$4.20); smørrebrød 20–30 kroner ($3.35–$5.05); hamburgers 32–38 kroner ($5.40–$6.40); sandwiches 29–35 kroner ($4.85–$5.90). No credit cards.
   Open: Daily 8am–7pm.

One of the best-known cafés along Strøget, near the Town Hall, Streckers is a two-in-one establishment. The street level of this old, traditional place still maintains its Danish menu and allure. Seated on garden-style iron chairs, you can order pastries, sandwiches, salads, or coffee. The upstairs balcony, however, is now an American diner. Breakfast and brunch are also available.

3. NEAR ROSENBORG SLOT

VERY EXPENSIVE

ST. GERTRUDS KLOSTER, Hauser Plads 32. Tel. 33-14-66-30.
   Cuisine: INTERNATIONAL. **Reservations:** Required. **Bus:** 4E, 7E, 14, 16.
$ **Prices:** Three-course menus 366–445 kroner ($61.55–$74.80); six-course menu dégustation 675 kroner ($113.45); appetizers 90–185 kroner ($15.15–$43.70); main dishes 188–260 kroner ($31.60–$43.70). AE, DC, MC, V.
   Open: Dinner only, daily 5–11:15pm.

Near Nørreport Station and south of Rosenborg Castle, this is the most romantic restaurant in Copenhagen. It is also one of the most expensive. There's no electricity in the labyrinth of 14th-century underground vaults, and the hundreds of flickering candles, open grill, iron sconces, and rough-hewn furniture create the most elegant medieval ambience. Have an apéritif in the darkly paneled library. Try the fresh homemade foie gras with black truffles, lobster served in a turbot bouillon, scallops sautéed with herbs in sauterne, venison (year round) with green asparagus and truffle sauce, or a fish-and-shellfish terrine studded with chunks of lobster and salmon.

EXPENSIVE

LES ETOILES ET UNE ROSE, Dronningens Tvaergade 43. Tel. 33-15-05-54.
   Cuisine: DANISH/FRENCH. **Reservations:** Required. **Bus:** 6, 8, 28, 41.
$ **Prices:** Six-course menu gourmet 395 kroner ($66.40); appetizers 62–92 kroner ($10.40–$15.45); main dishes 165–215 kroner ($27.75–$36.15). AE, DC, MC, V.
   Open: Lunch Mon–Fri noon–2pm; dinner Mon–Sat 5:30–10pm. **Closed:** First 2 weeks of Jan.

⭐ Hidden by a 1950s apartment complex, near the Royal Theatre, lies one of the top restaurants in Copenhagen. Inside, the Mandrup family operates an apéritif bar, a pale-green and white dining room, and an outdoor terrace for warm-weather meals. They earn their truly international reputation every night by serving such dishes as terrine of guinea fowl with truffles on a bed of spinach and honey-sautéed rhubard, ragoût of fresh seafood in puff pastry with root vegetables, and entrecôte of Danish lamb roasted with fresh herbs and covered in a mustard-cream sauce. The chef's "fish fantasy" combines seven different kinds of fish and shellfish.

4. AT GRÅBRØDRE TORV

MODERATE

BØF & OST, Gråbrødre Torv 13. Tel. 31-11-99-11.
  Cuisine: DANISH/FRENCH. **Reservations:** Required.
$ Prices: Fixed-price dinner 198 kroner ($33.30); appetizers 49–128 kroner ($8.25–$21.50); main dishes 115–159 kroner ($19.35–$26.75). DC, MC, V.
  Open: Mon–Sat 11:30am–midnight.
The "Beef and Cheese" is housed in a 1728 building, its cellars from a medieval monastery. In summer, there is a pleasant outdoor terrace, overlooking Grey Friars Square. Specialties include lobster soup, salmon savoie, Danish Heltling caviar, a cheese plate with six different selections, and some of the best grilled tenderloin in town. A salad with French dressing and roasted pine nuts is served with every meal. The beef dishes are considerably more expensive, but delicious. Desserts and a full wine list are also available.

PETER OXE'S RESTAURANT/VINKAELDER WINE BAR, Gråbrødre Torv 11. Tel. 33-11-00-77.
  Cuisine: DANISH. **Reservations:** Recommended. **Bus:** 5.
$ Prices: Appetizers 56–89 kroner ($9.40–$14.95); main dishes 85–139 kroner ($14.30–$23.35). DC, MC, V.
  Open: Daily noon–1am.
In the Middle Ages this was the site of a monastery, but the present building dates from the 1700s. The restaurant and wine bar was established in the 1970s, and continues in popularity among the young. A salad bar is included in the price of the main course, but it is so tempting that many opt to have it alone, costing 59 kroner ($9.90) per person. Dishes include lobster soup, salmon tartare, oysters, open-face sandwiches, hamburgers, and fresh fish. The Vinkaelder serves glasses, carafes, or bottles of wine from France, Spain, Italy, Germany, and Australia. A glass costs from 26 kroner ($4.35).

5. NEAR KULTORVET

INEXPENSIVE

RISTORANTE ITALIANO, Fiolstraede 2. Tel. 31-11-12-95.
  Cuisine: ITALIAN. **Reservations:** Recommended. **Bus:** 5.
$ Prices: Pizzas and pastas 39–59 kroner ($6.55–$9.90). AE, DC, MC, V.
  Open: Daily 11am–2am (kitchen closes at 1am).
This fun restaurant is patronized mainly by students from the nearby University of Copenhagen. Pizzas (Danish-Italian style) are featured, as well as lots of good pasta. Reasonably priced meat and fish courses are also available.

6. NEAR CHRISTIANSBORG

EXPENSIVE

KROGS FISKERESTAURANT, Gammel Strand 38. Tel. 33-15-89-15.
Cuisine: SEAFOOD. **Reservations:** Required. **Bus:** 2, 10, 16.
$ **Prices:** Fixed-price menu 325 kroner ($54.65) for three courses, 385 kroner ($64.70) for four courses; appetizers 78–155 kroner ($13.10–$26.05); main dishes 195–325 kroner ($32.80–$54.65). AE, DC, MC, V.
Open: Lunch Mon–Sat noon–3pm; dinner Mon–Sat 5–10pm.
Lying near Christianborg Castle, this 1789 building has been a restaurant since 1910, serving delectable seafood. Choices include lobster soup, bouillabaisse, natural oysters, mussels steamed in white wine, and poached salmon-trout. A limited selection of meat dishes is available.

NOUVELLE, Gammel Strand 34. Tel. 33-13-50-18.
Cuisine: DANISH. **Reservations:** Required. **Bus:** 28, 29, 41.
$ **Prices:** Four-course dinner 385 kroner ($64.70); three-course lunch 225 kroner ($37.80); appetizers 75–125 kroner ($12.60–$21); main dishes 175–218 kroner ($29.40–$36.65). AE, DC, MC, V.
Open: Lunch Mon–Fri 11:30am–3pm; dinner Mon–Sat 7:30–10pm.
⭐ In an elegant dining room setting Nouvelle is one of the capital's special restaurants. It lies on the first floor of a gray 1870 house beside a canal. The color scheme is dark and light tones of yellow, with gray and purple accents. The cuisine is modern Danish with such dishes as corn pie with Beluga caviar and cold bouillon-marinated vegetables, and cream of turbot soup spiced with sauterne. Try the fricassée of sole with mussels and pear or haunch of venison with damson plum sauce and a timbale of marrow. Finish with a selection of exotic cheese or a delectable house pastry.

MODERATE

DEN GYLDNE FORTUN, Ved Stranden 18. Tel. 33-12-20-11.
Cuisine: DANISH/SEAFOOD. **Reservations:** Recommended. **Bus:** 1, 6, 10.
$ **Prices:** Fixed-price meals 285 kroner ($47.90) at dinner, 135 kroner ($22.70) at lunch; appetizers 65–85 kroner ($10.95–$14.30); main dishes 135–295 kroner ($22.70–$49.60). AE, DC, MC.
Open: Mon–Fri noon–midnight, Sat–Sun 6–11pm.
Popular at lunchtime, this restaurant opposite Christiansborg Castle is a real "golden fortune," as the name translates. Dating from 1796, it has been visited by Hans Christian Andersen, Jenny Lind, and Henry Wadsworth Longfellow. You climb green marble stairs to enter the formal restaurant resembling an English club. Amid crystal chandeliers and modern lithographs, you'll enjoy good-tasting fresh fish. Look for daily specials or sample the herring, poached sole, Baltic salmon, or a Danish beef dish. Try a Scandinavian bouillabaisse.

FISKEKAELDEREN, Ved Stranden 18. Tel. 33-12-20-11.
Cuisine: SEAFOOD. **Reservations:** Required. **Bus:** 1, 6, 10.
$ **Prices:** Appetizers 55–88 kroner ($9.25–$14.80); main dishes 135–245 kroner ($22.70–$41.20). AE, DC, MC, V.
Open: Mon–Fri noon–11:30pm, Sat–Sun 5–10:30pm.
Though the building dates from 1750, this restaurant was established in 1975. It prides itself on very fresh fish either imported from the Mediterranean or caught in the waters of the North Atlantic. Warmly nautical in decor, it has a bubbling lobster tank and an ice table displaying the fish of the day. Try the terrine of smoked fish with seaweed and deep-fried artichokes, Danish fish soup, stuffed sole poached in white wine and glazed with hollandaise sauce, or fricassée of three types of fish in a

saffron-flavored bouillon with noodles. Some beef dishes, such as Charolais sirloin, are also served.

7. IN TIVOLI

Food prices inside Tivoli are about 30% higher than elsewhere. Try skipping dessert at a restaurant and picking up a less expensive treat at one of the many stands. Take bus 1, 6, 8, 30, 32, or 33 to reach the park and any of the following restaurants.

Note: These restaurants are open only from May to mid-September.

VERY EXPENSIVE

BELLE TERRASSE, Tivoli. Tel. 33-12-11-36.
   Cuisine: DANISH/FRENCH. **Reservations:** Required.
$ Prices: Fixed-price menu 275–435 kroner ($46.25–$73.10); appetizers 79–165 kroner ($13.30–$27.75); main dishes 215–275 kroner ($36.15–$46.25). AE, DC, MC, V.
   Open: Daily noon–11pm.
A seductive menu and a glamorous, flower-filled terrace lures diners to one of Tivoli's best restaurants. Guests such as Marlene Dietrich have enjoyed the Belle Epoque atmosphere in this octagonal greenhouselike dining room. The cuisine is refined and dignified, the service formal. Begin with the consommé of lobster soup with ravioli of chives, followed by salmon on a bed of leeks with saffron sauce or filet of veal with morels.

DIVAN II, Tivoli. Tel. 33-12-51-51.
   Cuisine: DANISH/FRENCH. **Reservations:** Required.
$ Prices: Appetizers 130–285 kroner ($21.85–$47.90); main dishes 198–295 kroner ($33.30–$49.60). AE, DC, MC, V.
   Open: Daily noon–midnight.
This may be the most expensive restaurant in Denmark. It's also the best. Service is impeccable in this exquisite gardenlike setting where the chef selects only the finest ingredients. Try the poached turbot with morels, Baltic salmon with glazed vegetables, or roast stuffed duckling with truffles.

EXPENSIVE

LA CREVETTE, Tivoli. Tel. 33-14-68-47.
   Cuisine: SEAFOOD. **Reservations:** Required.
$ Prices: Fixed-price meal 325 kroner ($54.65) at dinner, 198 kroner ($33.30) at lunch; appetizers 85–125 kroner ($14.30–$21); main dishes 145–225 kroner ($24.35–$37.80). AE, DC, MC, V.
   Open: Daily noon–11pm.
The only seafood restaurant in the Tivoli, it has an outdoor terrace and an elegant modern dining room. The seafood is prepared in a French international style. Specialties include salmon marinated in cognac, fish terrine, a three-herring platter, oven-baked turbot with tiny shrimp, grilled lobster, and a handful of well-seasoned meat dishes such as vegetable-stuffed breast of guinea fowl with a mushroom-and-boletus sauce. The best dessert is fresh berries with cream.

DIVAN I, Tivoli. Tel. 33-11-42-42.
   Cuisine: FRENCH. **Reservations:** Required.
$ Prices: Fixed-price meals 285–395 kroner ($47.90–$66.40) at dinner, 198 kroner ($33.30) at lunch; appetizers 59–185 kroner ($9.90–$31.10); main dishes 85–185 kroner ($14.30–$31.10). AE, DC, MC, V.
   Open: Daily noon–11pm (drinks until midnight).
Opened the same year as the Tivoli, this popular gardenlike restaurant has been run by

the same family ever since. Be assured of a refined French cuisine and service, and a good view of the Tivoli Gardens. Some Danish dishes are offered.

LOUISE NIMB, Tivoli. Tel. 33-14-60-03.
  Cuisine: DANISH/FRENCH. **Reservations:** Required.
$ **Prices:** Fixed-price menus 145–395 kroner ($24.35–$66.40); appetizers 110–400 kroner ($18.50–$67.25); main dishes 185–210 kroner ($31.10–$35.30). AE, DC, MC, V.
  Open: Lunch daily noon–4pm; dinner daily 5–11pm.
Next door to its companion restaurant La Crevette, this may be the most formal restaurant in Tivoli, styled like a Moorish pavilion. Dinner might include grilled salmon with red-wine butter, rib roast of beef, and tournedos in a calvados-based sauce. There is live piano music during dinner.

MODERATE

FAERGEKROEN, Tivoli. Tel. 33-12-94-12.
  Cuisine: DANISH. **Reservations:** Not required.
$ **Prices:** Appetizers 21–45 kroner ($3.55–$7.55); main dishes 60–130 kroner ($10.10–$21.85); fixed-price lunch 75 kroner ($12.60). DC, MC, V.
  Open: Daily 10am–midnight (hot food 11am–9:45pm).
Nestled amid a cluster of trees at the edge of the lake, this restaurant resembles a pink half-timbered Danish cottage. In warm weather, try to sit on the outside dining terrace. The menu offers drinks, snacks, and full meals. The latter might include an array of omelets, beef with horseradish, fried plaice with melted butter, pork chops with red cabbage, curried chicken, and fried meatballs. A pianist provides sing-along music every evening starting at 8pm.

GRØFTEN, Tivoli. Tel. 33-12-11-25.
  Cuisine: DANISH. **Reservations:** Not required.
$ **Prices:** Fixed-price menu 80 kroner ($13.45); appetizers 33–88 kroner ($5.55–$14.80); main dishes 65–140 kroner ($10.95–$23.55). DC, MC, V.
  Open: Daily 11am–11pm.
I think this is the best budget restaurant in Tivoli, offering a tourist menu that could be tomato soup with crisp French bread, followed by ground beef with gravy, grilled mushrooms, and tiny new potatoes. It's located next to the Peacock Theater, and most diners eat outside.

8. ON THE OUTSKIRTS

EXPENSIVE

RESTAURANT SAISON, in the Hotel Skovhoved, Strandvejen 267, Charlottenlund. Tel. 31-64-00-28.
  Cuisine: DANISH/FRENCH. **Reservations:** Required.
$ **Prices:** Fixed-price meals 215–465 kroner ($36.15–$78.15) at dinner, 170–275 kroner ($28.60–$46.25) at lunch; appetizers 85–105 kroner ($14.30–$17.65) at dinner, 45–95 kroner ($7.55–$15.95) at lunch; main dishes 180–225 kroner ($30.25–$37.80) at dinner, 175–225 kroner ($29.40–$37.80) at lunch. AE, DC, MC, V.
  Open: Lunch Mon–Sat noon–2pm; dinner Mon–Sat 5:30–10pm.
One of Denmark's finest restaurants lies 5 miles north of Copenhagen in a 1900 red-brick hotel. From the ground-floor dining room you can look across the water to Sweden. Guests can dine in either the white room or the red room, the latter painted with pseudo-Egyptian murals by turn-of-the-century students in exchange for a free room. There is also a glassed-in terrace. One fixed-price menu is devoted to local fare

such as a vegetable terrine with salted salmon or roast rabbit. Dishes change, but typical items include parsley-and-oyster soup, layered casserole of salmon and cabbage with a crab sauce, and sautéed halibut with forest mushrooms. Game, such as venison, is served in season.

SOLLERØD KRO, Sollerrødvej 35, Holte-Søllerød. Tel. 42-80-25-05.
   Cuisine: DANISH/INTERNATIONAL. **Reservations:** Required. **Directions:** Take highway E4 toward Holte and exit at Søllerød; or take the S-train to Holte and taxi the rest of the way.
$ **Prices:** Fixed-price dinner 525 kroner ($88.25); appetizers 120–145 kroner ($20.15–$24.35); main dishes 150–240 kroner ($25.20–$40.35). AE, DC, MC, V.
   Open: Daily 11:30am–10pm.
In a historic model village 11 miles north of Copenhagen, this traditional 1677 inn with a thatched roof and whitewashed walls is the top-rated restaurant of Zealand outside the capital. Located inside a flower-filled garden with outdoor courtyard dining, the setting is idyllic. Try such dishes as lobster bisque, filet of sole with Norwegian lobster and a lobster sauce, or loin of Danish lamb with herbs baked en croûte. From May to August, crevettes de fjord (shrimp from the fjord) is a feature.

MODERATE

RESTAURANT PAUSTIAN, Kalkbraenderiløbskaj 2. Tel. 31-18-55-01.
   Cuisine: DANISH. **Reservations:** Recommended.
$ **Prices:** Fixed-price lunch 175 kroner ($29.40); appetizers 55–95 kroner ($9.25–$15.95); main dishes 105–130 kroner ($17.65–$21.85). AE, DC, MC, V.
   Open: Lunch only, Mon–Fri noon–4pm, Sat noon–3pm.
Amid an industrial landscape 3 miles north of the city center along the North Harbor, this restaurant is part of the showroom for a large furniture outlet. In a futuristically modern building, it is worth the excursion. Combine lunch with a shopping trip to survey some of the finest Scandinavian furniture, including reproductions of the old masters such as Charles Eames and Alvar Aalto. The restaurant has cobalt-blue Majolica tile, high-tech lighting, and big windows framing cranes and masts of ships in the harbor. The cuisine uses the best of Danish produce. Begin with fresh oysters or mussel soup with leeks and garlic. Then try smoked salmon with spinach or veal kidney with mustard sauce.

9. SPECIALTY DINING

LOCAL FAVORITES

The favorite lunch of Scandinavians, particularly of Danes, is smørrebrød (an open-face sandwich). The purest form of smørrebrød is made with Danish dark rye bread, called *rugbrød,* although other types of bread are sometimes used. Most

---

 FROMMER'S COOL FOR KIDS
RESTAURANTS

City Rock Café (see p. 71) A busy café, rock 'n' roll music from the '60s to the '90s is played against a backdrop of banquettes made from a 1959 Cadillac and a Harley Davidson motorcycle.

Copenhagen Corner (see p. 70) A special children's menu with such dishes as shrimp cocktail and grilled rump steak are offered.

taverns and cafés offer smørrebrød, but there are also many places that just serve this on a take-out basis.

INEXPENSIVE

LILLE LAEKKERBISKEN, Gammel Strand 34. Tel. 33-32-04-00.
Cuisine: DANISH. **Reservations:** None. **Bus:** 28, 29, 41.
$ Prices: 32–88 kroner ($5.40–$14.80). AE, DC, MC, V.
Open: Lunch only, Mon–Sat 11:30am–4pm.

This lunch-only restaurant, in the same building as the elegant Nouvelle, has walls covered with 19th-century oil paintings and old tapestries. It offers a full array of smørrebrød along with such hot main dishes as fried plaice.

RESTAURANT OSTEHJØRNET, Store Kongensgade 56. Tel. 33-15-85-77.
Cuisine: DANISH. **Reservations:** Recommended. **Bus:** 1, 10.
$ Prices: Appetizers 50 kroner ($8.40); main dishes 70–85 kroner ($11.75–$14.30). DC, MC, V.
Open: June and Aug–Sept, Mon–Fri 11:30am–6pm; Oct–May, Mon–Fri 11:30am–6pm, Sat 11:30am–3pm. **Closed:** July.

Since this restaurant is so popular at lunchtime that a dozen or so diners are turned away, the secret is to arrive early or late. There are a variety of Danish specialties, but I prefer the seafood salads made fresh daily. I recommend the herring salad, the mussel salad, quiche Lorraine, veal Cordon Bleu, smoked turkey, sweetbreads, and the ham and cheese omelets. A smart dessert choice might be a delectable fruit tart with a hint of chocolate. The restaurant lies one floor above street level in an 18th-century building.

SLØTSKAELDEREN, Fortunstraede 4. Tel. 33-12-61-25.
Cuisine: DANISH. **Reservations:** Recommended. **Bus:** 1, 6, 10.
$ Prices: Smørrebrød (open-face sandwiches) 20–63 kroner ($3.35–$10.60). DC, MC, V.
Open: Tues–Sat 11am–3pm.

This is the star of the smørrebrød. This landmark opened in 1797, but since 1910 has been owned by the same family. Everything—the Danish wood trim, the framed old photographs, and the gold walls—add up to *hygge,* a coziness that has attracted such notables as the Prince of Denmark. Try the marinated salmon, fresh tiny shrimp, or hot frikadeller. The smoked-eel and scrambled-egg sandwich is said to be the best of its kind.

DINING COMPLEX

Scala, Axeltorv 2, was originally conceived in 1851 as the Danish National Amusement Center, a collection of shops, cafés, and amusement arcades for the wintertime. Close to the Tivoli, City Hall, and the Central Station, it thrived until 1958. In 1987 it was purchased and renovated, then reopened in 1989 as the most extensive range of bars, restaurants, cinemas, and nightlife possibilities in the Danish capital.

Restaurants in Scala are open daily from 11am to midnight or 1am. Reservations are almost never required. Establishments accept major credit cards (AE, DC, MC, V).

AFTERNOON TEA

LA GLACE, Skoubogade 3-5. Tel. 33-14-46-46.
Cuisine: PASTRIES. **Reservations:** None. **Bus:** 1, 6, 8.
$ Prices: Pastries 7.50–18 kroner ($1.25–$3.05). No credit cards.
Open: Daily 8am–6pm.

Open since 1879, this time-honored pastry shop offers a pot of coffee or chocolate for 21 kroner ($3.55), and a variety of cakes, pastries, and chocolates. Try a slice of sportskage (sportsman's cake), composed of whipped cream, crumbled nougat, macaroons, and profiteroles that have been glazed in caramel. If chocolate is your bag, you'll appreciate the Othellokage (macaroons, custard cream, and outrageous amounts of chocolate).

CAFES

CAFEEN NIKOLAJ, Nikolaj Plads 12. Tel. 33-11-63-13.
   Cuisine: DANISH. **Reservations:** None. **Bus:** 2, 6, 28, 41.
$ Prices: Appetizers 30–50 kroner ($5.05–$8.40); main dishes 45–88 kroner ($7.55–$14.80). No credit cards.
   Open: Mon–Sat noon–5pm.
This unusual café is located within the monument which, circa 1530, was the scene of the thundering sermons of Hans Tausen, a father of the Danish Reformation. It serves typically Danish lunches, including open-face sandwiches, soups, herring, and sliced ham and cheese.

SKINDBUKSEN, Lille Kongensgade 4, off Kongens Nytorv. Tel. 33-12-90-37.
   Cuisine: DANISH. **Reservations:** None. **Bus:** 9, 10.
$ Prices: Appetizers 29–45 kroner ($4.85–$7.55); main dishes 39–98 kroner ($6.55–$16.45). AE, DC.
   Open: Daily 11am–1am (kitchen closes at 8:45pm).
This atmospheric landmark, well known among the beer drinkers, serves lobscouse—a meat-and-potato stew (mainly potatoes). It's so popular that it is frequently sold out by noon. Smørrebrød is also available, costing from 20 kroner ($3.35). Other items include soups, pâtés, shrimp, and beef with béarnaise sauce.

STREET FOOD

Copenhagen has many hot-dog stands, chicken and fish grills, and smørrebrød counters, providing good, quick, and inexpensive meals.
   Hot-dog stands, especially those around the Rådhuspladsen, offer polser (steamed or grilled hot dogs) with shredded onions on top and pommes frites (french fries) on the side.
   The **bageri** or **konditori** (bakery) found on almost every block, sells fresh bread, rolls, and Danish pastries.
   Viktualiehandler (small food shops), throughout the city, are the closest thing to a New York deli. You can buy roast beef with løg (fried onions) included free. The best buy is smoked fish. Ask for a Bornholmer, a large, boneless sardine from the Danish island of Bornholm, or for røgost, a popular and inexpensive smoked cheese.
   Yogurt fans will be delighted to know that the Danish variety is cheap and tasty. It's available in small containers—just peel off the cover and drink it right out of the cup as the Danes do. Hytte ret (cottage cheese) is also good and cheap, but it's sold only in Irma stores.

PICNIC FARE & WHERE TO EAT IT

You can picnic in any of the city parks in the town center. Try Kongsgarten near Kongens Nytorv, the Kastellet area near *The Little Mermaid* statue, Botanisk Have (site of the Botanical Garden), the lakeside promenades in southeastern Copenhagen, and the old moat at Christianhavn. Remember not to litter.
   Pick up some Danish smørrebrød to take out. The most central location for this is **Centrum Smørrebrød,** Vesterbrogade 6 (tel. 33-12-80-76), which is open 24 hours a day. The location is near the Tivoli and the Central Rail Station. Sandwiches range from 16.50 to 33.50 kroner ($2.75 to $5.65).
   Another branch is **City Smørrebrød,** Gothersgade 12 (tel. 33-15-75-42), open daily from 8am to 8pm.

CHAPTER 7

WHAT TO SEE & DO IN COPENHAGEN

With all the emphasis on amusement parks, shopping expeditions, beer-drinking cellars and gardens, and bustling nighttime spots, some visitors to Copenhagen tend to overlook the galleries, museums, and castles that make the city so special. There are so many little hidden nooks of charm waiting to be explored that it's hard to decide what to do first.

1. SUGGESTED ITINERARIES

IF YOU HAVE 1 DAY

Day 1: Take Walking Tour 1 through the Old City (see below in this chapter), which will give you time to recover from jet lag. Spend the late afternoon at Christiansborg Castle on Slotsholmen island where the Queen of Denmark receives guests. Early in the evening head to the Tivoli.

IF YOU HAVE 2 DAYS

Day 1: See "If You Have 1 Day," above.
Day 2: Visit Amalienborg Palace, the queen's residence. Try to time your visit to witness the changing of the guard. Continue beyond the palace to *The Little Mermaid* statue. In the afternoon, see the art treasures of Ny Carlsberg Glyptotek. At night, visit Scala, the restaurant-and-shopping complex.

IF YOU HAVE 3 DAYS

Days 1 & 2: See "If You Have 2 Days," above.
Day 3: In the morning, visit the 17th-century Rosenborg Castle, summer palace of King Christian IV. Afterward, wander through the park and gardens. Have lunch at one of the restaurants lining the canal at Nyhavn, the traditional seamen's quarter of Copenhagen. In the afternoon, go to Rundetårn (Round Tower) for a panoramic view of the city, and if time remains, stop in at the National Museum and Denmark's Fight for Freedom Museum.

IF YOU HAVE 5 DAYS

Days 1–3: See "If You Have 3 Days," above.

Day 4: Head north from Copenhagen to Louisiana, the modern-art museum, and continue on to Helsingør to visit Kronborg Castle, famously associated with Shakespeare's Hamlet. Return by train to Copenhagen in time for a stroll along the Strøget, the longest walking street in Europe. For dinner, head to Dragør.

Day 5: Visit Frilandsmuseet, at Lyngby, a half-hour train ride from Copenhagen. Have lunch at the park. Return to Copenhagen and take another of our walking tours (see below in this chapter). If time remains, tour a beer factory, either Carlsberg or Tuborg. Pay a final visit to the Tivoli to cap your adventure in the Danish capital.

2. THE TOP ATTRACTIONS

TIVOLI GARDENS, Vesterbrogade 3. Tel. 33-15-10-01.

Since it opened in 1843, this 20-acre garden and amusement park in the center of Copenhagen has been a resounding success, with its merry-go-round of tiny Viking ships, its games of chance and skill (pinball arcades, slot machines, shooting galleries), and its Ferris wheel of hot-air balloons and cabin seats. There's even a playground for children.

An Arabian-style fantasy palace, with towers and arches, houses dancing halls and more than two dozen restaurants in all price ranges, from a lakeside inn to a beer garden. Take a walk around the edge of the tiny lake with its ducks, swans, and boats.

A parade of the red-uniformed Tivoli Boys Guard takes place on weekends at 6:30 and 8:30pm, and their regimental band gives concerts on Saturday at 3:30pm on the open-air stage. The oldest building at Tivoli, the Chinese-style Pantomime Theater, with its peacock curtain, stages pantomimes and ballets in the evening.

For more specifics on all the nighttime happenings in Tivoli—fireworks, brass bands, orchestras, discos, variety acts—see "Evening Entertainment," in this chapter.

Admission: 18 kroner ($3.05) adults 10am–1pm, 28 kroner ($4.70) 1pm–midnight; children half price. Each ride costs 7 kroner ($1.20); 115 kroner ($19.35) per person for Tivoli-Tour-Pass and for all 25 amusements.

Open: Daily 10am–midnight. **Closed:** Mid-Sept to late Apr. **Bus:** 1, 16, 29.

STATENS MUSEUM FOR KUNST (Royal Museum of Fine Arts), Sølvgade 48-50. Tel. 33-91-21-26.

This well-stocked art museum houses foreign painting and sculpture from the 13th century to the present. There are Dutch golden age landscapes and marine paintings by Rubens and his school plus portraits by Frans Hals and Rembrandt. The Danish golden age is represented by Eckersberg, Købke, and Hansen. French 20th-century art includes 20 works by Matisse. In the Royal Print Room are 300,000 drawings, prints, lithographs, and other works by such artists as Dürer, Rembrandt, Matisse, and Picasso.

Admission: Free.

Open: Tues–Sun 10am–4:30pm. **Bus:** 10, 24, 43, 84.

IMPRESSIONS

There is nothing of Hamlet in their character
—R.H. BRUCE LOCKHART, *MY EUROPE*, 1952

Copenhagen is the best-built city of the north
—WILLIAM COXE, *TRAVELS*, 1792

DENMARK

Copenhagen

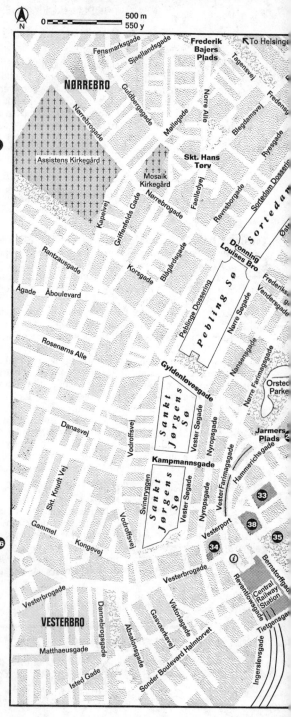

Hovedvej

Lille
Triangel

Gamisons
Kirkegård

Dag Hammerskjörds Alle

Kristianiagade

Østbanegade

Østerport
Station

Holmens
Kirkegård

Folke Bernadottes Alle

Forbindelsesvej

Øster Søgade

Oslo
Plads

Grønningen

Øster Farimagsgade

Stockholms Gade

Sortedam Dossering

Øster Søgade

Ryesgade

Damvej

Fredensbro

Søgade

Sø

S o r t e d a m s   S ø

Øster Farimagsgade

Gothersgade

Østre Anlæg

Sølvgade

Øster Voldgade

Suensonsgade

Store Kongensgade

Esplanaden

Gernersgade

Bredgade

Toldbodgade

Sølvgade

Klerkegade

Adelgade

Borgergade

Skt. Annae
Plads

Narre Voldgade

Åbenrå

Kronprinsessegade

Store Kongensgade

Gothersgade

Bredgade

Pilestræde

Krystalgade

Købmager gade

Kongens
Nytorv

Nyhavn

Nyhavn

Studiestræde

Vestergade

Østergade

Amagertorv

Højbro
Plads

Holbergsgade

Havnegade

Frederiksberggade

Gl. Strand

Holmens Kanal

Niels Juelsgade

I n d e r h a v n e n

Rådhus
Plads

Vester Voldgade

Kongens Tolnusgade

Knippelsbro

CHRISTIANSHAVN

H.C. Andersens Boulevard

Overgaden oven Vandet

Strandgade

Prinsessegade

Skt. Annae Gade

Christians Brygge

Mitchellegade

Hambrosgade

Langebro

Langebrogade

Torvegade

Prinsessegade

Christmas
Møllers
Plads

S y d b a v n e n

Thorshavnsgade

Amager Boulevard

s t a d s g r a v e n

Ved Stadsgraven

Amager Fælled Vej

To Airport

Church ✝

Post Office ⊠

Information ①

DEN HIRSCHSPRUNGSKE SAMLING (The Hirschsprung Collection), Stockholmsgade 20. Tel. 31-42-03-36.

This collection of Danish art from the 19th and early 20th centuries lies in Ostre Anlaeg, a park in the city center. Heinrich Hirschsprung (1836–1908), a tobacco merchant, created the collection and it has been growing ever since. The emphasis is on the Danish golden age with such artists as Eckersberg, Købke, Lundbye, and Marstrand. Some furnishings from the artists' homes are exhibited.

Admission: 20 kroner ($3.35) adults, free for children under 16.

Open: May–Sept, Wed–Sun 1–4pm; Oct–Apr, Wed 1–4pm and 7–10pm, Thurs–Sun 1–4pm. **Bus:** 10, 14, 24, 40.

ROSENBORG CASTLE, Øster Voldgade 4A. Tel. 33-15-32-86.

Founded by Christian IV in the 17th century, this red-brick Renaissance-style castle houses everything from narwhal-tusked and ivory coronation chairs to Frederik VII's baby shoes—all from the Danish Royal family. Officially, its biggest draws are the dazzling crown jewels and regalia in the basement Treasury, where a lavishly decorated coronation saddle from 1596 is also shown. Try to see the Knights Hall (Room 21), with its coronation seat, three silver lions, and relics from the 1700s. Another important attraction is Room 3 used by founding father Christian IV (lucky in love, unlucky in war), who died in this bedroom decorated with Asian lacquer art and a stucco ceiling. The King's Garden (Have) surrounds the castle, and the Botanical Gardens are across the street.

Admission: 30 kroner ($5.05) adults, 5 kroner (85¢) children under 15.

Open: Castle, Apr–May, daily 10am–3pm; June 2–Aug, daily 10am–4pm; Sept–Oct 21, daily 11am–3pm; Oct 22–Mar, Tues, Fri, and Sun 11am–2pm. Treasury and exhibition, Apr–May, daily 10am–3pm; June 2–Aug, daily 10am–4pm; Sept–Oct 21, daily 11am–3pm; Oct 22–Mar, Tues–Sun 11am–3pm. **Bus:** 5, 10, 14, 16.

CHRISTIANSBORG PALACE, Christiansborg Slotsplads. Tel. 33-92-64-92.

This granite-and-copper palace, located on the Slotsholmen—a small island that has been the center of political power in Denmark for more than 800 years—houses the Danish parliament, the Supreme Court, the prime minister's offices, and the Royal Reception Rooms. A guide will lead you through richly decorated rooms, including the Throne Room, banqueting hall, and Queen's Library. Before entering, you will be asked to put on soft overshoes to protect the floors.

On the grounds, visit the well-preserved ruins of the 1167 castle of Bishop Absalon, founder of Copenhagen.

Admission: Royal Reception Rooms, 22 kroner ($3.70) adults, 10 kroner ($1.70) children; parliament, free for all; castle ruins, 11 kroner ($1.85) adults, 5 kroner (85¢) children.

Open: Palace, May–Sept, English-language tours Tues–Sun at 11am, 1pm, and 3pm; Oct–Dec and Feb–Apr, English-language tours Tues–Fri and Sun at 11am and

---

IN THEIR FOOTSTEPS

Søren Kierkegaard (1813–55) The father of existentialism, Kierkegaard developed an almost-pathlogical sense of involvement in theology. His best-known work, *Either/Or*, written in 1843, shows his advocacy of a Christianity exclusively oriented to the Bible. "A melancholy Dane," he wrote many novels, including in 1849 *The Sickness Unto Death*.

- **Birthplace:** Born in Copenhagen, he was the seventh child of a prosperous wool merchant.
- **Residence:** A 19th-century house adjacent to the Court House building on Nytorv in Copenhagen.
- **Resting Place:** Assistens Kirkegård, Copenhagen.

1pm. Castle ruins, May–Sept, daily 9:30am–3:30pm; Oct–Apr, Mon–Fri and Sun 9:30am–3:30pm. **Closed:** Jan. English-language tours of the parliament are given mid-June to late Sept, Sun–Fri 10am–4pm. **Bus:** 1, 2, 5, 8, 9.

NY CARLSBERG GLYPTOTEK, Dantes Plads 7. Tel. 33-91-10-65.

The Glyptotek, behind the Tivoli, is one of the most important art museums in Scandinavia, founded by the 19th-century art collector Carl Jacobsen, Mr. Carlsberg beer himself. Located on the ground floor, the Egyptian collection, covering the entire civilization, is particularly outstanding. The most notable prize is a prehistoric hippopotamus, but some fine Greek originals (headless Apollo, Niobe's tragic children) and Roman copies of original Greek bronzes (4th-century Hercules) are also displayed, as are some of the noblest Roman busts—Pompey, Virgil, Augustus, Trajan. A favorite of mine is the Etruscan art display (sarcophagi, a winged lion, bronzes, pottery).

Upstairs are several masterpieces of the French impressionists including Manet (*The Absinthe Drinker*), Monet, Degas, and Renoir. Some 30 of Gauguin's works are here, as well as Cézanne's famous *Portrait of the Artist*. The French sculpture, such as Rodin's *The Citizens of Calais,* and the Degas bronze set, only add to the Glyptotek.

Admission: 15 kroner ($2.50) adults, free for children.

Open: May–Aug, Tues–Sun 10am–4pm; Sept–Apr, Tues–Sat noon–3pm, Sun 10am–4pm. **Bus:** 10, 24, 43, 84.

NATIONALMUSEET (National Museum), Frederiksholms Kanal 12, opposite Christiansborg Palace. Tel. 33-13-44-11.

A gigantic repository of anthropological artifacts, this museum is divided primarily into four departments. The Danish collections date from the Stone Age to the present and include Viking stones, helmets, and fragments of battle gear. Don't miss the "lur" horn, a Bronze Age musical instrument, among the most ancient instruments in Europe, and the world-famous "Sun Chariot," an elegant Bronze Age piece of pagan art.

The ecclesiastical art exhibit includes the 12th-century Lisbjerg Altar, a blending of pagan and Christian styles. Royal collections of medals and coins are also featured, as are the 3rd-century Gundestrup silver caldron, the Roman Hoby Cups depicting Homeric legends, and relics of the Eskimo culture and the people of Greenland.

Admission: Free.

Open: June 16–Sept 15, Tues–Sun 10am–4pm; Sept–June, Tues–Fri 11am–3pm, Sat–Sun noon–4pm. Guided tours Sun at 2pm. **Bus:** 1, 2, 5, 6, 10.

THORVALDSEN'S MUSEUM, Porthusgade 2. Tel. 33-32-15-32.

Located on Slotsholmen next door to Christiansborg, this great collection of Bertel Thorvaldsen (1770–1844) neoclassical sculpture represents the romanticism of the 18th and 19th centuries. The sculptor is famous for his classically restrained works and mythological subjects—Cupid and Psyche, Adonis, Jason, Hercules, Ganymede,

---

IN THEIR FOOTSTEPS

Hans Christian Andersen (1805–75) His first children's stories were published in 1835. The writer's goal was "to become famous," and some 168 fairy tales later, including *The Ugly Duckling, The Steadfast Tin Soldier,* and *The Little Mermaid,* Andersen got his wish.

● **Birthplace:** Born in the slums of Odense, Andersen had a poor cobbler for a father and a superstitious washerwoman for a mother.

● **Residences:** He traveled Europe, but lived at such addresses in Copenhagen as Nyhavn 67, Nyhavn 18, Nyhavn 20, and Vingårdsstraede 6.

● **Resting Place:** Assistens Kirkegård, Copenhagen.

Mercury—all of which are displayed at the museum. Thorvaldsen's personal collection of art is also shown, everything from Egyptian relics of Ptolemy to contemporary paintings. Thorvaldsen is buried in the courtyard of his museum.

Admission: Free.

Open: Tues–Sun 10am–5pm. **Bus:** 1, 2, 6, 8, 10.

FRIHEDSMUSEET (Museum of Denmark's Fight for Freedom, 1940–45), Churchillparken. Tel. 33-13-77-14.

This museum documents everything from the Danish tools of espionage and sabotage used to ward off Nazis, to World War II peace marches, to the highly skilled underground resistance movement.

On display are relics of torture and concentration camps, the equipment used for the wireless and illegal films, British propaganda leaflets, satirical caricatures of Hitler, information about Danish Jews and conversely about Danish Nazis, and the paralyzing nationwide strikes. An armed car, used against Danish Nazi informers and collaborators, is on the grounds.

Admission: Free.

Open: May to mid-Sept, Tues–Sat 10am–4pm, Sun 10am–5pm; Sept–May, Tues–Sat 11am–3pm, Sun 11am–4pm. Free guided tours given, May to mid-Sept, Sun and Thurs at 2pm. English-language tapes are also available. **Bus:** 1, 6, 9.

FRILANDMUSEET (Open-Air Museum), Kongevejen 100. Tel. 42-85-02-92.

This reconstructed village in Lyngboy, on the fringes of Copenhagen, recaptures Denmark's one-time rural character. The "museum" is nearly 90 acres, a 2-mile walk around the compound, and includes a dozen authentically re-created buildings— farmsteads, windmills, fishermen's cottages. Exhibits include a half-timbered 18th-century farmstead from one of the tiny windswept Danish islands, a primitive longhouse from the remote Faroe Islands, thatched fishermen's huts from Jutland, tower windmills, and a potter's workshop from the mid-19th century.

On summer afternoons, organized activities are staged. On a recent visit, folk dancers in native costume performed and there were demonstrations of lace making and loom weaving.

The park is about 9 miles from the Central Station. At the entryway to the museum is an old-style restaurant.

Admission: 15 kroner ($2.50) adults, 5 kroner (85¢) children.

Open: Mid-Apr to Sept, daily 10am–5pm; Oct 1–14, daily 10am–3pm; Oct 15–Apr 14, Sun 10am–3pm. **S-tog:** From the Central Station to Sorgenfri (leaving every 20 minutes).

3. MORE ATTRACTIONS

AMALIENBORG PALACE, Slotsplads.

These four 18th-century French-style rococo mansions—opening onto one of the most attractive squares (Amalienborg) in Europe—have been the home of the Danish royal family since 1794 when Christiansborg burned. Visitors are not allowed inside, but many flock to witness the changing of the guard at noon when the royal family is in residence. A swallowtail flag at mast signifies that the queen is in Copenhagen—and not at her North Zealand summer home, Fredensborg Palace.

The Royal Life Guard in black bearskin busbies (like the hussars) leaves Rosenborg Castle at 11:30am and marches along Gothersgade, Nørrevold, Frederiksborggade, Købmagergade, Østergade, Kongens Nytorv, Bredgade, Sankt Annae Plads, and Amaliegade to Amalienborg. After the event, the guard, still accompanied by the band, returns to Rosenborg Castle via Frederiksgade, Store Kongensgade, and Gothersgade.

Bus: 1, 6, 9, 10.

FROMMER'S FAVORITE
COPENHAGEN EXPERIENCES

Sitting at an Outdoor Café Because of Copenhagen's long gray winters, sitting at an outdoor café in the summer and drinking beer or eating is always a favorite pastime. The best spot is at Nyhavn (New Harbor), beginning at Kongens Nytorv. Enjoy ice cream while admiring the tall rigged ships with bow sprits moored in the canal.

Going to the Tivoli This is the quintessential summer adventure in Copenhagen, a tradition since 1843. It's an amusement park with a difference—even the merry-go-rounds are unusual, using a fleet of Viking ships instead of the usual horses.

Strolling the Strøget In Danish, the word *strøget* means "to stroll"— and that's exactly what all born-to-shop addicts do along this nearly three-quarter-mile stretch, from the Rådhuspladsen to Kongens Nytorv.

Exploring Alternative Life-Styles Not for everybody, but worth a look, is a trip to the Free City of Christiania, on the island of Christianshavn (take bus no. 8 from Rådhuspladsen). Since 1971, some 1,000 "squatters" have illegally declared themselves a free city, taking over 130 former army barracks spread across 20 acres. You can shop, dine, and talk to the natives about this experimental community with its own doctors, clubs, and stores. It even flies its own flag.

TØJHUSMUSEET (Royal Arsenal Museum), Tøjhusgade 3. Tel. 33-11-60-37.
On the grounds of Christiansborg, this museum features a fantastic display of weapons used for hunting and warfare. On the main floor—the longest vaulted Renaissance hall in Europe—is Cannon Hall, stocked with mortars, tanks, 1909 airplanes suspended from the ceiling, howitzers, a 21-ton German armored car, and a Nazi V-1 rocket. Above Cannon Hall is the impressive Arms Chamber, with one of the world's finest collections of hand-weapons. Many trophy banners hang above the wall cases of swords, and all Danish trophies since 1659 are kept in the museum. The museum building dates to 1598–1604.
Admission: 20 kroner ($3.35) adults, 10 kroner ($1.70) children.
Open: May–Sept, Tues–Sat 1–4pm, Sun 10am–4pm; Oct–Apr, Tues–Sat 1–3pm, Sun 11am–4pm. **Bus:** 1, 2, 5, 6, 8.

KUNSTINDUSTRIMUSEET (Museum of Decorative and Applied Art), Bredgade 68. Tel. 33-14-94-52.
Built between 1752 and 1757 under King Frederik V, this rococo building, houses European decorative and applied art from the Middle Ages to the present. Collections of furniture, tapestries, pottery, porcelain, glass, and silver are displayed, as are Chinese and Japanese art and handcrafts. The library contains around 63,000 books and periodicals dealing with arts and crafts, architecture, costumes, advertising, photography, and industrial design.
Admission: Museum, 20 kroner ($3.35) Sun, hols., and daily July–Aug; free other times. Library free.
Open: Museum, Tues–Sun 1–4pm; library, Tues–Sat 10am–4pm. **Bus:** 1, 6, 9. **Train:** Østerport.

RUNDETÅRN (Round Tower), Købmagergade 52A. Tel. 33-93-66-60.
This 17th-century public observatory, attached to a church, is visited by thousands who climb the spiral ramp (no steps) for a panoramic view of Copenhagen. The tower

is one of the crowning architectural achievements of the Christian IV era. Legend has it that Peter the Great, in Denmark for a state visit, galloped up the ramp on horseback, preceded by his carriage-drawn tsarina.

Admission: 10 kroner ($1.70) adults, 4 kroner (65¢) children.

Open: Apr–Oct, Mon–Sat 10am–5pm, Sun noon–4pm; Nov–Mar, Sat 10am–4pm, Sun noon–4pm. **Bus:** 5, 2, 14, 16, 17.

RÅDHUS (Town Hall), Rådhuspladsen. Tel. 33-15-38-00.

Built during the last years of Queen Victoria's reign, the Town Hall contains impressive statues of Hans Christian Andersen, and Niels Bohr, the Nobel Prize–winning Danish physicist, and Jens Olden's famous "World Clock," open for viewing Monday through Friday from 10:30am to 12:30pm and on Saturday at noon. King Frederik IX set the clock on December 15, 1955. The clockwork is so exact that the aberration in 300 years is 0.4 seconds. Climb the tower for an impressive view.

Admission: Rådhus, 10 kroner ($1.70); tower, 5 kroner (85¢).

Open: Rådhus, Mon–Wed and Fri 9:30am–3pm, Thurs 9:30am–4pm, Sat guided tour at 10am; tower, Mon–Fri at 11am and 2pm, Sat at 11am. **Bus:** 1, 6, 8.

VOR FRUE KIRKE (Copenhagen Cathedral), Nørregade. Tel. 33-14-41-28.

This Greek Renaissance-style church, built in the early 19th century near Copenhagen University, features Bertel Thorvaldsen's white marble neoclassical works including *Christ and the Apostles*. The funeral of Hans Christian Andersen took place here in 1875, and that of Søren Kierkegaard in 1855.

Admission: Free.

Open: Mon–Fri 9am–5pm. **Bus:** 5.

MARBLE CHURCH (or Frederik's Church), Frederiksgade 4. Tel. 33-15-37-63.

This 2-century-old church, with its green copper dome—one of the largest in the world—is a short walk from Amalienborg Palace. After an unsuccessful start during the neoclassical revival of the 1750s in Denmark, the church was finally completed in Roman baroque style in 1894. In many ways it is even more impressive than Copenhagen's cathedral.

Admission: Church, free; dome, 5 kroner (85¢).

Open: Church, Mon–Sat 11am–2pm; dome, Sat at 11am. **Bus:** 1, 6, 9, 10.

DEN LILLE HAVFRUE (*The Little Mermaid*), Langelinie.

The one statue *everybody* wants to see in Copenhagen is the life-size bronze of the *Den lille havfrue,* inspired by Hans Christian Andersen's *The Little Mermaid,* one of the world's most famous fairytales. The statue, unveiled in 1913, was sculpted by Edvard Erichsen. It rests on rocks right off the shore. The mermaid has been attacked more than once, losing an arm in one misadventure, decapitated in another.

Nearby is the **Gefion Fountain,** sculpted by Anders Bundgaard. Gefion, a Scandinavian mythological goddess, plowed Zealand away from Sweden by turning her sons into oxen. Also in the area is **Kastellet** at Langelinie (tel. 33-11-22-33). This ruined citadel was fortified in the 17th century, and can be explored daily from 6am to sunset. Admission is free.

In summer, a special "Mermaid Bus" leaves from Rådhuspladsen (Vester Volgade) at 10:30am (thereafter at half-hour intervals until 5:30pm). On the "Langelinie" bus there's a 20-minute stopover at *The Little Mermaid.* If you want more time, take bus no. 1, 6, or 9.

DAVIDS SAMLING, Kronprinsessegade 30. Tel. 33-13-55-64.

Its status as a privately funded museum, plus the excellence of its collection, make this a most unusual museum. Established by a Danish attorney, C. L. David (1878–1960), shortly after World War II on the premises of his private house across from the park surrounding Rosenborg Palace, the collection features European art, decorative art, and the largest collection—more than 400 items—of Islamic miniatures in the Nordic world. Dating from the 16th to the 19th century, they are mostly from India, Persia, and Turkey.

David's other major bequest to Denmark was his summer villa in the northern suburbs of Copenhagen at Marienborg, which is the year-round home of the Danish prime minister.

Admission: Free.
Open: Tues–Sun 1–4pm. **Bus:** 10, 17, 43.

BOTANISK HAVE (Botanical Gardens), Gothersgade 128. Tel. 33-12-74-60.

Planted from 1871 to 1874, the Botanical Gardens are located at a lake that was once part of the city's defensive moat. Across from Rosenborg Castle, it contains hothouses growing both tropical and subtropical plants. Special features include a cactus house and a palm house, all of which appear even more exotic in the far northern country of Denmark. An alpine garden contains mountain plants from all over the world.

Admission: Free.
Open: Summer, daily 8:30am–6pm; winter, daily 10am–3pm. **Bus:** 5, 7, 14, 16.

4. COOL FOR KIDS

Copenhagen is a wonderful place for children, and many of the so-called adult attractions also appeal to children. If you're traveling with children, don't miss the **Tivoli**, *The Little Mermaid* at Langelinie, and the changing of the Queen's Royal Life Guard at **Amalienborg Palace,** including the entire parade to and from that royal residence. Kids also enjoy **Frilandmuseet,** the open-air museum. (For details on the above sights, see "The Top Attractions" and "More Attractions," above.)

Other attractions great for kids include the following:

LEGETØJMUSEET (Danish Toy Museum), Valkendorfsgade 13. Tel. 33-14-10-09.

Come see a fascinating collection of toys from all over the world for children of all ages. Toys range from antique dolls and dollhouses to mechanical devices to games and books to hobbyhorses.

Admission: 20 kroner ($3.35) adults, 10 kroner ($1.70) children.
Open: Sat–Thurs 9–4pm. **S-tog:** Nørreport. **Bus:** 43.

LOUIS TUSSAUD WAX MUSEUM, H. C. Andersens Blvd. 22. Tel. 33-14-29-22.

Now a part of Tivoli, the Louis Tussaud Wax Museum is a major commercial attraction in Copenhagen. It features more than 200 wax figures, everybody from Danish kings and queens to Leonardo da Vinci. Children can visit the Snow Queen's Castle, or watch Frankenstein and Dracula guard the vampires and monsters.

Admission: 40 kroner ($6.70) adults, 17 kroner ($2.85) children.
Open: Apr 16–Sept 16, daily 10am–11pm; Sept 17–Apr 25, daily 10am–4:30pm. **Bus:** 1, 16, 29.

CIRKUS BENNEWEIS, Jernbanegade 8. Tel. 33-14-44-43.

The Benneweis Circus, opposite Tivoli Gardens, is one of the last grand-style circuses left in Europe. Five generations of Benneweises have run the circus nonstop in spite of two world wars. Bareback riders, tumblers, clowns, aerialists, trained seals—this is the real thing. Tickets can be purchased at the ticket office in the circus building between noon and 8pm.

Admission: 40–140 kroner ($6.70–$23.55).
Open: May–Aug, Tues–Fri at 8pm, Sat at 4 and 8pm, Sun at 4pm. **Bus:** 1, 2, 6, 8, 14, 16.

BAKKEN AMUSEMENT PARK, Dyrehavevej 62, Klampenborg. Tel. 31-63-35-44.

On the northern edge of Copenhagen, about 7½ miles from the city center, this amusement park was created 35 years before the Pilgrims landed at Plymouth Rock. It's a local favorite, featuring roller coasters, dancing, the tunnel of love, and a merry-go-round. Open-air restaurants are plentiful, as are snack bars and ice-cream booths. Proceeds from the amusements support this unspoiled natural preserve. There are no cars, only bicycles and horse-drawn carriages. Bakken is about a 20-minute ride from the Central Station.

Admission: Free.

Open: Late Mar to late Aug, daily 1pm–midnight. **Closed:** Late Aug to late Mar. **S-tog:** "Klampenborg" from Central Station to Klampenborg Station; then walk through Deer Park or take a horse-drawn cab.

TYCHO BRAHE PLANETARIUM, Gammel Kongevej 10. Tel. 33-12-12-24.

The marvel of the night sky, with its planets, galaxies, star clusters, and comets is created by a star projector using the planetarium dome as a screen and space theater. Named after the famed Danish astronomer, Tycho Brahe (1546–1601), the planetarium also stages Omnimax film productions. There's an information center and a restaurant.

Admission: 10 kroner ($1.70).

Open: Daily 10:30am–9:30pm. **Bus:** 1, 14.

THE ZOO, Roskildevej 32. Tel. 36-30-25-55.

With more than 2,000 animals from Greenland to Africa, this zoo boasts spacious new habitats for reindeer and the musk oxen as well as an open roaming area for the lions. Take a ride up the small wooden Eiffel Tower or walk across the street, and let your kids enjoy themselves in the petting zoo. The zoo is mobbed on Sunday.

Admission: 40 kroner ($6.70) adults, 20 kroner ($3.35) children.

Open: Daily 9am–sunset. **Bus:** 28, 41.

DENMARK'S AQUARIUM, Strandvejen, Charlottenlund. Tel. 31-62-32-83.

Opened in 1959, this is one of the most extensive aquariums in Europe. Its large tanks are famous for their decoration. Hundreds of salt and freshwater species are collected. One tank houses bloodthirsty piranha from South America. It's located in Charlottenlund Fort Park, north of Copenhagen.

Admission: 30 kroner ($5.05) adults, 15 kroner ($2.50) children.

Open: Mar–Oct, daily 10am–6pm; Nov–Feb, daily 10am–4pm. **S-tog:** Charlottenlund. **Bus:** 6.

5. SPECIAL-INTEREST SIGHTSEEING

FOR THE LITERARY ENTHUSIAST

Admirers of Hans Christian Andersen may want to seek out the various addresses at which he lived in Copenhagen. These include Nyhavn 18, Nyhavn 20, and Nyhavn 67. He also lived for a time at Vingårdestraede 6.

KØBENHAVNS BYMUSEUM (Copenhagen City Museum), Vesterbrogade 59. Tel. 31-21-07-72.

Devoted to Søren Kierkegaard (1813–55), the father of existentialism, this museum exhibits his drawings, letters, books, photographs, and personal belongings.

Admission: Free.

Open: Oct–Apr, daily 1–4pm; May–Sept, daily 10am–4pm. **Bus:** 6, 16, 28, 41.

ASSISTENS KIRKEGÅRD (Assistens Cemetery), Nørrebrogade/ Kapelvej.
The largest cemetery in Copenhagen, dating from 1711, it contains the tombs of Søren Kierkegaard, Hans Christian Andersen, and Martin Andersen Nexø, a famous novelist of the working class. The cemetery is now a public park.
Admission: Free.
Open: Sunrise–sunset. **Bus:** 5, 7, 16, 17, 18.

FOR THE ARCHITECTURE ENTHUSIAST

BØRSEN (Stock Exchange), Børsgade.
One of the most unusual buildings in Copenhagen, on Slotsholmen, it must be viewed from the outside, as its interior is not open to the public. Architects Hans and Lorenz Steenwinkel built the long, low Renaissance structure for Christian IV. The spire, 177 feet high, looks like a quartet of intertwined dragon tails. The Stock Exchange is no longer housed here; the building is now the headquarters of the Chamber of Commerce.
Bus: 1, 2, 5, 6, 8, 9.

GRUNDTVIGS KIRKE (Grundtvig Church), Pa Bjerget, Bispebjerg.
Resembling a huge organ, this church, built from 1921 to 1940, was designed by Jensen Klint, who died before it was completed. It is estimated that six million yellow bricks went into its construction. The interior is 250 feet wide and 115 feet high. The church is a popular venue for concerts.
Admission: Free.
Open: May 15–Sept 15, Mon–Sat 9am–4:45pm, Sun noon–4pm; Sept 16–May 15, Sun noon–1pm.

FOR BEER DRINKERS

CARLSBERG BREWERIES, Ny Carlsberg Vej 140. Tel. 31-21-12-21, ext. 1312.
A favorite tourist tradition is a visit to a world-famous Danish brewery: Carlsberg or Tuborg. The Carlsberg tour is more popular, lasting 90 minutes, not including the "beer party" at the end where guests sample the product. The Carlsberg plant stands on 62 acres of grounds, including a grain elevator, the tallest building in Copenhagen. Visitors are escorted through the brew houses, and are shown yeast cellars and storage basements. The swastika on the Carlsberg elephant doesn't mean they are Nazi sympathizers—Carlsberg used the sign long before Hitler. The factory turns out three million bottles of beer a day.
Admission: Free.
Open: Tours, Mon–Fri at 9am, 11am, and 2:30pm. **Bus:** 6 from Rådhuspladsen.

TUBORG BREWERIES, Strandvejen 54, Hellerup. Tel. 31-29-33-11, ext. 2212.
A modern brewery, Tuborg is actually jointly owned with Carlsberg, although they seemingly function as rivals. Each Dane has a favorite, but Tuborg has only 28% of the market, as opposed to 43% for Carlsberg. A highlight of the tour through the plant is the 85-foot beer bottle, the largest in the world. It could hold the contents of a million regular-size bottles.
Admission: Free.
Open: Tours, Mon–Thurs at 10am, 12:30pm, and 2:30pm, Fri at 10am, 1:30pm, and 2:30pm. **S-tog:** Hellerup.

WALKING TOUR 1 —— The Old City

Start: Rådhuspladsen.

Finish: Tivoli Gardens.
Time: 1½ hours.
Best time: Any sunny day.

An interesting walk starts at the:

1. **Rådhuspladsen** (Town Hall Square), in the center of Copenhagen. You can stop in at City Hall, but even more appealing is a bronze statue of Hans Christian Andersen, the spinner of fairytales, which stands near a boulevard bearing his name. Also on this square is a statue of two lur horn players that have stood here since 1914, and, as tradition has it, they will sound a note if a virgin should ever pass by.

   Bypassing the lur horn players, walk east along Vester Voldgade onto a narrow street on your left:

2. **Lavendelstraede.** Many houses along here date from the late 18th century. At Lavendelstraede 1, Mozart's widow (Constanze) lived with her second husband, Georg Nikolaus Nissen, a Danish diplomat, from 1812 to 1820.

   The little street quickly becomes Slutterigade.

3. **Courthouses** rise on both sides of this short street, joined by elevated walkways. Built between 1805 and 1815, this was Copenhagen's fourth town hall, now the city's major law courts. The main courthouse entrance is on Nytorv.

   Slutterigade will lead to:

4. **Nytorv,** a famous square where you can admire fine 19th-century houses. Søren Kierkegaard, the noted philosopher (1813–55), lived in a house adjacent to the courthouse. Cross Nytorv and veer slightly west or to your left until you reach Nygade, part of the famed:

5. **Strøget,** a traffic-free shopping street. At this point it goes under a different name. (It actually began at Rådhuspladsen and was called Frederiksberggade.) The major shopping street of Scandinavia, Strøget is a stroller's and a shopper's delight, following a three-quarter-mile trail through the heart of Copenhagen.

   Nygade is one of the five streets that comprise Strøget. Head northeast along this street, which quickly becomes the winding and narrow Vimmelskaftet, which turns into Amagertorv. Along Amagertorv, you'll come across the:

6. **Helligåndskirken** (Church of the Holy Ghost), on your left, with its 15th-century abbey, Helligåndshuset. This is the oldest church in Copenhagen, founded at the dawn of the 15th century. Partially destroyed in 1728, it was reconstructed in 1880 in a neoclassical style. Some of the buildings on this street are from 1616. The sales rooms of the Royal Porcelain Factory are at Amagertorv 6.

   Next you will come to Østergade, the last portion of Strøget. You'll see Illum's department store on your left.

   Østergade leads to:

7. **Kongens Nytorv,** Copenhagen's largest square, with many interesting buildings surrounding it and the equestrian statue of King Christian IV in the center. The statue is a bronze replica of a 1688 sculpture. (For more about this square, see Walking Tour 2, below.)

   At Kongens Nytorv, head right until you come to Laksegade. Then go south along this street until you reach the intersection of Nikolajgade. Turn right. This street will lead to:

8. **Skt. Nikoljk Church,** dating from 1530, and the scene of the thundering sermons of Hans Tausen, a father of the Danish Reformation.

REFUELING STOP The most famous pastry shop in Denmark, **9. La Glace** has a branch at Kongens Nytorv 2 (tel. 33-14-46-46). Since 1870 this place has been providing Danes with the best cakes and chocolates in town. Try sportskage (sportsman's cake) made of whipped cream, crumbled nougat, macaroons, and

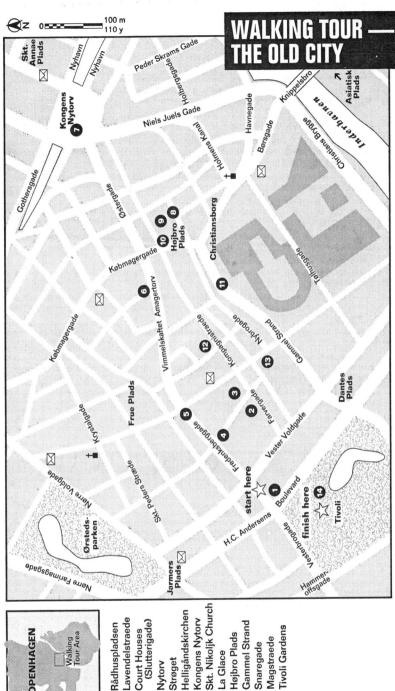

WALKING TOUR — THE OLD CITY

0 ⊢⊣⊢⊣⊢⊣ 100 m
110 y

Skt. Annae Plads

Nyhavn

Peder Skrams Gade

Holbergsgade

Havnegade

Knippelsbro

Asiatisk Plads

Inderhavnen

Christians Brygge

Kongens Nytorv ⑦

Niels Juels Gade

Gothersgade

Østergade

Holmens Kanal

Børsgade

Tøjhusgade

Christiansborg

Gammel Strand

Nybrogade

Købmagergade

⑨ ⑧
Højbro
⑩ Plads

⑥

⑪

Vimmelskaftet Amagertorv

Kompagnistraede

⑫

⑬

Frue Plads

⑤ ③
Frederiksberggade ④ ② Farvergade

Dantes Plads

Vester Voldgade

Krystalgade

Skt. Pejers Straede

Nørre Voldgade

Ørstedsparken

start here ① Boulevard

finish here ⑭

Tivoli

H.C. Andersens

Vesterbrogade

Hammer-offsgade

Jarmers Plads

Nørre Farimagsgade

Church ✝∎   Post Office ⊠

COPENHAGEN

Walking Tour Area

① Rådhuspladsen
② Lavendelstraede
③ Court Houses (Slutterigade)
④ Nytorv
⑤ Strøget
⑥ Helligåndskirchen
⑦ Kongens Nytorv
⑧ Skt. Nikolaj Church
⑨ La Glace
⑩ Højbro Plads
⑪ Gammel Strand
⑫ Snaregade
⑬ Magstraede
⑭ Tivoli Gardens

profiteroles glazed in caramel. The café is open Monday through Friday from 8am to 6pm, on Saturday from 8:30am to 6pm, and on Sunday from 10am to 10pm.

After viewing the church, head left down Fortunstraede to:

10. Højbro Plads, off Gammel Strand. You'll have a good view of Christiansborg Palace and Thorvaldsen's Museum on Slotsholmen. On Højbro Plads is an equestrian statue honoring Bishop Absalon, who founded Copenhagen in 1167. Several handsome buildings line the square. Continue west along:

11. Gammel Strand, which means "old shore." From this waterfront promenade, the former edge of Copenhagen, you'll have a good view across to Christiansborg Palace. A number of interesting old buildings line this street, and at the end you'll come upon the Ministry of Cultural Affairs, occupying a former government pawnbroking establishment, dating from 1730.

To the right of this building, walk up:

12. Snaregade, an old-fashioned provincial street, typical of the old city. Walk up until you reach Knabrostraede. Both of these streets boast structures built just after the great fire of 1795. Where the streets intersect, you'll see the Church of Our Lady.

Make your way back to Snaregade, and turn right to:

13. Magstraede, one of Copenhagen's best-preserved streets. Proceed along to Rådhusstraede. Right before you reach Rådhusstraede, notice the two buildings facing that street. These are the oldest structures in the city, dating from the 16th century.

Walk across Vandkunsten, a square at the end of Magstraede, then turn right down Gasegade, which doesn't go very far before you turn left along Farvergade. At this street's intersection with Vester Voldgade you'll see Vartov Church. Continue west until you reach Rådhuspladsen. Across the square, you'll see:

14. Tivoli Gardens, whose entrance is at Vesterbrogade 3. Drawing some 4.5 million visitors every summer, this amusement park has 25 different entertainments and attractions and an equal number of restaurants and beer gardens.

WALKING TOUR 2 — Kongens Nytorv To Langelinie

Start: Kongens Nytorv.
Finish: *The Little Mermaid.*
Time: 1½ hours.
Best time: Any sunny day.

Although the Nyhavn quarter, once a roistering sailors' town, has quieted down, it's still a charming part of old Copenhagen with its 1673 canal and 18th-century houses. To explore the area, begin at:

1. Kongens Nytorv, the biggest store in the capital, with an equestrian statue of King Christian IV. Meaning "King's New Market," Kongens Nytorv dates from 1680. On the northeast side of the square is:

2. Thott's Mansion, completed in 1685 for a Danish naval hero and restored in 1760. It now houses the French Embassy. Between Bredgade and Store Strandstraede, a little street angling to the right near Nyhavn, is **Kanneworff House,** a beautifully preserved privately owned house dating from 1782. On the west side of the square, at no. 34, is the Hotel d'Angleterre, considered the best in Copenhagen. Also here is an old anchor memorializing the Danish seamen who died in World War II.

On the southeast side of the square stands:

3. Theater Royal, founded in 1748, where ballet, opera, and plays are presented.

COPENHAGEN

Walking Tour Area

1. Kongens Nytorv
2. Thott's Mansion
3. Theater Royal
4. Nyhavn
5. Charlottenborg Palace
6. Skt. Annae Plads
7. Amalienborg Palace
8. Amaliehavn
9. Frederikskirke
10. The Medical History Museum
11. Café Lumskebugten
12. Frihedsmuseet
13. The Little Mermaid

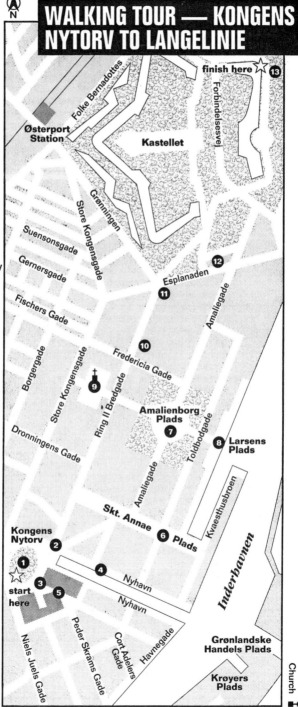

Statues of famous Danish dramatists are out front. The present theater, constructed in 1874, is in a Neo-Renaissance style.

With your back to the Hotel D'Angleterre, walk toward the water along:

4. Nyhavn, once filled with seamen's bars and lodgings, and ships' establishments. Nowadays it has become a restaurant row. First, walk along the north side (the left) of Nyhavn. In summer, café tables border the canal, taking on a festive atmosphere. At the port end of the canal you can see the Naval Dockyards, and Christianshavn across the harbor. High-speed craft come and go all day here, connecting Copenhagen with Malmö, Sweden.

On the quieter side of the canal (the south), you can see:

5. Charlottenborg Palace, now the Danish Academy of Fine Arts. A pure baroque work, it takes its name from Queen Charlotte Amalie, who lived there from 1700. Beautiful old homes, antique shops, and more restaurants line the southern flank. Nyhavn was also the home of Hans Christian Andersen at various times: no. 20 in 1835 where he wrote his first fairytales, no. 67 from 1845 to 1864, and no. 18 where he spent the last 2 years of his life, dying there in 1875.

Walk to the end of Nyhavn toward the harbor and turn left onto Kvaesthusgade, which will take you to:

6. Skt. Annae Plads, where ferries depart for Oslo. Many consulates, two hotels, and fine old buildings open onto this square. Walking inland along the plads, turn right onto Amaliegade, which leads under a colonnade into the cobbled Amalienborg Plads, site of:

7. Amalienborg Palace, with a statue of King Frederik V standing in its core. When the queen is in residence, there is a daily changing of the guard here at noon. The palace can only be viewed from the outside, as it is the official residence of the queen and her French prince. Four identical mansionlike palaces flank this square. The queen lives in the right wing next to the colonnade.

Between the square and the harbor are the gardens of:

8. Amaliehaven. Among the most beautiful in Copenhagen, these gardens were laid out by Jean Delogne, who made lavish use of Danish granite along with limestone imported from France. The bronze pillars around the fountain were the work of Arnaldo Pomodoro, an Italian sculptor.

After viewing the waterfront gardens, walk away from the water, crossing Amalienborg Plads and emerging onto Frederiksgade. Continue along this short street until you reach:

9. Frederikskirke, at no. 1. Often called Marmorkirken or "marble church," this building, begun in 1740, had to come to an end in 1770 because of the staggering costs. The church wasn't finished until 1894. It finally used Danish marble instead of the more expensive, imported Norwegian marble. The church was modeled on and planned to rival St. Peter's in Rome, and indeed ended up with some of the largest domes of any church in Europe. Supported on a dozen towering piers, the dome has a diameter of 108 feet.

Facing the church, turn right and head north along Bredgade, passing at no. 22:

10. Medicinsk-Historisk Museum (Medical History Museum), which traces the history of medicine. The collection is gruesome, with aborted fetuses, dissected heads, and the like.

REFUELING STOP Before you near *The Little Mermaid,* consider tea and a snack at **11. Café Lumskebugten,** Esplanaden 21 (see Chapter 6, "Copenhagen Dining"). Dating from 1854, this café offers a cold plate for 135 kroner ($22.70) and it's served throughout the afternoon. There are five specialties, including beef tartare, fish cakes with mustard sauce, marinated salmon, baked cod slices, and shrimp.

Bredgade comes to an end at the Esplanaden, which opens onto Churchhillparken, a green belt bordering water. Walk right along Esplanaden until you come to:

12. Frihedsmuseet, Churchillparken, the Danish Resistance Museum depicting the struggle of the Danish people against the Nazi's from 1940 to 1945.

After leaving the museum, walk toward the water along Langelinie where signs point the way to:

13. The Little Mermaid. Perched on rocks just off the harbor bank, *Den lille Havfrue* dates from 1913. The bronze figure, by Edvard Eriksen, was modeled after the figure of Ellen Price, a prima ballerina. In time, this much attacked and abused statue became the symbol of Copenhagen. It is the most photographed statue in all of Scandinavia.

6. ORGANIZED TOURS

BUS & BOAT TOURS   A number of sightseeing tours are offered in Copenhagen, either by boat or bus, ranging from get-acquainted jaunts to in-depth tours. Inexpensive bus tours depart from the lur horn-blowers statue at the City Hall Square, and boat trips leave either from Gammel Strand (the fish market) or Nyhavn.

For orientation, try the **1½-hour City Tour** (2½ hours with a visit to a brewery) which covers major scenic highlights like *The Little Mermaid*, Rosenborg Castle, and Amalienborg Palace. On workdays, tours visit either the Carlsberg or Tuborg brewery. Tours depart May 15 to September 15, daily at 10am and noon. The charge is 100 kroner ($16.80).

I heartily endorse the **City and Harbor Tour,** a 2½-hour trip by launch and bus, departing from Town Hall Square. The boat tours the city's main canals, passing *The Little Mermaid* and the Old Fish Market. It operates between May 1 to September 15, daily at 9:30am, 1pm, and 3pm, for 150 kroner ($25.20) per person.

Shakespeare buffs will be interested in an afternoon **Hamlet Tour,** a 5-hour trip to Hillerød, Frederiksborg Castle, and Elsinore, which leaves May 1 to September 30, daily at 1:30pm and costs 250 kroner ($42.05) per person.

Another popular trip is the **Hans Christian Andersen Tour,** an 11-hour journey to Roskilde, Egeskov Castle, and the house and museum of the storyteller in Odense. Tours depart May 15 to September 15, Sunday at 9am, for 420 kroner ($70.60) per person, not including lunch. Reserve in advance.

GUIDED WALKS   English-language guided walking tours of Copenhagen are offered during the summer. The price is 25 kroner ($4.20) for adults, 15 kroner ($2.50) for children. For information, contact **Danmarks Turistråd,** H. C. Andersens Blvd. 22 (tel. 33-11-13-25).

7. SPECIAL/FREE EVENTS

Much of Copenhagen is a summer festival, especially at the **Tivoli Gardens.** Although there's an entrance fee, many of the concerts and other presentations are free once inside. A total of 150 performances per summer are presented at the Concert Hall. Of these, more than 100 are free. Pantomime performances at the Pantomime Theater are also free. Performances on the open-air stage are free every night (closed Monday). Likewise, the other amusement park, **Bakken,** has many free events—and you don't have to pay an admission to enter—only if you patronize the various attractions.

The **birthday of Queen Margrethe** on April 16 is a celebration with the queen and the royal family driving through the pedestrian street, Strøget, in a stagecoach escorted by hussars in gala.

A **Ballet and Opera Festival** (mid-May to June) takes place at the Royal Theater, offering classical and modern dance, and operatic masterpieces.

Carnival in Copenhagen (June 2–4) is a great event where dressed-up Copenhageners move about the city in samba rhythm. The event is climaxed by a children's carnival on June 4.

The **Copenhagen Jazz Festival** (July 6–13) features the best of international jazz musicians.

The highly acclaimed Royal Danish Ballet performs at the Royal Theater for the **Fall Ballet Festival** (mid-August to September 1).

8. SAVVY SHOPPING

THE SHOPPING SCENE

Copenhagen is in the vanguard of shopping in Europe and much of the action takes place on **Strøget,** a pedestrian street in the heart of the capital. The Strøget begins on Frederiksberggade, north of Rådhuspladsen, and winds to Østergade, which opens onto Kongens Nytorv. This jam-packed street is lined with stores selling everything from porcelain statues of *Youthful Boldness* to Greenland shrimp to Kay Bojesen's teak monkeys.

Between stops, have a drink at an outdoor café, or just sit on a bench and watch the crowds.

Two other walking areas are nearby—**Grabrødertorv** and **Fiolstraede**— where you can browse through antiques shops and bookstores.

Bredgade, beginning at Kongens Nytorv, is the antiques district of Copenhagen. Prices tend to be very high. **Laederstraede** is another shopping street that competes with Bredgade for antiques.

BEST BUYS   In a country famed for its designers and craftspeople, you'll find your best buys in stainless steel, porcelain, china, glassware, toys (Kay Bojesen's wooden animals in particular), functionally designed furniture, textiles (napkins to rugs), and jewelry (decorative, silver, and semiprecious stones).

STORE HOURS   In general, shopping hours are Monday through Thursday from 9am to 5:30pm, until 7pm on Friday, and until 1pm on Saturday. Most shops are closed Sunday except the kiosks and supermarket at the Central Railroad Station. Here you can purchase food until 10pm or midnight. The Central Station's bakery is open until 9pm, and one of the kiosks at the Rådhuspladsen, selling papers, film, and souvenirs, is open 24 hours.

SHIPPING IT HOME & RECOVERING VAT   Denmark imposes a 22% tax on goods and services, a "Value-Added Tax" known in Denmark as Moms (pronounced "mumps"). However, special tax-free exports are possible. Many stores will mail goods to your home so as to avoid paying Moms. If you want to take your purchases with you, look for shops displaying DANISH TAX-FREE SHOPPING notices. Such shops offer tourists tax refunds for personal export. This refund applies to purchases over 600 kroner ($100.85) for visitors from the United States and Canada. Your tax-free invoice must be stamped by Danish Customs when you leave the country. You can receive your refund at Copenhagen's Kastrup International Airport when you depart. If you depart by land or by sea, you can receive your refund by mail. Requests for refunds are to be sent by mail to Danish Tax-Free Shopping A/S, 5 H. J. Holstvej, DK-2605 Brøndby, Denmark. You will be reimbursed by check, cash, or credit-card credit in the currency you wish.

The 600 kroner must be spent in one store for the refund to apply, but some major department stores allow purchases to be made over several days or even weeks, at the end of which the receipts will be tallied. Service and handling fees are deducted from the total, so actual refunds come to about 18%. Information on this program is available from the Danish Tourist Board (see "Fast Facts: Copenhagen" in Chapter 4).

SHOPPING A TO Z

ART GALLERIES & AUCTION HOUSES

ARNE BRUUN RASMUSSEN, Bredgade 33. Tel. 33-13-69-11.

Established shortly after World War II, this is the leading auction house in Denmark. The new season begins in August with an auction of paintings and fine artworks. July is usually quiet, although the premises remain open for appraisals and purchases. Viewing time is allowed before auctions, which take place about once a month. Auctions are also devoted to modern art, wine, coins, books, manuscripts, and antique weapons. Bus: 1, 6, 9, 10.

BRANNERS BIBLIOPHILE ANTIKVARIAT, Bredgade 10. Tel. 33-15-91-87.

If you're interested in engravings and woodcuts, this is the best place. Founded in 1946, this shop also sells maps, decorative prints, and rare books. Bus: 1, 6, 9, 10.

COURT GALLERY, Østergade 24. Tel. 33-11-20-50.

Located on the Strøget, this shop showcases contemporary art, both European and American. Summer exhibitions of graphics, oils, acrylics, sculpture, gouache, watercolors, and drawings can be seen. Bus: 1, 6, 9.

GALERIE ASBAEK, Ny Adelgade 8-10. Tel. 33-15-40-04.

This sophisticated art gallery is housed in a 1722 building that was Copenhagen's first theater. Galerie Asbaek has a five-floor permanent exhibition of the best local artists along with changing exhibitions of Scandinavian and foreign artists. There is a bookshop, a video room, and a café serving French-inspired Danish food. Graphics and posters are available for purchase. Bus: 1, 6, 9.

KUNSTHALLENS KUNSTAUKTIONER, Gothersgade 9. Tel. 33-13-85-69.

Established in 1926, this is Europe's leading dealer in the pan-European school of painting known as the COBRA School. (COBRA is derived from the combination of Copenhagen, Brussels, and Amsterdam, from which the artists originated.) These works, produced from 1948 to 1951, were an important precursor of abstract expressionism. The gallery holds 10 to 12 auctions yearly, of which six or seven deal with modern art; the others concentrate on the 19th century. July and August are slow, although the premises are open for inspection and appraisals. Bus: 1, 6, 9, 10.

BOOKSTORES

BOGHALLEN, Rådhuspladsen 37. Tel. 33-11-85-11.

This big store carries many books in English, as well as a wide selection of travel-related literature, including maps. You can also purchase books (in English) on Danish themes, such as the collected works of Hans Christian Andersen. The most centrally located shop is at Town Hall Square. Bus: 2, 8, 30.

DEPARTMENT STORES

ILLUM'S, Østergade 52. Tel. 33-14-40-02.

Another top department store, Illum's lies on the Strøget. Take time to browse through its vast world of Danish and Scandinavian design. The staff is helpful; nearly everybody speaks English. There is a restaurant. A special export cash desk at street level can help with your tax-free shopping. Bus: 1, 6, 9, 10.

MAGASIN, Kongens Nytorv 13. Tel. 33-11-44-33.

One of the most elegant department stores, Magasin is the biggest in Scandinavia.

Even the Queen of Denmark shops here without a bodyguard. It offers a complete assortment of Danish designer fashions, a large selection of glass and porcelain, and plenty of souvenirs. Goods are shipped abroad tax free. The main entrance to the store is opposite the Royal Theater. Bus: 1, 6, 9, 10.

FASHIONS

BRODRENE ANDERSEN, Østergade 7-9. Tel. 33-15-15-77.

A distinguished purveyor of "personal furnishings for gentlemen" (and increasingly for women), its atmosphere is of quiet dignity. An unquestionable Danish status symbol, the clothes are mostly German and Italian and, to a lesser degree, French. Bus: 1, 6, 9, 10.

GERA STOFFER, Østergade 36-38. Tel. 33-15-33-62.

This treasure house is unmatched in Scandinavia for the quality and beauty of its haute-couture fabrics. It is the third-largest fabric dealer in Europe. Bus: 43.

SWEATER MARKET, Frederiksberggade 15. Tel. 33-15-27-73.

Take your pick from top-grade cardigans, pullovers, hats, scarves, and mittens, hand-knitted in Denmark of 100% wool. There's also a large selection of Icelandic wool jackets and coats. Catalog sent upon request. Bus: 2, 8, 30.

HOME FURNISHINGS

ILLUMS BOLIGHUS, Amagertorv 10, on Strøget. Tel. 33-14-19-41.

A sophisticated center of modern design, this is one of Europe's finest showcases for household furnishings and accessories. Browse through furniture, lamps, rugs, textiles, bedding, glassware, kitchenware, flatware, china, jewelry, and ceramics. The store also sells fashions and accessories for women and men. There's even a gift shop. Bus: 28, 29, or 41.

LYSBERG, HANSEN & THERP, Bredgade 3. Tel. 33-14-47-87.

This 80-year-old shop is a great interior-decorating center offering fabrics, carpets, and furniture. Admire the decorated apartments furnished in impeccable taste. The company manufactures its own furniture in traditional design and imports fabrics, usually from Germany or France. Try to visit their gift shop which has many hard-to-find creations. Bus: 1, 6, 9, 10.

PAUSTIAN, Kalkbraenderiløbskaj 2. Tel. 31-18-45-11.

The leading furniture showroom in Copenhagen, located in the somewhat distant industrial Nordhavn section, this display house will ship anywhere in the world. The finest of Scandinavian design is on display, along with reproductions of the classics, from such designers as Alvar Aalto, the famed Finnish architect. Established in 1964, the store is definitely worth the trek. There's a well-recommended adjoining restaurant. S-tog: Nordhavn.

NEEDLEWORK

EVA ROSENSTAND A/S—CLARA WAEVER, Østergade 42. Tel. 33-13-29-40.

Danish-designed cross-stitch embroideries are sold here. The materials are usually linen in medium or coarser grades, but pure wool and cotton are also available. There is also an admission-free needlework museum, the only one of its kind in Europe. Bus: 1, 6, 9, 10.

PEWTER & SILVER

GEORG JENSEN, Østergade 40. Tel. 33-11-40-80.

The most regal silversmith in Copenhagen, the legendary Georg Jensen is known for its fine silver. For the connoisseur, there is no better address, for they display the largest and best collection of Jensen hollowware in Europe. Gold and silver jewelry in traditional and modern Danish design are also featured. A department specializing in secondhand Georg Jensen pieces is now open. Immediate delivery for place settings. Bus: 1, 6, 9, 10.

MUSIC

HMV SHOP, Axeltorv 2, Scala. Tel. 33-32-14-05.
Located on the third floor of the Scala complex, knowledgeable salespeople can help you select from the wide selection representing all schools, on both LPs and compact discs. Bus: 6, 16, 28.

PORCELAIN

HANS HANSEN SØV, Amagertorv 16. Tel. 33-15-60-67.
Less expensive than Georg Jensen, this is also a great silver shop, run by the same family since 1906. A high standard of craftsmanship is reflected in the contemporary silver pieces on sale. Some items are made of rosewood and inlaid with sterling silver. Gold jewelry is also sold. Bus: 28, 29, 41.

HOLMEGAARDS GLASVAERKER, Østergade 15. Tel. 33-12-44-77.
This is the only major producer of glasswork in Denmark. Its Wellington pattern, for example, was created in 1859 and is available once again. The Holmegaard glasses and the Regiment Bar set reflect solid craftsmanship. Bus: 1, 6, 9, 10.

PETER KROG, Bredgade 4. Tel. 33-12-45-55.
Peter Krog features fine silver, jewelry, and objets d'art of outstanding quality and value, bought up in the sales of large estates and reconditioned if necessary. Occasionally, among Russian works of art, he has works by Carl Fabergé, and the establishment is known for Georg Jensen used silver. Bus: 1, 6, 9, 10.

ROYAL COPENHAGEN AND BING & GRØNDAHL PORCELAIN, Amagertorv 6. Tel. 33-13-71-81.
Royal Copenhagen's trademark, three blue wavy lines, has come to symbolize quality in porcelain throughout the world. Founded in 1775, the factory was a royal possession for a century before passing into private hands in 1868. Royal Copenhagen's Christmas plates are a collector's item. The factory has turned out a new plate each year since 1908, most of the motifs depicting the Danish countryside in winter. On the top floor is a *huge* selection of seconds, and unless you're an expert, you can't tell. Visitors can inspect the factory at Smallegade 45 (tel. 31-86-48-48), where tours are given on Tuesday and Thursday at 9:45am. You can't make purchases at the factory. Bus: 28, 29, 41.

SKANDINAVISK GLAS/A.B. SCHOU, Ny Østergade 4. Tel. 33-13-80-95.
Porcelain pieces from Royal Copenhagen, Waterford crystal, porcelain from the Porsgrund factory in Norway, Lalique from Paris, Orrefors from Sweden, Lladró from Spain, and Wedgwood from England are all offered here. If you like to comparison-shop among famous competitors, this is the place. The exhibition of collectors' plates is the largest in Scandinavia. Bus: 1, 6, 9, 10.

TIN-CENTRET/THE PEWTER CENTRE, Ny Østergade 2. Tel. 33-14-82-00.
Scandinavia's largest selection of beautiful handmade pewter is found here, the exclusive sales outlet in Denmark for several Scandinavian and EC producers of high-quality handmade pewter. Apart from that, the outlet also sells Danish Flora Danica jewelry and German beer steins with pewter lids. Bus: 1, 9, 10.

SHOPPING CENTERS

COPENHAGEN AIRPORT SHOPPING CENTER
For excellent buys in Scandinavian merchandise, as well as tax-free goods, I recommend the shopping center at the airport. Scandinavian products here cannot be sold at higher prices than those in downtown Copenhagen, which means that if you

want to wait until the last minute to buy glass from Norway or Sweden, Icelandic wool items, furs, or arts and crafts from the five Scandinavian countries, you won't be at the mercy of comparative overpricing. A VAT-refund office is located nearby, so if you qualify for a refund (see "The Shopping Scene," above) you can secure it immediately.

SCALA, Axeltorv 2.
Across from the Tivoli Gardens, this is the densest collection of shops in Copenhagen. On five floors of stylish architecture it contains a full array of shops appealing to a wide variety of income levels. The complex is also loaded with restaurants and shops, offering both Danish and international food. A bevy of escalators carries shoppers up and down among the various floors. Bus: 6, 16, 28.

9. EVENING ENTERTAINMENT

Danes really know how to party. A good night means a late night, and on warm weekends, hundreds of rowdy revelers crowd Strøget until sunrise. Merrymaking in Copenhagen is not just for the younger crowd; jazz clubs, traditional beer houses, and wine cellars are routinely packed with people of all ages. Of course, the city has a more serious cultural side as well, exemplified by excellent theaters, operas, ballets, and a circus that shouldn't be missed.

THE ENTERTAINMENT SCENE

To find out what's happening at the time of your visit, pick up a free copy of *Copenhagen This Week* at the tourist information center. Ignore the "Copenhagen by Night" section, which is usually devoted to women advertising themselves as companions to visiting males. Turn instead to the section marked "Events Calendar," which has a week-by-week round-up of the most interesting entertainment and sightseeing events taking place in the Danish capital at the time of your visit.

THE PERFORMING ARTS

MERMAID THEATRE, Sankt Peders Straede 27B. Tel. 33-11-43-03.
Established in 1970, this is one of the three or four permanent English-language theaters in Europe outside the United Kingdom. It is committed to presenting exclusively English-language theatrical productions. Some of its plays are translated from other languages, including Chekhov's *The Harmfulness of Tobacco* and Hans Christian Andersen's *A Night in Roskilde*. Other presentations are American or British works. The box office is open Monday through Saturday from noon to 4pm. S-tog: Nørreport.
Admission: Tickets, 75–115 kroner ($12.60–$19.35).

ROYAL THEATRE, Kongens Nytorv. Tel. 33-14-17-66 on the day of performance, 33-14-17-65 for advance reservations.
A great winter bargain in Copenhagen is a performance by the world-renowned **Royal Danish Ballet** or **Royal Danish Opera.** Because the arts are state-subsidized in Denmark, ticket prices are comparatively low, and some seats are often available at the box office the day before a performance. The season lasts until May. Bus: 1, 6, 9, 10.
Admission: Tickets, 30–170 kroner ($5.05–$28.60).

THE CLUB & MUSIC SCENE
NIGHTCLUBS/CABARET

HAND I HANKE, Griffen Feldtsgade 20. Tel. 33-37-20-70.
This popular hangout for young people offers a pub upstairs and folk music, blues,

and rock on Tuesday, Thursday, Friday, and Saturday downstairs. There's no music in June and July, but otherwise everything is open all year. The pub is open daily from 2pm to 1:30am; downstairs, August to May, daily from 9pm to 1am. Beer costs 16 kroner ($2.70). Bus: 5, 7, 8, 16.

Admission: 25 kroner ($4.20).

FELLINI'S, in the SAS Royal Hotel, Hammerichsgade 1. Tel. 33-14-14-12.

Fellini's provides a sophisticated after-dark rendezvous, with excellent acoustics. Cavelike and intimate, it is dark with subtle lighting and strobes. Shows are presented around midnight. The upholstery is in vivid shades of red and black. Open Monday through Wednesday from 10pm to 3am, Thursday through Saturday from 10pm to 4:30am. Drinks cost 64 kroner ($10.75). Bus: 2, 8, 13.

Admission: 60 kroner ($10.10).

JAZZ & BLUES

DE TRE MUSKETERER (The Three Musketeers), Nikolaj Plads 25. Tel. 33-11-25-07.

Established in the 1970s, this is a leading jazz house, located in a building that was once the ticket office for the Danish State Railways. The establishment consists of a long and narrow room, with a gregarious bar. A different musical group is featured nightly. The venue is traditional jazz every night except Monday, when modern jazz is offered. A jazz band, such as the Red Hot Chili Peppers, plays nightly. Beer costs 23 to 26 kroner ($3.85 to $4.35); drinks, 25 kroner ($4.20). It's open Monday through Thursday from 8pm to 2am and on Friday and Saturday from 8pm to 3am. In winter there are also Sunday-afternoon jam sessions from 3 to 6pm.

Admission: 25–70 kroner ($4.20–$11.75), depending on the performance; Sun afternoons, free.

JAZZHUSET MONTMARTRE, Nørregade 41. Tel. 33-13-69-66.

Attracting music lovers of all ages, this is the center of modern jazz in Denmark, if not Europe, luring the finest jazz musicians from all over the world, including some all-time giants. During the week you can hear soul and funk as well. The club also houses the Café Monten, which provides piano concerts on Tuesday, Wednesday, and Thursday afternoons. The club is open Monday through Friday from 11pm to 5am and on Saturday and Sunday from 10pm to 5am. Beer costs 23 to 25 kroner ($3.85 to $4.20); drinks, 22 to 28 kroner ($3.70 to $4.70). Bus: 5, 7, 14, 16.

Admission: 50–250 kroner ($8.40–$42.05), depending on the performance.

LA FONTAINE, Kompagnistraede 11. Tel. 33-11-60-98.

This offbeat jazz house, a short walk to the northeast of Rådhuspladsen, has trio and jazz quartet performances that cater to a late-night clientele. Music starts at midnight. On Sunday night there is not a formal program—only a prolonged jam session whose venue depends on the inspiration of the moment. Jazz groups are usually Danish. Beer costs 20 kroner ($3.35). It's open Wednesday through Saturday from 11pm to 5am and on Sunday from 8pm to 2am. Bus: 28, 29, 41.

Admission: 20 kroner ($3.35).

RÅDHUSKROEN, Longangsstraede 21. Tel. 33-11-64-53.

Rådhuskroen is a candlelit drinking and dining spot that offers a variety of meals and large draft beers. Some of the best jazz in the city is played at this popular student hangout. It's open daily from 8pm to 3:30am; live music usually begins at 10pm. Bottled beer costs 20 kroner ($3.35). Bus: 2, 8, 30.

Admission: Free to 45 kroner ($7.55), depending on the performance.

DANCE CLUBS

AXEL DISCO, Axeltorv 2, Scala. Tel. 33-13-03-73.

Located in the Scala complex, this basement dance club attracts well-dressed clients over 20. Inside there's a large and electronically hip dance floor, a tequila bar, a beer bar, and a cocktail bar. Beer costs 20 to 31 kroner ($3.35 to $5.20), and drinks run 25 kroner ($4.20). The music is recorded. Men are encouraged to wear jackets. The place is open on Thursday from 11pm to 4am and on Friday and Saturday from 10pm to 5am. Bus: 6, 16, 28.

Admission: 40 kroner ($6.70) Fri–Sat; Thurs, 20 kroner ($3.35) for men, free for women.

CLUB EXALON, Frederiksberggade 38. Tel. 33-11-08-66.

In the city center on the Strøget, Club Exalon is decorated with dark-wood paneling, globe lighting, and striped banquettes. There is usually an hour of live music nightly, beginning at 10pm, and recorded dance music the rest of the night. The club is open daily from 10pm to 5am; beer costs 22 kroner ($3.70). Bus: 2, 8, 30.

Admission: 50 kroner ($8.40).

DADDY'S, Axeltorv 5. Tel. 33-11-67-91.

In the Palace Building across from the Scala complex, Daddy's has the most eye-catching facade of any club in town, painted in a vivid assortment of colors. The nightclub offers the largest dance floor and light show in Copenhagen, catering to a crowd in their 20s and 30s. Big-screen music videos are shown, and many fashion shows and modeling competitions take place here. An English-inspired buffet breakfast is served Sunday mornings from 5 to 7am, costing 30 kroner ($5.05) per person. Beer costs 20 to 30 kroner ($3.35 to $5.05). Daddy's is open on Thursday from 10pm to 3am, on Friday and Saturday from 11pm to 7am. Bus: 6, 16, 28.

Admission: 20–50 kroner ($3.35–$8.40).

DEN RØDE PIMPERNEL, H. C. Andersens Blvd. 7. Tel. 33-12-20-32.

The lively, clublike atmosphere of the Scarlet Pimpernel, near Rådhuspladsen, makes it a good place for dancing. It's the oldest club/restaurant in Copenhagen, established in 1939. People are admitted only after an inspection through a peephole. A live band plays a variety of dance music. It's open Tuesday through Thursday from 9pm to 3am and on Friday and Saturday from 9pm to 5am. A beer will set you back 24 kroner ($4.05) and mixed drinks run 48 kroner ($8.05). Bus: 2, 8, 30.

Admission: 30–40 kroner ($5.05–$6.70).

THE BAR SCENE

PUBS

DET LILLE APOTEK, Store Kannikestraede 15. Tel. 33-12-56-06.

This is a good spot for English-speaking foreign students to meet their Danish contemporaries. Platters of food—such as fish filet with asparagus and caviar, cold sliced salmon and caviar and chive sauce, seafood salad, and roast beef—are offered daily from 11am to 11pm, costing 59 to 79 kroner ($9.90 to $13.30). Beer runs 24 kroner ($4.05). It's open Monday through Wednesday from 11am to midnight, Thursday through Saturday from 11am to 2am, and on Sunday from 11am to midnight. Bus: 2, 8, 30.

DROP INN, Kompagnistraede 34. Tel. 33-11-24-04.

This is not a disco, but it does offer live and iconoclastic bands who perform for young people in their late teens and 20s. There's no dress code. The room combines antique and modern oil paintings and a long bar. It's open daily from 11pm to 4am. Beer costs 17 to 20 kroner ($2.85 to $3.35). Bus: 28, 29, 41.

Admission: Free.

LAURITS BETJENT, Ved Stranden 16. Tel. 33-12-03-01.

A popular nightspot has stood here since 1850. The ground floor is not all there is to this place. The upstairs attracts all ages who come to this barnlike place for the beer, which seems to be the favorite drink. While some dance to the recorded or live music, others chat near the long bar. Jazz, blues, and rock groups are featured every Friday and Saturday. It's open Monday through Saturday from 10pm to 5am. Beer costs 20 kroner ($3.35); drinks, 36 kroner ($6.05). Bus: 2, 6, 9, 43.

Admission: 20 kroner ($3.35) Fri–Sat.

LIBRARY BAR, in the Hotel Plaza, Bernstorffsgade 4. Tel. 33-14-92-62.
Frequently visited by celebrities and royalty, the Library Bar was once rated by Malcolm Forbes as one of the top five bars in the world. In a setting of antique books and works of art, you can order everything from a cappuccino to a cocktail. The setting is the lobby level of the landmark Plaza, commissioned in 1913 by King Frederik VIII. The bar was originally designed and built as the hotel's ballroom. Oregon pine was used for the paneling. The oversize mural of George Washington and his men is from 1910. It's open Monday through Saturday from 2pm to 1am and on Sunday from 2pm to midnight. Beer costs 20 kroner ($3.35); drinks begin at 35 kroner ($5.90). Bus: 1, 6.

NYHAVN 17, Nyhavn 17. Tel. 33-12-54-19.
This is the last of the honky-tonks that used to make up the former sailors' quarter. This café is a short walk from the patrician Kongens Nytorv and the d'Angleterre luxury hotel. In summer you can sit outside. It's open daily from 9am to 1am. Beer costs 20 kroner ($3.35) and drinks run 35 kroner ($5.90). Bus: 1, 6, 9, 10.

THE QUEEN'S PUB, in the Kong Frederik Hotel, Vester Voldgade 25. Tel. 33-12-59-02.
A popular spot, the Queen's Pub is connected to one of the city's most prestigious hotels. Amid English walnut paneling and mirrors etched with elaborate Victorian patterns, you can settle back and enjoy. It's open daily from 11:30am to 1am. Beer costs 17 to 24 kroner ($2.85 to $4.05). Bus: 2, 8.

VIN & OLGOD, Skindergade 45. Tel. 33-13-26-25.
A dancing, drinking, singing, and snacking complex, Vin & Olgod is complete with a tavern, a pub, a bodega, and a main beer hall. When the band plays on stage, everybody sings along. If you don't know the words, printed music sheets are provided. In any room, light beer and a variety of snacks are available. It's open Monday through Saturday from 8pm to 2am. A half liter of beer costs 36 kroner ($6.05) and drinks run 45 kroner ($7.55). Bus: 5, 7, 14.

WINE BARS

HVIIDS VINSTUE, Kongens Nytorv 19. Tel. 33-15-10-64.
Built in 1670, this old wine cellar is a dimly lit safe haven for an eclectic crowd. In December only, a combination of red wine and cognac is served. It's open Monday through Saturday from 10am to 1am; closed Sunday in July and August. Beer runs 17 to 22 kroner ($2.85 to $3.70); wine costs 24 kroner ($4.05). Bus: 1, 6, 9, 10.

THE GAY SCENE

AN ACTIVITIES CENTER

PAN SOCIETY, Knabrostraede 3. Tel. 33-13-19-48.
This nationwide organization was established in 1948 for the protection and advancement of gay rights. Its headquarters is inside a 19th-century yellow building off the Strøget. A dance club occupies three of its floors, and a modern café is on the ground floor. Thursday night is for women only. Every night is gay night, although a lot of straight people patronize the place because the music is so good.

Café Pan is open Monday through Thursday from noon to 3am, on Friday from noon to 5am, on Saturday from 11:30am to 5am, and on Sunday from 1pm to 3am. The dance club is open Sunday through Tuesday from 10pm to 3am, on Wednesday and Thursday from 10pm to 4am, and on Friday and Saturday from 10pm to 5am. Beer costs 20 kroner ($3.35); drinks, 36 kroner ($6.05).

Admission: Dance club, 50 kroner ($8.40).

BARS & PUBS

ERIK DEN RØDE, Amagerbrogade 40. Tel. 31-57-40-80.

At the corner of Holmbladgade, this pub has the interior of a cozy Danish *kro* (inn). It's a popular venue for gay businessmen who drop in to enjoy the frikadeller, filet of plaice, or grilled or roast beef. Appetizers cost around 35 kroner ($5.90); main dishes, 50 to 100 kroner ($8.40 to $16.60). A beer runs 20 kroner ($3.35). Bus: 2, 8, 11.

PINK CLUB, Farvergade 10. Tel. 33-11-26-07.

A new Copenhagen gay bar, it has a long bar with the atmosphere of a darkly upholstered private men's club. It's open daily from 4pm to 4am. Beer costs 16 to 19 kroner ($2.70 to $3.20). Bus: 2, 8, 30.

STABLE BAR, Teglgårdsstraede 3. Tel. 33-12-73-03.

This is the premier macho gay bar in town, filled with the usual collection of uniforms, leather, and levis. There's one bar and a decor outfitted in shades of gray, black, and stainless steel. It's open Sunday through Friday from 6pm to 2am and on Saturday from 10pm to 2am. A beer will set you back 15 to 18 kroner ($2.50 to $3.05). Bus: 2, 8, 30.

TIVOLI AT NIGHT

In the center of the gardens, the large **open-air stage** books vaudeville acts (tumbling clowns, acrobats, aerialists) who give two performances nightly, at 7 and 9pm (also at 5pm on the weekend). Spectators have to go through the turnstiles for seats, but there's an unobstructed view from the outside for standees. Special arrangements with jazz, beat, and folklore groups also take place during the season. Admission is free.

Near the Vesterbrogade entrance is the 100-year-old outdoor **Pantomime Theater,** with its Chinese stage and its peacock curtain that opens Monday through Saturday at 7:45pm, revealing a repertory of 16 different commedia dell'arte productions (the entertaining trio: Pierrot, Columbine, and Harlequin), authentic pantomimes that have been performed continuously in Copenhagen since 1801. Admission is free. Classic ballets, accompanied by the Tivoli Promenade Orchestra, are performed on the stage at 10pm.

The modern **Tivolis Koncertsal** (concert hall) is a great place to hear talented and famous artists, led by equally famous conductors. Inaugurated in 1956, the concert hall has a seating capacity of 2,000, and its season, lasting for more than 4 months beginning in May, has been called "the most extensive music festival in the world." Performances of everything from symphony to opera are held nightly at 7:30pm. Good seats are available at prices ranging from 30 to 80 kroner ($5.05 to $13.45) and up when major artists are performing—but most performances are free. Ballet usually costs 115 to 195 kroner ($19.35 to $32.80). Tickets are sold at the main booking office on Vesterbrogade (tel. 33-15-10-12).

Tivoli Glassalen (tel. 33-11-86-75) is housed in an octagonal gazebolike building with a glass, gilt-capped canopy. Depending on its repertoire, the program might interest you. Tickets range from 95 to 150 kroner ($15.95 to $25.20).

Jazzhus Slukefter (tel. 33-14-30-74) offers some of the best jazz in Copenhagen, often attracting big names from the United States. The club is open Monday through Saturday from 8pm to 2am. When the gardens close, you can enter from the street. Most concerts begin at 9:30pm, and the entrance fee ranges from free to 50 kroner ($8.40), depending on the performance. Beer costs 20 to 25 kroner ($3.35 to $4.20).

For dancing, head to **Dansetten** (tel. 33-14-06-99). Live bands, disco, video, and light and laser shows make for a lively evening. The place opens nightly at 8pm, closing at midnight on Sunday, Monday, Tuesday, and Wednesday, and at 2am on Thursday, Friday, and Saturday. A bottle of beer costs 23 kroner ($3.85), and admission is 50 kroner ($8.40). Guests can use the club's separate entrance.

10. EASY EXCURSIONS

BEACHES

The nearest beach to Copenhagen is **Bellevue** (take the S-train to Klampenborg), but the water is not recommended for swimming. If you like to swim at a sandy beach, take a trip (by train or car) to the beaches at North Zealand—**Gilleleje, Hornbaek, Liseleje,** and **Tisvildeleje.** Although these are family beaches, minimum bathing attire is worn.

To reach any of these beaches, take the train to Helsingør and then continue by bus. Or you can make connections by train to Hillerød and switch to a local train. Check at the railroad station for details. If you drive, you may want to stay for the evening discos at the little beach resort towns dotting the north coast of Zealand.

DRAGØR

Visit the past in this old seafaring town on the island of Amager, 3 miles south of Copenhagen's Kastrup Airport. It is filled with well-preserved half-timbered, ocher and pink 18th-century cottages with steep red-tile or thatch roofs, many of which are under the protection of the National Trust.

Dragør (pronounced *Drah*-wer) was a busy port on the herring-rich Baltic Sea in the early Middle Ages, and when fishing fell off, it became just another sleepy little waterfront village. After 1520, Amager Island and its villages—Dragør and Store Magleby—were inhabited by the Dutch, who brought their own customs, Low-German language, and agricultural expertise to Amager, especially their love of bulb flowers. In Copenhagen, you still see wooden-shoed Amager selling their hyacinths, tulips, daffodils, and lilies in the streets.

Dragør is a 35-minute trip on bus no. 30 or 33 from the Rådhuspladsen (Town Hall Square) in Copenhagen.

WHAT TO SEE & DO

DRAGØR MUSEUM, Havnepladsen 4. Tel. 31-53-41-06.
The exhibits at this harborfront museum show how the Amager Dutch lived from prehistoric times to the 20th century. Farming, goose breeding, seafaring, fishing, ship piloting, and ship salvage are delineated through pictures and artifacts.
Admission: 10 kroner ($1.70) adults, 5 kroner (85¢) children.
Open: May–Sept, Tues–Fri 2–5pm, Sat–Sun and hols. noon–6pm. **Bus:** 30, 33.

STUDIO OF CHRISTIAN MOLSTED, Blegerstraede 1. Tel. 31-53-41-06.
Next door to the Dragør Museum, visit the studio of noted Danish marine artist Christian Molsted (1862–1930), where many pictures and topographical drawings of Dragør are displayed.
Admission: 10 kroner ($1.70) adults, 5 kroner (85¢) children.
Open: May–Sept, Sat–Sun 2–5pm. **Bus:** 30, 33.

AMAGER MUSEUM, Hovedgaden 12 at Magleby. Tel. 31-53-02-50.
A rich trove of historic treasures is found in this museum outside Dragør. Exhibits reveal the affluence achieved by the Amager Dutch, with rich textiles, fine embroidery, and such amenities as carved silver buckles and buttons. Room interiors of a Dutch house are especially interesting, showing how these people decorated their homes and lived in comfort.

Admission: 10 kroner ($1.70) adults, 5 kroner (85¢) children.
Open: June–Aug, Wed–Sun 11am–3pm; Sept–May, Wed and Sun 11am–3pm.
Bus: 30, 33.

WHERE TO STAY

HOTEL DRAGØR, Drogdensvej 43, DK-2791 Dragør. Tel. 31-53-01-87.
24 rms (all with bath). TEL **Bus:** 30, 33.
$ **Rates:** 650–700 kroner ($109.25–$117.65) single; 660–730 kroner ($110.95–$122.70) double. AE, DC, MC.

Although most people visit this hotel for its food, it also offers comfortable old-fashioned bedrooms. You'll get a real feel for a country Danish inn, yet you're only 20 minutes from the Copenhagen Town Hall. Everything is clean and well kept, and the staff is friendly.

You can also enjoy the hotel's excellently prepared cuisine. There are six different preparations of herring, a Dragør Plate of mixed meats and pâtés, schnitzels, soups, and smørrebrød. Full meals begin at 190 kroner ($31.95), or you can order just a sandwich and salad at lunch. The dining room is open for lunch and dinner daily from 11am to 10pm.

WHERE TO DINE

CAFE BEGHUSET, Strandgade 14. Tel. 31-53-01-36.
Cuisine: DANISH/FRENCH. **Reservations:** Not required. **Bus:** 30, 33.
$ **Prices:** Appetizers 32–55 kroner ($5.40–$9.25); main dishes 85–135 kroner ($14.30–$22.70); three-course dinner 189 kroner ($31.75). DC, MC, V.
Open: Lunch daily noon–3pm; dinner daily 5:30–10pm.

This charming café on a cobblestone street in the center of town looks like an idyllic country cottage. The bar serves sophisticated drinks including Alabama Slammers, Blue Lagoons, and margaritas. Full meals include barbecued spareribs, gazpacho, mussels marinara, salad bar, marinated filet of beef, pepper steak, calves' liver, sorbets, and Irish coffee.

STRANDHOTEL, Strandlinbyn 9, Havnen. Tel. 31-53-00-75.
Cuisine: DANISH. **Reservations:** Recommended. **Bus:** 30, 33.
$ **Prices:** Appetizers 30–36 kroner ($5.05–$6.05); main dishes 85–135 kroner ($14.30–$22.70); lunch smørrebrød 32 kroner ($5.40). MC, V.
Open: Daily 11:30am–10:30pm.

Stop in here where King Frederik III ate his favorite eel soup and where Søren Kierkegaard dined as well. The building dates from 1840. You can enjoy full meals including filet of pork in paprika sauce, smoked eel, fried herring, filet of veal with foie gras, fried or poached plaice, and trout with almonds. At lunch, one of the best arrays of smørrebrød in town is served.

DRAGØR KRO, Kongvejen 23. Tel. 31-53-01-87.
Cuisine: DANISH/FRENCH. **Reservations:** Recommended. **Bus:** 30, 33.
$ **Prices:** Fixed-price dinner 109 kroner ($18.30) for two courses, 129 kroner ($20.85) for three courses; appetizers 35–70 kroner ($5.90–$11.75); main dishes 58–155 kroner ($9.75–$26.05). AE, MC, V.
Open: Daily noon–9:30pm (10:30pm in summer). **Closed:** Jan–Feb 8.

A series of half-paneled dining rooms are found in this 1721 building. There is a rose-filled courtyard for outdoor dining and drinking. You can select a fresh fish course with white wine sauce, or pepper steak, or perhaps filet of veal in mustard sauce. "Falling star" is a house specialty (boiled or fried fish with caviar and shrimp).

CHAPTER 8

ZEALAND & ITS ISLANDS

Although Copenhagen is Zealand's largest city, the island is rich with other attractions.

Many prefer to explore the island on day trips from the capital, since distances between attractions are short. The most popular day trip is a tour of three royal castles in North Zealand: Kronborg Castle at Shakespeare's Elsinore, the royal family's summer palace at Fredensborg, and the 17th-century castle of Frederiksborg at Hillerød.

Along the way, a popular stop is the Louisiana Museum, on the so-called Danish Riviera. The building is as architecturally interesting as the ever-changing exhibits of stunning modern art housed inside.

Once you've explored Hamlet's Castle, you might take a geological field trip to the white chalky cliffs and glacial deposits on the island of Møn.

SEEING ZEALAND & ITS ISLANDS

GETTING AROUND

Zealand is best explored by car, although it has an excellent bus and train network. By either bus or train you can reach all the important destinations outside Copenhagen in the following time periods: Helsingør, 50 minutes; Hillerød, 40 minutes; Roskilde, 20 minutes; Køge, 1 hour.

Inquire about schedule information at the Central Station in Copenhagen. At the information desk of the Danish State Railways you can request a round-trip ticket that will also include admission charges to certain major attractions.

The **Copenhagen Card** is a cost-saving device allowing unlimited travel on buses and trains in Copenhagen, North Zealand, Roskilde, and Køge. Without this card, travel can be pricey because there's no discount on round-trip tickets.

Many roads in Zealand have cycle tracks if you'd like to explore by bicycle. Most cars use the expressway highways, so it's safer to take the older secondary roads.

If you prefer an organized tour, inquire about the possibilities at the Copenhagen Tourist Office. The most popular tour is called the Castle Tour of North Zealand, visiting Kronborg, Fredensborg, and Frederiksborg. It takes 7 hours.

A SUGGESTED ITINERARY

Zealand can be explored from Copenhagen, but you'll get more of a feel for it by spending 2 or 3 nights in a Zealand *kro* (inn) or local hotel.

Day 1: Drive up the Danish Riviera coastline stopping at the Louisiana Art Museum, then continuing to Helsingør for the night.

Day 2: Explore Hamlet's Castle (Kronborg) and other attractions in the morning; then take a day trip on the ferry to Helsingborg, Sweden. Return to Helsingør for the night.

WHAT'S SPECIAL ABOUT ZEALAND

Beaches
- ☐ Denmark's Riviera is Strandvejen. Quiet, sandy beaches.
- ☐ The tranquil, sandy beaches of Møn, an island in the Baltic Sea.

Castles & Palaces
- ☐ Kronborg—"Hamlet's Castle"—the most visited place outside Copenhagen.
- ☐ Frederiksborg Castle, the premier castle of Scandinavia, called the Danish Versailles.
- ☐ Selsø Slot, the country's first Renaissance castle.

Great Cathedrals
- ☐ Roskilde Cathedral, resting place of 38 Danish kings and queens.

Ancient Ruins
- ☐ Five Viking vessels rescued from Roskilde Fjord on display near Roskilde.

Art Museums
- ☐ Louisiana Art Museum at Humlebaek, Denmark's most controversial modern-art museum.

Natural Attractions
- ☐ The white cliffs of Møn, created a million years ago by the sea.

Literary Pilgrimages
- ☐ Rungstedlund, home of Karen Blixen/Isak Dinesen, famed for *Out of Africa*.

Special Events
- ☐ Viking Pageant at Frederikssund, a 2-week festival (late June).
- ☐ Roskilde festival draws rock music lovers worldwide (early June).

Day 3: Stop off at the queen's summer home (outside visits only) at Fredensborg in the morning, then continue to Hillerød in the west to see Frederiksborg Castle. Drive to the Roskilde for the night.

Day 4: While in Roskilde, explore its attractions, including Roskilde Cathedral and the Viking Ship Museum. In the afternoon visit the Forsøgscenter, 5 miles west, site of a reconstructed Iron Age community.

Day 5: Drive to Køge, south of Copenhagen (take connecting Route 6). Have lunch, look around, and head for Stege, the capital of Møn, for the night. Explore the white cliffs, prehistoric burial sights, and medieval churches. Return to Copenhagen for the night.

1. RUNGSTEDLUND

15 miles north of Copenhagen

GETTING THERE   By Train   A Kystbanen train departs from Copenhagen's Central Station, taking 30 minutes.

By Bus   Buses for Rungstedlund leave from Copenhagen's Central Station.

By Car   Head north from Copenhagen along the E4 to Helsingør until you reach the turnoff east marked RUNGSTED.

Since the 1985 release of *Out of Africa*, starring Robert Redford and Meryl Streep, thousands of literary and movie fans have been visiting the former home of Karen Blixen, who wrote under the pen name Isak Dinesen. Her home, **Rungstedlund,** Runsted Strandvej III, is midway between Copenhagen and Helsingør on the coastal road.

Her father, Wilhelm Dinesen, purchased the estate in 1879. Blixen left in 1914 for

Kenya when she married Bror von Blixen Fenicke, but returned in 1931 and stayed until her death in 1962.

Blixen and her family in 1958 donated the family estate and its 40 acres to a private foundation, the Rungstedlund Fund. Following Blixen's death, the Danish Academy took over the house, closing it to the public. However, the grounds, maintained as a bird sanctuary, can be visited free daily until sunset. Blixen is buried in the grove at the foot of Edwaldshøj.

IN THEIR FOOTSTEPS

Karen Blixen/Isak Dinesen (1885–1962) Twice nominated for the Nobel Prize, Blixen, writing under the name Isak Dinesen, was a major 20th-century author. Her works included *Seven Gothic Tales* and her serene memoir, *Out of Africa*, about her life in Kenya.

• **Birthplace:** Born in Rungstedlund, she was the daughter of an aristocrat, Wilhelm Dinesen, soldier, sportsman, and writer.

• **Residences:** Her father's estate, Rungstedlund, in Zealand, and a Kenyan coffee plantation where she fell in love with Denys Finch Hatton.

• **Resting Place:** In the grove at the foot of Edwaldshøj, near her father's estate.

WHERE TO DINE

RESTAURANT NOKKEN, Rungsted Havn 44. Tel. 42-57-13-14.
   Cuisine: DANISH. **Reservations:** Recommended.
$ Prices: Appetizers 70–127 kroner ($11.75–$21.35); main dishes 98–198 kroner ($16.45–$33.30); two-course lunch 160 kroner ($26.90). AE, DC, MC, V.
   Open: Lunch daily noon–4pm; dinner daily 6–10pm (bar, daily noon–1am).
Amid light-grained paneling and whimsical nautical accessories, you can enjoy one of the best meals to be found along the Danish Riviera. A sweeping wall of windows encompasses the sea, the boats, and a view of the Swedish coast. Specialties include filet of prime beef with thyme and snails, double lamb chops with aromatic herbs, scampi orientale, oven-baked lemon sole, and heather-honey ice cream. The restaurant lies directly on the waterfront at Rungsted Pier.

2. HUMLEBAEK & LOUISIANA

20 miles north of Copenhagen

GETTING THERE   By Train   Humlebaek, the nearest town to Louisiana, may be reached by train from Copenhagen (København–Helsingør). Once at Humlebaek Station, the museum is a 10-minute walk.

By Bus   Take the S-train, Line A or B, to Lyngby station. From there, take bus no. 388 along the coast road. There is a bus stop at the museum.

By Car   Take the Strandvej (coastal road no. 152) from Copenhagen. The scenic drive takes about 45 minutes.

Established in 1958, the   ✪ **Louisiana Art Museum,** G. Strandvej 13 (tel. 42-19-07-19), is idyllically situated in a 19th-century mansion on the Danish Riviera surrounded by elegant gardens, opening directly onto the Oresund sound. The modern art displayed is paintings and sculptures by masters (Giacometti and Henry Moore, to name two) as well as the best and most controversial works of modern art. In particular, look for paintings by Carl-Henning Pedersen. Occasionally, there are Chinese or Egyptian art exhibits as well as concerts. The museum name came from the first owner of the estate, Alexander Brun, who had three wives, each named Louise. Admission is 40 kroner ($6.70) for adults, free for children. It's open Thursday through Tuesday from 10am to 5pm and on Wednesday from 10am to 10pm.

WHERE TO DINE

GAMLA HUMLEBAEK KRO, Ny Strandvej 2A. Tel. 42-19-05-69.
   Cuisine: DANISH. **Reservations:** Recommended.
$ Prices: Appetizers 36–55 kroner ($6.05–$9.25); main dishes 52–145 kroner ($8.75–$24.35). MC, V.
   Open: Daily noon–9:30pm.

A perfect lunch spot for visitors to the Louisiana Museum, the inn was built in 1722. Selections might include medallions of veal with morel sauce, stuffed filet of plaice, herring with sherry, marinated salmon, and a full array of continental wines. A fixed-price lunch costs 115 kroner ($19.35).

---

3. HELSINGØR (ELSINORE)

25 miles north of Copenhagen

GETTING THERE By Train There are frequent trains from Copenhagen taking 50 minutes.

By Bus Some 30 buses daily leave Copenhagen for the 1-hour trip to Helsingør.

By Car Take the E-4 north from Copenhagen.

ESSENTIALS The **Tourist Office** is at Havnepladsen (tel. 49-21-13-33), open daily from 9am to 5pm.

Helsingør (Elsinore in English) is visited chiefly for "Hamlet's Castle." Aside from its literary associations, the town has a certain charm: a quiet market square, medieval lanes, old half-timbered and brick buildings, remains of its once prosperous shipping industry.

In 1429 King Erik of Pomerania ruled that ships passing Helsingør had to pay sound dues. The town quickly developed into the focal point for international shipping, bringing in a lot of revenue. King Erik also built the Castle of Krogen, later rebuilt by Christian IV as the Castle of Kronborg. For a while Helsingør prospered and grew so much it was the second-largest town in the country.

WHAT TO SEE & DO

Guided tours of the city, costing 25 kroner ($4.20) per person, are conducted every Monday in July at 7pm.

KRONBORG CASTLE, Kronborg. Tel. 49-21-30-78.
   ✪ There is no evidence that Shakespeare ever saw this sandstone-and-copper Dutch Renaissance-style castle, full of intriguing secret passages and casemates, but he made it famous in *Hamlet*. According to 12th-century historian Saxo Grammaticus, though, if Hamlet had really existed, he would have been centuries before Kronborg was erected (1574–85). Over the years, some famous productions of the Shakespearian play have been staged here. One great performance was Derek Jacobi's interpretation in 1979. In 1954 the parts of Hamlet and Ophelia were played by Richard Burton and Claire Bloom.

The castle was restored in 1629 by Christian IV after it was gutted by fire. During its history, it has been looted, bombarded, occupied by Swedes, and used as a barracks from 1785 to 1922. Don't miss the starkly furnished Great Hall (the largest in northern Europe), the church with its original oak furnishings, and the royal chambers. Its bleak and austere atmosphere adds to its drama. Kronborg also contains a collection of wool and silk tapestries, great old oaken chests, and cupboards. In the basement sits Holger Danske, the mythological hero believed to aid Denmark when the country is threatened. The **Danish Maritime Museum** (tel. 49-21-06-85) is also on the premises, which explores the history of Danish shipping.

Guided tours are given every half hour October to April. In summer you can walk around on your own. The castle is half a mile from the rail station.

Admission: 20 kroner ($3.35) adults, 10 kroner ($1.70) children.

Open: May–Sept, daily 10:30am–5pm; Oct and Apr, Tues–Sun 11am–4pm; Nov–Mar, Tues–Sun 11am–3pm. **Closed:** Christmas Day.

KARMELITERKLOSTRET, Sct. Annagade 38. Tel. 49-21-17-74.

This well-preserved 15th-century former Carmelite monastery is the best of its kind in Scandinavia. It's located at the intersection of Havnegade and Kronborgvej.

Admission: 10 kroner ($1.70) adults, 5 kroner (85¢) children.

Open: Guided tours daily at 2pm (also at 11am from mid-Apr to mid-Oct). **Bus:** 801, 802, 803, 331.

SCT. MARIAE CHURCH, Sct. Annagade 38. Tel. 49-21-17-74.

A monastery complex with late 15th-century frescoes, St. Mary's also contains the organ played by baroque composer Diderik Buxtehude from 1660 to 1668 (still in use). The church lies near the intersection of Havnegade and Kronborgvej.

Admission: Free.

Open: Daily 1–4pm. **Bus:** 801, 802, 803, 331.

SAINT OLAI CHURCH, Sct. Annagade 12. Tel. 49-21-04-43.

Built between 1480 and 1559, this christening chapel is worth a visit. The interior of the church and the baptistry in particular are one-of-a-kind. The spired church is connected to the Carmelite cloisters. The church lies near the intersection of Havnegade and Kronborgvej.

Admission: Free.

Open: Mon–Sat 10am–4pm. **Bus:** 801, 802, 803, 331.

HELSINGØR BYMUSEUM, Sct. Annagade 36. Tel. 49-21-00-98.

Installed in part of the Carmelite monastery (see above), this museum houses the town's historic archives and various exhibits. In 1630 it was the local poorhouse, and for a long time a hospital, specializing in brain operations. Some tools used by these early surgeons are displayed, and are rather gruesome.

Admission: 5 kroner (85¢) adults, children free.

Open: Daily noon–4pm. **Bus:** 801, 802, 803, 331.

MARIENLYST SLOT, Marienlyst Allé 32. Tel. 49-21-00-98.

Another municipal museum, built in 1587 as a summer palace and rebuilt around 1760, Marienlyst Castle houses many of Helsingør's historic relics, with changing exhibits of arts and crafts.

Admission: 10 kroner ($1.70) adults, children free.

Open: June–Aug, Thurs–Tues noon–5pm, Wed noon–5pm and 7–10pm; Sept–May, Sat–Sun 2–5pm. **Bus:** 340, 801, 802.

DANMARKS TEKNISKE MUSEUM (Technical Museum of Denmark), Nodre Strandvej 23. Tel. 49-21-71-11.

This museum contains technical, industrial, scientific, and transportation exhibits, including the oldest Danish airplanes and trains, the world's first typewriter, and the world's first electromagnetic sound recorder (tape recorder). There's also an 1888 Danish automobile, Hammelvognen.

Admission: 20 kroner ($3.35) adults, 10 kroner ($1.70) children.

Open: Daily 10am–5pm. **Bus:** 340.

WHERE TO STAY

HOTEL HAMLET, Bramstraede 5, DK-3000 Helsingør. Tel. 49-21-05-91.
36 rms (all with bath). TV TEL **Bus:** 801, 802.
$ Rates (including breakfast): 595–695 kroner ($100–$116.85) single; 795–975 kroner ($133.65–$163.90) double. AE, DC, MC, V.

Each bedroom is carpeted and half-paneled, and has antique pinewood doors and English club-style furniture. The hotel's restaurant, Ophelia, is also recommended (see "Where to Dine," below). The hotel is well situated, lying close to Kronberg Castle and the ferry to Sweden.

HOTEL MARIENLYST, Nordre Standvej 2, DK-3000 Helsingør. Tel. 42-10-10-42. Fax 42-10-35-30. 209 rms (all with bath). TV TEL **Bus:** 340.
$ Rates (including breakfast): 750 kroner ($126.10) single; 1,050 kroner ($176.50) double. AE, DC, MC, V.

Located on the western outskirts of town beyond the castle, this hotel is about as close to Las Vegas as you'll get in Denmark. On the premises are a restaurant, bar, and casino. Some accommodations lie within apartmentlike annexes at the far end of an arched footbridge; others are in the main building.

Facilities include a sauna and an indoor swimming pool.

SKANDIA HOTEL, Bramstraede 1, DK-3000 Helsingør. Tel. 49-21-09-02. 46 rms (9 with bath). **Bus:** 801, 802.
$ Rates (including breakfast): 240 kroner ($40.35) single without bath, 320 kroner ($53.80) single with bath; 420 kroner ($70.60) double without bath, 620 kroner ($104.20) double with bath. AE, DC, MC, V.

The budget choice in town, the Skandia has relatively clean and spacious rooms filled with comfortable, albeit slightly dowdy, furniture. The hotel is set behind a red-brick facade along a street running parallel to the port. It's near the harbor and close to the ferry to Sweden.

WHERE TO DINE

Typical Danish hot meals, such as hakkebof (hamburger steak), frikadeller (Danish rissoles), rib roast with red cabbage, cooked or fried flounder or herring, and aeggekage (egg cake) with bacon, are served in the local restaurants. Some restaurants offer a *Danmenu*, a typical Danish meal. In Helsingør, you'll also find many fast-food places, and you won't want to miss the celebrated ice-cream wafers.

RESTAURANT FAERGAARDEN, Stengade 81B. Tel. 49-21-39-46.
Cuisine: DANISH. **Reservations:** Not required. **Bus:** 801, 802.
$ Prices: Appetizers 45–80 kroner ($7.55–$13.45); main dishes 135–175 kroner ($22.70–$29.40). MC, V.
Open: Daily 11am–10pm.

This restaurant, set in a former Customs house from 1770, serves tasty meals and generous portions of Danish specialties. You can order herring filets, steak tartare, a lunchtime platter of smoked eel with pâté and cheese, shrimp cocktail, plaice stuffed with shrimp, veal filet Cordon Bleu, and a full array of open-face sandwiches.

OPHELIA RESTAURANT, in the Hotel Hamlet, Bramstraede 3. Tel. 49-21-28-02.
Cuisine: DANISH/FRENCH. **Reservations:** Not required. **Bus:** 801, 802.
$ Prices: Appetizers 28–85 kroner ($4.70–$14.30); main dishes 118–248 kroner ($19.85–$41.70); two-course dinner 150 kroner ($25.20); fixed-price lunch 98 kroner ($16.45). AE, DC, MC, V.
Open: Daily 11:30am–10pm.

Ophelia is the most appealing restaurant in town. In the elegantly rustic dining room, photos of various world *Hamlet* productions line the brick walls. Specialties include butter-fried plaice with shrimp, pepper-pickled Baltic salmon, halibut cutlet with butter-sautéed spinach, steak with bordelaise sauce, and richly caloric desserts. Lunches will probably only set you back half as much as dinner.

In the basement is a tavern-style disco, the Shakespeare Club, where an over-30 crowd drinks and dances nightly except Tuesday, after 8pm. On weekends guests pay 25 kroner ($4.20) cover, and beer costs the same.

CAFETERIA SAN REMO, Stengade 53. Tel. 42-21-00-55.
  Cuisine: DANISH. **Reservations:** Not required. **Bus:** 801, 802.
$ Prices: Appetizers 20–45 kroner ($3.35–$7.55); main dishes 25–80 kroner ($4.20–$13.45). No credit cards.
  Open: June–July, daily 9am–9pm; Aug–May, daily 11am–6pm.

⑤ A down-to-earth self-service place with crystal chandeliers, the San Remo offers 35 different meals, including frikadeller (Ping-Pong meatballs) and potatoes. At the corner of Bjergegade, in a traffic-free shopping mall, the cafeteria lies half a block from the harbor. It dates from 1904 and is in a building with a Dutch architectural influence.

4. FREDENSBORG

6 miles west of Helsingør, 25 miles north of Copenhagen

GETTING THERE By Train From Copenhagen's Central Station, frequent trains run to Fredensborg.

By Bus Bus nos. 336 and 384 from Copenhagen's Central Station run to Fredensborg.

By Car From Copenhagen, head north on the E55 toward Helsingør, turning west on Route 6.

The splendid early 18th-century Italian-style **Fredensborg Palace** (tel. 42-28-00-25) is the summer home of the royal family. It was particularly celebrated during the reign of Christian IX, who assembled the greats of European royalty here in the days of Queen Victoria. Rooms open for public viewing are those actually used by the royal family. When the queen is in residence, visitors assemble at noon to watch the changing of the guard. On Thursday, except in July, the queen often appears to acknowledge a regimental band concert in her honor. Bus no. 336 stops nearby.

The palace can be visited only in July, daily from 1 to 5pm. Admission is 8 kroner ($1.35) for adults, 3 kroner (50¢) for children. The extensive grounds are open all summer.

WHERE TO STAY & DINE

HOTEL STORE KRO, Slotsgade 6, DK-3480 Fredensborg. Tel. 42-28-00-47. 49 rms (all with bath). TEL **Bus:** 336.
$ Rates (including breakfast): 550–700 kroner ($92.45–$117.65) single; 750–1,050 kroner ($126.10–$176.50) double. AE, DC, MC, V.
A 10-minute walk from the train station and only 5 minutes from Esrum Lake, the hotel was commissioned in 1723 by King Frederik IV. Well-furnished rooms, rich in character, reflect its proximity to the royal residence. Facilities include a sauna and a billiard and dart room. If you're stopping in for lunch, count on spending from 200 kroner ($33.60). Food is served daily from noon to 10pm.

5. HILLERØD

22 miles NW of Copenhagen

GETTING THERE By Train The S-train from Copenhagen's Central Station departs every 20 minutes and takes 35 minutes.

By Bus   From the Central Station in Copenhagen, take bus no. 701, 702, 703.

By Car   Take Route 16 north from Copenhagen.

ESSENTIALS   The **Tourist Office** is at Slotsgade 52 (tel. 42-26-28-52).

Hillerød offers some very interesting sights, including one of Scandinavia's most beautiful castles. It would be great to be in Hillerød at the time of the Viking festival in summer (see below).

WHAT TO SEE & DO

FREDERIKSBORG CASTLE, Fredensborgvej. Tel. 42-26-04-39.

⭐ This moated *slot* (castle), known as the Danish Versailles, is perhaps the major castle in all of Scandinavia. Like Kronborg, it was built in Dutch Renaissance style (red brick, copper roof, sandstone facade), and dates to 1560, the reign of Frederik II. However, his son, Christian IV, born at the castle, had most of the original edifice torn down and rebuilt in the early 17th century. In 1859 the castle was ravaged by fire, but it has been restored. Now it is a major national history museum.

Among its many sights are the sumptuously decorated and gilded chapel (be sure to see the king's pew and the wooden organ built by Esajas Compenius in 1610) where Danish kings were once crowned, and the Great Hall. In addition, Frederiksborg houses an extensive collection of portraits, historical paintings, and furnishings (ebony cabinets, four-poster beds, tapestries, enameled miniatures, coats-of-arms).

To reach the castle, it's a 15-minute walk from the train station or a short taxi ride.

Admission: 25 kroner ($4.20) adults, 5 kroner (85¢) children.

Open: May–Sept, daily 10am–5pm; Oct, daily 10am–4pm; Apr, daily 11am–4pm; Nov–Mar, daily 11am–3pm. **S-train:** Copenhagen to Hillerød.

NORDSJAELLANDSK FOLKEMUSEUM (North Zealand Folk Museum), Helsingørsgade 65. Tel. 42-26-43-79.

Collections depict the rural history of North Zealand, with special emphasis on the preindustrialization era. Native textiles and costumes are also exhibited.

There are supplementary displays at **Sophienborg,** Sophienborgvej 38 (tel. 42-26-43-79), an estate on the western outskirts of Hillerød. Sophienborg is easily reached by bus no. 734 from the Hillerød station. From there, it's an 8-minute walk. By car, take either Frederiksvaerksgade or Herredsvejen, turn right at Tulstrupvej, and follow signs to Sophienborg. It keeps the same hours as the folk museum, and admission is on the same ticket.

Admission: 10 kroner ($1.70) adults, children free.

Open: Museum and supplementary collections, June 24–Aug 26, Tues–Sun 11am–4pm; Aug 27–June 23, Tues–Sun 11am–4pm.

AEBELHOLT ABBEY, Aebelholtsvang 4, Meikse. Tel. 42-11-03-51.

This religious complex, 3½ miles west of Hillerød and founded in 1175 by Abbot Wilhelm, was one of Denmark's largest medieval ecclesiastical communities. The buildings were destroyed after the Reformation, but excavations have made it possible to establish the original outline of the complex. Numerous skeletons collected from the cemetery attest to the advanced medical knowledge of the monks who nursed people prior to their death. The skeletons are on view in a museum near the ruins.

Admission: 12 kroner ($2) adults, 5 kroner (85¢) children.

Open: Apr, Sat–Sun 1–4pm; May–Aug, Tues–Sun 10am–4pm; Sept, Tues–Sun 1–4pm; Oct, Sat–Sun 1–4pm. **Bus:** 124 from Hillerød.

A NEARBY VIKING PAGEANT

Frederikssund (not to be confused with Fredensborg or Frederiksborg) is a little town 8 miles southwest of Hillerød and 30 miles northwest of Copenhagen. It stages a 2-week Viking festival each summer where Nordic sagas are sometimes revived—and the record is set straight about who discovered America 5 centuries before Christopher Columbus. On other occasions, *Hamlet* is performed.

The festival begins the last week in June. The traditional pageant is performed nightly at 8pm and a Viking banquet follows. Tickets for the festival are 50 kroner ($8.40) for adults, 10 kroner ($1.70) for children. The banquet costs 90 kroner ($15.15) for adults (children are not invited to the banquet). You can take a train from Copenhagen's Central Station at 6:15pm Monday through Friday or at 5:57pm on Saturday and Sunday. From the station at Frederikssund, it's a 20-minute walk to the site of the pageant. For details, contact the Tourist Information Office in Copenhagen or phone 42-31-06-85, the Frederikssund Tourist Office.

WHERE TO DINE

LE BOEUF, Helsingørdgade 30. Tel. 48-24-30-30.
  Cuisine: DANISH/FRENCH. **Reservations:** Recommended.
$ **Prices:** Appetizers 39–52 kroner ($6.55–$8.75); main dishes 108–149 kroner ($18.35–$24.85); fixed-price dinner (sometimes) 98 kroner ($16.45). AE, DC, MC, V.
  Open: Mon–Sat 5–10pm.

In a commercial district of town, a 10-minute walk north of the rail station, this restaurant has white walls, dark rustic accessories, oil lamps on the walls, and candles flickering on the tables. The chef's specialty is steak, succulently grilled, including entrecôte, pepper steak, tournedos, and filet steak with a mustard sauce. Nonbeef-eaters can order the grilled salmon in a lemon-cream sauce. A salad bar is included in the price of the main course.

SLOTSHERRENS KRO, Frederiksborg Slot 5. Tel. 42-26-75-16.
  Cuisine: DANISH. **Reservations:** Not required.
$ **Prices:** Appetizers 28–75 kroner ($4.70–$12.60); main dishes 85–135 kroner ($14.30–$22.70).
  Open: Apr–Oct, daily 10am–9pm.

On the grounds of Frederiksborg Castle, a 15-minute walk from the train station, is a well-established inn that serves good, reliable Danish food. It's particularly busy in the summer.

AN EXCURSION TO SELSØ SLOT

Selsø Slot, Selsøvej 30 (tel. 42-32-01-71), is Denmark's first Renaissance castle, built in 1576 and renovated in the baroque style in 1733. Located at Hornsherred, east of Skibby, south of Skuldelev, and 35 miles west of Copenhagen, Selsø is one of the few private manor houses on Zealand that can be explored thoroughly.

The Great Hall and adjoining rooms are maintained as they were in 1733, with 14-foot-high marble panels, ornate plaster ceilings, and fine paintings. A children's room with hundreds of tin soldiers, the basement, vaults dating from around 1560, an old manor kitchen with open fireplace and a scullery, old tools, and a dungeon below the gatehouse are features worth seeing. Cultural events such as orchestra concerts are staged annually.

Admission is 25 kroner ($4.20) for adults, 10 kroner ($1.70) for children. The castle is open mid-June to mid-August, daily from 11am to 5pm; and May to October 1, on Saturday and Sunday only, from noon to 4pm (closed in early June and late August). To get there, take bus no. 318 from Frederikssund; or drive on Route 318 to Skibby and then follow the signs the 2 miles to Selsø.

6. ROSKILDE

20 miles west of Copenhagen

GETTING THERE By Train Trains leave three times an hour from Copenhagen's Central Station on the 35-minute trip to Roskilde.

By Bus Buses depart for Roskilde several times daily from Copenhagen's Central Station.

By Car Take the express highway 21 west from Copenhagen.

ESSENTIALS The **Roskilde Turistbureau,** Fondens Bro, DK-4000 Roskilde (tel. 42-35-27-00), provides a pamphlet with a walking tour of Roskilde. The office is open April to June, Monday through Friday from 9am to 5pm and on Saturday from 9am to 1pm; in July and August, Monday through Friday from 9am to 6pm, on Saturday from 9am to 2pm, and on Sunday from 11am to 2pm; in September and October, Monday through Friday from 9am to 5pm and on Saturday from 10am to 1pm; November to March, Monday through Thursday from 9am to 5pm and on Friday from 9am to 4pm.

SPECIAL EVENTS The **Roskilde Festival,** held outdoors on a large grassy field, draws pop, rock, and folk music lovers to town. To get information on the festival—dates and performers—call 42-36-66-13 (in May only) or write to the Roskilde Turistbureau (see above).

Roskilde, once a great ecclesiastical seat, was the country's leading city until the mid-15th century. Today its twin-spired cathedral is the major pilgrimage center of Denmark.

WHAT TO SEE & DO

LIFE-SEEING TOURS

The tourist office offers what they call "Life-Seeing Tours," matching North Americans with local people of similar interests and arranging trips to their homes, factories, and recreational places. These tours are for groups only, and must be arranged well in advance with the tourist office.

THE TOP ATTRACTIONS

ROSKILDE DOMKIRKE, Domkirkepladsen. Tel. 42-35-16-24.

Roskilde Cathedral is the resting place of 38 Danish kings and queens and countless noblemen and clergy. Their sarcophagi are placed in four chapels and behind the altar. In 1985 the burial site of King Frederik IX was added outside the cathedral, near the northwest tower. The present Gothic-Romanesque cathedral was constructed during the 12th century, and although damaged by a fire in 1968, it has since been restored, along with the magnificent altarpiece. In the cathedral, above the entrance door, clockwork toys, dating from around 1500, play a short tune.

Admission: 3 kroner (50¢) adults, 1 krone (15¢) children.

Open: Apr, Mon–Sat 9am–5:45pm, Sun 12:30–3:45pm; May–Aug, Mon–Sat 9am–5:45pm, Sun 12:30–5:45pm; Sept, Mon–Sat 9am–5:45pm, Sun 12:30–3:45pm; Oct–Mar, Mon–Sat 10am–5:45pm, Sun 12:30–3:45pm. **Bus:** 602, 603, 604.

VIKING SHIP MUSEUM, Strandengen. Tel. 42-35-65-55.

Five vessels found in Roskilde Fjord, and painstakingly pieced together from hundreds of pieces of wreckage, are on display here. It is presumed that the craft (dating from 1000–50) were deliberately sunk about 12.5 miles north of Roskilde at the narrowest section of the fjord. The discovery was relatively unprotected and unpublicized until 1957 when the Danish National Museum carried out a series of underwater excavations.

Also displayed is a merchant cargo ship used by the Vikings, a small ferry or fishing boat, and a Danish Viking warship similar to the ones portrayed in the Bayeux Tapestry. Also discovered was a "longship," a Viking man-of-war that terrorized European coasts. Copies of Viking jewelry may be purchased in the museum gift shop, and there is a cafeteria.

Admission: 20 kroner ($3.35) adults, 14 kroner ($2.35) children.

Open: Apr–Oct, daily 9am–5pm; Nov–Mar, daily 10am–4pm. **Bus:** 358.

THE ROSKILDE MUSEUM, Sankt Ols Gade 18. Tel. 42-36-60-44.

Located 100 yards from the Town Square, this museum, set in a former merchant's house, contains a collection of the celebrated Hedebo embroidery, regional costumes, and antique toys. Exhibits also include a skeleton of an aurochs, a unique Viking tomb, and a large number of medieval finds from the town. The museum also has a grocer's courtyard, with the shop in operation.

Admission: 5 kroner (85¢) adults, free for children.

Open: June–Aug, daily 11am–5pm; Sept–May, Mon–Sat 2–4pm, Sun 2–5pm. **Bus:** 602, 603, 604.

MORE ATTRACTIONS

The **St. Jørgensbjerg quarter** was originally a small fishing village, and a number of old, half-timbered houses, some with thatched roofs, remain. The houses cluster around St. Jørgensbjerg Church, Kirkegade, which dates from 1080. The church is open to visitors for part of June, all of July, and part of August, Monday through Saturday from 10am to 2pm.

Roskilde has a number of old springs, some once considered holy and thought to have healing powers. For a short period in the 1800s, the biggest spring, **Maglekilde,** was the center of a hydropathic establishment.

Roskilde Park offers a great view of the fjord, and during the summer contemporary music concerts are held here every Tuesday night. Also during the summer, the steamship *Skjelskor* takes passengers on tours of the fjord on Saturday and Sunday at 2 and 3:30pm.

Throughout the year, a **vegetable, flower, and flea market** is held at the Town Hall Square, Staendertorvet, Wednesday and Saturday morning.

NEARBY ATTRACTIONS

THE TRAMWAY MUSEUM, Skjoldenaesholm, Skjoldenaesvej 107. Tel. 53-62-88-33.

Some 10 miles southwest of Roskilde, in a pleasant woodland area close to Gyldenlveshj, the Tramway Museum is situated on the highest point on Zealand, 416 feet above sea level. To reach the museum, board an old tram at the entrance and travel the 1,000 feet to the main building.

Admission: 20 kroner ($3.35) adults, 10 kroner ($1.70) children.

Open: May–June 25 and Aug 10–Oct 21, Sat 1–5pm, Sun 10am–5pm; June 26–Aug 9, Tues–Thurs 10am–5pm, Sat 1–5pm, Sun 10am–5pm. **Closed:** Oct 22–Apr.

HISTORISK ARKAEOLOGISK FORSØGSCENTER, Slangeallen 2, DK-4323 Lejre. Tel. 42-38-02-45.

Five miles west of Roskilde, this archeological research center, Lejre Forsøgscenter, is the site of a reconstructed Iron Age community on 50 acres of woodland. The main feature is stone houses built with flint tools just as they were 4,000 years ago. Staffers re-create the physical plant and working conditions of primitive man: They thatch Iron Age huts, plow with "ards," harvest grain with flint sickles, weave, and make pottery by an open fire. They also sail in dugout canoes, grind corn with a stone, and bake in direct fire. Jutland black pottery is produced here, and at the gift shop ancientlike handcrafts are for sale. At the entrance to the village there are picnic tables and an old-style cafeteria offering light meals.

Admission: 35 kroner ($5.90) adults, 15 kroner ($2.50) children.

Open: May–Sept, daily 10am–5pm. **Closed:** Oct–Apr. **Transportation:** Take the train from Copenhagen to Lejre, then bus no. 233 to the center.

LEDREBORG GODSKONTOR (Ledreborg Manor), Allé 2, DK-4320 Lejre. Tel. 42-38-00-38.

A baroque manor house and French/English-style park 4½ miles southwest of Roskilde, Ledreborg Godskontor is one of the best-preserved monuments in Denmark. Near the manor is a passage grave dating from the late Stone Age, approximately 3000 B.C.

Admission: 25 kroner ($4.20) adults, 10 kroner ($1.70) children.

Open: July, daily 11am–4pm; June and Aug, Sun 11am–4pm. **Transportation:** From Copenhagen's Central Station, take the direct train to Lejre, leaving hourly and taking 35 minutes. From Lejre station, take the 3-minute bus ride to the castle and park.

WHERE TO STAY

EXPENSIVE

HOTEL PRINDSEN, Algade 13, DK-4000 Roskilde. Tel. 42-35-80-10. 52 rms (all with bath). MINIBAR TV TEL **Bus:** 602, 603.

$ Rates (including breakfast): 620 kroner ($104.20) single; 760–890 kroner ($127.75–$149.60) double. AE, DC, MC, V.

This century-old hotel is a good bet. A cozy, comfortable family hotel in the town center, a 5-minute walk from the cathedral, it's attractive and smartly furnished. Children under 12 stay free in their parents' room. At the ground floor restaurant, you can enjoy a wide selection of Danish dishes and international specialties.

SCANDIC HOTEL ROSKILDE, Søndre Ringvej 33. Tel. 46-32-46-32. Fax 46-32-02-32. 98 rms (all with bath). MINIBAR TV TEL

$ Rates (including breakfast): 640 kroner ($107.60) single; 855 kroner ($143.75) double. AE, DC, MC, V. **Parking:** Free.

Considered the best in Roskilde, this chain hotel offers a sleek modern decor and excellent facilities, including a spa pool, sauna, and solarium. The bedrooms are handsomely furnished and well equipped. The hotel also has a good restaurant, serving both Danish and international dishes, and a cocktail bar. Parking is free in front of the three-story hotel. It's located on the ring road directly south of the green belt, Roskilde Ring, on the southern outskirts of the city.

MODERATE

HOTEL & KURSUSCENTER, Maglegårdsvej 10, DK-4000 Roskilde. Tel. 42-35-66-88. Fax 42-35-85-86. 70 rms (all with bath). TV TEL **Bus:** 602.

$ Rates (including breakfast): 435 kroner ($73.10) single; 435–535 kroner ($73.10–$89.95) double. AE, DC, MC, V.

Not far from the A1 motorway, this Danish-modern hostelry offers clean, comfortable bedrooms. There's a restaurant and a living room with a billiard table.

ROSKILDE MOTOR HOTEL, Montelvej 28, DK-4000 Roskilde. Tel. 46-35-43-85. Fax 42-35-43-85. 54 rms (14 with bath).

$ Rates (including breakfast): 315 kroner ($52.95) single without bath, 485 kroner ($81.55) single with bath; 435 kroner ($73.10) double without bath, 640 kroner ($107.60) double with bath. DC, MC, V.

A 5-minute drive from the town center along Route 21, this popular motel has a dining room with excellent grilled chicken and meats. The motel basically offers no frills, but each of the modern rooms is comfortable and clean. The motel also has its own garage.

SVOGERSLEV KRO, Hovedgaden 45, Svogerslev, DK-4000 Roskilde.
Tel. 46-38-30-05. 18 rms (all with bath). TV TEL **Bus:** Hourly connections from the town center.
$ Rates (including breakfast): 400 kroner ($67.25) single; 500 kroner ($84.05) double. DC, MC, V.
This charmingly cozy inn is in an old fishing hamlet about 2½ miles from the town center. Rooms are handsomely furnished in a modern style and well kept. The kitchen serves Danish open-face sandwiches and an array of international dishes.

WHERE TO DINE

CLUB 42, Skomagergade 42. Tel. 42-35-17-64.
   Cuisine: DANISH/INTERNATIONAL. **Reservations:** Recommended.
$ Prices: Two-course fixed-price menu 85 kroner ($14.30); appetizers 32–99 kroner ($5.40–$16.65); main dishes 70–120 kroner ($11.75–$20.15). AE, DC, MC, V.
   Open: Lunch Mon–Sat 11am–4pm; dinner Mon–Sat 4–10pm.
In the center of town on a pedestrian street, 200 yards from the bus and train station, Club 42 has a large and impressive menu. Its best bargain is a two-course *Danmenu* offered at both lunch and dinner. Lunch includes a selection of cold dishes and open-face sandwiches. Dinner at this restaurant, often called Den Hvide Fugl, is a big affair, with fresh fish or charcoal-grilled items including pepper steak. Smoked eel and Norwegian crayfish are also featured. A children's menu is also offered, with dishes beginning at 22 kroner ($3.70). There is a large parking lot behind the restaurant.

RESTAURANT BYPARKEN, Frederiksborgvej. Tel. 42-35-05-72.
   Cuisine: INTERNATIONAL. **Reservations:** Recommended. **Bus:** 602, 603, 604.
$ Prices: Appetizers 32–85 kroner ($5.40–$14.30); main dishes 65–115 kroner ($10.95–$19.35). MC, V.
   Open: May–Sept, daily 11am–8pm. **Closed:** Oct–Apr.
The restaurant, set in a park north of the cathedral, overlooks the Roskilde Fjord. For your main course, select a fish or meat dish. It's often closed for special parties, so call in advance. During the summer, concerts are held in the park on Tuesday night.

RESTAURANT TOPPEN, Bymarken 37. Tel. 42-36-04-12.
   Cuisine: DANISH. **Reservations:** Recommended.
$ Prices: Appetizers 26–65 kroner ($4.35–$10.95); main dishes 65–120 kroner ($10.95–$20.15). MC, V.
   Open: Mon–Sat noon–10pm.
At the top of a water tower 274 feet above sea level, Restaurant Toppen offers a splendid view of the whole town, the surrounding country, and Roskilde Fjord—all from the dining room. Begin with a shrimp cocktail served with dill and lemon, which is accompanied by salad, bread, and butter. Main dishes are likely to include sirloin of pork à la Toppen with mushrooms and a béarnaise sauce, accompanied by a baked potato and salad, or perhaps tournedos, also served with béarnaise sauce, a baked potato, and salad. For dessert, try the chef's nut cake with fruit sauce and sour cream. The restaurant lies west of the town center between Vindingevej and Københavnsvej.

7. KØGE

25 miles south of Copenhagen

GETTING THERE   By Train   Take the S-railway extension from Copenhagen. Service is every 20 minutes throughout the day. The trip takes 1 hour.

By Bus   Buses depart frequently from Copenhagen's Central Station.

By Car   From Copenhagen, head south along the express highway E20/E55.

ESSENTIALS   Guided tours of Køge are arranged through the **Tourist Office,** Vestergade 1 (tel. 53-65-58-00). English is spoken.

Køge's controversial reputation as a witch-burning center makes it the Salem, Massachusetts, of Denmark. This old market town still retains a medieval aura, with its brick and half-timbered buildings. It's a convenient first stop if you're heading south from Copenhagen to the island of Møn.

WHAT TO SEE & DO

Walk down **Kirkestraede,** lined with graceful old houses. A small building, no. 20, near the church, is reputed to be "the oldest dated half-timbered house in Denmark," from 1527. In front of the house at Smedegarden 13, near an ancient tree, are a couple of porchstones from the Middle Ages, said to be the only pair in Denmark in their original position. Nearby is the attractive **St. Nicolai Church,** Kirkestraede 29 (tel. 53-65-13-59), open daily Sunday through Friday from 10am to noon (mid-June to early September, 10am to 4pm). Admission is free. Look for the carved angels on the pews, all without noses thanks to Swedish troops who came this way. Guided tours of the tower are given at 11am, noon, and 1pm Monday through Friday from June to September for 5 kroner (85¢).

THE KØGE MUSEUM, Nørregade 4. Tel. 53-65-02-62.

A fine provincial museum surrounded by a beautiful garden, the Køge is devoted to the history of culture in South Zealand. It consists of six well-furnished rooms and a kitchen with implements used between 1640 and 1899. Displays of costumes, textiles, carriages, farm equipment, crafts from artisans' guilds, and other historical artifacts of the area are featured. Curiously, there is a windowpane where Hans Christian Andersen scratched the words (translated, of course): "Oh, God, oh God in Køge." There's a collection of 322 coins from all over Scandinavia and Europe—the oldest coin is a Palatinate daler from 1548. The oldest house in Køge, from the early 16th century, was moved to this site from the main square. It's a 2-minute walk from the train station.

Admission: 10 kroner ($1.70) adults, 5 kroner (85¢) children.

Open: June–Aug, daily 10am–5pm; Sept–May, Mon–Fri 2–5pm, Sat–Sun 1–5pm.

KUNSTMUSEET KØGE SKITSESAMLING (Museum of Art), Nørregade 29. Tel. 53-66-24-14.

Mainly featuring 20th-century works, this museum near the train station also contains a collection of sketches and models showing the process of actualizing a work of art, from idea to final creation. In addition to the permanent collection, the museum arranges special exhibitions, films, and lectures.

Admission: 10 kroner ($1.70) adults, free for children.

Open: Tues–Sun 11am–5pm.

HEGNETSLUND KERAMIK, Teglvaerksvej 11. Tel. 53-67-45-71.

Founded in 1892, Hegnetslund Keramik features Danish arts and crafts. Stoneware, ceramics, terra-cotta pieces, and other products are for sale in the display room. The workshop can also be visited.

Admission: Free.

Open: Mon–Fri 10am–5pm. **Directions:** Head along Svansbjergvej over the viaduct (the second road to the left is Tegvaerksvej). The factory is opposite an Esso station on Vordingborgvej.

A NEARBY ATTRACTION

VALLØ CASTLE, Vallø.

This castle with French-style gardens was built between the 16th and the 18th century, and has been converted today into modern housing for old-age pensioners. Explore the sweeping gardens, with their lakes, moats, rare trees, and rose and dahlia flowerbeds. The castle is located 4 miles south of Køge between Herfølge and the east coast.

Admission: Free.
Open: Apr–Oct, daily 10am–sunset. **Closed:** Nov–Mar.

WHERE TO STAY

HOTEL HVIDE HUS, Strandvejen 111, DK-4600 Køge. Tel. 53-65-36-90.
Fax 53-66-33-14. 118 rms (all with bath). MINIBAR TV TEL
$ Rates (including breakfast): 580–690 kroner ($97.50–$116) single; 850–900 kroner ($142.90–$151.30) double. AE, DC, MC, V.
A great bet for an overnight stay or lunch visit, this attractive modern hotel has well-furnished bedrooms decorated in a Nordic style, many with balconies. The restaurant offers a view of Køge Bay, and there is also a bar and lounge. Other facilities include a sauna, solarium, and garage. The hotel lies east of the center along the water.

A NEARBY ACCOMMODATION

SØNDERGAARD, Krogen 15, DK-4632 Bjaeverskov. Tel. 53-67-00-15.
Fax 53-67-11-12. 32 rms (16 with bath). TV **Bus:** 246.
$ Rates (including breakfast): 360 kroner ($60.50) single without bath, 500 kroner ($84.05) single with bath; 525 kroner ($88.25) double without bath, 600 kroner ($100.85) double with bath. DC, MC, V.
About 25 miles from Copenhagen, between Køge and Ringsted, Søndergaard is a modern bed-and-breakfast family-style hotel with a heated swimming pool and sauna. The rooms are bright and simply furnished, and 21 have minibars and 9 contain phones. If you have a car, it's about a 10-minute drive to the beach.

8. MØN

80 miles south of Copenhagen

GETTING THERE   By Train   From Copenhagen's Central Station, take a train to Vordingborg in South Zealand. From there, take a bus to Stege, Møn's capital.

By Bus   Take bus no. 64 from Vordingborg in South Zealand to Stege. On the island, bus service is scarce. You'll need a car to explore.

By Car   Cross over from Zealand on the Dronning Alexandrines Bridge; then proceed through the old country town of Stege.

ESSENTIALS   The local tourist office is **Møns Turistforening,** Storegade 5, DK-4780 Stege (tel. 55-81-44-11).

In the southeast corner of Denmark, off Zealand, this little island's big attraction is 400-foot **Møns Klint,** 4 miles of white chalky cliffs that rise dramatically from the Baltic Sea. Møns Klint is cut by the Baltic Sea in a large pile of ice-transported chalk masses and glacial deposits. The chalk was formed from calcareous ooze 75 million years ago. The ooze that precipitated from the sea water enclosed shells of marine animals that are now fossils. The glacial deposits date from the last million years. They originated partly as boulder clay deposited by inland ice and partly as bedded clay and sand containing marine mussels. The boulders on the beach have dropped from the cliff and have been rounded by wave erosion.

WHAT TO SEE & DO

Møns Klint can be viewed from the east of the island if you have a car. Leave Stege, passing through Elmelunde. Once at Elmelunde, continue for another 6 miles east to the coast for the best view of the cliffs.

Stege, the capital of Møn, with a 16th-century Mill Gate, received its charter in 1268. During its turbulent history, it was often invaded, sometimes by Swedish mercenaries. Known for its primitive frescoes, **Stege Church** is one of the largest in the country, with a massive tower striped in brick and chalk. It is one of many whitewashed churches found on Møn that contain 14th-century frescoes depicting rural life.

Møn is known for the **prehistoric remains** that are scattered about the island. For detailed information, the Stege tourist office (see above) publishes a booklet called "Prehistoric Monuments of Møn." Several neolithic chambered tombs known as "giants' graves" were discovered. As the legend goes, the western part of the island was ruled by a "jolly green giant" called Green Huntsman and the eastern part of the island was the domain of another giant, Upsal.

After a visit to the cliffs, I suggest a short detour north to **Liselund,** a small thatched, palatial summer home from 1795 surrounded by lovely park grounds in the northeastern part of the little island. Hans Christian Andersen wrote *The Tinder Box* while staying in the Swiss cottage. The park is called a "folly" of the 18th century, when it was constructed by Bosc de la Calmette, a royal chamberlain who was inspired by Marie Antoinette's La Hameau at Versailles. You can buy refreshments at a small Swiss-style chalet filled with small antlers and antiques. The park is open daily until sunset all year.

The inveterate island collector may also want to explore two isolated communities, the islands of **Bogø** and **Nyord,** which are connected to Møn by bridge and causeway. Bogø has only one village, an old town that had shipping connections with Iceland in the 19th century. The other island, Nyord, off the northwest coast of Møn, has for 3 centuries been divided among just 20 farms. Cars are not allowed on Nyord.

WHERE TO STAY & DINE

HOTEL STEGE BUGT, Langelinie 48, DK-4780 Stege. Tel. 55-81-54-54.
Fax 55-81-58-90. 22 rms (all with bath). MINIBAR TV TEL.
$ Rates (including breakfast): 400–550 kroner ($67.25–$92.45) single; 525–750 kroner ($88.25–$126.10) double. AE, DC, MC, V.

One of the best hotels on the island, Stege Bugt is also the most central. Many of its modern and well-furnished bedrooms open onto balconies overlooking the sea. Bedrooms have many thoughtful amenities, and everything is well run and maintained. The hotel's restaurant offers a panoramic view and specializes in fresh fish and grill specialties. It serves meals daily until 10pm. A large park and mound are nearby.

CHAPTER 9

FUNEN

1. NYBORG
- **WHAT'S SPECIAL ABOUT FUNEN**

2. ODENSE

3. SVENDBORG

4. FAABORG

5. ÆRØ

Funen, the second-largest Danish island, separates Zealand from the mainland peninsula, Jutland. Both are filled with unique attractions, from a Viking ship to runic stones.

Hans Christian Andersen was born in Funen in the town of Odense. A visit to the storyteller's native island is a journey into a land of hop gardens and orchards along the roadsides, busy harbors, market towns, castles, and stately manor houses.

Funen has some 700 miles of coastline, with wide sandy beaches in some parts, while woods and grass grow all the way to the water's edge in others. Steep cliffs provide sweeping views of the Baltic or the Kattegat.

SEEING FUNEN
GETTING THERE

Funen is reached by the Little Belt bridges at Middelfart (Jutland), which is the road crossing from continental Europe, or by ferry from Nyborg-Korsør from the island of Zealand. An L-train from Copenhagen to Odense takes about 3 hours.

Once on the island, a private rented car is ideal, but the major towns, such as Svendborg and Faaborg, provide frequent bus service from the capital of Odense. Bus tickets can be bought on the bus; train tickets should be bought in advance at the train stations. Round-trip discounts are not granted, but 1-day tourist tickets are sold at the rail station in Odense.

To reach the island of Ærø, you'll need to take a ferry from Svendborg.

Because Funen is small and relatively flat, you might consider a bicycle itinerary provided by the local tourist office. Bicycles can be rented at train stations.

A SUGGESTED ITINERARY

After touring Zealand and Copenhagen, take the car-ferry from Korsør (on Zealand), landing at Nyborg on Funen in the west.

Day 1: Spend the morning exploring Nyborg Castle. Have lunch, and then travel west on the E20 (an express highway) to Odense.

Day 2: Explore Odense and its nearby attractions, including the Viking ship at Ladby and Egeskov Castle. Spend the night.

Day 3: Explore the port city of Svendborg, south of Odense, and its neighboring islands of Tåsinge and Thurø in the South Funen archipelago. Return to Odense and spend the night.

Day 4: Head west to Faaborg and walk around its Old Town. Ask at the tourist office about boat tours and maps outlining afternoon trips in the environs.

1. NYBORG
81 miles west of Copenhagen

GETTING THERE By Train Trains depart Copenhagen for Odense hourly with a stopover in Nyborg, where you take a ferry from Zealand to Funen.

WHAT'S SPECIAL ABOUT FUNEN

Beaches

☐ The most popular for swimming are at Kerteminde, Hasmark, Flyvesandet, Ristinge, Marstal, and Spodsbjerg.

Great Towns/Villages

☐ Odense, the capital, offering lots of attractions in the hometown of Hans Christian Andersen.

☐ Faaborg, an old seaport, idyllically set, one of Denmark's best-preserved market towns.

☐ Ærøskøbing, capital of the island of Ærø—a Lilliputian souvenir of the past.

Ancient Castles

☐ Egeskov Castle, the best-preserved Renaissance castle of its type in Europe.

☐ Valdemar's Slot on the island of Troense, built by King Christian IV in 1639.

☐ Nyborg Castle, its ramparts still intact, the oldest royal seat in Scandinavia.

Literary Pilgrimages

☐ H. C. Andersen's House at Odense, filled with memorabilia, like a walking stick and a top hat of the fairytale writer.

Idyllic Islands

☐ Ærø, the pearl of the South Funen archipelago, a sleepy memory of a maritime past.

☐ Tåsinge, the largest island in the South Funen archipelago, with its memories of Elvira Madigan, a doomed woman in love.

Special Events/Festivals

☐ Hans Christian Andersen's plays at the open-air theater in Funen Village, outside Odense (mid-July to mid-August).

☐ Annual July festival at Faaborg, with entertainment, dances, and an amusement park.

By Bus Buses run from Copenhagen to Odense, with a transfer through Nyborg via ferry.

By Car Take the E-20 expressway west from Copenhagen to Korsør in West Zealand. From there take a car-ferry (see below).

By Ferry Three lines run from Nyborg to Korsør on Zealand, with about 21 crossings a day, taking 50 minutes. The DSB car-ferries depart every 40 minutes (for information and reservations, call 65-31-40-54). Another car-ferry, Vognamnsruten (tel. 53-57-02-04), makes the run every hour on the half hour. Finally, DSB also runs a ferry for trains and foot passengers, hourly between Korsør and Nyborg (call 65-31-11-91 for information).

ESSENTIALS The **Nyborg Tourist Office** is located at Torvet 9 (tel. 65-31-02-80).

If you take a ferry linking Zealand and Funen, you'll dock at this old seaport and market town, a perfect place to explore before heading to Odense or Copenhagen.

Founded some 700 years ago, with a population today of 18,500, Nyborg is considered one of the oldest towns in Denmark. Its location in the middle of the trade route between Zealand in the east and Jutland in the west has helped boost its importance. In medieval times, from about 1200 to 1413, Nyborg was the capital of Denmark. Medieval buildings and well-preserved ramparts are testaments to that era. The town square of Nyborg, the **Torvet,** was formed in 1540, when a block of houses was demolished to make room for the royal tournaments of Christian III.

In 1988 one of the world's largest combined bridge-and-tunnel projects began. By 1993 trains will be able to cross **Store Baelt** (Great Belt), which separates Funen and Zealand. In 1996 it is anticipated that cars and trucks will also be able to cross. When this is completed, for the first time Copenhagen will be linked to continental Europe by road.

In summer, Denmark's oldest open-air theater, **Nyborg Voldspil,** performs an annual musical or operetta under the light beeches on the old castle ramparts. Throughout the summer the castle's Great Hall is the setting for concerts of classical music with international soloists. Inquire at the tourist office (see above) for more details.

WHAT TO SEE & DO

NYBORG CASTLE, Slotspadsen. Tel. 65-31-02-07.
Founded in 1170, Nyborg Castle, with its ramparts still intact, is the oldest royal seat in Scandinavia. Denmark's first constitution was signed in this moated castle by King Erik Glipping in 1282, and Nyborg Castle was the seat of the Danish parliament, the Danehof, until 1413. The present furnishings date primarily from the days of Christian IV, when Nyborg was a resplendent Renaissance palace. It's located directly north of the Torvet in the town center.
Admission: 10 kroner ($1.70) adults, 5 kroner (85¢) children.
Open: Mar–May and Sept–Oct, daily 10am–3pm; June–Aug, daily 10am–5pm.
Closed: Nov–Feb.

VOR FRUE KIRKE, Adelgade.
Dating from the late 14th and the early 15th century, the Church of Our Lady has a fine Gothic spire, three aisles, woodcarvings, old epitaphs, candelabra, and model ships. Nightly at 9:45, the Watchman's Bell from 1523 is rung—a tradition with origins far back in the town's history. Opposite the church is the 12th-century chapter house of the Order of St. John (Korsbrødregård), with a fine vaulted cellar now converted into a gift shop. The church is located at the end of the Kongegade in the town center.
Admission: Free.
Open: Mon–Sat 10am–2pm.

MADS LERCHES GÅRD (Nyborg Museum), Slotsgade 11. Tel. 65-31-26-19.
The Nyborg Museum is housed in a well-preserved half-timbered merchant's house built in 1601. You'll see interesting artifacts of the region from prehistoric to modern times.
Admission: 5 kroner (85¢) adults, 2 kroner (35¢) children.
Open: Mar–May and Sept–Oct, Tues–Sun 10am–3pm; June–Aug, daily 10am–4pm. **Closed:** Nov–Feb.

WHERE TO STAY

HOTEL HESSELET, Christianslundsvej 119, DK-5800 Nyborg. Tel. 65-31-30-29. 46 rms (all with bath). MINIBAR TV TEL **Bus:** 3.
$ Rates (including breakfast): 650 kroner ($109.25) single; 1,150–1,200 kroner ($193.30–$201.70) double. AE, DC, MC, V.
This is a splurge choice, classified as a Relais & Châteaux accommodation and the most stylish hotel in the region. Oriental carpets, leather couches, fireplaces, and sunken living rooms create a glamorous look. Spacious bedrooms include radios and TV hookups. An indoor swimming pool is ringed with semitropical plants. Six tennis courts and an 18-hole golf course lie within close reach. The hotel is known for its conference facilities. The hotel is about 2 miles northwest of the Knudshoved ferry terminal, a mile east of the rail station.

HOTEL NYBORG STRAND, Østersøvej 2, DK-5800 Nyborg. Tel. 65-31-31-31. 245 rms (all with bath). TV TEL **Bus:** 3.

$ Rates (including breakfast): 335 kroner ($56.30) single; 570 kroner ($95.80) double. AE, DC, MC, V.

Dating from 1899, Hotel Nyborg Strand is probably the largest and most popular conference hotel in Funen. Each well-furnished bedroom has a radio and TV hookup. On the premises are a pair of saunas, a bistro, a café, two restaurants, a private sand-and-pebble beach, an indoor swimming pool, plus 21 conference rooms in all shapes and sizes. The hotel is located a mile east of the rail station, near the beach.

2. ODENSE

97 miles west of Copenhagen

GETTING THERE   By Train   Some 32 trains daily leave Copenhagen's Central Station, taking 3 hours.

By Bus   Buses arrive frequently from Copenhagen, going by car-ferry from Korsør to Nyborg.

By Car   Take the E20 expressway west from Copenhagen to Korsør. There, board a car-ferry to Nyborg. Once on Funen, continue west on the E20.

ESSENTIALS   The **Odense Tourist Association,** Rådhuset (tel. 66-12-75-20), will help arrange excursions. The office also sells an **Odense Adventure Pass,** giving you access to 13 museums, the Odense Zoo, the Funen Tivoli, five indoor swimming pools, and the Hans Christian Andersen plays. You can also take a river cruise with the pass and travel free on the city buses and DSB trains within the municipality. The pass is valid for 2 days and costs 60 kroner ($37.20) for adults and 30 kroner ($18.60) for children.

This ancient town, the third largest in Denmark, has changed greatly since its famous citizen, Hans Christian Andersen, walked its streets. But it's still possible to discover a few unspoiled spots from yesteryear.

The capital is a smart base for exploring the rest of the island—trips north to the Viking ship at Ladby, or south to the château country and the archipelago.

WHAT TO SEE & DO

At the Odense Tourist Association, you can purchase tickets and receive information on a **2-hour sightseeing tour,** held daily except Sunday from June 25 to August 31. The charge is 50 kroner ($8.40) for adults, 25 kroner ($4.20) for children. Also at the tourist office, you can find out about the **Hans Christian Andersen plays** in the open-air theater in the Funen Village, presented from mid-July to mid-August. Tickets cost 35 kroner ($5.90) for adults, 20 kroner ($3.35) for children. During this time, Odense is overrun with fans of the storyteller. If no accommodations are available, the tourist office will book guests into private homes.

H. C. ANDERSENS HUS, Hans Jensensstraede 37-45. Tel. 66-13-13-72.
⭐ The object of most Funen pilgrimages is the "hus" and museum of Hans Christian Andersen, popular with both adults and children. Much H.C.A. memorabilia is here: his famous walking stick, top hat, battered portmanteau, plus letters to his dear friend Miss Jenny Lind and fellow writer Charles Dickens. In addition, hundreds of documents, manuscripts, and reprints of his books in dozens of languages are displayed.

Admission: 15 kroner ($2.50) adults, 3 kroner (50¢) children.
Open: Apr–May, daily 10am–5pm; June–Aug, daily 9am–6pm; Sept, daily 10am–5pm; Oct–Mar, daily 10am–3pm. **Bus:** 2.

H. C. ANDERSENS BARNDOMSHJEM (Andersen's Childhood Home), Munkemøllestraede 3. Tel. 66-13-13-72.

Visit Andersen's humble childhood home, where the fairytale writer lived between the ages of 2 and 14. From what is known of Andersen's childhood, his mother was a drunken, superstitious washerwoman, and Andersen was a gawky boy, lumbering and graceless, the victim of his fellow urchins' cruel jabs. However, all is serene at the cottage today; in fact, the little house has a certain unpretentious charm, and the "garden still blooms," as in *The Snow Queen*.

Admission: 2 kroner (35¢) adults, 1 krone (15¢) children.
Open: Apr–Sept, daily 10am–5pm; Oct–Mar, daily noon–3pm. **Bus:** 2.

ST. CANUTE'S CATHEDRAL, Klosterbakken 2. Tel. 66-12-03-92.

Despite its unimpressive facade, this is perhaps the most important Gothic-style building in Denmark. A popular feature of this 13th-century brick building is the elegant triptych gold altar screen, carved by Calus Berg in 1526 at the request of Queen Christine. King Canute, the patron of the church, was killed by angry Jutland taxpayers in 1086 and then canonized 15 years later. The church stands opposite the Town Hall. All city buses meet at Klingenberg, just by the cathedral.

Admission: Free.
Open: Mid-May to mid-Sept, Mon–Sat 10am–5pm, Sun and hols. 11:30am–3:30pm; mid-Sept to mid-May, Mon–Fri 10am–4pm, Sat 10am–noon.

FUNEN VILLAGE/DEN FYNSKE LANDSBY, Sejerskovvej 20. Tel. 66-13-13-72.

A big open-air regional culture museum, this is an archive of 18th- and 19th-century Funen life. Located in the Hunderup Woods, old buildings—a toll house, weaver's shop, windmill, farming homestead, jail, vicarage, village school, even a brickworks—were reassembled and authentically furnished. Plays and folk dances are staged at the Greek theater. In addition, you can visit workshops, see a coppersmith at work, as well as a basket maker, spoon cutter, blacksmith, and weaver.

Admission: 15 kroner ($2.50) adults, 5 kroner (85¢) children.
Open: Apr–May and Sept–Oct, daily 9am–4pm; June–Aug, daily 9am–6:30pm; Nov–Mar, Sun 10am–4pm. **Bus:** 2 from Flakhaven to museum, 1½ miles from the town center.

DANISH RAILWAY MUSEUM, Dannebrogsgade 24. Tel. 66-12-01-48.

Displayed are original locomotives and carriages from the past century depicting Denmark's railway history, including the first railroad acquired in 1847. One of the oldest locomotives in the collection, an "A-Machine," dates from 1888. Also on display are two royal coaches, a double-decker carriage, and a model railway. The museum is adjacent to the train station.

Admission: 15 kroner ($2.50) adults, 5 kroner (85¢) children.
Open: May–Sept, daily 10am–4pm; Oct–Apr, Sun 10am–3:30pm.

CARL NIELSEN MUSEET (Carl Nielsen Museum), Claus Bergsgade 11. Tel. 66-13-13-72.

Adjoining the Odense Concert Hall, this museum documents the life and work of composer Carl Nielsen and his wife, sculptress Anne Marie Nielsen. Visitors hear excerpts of Nielsen's music while they look at the exhibits and biographical slide show. Parking is available outside the concert hall. Elevator service available.

Admission: 10 kroner ($1.70) adults, 2 kroner (35¢) children.
Open: Summer, daily 10am–4pm. **Closed:** Winter. **Bus:** 2.

NEARBY ATTRACTIONS

LADBYSKIBET, Vikingevej 123, Ladby. Tel. 65-32-16-67.

Ladby, 12 miles northeast of Odense, is the site of a 72-foot-long 10th-century Viking ship, discovered in 1935. Remains of the ship are displayed along with replicas from the excavation (the genuine articles are in the National Museum in Copenhagen). A skeleton of the pagan chieftain buried in this looted ship was never found, just the bones of his nearly dozen horses and dogs.

Admission: 12 kroner ($2) adults, 5 kroner (85¢) children.

Open: May–Sept, Tues–Sun 10am–6pm; Oct–Apr, Tues–Sun 10am–3pm. **Bus:** 482 from Kerteminde, reached by bus from Odense.

EGESKOV CASTLE, Egeskovgade 18, Kvaerndrup. Tel. 62-27-10-16.

This 1554 Renaissance water castle with magnificent gardens, northeast of Faaborg at Kvaerndrup, is the most romantic and splendid of Denmark's fortified manors. The castle was built on oak pillars in the middle of a moat or small lake. International experts consider it the best-preserved Renaissance castle of its type in Europe.

Every year, some 200,000 visitors roam the 30-acre park and castle located on the main road between Svendborg and Odense. There's an automobile, horse carriage, and airplane museum on the grounds as well. Chamber-music concerts are held in the magnificent Great Hall of the castle on 10 summer Sundays beginning in late June, starting at 4pm.

The most dramatic story in the castle's history is about an unfortunate maiden, Rigborg, who was seduced by a young nobleman and bore him a child out of wedlock. Banished to the castle, she was imprisoned by her father in a tower from 1599 to 1604.

Admission: Castle, park, and museum, 60 kroner ($10.10) adults, 30 kroner ($5.05) children under 12; park and museum only, 40 kroner ($6.70) adults, 20 kroner ($3.35) children.

Open: Park, June–Aug, daily 9am–6pm; May and Sept, daily 10am–5pm. Castle, May–Aug, daily 10am–5pm. **Closed:** Park, Oct–Apr; castle, Sept–Apr.

FRYDENLUND, Skovvej 50, Naarup, DK-5690 Tommerup. Tel. 64-76-13-22.

This bird sanctuary and park is 12¼ miles southwest from Odense (signposted near the village of Tommerup). Some 200 different species of pheasants, ducks, geese, storks, ostriches, parrots, and owls, among others, from all parts of the world, live here. There are more than 120 aviaries and some 20 parkland areas in an old farm setting, with many flowers, bushes, and trees. You can enjoy coffee and homemade pastries in the café or bring your own lunch.

Admission: 20 kroner ($3.35) adults, 10 kroner ($1.70) children.

Open: Easter–May and Sept–Oct, daily 10am–4pm; June–Aug, daily 10am–6pm. **Closed:** Nov–Easter.

FUNEN AQUARIUM ROLD (Aquatic World), Roldvej 53, Rold, DK-5492 Vissenbjerg. Tel. 64-83-14-12.

The largest in Europe, this attraction consists of 30 aquariums. Some 3,000 specimens include 300 species of such fish as sharks, electric eels, piranhas, and dragon fish. There are also 20 large outdoor aviaries.

Admission: 30 kroner ($5.05) adults, 15 kroner ($2.50) children.

Open: Apr–Oct, daily 10am–7pm; Nov–Mar, daily 10am–6pm. **Directions:** Take the E20 express highway 10 miles west from Odense, until the turnoff to Vissenbjerg.

CARL NIELSEN'S BARNDOMSHJEM, Odensevej 2A, near Lyndelse. Tel. 66-13-13-72.

Eight miles from Odense, the childhood house of the famous composer is now a museum and archive of his life. Nielsen lived here during the last 5 years of his childhood until his confirmation in 1879. Two studies have been made into commemorative rooms, where the collections illustrate the composer's history.

Admission: 2 kroner (35¢) adults, 1 krone (15¢) children.

Open: May–Aug, 11am–3pm. **Closed:** Sept–Apr. **Bus:** 960, 962.

WHERE TO STAY

The easy-to-find hotels in Odense are clustered around the railway station.

EXPENSIVE

HOTEL H. C. ANDERSEN, Claus Bergsgade 7, DK-Odense C. Tel. 66-14-78-00. Fax 66-14-78-00. 148 rms (all with bath). MINIBAR TV TEL **Bus:** 4, 5.
$ Rates (including breakfast): 830 kroner ($139.50) single; 1,050 kroner ($176.50) double. AE, DC, MC, V. **Parking:** Free.
The Hotel H. C. Andersen is a first-class hostelry, with attractively furnished and comfortable bedrooms. You can dine in the Hans Christian Restaurant, have your drinks at the Fairy-Tale bar, and be entertained in the Nattergalen (Nightingale) nightclub, which has live music. The hotel has an exercise room, billiard tables, table tennis, a sauna, and a solarium.

ODENSE PLAZA HOTEL, Østre Stationsvej 24, DK-5000 Odense. Tel. 66-11-77-45. Fax 66-14-41-45. 70 rms (all with bath). MINIBAR TV TEL **Bus:** 4.
$ Rates (including breakfast): 650–1,100 kroner ($109.25–$184.90) single; 900–1,300 kroner ($151.30–$218.55) double. AE, DC, MC, V.
Completely renovated in 1985, this hotel is one of the most alluring upper-bracket hostelries in town. Each of the tastefully conservative bedrooms contains, among other amenities, a color TV with English-language video, and a hairdryer. Facilities include a sauna, solarium, and health club. Both laundry and room service are available.
A French-inspired restaurant with a modern cuisine and impeccable service draws diners from around the region.

SARA GRAND HOTEL, Jernbanegade 18, DK-5000 Odense. Tel. 66-11-71-71. Fax 66-14-11-71. 139 rms (all with bath). MINIBAR TV TEL.
$ Rates: 610–810 kroner ($102.55–$136.15) single; 810–1,010 kroner ($136.15–$169.80) double. AE, DC, MC, V.
This hotel's four-story 19th-century brick facade rises in a gabled Neo-Romanesque style from a street corner close to the center of town. The interior contains many traditional trappings, but public rooms are modernized. The plushly conservative bedrooms include a radio and color TV with video. Other facilities include a sauna, solarium, and high-ceilinged bar.
The hotel has a pleasant restaurant that opens onto an outdoor terrace in summer. There is occasional weekend dance music.

MODERATE

HOTEL ODENSE, Hunderupgade 2, DK-5000 Odense. Tel. 66-11-42-13. Fax 65-91-15-13. 62 rms (all with bath). TV TEL.
$ Rates (including breakfast): 490–620 kroner ($82.35–$104.20) single; 620–720 kroner ($104.20–$121.05) double. AE, DC, MC, V.
On Route A1 at the A9 junction, 1 mile from the town center, this 82-bed motel in a half-timbered renovated farmhouse offers compact and well-furnished bedrooms; 17 rooms have a minibar. A well-appointed first-class restaurant is on the premises, serving French and Danish cuisine.

MISSIONSHOTEL ANSGAR, Østre Stationsvej 32, DK-5000 Odense. Tel. 66-11-96-93. Fax 66-11-96-75. 44 rms (all with bath). TV TEL.
$ Rates (including breakfast): 335–425 kroner ($56.30–$71.45) single; 530–570 kroner ($89.10–$95.80) double. AE, DC, MC, V.
This hotel is conveniently located behind a stately stone-and-brick facade. Because of its good value, the hotel is often booked by Danes. A ground-floor restaurant serves

well-prepared and reasonably priced meals. In spite of the hotel's status as a Missions hostelry, the restaurant serves beer and wine.

WINDSOR HOTEL, Vindegade 45, DK-Odense C. Tel. 66-12-06-52. Fax 65-91-00-23. 62 rms (all with bath). TV TEL **Bus:** 4.
$ Rates (including breakfast): 500 kroner ($84.05) single; 650–1,050 kroner ($109.25–$176.50) double. AE, DC, MC, V.

Built in 1898, this cozy, well-furnished red-brick hotel occupies a quiet street corner close to the center of town near the rail station. High-ceilinged bedrooms are clean and comfortable, most with radios and minibars. They're furnished with well-crafted copies of 18th-century furniture. There's an elegant and stylish restaurant, a popular pub with exposed brick. Room and laundry service are provided.

WHERE TO DINE

UNDER LINDETRAEET, Ramsherred 2. Tel. 66-12-92-86.
Cuisine: DANISH/INTERNATIONAL. **Reservations:** Required. **Bus:** 2.
$ Prices: Fixed-price dinner 375 kroner ($63.05); appetizers 48–152 kroner ($8.05–$25.55); main dishes 122–204 kroner ($20.50–$34.30). DC, MC, V.
Open: Daily 9am–midnight. **Closed:** July 4–24.

This inn, 2½ centuries old, is located across the street from Hans Christian Andersen's house. For a quarter of a century, this has been a landmark restaurant in Odense, providing a menu based on fresh and high-quality ingredients. Many of the fish and meat dishes are Cordon Bleu–inspired. The atmosphere is old world, and in summer, meals and light refreshments are served outside under linden trees. Artists often sit here to sketch Andersen's house.

RODE 7, Østre Stationsvej 34. Tel. 66-12-30-99.
Cuisine: DANISH. **Reservations:** Recommended.
$ Prices: Three-course fixed-price menu (summer) 180 kroner ($30.25); appetizers 40–60 kroner ($6.70–$10.10); main dishes 120–160 kroner ($20.15–$26.90). DC, MC, V.
Open: Dinner only, Mon–Fri 5–11pm.

Installed in a century-old house with a lot of character, this is one of the city's leading restaurants, owned by culinary artist Anker Daugger. Specialties include steak au poivre, English beef, mixed grill, a marmite of calves' liver and sweetbreads, and herb-flavored lamb.

DEN GAMLE KRO, Overgade 23. Tel. 66-12-14-33.
Cuisine: DANISH/FRENCH. **Reservations:** Recommended. **Bus:** 4.
$ Prices: Fixed-price dinner 128 kroner ($21.50) for two courses, 189 kroner ($31.60) for three courses, 218 kroner ($36.65) for four courses; fixed-price lunches 95–155 kroner ($15.95–$26.05); appetizers 39–79 kroner ($6.55–$13.30); main dishes 108–185 kroner ($18.15–$31.10). DC, MC, V.
Open: Mon–Sat 11am–11pm, Sun 10am–9:30pm.

A well-preserved 1683 inn in the town center, its two dining rooms are cozy and furnished with antiques. Cozier still is the brick-vaulted cellar, with its oak tables and antique chairs. For a main course, try tournedos chasseur, pepper steak flambé, or salmon gratinée. In season, game dishes are a specialty. Dinners are accompanied by a covered loaf of hot French bread, cutting board provided. Luncheon-platter specials include marinated salmon with mustard dressing, herring, hot filet of plaice with tartar sauce, and roast beef with cold potato salad. The house's dessert special is crêpes Suzette. Fresh strawberries, topped with whipped cream, are usually offered in season.

SORTEBRO KRO, Sejerskovvej 20. Tel. 66-13-28-26.
Cuisine: DANISH. **Reservations:** Not required. **Bus:** 2 from Flakhaven.
$ Prices: Danish cold board 135 kroner ($22.70); appetizers 28–70 kroner ($4.70–$11.75); main dishes 75–120 kroner ($12.60–$20.15). MC, V.
Open: Daily 10am–11pm.

Outside the entrance to Funen Village, the open-air culture museum, Sortebro Kro is a coaching inn that dates from 1807. The interior is an attraction in its own right: long refectory tables, sagging ceilings with overhead beams, three-legged chairs, florid handmade chests, and crockery cupboards. Country meals are served featuring popular all-you-can-eat Danish cold board.

EVENING ENTERTAINMENT

NATTERGALEN, in the Hotel H. C. Andersen, Claus Bergsgade 7. Tel. 66-14-78-00.
This is the place to dance to live music. The crowd tends to be over 30. Beer costs 25 kroner ($4.20). It's open Monday through Wednesday from 10pm to 3am and Thursday through Saturday from 10pm to 4am. Bus: 4, 5.
Admission: Free.

3. SVENDBORG

27 miles south of Odense, 91 miles west of Copenhagen

GETTING THERE By Train Twenty trains a day leave from Odense's rail station, taking 1 hour to Svendborg.

By Bus Daily, 18 buses leave from Odense's bus station, taking 1 hour 30 minutes.

By Car Drive south from Odense along Route 9.

ESSENTIALS The **Svendborg Tourist Office** is at Møllergade 20, Torvet (tel. 62-21-09-80). It's open June 20 to mid-August, Monday through Friday from 9am to 5:30pm, on Saturday from 9am to 1pm, and on Sunday from 10am to noon; mid-March to mid-June and mid-August to mid-September, Monday through Friday from 9am to 5pm and on Saturday from 9am to noon; mid-September to mid-March, Monday through Friday from 9am to 5pm.

This old port on Svendborg Sound has long been a popular boating center where you can see yachts, ketches, and kayaks in the harbor. The town still retains some of its medieval heritage, but most of it has been torn down in the name of progress. Most visitors find that Svendborg makes a good base for touring the Danish château country and the South Funen archipelago as well.

Svendborg is a market town. On Saturday morning check out the cobblestone central plaza where flowers and fish are sold. Wander through the many winding streets where brick and half-timbered buildings still stand. On **Ragergade** you'll see the old homes of early seafarers. **Møllergade,** a pedestrian street, is one of the oldest streets in town, with about 100 different shops.

For the literary buff, the German writer Bertold Brecht lived at Skovsbo Strand west of Svendborg from 1933 to 1939, leaving at the outbreak of World War II. It was during this period that he wrote *Mother Courage and Her Children.*

WHAT TO SEE & DO

VIEBAELTEGÅRD, Grubbemøllevej 13. Tel. 62-21-02-61.
The headquarters for Svendborg County Museum's four branches, Viebaeltegård is housed in a former poorhouse/workhouse constructed in 1872, the only one of its kind still existing in a Danish town. These social-welfare buildings, including the garden, are now a historical monument. Inside, see displays from ancient times and the Middle Ages, including excavation finds from old Svendborg and South Funen. Crafts and other workshops are offered, including goldsmithing, pottery making, and printing. There is a big museum shop. You can picnic in the garden. The museum is located in the town center near the intersection with Dronningemaen.
Admission: 10 kroner ($1.70) adults, 5 kroner (85¢) children.

Open: May–Oct, Tues–Sun 10am–4pm; Nov–Dec and Feb–Mar, daily 1–4pm. **Closed:** Jan.

ANNE HVIDES GÅRD, Fruerstraede 3. Tel. 62-21-02-61.

The oldest secular house in Svendborg, another branch of the County Museum, it was built around 1558. It is a beautiful half-timbered structure with 18th- and 19th-century interiors, and collections of Svendborg silver, glass, copper, brass, and faïence. It is located in the direct center of Torvet.

Admission: 10 kroner ($1.70) adults, 5 kroner (85¢) children.

Open: May–Sept, Tues–Sun 10am–4pm; Oct–Apr, by arrangement with the main office.

SVENDBORG ZOOLOGISKE MUSEUM, Dronningemaen 30. Tel. 62-21-06-50.

Danish zoological specimens and large dioramas showing animal immigration and habitat are displayed. Many exhibits have sound effects. Make sure to stop in at the whale house where the skeleton of a 56-foot sei whale that beached itself on Tåsinge island in 1955 can be seen.

Admission: 10 kroner ($1.70) adults, 5 kroner (85¢) children.

Open: Apr–Sept, daily 9am–5pm; Oct–Mar, Mon–Fri 9am–4pm, Sat–Sun 10am–4pm. **Bus:** 205, 206, 208.

ST. NICOLAJ CHURCH, Sct. Nicolajgade 2B. Tel. 62-21-12-96.

On one of the city's oldest shopping streets stands Svendborg's oldest house of worship. Built before 1200 in the Romanesque style and last restored in 1892, its red-brick walls and white vaulting complement the fine altarpiece and stained-glass windows. The church is in a cluster of old houses off Kyseborgstraede, in the vicinity of Gerrits Plads. Enter through the south door.

Admission: Free.

Open: July–Aug, daily 8am–4pm; Sept–June, daily 8am–noon.

VOR FRUE SOGN, Frue Kirkestraede 4. Tel. 62-21-11-61.

On the hill where the old Castle Swineburg stood, this Romanesque-Gothic church, dating from 1253, has a carillon of 27 bells, played four times a day. Since 1660 the bells have rung at noon. From the tourist office at Torvet, walk up the steps leading to the rise on which the church stands, overlooking the Old Town and the harbor.

Admission: Free.

Open: Summer, daily 8am–5pm. **Closed:** Rest of year.

ST. JØRGEN'S CHURCH, Strandvej 97. Tel. 62-21-14-73.

St. George's Church, located below the Svendborgsund Bridge, is the medieval Sct. Jørgensgård, the leprosy hospital built outside the town. The core of the church is a Gothic longhouse with a three-sided chancel, probably from the late 13th century. During restoration of the church in 1961, an archeological dig of the floor disclosed traces of a wooden building believed to be a predecessor of the present house of worship. Note the lovely glass mosaics in the building.

Admission: Free.

Open: Summer, daily 8am–5pm. **Closed:** Rest of year.

NEARBY ATTRACTIONS

On Thurø

This horseshoe-shaped island, connected to Funen by a causeway, is filled with orchards and well-cared-for gardens, giving it the title "The Garden of Denmark." The island was once the property of the manor house, Bjornemose, but the Thurineans wanted liberty, so they joined together to buy back Thurø in 1810, an event commemorated by a stone proclaiming freedom from manorial domination.

There's a beautiful old church on Thurø, and good beaches can be found at Smørmosen, Thurø Rev, and Grasten.

On Tåsinge

The largest island in the South Funen archipelago, Tåsinge has been connected to Funen by the Svendborg Sound Bridge since 1966. **Troense,** the "skipper town" of Tåsinge, is one of the best-preserved villages in Denmark where many half-timbered houses still stand on Badstuen and Grønnegade, the latter declared Denmark's prettiest street.

The island was the setting for a famous tragic love story depicted in the film *Elvira Madigan.* After checking out of a hotel in Svendborg, Danish artist Elvira Madigan and her lover Sixten Sparre, a Swedish lieutenant, crossed by ferry to Tåsinge, where together they committed suicide. The "Romeo and Juliet" of Denmark were buried in the Landet churchyard in the middle of Tåsinge, where many brides, even today, throw their wedding bouquets on their graves. The centenary of these two lovers was widely observed in 1989 throughout Scandinavia and their death on a July day gave rise to many ballads.

The island is best explored by car—drive over the causeway (follow Route 9). However, the most important attraction, Valdemar's Slot, can be seen by taking the vintage steamer, M/S *Helge,* which departs several times daily from the harbor at Svendborg. Tickets are sold at **Svendborg Turiskkontor,** Torvet (tel. 62-21-09-80).

MARITIME MUSEUM, Strandgade 1, Troense. Tel. 62-22-52-32.

The Maritime Museum, the final branch of the County Museum, is housed in a 1790 school, and traces maritime history from the early 19th century to the present. Pictures of ships, panoramas, yachting models, and memorabilia of the trade routes to China and East India including Staffordshire figures, Liverpool ware, Sunderland china, ropework art, and ships in bottles are displayed.

Admission: 10 kroner ($1.70) adults, 5 kroner (85¢) children.

Open: May–Oct, Mon 2–5pm, Tues–Sun 9am–5pm; Nov–Dec and Feb–Apr, Mon–Fri 9am–5pm, Sat 9am–noon. **Closed:** Jan. **Directions:** Cross the causeway to Tåsinge, turn left and then left again, heading down Bregningevej toward the water. Turn right at Troensevej and follow signs to the old port of Troense and to the old village school (now the museum) on Strandgate.

VALDEMAR'S SLOT, Slotsalleen 100, Troense. Tel. 62-22-61-06.

Valdemar's Slot was built between 1639 and 1644 by orders of King Christian IV for his son, Valdemar Christian. In 1678 it was given to naval hero Niels Juel for his third victory over the Swedes in a Køge Bay battle. The Juel family still owns the *slot,* which is in considerably better condition than when the admiral arrived. He found that the enemy Swedes had occupied the estate, sending the copper roof home to make bullets and stabling horses in the church. The castle is now a museum.

Valdemar's Castle Church, in the south wing, was cleaned up by Admiral Juel, consecrated in 1687, and has been used for worship ever since. Two stories high, it's overarched by three star vaults and illuminated by Gothic windows.

Admission: 30 kroner ($5.05) adults, 10 kroner ($1.70) children.

Open: May–Sept, daily 10am–5pm; Easter–Apr and Oct, Sat–Sun and hols. 10am–5pm. **Closed:** Nov–Easter. **Directions:** Take the M/S *Helge* from Svendborg harbor. By car, from Troense follow Slotsallen to the castle.

TÅSINGE SKIPPERHJEM & FOLKEMINDESAMLINGEN, Kirkebakken 1, Bregninge. Tel. 62-22-71-44.

Set in an 1826 school building, this private historical collection contains model and bottled ships, a coin collection, and revealing archives of Tåsinge history. A small collection of memorabilia is associated with the tragic love drama of Elvira and Sixten. In another building, you can see what a typical sea captain's house looked like some 100 years ago.

Admission: 10 kroner ($1.70) adults, 5 kroner (85¢) children.

Open: Mid-June to mid-Aug, daily 10am–6pm; May to mid-June and mid-Aug to mid-Sept, Mon–Fri 10am–3:30pm, Sat–Sun 10am–5pm. **Closed:** Mid-Sept to Apr. **Bus:** 980 from Svendborg. **Directions:** From Valdemars Slot, turn right by two thatched cottages and left again at the next junction. Follow the signs to Bregninge.

BREGNINGE KIRKEBAKKE, Kirkebackken 1, Bregninge.
If the weather is clear, be sure to climb the Bregninge church tower for panoramic views of the island and the Funen archipelago. To the south are the Bregninge Hills, whose wooded slopes are popular for outings. Originally Romanesque, the church's porch dates from the 16th century and its north wing from the 18th century. Inside, you'll see a Romanesque granite font, a head of Christ on the north wall dating from about 1250, and a 1621 pulpit with rich ornamentation. In the porch is a tombstone with arcade decoration, the image of a vicar, and runic letters.
Admission: Free.
Open: Summer, Mon–Fri 8am–8pm; winter, Mon–Fri 8–11am and 1–4pm.
Bus: 980 from Svendborg.

WHERE TO STAY

HOTEL SVENDBORG, Centrumpladsen, DK-5700 Svendborg. Tel. 62-21-17-00. Fax 62-21-90-12. 87 rms (all with bath). A/C MINIBAR TV TEL **Bus:** 200, 208.
$ Rates (including breakfast): 585–650 kroner ($98.35–$109.25) single; 725–950 kroner ($121.85–$159.70) double. Summer discounts. AE, DC, MC, V.
This clean and stylish hotel offers the best accommodations in Svendborg. Bedrooms are modern, each well maintained, comfortable, and containing a number of amenities such as hairdryers. Room service is provided. Adjacent to the lobby is a café-bar with its own glassed-in front terrace and a modern high-ceilinged restaurant serving fresh food prepared from seasonal ingredients.

HOTEL TRE ROSER, Fåbborgvej 90, DK-5700 Svendborg. Tel. 62-21-64-26. Fax 62-21-15-26. 12 rms, 58 apartments (all with bath). TEL.
$ Rates (including breakfast): 425 kroner ($71.45) single; 600 kroner ($100.85) double; apartments 3,500 kroner ($588.35) weekly. DC, MC, V. **Parking:** Available.
Tre Roser offers attractively furnished apartments suitable for one to five people, with well-equipped kitchens. Most guests stay by the week, but apartments can be rented on a daily basis if available. The dozen bedrooms are furnished in a simple, functional, and modern style, short on frills but clean and comfortable.
In the main building is a reputable restaurant, TV room, sauna, billiard room, and table tennis. Outside is a big swimming pool, a paddling pool and playground for children, and patio. The hotel is located about 3 miles from the nearest bathing beaches. A 5-minute drive will bring you to the Svendborg Golf Course, where Tre Roser guests play free. There's plenty of parking space.

HOTEL ROYAL, Toldbodvej 5, DK-5700 Svendborg. Tel. 62-21-21-13. 24 rms (4 with bath). **Bus:** 200, 208, 980.
$ Rates: 190 kroner ($31.95) single without bath, 395 kroner ($66.40) single with bath; 295 kroner ($49.60) double without bath, 450 kroner ($75.65) double with bath. Breakfast costs 45 kroner ($7.55) extra. AE, DC, MC, V.
A 1930s hotel of modest comforts, this is for those who prefer a central location opposite the bus and rail stations. Rooms are simply furnished, each equipped with hot and cold running water. Adequate bathrooms are on each floor. Only breakfast is served, although a bar and café are on the premises.

MISSIONSHOTELLET STELLA MARIS, Kogtvedvaenget 3, DK-5700 Svendborg. Tel. 62-21-38-91. 28 rms (13 with bath). **Directions:** From Svendborg, head west along Kogtvedvej.
$ Rates (including breakfast): 250 kroner ($42.05) single without bath; 395 kroner ($66.40) double without bath, 415–515 kroner ($69.75–$86.55) double with shower or bath. No credit cards.
Missionshotellet Stella Maris is an old-fashioned place, the former dormer house of a large estate. The furniture may be dated, but all is comfortable, and the patina of time

has given the hotel a certain dignity. Sea-view units opening onto Svendborg Sound are more expensive. A private park leads directly to the sound. The restaurant serves typical regional dishes. Service is smooth.

NEARBY ACCOMMODATIONS
At Oure

MAJORGÅRDEN, Landevejen 155, DK-5883 Oure. Tel. 62-28-18-19. 4 rms (none with private bath). **Bus:** 910 running between Svendborg and Nyborg. **$ Rates** (including breakfast): 235 kroner ($39.50) single; 345 kroner ($58) double. DC, MC, V.

On the coast road, 7 miles from Svendborg and 20 miles from Nyborg, this 1761 white-brick inn has been cherished by such illustrious Danes as tenor Lauritz Melchior. Outside, a bower of roses grows against the walls, low white tables are on the lawn for coffee, and a little pond at the rear is filled with ducks. An old horse stable has been turned into a bar, complete with bowling lanes. The rooms sit cozily above the restaurant under the roofline. Two have old-fashioned fixtures and furnishings, and the others are much more modern. None of the bedrooms has phone or TV, but visitors still tend to find them charming.

If you're just driving by, stop in for a "plate of the inn"—two kinds of herring, plaice, meatballs, meat sausages, liverpaste, and cheese for 110 kroner ($18.50). A large selection of fish and meat dishes is also available, with meals costing 190 kroner ($31.95) and up.

At Stenstrup

STENSTRUP KRO, Gaestgivergård, DK-5771 Stenstrup. Tel. 62-26-15-14. 20 rms (11 with bath). **$ Rates:** 155 kroner ($26.05) single without bath, 275 kroner ($46.25) single with bath; 275 kroner ($46.25) double without bath, 375 kroner ($63.05) double with bath. Breakfast costs 40 kroner ($6.70) extra. No credit cards.

Located at the end of a side street at the edge of town, this is well known as a hotel and a popular restaurant. The building dates from the turn of the century. A motel wing, built in 1971, contains respectably conservative accomodations. The country-style restaurant serves lunch, drinks, snacks, and dinner every day of the year from noon to 9pm. Typical dishes include beef casserole, pork flavored with herbs, and the chef's special steak. Dinners cost from 150 kroner ($25.20). However, a special menu of luncheon platters ranges in price from 28 to 55 kroner ($4.70 to $9.25).

On Thurø

HOTEL & PENSION RØGERIET, Måroddevej 22 Thurø, DK-5700 Svendborg. Tel. 62-20-50-84. 16 rms (all with bath). **Bus:** 201. **$ Rates** (including breakfast): 280–360 kroner ($47.05–$60.50) single; 460–560 kroner ($77.35–$94.15) double. MC, V.

Three miles from Svendborg, on its own private beach, is this lovely old Danish compound, "The Smokehouse" in English, furnished in a homelike, personalized style. Comfortable chairs are set on the terraces so you may soak in the sound and the Isle of Tåsinge.

Rooms are well furnished with antiques, and most have balconies. Home-style Danish cooking is served in the cozy dining room. Paintings by the Funen artist Niels Hansen decorate the walls. Reservations are required during the summer.

On Tåsinge

HOTEL TROENSE, Strandgade 5, Troense, DK-5700 Svendborg. Tel. 62-22-54-12. Fax 62-22-78-12. 31 rms (27 with bath). TV **Bus:** 200. **$ Rates** (including breakfast): 410 kroner ($68.90) single; 640 kroner ($107.60) double. DC, MC, V.

Since 1905 this establishment has been well known as both a hotel and a restaurant.

All but a few of the bedrooms contain private baths, color TVs, and radios. Most are in the main white-walled building, and a few are in comfortable annexes nearby.

A fixed-price meal in the nautically designed dining room runs 165 kroner ($27.75) for two courses, 190 kroner ($31.95) for three courses. Specialties include filet of lemon sole; plaice stuffed with shrimp, asparagus, and mushrooms; medallions of pork with cream-and-curry sauce; stuffed tenderloin of pork; pepper steak flambé; and veal schnitzel. The restaurant is open for lunch and dinner every day of the year and offers a full wine list.

WHERE TO DINE

BORGEN, Faergevej 34. Tel. 62-21-29-76.
   Cuisine: DANISH. **Reservations:** Recommended.
$ Prices: Appetizers 31–62 kroner ($5.20–$10.40); main dishes 45–165 kroner ($7.55–$27.75). DC, MC, V.
   Open: Tues–Sun 11am–9:30pm. **Closed:** Mon in winter.

A four-story harborfront building, this restaurant has an outdoor terrace with views of the water and a separate bar. Built as a private house in 1916, it was sold to a Dane just before World War II. He was later accused of collaborating with the Nazis and quickly sold it to a private men's club, which has maintained a restaurant on the premises since 1946. The restaurant serves lobscous (Danish hash), steamed borgen (house) steak with elaborate garnishes, potato boats, and a herb sauce. The promotional meal of the chef offers a choice of six different kinds of steak for only 69 kroner ($11.60).

SUNDET, Havnpladsen 5A. Tel. 62-21-07-19.
   Cuisine: DANISH/FRENCH. **Reservations:** Recommended.
$ Prices: Appetizers 30–50 kroner ($5.05–$8.40); main dishes 45–100 kroner ($7.55–$16.80); lunch smørrebrød from 20 kroner ($3.35) each. No credit cards.
   Open: Daily 11am–midnight.

A 5-minute walk south of the commercial center, this waterfront restaurant is the oldest in town, built some 160 years ago in a stone house painted white. From its windows or summer terrace, you can see the harbor with its ferryboats, trawlers, and pleasure yachts. The chef specializes in fresh fish and meat, including a French-inspired bouillabaisse, T-bone steaks, and shrimp from the fjords of Greenland. The house flounder is the best in town—grilled with fennel and served with a butter sauce. They are proud not to serve french fries, offering traditional Danish new boiled potatoes sprinkled with parsley. They also have a separate bar popular with the locals.

NEARBY DINING
In Bregninge

BREGNINGE KRO, Sundbrovej 54. Tel. 62-22-54-75.
   Cuisine: DANISH/INTERNATIONAL. **Reservations:** Recommended. **Bus:** 980 from Svendborg.
$ Prices: Appetizers 39–45 kroner ($6.55–$7.55); main dishes 100–145 kroner ($16.80–$24.35). DC, MC, V.
   Open: Daily noon–9pm. **Closed:** Mon in winter.

Three miles south of Svendborg on the main road in the heart of the village is an old-fashioned 1864 country inn that has been serving abundant farm-style meals since the turn of the century. A large variety of Danish and international cuisine and wines are served. Dishes may include English-style curry soup, tournedos (perfectly prepared), or a local fish called "red tongue" in English, which is served as a filet with a mushroom-and-sherry sauce. Bregninge Kro is clean and makes for a pleasant and restful interlude.

In Vester Skerninge

VESTER SKERNINGE KRO, Krovej 9. Tel. 62-24-10-04.

Cuisine: DANISH. **Reservations:** Recommended.
$ Prices: Appetizers 32–50 kroner ($5.40–$8.40); main dishes 55–135 kroner ($9.25–$22.70). No credit cards.
Open: Wed–Mon 11am–9pm.
In the hamlet of Vester Skerninge, 7 miles west from Svendborg along Route 44, this *kro* (inn) was established in 1772, and has been dispensing generous portions of simple Danish food ever since. Behind a half-timbered facade, guests can order such dishes as clear or cream-based soups, English or French beefsteak, and wienerschnitzel. Passing motorists often drop in (without a reservation) for a hamburger.

4. FAABORG

17 miles west of Svendborg, 112 miles west of Copenhagen

GETTING THERE By Train Frequent trains connect Faaborg with both Odense and Svendborg. Connections can be made to Copenhagen.

By Bus Thirty buses a day run between Odense and Faaborg, taking 1 hour.

By Car From Svendborg, head west on Route 44; from Odense, go south on Route 43.

ESSENTIALS The **Faaborg and District Tourist Association,** Havnegade 2 (tel. 62-61-07-07), provides information on sightseeing and the annual July festival, beginning on the 4th, with entertainment, dances, an amusement park, and much more.

Faaborg (also written Fåborg), a small seaside town of red-roofed buildings, is a good base for exploring southwestern Funen. Crowned by an old belfry, Faaborg has a number of well-preserved buildings, among them the medieval **Vesterport,** all that's left of Faaborg's walled fortifications.

You'll find here one of the best collections of Funen paintings and sculpture, particularly the work of Kai Nielsen, an important modern Danish sculptor. One controversial sculpture by Nielsen that has been denounced as obscene by some and praised by others is **Ymerbrond** (Ymer Wall), displayed in the market square (a copy is in the Museum of Faaborg). The sculpture depicts a man drinking from the udder of a bony cow while the cow licks a baby.

WHAT TO SEE & DO

FAABORG MUSEUM, Grønnegade 75. Tel. 62-61-06-45.
Located near the bus station, this museum has a rich collection of work by Kai Nielsen. Aside from his works, the museum displays paintings by such outstanding local artists as Peter Hansen, Johannes Larsen, and Fritz Syberg. In the octagonal rotunda of the museum is a huge statue commissioned by Mads Rasmussen, a wealthy art patron who bore the nickname "Mads Tomato." The museum has a café, open from June to September, serving lunch and coffee.
Admission: 15 kroner ($2.50) adults, free for children.
Open: Apr–Oct, daily 10am–4pm; Nov–Mar, Sat–Sun and hols. 11am–3pm.

DEN GAMLE GAARD [The Old Merchant's House], Holkegade 1. Tel. 62-61-33-38.
This 1725 house was established as a municipal museum in 1932 and displays Faaborg life in the 18th and 19th centuries. Various furnishings (some of which were the property of Riborg Voight, an early love of Hans Christian Andersen's), glass,

china, and faïence indicating Faaborg's past importance as a trade and shipping center are also on view. Exhibits from Lyk, including beautiful textiles and embroidery, are in the back.

The museum lies in the town center near the marketplace and harbor.

Admission: 15 kroner ($2.50) adults, free for children.

Open: May 15–Sept 15, daily 10:30am–4:30pm. **Closed:** Sept 16–May 14.

KLOKKETÅRNET, Tarnstraede.

This old belfry is the landmark of Faaborg—it's all that's left of the 13th-century Church of Sct. Nicolai, the first church in town, which was demolished around 1600. The town's old fire sledge is also here. The carillon bells play hymns four times a day. The belfry is directly in the town center near the marketplace.

Admission: 2 kroner (35¢) adults, 1 krone (15¢) children.

Open: Mid-June to mid-Sept, Mon–Fri 10am–noon and 2–4pm, Sat 10am–noon. **Closed:** Mid-Sept to mid-June.

WHERE TO STAY

HOTEL FAABORG FJORD, Svendborgvej 175, DK-5600 Faaborg. Tel. 62-61-10-10. 132 rms (all with bath). TV TEL.

$ **Rates** (including breakfast): 500 kroner ($84.05) single; 760 kroner ($127.75) double. AE, DC, MC, V.

Set on its own park at the eastern edge of town, this modern year-round hotel has comfortable rooms, each with a balcony/terrace. An indoor swimming pool and sauna are among the amenities. The restaurant offers a magnificent sea view, good food, and an excellent wine cellar.

HOTEL-PENSION MOSEGÅRD, Nabgyden 31, DK-5600 Faaborg. Tel. 62-61-56-91. 22 rms (8 with bath). TV TEL.

$ **Rates** (including breakfast): 290 kroner ($48.75) single without bath, 400 kroner ($67.25) single with bath; 470 kroner ($79) double without bath, 580 kroner ($97.50) double with bath.

This is an oasis of charm and Danish comfort located near the beach 3 miles east of Faaborg. Many stay here on a weekly basis and full-board terms are available, but most guests prefer to tour during the day. Rooms are furnished in an old-fashioned country style—snug and comfortable.

NEARBY ACCOMMODATIONS

FALSLED KRO, Assensvej 513, Falsled, DK-5642 Millinge. Tel. 62-68-11-11. Fax 62-68-11-62. 14 rms (all with bath). TEL.

$ **Rates:** 750 kroner ($126.10) single; 1,500 kroner ($252.15) double. Breakfast costs 125 kroner ($21) extra. AE, DC, MC, V.

★ The epitome of a Danish roadside inn, a former 15th-century smugglers' inn, Falsled Kro has been converted into a premier small luxury hotel, the finest in Funen. A Relais & Châteaux, it offers tradition and quality in its colony of thatched buildings clustered around a cobbled courtyard with a fountain. Each accommodation is elegantly furnished and comfortable—some in converted outbuildings, others in cottages across the road. Eleven rooms have a TV and seven are fitted with minibars. A garden leads to the water and a yacht harbor. It's located west of Faaborg on Route 329.

Dining/Entertainment: Many critics rate the hotel restaurant the best in Denmark. Growing many of its own vegetables, the *kro* uses only fresh, seasonal produce. Inspired by France, cooking is in the modern style. The owners breed quail that are cooked and served with a port wine sauce. Sea trout and turbot are caught locally. The chef's seafood platter is perhaps the most outstanding in the country. Try salmon grilled or flamed over fennel. Game dishes predominate in autumn. The kitchen also bakes its own bread and cakes. The wine list is well chosen.

Services: Laundry, baby-sitting, room service, luggage service, translations and guide service.

Facilities: Tennis court 500 yards away, horseback riding 3 miles away, fishing and bathing areas, helipad, parking area.

STEENSGAARD HERREGÅRDSPENSION, Steensgaard, DK-5642
Millinge. Tel. 62-61-94-90. Fax 62-61-78-61. 15 rms (8 with bath). MINIBAR TEL **Bus:** 920, 930.

$ Rates (including breakfast): 350 kroner ($58.85) single without bath, 550 kroner ($92.45) single with bath; 550 kroner ($92.45) double without bath; 1,000 kroner ($168.10) double with bath. No credit cards.

Few places in Denmark are as evocative of bygone manorial life as this 12th-century brick-and-timber house. About 4 miles northwest of Faaborg, the oldest section of this hotel dates from 1310, possibly earlier. Bedrooms are comfortably furnished, often stylishly so with antiques.

You can eat here even if you are not a guest if you make reservations far enough in advance. Dinner is served at 7pm sharp. Fixed-price lunches go for 140 kroner ($23.55); dinners, 250 kroner ($42.05). Your meal might include champagne soup, roe deer with juniper berries, or salmon en papillote with local herbs.

KORINTH KRO, Reventlowsvej 10, DK-5600 Faaborg. Tel. 62-65-10-23.
32 rms (10 with bath). TV.

$ Rates (including breakfast): 280 kroner ($47.05) single without bath, 330 kroner ($55.45) single with bath; 385 kroner ($64.70) double without bath, 460 kroner ($77.35) double with bath. AE, DC, MC, V.

Four miles northeast of Faaborg along Route 8, this hotel features comfortably old-fashioned bedrooms, a sauna, solarium, children's playground, and rear garden. The building was originally intended as a school where local farm girls could learn weaving, but became an inn in 1801. Today, shielded from the main road by a screen of hollyhocks and evergreens, the inn sports a Victorian front porch loaded with architectural gingerbread, a red-tile roof, and scores of climbing vines. If you wish, you can just drop in for lunch or dinner.

WHERE TO DINE

RESTAURANT KLINTEN, Klintallée 1. Tel. 62-61-32-00.
Cuisine: DANISH. **Reservations:** Recommended.

$ Prices: Appetizers 35–45 kroner ($5.90–$7.55); main dishes 75–185 kroner ($12.60–$31.10). DC, MC, V.

Open: Daily 11am–9pm.

This simple but attractive restaurant, overlooking the water a quarter mile north of the commercial center, is a great place to eat in Faaborg. The kitchen is open until 9pm, but guests often stay much longer. Appetizers include smoked salmon with mustard sauce, avocado soup, perhaps marinated mushrooms, and such main dishes as chicken breast en papillote, entrecôte, or grilled salmon served with spinach.

5. AERØ

18 miles across the water south of Svendborg, 110 miles west of Copenhagen.

GETTING THERE By Car & Ferry If you're traveling by car from Copenhagen, make a reservation on the car-ferry. The trip to Ærø takes about an hour. From Svendborg, take a ferry to Ærøskøbing through the South Funen archipelago. The ferry makes six daily round-trips, carrying 700 passengers and 70 cars. There is a café on board. For a schedule, ask at the tourist office or at the ferry office at the harbor in Svendborg. Bookings are made through **A/S Dampskibsselskabet Ærø** in Ærøskøbing (tel. 62-52-10-18).

Getting Around If possible, take a car on the ferry since there is very limited bus service on Ærø. Bus no. 990 runs every hour on the hour in the afternoon between Ærøskøbing, Marstal, and Søby. Morning service is greatly curtailed.

Tourist offices (see below) provide bus schedules, which change seasonally. Tickets can be bought on the bus. For bus information in Ærøskøbing, call 62-52-11-03.

If you're interested in a **bus tour** of the island, call Mads "Bus" Jensen (tel. 62-58-13-13).

ESSENTIALS The **Marstal Tourist Office** is at Kirkestraede 29 (tel. 62-53-19-60), and the **Ærøskøbing Tourist Office** is at Torvet (tel. 62-52-13-00).

An interesting Denmark excursion is to the Baltic Sea island of Ærø, 22 miles long and 6 miles wide. The island has little seaside and country hamlets linked by winding, sometimes single-lane roads, with thatch-roofed farmhouses in pastures and cultivated fields. Ærø has both sand and pebble beaches.

There are many good places on Ærø to eat and sleep—cozy inns in the country and comfortable little hotels in town. Try some of the local rye bread; it's said to be the best in Denmark. With your aquavit (schnapps), ask for a dash of Riga balsam bitters, a tradition that started when Ærø men sailed to Riga, found these bitters, and used them ever since in their aquavit.

WHAT TO SEE & DO

ÆRØSKØBING

The neat little village of ✪ Ærøskøbing is a 13th-century market town, which came to be known as a skippers' town in the 17th century. Called "a lilliputian souvenir of the past," with its small gingerbread houses, intricately carved wooden doors, and cast-iron lamps, few Scandinavian towns have retained their heritage as much as Ærøskøbing. In the heyday of the windjammer, nearly 100 commercial sailing ships made Ærøskøbing their home port.

SØBY

The ferry from Faaborg docks at Søby, in the northwestern sector of the island. Before rushing to Ærøskøbing, visit a mellow manorial property, **Søbygård.** Now in ruins, this manor house is complete with moat and dank dungeons.

Photographers are fond of the local **church** with its octagonal steeple that dates to about 1200, with many later additions and alterations over the centuries. See, in particular, Claus Berg's triptych, a primitive rendition of the Crucifixion.

FLASKESKIBSSAMLINGEN, Smedegade 22. Tel. 62-52-29-51.

The seafaring life is documented in this museum of Peter Jacobsen's ships in bottles, which represents his life's work. Upon his death in 1960 at the age of 84, this former cook had crafted more than 1,600 bottled ships and some 150 model sailing vessels built to scale, earning him the reputation in Ærøskøbing of "the ancient mariner." The museum also has Ærø clocks, furniture, china, and carved works by sculptor H. C. Petersen.

Admission: 10 kroner ($1.70) adults, 5 kroner (85¢) children.
Open: May–Sept, daily 9am–5pm; Oct–Apr, daily 10am–4pm.

HAMMERICHS HUS, Brogade 3-5. Tel. 62-52-29-50.

This house is filled with 18th-century antiques and porcelain.
Admission: 5 kroner (85¢).
Open: Daily 10am–noon and 2–4pm.

MARSTAL

This thriving little port on the east coast of Ærø has had a reputation in sailors' circles since the days of the tall ships. The harbor, protected by a granite jetty, is still busy, with a shipyard producing steel and wooden vessels, an engine factory, a ferry terminal, and one of Denmark's biggest yacht basins. The street names of Marstal attest to its seafaring background: Skonnertvej, Barkvej, and Galeasevej (Schooner, Bark, and Ketch Road); Danish naval heroes; and seven Ferry Lanes.

Visit the **seamen's church** with a spire and illuminated clock in the town center. Inside are ship models and an altarpiece that depicts Christ stilling the tempest at sea.

Twice a day a mail boat takes a limited number of passengers on a 45-minute trip to tiny **Birkholm Island,** for swimming and exploration. There are no cars on Birkholm. Reservations on the mail boat can be made at the Marstal Tourist Office.

JENS HANSEN'S MARITIME MUSEUM, Prinsensgade 1. Tel. 62-53-23-31.

This museum contains collections of ship models, old maritime equipment, and objets d'art brought home by sailors from foreign shores.

Admission: 15 kroner ($2.50) adults, 6 kroner ($1) children.

Open: Apr to mid-May and mid-Aug to late Oct, daily 10am–4pm; mid-May to mid-Aug, daily 9am–5pm (also daily 7:30–10pm in June). **Closed:** Late Oct to mid-May.

MAREN MINORS MINDE, Teglgade 9.

This old skipper's house has been converted into a museum.

Admission: 5 kroner (85¢) adults, 2 kroner (35¢) children.

Open: Mid-Aug to late Oct, daily 9am–5pm. **Closed:** Late Oct to mid-Aug.

WHERE TO STAY

IN ÆRØSKØBING

HOTEL AERØHUS, Vestergade 38, DK-5970, Ærøskøbing. Tel. 62-52-10-03. 30 rms (18 with bath). MINIBAR TV TEL.

$ Rates (including breakfast): 230 kroner ($38.65) single without bath, 385–465 kroner ($64.70–$78.15) single with bath; 380 kroner ($63.85) double without bath, 625 kroner ($105.05) double with bath. AE.

Painted a salmon pink, this typical Danish inn has tile roofs and black half-timbers. Dormer windows peer like eyes from its steeply pitched roof. Inside it's charming, with many traditional features, such as copper kettles hanging from the ceiling and warm lamps glowing. Bedrooms are modernized but traditional—each clean and comfortable. You can also enjoy good Danish meals here. In summer, there's dining in the large garden. The hotel is a 3-minute walk from the harbor.

DET LILLE HOTEL, Smedegate 33, DK-5970 Ærøskøbing. Tel. 62-52-23-00. 6 rms (none with bath).

$ Rates (including breakfast): 225 kroner ($37.80) single; 380 kroner ($63.85) double. No credit cards. **Closed:** Mid-Oct to mid-Apr.

Det Lille Hotel has simple but cozy bedrooms. Frills are at a minimum but cleanliness and a warm welcome compensate. Meals at the terrace restaurant cost 120 kroner ($20.15) each and include pork chops with vegetables, ham cutlets with mushrooms and paprika-flavored potatoes, beef steak, fried chicken, and hash. Food is served daily from 11:30am to 2pm and 5:30 to 9pm. The hotel is 100 yards from the ferry and harbor.

Outside Town

VINDEBAL KRO, Vindeballe Gade 1, DK-5970 Ærøskøbing. Tel. 62-52-16-13. 5 bungalows (all with bath).

$ Rates: 250 kroner ($42.05) single; 400 kroner ($67.25) double. No credit cards.

This charming country inn, built in 1888, is located on the road between Søby and Marstal, close to the old town of Ærøskøbing. There are five comfortably modern bungalows with five beds and kitchenettes in each that are rented by the day or week. The bungalows are at the edge of an idyllic meadow, close to the seashore. You can drop in for a well-prepared meal, daily from 11am to 9:30pm, with a fixed-price meal costing 85 kroner ($14.30), and an à la carte meal going for 150 kroner ($22.50).

IN MARSTAL

AERØ KONGRESHOTEL, Egehovedvej 4, DK-5960 Marstal. Tel. 62-53-33-20. Fax 62-53-33-20. 102 rms, 20 suites. MINIBAR TV TEL **Bus:** 990 to Marstal.

$ Rates (including breakfast): 550 kroner ($92.45) single; 850 kroner ($142.90) double; suites from 1,100 kroner ($184.90). DC, MC, V.

A 5-minute walk south of the center of Marstal and a quarter mile from the beach, this hotel, opened in 1989, is the largest and most up-to-date on the island. Set in a windswept landscape of seagrass and sweeping vistas, rooms are first class, decorated in pastel colors, with all the amenities such as private baths. Suites are twice the size of regular rooms. To attract a weekend crowd, the hotel offers a Saturday-night special rate of 485 kroner ($81.55) per person, double occupancy, including a free dinner and access to the famous Saturday-night dance at the hotel. There is an excellent restaurant and one bar.

HOTEL MARSTAL, Droningsstraede 1A, DK-5960 Marstal. Tel. 62-53-13-52. 7 rms (none with bath).

$ Rates: 205 kroner ($34.45) single; 330 kroner ($55.45) double. No credit cards.

This old-fashioned hotel offers clean accommodations in a regional atmosphere. Most rooms have large windows and dark paneling. Full meals, served daily in the restaurant at lunch and dinner, cost 150 kroner ($25.20) and might include crab cocktail, salmon filet with French bread, pepper steak, or veal Cordon Bleu. Fixed-price two-course meals cost 85 kroner ($14.30), and special platters for children are available. The hotel is in the town center, 2 minutes from the harbor.

Outside Town

DUNKAER KRO, Dunkaervej 1, Dunkaer, DK-5970 Ærøskøbing. Tel. 62-52-15-54. 8 rms (none with bath).

$ Rates: 185 kroner ($31.10) single; 295 kroner ($49.60) double. Breakfast costs 45 kroner ($7.55) extra. No credit cards.

Located in the middle of the island, 5 miles outside Marstal on the road to Søby, this family-owned 1802 inn is a rambling, twin-gabled structure, with enough charm to suit the most ardent traditionalist. Quaintness prevails, from the thatched roof to the old grandfather clock standing in the dining room. Rooms are cozy and clean. In summer, food is served in an attractive old garden. Full-board rates of 795 kroner ($133.65) per person daily are only available after a 3-day stay. Otherwise you can order an old-fashioned Danish breakfast at an extra charge, or a hearty, filling dish of the day for 75 kroner ($12.60), complete with all the trimmings.

WHERE TO DINE

IN ÆRØSKØBING

RESTAURANT MUMM, Søndergade 12, Ærøskøbing. Tel. 62-52-12-12.
  Cuisine: AMERICAN/INTERNATIONAL. **Reservations:** Not required.
$ Prices: Appetizers 35–65 kroner ($5.90–$10.95); main dishes 45–85 kroner ($7.55–$14.30); fixed-price lunch 85 kroner ($14.30). AE, DC, MC, V.
  Open: Apr–Oct, daily 11am–11pm. **Closed:** Nov–Mar.

Restaurant Mumm, in the town center near the Torv, enjoys a reputation for well-prepared recipes that sometimes carry a North American flavor thanks to the long-ago sojourn of owner Grethe Mumm-Christensen in Salinas, California. Specialties include American filet steak, a salad buffet, mussel soup, lobster cocktail, grilled scampi, an array of fresh fish, and teriyaki steak.

IN MARSTAL

REGNBUEN RESTAURANT, Kirkestraede 7, Marstal. Tel. 62-53-32-83.
Cuisine: DANISH. **Reservations:** Recommended. **Bus:** 990.
$ Prices: Appetizers 35–50 kroner ($5.90–$8.40); main dishes 90–135 kroner ($15.15–$22.70). MC, V.
Open: June–Aug 15, daily noon–11pm; Aug 16–May, Fri–Sat 5–11pm.

Occupying a 1920s building in a pedestrian zone of Marstal, this restaurant serves good food, including fresh fish and Danish beefsteak. Try smoked salmon for an appetizer. The decor is mostly modern, with big-windowed views of a garden. There is also a cellar for after-dinner dancing. Entrance to the disco is free, and it's open from 8pm to 2am, with beer costing from 16 kroner ($2.70).

CHAPTER 10

JUTLAND

- **WHAT'S SPECIAL ABOUT JUTLAND**
- **1. JELLING**
- **2. RIBE**
- **3. ESBJERG**
- **4. FANØ**
- **5. ÅRHUS**
- **6. SILKEBORG**
- **7. EBELTOFT**
- **8. RANDERS**
- **9. MARIAGER**
- **10. AALBORG**
- **11. FREDERIKSHAVN**
- **12. SKAGEN**

Dramatically different from the rest of Denmark, Jutland is a peninsula of heather-covered moors, fjords, farmland, lakes, and sand dunes. Besides its three major tourist centers—Ribe in the south, and Århus and Aalborg in the north—there are countless old inns and off-the-beaten-path hamlets.

The mainland of Jutland lies between the North Sea, Skagerrak, and the Kattegat. It is 250 miles from the northern tip of Jutland, Skagen, to the German border in the south. The North Sea washes up on miles of sandy beaches, making this a favorite holiday place for Danes.

The meadows of Jutland are filled with rich birdlife and winding rivers; nature walks are an excellent way to spend time. The heart of Jutland is mainly beech forest and lakeland, sprinkled with some towns of modest size and light industry. Steep hills surround the deep fjords of the east coast. Gabled houses in the marshlands of South Jutland add to the charm of the peninsula. Two of the most popular vacation islands are Rømø and Fanø, off the southwest coast. Here, many traditional homes of fishermen and ship captains have been preserved.

Those who are heading to Germany after Denmark might want to make the northern swing first (Århus and Aalborg), stopping at Ribe on their way south. On the other hand, those heading north to Norway or Sweden should cross the mainland of Jutland into Ribe in the southeast, then steer north for the major sight at the top of the peninsula.

The Little Belt Bridge at Middlefart connects the island of Funen with the mainland, leading to Fredericia, where our tour begins.

SEEING JUTLAND

GETTING THERE

Flying into Jutland airports, primarily Århus, Billund, and Aalborg, is the fastest.

From Copenhagen, ferry links to North Jutland are possible from Kalundborg to Århus, Hundested to Grenå, Sjaellands Odde to Ebeltoft, and others. All these ferries transport cars.

Trains labeled "IC" or "L" offer the fastest service from Copenhagen to Jutland, taking 5 to 6 hours. Likewise, trains from the continent pass through northern Germany en route to Jutland.

Jutland is crisscrossed by a network of buses, most of which are operated by the Danish State Railways (DSB). No reductions are granted for round-trip tickets.

By car, take express highway E20 which runs across Funen. Motorists have to take

WHAT'S SPECIAL ABOUT JUTLAND

Beaches
- ☐ Fanø island's 11-mile sandy beach—something special.
- ☐ Rømø island's western shore, one of the North Sea's premier sandy beaches; nude bathing.

Great Towns/Villages
- ☐ Ribe, of stork's nest fame—once a Viking port, now the prettiest town in Denmark.
- ☐ Jelling, "the birthplace of Denmark," and Harold Bluetooth's favorite.
- ☐ Ebeltoft, Denmark's classic market town of cobbled streets and half-timbered houses.

Castles & Palaces
- ☐ Rosenholm, near Århus, a moated Renaissance manor set in 35 acres of parkland.
- ☐ Clausholm, near Århus, an early baroque palace, place of banishment for Queen Anna Sophie.

Churches & Abbeys
- ☐ The Rhineland-inspired Cathedral of Ribe, dating from 1150.
- ☐ The Black Friars St. Catherine's Church and Monastery, at Ribe, a well-preserved abbey.

Ace Attractions
- ☐ The 2,200-year-old Tollund Man at the Silkeborg Museum, prehistory's "most unspoiled face."
- ☐ Den Gamble By, a re-created Danish village in an open-air museum.

Special Events/Festivals
- ☐ Århus Festival, Scandinavia's biggest cultural event (early September).
- ☐ Ildfestregatta, Denmark's largest and oldest folk festival at Silkeborg, taking place on an excursion boat (early August).

a ferry from Korsør (Zealand), but can then drive all the way across the bridge into East Jutland.

Since Jutland is relatively flat, you may consider renting a bicycle. Tourist offices often rent them, or else will direct you to the nearest place that does.

A SUGGESTED ITINERARY

If pressed for time, consider the following route:

Day 1: Cross the bridge from Funen at Middlefart and head west across Jutland on Route 32 to the old town of Ribe. Spend the night.

Day 2: Drive north to Esbjerg and take the 20-minute ferry crossing to Fanø. Spend the night in Fanø at an old inn.

Day 3: Cross Jutland again, heading east for a night in Silkeborg.

Day 4: Explore Århus's attractions and old manors. Spend the night.

Day 5: Drive to Ebeltoft, northeast of Århus, for a night in this ideal market town.

Day 6: Head north, stopping for lunch in Randers. Plan an overnight stay in Aalborg, largest Jutland's city.

Day 7: Return to Copenhagen or spend another night in Jutland, heading to its "Land's End," Skagen, in the northeastern corner. At Frederikshavn, northeast of Aalborg, catch a car-ferry to Norway.

1. JELLING

7 miles west of Vejle; 90 miles west of Copenhagen

GETTING THERE   By Train   Jelling is a 20-minutes train ride from Vejle on the run to Struer and Herning. Trains depart about once an hour Monday through Friday, less frequently on weekends.

By Bus   Connections are possible from Vejle's bus station. Take bus no. 214.

By Car   From Vejle, take Route A18 north.

This sleepy little village is historically important as the 10th-century seat of Danish kings Gorm the Old and Harald Bluetooth, Gorm's son.

WHAT TO SEE & DO

In front of Jelling's village church stand two   ❂ **runic stones** that practically mark the beginning of recorded Danish history. (Don't expect Stonehenge.) One stone commemorates Queen Thyre, Gorm's wife and "Denmark's ornament." The other, a bigger, triangular hunk of granite, was ordered sculpted by Bluetooth to honor his father, although in fact it is a testimonial to his own conquests and the conversion of the Danes to Christianity.

The ancient tumuli (burial mounds) near the church are called **Gorm's Hill** and **Thyre's Hill.** A recent excavation revealed another burial chamber, under the site of the first **Jelling Church,** built around A.D. 960. It contained skeletons and large quantities of gold thread; Viking artifacts included silver figurines—all of which lead archeologists to believe that this burial chamber once housed royalty, perhaps even the earthly remains of Gorm and Thyre.

WHERE TO STAY

JELLING KRO, Gormsgade 16, DK-7300 Jelling. Tel. 75-87-10-06. Fax 75-87-25-75. 10 rms (5 with bath). **Bus:** 214.

$ Rates (including breakfast): 185 kroner ($31.10) single without bath; 350 kroner ($58.85) single with bath; 350 kroner ($58.85) double without bath; 540 kroner ($90.75) double with bath. AE, DC, MC, V.

In the center of the village, this 200-year-old *kro* (inn) is across the street from the famous burial hill where Denmark "began." Behind a yellow ocher facade, the main building contains five bathless rooms, charming but without many amenities. A recently constructed annex across the street offers modern accommodations with full baths, kitchenettes, and TVs. The hotel restaurant is open daily except Wednesday in winter. Food is served from 8am to 9:30pm, a three-course dinner costing 250 kroner ($42.05). Main dishes are likely to include sautéed breast of turkey, Danish beefsteak with fried onions and cucumber salad, and veal steak with mushrooms and leek bouillon.

TØSBY KRO, Bredsten Landevej 12, DK-7300 Jelling. Tel. 75-88-11-30. 6 rms (none with bath). **Bus:** 214 from Vejle.

$ Rates: 160 kroner ($26.90) single; 250 kroner ($42.05) double. Breakfast costs 40 kroner ($6.70) extra. No credit cards.

Only a few miles from the well-known Legoland i Billund and from the Lions Park in Givskud, 4 miles west of Jelling, this little 1882 inn is actually a boardinghouse where most guests are Norwegian or Danish. Rooms are pleasantly furnished and well kept. The Danish food served is well prepared. A generous lunch or dinner costs 85 kroner ($14.30).

---

2. RIBE

20 miles south of Esbjerg; 186 miles west of Copenhagen

GETTING THERE   By Train   Ribe is connected by hourly trains from Copenhagen via Bramming. Frequent connections are possible between Tønder (near the German border) and Esbjerg, a major part of the West Jutland coast.

By Bus There are frequent bus connections into Ribe from the following towns: Esbjerg, Åbenraa, Bramming, Gram, and Jels. Exact routings and times of departure are available at the tourist offices, and tickets can be bought on the bus.

By Car If you're crossing from East Jutland, take Route 32 cross country. If you're coming from mainland Europe, take Route 11 north from Tønder. Esbjerg is connected to Ribe by Route 24, which feeds into Route 11 south.

ESSENTIALS The **Ribe Tourist Office** is at Torvet 3–5 (tel. 75-42-15-00). It is one of the more helpful in Denmark.

Ribe, a town of narrow cobblestone lanes, half-timbered and crooked houses, became legendary because of the graceful storks that build their nests on top of the town's red-roofed medieval houses. Every year citizens in the oldest town of Denmark face the same question: Will the storks fly back in April?

This port was an important trading center during the Viking era in the 9th century and became an episcopal seat in 948, when one of the first Christian churches in Denmark was established here. It was also the royal residence of the ruling Valdemars around 1200.

In medieval days Ribe was linked by sea-trade routes to England, Germany, Friesland, the Mediterranean, and other ports, but then its waters receded. Today it is surrounded by marshes, much like a landlocked Moby-Dick. The town watchman still makes his rounds—armed with his lantern and trusty staff—since the ancient custom was revived in 1936.

At **Skibbroen,** you can see a full-size replica of an evert, a ship that used to carry much of Ribe's seafaring goods. Skibbroen is the harbor, used today only by pleasure craft and the excursion boat *Riberhus,* which operates from May to September, taking passengers through the marshlands around Ribe to the Kammerslusen (sluice) and the tidal flats.

WHAT TO SEE & DO

CATHEDRAL OF RIBE, Torvet. Tel. 75-42-06-19.

This stone-and-brick cathedral, the crowning achievement of this little town, was under construction from 1150 to 1175. Inspired by Rhineland architecture, it's a good example of the Romanesque influence on Danish architecture, despite its Gothic arches. A century later a tower was added: Climb it if you want to see how the storks view Ribe—and if you have the stamina. Try to see the legendary "Cat's Head Door," once the principal entranceway to the church, and the granite tympanum—*Removal of the Cross*—the most significant piece of medieval sculpture left in Denmark. Mosaics, stained glass, and frescoes recently done in the eastern apse are by artist Carl-Henning Pedersen. The church is located in the town center off Sønderportsgade.

Admission: 3 kroner (50¢) adults, 1 krone (15¢) children.

Open: Mid-May to Sept, Mon–Sat 10am–6pm, Sun noon–6pm; Oct to mid-May, Mon–Sat 10am–noon and 2–4pm, Sun 2–4pm.

ST. CATHERINE'S CHURCH AND MONASTERY, Sct. Catherine's Plads. Tel. 75-42-05-34.

The Black Friars (Dominicans) came to Ribe in 1228 and began constructing a church and chapter house (the east wing of a monastery), and parts of the original edifice can still be seen, especially the southern wall. The present church, near Dagmarsgade, with nave and aisles, dates from the first half of the 15th century, and the tower is from 1617. Extensive restorations have made this one of the best-preserved abbeys in Scandinavia. Only the monks' stalls and the Romanesque font remain from the Middle Ages. The handsome pulpit dates from 1591 and the altarpiece from 1650.

You can walk through the cloisters and see ship models and religious paintings hanging in the southern aisle. Tombstones of Ribe citizens from the Reformation and later are along the outer walls of the church.

Across the street is the smallest house in Ribe, a brick-and-timber structure, a private home not open to the public. For information, phone the tourist office (tel. 75-42-15-00).

Admission: Church, free; cloisters, 2 kroner (35¢) adults, .50 krone (10¢) children.

Open: May–Sept, daily 10am–noon and 2–5pm; Oct–Apr, daily 2–4pm. **Bus:** 19.

HANS TAUSEN'S HOUSE, Sct. Skolegade.

The history of the Ribe area from the Stone Age (some 10,000 years ago) to today is exhibited along with finds from the Viking Age dating back to the earliest days of Ribe, between 700 and 800. Hans Tausen's House faces the cathedral.

Admission: 8 kroner ($1.35) adults, 3 kroner (50¢) children.

Open: Summer, daily 10am–5pm; autumn and spring, Tues–Sun 11am–3pm; winter, Tues–Sun 11am–1pm. **Closed:** Mon Sept–May.

RIBE RÅDHUSSAMLING (Town Hall Museum), Stenbogade.

The oldest existing town hall in Denmark, originally built in 1496, the medieval Town Hall Museum houses the town's artifacts and archives. Included are a 16th-century executioner's sword, ceremonial swords, the town's money chest, antique tradesmen's signs, and a depiction of the "iron hand," still a symbol of police authority. Enter from Støckens Plads.

Admission: 5 kroner (85¢) adults, 3 kroner (50¢) children.

Open: May–Sept, Mon–Fri 1–3pm. **Closed:** Oct–Apr.

RIBE KUNSTMUSEUM, Sct. Nicolaigade 10. Tel. 75-42-03-62.

An extensive collection of Danish art is displayed at the Ribe Kunstmuseum including works of acclaimed Danish artists like Eckersberg, Kobke, C. A. Jensen, Hammershøj, and Juel. Housed in a stately mid-19th-century villa in a garden on the Ribe River, many paintings are from the Golden Age of Danish art. Occasionally the museum changes exhibitions.

Admission: 10 kroner ($1.70) adults, free for children.

Open: June 15–Sept 14, daily 11am–4pm; Sept 15–June 14, Tues–Sun 1–4pm.

WHERE TO STAY

HOTEL DAGMAR, Torvet 1, DK-6760 Ribe. Tel. 75-42-00-33. Fax 75-42-36-52. 50 rms (all with bath). MINIBAR TV TEL.

$ Rates (including breakfast): May–Aug, 525–625 kroner ($88.25–$105.05) single; 725–850 kroner ($121.85–$142.90) double. Sept–Apr, 480–580 kroner ($80.70–$97.50) single; 680–780 kroner ($114.30–$131.10) double. AE, DC, MC, V.

A Denmark legend, this historic 1581 hotel claims the most glamorous address in the region. Converted from a private home in 1850, it's named after a medieval Danish queen. Bedrooms are well furnished and comfortable, with traditional yet modern styling. Every Friday and Saturday night except in summer there is music and dancing. The hotel's restaurant, recommended below, was lightly renovated in 1988 so the atmosphere could still be preserved.

SØNDER HOTEL JYLLAND, 22 Sønderportsgade, DK-6760 Ribe. Tel. 75-42-04-66. 8 rms (none with bath).

$ Rates (including breakfast): 210 kroner ($35.30) single; 420 kroner ($70.60) double. AE, MC, V.

Located behind a century-old red-brick facade, 100 yards south of the cathedral, this hotel is respectable and clean. None of the simple rooms has a private bath, but because of the lack of hotels in Ribe, it's often fully booked. The spacious dining room serves well-prepared and generous portions of Danish specialties every day at lunch and dinner.

KALVSLUND KRO, Koldingvej 105 at Kalvslund, DK-6760 Ribe. Tel.
75-43-70-12. 6 rms (none with bath). **Bus:** 57 or 921 from Ribe.
$ Rates (including breakfast): 175 kroner ($29.40) single; 325 kroner ($54.65)
double. No credit cards.

An 1865 Danish inn 5½ miles north of Ribe on Route 11, the Kalvslund Kro offers
clean and comfortable rooms but few frills. The furniture, according to the
management, "is old but not antique." Breakfast is served, but it costs extra.

The restaurant serves home-style cooking. The food I've sampled was well
prepared and well presented. Dishes are straightforward, the meat of good quality.
Full meals cost 75 to 110 kroner ($12.60 to $18.50), including such dishes as
asparagus soup, Danish beef with sautéed onions, and pork cutlets. It's open daily in
summer, from 8am to 10pm, but only on Friday, Saturday, and Sunday in winter.

WHERE TO DINE

HOTEL DAGMAR, Torvet 1. Tel. 75-42-00-33.
   Cuisine: DANISH/INTERNATIONAL. **Reservations:** Required.
$ Prices: Fixed-price meals, 295–325 kroner ($49.60–$54.65) at dinner, 126–176
kroner ($21.20–$29.60) at lunch; appetizers 78–108 kroner ($13.10–$18.15);
main dishes 192–208 kroner ($32.30–$34.95). AE, DC, MC, V.
   Open: Daily noon–10pm.

Opposite the cathedral near the train station, the Hotel Dagmar's four dining rooms
are a 19th-century dream of ornate furnishings and accessories. The international
cuisine is the best in town, and it's impeccably served and complemented by a
sophisticated wine list. There are also two informal, cozy cellar restaurants.

WEIS' STUE, Torvet 2, DK-6760 Ribe. Tel. 75-42-07-00.
   Cuisine: DANISH. **Reservations:** Recommended.
$ Prices: Appetizers 30–45 kroner ($5.05–$7.55); main dishes 55–160 kroner
($9.25–$26.90). No credit cards.
   Open: Daily 11am–9pm.

This 200-year-old brick-and-timber Lilliput inn, on the market square across from the
cathedral, serves scrumptious food. My most recent dinner here consisted of
marinated herring with raw onions, shrimp with mayonnaise and lemon, smoked
Greenland halibut with scrambled eggs, liverpaste with mushrooms, sliced ham and
Italian salad, filet with onions, and two sorts of cheese with bread and butter.

The inn also rents four bathless rooms, charging 200 kroner ($33.60) for the one
very cramped single and 450 kroner ($75.65) for the other three doubles. Rates
include breakfast.

VAERTSHUSET SAELHUNDEN, Skibbroen 13. Tel. 75-42-09-46.
   Cuisine: DANISH. **Reservations:** Not required.
$ Prices: Appetizers 16–22 kroner ($2.70–$3.70); main dishes 52–118 kroner
($8.75–$19.85). DC, MC, V.
   Open: Daily noon–8:45pm.

This charming little restaurant stands amid stately trees near the edge of the town's
narrow canal just north of the cathedral. The low-slung brick building dates from the
1600s, although in the 18th and 19th centuries it was the town's shoe factory. The
dining room, the Seals Room, is decorated with many pictures and seal skins.
Regional dishes include Skipperlavskovs (beef, potatoes, and onions concocted into a
hash) served with brown bread and a beetroot salad. Also featured are ox tenderloin,
clear bouillon with meatballs, and fried filet of plaice. In summer, you can sit in the
cozy yard.

EASY EXCURSIONS FROM RIBE

Off the west coast of Jutland, **Rømø,** a North Frisian island, is the largest Danish
island in the North Sea. It is about 5½ miles long and 4 miles wide. The western shore
opens onto the North Sea, whereas the east coast facing the mainland is bounded by
tidal shallows. The northwest corner of the island is a restricted military zone.

The island, which is separated from the German island of Sylt by the Lister Deep, has a wild, windswept appearance and is particularly known for its nude sunbathing, as is the German island of Sylt. In summer, Rømø is filled with tourists, especially Germans, but off-season it's one of the sleepiest places in Europe.

To reach Rømø, take the 6-mile stone causeway from mainland Jutland. You can take a bus south from Ribe to Skaerbaek and then bus no. 29 across the tidal flats to Rømø.

If you'd like to continue your trip to Sylt from Rømø, take a car-ferry from the Danish fishing village of Havneby to the far northern German town of List.

---

3. ESBJERG

58 miles west of Vejle, 105 miles SW of Århus,
173 miles west of Copenhagen.

GETTING THERE By Plane Flights arrive at Esbjerg from Aberdeen and Dundee in Scotland and also from Humberside in England. Flights also arrive from London at Billund Airport, where a taxi to Esbjerg costs 460 kroner ($77.35). There is also air service several times a day to Copenhagen.

By Train Connections are possible almost hourly from Copenhagen and Frederikshavn via Fredericia.

By Bus About three buses daily depart for Esbjerg from Frederikshavn, Aalborg, Viborg, and Herning.

By Car From all corners of Denmark, highways lead to Esbjerg. From the German border in the south, take Route 11 north, heading left at the junction with Route 24. From Funen in the east, take the E20 express highway west across Jutland.

By Ferry Esbjerg has three weekly ferry departures heading for Harwich in England all year. Summer ferries connect Esbjerg with Newcastle.

ESSENTIALS The **Esbjerg Tourist Office,** Skolegade 33 (tel. 75-12-55-89), is open Monday through Friday from 9am to 5pm and on Saturday from 9am to noon.

Esbjerg's harbor, with its easy accessibility to the North Sea, is a perfect shipping point for large agricultural exports to Great Britain, making it Denmark's largest fishing port. In recent years the oil and natural gas deposits in the North Sea have made Esbjerg the country's oil city. Many ships here are used as supply vessels for the Danish oil rigs.

Esbjerg is laid out with straight, wide streets, square town sections, and a large town square. There is a long pedestrian street, plus many specialty shops and large shopping centers.

Buses service the town, and you can make connections to other parts of the country. From the harbor, you can take a ferry year round to Harwich, England, and to Newcastle, England, and the Faroe Islands in summer. For information, contact **DFDS,** Englands-terminalen (tel. 75-12-48-00). You can also connect by ferry with Fanø (see below), a 20-minute crossing made every 30 minutes in summer, hourly in winter. Information is available from **Fanø-overfarten** (tel. 75-12-00-00).

WHAT TO SEE & DO

BOGTRYKMUSEET, Borgergade 6. Tel. 75-13-53-63.
The largest working presswork museum in Denmark, it's built and furnished like a

medium-size Danish printing office. Exhibits of printed work and presses trace the craft of printing through 500 years. You can see the process as it developed from handset type and printing on cumbersome man-powered presses to the fast, accurate production with modern state-of-the-art equipment.

Admission: 10 kroner ($1.70) adults, 5 kroner (85¢) children.
Open: May–Sept, Mon–Fri 2–5pm. **Closed:** Oct–Apr. **Bus:** 1, 5, 6, 8, 9.

ESBJERG MUSEUM, Nørregade 25. Tel. 75-12-78-11.

Exhibits at the Esbjerg Museum chronicle the prehistoric periods in Southwest Jutland and the history of the region. Check out the beautiful collection of costumes. From the bus and train stations, follow signs for a quarter mile; the museum lies off Torvetgade.

Admission: 10 kroner ($1.70) adults, free for children.
Open: Tues–Sun 10am–4pm.

FISKERI-OG-SØFARTSMUSEET, SALT-VANDSAKVARIET, AND SAE-LARIUM, Tarphagvej. Tel. 75-15-06-66.

In this huge open-air tank the animals are fed daily at 11am and 2:30pm. Down below, you can watch the antics of the seals underwater through the glass.

Admission: 25 kroner ($4.20) adults, 15 kroner ($2.50) children.
Open: Daily 10am–5pm. **Bus:** 22, 23, 30.

WHERE TO STAY

SCANDIC HOTEL OLYMPIC, Strandbygade 3, DK-6700 Esbjerg. Tel. 75-18-11-88. Fax 75-18-11-08. 87 rms (all with bath). MINIBAR TV TEL. **Bus:** 1, 11, 12.

$ Rates (including breakfast): 650 kroner ($109.25) single; 855 kroner ($143.75) double. AE, DC, MC, V.

On a tree-lined street in the center of town, this impressively bulky hotel is a member of a Scandinavian chain. You don't get surprises in decor or amenities, but you get dependable comfort in its well-furnished bedrooms. Each has comfortable modern furniture and a number of amenities. Facilities include a sauna, solarium, ample parking, and some shops and kiosks.

HOTEL BRITANNIA, Torvet, DK-6701 Esbjerg. Tel. 75-13-01-11. Fax 75-45-20-85. 79 rms (all with bath). MINIBAR TV TEL **Bus:** 22.

$ Rates (including breakfast): 450–550 kroner ($75.65–$92.45) single; 580–660 kroner ($97.50–$110.95) double. AE, DC, MC, V.

Considered one of the best hotels in town, rooms here are comfortably furnished. Among other amenities, they contain radios and TVs with video movies. On the premises are a tastefully decorated modern restaurant and pub.

ANSGAR HOTEL, Skolegade 36, DK-6700 Esbjerg. Tel. 75-12-82-44. Fax 75-13-95-40. 65 rms (all with bath). MINIBAR TV TEL **Bus:** 1, 5, 6, 9, 21.

$ Rates (including breakfast): 370–390 kroner ($62.20–$65.55) single; 500–520 kroner ($84.05–$87.40) double. AE, DC, MC. **Parking:** Available.

This well-established three-story hotel, in the center of town overlooking the square, is near the pedestrian shopping street. Rooms are modern and comfortable. The hotel's restaurant serves international as well as Danish fare, and there is also a lounge. An elevator serves the three floors, and there is parking in the back.

WHERE TO DINE

RESTAURANT PAKHUSET, Dokvej 3. Tel. 75-12-74-55.

Cuisine: DANISH. **Reservations:** Required. **Bus:** 5.

$ Prices: Five-course fixed-price dinner 310 kroner ($52.10); appetizers 65–98 kroner ($10.95–$16.45); main dishes 140–192 kroner ($23.55–$32.30). DC, MC, V.

Open: Lunch Mon–Sat noon–3pm; dinner Mon–Sat 5:30–11pm.

An interesting, charming restaurant near the ferry to Fanø, Pakhuset uses fresh ingredients to prepare Danish specialties. Fresh fish is featured. An art gallery is housed in the restaurant.

---

4. FANØ

10 miles west of Esbjerg to Sønderho, 1 mile west of Esbjerg to Nordby, 176 miles west of Copenhagen to Nordby

GETTING THERE   By Car   At Esbjerg you can board a ferry (see below) for the trip to Fanø, which has one main road, stretching from Nordby in the north to Sønderho in the south.

By Ferry   Ferries depart from the harbor of Esbjerg in West Jutland for the island of Fanø, taking 20 minutes. Ferries leave every 30 minutes in summer and every hour in winter. The price of a one-way ticket is 17 kroner ($2.85) for adults and 9 kroner ($1.50) for children. For more information, call DSB at 75-12-00-00.

A 20-minute ferry ride from Esbjerg will take you to **Nordby,** a logical starting point for an exploration of Fanø, where you'll find heather-covered moors, windswept sand dunes, fir trees, wild deer, and bird sanctuaries. From Ribe, Fanø makes for a great day's excursion (or longer if there's time).

Fanø is a popular summer resort among the Danes, Germans, and English. **Sønderho,** on the southern tip, with its memorial to sailors drowned at sea, is my favorite spot—somewhat desolate, but that's its charm.

WHAT TO SEE & DO

A summer highlight on Fanø is the **Fannikerdagene** festival, the first weekend in July, which offers traditional dancing, costumes, and events connected with the days when sailing ships played a major part in community life.

If you miss the festival, try to be on Fanø the third Sunday in July for **Sønderho Day.** High point of the festive day is a wedding procession that passes through the town to the square by the old mill. Traditional costumes and bridal dances are some of the attractions.

WHERE TO STAY & DINE

SØNDERHO KRO, Kropladsen 11, Sønderho, DK-6720 Fanø. Tel. 75-16-40-09. 7 rms (all with bath). TEL.

$ Rates: 450–575 kroner ($75.65–$96.65) single; 560–800 kroner ($94.15–$134.50) double. Breakfast costs 60 kroner ($10.10) extra; half board, 575 kroner ($96.65) per person. AE, DC, MC, V.

A 1722 thatch-roofed, ivy-covered inn, this National Trust House nestled behind the sand dunes is an unbeatable choice. Each of the rooms has its own distinctive character, yet all fit into the traditional atmosphere of the inn. Antiques add a final touch. The first-floor lounge has views of the tidal flats, and the dining room is atmospheric as well. The cuisine is superb and plentiful, with meals beginning at 250 kroner ($42.05). Sønderho Kro is 8 miles south of the Nordby ferry dock; a bus connects with ferry arrivals.

FANØ KROGAARD, Langelinie 11, Nordby, DK-6720 Fanø. Tel. 75-16-20-52. Fax 75-16-23-00. 18 rms (3 with bath).

$ Rates (including breakfast): 300 kroner ($50.45) single without bath, 400 kroner ($67.25) single with bath; 400 kroner ($67.25) double without bath, 600 kroner ($100.85) double with bath. MC, V.

This old-fashioned inn, originally constructed in 1624, has been welcoming wayfarers ever since. Located 100 yards from the ferry dock, rooms are simple but cozy, comfortable, and nautical. The owner, Jorn Fischer, is also a fisherman, and the fish he serves in his restaurant is considered the freshest on the island. Specialties vary according to the catch of the day. Meals begin at 180 kroner ($30.25), and the kitchen serves daily from 11am to 9:30pm. There is also a bar, very popular in Nordby, open from 8am to midnight, and an outdoor terrace used in summer. There's also a disco in the cellar open on Friday and Saturday nights from 11pm to 5am; entrance is free but beer costs 16 kroner ($2.70) a bottle.

5. ÅRHUS

43 miles south of Aalborg, 109 miles west of Copenhagen

GETTING THERE   By Plane   Both SAS and Danair fly from Copenhagen to Århus, a total of 12 flights daily Monday through Friday and 5 flights on Saturday and Sunday. Flights arrive daily from London, Oslo, and Malmö, Sweden. An airport bus runs directly from the airport to the Central Station in Århus.

By Train   About 5 or 6 trains a day make the 5-hour trip from Århus to Copenhagen. Some 20 trains a day connect Aalborg with Århus, taking 1 hour 40 minutes. From Frederikshavn, the North Jutland port and ferry-arrival point from Norway, some 20 trains a day run to Århus, taking 3 hours.

By Bus   Two buses daily make the 4-hour run to Århus from Copenhagen.

By Car   From the east, cross Funen on the E20 express highway, heading north at the junction with the E45. From the north German border, head north all the way along the E45. From Frederikshavn and Aalborg in the north, head south along the E45.

ESSENTIALS   Tourist Information   The tourist office, **Århus Turist-forening,** is located in the Town Hall at Rådhuset, DK-8000 Århus C (tel. 86-12-16-00).

GETTING AROUND   A **Tourist Ticket,** costing 25 kroner ($4.20), can be purchased from a vending machine on the rear platform of the Central Bus Station (tel. 86-12-86-22)—bus drivers do not sell this ticket. This ticket, valid for 24 hours, is for an unlimited number of rides on all bus routes within Zones 1 to 4. The ticket is also valid for the special 2-hour guided sightseeing tour of Århus. Two children under 12 can travel on one Tourist Ticket.

Jutland's capital, the second-largest city in Denmark, Århus is a cultural center, a university town combined with a lively port. Aside from enjoying the city's many restaurants, hotels, and nighttime amusements, you can use Århus as a good base for excursions to Silkeborg, Ebeltoft, and the moated manors and castles to the north.

WHAT TO SEE & DO

For the best introduction to Århus, head for the town hall's tourist office, where a 2½-hour **sightseeing tour** leaves daily at 10am from June 25 to September 8, costing 25 kroner ($4.20) per person.

DEN GAMLE BY, Vesterbrogade. Tel. 86-12-31-88.

The top sight in Århus, Den Gamle By displays more than 65 buildings representing Danish life from the 16th to the mid-19th century, re-created in a botanical garden. This open-air museum is different from similar museums near Copenhagen and Odense, where the emphasis is on rural life. Visitors walk through the authentic-looking workshops of bookbinders, carpenters, hatters, and more. A popular attraction is the Burgomaster's House, a wealthy merchant's antique-stuffed, half-timbered home, built at the end of the 16th century. Make sure to see the Textile Collection and the Old Elsinore Theater, erected in the early 19th century. Inquire at the ticket office about summer programs staged here—chamber music, opera, and the like. There's a restaurant on the grounds.

Admission: 30 kroner ($5.05).

Open: May to mid-Oct, daily 9am–5pm; spring and fall, daily 11am–3pm; winter, daily 11am–1pm. **Bus:** 3.

CATHEDRAL OF ST. CLEMENS, Bispetorvet. Tel. 86-123-845.

This late Gothic red-brick, copper-roofed cathedral, crowned by a 315-foot spire, begun at the beginning of the 13th century and completed in the 15th, is the longest cathedral in Denmark, practically as deep as its spire is tall. Of chief interest here is the Renaissance pulpit, 15th-century triptych, and 18th-century pipe organ. (After the cathedral, I suggest a visit to the nearby medievalesque arcade at Vestergade 3, with its half-timbered buildings, rock garden, cobblestone courtyard, aviary, and excellent display of antique interiors.)

Admission: Free.

Open: May–Sept, Mon–Fri (if no ceremonies are being held) 9:30am–4pm; Oct–Apr, Mon–Fri 10am–3pm. **Bus:** 3, 11, 54, 56.

VIKINGEMUSEET, St. Clemens Torv 6. Tel. 86-272-433.

Down the steps to the left of the cathedral is a Viking Museum where the remains of the town's old Viking walls have been found. After seeing the museum, visitors are invited to enter the bank. There is always an admission-free exhibition of Danish artists in the basement next to the storage room.

Admission: Free.

Open: Mon–Wed and Fri 9:30am–4pm, Thurs 9:30am–6pm. **Bus:** 3, 11, 54, 56.

VOR FRUE KIRKE, Frue Kirkeplads. Tel. 86-121-243.

A 13th-century church, this was the former abbey church of the Dominican brothers (1240). Worth inspection is St. Nicholas Church under the chancel, the oldest stone church in Scandinavia, dating back to Viking days (1060). On Sunday there are services at 9 and 10am.

Admission: Free.

Open: May–Oct, Mon–Sat 9:30am–4pm; Nov–Apr, Mon–Sat 10am–3pm. **Bus:** 7, 10, 17.

RÅDHUSET, Park Allé. Tel. 86-132-000.

A crowning architectural achievement in the center of Århus, the Rådhuset, or Town Hall, was built between 1936 and 1941 to commemorate the 500th anniversary of the Århus charter. Arne Jacobsen was one of the designers—and it's been the subject of controversy ever since. The modern marble-plated structure with lots of airy space and plenty of glass can be seen on a free guided tour. The tour starts at the tourist office at the tower entrance. I prefer to take the elevator (346 steps for those who dare) to the top of the 197-foot tower, where a carillon rings every now and then. From here you can see the entire city of Århus and the busy harbor.

Admission: Free.

Open: June 20–Sept, Mon–Fri at noon and 2pm, Sat–Sun at noon. **Bus:** 3, 4, 5, 14.

FORHISTORISK MUSEUM—MOESGÅRD, Moesgård Manor. Tel. 86-272-433.

The former Århus Museum is now an archeological and ethnographic museum in a country setting about 5 miles from the town, at Moesgård Manor. Focusing on prehistory, the museum is a major attraction, drawing visitors from all over. It owns the incredibly well-preserved 2,000-year-old Grauballe man, who had lain since the Iron Age in a bog in central Jutland. Outside in the park and woods is an open-air museum that displays prehistoric reconstructions and a prehistoric "trackway."

Admission: 20 kroner ($3.35) adults, free for children under 15 accompanied by an adult.

Open: Apr–Sept, daily 10am–5pm; Oct–Mar, Tues–Sun 10am–5pm. **Bus:** 6 from the railway station.

NEARBY ATTRACTIONS

LEGOLAND, Nordmarksvej, 7190 Billund. Tel. 75-33-13-33.
At this family amusement park, the main attraction is Miniland, a landscape built of approximately 33 million Lego bricks showing the world's famous landscapes and buildings in miniature. There is also a real Wild West town where you can see a copy of the monument at Mount Rushmore, and a 45-foot monument of Chief Sitting Bull. Visit the world-famous antique doll and dollhouse collection, mechanical toys, various educational exhibitions, and of course all the adult and kiddie rides. Other attractions include Titania's Palace, the largest and most expensive miniature palace in the world, and an antique collection of gadgets. To reach Legoland, head south from Århus along Route E45 toward Vejle. At Billund center, travel along Åstvej.
   Admission: 40 kroner ($6.70) adults, 20 kroner ($3.35) children.
   Open: May to mid-Sept, daily 10am–8pm. **Closed:** Mid-Sept to Apr.

JYSK AUTOMOBILMUSEUM (Jutland Car Museum), DK-8883 Gjern. Tel. 86-87-50-50.
Near Silkeborg at Gjern, this is the only automobile museum in Jutland, featuring 135 vintage automobiles dating from 1900 to 1948. Sixty-five different makes are represented, among them the V12-cylinder Auburn, V12-cylinder Cadillac, 1947 Crosley, the famous Renault Taxis de la Marne, Kissel, Hotchkiss, Jordan, Vivinus, Rolls-Royce, and Maserati. A number of motorcycles are also displayed.
   Admission: 30 kroner ($5.05) adults, 15 kroner ($2.50) children.
   Open: Apr, Sat–Sun 10am–5pm; May–Sept 15, daily 10am–6pm; Sept 16–Nov 1, Sat–Sun 10am–5pm. **Closed:** Nov 2–Mar. **Bus:** Silkeborg–Gjern.

ØM KLOSTER MUSEUM, Emborg ner Gamle Ry, DK-8660 Skanderborg. Tel. 86-89-81-94.
At Emborg, on the north bank of a lake, are the ruins of a Cistercian monastery dating from 1172. Skeletons from the monastery hospital are displayed for those inclined to view them. Besides the church site and monks' graves there is a medicinal herb garden.
   Admission: 15 kroner ($2.50) adults, 7 kroner ($1.20) children.
   Open: May–Aug, Tues–Sun 9am–6pm; Apr and Sept, Tues–Sun 9am–5pm; Oct 1–21, Tues–Sun 9am–4pm. **Closed:** Late Oct to Mar. **Bus:** 15, 59, 94, 95.

WHERE TO STAY

Low-cost accommodations in this lively university city are limited. Those on strict budgets should go to the tourist office in the Town Hall (tel. 86-12-16-00) for bookings in **private homes.** Office hours mid-June to the end of August, are daily from 9am to 9pm; the first 2 weeks of September, daily from 9am to 7pm; from mid-September to mid-June, Monday through Friday from 9am to 5pm and on Saturday from 9am to noon.

EXPENSIVE

ATLANTIC HOTEL, Europaplads 12-14, DK-8000 Århus C. Tel. 86-13-11-11. Fax 86-13-23-43. 107 rms (all with bath). MINIBAR TV TEL. **Bus:** 6.
   $ Rates (including breakfast): 750–1,045 kroner ($126.10–$175.65) single; 950–1,045 kroner ($159.70–$175.65) double. AE, DC, MC, V.
A favorite of commercial travelers, the Atlantic has comfortably streamlined bedrooms, each with a balcony, radio, and color TV with video. There is also an attractively decorated restaurant, plus a Scottish-style pub.

HOTEL ROYAL, Stove Torv 4, DK-8000 Århus C. Tel. 86-12-00-11. 111 rms (all with bath). MINIBAR TV TEL. **Bus:** 56, 58.
   $ Rates (including breakfast): 800–1,500 kroner ($134.50–$252.15) single; 1,000–1,800 kroner ($168.10–$302.60) double. Weekend discounts. AE, DC, MC, V.
This is the most glamorous place to stay in town. The date established in gilt letters on

its neobaroque facade commemorates the hotel's establishment in 1838. There have been numerous additions and upgradings since. The Royal stands close to the city's symbol, its cathedral. After you've registered, a vintage elevator will take you to one of the bedrooms, many quite spacious. Bedroom amenities include color TV with video and radio. You can enjoy Danish meals in the mezzanine-level greenhouse restaurant, the Queen's Garden.

MODERATE

MISSIONSHOTELLET ANSGAR, Banegårdsplads 14, DK-8100 Århus C. Tel. 86-12-41-22. Fax 86-20-29-04. 169 rms (153 with bath). TEL **Bus:** 3, 17, 56, 58.
$ Rates (including breakfast): Old wing: 250 kroner ($42) single without bath; 485 kroner ($81.55) double without bath. New wing: 500 kroner ($84.05) single with bath; 750 kroner ($126.10) double with bath. DC, MC, V.
A dignified and traditional hotel, convenient to the Town Hall, it offers a full range of rooms in different price ranges. Bedrooms are all tastefully decorated, many with modern furnishings. There's plenty of lounging room, and the food and service in the dining room are quite fine.

BUDGET

ERIKSEN'S HOTEL, Banegårdsgade 6-8, DK-8000 Århus C. Tel. 86-13-62-96. Fax 86-13-76-76. 40 rms (none with bath). **Bus:** 16, 17.
$ Rates: 230 kroner ($38.65) single; 350 kroner ($58.85) double. Breakfast costs 30 kroner ($5.05) extra. MC, V.

This hotel is the best bargain in the vicinity of the rail station. More rooming house than hotel, Eriksen's is utilitarian, clean, and recently modernized. Showers are just outside the rooms. In addition to breakfast, the hotel also serves a quick lunch and is licensed for beer.

PARK HOTEL, Sonder Allé 3, DK-8000 Århus C. Tel. 86-12-32-31. 14 rms (none with bath).
$ Rates: 225–235 kroner ($37.80–$39.50) single; 330–365 kroner ($55.45–$61.35) double. Breakfast costs 40 kroner ($6.70) extra. DC, MC, V.
On two floors of a 1930s apartment building, the Park has an upper-story reception area located in a sunny pair of comfortably old-fashioned rooms with a corner bar. Rooms are clean and bright, with built-in light-grained furniture and big windows. The hotel, open all year, is near a busy commercial street on a corner at Town Hall Square.

WHERE TO DINE

EXPENSIVE

GAMMEL ÅBYHOJ, Bakkeallé I, Åbyhoj. Tel. 86-15-77-33.
Cuisine: FRENCH. **Reservations:** Required. **Bus:** 5, 10, 16, 94, 17.
$ Prices: Fixed-price meals 385 kroner ($64.70) at dinner, 275 kroner ($46.25) at lunch; appetizers 85–180 kroner ($14.30–$30.25); main dishes 155–210 kroner ($26.05–$35.30). AE, DC, MC, V.
Open: Mon–Sat 11:30am–midnight.

One of the few Relais & Châteaux in Denmark, the ritzy Gammel Åbyhoj lies in an affluent suburb about a mile west of the town center. The building dates from 1909 when it was a private residence for a city railway tycoon. Since 1989 it has been run by the French-born chef, Michel Michaud. First enjoy a drink in the lounge, where the built-in furniture carries a hint of art deco styling. Cold-weather fires illuminate the hardwood and French chairs in the twin dining rooms. There's even a walnut-shaded courtyard and arbor-covered solarium for warm-weather dining.

The limited menu is based on very fresh ingredients. Typical dishes might include veal filet with braised endive, terrine of foie gras, a succulent version of tournedos, and sophisticated preparations of salmon, lamb, sweetbreads, and fish, along with such rich desserts as a chocolate marquise with a kiwi-cream sauce.

RESTAURANT DE 4 ÅRSTIDER (The Four Seasons), Aboulevarden 47. Tel. 86-19-96-96.
  Cuisine: FRENCH. **Reservations:** Required. **Bus:** 24, 52.
$ Prices: Fixed-price meals 225 kroner ($37.80) for a four-course vegetarian meal, 250 kroner ($42.05) for a four-course dinner, 420 kroner ($70.60) for a five-course "surprise" meal; appetizers 78–98 kroner ($13.10–$16.45); main dishes 188–198 kroner ($31.60–$33.30).
  Open: Lunch Mon–Sat noon–2:30pm; dinner Mon–Sat 6–10:30pm. **Closed:** July.

Easily the most charming restaurant in the city center, lying beside the Århus Canal, the property is co-owned by maître d' and artist Ulrik Witt, whose whimsical abstract paintings line paneled walls. His co-owner, Jonna Hald, is probably the best-known female chef in Denmark. Some of the carefully presented specialties include fresh asparagus with foie gras and butter sauce, filet of red snapper with pink peppercorns, lobster with tomato sauce, and succulent preparations of lamb and veal. In the autumn, you can enjoy game dishes, including breast of wild duckling with red wine sauce or fresh wild pheasant with hazelnuts and cream sauce. You can order an apéritif in the lounge amid 19th-century antique chests and comfortable settees.

RESTAURANT MAHLER, Vestergade 39. Tel. 86-19-06-96.
  Cuisine: DANISH/FRENCH. **Reservations:** Required. **Bus:** 7, 10, 17.
$ Prices: Three-course fixed-price dinner 235 kroner ($39.50); appetizers 55–98 kroner ($9.25–$16.45); main dishes 155–185 kroner ($26.05–$31.10). DC, MC, V.
  Open: Dinner Tues–Sat 6pm–midnight. **Closed:** 3 weeks in July.

This pleasant restaurant in the center of town offers a different menu every 2 weeks. You might find sweetbreads, filet mignon, filet of veal with tomato sauce, quenelles of pike-perch in saffron sauce, or partridge with cranberries and stuffed cabbage. On Friday and Saturday nights the chef turns to a particular region of Europe, usually France, and prepares the specialties of that area, perhaps Alsace or the Loire Valley.

MODERATE

FLASKEHALSEN, Østergade 12. Tel. 86-13-99-63.
  Cuisine: DANISH. **Reservations:** Recommended. **Bus:** 2, 6, 17.
$ Prices: Appetizers 35–60 kroner ($5.90–$10.10); main dishes 69–160 kroner ($11.60–$26.90). AE, DC, MC, V.
  Open: Mon–Sat 11:30am–11:30pm.

Motifs of Hans Christian Andersen line the walls at Flaskehalsen, and some of the dishes are named after the Danish writer's adventure stories. Meals are moderately priced. A hearty fish dinner with potatoes and vegetables is the most popular dinner. Enjoy the salad bar—it's one of the best in town.

GULDHORNET, Banegardsplads 10. Tel. 86-12-02-62.
  Cuisine: DANISH/FRENCH. **Reservations:** Recommended. **Bus:** 3, 17, 56, 58.
$ Prices: Three-course fixed-price lunch or dinner 119 kroner ($20); appetizers 34–59 kroner ($5.70–$9.90); main dishes 56–158 kroner ($9.40–$26.55). AE, DC, MC, V.
  Open: Daily 10am–11pm.

Immediately to your left as you exit the Århus Railway Station stands Guldhornet, warm and cozy, with hanging lamps and brightly colored tables. The fixed-price meal is a good value, including, for example, marinated salmon, beefsteak, salad bar, and ice cream. Some French specialties include chateaubriand or pepper steak flambéed in cognac at your table. A Danish specialty worth trying is Guldhornet Sorte Grude, a stew bowl filled with succulent chunks of beef with onions and mushrooms cooked in a thick broth and usually served with rice. The chef also makes Danish hash.

TEATER BODEGA, Skolegade 7. Tel. 86-12-19-17.
 Cuisine: DANISH. **Reservations:** Recommended. **Bus:** 6.
$ **Prices:** Appetizers 27–50 kroner ($4.55–$8.40); main dishes 65–149 kroner ($10.95–$25.05); lunchtime smørrebrød 25–60 kroner ($4.20–$10.10). DC, MC, V.
 Open: Mon–Sat 11am–11:30pm. **Closed:** July.

Originally established at a different address in 1907, Teater Bodega in 1951 moved across the street from both the Århus Dramatic Theater and the Århus Cathedral. It tries to provide an amusing dining ambience for theater and art lovers. The walls are covered with illustrations of theatrical costumes along with other thespian memorabilia. The food is solid and flavorful in the Danish country style. Various kinds of Danish hash, including biksemad, are served along with regular or large portions of Danish roast beef. There's also English and French beef, fried plaice, and flounder.

BUDGET

MUNKESTUEN, Klostertorvet 5. Tel. 86-12-95-67.
 Cuisine: DANISH/INTERNATIONAL. **Reservations:** None. **Bus:** 1, 2, 6, 9.
$ **Prices:** Appetizers 22 kroner ($3.70); main dishes 36–90 kroner ($6.05–$15.35). No credit cards.
 Open: Daily 11am–midnight.

You almost invariably stumble upon this charming old place if you're out sightseeing. This small and cozy inn with a courtyard is in the old Klostertorv across from Frue Kloster Abbey. Dishes depend on seasonal fresh produce. The owner, Lise Poulsen, says she gets inspiration from the culinary traditions of the world, but still cooks everything "the Danish way."

EVENING ENTERTAINMENT

MUSIKHUSET ÅRHUS, Thomas Jensens Allé. Tel. 86-134-344.

Opened in 1982, this concert hall is the home of the Århus Symphony Orchestra, the Danish National Opera, and the Århus Festival. Events range from ballets to musicals to symphony concerts. Programs are presented on the great stage, the small stage, and the cabaret stage, as well as in the amphitheater and on the foyer stages where free performances are held year round. The foyer, open daily from 11am to curtain time, is where the booking office, information desk, café/restaurant, and record and souvenir shops are located. The foyer is open daily from 9am to 11pm. For information, and to purchase tickets, ask in the foyer or at the tourist bureau. Bus: 16, 17.
 Admission: Foyer, free; performances, ticket prices depend on the event.

TIVOLI-FRIHEDEN, Skovbrynet. Tel. 86-14-73-00.

Århus's version of Copenhagen's Tivoli, Tivoli-Friheden has its own particular character. Located in a forest, it is bright and modern, almost like a nighttime fairyland. Entertainment includes an open-air theater, art shows, concerts, and clowns. It's open late April to mid-August, daily from 10am to 11pm. Bus: 4.
 Admission: 20 kroner ($3.35) adults, 10 kroner ($1.70) children.

6. SILKEBORG

27 miles west of Århus, 174 miles west of Copenhagen

GETTING THERE   By Train   Trains run frequently throughout the day between Århus and Silkeborg and between Copenhagen (via Fredericia) and Silkeborg.

By Bus   Frequent buses run daily connecting Silkeborg with Århus.

By Car From Århus, head west along Route 15.

ESSENTIALS The tourist office, **Silkeborg Turistbureau,** is located at Torvet 9, DK-8600 Silkeborg (tel. 86-82-19-11).

The center of the Danish Lake District, it's definitely worth a 1-day jaunt west from Århus to visit the riverside town of Silkeborg. Lying in the midst of some of Denmark's most beautiful scenery, it's a great spot to explore **Himmelbjerget** (Sky Mountain), the highest peak in low-lying Denmark. But be warned: The "mountain" is less than 500 feet high and won't dazzle those who've just come from Norway.

WHAT TO SEE & DO

The most intriguing way to see Sky Mountain and the surrounding countryside is aboard the paddle steamer *Hjejle,* operating since 1861, and sailing frequently in summer. For schedules and information, call **Hjejle Co. Ltd.** (tel. 86-82-07-66).

SILKEBORG CULTURAL MUSEUM, Hovegardsvej 7. Tel. 86-82-14-99.
This 18th-century manor by the Guden River, directly east of Torvet, houses the 2,200-year-old **Tollund Man,** discovered in a peat bog in 1950. His face is considered the most unspoiled of all man's early ancestors. The body was so well preserved, in fact, that scientists were able to determine the contents of his last supper: flax, barley, and oats. His head capped by fur, the Tollund Man was strangled by a plaited leather string—probably the victim of a ritual sacrifice. An equally well preserved body, known as the Elling Girl, was found near the same spot. Scientists estimate she was about 25 years old when she died in 210 B.C.
The museum also has a special exhibition of old Danish glass, a clogmaker's workshop, a collection of stone implements, antique jewelry, and artifacts from the ruins of Silkeborg Castle.
Admission: 15 kroner ($2.50) adults, 5 kroner (85¢) children.
Open: Apr to mid-Oct, daily 10am–5pm; Oct to mid-Apr, Wed and Sat, Sun noon–4pm.

SILKEBORG KUNSTMUSEUM, Gudenavej 7-9. Tel. 86-82-53-88.
This museum offers unique exhibitions, including Asger Jorn's paintings and ceramics.
Admission: 10 kroner ($1.70) adults, free for children.
Open: Apr–Oct, Tues–Sun 10am–5pm; Nov–Mar, Tues–Sun noon–4pm. **Bus:** 10.

NEARBY ATTRACTIONS

The **triangle tour** of three of East Jutland's most attractive manor houses is one of the greatest treasures on the Danish peninsula.

ROSENHOLM SLOT, DK-8543 Hornslet. Tel. 86-99-40-10.
On an islet 13 miles north of Århus and half a mile north of Hornslet, this moated Renaissance manor has been the home of the Rosenkrantzes for 4 centuries. The four-winged castle, encircled by about 35 acres of parkland, houses a Great Hall (its most important room), as well as a large collection of Flemish woven and gilded leather tapestries, old paintings, Spanish furniture, a vaulted gallery walk, and pigskin-bound folios.
Admission: 40 kroner ($6.70) adults, 10 kroner ($1.70) children.
Open: June 20–Aug 5, Mon–Fri 10am–5pm. **Closed:** Aug 6–June 19. **Bus:** 119, 121 from Århus's Central Bus Station.

CLAUSHOLM, Voldum, DK-8370 Hadsten. Tel. 86-49-10-40.
Eight miles southeast of Randers and 19 miles north of Århus, 17th-century Clausholm is a splendid baroque palace—one of the earliest in Denmark. It was

commissioned by King Frederik IV's chancellor, whose teenage daughter, Anna Sophie, married the king. When Frederik died, his son by his first marriage banished the queen to Clausholm, where she lived with her own court until her death in 1743.

The rooms of the castle are basically unaltered since Anna Sophie's day, but few of the original furnishings remain. The salons and ballroom feature elaborate stucco ceilings and decorated panels, and there is an excellent collection of Danish rococo and Empire furnishings that have replaced the original pieces. The Queen's Chapel, where Anna Sophie and her court worshipped, is unchanged and contains the oldest organ in Denmark. In 1976 the Italian baroque gardens were reopened, complete with a symmetrically designed fountain system. Visitors can snack at the cafeteria in the vaulted cellars of the castle.

With sufficient notice, arrangements can be made for a special tour of the castle conducted by one of the owners, followed by either lunch or dinner, served in the elaborate ballroom. Prices are 900 kroner ($151.30) per person. If you arrange for it several months in advance, you may even reserve a concert on the old organ in the chapel, or a chamber-music recital in the grand ballroom.

Admission (including a guided tour): 25 kroner ($4.20) adults, 15 kroner ($2.50) children.

Open: June–Aug 15, daily 11am–5pm; Aug 16–May, Sat 2–5pm, Sun 11am–5pm. **Bus:** 221 from Randers.

GAMMEL ESTRUP, Jyllands Herregårdsmuseum, Randersvej 2, DK-8983 Auning.
This Renaissance manor was owned by two families for 6 centuries, but today it houses the **Jutland Manor House Museum** (tel. 86-48-30-01) in the main building and the **Danish Agricultural Museum** (tel. 86-48-34-44) in the earlier drift buildings. Built on medieval fortified grounds, the origins of Gammel Estrup go back to the 14th century, with major rebuilding of the present structure in the early 1600s. The Manor House Museum, with Great Hall, chapel, and many other rooms, is richly decorated with stucco ceilings, tapestries, and paintings from the 17th and 18th centuries. The Agricultural Museum has tools and machines used over several centuries and a special exhibition showing "the year of the farmer."

Admission: For each museum, 15 kroner ($2.50) adults, 5 kroner (85¢) children.

Open: Apr–Sept, daily 10am–5pm; Oct–Mar, Tues–Sun 11am–3pm. **Directions:** From Silkeborg, take Route 46 northeast to Randers; from there, Route 16 east to Auning. **Bus:** 214.

WHERE TO STAY

The **Silkeborg Turistbureau,** at Torvet 9 (tel. 86-82-19-11), can book you into nearby **private homes.** The office is open Monday through Friday from 9am to 5pm and Saturday from 9am to noon.

SCANDIC HOTEL SILKEBORG, Udgårdsvej 2, DK-8600 Silkeborg. Tel. 86-80-35-33. Fax 86-80-35-06. 117 rms (all with bath). A/C MINIBAR TV TEL **Bus:** 3 from the rail station.
$ Rates (including breakfast): 745 kroner ($125.25) single; 945 kroner ($158.85) double. AE, DC, MC, V.
This is the newest (1990) and largest hotel in Silkeborg, 1½ miles from the town center in a residential neighborhood surrounded by fields and forests. Each room is well furnished and decorated in strong violets, reds, and blues. On the premises are two restaurants, an indoor pool, and a sauna. The most glamorous restaurant, Guldenanden (Golden Duck), is open for lunch and dinner daily, with full meals costing 180 to 250 kroner ($30.25 to $42.05).

HOTEL IMPALA, Vestre Ringvej 53, DK-8600 Silkeborg. Tel. 86-82-03-00. Fax 86-81-40-66. 60 rms (all with bath). MINIBAR TV TEL.
$ Rates: 435–450 kroner ($73.10–$75.65) single; 660–720 kroner ($110.95–$121.05) double. AE, DC, MC, V.
One of the best hotels in the area, the Impala has streamlined rooms with angular

Danish-modern furniture and private balconies. Outside, gardens slope past an artificial pond to the highway. Its rustic core was built as a farmhouse in 1890, and several modern chalet extensions were added in 1975 when it became a hotel. It's located west of Langsø Lake.

Lunch and dinner are served daily in the upstairs dining room to drop-ins as well as to hotel guests. Specialties include braised halibut with spinach and saffron, lemon sole and freshwater crayfish à la nage, turbot and lobster with fines herbes and truffles, breast of duck with cherry sauce, and pepper steak flambé. A full list of European wines is available. Full meals cost from 235 kroner ($39.50).

HOTEL DANIA, Torvet 5, DK-8600 Silkeborg. Tel. 86-82-01-11. Fax 86-80-20-04. 47 rms (all with bath). TV TEL.
$ Rates (including breakfast): 540 kroner ($90.75) single; 685 kroner ($115.15) double. AE, DC, MC, V. **Parking:** Free.

Right on the marketplace and 5 minutes from the railway station, the Dania has been a tradition since it was built in 1848. While antiques fill the corridors and reception lounge, the rooms have been completely renovated in a functional, modern style. Outdoor dining on the square is popular in summer, and the hotel has the longest outdoor restaurant in Denmark, serving typical Danish food along with Scandinavian and French dishes. On Thursday, Friday, and Saturday nights, a bar with disco dancing is popular, and there is live entertainment on Friday and Saturday. Ample free parking is provided.

SVOSTRUP KRO, Svostrupvej 60, Svostrup DK-8600 Silkeborg. Tel. 86-87-70-04. 14 rms (4 with bath). **Bus:** 313 from Silkeborg.
$ Rates: 128 kroner ($21.50) single without bath, 440 kroner ($73.95) single with bath; 340 kroner ($57.15) double without bath, 500 kroner ($84.05) double with bath. Breakfast costs 35 kroner ($5.90) extra. DC, MC, V.

In the center of Svostrup, 6 miles north of Silkeborg, this stylish hotel is a former bargeman's inn built in 1832. Situated on farmland between the Guden River and the Gjern Hills, rooms are comfortable. The inn also has a good restaurant, open daily from 7am to midnight, with meals beginning at 150 kroner ($25.20). The kitchen specializes in fish, including many different preparations of salmon, but also excellent steaks and chateaubriand.

NEARBY ACCOMMODATIONS

In Ry

GAMMEL RYE KRO, Ryesgade 8, Gammel Ry, DK-8680 Ry. Tel. 86-89-80-42. Fax 86-89-85-46. 15 rms (all with bath). TV **Bus:** 311 from Århus.
$ Rates (including breakfast): 385 kroner ($64.70) single; 620 kroner ($104.20) double. DC, MC, V.

This historic inn near the main square of Old (Gammel) Ry is typical of the dozens of unpretentious, simply furnished, but modernized inns of the Jutland countryside. The place looks like a large white farmhouse, set 200 yards north of the village church and the town market square. Its history goes back 400 years to other inns set on the same spot, although Gammel Rye Kro is about 150 years old.

The restaurant offers two-course fixed-price lunches or dinners for 80 kroner ($13.45). Food is served daily from 7am to 11pm. Dishes include such typical Danish specialties as fish filet with béarnaise sauce, local beef with onion, fried eel, and an old-fashioned hash, biksemad.

In Ans

KONGENSBRO KRO, Gamle Kongevej 70, DK-8643 Ans. Tel. 86-87-01-77. 16 rms (all with bath). TEL.
$ Rates (including half board): 450–500 kroner ($75.65–$84.05) per person. AE, DC, MC, V.

This charming place lies between Ans and Århus, about a 10-mile drive north of Silkeborg. Accommodations are pleasantly cozy, and some rooms have TVs.

Since 1949 it has been the property of the Andersens, a family of well-known chefs (matriarch, Else, is the author of five Danish cookbooks). Meals are served daily from noon to 3pm and 6 to 9pm. A midday two-course meal begins at 85 kroner ($14.30). Specialties include frikadeller with red cabbage, quail with a port wine sauce, succulent beef dishes, and locally caught trout in puff pastry with dill sauce.

7. EBELTOFT

33 miles NE of Århus, 209 miles west of Copenhagen

GETTING THERE By Train Go as far as Århus by train, connecting to Copenhagen via Fredericia. At Århus Central Station, board bus no. 123 for Ebeltoft.

By Bus Bus no. 123 runs from Århus to Ebeltoft and Randers.

By Car Take Route 15 northeast from Århus, cutting south onto Route 21.

ESSENTIALS The **Ebeltoft Turistbureau** is at Torvet 9–11 (tel. 86-34-14-00).

A well-preserved town of half-timbered buildings, Ebeltoft ("apple orchard" in English) is the capital of the Mols hill country. This is a village of cobblestone streets, hidden-away lanes, old inns, and ruddy-faced fishermen who still carry on the profession of their ancestors.

WHAT TO SEE & DO

FRIGATE *JYLLAND,* Strandvejen 4. Tel. 86-34-10-99.

The *Jylland,* dating from 1860, is the oldest man-of-war in Denmark and the world's longest wooden ship. The frigate is moored in the harbor.
Admission: 15 kroner ($2.50) adults, 5 kroner (85¢) children.
Open: Apr–Sept, daily 10am–5pm. **Closed:** Oct–Mar.

DET GAMLE RÅDHUS, Torvet. Tel. 86-34-13-82.

The Town Hall looks as if it had been erected just for kindergarten children to play in—don't miss this 1789 building, a museum housing an ethnographical collection from Thailand and an old post office. It's located in the town center north of Strandvejen.
Admission: 10 kroner ($1.70) adults, 5 kroner (85¢) children.
Open: June–Aug, Tues–Sun 10am–5pm; Sept–May, Tues–Sun 11am–3pm.

FARVERGÅRDEN, Adelgade 13-15. Tel. 86-34-13-82.

Dating from 1772, the oldest part of this dyeworks is from 1683. Exhibits include the living quarters with original furniture, the dye facilities with a pressing room, a dye room with boilers, a printing room, and a stable wing with a coach house dating from the early 18th century. It's located directly west of Torvet in the town center.
Admission: 10 kroner ($1.70) adults, 5 kroner (85¢) children.
Open: Mid-May to late May and the first 2 weeks in Sept, daily 11am–3pm; June and Aug, daily 10am–4pm; July, daily 10am–5pm; mid-Sept to Off-season, by special arrangement only.

WHERE TO STAY & DINE

HOTEL HVIDE HUS, Strandgårdshøj 1, DK-8400 Ebeltoft. Tel. 86-34-14-66. Fax 86-34-49-69. 100 rms (all with bath). MINIBAR TV TEL **Bus:** 123 from Århus.

$ Rates (including breakfast): 640 kroner ($107.60) single; 840 kroner ($141.20) double. AE, DC, MC, V.

An elegant establishment built in 1963, the Hvide Hus provides comfortable and well-furnished rooms with terraces, radios, and refrigerators. Recreational facilities include an exercise room, sauna, solarium, swimming pool, and golf course. A nightclub, Molbostuen, is also on the premises, as is a restaurant open until midnight.

HOTEL EBELTOFT STRAND, Nordre Strandvej 3, DK-8400 Ebeltoft. Tel. 86-34-33-00. Fax 86-34-46-36. 68 rms (all with bath). MINIBAR TV TEL **Bus: 123.**

$ Rates (including breakfast): 550 kroner ($92.45) single; 825 kroner ($138.70) double. AE, DC, MC, V.

Centrally located, this late-1970s hostelry has rooms overlooking Ebeltoft Bay. The comfortably furnished bedrooms all have radios, color TVs with hotel video, and balconies or terraces. Facilities include tennis courts, horseback riding, an indoor swimming pool, and a sauna. The hotel also has a restaurant, bar, TV lounge, open fireplace, lobby and sitting lounge, and playground. The location is a 5-minute drive to the ferry and 15 minutes to Tirstrup Airport.

EBELTOFT PARKHOTEL, Vibaek Strandvej 4, DK-8400 Ebeltoft. Tel. 86-34-32-22. Fax 86-34-09-41. 70 rms (all with bath). TEL.

$ Rates (including breakfast): 400 kroner ($67.25) single; 580 kroner ($97.50) double. AE, DC, MC, V.

The Ebeltoft, a hotel built in the 1960s and modernized since then, is about 1,000 feet from a fine, sandy beach, and a brisk 20-minute walk from the Old Town. All rooms have radios and most have TVs. For recreation, use the sauna, swimming pool, and bicycle trainers, or play table tennis and billiards. The hotel has both a bar and a restaurant. As you enter Ebeltoft, the hotel is on the left side at the town entrance.

MOLS KROEN, Hovegaden 16, Femmoller Strand, DK-8400 Ebeltoft. Tel. 86-36-22-00. 25 rms (17 with bath). **Bus:** 123 from Århus.

$ Rates (including breakfast): 240 kroner ($40.35) single without bath, 360 kroner ($60.50) single with bath; 370 kroner ($62.20) double without bath, 565 kroner ($95) double with bath. AE, DC, MC, V.

Combining 1920s nostalgia with modernity, the attractive rooms here have half-canopied beds and some open onto terraces that overlook the Mols Hills. A fine white beach is just 350 feet away.

The hotel restaurant ranks as one of the finest in the area. The staff takes time to present the food with some flourish, and the quality is first class. On a special weekend arrangement, you get 5 o'clock tea, a three-course dinner, a dance, a bed for the night, and a brunch the following morning—all for 395 kroner ($66.40) per person.

---

8. RANDERS

23 miles north of Århus, 200 miles west of Copenhagen

GETTING THERE By Train Trains run hourly between Copenhagen and Randers. There are rail links with Aalborg and Århus.

By Bus There is frequent bus service (no. 118) between Århus and Randers. It takes only 50 minutes to reach Randers from Århus. Bus tickets can be purchased once you board.

By Car Head north from Århus along the E45.

ESSENTIALS The **Randers Tourist Office** (Hellgåndshuset) is at Erik Menveds Plads 1 (tel. 86-42-44-77).

The sixth-largest town in Denmark, with 60,000 inhabitants, Randers was founded at the point where Denmark's longest river, the Gudenå, becomes a natural fjord for the traffic between the northern and southern parts of Denmark.

WHAT TO SEE & DO

As you stroll through the medieval streets and lanes of Randers, you'll see several beautiful, well-preserved half-timbered houses from the 16th and 17th centuries that were originally built by prosperous merchants.

The tourist office, on Erik Menveds Plads, lies in one of the town's most famous buildings, **Helligåndshuset,** or the House of the Holy Ghost. Constructed around 1500 by monks, it was a home for the aged until the Reformation in 1536.

Armed with a map from the tourist office, walk from here along Denmark's first pedestrian street, **Houmeden,** inaugurated in 1963. The half-timbered houses on the north side of the street date from around 1560. You come out at **Town Hall Square,** center of Randers. On the western side of the square is the oldest stone house in Randers, dating from 1468. Town Hall, on the east side of the square, was built in 1778.

Heading east behind Town Hall, continue down Rosengade and Nygade. On the corner is **Fideikommishuset,** constructed in 1833 by Joseph Carl Wulff, a prominent Jew. This was a large Jewish quarter until the 19th century. Nygade 4 is the oldest half-timbered house in Randers, from 1550.

Turn right onto Østervold, which more or less follows the line of the old moat that used to exist in Randers running along the ramparts. At the northern end, Nørrestraede climbs to the town's courthouse and prison. On the corner of Nørrestraede and Østervold is one of the oldest school buildings in Randers, from 1861.

For a final look, visit **St. Mortens Church,** along Kirkegade. Built as the church for the Holy Ghost monastery around 1500, it is considered one of Denmark's most attractive town churches. Note the beautifully carved doors to the main entrance.

If time allows, visit the city's numerous green areas and parks for peaceful walks or jogging. In particular, the **Gudenå Valley** is idyllic.

WHERE TO STAY

HOTEL RANDERS, Torvetgade 11, DK-8900 Randers. Tel. 86-42-34-22.
   Fax 86-40-15-86. 69 rms, 6 suites (all with bath). TV TEL **Bus:** 2, 10, 11.
$ Rates (including breakfast): 500–600 kroner ($84.05–$100.85) single; 645–800 kroner ($108.40–$134.50) double; suites from 1,100 kroner ($184.90). AE, DC, MC, V.

Popular with American tourists, this beautiful, historic 1856 hotel has kept its original charm, combining elegant style and old Danish tradition. American Express awarded the hotel for its fine service. The rooms are tastefully furnished, with radio and video. There are two restaurants and a grill room, serving Danish and international food. The Maritim Bar is a charming rendezvous spot. Services include room service, laundry and dry-cleaning service, and baby-sitting. Car rentals can also be arranged.

MISSIONSHOTEL/RANDERS SØMANDSHJEM, Østervold 42, DK-8900 Randers. Tel. 86-43-77-88. 20 rms (all with bath). TV TEL **Bus:** 2, 10, 11.
$ Rates (including buffet breakfast): 385 kroner ($64.70) single; 620 kroner ($104.20) double. Discounts Fri–Sat nights, 200 kroner ($33.60) per person. AE, DC, MC, V. **Parking:** Available.

In the center of town, a 2-minute walk from the bus station, the shopping district, and the restaurants and sights of Randers, this completely renovated hotel offers bright, well-furnished bedrooms with private baths and views of the harbor. There is a cozy lounge where you can watch TV and video. Private parking is provided for guests.

WHERE TO DINE

HVIDSTEN KRO, Mariagevej 450, Hvidsten, DK-8981 Spentrup. Tel. 86-47-70-22.
   Cuisine: DANISH. **Reservations:** Required in summer. **Bus:** 235.

$ Prices: Fixed-price menu 85–150 kroner ($14.30–$25.20); appetizers 35–55 kroner ($5.90–$9.25); main dishes 45–150 kroner ($7.55–$25.20). DC, MC, V. **Open:** Tues–Sun 11:30am–7:30pm. **Closed:** Sept–May.

A thatched farmhouse between Randers and Mariager, this establishment has doubled as a country inn since 1634, making it one of the oldest in Denmark. The furnishings at the five-room main inn, used only for dining, are memorable: copper, brass, ceramics, samovars, deeply recessed windows, old sea chests, and walls painted with primitive murals. Waitresses wear floor-length, cotton checked kitchen aprons.

For a stopover or for a home-cooked, farm-style meal, Hvidsten Kro is unbeatable. One of the reasons for its fame is its five-course "Gudruns Recipe" meal, which costs only 150 kroner ($25.20). It's possible, too, to order only a half recipe—herring, bacon omelet, and the Dansk koldt bord—for 85 kroner ($14.30), a huge meal in itself.

The bedrooms in the guesthouse out back are bright and clean, but small, containing hot and cold running water. Singles go for 120 kroner ($20.15); doubles are 220 kroner ($37).

9. MARIAGER

36 miles north of Århus, 213 miles west of Copenhagen

GETTING THERE By Train There is no direct train to Mariager. Trains run from Aalborg to Hobro, east of Mariager, every 30 minutes, and trains from Århus to Hobro run hourly. Take the bus from Hobro.

By Bus Buses to Mariager run hourly from Hadsun, Hobro, or Randers. The ride from all three takes about half an hour.

By Car Take the E45 north from Randers and head east at the junction of Route 555.

ESSENTIALS The **Mariager Tourist Association** is located at Torvet 4, DK-9550 Mariager (tel. 98-54-13-77).

WHAT TO SEE & DO

Aalborg-bound motorists with time should stop over at Mariager, "the city of the roses." In a charming setting overlooking Mariager Fjord, the town has quaint cobblestone streets and half-timbered, red-roofed buildings.

Eight miles east of Hobro, at the western end of the Mariager Fjord, Mariager (Maria's Field) is the tiniest town in Denmark. It was only a little fishing hamlet with ferry service on the way between Randers and Aalborg before the founding of the Brigettine Abbey around 1410, after which it became an active commercial and trading center. Many buildings have been preserved from this era, among them the **abbey church,** which may be seen as you walk around the paved streets of the town.

An **18th-century merchant's house,** considered one of the most beautiful buildings in Mariager, houses a museum, art gallery, and parish community center. In the courtyard, there's a well-preserved long gallery.

WHERE TO STAY

If you can't find a hotel room, the Mariager Tourist Association will help book you in a **private home** or boardinghouse.

HOTEL POSTGARDEN, Torvet 6A, DK-9550 Mariager. Tel. 98-54-10-12.
Fax 98-54-24-64. 14 rms (all with bath). TV TEL **Bus:** "Mariager" bus from Randers or Århus.

$ Rates (including breakfast): 395 kroner ($66.40) single; 580 kroner ($97.50) double. AE, DC, MC, V.

If you're passing through Mariager, the road will take you right past the Hotel Postgarden, which looks out onto the marketplace and the small Town Hall. Dating from 1710, this hotel was restored in 1982 and rents out lovely rooms. Locals meet for drinks at the popular hotel pub.

LANDGANGEN, Oxendalen 1, DK-9550 Mariager. Tel. 98-54-11-22. 11 rms (7 with bath).

$ Rates (including breakfast): 250 kroner ($42.05) single without bath, 300 kroner ($50.45) single with bath; 350 kroner ($58.85) double without bath, 420 kroner ($70.60) double with bath. AE, DC, MC, V.

Set beside the river a 5-minute walk north of the cathedral, the white exterior and simple architecture of this building dates from the late 1960s. Rooms are clean and neat, although relatively simple. The ones with private bath also have telephone and TV; the bathless ones do not. The place is even better known as a restaurant, which is open in summer, daily from noon to 9pm, and in winter, Wednesday through Monday from noon to 8pm. Its dining room features Danish specialties and cozy furniture with a view of the water. Full meals range from 150 to 220 kroner ($25.20 to $37).

---

10. AALBORG

69 miles north of Århus, 238 miles west of Copenhagen

GETTING THERE By Plane Aalborg airport, 3 miles from the city center, has many daily connections to Copenhagen.

By Train Twenty trains a day connect Aalborg and Århus, taking 40 minutes. Some 25 connecting daily trains at Århus go to Copenhagen via Fredericia.

By Bus Frequent buses run between Århus and Aalborg. The bus station in Aalborg is the transport center for all of northern Jutland, with buses fanning out in all directions. For all bus information in the area, call **Nordjyllands Trafikselskab** (tel. 98-12-96-12).

ESSENTIALS The **Aalborg Tourist Bureau** is located at Østerågade 8, DK-9000 Aalborg (tel. 98-12-60-22).

The largest city of northern Jutland, Aalborg has a worldwide reputation as a producer of aquavit. Although essentially a shipping town and commercial center, it makes a good base for sightseers, with its many hotels, attractions (a blend of old and new), its more than 200 restaurants, and its nightlife.

History is a living reality in Aalborg. The city was founded 1,000 years ago when the Viking fleets assembled in these parts before sailing on their predatory expeditions. The original atmosphere of Aalborg is preserved in its old streets and alleys. Near the Church of Our Lady are many beautifully restored and reconstructed houses, some of which date from the 16th century.

Denmark's largest forest, **Rold,** where robber-bandits once roamed as they did in Sherwood, is right outside town. Also, **Rebild National Park** is the site of the yearly American Fourth of July celebration.

Not far from Aalborg, on the west coast of northern Jutland, are some of the finest beaches in northern Europe, stretching from Slettestrand to Skagen. The beach-resort towns of **Blokhus** and **Løkken** are especially popular with Danes, Germans, and Swedes. Blokhus is about 18 miles from Aalborg.

WHAT TO SEE & DO

JENS BANG'S STONEHOUSE, Østerågade 9.

This six-floor mansion, built in 1624 in a glittering Renaissance style, once belonged to a wealthy merchant. The historic wine cellar, Duus Vinkjaelder (see "Where to Dine," below), is the meeting place of the Guild of Christian IV. On the ground floor is an old apothecary shop. The mansion itself is still privately owned and is not open to the public.

BUDOLFI KIRKE, Algade.

This elaborately decorated cathedral is dedicated to St. Botolph, patron saint of sailors. Inside the church, which dates from 1500, are unusual pews, paintings from the 16th to the 18th century, Renaissance pulpits, and a baroque font. The spire was built in the 1700s. A carillon sounds daily, every hour from 9am to 10pm.

Admission: Free.

Open: Mon–Fri 9am–3pm, Sat 9am–noon.

NORDJYLLANDS KUNSTMUSEUM (North Jutland Museum of Modern and Contemporary Art), Kong Christians Allé 50. Tel. 98-13-80-88.

The museum building is a prime example of modern Scandinavian architecture. Built from 1968 to 1972, it was designed by Elissa and Alvar Aalto and Jean-Jacques Baruel as a showplace for 20th-century Danish and international art, with changing exhibitions. There are galleries, sculpture gardens, two auditoriums, a children's museum, an outdoor amphitheater, and a restaurant, the Museumscafeen.

Admission: 20 kroner ($3.35) adults, free for students and children.

Open: Mid-May to mid-Sept, daily 10am–5pm; mid-Sept to mid-May, Tues–Sun 10am–5pm.

AALBORG TOWER, Søndre Skovvej, at Skovbakken. Tel. 98-12-01-02.

From this tower rising 325 feet above sea level, there's a perfect view of the city and the fjord.

Admission: 10 kroner ($1.70) adults, 5 kroner (85¢) children.

Open: Apr 12–June 15 and Aug 16–Sept 1, daily 10am–5pm; June 16–Aug 15, daily 10am–7pm. **Closed:** Sept 2–Apr 11.

AALBORG ZOOLOGISKE HAVE, Mølleparkvej 63. Tel. 98-13-07-33.

Mølleparken is a large park with a lookout where you can see most of Aalborg and the Isle of Egholm (look for Roda Reilinger's sculpture *Noah's Ark*). In the park is the second-largest zoo in Scandinavia, where animal specimens from all over the world wander freely in surroundings designed to duplicate an open African range. Apes and beasts of prey are kept under minimal restrictions. There is a good restaurant inside the zoo, and snack bars here and there.

Admission: 36 kroner ($6.05) adults, 20 kroner ($3.35) children 4–12.

Open: Mar–Nov, daily 9am–5pm. **Closed:** Dec–Feb. **Bus:** 8.

MONASTERY OF THE HOLY GHOST, C. W. Obels Plads.

This vine-covered monastery is the oldest social-welfare institution in Denmark, as well as the oldest building in Aalborg, dating back to 1431. The step-gabled monastery, in the heart of the shopping malls, is well preserved. See the refectory, the vaulted storage cellars and "prison," the whitewashed cloisters, and the chapter house with its 16th-century frescoes.

Admission: Guided tour, 10 kroner ($1.70) adults, 5 kroner (85¢) children.

Open: Guided tour, late June to mid-Aug, Mon–Fri at 2pm; mid-Aug to late June, arrangements can be made through the Aalborg Tourist Bureau.

A WATER-SPORTS PARK

WATERLAND, Vandmanden 5. Tel. 98-18-92-00.

Aalborg's 6,600-square-yard indoor water-sports park offers a 650-foot water chute, wave and bubble pools, grottoes, and waterfalls to swim under, plus tideways, fountains, sauna, sunlamps, and an exercise room. An open-air swimming pool heated in winter to between 90°F and 95°F is connected by channels to an indoor pool, so you can swim indoors and outdoors year round. There is also a cafeteria.

Admission: 30 kroner ($5.05) for 1 hour, 50 kroner ($8.40) for 2 hours, 60 kroner ($10.10) for 3 hours.

Open: Mon–Thurs 8am–10pm, Fri–Sat 8am–midnight, Sun 9am–10pm.

AALBORG TOURS

From late June to mid-August you can take an English-language bus tour to see the sights of Greater Aalborg. The 2½-hour tour costs 15 kroner ($2.50) for adults and 5 kroner (85¢) for children. Information and tickets are available at the Aalborg Tourist Bureau, Østerågade 8 (tel. 98-12-60-22).

Another possibility is your English-speaking taxi driver, who will take you past the city highlights. The maximum number of passengers is four and the tour lasts 1½ hours. The price for four people is 375 kroner ($63.05). For details, ask at the Aalborg Tourist Bureau.

NEARBY ATTRACTIONS

The remains of a Viking hamlet and the largest burial site from the Germanic Iron Age (more than 700 cremation graves, including about 150 ship settings) have been excavated at **Lindholm Høje,** near Nørresundby, north of Aalborg. Set in park surroundings, the excavations are open to the public year round. Finds from the site are on view at the **Aalborg Historical Museum,** Algade 48 (tel. 98-12-45-22). The site is open daily from 10am to 5pm; admission is free. Take a 10-minute bus ride (bus no. 1, which leaves every 10 minutes during the day) from the Aalborg town center; then it's a 10-minute walk.

A magnificent Renaissance castle dating from 1588, **Voergård Slot,** Flauenskjold (tel. 98-86-71-08), is filled with sculpture, Louis XVI furnishings, a banqueting hall, grand salon, and works by Goya and Rubens. Admission is 25 kroner ($4.20) for adults, 10 kroner ($1.70) for children. Take the E45 north from Aalborg, cutting east on Route 559 to Dronningland. Follow signs from there. It's open June to August, Monday through Saturday from 2 to 5pm and on Sunday from 10am to 5pm; May to September, Monday through Saturday from 2 to 5pm and on Sunday and holidays from 10am to 5pm; Easter holidays, 10am to 5pm (Easter Eve, 2 to 5pm).

Americans who are in Jutland on the Fourth of July should make a beeline to the **Rebild National Park,** 18 miles south of Aalborg. On these heather dunes, Danes, Danish-Americans, and Americans celebrate American Independence Day. The program often features opera singers, folk dancers, choirs, and glee clubs, together with well-known speakers. In the park is the **Lincoln Memorial Log Cabin and Immigrant Museum,** devoted to mementos of Danish immigration to the United States.

A 1-hour bus ride takes you to the resort town of **Blokhus** and the broad white beaches of the North Sea coast. Not far from here is a 124-acre amusement park, **Fårup Sommerland and Waterpark,** Pirupvejen, DK-9493 Saltum (tel. 08-88-16-00), which offers many possibilities of fun and relaxation for both children and adults. The water park, largest of its kind in Denmark, has wild rivers, a speed slide, a surf hill, and water slides. Admission is 70 kroner ($11.75) for adults or children (children under 4, free). It's open mid-May to August, daily from 10am to 7pm.

WHERE TO STAY

EXPENSIVE

HOTEL PHØNIX, Vesterbro 77, DK-9000 Aalborg. Tel. 98-12-00-11. Fax 98-16-31-66. 185 rms (all with bath). MINIBAR TV TEL **Bus:** 1, 3, 5.
$ **Rates** (including breakfast): 640 kroner ($107.60) single; 930 kroner ($156.35) double. AE, DC, MC, V

This is a first-class hotel in the former residence of 18th-century Brigadier William von Halling, who led a questionable life but had good taste in building and the arts. Many heads of state have stayed in this traditional and comfortable hostelry with a high standard of service. It has several restaurants and bars as well as recreational facilities.

LIMSFORDSHOTELLET, Ved Stranden 14-16, DK-9000 Aalborg. Tel. 98-16-43-33. Fax 98-16-17-47. 180 rms (all with bath). MINIBAR TV TEL **Bus:** 1, 4, 40, 46.

$ Rates (including breakfast): 660–710 kroner ($110.95–$119.35) single; 920 kroner ($154.65) double. AE, DC, MC, V.

With its daring design, this is the most avant-garde hotel in town. It's located near Jomfru Anegade, a street packed with bars and restaurants. In the center of town, within a 3-minute walk east of the cathedral, the hotel opens onto the famous Limsjorden Canal. The public rooms are sparsely furnished with modern, streamlined furniture. The hotel has a handful of bars and restaurants and a sauna. Many of the comfortable bedrooms overlook the harbor. During the lifetime of this edition, the hotel will be expanding with a goal of becoming the largest hotel in Aalborg. In the basement is a piano bar, an autumnal fantasy of warm shades of brown, open from 5pm to 1 or 2am.

SLOTSHOTELLET, Rendsburggade 5, DK-9100 Aalborg. Tel. 98-10-14-00. Fax 98-11-65-70. 144 rms (all with bath). TV TEL **Bus:** 1, 2, 4, 5, 6.

$ Rates (including breakfast): 700 kroner ($117.65) single; 900 kroner ($151.30) double. AE, DC, MC, V.

Stylish and comfortable, this tasteful and well-designed hotel opened in 1986, and it is located a few blocks from the town center within view of the harbor. The hotel lies adjacent to the most important waterway in Aalborg, the Limsjorden Canal, and it is about a 2-minute walk east from the cathedral. There is a café and bar, and the bedrooms are modern, with color TV, radio, and comfortable beds. A large, varied breakfast is served daily. Facilities include a solarium, fitness room, sauna, and table tennis. Handicap facilities are provided. On each floor are ice and shoe-polishing machines.

MODERATE

AALBORG SØMANDSHJEM, Østerbro 27, DK-9000 Aalborg. Tel. 98-12-19-00. Fax 98-11-76-97. 56 rms (47 with bath). TV **Bus:** 1, 3, 7, 8, 13, 19.

$ Rates (including breakfast): 250 kroner ($42.05) single without bath, 400 kroner ($67.25) single with bath; 460 kroner ($77.35) double with shower, 580 kroner ($97.50) double with shower and toilet. AE, DC, MC, V.

The 1956 exterior is functional and businesslike, but the public rooms are simple and welcoming. Rooms are light and airy, but not stylishly decorated, and the bathrooms are small and adequate. The hotel was completely renovated in 1988, and some rooms were equipped with phones. The rooms without bath or shower are small singles. The hotel restaurant does not serve alcohol, but offers a daily two-course lunch or dinner for 55 kroner ($9.25). The hotel is a 20-minute walk east of the railway station on the eastern outskirts of town, close to the Tivoli amusement park.

HOTEL ANSGAR, Prinsensgade 14-16, DK-9000 Aalborg. Tel. 98-13-37-33. Fax 98-16-52-82. 40 rms (30 with bath). MINIBAR TV TEL **Bus:** 2, 12, 54.

$ Rates (including breakfast): 315 kroner ($52.95) single without bath, 470 kroner ($79) single with bath; 500 kroner ($84.05) double without bath, 675 kroner ($113.45) double with bath. AE, DC, MC, V.

Opposite the railway station, this 1906 landmark hotel offers rooms that have recently been redecorated in a light, modern style and include, among other amenities, radios and videos. The hotel has a garden patio, exercise room, sauna, solarium, Jacuzzi, and table tennis. Other than a breakfast room, there is no restaurant, although the hotel has a bar.

PARK HOTEL, Boulevarden 41, DK-9000 Aalborg. Tel. 98-12-31-33. Fax 89-13-31-66. 81 rms (all with bath). TV TEL.
$ **Rates** (including breakfast): 525–625 kroner ($88.25–$105.06) single; 610–730 kroner ($102.55–$122.70) double. AE, DC, MC, V. **Parking:** Available.

The original 18th-century atmosphere has been preserved but the hotel has been carefully modernized throughout the years. Rooms are clean, comfortable, and modern. The hotel also has a restaurant serving both Scandinavian and international food, but the major restaurant street of Aalborg is just a 5-minute walk from the Park. Room service is provided, as is baby-sitting. Facilities include a parking garage and a health club.

NEARBY ACCOMMODATIONS

HOTEL SCHEELSMINDE, Scheelsmindevej 35, DK-9100 Aalborg. Tel. 98-18-32-33. Fax 98-18-33-34. 70 rms (all with bath). TV TEL **Bus:** 4, 6, 41, 42.
$ **Rates** (including breakfast): 550 kroner ($92.45) single; 820 kroner ($137.85) double. AE, DC, MC, V.

This is one of my favorite hotels in the city, and it should appeal to motorists in particular. In classic surroundings, you can escape the noise of Aalborg and wander at leisure through the hotel's large private grounds. Each room is decorated in pastel colors with a light modern decor. Reservations are strongly advised during peak season, because of the hotel's popularity.

You might also like to dine here, since the hotel chef is equally at home with Danish and international specialties. The restaurant was designed with large windows overlooking the park. It is open daily from 11am to 10pm, offering fixed-price meals at 98 kroner ($16.45) for two courses and 125 kroner ($21) for three courses. Facilities include an indoor swimming pool, Jacuzzi, and sauna.

WHERE TO DINE

As previously mentioned, a number of restaurants throughout Denmark, including some in Aalborg, serve a **Danmenu,** a two-course lunch or dinner of traditional Danish food with local specialties, going for around 85 kroner ($14.30). These restaurants are easy to find, identifiable by the special Danmenu sign. **Jomfru Anegade** is perhaps the most famous restaurant street in Denmark. The cooking, I've found, is some of the best in Jutland.

MODERATE

FYRTØJET, Jomfru Anegade 17. Tel. 98-13-73-77.
Cuisine: DANISH/INTERNATIONAL. **Reservations:** Recommended. **Bus:** 1, 3, 5.
$ **Prices:** Appetizers 30–50 kroner ($5.05–$8.40); main dishes 70–140 kroner ($11.75–$23.55). DC, MC, V.
Open: Mon–Sat 11:30am–midnight, Sun 5–11pm.

S A cozy, small restaurant in the center of town, Fyrtøjet serves at outdoor tables in summer. I suggest the almueplatte, a Danish specialty, a so-called peasant's plate, with marinated herring with curry salad, two warm rissoles, cold potato salad and chives, and deep-fried Camembert cheese with blackcurrant jam. Other main dishes include stuffed plaice with shrimp, pepper steak, tournedos béarnaise, salmon cutlet, and breast of duck. A three-course lunch costs from 60 kroner ($10.10).

LAYALINA, Ved Stranden 7. Tel. 98-11-60-56.
Cuisine: LEBANESE/INTERNATIONAL. **Reservations:** Not required. **Bus:** 1, 3, 5.
$ **Prices:** Fixed-price dinner 79–195 kroner ($13.30–$32.80); appetizers 29–69 kroner ($4.85–$11.60); main dishes 69–169 kroner ($11.60–$28.40). AE, DC, MC, V.
Open: Daily 5pm–midnight.

Layalina means "our pleasant nights" in Arabic. Its owners are Lebanese, and they have decorated the restaurant warmly, with Middle Eastern handmade artifacts. Exotic dishes such as shish kebab and hummus are served in an atmosphere of genuine Middle Eastern hospitality. The house special is three brochettes with lamb, meatballs, and spicy sausage, served with rice, Oriental sauce, salad, and fried potatoes.

REGENSEN, Jomfru Anegade 16. Tel. 98-12-59-77.
    Cuisine: DANISH. **Reservations:** Not required. **Bus:** 1, 3, 5.
$ **Prices:** Fixed-price menus 98–218 kroner ($16.45–$36.65). AE, DC, MC, V.
    Open: Daily 11am–1am.

A family-type restaurant a 5-minute walk east of Nytorv, this is a good bet for reasonably priced meals. The cavernous brick dining room is usually lively with a crowd of locals and tourists. The restaurant is housed on the ground level of one of the street's oldest buildings dating from around the turn of the century. The kitchen favors a series of fixed-price meals, always a good value. You are likely to be offered typical Danish fare, including herring, pepper steak flambé, cold roast beef, and the fresh fish of the day. A salad buffet is offered daily.

RESTAURANT CAFEEN AND DUFY, Jomfru Anegade 8. Tel. 98-16-34-44.
    Cuisine: DANISH. **Reservations:** Recommended. **Bus:** 1, 3, 5.
$ **Prices:** Fixed-price meals 59 kroner ($9.90) at lunch, 89 kroner ($14.95) at dinner; appetizers 35–55 kroner ($5.90–$9.25); main dishes 119–150 kroner ($20–$25.20). DC, MC, V.
    Open: Mon–Sat 11:30am–10:30pm, Sun 11:30am–10pm.

The sophisticated decor, attentive service, and superb cuisine make this glistening pair of restaurants the very best on a street crammed with places to eat. The same kitchen prepares the tempting specialties served in the downstairs bistro and in the more formal upstairs restaurant. The menu and prices are the same in both restaurants. Choices might include the best chunky lobster soup in the region, served with sour cream, followed by sautéed Skagen shrimp, fish of the day, fish pâté, chateaubriand with bordelaise sauce, roast breast of duck with madeira sauce, or Dijon-style beef. There's dining on the outdoor terrace in summer.

BUDGET

HOLLES VINSTUE, Algade 57. Tel. 98-13-84-88.
    Cuisine: DANISH. **Reservations:** Not required. **Bus:** 1, 3, 5.
$ **Prices:** Appetizers 20–30 kroner ($3.35–$5.05); main dishes 38–58 kroner ($6.40–$9.75); smørrebrød 19 kroner ($3.20). No credit cards.
    Open: Mon–Fri 10am–midnight, Sat 10am–4pm.

A 4-minute walk west of Nytorv, this is a popular wine bar and restaurant with an inviting atmosphere. The owners sell wine by the bottle or glass, usually French, although many German vintages appear on the list. A glass of house wine costs 18 kroner ($3.05). You can order hefty smørrebrød (open-face sandwiches) to accompany it, or you can ask for more substantial meals, including a wienerschnitzel, various omelets, some Danish stews or hashes, and two fish filets served with french fries.

FOR LIGHT MEALS & SNACKS

DUUS VINKJAELDER, Østeràgade 9. Tel. 98-12-50-56.
    Cuisine: DANISH. **Reservations:** Not required. **Bus:** 1, 3, 5.
$ **Prices:** Snacks 14–37 kroner ($2.35–$6.20); wine by the glass 18 kroner ($3.05). MC, V.
    Open: Mon–Fri 11–1am, Sat 10am–2am.

This old-world 1624 cellar lies beneath one of the most famous private Renaissance mansions (Jens Bang's Stonehouse), a 2-minute walk east of the cathedral. It features a selection of beer and wine (ever had Rainwater Madeira?), but it's a bit skimpy on the food. It's more of a snack restaurant and a wine bar than a full-fledged restaurant.

However, you can order a plate of Danish hash (biksemel), or a burger, perhaps some pâté. Most wines are French.

EVENING ENTERTAINMENT

TIVOLILAND, Karolinelundsvej. Tel. 98-12-33-15.
Tivoliland has lots of snap and sparkle, even though it is a copy of the more famous gardens of Copenhagen. A "China Town" theme park, an open-air stage, good restaurants, a pizzeria, dancing, sing-alongs, Scandinavia's only boomerang roller coaster (with screws and loops both forward and backward), a roundabout vertical ride, and a cinema with a 180° screen are some of the 80 attractions. It's open April to September, daily from 10am to 10pm. Bus: 1, 8, 13, 19.
Admission: 30 kroner ($5.05) adults, 20 kroner ($3.35) children.

DANCING PALACE, Vesterbro 76. Tel. 98-12-62-22.
The closest thing in town to a 1940s dance palace, this complex spreading across three floors is advertised as "the largest of its kind in the city." At street level is a stage with live bands playing popular dance music, where beer costs 22 kroner ($3.70). One flight above is a restaurant, serving international meals costing 160 to 250 kroner ($26.90 to $42.05) in a supper-club atmosphere. The street-level club and restaurant are open on Friday and Saturday from 7:30pm to 2am. The topmost floor is a disco for young people, open Tuesday through Saturday from 7:30pm to 2am. Bus: 1, 3, 5.
Admission: 45–70 kroner ($7.55–$11.75).

---

11. FREDERIKSHAVN

40 miles NE of Aalborg, 238 miles west of Copenhagen

GETTING THERE By Train From Århus, 20 daily trains run north to Frederikshavn, the trip taking 3 hours.

By Bus Frequent buses run between Aalborg and Frederikshavn.

By Car Head north from Aalborg along the E45 to Frederikshavn.

ESSENTIALS The **Frederikshavn Turistbureau,** Brotorvet 1, DK-9900 Frederikshavn (tel. 98-42-32-66), near the ferry dock, is open daily during the summer season from 8:30am to 8:30pm (on Sunday from 8:30 to 11am and 4 to 8:30pm); the rest of the year, Monday through Saturday from 9am to 4pm.

For many, this eastern coastal town is a final stopover in Denmark. Ferry connections with Sweden (Gothenburg) or Norway (Oslo, Moss, and Larvik) make it the gateway city to these other Scandinavian countries. The **Swedish Stena Line** (tel. 98-42-43-66) maintains luxury ferry service with sailings from Frederikshavn to Gothenburg and Oslo.

WHAT TO SEE & DO

BANGSBO MUSEUM, Dronning Margrethsvej 1. Tel. 98-43-31-11.
In a wooded area beside the Deer Park at the edge of town, 18th-century buildings were constructed on the site of a 1364 manor house. The old barn, from 1580, one of the oldest in Denmark, houses antique farm equipment and implements. The main house has a collection of handcrafts made from human hair, a large display of relics from World War II, and a nautical section including ship models, figureheads, and

other mementos. An early medieval ship similar to the vessels used by the Vikings is in one of the stable buildings.

Admission: 15 kroner ($2.50) adults, 5 kroner (85¢) children.

Open: Apr–Oct, daily 10am–5pm; Nov–Mar, Tues–Sun 10am–5pm. **Bus:** 1, 2.

CLOOSTÅRNET, Brønderslevvej. Tel. 98-48-60-69.

Near the Bangsbo Museum, this nearly 200-foot tower west of the town center offers extensive views, and in good weather you can see most of Vendsyssel. An elevator takes you up.

Admission: 10 kroner ($1.70) adults, 2 kroner (35¢) children.

Open: May to mid-June, Mon–Fri 1–6pm, Sat–Sun 10am–6pm; mid-June to mid-Aug, daily 10am–8pm; mid-Aug to late Aug, Tues–Sun 1–6pm. **Closed:** Late Aug to Apr. **Bus:** 210, 225.

WHERE TO STAY

In case you miss the boat and need a room, the **Frederikshavn Turistbureau** (tel. 98-42-32-66) will book you into a private home, from 160 kroner ($26.90) for a double.

EXPENSIVE

FREDERIKSHAVN SØMANDSHJEM, Tordenskjoldsgade 14, DK-9910
Frederikshavn. Tel. 98-42-98-10. Fax 98-43-33-11. 192 rms (all with bath), 23 suites. MINIBAR TV TEL **Bus:** 1, 2.

$ Rates (including breakfast): 850 kroner ($142.90) single; 1,150 kroner ($193.30) double; suites from 1,750 kroner ($294.20). AE, DC, MC, V.

In the center of town, near the pedestrian shopping area and not far from the harbor, this hotel has a heated pool, Jacuzzis, saunas, fitness facilities, and a solarium. It is the largest hotel in Denmark outside Copenhagen, having been constructed near the harbor in 1987. Some units can be converted into three- and four-bed accommodations, suitable for families, and a number of rooms are equipped for handicapped persons. All rooms have hairdryers. Good food is served in the gourmet restaurant, the luncheon room, and the pool coffeeshop. There is also a nightclub on the premises.

HOTEL JUTLANDIA, Havnepladsen 1, DK-9900 Frederikshavn. Tel. 98-42-42-00. Fax 98-42-38-72. 105 rms (all with bath). MINIBAR TV TEL **Bus:** 1, 2.

$ Rates (including breakfast): 650–950 kroner ($109.25–$159.70) single; 880–1,550 kroner ($147.95–$260.55) double. AE, DC, MC, V. **Parking:** Available.

Opposite the harbor, the Jutlandia has a splendid view. The hotel is well managed and maintained. Bedrooms are furnished in contemporary styling, each one comfortable and inviting. Jutlandia also has a good restaurant. Your car will be safe in the locked basement garage.

PARK HOTEL, Jernbanegade 7, DK-9900 Frederikshavn. Tel. 98-42-22-55. Fax 98-42-20-36. 30 rms (17 with bath). TEL **Bus:** 1, 2.

$ Rates (including breakfast): 350 kroner ($58.85) single without bath, 600 kroner ($100.85) single with bath; 600 kroner ($100.85) double without bath, 820 kroner ($137.85) double with bath. AE, DC, MC, V.

An atmospheric choice with a certain charm, this is a member of the Romantic Hotels & Restaurants of Europe built in 1880 in an old French and English style. Many of the handsomely furnished traditional bedrooms have marble bathrooms and a private terrace. Some rooms contain a minibar and TV. The Park is especially noted for its gourmet restaurant, Gastronomen, which serves an international cuisine. Laundry and room service are provided. A swimming pool and health club are next door.

MODERATE

HOFFMANS HOTEL, Tordenskjoldsgade 1, DK-9900 Frederikshavn. Tel. 98-42-21-66. 74 rms (37 with bath). TV TEL **Bus:** 1, 2.

$ Rates (including breakfast): 325 kroner ($54.65) single without bath, 420 kroner ($70.60) single with bath; 520 kroner ($87.40) double without bath, 600 kroner ($100.85) double with bath. AE, DC, MC, V. **Parking:** Available.

In the center of Frederikshavn (the car park at the rear is convenient for ferry departures), rooms here are comfortable and attractively furnished. You can have lunch or dinner in the hotel's cafeteria, open May to September, daily from 8am to 6pm.

HOTEL MARIEHØNEN, Danmarksgade 40, DK-9900 Frederikshavn. Tel. 98-42-01-22. 32 rms (all with bath). TEL **Bus:** 1, 2.

$ Rates (including breakfast): 380 kroner ($63.90) single; 640 kroner ($107.60) double. **Closed:** Sept–May. AE, DC, V.

Right in the heart of Frederikshavn, this is an old but pleasant hostelry. In summer, it receives passengers mainly going to either Oslo or Gothenburg. Rooms are not stylish, but are clean and comfortable. The hotel also operates a good restaurant.

WHERE TO DINE

RESTAURANT VINKAELDEREN, Havnegade 8. Tel. 98-42-02-70.
Cuisine: DANISH. **Reservations:** Not required. **Bus:** 1, 2.
$ Prices: Three-course fixed-price meal 84 kroner ($14.10); appetizers 28–65 kroner ($4.70–$10.95); main dishes 65–160 kroner ($10.95–$26.90). AE, DC, MC, V.
Open: Daily 11am–midnight.

Lying midway between the harbor and the center of town, this restaurant is recognized by its red-brick facade, bull's-eye glass windows, and multiple carriage lamps. Originally established after World War II, it has a warmly rustic coziness enhanced by the racks of European wines on the walls. House wine costs 22 kroner ($3.70) per glass. Fresh fish and Danish beef dishes are a specialty. The fixed-price menu is served day and night.

FLADSTRAND, Rimmensgade 2. Tel. 98-42-24-27.
Cuisine: DANISH. **Reservations:** Not required. **Bus:** 1, 2.
$ Prices: Appetizers 20–35 kroner ($3.35–$5.90); main dishes 40–100 kroner ($6.70–$16.80). No credit cards.
Open: Sun–Thurs 8am–10pm, Fri–Sat 8am–midnight.

Named after the historic center of town, this popular and unpretentious restaurant was established more than 70 years ago. It's a charming and old-fashioned place. The kitchen serves generous portions of hearty fare, including a herring plate, wienerschnitzel, fresh fish, and Danish beef dishes. It feeds a sizable number of city residents at breakfast at 8 each morning, offering bacon and eggs for 45 kroner ($7.55).

12. SKAGEN

25 miles north of Frederikshavn, 303 miles west of Copenhagen

GETTING THERE **By Train** Twelve trains a day depart from Frederikshavn for Skagen, taking 40 minutes.

By Bus Eleven buses a day leave from Frederikshavn for Skagen, taking 1 hour.

By Car Head north from Frederikshavn along the E45.

ESSENTIALS The **Tourist Office** is at Skt. Laurentii Vej 18 (tel. 98-44-13-77). It's open Monday through Saturday from 9am to 5pm.

Skagen is the "Land's End" of Denmark—the far northern stretches of mainland Jutland on its eastern coast. It has been compared to a "bony finger" pointing into the North Sea. Pronounced "skane," Skagen is the second-biggest fishing port in Denmark. In recent years it has attracted a thriving little artists' colony that has done much to enliven the town.

WHAT TO SEE & DO

If you walk to a point of land called **Grenener,** you will be at the top of the continent of mainland Europe and can tip your toes into the Skagerrak and Kattegat seas. Another charming oasis to seek out is **Gammel Skagen,** a little seaside resort set against a backdrop of dunes and sea grass.

SKAGEN MUSEUM, Brøndumsvej. Tel. 98-44-64-44.

The most important attraction of the town, this museum displays the works of local artists, many from the 1930s when Skagen was a thriving art colony. You'll see many paintings by P. S. Krøyer (1851–1909) and Michael Ancher (1849–1909) and Anna Ancher (1859–1935).

Admission: 25 kroner ($4.20) adults, free for children.

Open: Apr and Oct, daily 11am–3pm; May and Sept, daily 10am–5pm; June–Aug, daily 10am–6pm; Nov–Mar, Wed–Fri 1–3pm, Sat–Sun 11am–3pm.

HOME OF MICHAEL AND ANNA ANCHER, Markvej 2. Tel. 98-44-30-09.

You can visit the home of these artists whose work is on display in the Skagen Museum.

Admission: 20 kroner ($3.35) adults, 10 kroner ($1.70) children.

Open: Apr and Oct, daily 11am–3pm; May–June 20 and Aug 16–Sept, daily 10am–5pm; June 21–Aug 15, daily 10am–6pm; Nov–Mar, Sat–Sun 11am–3pm.

WHERE TO STAY & DINE

HOTEL SKAGEN, Gammel Landevej 39, DK-9990, Skagen. Tel. 98-44-22-33. Fax 98-44-21-34. 105 rms (all with bath). TV TEL.

$ Rates (including breakfast): 640 kroner ($107.60) single; 1,000 kroner ($168.10) double. AE, DC, MC, V.

One of the best hotels in the area, it was completely rebuilt after a fire in 1986. Today, better than ever, bedrooms are modern, attractive, and functionally furnished. Each is comfortable and well maintained, drawing mainly a summer business. The hotel also offers a restaurant and bar. It's located beside the main road to the south, a 10-minute walk from the city center.

SKAGEN FISKE RESTAURANT, Fiskehuskaj 13. Tel. 98-44-68-54.

Cuisine: DANISH. **Reservations:** Recommended.

$ Prices: Appetizers 35–85 kroner ($5.90–$14.30); main dishes 55–105 kroner ($9.25–$17.65). No credit cards.

Open: Daily 11am–10pm.

Considered the best in town, this restaurant stands in a row of little, peak-roofed fishermen's cottages at the fish harbor. Here the yachting crowd from Skagen harbor often crowds into the downstairs tavern with its sand-covered floor. Large plates of shrimp are served at bare tables, or you can eat outside in fair weather at picnic tables. Many patrons show up here at happy hour to watch the sunset. At the more formal restaurant upstairs, you can enjoy such dishes as salmon tartare or sea salmon cooked in red wine. In summer, folk singers often entertain.

CHAPTER 11

GETTING TO KNOW NORWAY

Land of the midnight sun and glacier-born fjords, Norway is a special experience.

The name Norway (in Norwegian, Norge or Noreg) is derived from *Nordvegr,* meaning "the way of the north." The term was used by the Vikings more than 1,000 years ago for the shipping route along the Norwegian west coast. For the 4 million Norwegians—seafarers since the dawn of history— it seems natural to give the country a nautical name.

To the ancients, Norway was a mythical land. A journey to it was laden with unspeakable perils. Writers called the mythical land Ultima Thule, and feared that it was inhabited by strange, barbaric, even fabulous creatures. In the 4th century B.C. the Greek writer Pytheas thought the laws of nature did not apply there, claiming that everything—water, earth—floated in mid-air. Herodotus claimed that in Norway feathers were constantly being blown into one's face and that feathers covered everything—an early attempt perhaps to describe a snowstorm.

Norway is a land of tradition, as exemplified by its rustic stave churches and folk dances stepped to the airs of a fiddler. But Norway is also modern. It is a technologically advanced nation, rich in petroleum and hydroelectric energy. Norwegians also enjoy a well-developed public system of social insurance, comprising old-age pensions, health insurance, unemployment insurance, and rehabilitation assistance. The system is financed by contributions from the insured, which makes Norway one of the most heavily taxed nations on earth.

One of the last great natural frontiers of the world, Norway invites exploration, with its steep and jagged fjords, salmon-teeming rivers, glaciers, mountains, and meadows. In winter the shimmering aurora borealis is the lure, giving way to the midnight sun of summer.

1. GEOGRAPHY, HISTORY & POLITICS

GEOGRAPHY

Norway measures some 1,100 miles in length, but it is an extremely narrow mountainous country: 70% of the land is covered by mountains, glaciers, lakes, and wasteland, and less than 4% of the territory is arable. In the Jotunheimen

NORWAY
N
0
150 km
93 mi
Arctic Ocean
North Cape
Honningsvåg
Vardø
Vadsø
Hammerfest
Kirkenes
Lakselv
Alta
E6
Karasjok
Norwegian Sea
Tromsø
Kautokeino
Lofoten Islands
Harstad
Narvik
Bjorkliden
Kiruna
FINLAND
Atlantic Ocean
Bodø
ARCTIC CIRCLE
Luleå
NORWAY
SWEDEN
Gulf of Botbnia
Umea
Kristiansund
Trondheim
Røros
Sundsvall
Molde
Andalsnes
Oppdal
Dovrefjeld Mountains
Geiranger
E69
Alesund
Seljestad
Fjaerland
Jostedal Glacier
Beitostølen
Lillehammer
Gävle
Balestrand
Solvorn
Gjøvik
E68
Flåm
Voss
Ulvik
Glittertind Mountains
Uppsala
Lofthus
Bergen
Eidfjord
Geilo
Utne
OSLO
STOCKHOLM
Kinsarvik
Karlstad
Hardanger Mountains
Sandefjord
Skara
Fredrikstad
Stavanger
Gotland
E18
Gothenburg

?DID YOU KNOW . . . ?

- Norwegians have one of the highest per capita incomes in the world.
- While medieval alchemists were trying to make gold, they instead discovered *akevitt* (aquavit, or schnapps), the national "firewater" of Norway.
- Norway has the world's largest foreign trade per capita.
- The average population density of Norway is only 13 inhabitants per square kilometer, compared to 96 for Europe as a whole.
- Norway, sharing a 1,055-mile border with the Soviet Union, disputes control of a sea area the size of Belgium, Switzerland, and Austria combined.
- Hammerfest in northern Norway is the northernmost town in the world.
- More people of Norwegian descent (five million) live in the United States than in Norway itself.

range in south-central Norway are the highest mountain peaks in Europe north of the Alps. The country has some 1,700 glaciers. Along the coast a string of about 50,000 islands shelter the mainland against the worst effects of Atlantic storms. The largest tracts of agricultural land are found in south-central Norway: north and south of Oslo, south of the city of Stavanger on the west coast, around the Trondheim fjord in central Norway, and also in the country of Troms in the far north.

WESTERN NORWAY   Western Norway is fabled for its fjords. A fjord is a saltwater arm of the sea, stretching inland, and many date from the end of the Ice Age. Some fjords cut their way into mountain ranges as high as 3,300 feet. The longest fjord in western Norway is the **Sognefjord,** north of Bergen, winding its way 110 miles inland. Other major fjords in the district are Nordfjord, Geirangerfjord, and Hardangerfjord. The capital of the fjord district is **Bergen,** the second-largest city in Norway but the largest on the west coast. It is the best starting point for trips through the fjord district.

CENTRAL NORWAY   Fjords are also common in central Norway, the largest being **Trondheimsfjord** and **Narnsfjord.** It's not unusual for roads to pass waterfalls that cascade straight down into the fjords. Central Norway is filled with many thick forests and snow-capped peaks. **Trondheim** is its largest city and the most interesting in Norway to visit after Oslo and Bergen. **Ålesund** is also a tourist center with its own charm, as is **Molde.** Both are good centers for exploring the district.

EASTERN NORWAY   Eastern Norway, bordering Sweden, has gentler land than the west. It is characterized by its clear blue lakes, rolling hills, and green valleys. In some ways it's the most traditional part of the country. It contains many fertile valleys, and, because of that, was one of the first to be populated. Some of the biggest valleys are Valdres, Osterdal, Hallingdal, Numedal, and Gudbrandsdalen. Campers and hikers in summer frequent the great forests of the Hedmark region, site of Norway's longest river, the Glomma, flowing for some 360 miles. Many ski resorts are found in the area, none more notable than **Geilo** and **Lillehammer,** the latter the scheduled site of the 1994 Olympics. Of course, the greatest attraction of Norway—and its most visited destination—is the capital, **Oslo,** rising from the shores of Oslofjord. But much, much more about that later.

SOUTHERN NORWAY   Southern Norway is sometimes called the Riviera of Norway, because of its unspoiled and uncrowded beaches. It's also a favorite port of call for the yachting crowd. **Stavanger** is the largest city of southern Norway, and also the most visited. But there is much more to explore in this Telemark region, which is filled with lakes and canals used for canoeing and boating in summer. In **Skien,** lake steamers are boarded for trips on an inland series of canals. The southern

IMPRESSIONS

I would not enter Norway again for all the firs in Scandinavia. The blight of temperance has settled on the place.
—ARCHER GRANT OF STROUD, GLOUCESTERSHIRE, 1912.

November always seemed to me the Norway of the year.
—EMILY DICKINSON, 1864.

---

part of **Kristiansand** is a link between Norway and continental Europe. Ferries from abroad dock here. In the area is **Hamresanden Beach,** stretching for 6 miles, one of the longest stretches of uninterrupted beachfront in Europe. Along the western half of the district are found more fjords, notably Lysefjord, Sandefjord, and Vindefjord.

NORTHERN NORWAY Northern Norway, the "Land of the Midnight Sun," lies near the top of the earth. It's a region of craggy cliffs that soar down into the sea and of deep fertile valleys along with deserted moors. It has islands with sparse, if any, population where life has remained unchanged for generations. The capital of the Nordland region is **Bodø,** a base for Arctic fishing trips and visits to the wild Glomfjord whose glacier water is chilled year round. Norway's second-largest glacier, Svartisen, is also in this region, as is the city of **Narvik,** a major Arctic port and the gateway to the Lofoten islands, which are filled with fishing villages.

TROMS The main city in the region of Troms is **Tromsø,** from which polar explorations are launched. Troms contains one of Norway's most impressive mountain ranges, the **Lyngs Alps,** drawing skiers in winter and hikers in summer.

FINNMARK At the very top of Norway is the Finnmark region, home of the Samis or Lapps. Centers here include the Lapp town of **Kautokeino** and **Hammerfest,** the northernmost city of the world. Most tourists visit Finnmark to see the **North Cape,** the northernmost point in Europe and an ideal viewing spot for the Midnight Sun.

HISTORY

Norway has been inhabited since around 14,000 B.C., the first people appearing as the ice sheets melted over Scandinavia. The early settlers hunted reindeer and other game in these northern lands. Some 5,000 to 6,000 years ago, settlers turned to agriculture, especially around the Oslofjord. In the Roman era, there were links to the countries of the south, as unearthed artifacts have disclosed.

THE AGE OF THE VIKINGS Prehistory came to an end during the Viking era, roughly 800 to 1050 A.D. Much of what is known about this era wasn't written down, but has been revealed through sagas passed by word of mouth or by archeological digs. Some scholars date the looting of the Lindisfarne monastery in northern England in 793 as the beginning of the "age of the Vikings."

"The Vikings are coming!" became a dreadful cry along the coastlines of Europe. The victims expected fire and

DATELINE

• **800–1050** The age of the Vikings, when Norsemen terrorized European coastlines.

• **872** Harald Fairhair conquers many small provinces and reigns as first king.

• **1001** Leif Eriksson discovers America (or so the sagas claim).

• **1030** Christianity is firmly estab-

(continues)

182 • NORWAY

DATELINE

- lished; Olaf II is declared a saint.
- **1066** The Viking age ends with the defeat of King Harald III in England.
- **1350** The Black Death wipes out much of the population.
- **1397** Margaret becomes Queen of Norway, Denmark, and Sweden at the Union of Kalmar.
- **1439** Danish rule is imposed on Norway.
- **1814** Norway breaks from Denmark and adopts a constitution, but comes under Swedish rule.
- **1905** The Norwegian parliament breaks from Sweden and declares independence.
- **1914** Norway declares its neutrality in World War I.
- **1920** Norway joins the League of Nations, ending isolation.
- **1940** Nazi troops invade Norway; the king and government flee.
- **1945** Norway regains independence and executes its Nazi puppet ruler Quisling.
- **1960s** Oil boom hits Norway.
- **1986** Labor party votes first woman prime minister, who names seven women to her 18-member cabinet.

(continues)

sword. Scandinavian historians are usually kinder to the Vikings, citing the fact they often came to trade and colonize. From Norway, the Vikings branched out to settle in the Orkney and Shetland Islands (now part of Scotland). They also settled in the Scottish Hebrides and on the Isle of Man. Settlements were made on Greenland and Iceland, which the Vikings found uninhabited. Norse communities on Greenland eventually died out. The sagas claim that Leif Eriksson discovered "wineland of the good" in 1001, a reference to the American continent. Many scholars, however, claimed that Vikings in their seaworthy long ships navigated to America long before Leif Eriksson. The end of the Viking age was said to have come in 1066, when King Harald III of Norway lost the Battle of Stamford Bridge in England.

The road to unifying Norway was rough. In 872 Harald Fairhair, winning a battle near Stavanger, conquered many of the provinces of Norway, but other battles for unification would take decades. Harald was followed by his son, Eric I, or "Bloddy Axe" as his enemies called him. Eric began his reign by assassinating two of his eight brothers. He later killed five other brothers, leaving only one, before he himself died in Cumberland (England) in 954. Eric was followed by his brother, Haakon, who became king. Haakon tried to convert Norwegians to Christianity but did not succeed. Eric's sons schemed to capture Haakon so that one of them could become king. The rulers of Denmark aided the heirs and Haakon died in 960 in the Battle of Fitjar. Harald II Graafell, one of Eric's sons, became king of Norway. Cruel and oppressive, he died in a battle in 970.

Haakon, son of Sigurd of Lade, next became king of Norway. He resisted Danish attacks and ruled for around 25 years, dying in a peasant riot in 995. He was followed by Olaf I Trygvasson, who continued the spread of Christianity throughout Norway, trying to convert Greenland and Iceland as well. At war with Denmark, he died in the battle of Swold in 1000, and Norway was divided between Denmark and the Jarl of Lade.

Olaf II Haraldsson was a Viking until 1015, when he became king of all Norway. Although oppressive and often cruel, he continued the spread of Christianity. Canute of Denmark invaded Norway in 1028, sending Olaf fleeing to England. Upon his return in 1030, he died in the Battle of Stirklestad. Canute's son, Sweyn, ruled Norway from 1028 to 1035. Sweyn was forced out when Olaf II was proclaimed a saint and his son, Magnus I, was made king. Magnus was also king of Denmark, a position he lost when Canute's nephew led a revolt against him and was killed. With the sainthood of Olaf, Christianity was firmly established in Norway.

Harald Sigurdsson ruled Norway from 1046, known as Harald III. He was king of Norway and Denmark, but died in 1066, at the close of the Viking age.

THE MIDDLE AGES Kings came and went, winning and losing battles, dying on the field. Wars with Denmark continued, and civil wars raged from 1130 to 1227. But through it all, towns and the church continued to grow. Under King Haakon V in the 13th century, Oslo became the capital of Norway. The Black Death reached Norway in 1350 and wiped out much of the population.

From 1319 to 1343 Norway and Sweden had a joint monarch, Haakon VI (1340–80), son of the Swedish king, Magnus Eriksson. Haakon was the lawful heir to the throne of Norway. He married Margaret, daughter of Danish king Valdemar Atterdag. Their son, Olaf, was chosen to be the Danish king upon the death of Valdemar in 1375. He inherited the throne of Norway after his father died in 1380, thus bringing Norway into a union with Denmark. This union was to last until 1814.

DATELINE

• **1989** Center-right coalition regains power.
• **1990** Ms. Brundtland becomes prime minister once again.

UNION WITH DENMARK   Olaf died at the age of 17, and Margaret ruled as regent of Norway, Denmark, and Sweden. She ruled through her nephew, Eric of Pomerania, who had become king of Norway in 1389. He was recognized as a joint ruler at Kalmar. Margaret, however, actually ruled the country until her death in 1412.

Eric of Pomerania tried to continue to rule the three countries, but Sweden and Norway rebelled. Eric fled in 1439 and Christopher III of Bavaria became the ruler, imposing Danish rule over Norway.

Norway slowly disintegrated under Danish rule. Denmark led Norway into the Seven Years' War in 1563, and took unfair advantage of its position in trade, in the military, even in surrendering Norwegian land to Sweden. In the Napoleonic wars, from 1807 to 1814, Denmark and Norway were allied with France, although this brought them much economic hardship. Famine was widespread.

By 1813 Sweden wanted to take Norway, having lost Finland to the Russian tsar in the east. In 1814 Frederik VI surrendered to the allies against Napoleon and handed Norway over to his Swedish opponents. That officially ended 434 years of Danish rule.

SECESSION FROM DENMARK   On May 17, 1814, at a meeting at Eidsvoll, an assembly adopted a constitution and chose Christian Frederik as the Norwegian king. May 17, to this day, is celebrated as the Norwegian national day. The Swedes objected and launched a military campaign, eventually subduing the Norwegians. The Swedes accepted the Norwegian constitution, but only within a union of the two kingdoms. Christian Frederik fled.

In the immediate years to come, Norway suffered through one of its greatest depressions. Norway's parliamentary assembly, the Storting, engaged in repeated conflicts with Swedish monarchs. Bernadotte ruled over both Norway and Sweden as King Charles XIV in 1818.

By the 1830s the economy of Norway had improved. The first railway line was laid in 1854. Its merchant fleet drastically increased between 1850 and 1880.

From the 1880s on, the Liberals in the Norwegian Storting brought much-needed reform to the country. But by the end of the century the conflict with Sweden was growing, as more and more Norwegians demanded independence.

In August 1905 the Storting decided to dissolve the union with Sweden. Sweden agreed to let Norway rule itself. In October 1905 an election took place in Norway and the son of Denmark's king was proclaimed king of Norway. He chose the name Haakon VII.

AN INDEPENDENT NORWAY   Free at last, Norway enjoyed peace and prosper-

---

IMPRESSIONS

Norway is a hard country: hard to know, hard to shoot over, and hard—very hard—to fall down on: but hard to forsake and harder to forget.
—J. A. LEES, *PEAKS AND PINES, ANOTHER NORWAY BOOK, 1899.*

ity until the beginning of World War I. Even though the economy was progressing, thousands of Norwegians emigrated to the United States around the turn of the century. In 1914 Norway joined with Sweden and Denmark in declaring a policy of neutrality. Despite this declaration, around 2,000 Norwegian seamen lost their lives in World War I because of submarine attacks and underwater mines.

In 1920 Norway became a member of the League of Nations, ending its policy of isolation. At the outbreak of World War II, Norway again declared its neutrality. Nonetheless, Allied forces mined Norway's waters in 1940, and the Nazis attacked on April 9, 1940. Great Britain and France provided some military assistance, but Norway fell after a 2-month struggle. The government and the royal family fled into exile in England. With them they brought 1,000 ships of the Norwegian merchant fleet. In spite of the resistance movement, Norway was occupied until the end of the war in 1945, with Vidkun Quisling, the Norwegian minister of defense in the 1930s, serving the Nazis as leader of the puppet government.

Quisling was executed following the Nazi retreat from Norway. On June 7 of that year the government in exile returned from Britain. The retreating Germans had followed a scorched-earth policy in Finnmark, destroying almost everything of value. In the late 1940s Norway began to rebuild its shattered economy.

After an abortive attempt to form a Nordic defense alliance, Norway, along with Denmark, joined NATO in 1949. The Communist party tried to gain influence in Norway, but failed.

By the 1960s oil prospecting in the North Sea had yielded rich finds; this resulted in a profound restructuring of Norwegian trade and industry. In 1972 Norway voted not to enter the Common Market, following a bitter political dispute.

Norway had a nonsocialist government from 1981 to 1986. In 1986 Labor party leader Gro Harlem Brundtland headed a minority government as Norway's first female prime minister, and introduced seven women into her 18-member cabinet. Soon, however, tumbling oil prices and the subsequent unemployment that it brought led to a recession. The Labor government lost the 1989 elections. A center-right coalition took over the government, composed of the Center party, Conservatives, and the Christian Democrats.

However, in November of 1990, Ms. Brundtland was returned to office as prime minister, this time with nine women in her 19-member cabinet.

Today the government of Norway faces problems familiar in many parts of the world: violent crime, drugs, immigration control, unemployment, and acid rain and pollution, much of it coming from Great Britain. Concern about acid rain and pollution from Britain was so severe that a 1987 visit from Margaret Thatcher brought out the riot police.

New elections are slated for 1993, as EC membership continues to be a burning issue.

POLITICS

Norway is a constitutional monarchy, with the 150-member National Assembly (Storting) exercising legislative power. But the country is in the vanguard of the advanced socialized nations, with compulsory national insurance, old-age pensions, unemployment insurance, family allowances, and holidays with pay for all workers.

2. FAMOUS NORWEGIANS

Bjørnstjerne Bjørnson (1832–1910) A great Norwegian writer, he wrote many folk tales that inspired Henrik Ibsen. In 1857, he took over Ibsen's job as director of the Bergen Theater. His historical plays brought him world acclaim, and he became radically involved in Norwegian nationalism, campaigning for an independent

IMPRESSIONS

I know the Norwegians from Illinois, and I know that no immigrants have advanced America more than they.
—ABRAHAM LINCOLN

country. One of his poems became the national anthem of Norway, *Ja, vi elsker dette landet* (Yes, I Love This Land). He won the Nobel Prize in 1903.

Kirsten Flagstad (1895–1962) This great Wagnerian singer in the history of opera was born in Hagmar, Norway. Her 1933 performance at the Wagner Festival in Bayreuth, Germany brought her world acclaim. She made her debut at the Metropolitan Opera House in New York City in 1935 as Sieglinde in *Die Walküre.*

Edvard Grieg (1843–1907) "The Chopin of the North." Norway's national composer who adapted themes from folk music in *Peer Gynt Suite* for example. Born in Bergen to an English father and Norwegian mother.

Knut Hamsun (1859–1952) At age 19, in 1888, a Danish magazine published a portion of his novel, *Hunger.* This novel, along with *Growth of the Soil* and *The Women at the Well,* earned him international fame. In 1920 he won the Nobel Prize for literature.

Thor Heyerdahl (1914–   ) This ethnologist began in 1937 the first expedition in the Pacific. In 1947, he led the celebrated *Kon-Tiki* expedition from Peru to Polynesia, and in 1951 won an Academy Award for his documentary (see the Kon-Tiki Museum in Chapter 14). In 1969 and 1970, he led two *Ra* expeditions. Many of his books have become bestsellers, including *Aku Aku,* a study of Easter Island translated into 32 languages.

Sigurd Hoel (1890–1960) Writer whose best known work is *One Day in October* (1931).

Henrik Ibsen (1828–1906) Great modernist-realist playwright. Author of *A Doll's House, Hedda Gabler, The Mater Builder,* and *Peer Gynt.*

Trygve Lie (1896–1968) A leading labor party lawyer and politician, in 1940 Lie was named foreign minister of a Norwegian government in exile during the Nazi occupation. In 1946, he was elected Secretary-General of the United Nations for five years. In 1950 he undertook a "great peace mission," and also supported the United Nations effort to send troops to Korea. In 1951, his term was extended as Secretary-General, but he resigned because of continuous Soviet refusal to recognize him.

Edvard Munch (1863–1944) The greatest Scandinavian painter. His famous works include the gut-wrenching *The Cry* (1985) and *The Bridge* (1901). See his murals at Oslo University.

Fridtjof Nansen (1861–1930) A great world explorer, he dreamed of crossing the ice caps of Greenland, a remarkable feat that brought him glory in 1889. He led the Norwegian delegation to the first assembly of the League of Nations in 1920, and in 1922 was awarded the Nobel Peace Prize for his work repatriating prisoners of war.

Liv Ullmann (1938–   ) The most famous Norwegian actress made her stage debut in 1957, and became known in the 1960s for her work with the National Theater. World acclaim came through her roles in the films of Ingmar Bergman, her lover at the time. These included *Cries and Whispers, Scenes from a Marriage,* and *Persona.* She's appeared on Broadway and has written two volumes of impressionistic memoirs.

Sigrid Undset (1882–1949) Writer. *Kristen Lavransdatter* is considered her masterpiece.

Adolf Gustav Vigeland (1869–1943) Sculptor whose monumental works are one of Oslo's major sights. A controversial artist—some claim a genius, others a madman. See the obelisk in Frognerpark.

3. SPORTS & RECREATION

BICYCLING Bikes can be rented virtually anywhere in Norway. Inquire at your hotel or the local tourist office. The Norwegian Mountain Touring Association (see "Hiking," below, for address) provides inexpensive lodging for people taking overnight bike trips. For suggestions of tours, maps, and brochures, contact **Skylistenes Landsforening,** Majorstuveien 20, N-0367 Oslo 3 (tel. 02/44-27-31).

CANOEING/KAYAKING/RAFTING There are thousands of lakes, streams, and rivers in Norway suitable for these activities. Canoeing under the Midnight Sun in northern Norway is particularly popular. Canoe tours are arranged by the **Norwegian Youth Hostel Association,** Dronningensgaten 26, N-0154 Oslo 1 (tel. 02/42-14-10).

DIVING Excellent diving centers provide diving trips, instruction, and rental of equipment. Divers into harpooning often catch their own dinner, with many kinds of fish from which to make a selection. Conditions for submarine photography are generally good, with an underwater visibility of 30 to 100 feet. Many shipwrecks are found along Norway's extensive coastline and fjords. Diving vacation packages are provided by **Barmanns Dykkesenter,** Langveien 72B, N-6500 Kristiansund N (tel. 073/71-649).

FISHING Norway is long famous for its grand salmon and trout fishing. The main season for salmon fishing lasts from June to August, though June and July are the best months. Sea trout fishing takes place from June to September, but is best in August. The season for brown trout fishing varies with altitude.

People 16 years of age or older must purchase a fishing license for 60 kroner ($9.95). National fishing licenses can be purchased at local post offices; fishing in the ocean is free.

Some companies even arrange fishing tours in Norway, including **Passage Tours of Scandinavia.** (Tel. toll free 800/548-5960 in the U.S. for more information.)

GOLF Many golf clubs in Norway open their greens to foreign guests. Unlike some countries, greens fees in Norway tend to be moderate. Clubs include the **Oslo Golf Club** (18 holes) at Bogstad, Oslo (tel. 02/50-44-02), and the **Bergen Golf Club** (9 holes), Aastvedt, Ovre Ervik, at Bergen (tel. 05/18-20-77).

IMPRESSIONS

I have saved the world from a mediocre painter and given the world a literary genius.
—HENRIK IBSEN'S WIFE

Only when you see the provincialism of Oslo do you appreciate the wonderfulness of Ibsen.
—ARNOLD BENNETT, *JOURNAL 1929*

IMPRESSIONS

People shall be made to understand the greatness of my art; when facing it, they shall learn to remove their hats, as if in a cathedral.
—EDVARD MUNCH

HIKING Much of Norway is made up of mountains and wilderness, so hiking is a favorite pastime, enjoyed by the Norwegians themselves as much as visitors. The Norwegian Mountain Touring Association provides guided hikes lasting from 1 to 2 weeks. Of course, hikes are for people in at least average physical condition. The cost for a 1-week hiking tour, including meals and overnight stays, ranges from 2,400 to 3,000 kroner ($398.15 to $497.70). More information is available from the **Norwegian Mountain Touring Association,** Box 1963 Vika, N-0125 Oslo 1 (tel. 02/41-80-20).

HORSEBACK RIDING Many companies offer tours of Norway's wilderness, taking in some of its more spectacular natural scenes. These can range from a few hours to a full week, and they're available all over Norway. Luggage is transported by car. Some of the candidates that offer such tours are **Norefjell Hestesenter,** Dynge Gård, N-3516 Noresund (tel. 067/46-184), and **Dyrhaugs Ridesenter,** N-7590 Tydal (tel. 07/81-53-82).

SAILING In summer, the long coast of Norway can be a yachting person's challenge. The most tranquil havens are along the southern coast. For information on yacht and sailboat rentals, contact local tourist offices or the **Norway Yacht Charter,** Postboks 91-Sentrum, N-0101 Oslo 1 (tel. 02/42-64-98).

SKIING Norway's skiing terrain is among the best in the world. The optimum times for skiing are in February and March (the first 2 weeks in April are usually good also). Two of the principal resorts, **Geilo** and **Voss,** lie on the Oslo–Bergen rail line. The most famous and easily accessible resort is **Lillehammer,** north of Oslo. In and around the Norwegian capital skiing is common; the deservedly famed ski jump, **Holmenkollen,** with its companion ski museum, is minutes from the heart of Oslo. The yearly ski championship here in March draws ace skiers from all over Europe and North America.

Norwegian ski resorts are known for their informality, evident both in the ski schools and in the atmosphere. Simple folklore and hearty good fun replace the sophisticated après-ski life often found in alpine resorts. Incidentally, "ski" is an Old Norse word, as is "slalom."

A great part of the Norwegian skiing is cross country, perfect for the amateur. But there is plentiful terrain for the more skilled. Curling, sleigh rides, and skating also are popular winter sports. All major centers have ski lifts, and equipment in Norway is much cheaper to rent than it is in luxury resorts like St. Moritz.

Skiing is not only a winter sport in Norway. Summer skiing, both downhill and cross country, normally takes place at summer ski centers near glaciers. Several establishments provide information about this type of skiing. They include **Galdhopiggen,** Sommerskisenter, N-2687 Boverdalen (tel. 062/12-142), and **Vargebreen Sommarski,** N-5727 Jondal (tel. 056/33-220).

---

4. FOOD & DRINK

FOOD

MEALS & DINING CUSTOMS Most working Norwegians seldom eat lunch, grabbing a quick open-face sandwich, or smørbrød, at their offices. But in major towns and cities, lunch is generally served from 1 to 3pm. The *middag,* the main meal of the day, is generally eaten between 4:30 and 6pm. Many restaurants serve this popular middag from 1 to 8pm. In late-closing restaurants it's possible to dine much later, until around midnight in Oslo. Long after middag time a Norwegian family will have *aftens,* a smørbrød supper that will see them through the night.

THE CUISINE   The chief criticism leveled against Norwegian cooking is that it's too bland. The food is always abundant (the Norwegians are known for their second helpings), substantial, and well prepared—but no threat to the French for a Cordon Bleu prize.

Norwegians are proud—and rightly so—of many of their tempting specialties, ranging from **boiled cod** (believe it or not, this is considered a delicacy) to reindeer steak smothered in brown gravy and accompanied by tart little lingonberries (which resemble wild cranberries).

Norway relies on fish, both freshwater and saltwater, for much of its food supply. Prepared in countless ways, fish is usually well cooked—and always fresh, a good bet indeed. Try, in particular, the aforementioned boiled cod; it's always—but always—served with boiled potatoes.

In early summer, **kokt laks** (boiled salmon) is a highly rated delicacy. **Kreps** (crayfish) is another big production as it is in Finland, and **ørret** (mountain trout), preferably broiled and served with fresh lemon, is a guaranteed treat. A recommendation for top-notch fare: **fiske-gratin** (fish soufflé), delicately seasoned.

Norwegians love their fatty smoked eel (**røket al**), although many foreigners have a tendency to whip by this one on the smörgåsbord table. The national appetizer is brine-cured herring with raw onions.

You may want to try a **reindeer steak,** or else **faar-i-kaal,** the national dish, a heavily peppered cabbage-and-mutton stew served with boiled potatoes. A fisherman's or a farmer's favorite is **lapskus** (hash, to us), prepared with whatever's left over in the kitchen. The North American palate seems to take kindly to **kjøttkaker,** the Norwegian hamburger—often pork patties—served with sautéed onions, brown gravy, and boiled potatoes.

The **boiled potato** is ubiquitous. Incidentally, the Norwegian prefers it without butter—just a bit of parsley. Nowadays fresh vegetables and crisp salads are a regular feature of the Norwegian diet as well.

   FROMMER'S SMART TRAVELER: RESTAURANTS

VALUE-CONSCIOUS DINERS MAY WANT TO CONSIDER THE FOLLOWING:

1. Look for the *dagens menu* or daily special that is reasonable in price and was prepared fresh that day.
2. Order fixed-priced menus, especially at lunch. Often you can dine in some of the most expensive restaurants by patronizing them at lunch and ordering from the set menu.
3. Do as the Norwegians do: Prepare one or two *smørbrød* (open-faced sandwiches) for lunch.
4. Watch the booze—it can add greatly to the cost of any meal.
5. Go ethnic—there are some great inexpensive foreign dining spots. Norwegian restaurants tend to be expensive.
6. Best bet for a quick and inexpensive meal is a *konditori*, or bakery tearoom. Look for the cafeterias as well.
7. Fill up at the traditional Norwegian *koldtbord* (cold board) at breakfast buffets, so you'll need only a light lunch.

Rommegrøt is a sour-cream porridge covered with melted butter, brown sugar, and cinnamon. If they're in season, try the good-tasting, amber-colored **multer** (cloudberries). An additional treat, well made in Norway, is a pancake accompanied by **lingonberries.**

Frokost (breakfast) is often a whopping **koldtbord,** the famous cold board consisting of herring and goat's cheese, and often such fare as salmon and soft-boiled eggs, plus **wienerbrød** (Danish pastry). At this time, most tourists encounter the ever-popular **flatbrød,** paper-thin crisp rye bread. Many visitors may not want to spend the extra kroner for this big spread, but those going on glacier expeditions need this early-morning fortification.

Incidentally, **smörgåsbord** and smørrebrød (**smørbrød** in Norway) are very popular in Norway, although they seem to be served here without the elaborate ritual typical of Denmark and Sweden. Customarily, smörgåsbord in Norway is only a prelude to the main meal.

DRINK

Norway has strict laws regarding the sale of alcohol. Beer and wine may be served in hotels and restaurants 7 days a week, but hard liquor can be sold only between 3 and 11:45pm—and never on Sunday. Visitors can buy the precious stuff from the Vinmonopolet, the big-brother state liquor-and-wine monopoly (see below). The restriction on hard liquor may be a bonus for budgeteers, since Norwegian prices are sky-high, in line with all the Scandinavian countries. *Warning:* Unless visitors ask for a favorite brand of gin or scotch, they may be served a sour-tasting Norwegian home brew.

The Norwegians, like the Danes, are essentially beer drinkers. Low in alcohol content is **pils,** a light lager, but the **lagerøl** is so low in alcoholic content (less than 2.5%) that it's a substitute for water only. The stronger Norwegian beer is the export, available at higher prices. Two other types of beer are Brigg and Zero.

The other national drink is **akevitt** (sometimes written as aquavit or schnapps). Who would ever think that potatoes and caraway seeds could knock a person under the table? It's that potent, although it's misnamed the "water of life." Norwegians gulp down beer as a chaser. Aquavit (try Linie Akevitt) is sloshed around in oak vats all the way to Australia and back—for added flavor.

The stores of **Vinmonopolet,** the monopoly that sells wines and spirits, are open Monday through Wednesday from 10am to 5pm, on Thursday from 9am to 6pm, and on Friday from 9am to 5pm. The Vinmonopolet is closed on Saturday in all towns except Kirkenes, Bodø, Ålesund, Trondheim, Haugesund, and Arendal. Alcoholic beverages are not sold to anyone under 20 years of age.

5. RECOMMENDED BOOKS, FILMS & RECORDINGS

BOOKS

HISTORY & MYTHOLOGY   *The Vikings,* by Johannes Brøndsted (Penguin), is one of the most enjoyable and best-written documents of the Age of the Vikings. The good, the bad, and the ugly come alive in these pages.

Quisling: A Study in Treason, by Oddvar K. Hoidal (OUP), studies the world's most famous traitor, Quisling, who was executed by the Norwegians for running the Nazi puppet government there. A tremendous portrait of this dreadful man and his era emerge in this long-winded book. But at a retail price of $75, you'd better check it out of the library.

The Vinland Sagas: The Norse Discovery of America, translated by Magnús Magnússon and Hermann Palsson (Penguin). Viking fans will not put down this incredible saga, detailing how Viking Norwegians sailed in their longships to the eastern coast of "Vinland" (America) as early as the 10th century.

The Norwegians, by Arthur Spencer (David & Charles), is the best book on the market today for understanding the Norwegian people and their advanced society.

ADVENTURE *The Kon-Tiki Expedition,* by Thor Heyerdahl (Washington Square Press), once made into a film, details the saga of today's modern Norwegian "Viking," who set out on a raft with five comrades and sailed 4,300 miles in 1947—all the way from Peru to Polynesia.

LITERATURE & THEATER *The Governor's Daughter,* by Camilla Collett (in several editions), is called the first modern Norwegian novel. Although published in 1854, it still reads like a modern novel.

Ibsen Plays; One to Six, by Henrik Ibsen (Heinemann Educational and countless other volumes). The works of Norway's greatest playwright live on in this six-volume set. Works include *A Doll's House* and *Hedda Gabler.*

The Ferry Crossing, by Edvard Hoem (New York: Garland), was a success in 1989. The book depicts a tiny Norwegian coastal village in an unorthodox story form.

FILMS

Norwegian filmmakers have yet to equal the success of *Pathfinder* in the late 1980s, which was nominated for an Academy Award as best foreign film.

The most recent best film to come out of Norway (available on video) is *Karachi,* directed by Oddvar Einarson (his *X* won an award at the Venice Film Festival in 1987). *Karachi* deals with drug trafficking between Pakistan and Scandinavia.

RECORDINGS

CLASSICAL *Peer Gynt,* by Edvard Grieg, performed by the Oslo Philharmonic Orchestra, conducted by Esa-Pekka Salonen.

Violin Interpretations, by Terje Tønnesen. Along with Lars Anders Tomter (viola) and Reidun Askeland (piano), this Norwegian violinist plays interpretations of Grieg's Violin Sonata, interpretations of Norwegian composer Johan Halvorsen's adaptations of Handel's violin works, and interpretations of Bjarne Brustad's compositions for solo violin.

MODERN OPERA *Which Witch,* a recently written rock opera, is performed by the musical group Dollie de Luxe, which received favorable critical reviews in Stratford-upon-Avon in England. Most of it was composed by Norwegian singer/composer Benedicte Adrian. Accompanying her on keyboard is Ingrid Bjornow.

FOLK *Norwegian Peasant Dances* (Opus 72), by Edvard Grieg, with original fiddle tunes from Telemark, is a musical oddity, even in Norway. This recording alternates Grieg's peasant dances between violin renditions by Norwegian Knut Buen and piano interpretations of the same melody by Norwegian Einar Steen-Nøkleberg.

Rosensfole, Agnes Buen. Known as a "natural" singer, Ms. Buen is accompanied by Norway's best saxophonist, Jan Garbarek, who is better known for his jazz interpretations. He adds texture and greater depth to Ms. Buen's renditions of Norwegian folk melodies.

JAZZ *Norske Rytmekonger,* by Norske Rytmekonger (the Norwegian Rhythm Kings), is the popular band featured on this enormously successful recording. They are considered Norway's finest interpreters of New Orleans–style jazz.

Cherokee, by Egil Kapstad. Kapstad interprets jazz on his piano, including bee-bop, and is considered among Norway's top jazz musicians.

URBAN ROCK 'N' ROLL *The Dum Dum Boys,* by the Dum Dum Boys. Norwegian-language lyrics are printed on the inside cover of this album by an all-Norwegian group, considered a leader in their field. Their most famous single recording is *Chop Suey* (CBS Records, 1990).

CHAPTER 12

PLANNING A TRIP TO NORWAY

This chapter is devoted to the nitty gritty of planning a trip to Norway—costs, events, itineraries, and detailed practicalities like taxes, tipping, and emergencies. It should be read in conjuction with Chapter 1.

1. CURRENCY & COSTS

CURRENCY The Norwegians use the **kroner** and **øre**—simple for those who have mastered the Danish currency system. Bank notes are issued in 10, 50, 100, 500, and 1,000 kroner. Nickel coins are issued in 10 and 50 øre, 1 krone, and 5 and 10 kroner.

Warning: The Norwegian krone (sometimes abbreviated NOK) differs in value from the krone used in Denmark, Iceland, and Sweden. Travelers entering Norway from one of those countries should be aware that those currencies are not accepted in Norway as payment for goods and services.

WHAT THINGS COST IN OSLO	U.S. $
Taxi from Fornebu Airport to the city center	18.00
Bus from Fornebu Airport to the city center	4.00
Local telephone call	.35
Double room at the Grand Hotel (deluxe)	332.00
Double room at the Hotel Stefan (moderate)	204.00
Double room at the Ansgar Hotel (budget)	125.00
Continental breakfast	5.00
Lunch for one at Bristol Grill (moderate)	25.00
Lunch for one at Storstova (budget)	12.00
Dinner for one, without wine, at Etoile (deluxe)	50.00
Dinner for one, without wine, at D.S. Louise (moderate)	35.00
Dinner for one, without wine, at Gamla Rådhus (budget)	20.00
Pint of beer (draft pilsner)	6.00
Coca-Cola (in a restaurant)	3.00
Cup of coffee	1.35
Roll of Kodacolor film, 24 exposures	10.00
Admission to a museum	1.65–3.35
Movie ticket	6.80
Theater ticket (at National Theater)	12.00

THE KRONE & THE DOLLAR

At this writing $1 = 6 Norwegian kroner (or 1 Norwegian krone = 16.6¢), and this was the rate of exchange used to calculate the dollar values given in the Norway chapters (rounded to the nearest nickel). This rate fluctuates from time to time and may not be the same when you travel to Norway. Therefore the following table should be used only as a guide:

Kroner	U.S. $	Kroner	U.S. $
0.25	0.04	125	20.75
0.50	0.08	150	24.90
1	0.17	175	29.05
5	0.83	200	33.20
10	1.65	225	37.35
15	2.50	250	41.50
20	3.30	300	49.80
25	4.15	350	58.10
30	5.00	400	66.40
40	6.65	450	74.70
50	8.30	500	83.00
60	9.95	600	99.60
70	11.60	700	116.20
80	13.25	800	132.80
90	14.95	900	149.40
100	16.60	1,000	166.00

WHAT THINGS COST IN BERGEN

	U.S. $
Taxi from Bergen Airport to the city center	26.50
Bus from Bergen Airport to the city center	6.00
Local telephone call	.35
Double room at the Norge Hotel (deluxe)	231.00
Double room at the Bryggen Orion (moderate)	158.00
Double room at the Park Pensjon (budget)	106.00
Continental breakfast	6.00
Smörgasbord lunch for one at Ole Bull Restaurant	26.00
Lunch for one at Dickens (budget)	22.00
Dinner for one, without wine, at Bellevue (deluxe)	66.50
Dinner for one, without wine, at Enhjørningen (moderate)	27.00
Dinner for one, without wine, at Kaffistova (budget)	17.00
Pint of beer (draft pilsner)	6.00
Coca-Cola (in a restaurant)	3.00
Cup of coffee	1.25
Roll of Kodacolor film, 24 exposures	8.00
Admission to a museum	1.65
Movie ticket	6.50
Theater ticket (at Den National Scene)	17.00

2. WHEN TO GO — CLIMATE, HOLIDAYS & EVENTS

CLIMATE

In summer the average temperature in Oslo ranges from 57°F to 65°F. In January it hovers around 27°F—ideal for winter sports.

The western coast of Norway is warmed by the Gulf Stream, and winters tend to be temperate. Rainfall, however, is heavy.

Above the Arctic Circle, the sun shines night and day from mid-May until late July. In contrast, the North Cape plunges into darkness for about 2 months in winter.

Norway's Average Daytime Temperatures (°F)

	Jan	Feb	Mar	Apr	May	June	July	Aug	Sept	Oct	Nov	Dec
Oslo	25	26	32	41	51	60	64	61	53	42	33	27
Bergen/ Stavanger	35	35	38	41	40	55	59	58	54	47	42	38
Trondheim	27	27	31	38	47	53	58	57	50	42	35	31

MIDNIGHT SUN   Norway is the land of the Midnight Sun. In summer the sun never fully sets in the northern part of the nation and even in the south there is daylight as late as 11pm and the sun rises around 3am.

The best vantage points and dates in Norway on which to see the spectacle of the Midnight Sun are as follows: **North Cape,** May 12 to August 1; **Hammerfest,** May 14 to July 30; **Tromsø,** May 19 to July 26; **Lofoten Islands,** May 23 to July 17; **Harstad,** May 23 to July 22. All locations can be reached by public transportation.

Keep in mind that although the sun may be shining at midnight, it's not as strong as at midday. Bring along a warm jacket or sweater.

HOLIDAYS

Norway celebrates the following public holidays: January 1 (New Year's Day), Maundy Thursday, Good Friday, Easter, May 1 (Labor Day), Ascension Day, May 17 (Independence Day), Whitmonday, December 25 (Christmas), and December 26 (Boxing Day).

NORWAY CALENDAR OF EVENTS

Dates given may not be exact; they only give a general indication of time. Check with the tourist office before planning to attend an actual event.

JANUARY

☐ **Northern Lights Festival,** Tromsø. Classical and contemporary music performances by musicians from Norway and abroad. January 18–21.

FEBRUARY

☐ **Kristiansund Opera Festival.** Featuring Kristiansund Opera's own productions of opera and ballet, including art exhibitions, concerts, and other types of information. February 2–11.

MARCH

☐ **Birkebeiner Race.** This historic and international ski race crosses the mountains between Rena and Lillehammer, site of the 1944 Olympics, in a 33-mile cross-country trek. March 18.

☐ **Narvik Winter Festival,** Narvik. Sports events, carnivals, concerts, and opera performances highlight this festival dedicated to the people who built the railway across northern Norway and Sweden. March 24–April 1.

☐ **Nordic Film Festival,** Kristiansand. The public is invited to screenings of Nordic films. March 28–April 1.

APRIL

☐ **Voss Jazz Festival,** Voss. Three days of jazz and folk-music performances are presented by European and American artists. April 6–8.

MAY

☐ **The Viking Run.** An international half-marathon is staged in the Sognefjord with marathon queen Grete Waitz. Some participants stay over for summer skiing, glacier climbing, biking, boating, and mountain climbing. May 26.

✪ *BERGEN INTERNATIONAL FESTIVAL   A world-class music event that features artists from Norway and around the world. This is one of the largest annual musical events in Scandinavia.*
*   **Where:** Various venues at Bergen. **When:** May 23–June 3. **How:** Details about the events and where and how to attend them are supplied by the Bergen International Festival, Box 183, N-5001 Bergen (tel. 05/32-04-00).*

JUNE

☐ **Emigration Festival,** Stavanger. Commemoration of Norwegian immigration to North America. Exhibitions, concerts, theater, folklore. June 7–21.

☐ **Folk Music Festival,** Nesbyen. Traditional Norwegian folk music is performed. June 8–10.

☐ **North Cape March.** This trek from Honningsvåg to the North Cape is one of the world's toughest. Round-trip march is 42 miles. June 16.

☐ **Midsummer Night.** Celebrations and bonfires all over Norway. June 23.

☐ **Emigration Festival,** Kvinesdal. Commemorates the Norwegian immigration to the United States. June 26–July 1.

☐ **International Choir Festival,** Leirvik. Choirs from Europe and the United States participate in this festival. June 28–July 1.

JULY

☐ **Kongsberg Jazz Festival.** International artists participate in one of the most important jazz festivals in Scandinavia, with open-air concerts. July 4–8.

☐ **Midnight Sun Marathon.** The marathon takes place in Tromsø in northern Norway and starts at midnight. July 7.

☼ *MOLDE INTERNATIONAL JAZZ FESTIVAL* The "City of Roses" is
the site of Norway's oldest jazz festival, annually attracting international
stars from both sides of the Atlantic.
 Where: Venues in Molde. *When:* July 16–21. *How:* For details about
the events and how to attend them, contact the Molde Jazz Festival, Box
261, N-6401 Molde (tel. 072/53-779).

AUGUST

☐ **The Peer Gynt Festival,** Vinstra. Art exhibitions, evenings of music and song,
parades in national costumes, and other events honor the fictional character Peer Gynt,
from the Ibsen play of the same name. August 3–12.
☐ **Telemark Festival.** International festival of folk music and folk dance taking place
in Bo where many famous fiddlers, dancers, and singers live. August 9–12.

SEPTEMBER

☐ **International Salmon Fishing Festival,** Suldalslagen. Takes place outside
Stavanger in western Norway; participants come from Norway and abroad.

OSLO
CALENDAR OF EVENTS

MARCH

☼ *HOLMENKOLLEN SKI FESTIVAL* One of Europe's largest ski
festivals, with World Cup Nordic skiing and biathlons, international
ski-jumping competitions, and Norway's largest cross-country race for
amateurs.
 Where: Holmenkollen Ski Jump on the outskirts of Oslo. *When:* March
12–18. *How:* Contact Skiforeningen, Kongevn. 5, Holmenkollen, N-0390
Oslo 3 (tel. 02/14-16-90), for details about participating or attending.

MAY

☐ **The Grete Waitz Run.** A run for women only through the streets of Oslo, with
participation by marathon queen Grete Waitz. May 12.

JUNE

☐ **The Faerder Sailing Race.** Some 1,000 sailing boats participate in this race,
ending in Borre, by the Oslofjord. June 9.

JULY

☐ **Mobil Bislett Games.** International athletic competitions in Oslo are staged, with
professional participants from all over the world. July 14.
☐ **Norway Cup International Youth Soccer Tournament.** The world's largest
youth soccer tournament draws 1,000 teams from around the world to Oslo. July
28–August 4.

AUGUST

☐ **Chamber Music Festival.** Oslo is host to chamber music concerts by both
Norwegian and foreign musicians in Akershus Castle and Fortress, which dates from
A.D. 1300. August 3–12.

- ☐ **The Oslo Jazz Festival.** Annual jazz festival in Oslo featuring music from the earliest years of jazz, the 1920 to 1925 era, with classical concerts, opera, and ballet. August 8–12.
- ☐ **World Cup Summer Ski Jumping.** Takes place in Marikollen, Raelingen, just outside the center of Oslo. August 19.

SEPTEMBER

- ☐ **Oslo Marathon.** An annual event drawing some of Norway's best long-distance runners. September 8.

DECEMBER

☉ *NOBEL PEACE PRIZE CEREMONY* *The major event on the Oslo calendar, drawing the most world interest. Winners have included everybody from Mother Teresa to Gorbachev.*
   Where: Oslo City Hall. When: December 10. How: Attendance by invitation only. Information available at Nobel Institute, Drammensvn. 19, N-0255 Oslo 2 (tel. 02/44-36-80).

3. GETTING AROUND

BY PLANE

Norway has excellent air service. In addition to SAS, two independent airways, Braathens SAFE and Wideroe Flyveselskap, provide a quick and convenient means of getting around a large country with many hard-to-reach areas. All three airlines offer mini-fares, reduced rates available when booked outside Norway.

BRAATHENS SAFE A top-notch independent airline, the Norwegian flag carrier Braathens SAFE (tel. 02/12-20-70 in Oslo or 05/23-23-25 in Bergen), carries more passengers on domestic routes than any other airline in Norway. The company has more than 2,500 employees and carries 2.8 million passengers a year. It operates charter flights throughout Europe and North Africa and has regularly scheduled routings inside Norway, linking major cities as well as more remote places not covered by other airlines. Its air routes directly link Oslo to all major cities in the country along with frequent flights along the coast from Oslo to Tromsø and farther north to Longyearbyen on the island of Spitsbergen.

You might also inquire about the **Visit Norway Pass** offered by Braathens SAFE, which grants reductions and is valid for 1 month. For example, you're given two flight coupons within Norway for $105 (U.S.), four coupons for $200. However, these are valid only from May 1 until September 30. The Visit Norway Pass also entitles you to a free Scandinavian Bonus Pass valid from June 1 to September 1 and worth 150 kroner ($24.90). It offers substantial discounts at 43 Inter Nor Hotels in Norway. The Visit Norway Pass is sold by airlines that have agreements with Braathens SAFE. It is also sold at Scanam/STC, 8939 Sepulveda Blvd., Suite 220, Los Angeles, CA 90045 (tel. toll free 800/272-2626, 800/972-2626 in California).

SAS SAS crisscrosses Norway with a number of regularly scheduled domestic flights, connecting Bergen, Oslo, Trondheim, and Bodø. It's also possible to fly to the Arctic gateway of Tromsø; to Alta in Finnmark, the heart of Lapland; and to Kirkenes, near the Russian border.

SAS offers a **Visit Scandinavia Fare,** a five-coupon $250 ticket valid for travel on all SAS flights within and between Norway, Denmark, and Sweden from July 1 to August 14.

WIDE ROE FLYVESELSKAP An **Air Pass** offered by Wideroe is valid for 14 days for 1,900 kroner ($315.20) on the airline's routes within Norway—some 39 destinations—from June 16 to August 20. Children pay 1,200 kroner ($199.10). The Air Pass is sold by Norwegian travel agencies and can also be obtained at 39 domestic airports. Tickets are standby and cannot be booked in advance. As an added allure, the Air Pass also entitles you to the Nordic Hotel Pass.

BY TRAIN

Norway is crisscrossed by a network of electric and diesel-electric trains that run as far as Bodø, 62 miles beyond the Arctic Circle. (After that, visitors have to take a coastal steamer, plane, or bus along the run to Tromsø and the North Cape.)

The most popular run is between Oslo and Bergen, a distance of 300 miles. Often visitors with limited time choose this train route for its fabled mountains, gorges, white-water rivers, and fjords. Conductors often stop for major scenic views.

Second-class travel on Norwegian trains is recommended. In fact, second class in Norway is as good as or better than second-class travel anywhere else in Europe, with reclining seats and lots of unexpected comforts. The one-way second-class fare to Bergen from Oslo is $57, and $85 in first class. Another popular run, from Oslo to the railway's northern terminus at Bodø, some 800 rail miles, costs $105 one way in second class or $157 in first class.

One of the country's logical scenic trips—from Bergen to Bodø—is not possible because of the terrain, so trains to Bodø leave from Oslo, not Bergen. The express trains are called *Hurtigtog/Ekspress,* while regular trains are called *Persontog* (usually second-class seats only).

On express and other main trains you have to reserve seats at the train's starting station for a 13-krone ($2.15) fee per person. Sleepers and seats are priced per person and evaluated by the number of berths in each compartment. In addition to the basic rail fare, there is a $48 charge in a single sleeper compartment, $24 in a double sleeper compartment, and $12 in a triple sleeper compartment. Children under 4 years of age travel free when not occupying a seat. Children 4 to 15 years of age and senior citizens pay 50% of the regular adult fare. Group and midweek tickets are also available.

There are special compartments for the physically handicapped on most medium- and long-distance trains. These may be used by persons in wheelchairs and others with physical handicaps as well as their companions. Children under 4 travel free if they do not occupy a separate seat. Passengers between 4 and 15 years of age pay half fare.

Travelers over age 67 are entitled to a 50% discount, called an **Honnorrabatt,** on Norwegian train journeys of over 31 miles. During special periods, reductions are also offered on the popular coastal steamers. The spouse of someone over 67 can also receive the 50% discount.

The **Norwegian Bargain Rail Pass** is a one-way second-class ticket valid for 7 2days. There is no mileage limitation, and stopovers are allowed within the 7-day period. Tickets may be used only Monday through Thursday and not during the Christmas or Easter holidays. The price is about $60, and the pass may be purchased at any rail station in Norway.

For travelers who can plan their stopovers with long relaxing weekends in mind, the **Midtukebillet** (midweek ticket) may be suitable. It's valid for second-class travel between Monday and Friday anywhere in Norway during a 1-week period. The price is 360 kroner ($59.70), which is less than half the price of a second-class one-way ticket between Oslo and Bodø. The only drawback is that a passenger can never repeat a leg of the journey in reverse order, but must continue inexorably north or south until the end of the designated week.

For tickets, go to the **NSB Reisebyra,** Stortingsgate 28, N-0161 Oslo 1 (tel. 02/42-94-60), or write the office.

For **information** about Norwegian trains, call 02/42-19-19, a central number in Oslo.

BY BUS

Where the train or coastal steamer stops, a scenic bus is usually waiting to take passengers the rest of the way. Norway's bus system is excellent, linking remote, off-the-beaten-path villages along the fjords. Numerous all-inclusive motorcoach tours—often combined with steamer travel—are offered from Bergen or Oslo in summer. The train ends its northward run in Bodø, but it's possible to take the Polar Express bus, 39 miles east of Bodø in Fauske. This fascinating bus trip spans the distance along the Arctic Highway through Finnmark (Lapland) to Kirkenes near the Russian border and back. The Kirkenes run operates from June to October, but the service is year round from Fauske to Alta in Finnmark. Passengers are guaranteed hotel accommodations along the way.

Buses are equipped with air conditioning, toilets, adjustable seats, reading lights, and telephone. Reservations are not accepted on most buses, and payment is made to the driver on board. Fares depend on the distance traveled. Children under 4 travel free, and children 4 to 16 and senior citizens pay half price. For the Oslo–Sweden–Hammerfest "Express 2000," a 30-hour trip, reservations must be made in advance.

The **Bus Pass** is a discount card costing 1,000 kroner ($165.90) and giving a 33% discount on travel on the Nor-Way Bussekspress domestic routes and on routes to 200 destinations elsewhere in Europe. The Bus Pass may be purchased at Norwegian travel agencies and post offices. For more information, the sales office in Oslo is Nor-Way Bussekspress Jernbanetorget, Oslo 1 (tel. 02/33-08-64).

BY CAR & FERRY

Dazzling scenery awaits you at nearly every turn. Some of the roads are less than perfect (often dirt or gravel) but passable. Most mountain roads are open by May 1; the so-called motoring season lasts from mid-May to the end of September. In western Norway hairpin curves are common, but if you're willing to settle for doing less than 150 miles a day you needn't worry. The easiest and most convenient touring territory is in and around Oslo and the trek southward, from the capital to Stavanger. You can drive to the North Cape by car.

Bringing a car into Norway is not a problem. Drivers must have their national driver's license, car registration book, "warning triangle," and an insurance "Green Card" (obtainable from Customs upon entering Norway).

Mostly privately run, car-ferries in the western fjord country and in the north are essential to transportation. Motorists should ask the tourist bureau for a free map, "Norway By Car," and a timetable outlining car-ferry services. Some ferries will accept advance reservations. Since the ferries are vital to the transportation system— and are mostly used by Norwegians—the cost for passengers or for car transport is low.

RENTALS   Hertz, Avis, and Budget offer well-serviced, well-maintained fleets of rental cars within Norway.

The cheapest **Budget Rent-a-Car** (tel. toll free 800/527-0700 in the U.S.) car, a Ford Fiesta, requires a 2-day advance reservation, a valid driver's license, and a payment of $324 per week, with unlimited mileage, plus 20% Norwegian tax. Budget's offices are at Fornebu Airport (tel. 02/53-79-24) and downtown at the Oslo Plaza Hotel (tel. 02/17-11-80).

Hertz (tel. toll-free 800/654-3001 in the U.S.) offers a wide selection of cars from a manual-shift Ford Fiesta to a Volvo and a large Mercedes with automatic transmission. For the lowest rates you need to reserve a car 21 days before the anticipated departure (*not* 21 days before the anticipated pickup of the car). With this 21-day advance booking, as part of its "World on Wheels" promotion, Hertz charges $427 per week for its smallest car, a Ford Fiesta, including government tax and all necessary insurance premiums (including the cost of a collision-damage waiver). Hertz's main office in Oslo is at Fornebu Airport (tel. 02/53-36-47), and in central Oslo at Holbergsgate 30 (tel. 02/20-01-21).

The smallest **Avis** (tel. toll free 800/331-2112 in the U.S.) car, the Ford Fiesta, is available for $364 per week, mileage included. Rentals at Avis require only a 2-day advance booking from the U.S. Like its competitor, Avis builds all insurance premiums into its rates. But unlike Hertz, Avis charges 20% extra for tax. Avis's offices are at Fornebu Airport (tel. 02/53-05-57), at Gardemoen Airport (tel. 06/97-84-48), and in central Oslo at Munkedamsveien 27 (tel. 02/83-58-00).

One final company, sometimes offering short-term car rentals through European-based car-rental outfits, is **Kemwell,** a small but reliable company based in Harrison, New York. For information on its sometimes unusual discounts, call Kemwell (tel. toll free 800/678-0678).

Insurance Budget builds a nominal insurance coverage into its rates but it's probably not sufficient for most drivers and most accidents. If you have a mishap and didn't purchase additional insurance, you'll be responsible for the first $1,333 of repairs to your car. You can waive all but $100 of financial responsibility by accepting an optional insurance policy offered by Budget. If you accept it, the counter attendant will have you sign a collision-damage waiver, which will add around $12 per day to your rental bill. It may be worth it. You can also sign up for additional personal accident insurance (which will cover most hospital bills in the event of injury) for an extra $4 per day.

GASOLINE In and around Oslo you'll find plenty of gasoline stations. However, if you're planning long drives on offbeat roads, always ask where the next station is. For a liter of super-grade gasoline in Norway, expect to pay 6 to 7 kroner ($1 to $1.15) per ~~gallon~~ liter. Prices are likely to be higher in the north. *$4 -$5 a gallon*

DRIVING RULES Don't drink and drive. All Scandinavian countries are fanatically strict about drunken drivers.

It is mandatory for all cars and trucks in Norway to have their headlights on—day and night—as a safety measure.

Cars are driven on the right-hand side of the road.

ROAD MAPS Ask for road maps at local tourist offices, bookstores, or the **Norwegian Automobile Club,** Storgata 2, N-0155 Oslo 1 (tel. 02/42-94-00). The best commercial road maps on Norway are published by Hallweg.

BREAKDOWNS/ASSISTANCE If your rental car breaks down in Norway, call the rental company first. Otherwise, contact one of the following:

In Oslo: Falken Rescue Service (tel. 02/23-25-85, 24 hours daily), NAF Alarm (tel. 02/42-94-00, 24 hours daily), or Viking Rescue Reserve (tel. 02/60-60-90, 24 hours daily).
In Bergen: Falken Rescue Service (tel. 05/32-62-00) or Viking Rescue Service (tel. 05/29-22-22).

In Stavanger: Falken Rescue Service (tel. 04/58-60-20, 24 hours daily) or Viking (tel. 04/58-29-00, 24 hours daily).

BY RV   By law, trailers rented in Norway cannot be wider than 7½ feet and the combined length of car and trailer cannot be longer than 59 feet. Some roads are not suitable for such recreational vehicles. Inquire at the rental agency about the route you plan to take.

Contact one of the following: **InterRent Kloppavn 20,** N-1473 Skårer (tel. 02/70-04-00); **Ostlandske Bil og Camping,** Nye Vakasvn 55, N-1364 Hvalstad (tel. 02/98-03-87); and **Bergen Caravan,** Liamyrane 6, N-5090 Nyborg (tel. 05/18-92-30).

BY STEAMER

For a look at the fjords of western Norway, nothing tops the indomitable steamer. In northern Norway, too, those with the time can take a tiny cargo or mail steamer to one of the remote offshore fishing villages, a marvelously cheap and offbeat adventure. Some of the most popular sea trips in Europe are the 12-day, all-inclusive round-trip steamer trips from Bergen to Kirkenes (near the Russian border), some 2,500 miles of scenic coastline.

It's cheaper to book passage in the spring (April), early summer, late summer, and autumn, when the fares are considerably reduced. From late May to the end of August is high season. Depending on the accommodations and the time of year, fares range from $720 to $1,770 per person. Bookings are tight during peak months, so reserve in advance. Children under 12 get a 25% discount on round-trip voyages, and a 50% discount on port-to-port sailings. Children under 4 years of age are not charged if berths are shared with their parents. Tours are offered by **Bergen Line,** and reservations may be made at their agent's office at 505 Fifth Ave., New York, NY 10017 (tel. 212/986-2711, or toll free 800/323-7436).

SUGGESTED ITINERARIES

IF YOU HAVE 1 WEEK

Day 1: Fly to Oslo, check into a hotel, and relax. Few can fight the jetlag on their first day in the Norwegian capital.

Day 2: After breakfast in Oslo, take the ferry to the Bygdøy peninsula for a look in the Kon Tiki Museum, the polar ship *Fram,* the Viking ships, and the Norwegian Folk Museum, breaking for lunch when ready.

Day 3: While still in Oslo, visit the 75-acre Frogner Park to see the Vigeland sculptures and view the collection of paintings by Edvard Munch. You should have enough time to see the Henie-Onstad Foundation art center 7 miles from Oslo. Return in time to go to the Lookout Tower and Ski Jump at Holmenkollen where you can dine, enjoying a superb view of Oslo.

Day 4: Head south on a fascinating day trip from Oslo to some of the major towns along the Oslofjord. In the morning, drive to Fredrikstad on the Glomma River, taking in its Old Town and visiting Norway Silver Designs, its handcraft center. Drive back to Moss and take a ferry across the fjord. From Horten on the west bank, drive south to Tønsberg, Norway's oldest town (visit the Vestfold Folk Museum), and then on to Sandefjord, the former whaling capital with a whaling museum. Drive back to Oslo for dinner.

Day 5: Leaving Oslo by train, head west for Bergen on a 300-mile "day trip"—one of the highlights of European travel. You literally go across the rooftop of Norway, past the ski resorts of Geilo and Voss. After this dramatic trip, you'll arrive in Bergen.

Day 6: Explore Bergen's many attractions, such as the Fantoft Stave Church and Trolls' Hill (the summer villa of composer Edvard Grieg).

Day 7: For 1 day and night, go to Ulvik on the Hardangerfjord in the western fjord district, reached by public transport from Bergen. This beautiful town is typical of the fjord towns in the entire district.

IF YOU HAVE 2 WEEKS

Days 1–7: Spend the first week as described above.

Day 8: While still based in Ulvik (see "Day 7," above), continue to explore the fjord district.

Day 9: Return to Bergen, then fly to Trondheim, also a major sightseeing attraction.

Day 10: If it's summer, take a 13-hour train ride from Trondheim to Bodø on the Midnight Sun Special. Spend the night in Bodø, north of the Arctic Circle.

Day 11: From Bodø, fly to Tromsø, 250 miles north of the Arctic Circle (it does not have rail service). Stay overnight in Tromsø and see its limited, but interesting, attractions.

Day 12: Rent a car in Tromsø and head north for the last leg of the trip: a 280-mile run over the Arctic Highway. I suggest that you spend the night in Alta. The road is slow-going, as it wraps itself around inlets and fjords.

Day 13: Continue driving north to Hammerfest, the most northerly town in the world of any major size. Stay overnight.

Day 14: From Hammerfest, take an excursion boat directly to the North Cape. Those with more time can drive to Honningsvåg, the world's northernmost village, the gateway to the North Cape. Buses leave from its marketplace daily, heading for the cape, a 22-mile run.

Return to Tromsø where air connections can be made to Oslo and your return flight to North America or to another Scandinavian capital.

IF YOU HAVE 3 WEEKS

Days 1–4: Spend the first 4 days as described in "If You Have 1 Week," above.

Day 5: Explore Oslo in greater depth, visiting Akershus Castle, with its Norwegian Resistance Museum, and the National Gallery. Take one of the walking tours mapped out for Oslo—two if you have the time and the stamina (see Chapter 14).

Day 6: Drive north from Oslo along the E6 to the ski resort of Lillehammer, site of the 1994 Winter Olympics. Stop for lunch at Gjøvik, "the white town on Lake Mjøsa," arriving in Lillehammer in time to view the Sandvig Collections. Either overnight in Lillehammer or return to Oslo.

Day 7: Leave either Oslo or Lillehammer by train, depending on where you spent the night, heading west for Bergen across the rooftop of Europe.

Day 8: Spend the day sightseeing in Bergen, visiting the Fantoft Stave Church and Trolls' Hill (the summer villa of composer Edvard Grieg).

Day 9: Take a trip to the Hardangerfjord and the Folgefonn glacier. Bus trips depart from Bergen for this full-day tour.

Day 10: Board an express steamer from Bergen to Gudvangen to see the Sognefjord, the longest fjord in Norway. From Gudvangen, go by bus to Voss, a famous ski resort.

Day 11: Spend another day in Voss taking excursions and exploring the area.

Day 12: Return to Bergen for an overnight stay. Relax.

Day 13: From Bergen, go to Ålesund at the top of the fjord country and explore the town.

Day 14: While still in Ålesund, take a sightseeing tour for the day to Geiranger, one of the most famous resorts in the fjord country. Waterfalls are in and around the area. Return to Ålesund for the night.

Day 15: From Ålesund, make air connections to Trondheim, the third-largest city of Norway and a historic capital. Explore some of its attractions.

Day 16: Explore Trondheim fully and spend the night.
Day 17–21: Follow the schedule outlined for Days 10 to 14 listed in "If You Have 2 Weeks," above.

FAST FACTS: NORWAY

Business Hours Most **banks** are open Monday through Friday from 8:15am to 3:30pm (on Thursday to 5pm); closed Saturday and Sunday. The **Fellesbanken's Exchange** at the Oslo Central Railway Station (tel. 02/41-26-11) is open Monday through Friday from 8am to midnight, on Saturday from 8am to 7pm, and on Sunday from 8am to noon. There's a bank at Fornebu Airport, open daily from 7am to 10:30pm. There is also a bank at Gardermoen Airport. Most **businesses** are open Monday through Friday from 9am to 4pm. **Stores** are generally open Monday through Friday from 9am to 5pm (many stay open late on Thursday until 6pm or 7pm) and on Saturday from 9am to 1 or 2pm. Sunday closings are observed.

Cigarettes Tobacco kiosks carry Norwegian brands of American-blended cigarettes that are cheaper than the British and American brands on sale.

Currency See "Currency & Costs," above.

Customs With certain food exceptions, personal effects, intended for your own use, can be brought into Norway. If you take them with you when you leave, you can bring in cameras, binoculars, radios, portable TV sets, and the like, as well as fishing and camping equipment. Americans or Canadians can bring in 400 cigarettes, or 500 grams of tobacco and 200 sheets of cigarette paper, or 50 cigars; and 1 liter of spirits or 1 liter of wine. Britons can bring in 200 cigarettes, or 250 grams of tobacco and 200 sheets of cigarette paper; 1 liter of spirits; and 1 liter of wine.

Upon leaving, you can hold up to 5,000 kroner ($829.50) in Norwegian cash.

Dentists For emergency dental services, ask your hotel or host for the nearest dentist. Most Norwegian dentists speak English.

Doctors If you become ill or injured while in Norway, hotel staffs can refer you to a local doctor, nearly all of whom speak English. If not at a hotel, call the nearest 24-hour emergency medical phone number: 02/20-10-90 in Oslo, 05/32-11-20 in Bergen, 07/59-88-00 in Trondheim, 04/53-33-33 in Stavanger, and 083/83-000 in Tromsø.

Driving Rules See "Getting Around," above.

Drug Laws There are severe penalties in Norway for any activities related to the possession, use, purchase, sale, or manufacturing of drugs. Penalties are often based on quantity, but that can vary. Possession of what is deemed a small amount of drugs, either hard or soft, can lead to a heavy fine and deportation. Possession of a "large" amount of drugs can elicit a prison term ranging anywhere from 3 months to 15 years, depending on the circumstances. Norwegian police are particularly strict with any cases involving sales of drugs to children, and the courts tend to impose maximum prison terms in such cases.

Drugstores Drugstores, called *Apotek,* are open during normal business hours.

Electricity Norway has 220 volts, 50–30 cycles, A.C., and standard continental two-pin plugs are used. Transformers and adapters will be needed with Canadian and American equipment. Always inquire at your hotel before plugging in any electrical equipment.

Embassies & Consulates In case you lose your passport or have some other emergency, contact your national embassy in Oslo. The **U.S. Embassy** is at Drammensveien 18, N-0255 Oslo 2 (tel. 02/44-85-50); the **British Embassy,** at Thomas Heftyes Gate 8, N-0264 Oslo 2 (tel. 02/55-24-00); and the **Canadian Embassy,** at Oscarsgate 20, N-0352 Oslo 3 (tel. 02/46-69-55). Travelers from Australia, Ireland, and New Zealand should contact the British Embassy. The **British consulate** is at Strandgaten 18 in Bergen (tel. 32-70-11).

Emergencies   Hotel staffs can usually refer you to a local doctor. If you're not at a hotel, call the nearest 24-hour emergency medical phone number: 02/20-10-90 in Oslo, 05/32-12-10 in Bergen, 07/59-88-00 in Trondheim, 04/53-33-33 in Stavanger, and 083/83-000 in Tromsø.

Etiquette   Norwegians, for the most part, are well mannered, and expect you to be too. "Good day" is said to everyone, and "Thank you" is said even for a simple service or favor. You should always bring flowers or candy if invited to a private home for dinner. Shaking hands is a ritual when you meet someone or take leave. Both women and men shake hands.

Gasoline   See "Getting Around," above.

Hitchhiking   Look clean and you'll find it an acceptable custom. If you're heading from Oslo to Bergen and the western fjord district, board the local train to Skøyen and then try to hitch a ride from Drammensveien. From Trondheim and points north, catch the T-bane train to Carl Berners Plads and position yourself along the Trondheimsveien.

Language   A nationwide controversy: Danish–Norwegian (*riksmaal*) is commonly spoken, but a rise of patriotic spirit has caused Norwegians to turn to New Norwegian (*landsmaal*). But English is spoken almost universally in Norway, certainly by most people engaged in the tourist business. For the best phrase book, purchase a copy of *Norwegian for Travellers,* published by Berlitz.

Laundry/Dry Cleaning   Laundry and dry-cleaning services are provided at most hotels. There are coin-operated laundries and dry-cleaners in most Norwegian cities.

Liquor Laws   Most restaurants, pubs, and bars in Norway are licensed to serve liquor, wine, and beer. The drinking age in Norway is 18 for beer and wine and 20 for liquor.

Mail   At press time, airmail letters to the United States and Canada cost 5 kroner (85¢) for up to 20 grams; postcards, 4 kroner (65¢). It takes an airmail letter 7 to 10 days to reach Norway from the U.S. or vice versa. Norway's mail is handled by the **General Directorate of Posts,** Box 1181 Sentrum, N-0107 Oslo 1 (tel. 02/40-90-50). Mailboxes are a vibrant red, embossed with the trumpet symbol of the Norwegian postal service. They are found on walls, at chest level, in various places throughout cities and towns. Stamps can be bought at magazine kiosks or from town merchants.

Only the post office can weigh, evaluate, and tell you the different options for time or the various regulations that apply to parcels. Shipments to places outside Norway require a declaration on a pre-printed form, stating the contents and value of the package.

Maps   Many tourist offices supply free maps of their district. You can also contact the **Norwegian Automobile Club,** Storgata 2, N-0155 Oslo 1 (tel. 02/42-94-00). Bookstores throughout Norway always sell detailed maps of the country for those planning extensive touring. The most reliable ones are published by **Hallweg.**

Pets   Leave your pet at home. Fearing the risk of rabies, Norway does not allow dogs, cats, and other domestic animals into the country without a permit from the Ministry of Agriculture. The quarantine period for dogs and cats is 4 months.

Police   Dial **000** nationwide for police assistance.

Radio/TV   Radio and television broadcasts are in Norwegian. However, Norwegian National Radio (NRK) has news summaries in English several times weekly.

Rest Rooms   All terminals, big city squares, and the like have public lavatories. In small towns and villages, head for the marketplace. Hygienic standards are usually adequate. If you patronize the toilets in a privately run establishment, such as a café, it is considered polite to buy a small pastry or coffee.

Safety   Whenever you're traveling in an unfamiliar city or country, stay alert. Be aware of your immediate surroundings. Wear a moneybelt and don't sling your camera or purse over your shoulder; wear the strap diagonally across your body. This will minimize the possibility of your becoming a victim of crime. Every society has its criminals. It's your responsibility to be aware and alert even in the most heavily touristed areas.

Taxes   Norway is not a member of the European Community, but it imposes a 20% value-added tax on most goods and services, which is figured into your final bill. However, if you make your purchases in any store bearing the TAX-FREE sign, you will be entitled to a 10% to 14% refund in cash for purchases over 300 kroner ($49.75). Just ask the shop assistant for a tax-free shopping check, showing your passport to indicate that you're from the United States or Canada. You may not use the articles purchased before leaving Norway, and they must be taken out of the country within 4 weeks of purchase. Complete the information required on the back of the check you are given at the store, and then report at your point of departure at an area marked by the TAX-FREE sign, not at Customs. Your refund check will be exchanged there in kroner for the amount due you. Norway's tax-free checks can also be repaid in Sweden, Finland, and Denmark. Refunds are available at all points of departure— airports, ferry and cruise-ship terminals, borders, and train stations.

Telephone/Telegrams   Direct-dial long-distance calls can be made to the United States and Canada from most phones in Norway by dialing 095, then the country code (1 for the U.S. and Canada), and the area code and phone number you wish to reach. Check at the hotel front desk before placing a call. Norwegian coins of 1 krone (15¢) and 5 kroner (85¢) are used in pay phones in Norway.

Telegrams can be sent from private or public phones by dialing 0138.

Time   At noon, eastern standard time (EST) in New York City, it's 6pm in Norway. Norway goes on summer time around March 28 (the date varies every year), until around September 26.

Tipping   Hotels, depending on their classification, add 10% to 15% to your bill, which handles most matters, unless someone on staff has done some special service for you. Most bellhops get at least 3 kroner (50¢) per suitcase. Nearly all **restaurants** add a service charge of up to 15% to your bill, but it's still customary to leave small change. **Bartenders** get about 5% of the bill. **Barbers and hairdressers** aren't usually tipped, but **toilet attendants and hatcheck people** expect at least 2 kroner (35¢). Don't tip theater ushers. **Taxi drivers** do not expect tips unless they handle heavy luggage.

Water   Water is generally safe to drink throughout Norway.

Yellow Pages   It's often difficult to find a listing, especially if you don't know the Norwegian name for the service you are seeking. Hotel desks tend to be helpful.

INTRODUCING OSLO

O slo was founded in the mid-11th century by a Viking king and became the capital around 1300 under King Haakon V. In the course of its history the city burned down several times, and was completely destroyed by fire in 1824. However, the master builder, Christian IV, King of Denmark and Norway, ordered the town rebuilt near the Akershus Castle. He named the new town Christiania, after himself, and that was its official name until 1924, when the city celebrated its 300-year jubilee and reverted to the old name of Oslo.

In 1814 Norway was separated from Denmark and united with Sweden, a union that lasted until 1905. During that period, the Royal Palace, the House of Parliament, the old university, the National Theater, and the National Gallery were built.

After World War II, Oslo grew to 175 square miles. It's one of the 10 largest capitals in the world in sheer area. The city is one of the most heavily forested on earth—in all this land area fewer than half a million Norwegians live and work.

One of the oldest Scandinavian capital cities, Oslo has never been a mainstream European tourist site. Many have the impression that it's lean on attractions. In fact, it is a culturally rich capital with many diversions, enough to fill at least 3 or 4 busy days. It is also the center for many easy excursions along the Oslofjord or to towns and villages in its environs, both north and south.

In recent years Oslo has surprisingly grown from what even the Scandinavians viewed as a Nordic backwater to one of the most happening cities of Europe. Restaurants, nightclubs, cafés, shopping complexes, and other venues have opened as never before. A kind of Nordic joie de vivre permeates the city. The only problem is that it's expensive, one of the most expensive cities of Europe. Proceed with caution if you're on a strict budget.

One final point: Every inhabitant of Oslo is a nature lover. Locals spend much time devoted to pursuits in the forest or on the fjord. It takes only half an hour by tram into the hills from Parliament or the Royal Palace to the 154-foot Tryvann Observation Tower where you have a view over the lushest part of the capital—Oslo Marka, the giant forest. It was here in the Krogskogen forests that many Norwegian folktales took place—tales of princesses, kings, penniless heroes, and the inevitable forest "trolls." And from the same tower in summer you can look down on hundreds of sailboats, motorboats, and windsurfers enjoying the numerous islands of the Oslo archipelago.

1. ORIENTATION

ARRIVING

BY PLANE The domestic airport, **Fornebu** (tel. 02/59-33-40), at Snaroya, is 5½ miles from Oslo. The international airport, **Gardermoen** (tel. 06/97-80-20), 1 hour

WHAT'S SPECIAL ABOUT OSLO

Beaches
☐ Oslo's archipelago of islands in the inner fjord is a summer playground. Take a ferry to the beach.

Monuments/Buildings
☐ Akershus Castle and Fortress, dating from 1300 but rebuilt in the 17th century. Walk its ramparts.

☐ City Hall (Rådhus), inaugurated in 1950 and decorated by the country's leading painters and sculptors, honors Oslo's 900th anniversary.

Museums
☐ Folk Museum, 170 buildings from all over Norway, including a 1200 stave church, were moved here. Life in the 18th century goes on.

☐ Munch Museum, showcasing Edvard Munch, Scandinavia's greatest painter.

☐ Viking Ship Museum, housing the *Oseberg, Gokstad,* and *Tune* ships from A.D. 800–900.

Parks/Gardens
☐ Vigeland Sculpture Park, where the often-bizarre world of sculptor Gustaf Vigeland is depicted.

For the Kids
☐ *Kon Tiki* Museum, displaying the balsa raft that Thor Heyerdahl used to make a dangerous voyage across the Pacific.

Offbeat Oddities
☐ Ski Museum, the world's oldest, containing everything from a 2,500-year-old ski to a polar ski.

Scenic Vistas
☐ The Tryvann Observation Tower, the highest point in Oslo, offering some 30,000 square miles of fjord country spread before you.

Special Events/Festivals
☐ Holmenkollen Ski Festival, attracting the best world's cross-country skiers and jumpers (early March).

from the city center, receives mostly TWA, Pan Am, and charter flights. If you have a choice, it's far better—and less expensive—to arrive at Fornebu, because of its more convenient location. Fornebu services both domestic and international flights of SAS and other intra-European airlines, including British Airways and Icelandair.

SAS operates a bus service from both terminals to the Central Railway Station and other points in Oslo every 15 minutes. The fare is 60 kroner ($9.95) to and from Gardermoen and 25 kroner ($4.15) to and from Fornebu.

BY TRAIN Trains from the continent and from Sweden or Copenhagen pull into **Oslo Sentralstasjon,** at the beginning of Karl Johans Gate, in the center of the city. The station is open daily from 7am to 11pm. From the Central Station, you can catch trains heading for Bergen, Trondheim, "end-of-the-line" Bodø, and all other rail links in Norway. You can also take trams to all major parts of Oslo. Lockers and a luggage office are available at the station, and you can also exchange money here. For train information, call 17-14-00.

BY CAR If you're driving from mainland Europe, the fastest way to reach Oslo is to take the car-ferry from Frederikshavn (Denmark). You can also take a car-ferry from Copenhagen, or drive from Copenhagen by crossing over to Helsingborg (Sweden) from Helsingør (Denmark). Once at Helsingborg, take the E6 north all the way to Stockholm. If you're driving from Stockholm to Oslo, take the E18 west all the way. Once you near the outskirts of Oslo from any direction, follow the signs into the Sentrum.

BY FERRY Ferries from Europe arrive at the Oslo port, a 15-minute walk (or a short taxi ride) from the center. From Denmark, Scandinavia's link with the continent, ferries depart for Oslo from Copenhagen, Hirtshals, and Frederikshavn. From

Strømstad (Sweden), there is a daily crossing in summer to Sandefjord (Norway), taking 2½ hours; from Sandefjord, it's an easy drive or train ride north to Oslo.

TOURIST INFORMATION

Assistance and information for visitors is available at **Rådhuset** (City Hall), Rådhusgaten 19, N-0037 Oslo 1 (tel. 02/33-43-86). Entrance is on the harborside. Free maps, brochures, sightseeing tickets, and guide services are available. The office is open mid-May to mid-September, Monday through Saturday from 8:30am to 4pm and on Sunday from 9am to 5pm; late September to early May, Monday through Friday from 8:30am to 4pm and on Saturday from 8:30am to 2:30pm.

There is also an information office at the central station, **Oslo Sentralstasjon,** at the beginning of Karl Johans Gate (tel. 17-11-24), open daily from 8am to 11pm.

CITY LAYOUT
MAIN ARTERIES & STREETS

Oslo is at the mouth of the 60-mile-long Oslofjord. Opening onto the harbor is **Rådhusplassen,** dominated by the modern **City Hall,** a major attraction. Guided bus tours leave from this point, and the launches that cruise the fjords depart from the pier facing the municipal building (it's possible to catch Bygdøy-bound ferries from the quay at Rådhusplassen).

Out on a promontory to the east is **Akershus Castle.** At **Bygdøy,** the much larger peninsula which juts out to the west, four of Oslo's major attractions can be found: the Viking ships, the *Fram* Museum, *Kon-Tiki* raft, and the Folk Museum.

Karl Johans Gate, Oslo's main street, mainly for shopping and strolling, is north of City Hall Square. This boulevard begins at Ostbanesstasjonen (East Station) and stretches all the way to the 19th-century **Royal Palace** at the western end.

A short walk from the palace is the famed **Students' Grove** (the University of Oslo is nearby), where everybody gathers on a summer day to socialize. Dominating this center is the **National Theater,** guarded by statues of Ibsen and Bjørnson, the two greatest names in Norwegian theater. South of the theater and near the harbor is **Stortingsgate,** another shop-filled street.

The main city square is **Stortorvet,** although it is no longer the center of city life, having lost that position to Karl Johans Gate.

At a subway stop near the National Theater, it's possible to head out for **Tryvasstårnet,** the loftiest lookout town in Scandinavia, and to the **Holmenkollen Ski Jump.**

FINDING AN ADDRESS

Street numbers begin on the south side of streets running on a north-south axis, and on the eastern end of streets running on an east-west axis. All odd numbers lie on one side of the street, and all even numbers are on the opposite side of the street. In some cases, a large building contains several establishments, and different addresses are designated as 3A, 3B, and 3C.

NEIGHBORHOODS IN BRIEF

Oslo is made for walking—in fact, you can walk from the Central Station all the way to the Royal Palace (Slottet) in a straight line. Except for excursions to museum-loaded Bygdøy peninsula and the Holmenkollen Ski Jump, most attractions can be covered on foot.

Oslo does not break up into separate neighborhoods or districts like London and Paris. It consists mainly of **central Oslo,** with the Central Station on the eastern side of the city center and the Royal Palace on the west. Karl Johans Gate, the main street, connects these two points. There are almost 50 museums and galleries in Central Oslo, enough to fill many a rainy day. The most interesting include Akershus Castle, the Norwegian Resistance Museum, and the National Gallery.

The streets Drammensvei and Frognervei lead northwest to **Frognerpark** (whose main entrance is on Kirkevei). Site of the Vigeland Sculpture Park, which brings together some masterpieces of Gustav Vigeland (1869–1943), this is a delightful area.

Old Town or Gamlebyen lies south of the Parliament Building (the Storting) and Karl Johans Gate. This section contains some of the most old-fashioned restaurants of Oslo, along with the Norwegian Resistance Museum and the Old Town Hall.

Aker Brygge, the newest neighborhood of Oslo, sprouted up in the old wharf area down by the mouth of the Oslofjord, land formerly reserved for shipbuilding yards. Fueled by oil wealth, steel-and-glass buildings rise from what was a relatively dilapidated section. Now some of the best shops, theaters, restaurants, and cultural attractions are here, along with apartments for such well-heeled owners as Diana Ross.

In **eastern Oslo** the neighborhood centers around the Botanisk Have (Botanic Garden), the Zoological Museum, and the Munch Museum in Tøyen.

To the west of Oslo, 4 miles by car but better reached by car-ferry, is the **Bygdøy peninsula,** containing important city attractions like the Norwegian Folk Museum, the Viking Ships, the *Fram* Museum, and *Kon-Tiki.*

Many neighborhoods of Oslo lie along the **Oslofjord,** which stretches for more than 60 miles northward from the Skagerrak to Oslo, filled with basins which are dotted with islands. (There are 40 islands alone in the immediate Oslo archipelago.)

Nearly all visitors to Oslo head for **Holmenkollen,** a wooded range of hills northwest of the town rising to about 1,740 feet. It can be reached by electric train from the National Theater in the center of Oslo in 35 minutes.

Marka, Oslo's forest, is a great recreation area, offering hiking, bicycle riding, skiing, fishing, wild berry picking, jogging trails, and more. It contains 343 lakes, 310 miles of ski trails, 387 miles of trails and roads, 11 sports chalets, and 24 ski jumps and alpine slopes.

STREET MAPS

Maps of Oslo are distributed free at the tourist office (see above). For extensive exploring, especially of some of the back streets of Oslo, you may need a more detailed map. The best and most comprehensive is *Falk Plan,* a pocket-size map with a street index that can be opened and folded like a wallet. It is sold at most newsstands in central Oslo. If you don't find it, go to the city's most central bookstore, **Tanum Libris,** Karl Johans Gate 43 (tel. 42-93-10).

2. GETTING AROUND

BY PUBLIC TRANSPORTATION

Oslo has an efficient citywide network of buses, trams (streetcars), and subways. Buses and electric trains take passengers to the suburbs; ferry departures to Bygdøy from May to October are from the harbor in front of Oslo Rådhuset (City Hall).

DISCOUNT PASSES

The **Oslo Card (Oslo-Kortet)** is offered to help you become acquainted with the city at a fraction of normal costs. It allows free travel on public transport, free admission to famous museums and other top sights, favorable rates on sightseeing buses and boats, a rebate on your car rental, special treats in restaurants, and reduced rates in any of 23 hotels in the Oslo area, including some of the finest. You may purchase the card in hotels and fine stores, from travel agents, at tourist information offices, and in the branches of Sparebanken Oslo Akershus. It costs 80 kroner ($13.25) for adults for 1 day, 120 kroner ($19.90) for 2 days, and 150 kroner ($24.90) for 3 days. Children pay 40 kroner ($6.65), 60 kroner ($9.95), and 75 kroner ($12.45), respectively.

Convenient for visitors who do not purchase the Oslo Card is the 24-hour **Tourist**

Ticket (Turistkort), which lets you travel anywhere in Oslo whenever you wish, by bus, tram, subway, local railways, or boat, including the Bygdøy ferries in summer. The Tourist Ticket costs 40 kroner ($6.65) for adults, half fare for children under 16 (children under 4 travel free). The ticket will be stamped when it's used for the first time and will then be good for the next 24 hours.

BY BUS, TRAM & SUBWAY

Jernbanetorget is the major bus and tram terminal stop in Oslo. Most buses and trams passing through the heart of town stop at Wessels Plass, next to the Parliament, or at Stortorget, the main marketplace. Many also stop at the National Theater or University Square on Karl Johans Gate as well as Oslo's suburbs.

By subway, the T-banen has four branch lines east and the Western Suburban route (including Holmenkollen) has four lines to the residential sections and recreation grounds west and north of the city. Subways and trains to Oslo's environs leave from near the National Theater on Karl Johans Gate.

For **information** about timetables and fares, call **Trafikanten** at 17-70-30.

Automated machines cancel prebought tickets. Single-journey tickets are also sold by the drivers for 13 kroner ($2.15). Children travel for half fare. A 12-coupon "Maxi" card costs 135 kroner ($22.40), and a four-coupon "Mini" card goes for 60 kroner ($9.95); both are half price for children. Maxi and Mini cards can be used for unlimited transfers within 1 hour of the time the ticket is stamped.

BY TAXI

If you need to order a taxi in advance, call 38-80-70 24 hours a day. Reserve at least 1 hour in advance.

The approximate fare from Gardermoen to Oslo is 510 kroner ($84.60), and from Fornebu, 80 kroner ($13.25) to 120 kroner ($19.90). (The fare for Gardermoen can be greatly reduced if you order the taxi in advance.)

All taxis are equipped with an official taxi meter, and Norwegian cab drivers are honest. When a car is available, a roof light goes on. Taxis can be hailed on the street, providing they are more than 100 yards from a rank. The worst time to hail a taxi is Monday through Saturday from 8:30 to 10am and Monday through Friday from 3 to 5pm.

BY CAR

This is not a practical means of getting around Oslo because parking is limited. Besides, an efficient network of public transportation makes use of a private car unnecessary. You can even reach the most isolated sights in the environs by public transportation.

Cars are towed away if found illegally parked. There are multistory parking lots in the city center including **Vika Park og Service,** Munkedamsveien 27 (tel. 83-26-19), and **Vestre Vika Bilpark,** Dronning Mauds Gate (tel. 83-35-35). For car problems, call the **NAF Alarm Center** (tel. 42-94-00), open 24 hours a day.

For more information see "Getting Around," in Chapter 12.

BY FERRY

In summer, beginning in mid-April, ferries depart for Bygdøy from Pier 3 in front of the Oslo Rådhuset. For schedule information, call **Båtservice** (tel. 20-07-15). It's recommended that you use a ferry or bus to Bygdøy since parking conditions there are crowded. Other ferries leave for various parts of the Oslofjord. Inquire at the **Tourist Information Office** at Rådhuset (tel. 33-43-86).

BY BICYCLE

Den Rustne Eike, Oscarsgate 32 (tel. 44-18-80), behind the Royal Palace, rents bicycles at moderate rates, complete with free maps of interesting routes in Oslo and its environs. The cost is 60 kroner ($9.95) per day or 300 kroner ($49.75) per week, with a 500-krone ($82.95) deposit required. It's open Monday through Friday from 8am to 4:30pm; in summer, sometimes also on Saturday from 10am to 2pm, but call first.

FAST FACTS: OSLO

American Express The representative is **Winge Reisebyrå,** Karl Johans Gate 33 (tel. 42-91-50), Open Monday through Friday from 8:30am to 5pm.

Area Code The telephone area code for Oslo is 02.

Baby-Sitters Oslovian hotels are often helpful in enlisting the help of a chambermaid for "child-minding." Give at least a day's notice, two if you can. You can also contact the tourist office (see above) where a list of available sitters is kept on file and updated frequently. The cost varies, but it's often 65 kroner ($10.80) per hour.

Bookstores Oslo has a number of bookstores throughout the city. The most central (also one of the best stocked) is **Tanum Libris,** Karl Johans Gate 43 (tel. 42-93-10).

Currency Exchange **Banks** will exchange most foreign currencies or cash traveler's checks (bring your passport). If banks are closed, try the **Currency Exchange Office** at the Oslo Sentralstasjon (tel. 17-14-00), open June to September, daily from 7am to 11pm; October to May, Monday through Friday from 8am to noon and 1:30 to 8:30pm, on Saturday from 8am to 7pm, and on Sunday from 8am to noon.

Dentists In an emergency contact **Tøyen Senter,** Kolstadgate 18 (tel. 67-48-46), open Monday through Friday from 8 to 11pm and on Saturday, Sunday, and holidays from 11am to 2pm. Private dentists may also be called if you can wait (in volume 1B of the telephone directory, look under "Tannleger"); there's rarely a language barrier.

Doctors There are two emergency clinics. The 24-hour **Oslo Municipal Casualty Clinic** is at Storgata 40 (tel. 20-10-90); equipped with ambulances, it handles mainly accident cases. For more routine medical assistance you can contact the biggest hospital in Oslo, **Ullaval,** Kirkeveien 166 (tel. 11-80-80). To consult a private doctor, nearly all of whom speak English, see the telephone directory (look in volume 1B under "Leger") or ask at your hotel for a doctor recommendation. Some larger hotels have arrangements with doctors in case a guest becomes ill.

Drugstores An all-night pharmacy is **Jernbanetorvets Apotek,** Jernbanetorget 4A (tel. 41-24-82).

Embassies & Consulates See "Fast Facts: Norway," in Chapter 12.

Emergencies Dial the Oslo **police** at 002 or 66-90-51; report a **fire** at 42-99-00; call an **ambulance** at 20-10-90.

Eyeglasses **Optiker,** Karl Johans Gate 20 (tel. 41-53-93), is a big supplier, and very centrally located. Most contact lenses are immediately in stock. It takes about 2 days for unusual prescriptions.

Gasoline The Esso station, **Abelhaugen,** Haakon VII Gate 9 (tel. 11-23-26), is open 24 hours.

Hairdressers/Barbers One floor above street level, **Saxophone,** Karl Johans Gate 20 (tel. 41-50-47), accepts both men and women, charging 260 kroner ($43.15) for a woman's cut and 200 kroner ($33.20) for a man's cut. It's open Monday through Friday from 9am to 8pm and on Saturday from 9am to 5pm.

Information See "Tourist Information" in "Orientation," in this chapter.

Laundry A self-service laundry is **Majorstua Mynstvaskeri,** Vibes Gate 15 (tel. 69-43-17), open Monday through Friday from 8am to 8pm and on Saturday from 8am to 5pm. Washing and drying are usually finished in 1 hour. You must have your coins ready to put in the machines.

Libraries The Oslo municipal library, **Diechmann Library,** Henrik Ibsens Gate 1 (tel. 20-43-63), is the largest in Norway, containing many English-language volumes, a children's department, and a music department. It's open Monday through Friday from 8:15am to 8pm (to 6pm in summer) and on Saturday from 8:15am to 3pm.

Lost Property   The Lost and Found Office, **Hittegodskontoret,** at Grønlandsleiret 44 (tel. 66-98-65), is open May 15 to September 15, Monday through Friday from 8:15am to 2:15pm; September 16 to May 14, Monday through Friday from 8:15am to 3:15pm.

Luggage Storage/Lockers   Facilities for luggage storage are available at the **Oslo Sentralstasjon,** at the beginning of Karl Johans Gate (tel. 17-14-00), open daily from 7am to 11pm. Lockers cost 5 to 20 kroner (85¢ to $3.30), depending on size.

Newspapers/Magazines   English-language newspapers and magazines are sold (at least in the summer months) at newsstands (kiosks) throughout Oslo. International editions, including the *International Herald-Tribune,* are always available.

Photographic Needs   Try **Foto Service,** at Karl Johans Gate 33 (tel. 42-98-04), for supplies, including black-and-white and color film. Film can be developed in 3 hours. It's open Monday through Friday from 9am to 5pm and on Saturday from 10am to 2pm.

Police   Dial 002 or 66-90-51.

Post Office   The **Oslo General Post Office** is at Dronningensgate 15, with its entrance at the corner of Prinsensgate (tel. 40-78-23). It's open Monday through Friday from 8am to 8pm and on Saturday from 9am to 3pm; closed Sunday and public holidays. If you've sent your mail general delivery (mark it POSTE RESTANTE), you can collect it here, providing you have your passport.

Radio/TV   The most important broadcaster is the Norwegian government, which owns and controls emissions on the NRK station. Oslo receives many signals from other countries, including BBC broadcasts from London. Radio Norway International broadcasts on MHz frequency.

Religious Services   Evangelical Lutheran is the official state religion, but there is complete religious freedom for all. The **American Lutheran Church** is at Fritznersgate 15 (tel. 44-35-84). Masses are in English at **Eikeli Catholic Church,** Vestsen 18 (tel. 24-25-69). Other churches (with services in Norwegian) include **St. Olav's Church,** which has mass for Roman Catholics, at Akersveien 5 (tel. 20-72-26). There's a Baptist church, **Baptistmenighet,** at Hausmannsgate 22 (tel. 20-76-49), and a Methodist church, **Centralkirken,** St. Olavsgate 28 (tel. 20-03-01). A **synagogue** is at Bergstien 13-15 (tel. 69-29-66).

Rest Rooms   Clean public toilets can be found throughout the city center, as well as in parks, and all bus, rail, and air terminals. For a detailed list, contact the Tourist Information Office.

Safety   Whenever you're traveling in an unfamiliar city or country, stay alert. Be aware of your immediate surroundings. Wear a moneybelt and don't sling your camera or purse over your shoulder; wear the strap diagonally across your body. This will minimize the possibility of your becoming a victim of crime. Every society has its criminals. It's your responsibility to be aware and alert even in the most heavily touristed areas.

Shoe Repairs   The best service is in the basement of **Steen & Strøm,** Kongensgate (tel. 41-68-00), the city's leading department store. Unless there's a rush, routine service can often be rendered on the spot.

Taxes   Oslo has no special city taxes. You pay the same "Value-Added Tax" throughout the country (see "Fast Facts: Norway" in Chapter 12).

Taxis   See "Getting Around," in this chapter.

Telephones, Telegrams, Telex   Phone calls can be made and telegrams and Telexes can be sent daily from 8am to 10pm at Kongensgate 12 and nightly from 10pm to 8am at Kongensgate 21. The entrance is from Prinsensgate. For operator assistance in English, dial 093. To send telegrams, dial 013. Try not to make long-distance calls from your hotel, where the charges are often doubled or tripled. For assistance in dialing abroad, call 0115, or ask the hotel operator for help.

Transit Information   For information about tram and bus travel, call

Trafikanten (tel. 17-70-30), located in front of the Central Station. For information about train travel, go to the Central Station or call 17-14-00.

Weather   See temperature and rainfall chart in Chapter 12.

3. NETWORKS & RESOURCES

FOR STUDENTS   Oslo's **Ungdomsinformasjonen** (Oslo Municipal Youth Information Office) at Akersgaten 57 (tel. 11-04-09) is great if you're planning to hitchhike through Norway because it can often match riders and drivers. The center will also dispense information about youth-oriented activities, cheap accommodations, low-cost restaurants, and more.

The **University of Oslo** sponsors a 6-week International Summer School from June 29 to August 9. It is open to qualified participants from all over the world. Courses are offered in humanities, social sciences, and environmental protection. The fee of $2,120 covers field trips, registration, and room and board at Blindern Student Home. You can receive a detailed catalog and application form from: Oslo International Summer School, North American Admissions Office, c/o Saint Olaf College, 1520 Saint Olaf Avenue, Northfield MN 55057-1098 (tel. 507/663-3269).

FOR GAY MEN & LESBIANS   Call the **Gay Switchboard** (tel. 38-22-28) any time daily between 8 and 11pm. An English-speaking representative will provide you with the latest details about gay and lesbian life in Oslo as well as what clubs are currently in vogue.

Tromso Bokhandel, Kristian Augustsgate 19 (tel. 20-25-09), sells a wide range of gay and lesbian books.

FOR WOMEN   The Women's Center in Oslo burned down in 1990. Check with the tourist office (see above) to see if a new one has opened by the time of your visit.

Violent crimes against women, including rape, are extremely rare in Norway—virtually nonexistent in most parts of the country. However, the usual precautions and discretion smart women would exercise anywhere should be followed in Norway. Norway has a rape crisis center called **Krisesenteret** (tel. 35-00-48). Only the telephone number is given out. Victims calling this number are "screened" on the phone before they are given the address of the center. This is done for security reasons.

Oslo has no hotels set aside for women only.

CHAPTER 14

OSLO ACCOMMODATIONS & DINING

1. OSLO ACCOMMODATIONS

- **FROMMER'S COOL FOR KIDS: HOTELS**

2. OSLO DINING

- **FROMMER'S COOL FOR KIDS: RESTAURANTS**

In recent years, many of Oslo's major hotels and restaurants have been completely restored or rebuilt, and now the city offers some of the finest in European accommodations and dining. This is not to mention the many establishments that have opened for the first time in Oslo, bringing to the city a more modern and international flair.

1. OSLO ACCOMMODATIONS

By the standards of many cities in the United States or Canada, hotels in Oslo are very expensive indeed, even the so-called moderate ones. Therefore, the category of "moderate" means it's moderate for Oslo. In your hometown, the moderate price might buy you luxury.

Hotels labeled "Very Expensive" charge $280 to $330 a night for a double; "Expensive," $215 to $260; "Moderate," $130 to $180; and "Inexpensive," $95 to $125. Breakfast is almost always included in these prices, and it's usually a generous Norwegian buffet. Budget is a special category; the cheapest of all is a youth hostel.

Before these high prices make you cancel your trip, read on. Oslovian hotels lose most of their business travelers—the main source of their revenue—during the peak tourist visiting months of midsummer. Even though the town is filled with visitors at this time, many hoteliers slash their prices. July is always a month for discounts. Some hotels extend their discounts from June 21 to mid-August. Regular pricing usually begins in mid-August. For exact dates of these discounts, check with the hotel.

Likewise, hoteliers slash prices on weekends. A weekend is most often defined as Friday and Saturday, maybe Sunday. Sometimes regular prices are charged on Sunday night. Again, hotels often change their policies, so it's best to check what the price scale is going to be when making reservations. Don't always count on a discount; a sudden conference in the city could result in increased prices.

The most economy-minded tourists will cut prices even more by booking into one of the more old-fashioned hotels that still offer a number of rooms without private bath. Sometimes a shower is included in a room, but no toilet. In most cases, corridor toilets and bathrooms are in adequate supply. Even the bathless rooms will usually offer a sink with hot and cold running water.

HOTEL RESERVATIONS   The worst months for finding a place to stay in Oslo are May, June, September, and October, since many business conferences are held at this time. July and August are better, even though that's the peak time of the summer tourist invasion.

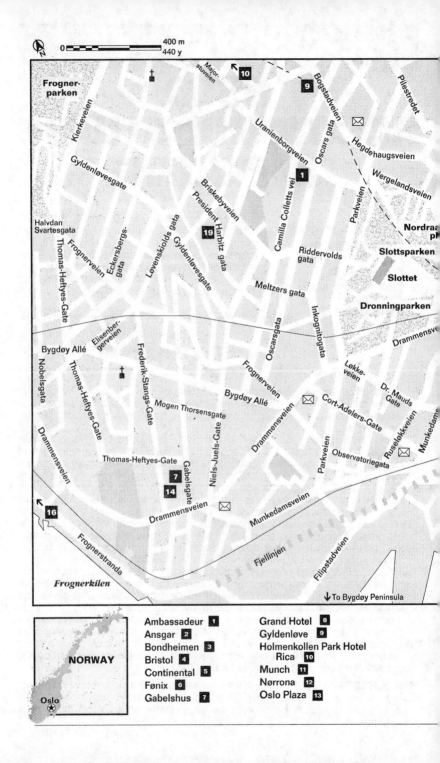

0 ⊢━━━━━━┤ 400 m
          440 y

Frogner-
parken

Major-
stua veien

10

9

Bogstadveien

Pilestredet

Kierkeveien

Uranienborgveien

Oscars gata

Hegdehaugsveien

Gyldenløvesgate

Wergelandsveien

Briskebyveien

1

Camilla Colletts vei

Parkveien

**Nordraa
p**

President Harbitz gata

Halvdan
Svartesgata

Eckersbergs-
gata

Løvenskiolds gata

Gyldenløvesgate

19

Riddervolds
gata

Slottsparken

Thomas-Heftyes-Gate

Frognerveien

Meltzers gata

Slottet

Inkognitogata

Dronningparken

Elisenber-
gerveien

Oscarsgata

Drammensv

Bygdøy Allé

Frognerveien

Frederik-Stangs-Gate

Løkke-
veien

Dr. Mauds
Gate

Nobelsgata

Thomas-Heftyes-Gate

Mogen Thorsensgate

Bygdøy Allé

Cort-Adelers-Gate

Ruseløkkveien

Munkedams

Drammensveien

Drammensveien

Niels-Juels-Gate

Parkveien

Observatoriegata

7

Gabelsgate

14

Thomas-Heftyes-Gate

Munkedamsveien

16

Drammensveien

Frognerstranda

Fjellinjen

Filipstadveien

Frognerkilen

↓To Bygdøy Peninsula

NORWAY

Oslo
☆

Ambassadeur **1**

Ansgar **2**

Bondheimen **3**

Bristol **4**

Continental **5**

Fønix **6**

Gabelshus **7**

Grand Hotel **8**

Gyldenløve **9**

Holmenkollen Park Hotel
　Rica **10**

Munch **11**

Nørrona **12**

Oslo Plaza **13**

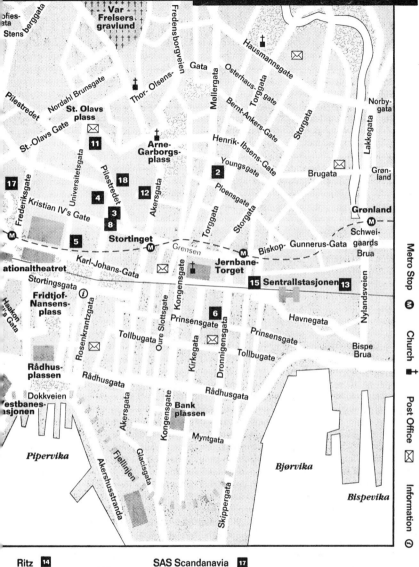

Var
Frelsers
gravlund

ofies-
ata
Stens berggata

Fredensborgveien

Gata

Hausmannsgate

Norby-
gata

Lakkegata

Nordahl Brunsgate

Thor- Olsens-

Møllergata

Osterhaus-

Torggate

gate

Storgata

Bernt-Ankers-Gate

Pilestredet

St. Olavs
plass

St.-Olavs Gate

**St. Olavs
plass**

11

Arne-
Garborgs-
plass

Henrik- Ibsens-Gate

Brugata

Grøn-
land

Universitetsgata

Pilestredet

Akersgata

Youngsgate

2

17

Frederiksgate

Kristian IV's Gate

18

4

12

Ploensgate

Grønland

M

3

Torggata

Storgata

Schwei-
gaards
Brua

8

5

Stortinget

M

Grensen

Biskop- Gunnerus-Gata

Karl-Johans-Gata

Kongensgate

**Jernbane-
Torget**

M

ationaltheatret

Stortingsgata

15 **Sentralstasjonen** 13

**Fridtjof-
Nansens-
plass**

Rosenkrantzgata

Oure Slottsgate

Prinsensgate

6

Dronnigensgata

Prinsensgate

Havnegata

Nylandsveien

Bispe
Brua

Tollbugata

Kirkegata

Tollbugate

**Rådhus-
plassen**

Rådhusgata

Rådhusgata

Akersgata

Kongensgate

**Bank
plassen**

Dokkveien

estbanes-
asjonen

Myntgata

Haakon
I's Gata

Pipervika

Fjellinjen

Glacisgata

Akershusstranda

Bjørvika

Skippergata

Bispevika

The **Innkvartering** kiosk at the Central Station (tel. 17-11-24) will help visitors who need a room in a hurry upon arrival. If they can't find a hotel in the price range you specify, they'll book you into a private home or apartment. That will cost from 225 kroner ($37.35) for a bathless double, from 140 kroner ($23.25) for a single. The service charge for on-the-spot booking is 15 kroner ($2.50) per adult, 5 kroner (85¢) per child, plus a small deposit. Minimum stay is 2 days.

The accommodation center is open May to the end of September, daily from 7am to 11pm, and October to the end of April, daily from 8am to 11pm. It is closed on some holidays.

Oslo Promotion, Rådhusgaten 19 (tel. 33-43-86), can assist visitors with overnight accommodation in hotels and boardinghouses. Advance booking must be requested in a written application to Oslo Promotion, Rådhusgaten 23, N-0158 Oslo 1, Norway, 21 days before your arrival date and must contain the following: name and address, dates of arrival and departure, required standard and price class, and a bank draft for 100 kroner ($16.60) per person. This payment includes a booking fee of 30 kroner ($5) and a deposit to the establishment in which your rooms are reserved. The deposit will be deducted from your bill upon departure. Cancellations must be made in writing at least 8 days before the date of arrival and sent directly to the accommodation address. A full refund cannot be guaranteed. Visitors will receive a written confirmation of their reservations with a receipt for the advance payment. Hotel rates are given in the group's price list. Boardinghouses cost 180 to 250 kroner ($29.85 to $41.50) for a single room, 300 to 450 kroner ($49.75 to $74.65) for a double. Private home accommodations cannot be booked in advance, but are handled upon your arrival at the accommodation office at the Central Station.

The office is open May 1 to the end of September, daily from 7am to 11pm; October to April, daily from 8am to 11pm.

Note: Tariffs quoted below for hotels include service charge and tax.

IN THE CENTER

VERY EXPENSIVE

GRAND HOTEL, Karl Johans Gate 31, N-0159 Oslo 1. Tel. 02/42-93-90, or toll free 800/223-5652 in the U.S. Fax 02/42-12-25. 290 rms, 50 suites. MINIBAR TV TEL **Metro:** Sentrum.

$ Rates (including buffet breakfast): Mon–Thurs, 1,800 kroner ($298.60) single; 2,000 kroner ($331.80) double. Fri–Sun, 700 kroner ($116.15) single; 1,000 kroner ($165.90) double. From 2,500 kroner ($414.75) suites. AE, DC, MC, V.

Norway's leading hotel, located on the wide boulevard that leads to the Royal Palace, this stone-walled hotel with its mansard gables and copper tower has been an integral part of Oslo life since it was built in 1874. Famous guests include Arctic explorer Roald Amundsen, Edvard Munch, Gen. Dwight Eisenhower, Charlie Chaplin, Henry Ford, and Henrik Ibsen, who was especially fond of the place.

Bedrooms are either in the 19th-century core or in one of the tasteful new additions. The modern rooms contain plush facilities and electronic amenities, and the older ones have been completely modernized as well to offer luxurious comfort. Some accommodations have air conditioning.

Dining/Entertainment: The hotel has several restaurants, serving both international and Scandinavian food. Two, the Palmen and the Grand Café, offer live entertainment. The Grand Café is the most famous in Oslo, but you can also partake of the French-inspired cuisine at Etoile or enjoy the British clublike atmosphere of the Grand Grill. The Bonanza, a night restaurant with dancing, specializes in steaks. The lobby-level Limelight Bar is connected to the Oslo Nyte Teater next door, and the Etoile Bar is an informal meeting place next to the swimming pool.

Services: Laundry and room service, guide services, message desk, express checkout, safety deposit boxes, and a sophisticated concierge.

Facilities: Indoor swimming pool, sauna, solarium, boutiques, car-rental desk.

HOTEL CONTINENTAL, Stortingsgaten 24-26, N-0117 Oslo 1. Tel.

02/41-90-60. Fax 02/42-96-89. 170 rms (all with bath), 12 suites. A/C MINIBAR TV TEL **Metro:** Sentrum.

$ **Rates** (including breakfast): Winter, 1,450–1,650 kroner ($240.55–$273.75) single; 1,750–1,850 kroner ($240.55–$273.53) double; from 2,500 kroner ($414.75) suite. Summer, 575 kroner ($95.40) single; 930 kroner ($154.30) double. AE, DC, MC, V. **Parking:** Garage available.

One of the leading hotels of Europe, right in the city center midway between the Royal Palace and the City Hall, the Continental is rich in tradition and quality. Built in 1900, it has been owned by the same family for four generations. Personal service is a hallmark of the hotel. Bedrooms have style and grace and are furnished in light Nordic tones with many amenities.

Dining/Entertainment: Annen Etage is a gourmet restaurant, one of the finest in Norway. The Tivoligrillen is more moderately priced with an excellent grill menu, and the Theatercafeen is northern Europe's only surviving Viennese café. The Continental Bar contains Norway's largest privately owned collection of Edvard Munch paintings, and the Loftet is the hotel's disco, built like an attic. Breakfast is served at Carolines.

Services: Baby-sitter upon request, laundry.

Facilities: Private underground garage, newsstand, perfumery, men's hairdresser.

SAS SCANDINAVIA, Holbergsgate 30, N-0166 Oslo 1. Tel. 02/11-30-00. Fax 02/11-30-17. 487 rms (all with bath), 4 suites. A/C MINIBAR TV TEL **Bus:** 17, 76.

$ **Rates** (including breakfast): Standard rooms: Mon–Thurs, 1,460 kroner ($242.20) single; 1,680 kroner ($278.70) double. Fri–Sun, 775 kroner ($125.55) single; 930 kroner ($154.30) double. Children under 15 free. Royal Club: Mon–Thurs, 1,780 kroner ($295.30) single, 1,990 kroner ($330.15) double; Fri–Sun, 1,280 kroner ($212.35) single, 1,420 kroner ($235.60) double. From 3,000 kroner ($497.70) suite. AE, DC, MC, V.

Near the Royal Palace, this is one of two hotels in the Oslo area operated by Scandinavian Airlines (the other is at the airport). The hotel is a well-managed and attractive place, drawing mainly business clients in the winter and tourists in the summer. From many of its nicely decorated and well-furnished bedrooms, there are views of the fjord. Rooms have several amenities including video, hairdryer, and trouser press. The best rooms are in the Royal Club, spread across three separate floors with their own breakfast lounge, electronic safe, and such extra touches as bathrobes, slippers, and fruit baskets.

Dining/Entertainment: The hotel operates five restaurants, including the Holberg, widely regarded as Oslo's best restaurant. Less expensive, the Brasseriet serves from an excellent menu amid an art deco–inspired chic. You can drink and eat at Charly's and the Galaxy. The Summit 21 is spectacular, a "sky bar" on the 21st floor with views over the city.

Services: Room service, baby-sitting, express laundry service, complete business services, express SAS airline check-ins.

Facilities: Health club, exercise room, swimming pool, sauna.

EXPENSIVE

BRISTOL, Kristian IV's Gate 7, N-0164 Oslo 1. Tel. 02/41-58-40. Fax 02/42-85-51. 141 rms (all with bath) 4 suites. A/C MINIBAR TV TEL **Metro:** Sentrum.

$ **Rates** (including breakfast): Mon–Thurs (except July), 1,190–1,350 kroner ($197.40–$223.95) single; 1,490 kroner ($247.20) double. July and weekends year round, 500 kroner ($82.95) single; 750 kroner ($124.45) double. AE, DC, MC, V.

In the heart of the city, on a side street north of Karl Johans Gate, the Bristol is the choice of many a discriminating traveler. Traditional in style, this 1920s-era hotel is warm, inviting, and luxurious. The Moorish-inspired lobby, with its

Winter Garden and Library Bar, sets the elegant tone. Bedrooms have special character, most often furnished in light Nordic pastels, homelike and comfortable. Many thoughtful amenities are installed, including hairdryers and trouser presses.

Dining/Entertainment. The Bristol has several drinking and dining possibilities, including the intimate Bristol Grill, featuring meats grilled over charcoal. El Toro is a dine-and-dance restaurant, with live bands and a welcoming bar. You can also enjoy a drink at the Bristol Lounge.

Services: Room service, laundry and dry-cleaning service, baby-sitting.

Facilities: Studio Bristol for hair and skin care.

MODERATE

BONDHEIMEN, Rosenkrantzgate 8, N-0159 Oslo 1. Tel. 02/42-95-30.
Fax 02/41-94-37. 76 rms (all with bath). MINIBAR TV TEL **Tram:** 7, 11.

$ **Rates** (including breakfast): Sun–Thurs (except July), 1,000 kroner ($165.90) single; 1,140 kroner ($189.15) double. July and year round, Fri–Sat 560 kroner ($92.90) single; 720 kroner ($119.45) double. AE, DC, MC, V.

In the city center, only a short block from the Students' Grove at Karl Johans Gate, the Bondheimen was built in 1913 by a cooperative of farmers and students to provide inexpensive, clean, and safe accommodations when they visited Oslo from the countryside. Each bedroom is outfitted with modern Norwegian furniture and contains such extras as a trouser press. The minibar has drinks but no alcohol, as the hotel is alcohol-free. At street level is a self-service Kaffistova (cafeteria), dispensing good Norwegian food to its cost-conscious clients.

STEFAN HOTEL, Rosenkrantzgate 1, N-0159 Oslo 1. Tel. 02/42-92-50.
Fax 02/33-70-22. 130 rms (all with bath). MINIBAR TV TEL **Tram:** 7, 11.

$ **Rates** (including breakfast): Sun–Thurs (except July), 1,125 kroner ($186.65) single; 1,225 kroner ($203.25) double. July and Fri–Sat year round, 500 kroner ($82.95) single; 740 kroner ($122.75) double. AE, DC, MC, V.

In an excellent location in the center of the city, this hotel is clean, comfortable, and unpretentious. Built in 1952, it has been modernized and much improved since then. Bedrooms are well furnished and maintained, and are comfortably and tastefully decorated. Facilities for the handicapped are available in two of the bedrooms. Its eighth-floor restaurant is one of the city's lunchtime landmarks (see "Oslo Dining," in this chapter).

INEXPENSIVE

ANSGAR HOTEL, Møllergaten 26, N-0179 Oslo 1. Tel. 02/20-47-35. Fax 02/20-54-53. 58 rms (18 with shower). TEL **Tram:** 2, 7, 11.

$ **Rates** (including breakfast): Mon–Thurs in winter, 500 kroner ($82.95) single without bath, 620 kroner ($102.85) single with shower; 650 kroner ($107.85) double without bath, 750 kroner ($124.45) double with shower. Summer and Fri–Sun year round, 375 single ($62.20) without bath, 475 kroner ($78.80) single with shower; 475 kroner ($78.80) double without bath, 575 kroner ($95.40) double with shower. AE, DC, MC, V.

⑤ Well built and well decorated, the Ansgar, located off Youngstorget, a 2-minute walk from the Opera House, draws a conservative clientele who want good, plain comfort. All rooms were last renovated in 1987. The hotel has an indoor garage. No alcohol is served.

MUNCH, Munchsgatan 5, N-0130 Oslo 1. Tel. 02/42-42-75. Fax 02/20-64-69. 180 rms (all with bath). MINIBAR TV TEL **Metro:** Sentrum.

$ **Rates** (including breakfast): Mon–Thurs in winter, 620 kroner ($102.85) single; 725 kroner ($120.30) double. Summer and Fri–Sun year round, 350 kroner ($58.05) single; 460 kroner ($76.30) double. AE, DC, MC, V.

⑤ Five minutes north of Karl Johans Gate is this good one-star hotel—really like a bed-and-breakfast. Built in 1983, it offers comfortably furnished, well-maintained, and functional bedrooms, decorated with reproductions of Edvard

Munch paintings. There is no bar or restaurant, but the surrounding neighborhood is well supplied.

NORRØNA, Grensen 19, N-0159 Oslo 1. Tel. 02/42-64-00. Fax 02/33-25-65. 40 rms (all with bath). TV TEL **Bus:** 17. **Tram:** 1, 7.

$ Rates (including breakfast): Sun–Thurs in winter, 660 kroner ($109.50) single; 780 kroner ($129.40) double. Summer and Fri–Sat year round, 525 kroner ($87.10) single; 625 kroner ($103.70) double. AE, DC, MC, V.

⑤ In the heart of Oslo's old section, occupying the upper floors of a modernized building, this hotel is great for families. It's a safe, clean haven, with a reasonably priced cafeteria. Convenient to both sightseeing and shopping, it offers well-equipped rooms furnished in Scandinavia modern, a few with private balconies. The lounge is homelike and informal.

IN THE WEST END

EXPENSIVE

HOTEL AMBASSADEUR, Camilla Colletts Vei 15, N-0258 Oslo 2. Tel. 02/44-18-35. Fax 02/44-47-91. 42 rms (all with bath), 8 suites. MINIBAR TV TEL **Bus:** 1, 11.

$ Rates (including breakfast): Mon–Thurs Sept–May, 1,150 kroner ($190.80) single; 1,370 kroner ($227.30) double; from 1,500 kroner ($248.85) suite. June–Aug and weekends year round, 550 kroner ($91.25) single; 700 kroner ($116.15) double. AE, DC, MC, V.

Located in the west end in the vicinity of the Royal Palace, this hotel is considered intimate by Oslo standards. Sometimes attracting diplomats, it is a first-class executive hotel with personalized service. Each room is decorated in a different style, evoking such places as classical Rome or colonial Shanghai. Particularly attractive is the hotel's basement bar, with an English club atmosphere. The sophisticated restaurant, Sabroso, offers full meals, such as marinated salmon and smoked filet of partridge, priced from 335 kroner ($55.60). It is one of Oslo's best restaurants, decorated with paintings and an elegant decor. A swimming pool and sauna are on the lower ground floor.

MODERATE

FØNIX, Dronningensgate 19, N-0154 Oslo 1. Tel. 02/42-59-57. Fax 02/33-12-10. 67 rms (17 with bath). TEL **Metro:** Jernbanetorget.

$ Rates (including breakfast): 300–370 kroner ($49.75–$61.40) single without bath, 400–460 kroner ($66.35–$76.30) single with bath; 500–600 kroner ($82.95–$99.55) double without bath, 850 kroner ($141) double with bath. Extra bed 200 kroner ($33.20). AE, MC, DC, V.

A 3-minute walk from the Central Station, the Hotel Fønix offers great value. Though constructed in 1924, the hotel has been frequently redecorated. For the single traveler on a budget, the hotel is a good bet, as it offers 38 single rooms without bath. Breakfast is served in its restaurant, Kristine, furnished with turn-of-the-century oak dining suites. The hotel is fully licensed and serves an international cuisine.

GABELSHUS, Gabels Gate 16, N-0205 Oslo 2. Tel. 02/55-22-60. Fax 02/44-27-30. 45 rms (all with bath). TV TEL **Bus:** 9.

$ Rates (including breakfast): Mon–Thurs, 800 kroner ($132.70) single; 1,000 kroner ($165.90) double. Fri–Sun, 550 kroner ($91.25) single; 750 kroner ($124.45) double. Summer discounts available. AE, DC, MC, V.

Lying on a quiet, tree-lined street in the west end, this hotel building dates from 1912 and it has been a small hotel since 1945. Discreetly conservative, the look is that of an English manor house, laced with climbing ivy. Public rooms are filled with antiques, art, burnished copper, and working fireplaces. Each of the bedrooms is decorated with tasteful colors and textiles, some with private baths and terraces. The elegant restaurant serves meals costing from 150 kroner ($24.90). It's a brisk 15-minute walk from the town center.

RITZ HOTEL, Frederick Stangs Gate 3, N-0272 Oslo 2. Tel. 02/44-39-60. Fax 02/44-67-13. 52 rooms (all with bath). TV TEL **Tram:** 9.
$ Rates (including breakfast): Mon–Thurs, 800 kroner ($132.70) single; 1,000 kroner ($165.90) double. Fri–Sun, 550 kroner ($91.25) single; 650 kroner ($107.85) double. AE, DC, MC, V. **Parking:** Available.

On the western outskirts of Oslo, a 2-minute walk from the British Embassy, this well-run 1915 hotel is owned by the slightly more upscale Gabelshus (see above). In an area of expensive private villas, it offers good value for the neighborhood. Rooms are well maintained and comfortable. Drinks are served in the rooms at all hours. The hotel's restaurant serves meals for 260 kroner ($43.15). The Ritz shares a parking lot with the Gabelshus.

WHITE HOUSE, President Harbitzgatan 18, N-0259 Oslo 2. Tel. 02/14-19-60. 21 rms (all with bath). MINIBAR TV TEL **Tram:** 1.
$ Rates (including breakfast): Sun–Thurs in winter, 650 kroner ($107.85) single; 800 kroner ($132.70) double. Summer and Fri–Sat year round, 450 kroner ($74.65) single; 600 kroner ($99.55) double. AE, DC, MC, V.

Only 15 minutes by foot from the city center, the White House is in Breskeby, a comfortable residential section in back of the Royal Palace. It was built around 1900 as a private house, but has been greatly modernized since. Rooms are simply furnished, but comfortable, and all are well maintained. There's a fondue restaurant, Den Lille Fondue, where you can dine inside or on an outdoor wooden platform overlooking the street in summer. It is open daily from 5 to 11pm.

INEXPENSIVE

GYLDENLØVE, Bogstadveien 20, N-0355 Oslo 3. Tel. 02/60-10-90. Fax 02/60-33-90. 168 rms (133 with shower). MINIBAR TV TEL **Tram:** 1, 11.
$ Rates (including breakfast): Sun–Thurs in winter, 350 kroner ($58.05) single without shower; 475–675 kroner ($78.80–$112) single with shower; 520 kroner ($86.25) double without shower, 620–880 kroner ($102.85–$146) double with shower. July and Fri–Sat year round, 275 kroner ($45.60) single without shower; 320–420 kroner ($53.10–$69.70) single with shower; 350 kroner ($58.05) double without shower, 490–540 kroner ($81.30–$89.60) double with shower. AE, DC, MC, V.

Built in 1937, this eight-story modern *hospits* offers spacious, comfortably designed rooms. Most bedrooms are completely furnished, with wood-grained units and wall-to-wall draperies. Note that 48 of the bedrooms that have a private shower do not have a sink or toilet, although corridor facilities are adequate. The hotel is a 10-minute walk from the grounds of the Royal Palace.

NEAR THE CENTRAL STATION

VERY EXPENSIVE

OSLO PLAZA HOTEL, Sonja Henies Plads 3, N-0107 Oslo 1. Tel. 02/17-10-00. Fax 02/17-73-00. 650 rms (all with bath), 19 suites. A/C MINIBAR TV TEL **Bus:** 14, 24, 71.
$ Rates (including breakfast): Standard rooms: Sun–Thurs (except midsummer), 1,490 kroner ($247.20) single; 1,690 kroner ($280.35) double. Midsummer and Fri–Sat (sometimes Sun) year round, 675 kroner ($112) single; 925 kroner ($153.45) double; from 2,500 kroner ($414.75) suite. Plaza Tower: 1,690–1,790

kroner ($280.35–$296.95) single; 1,940–2,040 kroner ($321.85–$338.45) double. AE, DC, MC, V.

Opened by the late King Olav V in 1990, this 37-floor "skyscraper" stands in the Vaterland district, near the railway station. It is the largest hotel in northern Europe, with its public Skywalk on the top floor, the highest viewing point. Guests flock to Scandinavia's tallest building for rooms, dining, and entertainment. Plaza Tower is a hotel within a hotel, with greater service, comfort, and quality in the bedrooms. All rooms are tastefully furnished in modern colors, with a number of amenities. Much of the hotel is decorated with original art, including many paintings by prominent Norwegian artists.

Dining/Entertainment: Brasserie Abelone is a popular French brasserie and Ristorante Lakata is a classical Italian restaurant serving dinner only. The Jens Jap Bar is decorated like an English library, and Lilletorvet in the lobby lounge serves homemade pastries. The Skybar is the highest supperclub in Scandinavia.

Services: Baby-sitting, room service, laundry and dry cleaning, business services.

Facilities: Health center, largest convention center in northern Europe, Sonja Henie Ballroom (named after the famous Norwegian skating champion and film star).

ROYAL CHRISTIANIA, Biskop Gunnerus Gate 3, N-0106 Oslo 1. Tel. 02/42-94-10. Fax 02/42-46-22. 456 rms (all with bath). A/C MINIBAR TV TEL **Bus:** 30, 31, 41. **Tram:** 2.

$ Rates (including breakfast): Winter, Mon–Thurs, 1,550 kroner ($257.15) single, 1,750 kroner ($290.35) double; Fri–Sun, 900 kroner ($149.30) single, 1,050 kroner ($174.20) double. Summer, 550 kroner ($91.25) single; 920 kroner ($152.65) double. AE, DC, MC, V. **Parking:** Available in the basement.

Fifty yards from the rail station, this is a five-star luxury hotel that opened in 1990 in the Vaterland district following a total rebuilding. The hotel was originally constructed for the 1952 Oslo Winter Olympics. Now it is one of Norway's finest hotels. Rooms are quiet, comfortable, and tastefully designed, and round-the-clock room service is provided.

Dining/Entertainment: The Christiania has three restaurants and five bars, serving international, American, Italian, and Scandinavian food. The Atrium opens onto a view of a "forest" of greenery with a waterfall, La Trattoria serves excellent pasta and meat dishes, and Christian IV is the classic choice with top-notch service. Guests in winter can enjoy a drink in front of the fireplace in the Library, or patronize the Frederik Piano Bar. Vintage wine is served at Baccus, the pub is called Off-Side, and Clockworks is the late-night café and disco.

Services: 24-hour room service, baby-sitting, massage, business services.

Facilities: Circular pool with wave machine, solarium, Finnish sauna, Turkish bath, boutiques, basement parking.

NEAR THE HOLMENKOLLEN SKI JUMP

EXPENSIVE

HOLMENKOLLEN PARK HOTEL RICA, Kongeveien 26, N-0390 Oslo 3. Tel. 02/14-60-90, or toll free 800/223-5652 in the U.S. Fax 02/14-61-92. 191 rms (all with bath). A/C MINIBAR TV TEL **Bus:** Holmenkollen, from the center.

$ Rates (including breakfast): Mon–Thurs in winter, 1,195 kroner ($198.25) single; 1,295 kroner ($214.85) double. Summer and Fri–Sun year round, 745 kroner ($123.60) single; 845 kroner ($140.20) double. AE, DC, MC, V.

Holmenkollen Park Hotel Rica lies on Holmenkollen hill near the famous Ski Jump, only 15 minutes from the city center. Opened in 1982 as an enlargement of an original timber building, the hotel has Viking carvings and characteristic turrets dating back to 1894. Holm Munthe, the architect, was a modern pioneer in the "dragon motif" and the hotel itself is a work of art, with paintings and decorations by famous Norwegian

FROMMER'S COOL FOR KIDS
HOTELS

Bristol *(see p. 217)* One of the most elegant and comfortable hotels of Oslo welcomes children and lets those under 15 stay free in their parents' room. The chef will even put a "junior steak" on the grill.

Holmenkollen Park Hotel Rica *(see p. 221)* A kid-pleaser if there ever was one in both summer and winter. It's near the famous ski jump and has its own swimming pool and sports facilities. Children under 4 stay free; those 4 to 16 get a 50% discount in three- or four-bedded rooms.

Norønna *(see p. 219)* A reliable choice, attracting the economy-minded family trade. An extra bed in a parent's room costs 125 kroner ($20.75), and there's a moderately priced café on the premises.

Royal Christiania *(see p. 221)* Kids delight in the circular pool with a wave machine. Fruit juices and snacks are served in the afternoon. Baby-sitting can be arranged.

---

artists, including Munthe and Weidemann. The hotel's panoramic views open onto the greater Oslo area, with its fjords. Most bedrooms are in new wings that have been added to the original structure. Each is well furnished and equipped with modern amenities.

Dining/Entertainment: In the old part, the gourmet restaurant is De Fem Stuer (The Five Rooms), which is beautifully decorated in the old Norwegian style with lots of paneling and elegant accessories. Meals are also served in the Bakeriet (The Bakery), with grill specialties and a copious salad bar. Drinks are offered in the Atrium, with green plants and forest views. There is also a lobby bar and nightclub.

Services: Baby-sitting, room service.

Facilities: Swimming pool, saunas, whirlpool, illuminated ski tracks outside the door.

FORNEBU AIRPORT

EXPENSIVE

SAS PARK ROYAL, Fornebuparken, N-1324 Lysaker-Oslo. Tel. 02/12-02-20. Fax 02/12-00-11. 254 rms (all with bath). A/C MINIBAR TV TEL.
$ Rates (including breakfast): Standard rooms, Mon–Thurs, 1,295 kroner ($214.85) single, 1,490 kroner ($247.20) double; weekends, 770 kroner ($127.75) single, 910 kroner ($150.95) double. Royal Club, 1,610 kroner ($267.10) single; 1,860 kroner ($308.60) double. AE, DC, MC, V.

In Fornebu Park close to the Oslofjord and 2 minutes by car from the airport, this hotel opened in 1971 as a member of SAS International Hotels. Aimed primarily at business clients, it also welcomes sightseers, especially those who want to be near the airport for convenient departures. Bedrooms have attractive styling and furnishings, often in autumnal tones. The Royal Club, a hotel within the hotel, has upgraded services and facilities.

Dining/Entertainment: The hotel has one restaurant, Fornebu Park, known for its international kitchen and Scandinavian specialties. There is also the Symphony Bar, offering sandwiches and a light lunch menu.

Services: Laundry service, SAS Euroclass check-in, SAS Service Center (hotel reservations, air tickets, car rental, and the like).

Facilities: Health club, sauna, whirlpool, lobby shop with newsstand, tennis court, solarium.

2. OSLO DINING

In the past few years Oslo has had an explosion of restaurants unprecedented in Scandinavia. You can now "dine around the world" without leaving Oslo. The biggest concentration of restaurants is at Aker Brygge, a former shipbuilding yard on the harborfront—now turned into the smartest dining and shopping complex in Norway.

Not all restaurants in Oslo are new. Some have long associations with artists and writers, like the Grand Café, former stamping ground of Henrik Ibsen and Edvard Munch, and the Theatercafeen and Blom.

The influx of foreigners in recent years has led to the growth of international restaurants, represented by Mexico, Turkey, Morocco, China, Greece, and others. Among the European cuisines, French and Italian are the most popular; many restaurants offer American-style food as well.

At nearly all restaurants recommended below, a 15% service charge is included, as is the 20% Value-Added Tax. No further tipping is required, although it is customary to leave some small change if service has been good. Of course, that added 35% means that many restaurant tabs appear unreasonably high.

The "Very Expensive" category indicates meals that generally cost $60 or more; "Expensive," $40 to $50; "Moderate," $20 to $25; and "Inexpensive" is anything under $20. Wine and beer can be lethal to your final bill, so be careful.

IN THE CENTER

VERY EXPENSIVE

D'ARTAGNAN, Øvre Slottsgate 16. Tel. 41-50-62.
   Cuisine: FRENCH. **Reservations:** Required. **Bus:** 27, 29, 30, 41, 61.
$ Prices: Fixed-price menu 550 kroner ($91.25), appetizers 100–155 kroner ($16.60–$25.70); main dishes 220–255 kroner ($36.50–$42.30). AE, DC, MC, V.
   Open: Dinner only, Mon–Fri (also Sat Oct–Christmas) 4:30pm–midnight.
   Closed: July.

Named after one of the dashing three musketeers, the owner's childhood hero, this is a temple of gastronomy. Freddie Neilsen uses some of the best Norwegian ingredients for his menu, which changes four or five times a year, as the seasons do. There's no sign in front, giving the restaurant the allure of a private club, but a discreet brass plaque announces the place, and you ring a bell to enter. One flight up is a bar with Chesterfield sofas where you can order an apéritif and peruse the menu.

The dining room is up another flight of stairs, with pink marble tables, a royal-blue color scheme, and lots of silver accents. Selections include sole baked in shellfish in spiced butter (a favorite of Harry Belafonte), reindeer with white sherry sauce, quail in filo pastry with duck-liver sauce, and an appetizer of Norwegian bouillabaisse, cooled and refrigerated until it congeals into a terrine. It's served with a garlicky rouille and a saffron-flavored vinaigrette.

HOLBERG, in the SAS Scandinavia Hotel, Holbergsgate 30. Tel. 11-30-00.
   Cuisine: FRENCH. **Reservations:** Required. **Bus:** 17, 76.
$ Prices: Fixed-priced menu 385 kroner ($63.85) for three courses, 525 kroner

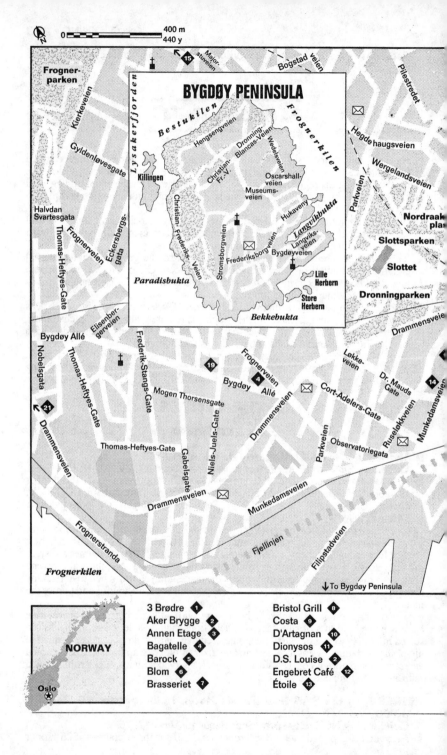

0 400 m
   440 y

BYGDØY PENINSULA

Frogner-
parken

Major-
stuveien

Bogstad veien

Pilestredet

Lysakerfjorden

Bestukilen

Frognerkilen

Hegde haugsveien

Wergelandsveien

Kierkeveien

Gyldenløvesgate

Hengsengveien

Dronning-
Blancas-Veien

Christian-
Fr.-V.

Wedelsveien

Oscarshall-
veien

Museums-
veien

Killingen

Parkveien

Nordraak
plas

Halvdan
Svartesgata

Eckersbergs-
gata

Frognerveien

Hukaveny

Langvikbukta

Slottsparken

Christian-
frederiks-
Veien

Stromsborgveien

Frederiksborgveien

Langviks-
veien

Slottet

Thomas-Heftyes-Gate

Paradisbukta

Bygdøyveien

Lille
Herbern

Dronningparken

Store
Herbern

Bekkebukta

Drammensveie

Bygdøy Allé

Elisenber-
gerveien

Frognerveien

Løkke-
veien

Nobelsgata

Thomas-Heftyes-Gate

Frederik-Stangs-Gate

19

Bygdøy **4** Allé

Dr. Mauds
Gate

14

Mogen Thorsensgate

Cort-Adelers-Gate

Ruseløkkveien

Munkedamsveien

21

Niels-Juels-Gate

Drammensveien

Parkveien

Observatoriegata

Thomas-Heftyes-Gate

Gabelsgate

Drammensveien

Drammensveien

Munkedamsveien

Frognerstranda

Fjellinjen

Filipstadveien

Frognerkilen

↓To Bygdøy Peninsula

NORWAY

Oslo

3 Brødre **1**

Aker Brygge **2**

Annen Etage **3**

Bagatelle **4**

Barock **5**

Blom **6**

Brasseriet **7**

Bristol Grill **8**

Costa **9**

D'Artagnan **10**

Dionysos **11**

D.S. Louise **2**

Engebret Café **12**

Étoile **13**

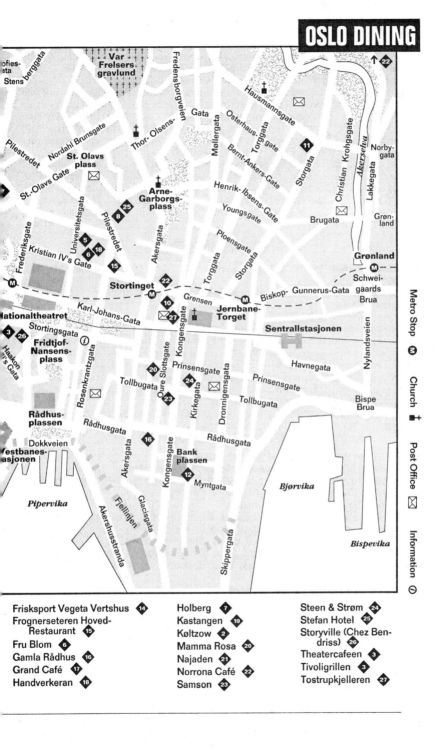

Metro Stop Ⓜ

Church ⛪

Post Office ✉

Information ⓘ

Frisksport Vegeta Vertshus **14**
Frognerseteren Hoved-
    Restaurant **15**
Fru Blom **6**
Gamla Rådhus **16**
Grand Café **17**
Handverkeran **18**

Holberg **7**
Kastangen **19**
Køltzow **2**
Mamma Rosa **20**
Najaden **21**
Norrona Café **22**
Samson **23**

Steen & Strøm **24**
Stefan Hotel **25**
Storyville (Chez Ben-
    driss) **26**
Theatercafeen **3**
Tivoligrillen **3**
Tostrupkjelleren **27**

($87.10) for the six-course "symphony"; appetizers 98–136 kroner ($16.25–$22.55); main dishes 225–275 kroner ($37.35–$45.60). AE, DC, MC, V.
Open: Dinner only, Tues–Sat 7–11pm. **Closed:** July.

✪ Generally acclaimed as one of the finest restaurants in Oslo—if not the finest—this restaurant is on the ground floor of the SAS Scandinavia Hotel (see "Oslo Accommodations," in this chapter). Enjoy an apéritif in the Klim Bar, then head to the intensely formal dining room ringed with costumes draped on mannequins honoring characters in various plays by Holberg, for whom the restaurant is named. Service is formal and the trappings are elegant.

The menu changes based on seasonal ingredients, but you are likely to be offered such appetizers as fricassée of mushrooms with smoked mussels or a tureen of eel with horseradish sauce and herbs. For a main dish, try fricassée of angler fish and crab with fine vegetables and saffron, or breast of duck with glazed apples in a cider sauce. Desserts are elegant, including apples gratinée with raisins in a cinnamon-flavored ice cream.

EXPENSIVE

ANNEN ETAGE, in the Hotel Continental, Stortingsgaten 24-26. Tel. 41-90-60.
Cuisine: FRENCH. **Reservations:** Required. **Metro:** Sentrum.
$ Prices: Appetizers 80–200 kroner ($13.25–$33.20); main dishes 170–260 kroner ($28.20–$43.15). AE, DC, MC, V.
Open: Mon–Fri 4–10:40pm, Sun 3–7pm.

In one of the grandest Norwegian hotels, the name of this restaurant—"second floor" in English—hardly prepares you for the refined service, elegant decor, and quality food. The restaurant still retains its Belle Epoque ambience of gilded Corinthian columns and pink, red, and white floral patterns. Clients have included the royal families of Norway, Denmark, and Sweden, along with Liv Ullmann, Norwegian parliamentarians, and a bevy of oil millionaires.

The menu is seasonally adjusted, but you are likely to be offered game pâté, followed by rack of reindeer with chanterelles, breast of black grouse with red wine sauce, grilled salmon, or rack of lamb with parsley and artichokes.

BLOM, Karl Johans Gate 41B. Tel. 42-73-00.
Cuisine: NORWEGIAN. **Reservations:** Required. **Metro:** Sentrum.
$ Prices: Appetizers 38–85 kroner ($6.30–$14.10); main dishes 146–235 kroner ($24.25–$39). AE, DC, MC, V.
Open: Mon–Sat 11:30am–midnight.

Considered a cultural and architectural landmark, this restaurant was recently painstakingly re-created to its original glory as the symbol of bohemian life in the early 20th century. All the cultural giants dined here, including Charlie Chaplin, Edvard Grieg, Henrik Ibsen, Edvard Munch, and Gustav Vigeland—and they are commemorated by heraldic plaques, each depicting important symbols of their careers.

Food is tasty and well prepared. At dinner, full meals might include marinated filet of reindeer with a morel-cream sauce, lamb cutlet with lamb medallions in a Dijon mustard and rosemary sauce, beef tenderloin with red wine and onions, and a host of fresh fish dishes. The wine list is one of the most complete in Oslo. A smörgåsbord is priced on a per-portion basis, unless you select from an array of open-face sandwiches priced from 46 kroner ($7.65) to 88 kroner ($14.60) each.

BRASSERIET, in the SAS Scandinavia Hotel, Holbersgate 30. Tel. 11-30-00.
Cuisine: FRENCH. **Reservations:** Not required. **Bus:** 17, 76.
$ Prices: Appetizers 45–98 kroner ($7.45–$16.25); main dishes 153–185 kroner ($25.40–$30.70). AE, DC, MC, V.
Open: Lunch, daily noon to 3pm; dinner 6–10:30pm.

Many prefer this simpler and more reasonably priced fare to that of the more elegant

Holberg, also in the SAS Scandinavia. After passing through the modern bar, Le Bar, where you'll often hear a pianist, you enter this large French-style brasserie, with potted palms and art deco accents. The salad bar is extremely fresh. Behind a visible grill, a battalion of uniformed chefs produce your dinner, turning out such selections as Norwegian salmon with mustard sauce, jumbo shrimp with Pernod (prepared at your table), wienerschnitzel, and spinach pasta with smoked salmon.

ETOILE, in the Grand Hotel, Karl Johans Gate 31. Tel. 42-93-90.
   Cuisine: FRENCH. **Reservations:** Required. **Metro:** Sentrum.
$ **Prices:** Fixed-price dinner 350 kroner ($58.05); appetizers 51–96 kroner ($8.45–$15.95) (more for caviar); main dishes 150–245 kroner ($24.90–$40.65); lunch buffet 165 kroner ($27.35). AE, DC, MC, V.
   Open: Lunch Mon–Sat noon–3pm; dinner Mon–Sat 4–11:15pm.
On the sixth floor of the new wing of Oslo's Grand Hotel, this restaurant is distinctively modern and serves a fine cuisine. To reach it, take a special elevator to the right of the hotel entrance. Sloping walls of glass open onto views of Oslo's historic district, and the place is illuminated in the evening by candlelight. The lunchtime buffet is popular, offering two hot courses plus salads and cheese. In the evening, you can enjoy such à la carte dishes as tartare of both smoked and fresh salmon with chopped onion and sour cream, filet of wild boar with pommes dauphinoise, medallions of venison in Pernod, and cloudberries with cream.

MODERATE

BAROCK, Universitetsgata 26. Tel. 42-44-20.
   Cuisine: NORWEGIAN. **Reservations:** Required on weekends. **Metro:** Sentrum.
$ **Prices:** Appetizers 62–78 kroner ($10.30–$12.95); main dishes 152–225 kroner ($25.20–$37.35). AE, DC, MC, V.
   Open: Dinner only, Tues–Sat 6pm–12:30am, Sun–Mon 8pm–12:30am.
A glamorous café/restaurant, Barock is decorated in a Neo-Edwardian style with palms, faux marbre columns, and crystal chandeliers. You can enjoy smoked breast of duckling with vinaigrette sauce and mango, filet of venison with mushrooms and cream sauce, and baked halibut with lemon-cream sauce and garlic. After dinner, you will be admitted free to the adjacent nightclub, Humla (see "Evening Entertainment," in Chapter 15).

BRISTOL GRILL, in the Bristol Hotel, Kristian IV's Gate. Tel. 41-58-40.
   Cuisine: FRENCH. **Reservations:** Required. **Metro:** Sentrum.
$ **Prices:** Appetizers 48–88 kroner ($7.95–$14.60); main dishes 95–228 kroner ($15.75–$37.85); lunch buffet 150 kroner ($24.90). AE, DC, MC, V.
   Open: Lunch buffet, Mon–Fri 11:30am–2:30pm; restaurant, daily 11:30am–midnight.
Set in this 1920s hotel (see "Oslo Accommodations," in this chapter), this street-level restaurant has a rich decor with great charm and paneled walls. The buffet is one of the best food values in town. Try such appetizers as mousse of pheasant Périgord and follow with such a dish as marinated halibut in a mustard sauce or bouillabaisse provençale. Another dish is fried sea devil with a timbale of salmon and a lobster-cream sauce; a specialty is sailor's wife casserole with white wine. You can also enjoy grilled trout with a Cumberland salad.

COSTA, Klingenberg 4. Tel. 42-41-30.
   Cuisine: ITALIAN. **Reservations:** Recommended. **Bus:** 27, 29.
$ **Prices:** Antipasti 38–78 kroner ($6.30–$12.95); pastas 68–78 kroner ($11.30–$12.95); main dishes 145–165 kroner ($24.05–$27.35). AE, DC, MC, V.
   Open: Restaurant, summer, daily 4–11:30pm; winter, daily 3–11:30pm. Café/bar, summer, daily 4pm–1:30am; winter, daily 3pm–1:30am.
Owned by Italian-born Constantino Lemme, who has made a lifetime endeavor of establishing Italian restaurants in Norway, including Mamma Rosa (see below), this fashionable place serves the finest Italian food in Oslo. The trappings are elegant, and

the service excellent. Guests enter through a bar and café where they can either order drinks or order from the full menu at prices 10% to 15% lower than in the main and more formal restaurant. Try such dishes as tenderloin of beef with forest mushrooms in a brandy-cream sauce, filet of hare with rosemary, penne with salmon, veal scaloppine, or pâté of pheasant. The antipasti are always a temptation, as is the array of pasta and fresh fish dishes.

D. S. LOUISE, Stranden 3, Aker Brygge. Tel. 83-00-60.
   Cuisine: NORWEGIAN. **Reservations:** Recommended. **Bus:** 27.
$ **Prices:** Fixed-price menus 119–350 kroner ($19.75–$58.05); appetizers 60–75 kroner ($9.95–$12.45); main dishes 120–190 kroner ($19.90–$31.50). AE, DC, MC, V.
   Open: Mon–Sat 11:30am–11pm, Sun 2–11pm.
By most standards, this is judged to be the best restaurant in the harborfront shopping-and-dining complex, Aker Brygge. On street level and outfitted in a warmly textured sheathing of hardwood, with lots of nautical accents, it takes its name from a 19th-century Norwegian steamboat. The chef prepares such specialties as braised hare with brussels sprouts and stewed mushrooms and cranberries, and a "cold symphony" of shrimp, salmon, hare, roast beef, potato salad, and cheese. It's a meal unto itself. A house specialty, also a meal unto itself, is the Brygge Tallerken, fried horsemeat with stewed mushrooms.

GRAND CAFÉ, in the Grand Hotel, Karl Johans Gate 31. Tel. 33-48-70.
   Cuisine: NORWEGIAN. **Reservations:** Recommended. **Metro:** Sentrum.
$ **Prices:** Appetizers 33–75 kroner ($5.45–$12.45); main dishes 83–139 kroner ($13.75–$23.05). AE, DC, MC, V.
   Open: Mon–Sat 11am–11:30pm, Sun noon–11:30pm.
This is the grand old café of Oslo, steeped in legend and tradition. Ibsen, who used to patronize the Grand Café, enjoying whale steaks, is depicted, along with Edvard Munch and many others, in a large mural on one wall. A postcard sold at the reception desk will identify them in the mural.
   Food can include everything from a napoleon with coffee to a full meal. Dishes include fried stingray, standard veal and beef dishes, reindeer steaks, and elk stew. Sandwiches are also available, costing 38 to 69 kroner ($6.30 to $11.45). Sunday jazz buffets with live music cost 175 kroner ($29.05) per person and are performed from January to May and September to Christmas.

STORYVILLE [CHEZ BENDRISS], Universitetsgata 26. Tel. 42-96-35.
   Cuisine: CREOLE. **Reservations:** Recommended. **Metro:** Sentrum.

IN THEIR FOOTSTEPS

Edvard Munch (1863–1944) The "world's greatest expressionist" and "the handsomest man in Norway" wrote, "Illness, madness, and death were the black angels who stood guard over my cot, and they have followed me throughout my life." A one-man show in 1889 at the age of 25 launched his career. His influence on the development of modern expressionism was considered as great as that of van Gogh. He became Scandinavia's greatest painter, and his series of paintings, entitled *From Modern Spiritual Life*, established his genius.
   • **Birthplace:** December 12, 1863, at Loten, Norway.
   • **Favorite Haunts:** Grand Café in Oslo where he joined a group "of radical Bohemians"; provincial towns along the Oslofjord.
   • **Resting Place:** Ground of Honor, Vår Frelsers Gravlund, Oslo, where he was buried in an unadorned tomb, his sister refusing a request from the German command for a state funeral.

$ Prices: Appetizers 48–70 kroner ($7.95–$11.60); main dishes 115–165 kroner ($19.10–$27.35). AE, DC, MC, V.

Open: Dinner only, Mon–Thurs 4–10:30pm, Fri–Sat 5–11pm.

Located in a cellar hideaway in the town center, this restaurant, with its scarlet wallpaper, sounds of Bourbon Street jazz, gilded mirrors, and Edwardian palms, re-creates the New Orleans Dixieland era. You can enjoy Créole dishes, including Créole gumbo, crayfish bisque, stuffed crabs, and Créole casserole with cayenne pepper, along with jambalaya, southern fried chicken, and barbecued spareribs.

3 BRØDRE, Øvre Slottsgate 14. Tel. 42-39-00.

Cuisine: NORWEGIAN. **Reservations:** Not required. **Bus:** 27, 29, 30.

$ Prices: Restaurant, appetizers 47–72 kroner ($7.80–$11.95); main dishes 127–180 kroner ($21.05–$29.85). Kaelleren, soup 48 kroner ($7.95); cheese and meat fondues 80–120 kroner ($13.25–$19.90). AE, DC, MC, V.

Open: Restaurant, Mon–Thurs noon–10:45pm, Fri–Sat 11am–2:30am, Sun 3pm–12:30am; Kaelleren, Sun–Thurs 6pm–10:30pm, Fri–Sat 6pm–12:30am.

This three-in-one establishment, Three Brothers is named after the original glove manufacturers who once occupied the building. The street level is devoted to a bustling pub. The Kaelleren, downstairs, serves soup as an appetizer, followed by cheese and meat fondues. The upstairs restaurant is more formal and expensive. You might begin with Norwegian salmon tartare or snails, and follow with an almond-and-garlic gratinée. The most popular appetizer is a selection of fresh mussels poached with leek, parsley, garlic, and cream. For a main course, try the fried catfish with prawns, mussels, red pepper, and capers, or beefsteak with béarnaise sauce.

INEXPENSIVE

DIONYSOS, Calmeyersgate 11. Tel. 60-78-64.

Cuisine: GREEK. **Reservations:** Recommended. **Tram:** 1, 2, 11.

$ Prices: Appetizers 35–58 kroner ($5.80–$9.60); main dishes 80–120 kroner ($13.25–$19.90). AE, MC, V.

Open: Daily 3–11pm.

The decor is similar to a family-oriented tavern in Athens. Specialties include dishes from Cyprus, Crete, Thessalonika, and the Pelopponese. An exuberant group of Greek-born waiters serve such dishes as Gastra Manis (from northern Greece, made with oxmeat and eggplant, pepperoni, vegetable, and potatoes), moussaka, souvlaki, and a wide selection of kebabs. For an appetizer, try a mixed platter of Greek appetizers, such as taramosalata and feta cheese. Recorded bouzouki music begins at 8pm, and the bar stays open until 1am.

GAMLA RÅDHUS (Old Town Hall), Nedre Slottsgate 1. Tel. 42-01-07.

Cuisine: NORWEGIAN. **Reservations:** Recommended. **Bus:** 27, 29, 30, 41,

IN THEIR FOOTSTEPS

Henrik Ibsen (1828–1906) Ibsen attained towering stature as a world dramatist. *Brand* (1866) and *Peer Gynt* (1867) are recognized as two of the finest plays of the 19th century. *A Doll's House* (1879) was his word on the hollowness of the marriage morality of his day. Other masterpieces include *Ghosts* (1881), *Hedda Gabler* (1890), and *The Master Builder* (1892).

• **Birthplace:** Born March 20, 1828, at Skien, Norway.

• **Favorite Haunts:** The Bergen Theater (1851–57); Dresden, Germany (1868–91); Oslo (1891–1906), where he patronized the Grand Café twice a day.

• **Resting Place:** The Ground of Honor, Vår Frelsers Gravlund, in Oslo.

61.

$ **Prices:** Appetizers 35–65 kroner ($5.80–$10.95); main dishes 50–146 kroner ($8.30–$24.25). AE, DC, MC, V.

Open: Mon–Fri 11am–11pm, Sat 4–11pm.

The oldest restaurant in Oslo, Gamla Rådhus is located in what in 1641 was Oslo's Town Hall. In the spacious dining room, a fixed-price noon meal is served as well as a full array of smørbrød (open-face sandwiches). A la carte dinner selections can be made from a varied menu including fresh fish, game, and Norwegian specialties. If you're watching your budget, enjoy your plate of food with a glass of beer or mineral water at the wood-paneled Kroen Bar.

MAMMA ROSA, Øvre Slottsgate 12. Tel. 42-01-30.

Cuisine: ITALIAN. **Reservations:** Not required. **Metro:** Sentrum.

$ **Prices:** Appetizers 35–66 kroner ($5.80–$10.95); main dishes 50–146 kroner ($8.30–$24.75). AE, DC, MC, V.

Open: Mon–Sat 11am–11:30pm, Sun 1–10:30pm.

The popularity of this Italian-style trattoria is a good indication of Norwegians' changing tastes. The dining room's decor is a "reproduction rococo," and it lies one floor above street level. You can order 10 kinds of pizzas, fried scampi and squid, rigatoni of the house, pasta Mamma Rosa (three kinds of pasta with three sauces), grilled steaks, and Italian ice creams.

THEATERCAFEEN, in the Hotel Continental, Stortingsgate 24. Tel. 41-90-60.

Cuisine: NORWEGIAN. **Reservations:** Recommended. **Metro:** Sentrum. **Tram:** 1, 2.

$ **Prices:** Fixed-price meals 170 kroner ($28.20) at dinner, 145 kroner ($24.05) at lunch; appetizers 30–95 kroner ($5–$15.75); main dishes 85–235 kroner ($14.10–$39). AE, DC, MC, V.

Open: Mon–Sat 11am–10:45pm, Sun noon–9:45pm.

The last of the grand Viennese cafés, Theatercafeen competes with the Grand Café for theater goers, present-day *boulevardiers*, and businesspeople. With soft lighting, antique bronze, cut-glass lighting fixtures, and art nouveau mirrors, this large and sophisticated restaurant is beautiful. A bar area plus a musicians' gallery complete the ambience. Music is usually performed from 4 to 6pm and 8 to 11pm. Daily specials are served only from 3 to 7pm.

You can enjoy shrimp cocktail, Norwegian fjord salmon, reindeer with mushrooms, mussels with white wine in sour cream, and a "fish and sea fruit" pot.

IN THE WEST END

VERY EXPENSIVE

BAGATELLE, Bygdøy Allé 3. Tel. 44-63-97.

Cuisine: FRENCH. **Reservations:** Required. **Bus:** 30, 31, 41, 72, 73.

$ **Prices:** Fixed-price meals 450–500 kroner ($74.65–$82.95) at dinner, 150–200 kroner ($24.90–$33.20) at lunch; appetizers 100–150 kroner ($16.60–$24.90); main dishes 200–250 kroner ($33.20–$41.50). AE, DC, MC, V.

Open: Lunch Mon–Fri 11:30am–2pm; dinner Tues–Sat 6–10pm. **Closed:** July.

This contemporary, informal French restaurant in the west end is widely regarded as the premier dining choice in Oslo. For most of this century there has been a French restaurant on this spot, but in 1982 it reformed itself and introduced a light, modern cuisine, based on market-fresh ingredients. Fish and seafood are featured, but the menu changes daily, depending on the market and the whim of its owner and chef, Eyvind Hellstrøm. You are likely to sample such superb dishes as a Norwegian lobster salad, paupiettes of sole with chives, or calf's head with tarragon butter.

MODERATE

KASTANJEN, Bygdøy Allé 18. Tel. 43-44-67.
  Cuisine: NORWEGIAN. **Reservations:** Required on weekends. **Tram:** 30.
$ **Prices:** Appetizers 50–60 kroner ($8.30–$9.95); main dishes 95–190 kroner
  ($15.75–$31.50). AE, DC, MC, V.
  Open: Mon–Sat 4–10pm. **Closed:** July.

Named for the chestnut trees that line the street on which it sits, this restaurant lies in
the western residential section of Oslo, near several embassies. The decor is modern,
warm, and unpretentious. The menu, illuminated by candlelight, changes monthly,
and is based on seasonal ingredients. Six or seven dishes every night could, depending
on their size, be ordered as either appetizers or main courses, including salmon with
crayfish. There are one or two luxurious items among the main-dish selections, but
most courses are priced at 95 kroner ($15.75). Monkfish is sautéed and served with a
crayfish sauce, or you might order reindeer, which is first sautéed, then baked, and
finally served with reindeer gravy and red currants. Smoked codfish with mustard
sauce is another favorite.

NEAR THE HOLMENKOLLEN SKI JUMP

EXPENSIVE

**FROGNERSETEREN HOVED-RESTAURANT, Holmenkollveien 200. Tel.
14-37-36.**
  Cuisine: NORWEGIAN. **Reservations:** Recommended. **Tram:** Frognerseter-
banen.
$ **Prices:** Fixed-priced menus 180–270 kroner ($29.85–$44.80); appetizers 60–
130 kroner ($9.95–$21.55); main dishes 155–230 kroner ($25.70–$38.15). AE,
DC, MC, V.
  Open: Daily noon–midnight.

On a mountain ledge, this log Norse lodge, furnished like a grand chalet, offers a
spectacular view of Oslo and the fjord. In addition to the dining room, there is a café
with prices about 10% lower, as well as a breezy outdoor terrace for snacks and beer.
The chef specializes in game, including pheasant pâté with Cumberland sauce,
medallions of reindeer, and filet of elk fried in honey and nuts. You can also order
Norwegian salmon—poached, marinated, or smoked. For dessert, try the chef's
well-known apple cake. Cloudberries with whipped cream are sometimes available.

The restaurant is a 30-minute ride to the terminal stop some 1,600 feet above sea
level. Be warned: It is about 1,000 feet downhill to the restaurant from the
Holmenkollen railway stop.

AT BYGDØY

MODERATE

NAJADEN, Bygdøynesveien 37. Tel. 43-81-80.
  Cuisine: NORWEGIAN. **Reservations:** Recommended. **Bus:** 30. **Ferry:**
Bygdøy.
$ **Prices:** Appetizers 55–60 kroner ($9.10–$9.95); main dishes 145–200 kroner
($24.05–$33.20); dinner fish buffet 180 kroner ($29.85); summer lunch buffet 150
kroner ($24.90). AE, DC, MC, V.
  Open: Summer, Mon–Sat 11am–10pm, Sun noon–5pm; spring and autumn,
Mon–Sat 11am–8pm, Sun noon–5pm; winter, Mon–Sat 11am–8pm, Sun noon–
5pm.

In the Norwegian Shipping Museum, this restaurant overlooks an exhibition room of
sculptures removed from 19th-century clipper ships. The popular summer luncheon
buffet offers an elaborate array of fish and meat dishes, open from 11am to 3pm; the
rest of the year, à la carte lunch service is featured. Children under 16 pay half price.
In the evening, a more expensive—and more elaborate—fish table is laid out

containing more than 40 different preparations of seafood. A Sunday buffet is available year round.

SPECIALTY DINING

SELF-SERVICE CAFETERIAS

NØRRONA CAFE, Grensen 19. Tel. 42-72-88.
   Cuisine: NORWEGIAN. **Reservations:** Not required. **Tram:** 2, 11.
   $ Prices: Smørbrød 25–37 kroner ($4.15–$6.15); salads and soups 22–37 kroner ($3.65–$6.15); main dishes 58–82 kroner ($9.60–$13.60). No credit cards.
   Open: Mon 10am–6pm, Tues–Fri 8am–6:15pm, Sat 9am–4pm, Sun noon–5pm.
In high-priced Oslo it is no wonder that this cost-conscious cafeteria survives here, one floor above street level in the commercial center of town. Many shoppers prefer to drop in here for a smørbrød (open-face sandwich). Full hot meals are also served, including Norwegian fish soup and pork cutlets, as well as salads. You might finish off with one of the freshly made desserts. On Sunday, one main course plus dessert is a bargain at 80 kroner ($13.25).

SAMSON, Øvre Slottsgate 21. Tel. 42-55-62.
   Cuisine: NORWEGIAN. **Reservations:** Not required. **Bus:** 27.
   $ Prices: Appetizers 25–50 kroner ($4.15–$8.30); main dishes 55–115 kroner ($9.10–$19.10). No credit cards.
   Open: Mon–Wed and Fri–Sat 8am–7pm, Thurs 8am–8pm.
At the corner of Karl Johans Gate in an 1894 building, this modern big-windowed cafeteria overlooks a pedestrian street. Its familiar dishes include filet mignon, pepper steak, wienerschnitzel, and beef Stroganoff. You pay for your meal at a counter and the waitress carries it to your table. Samson earned its good reputation from the dozen or so bakeries and pastry shops it operates throughout Oslo, so you can always be sure the pastries are fresh.

DEPARTMENT STORE DINING

STEEN & STRØM, Kongensgate 23. Tel. 41-68-00.
   Cuisine: NORWEGIAN. **Reservations:** Not required. **Bus:** 27, 29, 30, 31, 41.
   $ Prices: Cafeteria, hot platters 47–90 kroner ($7.80–$14.95); sandwiches 25–39 kroner ($4.15–$6.45). Gamlestua, appetizers 33–43 kroner ($5.45–$7.15); main dishes 79–135 kroner ($13.10–$22.40). AE, DC, MC, V.
   Open: Cafeteria, Mon–Fri 9am–5:30pm, Sat 9am–3:30pm; Gamlestua, Mon–Fri 11am–5:30pm, Sat 11am–3pm.
On the top floor of Norway's largest department store is a self-service cafeteria and an Old Norse dining room. The cafeteria has a wide selection of open-face sandwiches and cakes. I recently had a roast beef delight with remoulade sauce. The elegant and

---

 FROMMER'S COOL FOR KIDS

RESTAURANTS

Mamma Rosa (see p. 230) The best place to fill up on 10 kinds of pizzas or one of the pasta dishes, each a meal in itself.

Najaden (see p. 231) As if being housed in the Norwegian Ship Museum weren't attraction enough for kids, they can also enjoy an elaborate summer buffet at half price. But they must be under 16.

more formal Gamlestua specializes in Norwegian recipes, and meals can include lamb chops, fried liver, and fresh fish, topped off with either Norwegian sour-cream pudding or almond cake.

SMÖRGÅSBORD

STEFAN HOTEL, Rosenkrantzgate 1. Tel. 42-92-50.
   Cuisine: NORWEGIAN. **Reservations:** Recommended. **Tram:** 17.
$ Prices: Appetizers 38–65 kroner ($6.30–$10.80); main dishes 125–155 kroner ($20.75–$25.70); lunch buffet 195 kroner ($32.35). AE, DC, MC, V.
   Open: Lunch Mon–Fri 11:30am–3pm, Sat noon–3pm; dinner daily 4–9:30pm.

   The Stefan Hotel (see "Oslo Accommodations," in this chapter) is widely known for a luncheon smörgåsbord that includes at least 50 different dishes. Go early, when the food is first put on the table. My Norwegian friends consider this the best luncheon buffet in the capital, and I concur. The assortment usually includes cucumber salad, fish and meat salads, sausages, meatballs, potato salad, smoked fish, and a selection of Norwegian cheese. Desserts are also good. Beer and wine are served. You can also return in the evening to enjoy an excellent selection of à la carte Norwegian food. Dishes are likely to include marinated filet of sea perch served with a mustard-dill sauce, baked beef with a sweet-and-sour onion sauce, and smoked leg of lamb. A specialty is hot smoked moosemeat served with rowan jelly and broccoli. For dessert, try the ice-cream soufflé with chocolate sauce.

VEGETARIAN

ENGEBRET CAFÉ, Bankplassen 1. Tel. 33-66-94.
   Cuisine: NORWEGIAN. **Reservations:** Recommended. **Bus:** 27, 29, 30.
$ Prices: Appetizers 58–76 kroner ($9.60–$12.60); main dishes 162–178 kroner ($26.85–$29.55); lunch smørbrød 29–86 kroner ($4.80–$14.25); *dagens menu* 75 kroner ($12.45). AE, DC, MC, V.
   Open: Mon–Fri 11am–midnight, Sat noon–midnight.

An enduring Oslovian favorite since it was established in 1857, this restaurant is housed in two landmark buildings joined together and lying directly north of Akershus Castle. It has an old-fashioned atmosphere and good food. From noon to 6pm, a *dagens menu* (daily menu) is good value. You get one course, perhaps Norwegian shark in a butter sauce, plus coffee. During lunch, a tempting selection of open-face sandwiches is available. The menu grows more elaborate in the evening when you might begin with a terrine of game with blackberry port wine sauce or Engebret's fish soup. You can go on to order such dishes as red wild boar with whortleberry sauce or Engebret's big fishpot. For dessert, try the cloudberry parfait (known as a Lakkasabayonne) served with a cloudberry liqueur.

TOSTRUPKJELLEREN, Karl Johans Gate 25. Tel. 42-14-70.
   Cuisine: NORWEGIAN. **Reservations:** Recommended. **Metro:** Sentrum.
$ Prices: Appetizers 45–88 kroner ($7.45–$14.60); main dishes 115–205 kroner ($19.10–$34). AE, DC, MC, V.
   Open: Mon–Sat 4–11pm.

Set only a few paces from the Norwegian Parliament building, this restaurant is considered the best of Oslo's cellar restaurants. At least most members of the Norwegian Parliament seem to agree, as many of them eat here weekdays. Journalists also frequent the place, perhaps hoping to pick up a story. The antique restaurant dates from 1897, and it is accessible via a narrow outside staircase. It has sturdy furniture and a venerable decor like a Teutonic beer hall. Try one of the seafood platters or grilled filet of beef. Catch of the day is also available.

HANDVERKERAN, Rosenkrantzgate 7. Tel. 42-07-50.
   Cuisine: NORWEGIAN. **Reservations:** None. **Tram:** 7, 11.
$ Prices: Appetizers 55–70 kroner ($9.10–$11.60); main dishes 95–160 kroner ($15.75–$26.55); lunch platters 48–90 kroner ($7.95–$14.95); sandwiches 40–52 kroner ($6.65–$8.65). AE, DC, MC, V.

Open: Lunch Mon–Sat 11am–2pm; à la carte meals Mon–Sat 2–11pm.
Lying right off Karl Johans Gate, the Carpenter's Restaurant (its English name) attracts many journalists and politicians. Except for an occasional "brightening up," the place is much as it was when it was first established in 1900. Sandwiches and hot food are served until 2pm; after that, the à la carte menu becomes available. Dishes include both cured and smoked salmon, reindeer steak with cream sauce and potatoes, and leg of lamb. Specialties are "sea devil" and beefsteaks.

FRISKSPORT VEGETA VERTSHUS, Munkedamsveien 3B. Tel. 83-42-32.
   Cuisine: VEGETARIAN. **Reservations:** Not required. **Bus:** 27.
$ **Prices:** Soups and salads 20 kroner ($3.30); unlimited buffet 58–98 kroner ($9.60–$16.25). AE, DC, MC, V.
   Open: Daily 10am–11pm.

Since 1938 this basement cafeteria near the Rådhus, a stronghold of social activism and news of countercultural activities, is the only major vegetarian restaurant in town. At street level is a café where you help yourself to a buffet of 30 salad dishes and a large number of hot dishes, along with bread, butter, cheese, and coffee. The kitchen is also proud of its pizzas. You eat as much as you want. You can order juices, mineral water, soft drinks, or nonalcoholic wine.

BUFFETS

TIVOLIGRILLEN, in the Hotel Continental, Stortingsgaten 26. Tel. 41-90-60.
   Cuisine: NORWEGIAN. **Reservations:** Recommended. **Metro:** Sentrum.
$ **Prices:** Appetizers 38–98 kroner ($6.30–$16.25); main dishes 89–156 kroner ($14.75–$25.90). AE, DC, MC, V.
   Open: Mon–Sat noon–11:30pm, Sun 1–10pm.
In the Hotel Continental, with an entrance around the corner on Roald Amundsens Gate, Tivoligrillen serves good, reasonably priced food. Menu items include pepper steak, herring with sour cream and rye bread, a gratinée of mussels, and Swedish caviar with onions and sour cream. The house specialty is poached filet of trout with stewed mushrooms and a mousseline sauce. Also popular is a salad-and-sandwich buffet offered Monday through Saturday from 11am to 2pm. Sandwiches cost 23 to 49 kroner ($3.80 to $8.15).

WINE STUBE

FRU BLOM, Karl Johans Gate 41B. Tel. 42-73-00.
   Cuisine: NORWEGIAN. **Reservations:** Recommended. **Metro:** Sentrum.
$ **Prices:** Appetizers 35–60 kroner ($5.80–$9.95); main dishes 50–120 kroner ($8.30–$19.90). AE, DC, MC, V.
   Open: Mon–Sat 11:30am–1am, Sun 5pm–midnight.
Set in a commercial shopping arcade midway between the Royal Castle and Parliament, this informal wine stube has a darkly paneled dining room, a prominent stand-up bar, and a cluster of dining tables set out in front beneath a glassed-in roof. It is run by the owners of one of the most famous restaurants of Oslo (Blom), although here the prices are a lot lower. You can order just a beer or wine, or a full meal. Menu items include lasagne, salmon prepared three different ways, seafood bouillon with garlic croûtons, the catch of the day (seafood), and lingonberry ice-cream parfait. Cappuccino and espresso are also served.

DINING CLUSTERS

One of the Oslovian's favorite pastimes is to visit **Aker Brygge,** a waterfront plot of land which, until developers restored it, was a dilapidated shipbuilding yard, lying directly west of the Rådhus. The design is postmodern and futuristic, combining more shopping, entertainment, and dining diversions into one area than anywhere else in Norway. Many people, some of them *en famille,* come here to sample the various restaurants and cafés, watch the people, and listen to the array of music playing in the bars. Part of the fun is strolling through the complex and picking the restaurant of your choice. Norwegian food is served along with a representative selection of foreign food offerings, including American. Especially recommendable is **D. S. Louise.** In summer, both foreigners and locals fill the outdoor tables overlooking the active harbor life. Many nightlife possibilities exist here (see "Evening Entertainment," in Chapter 15). To reach it, take bus no. 27 or walk down from the center.

PICNIC FARE & WHERE TO EAT IT

Oslo is filled with picture-perfect vistas that call for a bottle of wine and a picnic. Delicatessens are scattered throughout the city. One of the best is **Køltzow, Verkstedhallen,** Stranden 3, in Aker Brygge (tel. 83-00-70). Here you can order a platter of fresh oysters to take out or a paper bag loaded with ready-to-eat cooked shrimp and a container of salt. Buy a loaf of bread, select some bite-sized portions of butter, pick up plastic utensils, and head for the Bygdøy peninsula. You can also order fancy fare as well, including salmon pâté, shellfish pâté, or a vegetable pâté studded with crabmeat. There is also an array of sandwiches priced from 50 to 65 kroner ($8.30 to $10.80) each. It's open Monday through Friday from 10am to 8pm, on Saturday from 10am to 6pm, and on Sunday from 1 to 6pm. Ferries for Bygdøy depart just a short walk from this deli. **Bus:** 27.

In the area, right in front of Rådhuset, you can join Oslovians for a special picnic treat. From 7 to 8am, shrimp fishermen pull their fishing boats into harbor having just caught and cooked a fresh batch of shrimp after a night at sea. You can order shrimp in bags, coming in two sizes, priced from 25 to 40 kroner ($4.15 to $6.65). Seafood fanciers take their shrimp to the dock's edge, remove the shells, and feast away. The fishermen usually stick around all day until they've sold the last batch—saving just enough for their own family.

CHAPTER 15

WHAT TO SEE & DO IN OSLO

1. **SUGGESTED ITINERARIES**
2. **THE TOP ATTRACTIONS**
• **FROMMER'S FAVORITE OSLO EXPERIENCES**
3. **MORE ATTRACTIONS**
4. **COOL FOR KIDS**
5. **SPECIAL-INTEREST SIGHTSEEING**
• **WALKING TOURS**
6. **ORGANIZED TOURS**
7. **SPECIAL/FREE EVENTS**
8. **SPORTS/RECREATION**
9. **SAVVY SHOPPING**
10. **EVENING ENTERTAINMENT**

Some would be happy to come to Oslo just for the views of the harborfront city and Oslofjord. Panoramas are a major attraction, especially that from Tryvannstårnet, a 390-foot observation tower atop 1,900-foot-high Tryvann Hill in the environs (see below). But there are many man-made attractions worthy of your time and exploration. The beautiful surroundings make these sights even more appealing.

1. SUGGESTED ITINERARIES

IF YOU HAVE 1 DAY

Arm yourself with a bag of freshly cooked shrimp—purchased right off the shrimp boats at the harbor in front of the Rådhus—and take a ferry over to the Bygdøy peninsula. Explore some of Oslo's major attractions—they're within walking distance of each other. Explore the Viking ships, the polar ship *Fram*, the *Kon-Tiki* Museum, the Norwegian Maritime Museum, and the Norwegian Folk Museum. In the late afternoon, go to Frogner Park to admire the Vigeland sculptures.

IF YOU HAVE 2 DAYS

Day 1: See "If You Have 1 Day," above.
Day 2: Take a Frommer walking tour (see below), have lunch in a Norwegian restaurant, and explore the Edvard Munch Museum in the afternoon. In summer, visit Studenter Lunden, the students' grove near the National Theater for some beer and fresh air.

IF YOU HAVE 3 DAYS

Days 1 & 2: See "If You Have 2 Days," above.
Day 3: Take another Frommer walking tour (see below), eating lunch along the way. Explore Akershus Castle and the adjoining Norwegian Resistance Museum in the afternoon. By late afternoon, visit the lofty lookout tower at Tryvannstårnet and see the Skimuseet at Holmenkollen, taking in a view of Oslo's environs. Have dinner at Holmenkollen.

IF YOU HAVE 5 DAYS

Days 1–3: See "If You Have 3 Days," above.
Day 4: Head south from Oslo for a 1-day excursion to the Oslofjord country, with

stopovers at the Old Town at Fredrikstad; Tønsberg, Norway's oldest town, and Sandefjord, an old whaling town. Head back to Oslo for the night.

Day 5: See the rest of Oslo's major sights, like the National Gallery, the Historical Museum, and the Henie-Onstad Foundation 7 miles from Oslo—a stunning museum of modern art.

2. THE TOP ATTRACTIONS

VIKINGSKIPHUSET (Viking Ship Museum), Huk Aveny 35, Bygdøy. Tel. 43-83-79.

Displayed here are three Viking burial vessels, excavated on the shores of the Oslofjord and preserved in clay. The most spectacular find is the 9th-century *Oseberg,* discovered near Norway's oldest town. This 64-foot dragon ship features a wealth of ornaments and is believed to have been the burial chamber of Harald Fairhair's grandmother and her slave.

The *Gokstad* find is a great example of Viking vessels because it's so well preserved. The smaller *Tune* ship was never restored. Look for the Oseberg animal-head post, the elegantly carved sleigh used by Viking royalty, and the Oseberg four-wheeled cart.

Admission: 15 kroner ($2.50) adults, 7 kroner ($1.15) children.

Open: May–Aug, daily 10am–6pm; Sept, daily 11am–5pm; April and Oct, daily 11am–4pm; Nov–Mar, daily 11am–3pm. **Ferry:** In summer, leaves from Pier 3 facing Rådhuset. **Bus:** 30 from the National Theater to polar ship *Fram* and *Kon-Tiki* Museum (see below).

POLAR SHIP *FRAM,* Bygdøynes. Tel. 55-74-64.

A long walk from the Viking ships, the Frammuseum contains the sturdy polar exploration ship *Fram,* which Fridtjof Nansen sailed across the Arctic (1893–96). The vessel was later used by the famed Norwegian explorer Roald Amundsen, the first man to reach the South Pole (1911).

Admission: 10 kroner ($1.65) adults, 5 kroner (85¢) children.

Open: May–Aug, daily 10am–5:45pm; Sept, daily 1–4:45pm; Oct, daily noon–2:45pm; Mar 23–Apr, daily 11am–2:45pm. **Closed:** Nov–Mar 22. **Ferry:** In summer, leaves from Pier 3 facing Rådhuset. **Bus:** 30 from the National Theater.

KON TIKI MUSEUM, Bygdøynesveien 36. Tel. 43-80-50.

Kon Tiki is the world-famed balsa-log raft that the young Norwegian scientist, Thor Heyerdahl, and his five comrades sailed in for 4,300 miles in 1947—all the way from Callao, Peru, to Raroia, Polynesia.

Besides the raft, there are other exhibits from Heyerdahl's subsequent visit to Easter Island: casts of stone giants and small originals, a facsimile of the whale shark, and an Easter Island family cave, with a collection of sacred lava figurines hoarded in secret underground passages by inhabitants of that island. The museum also houses the original papyrus *Ra II* in which Heyerdahl crossed the Atlantic in 1970.

Admission: 15 kroner ($2.50) adults, 8 kroner ($1.35) children.

Open: Mid-May to Aug, daily 10am–6pm; Sept–Oct and Apr to mid-May, daily 10:30am–5pm; Nov–Mar, daily 10:30am–4pm. **Ferry:** In summer, leaves from Pier 3 facing Rådhuset. **Bus:** 30 from the National Theater.

NORSK SJØFARTSMUSEUM, Bygdøynesveien 37. Tel. 43-82-40.

This museum chronicles the maritime history and culture of Norway, complete with a ship's deck with helm and chart house. There is also a three-deck-high section of the passenger steamer *Sandnaes.*

The Boat Hall features a fine collection of original small craft, including the fully restored polar vessel *Gjoa,* used by Roald Amundsen in his search for America's Northwest Passage. The three-masted schooner *Svanen* (Swan) is moored at the museum. Built in Svendborg, Denmark, in 1916 and later sailing under both

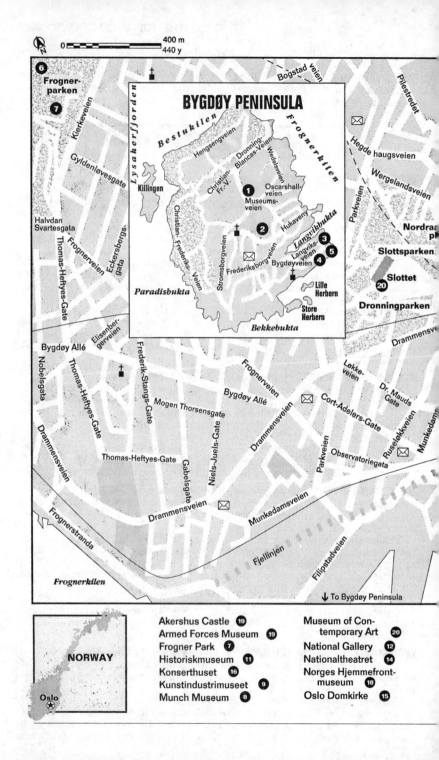

0 | 400 m
| 440 y

Frognerfjorden

Bogstad veien

Pilestredet

Frogner-parken 6
7

Kierkeveien

BYGDØY PENINSULA

Hegde haugsveien

Gyldenløvesgate

Bestukilen

Hengsengveien

Wergelandsveien

Lysakerfjorden

Dronning-
Blancas-Veien
Christian-
Fr.-V.

Wedelsveien

Parkveien

Nordraa
pl

Halvdan
Svartesgata

Killingen

Oscarshall-
veien 1
Museums-
veien

Slottsparken

Eckersbergs-gata

Christian-
Frederiks-
Veien

Christian-
Fr.

2

Hukavøny

Langvikbukta

Slottet
20

Thomas-Heftyes-Gate

Frognerveien

Strømsborgveien

Langviks-
veien 3
5
4

Dronningparken

Paradisbukta

Frederiksborg veien

Bygdøyveien

Lille
Herbern

Drammensv

Bekkebukta

Store
Herbern

Elisenber-gerveien

Bygdøy Allé

Frognerveien

Løkke-
veien

Dr. Mauds
Gate

Nobelsgata

Thomas-Heftyes-Gate

Frederik-Stangs-Gate

Bygdøy Allé

Cort-Adelers-Gate

Ruseløkkveien

Munkedam

Mogen Thorsensgate

Drammensveien

Parkveien

Observatoriegata

Thomas-Heftyes-Gate

Gabelsgate

Niels-Juels-Gate

Munkedamsveien

Drammensveien

Drammensveien

Frognerstranda

Fjellinjen

Filipstadveien

Frognerkilen

↓ To Bygdøy Peninsula

NORWAY

Oslo
★

Akershus Castle 19	Museum of Con-temporary Art 20
Armed Forces Museum 19	National Gallery 12
Frogner Park 7	Nationaltheatret 14
Historiskmuseum 11	Norges Hjemmefront-museum 18
Konserthuset 16	Oslo Domkirke 15
Kunstindustrimuseet 9	
Munch Museum 8	

OSLO ATTRACTIONS

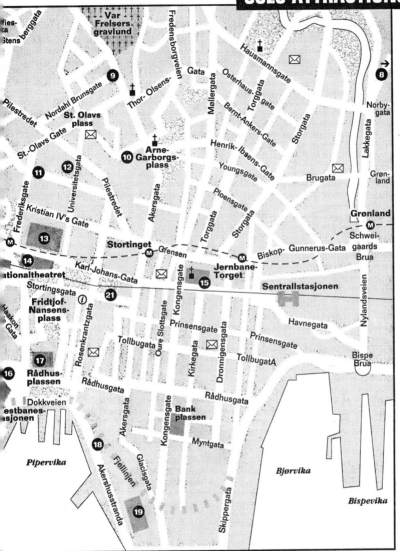

Metro Stop Ⓜ   Church ✝   Post Office ✉   Information ①

Oslo Universitet ⑬

Rådhuset ⑰

Royal Palace (Slottet) ⑳

Stortinget (Parliament) ㉑

Trefoldighetskirken ⑩

Vigeland Sculpture
    Garten ⑥

BYGDØY PENINSULA:

Frammuseet ⑤

Kon-Tiki Museum ③

Norsk Folkemuseum ①

Norsk Sjøfartsmuseum ④

Vikingskiphuset ②

Norwegian and Swedish flags, the ship now belongs to the museum and is used as a training vessel and school ship for young people.

Admission: Museum and boat hall, 15 kroner ($2.50) adults, 6 kroner ($1) children. Family ticket for two adults and two or three children, 35 kroner ($5.80).

Open: May–Sept, daily 10am–8pm; Oct–Apr, Mon–Sat 10:30am–4pm, Sun 10:30am–5pm. **Ferry:** In summer, leaves from Pier 3 facing Rådhuset. **Bus:** 30 from the National Theater.

NORWEGIAN FOLK MUSEUM, Museumsveien 10. Tel. 43-70-20.

From all over Norway, 170 original buildings have been transported and reassembled on 35 acres on the Bygdøy Peninsula. This open-air folk museum, the oldest of its kind in the country, includes a number of medieval buildings, such as the Raulandstua, one of the oldest wooden dwellings still standing in Norway, and a stave church from about 1200. The rural buildings are grouped together by region of origin, while the urban houses have been laid out in the form of an old town.

Inside, the museum has 200,000 exhibits, capturing every imaginable facet of Norwegian life, past and present. Furniture, household utensils, clothing, woven fabrics, and tapestries are displayed, along with fine examples of rose painting and wood carving. Farming implements and logging gear pay tribute to the development of agriculture and forestry in Norway. One of the most celebrated displays is Henrik Ibsen's completely reassembled study, transported from his home at Arbiens Gate 1 in Oslo, where he lived until his death in 1906. Also look for the outstanding exhibition on Norway's Lapp population.

The museum also contains a fascinating musical and ecclesiastical section. Recitals are frequently held here using the historic instruments from the museum collection.

Admission: 35 kroner ($5.80) adults, 15 kroner ($2.50) children.

Open: Mon–Sat 10am–6pm, Sun 11am–6pm. **Ferry:** In summer, leaves from Pier 3 in front of Rådhuset to Dronningen Pier. **Bus:** 30 from the National Theater.

THE VIGELAND SCULPTURES, Frogner Park. Tel. 55-28-84.

The lifetime work of Gustav Vigeland, Norway's greatest sculptor, is displayed in the 75-acre Frogner Park in western Oslo. Nearly 175 sculptures in granite, bronze, and iron can be admired. See in particular his four granite columns, symbolizing the fight between humanity and evil (a dragon, the embodiment of evil, embraces a woman). The angry boy is perhaps the most photographed statue in the park, but the really celebrated work is the 52-foot-high monolith, composed of 121 figures of colossal size—all carved into one piece of stone, depicting the struggle of life (Vigeland made the plaster model, and it took three men 14 years to carve it).

Nearby, the **Vigeland Museum,** at Nobelsgate 32 (tel. 44-23-06), is the sculptor's former studio, containing more of his works, sketches, and woodcuts.

Admission: Park, free; museum, 20 kroner ($3.30) adults, 10 kroner ($1.65) children.

Open: Park, daily 24 hours. Museum, May–Sept, Tues–Sat 10am–6pm, Sun noon–7pm; Oct–Apr, Tues–Sat noon–4pm; Sun noon–6pm. **Metro:** Frogner. **Bus:** 72. **Tram:** 2.

EDVARD MUNCH MUSEUM, Tøyengate 53. Tel. 67-37-74.

Devoted exclusively to the works of Edvard Munch (1863–1944), considered the leading painter of Scandinavia, the exhibit, his gift to the city, traces his work from early realism to his latter-day expressionism. The collection comprises 1,100 paintings, some 4,500 drawings, around 18,000 prints, numerous graphic plates, six sculptures, and important documentary material. The pictures are changed periodically.

Admission: 20 kroner ($3.30) adults, 10 kroner ($1.65) children.

Open: May–Sept, Mon–Sat 10am–8pm, Sun noon–8pm; Oct–Apr, Tues–Sat 10am–4pm, Sun noon–8pm. **Metro:** Tøyen. **Bus:** 29 from Rådhusplassen.

RÅDHUSET (City Hall), Rådhusplassen. Tel. 41-00-90.

Called everything from "aggressively ugly" to the "pride of Norway," the modern city hall, inaugurated in 1950, must be seen to be judged. Its simple brick exterior with double towers houses, among other things, the stunning troll-size (85 by 43 feet) wall painted by Henrik Sørensen and the mural *Life* by Edvard Munch. The rest of the city hall contains tapestries, frescoes, sculpture, and wood carvings by Dagfin Werenskiold. Guided tours in English are available. In the courtyard, you can see the astronomical clock and Dyre Vaa's swan fountain.

Admission: Free.

Open: Apr–Sept, Mon–Sat 10am–3pm, Sun noon–3pm; Oct–Mar, Mon–Sat 11am–2pm, Sun noon–3pm. **Bus:** 27.

AKERSHUS CASTLE, Festnings-Plassen. Tel. 41-25-21.

One of the oldest historical monuments in Oslo, Akershus Castle was built in 1300 by King Haakon V Magnusson. It was a fortress and a royal residence for several centuries. A fire in 1527 devastated the northern wing, and the castle was rebuilt and transformed into a royal Renaissance palace under the Danish-Norwegian king, Christian IV. Now it's used by the Norwegian government for state occasions. Guided tours are offered at 11am, 1pm, and 3pm (on Sunday at 1 and 3pm).

Admission: 10 kroner ($1.65) adults, 5 kroner (85¢) children.

Open: Apr 14–30, Sun 12:30–4pm; May–Sept 15, Mon–Sat 10am–4pm, Sun 12:30–4pm; Sept 16–Oct, Sun 12:30–4pm. **Closed:** Nov–Apr 13.

NORGES HJEMMEFRONTMUSEUM (Norway's Resistance Museum), Akershus Fortress. Tel. 40-31-38.

From underground printing presses to radio transmitters, beginning with the German attack in 1940 until the liberation in 1945, this museum documents World War II resistance activities. Outside is a monument dedicated to Norwegian patriots, many of whom were executed at this spot by the Nazis during the war.

Admission: 15 kroner ($2.50) adults, 5 kroner (85¢) children.

Open: Mid-Apr to Sept, daily 10am–4pm; Oct to mid-Apr, Mon–Sat 10am–3pm, Sun 11am–4pm. **Tram:** 1, 2, 9.

FORSVARSMUSEET (Armed Forces Museum), Akershus Fortress. Tel. 40-35-82.

While in the area of Akershus Fortress, you can also explore this museum documenting Norwegian military history from the dawn of the 16th century to 1950. Guns, tanks, bombs, and planes are all here, from a fighter plane left over from the "Great War" to a Spitfire from World War II. All these weapons and modern artillery are housed in a former military arsenal. The museum has its own cafeteria.

Admission: Free.

Open: May 15–Sept 15, Mon, Wed, and Fri 10am–3pm; Tues and Thurs 10am–8pm; Sat–Sun 11am–4pm. Sept 16–May 14, Mon–Fri 10am–3pm, Sat–Sun 11am–4pm. **Tram:** 1, 2, 9.

TRYVANNSTÅRNET (Lookout Tower and Ski Jump), Voksenkollen. Tel. 14-67-11.

The loftiest lookout tower in Scandinavia—the gallery is approximately 1,900 feet above sea level—offers a view of the Olsofjord with Sweden to the east.

A walk down the hill takes us back to Frognerseteren (see "Oslo Dining" in Chapter 14). You can take another 20-minute walk down the hill to the Holmenkollen ski jump, the site of the 1952 Olympic competitions. It's also the site of Norway's highlight of wintersports, the **Holmenkollen Ski Festival** where elite skiers of the world gather for competitions in downhill, slalom, giant slalom, cross-country ski races, and jumping.

Admission: 15 kroner ($2.50) adults, 10 kroner ($1.65) children.

Open: Mar–Apr, Tues–Sun 10am–6pm; May and Aug, daily 10am–8pm; June–July, daily 9:30am–10pm; Sept, daily 10am–6pm; Oct, Tues–Sun 10am–4pm.

FROMMER'S FAVORITE
OSLO EXPERIENCES

Enjoying Fresh Shrimp off the Boats Head for the harbor in front of Rådhuset and buy a bag of freshly caught and cooked shrimp from a shrimp fisherman. Get a beer at an Aker Brygge Café and shell and eat your shrimp along the harbor.

Experiencing Life of the Fjords In summer, head for the harbor where boats wait to take you sightseeing, fishing, or to the beaches.

Hanging Out in Students' Grove Summer is short in Oslo, and it's savored. Late-night drinkers sit in open-air beer gardens, enjoying the pale nights that have no end.

Listening to the Street Musicians By the hundreds, musicians flock to Oslo in summer. You can enjoy their music along Karl Johans Gate and at the Marketplace.

Taking the Ferry to Bygdøy Bygdøy peninsula is a treasure trove of Viking ships, Thor Heyerdahl's *Kon Tiki*, seafood buffets, a sailboat harbor, bathing beaches, and a folk museum with old farmsteads, houses, and often folk dancing.

Subway: Holmenkollen SST Line 15 from near the National Theater to Voksenkollen, a 30-minute ride; then an uphill 15-minute walk.

SKIMUSEET (Ski Museum), Kon Geveien 5, Holmenkollen. Tel. 14-16-90.

At Holmenkollen, an elevator takes visitors up another tower for a view of Oslo and the fjord. At the base of the ski jump is the Ski Museum (Skimuseet), displaying a wide range of exhibits including a 4,000-year-old pictograph from Rodoy in Nordland, which documents skiing's thousand-year-old history. The oldest ski in the museum dates from around A.D. 600. The museum has exhibits of Nansen's and Amundsen's polar expeditions, plus skis and historical items from various parts of Norway, including the first "modern" skis dating from around 1870.

Admission: Museum and ski jump, 15 kroner ($2.50) adults, 10 kroner ($1.65) children.

Open: May–June and Aug–Sept, daily 10am–7pm; July, daily 9am–10pm; Oct–Apr, daily 10am–4pm. **Transportation:** See the Lookout Tower and Ski Jump, above.

3. MORE ATTRACTIONS

NASJONALGALLERIET (National Gallery), Universitetsgaten 13. Tel. 20-04-04.

This state museum, a short walk from Students' Grove, has a good collection of works by world-famous artists, including Cézanne and Matisse, but it is recommended chiefly for its paintings by Norwegians—particularly the leading Romantic landscape painter, Johan Christian Dahl, who flourished in the early 19th century. Three other outstanding Norwegian artists were highly valued for their realistic works: Harriet Backer (a leading painter in the 1880s famous for interior portraits of Norwegian life), Christian Krohg (subjects from seafarers to prostitutes), and Erik

Werenskiold (see his *Peasant Funeral*). On the main staircase is a display of Norwegian sculpture from 1910 to 1945. See particularly the works of Gustav Vigeland and the two rooms devoted to Edvard Munch (see his much-reproduced *The Scream,* painted in 1893).

Admission: Free.

Open: Mon–Wed and Fri–Sat 10am–4pm, Thurs 10am–8pm, Sun 11am–3pm. **Tram:** 7, 11.

OSLO DOMKIRCHE (Oslo Cathedral), Stortovet 1. Tel. 41-27-93.

Oslo's 17th-century cathedral at Stortovet (the Marketplace) was restored in 1950, when its modern tempera ceiling decorations were completed by Hugo Lous Mohr. The cathedral contains works by 20th-century Norwegian artists, including bronze doors by Dagfin Werenskiold. Don't miss the pulpit and altar dating from the cathedral's earliest days, its stained-glass windows by Emanuel Vigeland (not to be confused with the sculptor, Gustav) in the choir and Borgar Hauglid in the transepts, and its five-story-tall organ. Services are held on Sunday at 11am and 7:30pm, with church music and prayer on Saturday at noon and Wednesday at 7:30pm.

Admission: Free.

Open: Mon–Fri 10am–1pm. **Tram:** 7, 11.

HISTORISK MUSEUM (Historical Museum), Frederiksgate 2. Tel. 41-63-00.

Devoted to ethnography, antiquities, and numismatics, this museum near Karl Johans Gate houses an interesting collection of antiquities on the ground floor, with Viking artifacts, and a display of gold and silver from the 5th through the 13th century in the Treasure House. The collection also contains gold objects from about A.D. 400 to 600, and iron objects from about A.D. 600 to 800. Don't miss the reddish Ringerike Alstad Stone in the medieval hall, which was carved in relief; and the Dynna Stone, an 11th-century runic stone honoring the fairest maiden in Hadeland. There is also a rich collection of ecclesiastical art in a series of portals from stave churches. The museum is operated by the University of Oslo Universitetets Oldsaksamling.

Admission: Free.

Open: May 15–Sept 14, Tues–Sun 11am–3pm; Sept 16–May 14, Tues–Sun noon–3pm. **Tram:** 7, 11.

HENIE-ONSTAD KUNSTENTER (Henie-Onstad Foundations), N-1311 Hkvikodden, Baerum. Tel. 54-30-50.

On a handsome site beside Oslofjord, 7 miles from Oslo, ex-movie star and skating champion Sonja Henie and her husband Niels Onstad, the shipping tycoon, opened a museum to combine and display their art collection. An especially good 20th-century collection, there are some 1,800 works by Munch, Picasso, Matisse, Léger, Bonnard, and Miró. Miss Henie's contributions can be seen in her Trophy Room (three Olympic gold medals—she was the star at the 1936 competition—and 10 world skating championships). In all, she garnered 600 trophies and medals.

Besides the permanent collection, there are plays, concerts, films, and special exhibitions. An open-air theater-in-the-round is used in summer for folklore programs, jazz concerts, and song recitals. On the premises is a top-notch, partly self-service, grill restaurant, the **Piruetten,** for the budget traveler.

Admission: 20 kroner ($3.30) adults, 10 kroner ($1.65) children.

Open: Jan–May and Sept–Dec, Mon 11am–5pm; Tues–Fri 9am–9pm, Sat–Sun 11am–5pm; June–Aug, Mon 11am–5pm, Tues–Fri 9am–9pm, Sat–Sun 11am–7pm. **Bus:** 161, 162, 251, 261 from the old university at Karl Johans Gate; then about a 5-minute walk.

KUNSTINDUSTRIMUSEET (Museum of Applied Art), St. Olavs Gate 1. Tel. 20-35-78.

Founded in 1876, this is one of the oldest museums in Norway and among the oldest applied arts museums in Europe. Extensive collections of handcrafts and industrial designs from both Norway and abroad range from the 7th century to today, including exhibitions of furniture, glass, metal, ceramic ware, textiles, and fashion.

The collections include some 35,000 objects covering a period of 2,500 years. The first floor is devoted to temporary exhibitions of modern crafts and design. The museum gives lectures and guided tours, and also holds concerts in its Norwegian gallery.

Admission: 15 kroner ($2.50) adults, 8 kroner ($1.35) children.

Open: Tues–Fri 11am–3pm, Sat–Sun noon–4pm. **Metro:** Sentrum. **Bus:** 17.

MUSEET FOR SAMTIDSKUNST (Museum of Contemporary Art), Bankplassen 4. Tel. 33-58-20.

One of Oslo's newest museums, this collection acquired by the state in postwar years, opened in 1990 presenting an array of international and Norwegian contemporary art. Once grouped together in the National Gallery, it now has more room to "breathe" in its new home.

Admission: Free.

Open: Tues–Fri 11am–7pm, Sat–Sun 11am–4pm. **Tram:** 1, 2, 9. **Bus:** 18, 29.

STORTINGET (Parliament), Karl Johans Gate 22. Tel. 31-30-50.

Constructed in 1861 to 1866, the Norwegian Parliament in the center of town was richly decorated by contemporary Norwegian artists. The style is Neo-Romanesque. Guided tours are obligatory.

Admission: Free.

Open: Guided tours, July–Aug, Mon–Fri at 11am, noon, and 1pm. **Closed:** Sept–June. **Metro:** Sentrum.

PARKS & GARDENS

Marka, the thick forest that surrounds Oslo, might be considered a giant pleasure park, but there are others.

BOTANISK HAGE OG MUSEUM (Botanical Gardens), Sarsgate 1. Tel. 68-69-60.

At Tøyen, near the Munch Museum, this is an oasis in the heart of Oslo. In this far northern clime, many exotic plants grow, including cacti, orchids, and palms. More than 1,000 different mountain plants can be viewed in the rock garden, with its waterfalls. There is also a museum in the park, with a botanical art exhibition.

Admission: Free.

Open: May–Aug 15, Mon–Fri 7am–8pm, Sat–Sun 10am–8pm; Aug 16–Sept, Mon–Fri 7am–7pm, Sat–Sun 10am–7pm; Oct–Mar, Mon–Fri 7am–5pm, Sat–Sun 10am–5pm; Apr, Mon–Fri 7am–6pm, Sat–Sun 10am–6pm. **Bus:** 20.

SLOTTSPARKEN, Drammensveien 1.

Unlike Buckingham Palace, the park surrounding the Royal Palace (*Slottet*) is open to the public year round. The changing of the guard takes place daily at 1:30pm. When the king is in residence, the Royal Guard band plays Monday through Friday.

The palace was constructed from 1825 to 1848. Some first-time visitors are surprised at how open and relatively unguarded the palace is, standing without walls or rails. You can walk through the grounds, but can't go inside unless you have an invitation from the king. The statue at the front of the castle, at the end of Karl Johans Gate, is of Karl XIV Johan himself, who ruled over both Norway and Sweden. He ordered the palace constructed, but died before it was finished.

Admission: Free.

Open: Daily dawn–dusk. **Metro:** Sentrum.

4. COOL FOR KIDS

Oslo rivals Copenhagen when it comes to attractions suitable for both children and grownups. The top thrill of a trip in the fjord is, I am sure, seeing the Viking burial ships that have been excavated on the Bygdøy Peninsula, and the Norwegian Maritime Museum and Boat Hall.

Other sights, already discussed, that are of special interest to children include: the polar exploration ship *Fram,* which bore both Nansen and Amundsen on their ventures to the North and South Poles; the balsa-log raft *Kon Tiki,* in which Thor Heyerdahl made his historic journey across the Pacific; the lookout tower, ski jump, and Ski Museum at Holmenkollen; the folk museum, depicting life in Norway since the Middle Ages; and the ancient fortress on the Oslofjord, Akershus Castle.

NORGESPARKEN TUSENFRYD, Vinterbro by the E6/E18/Mosseveien. Tel. 09/94-63-63.

It's not the Tivoli Gardens of Copenhagen, but this family amusement park, 12 miles from the Central Station, is lots of fun, nevertheless. It offers more than 20 attractions, including a roller coaster with a loop and corkscrew, a log run, an amphitheater with all-day entertainment, and many games of skill or chance.

Admission: 110 kroner ($18.25) adults, 85 kroner ($14.10) children.

Open: June 4–Aug 14, daily 11am–8:30pm; Aug 15–Sept 9, Sat–Sun 11am–8:30pm. **Closed:** Sept 10–June 3. **Bus:** 541.

BARNEKUNST MUSEUM (International Children's Art), Lille Frøensveien 4. Tel. 46-85-73.

From more than 130 countries, the collection in this unique museum is children's art—drawings, paintings, ceramics, sculpture, tapestries, and handcrafts. Some I inspected would have pleased Picasso, I'm certain. There is also a children's workshop devoted to paintings, drawings, music, and dancing.

Admission: 20 kroner ($3.30) adults, 15 kroner ($2.50) children.

Open: June 5–Aug 8, Mon–Fri 11am–5pm; during the school year, Tues–Thurs 9:30am–2pm. **Bus:** 72.

5. SPECIAL-INTEREST SIGHTSEEING

FOR THE ART LOVER

AULA (Great Hall), Oslo University, Karl Johans Gate 47. Tel. 42-90-10 ext. 756.

Devotees of the work of Edvard Munch will not only want to see the Munch Museum but the Great Hall of the university where Scandinavia's greatest artist painted murals on the walls. Regrettably, it is open only in July.

Admission: Free.

Open: July only, Mon–Fri noon–2pm. **Metro:** Sentrum.

FOR THE LITERARY ENTHUSIAST

Consider Walking Tour 2, below, which follows in the footsteps of Ibsen.

MUNCH MUSEUM, Tøyengate 53. Tel. 67-37-74.

This repository of much of the life's work of Edvard Munch, has already been previewed. But a special exhibition focuses on Munch's stage designs for the plays of Henrik Ibsen, including two of his most popular works, *Hedda Gabler* and *Ghosts.* Woodcuts are preserved that were based on *The Pretenders* and there is also a series of drawings related to *Peer Gynt* and the production of *When We Dead Awaken.* Look, also, for Munch's painting of Ibsen at his favorite table at the Grand Café.

Admission: 20 kroner ($3.30) adults, 10 kroner ($1.65) children.

Open: May–Sept, Mon–Sat 10am–8pm, Sun noon–8pm; Oct–Apr, Tues–Sat 10am–4pm, Sun noon–8pm. **Metro:** Tøyen. **Bus:** 29 from Rådhusplassen.

OSLO BYMUSEUM (City Museum), Frognerveien 67. Tel. 43-06-45.

Housed in the 1790 Frogner Manor at Frogner Park, site of the Vigeland sculptures, this museum surveys the history of Oslo, of interest in itself. But it also contains mementos of Henrik Ibsen, like the chair and marble-top table where he sat at the Grand Café. Four glasses from which he drank are engraved with his name.

Admission: 15 kroner ($2.50) adults, 5 kroner (85¢) children.

Open: June–Aug, Mon–Fri 10am–6pm, Sat–Sun 10am–5pm; Sept–May, Mon–Fri 10am–4pm, Sat–Sun 11am–4pm.

FOR THE ARCHITECTURE LOVER

Those interested in modern architecture should head to **Vaterland,** in East Oslo. One of Oslo's major development sites, launched in the 1980s, this "city within a city" includes a 9,000-seat hall for musical and sporting events, an art gallery, a train station (scheduled for completion in 1991), and large conference facilities.

Those interested in recycling old districts will also want to explore **Aker Brygge,** west of City Hall. Located along the harbor, "the Fisherman's Wharf of Oslo" opened in 1986 in what had been former shipbuilding yards. Today it is a modern complex of shops, nightspots, restaurants, delis, wine bars, and ice-cream parlors.

ARKITEKTURMUSEUM (Architecture Museum), Josefinesgate 32-34. Tel. 60-22-90.

Located in Homans byen, a residential area from the 19th century, this museum has alternating architectural exhibits and a library.

Admission: Free.

Open: Sept–May 15, Mon–Wed and Fri 9am–3pm, Thurs 9am–8pm; May 16–Aug, Mon–Fri 9am–3pm. **Tram:** 7, 11.

CHRISTIANIA BYMODELL, Høymagasinet, Akershus Festning. Tel. 33-31-47.

Norway's capital was first called Oslo, then Christiania, then Oslo again. Today an area in the historic district, this architectural model of the city of Christiania in the year 1838 is part of a multimedia program shown on screen tracing the city's history from its foundation in 1624 until 1840.

Admission: 30 kroner ($5) adults, 10 kroner ($1.65) children.

Open: June–Sept 15, Tues–Sun 11am–5pm. **Closed:** Sept 16–May. **Tram:** 1, 2, 9.

GAMLE AKER KIRKE (Old Aker Church), Geitemyrsveien 7D. Tel. 46-11-68.

Originally constructed in 1100, this is the oldest stone church in Scandinavia still in use as a parish church. Guided tours are conducted year round.

Admission: Free.

Open: Mon–Thurs noon–2pm; guided tours Sat at 11am and Sun at 6pm.

WALKING TOUR 1 —— Historic Oslo

Start: Aker Brygge.
Finish: Royal Palace.
Time: 2½ hours.
Best Time: Any day it's not raining.

Start at the:

1. **Harbor of Aker Brygge,** to the west of Rådhuset, with its fine view of Akershus Castle. This steel-and-glass complex is a rebuilt district of shops and restaurants that was developed from the old shipbuilding grounds of Oslo. From Aker Brygge, head east along Rådhusplassen, looking at:

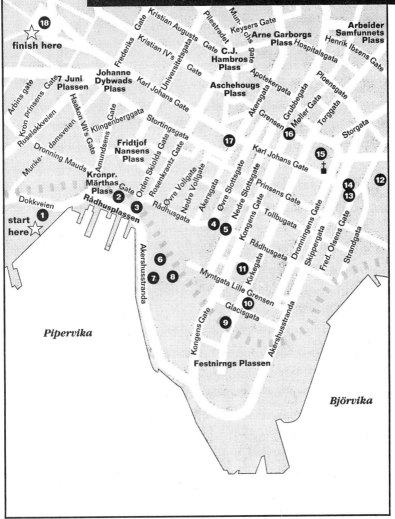

2. Rådhuset, on your left. The city hall of Oslo, built in 1950 with double towers, is decorated with artwork by Norwegian artists. Climb the steps at the east end of the square to see the:

3. statue of Franklin D. Roosevelt (you have to climb a slight hill). Eleanor Roosevelt flew to Oslo to dedicate the statue.

As you traverse this area, you will be in the heart of the Renaissance city from the 1600s. Take Rådhusgata east to:

4. Christiania Torv, a traffic hub. The yellow house on your left is the Young Artists Association, but once it was the home of the dreaded executioner. His fee depended on the type of execution performed.

REFUELING STOP   To the right of the Young Artists Association is the **5. Kafé Celsius,** Rådhusgata 19 (tel. 42-45-39), Oslo's oldest residential house. Today it is a charming arts-oriented café serving tasty food, with sandwiches costing from 35 kroner ($5.80). You can also order pasta salads and such dishes as ratatouille or tortellini. On cold days, a fireplace burns.

Continue along Rådhusgata, turning right onto Nedre Slottsgate. Walk to the end of the street. At Myntgata, turn right and pass through a gate. You are now on the greater grounds of Akershus Castle. The first building on the right is the:

6. Norwegian Resistance Museum, which has displays of events related to the Nazi occupation of Norway from 1940 to 1945. Also at the site is:

7. Akershus Castle and Fortress, dating from 1300 but rebuilt in the 17th century. Take a guided tour of the fortress and walk its ramparts. Pause on the grounds to look at the:

8. Execution Site in front of the Norwegian Resistance Museum. Nazis took prisoners here, often Norwegian freedom fighters, and shot them. There's a memorial to the resistance movement, and you'll have a good view of the harbor in the distance.

Cross the drawbridge to the east and continue through the castle grounds to the:

9. National Monument to the German Occupation commemorating the suffering the country endured at the hands of the Nazis. After seeing the monument, turn north into:

10. Grev Wedels Plass, the site of Den Gamle Logen (freemason's lodge) where in 1850 Ibsen wrote poems. Head north along Kirkegata until you reach:

11. Bankplassen, site of the old Bank of Norway. Today the old bank is now the Museum of Contemporary Art, Bankplassen 4, with the state collection of international and Norwegian modern art gathered since World War II. This square was once the social center of Oslo, and Ibsen staged his first play here in 1851 at a theater that later burned down in 1877.

From Bankplassen, turn right onto Revierstredet and left again onto Dronningens Gate. At one time the waterfront came up to this point. Go right at Tollbugata at the Central Post Office. At the intersection with Fred Olsens Gate, turn left and walk to the:

12. Oslo Sentralstasjon, Oslo's rail hub, where trains arrive from the continent and also depart from all points linked by train in Norway. Turn left onto:

13. Karl Johans Gate, the main pedestrian-free street that stretches from the Central Station in the east and to the Royal Palace in the west end. On your right, you pass:

14. Basarhallene, a huge complex filled with boutiques and various shops.

Turn right at Kirkegata heading for:

15. Oslo Domkirche, Stortovet, the 17th-century cathedral at Oslo's old marketplace. Like the city hall, the cathedral is decorated with outstanding works by Norwegian artists.

From Stortovet, walk west along Grensen until you reach the following stopover.

REFUELING STOP   The atmosphere of old Oslo lives on at the **16. Stortovets Gjaestgiveri,** Grensen 1 (tel. 42-88-63), located on a busy commercial street. This drinking and dining emporium, dating from the 1600s, is often filled with spirited beer drinkers. It may not be everyone's favorite, but it has a list of devotees who don't want to change a thing. You can get snacks or complete meals, along with an assortment of drinks.

Continue west on Grensen until you reach Lille Grensen. Cut left onto this street, returning to Karl Johans Gate. On your left will be the:
17. **Norwegian Parliament (Stortinget),** Karl Johans Gate 22. Constructed in 1861 to 1866, it is richly decorated by contemporary Norwegian artists.

Continue west along Karl Johans Gate, passing many of the monuments covered on Walking Tour 2 (see below). Eventually you reach the:
18. **Royal Palace (Slottet),** Drammensveien 1, residence of the King of Norway. Public access is possible only to the park.

WALKING TOUR 2 —— In the Footsteps of Ibsen & Munch

Start: National Theater.
Finish: National Gallery.
Time: 2 hours.
Best Time: Any day it's not raining.

The tour begins at:
1. **National Theatret,** Stortingsgaten 15, lying off Karl Johans Gate near Studenter Lunden (Students' Grove) in Oslo's center. Study your map in front of the Henrik Ibsen statue at the theater where many of his plays were first performed and are still being presented. The Norwegian National Theater (tel. 41-27-10), inaugurated in 1899 with a rococo salon in gold and red, is considered one of the most beautiful in Europe. Guided tours are possible year round on Monday at 6pm. From June 15 to July 8, daily tours are given at 6pm. Tours cost 15 kroner ($2.50) for adults and 8 kroner ($1.35) for children. Phone for information.

Facing the statue of Ibsen, continue up the Stortingsgaten in the direction of the Royal Palace (Slottet). Cut left at the intersection and walk along Ruselokkveien. The Vika Shopping Terraces, an unattractive row of modern storefronts tacked onto an elegant 1880 Victorian terrace, used to be among Oslo's grandest apartments. In World War II it was the Nazi headquarters. Continue along this complex to the end, turning right onto Dronnings Mauds Gate, which quickly becomes Lokkeveien.

At the first building on the right, you come to the:
2. **Private apartment of Ibsen.** Look for the blue plaque marking the building. The playwright lived here from 1891 to 1899, moving when his wife complained she didn't like the address, even though it was one of Oslo's most elegant. Ibsen wrote two plays while living here.

Turn right onto Arbinsgate and walk to the end of the street until you reach Drammensveien:
3. **Ibsen's last address.** At the first building on the left, at the corner of Arbinsgate and Drammensveien, you will see an Omega store, but look for the blue plaque on the building. Ibsen lived here from 1895 until his death. He often

sat in the window, a light casting a glow over his white hair. People lined up in the street below to get a look at him. The great Italian actress, Eleanora Duse, came this way to bid him a final *adieu,* but he was too ill to see her. She stood outside in the snow and blew him kisses.

The King of Norway used to give Ibsen a key to enter the private gardens surrounding the Royal Palace (everybody has that privilege today).

Turn right on Drammensveien and continue back to the National Theater. Take Karl Johans Gate, on the left side of the theater, and walk east. On your left, you'll pass the:

4. University of Oslo, Karl Johans Gate 47 (tel. 42-90-91), where Aula, the great hall of the university, was decorated with murals by Edvard Munch. The hall is open to the public only in July.

Twice a day Ibsen walked along this same sidewalk to the Grand Café. Admirers often threw rose petals in his path, but he pretended not to see them. He was called "the Sphinx," because he wouldn't talk to anybody.

REFUELING STOP   The **5. Grand Café,** Karl Johans Gate 31, was the center of social life for the literati and the artistic elite, including Munch. It was—and is—the most fashionable café in Oslo (see Chapter 14). At the far wall of the café, you can see Per Krogh's famous mural painted in 1928. Ibsen, the man in the top hat and the gray beard, is at the far left, and Munch—called the handsomest man in Norway—is seated at the second window from the right at the far right of the window. The poet and playwright, Bjørnstjerne Bjørnson, can be spotted on the street outside (second window from the left, wearing a top hat)—he wouldn't deign to come into the café. At the café you can order food and drink, a big meal or a snack.

Returning to the street outside, note the National Parliament Building (Stortinget) on your left.

Proceed left and turn left onto Lillegrensen. Cross the major boulevard, Grensen, and walk straight to:

6. Akersgata, the street of the funeral cortège of Ibsen. Services were conducted at the Holy Trinity Church on June 1, 1906. Veer left to see the:

7. Birthplace of Ibsen's son. On your left, at the corner of Teatergata and Akersgata, is the site of the famous Strømberg Theater, which burned down in 1835. It was also a residence: Ibsen's son was born here in 1859.

Also on Askersgata is:

8. Trefoldighetskirken (Holy Trinity Church), site of Ibsen's funeral. A little farther along Akersgata is St. Olav's Church. Turn on the right side of this imposing house of worship onto Akersveien and go to:

9. Damplassen, a small square—one of the most charming in Oslo—that doesn't appear on most maps. Norway's greatest poet, Henrik Wergeland, lived in the pink house on this square from 1839 to 1841.

Take a right at the square and head down:

10. Damstredet, a typical old Oslo street, with antique wooden houses mainly occupied by artists.

Damstredet winds downhill to Fredensborgveien, where a left turn and a short walk will take you to Maridalsveien, a busy but dull thoroughfare. As you walk north along this street, on the west side, look for a large, unmarked gateway, inside of which are wide stone steps. Climb to the top, follow a little pathway, and go past gardens and flower beds. Pass a set of brick apartment buildings on the left, and proceed instead to a little street:

11. Telthusbakken, where you'll see a whole row of early Oslo wooden houses. Look right in the far distance at the green building where Munch used to live. Telthusbakken leads to Akersveien and on your left you can see:

12. Gamle Aker Kirke (Old Aker Church) (tel. 46-11-68). Enter at Akersbakken, where Akersveien and Akersbakken intersect. Built in 1100, this is the oldest stone parish church in Scandinavia still in use. It stands on a green hill with an old graveyard around it, inside a stone wall.

A short block from the church along Akersbakken (veer left outside the front of the church and go around a corner), you come to the north entrance of:

13. Vår Frelsers Gravlund (Our Savior's Cemetery), the city's expansive burial ground. In a section designated the Ground of Honor, famous Norwegians are buried, including Munch, Ibsen, and Bjørnson. Signs do not point the way, but it's easy to see a tall obelisk. This is the:

14. Tomb of Ibsen. His wife, Susannah, whom he called "the cat," is buried to the playwright's immediate left. She died in 1914. The hammer on the obelisk is symbolic of his work *The Miner,* indicating how he "dug deep" into the soul of Norway.

To the right of Ibsen's tomb is the:

15. Tomb of Bjørnson (1832–1910), who once raised money to send Ibsen to Italy. Before the birth of their children, Ibsen and Bjørnson agreed that one would have a son and the other a daughter, and they would both grow up to get married. Miraculously, Ibsen had a son, Bjørnson a daughter, and they did grow up to get married. Bjørnson wrote the national anthem of Norway, and his tomb is draped in a stone representation of a Norwegian flag.

To the far right of Bjørnson's tomb is the:

16. Tomb of Edvard Munch. Scandinavia's greatest painter (born 1863) has a completely unadorned tomb. If you're visiting on a snowy day, it will be completely buried, as its marker lies close to the earth. Munch died in 1944 during the darkest days of the Nazi occupation of Norway. His sister turned down a request from the German command to give Munch a state funeral, feeling that it would be inappropriate. The grave has remained unadorned since 1944.

On the west side of the cemetery, you'll come to Ullevålsveien. Turn left on this busy street and go back south toward the center of Oslo. You'll soon see St. Olav's Church, this time on your left. But stay on the west side of the street where Ullevålsveien intersects with St. Olavs Gate.

17. Kunstindustrimuseet, St. Olavs Gate 1, is the museum of applied art (see "More Attractions," above). Even if you don't have time to visit the museum, you may want to go inside to patronize its café.

After visiting the museum, continue along St. Olavs to:

18. Pilestredet. Look to your immediate right. A wall plaque on a decaying building commemorates the fact that Munch lived here from 1868 to 1875. When demolition teams started to raze the building, counter-culture groups illegally took it over and have been occupying the building ever since. On its brick wall side, the Munch masterpiece, *The Scream,* has been re-created in spray paint. Munch came to this building when he was 5, and many of his "memory paintings" were of the interior.

At Pilestredet, turn left. One block later, turn right onto Universitetsgate, heading south toward Karl Johans Gate. You'll pass a number of architecturally interesting buildings, and will eventually arrive at the:

19. National Gallery, Universitetsgata 13, where the state has deposited the largest collection of Norwegian and foreign art. A separate room is devoted solely to masterpieces by Munch.

6. ORGANIZED TOURS

CRUISES AROUND THE FJORD Departing from Pier 3 in front of Oslo Rådhuset (city hall), **Båtservice Sightseeing,** Rådhusbrygge 3, Rådhusplassen (tel. 20-07-17), offers a 50-minute mini-cruise boat tour, with a view of the harbor and the city, including the ancient fortress of Akershus and the islands in the inner part of Oslofjord. Cruises depart mid-May to late August, daily on the hour from 10am to 8pm (limited sailing at the beginning and end of the season). Adults pay 45 kroner ($7.45); children, 22 kroner ($3.65).

If you have more time, take the 2-hour fjord cruise through the maze of islands and narrow sounds in the fjord. Departures are May 1 to mid-September, daily at 10:30am and 1, 3:30, and 5:45pm; the cost is 90 kroner ($14.95) for adults, 45 kroner ($7.45) for children. Refreshments available on board. There are variants of this cruise, such as the fjord cruise with lunch, also 2 hours, leaving May 1 to mid-September, daily at 10:30am, and costing 190 kroner ($31.50) for adults, 95 kroner ($15.75) for children. After the 2-hour fjord cruise, the boat anchors so passengers can go ashore for lunch at Najaden restaurant.

An evening fjord cruise, including a maritime buffet, also at the Najaden, leaves from late June to the end of August, daily except Sunday at 5:45pm. Prices are 270 kroner ($44.80) for adults, 135 kroner ($22.40) for children. Another evening cruise is a 2-hour fjord cruise with a prawn party, taking place from early July to the second week of August, Tuesday and Friday at 6:30pm. Passengers peel red prawns which are served with white wine or beer. If you're not big on prawns, a dish of Norwegian cured meat is also offered. Adults pay 180 kroner ($29.85); children, 90 kroner ($14.95).

CITY TOURS   HMK tours has been showing visitors around Oslo for more than a century. From May 1 to September 30, they have a 3-hour morning sightseeing jaunt that costs 130 kroner ($21.55) for adults and 65 kroner ($10.80) for children. The bus visits Akershus, Frogner Park and the Vigeland sculptures, and then the Holmenkollen Ski Jump for a view of Oslo and its fjord, before going on to the Munch Museum.

You might also want to take the 3-hour afternoon tour, costing 150 kroner ($24.90) for adults, 75 kroner ($12.45) for children. Leaving at 2:30pm, it concentrates on the museums on Bygdøy, including the Museum of Norwegian Folklore and the Viking ships, as well as *Fram* and *Kon Tiki*.

Starting point is the harbor side of Rådhuset, and passengers should arrive 15 minutes before departure. Authorized guides speak English. The tours are operated by **H. M. Kristiansens Automobilbyrå,** Hegdehausveien 4 (tel. 20-82-06).

7. SPECIAL/FREE EVENTS

Always check at the **tourist office** for a list of events likely to be planned during the week of your visit. Many are free, including summer jazz concerts at the National Theater. In front of the theater, along Students' Grove, you'll see much street entertainment, including singers, clowns, musicians, and jugglers.

Concerts are presented in the chapel of **Akershus Castle** and Fortress, Akershus Command, on Sunday at 2pm. During the summer, promenade music, parades, drill marches, exhibitions, and various theatrical performances are also presented on the castle grounds.

The March **Holmenkollen Ski Festival** is one of the most exciting times to visit the Norwegian capital. On the last day, the world's most thrilling ski jumps are presented.

In June, the **Faerder sailing race** attracts some 1,000 sailboats that compete on the Oslofjord.

Constitution Day, July 4, brings out a parade of colorfully costumed children marching through Oslo.

In August, the **Chamber Music Festival** at Akershus Castle and Fortress presents concerts by both Norwegian and foreign musicians.

The **Oslo Jazz Festival,** also in August, includes not only old-time jazz, but classical concerts, opera, and ballet performances as well.

8. SPORTS/RECREATION

From spring to fall, the Oslofjord is a mecca for swimming, sailing, windsurfing, and angling. Daily excursions are arranged by motor launch at the harbor. Surburban forest areas await hikers, bicyclists, and anglers in summer. In winter, the area is ideal terrain for cross-country skiing on marked trails illuminated at night, as well as downhill or slalom, tobogganning, skating, and more. Safaris by Land Rover are arranged year round.

BEACHES Avoid the inner-harbor area because of pollution. The nearest and most popular beach is at **Hovedøya,** which is also the site of the 12th-century Cistercian monastery erected by English monks. Swimming is from a rocky shore. Also try **Drøbak,** 24 miles south of Oslo (take bus no. 541).

Oslovian beach devotees cite **Gressholmen** and **Langøyene,** a 15-minute ride from Vippetangen, as having the finest beaches in the Oslo environs. Nudism is practiced at beaches on the southern side of Langøyene.

The closest safe beaches are those on the west of Bygdøy peninsula, the museum island reached by bus no. 30 from the National Theater. These include **Huk** and **Paradisbukta.** There's nude bathing at Huk. Beaches are also at **Langåra,** lying 10 miles west of Oslo. Take the local train to Sandvika and make ferry connections from there.

On the east side of the fjord, an array of beaches is reached by taking bus no. 75B from Jernbanetorget in East Oslo. Departures are about every hour on weekends. The closest beach, a 12-minute ride, is **Ulvøya,** which is one of the best and considered the safest for children. Nudists journey on to **Standskogen.**

FISHING The fishing is just great in Oslofjord and the forest lakes of Marka. However, you need a fishing permit, which can be purchased in most shops at a cost of 90 kroner ($14.95). A state fee of 60 kroner ($9.95) must also be paid at any local post office.

GOLF Members of recognized golf clubs are allowed to play at **Oslo Golfklubb,** Bogstad (tel. 50-44-020). In addition to charging greens fees ranging from 100 to 120 kroner ($16.60 to $19.90), the club will also rent clubs and equipment.

GYMS One of the best is **Harald's Gym,** Hausmannsgate 6 (tel. 20-34-96), which accepts nonmembers, charging 40 kroner ($6.65) entrance, plus another 40 kroner ($6.65) for use of the solarium. It is open Monday through Friday from 9am to 9pm and on Saturday and Sunday from 10am to 5pm.

HORSE RACING The **Øvrevoll Racecourse,** Vollsveien 132 (tel. 24-01-90), is open from mid-April to mid-November, with races on Monday and Thursday at 6pm. Take bus no. 131 to Eiksmarka.

SKIING A 15-minute tram or bus ride from central Oslo will take you to Oslo's winter wonderland, a 1,612-mile ski-track network, estimated to be the distance between Oslo and Tunis in North Africa. Many ski schools and instructors operate in winter. You can even go on a sleighride wrapped in sheepskin. Other activities include dogsled rides, snowshoe trekking, and Marka forest safaris. There is a total of 14 slalom slopes to select from, along with ski jumps in all shapes and sizes, including the most famous one at Holmenkollen. The tourist authorities at Oslo Promotion will provide specific details about changing venues from many of these activities.

SWIMMING POOLS & BATHS The most centrally located municipal bath is **Vestkantbadet,** Sommerogate 1 (tel. 44-07-26), offering Finnish sauna or Roman baths Monday to Saturday from 7:30am to 7:30pm. It costs 29 kroner ($4.80) for use of the pool and use of the large sauna. For 170 kroner ($28.20) you get use of the pool, an upgraded sauna, and a scrub and massage. For this special sauna, call in advance for a reservation. The pool is reserved for men on Monday, Wednesday, and Friday and for women on Tuesday, Thursday, and Saturday. It's located near the American Embassy, about a mile north of Oslo's center. The baths are closed during most of July and part of August.

For outdoor swimming, **Frognerbadet,** Middelthunsgate 28 (tel. 44-07-26), in Frogner Park, has an open-air pool near the Vigeland sculptures (take tram no. 2 from the National Theater). The entrance fee is 29 kroner ($4.80) for adults, 12 kroner ($2) for children. It's open mid-May to mid-September, Monday through Friday from 7am to 8pm.

TENNIS The municipal courts at **Frogner Park** are usually fully booked for the season by the locals, but apply at the kiosk about a vacancy that might become available.

One of your best bets is **Njårdhallen,** Sorkedalsveien 106 (tel. 14-15-92), which is open Monday through Friday from 7am to 2pm, providing both indoor and outdoor courts.

WINDSURFING You can rent windsurfing equipment at **Sport Windsurfing Center,** Bygdøy Allé 60A (tel. 44-79-28). They will also inform you on the best places to windsurf and other such details.

9. SAVVY SHOPPING

THE SHOPPING SCENE **The best buys** include sportswear, silver and enamelware, traditional handcrafts, pewter, glass by Hadelands Glassverk (founded in 1762), teak furniture, and stainless steel.

Oslo has many **traffic-free streets** for strollers and shoppers. The heart of this district is the **Strøget,** where more than two dozen shops sell everything from Norwegian handcrafts to enameled silver jewelry. At the marketplace on Strøget, you can, in fair weather, stop for a glass of beer at an open-air restaurant. Many stores are clustered along **Karl Johans Gate** and the streets branching off from it.

Hours: Shops are generally open Monday through Friday from 9am to 5pm (in summer until 4pm). On Saturday most close by 1pm (2 or 3pm at some larger stores), and they are closed on Sunday.

Shipping It Home and Recovering VAT: Norway imposes a 20% Value Added Tax (called VAT) on goods purchased. But there are ways of avoiding paying this tax. See "Taxes" in "Fast Facts: Norway" in Chapter 12.

Special tax-free exports are possible, with many stores mailing goods home to you, which makes the payment of tax and its recovery unnecessary.

SHOPPING A TO Z
ARTS & CRAFTS

NORWAY DESIGNS, Stortingsgaten 28. Tel. 83-11-00.

This is the country's headquarters for high-quality Norwegian and Scandinavian arts and crafts. An ideal shopping center for ceramics, glassware, pottery, textiles (there's a fashion shop), rugs, souvenirs, silverware, and furniture. Norway Designs has all the crafts that have given Norwegians an international reputation as outstanding designers. Metro: Sentrum.

DEN NORSKE HUSFLIDSFORENING, Møllergata 4. Tel. 42-10-75.

Near the Marketplace and the cathedral, Husfliden, as it's called, is the display and retail center for the Norwegian Association of Home Arts and Crafts, founded in 1891. Today it is almost eight times larger than any of its competitors, offering an unparalleled opportunity to see assembled over two floors the very finest of Norwegian design in ceramics, glassware, furniture, and woodworking. You can also purchase souvenirs, gifts, textiles, rugs, knotted Rya rugs, embroidery, wrought iron, and fabrics by the yard. Goods are shipped all over the world. Metro: Sentrum.

BOOKS

DAMMS ANTIKVARIAT, Tollbodgaten 25-27. Tel. 41-04-02.
A bookshop since 1843 specializes in old and rare books, atlases and maps, and nautical prints. Metro: Sentrum.

TANUM KARL JOHAN, Karl Johans Gate. Tel. 42-93-10.
A fine Oslo bookstore, lying in the center of town, it offers a staggering selection, including many English titles. Metro: Sentrum.

TANUM LIBRIS, Karl Johans Gate 43. Tel. 42-93-10.
A leading Oslo bookstore, well stocked in English titles, both fiction and nonfiction. It is particularly known for its selection of travel guides, including maps of Oslo and Norway. Metro: Sentrum.

CHILDREN'S WEAR

KID COOL, Stranden 1, Aker Brygge. Tel. 83-17-84.
This is a well-stocked branch of a leading children's clothing manufacturer in Oslo. Set in the shopping and restaurant complex west of Rådhuset, it has an impressive array of merchandise, including blouses, pants, hats, sweatsuits, sweaters, skirts, shoes, and belts, along with many accessories for children aged 1 to 12. Bus: 27.

DEPARTMENT STORES

GLASMAGASINET, Stortovet 9. Tel. 11-40-80.
Claiming that smaller boutiques tend to charge more, locals usually head for this big department store, specializing in unusual accessories for the home and kitchen. It might qualify as the biggest outlet of the Hadelands Glassverk (Glassworks) in all of Norway. It also contains a ground-floor coffee shop and restaurants on both the second and third floors. Metro: Sentrum.

STEEN & STRØM, Kongensgate 23. Tel. 41-68-00.
The largest department store in Norway, Steen & Strøm is a treasure house of hundreds of Nordic items—from the ground-floor souvenir shop to the sales departments on the top floors. Look for hand-knitted sweaters, hand-painted wooden dishes reflecting traditional Norwegian art, hand-knitted caps, and pewter dinner plates made from old molds. Metro: Sentrum.

FOLK COSTUMES

HEIMEN, Rosenkrantzgate 8. Tel. 11-11-25.
A leading purveyor of both modern and traditional Norwegian handcrafts and costumes, Heimen carries folk costumes, antiques and reproductions, along with a choice of more than three dozen different *bunads* or styles for the family to select from, including different regions of Norway, both north and south. Clothing is sold for women, men, and children. Hand-knitted sweaters in traditional Norwegian patterns are a special item, as are pewter and brass items. It's about a block from Karl Johans Gate. Metro: Sentrum.

GLASS

HADELAND GLASSVERK, N-3520 Jevnaker. Tel. 47-63-11.
The most famous name in Norwegian glass, dating from 1762, can easily be reached by public transportation. You can see glass being blown and shaped, and visit a glass museum and a gallery with changing exhibitions. You can also purchase Hadeland's complete collection, and "seconds" are sold at reduced prices. There's a restaurant on the premises. The complex is also open on Sunday from noon to 6pm. Bus: Take the Hønefoss/Jevnaker bus from Vaterland, leaving hourly; phone 19-92-38 for the bus schedule.

JEWELRY, ENAMELWARE & SILVER

DAVID-ANDERSEN, Karl Johans Gate 20. Tel. 41-69-55.
This outstanding Norway jeweler, established more than a century ago, distributes enameled demitasse spoons and sterling-silver bracelets with enamel, available in many stunning colors such as turquoise and dark blue. The multicolored butterfly pins are also popular in sterling silver (gold-plated) with enamel. David-Andersen's collection of Saga silver is inspired by traditional features in Norwegian folklore and from Viking designs, combined with the pristine beauty of today's design. The store now offers an exquisite collection of pewter items. Metro: Sentrum.

MUSIC

NORSK MUSIKFORLAG, Karl Johans Gate 39. Tel. 42-53-67.
Set in the town center on the main street, this store's selection isn't the largest, but its staff, all of whom speak English, claim with justification that its stock of classical, jazz, popular, and rock selections is the most carefully chosen in Oslo. The store stocks both LPs and compact discs. Metro: Sentrum.

PEWTER

TINNBODEN, Tordenskioldsgate 7. Tel. 42-24-61.
Some of the best pewter dinnerware available in Oslo is offered here, near Rådhuset close to the harbor. The shop also sells gift articles and souvenirs. It has no annual closing. Tram: 1, 2, 9.

HEYERDAHL, Fridtjof Nansens Plass 6. Tel. 41-59-18.
Next to the Rådhusplassen, this store offers one of the city's most imaginative collections of pewter. You can buy a menagerie of Arctic animals fashioned from walrus tusk, stone and brass vessels, and ashtrays made of a glistening form of copper ore mined in northern Norway. There's also gold and silver jewelry. Metro: Sentrum.

SHOPPING MALLS

Oslo has three large shopping arcades, including Aker Brygge at the west side of the harbor, a short walk from Rådhuset; and Oslo City and Galleri Oslo, both near the Central Station.

Oslo City, Stenersgate 1, opposite the Central Station, has become the biggest shopping center in Norway, with an array of shops selling all types of merchandise. You can also dine here in a number of restaurants.

Also near the Central Station, **Galleri Oslo,** at Vaterland, has been called Europe's longest indoor shopping street. You can find everything in the same complex. Activity goes on day and evening until midnight, including Sunday. A walkway connects Galleri Oslo to the Central Station.

Aker Brygge is a unique shopping venue by the Oslofjord. It is virtually a city within a city, with a wide array of merchandise. The complex also includes restaurants, theaters, cinemas, and cafés.

SWEATERS

OSLO SWEATER SHOP, in the SAS Hotel Scandinavia, Holbergsgate 30. Tel. 11-29-22.
Some 5,000 handcrafted sweaters, one of the best collections in Norway, are stocked here close to the Royal Palace. Since the sweaters are handmade, it's important to try them on before you buy. The sales staff is helpful. Metro: Sentrum.

SOUVENIRS & GIFTS

WILLIAM SCHMIDT, Karl Johans Gate 41. Tel. 42-02-88.
Established in 1853, William Schmidt is a leading purveyor of unique souvenirs, including pewter items (everything from Viking ships to beer goblets), Norwegian

dolls in national costumes, wood carvings (the troll collection is the most outstanding in Oslo), and sealskin items such as moccasins and handbags. The shop specializes in hand-knitted cardigans, pullovers, gloves, and caps. Sweaters are made from moth-proofed 100% Norwegian wool. Metro: Sentrum.

10. EVENING ENTERTAINMENT

Oslo is fast emerging as a bustling nightlife city. Midnight is no longer a hint for everybody to call it a night. Today, Oslo boasts 100 night cafés, clubs, and restaurants—and 34 of these stay open until 4 in the morning.

The autumn and winter seasons are for cabarets, theater, and concerts. There are four cabaret stages and nine theater stages, all offering productions except in summer. Oslo is also a favorite destination of international performing artists in classical music, pop, rock, and jazz.

For movie lovers, Oslo has a lot to offer. The city is now considered to have the best and most extensive selection of movies in Europe, with 30 screens and five large film complexes. All films are shown in their original languages, with subtitles.

THE ENTERTAINMENT SCENE

The best way to find out what's happening at the time of your visit is to pick up a copy of **What's On in Oslo,** detailing concerts and theaters and other useful information.

Oslo doesn't offer any agents specializing in discounted tickets, as they do in such cities as London. However, to compensate, it offers an exceptional number of free events. These are documented in the monthly "diary" of *What's On in Oslo.* The guide also lists the latest exhibitions at art galleries, which might be a delightful way to spend the early part of an evening.

You don't always have to go to the theater to purchase tickets. Tickets to the theater, ballet, and opera are sold at **Billettsentralen,** Karl Johans Gate 35 (tel. 44-76-77).

The **Oslo Philharmonic,** now world famous, plays regularly under the leadership of Mariss Janson. Regrettably, you cannot hear them from June 20 until the first of September.

If you visit Oslo sometime other than summer, you also have a chance to see its thriving opera and ballet company, **Den Norske Opera.** Unfortunately for those who don't speak Norwegian, performances at the **Nationaltheatret,** which is always presenting Ibsen, are in Norwegian. However some devotees who know Ibsen plays well in their own language have attended performances just to hear what Ibsen sounded like in the original version.

THE PERFORMING ARTS

THE MAJOR CONCERT/PERFORMANCE HALLS

Konserthus, Munkedamsveien 15 (tel. 41-60-65). Home of the Oslo Philharmonic. Metro: Sentrum.

Nationaltheatret (National Theater), Stortingsgaten 15 (tel. 41-27-10). Ibsen and Bjørnson in the original.

Den Norske Opera (Norwegian National Opera), Storgaten 23C (tel. 42-77-00 for information, 42-77-24 to order tickets). Norwegian opera and ballet.

CLASSICAL MUSIC

KONSERTHUS, Munkedamsveien 15. Tel. 41-60-65.

Two blocks from the National Theater, this is the home of the widely acclaimed Oslo Philharmonic. Performances are given autumn to spring, on Thursday and Friday. Guest companies from around the world often appear on other nights. The hall is closed from June 20 until the middle of August, except for occasional folkloric groups whose appearances are announced in *What's On in Oslo*. Metro: Sentrum.
Prices: Tickets, 85–110 kroner ($14.10–$18.25).

VIGELAND MUSEUM, Nobels Gate 32. Tel. 44-11-36.
In summer, there are concerts in the courtyard, usually Wednesday evening at 7pm and Sunday at 1pm. Performances are advertised in *What's On in Oslo*. Tram: 2.
Prices: Tickets, 20–35 kroner ($3.30–$5.80).

THEATER

NATIONALTHEATRET (National Theater), Stortingsgaten 15. Tel. 41-27-10.
At the upper end of the Students' Grove, this theater opens in August, so it may be of interest to off-season theater lovers who want to hear Ibsen and Bjørnson in the original. Avant-garde productions get a fair trial at the **Amfiscenen** in the same building. There are no performances in July. Guest companies often perform plays in English. Metro: Sentrum.
Prices: Tickets, 100–250 kroner ($16.60–$41.50).

OPERA & DANCE

DEN NORSKE OPERA (Norwegian National Opera), Storgaten 23C. Tel. 42-77-00 for information, 42-77-24 to order tickets.
The 1931 building, originally a movie theater, was adapted for better acoustics and dedicated in 1959 to the Norwegian National Opera. Besides opera, it is also the leading venue for ballet. The Norwegian opera and ballet troupes combined to form Den Norske Opera. The company performs some 20 different operas and operettas every year. Ballet performances alternate with opera presentations. There are no performances in July. Unlike some European opera companies, tickets are generally available to nonsubscribers. Bus: 56, 62, 66.
Prices: Tickets, 50–190 kroner ($8.30–$31.50), except for galas when tickets climb to 790 kroner ($131.05) and beyond. Seats can be reserved in advance and paid for with credit cards.

SUMMER CULTURAL ENTERTAINMENT

The **Bondeungdomslaget (Folk Dance Group of the Young Farmers' Union)** performs in July and August at the Oslo Concert Hall, Munkedamsveien 14 (tel. 20-60-20). The 1-hour performances are given on Monday and Thursday at 9pm. Tickets cost 70 kroner ($11.60) for adults and 40 kroner ($6.65) for children. Metro: Sentrum.
The **Norwegian Folk Museum** on Bygdøy presents folk-dance performances by its own ensemble in summer at the museum's open-air theater (see *What's On in Oslo* for details). Tickets are 70 kroner ($11.60) for adults, 40 kroner ($6.65) for children. Take the ferry from Pier 3 near Rådhuset.

THE CLUB & MUSIC SCENE
NIGHTCLUBS/CABARET

GLEDES HUSET LUDVIK (Ludvik's Fun House), Torggata 16. Tel. 42-88-80.
One of Oslo's most unusual clubs is set within the high-ceilinged premises of what was the city's busiest 19th-century public bathhouse. The difficult-to-find entrance is on Henrik Ibsens Gate, around the corner from the official address. You traverse a trompe-l'oeil footbridge and enter a zany world of scantily clad plastic mannequins, antique sleighs, rocking chairs, brass horns, and old-time memorabilia attached to the

ceiling. The place is a full-fledged restaurant, serving such dishes as peppersteak, cured salmon with mustard sauce, and cured elkmeat steak. The last food orders go in at 11pm, but the singing and drinking continue until 2am. The club often features cabaret but the schedule varies, especially in the slower summer months. On most nights they host *Karaoke* parties. This is a Japanese nightlife craze where members of the audience, microphone in hand, sing to an orchestral track while reading the lyrics from a TV monitor above the stage. Ludvik's is open daily from 5pm to 2am. Meals cost 150 kroner ($24.90); beer, 33 kroner ($5.45). Tram: 1, 2, 7, 11.

Admission: 50–100 kroner ($8.30–$16.60) on cabaret nights, free other nights.

HUMLA, Universitetsgaten 26. Tel. 42-44-20.

A labyrinth of hallways, dance areas, and bars, Humla contains one of the best restaurants in Oslo, the Barock (see Chapter 14). The interior is strikingly stylish. You can dine at café tables on a carpeted balcony overlooking a theater where acts are interspersed with disco music. At the **Dizzie Theater and the Humla Restaurant,** the stage features cabaret acts which usually last for 90 minutes including drag, pop-rock nostalgic revues, and Norwegian comedy. The program changes monthly. Tables are cleared away and disco music plays until 3:30am. You can also dine on the mezzanine.

John's Bar, thanks to its murals, pays tribute to a 19th-century folk legend about a Norwegian and two Swedes who set off together to see the world. The **Exit Disco,** which is open very late, lies four floors above the street. The joke in Oslo is, if you're drunk by the time you start up, you will have sobered by the time you reach the top, as there is no elevator. The decor includes potted cactus, Oriental carpets, and a DJ playing from the chassis of an old American car.

The Dizzie Theater and Humla Restaurant are open Tuesday through Saturday from 8pm to 3:30am; John's Bar, Wednesday through Monday from 6pm to 12:30am; the Exit Disco, on Wednesday from midnight to 3:30am, on Friday and Saturday from 11pm to 3:30am, and on Sunday from 12:30 to 3:30am. A beer in John's Bar will cost 29 kroner ($4.80); in the Exit Disco, 34 kroner ($5.65). Metro: Sentrum.

Admission: Dizzie Theater, 225–270 kroner ($37.35–$44.80) for dinner and show; the Exit Disco, 30 kroner ($5) cover charge Fri–Sat.

DANCE CLUBS/DISCOS

LOFTET, in the Hotel Continental, Stortingsgaten 26 (entrance on Roald Amundsens Gate). Tel. 41-90-60.

This disco has a unique setting: five small rooms built as a loft, each having a different decor. You have to be 22 years of age to get in, and on weekends you should arrive by 8pm or else be prepared to wait in line. Open Tuesday through Thursday from 8pm to 2am, on Friday and Saturday from 8pm to 4am. A half liter of *pils* will cost 35 kroner ($5.80). Metro: Sentrum.

Admission: 20–50 kroner ($3.30–$8.30) cover charge.

BONANZA BAR, in the Grand Hotel, Karl Johans Gate 31. Tel. 42-93-90.

Bonanza is a very crowded bar, restaurant, and disco in the vaulted cellars of the luxurious Grand Hotel. You descend a stairway into a series of candlelit rooms. The DJ plays music geared to the over-30 conservative crowd, and almost any request will be honored. It's open Monday through Saturday from 8pm to 2:30am. Beer costs 37 kroner ($6.15); mixed drinks, 55 kroner ($9.10). Metro: Sentrum.

Admission: 40–55 kroner ($6.65–$9.10).

GALAXY, in the SAS Scandinavia Hotel, Holbergsgate 30. Tel. 11-30-00.

This glistening black-and-mirrored dance club is designed for the conservatively affluent clientele who stay at this upscale hotel. The place caters to an over-30 crowd. Disco music features recent releases from Los Angeles, Paris, or New York, and the sound system is focused so that you can actually talk normally. It's open Tuesday through Sunday from 10pm to 4am. Beer costs 33 to 38 kroner ($5.45 to $6.30). Metro: Sentrum.

Admission: 50 kroner ($8.30) cover charge.

JAZZ/ROCK

CAFE ENGEBRET, Bankplassen 1. Tel. 33-66-94.

Most of this landmark café's income is derived from its status as a popular restaurant (see Chapter 14). But it also doubles every night as a jazz club. Set near Akershus Castle, it's on the upper floor of a pair of low-slung 19th-century buildings. In a world completely divorced from the food service downstairs, the sounds of hot jazz and cool blues can be heard. It's open Wednesday through Saturday from 9am to 1:30am. A beer will set you back 32 kroner ($5.30). Bus: 18.

Admission: 20–50 kroner ($3.30–$8.30), depending on the group.

ROCKEFELLER MUSIC HALL, Torggate 16. Tel. 20-32-32.

With a capacity for 100 patrons, this is one of the largest establishments of its kind in Oslo, calling itself both a concert hall and a club. It lies one floor above street level in a 1910 building, originally a boathouse. Three nights a week (call for dates) live concerts are presented. Musical forms include everything from reggae to rock to jazz. On nights when no concert is given, films of the world's great video concerts are shown on a wide screen. Small dishes of food, such as pastas and sandwiches, are available in the café section. Most of the crowd seems in the 18 to 37 age bracket. It's open Sunday through Thursday from 8pm to 1am and on Friday and Saturday from 9pm to 4am. A beer will cost 29 to 36 kroner ($4.80 to $5.95); snacks, 20 to 60 kroner ($3.30 to $9.95). Metro: Sentrum.

Admission: 40–200 kroner ($6.65–$33.20) cover charge, depending on the entertainment.

THE BAR SCENE

PUBS/BARS

LIMELIGHT, in the Grand Hotel, Karl Johans Gate 31. Tel. 42-93-90.

Steeped in the atmosphere of the theater, this fashionable Oslo bar has a connecting passage to the theater next door (Oslo Nye Teater). It's a favorite rendezvous for drinks before or after a show. Open daily from 3pm to midnight. A beer or mixed drink costs 35 kroner ($5.80). Metro: Sentrum.

LIBRARY BAR, in the Hotel Bristol, Kristan IV's Gate 7. Tel. 41-58-40.

This may be the best spot in the Bristol for people-watching, in a lobby reminiscent of the Edwardian era. You'll be sheltered behind racks and racks of leather-bound books, which you can actually remove and read. The total effect is like being inside a well-furnished private club, with potted palms. Live piano music is presented at lunchtime when you can order from a selection of open-faced sandwiches for 39 to 66 kroner ($6.45 to $10.95). Specialty cocktails have such demure names as "Take Me Home," "Norwegian Kiss," and "Prince of Norway." It's open daily from 10am to 2:30am; alcohol is served from 1pm to midnight. A beer will cost you 35 kroner ($5.80); mixed drinks, 45 kroner ($7.45). Metro: Sentrum.

SKY BAR, in the Oslo Plaza Hotel, Sonja Henies Plads 3. Tel. 17-10-00.

The loftiest bar in Norway, this aptly named place crowns the 37-floor deluxe Oslo Plaza Hotel. To reach it, you take a glassed-in elevator from a separate entrance outside the hotel. Upstairs, the view is spectacular, and the decor has lots of black granite and russet-colored marble, a bar very much of the 1990s. It has both bustling standup areas and sitdown couches, with a piano perched amid the hubbub. On weekends, the line is long at the elevator. The bartender's special is the "Oslo Plaza," made with vodka, amaretto, and Coca-Cola, topped off with cream. It's open daily from 5pm to 3:30am. Beer costs 35 kroner ($5.80); mixed drinks, 45 kroner ($7.45). Bus: 14, 24, 71.

Admission: 4 kroner (65¢) cover charge after 10pm.

ETOILE BAR, in the Grand Hotel, Karl Johans Gate 31. Tel. 42-93-90.

Drawing members of Parliament across the street, this is a grand bar attached to an equally grand restaurant in a new wing of Norway's greatest hotel, the Grand. It is encased with windows opening onto views of historic Oslo and close to the hotel's swimming pool and sauna. The appearances and interests of the clients change visibly throughout the day, from businesspeople during the day to a more spirited crowd at night. To reach it, you take a special elevator that departs from the right of the hotel entrance. Drinks include brandy sours, several Caribbean-inspired rum drinks, and the house special, a "Yellow Sweater." You'll pay 31 kroner ($5.15) for a beer, 44 to 61 kroner ($7.30 to $10.10) for a more potent libation. This Star is open Monday through Saturday from 3pm to 12:30am. Metro: Sentrum.

KLIMS BAR, in the SAS Scandinavia Hotel, Holbergsgate 30. Tel. 11-30-00.

On the ground level of this first-class hotel, Klims was designed as an apéritif bar for what many consider Oslo's best restaurant, the Holberg. But the fact that it contains some exceptional murals has turned it into a bit of a drinking haven in its own right. The murals were painted by the Danish-born artist, Bjørd Viinblad in 1975, showing an allegorical and fantastical menagerie of dragons, flying leopards, and talking flowers. The characters portray the childhood legend of Nils Klims, a story originally written by Holberg that is dear to the hearts of every Scandinavian child. Enjoy a drink at the marble-top bar: beer is 32 kroner ($5.30); a mixed drink, 45 kroner ($7.45). Klims is open Tuesday through Saturday from 5pm to midnight. Bus: 17, 76.

CONTINENTAL BAR, in the Hotel Continental, Stortingsgaten 24-26. Tel. 41-90-60.

On the street level of the Hotel Continental (see Chapter 14) near the National Theater, this is an oval room with a bronze statue of a musician in the center. It's a chic and sophisticated place. The walls are hung with the largest collection of Munch paintings in the world outside museums. Many were purchased in 1934. For fear of theft (several paintings were stolen, and later recovered), two or three of the works are now judicious copies. The bar is open Monday through Saturday from 3 to 11:30pm. Sandwiches are available for 56 to 69 kroner ($9.30 to $11.45); drinks begin at 40 kroner ($6.65). Metro: Sentrum.

SUPPER CLUBS

EL TORO, in the Hotel Bristol, Kristan IV's Gate 7. Tel. 41-58-40.

The entrance to El Toro is clearly visible from the sidewalk near the main entrance to the hotel. A popular bar with an intimately lit restaurant, a dance floor, and an Iberian decor, this has become one of the most popular places in Oslo. Conservative dress is suggested. A dance band provides the music from 8pm. Main dishes include poached salmon with butter-cream sauce, chateaubriand with béarnaise sauce, filet of veal Oscar with asparagus, and a mixed grill. Cocktails include tequila sunrises, margaritas, and a Norwegian high-powered bomb, Fjellbekk (mountain stream), made with aquavit, vodka, lime juice, and Sprite. Meals cost around 250 kroner ($41.50); drinks, 45 kroner ($7.45). It's open Tuesday through Thursday from 7pm to 1am and on Friday and Saturday from 7pm to 2am. Reservations are recommended. Metro: Sentrum.

THE OYSTER BAR, in the Oslo Plaza Hotel, Sonja Henies Plads 3. Tel. 17-10-00.

Adjoining the Penthouse Sky Bar (see above), this is a pocket of posh, a late-night supper club specializing in seafood delicacies. Don't expect a full and hearty meal on the top floor of this five-star hotel. More likely, the menu will contain a limited selection of very fresh fish served on beds of seaweed. The menu is short, no more than four or five choices a night. Everything is based on the catch of the day. You might enjoy steamed black-shell mussels on a bed of egg yolk and cream, warm crayfish tails on a bed of sautéed spinach leaves, or half a Norwegian lobster. The pièce de la résistance is a shellfish platter with several different sauces. Seafood dishes run 75 to 275 kroner ($12.45 to $45.60). Oysters are sold by the half dozen, and there's a limited but carefully chosen wine list. The seafood is served Monday through Saturday from 5pm to 2am. Bus: 14, 24, 71.

NIGHT CAFES

CRUISE CAFE, Stranden 3, Aker Brygge. Tel. 83-64-30.

The most popular bar in this dining-and-shopping complex west of Rådhuset is packed with a devoted clientele who like the woodsy decor, the music (often live), and the conviviality. Sometimes there's a live concert, at which time a cover charge is imposed. The culinary venue is burgers and beers—a Cruiseburger costs 65 kroner ($10.80)—with a handful of Norwegian dishes thrown in. It's open on Monday and Tuesday from noon to 1am, on Wednesday and Thursday from noon to 2am, on Friday and Saturday from 1pm to 4am, and on Sunday from 1pm to 1am. Bus: 27.

Admission: 50–240 kroner ($8.30–$39.80) cover charge, when there's live music, depending on the band.

BROKER CAFE, Bogstadveien 27. Tel. 69-36-47.

By day this is a somewhat demure café serving morning coffee and light meals. Its greatest panache, however, occurs later in the evening when a rock-conscious, hip crowd convenes for drink, conversation, and food. The decor dates from around the turn of the century, including lots of mirrors and Belle Epoque trappings. The food includes lasagne, sandwiches, and salads, for 49 to 75 kroner ($8.15 to $12.45); a beer costs 30 to 35 kroner ($5 to $5.80). The café is open Monday through Thursday from 10am to 1am, on Friday and Saturday from 10am to 2:30am, and on Sunday from noon to 1am. Tram: 11.

CAFE LORRY, Parkveien 12. Tel. 69-69-04.

This café prides itself on stocking more kinds of beer—81 in all—than any other nightclub in Norway. Most of the brands are made in Norway, and many are so esoteric that they're known only to the most dedicated Norwegian beer drinker. Ask a member of the staff for a recommendation. Sometimes a paid performer is at the piano; at other times, customers who think they're musically talented. The serious drinking begins after 5pm, and the decor is rustic and "sudsy." Beer costs 28.50 to 36 kroner ($4.75 to $5.95). The place can be fun. It's open Monday through Saturday from 8am to 2:30am and on Sunday from 9am to 2:30am. Tram: 11.

AFTER-HOURS DRINKING & DINING

MARIA VON TRAPP, Møllergata 23. Tel. 11-05-60.

This establishment shares a building (but not necessarily the clientele) with the premier gay bar of Oslo, Den Sorte Enke. Hours are geared to coincide with the hunger pangs of late-night Oslovian society, who might yearn for hamburgers and snacks at impossibly late hours. Hamburgers cost 52 kroner ($8.65) and beer runs 25 to 30 kroner ($4.15 to $5). Don't expect a conservative clientele. The largest wall sports a life-size mural of a guitar-toting Julie Andrews skipping over an Austrian Alp. The place is open daily from 11pm to 4am. Metro: Sentrum.

GAY & LESBIAN DRINKING & DINING

DEN SORTE ENKE (Black Widow), Møllergata 23. Tel. 11-05-60.

This is the premier gay bar of Norway. Its street-level cocktail and beer bar is a major gathering place for young gay people. Lesbians are welcome, but the clientele is mostly male. Downstairs is a disco, and a few steps away, a dungeonlike leather bar consciously decorated like an S&M parlor. Beer costs 33 kroner ($5.45). It's open daily from 6pm to 4am. Metro: Sentrum.

Admission: Free for the bar, 30–40 kroner ($5–$6.65) for the disco.

JOY'S CLUB, Kongensgate 6. Tel. 42-66-22.

This club divides its clientele about half and half between lesbians and gay men. Large and labyrinthine, it has lots of secluded corners for dialogues, as well as a disco and dance floor. The atmosphere is cruisy, but it's a clean, safe haven. Beer costs 24 kroner ($4) before midnight, 33 kroner ($5.45) after. The bar is open daily from 6pm to 4am; the disco operates Wednesday through Saturday from 10pm to 4am. Bus: 27, 29, 30.

Admission: Free for the bar, 40 kroner ($6.65) for the disco.

DIVINE, Pilestraede 9. Tel. 42-22-30.

The second floor contains the leading gay restaurant of Oslo, but many clients visit just to patronize the street-level disco and the high-tech bars. In the modern restaurant, the color scheme is black with high-voltage pinpoint lighting. The food is international and Norwegian, the most popular dish being a platter of lemon-marinated shrimp and blue oysters and crayfish. Other popular dishes include filet of fish, chili, and a marinated filet of lamb in herb sauce. Light snacks are also available. Meals cost about 160 kroner ($26.55), snacks run 25 to 65 kroner ($4.15 to $10.80), and a beer costs 33 kroner ($5.45). The restaurant is open Sunday through Thursday from 3pm to 1am and on Friday and Saturday from 3pm to 3am. The disco is one of the liveliest in Oslo, especially on weekends; it's open daily from 10pm to 4am. Metro: Jernbanetorget.

Admission: 40 kroner ($6.65) for the disco.

SHAME, Rosenkrantzgate 10.

Gay men are welcome, but this place caters mainly to lesbians. With a prominent flag displayed in front advertising its "Shame" to passersby, this club is set on a side street off Karl Johans Gate, near both the Bristol and Grand Hotels. Open Wednesday through Sunday from 10pm to 4am, it's especially active on Friday and Saturday nights. Beer costs 28 kroner ($4.65). Metro: Sentrum.

Admission: Free.

MOVIES

American or British import films are shown in English, with Norwegian subtitles. Patrons line up at the cinemas for tickets in the same way that Americans might frequent Broadway shows. Tickets are sold for specific performances only. Many theaters have three showings nightly, at 5, 7, and 9pm, but the big road-show specials usually are shown only once in an evening, generally at 7:30pm. One of the most centrally located cinemas, showing first-run features, is the **Colosseum,** Fridtjof Nansensvei 8 (tel. 46-39-60). Tram: 1, 2, 11.

CHAPTER 16

EASY EXCURSIONS FROM OSLO

1. **FREDRIKSTAD**
- **WHAT'S SPECIAL ABOUT THE ENVIRONS OF OSLO**
2. **TØNSBERG**
3. **SANDEFJORD**
4. **LILLEHAMMER**
5. **THE PEER GYNT ROAD**

The environs of Oslo offer an array of 1-day excursions available to visitors either by boat, car, or bus.

The chief center is Fredrikstad, in Østfold on the east bank of Oslofjord. A trip here can be combined—all in 1 day—with visits to the ports of Tønsberg and Sandefjord, on the west bank, by crossing over on the ferry from Moss to Horten, then heading south.

The major center in the north is the summer resort and ski center of Lillehammer, site of the 1994 Olympics. Those who overnight in the area can also take the famous Peer Gynt Road the following day, a route Ibsen traveled while researching his masterpiece, *Peer Gynt*. Other suitable centers include Gløvik on Lake Mjøsa and the alpine village of Beitostølen.

SEEING OSLO'S ENVIRONS

GETTING THERE Both sides of the Oslofjord south of Oslo are serviced by frequent trains from the capital. Trains go down the eastern side to Moss, Fredrikstad, and Halden, and trains traverse the western side to Drammen, Tønsberg, Sandefjord, and Larvik.

If you want to cross the fjord, on either side, go to Moss or Horten. A 40-minute car-and-passenger ferry plies the fjord connecting both banks. In summer it's also possible to cross from Strømstad, Sweden, to Sandefjord. Frequent trains also run north from Oslo to Lillehammer, which is the best center for touring the many attractions north of Oslo, including the Peer Gynt Road.

A SUGGESTED ITINERARY Go south from Oslo for 2 nights, taking your time exploring the old towns of Fredrikstad, Tønsberg, and Sandefjord. On the third day, drive north to Lillehammer where you can easily spend 3 days, exploring not only the attractions of this summer-and-winter resort, but using it as a base for driving around Peer Gynt country and other sights, including museum-filled Hamar.

---

1. FREDRIKSTAD

60 miles south of Oslo

GETTING THERE By Train Trains from Oslo's Central Station depart for Fredrikstad in the south about every 2 hours.

By Bus There is frequent bus service daily from Oslo to Fredrikstad.

By Car Take Highway E6 south from Oslo heading toward Moss. Continue past Moss until you reach the junction at Route 110, which is signposted south to Frederikstad.

WHAT'S SPECIAL ABOUT THE ENVIRONS OF OSLO

Great Towns/Villages

- ☐ Tønsberg, the oldest town in Norway, with historic districts and a folk museum.
- ☐ Fredrikstad, a well-preserved fortress town with an artisan quarter.
- ☐ Lillehammer, a premier European ski resort, site of the 1994 Winter Olympics.

Scenic Drives

- ☐ The Peer Gynt Road, northwest of Lillehammer—immortalized by Henrik Ibsen.
- ☐ Oldtidsveien, the highway of the ancients, near Fredrikstad—the most concentrated collection of archeological monuments in Norway.

For the Kids

- ☐ Hunderfossen Family Park, near Lillehammer—50 activities for both children and adults.

Museums

- ☐ The Sandvig collections at Lillehammer—150 old buildings recreate the Norway of yesterday.
- ☐ Vestfold Folk Museum at Tønsberg, with many Viking and whaling treasures.
- ☐ Commander Christensen's Whaling Museum at Sandefjord, with memorabilia of the great whaling days.

ESSENTIALS   For information, the **Fredrikstad turistkontor** is on Østre Brohode in Gamle Fredrikstad (tel. 09/32-03-30). The **telephone area code** for Fredrikstad is 09.

In recent years Fredrikstad has become a major tourist center, thanks to its Old Town and 17th-century fortress. Across the river on the west bank is a modern industrial section, and although a bridge links the two sections, the best way to reach the Old Town is by ferry, costing 2 kroner (35¢). The departure point is about four blocks from the Fredrikstad railroad station—simply follow the crowd out the main door of the station and make an obvious left turn and continue down to the shore of the river.

WHAT TO SEE & DO

Frederikstad was founded in 1567 as a market town on the Glomma River. **Fredrikstad Fortress,** in use until 1903 and boasting some 200 cannons at its peak, is still used by Norway's military forces. The main guardroom and old convict prison are now the **Municipal Museum,** Gamleslaveri, open June to August, Monday through Saturday from 10am to 4pm and on Sunday from noon to 5pm; during the rest of the year it's open only on Saturday and Sunday. Admission is 5 kroner (85¢).

Outside the gates of the Old Town is **Kongsten Fort,** on what was first called Gallows Hill, an execution site. When Fredrikstad Fortress was built, it was provisionally fortified in 1677, becoming known as Svenskeskremme (Swede Scarer). Today's Kongsten Fort was subsequently built there, with 20 cannons, underground chambers, passages, and countermines.

You can take guided tours in the Old Town to visit the church, the museum, and the glass-blowing and silver-design operations belonging to **Norway Silver Designs,** a society of artists and artisans. Its headquarters are in one of the old houses in the Old Town at Kirkegaten 28A (tel. 32-06-78), open Monday through Friday from 9am to 4pm and on Saturday from 9am to 1pm. You can visit its showrooms anytime during these hours, but to see the actual products being made and the place where classes are given, you must take a 1-hour guided tour for 16 kroner ($2.65). Tours are given Monday through Friday at 9:30am, 11am, 12:30pm, and 2pm.

After leaving Fredrikstad, take a drive along the **Oldtidsveien,** or the "highway of the ancients," the most concentrated collection of archeological monuments in Norway. It lies along Highway 110 between Fredrikstad and Skjeberg. The ancient monuments include 3,000-year-old rock carvings at Begby, Hornes, and Solberg, and 2,000-year-old burial grounds at Hunn with stone circles.

Other attractions include **Tomta** (tel. 34-50-33), the 1872 birthplace of explorer Roald Amundsen, at Borge, where a museum and monument are now dedicated to him. They are located between Fredrikstad and Sarpsborg, off the E6, and the house is usually open Monday through Friday from 2 to 6pm.

WHERE TO STAY

HOTEL CITY, Nygård 44-46, N-1600 Fredrikstad. Tel. 09/31-77-50. Fax 09/31-77-50. 102 rms (all with bath). MINIBAR TV TEL **Bus:** 31.

$ Rates (including breakfast): 450–950 kroner ($74.65–$157.60) single; 560–1,150 kroner ($92.90–$190.80) double. AE, DC, MC, V.

Located in the town center, about 500 yards from the rail station, this is a stylish hotel, in spite of an exterior that looks like an office building. The interior has a quasi high-tech decor, and each of the comfortable bedrooms, furnished in good taste, has a radio and color TV with video movies. On the premises are a basement restaurant with a nightclub and dance music, three bars, and a winter-garden café with marble sheathing. There is also a private indoor parking area.

VICTORIA HOTEL, Turngaten 3, N-1600 Fredrikstad. Tel. 09/31-11-65. Fax 09/31-11-65. 55 rms (all with bath). TV TEL **Bus:** 31.

$ Rates (including breakfast): 465–580 kroner ($77.15–$96.20) single; 535–700 kroner ($88.75–$116.15) double. AE, DC, MC, V.

The oldest hotel in town, originally established in 1883, the Victoria was completely renovated in 1989. It overlooks the most idyllic park in town. Bedrooms are comfortable, and a restaurant and bar are on the premises. It's located near the train station.

WHERE TO DINE

RESTAURANT TAMBUREN, Faergeportgate 78. Tel. 32-03-13.

Cuisine: NORWEGIAN. **Reservations:** Recommended. **Bus:** Marked "Gamlebyen" from the center.

$ Prices: Appetizers 45–65 kroner ($7.45–$10.80); main dishes 85–175 kroner ($14.10–$29.05). AE, DC, MC, V.

Open: Pub, daily 6pm–midnight. Dining room, May–Sept, daily 11am–11pm; Oct–Apr, daily 3–11pm.

For tradition and atmosphere, this restaurant has no competition within the Old Town. Originally built in the 19th century as the home of a village priest, the rebuilt Gothic-inspired structure has a popular courtyard for warm-weather outdoor dining. The basement pub has an open fireplace. Served in the dining room are well-prepared meals that include two kinds of entrecôte, beef, and pork, along with mixed grills, fish, and five kinds of open-face sandwiches. On summer weekends there's live music nightly after 9pm.

2. TØNSBERG

64 miles south of Oslo

GETTING THERE   By Plane   The nearest air service is at Torp Airport, lying halfway between Sandefjord and Tønsberg. It has connections to Bergen, Stavanger, and Copenhagen.

By Train   Tønsberg is about 1½ hours by train from Oslo, and 16 trains arrive daily from Oslo. The train station is in the city center.

By Bus   Frequent buses arrive from Oslo, and the Tønsberg district has good connections to Sandefjord (see below). Buses usually leave Tønsberg hourly, traversing the district, including stops at Horten.

By Car   Take Highway 18 south from Oslo via Drammen.

By Boat   From mid-June until the last week in August, Tønsberg has a hydrofoil connection with Oslo, twice daily.

ESSENTIALS   For information, go to **Tourist Information,** Storgaten 55 (tel. 033/14-819). The **telephone area code** for Tønsberg is 033.

B ordering the western bank of the Oslofjord, Tønsberg is Norway's oldest town. It is divided into a historic area, filled with old clapboard-sided houses, and the commercial center, where the marketplace is located. The 40-square-mile town has some 31,000 inhabitants.

Tønsberg was founded a year before King Harald Fairhair united parts of the country in 872, and this Viking town became a royal coronation site. Svend Foyn, the man who invented modern whaling and seal hunting, was born here.

WHAT TO SEE & DO

Slottsfjellet, a huge hill fortress directly ahead of the train station, is touted as "the Acropolis of Norway." But it has only some meager ruins, and people mostly come here for the view from the lookout tower. Built in 1888, **Slottsfjelltårnet** is open May 18 to June 23, Monday through Friday from 10am to 3pm; June 24 to mid-August, Monday through Friday from 11am to 6pm and on Sunday from 1 to 6pm; mid-August to mid-September, Monday through Friday from 10am to 2pm and on Saturday and Sunday from noon to 2pm. Admission is 7 kroner ($1.15) for adults and 2 kroner (35¢) for children.

Nordbyen is the old and scenic part of town, with well-preserved houses. **Haugar** cemetery at Møllebakken, is right in the center of town, with the Viking graves of King Harald's sons, Olav and Sigrød.

Sem Church, the oldest in Vestfold, was built of stone in the Romanesque style around 1100. It is open Tuesday through Friday from 9am to 2pm; inquire at the verger.

You should also see **Fjerdingen,** a street of charming restored houses near the mountain farmstead. Tønsberg was also a Hanseatic town during the Middle Ages, and some houses have been redone in typical Hanseatic style.

In the **Vestfold Folk Museum,** Framannsveien 30 (tel. 12-919), there are many Viking and whaling treasures. One of the chief sights is the skeleton of a blue whale, the largest animal the world has ever known (sometimes weighing up to 150 tons). There is also a real Viking ship displayed, the *Klastad* from Tjolling, built about A.D. 800.

In the rural section of the museum, visit the **Vestfold Farm,** which includes a 1600 Hynne house, a timbered barn from Bøen, a storehouse from Fadum (with the characteristic apron), the Heierstadloft (oldest preserved timbered building in Vestfold, c. 1350), a smithy with a charcoal shed, a grain-drying house, a mountain farmstead, and two cow sheds.

Still at the museum, have lunch at a real mountain farmstead—a typical meal, with rømmegrøt (porridge made with sour cream) and other farm foods. The area is perfect for a picnic.

Admission is 10 kroner ($1.65) for adults, 5 kroner (85¢) for children. In the summer, it is open Monday through Saturday from 10am to 5pm and on Sunday and holidays from 1 to 5pm; from mid-September to mid-May, Monday through Friday from 10am to 2pm and on Sunday from noon to 5pm.

WHERE TO STAY

HOTEL KLUBBEN, Nedre Langgate 49, N-3100 Tønsberg. Tel. 033/11-51-11. Fax 033/13-199. 94 rms (all with bath). MINIBAR TV TEL
$ Rates (including breakfast): 725–1,045 kroner ($120.30–$172.55) single; 1,045–1,150 kroner ($172.55–$190.80) double. AE, DC, MC, V.

Part of a well-known Norwegian chain, this balconied 1968 hotel, east of Storgaten, has a glassed-in restaurant-terrace overlooking the water. The bedrooms are comfortable and well furnished. There are a handful of bars and restaurants, and a small art gallery. You'll also have access to the town's modern theater.

GRAND HOTEL, Øvre Langgate 65, N-3100 Tønsberg. Tel. 033/12-203. Fax 033/12-892. 63 rms (all with bath). MINIBAR TV TEL
$ Rates (including breakfast): Summer and weekends year round, 590 kroner ($97.90) single; 680 kroner ($112.80) double. Winter, Mon–Fri, 660–890 kroner ($109.50–$147.65) single; 760–1,000 kroner ($126.10–$165.90) double. AE, DC, MC, V.

The Grand Hotel's elaborate exterior is a reminder of this hotel's pretensions when it was built in 1931. The interior has been modernized and the rooms are comfortably contemporary. On the premises are two restaurants and a nightclub. The hotel has a health studio and a sauna. It's located in the town center directly south of Hauger.

HOTEL MARITIM, Storgaten 17, N-3100 Tønsberg. Tel. 033/17-100. 35 rms (all with bath). TV TEL **Directions:** See below.
$ Rates (including breakfast): Summer, 420 kroner ($69.70) single; 600 kroner ($99.55) double. Winter, 550 kroner ($91.25) single, 750 kroner ($124.45) double. AE, DC, MC, V.

This 1955 hotel is owned and operated by one of Norway's seamen's associations. Located on a square sloping down to the harbor, it occupies a four-story building, with the reception area on the third floor. Each room is well furnished and has a color scheme of either pink or white. Some rooms overlook the harbor, and all of them have carpeting and a comfortably modernized decor. It's a 10-minute walk east of the rail station on the main pedestrian street.

WHERE TO DINE

FREGATTEN, Storgaten 17. Tel. 14-776.
Cuisine: NORWEGIAN. **Reservations:** Not required. **Directions:** See below.
$ Prices: Appetizers 28–60 kroner ($4.65–$9.95); main dishes 45–190 kroner ($7.45–$31.50); fixed-price one-course lunch 65 kroner ($10.80). AE, DC, MC, V.
Open: Mon–Sat noon–10pm.

In the town center, in the Hotel Maritim building, Fregatten is one of the best restaurants in Tønsberg. In a pleasant, nautical dining room, soups such as fresh mushroom, and main courses such as filet steak, pepper steak, and entrecôte, are served. If you don't want beef, you'll find a fresh fish of the day (often served with shrimp-and-lobster sauce). For dessert, try an Irish coffee or vanilla pudding with sorbet. It's a 10-minute walk east of the railstation.

HÅNDVERKEREN, Møllergate 6. Tel. 12-388.
Cuisine: NORWEGIAN. **Reservations:** Not required.
$ Prices: Appetizers 45–69 kroner ($7.45–$11.45); main dishes 65–160 kroner ($10.80–$26.55); Sunday fixed-price menu 114 kroner ($18.90). AE, DC, MC, V.
Open: Mon–Sat 9:30am–11pm, Sun 1–11pm.

In an 1890 clapboard-sided house, this establishment has a tastefully decorated dining room and a summer cafe. A preferred dining room is richly paneled and carpeted. A three-course meal could include shrimp cocktail, fresh fish of the day, T-bone steak with béarnaise sauce, beef with onions, entrecôte with salad, and foaming mugs of

Norwegian beer. Filet of reindeer is a specialty. One part of the restaurant has been transformed into a popular pub, keeping the same hours and charging 38 kroner ($6.30) for a half liter of beer.

3. SANDEFJORD

68 miles south of Oslo, 15 miles south of Tønsberg, 9 miles north of Larvik

GETTING THERE **By Train** There are five daily express trains from Oslo, reaching Sandefjord in about 2 hours.

By Bus Frequent buses run between Oslo and Sandefjord daily. There are also good bus connections between Tønsberg and Sandefjord.

By Car Take the E18 south from Oslo all the way to Sandefjord.

By Ferry There is a daily ferry connection to Strømstad, Sweden, taking 2½ hours. For information, call **Scandi Line,** Tollbugata 5 (tel. 034/60-800).

ESSENTIALS For information, go to **Sandefjord Reiselivsforening,** Hjertnespromenaden (tel. 034/60-590). The **telephone area code** for Sandefjord is 034.

A summer resort, Sandefjord takes its name from a 6-mile fjord. Once a major whaling town, Sandefjord has built up the third-largest merchant fleet in Norway.

WHAT TO SEE & DO

At the southern end of Jernbanealleen, near a marina for pleasure craft, stands the great **Whaling Monument,** dedicated to the industry on which modern Sandefjord was founded.

Lying off Storgata, **Commander Christensen's Whaling Museum,** Museumsgaten 39 (tel. 63-251), has a replica of the mighty blue whale (its tongue weighs 3½ tons). Visiting hours are May to October daily from 11am to 4pm; in winter, on Sunday only, from 1 to 5pm. Admission is 10 kroner ($1.65) for adults, free for children.

Sandefjord has several charming parks. **Bugårdsparken** is a sports and leisure center with a playground for children, a swan lake, and a duck pond.

Also worth a visit is the royal burial mound at **Gokstad,** 2 miles east of the town center, where the Gokstad Viking ship (now at the Vikingskiphuset in Oslo) was found.

WHERE TO STAY

RICA PARK HOTEL, Strand Promenaden 9, N-3200 Sandefjord. Tel. 034/65-550. Fax 034/65-550. 160 rms (all with bath). MINIBAR TV TEL
$ Rates (including breakfast): 900–1,100 kroner ($149.30–$182.50) single; 1,140–1,440 kroner ($189.15–$238.90) double. AE, DC, MC.

By far the most stylish, comfortable, and prestigious hotel in the region, the Rica Park overlooks the harbor and a city meadow. Each of the bedrooms is unusually opulent, filled with rich fabrics, carpeting, and furniture. The sophisticated public rooms include a library-style bar, an elegant restaurant, and a handful of formal salons. On the premises is a disco and a saltwater swimming pool. It's located off Hystadveien.

ATLANTIC HOME HOTEL, Jernbanealléen 33, N-3200 Sandefjord. Tel. 034/68-000. Fax 034/68-020. 74 rms (all with bath), 5 suites. MINIBAR TV TEL
$ Rates (including breakfast): Summer and weekends year round, 590 kroner ($97.90) single; 690 kroner ($114.45) double. Winter Mon–Fri, 850 kroner ($141) single; 950 kroner ($157.60) double; suites from 1,090 kroner ($180.85). AE, DC, MC, V.

Built on the site of an older structure, this hotel respected its 1914 origins in its new design. The tasteful interior takes the whaling theme as its motif. Bedrooms have sleek modern styling and a number of amenities. Suites have their own fireplaces and Jacuzzi's, and three rooms are equipped for the handicapped. Children under 4 stay free, and children 4 to 16 are charged half price, in their parents' room. The hotel's Bistro La Coquille is furnished in a French provincial style, offering excellent food and service. The hotel is in the town center off Storgata.

HOTEL KONG CARL, Torvgaten 9, N-3200 Sandefjord. Tel. 034/63-117.
29 rms (all with bath). TV TEL
$ Rates (including breakfast): 380–520 kroner ($63.05–$86.25) single; 530–660 kroner ($87.95–$109.50) double. DC, MC, V.

Near the town center and marketplace, the country Victorian white clapboard-sided house dates from 1690. The hotel's cathedral-ceilinged annex is used extensively as a conference center. Bedrooms are simply furnished, but comfortable and inviting. Four contain a minibar. Lunch and dinner in the unpretentious Norwegian-style restaurant cost from 140 kroner ($23.25) each, served daily except Sunday. You can have a beer on the terrace in the summer. There is a parking space for 20 cars.

WHERE TO DINE

EDGAR LUDI'S GOURMET, Rådhusgaten 7. Tel. 62-741.
Cuisine: NORWEGIAN. **Reservations:** Recommended.
$ Prices: Appetizers 49–65 kroner ($8.15–$10.80); main dishes 100–175 kroner ($16.60–$29.05). AE, DC, MC, V.
Open: Daily noon–11pm.

This pleasant, sunny restaurant, in a new building in the center of the Old Town off Torggata, is one of the best dining spots around. Amid carefully focused lighting, mirrors, and palms, you can enjoy beef filet with green peppercorns, lamb filet with spinach and lemon sauce, turbot with Noilly Prat, burgundy snails in puff pastry, warm salmon soufflé, and veal with basil sauce.

---

4. LILLEHAMMER

105 miles north of Oslo, 226 miles south of Trondheim

GETTING THERE By Plane Visitors fly to either Fornebu or Gardermoen airport in the Oslo area, then go by bus or train to Lillehammer.

By Train Express trains from Oslo take about 2 hours and 20 minutes, and local trains take around 3 hours. Depending on the time of year, five to eight trains per day leave Oslo for Lillehammer.

By Bus Frequent buses run between Oslo and Lillehammer.

By Car Head north from Oslo along the E6.

ESSENTIALS The **Lillehammer Tourist Office** is at Jernbanegaten 2 (tel. 062/59-299). The **telephone area code** is 062.

SPECIAL EVENTS The 17th **Olympic Winter Games** is scheduled to begin in Lillehammer on February 12, 1994. It will represent the largest sports event Norway has ever organized. For 16 days, world attention will focus on Lillehammer, which is the smallest town ever to be asked to host the Olympics. Details can be obtained by contacting the **Lillehammer Olympic Organizing Committee,** Elvegata 19 (P.O. Box 106), N-2601 Lillehammer, Norway (tel. 062/71-994).

Surrounded by mountains, Lillehammer, a favorite resort for Europeans, is at the head of Lake Mjøsa. Host to the 1994 Winter Olympics, the town is already busy preparing.

The Hafjell Alpine Center, the main venue for alpine competitions in 1994, is situated about 9 miles away from the center of Lillehammer, with seven lifts and 12 miles of alpine slopes. Lillehammer is also the starting point for 250 miles of prepared tracks, 3 miles of which are illuminated. The Ski Center has three lifts and 2 miles of alpine slopes.

Lillehammer gears up for its winter sports season in December. In addition to its ski center, Lillehammer has an important admission-free skating rink (open in winter Monday through Friday from 11am to 9pm and on Sunday from 11am to 5pm). All this activity is supplemented in winter by festivals, folklore nights, and ski races.

WHAT TO SEE & DO

During the peak summer season, usually June 20 to August 20, the tourist bureau schedules several excursions, including one to the **Maihaugen Open-Air Museum (the Sandvig Collections)** and one on **Lake Mjøsa** on board the *White Swan of Lake Mjøsa*, a 135-year-old paddle steamer. Ask the tourist bureau (see above) for a list of activities.

MAIHAUGEN OPEN-AIR MUSEUM (The Sandvig Collections), Maihaugveien 1. Tel. 50-135.

This museum of provincial culture has assembled 150 buildings (more than 30,000 exhibits), ranging from manor farms to the cottage of the poorest yeoman worker. The houses, reassembled here and furnished in 17th- to 18th-century styles, came from all over the Gudbrandsdal Valley. See, in particular, the Garmo Stave Church and the Old Workshops, which range from gun smithing to wood-engraving. It's located southeast of Lillehammer, about half a mile from the town center.

Admission: 35 kroner ($5.80) adults, 15 kroner ($2.50) children.

Open: May and Sept, daily 10am–4pm; June–Aug, daily 10am–6pm; Oct–Apr, old workshops and indoor museum only, daily 11am–2pm. **Bus:** Route 007 (Nybu).

LILLEHAMMER BYS MALERISAMLING (Lillehammer Town Art Museum), Kirkegata 69. Tel. 51-944.

Founded in 1921, Norway's third-largest gallery has more than 800 works of Norwegian art dating from the early 19th century through the present. From September to April, lectures and various music performances are given. It lies on the north side of the main square, Stortorget.

Admission: 20 kroner ($3.30) adults, free for children under 12.

Open: June–Aug, Tues–Fri 11am–4pm, Sat 10am–2pm, Sun noon–4pm.

LILLEPUTTHAMMER, Øyergjestegård, Øyer. Tel. 78-335.

Adjoining the Øyer Inn is a miniature town depicting Lillehammer around the turn of the century. Some houses are populated with mechanical dolls in old-fashioned costumes; there's a small moving-picture theater in another. In another house, real children can play, paint, and draw. A minitrain goes through a park that has play areas and ponies for children to ride. There is a cafeteria and gift shop. It's located 10½ miles north of Lillehammer.

Admission: 15 kroner ($2.50) adults, 10 kroner ($1.65) children.

Open: June 16–Aug 12, daily 10am–7pm. **Closed:** Aug 13–June 15.

HUNDERFOSSEN FAMILY PARK, N-2638 Fåberg. Tel. 74-222.

Here you will find an interesting presentation of the most popular Norwegian fairytales, as well as more than 50 activities for both children and adults, and lots of space just to roam around. There is a cafeteria and swimming pool. A 40-foot troll at the gate welcomes visitors. The park is 7½ miles north of Lillehammer on the E6.

Admission: 85 kroner ($14.10) adults, 70 kroner ($11.60) children.

Open: Mid-June to mid-Aug, daily 10am–7pm. **Closed:** Mid-May to mid-June.

MUSEUM OF NORWEGIAN VEHICLE HISTORY, Lilletorget. Tel. 56-165.

Norway's only vehicle museum shows the development of transportation from the first sledges and wagons to the car of today. It's west of the town center; from the bus station, head out Elvegata.

Admission: 25 kroner ($4.15) adults, 12 kroner ($2) children.

Open: Mid-June to Aug, Mon–Fri 10am–6pm; Sept to mid-June, Mon–Fri 10am–2pm, Sat–Sun 10am–4pm.

SPORTS/RECREATION IN LILLEHAMMER

SKIING Ideal for both professional and neophyte skiers, Lillehammer has a 307-foot slope for the show-offs, and a smaller jump suitable for amateurs. Ski lifts take skiers 1,500 feet above sea level up the slalom slope, and more than 250 miles of marked skiing trails are packed by machines. Daily skiing classes are offered at the Lillehammer Ski School, and several cross-country tours are held weekly. Ask at the tourist office (see above) for details.

SPORTS FACILITIES The first hall erected for the 1994 Olympics, **Kristins Hall,** Stampesletta (tel. 66-424), has an ice rink, a sports hall, a curling rink, and an athletic track.

The hall stands at the **Stampesletta Central Sports Stadium,** an extensive sports grounds behind the town center. The stadium has three grass playing fields, one gravel field, two handball courts, an athletic track, and a show-jumping ring. It will be the central stadium for the Olympics.

The **Kringsjå Indoor Tennis Courts** are at Hammersengveien. Call the Lillehammer Tennis Club (tel. 60-065) for details about how to play.

NEARBY ATTRACTIONS

In Follebu

AULESTAD, N-2620 Follebu. Tel. 062/20-326.

Only 12 miles from Lillehammer, Aulestad is the home of Norway's Nobel Prize–winning poet Bjørnstjerne Bjørnson (1832–1910). He purchased the farm in 1875 and was living here when he learned of his Nobel laurels in 1903. The home is now a national museum.

Admission: 15 kroner ($2.50) adults, 7 kroner ($1.15) children.

Open: Mid-May to June and the first 2 weeks of Sept, daily 11am–2:30pm; in June and Aug, daily 10am–4pm; in July, daily 10am–5:30pm. **Closed:** Mid-Sept to mid-May

In Hamar

Some 36 miles from Lillehammer, in the heart of rich farmland, is Hamar, Norway's largest inland town, and the home of Kirsten Flagstad, the famous operatic soprano, born here in 1885. In addition to the following attractions, Hamar also has the remains of a medieval cathedral, from around 1150, and a bishop's palace.

KIRSTEN FLAGSTAD MUSEUM, Kirkegate 11. Tel. 065/27-660.

Lying 50 yards from the marketplace and 10 minutes from the railroad station, this museum contains Flagstad's memorial collection. The Metropolitan Opera in New York City contributed items, including some of the gowns she wore in her famous operatic roles. Flagstad recordings can be heard in a special room of the museum.

Admission: 10 kroner ($1.65) adults, 5 kroner (85¢) children.

Open: June 15–Aug 10, daily 10am–4pm. **Closed:** Aug 11–June 14.

NSB JERNBANEMUSEET, Strandvegen 132. Tel. 065/21-560.

This museum collects and displays bits of Norwegian rail history since its beginning in the 1840s. Vehicles include models from 1861 to 1950, among them three royal coaches and several steam locomotives weighing up to 150 tons. There is a museum park with several station buildings, railway tracks, and other exhibits, as well as a "dining car" serving snacks and refreshments. A small train travels along the grounds of the amusement park; trips cost 10 kroner ($1.65) for adults and 5 kroner (85¢) for children.

Admission: 20 kroner ($3.30) adults, 10 kroner ($1.65) children.

Open: May 20–Oct 1, daily 10am–6pm. **Closed:** Oct 2–May 19. **Directions:** Bus no. 1 from the railroad station runs here, or it's a 30-minute walk from the town center heading north along the shore of Lake Mjøsa.

INTERFERENS HOLOGRAFI, Strandveien 100, Domkirkeodden. Tel. 065/25-050.

At Domkirkeodden, Hamar's museum and recreation area, about a mile from the town center and rail station, Mr. and Mrs. Olav Skipnes have assembled Norway's first and largest exhibition of holography. The projected holographic images are created by a special laser technique and give the observer an illusion of seeing objects in their natural three dimensions. They sometimes seem to penetrate out of the image plane and float in the air. The exhibition comprises some 100 holograms.

Admission: 20 kroner ($3.30) adults, 10 kroner (85¢) children.

Open: Mid-May to mid-June, Tues–Sun 11am–4pm; mid-June through Aug, Tues–Sun 11am–6pm; Sept to mid-May, Sat–Sun 11am–4pm. **Directions:** You can reach the exhibition by taxi, on foot, or by renting a bicycle at the rail or bus station. From the center, starting at the quay of the old paddlewheel steamer *Skibladner,* a promenade path along the shore of Lake Mjøsa leads to the area.

HEDMARK KUNSTNERSENTER (Hedmark Artists' Center), Strandveien 98. Tel. 065/30-010.

This center offers changing exhibitions of local artworks. It's beautifully situated by Lake Mjøsa west of town, which makes for a pleasant walk along the lake.

Admission: 10 kroner ($1.65) adults, free for children.

Open: Mon–Fri 9am–3pm.

WHERE TO STAY

EXPENSIVE

LILLEHAMMER HOTEL, Turisthotellveien 27B, N-2600 Lillehammer. Tel. 062/54-800. Fax 062/57-333. 166 rms (all with bath). MINIBAR TV TEL

$ Rates (including breakfast): 820 kroner ($136.05) single; 1,050 kroner ($174.20) double. AE, DC, MC, V.

A luxurious and sports-oriented hotel, this establishment is located in a forested 8-acre park near the Lillehammer ski center and the Maihaugen Open-Air Museum. Bedrooms are tastefully modern, some equipped for the handicapped. The hotel has three restaurants featuring both evening dance music and buffets. On the premises are conference facilities, and outdoor and indoor pools, with saunas and a solarium. The wood and marble-trimmed public areas are among the most glamorous in the region.

About a mile away across Lake Mjøsa, the hotel maintains its own sports center with a terrace, where you can rent sailboats and canoes, waterski, or sit on the flower-strewn terrace to enjoy the view. To reach the hotel, take a taxi from the rail station.

RICA VICTORIA HOTEL, Storgate 84B, N-2600 Lillehammer. Tel. 062/50-049. Fax 062/52-474. 92 rms (all with bath). TV TEL

$ Rates (including breakfast): Mid-June to mid-August and weekends year round, 580 kroner ($96.20) single; 850 kroner ($141) double. Mid-Aug to mid-June, Mon–Fri, 900 kroner ($149.30) single; 1,050 kroner ($174.20) double. AE, DC, MC, V.

One of the largest and most modern hotels in town, the Rica Victoria was established in 1872, but new wings filled with modern comfort were extended in 1963 and 1976. Each of the well-furnished bedrooms contains comfortably upholstered chairs and sofas. Known for its conference facilities, the hotel also has a bar, blazing fireplaces, and several restaurants, including the Victorianhjørnet, seating 100 guests, and the regular dining room seating 180 guests. Guests also enjoy dancing in the Rica Plaza Dancing Club. The hotel is 300 yards from the rail station.

MODERATE

OPPLAND HOTEL, Hamarveien 2, N-2600 Lillehammer. Tel. 062/58-500. Fax 062/55-325. 75 rms (all with bath). MINIBAR TV TEL
$ Rates (including breakfast): Summer, 540 kroner ($89.60) single; 700 kroner ($116.15) double. Winter, 800–900 kroner ($132.70–$149.30) single; 600–840 kroner ($99.55–$139.35) double. AE, DC, MC, V.

Constructed in 1951, this hotel was later extended in two different decades and was completely modernized again in 1990. Half a mile south of the rail station, it is near the Ski Center and is a good starting point for cross-country skiing. It offers modern, comfortable, and well-furnished bedrooms. The hotel also makes a good drinking and dining center (see Baccus Bar and Halvadans Stue, below).

INEXPENSIVE

DØLAHEIMEN HOTELL & KAFETERIA, Jernbanegaten 3, N-2601 Lillehammer. Tel. 062/58-866. 21 rms (all with bath). TV TEL
$ Rates: 420 kroner ($69.70) single; 580 kroner ($96.20) double. Breakfast costs 41 kroner ($6.80) extra. V.

A modern hotel and cafeteria in the center of Lillehammer at the rail and bus stations, the Dølaheimen is usually heavily booked in July and early August, so reservations are important. An informal, family atmosphere prevails; children are welcome. Rooms are sleek, functional, and comfortable. There's a large air-conditioned cafeteria with a separate room for nonsmokers, a sitting room, and an upstairs TV lounge. Parking is available for the handicapped.

GJESTEHUSET ERSGAARD, Nordsetervn 201, N-2600 Lillehammer. Tel. 062/50-684. Fax 062/53-109. 30 rms (16 with shower). **Directions:** See below.
$ Rates (including breakfast): 300 kroner ($49.75) single without bath, 430 kroner ($71.35) single with bath; 500 kroner ($82.95) double without bath, 580 kroner ($96.20) double with bath. MC, V.

 A pleasant family hotel created from a 1570 farm on the outskirts of town, Ersgaard sits atop a mountain overlooking the resort and Lake Mjøsa. If you have a car, this makes for a pleasant stay. Bedrooms are modest but adequately furnished. The Norwegian buffet breakfast features assorted jams, cheese (even goat), Norwegian herring, cold cuts, fresh bread, boiled eggs, a choice of cereal, and coffee, tea, milk, or juice. A complete lunch or dinner will cost from 125 kroner ($20.75). Bus service from Lillehammer is available twice a day. The hotel is 1 mile from the town center in the center of the Olympic Park; follow signs to Nordseter.

NEARBY PLACES TO STAY

RUSTAD HOTELL AND FJELLSTUE, N-2612 Sjusjøen. Tel. 065/63-408. Fax 065/63-574. 52 rms (36 with bath). **Bus:** Sjusjøen from Lillehammer.
$ Rates (including breakfast): 235 kroner ($39) single without bath, 375 kroner ($62.20) single with bath; 440 kroner ($73) double without bath, 720 kroner ($119.45) double with bath. No credit cards.

 Some visitors might want to settle in the wilderness at this favorite spot, about 14 miles north of Lillehammer. This log-and-timber chalet is on the edge of a lake (there's a dock for swimming and boats) and surrounded by private grounds. The well-furnished bedrooms have views of the lake or mountains, and more than half have private showers and toilets (all come equipped with hot and cold running water). Country-style meals are served. In winter, people enjoy one of the best ski terrains in Norway, and there's horseback riding in summer. The public rooms are furnished in antiques.

WHERE TO DINE

HALVDANS STUE, in the Oppland Hotel, Hamarveien 2. Tel. 58-500.
Cuisine: NORWEGIAN. **Reservations:** Not required.
$ Prices: Appetizers 48–75 kroner ($7.95–$12.45); main dishes 146–198 kroner ($24.25–$32.85). AE, DC, MC, V.
Open: Daily 7am–10:30pm.
Located in the Oppland Hotel (see "Where to Stay," above), a half mile south of the rail station, this restaurant is popular with visitors and locals. The decor is warmly traditional, with a color scheme of pink and brown. The food is good, the service helpful, and the portions generous. Try such dishes as filet of codfish with beetroot and leek sauce or roast duckling with orange sauce. It's possible to order a one-course supper for only 38 kroner ($6.30).

QUEEN RESTAURANT, in the Rica Victoria Hotel, Storgate 84B Tel. 50-049.
Cuisine: NORWEGIAN/INTERNATIONAL. **Reservations:** Recommended.
$ Prices: Appetizers 39–45 kroner ($6.45–$7.45); main dishes 79–225 kroner ($13.10–$37.35); two-course lunch with coffee 145 kroner ($24.05); three-course dinner with coffee 185 kroner ($30.70). AE, DC, MC, V.
Open: Lunch, daily 11am–3pm; dinner, daily 3pm–11pm.
Considered one of the best restaurants of town, the Queen occupies lobby-level premises at the Rica Victoria Hotel (see "Where to Stay" above). Its windows overlook the city center. The decor is modern, with a color scheme of pastel blues and greens, with touches of pale pink. Specialties include mountain trout fried in sour cream and boiled catfish with butter sauce and cucumber salad. Main dishes range from frikadeller (meatballs), the cheapest item on the menu, to chateaubriand, the most expensive. The set menus are good value. A cold buffet is served for the same cost as the fixed-price lunch, and a warm buffet is offered at night for the same price as the set dinner. It's a 3-minute walk north of the rail station.

VICTORIANHJØRNET (Victorian Corner), in the Rica Victoria Hotel, Storgate 84B. Tel. 50-049.
Cuisine: STEAKS/PIZZA. **Reservations:** Not required.
$ Prices: Pizzas 64–135 kroner ($10.60–$22.40); main dishes 119–138 kroner ($19.75–22.90); deli specials, served until 7pm, 64 kroner ($10.60) per platter. AE, DC, MC, V.
Open: Sun–Fri noon–midnight, Sat 11am–midnight.
One floor above lobby level in the Rica Victoria Hotel (see "Where to Stay," above) is a bistro, pizzeria, and steakhouse serving good and reasonably priced meals. The decor is red and white with an old-fashioned woodsy ambience. The place doubles as a pub, but is better known as a steakhouse. Both pizzas and steaks come in different sizes and are priced accordingly. It's a 3-minute walk north of the rail station.

BRYGGERIKJELLERN, Elwagata 19. Tel. 53-956.
Cuisine: NORWEGIAN. **Reservations:** Not required.
$ Prices: Salad 50 kroner ($8.30); main dishes 49–98 kroner ($8.15–$16.25). AE, DC, MC, V.
Open: Mon 6–11pm, Tues–Fri 6pm–1am, Sat 1pm–1am, Sun 3pm–1am.
In 1969 this 1814 brewery, a 7-minute walk east of the rail station, was transformed into a pub/restaurant serving beer, steaks, and main dishes, and it has done a roaring business ever since. It's especially popular in winter with skiers. Salads are the only appetizers. Many people come here just to drink, paying 35.50 kroner ($5.90) for a half liter of beer. A disco connected with the pub is open Wednesday through Saturday from 9pm to 1am. Admission is 50 kroner ($8.30).

NEARBY PLACES TO DINE

KIRKESTUEN CAFETERIA, Maihaugveien 1. Tel. 50-135.
   Cuisine: NORWEGIAN. **Reservations:** Not required. **Bus:** 007 (Nybu) for half
   a mile southeast of the town center.
$ Prices: Appetizers 35–45 kroner ($5.80–$7.45); main dishes 50–100 kroner
   ($8.30–$16.60). AE, MC, V.
   Open: June 15–Aug 20, daily 11am–5:30pm. **Closed:** Aug 20–June 14.
This cafeteria is located in an old hillside country inn, among the ancient buildings of
a folk museum. Traditional Norwegian dishes and a wide selection of open-face
sandwiches are featured. You can order such typical dishes as rømmergrøt, sour-
cream porridge, followed by fried trout with salad and potatoes.

EVENING ENTERTAINMENT

In addition to the disco at the Bryggerikjellern (see "Where to Dine," above), you
might try the following two establishments.

BACCUS BAR, in the Oppland Hotel, Hamarveien 2. Tel. 58-500.
   This pub serves no food, but is a musical bar, one of the few live-music places in
Lillehammer. It lies in the cellar beneath the Oppland Hotel, a half mile south of the
rail station. Beer costs 35 kroner ($5.80). It's open Monday through Saturday from
6pm to 1am; music begins at 8:30pm.
   Admission: 25–35 kroner ($4.15–$5.80).

RICA VICTORIA HOTEL, Storgate 84B. Tel. 50-049.
   The minimum age at this hotel dancing club is 21. It's accessible through the hotel
lobby or by a separate entrance. Inside, the decor is rustic and couples—mostly in
their 20s and 30s—dance to recorded music. It's open Monday through Saturday
from 8pm to 1am. A beer costs 25 kroner ($4.15).
   Admission: 40 kroner ($6.65); free for hotel residents.

5. THE PEER GYNT ROAD

The road between Lillehammer and the town of Vinstra, 38 miles long (not counting
detours), takes you right into the heart of Peer Gynt country. Henrik Ibsen came this
way when he was researching his masterpiece *Peer Gynt,* published in 1867 and later
set to music by Edvard Grieg. Ibsen based his tale in part on the exploits of one Per
(spelled with only one *e*) Gynt Haga, a real-life Norwegian folk hero noted for such
exploits as riding on the backs of reindeer at breakneck speed.
   As you drive through the Gudrandsdal (Gudrands Valley), you can travel the same
route that bewitched the original hero, and outside Vinstra you can visit the
monument to Per Gynt Haga, the Peer Gynt prototype, in the cemetery adjoining the
Sødorp Church, 1 mile south of town.
   The Peer Gynt country is a magnificent unspoiled mountain region with altitudes
varying from 2,526 to 4,920 feet. This is one of Norway's oldest and best-known
sports districts. The skiing center at Fefor was opened as early as 1904, and it was here
that the adventurous Capt. Robert Falcon Scott tested the equipment for his
expedition to the South Pole.
   Here a respect for tradition is combined with modern skiing facilities. The area
features 248 miles of prepared double track for cross-country skiing and 10 ski-lift
and downhill facilities. It's suitable for those who'd like to combine cross-country and
alpine skiing.
   The region is also a lure to summer travelers, as the Peer Gynt Road passes
mountains, farmsteads, fish-filled lakes, wild game, and alpine flowers.
   The best source of information about touring in the area is the **Vinstra
Turistkontor,** Nedre Gate 2 (tel. 062/90-166), at the northern end of the road in

Vinstra. For a suggested tour of the area in more detail, see "Suggested Itineraries" in Chapter 12, "Planning a Trip to Norway."

WHERE TO STAY IN PEER GYNT COUNTRY

Most people travel the Peer Gynt Road as an excursion from Lillehammer. But if you'd like to stay around for a few days, here are several recommended accommodations, all in the moderate price range.

DALSETER HØYFJELLSHOTELL, Gudbrandsdalen, N-2628 Espedalen. Tel. 062/99-910. Fax 062/99-941. 90 rms (81 with bath). TEL **Bus:** Espedalen bus from Lillehammer.

$ Rates (including breakfast): 440 kroner ($73) single without bath, 540 kroner ($89.60) single with bath; 620 kroner ($102.85) double without bath, 720 kroner ($119.45) double with bath. MC, V.

This 1963 hotel set on a hillside overlooking forests and mountains caters to families. The views are stunning. Bedrooms are outfitted in a cozy, comfortable Norwegian style, with lots of heat in winter. Meals in the warm, contemporary dining room are well prepared. Evening dance music contributes to the ambience. There's a dining room, an indoor swimming pool, a gymnasium, an intricate network of well-marked hiking or skiing trails, and fishing facilities.

FEFOR HIFJELLSHOTELL, Fefor, N-2640 Vinstra. Tel. 062/90-099. 128 rms (all with bath). TEL

$ Rates: Summer, 460 kroner ($76.30) single; 640–730 kroner ($106.20–$121.10) double. Winter (with full board and 5-night minimum stay), 810 kroner ($134.40) per person daily. AE, DC, MC, V.

This hotel's interesting exterior features red Nordic dragons on the roof of its older wing, dating from 1891. The modern addition has the best rooms, but there are magnificent views in each section. The public rooms feature fireplaces, heavy iron chandeliers, and lots of comfortable nooks and cubbyholes. There's an indoor and an outdoor swimming pool, ski runs, boating facilities, organized children's activities, and an ice skating rink. It's located on the shores of Lake Fefor.

GAUSDAL HIFJELLSHOTELL, Gausdal, N-26220 Svingvoll. Tel. 062/28-500. Fax 062/28-500. 125 rms (all with bath). TEL

$ Rates: Summer (including breakfast): 500 kroner ($82.95) single; 800 kroner ($132.70) double. Winter (with breakfast and a 5-night minimum stay), 650 kroner ($107.85) single; 1,100 kroner ($182.50) double. Half board costs 100 kroner ($16.60) per person extra. AE, DC, MC, V.

The hotel sits in the center of the small but popular mountain resort of Gausdal, 10 miles west of Tretten, the nearest rail station, and the owners will send a car to pick you up there. Originally built in 1876, it was set afire by the Nazis in 1944. In 1956, it rose again as a hotel, with attractively furnished and modernized bedrooms, many opening onto views of the mountains. There are facilities for tennis, swimming, a sauna, and a pool. Miles of hiking or ski trails surround the hotel, and provisions are made for downhill and cross-country skiing, horseback riding, and hill climbing. The hotel is especially popular as a ski center in winter.

If you're just passing through Gausdal, you can patronize a lunchtime smörgåsbord for 140 kroner ($23.25) per person or a fixed-price dinner for 175 kroner ($29.05).

SKEIKAMPEN HØIFJELLSHOTELL, N-2622 Skeikampen. Tel. 062/28-505. Fax 062/27-520. 83 rms (all with bath). TV TEL **Train:** Dovrebanen Railway from Lillehammer to the Tretten station.

$ Rates (including breakfast): Summer, 385 kroner ($63.85) single; 620 kroner ($102.85) double. Winter (with 2-day minimum stay), 520–720 kroner ($86.25–$119.45) per person. AE, DC, MC, V.

In many ways, this is the best hotel in the region, with attractive public rooms filled with antique and modern Scandinavian furniture and acres of woodland grounds. The snug and cozy bedrooms, decorated in "Nordic light" pastels, are distributed in such a way that most of them open onto scenic views. Sports lovers will find an indoor pool, a sauna, a ski lift adjacent to a smaller rope tow for beginners, and a ski school with child-care facilities. As the hotel is right at the timber line, both forested and rocky paths are well marked for climbers.

On the premises is a Spanish-influenced bodega, with the best wine stock in the region. Wine-testing parties and semiformal dinners are held here at least three times a week. A lunch buffet costs 150 kroner ($24.90).

WADAHL HIFJELLSHOTELL, N-2645 Harpefoss. Tel. 062/98-300. Fax 062/98-360. 90 rms (all with bath). MINIBAR TV TEL
$ Rates: Summer, 500 kroner ($82.95) single; 800 kroner ($132.70) double. Winter (with full board and 3-night minimum stay), 650 kroner ($107.85) per person. MC, V.

Originally established in 1900 as a survival station for the high mountains around it, it became a hotel in 1930 and has been enlarged several times since. Rooms are comfortably furnished and modernized. Winter is high season, and because of the hotel's isolation, guests usually plan to eat here. Patrons enjoy the tasty dinners and evening dance music here. Facilities include a large outdoor pool, an indoor pool, tennis courts, horseback-riding facilities, saunas, and a year-round sun terrace. The hotel is 11 miles southwest of Vinstra, the nearest rail station, and 9 miles northwest of Harpefoss, which has no rail link. There is no public transort to the hotel, but arrangements can be made to have you picked up at the rail station.

BERGEN

In western Norway the landscape takes on an awesome beauty, with iridescent glaciers, deep fjords that slash into rugged, snow-capped mountains, roaring waterfalls, and secluded valleys that lie at the end of corkscrew-twisting roads. From Bergen the most beautiful fjords to visit are: Hardanger (best at blossom time, May and early June) to the south; Sogne, Norway's longest fjord, immediately to the north; and the Nord fjord north of that. A popular excursion on the Nordfjord takes visitors from Loen to Olden along rivers and lakes to the Brixdal Glacier.

If you have time, on Hardangerfjord you can stop over at one of the fjord resorts like Ulvik or Lofthus. From many vantage points it's possible to see the Folgefonn Glacier, Norway's second-largest ice field, which spans more than 100 square miles. Other stopover suggestions include the summer resorts (winter ski centers) of Voss and Geilo.

Bergen, with its many sightseeing attractions, good hotels, boardinghouses, and restaurants, and its excellent boat, rail, and coach connections, makes the best center in the fjord district.

It's an ancient city that looms large in Viking sagas. Until the 14th century it was the seat of the medieval kingdom of Norway. The Hanseatic merchants established a major trading post here, holding sway until the 18th century.

Bergen has survived many disasters, including several fires and the explosion of a Nazi ship during World War II. It's a town with important traditions in shipping, banking, and insurance, and its modern industries are expanding rapidly.

1. ORIENTATION

ARRIVING

BY PLANE **Bergen Airport** (tel. 99-82-50), at Flesland, is 12 miles south of the city. It offers intercontinental routes to and from New York, Los Angeles, Seattle, Chicago, and Montréal.

Frequent **airport bus** service makes a circuit from the airport to the SAS Royal Hotel, Braathens SAFE's office at the Hotel Norge, and the city bus station. For departure times, inquire at the airlines or at the Tourist Information Center. One way fare on the airport bus is 35 kroner ($5.80).

WHAT'S SPECIAL ABOUT BERGEN

Historic Districts
☐ Bryggen, where warehouses and commercial buildings of the Hanse-atic trading days are re-created along the harborfront.

Museums
☐ Bryggens Museum, a cultural-history museum based on extensive excava-tions of Bergen of the Middle Ages.
☐ Gamle Bergen, an open-air museum with around 35 wooden houses—a living example of Bergen architec-ture during the 18th and 19th cen-turies.

Ancient Buildings
☐ The Fantoft Stave Church, a Norwe-gian stave church of the early 12th century in the Sognefjord area.
☐ Rosenkrantz Tower, erected as a for-tified official residence by a feudal lord in the 1560s.

Musical Shrines
☐ Troldhaugen, home of the great composer Edvard Grieg for 22 years, where some of his best-known works were composed.

Scenic Tours
☐ "Norway in a Nutshell," a do-it-yourself tour that encapsulates the best of Norway in 12 hours.
☐ An express steamer to Gudvangen to view Norway's longest fjord, Sognefjord.

Special Events/Festivals
☐ A calvacade of music, drama, opera, ballet, and folklore, including perfor-mances of Grieg's works (late May to early June).
☐ Fana Folklore, a tradition-laden coun-try festival staged throughout the summer.

BY TRAIN Day and night trains arrive from Oslo and stations en route. For information, phone 05/31-96-40 or 05/31-93-05. Trip time is 8½ hours from Oslo to Bergen.

BY BUS Express buses travel to Bergen from Oslo, Trondheim, Ålesund, and the Nordfjord area. Trip time from Oslo is 11 hours.

BY CAR A toll is charged on all vehicles driven *into* the city center Monday through Friday from 6am to 10pm. A single ticket costs 5 kroner (85¢); a book of 20 tickets, 90 kroner ($14.95).

To cross from Oslo to Bergen is a long and tedious mountain drive, although filled with dramatic scenery. Since the country is split by mountains, there is no direct road. You can take the southern route, the E76, going through mountain passes until the junction with Route 47; then head north to the ferry crossing at Kinsarvik that goes across the fjords to the E68 leading west to Bergen. The northern route is via Highway 7, going through the resort of Geilø, to the junction with Route 47; then head south to Kinsarvik. After crossing on the ferry, you arrive at the E68. Head west to reach Bergen.

TOURIST INFORMATION

For information, maps, and brochures about Bergen and its environs, the **Tourist Information Center,** on Torgalmenning (tel. 05/32-14-80), in the heart of town, is open from the last week in April to the last week in May and mid-September to mid-October, Monday through Saturday from 8:30am to 8pm and on Sunday from 9:30am to 8pm; from the last week in May to mid-September, Monday through Saturday from 8:30am to 10pm and on Sunday from 9:30am to 10pm. Off-season, it is closed Sunday but open other days from 10am to 3pm.

The Tourist Information Center will also help you find accommodations (see below), exchange foreign currency, and cash traveler's checks when banks are closed.

CITY LAYOUT

Bergen is squeezed between mountain ranges and bounded by water. The center of the city lies between the harbor, **Bryggen** (see below), the railway station, and the main square, called **Torgalmenningen.**

Like Rome, Bergen is said to have grown up around seven hills. For the best overall view, take the funicular to **Fløien** (see "More Attractions," below). The northern-most section of the city is **Sandviken,** filled with old warehouses. The area south of central Bergen has recently developed at an incredible rate.

In the center of Bergen, you will be caught up in the charm of cobblestone streets as you explore the quayside with its medieval houses, the open-air fish market, the city center with its colonnaded shops and cafés, and **Gamle Bergen,** where you can step back to the early 19th century.

2. GETTING AROUND

BY BUS

The **Central Bus Station (Bystasjonen),** Strømgaten 8 (tel. 32-67-80), is the terminal for all buses serving the environs of Bergen and the Hardanger area, as well as the airport bus. The station has luggage storage, shops, and a restaurant. City buses are all marked with their destination and route number.

Special 48-hour **tourist tickets** for unlimited travel are available at the Tourist Information Office on Torgalmenningen (see below). A 1-day ticket for Bergen costs 48 kroner ($7.95), 60 kroner ($9.95) if the environs are included. The offer is valid May through September.

BY TAXI

Taxis are readily available at the airport, or phone 99-09-90. A ride from the Bergen Airport to the center costs 160 kroner ($26.55). Sightseeing by taxi costs 250 kroner ($41.50) per hour.

BY CAR

For convenient indoor parking, try the **Bygarasjen Busstation** (tel. 32-53-60), a large indoor garage near the bus and train stations, about a 5-minute walk from the city center. It's open 24 hours a day and charges 5 kroner (85¢) per hour from 7am to 5pm or a maximum of 30 kroner ($5). From 5pm to 7am, the charge is only 2 kroner (35¢) per hour. You can park 24 hours a day for 45 kroner ($7.45).

BERGEN RENTAL CARS **Hertz** in Bergen is at the airport (tel. 32-79-20, or toll free 800/654-3001 in North America) and downtown at Nygårddsgate 89 (same phone). For a 2-day rental, the smallest car is a Ford Fiesta or Peugeot 205, costing 425 kroner ($70.50) per day, plus 4.75 kroner (80¢) per kilometer, plus 20% tax.

Avis is at the Bergen airport (tel. 22-76-18) and downtown at Lars Hillesgate 20 (tel. 32-01-30, or toll free 800/331-2112 in North America). For a 2-day rental, their smallest car is a Ford Fiesta or a Renault 5, costing 450 kroner ($74.65) per day, plus 4.95 kroner (90¢) per kilometer, plus 20% tax.

Budget is at the Bergen airport (tel. 22-75-27) or downtown at Tide Auto, A/S Nordnes (tel. 31-14-13, or toll free 800/472-3323 in North America). Budget is the least expensive of the three companies, with a Ford Fiesta costing 355 kroner ($58.70) per day, plus 3.85 kroner (65¢) per kilometer, plus 20% tax, plus an optional collision-damage waiver.

BY FERRY

You can take a ferry across the harbor Monday through Friday from 6:45am to 4:15pm, but they don't run on Saturday and Sunday. One-way fares are 7 kroner ($1.15) for adults, 4 kroner (65¢) for children.

COASTAL STEAMERS

Express boats leave from Munkebryggen (tel. 32-65-60 for departure information), heading for Hardanger Fjord and Sunnhordland. Steamers leave from Möhlenspris-kaien (tel. 32-40-15) heading for Sognefjord, Nordfjord, and Sunnfjord. Local steamers serving the island and fjords immediately north of Bergen dock at the inner harbor on the left-hand side of the Fish Market at Strandkaiterminalen.

FAST FACTS: BERGEN

American Express   In Bergen, it's represented by **Winge Travel Bureau,** Christian Michelsen Gate 1-3 (tel. 32-59-59), open Monday through Friday from 8:30am to 4pm and on Saturday from 8:30am to 1pm.

Area Code   The telephone area code for Bergen is 05.

Banks   Banking transactions can be handled at **Fokus Bank,** Rådstuplass 2-3 (tel. 21-86-00), with branches at Bystasjonen (the Central Bus Station), Strømgate 8, and Strandgaten 77.

Bookstores   One of the best, with a wide range of books in English, is **F. Beyer Bok-og Papirhandel,** Strandgaten 4 (tel. 32-11-80).

Business Hours   **Banks** are usually open Monday through Friday from 8:15am to 3:30pm, and on Thursday until 6pm. Most **businesses** are open Monday through Friday from 9am to 4pm. **Shops** are generally open on Monday through Friday from 9am to 4:30pm, and on Thursday until 7pm (sometimes also on Friday until 7pm); Saturday hours are 9am to 2pm.

Car Rentals   See "Getting Around" in this chapter.

Currency Exchange   There is a currency exchange at the Bergen Airport. In town, you can exchange money at any one of several banks. When banks are closed, you can exchange money at the tourist office (see above).

Dentist   Emergency care is available at Lars Hillesgate 30 (tel. 32-11-20), daily from 10 to 11am and 7 to 9pm.

Doctor   For medical assistance, call **Accident Clinic,** Lars Hillesgate 30 (tel. 32-11-00), which is open 24 hours. Your hotel will also set up an appointment with an English-speaking doctor if it is not an emergency.

Drugstores   A 24-hour pharmacy is **Apoteket Nordstjernen,** at the Central Bus Station (tel. 31-68-84).

Embassies/Consulates   Most foreign nationals will have to go to their embassies in Oslo if they have a problem; only Great Britain maintains a consulate in Bergen, at Strandgaten 18 (tel. 32-70-11).

Emergencies   For the **police,** dial 002; to report a **fire,** call 001; for an **ambulance,** dial 003.

Eyeglasses   A good optician is **Optiker Svabø,** Strandgaten 18 (tel. 31-69-51).

Hairdressers/Barbers   Try **Prikken Fisørsalong,** Strandkaien 2 (tel. 32-31-51).

Hospitals   A medical center, **Accident Clinic,** open day and night, is located at Lars Hillesgate 30 (tel. 32-11-20). There is a general hospital, but you can't go directly there. You must either go through the Accident Clinic or call Sykebesøkformidling (Sick Call Help) at 32-40-60.

Laundry/Dry Cleaning   Try **Jarlens Vaskoteque,** Lille Øvregate 17 (tel. 32-55-04), near the Hotel Victoria in a little alley about 50 yards northeast of the 17th-century church, Korskirken, off Kong Oscars Gate.

Libraries   The **Bergen Public Library,** Strømgaten (tel. 31-97-50), is open in July and August on Tuesday, Wednesday, and Friday from 9am to 3pm, on Monday and Thursday from 9am to 7pm, and on Saturday from 9am to 1pm; the rest of the year, Monday through Friday from 9am to 8pm and on Saturday from 9am to 2pm.

Lost Property   This problem is handled by **Hittegodskontoret,** Nygaten 1 (tel. 21-66-00), open Monday through Saturday from 9am to 2pm.

Luggage Storage/Lockers   Both locker rental and luggage storage are available at **Jernbanestasjonen (Railway Station),** Strømgaten 1 (tel. 31-96-40), open daily from 6:45am to 11pm.

Photographic Needs   Go to **Foto Knutsen,** Galleriet, Torgalmenningen 8 (tel. 31-16-78), next to Tourist Information.

Police   Call 002.

Post Office   The main post office, Byparken (by the City Park; tel. 31-81-00), is open Monday through Friday from 8am to 5pm (to 7pm on Thursday) and on Saturday from 9am to 1pm.

Religious Services   Lutheran services are held in English in the **Domkirken,** the Norwegian state church's cathedral, Kong Oscars Gate (tel. 31-04-70), at 9:30am on Sunday in June, July, and August. **St. Paul's Roman Catholic Church,** Christiesgate 16 (tel. 32-54-10), celebrates masses in English on Sunday at 10am.

Shoe Repairs   Try **Mr. Minit Sko & Nøkkelservice,** Galleriet, Torgalmenningen (tel. 96-06-40), open Monday through Saturday from 9am to 8pm.

Taxes   Bergen imposes no city taxes other than the Value Added Tax on all goods and services in Norway.

Taxis   See "Getting Around" in this chapter.

Telegram   Dial 0138 to send a telegram. The **Telegraph Building,** Byparken (by the City Park), is open Monday through Saturday from 8am to 8pm and on Sunday from 2 to 7pm.

Telephone   Public telephones take 1-krone (17¢) coins. Local calls cost 2 kroner (35¢). To call abroad, dial 0115.

3. ACCOMMODATIONS

Easily found in the center of Torgalmennigen, the **Tourist Information Center** (see above) not only books guests into hotels but secures accommodations in private homes. More than 30 families take in guests during the summer months.

The booking service costs 10 to 20 kroner ($1.65 to $3.30), but prospective guests also pay a deposit that is deducted from the final bill. Rooms in private homes are usually priced at 130 to 150 kroner ($21.55 to $24.80) single, 200 to 240 kroner ($33.20 to $39.80) double, with no service charge. Breakfast costs around 50 kroner ($8.30) extra.

Rates quoted for the hotels below include service and tax. Hotels ranked "Very Expensive" charge $200 to $270 a night for a double room; "Expensive," $186 to $190; "Moderate," $132 to $165; "Inexpensive," $82 to $106. "Budget" is a specialty category—in this case boarding houses charging $40 to $66 a night for a double.

Many of the deluxe and first-class places lower their tariffs considerably on weekends and at midsummer. Reductions, when available, are cited under rates.

VERY EXPENSIVE

HOTEL ADMIRAL, Sundtsgata 9, N-5001 Bergen. Tel. 05/32-47-30. Fax 05/23-30-92. 107 rms (all with bath). MINIBAR TV TEL **Bus:** 2, 3, 4.

$ Rates (including breakfast): Summer Mon-Thurs, 380 kroner ($63.05) per person double. Winter Mon-Thurs 920–1,050 kroner ($152.65–$174.20) single; 1,190–1,290 kroner ($197.40–$214) double. Weekends year round, 580 kroner ($96.20) single; 720 kroner ($119.45) double. AE, DC, MC, V.

This is one of the town's most unusual hotels, originally built in 1906 but renovated in 1987. The bedrooms are comfortable, well furnished, and also well maintained. There is an attractive piano bar off the lobby, as well as a first-class restaurant, Emily, known for its seafood.

HOTEL NORGE, Ole Bulls Plass 2-4, N-5001 Bergen. Tel. 05/21-01-00, or toll free 800/223-5652 in North America. Fax 05/21-02-99. 347 rms (all with bath); 12 suites. MINIBAR TV TEL **Bus:** 2, 3, 4.

$ Rates (including breakfast): Weekdays, 1,125–1,390 kroner ($186.65–$230.60) single; 1,390–1,540 kroner ($230.60–$255.50) double. Weekends, 640–910 kroner ($106.20–$150.95) single; 830–1,050 kroner ($137.70–$174.20) double. Suites from 3,100 kroner ($514.30). Children under 12 stay free in their parents' room. DC, MC, V.

⭐ In the city center, near Torgalmenningen, the Norge has been a Bergen tradition since 1885. In World War II the Gestapo made it their headquarters, but it reopened as a hotel after the war. Because of structural flaws, it was torn down and rebuilt in 1962, and then reopened to play host to everybody from the Crown Prince of Japan to the Shah of Iran. It still remains a favorite with today's visiting celebrities.

Each accommodation has a radio, TV with in-house videos, and in some cases, oversize bathtubs big enough for two. Some of the units open onto private balconies overlooking the begonia-ringed borders of a nearby park. The hotel is a member of the Steingenberger Reservations System.

Dining/Entertainment: The hotel offers the widest array of drinking and dining establishments in Bergen, including its gourmet restaurant, Grillen, and Ole Bull's, an informal place for lunch and light meals. Homemade pastries are served in the morning at Bakdakinen, and à la carte meals are available there at lunch and dinner. The Cafe 003 is a night café. Drinking places include the Balcony Bar, Koggen Piano Bar, and Bull's Eye, the last an English pub on the corner. The Pandora Night Club is a leading nightlife venue.

Services: 24-hour room service.

Facilities: Swimming pool, solarium, sauna, Jacuzzi, gym, garage.

NEPTUN, Walckendorffsgate 8, N-5001 Bergen. Tel. 05/90-10-00. Fax 05/23-32-02. 121 rms (all with bath). MINIBAR TV TEL **Bus:** 1, 5, 9.

$ Rates (including breakfast): Summer and Fri–Sun year round, 600 kroner ($99.55) single; 800 kroner ($132.70) double. Winter Mon–Thurs, 1,050 kroner ($174.20) single; 1,350 kroner ($223.95) double. AE, DC, MC, V.

Close to the harbor and fish market, this is a modern and handsomely decorated hotel in the city center, known for its collection of Norwegian modern art. The owner, Hans Inge Bruarøy, is head of the Bergen Arts Society and collecting paintings is his passion. The hotel was recently expanded, a new floor of upgraded accommodations added. Many prefer its comfortable and spacious accommodations to all others in Bergen. Each room is attractively styled and well maintained.

Dining and drinking facilities include the Restaurant Lucullus, the Ludvig Bar, and the Bistro Pascal. There is a 20-car basement garage.

SAS ROYAL HOTEL, Bryggen, N-5000 Bergen. Tel. 05/31-80-00. Fax 05/32-48-08. 300 rms (all with bath). A/C MINIBAR TV TEL **Bus:** 1, 5, 9.

$ Rates (including breakfast): Summer, 650 kroner ($107.85) single; 820 kroner ($136.05) double. Winter, 1,290–1,490 kroner ($214–$247.20) single; 1,440–1,640 kroner ($238.90–$272.10) double. AE, DC, MC, V.

⭐ Opened in 1982, this hotel stands on ancient ground, having been built on the fire-ravaged site of old warehouses that stood here since 1170. Houses along Bryggen (The Quay) were reconstructed in the old style and SAS maintained the spirit of the architecture in creating this excellent hotel. During construction, many Hanseatic artifacts were unearthed and are on display.

The hotel is completely modernized with what is considered almost the finest services and amenities in Bergen. Bedrooms are beautifully maintained, each with lithographs and comfortably upholstered furniture. Sixty rooms are reserved for nonsmokers. The hotel attracts mainly commercial clients in winter.

Dining/Entertainment: Guests can dine in the hotel's Gourmet Restaurant, after enjoying drinks in the cocktail lounge. There is also a Café Royal. The hotel has a nightclub, Engelen, and a pub, Madam Felle.

Services: Business service center, secretarial service, 24-hour room service, SAS Euroclass check-in.

Facilities: Indoor swimming pool, sauna, health club, private basement garage, laundry, car-rental desk.

EXPENSIVE

GRAND HOTEL TERMINUS, Kong Oscars Gate 71, N-5018 Bergen. Tel. 05/31-16-55. Fax 05/31-85-76. 130 rms (all with bath). TV TEL **Bus:** 2, 4.
$ Rates (including breakfast): 850 kroner ($141) single; 1,150 kroner ($190.80) double. AE, DC, MC, V.

A Bergen landmark since 1928, this hotel, located between the bus and rail stations, offers quality and tradition. Bedrooms are modernized and furnished attractively in light Nordic pastels, containing such extra amenities as radios and hairdryers. The hotel offers an excellent restaurant and often presents Norwegian buffets. Guests gather in the lounge after dinner for coffee.

SUITELL EDVARD GRIEG, Sandsliåsen 50, N-5049 Sandsli. Tel. 05/22-99-01. Fax 05/22-99-85. 148 suites (all with bath). **Bus:** From Platform 16 at the Bergen bus station, take any bus marked "Milde/Hjellstad (Øvre Nestun)."
$ Rates (including breakfast): Midsummer and Fri–Sat year round, 750 kroner ($124.45) single or double. The rest of the year, Sun–Thurs, 1,120 kroner ($185.80) single or double. AE, DC, MC, V.

Norway's first all-suite hotel lies 12 miles south of Bergen and 3 miles from the Bergen airport. Opened in 1987, it has a modern design, with walls of glass illuminating the lobby. Each suite has a bedroom, bathroom, and lounge, and each is luxuriously furnished. Three suites are equipped for wheelchair guests. Monday through Friday guests can dine in the intimate and expensive Mozart Restaurant, or can enjoy Norwegian and international food in the H. C. Andersen restaurant. The lobby bar, Nordraak, is a cozy rendezvous, and patrons can also dance at the Liszt nightclub. Free airport transfers are arranged for arriving and departing guests.

MODERATE

AUGUSTIN HOTEL, C. Sundtsgate 24, N-5004 Bergen. Tel. 05/23-00-25. Fax 05/23-31-30. 38 rms (all with bath). TV TEL **Bus:** 1, 5, 9.
$ Rates (including breakfast): Summer and Fri–Sat year round, 480 kroner ($79.65) single; 620 kroner ($102.85) double. Winter Sun–Thurs, 550 kroner ($91.25) single; 800 kroner ($132.70) double. AE, DC, MC, V.

The Augustin Hotel, a 5-minute walk west of the harborfront, has been a family favorite since 1917. The rooms were remodeled in the mid-1980s, and are pleasantly furnished. A good Norwegian breakfast is served in the residents' breakfast room. The hotel also has a traditional patisserie, Augusta, serving hot and cold dishes, and an attractive bistro for light lunches, hot meals, salads, and sandwiches. It serves only beer.

ROSENKRANTZ, Rosenkrantzgate 7, N-5003 Bergen. Tel. 05/31-50-00. Fax 05/31-47-76. 129 rms (all with bath). MINIBAR TV TEL **Bus:** 1, 5, 9.
$ Rates (including breakfast): 820 kroner ($136.05) single; 950 kroner ($157.60) double. AE, DC, MC, V.

This 1921 hotel stands near Bryggen in the city center. The lobby, sheathed in white marble, leads to a comfortable dining room and bar. Rooms are pleasantly furnished, all updated and equipped with modern amenities including hairdryers. Twenty rooms are reserved for nonsmokers. Facilities include a TV lounge, a piano bar, a restaurant, Harmoni, and a nightclub, Rubinen, with live music. Next door to the hotel is a covered parking garage.

VICTORIA HOTEL, Kong Oscars Gate 29, N-5017 Bergen. Tel. 05/31-50-30. Fax 05/32-81-78. 43 rms (all with bath). MINIBAR TV TEL **Bus:** 2, 4.

$ Rates (including breakfast): Summer and Fri–Sat year round, 540 kroner ($89.60) single; 740 kroner ($122.75) double. Winter Mon–Thurs, 840 kroner ($139.35) single; 1,000 kroner ($165.07) double. AE, DC, MC, V.

Midway between the harbor and the railway station, this hotel, constructed around 1912 but completely rebuilt in 1985, is a longtime favorite, for both its comfort and its tradition. Each of the well-furnished bedrooms has a distinct color theme of red, yellow, orange, blue, or green. Five rooms are for nonsmokers. The hotel's restaurant, Kong Oscar, is the only Spanish restaurant in Bergen. There is also a breakfast room and a lounge with an open fireplace. The Victoria is licensed to sell beer and wine.

INEXPENSIVE

HOTELL HORDAHEIMEN, C. Sundstgate 18, N-5004 Bergen. Tel. 05/23-23-20. Fax 05/23-49-50. 69 rms (60 with bath). TV TEL **Bus:** 1, 5, 9.

$ Rates (including breakfast): 345 kroner ($57.25) single without shower, 640 kroner ($106.20) single with shower; 500 kroner ($82.95) double with shower. AE, DC, MC, V.

Operated by the Bondeungdomslaget i Bergen, an association that sponsors cultural and folklore programs, the hotel has become a Bergen base for many young people from nearby districts. The lounge and dining rooms have been tastefully designed and coordinated, and the bedrooms—simple and utilitarian—are immaculate. A room without bath has a hot- and cold-water basin. Reasonably priced meals are served in the restaurant one flight up. No alcohol is served.

PARK PENSJON, Harald Hårfagresgaten 35 and Parkveien 22, N-5007 Bergen. Tel. 05/32-09-60. Fax 05/31-03-34. 50 rms (all with bath). TV TEL **Bus:** 2, 3, 4.

$ Rates (including breakfast): 540 kroner ($89.60) single; 640 kroner ($106.20) double. MC, V.

Located in an attractive university area, this is a converted 1890 town house. Rooms are comfortable and traditionally furnished. In summer, reserve well in advance—you'll get a prompt reply, with instructions for a deposit to cover the first night's rent. The park is a 10-minute walk from the train and bus stations.

BUDGET

FAGERHEIM PENSJON, Kalvedalsveien 49A, N-5018 Bergen. Tel. 05/31-01-72. 12 rms (none with bath). **Bus:** 2, 4, 7, 11 from the post office.

$ Rates: 190–230 kroner ($31.50–$38.15) single; 300–340 kroner ($49.75–$56.40) double. Extra bed 80 kroner ($13.25). Breakfast costs 35 kroner ($5.80) extra. No credit cards.

This attractively old-fashioned 1900 hillside house lies about 6 minutes from the town center. A few of the homelike bedrooms have small kitchens. Most accommodations have a view of the water and city. A garden surrounds the house.

MYKLEBUST PENSION, Rosenbergsgate 19, N-5015 Bergen. Tel. 05/90-16-70. 6 rms (2 with bath). TV **Bus:** 2, 3, 4.

$ Rates: 320 kroner ($53.10) single without bath (available only May–Sept); 370 kroner ($61.40) double without bath, 400 kroner ($66.30) double with bath. Breakfast costs 45 kroner ($7.45) extra. No credit cards.

A 15-minute walk from the rail station, rooms in this boarding house are furnished in contemporary Norwegian style, and all have hot and cold running water, with shower and toilet close by. Breakfast, brought to your room at the time you request, costs extra and consists of ham, cheese, egg, bread, rolls, marmalade, butter, jam, coffee, milk, and juice. In a central hallway, guests may use a stove, refrigerator, washing machine, and dishes and utensils.

SORTLAND PENSJON, Vestre Torggate 20B, N-5015 Bergen. Tel. 05/31-88-67. 7 rms (none with bath). **Bus:** 2, 3, 4.

$ Rates: 180 kroner ($29.85) single; 240 kroner ($39.80) double. No credit cards.

Ⓢ This economy find lies right in the center of Bergen, a 2-minute walk west of Ole Bull's Plass and the landmark Hotel Norge, midway between the Tourist Information Office and Johanneskirchen. Originally built as a private family home in 1906, it has been converted to receive guests. Rooms are simply furnished, but clean and comfortable, and adequate showers are in the corridor. Mr. Sortland is your English-speaking host. No breakfast is served, but many cafés lie nearby.

4. DINING

Restaurants classified as "Very Expensive" charge $61 to $82 for a meal; "Expensive," $44 to $59; "Moderate," $23 to $28; and "Inexpensive," around $16.

VERY EXPENSIVE

BANCO ROTTO, Vagsalmenningen 14-22. Tel. 32-75-20.
Cuisine: NORWEGIAN. **Reservations:** Required. **Bus:** 1, 5, 9.
$ Prices: Appetizers 55–74 kroner ($9.10–$12.30); main dishes 135–220 kroner ($22.40–$36.50); fixed-price lunch platter 75 kroner ($12.45); fixed-price evening platter 100 kroner ($16.60). AE, DC, MC, V.
Open: Daily 11am–11:15pm (bar, daily 6pm–12:30am). **Closed:** Sun in winter.
You'll pass between ornate iron lampposts to reach the interior of this restaurant, housed in a former 1875 bank. A 2-minute walk from the harborfront, this dignified restaurant serves specialties that include scampi with scallops in vermouth sauce, North Cape catfish, roast sirloin of beef, medallions of reindeer, hot apple cake, and a wide selection of wines. A luxurious bar adjoins the restaurant, with drinks costing from 49 kroner ($8.15).

RESTAURANT BELLEVUE, Bellevuebakken 9. Tel. 31-02-40.
Cuisine: NORWEGIAN. **Reservations:** Required. **Bus:** 11.
$ Prices: Appetizers 55–115 kroner ($9.10–$19.10); main dishes 185–255 kroner ($30.70–$42.30); five-course dinner 475 kroner ($78.80). AE, DC, MC, V.
Open: Daily 6–11pm. **Closed:** May 2–9.
A stylish panoramic restaurant high on a hill, the Bellevue was originally built as a midsummer retreat in 1796. Have predinner drinks in the bar and follow with a meal of warm fish mousse stuffed with shellfish-and-lobster sauce, a terrine of vegetables with herb sauce, tournedos garnished with lobster, or a "symphony" of fresh fish and shellfish. The homemade ice cream studded with seasonal berries makes for a refreshing dessert.

ZACCHARIASBRYGGE, Zacchariasbrygge. Tel. 31-75-66.

Cuisine: FISH/SHELLFISH. **Reservations:** Not required. **Bus:** 1, 5, 9.
$ Prices: Appetizers 40–60 kroner ($6.65–$9.95); main dishes 150–250 kroner ($24.90–$41.50). AE, DC, MC, V.
Open: Daily 3–11:30pm.

This highly recommended restaurant at the harborfront occupies the street level of a large, clapboard-sided building, once a 19th-century warehouse destroyed by the Nazis in World War II. The present building, painted a deep reddish brown, is an authentic re-creation. Specialties are fish and shellfish, often pulled directly from a holding tank as you watch. Fish is prepared in many different variations. In autumn, game is featured.

EXPENSIVE

BRYGGELOFTET/BRUGGESTUEN, Bryggen 6. Tel. 31-06-30.
Cuisine: NORWEGIAN. **Reservations:** Not required. **Bus:** 1, 5, 9.
$ Prices: Appetizers 28–49 kroner ($4.65–$8.15); main dishes 65–160 kroner ($10.80–$26.55); lunchtime smørbrød 25–59 kroner ($4.15–$9.80). AE, DC, MC, V.
Open: Mon–Sat 10am–11:30pm, Sun 1–11:30pm.

Bryggeloftet/Bruggestuen is the best-established restaurant along the harborfront. At street level the Bruggestuen has low ceiling beams, carved banquettes, and 19th-century murals of old Bergen, along with dozens of clipper-ship models. For a more formal meal, head upstairs for the Bryggeloftet, with its high ceilings and wood paneling. A dinner in either section might include grilled porbeagle (a form of whitefish) served with shrimp, mussels, and a white wine sauce, roast reindeer with cream sauce, or pepper steak with a salad. Several different preparations of salmon and herring are featured, along with roast pork with Norwegian sour cabbage.

OLE BULL RESTAURANT, in the Hotel Norge, Ole Bulls Plass 2-4. Tel. 21-01-00.
Cuisine: NORWEGIAN. **Reservations:** Recommended. **Bus:** 2, 3, 4.
$ Prices: Smörgåsbord 155 kroner ($25.70) per person; appetizers 55–85 kroner ($9.10–$14.10); main dishes 135–185 kroner ($22.40–$30.70). AE, DC, MC, V.
Open: Daily noon–11pm.

This well-managed restaurant offers the best smörgåsbord in town, served daily from noon to 6pm. Time-tested Norwegian dishes are also served—platter after platter of freshly prepared meat and fish dishes. You can also dine à la carte in the evening. Try the fresh fish—it's always reliable.

MODERATE

ENHJØRNINGEN, Enhjørningsgården Bryggen. Tel. 32-79-19.
Cuisine: SEAFOOD. **Reservations:** Recommended. **Bus:** 1, 5, 9.
$ Prices: Lunch seafood buffet 145 kroner ($24.05); appetizers 58–85 kroner ($9.60–$14.10); main dishes 78–135 kroner ($12.95–$22.40). AE, DC, MC, V.
Open: Lunch, May–Oct, daily noon–4pm. Dinner, May–Aug, daily 4–11pm; Sept–Apr, Mon–Sat 4–11pm.

Enhjørningen is Bergen's major seafood restaurant. Within its handful of dining rooms, you'll find a Neo-Victorian decor, plants, and well-prepared seafood specialties. Go for the all-you-can eat seafood luncheon buffet.

HOLBERG-STUEN, Torgalmenningen 6. Tel. 31-80-15.
Cuisine: NORWEGIAN. **Reservations:** Not required. **Bus:** 1, 5, 9.
$ Prices: Appetizers 50–60 kroner ($8.30–$9.95); main dishes 70–125 kroner ($11.60–$20.75). AE, DC, MC, V.
Open: Mon–Sat 10am–12:30am, Sun 1pm–12:30am.

One floor above street level, this 1927 restaurant lies midway between the harborfront fish market and Ole Bulls Plass. It has a beer cellar atmosphere, with beamed ceilings, an open log fire, leaded-glass casement windows, high-back settles, and armchairs.

IMPRESSIONS

Reaching Bergen we fail to find it particularly attractive. Everything is fishy. You eat fish and drink fish and smell fish and breathe fish.
—LILIAM LELAND, *TRAVELLING ALONE, A WOMAN'S JOURNEY ROUND THE WORLD,*
1890.

Hearty diners devour fish filet in white wine sauce, accompanied by prawns, mushrooms, and asparagus. Good for late-night drinking.

WESSEL-STUEN, Engen 14. Tel. 90-08-20.
   Cuisine: NORWEGIAN. **Reservations:** Not required. **Bus:** 2, 3, 4.
$ Prices: Appetizers 28–47 kroner ($4.65–$7.80); main dishes 94–136 kroner ($15.60–$22.55); one-course *dagens* menu 50–80 kroner ($8.30–$13.25). AE, DC, MC, V.
   Open: Daily 11:30am–12:30am.

This bodega-style restaurant has all the trappings of an 18th-century wine cellar and was named for the humorist Johan Herman Wessel, who wrote such works as *Love Without Stockings.* The restaurant is decorated in old tavern style with beamed ceilings, and its adjoining pub is a famous meeting place for locals. Meals are likely to include such dishes as pan-fried cod tongues, black-pepper steak, sautéed salmon with shrimp, spaghetti Napoli, and barbecued spareribs. Every day the chef features a different steak special, one of the most popular dishes in town.

INEXPENSIVE

CAFETERIA KAFFISTOVA, Torget 1. Tel. 31-66-27.
   Cuisine: NORWEGIAN. **Reservations:** Not required. **Bus:** 1, 5, 9.
$ Prices: Cafeteria, 23–42 kroner ($3.80–$6.95) smørbrød; 45–55 kroner ($7.45–$9.10) main dishes. Restaurant, 50–85 kroner ($8.30–$14.10) main dishes. No credit cards.
   Open: Summer, daily 8am–10pm; winter, Mon–Fri 8am–7pm, Sat 9am–4pm, Sun 11am–6pm.

A great all-around choice for economy dining in Bergen, this place has a modern self-service cafeteria on the lower floor and, one floor above street level, a full-fledged restaurant. There are no particular appetizers, since the price of your main course includes either soup or coffee, which makes this place a real bargain for Bergen. Many interesting smørbrød concoctions are served along with hot dishes. Among the à la carte offerings are rømmergrøt (sour cream porridge), cured mutton, and trout.

---

5. ATTRACTIONS

SUGGESTED ITINERARIES

IF YOU HAVE 1 DAY

Take in all the top attractions of Bergen, including the old Hanseatic Bryggen, with its nearby museums; explore the shops and artisan workshops along the harbor; and, to cap your day, take the funicular to Floien for a panoramic view.

IF YOU HAVE 2 DAYS

Day 1: See "If You Have 1 Day," above.
Day 2: Head for the environs of Bergen, which can be reached by public transporta-

tion. Visit the Fantoft Stave Church and Troldhaugen, Edvard Grieg's former home. In the afternoon, journey to Ole Bull's Villa, 16 miles south of Bergen.

IF YOU HAVE 3 DAYS

Days 1 & 2: See "If You Have 2 Days," above.
Day 3: Take the 12-hour "Norway in a Nutshell" tour (see below).

IF YOU HAVE 5 DAYS

Days 1–3: See "If You Have 3 Days," above.
Day 4: Explore the Hardanger fjord and the Folgefonn glacier by round-trip coach from Bergen (see "Easy Excursions," below).
Day 5: Explore Sognefjord by express steamer, going by bus via Voss, and returning by train to Bergen (see "Easy Excursions," below).

THE TOP ATTRACTIONS

In addition to the sights below, take a stroll around ✪ **Bryggen.** This row of Hanseatic timbered houses, rebuilt along the waterfront after the disastrous fire of 1702, is what remains of medieval Bergen. The northern half burned to the ground as late as 1955. Bryggen has been incorporated into UNESCO's World Heritage List as one of the world's most significant cultural and historical re-creations of a medieval settlement, skillfully incorporated in the surroundings of modern Bergen. It is a center for arts and crafts, where painters, weavers, and craftspeople have their workshops. As you stroll along, you'll see that some of these workshops are open to the public.

DET HANSEATISKE MUSEUM, Finnegårdsgaten 1A, Bryggen. Tel. 31-41-89.

✪ In one of the best-preserved wooden buildings at Bryggen, this museum illustrates Bergen's commercial life on the wharf centuries ago. German merchants, representatives of the Hanseatic League centered in Lübeck, lived in these medieval houses built in long rows up from the harbor. With dried cod, grain, and salt as articles of exchange, fishermen from northern Norway met German merchants during the busy summer season. The museum is furnished with authentic articles dating from 1704.
Admission: 10 kroner ($1.65) adults, 5 kroner (85¢) children (free for children Oct–Apr).
Open: June–Aug, daily 10am–4pm; May and Sept, daily 11am–2pm; Oct–Apr, Sun–Wed and Fri 11am–2pm. **Bus:** 1, 5, 9.

MARIAKIRKE (St. Mary's Church), Dreggen. Tel. 31-59-60.

The oldest building in Bergen (its exact date is unknown, but perhaps from the mid-12th century) is this Romanesque church, one of the most beautiful in Norway. Its altar is the oldest ornament in the church, and there's a baroque pulpit donated by Hanseatic merchants with carved figures depicting everything from Chastity to Naked Truth. Organ concerts are given from May to the end of September at 7:30pm on Tuesday for 30 kroner ($5); on Thursday they're free.
Admission: Free.
Open: May–Sept, Mon–Fri 11am–4pm; Oct–Apr, Sun and Tues–Fri 11am–4pm, Mon and Sat noon–1:30pm. **Bus:** 1, 5, 9.

RASMUS MEYERS COLLECTIONS, Rasmus Meyers Allé. Tel. 31-11-30.

Within walking distance of the fish market, this museum houses an excellent display of Norwegian paintings. The star attractions are the egg-shaped figures of Edvard Munch, but two important 19th-century artists, Christian Krohg and Harriet Backer, are also represented.

Admission: Summer, 10 kroner ($1.65); winter, free.
Open: Mid-May to mid-Sept, Mon–Sat 11am–4pm, Sun noon–3pm; late Sept to early May, Wed–Mon noon–3pm. **Bus:** 1, 5, 9.

HÅKONSHALLEN (King's Tower), Bradbenken. Tel. 31-60-67.

If you walk along the water from Bryggen, you come upon the Håkonshallen, built between 1247 and 1261, later restored following damage in a 1944 fire. This is the largest and most imposing building remaining on the site of the royal residence of Bergen, and was the political center of the 13th-century kingdom of Norway. Guided tours are conducted hourly.
Admission: 10 kroner ($1.65) adults, 5 kroner (85¢) children.
Open: Mid-May to mid-Sept, daily 10am–4pm. **Closed:** Late Sept to early May. **Bus:** 1, 5, 9.

ROSENKRANTZ TOWER, Bradbenken. Tel. 31-43-80.

Originally a fortified royal residence in the 13th century, Rosenkrantz Tower was rebuilt and enlarged in the 1560s. It was constructed by the governor of Bergenhus (Bergen Castle), Erik Rosenkrantz, as a combined defense and residential tower. It has been restored. Two older structures were incorporated into the tower: King Magnus the Lawmender's keep from about 1260 and Jørgen Hanssøn's keep from about 1520. Guided tours of the tower and Håkonshallen (see above) leave about every hour.
Admission: 10 kroner ($1.65) adults, 5 kroner (85¢) children.
Open: May 15–Sept 14, daily 10am–4pm. **Closed:** Sept 15–May 14. **Bus:** 1, 5, 9.

MORE ATTRACTIONS

FUNICULAR TO FLØIEN

A short walk from the fish market is the station where the funicular heads up to Fløien, the most famous of Bergen's seven hills. At 1,050 feet, the view of city, the neighboring hills and the harbor is worth every ore.
Admission: 26 kroner ($4.30) adults, 12 kroner ($2) children, round-trip.
Open: Daily 8am–11pm, with departures every 30 minutes. **Bus:** 1, 5, 9.

BRYGGENS MUSEUM, Bryggen. Tel. 31-67-10.

Displaying artifacts unearthed during extensive archeological excavations of Bryggen from 1955 to 1972, exhibits include remains of the oldest buildings in Bergen, dating from the 12th century, in their original settings. You can also see runic inscriptions. The museum, sponsored by the Erling Dekke Naess Institute for Medieval Archeology, illustrates the daily and cultural life of Bergen in the Middle Ages.
Admission: 10 kroner ($1.65) adults, free for children.
Open: May–Aug, Mon, Wed, and Fri 10am–4pm, Tues and Thurs 10am–8pm, Sat–Sun 11am–3pm; Sept–Apr, Mon–Fri 11am–3pm, Sat noon–3pm, Sun noon–4pm. **Bus:** 1, 5, 9.

BERGEN AQUARIUM, Nordesparken 2. Tel. 23-85-00.

A 15-minute walk from the city center, this aquarium is one of the largest and finest in Scandinavia. The marine life is exceptional, including seals, penguins, lobsters, and piranhas. In the outer hall you can dip your hand into the shallow pool and literally get the feel of the fish in unpolluted water pumped up from a depth of 400 feet in the fjord outside. As you step into the twilight of the main aquarium hall, you plunge into the sea in a giant diving bell. Nine glassed-in tanks, each containing about 62,500 gallons of water, ring the hall. Downstairs is a wide range of marine life in 42 small aquaria demonstrating many colorful forms of sea life and illustrating evolutionary development.
Admission: 10 kroner ($1.65) adults, free for children.
Open: May–Sept, daily 9am–8pm; Oct–Apr, daily 10am–6pm. **Bus:** 4 from the town center.

FANTOFT STAVE CHURCH, Paradis. Tel. 28-07-10.

★ Constructed on the principle of a Viking ship, this well-preserved 1150 stave church at Fantoft, near Grieg's home, is richly decorated with both pagan and Christian elements.

Admission: 7 kroner ($1.15) adults, free for children.

Open: Mid-May to mid-Sept, daily 10:30am–1:30pm and 2:30–5:30pm. **Closed:** Late Sept to early May. **Bus:** From Bergen station Platforms 18–20, to Paradis on the Fantoft bus, a 10-minute ride, plus a 10-minute walk from the bus stop.

TROLDHAUGEN (Trolls' Hill) at Troldhaugen, Hop. Tel. 91-17-91.

★ This Victorian house, in beautiful rural surroundings at Hop, near Bergen, was the summer villa of composer Edvard Grieg. The house still contains Grieg's own furniture, paintings, and other mementos. His Steinway grand piano is frequently used at concerts given in the house during the annual Bergen Festival, as well as at Troldhaugen's own summer concerts. Grieg and his wife, Nina, are buried in a cliff grotto on the estate. At his cottage by the sea, he composed many of his famous works.

Admission: 10 kroner ($1.65) adults, 5 kroner (85¢) children.

Open: May 2–Oct 1, daily 10:30am–1:30pm and 2:30–5:30pm. **Closed:** Oct 2–May 1. **Bus:** Hop-bound buses leave from the bus station at Bergen (Platforms 18–20). Once the bus lets you off, turn right, walk about 200 yards, then turn left at Hopsvegen. From there just follow the signs to Troldhaugen, a 20- to 30-minute walk.

GAMLE BERGEN, Elsesro, Sandviken. Tel. 25-63-07.

At Elsero and Sandviken is a collection of houses set in a park from the 18th and 19th centuries. The Old Town is complete with streets, an open square, and narrow alleyways. Some of the interiors are exceptional, including a merchant's living room in the typical style of the 1870s—with padded sofas, heavy curtains, potted plants—a perfect setting for Ibsen's *A Doll's House.*

Admission: 20 kroner ($3.30) adults, 10 kroner ($1.65) children.

Open: Houses, mid-May to mid-Sept, guided tours every hour noon–6pm. Park and restaurant, daily 11am–10pm. **Closed:** Late Sept to early May. **Bus:** 1 or 9 from the Bergen post office leaves every 10 minutes.

GAMLEHAUGEN, Fjøsanger. Tel. 91-19-50.

Gamlehaugen is the king's Bergen residence, and was the home of the late prime minister, Christian Michelsen. The garden is always open to the public.

Admission: 10 kroner ($1.65) adults, 5 kroner (85¢) children.

Open: June-Sept, Mon–Fri 10am–noon. **Bus:** Fjøsanger bound bus from Central Station.

IN NEARBY LYSØEN

MUSEET LYSØEN/OLE BULL'S VILLA, Lysøen. Tel. 30-90-77.

On the island of Lysøen, 16 miles south of Bergen, stands the villa and concert hall built in 1872 to 1873 for the world-famous violin virtuoso and Norwegian national hero, Ole Bull. The building, now a national monument, is just as it was when the musician died in 1880. Eight miles of trails built by Bull meander around the island.

Admission: 15 kroner ($2.50) adults, 5 kroner (85¢) children.

Open: Guided tours of villa, mid-May to Sept, Mon–Sat noon–4pm, Sun 11am–5pm. **Closed:** Oct to early May. **Directions:** Drive or take a bus (from Platform 20 at the Bergen bus station; marked "Fana-Os-Milde") to Sørestraumen on road 553; then take the Ole Bull ferry from Sørestraumen, Buena Kai. Round-trip ferryboat fare is 25 kroner ($4.15) adults, 10 kroner ($1.65) children.

ORGANIZED TOURS

Bergen has a good list of **motorcoach city tours,** all departing from the Hotel Norge in the city center. A 1-hour orientation tour of old and new Bergen is offered June 1 to August 15 daily, departing at 9:30am and costing 60 kroner ($9.95) per person. But the best tour of Bergen is the 11am, 2-hour tour of the city, covering all the major sightseeing attractions, among them the Hanseatic Museum and 12th-century St. Mary's Church. The tour operates daily from May 2 to September 30 and costs 90 kroner ($14.95).

Another tour, offered daily from May 2 to the end of September, taking 3 hours, calls at Grieg's home and the Fantoft stave church. It leaves at 3:30pm and costs 125 kroner ($20.75).

Reservations for all three tours can be made through **Unitur,** Strandgaten 191 (tel. 32-35-30), on the ground floor facing the harbor.

6. SPECIAL/FREE EVENTS

The jam-packed **Bergen International Festival,** usually scheduled during the last week of May and the first days of June, is famous for its performances of music, drama, opera, ballet, and folklore. The works of Edvard Grieg dominate the festivities. Concerts are held daily at his former home, Troldhaugen, and the modern concert hall bearing his name, featuring such international artists as André Previn and Murray Perahia. Concerts are also given in the 700-year-old Håkonshallen or in the 12th-century St. Mary's Church, and folklore performances round out the events. Den Nationale Scene performs Ibsen and contemporary plays. In the last few years, concerts have also been held at Lysøen, former home of the 19th-century Bergen-born violin virtuoso, Ole Bull. For festival information, contact Greig Hall, Lars Hillesgate 3A (Box 183), N-5001 Bergen (tel. 05/32-04-00).

From June 24 to August 1 recitals are held at **Troldhaugen,** Edvard Grieg's former home, every Wednesday and Sunday at 8pm. From early September to mid-October, there are also Sunday matinees at 1pm. Tickets are available from the Tourist Information Center (see above) or at the entrance.

Visitors are invited by **Fana Folklore** to a traditional Norwegian country festival that takes place in an 800-year-old Fana church where the organist plays a miniconcert of hymns. Then you'll be taken to a private home where you're treated like friends of the family with true Norwegian farm hospitality, to join in their festivals following old customs and accompanied by plenty of food, song, music, and lively dances.

Buses leave from Festplassen in Bergen June 5 to August 31 on Monday, Tuesday, Thursday, and Friday at 7pm (extra evenings in May and September). The price, which includes everything—and that means a full meal—is 160 kroner ($26.55). Tickets are sold at most hotel reception desks, at travel agents, and from the Tourist Information Centre (see above).

7. SPORTS/RECREATION

FISHING   Fishing permits and pertinent information may be obtained from the **Bergen Angling Club,** Fosswinckelsgate 37 (tel. 32-11-64). Sea fishing is free.

GOLF   The **Åstveit Golf Course** (tel. 18-20-77) has nine holes and allows nonmembers, but call in advance. It's a 15-minute drive north of Bergen on Route 14. You can also take the Åsane bus from the central station in Bergen.

SWIMMING   Swim in the heated saltwater pool at the **Sentralbadet,** Teatersgaten 9 (tel. 23-10-34). For hours, check with the tourist office. Adults pay 25 kroner ($4.15); children, 8 kroner ($1.35).

For open-air swimming, go to **Tømmersvagen,** 15 minutes from the center by the Eidsvåg bus.

TENNIS   The **Bergen Tennis Club,** with courts at Årstad, allows nonmembers to play. Phone 29-91-67 for details. Take bus no. 2.

WALKING   Only 10 minutes away from town by the funicular, several roads and footpaths lead to **Mount Fløien,** an unspoiled wood and mountain terrace with lakes and rivers.

The **Bergen Touring Club,** C. Sundtsgate 3 (tel. 32-22-30), arranges walking tours farther afield and supplies information on huts and mountain routes all over Norway.

8. SAVVY SHOPPING

As mentioned, shoppers who live outside Scandinavia who spend more than 300 kroner ($49.75) in a tax-free tourist shop get between 10% and 15% of the purchase price refunded when they leave Norway. You will receive your refund in cash even if you have used a credit card.

THE SHOPPING SCENE

Real bargain sleuths head to the **Marketplace,** where many local handcrafts from the western fjord district are displayed, including rugs and handmade tablecloths. This is one of the few places in Norway where bargaining is welcomed. The market keeps no set hours, but is best visited between 8am and noon. Take bus 1, 5, or 9.

Hours   Stores are generally open Monday through Friday from 9am to 4:30pm (to 7pm on Thursday; some shops also on Friday) and on Saturday from 9am to 2pm (some to 1pm). Shopping centers outside the city are open Monday through Friday from 10am to 8pm and on Saturday from 9am to 4pm. Some food stores stay open until 8pm Monday through Friday, to 6pm on Saturday.

SHOPPING A TO Z
DEPARTMENT STORES

SUNDT & CO., Torgalmenningen 14. Tel. 38-80-20.
   Bergen's leading department store stands near the tourist information booth. Excellent buys include linen tablecloths, purses for women, and Norwegian knitwear, plus a vast array of souvenirs.

FASHION

KLØVERHUSET, Strandkaien 10. Tel. 32-77-20.
   Next to the fish market on the harbor, this four-story shopping center has been Bergen's largest fashion store since 1923. Besides the latest in modern design, it also offers good bargains, such as moderately priced and attractively designed knitted sweaters, gloves, and Lapp jackets. There's a special gift shop open only in summer.

HANDCRAFTS

Aside from the stores listed below, in and around Bryggen Brukskunst, the restored Old Town near the wharf, many craftspeople have taken over old houses to ply the ancient Norwegian trades. Crafts boutiques here often display Bergen souvenirs, many based on designs 300 to 1,500 years old. For example, I purchased a reproduction of a cruciform pilgrim's badge (Romanesque in style). Other tempting items are likely to include sheepskin-lined booties or exquisitely styled hand-woven woolen dresses.

HUSFLIDEN I BERGEN, Vågsalmenning 3. Tel. 31-78-70.
   You'll find the widest selection of national handcrafts here—the finest handmade knitwear from the western fjord district, along with woodwork, brass, and pewterware.

PRYDKUNST-HJERTHOLM, Olav Kyrres Gate 7. Tel. 31-70-27.

The leading outlet for glassware and ceramics, it purchases much of its merchandise directly from the studios of artisans who turn out quality goods not only in glass and ceramics, but also in pewter, wood, and textiles. Gift articles and souvenirs are also sold. It's a 2-minute walk from the Tourist Information Center.

JEWELRY

DAVID-ANDERSEN, Torgalvalmenning 10. Tel. 31-00-80.
This is the Bergen branch of the most famous jewelry store in Norway. Its better-stocked store was previewed under "Savvy Shopping" in Chapter 15. The collection of hand-painted enamel on sterling silver is exceptional, although they have far more expensive items as well.

SHOPPING MALLS

GALLERIET, Torgalmenningen.
This is the most important shopping complex in the Bergen area, with 60 different stores offering tax-free shopping. Close to Bergen's fish market, it offers a wide array of various kinds of merchandise, and features summer sales and special exhibitions. It also has several fast-food places. Open Monday through Friday from 9am to 8pm and on Saturday from 9am to 4pm.

9. EVENING ENTERTAINMENT

THE PERFORMING ARTS

GRIEGHALLEN, Lars Hillesgate 3A. Tel. 21-61-00.
Opened in mid-1978, the modern Grieg Hall is Bergen's monumental showcase for music, drama, and a host of other cultural events. The stage is large enough to accommodate an entire grand opera production, and the main foyer will comfortably seat 1,500 guests for lunch or dinner. Snack bars provide drinks and light snacks throughout the performances. On the street level the building features an arcade of shops, and the upper floors house the offices of the Philharmonic Orchestra and the Bergen International Festival.

The Bergen Symphony Orchestra, founded in 1765, performs here from August to May, on Thursday at 7:30pm and often on Saturday at 12:30pm. Its repertoire consists of classical and contemporary music, as well as visiting productions of opera. International conductors and soloists perform.

Prices: Tickets, 100–200 kroner ($16.60–$33.20). **Bus:** 2, 3, 4.

DEN NATIONAL SCENE, Engen 1. Tel. 90-17-88.
September to June is the season for Norway's oldest theater, founded in the

IN THEIR FOOTSTEPS

Edvard Grieg (1843–1907) "The Chopin of the North," Grieg wrote his first composition at the age of nine, and in time he became a romantic musician under Mendelssohn and Schumann. Themes from folk music are successfully exploited in the *Peer Gynt Suite* (1888). He was Norway's first composer to become famous throughout Europe.

• **Birthplace:** June 15, 1843, in Bergen.

• **Favorite Haunts:** Rome where he met Franz Liszt; Christiania (now Oslo) where he became a member of the Royal Musical Academy of Sweden in 1872, and his beloved Troldhaugen (Troll's Hill) outside Bergen.

• **Resting Place:** He died on September 4, 1907, and was buried in a cliff grotto at Troldhaugen (open to the public).

mid-19th century. Its repertoire consists of classical Norwegian and international drama, contemporary plays, frequent productions of music drama, as well as visiting productions of opera and ballet.

Prices: Tickets, 100–200 kroner ($16.60–$33.20). **Bus:** 2, 3, 4.

SUMMER CULTURAL ENTERTAINMENT

BERGEN FOLKLORE, Bryggens Museum, Bryggen. Tel. 31-67-10; for reservations, 24-89-29 or 13-00-79.

The Bjørgvin Regional folk-dancing troupe arranges a folklore program at this museum mid-June to mid-August, on Monday and Wednesday at 8:30pm. The program lasts about an hour, consisting of traditional folk dances and music from rural Norway. Tickets are on sale at the Tourist Information Center or at the door.

Admission: 60 kroner ($9.95). **Bus:** 1, 5, 9.

THE CLUB & MUSIC SCENE

RUBINEN, Rosenkrantzgate 7. Tel. 31-50-00.

Rubinen is one of Bergen's most popular nightclubs. It plays all kinds of danceable and drinkable music, including country-western and rock 'n roll. Drinks cost about 45 kroner ($7.45). It's open Tuesday through Sunday from 8pm to 3am, with live music nightly. Bus: 2, 3, 4.

Admission: 50 kroner ($8.30).

PANDORA NIGHT CLUB, in the Hotel Norge, Ole Bulls Plass 2-4. Tel. 21-01-00.

Close to Torgalmenningen, this disco and dance bar caters to an over-30 crowd in relatively plush comfort. If you want to hear the latest music from New York or London, this is the place. A scotch and soda costs 54 kroner ($8.95); a beer, 45 kroner ($7.45). It's open Monday through Saturday from 9pm to 3am; live music is occasionally presented on Tuesday and Wednesday. Bus: 2, 3, 4.

Admission: 50 kroner ($8.30) Wed–Sat.

ENGELEN, in the SAS Royal Hotel, Bryggen. Tel. 31-80-00.

This is one of Bergen's more affluent and elegant discos. Its music features the latest releases. Light meals are available, and drinks cost 45 kroner ($7.45). It's open Tuesday through Saturday from 8pm to 2:30am. Bus: 1, 5, 9.

Admission: 50 kroner ($8.30).

THE BAR SCENE

BULL'S EYE PUB, in the Hotel Norge, Ole Bulls Plass 2-4. Tel. 21-01-00.

The huge Bull's Eye Pub is decked out like a Victorian pub with lots of polished hardwood and red-flecked wallpaper. This is the most famous drinking spot in Bergen. The live music helps fill its 200 seats to capacity. A half liter of beer will set you back 35 kroner ($5.80). It's open daily from noon to 1am. Bus: 2, 3, 4.

KONTORET PUB, Ole Bulls Plass 8-10. Tel. 90-07-60.

Perhaps the most frequented pub in the town center, the Kontoret is located in the Hotel Norge next to the Dickens restaurant and pub. Drinkers can wander freely between the two places, as they are interconnected and are also accessible through exterior doors. In the Kontoret Pub you can order the same food served at Dickens, although most people seem to come here to drink. The local brew is called Hansa; a half liter of draft beer is 37 kroner ($6.15). The pub is open Sunday through Friday from 4pm to 12:30am and on Saturday from noon to 12:30am. Bus: 2, 3, 4.

ZACCHARIASBRYGGE PUB, Zacchariasbrygge. Tel. 31-03-60.

Set on the harborfront of Old Bergen, in the same oxblood-colored former warehouse as the restaurant Zacchariasbrygge (see "Dining," above), this place is one of Bergen's most popular, and sometimes noisiest, pubs. Mingling with copious quantities of flowing suds at 38.50 kroner ($6.40) for a half pint of lage and Italian wines for 36 kroner ($5.95) a glass—are the sounds of pian live singer. There's additional seating on the upper floor. The pub is op 11am to 1am. Bus: 1, 5, 9.

MOVIES

Bergen has a number of movie theaters, such as **Konsertpaleet,** Neumannsgate 3 (tel. 31-96-20), and **Forum,** in Danmarkplass (tel. 29-80-70), showing all films in the original versions. The earliest performance is at 11am; the latest at 11pm.

10. NETWORKS & RESOURCES

FOR STUDENTS   About a 12-minute walk from Torvalmenning, **Universite-tenes Travel Bureau,** Studentsamskipnaden, Parkveien (tel. 32-64-00), sells discount tickets on both planes and boats. For example, you might get discounts ranging up to 50% on flights to either Stockholm or Copenhagen. You can also get discounts on steamers to Newcastle in northeastern England. Some of these discounts range as high as 25% off regular prices. You must be under 26 years of age.

FOR GAY MEN & LESBIANS   The **Gay Switchboard** in Bergen (tel. 31-05-77) is open only on Wednesday from 7 to 11pm.

You might call one of the gay liberation organizations for information about activities in Bergen. Try **DNF-48,** Kalfarveien 32A (tel. 31-05-77), open Monday through Friday from 10am to 4pm.

Homofil Bevegelse i Bergen (HBB), 5013 Bergen-Nygårdstangen (tel. 31-21-39), is a gay rights movement serving Bergen and western Norway. Call for information about its disco, operated on Saturday from 10pm to 2am. An open house is staged at its office and café on Thursday from 7 to 10pm and on Saturday from 2 to 5pm.

FOR WOMEN   The local branch of the International Women's Organization is **Zonta,** St. Hanshaugen 56, Fyllingsdalen (tel. 16-19-92). The contact in Bergen is Berit Wollan.

11. EASY EXCURSIONS

Two of Norway's most famous fjords, the **Hardanger** and the **Sognefjord,** can easily be explored from Bergen. The least expensive way to see the Hardanger fjord and the **Folgefonn Glacier** is to take a round-trip coach from the Central Bus Station, Strømgaten 8, leaving from Platform 1 daily at 7:45am all year. The full-day independent tour includes a luncheon stopover at Utne or Lofthus and returns to Bergen around 9pm; round-trip fare is 260 kroner ($43.15), excluding lunch.

Norway's longest fjord, Sognefjord, can be crossed by express steamer to **Gudvangen.** From Gudvangen, passengers go to Flåm. From Flåm, a train runs back to Bergen. The round-trip fare, excluding lunch, is 425 kroner ($70.50) for adults, 213 kroner ($35.35) for children. Departures from Bergen, June 1 to August 31, are daily at 8:10am.

NORWAY IN A NUTSHELL

This 12-hour tour is the most exciting 1-day tour in the country, encompassing two arms of **Sognefjord,** and the train ride from **Myrdal** down to **Flåm** (a drop of 2,900 feet, past seemingly endless waterfalls). In June, July, and August, the tour aves at 9:15am from the Bergen railway station; guests have lunch at Flåm, then board a river steamer for Gudvangen, where they hop on a bus to Voss, then a train back to Bergen. The round-trip fare, excluding meals, is 280 kroner ($46.45) for adults, 140 kroner ($23.25) for children.

JOSTEDAL GLACIER

One of Norway's most outstanding sights is the Jostedal Glacier, the largest in Europe and second largest in the world. Between the Sognefjord and the Nordfjord, above a valley called Briksdal, the glacier is about a mile above sea level and almost 350 feet long. Most of the icy giant can be circled by visitors, depending on the choice of route.

Most people are satisfied simply to go by excursion boat from Bergen and up the Nordfjord. Boats enter the fjord from the Norwegian Sea some 40 miles south of Ålesund.

For a more complete view, however, you can approach Jostedal by road, going about 65 miles north from the Sognefjord to reach the roads that go around the ice mass.

Medium-size cruise liners make their way up the Nordfjord to dock at the little town of Olden at the fjord's head. From Olden, a road leads to the Briksdal Valley and the **Briksdal Mountain Lodge,** about a 45-minute bus or car trip. From the lodge, you can walk to the base of the glacier or go in a two-wheel cart the lodge will supply. Up to five people can ride in the horse-drawn carts. If you're adventurous you may choose to go on foot, but the road is rough and muddy and should only be tackled by the hearty. Walk across the bridge, then follow a trail up to Jostedal Glacier. Wrap up in foul-weather gear, as it's cool and misty in the area.

The portion of the glacier visited from Olden is just one of the seven arms of the mighty ice giant, a remnant of the frigid coat that once covered all of Norway.

CHAPTER 18

THE FJORD DISTRICT

Western Norway is the heart of fjord country. Norwegian fjords are narrow arms of the sea, snaking their way inland. It took three million years to form the furrows and fissures that give western Norway its distinctive look. At some points the fjords become so narrow that a boat can hardly wedge between the mountainsides.

Bergen is the best departure point for trips to the fjords: to the south lies the famous Hardangerfjord and to the north the Sognefjord, cutting 111 miles inland.

About 1½ hours from Bergen, Voss is a famous ski resort that is also well situated between both the Hardangerfjord and the Sognefjord.

We'll start in the towns around the Hardangerfjord—Lofthus, Kinsarvik, Eidfjord and Ulvik, make a detour to Voss, and then move north to the towns around the Sognefjord like Balestrand and Flåm.

SEEING THE FJORD DISTRICT
GETTING THERE

Bergen is the traditional gateway to the fjord country. From Bergen, you have a choice of several options for getting about the district; the most expensive is by private car. Most of the towns and villages have road connections, although you'll have to take several car-ferries to cross the fjords. Boat excursions, many of which leave from Bergen, are the traditional way to see the fjords. In summer, dozens of possibilities await you. Contact the Bergen Tourist Office for details.

Of the towns recommended in this chapter, Voss and Geilo, both winter ski centers and summer mountain resorts, have the best rail connections with Oslo and Bergen. But all the fjord towns and villages are connected by buses which make their way carefully through the mountains and along the fjords, with vistas in all directions. Of course, travel by bus from place to place is time-consuming and often there are only two to five departures a day, depending on business, so you have to plan your connections in advance. Details about bus routes in the fjord district are available at the Central Station in Bergen.

A SUGGESTED ITINERARY

Days 1 & 2: From Bergen, explore the Hardangerfjord first and plan a 2-night stopover in one of these fjord villages: Utne, Lofthus, Kinsarvik, or Ulvik. Many visitors think Ulvik is the prettiest place. Explore some folk museums in the region and take long walks along the fjords.

Day 3: Journey to Voss for the night.

Day 4: Take the electric tram to Flåm for an overnight stay.

Day 5: Travel to Balestrand for the night.

WHAT'S SPECIAL ABOUT THE FJORD DISTRICT

Great Towns/Villages

☐ Lofthus, in the Hardanger fjord district, once the haunt of Edvard Grieg and other artists.

☐ Ulvik, on an arm of the Hardangerfjord, everybody's fantasy of a Norwegian fjord village.

Great Resorts

☐ Voss, a folkloric resort popular year round; winter sports enthusiasts join its "ski circus."

☐ Geilo, in the Hol mountain district, with 81 miles of marked tracks for cross-country skiing.

The Fjords

☐ Sognefjord, cutting 111 miles inland, the longest and most strident of Norway's fjords.

☐ Hardangerfjord, extending for 75 miles; its shores contain fruit plantations, and blossom time is when to go.

Scenic Wonders

☐ Hardangervidda National Park, on the largest high mountain plateau in Europe, home to 20,000 wild reindeer.

Museums

☐ Hardanger Folk Museum at Utne, where old timbered houses from fjord villages have been preserved.

☐ Voss Folk Museum at Mølster, a time capsule preserving the old ways of Norwegian farmlife.

Churches

☐ Kinsarvik Church, dating from the 12th century, one of Norway's oldest stone churches.

Day 6: Still in Balestrand, take an excursion on the Sognefjord, Norway's longest fjord.

Day 7: Return to Voss from Balestrand and take the train east for a final stopover in Geilo, from which you can easily journey to Oslo and your next destination.

---

1. UTNE

81 miles east of Bergen, 28 miles north of Odda

GETTING THERE   By Ferry   In the west board the ferry at Kvanndal; in the east, at Kinsarvik. There are frequent departures.

By Train   Connections are possible from Voss 24 miles in the east, on the main Bergen–Oslo line.

By Bus   Connections are made via Odda in the south and from Bergen in the west.

By Car   Head east from Bergen along the E68. At Kvanndal, board the ferry for Utne.

ESSENTIALS   The telephone area code for Utne is 054.

Utne has a view of the entrances to three fjords: Indre Samla, Granvin, and Eid. Across Utnefjorden, the formidable bulk of Oksen (7,953 feet) rises from the headland separating the Granvin and the Eid fjords. A great ravine breaches the steep slope of Oksen. Utnefjorden is almost 2 miles wide opposite Utne and nearly 2,700 feet deep in places, making it deeper than any other part of the Hardangerfjord.

Utne is at the northern end of the Folgefonn peninsula, with mountains looming nearby. Two valleys converge on the town, Utnedalen to the east and Fossdalen to the west. The river through Fossdalen forms fine falls as it drops through the woods toward the end of its course, dividing into two branches as it reaches the fjord.

WHAT TO SEE & DO

The **Hardanger Folk Museum** (tel. 66-900), founded in 1911, exhibits old timber buildings, furnished according to their eras, from several parts of Inner Hardanger. By the fjord are old boathouses and a general store that once stood on the quayside. Twenty wooden houses are in the open-air portion of the museum. In the administrative building are local arts and crafts, national costumes, data on the fruit-growing industry, and a review of tourism in the 18th and 19th centuries.

The museum is open daily from 8am to 4pm, charging 20 kroner ($3.30) for adults, free for children. There are two branch museums, one near Lofthus and one between Kinsarvik and Eidfjord (see below).

When fjords were the highways of western Norway, Utne was an important junction. The **Utne Hotel** (see below) opened in 1722.

About 10 miles away from Utne lies **Agatunet,** a small village of buildings preserved on their original sites. The oldest building is **Lagmannstova,** the 13th-century Judge's House. Agatunet is open mid-May to mid-September, daily from 10am to noon and 2 to 4pm. Admission is 6 kroner ($1) for adults, 3 kroner (50¢) for children.

WHERE TO STAY

ROMANTIK UTNE HOTEL, N-5797 Utne i Hardanger. Tel. 054/66-983. Fax 054/69-950. 23 rms (19 with bath).

$ Rates (including breakfast): 380 kroner ($63.05) single without bath, 500 kroner ($82.95) single with bath; 600 kroner ($99.55) double without bath, 750 kroner ($124.45) double with bath. AE, DC, MC, V.

The 1772 Utne Hotel is the oldest hotel in Norway still in operation—for five generations the proprietors have devotedly served their guests. If you'd like to relax in a comfortable, antique-filled atmosphere of hospitality, this is the place, just a few minutes from the ferry quay. You can have lunch à la carte, and dinner for 180 kroner ($29.85) and up.

2. LOFTHUS

236 miles west of Oslo, 87 miles east of Bergen

GETTING THERE   By Ferry   Board the ferry at Kvanndal for Kinsarvik where you can make bus connections south to Lofthus.

By Train   Connections are possible from Voss, 31 miles to the east, on the main Bergen–Oslo line.

By Bus   Bus service takes 1 hour from Odda in the south, 15 minutes from Kinsarvik in the north. From Bergen you can go by express bus/boat in 2½ hours.

By Car   Take the E68 east from Bergen to Kvanndal, where you can board a car-ferry to Kinsarvik. At Kinsarvik, head south on Route 47 to Lofthus.

ESSENTIALS   You can write for information from **Ullensvang Tourist Association,** Box 73, N-5780 Kinsarvik (tel. 054/63-112). The **telephone area code** for Ullensvang is 054.

A favorite spot in the Hardanger district is sleepy Lofthus, once the haunt of Edvard Grieg and other artists. On the fjord, the resort is enveloped by snow-capped mountains, farms, and orchards. Hovering in the background is the Folgefonn Glacier.

Lofthus is actually the collective name for several groups of farms—Helleland, Eidnes, Lofthus, Opedal, Århus, and Ullensvang—extending from north to south along the eastern coastal slopes of Sørfjorden, 4 to 5 miles south of Kinsarvik Bay.

The discovery of a runic stone at Pedal, the oldest and largest group of farms, established that the area has been peopled since about 600 A.D. Cistercian monks came to Opedal seven centuries later and pioneered a fruit-growing industry. Their footpaths are still used and many have benefited from the 616 steps, the Monks' Staircase, that makes its way up the steep gradient to the Vidda.

The church and buildings of Ullensvang lie around the mouth of the Opo River. The Gothic stone church was probably built at the end of the 13th century, and the builders may have been Scottish masons. Ullensvang was the name of the ancient farm where the *prestegård* (church farm) stands facing the church. It is now the name of the church, the hamlet, the parish, and the *kommune*, and the site of the most famous hotel in the region (see below).

WHAT TO SEE & DO

Almost 4 miles from Kinsarvik on Route 47 to Odda, a minor road forks left providing an alternative route to Lofthus. A short distance from the fork is the **Skredhaugen Museum** (tel. 66-927), a branch of the Hardanger Folk Museum at Utne. Greve's collection of 10 timber houses gathered from the area and furnished according to their period can be seen. There's also an art gallery filled with 19th-century works. The museum is open from late May to late August, Monday through Saturday from 11am to 4pm and on Sunday from noon to 4pm. Admission is 20 kroner ($3.30) for adults, free for children.

WHERE TO STAY

HOTEL ULLENSVANG, N-5774 Lofthus i Hardanger. Tel. 054/61-100.
130 rms (all with bath). TV TEL
$ **Rates** (including breakfast): 775 kroner ($128.55) standard single, 1,000 kroner ($165.90) deluxe single; 850 kroner ($141) standard double, 1,400 kroner ($232.25) deluxe twin. AE, DC, MC, V.

Once a romantic inn on the edge of the Hardangerfjord, a retreat of Edvard Grieg—his piano is still kept in a cottage on the grounds—it was greatly expanded in the 1970s and is now the best-known "health farm" in Norway. "Farm" is hardly the word for this place, however. It's a beautifully equipped modern structure with a garden opening onto the shoreline, with views of the Folgefonn Glacier. Run by the Utne family for four generations, it offers rooms ranging from standard to deluxe. All are handsomely furnished with a number of amenities. The modest beginning in 1846 as a guesthouse has given way to a modern resort hotel, but an old-fashioned tradition of hospitality remains. Scandinavian kings, Emperor Wilhelm II, and European nobility have patronized the hotel.

Dining/Entertainment: The dining room seats 500 people (see "Where to Dine," below). International bands are often brought in to entertain guests. The hotel has a modern cocktail bar.

Services: Hairdresser, room service.

Facilities: Rowboats for fjord cruises, sail boats, heated swimming pool, whirlpool, game room, solarium, sauna, gym, jet spa, tennis court, squash court.

ULLENSVANG GJESTEHEIM, N-5774 Loftus i Hardanger. Tel. 054/61-236. 17 rms (none with bath).
$ **Rates** (including breakfast): 230 kroner ($38.15) single; 380 kroner ($63.05) double; 490 kroner ($81.30) triple. No credit cards.

Ullensvang Gjesteheim is a cozy, homelike guesthouse in the town center, furnished with a personal touch. Rooms are quiet and have hot and cold running water. Close to the rooms are shared baths. The dining room serves the

Norwegian *koldbord* for breakfast, and Norwegian specialties at lunch and dinner. You will relish their home-cooked food—both lunch and dinner go for 130 kroner ($21.55). In the garden are two old houses of the 16th century, the Borvehouse and Bleiehouse, which guests may visit.

WHERE TO DINE

RESTAURANT ULLENSVANG, Lofthus i Hardanger. Tel. 61-100.
   Cuisine: NORWEGIAN. **Reservations:** Recommended.
$ Prices: Dinner buffet 220 kroner ($36.50); three-course lunch 150 kroner ($24.90). Appetizers 55–65 kroner ($9.10–$10.80); main dishes 120–175 kroner ($19.90–$29.05). AE, DC, MC, V.
   Open: Lunch daily 1–3pm; dinner daily 7–9:30pm.

A hearty three-course Norwegian lunch is offered here, but most guests come in for the buffet dinner spread of at least 65 dishes—everything from jellied salmon to homemade cakes. Occasionally folk dancing is staged, and guests are invited to join in. Six nights a week there's a live band for dancing. It's located in the town center on the edge of the Hardangerfjord.

---

3. KINSARVIK

74 miles east of Bergen, 24 miles south of Voss, 223 miles west of Oslo

GETTING THERE   By Train   The Bergen Railroad running between Bergen and Oslo will take you to the Voss station, the nearest terminal to Kinsarvik. There are 14 arrivals and departures a day. From Voss, you can journey to Kinsarvik by bus. Trip time from Oslo to Voss is 5½ hours.

By Bus   Bus service takes 1¼ hours from Odda, 15 minutes from Lofthus. The bus trip from Bergen takes 2½ hours, and 50 minutes from Voss, the nearest rail connection.

By Boat   Boats leaving from Kvanndal on the northern coast of the Hardangerfjord take about 45 minutes.

ESSENTIALS   The tourist office is at **Ullensvang Reiselivslag,** N-5780 Kinsarvik (tel. 054/63-112). The **telephone area code** for Kinsarvik is 054.

The main village of Kinsarvik stands on a glacier-formed ridge at the mouth of the Kinso River, which flows into four magnificent waterfalls as it drops from the plateau to Husedalen on its way to the sea. From early times Kinsarvik was the marketplace for the region.

Kinsarvik was the principal timber port of Hardanger in the 17th and early 18th century. When the export of timber was transferred to Bergen in 1750, Kinsarvik developed a shipbuilding industry that continued until 1870, when it became a center for wood carving. Today a pewter factory is one of its principal industries.

WHAT TO SEE & DO

The plot of grass that slopes to a stony beach near the Kinsarvik ferry terminal is **Skiperstod,** site of a boathouse for naval longships from about 900 until 1350.

   Borstova, the building on the fjord side of the green facing the church, was constructed partly from the timbers of St. Olav's Guildhall, the meeting place of the local guild until 1680. It is now a council chamber and social center.

Kinsarvik Church, said to have been built by Scottish masterbuilders at the end of the 12th century, is one of the oldest stone churches in Norway. The interior was restored in 1961 to its pre-Reformation condition. It has a 17th-century pulpit painted by Peter Reimers, a painted and carved altarpiece, and medieval frescoes.

The stone column (*minnestein*) on the green commemorates the local men who fought in the wars that led to the end of the union with Denmark in 1814.

The **Hardanger Recreation Park (Tillegg i tekst),** in the middle of Kinsarvik, is open on Saturday and Sunday from May to the end of September, daily from mid-June to the end of August.

About 9 miles from Kinsarvik en route to Eidfjord, off Highway 7, the **Bu Museum** has three old houses containing furniture and domestic and craft equipment. The basement of an old farmhouse is filled with artifacts dating from the Stone Age to modern times. The museum also has a collection of national costumes from the Hardanger area. It is open late May to late August, daily from 9am to 5pm. For more information, phone the main museum in Utne (tel. 054/66-900). Admission is 10 kroner ($1.65).

WHERE TO STAY

KINSARVIK FJORD HOTEL, N-5780 Kinsarvik. Tel. 054/63-100. Fax 054/63-3740. 75 rms (62 with bath). TV TEL
$ Rates (including breakfast): 480 kroner ($79.65) single without bath, 530 kroner ($87.95) single with bath; 640 kroner ($106.20) double without bath, 700 kroner ($116.15) double with bath. AE, DC, MC, V.

Modern and well equipped, this is a family-type place. Both the public rooms and guest bedrooms have attractive modern styling, many opening onto views. Rooms are well maintained and comfortably furnished, and children sharing a room with their parents get a 50% reduction on meals.

Even if you don't stay here, you might like to have lunch for 165 kroner ($27.35) or dinner for 180 kroner ($29.85) in the pleasant dining room. The hotel is known for its generous buffets. There's a fully licensed bar, and an orchestra plays for the guests. A separate cafeteria bar is on the premises.

It's located near the traffic junction of the main road (RV7) over the Hardanger plateau and the E76 over Haukeli.

HARDING MOTELL & HYTTETUN, N-5780 Kinsarvik. Tel. 054/63-182. 7 chalets. TV
$ Rates: 585 kroner ($97.05) six-bed room; 700 kroner ($116.15) eight-bed room. No credit cards.

⑤ The Harding Motell & Hyttetun is a chalet village containing 27 units and a main building with a cafeteria. The chalets are well equipped with kitchens, bedrooms, baths, and living rooms with TV and video. An activity area includes a heated swimming pool, solarium, sauna, and jet-spa. The Harding is near the traffic junction of the main road (RV7) over the Hardanger plateau and the E76 over Haukeli.

---

4. EIDFJORD

93 miles east of Bergen, 209 miles west of Oslo

GETTING THERE   By Train   Take the train from Bergen to Voss, where a connecting bus will take you the rest of the way.

By Bus   Buses for Eidfjord depart three or four times a day from Voss, taking 1¾ hours. Part of the route across the Eidfjord itself requires a 10-minute ferryboat ride. In summer the ferry departs every 10 minutes, and in winter every 40 minutes.

By Car   From Odda in the south, take Route 47 north; from Geilo in the east, take Route 7 west. The drive takes an hour.

ESSENTIALS   The **tourist office** is located in the town center (tel. 054/65-177). There are no street names. The **telephone area code** for Eidfjord is 054.

At the northern tip of the Hardangerfjord lies the Eidfjord district. Approximately 1,000 people live here, supporting themselves with agriculture, tourism, and cottage industries. The area is a paradise for hikers and home to the continent's largest herd of wild reindeer. Mountain trout with sour cream is a regional food specialty.

WHAT TO SEE & DO

The county contains nearly one-quarter of **Hardangervidda National Park,** which is on the largest high-mountain plateau in Europe, home to 20,000 wild reindeer. Well-marked hiking trails connect a series of 15 tourist huts.

Several canyons, including the renowned **Måbø Valley,** lead down from the plateau to the fjords. Here you'll see the famous 550-foot Voringfoss waterfall; the Valurefoss in Hjømo Valley has a free fall of almost 800 feet.

Part of the 1,000-year-old road across Norway, traversing the Måbø Valley, has been restored for hardy hikers.

In Sima Valley, about 3¾ miles from the center of Eidfjord, you can visit the **Sima Power Plant,** one of the largest hydroelectric plants in Europe. Guided tours are given, and one of the dams built for the plant, the enormous Sysendam, can be seen from the R7 road.

A small mountain farm, **Kjeaasen,** nearly 2,000 feet above sea level, can be reached by car. From Kjeaasen you have a splendid view. The footpath is recommended only to those in good physical condition.

The 14th-century stone **Eidfjord Old Church** can be visited with a guide— make arrangements at the tourist office.

Numerous lakes and rivers offer good trout fishing, and in two rivers, the Eio and the Bjoreio, as well as in the Eidfjord Lake, you can fish for salmon. The local tourist office has rowboats and bicycles for rent.

WHERE TO STAY

HOTELL VØRINGSFOSS, N-5783 Eidfjord. Tel. 054/65-184. Fax 054/65-505. 50 rms (all with bath).

$ Rates (including breakfast): 275–325 kroner ($45.60–$53.90) single; 400 kroner ($66.35) double. AE, DC, MC, V.

Hotel Vøringsfoss lies by the fjord in Nedre Eidfjord, 20 paces from the bus station. The hotel represents a pleasing combination of the old and the new, as it has been accommodating guests since the 1880s but was extended and modernized over the years. Six of the bedrooms are modern, while the others are more old-fashioned but with comfortable furniture. Many open onto views of Eidfjord, and 40 of the bedrooms have TV and phone.

The hotel contains four restaurants, ranging from an unpretentious pub to a more upscale place. Price of a two-course lunch ranges from 60 to 70 kroner ($9.95 to $11.60), with dinner costing 150 to 250 kroner ($24.90 to $41.50).

5. ULVIK

93 miles east of Bergen, 64 miles west of Geilo, 25 miles west of Voss

GETTING THERE   By Train and Bus   From Bergen or Oslo, take the train to Voss where you can catch a bus for the 25-mile ride to Ulvik (45 minutes). There are five daily buses in summer from Voss and three daily buses in winter. Buses stop in front of the Ulvik church in the town center (there is no formal bus station).

By Car   From Voss, head east on the E68, continuing east at the junction with Route 572.

ESSENTIALS The **Ulvik tourist office** (tel. 05/52-63-60) is in the center of town and will arrange any number of excursions—from trips on fjord steamers to bus tours to the Osa Mountains. The **telephone area code** for Ulvik is 05.

Ulvik is that rarity—an unspoiled resort—lying like a fist at the end of an arm of the Hardangerfjord surrounded in summer by misty peaks and fruit farms.

The village's century-old church is attractively decorated in the style of the region.

WHERE TO STAY

BRAKANES HOTEL, N-5730 Ulvik. Tel. 05/52-61-05. Fax 05/52-64-10. 100 rms (all with bath). MINIBAR TV TEL

$ **Rates** (including breakfast): May 20–Sept 1,750 kroner ($124.45) single; 1,050–1,200 kroner ($174.20–$199.10) double. Sept 2–May 19, 650 kroner ($107.85) single; 900–1,050 kroner ($149.30–$174.20) double. AE, DC, MC, V.

The view of the Hardangerfjord and the surrounding forest is famous from this well-recommended hotel near the town center at the edge of the fjord. Originally built 130 years ago, all that remains of the original building is one small dining room. The balconied and skylight-covered modern building you see today evolved from a series of reconstructions beginning in the 1960s. Bedrooms are comfortably furnished and beautifully maintained. Facilities include a sauna, pool room, and tennis courts. In summer plane rides can be arranged over the fjords. Windsurfing and boat rentals are available. The hotel also offers the area's best-known nightlife choice.

STRAND HOTEL OG MOTEL, N-5730 Ulvik. Tel. 05/52-63-05. Fax 05/52-64-10. 41 rms (all with bath).

$ **Rates** (including breakfast): 575 kroner ($95.40) single; 840 kroner ($139.35) double. AE, DC, MC, V. **Closed:** Mid-Oct to late Apr.

This hotel, fronting the fjord, is a bungalow-style building. All bedrooms are completely up-to-date and overlook the fjord. The owners have added a motel with a dozen rooms; seven of these newer units contain private balconies, and four have private terraces. It is licensed for beer and wine, and has a dining room where you can order meals for 85 to 180 kroner ($14.10 to $29.85). Waterskiing, motorboat rides, and rowing are available. There's also a heated indoor swimming pool and sauna. It's a 5-minute walk from the town center.

ULVIK HOTEL, N-5730 Ulvik. Tel. 05/52-62-00. Fax 05/52-66-41. 56 rms (all with bath). TEL

$ **Rates** (including half board): Summer, 480 kroner ($79.65) single; 760 kroner ($126.10) double. Winter, 450 kroner ($74.65) single; 700 kroner ($116.15) double. AE, DC, MC, V.

The hotel was built in 1946, with a significant addition in 1972; the garden is separated from the fjord only by a road. Bedrooms are modern and comfortable, painted in light pastels. More than half of them overlook the fjord. A dining room is reserved for boarding guests, but the A La Carte Restaurant (that's its name) set on the hotel's street level is more stylish, serving excellent Norwegian food. Shrimp and salmon are the most popular items on the menu. Live music and a nightclub format are presented Wednesday through Sunday from 9pm to either midnight or 1am. It's located on the fjord in the town center.

ULVIK FJORD PENSJONAT, N-5730 Ulvik. Tel. 05/52-61-70. Fax 05/52-61-60. 20 rms (17 with bath). TEL

$ **Rates** (including breakfast): 275 kroner ($45.60) single without bath, 375 kroner ($62.20) single with shower; 450 kroner ($74.65) double without bath, 550 kroner ($91.25) double with bath. V.

Ⓢ Ulvik Fjord Pensjonat, constructed in two stages, in 1946 and 1977, is one of the finest guesthouses along the Hardangerfjord. Rooms are spacious and pleasantly furnished in a regional Norwegian style. You are welcomed by the Hammer family, who won the Norwegian Hospitality Prize of 1989. They invite you to use their sauna and solarium and to partake in their good-tasting fjord cooking. The lounge, called Ulvestova (Wolf's Den), is decorated with a large collection of stuffed wild animals and birds. It's 700 yards from the town center.

6. VOSS

78 miles east of Bergen, 255 miles west of Oslo

GETTING THERE   By Train   Train service takes about 1½ hours from Bergen, 1½ hours from Myrdal, and 2¼ hours from Flåm. About 14 trains running between Bergen and Oslo stop daily at Voss. Trip time between Voss and Oslo is 8½ hours.

By Bus   One bus daily runs between Bergen and Voss, taking 2¼ hours; and between Voss and Oslo, taking 11 hours.

By Car   From Bergen, take the E68 east all the way to Voss.

ESSENTIALS: For information, go to **Voss Turistkontor,** Vangsgate 81 (tel. 05/51-17-16). The **telephone area code** is 05.

Between the Sogne and Hardanger fjords, Voss is a famous year-round resort, also known for its folklore. Maybe the trolls don't strike fear into the hearts of farm children any more, but they are still called out of hiding to give the visitors a little fun.

Voss is a natural base for exploring the two largest fjords in Norway, the Sognefjord to the north and the Hardangerfjord to the south. In and around Voss are glaciers, mountains, fjords, waterfalls, orchards, rivers, and lakes.

WHAT TO SEE & DO

In addition to the attractions below, don't miss seeing **St. Olav's Cross,** Skulegata, near the Voss Cinema. It's the oldest historic relic in Voss, believed to have been raised when the townspeople adopted Christianity in 1023.

A ride on the **Hangursbanen Cable Car** (tel. 51-18-17) will be a memorable part of your visit, offering beautiful views of Voss and the environs. Refreshments or meals are available at the mountaintop restaurant. The hardy take the cable up, then spend the rest of the afternoon strolling leisurely down the mountain. A round-trip ride costs 35 kroner ($5.80) for adults, 25 kroner ($4.15) for children. Entrance to the cable car is on a hillside after a 10-minute walk north of the center.

VANGSKYRKJE, Vangsgata 3. Tel. 51-22-78.
This 13th-century church with a timbered tower in the center of Voss contains a

IN THEIR FOOTSTEPS

Ludvig Holberg (1684–1754) After various careers, Holberg achieved major success in Copenhagen, writing Danish comedies. His most famous, produced in 1724, was called *Henrik and Pernille*. The 32 comedies he produced are largely responsible for his reputation as "the father of Danish literature," although he was Norwegian born.
   • **Birthplace:** December 3, 1684, in Bergen, where he was soon orphaned.
   • **Residences:** Voss (Norway), Oxford (England), and Copenhagen where he was to know his greatest success.
   • **Resting Place:** Dying in Copenhagen on January 27, 1754, at the age of 70, he was buried at Sorø in Zealand.

striking Renaissance pulpit, stone altar and triptych, fine wood carvings, and a painted ceiling. It's a 5-minute walk east of the rail station.
Admission: Free.
Open: Summer, daily 9am–7pm. **Closed:** Winter.

FINNESLOFTET, Finne. Tel. 51-11-00.
About a mile west of Voss in Finne, Finnesloftet is one of the oldest timbered houses in Norway, dating from the mid-13th century. It's a 15-minute walk west of the rail station.
Admission: 15 kroner ($2.50).
Open: Summer, daily 10am–3:30pm. **Closed:** Winter.

VOSS FOLKEMUSEUM, Mølster. Tel. 51-15-11.
A collection of authentically furnished houses, this museum shows what early farm life was like. The new building also displays selected items from the museum's collection of home crafts. Take a taxi from the center: Only those who are part goat should attempt the uphill climb.
Admission: 15 kroner ($2.50) adults, free for children.
Open: May–Sept, daily 10am–5pm; Oct–Apr, Mon–Fri 10am–3pm.

SKIING

Voss is continually adding to its facilities, and is definitely in the race to overtake Geilo and Lillehammer as Norway's most popular winter playground. Its chair lifts, ski lifts, and aerial cableway carry passengers up 2,625 feet.

The town offers what it calls a "ski circus": Beginners take the Hangursbanen cable car; one ski lift (3,000 feet long) goes from Traastolen to the top of Slettafjell (with a wide choice of downhill runs); the Bavallen lift is for the slalom slopes; and the downhill runs are at Lonehorgi.

Lessons at the **Ski School** (tel. 51-18-17), at the end of the cable-car run, are moderate in cost. The tourist office and hotels can arrange bookings.

Parents can park children ages 3 to 7 in a "snow nursery" while they spend the day skiing. Kids over 7 can ski. A special branch of the Ski School handles these youngsters. Ski equipment—everything from boots to touring skis—can be rented.

WHERE TO STAY

EXPENSIVE

FLEISCHERS HOTEL, Evangerveiten 13, N-5700 Voss. Tel. 05/51-11-55
Fax 05/51-22-89. 71 rms (all with bath). TV TEL
$ Rates (including breakfast): 800 kroner ($132.70) single; 940 kroner ($155.95) double. AE, DC, MC, V.
On the lakefront right beside the Voss Rail Station, Fleischers couldn't be more convenient: The Bergen–Oslo train stops out back. The traditional choice for Voss, this gracious 1889 frame hotel added a modern wing that has 30 units, all with private showers, toilets, kitchenettes, and terraces overlooking the lake. Several rooms contain minibars. In the old part of the hotel, the rooms are old-fashioned. The fully licensed hotel features a dining room, billiard room, library, two bars, band dancing, films, and occasional folk dancing.

HOTEL JARL, Voss Sentrum, N-5700 Voss. Tel. 05/51-19-33. Fax 05/51-37-69. 80 rms (all with bath). MINIBAR TV TEL
$ Rates (including breakfast): 750 kroner ($119.45) single; 1,140 kroner ($189.25) double; 1,300 kroner ($215.65) family room. AE, DC, MC, V.
In this centrally situated hotel are singles, doubles, and family rooms, each furnished with comfortably modern styling. Other facilities include attractive public rooms, an indoor swimming pool, a sauna bath, an English pub, game room, and a popular nightclub, Knight's Club. You can take your meals in the pleasant dining room, or

relax in an intimate bistro and bar, with dinner costing 130 to 175 kroner ($21.55 to $29.05). The Hotel Jarl is in the town center by the bridges, 800 yards from the rail station.

PARK HOTEL VOSSEVANGEN, Uttrågate, N-5701 Voss. Tel. 05/51-13-22. Fax 05/50-00-39. 63 rms (all with bath). MINIBAR TV TEL

$ Rates (including breakfast): Summer, 550 kroner ($91.25) single; 650 kroner ($107.85) double. Winter, 725 kroner ($120.30) single; 900 kroner ($149.30) double. Half board costs 195 kroner ($32.35) extra. AE, DC, MC, V.

In 1990 this hotel merged itself architecturally with its neighbor, the Vossevangen Hotel. Shortly after their union, an architect joined the two sections with a covered passageway. The Park was built in 1961 and the Vossevangen in 1954. Presently, the Park is the more luxurious of the two, but the Vossevangen will be restored until it has the same standard. Bedrooms are comfortably and attractively furnished. The hotel is family owned and contains the best restaurant in town, the Elysée (see "Where to Dine," below). Facilities include the Café Stationen, the Pentagon Dance Bar, and the Pianissimo Bar. It's located in the center, about 100 yards from the rail station.

INEXPENSIVE

BAVALLSTOVA PENSJONAT, Bavallsuegen 272 (Postboks 179 Bavallen), N-5700 Voss. Tel. 05/51-18-73. 17 rms (all with bath).

$ Rates: 380 kroner ($63.05) double. Breakfast costs 50 kroner ($8.30) extra. No credit cards.

This is an immaculate and comfortable boarding house, about 3¼ miles from the center of Voss, near the Bavellen ski lift. Rebuilt in 1982, it has tasteful, restful bedrooms, all doubles. The bright cafeteria has a panoramic view of Voss, the lake below, and the mountains beyond. There is a large lounge with an open fireplace. The hostess speaks English.

KRINGSJÅ PENSION, Voss Sentrum, N-5700 Voss. Tel. 05/51-16-27.

$ Rates (including breakfast): 680 kroner ($112.80) single; 560 kroner ($92.90) double. AE, DC, MC, V.

Kringsjå Pension is an inviting modern guesthouse. The public rooms are spacious and airy, and the bedrooms, all twins, are plainly decorated and functionally furnished. You'll pay from 135 kroner ($22.40) for a good Norwegian lunch or dinner.

NØRING PENSION, Uttrågate 41, N-5700 Voss. Tel. 05/51-12-11. 21 rms (none with bath).

$ Rates (including breakfast): 350 kroner ($58.05) single; 540 kroner ($89.60) double. AE, DC, MC, V.

Ⓢ Nøring Pension is a first-class pension built near the river in 1949, about a 10-minute walk from the town center, providing clean, functional accommodations. Half the rooms face the mountains. Licensed for beer and wine, the boardinghouse serves good hearty breakfasts. The Nøring is open in both summer and winter (ski boots are available). The lounge opens onto a terrace with summer garden furniture.

WHERE TO DINE

ELYSEE, in the Park Hotel Vossevangen, Uttrågate. Tel. 51-13-22.
   Cuisine: FRENCH/NORWEGIAN. **Reservations:** Recommended.
$ Prices: Appetizers 30–50 kroner ($5–$8.30); main dishes 135–200 kroner ($22.40–$33.20); lunch smörgåsbord 150 kroner ($24.90) per person. AE, DC, MC, V.
   Open: Daily noon–11pm.

This is the prestige restaurant of town, with more than 10,000 bottles of wine in inventory, the finest list in the fjord district. The decor is neoclassical, modeled on Greek motifs, and the location is on the lobby level of the Park Hotel Vossevangen (see "Where to Stay," above). Fresh Norwegian salmon is poached in white wine and served with a herb sauce, or you can order such typical dishes as filet of lamb provençale or filet of roast venison with lingonberry sauce. The lunchtime smörgåsbord—cold dishes only—is a great food value. The restaurant is in the town center, 100 yards from the rail station.

FLEISCHERS RESTAURANT, Evangerveiten 13. Tel. 51-11-55
   Cuisine: NORWEGIAN. **Reservations:** Recommended.
$ **Prices:** Appetizers 45–65 kroner ($7.45–$10.80); main dishes 155–175 kroner ($25.70–$29.05); lunch smörgåsbord 145 kroner ($24.05); four-course fixed-price dinner 190 kroner ($31.50). AE, DC, MC, V.
   Open: Mon–Sat 1–10:30pm, Sun 1–9:45pm.
The dining room of this landmark hotel, a few steps away from the Voss Rail Station, hasn't been altered since the hotel opened a century ago. The colors are dark reds and dark greens, a medley of Victorian tradition. Long the leading restaurant in the Voss area, Fleischers remains the favorite of the traditionalist. Its lunchtime smörgåsbord is a lavish array of all-you-can-eat Norwegian delicacies. Specialties include smoked salmon, filet of beef, gratinated filet of lamb, and filets of pork and veal.

VANGEN CAFE, Vangen Super-Market, Vangsgate. Tel. 51-12-05.
   Cuisine: NORWEGIAN. **Reservations:** Not required.
$ **Prices:** Soup 17 kroner ($2.80); smørbrød 26–30 kroner ($4.30–$5); two-course *dagens* menu 50–70 kroner ($8.30–$11.60). No credit cards.
   Open: Mon–Fri 9:30am–6pm, Sat 9:30am–3pm, Sun noon–6pm.
This is the least expensive cafeteria-style outlet in Voss, sitting one floor above street level over a small souvenir shop and food market in the center of town, a 5-minute walk south of the rail station. Soft drinks and fruit juices are sold, but no alcohol, not even beer or wine. The daily *dagens* menu is the best food value in town, and a selection of smørbrød is available throughout the day.

EVENING ENTERTAINMENT

FLEISCHERS TOP SPOT NIGHTCLUB, in Fleischers Hotel, Evangerveiten 13. Tel. 51-11-55.
   In the cellar of Fleischers Hotel (see "Where to Stay," above), this is the best-established nightlife spot in Voss. Dance bands play nightly for an older crowd who believe in dressing up a bit for the occasion. Many people come here just to drink—beer costs 37 kroner ($6.15)—but it's also possible to order full meals, for 150 to 225 kroner ($24.90 to $37.35). Steak platters are a feature. It's open Monday through Thursday from 9pm to 1am and on Friday and Saturday from 9pm to 3am.
   Admission: 25–50 kroner ($4.15–$8.30).

AN EXCURSION TO THE SOGNEFJORD

Motorists with more time may want to visit the Sognefjord district, the largest of all Norwegian fjords. From Voss the northern route leads to **Vik.** The scenery is beautiful, and the road goes along for miles across a desolate tableland at 3,000 feet above sea level. The lakes on a summer day appear green, and on the distant slopes is snow.
   In Vik, try to see the stave church, one of the most attractive in Norway. Then take the road to **Vangsnes,** where you can make ferry connections across the Sognefjord to Balestrand or Dragsvik. Once across, take Route 5 north. The highway is steep, bringing you through pleasant countryside with waterfalls until you reach **Viksdalen,** about 40 miles from Dragsvik.

---

7. FLÅM

40 miles east of Voss, 217 miles west of Oslo

GETTING THERE By Train The best—and most exciting—approach to Flåm is aboard the ✪ **electric train from Myrdal,** which has good connections from both Bergen and Oslo. The electric train follows a 12-mile route overlooking a 2,844-foot drop, stopping occasionally for passengers to photograph spectacular waterfalls. Trip time is 50 minutes. In winter, about four or five trains a day make the run to Flåm. In summer, depending on business, they are much more frequent, beginning at 4am and running throughout the day.

By Bus Monday through Saturday, one bus daily runs between Aurland and Flåm, taking 30 minutes.

By Ferry May to September, two fjord ferries per day cross between Aurland and Flåm, taking 30 minutes.

By Car Road links are possible from Aurland in the north (take Route 601 south).

ESSENTIALS The **telephone area code** for Flåm is 056.

Flåm (pronounced Flawm) lies on the Aurlands Fjord, a tip of the more famous Sognefjord. In the village you can visit the old church dating from 1667, with painted walls done in typical Norwegian country style.

WHERE TO STAY

FRETHEIM HOTELL, N-5743 Flåm. Tel. 056/32-200. Fax 056/32-303. 75 rms (70 with bath). TV TEL
$ Rates (including breakfast): 435 kroner ($72.15) single without bath, 520 kroner ($86.25) single with bath; 820 kroner ($136.05) double without bath, 880 kroner ($146) double with bath. Half board costs 395 kroner ($65.55) per person extra. AE, MC, V.
Dating from the 1860s, this is one of the oldest and most historic hotels in the region. Although its bedrooms have been modernized, its lounges, dining rooms, and public areas have retained the high ceilings, wood paneling, and old-fashioned details of the original construction. In addition to its restaurant (open to nonguests), the hotel also has a moderately priced cafeteria and a bar. It's located across the street from the rail station.

HEIMLY LODGE AND MARINA, N-5743 Flåm. Tel. 056/32-241. 36 rms (8 with bath).
$ Rates (including breakfast): 375 kroner ($62.20) single without bath, 425 kroner ($70.50) single with bath; 575 kroner ($95.40) double without bath, 620 kroner ($102.85) double with bath. AE, MC, V. **Closed:** Nov–Apr.
S Near the end of the electric railway, this lodge was created by Dr. Otto Tokvam some 45 years ago as a ski school. But demand for accommodations in the area led him to create this place which he filled in part with antiques and old-fashioned pieces. It is a frame chalet, with views in many directions. Bedrooms are comfortable and cozy. Tennis, badminton, swimming, waterskiing, salmon and trout fishing, and motorboating along the fjords are all available. Facilities also include a cafeteria with salad bar, and a pub. Lunches begin at 125 kroner ($20.75), and dinner at 140 kroner ($23.25).

---

8. GEILO
149 miles west of Oslo, 149 miles east of Bergen

GETTING THERE By Air Degali Airport is 16 miles from Geilo. **Nørving Airlines** has scheduled flights daily from Oslo, taking 30 minutes, and from Bergen, taking 35 minutes.

By Train Train service takes 2¼ hours from Flåm, 1½ hours from Myrdal, and 4 hours from Oslo or Bergen. Four trains run from either Bergen or Oslo daily.

By Bus Bus connections are possible from Oslo's Central Station, but tourist officials recommend the train as Geilo is on the main rail link between Bergen and Oslo.

By Car From Oslo, head west on Route 7 all the way.

ESSENTIALS The **Turistkontoret** for Geilo (tel. 067/85-206) is in the town center. The **telephone area code** for Geilo is 067. The town doesn't use street addresses, but everything is easy to find.

One of Norway's best-known ski resorts, Geilo, some 2,600 feet above sea level in the Hol mountain district, is also an attractive summer resort. Although it is not in the fjord country, it is included in this chapter because it is a "gateway" to the fjord country on the route from Oslo to Bergen. Geilo lies halfway between Oslo and Bergen.

In the Geilo area, there are 81 miles of marked tracks for cross-country skiing in winter.

WHAT TO SEE & DO

The main ski season is January through March. The **Ski School** has more than two dozen instructors, known for their patience with amateurs. Other amusements include sleigh rides, curling, and skating at the **Geilo Stadium**.

From here you can visit the historical museum in **Hol,** 6 miles northeast of Geilo, to see 16th-century wood carvings, as well as a 12th-century stave church. Another destination is the ancient Viking burial ground at **Fekjo.**

Of course, the chair-lift ride is good for scenery—mountain plateau and fjord. The terminal for the lift is a short walk from the railway station.

WHERE TO STAY

VERY EXPENSIVE

DR. HOLMS HOTEL, N-3580 Geilo. Tel. 067/85-622. Fax 067/86-620. 110 rms (all with bath); 14 suites. MINIBAR TV TEL

$ Rates: Summer (including breakfast), 890 kroner ($147.65) single; 1,580 kroner ($262.15) double. Winter (including half board), 990–1,150 kroner ($164.25–$190.80) single; 1,780–2,060 kroner ($295.30–$341.75) double. Suite supplement from 300 kroner ($49.75) per person. AE, DC, MC, V.

One of the most famous resort hotels in Norway, Dr. Holms is the finest place to stay in the area. Located near the rail station, you get elegance, comfort, and traditional styling. Dr. J. C. Holm opened the hotel in 1909 but since then there has been a lot of changes, including the addition of two completely new wings and a swimming complex. The final facelift was in 1989. The original works of art decorating the hotel have been retained. Rooms are beautifully furnished with traditional styling and many amenities, such as trouser press, radio, and TV with satellite and video channels. Rates can go higher on special weekends in winter.

Over the years many famous guests have stayed here, including ski queen and movie star Sonja Henie, even two generations of Norwegian kings. The Baron Philippe de Rothschild has checked in, as did Emperor Akihito of Japan.

Dining/Entertainment: In days gone by, a world-famous violinist Garaguli performed *Ave Maria* in the main lounge. Artists still perform in the main lounge, or you can enjoy drinks in the three bars, including the Skiers' Bar, the après-ski favorite. Guests can dine in the 400-seat dining room or book a table in the 40-seat Le Monarque, the hotel's specialty restaurant. Camus is the hotel's nightlife venue.

Services: 24-hour room service, baby-sitting.

Facilities: Swimming pool, gym, sauna, library, conservatory, conference center, tennis courts, heated ski stall.

EXPENSIVE

HOTELL ALPIN, N-3580 Geilo. Tel. 067/85-544. 27 rms (all with bath). TV
$ Rates: Summer (including breakfast), 300 kroner ($49.75) single; 380 kroner ($63.05) double. Winter (with half board), 480–1,300 kroner ($79.65–$215.65) single; 700–2,000 kroner ($116.15–$331.80) double. AE, DC, MC, V.
In the center of the village, 500 yards east of the rail station, the Hotell Alpin has an intimate atmosphere with soft lighting and wood paneling in the halls and smaller lounges. The restaurant offers a good à la carte menu, and there's music and dancing during the evening in season. Views from the windows open to the mountains and rivers.

BARDØLA HØYFJELLSHOTEL, N-3580 Geilo. Tel. 067/85-400. Fax 067/86-679. 57 rms (all with bath), 45 suites. MINIBAR TV TEL
$ Rates: Summer (including breakfast), 450–870 kroner ($74.65–$144.35) single; 700–1,295 kroner ($116.15–$214.85) double. Winter (with half board), 670–770 kroner ($111.15–$127.75) per person. Suite supplement 175 kroner ($29.05) per person. AE, DC, MC, V.
In tranquil surroundings in the environs of Geilo, less than a mile from the Geilo rail station, this well-run hotel is inviting in both summer and winter. It has a high standard of comfort, and the largest number of suites of any hotel in the area. Bedrooms and suites are attractively styled and comfortably furnished. On certain winter weekends rates may rise sharply; check carefully when making a booking. Inside is a swimming pool, a Jacuzzi, massage parlor, sun studio, and a hairdressing salon. Outdoor facilities include a heated pool and tennis courts. The hotel enjoys a good reputation for its Chaîne des rôtisseurs cookery. An international band provides entertainment 6 nights a week.

GEILO HOTEL, P.O. Box 113, N-3581 Geilo. Tel. 067/85-511. Fax 067/86-730. 72 rms (all with bath). MINIBAR TV TEL
$ Rates: Summer (including breakfast), 485–625 kroner ($80.45–$103.70) single; 700–800 kroner ($116.15–$132.70) double. Winter (with half board), 625–760 kroner ($103.70–$126.10) single; 990–1,260 kroner ($164.25–$209.05) double. AE, DC, MC, V.
This was the first hotel to open in Geilo, and its oldest part dates from 1880. It was renovated in the summer of 1990 and now its accommodations are better than ever. Rooms are attractively furnished and comfortably appointed. The nearest ski lift is about 200 yards from the hotel. The hotel offers room service and baby-sitting, and has such facilities as a sauna, whirlpool, one restaurant serving Scandinavian food, and two bars. The hotel is 300 yards from the rail station.

MODERATE

VESTLIA HØYFJELLSHOTELL, N-3580 Geilo. Tel. 067/85-611. Fax 067/86-689. 37 rms (all with bath), 38 demi-suites. MINIBAR TV
$ Rates (including breakfast): Summer, 630 kroner ($104.50) double; winter, 900 kroner ($149.30) double. Suite 200 kroner ($33.20) per person. AE, DC, MC, V.
This is not a big fancy hotel, but guests keep coming back. The location is 200 yards from the ski lifts and cross-country slopes, 1 miles from the Geilo rail station. It is also a good summertime choice, as guests go hiking, boating, or even horseback riding. Regular bedrooms, all doubles, are furnished in an attractive ski-chalet style, with lots of wood. Some big family rooms with four beds are available, which cost the same as the regular hotel rooms. The hotel has a swimming pool, sauna, and solarium, plus two restaurants. Scandinavian buffets are served, and live dance music is provided.

INEXPENSIVE

GEILO HØYFJELLSPENSJONAT, N-3581 Geilo. Tel. 067/85-036. Fax 067/86-916. 11 rms (all with bath).
$ Rates: Summer (including breakfast), 280 kroner ($46.45) single; 380 kroner

($63.05) double. Winter (with half board), 340 kroner ($56.40) per person. AE, MC, V.

This boardinghouse is small but rents immaculately clean rooms. It has received guests since 1930 and was renovated in 1989. Families with children are welcomed. Good homemade cooking is offered in the restaurant. Lunch is not served—but instead there are Norwegian open-face sandwiches, with coffee or tea. It's located in the town center, 500 yards from the rail station.

WHERE TO DINE

LE MONARQUE, in the Dr. Holms Hotel. Tel. 85-622.
Cuisine: FRENCH. **Reservations:** Required.
$ Prices: Appetizers 80–150 kroner ($13.25–$24.90); main dishes 190–300 kroner ($31.50–$49.75). AE, DC, MC, V.
Open: Dinner only, daily 7–11pm.

This is the premier restaurant of Geilo, 200 yards from the rail station, long enjoying a reputation for quality food. It is the most exclusive dining spot at the resort, and the decor is richly warm and formal. It lies one floor above street level at Dr. Holms Hotel (see "Where to Stay," above). Main dishes change with the season, but filet of reindeer is a specialty. The finest of European wines is served, including the hotel's own vintage, Château Dr. Holms, produced in the vineyards of France.

GRILL ALPIN, near the tourist office. Tel. 85-384.
Cuisine: STEAKS. **Reservations:** Not required.
$ Prices: Appetizers 45–60 kroner ($7.45–$9.95); main dishes 55–156 kroner ($9.10–$25.90). AE, DC, MC, V.
Open: Dinner only, Tues–Sat 4–10:30pm.

This is a cozy little grill, specializing in steak, located across from the rail station, on the premises of Café Alpin. Other selections include lamb chops, grilled elk steak, and Norwegian-style mutton stew.

CAFE ALPIN, near the tourist office. Tel. 85-384.
Cuisine: NORWEGIAN. **Reservations:** Not required.
$ Prices: Appetizers 22–55 kroner ($3.65–$9.10); main dishes 35–114 kroner ($5.80–$18.90). AE, DC, MC, V.
Open: Mon–Sat 9am–7pm, Sun 11am–7pm.

On the second floor, above the bank and next to the tourist bureau, this café is the best economy dining choice in town. It's good for coffee, sandwiches, or a hot meal. The cafeteria serves a three-course dinner from noon, and diners may order from the à la carte menu until 10pm in the grill room.

If it's on the menu, try the creamed fish soup. For main dishes, you may want to try such Norwegian specialties as chopped reindeer meatcakes with mixed vegetables or cured herring with sliced beets, raw onions, and boiled potatoes. For dessert, a tempting selection of Norwegian pastries is offered.

EVENING ENTERTAINMENT

NIGHTCLUB CAMUS, in the Dr. Holms Hotel. Tel. 85-622.
Open only in winter, this is the chic dance club of the resort. It's likely to feature either recorded or live music in a sophisticated ambience on the lobby level of the Dr. Holms Hotel (see "Where to Stay," above), 200 yards from the rail station. No jeans are permitted, and it's best to dress up a bit. A beer will cost 35 kroner ($5.80). It's open October to April, Monday through Saturday from 9pm to 2am.
Admission: 40 kroner ($6.65); free for hotel residents.

CHAPTER 19

KRISTIANSAND S, STAVANGER & SOUTHERN NORWAY

The coastal lands of southern Norway, shaped geographically like a half moon, are often called Norway's Riviera because of their beaches, bays, and sailing opportunities. Within this area, the Telemark region is known for its lakes and canals which are used for summer boating and canoeing. From Skien visitors can explore this water network. Arendal is a charming old town with a harbor near some of the best beaches. Kristiansand S is a link between Norway and the rest of Europe. The Christiansholm Fortress has stood here since 1674, and the town is near a 6-mile-long beach, Haresanden. In the western part of the region, the Lysefjord, Sandefjord, and the Vindefjord are easily accessible from Stavanger, the largest city in southern Norway.

The southern part of Norway is called Sørlandet, a land of hills, valleys, mountains, rivers, and lakes. The area gets more sunshine than any other place in Norway and northern Europe. Gulf Stream temperatures make bathing possible in summer. This section is the major domestic vacation choice for Norwegians.

Rogaland is the southwestern part of the country, and it has been called "Norway in a nutshell" because of its great variety of nature. Fjords, mountains, green valleys, beaches, old towns and villages, a mild climate, and countless fishing possibilities make this a vacation land.

The district lives today in the technological future, thanks to its oil industry, but it also harks back to the country's oldest inhabitants. Here, the Viking king Harald Fairhair gathered most of Norway into one kingdom in A.D. 872. The locals say that it was from here that the Vikings sailed to discover America.

Rogaland also consists of the hilly Dalane in the south, the flat Jaeren (farmland), the beautiful Ryfylke, and in the north, Karmøy and Haugesund.

SEEING SOUTHERN NORWAY
GETTING THERE

If you're flying or taking the train, Stavanger in the southwest or Kristiansand S in the center of the southern coast make the best gateways to the area and also have the most frequent connections. Fred Olsen Lines sails between Denmark and Kristiansand S daily all year if you're in Denmark and want to begin your exploration of Norway in its southern tier.

If you're driving from Oslo, you can travel all the way to Stavanger on a good

WHAT'S SPECIAL ABOUT SOUTHERN NORWAY

Great Towns/Villages
- ☐ Skien, Henrik Ibsen's hometown, the best center for touring the old and historic county of Telemark.
- ☐ Stavanger, a historic, well-preserved old town, an oil boom center, and an excursion base for fjord tours.
- ☐ Kristiansand S, founded by Christian IV, the best center for exploring the "Norwegian Riviera."

Museums
- ☐ Aust-Agder Museet, at Arendal, one of the country's oldest, showcasing the folklore of the Norwegian south.
- ☐ Vest Agder Fylkes, at Kristiansand S, one of Norway's largest open-air museums.

Ancient Monuments
- ☐ The Heddal Stave Church, at Heddal, dating from the 1240s, one of Norway's best preserved.

Scenic Wonders
- ☐ The Telemark Canal, a scenic journey through lock and lake deep in the heart of folkloric region.
- ☐ Pulpit Rock, outside Stavanger, towering 1,800 feet above the Lysefjord.

Cool for Kids
- ☐ Kristiansand S Zoo, set on 100 acres, with many exotic animals and many from the Nordic climes.

Literary Pilgrimages
- ☐ Venstøp Farm, near Skien, the childhood home of Henrik Ibsen, filled with family memorabilia.

Special Events/Festivals
- ☐ The North Sea Festival, a sea-fishing festival at Haugesund in June.

---

express highway, the E18. It or its subsidiary routes connect most of the places recommended in this chapter.

If you're in the west of Norway at Bergen, it's best either to fly to Stavanger or to take the hydrofoil or car-ferry.

A SUGGESTED ITINERARY

Day 1: From Oslo, go south to Ibsen's hometown of Skien for a 2-night stopover. See the sights of Skien.

Day 2: Take the 10-hour trip up the Telemark Canal.

Day 3: Returning to the E18, continue southwest for a third night in the Arendal area which has many interesting sights.

Day 4: Explore Kristiansand S and spend the night.

Day 5 & 6: Drive or board the train to Stavanger, taking fjord cruises and exploring its Old Town.

---

1. SKIEN

86 miles south of Oslo, 19 miles west of
the Larvik–Frederikshavn (Denmark) ferry connection

GETTING THERE   By Plane   Daily flights arrive from Oslo at Skien Airport, 2 miles from the town center.

By Train   From Oslo's Central Station, the Vestfold express train goes first to Larvik and then to Skien. Skien is also the beginning of another rail link to Oslo via Kongsberg and Drammen. Trip time to Oslo is 3 hours.

By Bus   Daily buses arrive from the Central Station in Oslo. Skien is also the center for buses branching out to the Telemark district. If you plan to tour Telemark by bus, call Ruteopplysningen (tel. 52-79-74) for schedules.

By Car   Take the E18 south from Oslo.

ESSENTIALS   The **Skien Turistkontor** is at Kongensgate 31 (tel. 03/52-82-27). The **telephone area code** for Skien is 03.

Skien is a bustling industrial town and the administrative capital of Telemark county. Long proud of its association with playwright Henrik Ibsen (1828–1906), a native of Skien, it is visited not only for its Ibsen associations, but because it is the principal gateway to Telemark.

Skien is an old town, dating from 1100, although it wasn't until 1358 that it received its royal charter. It has been ravished by fire and floods over the centuries, several of which destroyed the town. The last disastrous fire occurred in 1886, and a new town had to be created out of the debris. Skien covers an area of 489 square miles, with nearly 50,000 inhabitants.

WHAT TO SEE & DO

Ibsen left Skien in 1843 when he was 15 years old, returning only briefly as part of an unsuccessful attempt to borrow some money to enter prep school in Oslo. He lived at several addresses in Skien, including a small house in an old neighborhood, Snipetorp 27, near the town center. The house on Snipetorp is one of several in the neighborhood that have been proclaimed protected monuments. Ibsen's former home is now a cultural center and an art gallery.

VENSTØP FARM, Venstøp. Tel. 52-57-49.

Ibsen's childhood home, Venstøp Farm is furnished with objects actually used by the Ibsen family as well as period pieces. The building dates from the early 1800s. Two paintings are by Ibsen—he had originally wanted to become an artist, but his wife ("the cat") insisted that he be a playwright, thus (in her words) giving the world a great dramatic talent but sparing it a mediocre artist. The farm is 3 miles north of the town center.

Admission: 10 kroner ($1.65) adults, 5 kroner (85¢) children.

Open: June–Sept 1, daily noon–4pm. **Closed:** Sept 2–May.

HISTORICAL MUSEUM OF TELEMARK, Brekkepark. Tel. 52-35-94.

This museum displays some 20 old buildings from different districts of Telemark. The museum collections feature folk and national costumes, textiles, handcrafts, and woodcarving. Some buildings are furnished with authentic pieces, ranging from the Renaissance to Victorian days. A special section is centered on Henrik Ibsen. A restaurant and open-air theater are found in the park.

Admission: 10 kroner ($1.65) adults, 5 kroner (85¢) children.

Open: May 12–June 23, Tues–Sat 10am–2pm, Sun noon–6pm; June 24–Sept 1, Tues–Sat noon–4pm, Sun noon–6pm. **Closed:** Sept 2–May 11.

WHERE TO STAY

RICA IBSEN HOTEL, Kongensgate 33, N-3700 Skien. Tel. 03/52-49-90.
Fax 03/52-61-86. 199 rms (all with bath). MINIBAR TV TEL.

$ Rates (including breakfast): Mon–Thurs (except midsummer), 950 kroner ($157.60) single; 1,100 kroner ($182.50) double. Midsummer and Fri–Sun year round, 575 kroner ($95.40) single; 750 kroner ($124.40) double. AE, DC, MC, V.

Parking: Garage available.

This well-rated hotel stands near Brekkepark where Ibsen is said to have received much of his early inspiration. A stylish hotel, considered the best in town, it was designed and built in 1979 of red brick and panes of insulated glass. It boasts an interior jammed with many trees, creating a greenhouse. Each room is well furnished and maintained and decorated with contemporary styling. Twelve rooms are reserved for nonsmokers and there is also a no-smoking area in the breakfast room. It's located in the center of Skien, a quarter mile from the rail station.

Dining/Entertainment: The hotel restaurant is Susannah's (see "Where to Dine," below), and there's also a dance bar (Susi), a bar lounge, and a nightclub.

Services: Room service.

Facilities: Indoor swimming pool, sauna, solarium, private garage.

HØYERS HOTELL, Kongensgate 6, N-3701 Skien. Tel. 03/52-05-40. Fax 03/52-26-08. 70 rms (all with bath). MINIBAR TV TEL.

$ Rates (including breakfast): Mon–Thurs (except midsummer), 620 kroner ($102.85) single; 780 kroner ($129.40) double. Midsummer and Fri–Sun year round, 420 kroner ($69.70) single; 520 kroner ($86.25) double. AE, DC, MC, V.

Long a traditional favorite, the hotel was originally built in 1900, and it stands today in the center of gardens stretching to the water. A 3-minute taxi ride from the rail station, it offers some of the best bedrooms in town, each comfortably and attractively furnished. Five are reserved for nonsmokers. Facilities include a dance restaurant (see "Where to Dine," below), a fully licensed bar, and a solarium.

WHERE TO DINE

BODEN SPISERI, Langbryggene 5. Tel. 52-61-70.
   Cuisine: NORWEGIAN. **Reservations:** Required.
$ Prices: Appetizers 40–60 kroner ($6.65–$9.95); main dishes 120–190 kroner ($19.90–$31.50). AE, DC, MC, V.
   Open: Dinner only, Mon–Fri 3:30pm–midnight, Sat 6pm–midnight, Sun 3–9pm.

⭐ Although it was established as recently as 1987, this quickly became known as the town's most charmingly old-fashioned restaurant. A 10-minute walk south of the station, it's in a clapboard-sided building originally erected as a harborfront warehouse more than a century ago. The staff speaks English. For their specialties, try cured filet of venison in thin slices as an appetizer, followed perhaps by filet of reindeer with juniper berries, and a medley of fresh vegetables: broccoli, cauliflower, and grilled tomatoes. The preferred dish of many clients is a three-fish casserole studded with mussels and shrimp and served in a wine-based cream sauce.

SUSANNAH'S RESTAURANT, in the Rica Ibsen Hotel, Kongensgate 33. Tel. 52-49-90.
   Cuisine: NORWEGIAN. **Reservations:** Recommended.
$ Prices: Appetizers 50–90 kroner ($8.30–$14.95); main dishes 110–220 kroner ($18.25–$36.50). AE, DC, MC, V.
   Open: Daily 11am–11pm.

This restaurant is filled with the same bounty of trees and flowers that adorn the "greenhouse lobby." It is a big-windowed restaurant that later in the evening becomes a dance place where older, conservative couples come to have a good time. Fresh fish, lamb, and Norwegian beef are featured. It's on the ground floor of the Rica Ibsen Hotel (see "Where to Stay," above), in the center of Skien a quarter mile from the train station.

RESTAURANT COUENAR, in the Høyers Hotell, Kongensgate 6. Tel. 52-05-40.
   Cuisine: NORWEGIAN. **Reservations:** Recommended.
$ Prices: Appetizers 45–55 kroner ($7.45–$9.10); main dishes 78–110 kroner ($12.95–$18.25); smørbrød 20–70 kroner ($3.30–$11.60). AE, DC, MC, V.
   Open: Daily 11am–11pm.

This is a good choice for moderately priced food served at the oldest and most traditional hotel in town half a mile south of the rail station. During the day many locals drop in for smørbrød. But the kitchen also prepares substantial meals, including excellent Norwegian fish dishes, such as river salmon and fjord shrimp. Reindeer and game are also featured. After 10pm, the restaurant becomes a nightclub. Hotel guests are admitted free, but others pay a 70-krone ($11.60) cover charge.

EASY EXCURSIONS IN TELEMARK

From Skien you can take a famous boat tour up the ✪ **Telemark Canal.** Both the M/S *Victoria* and the M/S *Telemarken* run the stretch between Skien and Dalen, deep in Telemark, a 10-hour trip on this inland waterway, at a cost of 150 kroner ($24.90). You go through lock and lake. Departures from Skien are at 8:30am. When the boat stops to negotiate the locks, you are allowed to get off and stroll the canal banks. Bookings are possible in Skien through **Telemarksreiser,** Nedre Hjellegate 18 (tel. 52-92-05).

Once at Dalen, Route 37 leads north to **Rjukan,** the center of southern Norway. This sleepy town once played a major role in world history, as depicted in the Kirk Douglas film *The Heroes of Telemark*. In 1943 the valley was heavily guarded by Nazi troops, as the Germans were working here on the first atomic bomb experiments to develop "heavy water." Norwegian saboteurs, in the face of incredible odds, managed to climb down the steep, icy gulch to blow up the Vemork Plant of Norsk Hydro. The towering peak of Mount Gausta at 6,000 feet prevents the sun from shining on Rjukan for 5 months every year.

Alternatively, near Dalen, you can join the E76 leading east back to Oslo. But stop at the ✪ **Heddal Stave Church,** in Heddal, directly west of Notodden (tel. 036/20-250 for information). This is the largest of the preserved Norwegian stave churches. Erected in the 1240s and dedicated to the Virgin Mary, it has fine carved portals with traditional dragon-and-tendril ornamentations and fantastic human figures. The structure is 85 feet high and 65 feet long, and contains a dozen columns inside. It is considered the architectural wonder of southern Norway. The bishop's chair inside is from the end of the 17th century. It is open May 15 to June 20, daily from 10am to 5pm; June 21 to August 25, daily from 9am to 7pm; and August 26 to September 15, daily from 10am to 5pm (closed September 15 to May 14). Admission is 12 kroner ($2) for adults, free for children.

2. ARENDAL

149 miles SW of Oslo, 43 miles east of Kristiansand S

GETTING THERE   By Train   Four trains a day arrive from Oslo, requiring a change of trains at Nelaug. Trip time, including the transfer, is 4½ hours.

By Bus   There is direct bus service daily from Oslo, with two or three stops along the way; trip time is 4 hours. The name of the bus leaving from Oslo is Sorlandsekpressen, destination Oslo/Arendal/Kristiansand S.

By Hydrofoil   From June 15 to August 15, hydrofoils link Arendal and Oslo. Departures are at 9am from in front of the Rådhuset in Oslo and take 5 hours. The cost is 220 kroner ($36.50) each way. The scenery is breathtaking.

By Car   Take the E18 west from Oslo.

ESSENTIALS   The **Arendal Tourist Office** lies in the heart of the Old Town at Nedre Tyholmsveien 7B (tel. 041/22-193). The **telephone area code** for Arendal is 041.

The administrative center of the Aust-Agder district, this southern port city was once known as "the Venice of Scandinavia," because of its canals. But following a disastrous fire, they were turned into wide streets. Its sheltered harbor is one of the most colorful along the coast.

For the best look at old Arendal, go to **Tyholmen** in the center, with its handsomely preserved wooden houses of the 18th century. In summer, the harbor, **Pollen,** is filled with boats and people, as this is one of the most popular centers for domestic tourism in Norway. Many Norwegians come here to take boat trips among the neighboring skerries, and they also traverse the delta of the Nid River.

WHAT TO SEE & DO

ARENDAL RÅDHUSET, Rådhusgate 10. Tel. 22-980.

The Rådhuset, or Town Hall, in the center of town, still houses the administrative offices of the city. It's better known as the second-largest timber building in Norway and the country's single tallest timber structure. Built in 1815, the building has some 300 antique portraits, most of them painted in the 19th century, the largest such collection in Norway.

Admission: Free. English-language guided tours cost 15 kroner ($2.50).
Open: Mon–Fri 9am–3pm.

AUST-AGDER MUSEET, Parkveien 16. Tel. 22-422.

This museum, established in 1858, is one of the largest and most important in the country. Showcasing the folklore of the region, it is filled with memorabilia of the history of the town, mainly artifacts relating to its seafaring heyday. The museum is 1 mile north of the town center; to reach it, follow the signs in the direction of Oslo.

Admission: 10 kroner ($1.65).
Open: Mon–Fri 8:30am–3:30pm, Sat–Sun noon–3pm.

WHERE TO STAY

TYHOLMEN HOTEL, Teaterplassen 2, N-4800 Arendal. Tel. 041/26-800.

Fax 041/26-801. 54 rms (all with bath). TV TEL.
$ Rates (including breakfast): Sun–Thurs Sept–May, 940 kroner ($155.95) single; 1,100 kroner ($182.50) double. June–Aug and Fri–Sat year round, 580 kroner ($96.20) single; 720 kroner ($119.45) double. AE, DC, MC, V.

Enjoying dramatic views of one of Norway's loveliest harbors, this hotel is the most interesting in town. Architecturally, it was inspired by the 1800s, the heyday of the sailing vessels that put Arendal on the map. It offers handsomely furnished and comfortably appointed bedrooms—try for a harbor view. The hotel has an outdoor restaurant, Bryggekanten, which is a summer favorite, and a lounge bar, Åtte Glass. There is also a coffee shop, Spiseriet. Its glamorous restaurant, Tre Seil, and its steakhouse, Ruffan, are recommended separately (see "Where to Dine," below). It's a 2-minute walk south of the bus station.

WHERE TO DINE

RUFFAN, in the Tyholmen Hotel, Teaterplassen 2. Tel. 26-800.

Cuisine: STEAKS. **Reservations:** Recommended.
$ Prices: Appetizers 62–119 kroner ($10.30–$19.75); main dishes 170–260 kroner ($28.20–$43.15). AE, DC, MC, V.
Open: Dinner only, daily 6–11pm.

For people with hearty appetites, this is one of the favored dining spots of town, a 2-minute walk south of the bus station. It is a cozy cellar kind of place located in the Tyholmen Hotel (see "Where to Stay," above). Its decor is strongly nautical. Appetizers might include a West Indian–inspired dish of minced shrimp with chili peppers toasted with grilled avocado and served with soy sauce. The chef makes excellent stuffed baked potatoes and such standard fare as lamb chops and chicken. But most guests visit for the specialty, grilled steaks, coming in many different sizes and cuts.

TRE SEIL, in the Tyholmen Hotel, Teaterplassen 2. Tel. 26-800.

Cuisine: NORWEGIAN. **Reservations:** Recommended.
$ Prices: Appetizers 62–119 kroner ($10.30–$19.75); main dishes 150–160 kroner ($24.90–$26.55). AE, DC, MC, V.
Open: Dinner only, Mon–Sat 6–11pm, Sun 1–6pm.

"Three Sails" is the most prestigious restaurant in town, a 2-minute walk south of the bus station. Its decor is nautical, and big windows look out over the moored yachts and boats in the harbor. You can enjoy excellent cuisine and formal service. Try, for example, salmon with sour-cream sauce and Norwegian crabs; large prawns gratinée with garlic, herbs, and butter; or an unusual dish from north-central Norway—grilled filet of reindeer saddle served next to grilled filet of salmon and accompanied by sautéed mushrooms and vegetables.

BOTANICA, in the Phønix Hotel, Tyholmen. Tel. 25-160.
   Cuisine: NORWEGIAN/FRENCH. **Reservations:** Not required.
$ **Prices:** Appetizers 58–65 kroner ($9.60–$10.80); main dishes 80–185 kroner ($14.75–$30.70); smørbrød 20–70 kroner ($3.30–$11.60). DC, MC, V.
   Open: Mon–Sat 10am–midnight, Sun 1pm–midnight.
The decor, as befits the restaurant's name, has plants and a red-and-green color scheme. Lunch here is unpretentious and simple. Many prefer to take one of the selections of smørbrød. There is also an impressive salad bar priced at 49 kroner ($8.15) if you'd like to make a main meal of it. Dinner is more elaborate, including such dishes as prawn cocktail or escargots bourguignons to get you going, followed by such tasty dishes as deep-fried scrod or pepper steak. The place is a quarter mile from the train station.

EASY EXCURSIONS

In the bay of Arendal, **Merdøy Island** is like getting caught in a time capsule. It is virtually intact architecturally from its prosperous 19th-century seafaring days. Today its clapboard-sided houses still have their allure.

There are no restaurants, only a small café, and lovely bathing beach.

The **Merdøgård Museum** on the island is run by the Aust-Agder Museum (see "What to See & Do," above), which you should call for information. This museum is a perfectly preserved early 19th-century house, with the furnishings intact, of a long-departed sea captain. A guardian lives on the premises to show you around. It's open from early June to late August, daily from 8:30am to 3:30pm, charging 10 kroner ($1.65) for admission.

To reach the island, take a ferry departing from Pollen at Arendal's harborfront. Departures are three or four times daily, and the boat makes stops at two or three other islands before reaching Merdøy. The ferry costs 15 kroner ($2.50) each way, and the trip takes 20 minutes. The tourist office (see above) will supply you with exact departure times, which change frequently.

Twelve miles west of the center of Arendal is Grimstad, site of the **Grimstad Bymuseum-Ibsenhuset,** on Henrik Ibsen Gate, in the center of town. Henrik Ibsen worked in this town at a pharmacy, while pressing his suit for the pharmacist's daughter. Ibsen wrote his first play, *Catalina,* here. The Grimstad museum includes the old pharmacy and Ibsen's house. It's open May to September, daily from 9am to 8pm. Admission is 20 kroner ($3.30).

Farther afield, **Northølm,** Route 7, E18 (N-4890 Grimstad), 4 miles west of Grimstad, is open June to August, Monday through Friday from 9am to 3pm, charging 10 kroner ($1.65) for admission. The former home of Knut Hamsun is today privately owned, so hours are subject to change. Winning the Nobel Prize in 1918, this writer, called the "Balzac of Norway," purchased this residence, which he turned into a model farm. His novels gave a vivid portrait of 19th-century Norwegian values. Much memorabilia of Hamsun remains in the house. His works are still very popular in Germany, almost more so than they are in Norway.

3. KRISTIANSAND S

213 miles west of Oslo
327 miles east of Bergen, 213 miles west of Oslo

GETTING THERE **By Plane** Kristiansand Municipal Airport is located at Kjevik, 10 miles out of town. Both Braathens SAFE and SAS airlines service the town.

By Train   Five trains a day connect Kristiansand S with Oslo, taking 4 to 5 hours, depending on the train.

By Bus   Kristiansand S is connected by bus to Oslo, with one departure daily, taking 7½ hours.

By Ferry   International ferries link Kristiansand S to Hirtshals, in the northern part of Jutland in Denmark. Ferries cross once or twice daily, depending on the time of year, taking 4 hours.

By Car   Take the E18 west from Oslo or the E18 east from Stavanger.

ESSENTIALS   Go to **Turist information,** Henrik Wergelandsgata 17 (tel. 042/95-369). The **telephone area code** for Kristianstand S is 042.

People heading to Bergen and the fjord country often arrive in Norway at Kristiansand S (not to be confused with Kristiansand N in the north). The biggest city and an important port of Sørlandet (the south coast), Kristiansand S has been called "the pearl of the Norwegian Riviera."

Founded by King Christian in 1641, Kristiansand S is a busy port and industrial center, yet it has many charming old streets and antique houses clustered cozily together. Water surrounds the city.

Kristiansand S is the largest town in the south and Norway's largest ferry port. **Kvadraturen,** "the quadrant," is known for its right-angled street plan that was influenced by the Renaissance period's strict adherence to form. **Markens** is the town's pedestrian precinct and meeting place.

WHAT TO SEE & DO

It's worth a visit to **Christiansholm Fort,** at Østre Havn, dating back to 1674 and often the center of local handcraft exhibitions; the **Fish Quay,** with its troughs and tanks full of live fish; and **Kristiansand Cathedral,** Kirkegaten (tel. 24-789), one of the largest churches in Norway. Built in the Neo-Gothic style, it was dedicated in 1885. It is open May 1 to September 1, daily from 10am to 4pm.

One of the oldest and most beautiful parish churches in the area is **Oddernes Klokkerkontor,** Jegersbergeveien 6, a mile from the town center, reached by bus no. 22. The midnave and choir were built around 1040. May to early September, the church is open Monday through Friday from 9am to 2pm; to visit it at other times, call 90-187 at least a day in advance.

VEST AGDER FYLKES-MUSEUM, Kongsgard, Vigeveien 22B. Tel. 90-228.

One of the largest open-air museums in Norway, it contains nearly 30 farm and city buildings moved to the site. Some are equipped with provincial furnishings, glass, and stoneware. It's a short distance from the town center.

Admission: 5 kroner (85¢) adults, 2 kroner (35¢) children.

Open: June 20–Aug 20, Mon–Sat 10am–6pm, Sun noon–6pm. **Closed:** Aug 21–June 19.

GIMLE GÅRD MUSEUM, Gimleveien 23. Tel. 92-388.

Built in the early 1800s, this museum contains 18th-century furniture and 17th- and 18th-century European paintings. It's a mile east of Kristiansand S, near the E18 and the Oddernes Church.

Admission: 20 kroner ($3.30) adults, 5 kroner (85¢) children.

Open: May–Sept, Tues–Sun noon–3pm. **Closed:** Oct–Apr.

KRISTIANSAND ZOO. Tel. 46-200.

This 100-acre **zoo** contains many exotic specimens, including some Nordic species. Animals roam in large open enclosures. Norway's biggest **amusement park** is on the same grounds, containing "Troll Valley," a playland, a bobsled track, a water slide, an amphitheater, and a goldmining town. It's located 7 miles east of Kristiansand S on the E18.

Admission: 100 kroner ($16.60) adults, 80 kroner ($13.25) children.
Open: Zoo and park, summer, daily 10am–7pm; winter, daily 10am–4pm.

NEARBY ATTRACTIONS

The **Setesdalsbanen** (tel. 56-482) runs a steam train along 3 miles of narrow-gauge track. The locomotive, dating from 1901, starts its run at Grovane, 12½ miles from Kristiansand, leaving at 11:30am, 1pm and 2:30pm on Sunday from mid-June to the end of August. Fares are 25 kroner ($4.15) for adults and 15 kroner ($2.50) for children along the Grovane–Beihklen run. Take bus no. 30 or 31.

The countryside surrounding Kristiansand consists of rolling meadows, birch-clad hills, deep valleys, and mountain moors; you'll see the nicest scenery along the E18 either going east or west.

West of **Mandal** stands Norway's southernmost point, with a lighthouse dating from 1655. The Dutch town of **Flekkefjord** on the Grise Fjord, with its low wooden buildings, narrow twisting streets, and warehouses, is particularly worth seeing.

A drive along Route 9 toward the **Setesdal and Sirdal moors** offers a variety of scenery and the chance to view traditional Norwegian life.

Kristiansand's sightseeing boat, **M/B Maarten,** tours the idyllic offshore islands leaving mid-June to mid-August, weekdays from the fish quay at 10am. In July there are also departures at 1 and 3pm.

WHERE TO STAY

Some hotels in Kristiansand offer up to a 40% discount from mid-June to mid-August. The prices include rooms with bath or shower, toilet, and breakfast—sometimes even the luncheon buffet.

EXPENSIVE

CALEDONIEN, Vestre Strandgate 7, N-4601 Kristiansand S. Tel. 042/ 29-100. Fax 042/25-990. 205 rms (all with bath). MINIBAR TV TEL.
$ **Rates** (including breakfast): Mon–Thurs (except midsummer), 1,095 kroner ($181.65) single; 1,230 kroner ($204.05) double. Midsummer and weekends year round, 550 kroner ($91.25) single; 740 kroner ($122.75) double. AE, DC, MC, V.

This prestigious hotel is considered the largest full-service hotel in the southern part of Norway, and it's within walking distance of the rail station, bus station, and ferry terminal. Theater, cinema, and shopping areas are nearby. Bedrooms are modern and stylish, and each is equipped with a number of amenities.

Dining/Entertainment: The hotel's Café Jens is a popular all-day rendezvous for light meals and drink, and the Constance Restaurant seats 170, serving both international and Norwegian food. Other nighttime venues include the Carat Dance Bar, the DeCapo Piano Bar, the CD Discothèque, and Telford's Pub.

Services: Room service, baby-sitting.
Facilities: Garage, wheelchair access.

ERNST PARK HOTEL, Rådhusgata 2, N-4601 Kristiansand S. Tel. 042/ 21-400. Fax 042/20-307. 109 rms (all with bath), 4 suites. MINIBAR TV TEL.
$ **Rates** (including breakfast): 790–1,045 kroner ($131.05–$173.35) single; 995–1,150 kroner ($165.05–$190.80) doubles; from 1,300 kroner ($215.65) suites. Special summer discounts granted on request (variable). AE, DC, MC, V.

Since this hotel opened more than 130 years ago, it has been the traditional favorite for a southern stopover. The hotel was completely renovated in 1988, but care was taken to preserve its classic look. The hotel is beautifully run and managed, and the bedrooms have contemporary styling and many amenities for a comfortable stay. Each has video, trouser press, and hairdryer. It's 200 yards from the central bus terminal, rail station, and ferry dock.

Dining/Entertainment: The Restaurant Børsen, the main restaurant of the hotel, has an English atmosphere, whereas the Brasserie Børsen is an informal indoor/outdoor restaurant with a conservatory. The lobby bar, near the conservatory, is called the Børsen Bar, and the hotel's nightclub is Night Ca. On the ground floor is a pub, Øl & Vinstuen.

Services: Laundry/dry cleaning, secretarial services, room service; helpful reception desk.

Facilities: Basement parking (request when booking room), *biblioteket* (library).

MODERATE

RICA FREGATTAN HOTEL, Dronningensgata 66-68, N-4601 Kristiansand S. Tel. 042/21-500. 47 rms (all with bath). TV TEL.

$ Rates: 520 kroner ($86.25) single; 680 kroner ($112.80) double. AE, DC, MC, V.

Its proximity to the water makes the Rica Fregattan a good choice for boaters. The bedrooms have modern furnishings. The establishment's social center is a pub with brass embellishments. It's in the town center, a half mile from the rail station.

INEXPENSIVE

HOTEL BONDEHEIMEN, Kirkegaten 15, N-4611 Kristiansand S. Tel. 042/24-440. 36 rms (all with bath). TEL.

$ Rates (including breakfast): Mon–Thurs Aug 21–June 24, 340–480 kroner ($56.40–$79.65) single; 620 kroner ($102.85) double. June 25–Aug 20 and weekends year round, 280–340 kroner ($46.45–$56.40); 540 kroner ($89.60) double. AE, MC, V. **Parking:** Available.

In the town center near the bus terminal, the Bondeheimen has comfortable and adequately furnished rooms. It has lounges and a cafeteria offering Norwegian food until 5pm.

WHERE TO DINE

BAKGÅRDEN, Tollbodgate 5. Tel. 27-955.
   Cuisine: NORWEGIAN/INTERNATIONAL. **Reservations:** Required. **Bus:** 1, 10.
   $ Prices: Appetizers 48–64 kroner ($7.95–$10.60); main dishes 147–190 kroner ($24.40–$31.50). AE, DC, MC, V.
   Open: Dinner only, Mon–Sat 6–11pm.

This is a well-established and good restaurant lying in a turn-of-the-century building whose interior is accented with bare wooden tables, wooden chairs, and a collection of oil-burning lamps. The food is an unending festival celebrating southern Europe, with additional flair added by borrowing recipes from around the world, although dishes are tailored to local palates. Appetizers might include a Mexican ceviche, or snails in garlic butter followed by grilled filet of pheasant with grapes or tenderloin steak with mussels. The food is the most imaginative in town.

SJØHUSET (Sea House), Østre Strandgate 12A. Tel. 26-260.
   Cuisine: NORWEGIAN/FRENCH. **Reservations:** Required in midsummer. **Bus:** 1, 10.
   $ Prices: Appetizers 50–60 kroner ($8.30–$9.95); main dishes 150–190 kroner ($24.90–$31.50). AE, DC, MC, V.
   Open: June–July, daily 11:30am–midnight; Aug–May, Mon–Sat 3pm–midnight.

Set directly on the harborfront in the center of town, this restaurant is in a century-old former warehouse whose oxblood-red clapboard-sided walls are still distinctive. Inside, you see the massive structural beams of its original construction and a blazing stone-sided fireplace. In summer, guests prefer the waterfront terrace instead. Specialties include an assorted platter of fish, including anglerfish, salmon, and a third type determined by the day's catch. The fish is poached in white wine and served with a Noilly Prat sauce along with shrimp, asparagus, and rice. The meat specialty is chateaubriand with a béarnaise sauce.

4. STAVANGER

100 miles south of Bergen, 376 miles west of Oslo

GETTING THERE By Plane Flights land at **Stavanger International Airport** at Sola from Copenhagen, Esbjerg/Århus, Gothenburg, London, Newcastle, Glasgow, Aberdeen, Amsterdam, and Paris, with good connections from Bergen and Oslo. An SAS bus will take you to the town center 25 kroner ($4.15).

By Train Three trains a day cross Norway from Oslo to Stavanger, taking 9 hours.

By Bus Stavanger has bus links with Kristiansand S, running once or twice a day, taking 5 hours.

By Ferry In Bergen, it's better to take a car-ferry, the *Kystveien* to Stavanger, as driving there will take you on a 93-mile detour that includes three ferry crossings. In Bergen tickets are issued on board, but vehicles must be booked in advance (tel. 05/14-11-00 between 8am and 3:30pm). The fare is 160 kroner ($26.55) for adults and 100 kroner ($16.60) for children. The ferry lands at Randaberg, north of Stavanger. Route 14 takes you the rest of the way there.

By Car From Kristiansand S, continue west until you reach the end of the E18 in Stavanger.

By Hydrofoil From Bergen, connections take 4½ hours. There are two or three daily departures.

ESSENTIALS The **Tourist Pavilion,** Box 11, N-4001 Stavanger (tel. 04/53-51-00), is next to the railway station. The **telephone area code** for Stavanger is 04.
 A **Stavanger Card,** free to visitors staying in Stavanger hotels, offers a 50% reduction on Flaggrutens high-speed boats between Stavanger and Bergen, the same discount on all scheduled buses in Stavanger, and a 25% discount on Westamaran services. The card, obtainable only in Stavanger (ask at your hotel) also grants discounts at cinemas, theaters, museums, car-rental agencies, city and fjord sightseeing trips, and the Kongeparken amusement park.

Stavanger, Norway's fourth-largest town, on the Ryfylkefjord, has always been a bustling seaport with a thriving fish-canning industry. Today it's also the oil capital of Norway—although this has made it more cosmopolitan, it remains a charming seaport amid beautiful surroundings. The old marketplace, where fish and vegetables have been sold since the 9th century, is set against the cathedral, dating from 1125.

WHAT TO SEE & DO

Gamle Stavanger, in the heart of town, is filled with some 150 wooden houses, cobblestone streets, climbing steep hills, fascinating quays, and well-preserved old homes, some with picket fences. It is considered northern Europe's best-preserved wooden-house settlement. It was built at the end of the 17th and 18th centuries with money brought home by seafarers.
 The **Stavanger Domkirke,** Haakon VII's Gate 7 (tel. 52-42-61), which faces the marketplace, is one of Norway's most outstanding medieval monuments, dedicated around 1125. After a fire in 1272, the Gothic-style chancel was added. The magnificent 1125 Norman-style nave remains. See the fine memorial tablets and the enormous pulpit, outstanding examples of baroque art in Norway.
 It's open mid-May to mid-September, Monday through Saturday from 9am to

6pm and on Sunday from 1 to 6pm; in other months, daily from 9am to 2pm. Sunday service is at 11am.

There are many opportunities to see goldsmiths, silversmiths, and enamel workers at their crafts in and around Stavanger. For details, call the tourist office (see above).

The **Stavanger Museum** consists of three parts. Archeology, zoology, cultural history, and local crafts exhibits can be seen at **Musegate 16.** The **Maritime Museum,** Nedre Strandgaten 17–19, contains exhibits on local shipbuilding, the Stavanger harbor, the herring room (1808–70), a general store, and a ship/store owner's dwelling. The **Canning Museum,** Øvre Strandgaten 88, is a restored canning factory with production facilities intact. For information about the museums or the mansions below, phone 52-60-35. All are open mid-June to mid-August, Tuesday through Sunday from 11am to 3pm; the remainder of the year, Sunday only, from 11am to 3pm. Admission is 10 kroner ($1.65) for adults, free for children.

The **Ullandhaugh Tower,** 3 miles from the center, offers a gorgeous view. Take bus no. 10, departing from St. Olavsgården and heading for Gosen. The one-way fare is 10 kroner ($1.65).

The **Norwegian Emigration Center,** Bergjelandsgata 30 (tel. 50-12-67), is the headquarters for tracing ancestors who went from Norway to America or Canada. Its archives are based on sources from throughout Norway. It's open Monday through Friday from 9am to 3pm.

The **Ledaal Mansion,** built in 1800, is now the local royal residence, belonging to the Stavanger Museum. The mansion can be reached by walking a quarter of a mile from the railway station. It is open June 1 to August 31, Tuesday through Saturday from 11am to 5pm and on Sunday from 11am to 4pm. Admission is 10 kroner ($1.65) for adults, free for children.

Breidablikk, built in 1880, is another patrician mansion run by the Stavanger Museum. It keeps the same hours and charges the same admission as Ledaal (see above).

TOURS

For a 2-hour tour of the **sights of Stavanger,** including the Ryfylkefjord, a guided motorcoach tour leaves June 1 to August 31, Monday through Saturday at 1pm from in front of the cathedral (visited at the end of the tour). Cost is 95 kroner ($15.75) for adults, 60 kroner ($9.95) for children.

For an economy tour, take bus no. 10, 12, 17, 40, or 50 from St. Olavsgården for a circular ride around Stavanger. The 1-hour ride costs 12 kroner ($2).

Pulpit Rock (Prejestolen) is a landmark towering 1,800 feet above Lysefjord; it can be visited on either a boat or a bus trip, or by a car-ferry trip and short drive, taking about 45 minutes from Stavanger. If you want to climb the rock, you can take a boat-bus-hiking jaunt; a pathway leads to the top. The boat trip, lasting 2½ to 3 hours, leaves Skagen Quai in June, July, and August, on Monday, Tuesday, Thursday, Friday, and Saturday at 10am. From July 1 to August 20, there is also an afternoon departure on Monday, Tuesday, Thursday, Friday, and Saturday at 3pm, plus a sailing on Wednesday and Sunday at 5pm. The trip costs 175 kroner ($29.05) for adults, 85 kroner ($14.10) for children.

For the same prices, a longer trip is offered from July 1 to August 20, leaving on Monday and Saturday at 10:30am from Skagenkaien, and lasting about 8 hours. The tour starts by boat to Meling and continues by bus to Prekestolhytten (the Pulpit Cabin), from which a 4-hour hike up and down Pulpit Rock allows you to see the impressive Lysefjord. There is no tour leader.

Finally, you can take any number of independent fjord excursions on one of the ships of the White Fleet that traverse the Ryfylkefjords. For tickets and help with itineraries, go to the **Rødne Clipperkontoret,** Skagenkaien 18 (tel. 52-02-67).

WHERE TO STAY

The local tourist office, the **Tourist Pavilion,** next to the railway station, (Box 11, N-4001 Stavanger; tel. 53-51-00), will book you into a private home at 150 kroner

($24.90) and up per person for a night. The office is open June to late August, Monday through Friday from 9am to 6pm, on Saturday from 9am to 4pm and on Sunday from 10am to 4pm; September 1 to the end of May, Monday through Friday from 9am to 4pm and on Saturday from 9am to 1pm.

VERY EXPENSIVE

ATLANTIC HOTEL, Jernbaneveien 1, N-4001 Stavanger. Tel. 04/52-75-20. Fax 04/53-48-69. 36 rms (all with bath). A/C MINIBAR TV TEL.
$ Rates (including breakfast): Summer, 580 kroner ($96.20) single; 600 kroner ($99.55) double. Winter, 1,160 kroner ($192.45) single; 1,350 kroner ($223.95) double. AE, DC, MC, V.
The Atlantic Hotel has long been the leading choice of Stavanger hotels. A member of Reso Hotels, a Norwegian chain, it stands right in the heart of town a 2-minute walk from the Old Town, with views of Lake Breiavatnet. The hotel offers spacious and well-furnished bedrooms and a wide array of nightlife and dining facilities. Some of its restaurants are recommended below (see "Where to Dine"), including its Antique Restaurant for gourmet dining. Its Mortepumpen Grill and Fish Restaurant offers seafood. It also has two English-style pubs and bars, including King Oscar and Alexander.

KNA HOTELLET, Lagårdsveien 61, N-4001 Stavanger. Tel. 04/52-85-00. Fax 04/53-59-97.
$ Rates (including breakfast): Winter weekends and summer, 550 kroner ($91.25) single; 600 kroner ($99.54) double. Winter weekdays, 850–1,050 kroner ($141–$174.20) single, 1,000–1,245 kroner ($165.90–$206.50) double. AE, DC, MC, V.
Parking: Garage available.
Centrally located 900 yards from the Market Place, this Reso Hotels chain member was built in 1959 and completely modernized in the 1980s, with a new wing added with 120 extra rooms. Bedrooms are comfortably and attractively furnished with many amenities. Two floors are reserved for nonsmokers. The hotel is known for its food, which is served in the Grillen, the Havestuen, and the Stavangerstuen. After-dark hours are spent at the Monte Carlo nightclub, where food is also served. Guests meet for drinks in the Bar Ocean. The hotel also has a garage for 130 cars.

SAS ROYAL HOTEL, Lokkeveien 26, N-4001 Stavanger. Tel. 04/56-70-00, or toll free 800/221-2350 in the U.S. Fax 04/56-74-60. 204 rms (all with bath), 8 suites. A/C MINIBAR TV TEL **Bus:** 5, 15.
$ Rates (including breakfast): Summer and Fri–Sat year round, 720 kroner ($119.45) single; 800–900 kroner ($132.70–$149.30) double. Winter, 1,250 kroner ($207.40) single; 1,400–1,500 kroner ($232.25–$248.85) double; 1,650–3,350 kroner ($273.75–$555.75) suites. AE, DC, MC, V.
Erected in 1987, this distinctively stylish hotel is a 4-minute walk from the town center. Its bedrooms, which rise in balconied tiers above an atrium core, are designed with either an Italian, Japanese, American, or Scandinavian flair. The American rooms are clean, conservatively elegant, and comfortable; Italian units appear to have emerged straight from a Milanese design showcase; and the Japanese rooms are complete with lacquer screens and lots of light-grained pieces (even rice-paper window blinds). Rooms contain hairdryers and trouser presses.
Dining/Entertainment: The Harlequin Lobby Restaurant, serving three meals a day, has a seven-story-high ceiling. The Chicago Bar & Grill is recommended separately (see "Where to Dine," below).
Services: SAS airline check-in in the hotel lobby, "office-for-a-day" center, 24-hour room service, 3-hour express laundry.
Facilities: Swimming pool, sauna, solarium, whirlpool.

EXPENSIVE

VICTORIA HOTEL, Skansegate 1, N-4001 Stavanger. Tel. 04/52-05-26. Fax 04/52-71-48. 108 rms (all with bath). A/C MINIBAR TV TEL.

$ Rates (including breakfast): Summer, 460 kroner ($76.30) single; 560 kroner ($92.90) double. Winter, 1,050 kroner ($174.20) single; 1,175 kroner ($194.95) double. AE, DC, MC, V.

Dating from 1900, this hotel was built with a brick facade and an ornate portico in the city center. In spite of modernizations, much original ornamentation has remained, and it is still the preferred choice for the traditionalist. It is a first-class hotel with views over the harbor. Bedrooms are well furnished and attractively styled, and extra amenities include trouser press and hairdryer. Furnishings, color schemes, and room sizes vary in different parts of the hotel. The Victoria Steakhouse offers the finest beef in town, and you can arrive early for an apéritif in the English-style Queen Victoria Bar. Parking is available near the hotel, and services include laundry facilities and room service. It's directly east of Stavanger Cathedral.

MODERATE

HUMMEREN HOTEL, Havneveien 4, N-4056 Tananger. Tel. 04/69-93-90. Fax 04/69-93-30. 33 rms (all with bath). A/C MINIBAR TV TEL **Bus:** 152.
$ Rates (including breakfast): Mid-June to mid-Aug, 450 kroner ($74.65) single; 550 kroner ($91.25) double. Winter, 785–900 kroner ($130.25–$149.30) single; 900–1,000 kroner ($149.30–$165.90) double. AE, DC, MC, V.

Lying 3 miles from the airport and 9 miles from Stavanger, the Hummeren, opened in 1987, looks a lot like a quaint little hotel in Newport, Rhode Island, with a distinct nautical flavor. Each bedroom combines lots of varnished mahogany and brass with views of the harbor. Some rooms have waterside balconies. Live entertainment is provided on weekends.

The first Hummeren Restaurant opened on this site in 1935. A smörgåsbord buffet, served from 11:30am to 2pm, featuring platters of lobster and crab among other ingredients, costs 160 kroner ($26.55) and is one of the best food values in the area. Lobsters come fresh from a tank.

INEXPENSIVE

BERGELAND GJESTGIVERI, Vikedalsgate 1A, N-4000 Stavanger. Tel. 04/53-41-10. Fax 04/53-35-99. 62 rms (all with shower).
$ Rates (including breakfast): Sept 16–June 14, 450–500 kroner ($74.65–$82.95) single; 550–650 kroner ($91.25–$107.85) double. June 15–Sept 15, 200 kroner ($33.20) per person. AE, MC, V.

This is a modest, comfortable boardinghouse in a quiet residential area 450 yards from the rail station. All rooms have showers. The hotel serves a good Norwegian dinner daily from 5 to 8pm, and offers à la carte service 24 hours.

ROGALANDSHEIMEN GJESTGIVERI, Musegatan 18, N-4000 Stavanger. Tel. 04/52-01-88. 15 rms (none with bath). **Bus:** 4.
$ Rates (including breakfast): 250–320 kroner ($41.50–$53.10) single; 370–420 kroner ($61.40–$69.70) double. Discounts available for children. AE, V.

This 1890 Norwegian guesthouse has old-fashioned, comfortable rooms. Although only breakfast is available, their guesthouse is only a few minutes walk to the center of Stavanger.

WHERE TO DINE
EXPENSIVE

ANTIQUE, in the Atlantic Hotel, Jernbaneveien 1. Tel. 52-75-20.
Cuisine: FRENCH/NORWEGIAN. **Reservations:** Required.
$ Prices: Appetizers 50–55 kroner ($8.30–$9.10) at dinner, 15–50 kroner ($2.50–$8.30) at lunch; main dishes 75–90 kroner ($12.45–$14.95) vegetarian at dinner, 190–210 kroner ($31.50–$34.85) meat at dinner, 120–140 kroner ($19.90–$23.25) at lunch; *dagens menu* (one-course lunch) 70 kroner ($11.60). AE, DC, MC, V.

Open: Mon–Fri noon–midnight, Sat 5pm–midnight, Sun noon–11pm.
Next to the city park with views of the small lake, Breiavannet, this is one of the finest dining rooms in Stavanger. In spite of the name, Antique, the decor of the restaurant is modern. Every night the restaurant offers four different types of freshly caught fish. The chef is also known for his lamb dishes. Mostly the cookery is French inspired, but also includes some Norwegian specialties. The restaurant has a cellar filled with exotic wines. Clients are sometimes invited downstairs for a look at the vintages and a taste of "this or that." Try the pepper steak Armanac flambé, finishing with crêpes Suzettes.

CHICAGO BAR & GRILL, in the SAS Royal Hotel, Lokkeveien 26. Tel. 56-70-00.
Cuisine: AMERICAN. **Reservations:** Not required. **Bus:** 5, 15.
$ Prices: Appetizers 65–78 kroner ($10.80–$12.95); main dishes 145–246 kroner ($24.05–$40.80). AE, DC, MC, V.
Open: Mon–Sat 11:30am–11:30pm.
On the lobby level of the SAS Royal Hotel (see "Where to Stay," above), this sophisticated dining spot is a 4-minute walk from the old town center. The decor is inspired by the U.S. gangster era of Chicago in the 1930s. The kitchen imports the biggest volume of U.S.-bred beef in the region, including prime tenderloin, sirloin steaks, and filet steaks—the full range of American beef grilled to your request and served on a sizzling hot platter. For appetizers, try either the Manhattan clam chowder or seafood Charleston. Some patrons come just to drink at the adjoining bar where a half liter of beer costs 38 kroner ($6.30).

JANS MATS & VINHUS, Breitorget. Tel. 52-45-02.
Cuisine: NORWEGIAN/FRENCH. **Reservations:** Required. **Bus:** 2, 5, 12.
$ Prices: Fixed-price menu 350 kroner ($58.05); appetizers 65–80 kroner ($10.80–$13.25); main dishes 200–245 kroner ($33.20–$40.65). AE, DC, MC, V.
Open: Dinner only, Mon–Sat 6–10:30pm.
This establishment, considered by some as the best restaurant in Stavanger, occupies a well-accessorized underground cellar whose stone walls were originally laid in 1850. The color scheme includes candlelight, and the wine list is extensive. The daily menu changes frequently but is likely to include such dishes as salmon à la nage, pan-fried filet of monkfish on a bed of fresh spinach with a saffron-cream sauce, and tenderloin of beef with a fresh mushroom sauce and fresh vegetables. For dessert, choose from an assiette of homemade ice creams and sherbets with fresh seasonal berries. You can reach it by walking north of the rail station. It's in a small shopping complex in the city center.

STRAEN, Nedre Strandgate 15. Tel. 52-61-00.
Cuisine: SEAFOOD. **Reservations:** Recommended.
$ Prices: Fixed-price menu 285 kroner ($47.30); appetizers 76–95 kroner ($12.60–$15.75); main dishes 169–218 kroner ($28.05–$36.15). AE, DC, MC, V.
Open: Dinner only, Mon–Sat 5–11pm.
Straen is the leading seafood restaurant in Stavanger, its windows opening onto a view of Vägen Harbor. In a complex that includes a café, outdoor restaurant, small bar, and nightspot, it is reached by crossing a cobblestone courtyard. You can order homemade cream of fish soup, fresh mussels in white wine, steamed or fried halibut, or baked filet of codfish, all delectable. A famous specialty is the "fish symphony." Straen is located in the town center on the west side of the main quay.

MODERATE

SJOHUSET SKAGEN, Skagenkaien 16. Tel. 52-61-90.
Cuisine: INTERNATIONAL. **Reservations:** Recommended.
$ Prices: Fixed-price menu 150 kroner ($24.90); appetizers 20–67 kroner ($3.30–$11.10); main dishes 48–161 kroner ($7.95–$26.80). AE, DC, MC, V.
Open: Daily 11:30am–11:30pm.

⑤ This first-class restaurant at the harbor, packed with antiques, is in an old timbered boathouse. The decor is nautical, ranging from models of sailing ships to fishing equipment. Naturally, the kitchen specializes in fresh fish dishes. Try the grilled Norwegian salmon, or sautéed filets of monkfish. You can also order meat dishes, including grilled filet of reindeer and steak chasseur.

INEXPENSIVE

LA GONDOLA, Nytorget 8. Tel. 53-42-35.
 Cuisine: ITALIAN. **Reservations:** Recommended.
$ Prices: Appetizers 25–45 kroner ($4.15–$7.45); main dishes 56–119 kroner ($9.30–$19.75); pizzas from 45 kroner ($7.45). AE, DC, MC, V.
 Open: Mon–Sat 11:30am–11pm, Sun 1–11pm.
La Gondola is a steakhouse and pizzeria connected to the more formal Mongolian Grill and Chinese Restaurant. Its best value is its Sunday buffet from 1 to 7pm, costing 88 kroner ($14.60) for adults and 44 kroner ($7.30) for children. The pizza oven is fired for lunch as well as dinner, and you can also order pizzas to take out. If you'd like more formal food, order one of the grills, including a T-bone steak Florentine style. Other Italian dishes are offered, including scaloppine alla boscaiola (filets of pork with tomato sauce and mushrooms) and veal with shrimp, asparagus, and béarnaise sauce. It's in the town center across from the police station.

EVENING ENTERTAINMENT

COBRA CLUB, in the Atlantic Hotel, Jernbaneveien 1. Tel. 52-75-20.
 A leading nighttime rendezvous, the Cobra Club bills itself as an "adult disco." You can dance to the latest music or drink in an elegantly decorated setting. Technically, this is a members-only club, but visitors to Stavanger are often allowed in. It's in the cellar of the Atlantic Hotel (see "Where to Stay," above), a 2-minute walk from the Old Town. The club is open Monday through Saturday from 10pm to 4am, and no jeans are allowed. Beer costs 38 kroner ($6.30), and mixed drinks go for 30 to 55 kroner ($5 to $9.10).
 Admission: 50 kroner ($8.30).

AMADEUS DANCING, in the Atlantic Hotel, Jernbaneveien 1. Tel. 52-75-20.
 A "grownup" dance bar for people over 25 years old, Amadeus Dancing is adjacent to the Antique restaurant (see "Where to Dine," above). Part of a supper club, it's open for disco dancing only 4 nights a week: Tuesday, Wednesday, Friday, and Saturday from 9pm to 2am. The minimum age is 23, and no jeans are allowed. A beer will set you back 38 kroner ($6.30); mixed drinks, 30 to 55 kroner ($5 to $9.10).
 Admission: 50 kroner ($8.30); free for diners at the Antique restaurant.

---

5. HAUGESUND

35 miles north of Stavanger, 65 miles south of Bergen, 295 miles west of Oslo

GETTING THERE **By Plane.** Flights arrive at Haugesund Airport in Karmøy. There are seven daily flights from Oslo, and two flights each from Bergen and Stavanger.

By Train There is no train service. The nearest rail depot is at Stavanger, from which you can reach Haugesund by express boat (see below).

By Bus There is bus service daily from Oslo to Haugesund, taking 9 hours.

By Car The E76 Haukeli Highway, known as "the road of the conquerors," runs from Oslo in the east across Norway, ending at Haugesund. You go through varied and dramatic scenery from the fields of eastern Norway, through the valleys of

Telemark, over the mountain plateau of Haukeli at a height of 3,300 feet, finally reaching the fjords of western Norway. Allow about 10 hours for this drive, one of the most famous in Europe.

By Boat Three express boats make the 1½-hour run daily from Stavanger to Haugesund. Express boats from Bergen also make the trip, taking 3 hours.

ESSENTIALS For information, go to **Reisetrafikkforeningen for Hauge-sund og Distriktene,** Smedesundet 90 (tel. 04/72-52-55). The **telephone area code** for Haugesund is 04.

Haugesund is a shipping port with century-old herring fisheries. Hardangerfjord lies to the north and Ryfylke to the south.

Haugesund is also a center of the offshore oil industry which has brought prosperity to the region. In many ways it's a typical urban center of western Norway, lying in the region between the Hardangerfjord and Boknafjord. There's always something interesting to watch in the Haugesund harbor, plus opportunities for fishing trips and excursions into the nearby fjord district.

WHAT TO SEE & DO

The most interesting sight is the raspberry-pink **Town Hall,** with its flower-filled square and cobbled marketplace. The gift of a local shipping magnate, the Haugesund Town Hall continues a Norwegian tradition of having local artists decorate municipal buildings.

About a mile north of the town is a 55-foot granite obelisk, **Haraldhaugen,** erected in 1872 in honor of Norway's unification under Harald Fairhair (his burial mound is believed to be on the spot). Each county (*fylke*) contributed a stone pillar.

For information about any number of day tours from Haugesund, go to the **tourist bureau** (see above). A popular round-trip excursion is to Norway's most populous island, **Karmøy,** south of Haugesund. This island was strategic in Viking times, and is linked to the mainland today by Karmsund Bridge, one of the largest in the country.

WHERE TO STAY

RICA MARITIM HOTELL, Asbygata 3, N-5500 Haugesund. Tel. 04/71-11-00. Fax 04/71-64-77. 247 rms (all with bath). MINIBAR TV TEL.
$ Rates (including breakfast): Weekdays (except midsummer), 850 kroner ($141) single; 1,220 kroner ($202.40) double. Midsummer and weekends year round, 480 kroner ($79.65) single; 720 kroner ($119.45) double. AE, DC, MC, V.

The most distinctively modern building along the harbor, this is the biggest hotel in Haugesund. In August it's especially crowded with people connected with the Norwegian film industry—the Amanda (the Norwegian equivalent of the Oscar) is presented here at the hotel. The most palatial quarters at the hotel are named for actress Liv Ullmann. Bedrooms are plush and modern with many amenities. A bar to the left of the lobby has a live pianist playing till midnight. The hotel has a dining room seating 200 and a nightclub.

AMANDA HOME HOTEL, Smedasundet 93, N-5000 Haugesund. Tel. 04/71-74-00. Fax 04/72-86-21. 77 rms (all with bath), 2 suites. A/C MINIBAR TV TEL.
$ Rates (including breakfast): Mon–Thurs in winter, 840 kroner ($139.35) single; 1,050 kroner ($174.20) double. Summer and weekends year round, 450 kroner ($74.65) single; 575 kroner ($95.40) double. Suites 1,000–1,300 kroner ($165.90–$215.65). AE, DC, MC, V.

This imposingly old-fashioned building, constructed in the early 20th century, was once an office building. In 1989 its owners converted it to a hotel and added an extension with details similar to the old structure. It has as a central theme the history of motion pictures and the Amanda statuette, Norway's equivalent of Hollywood's Oscar. Each bedroom has an individual decor based on stills and movie posters. Most of the comfortable and attractively furnished rooms open onto the waterfront. Breakfast is the only meal served. The Amanda is in the town center on the waterfront

HOTEL NEPTUN, Haraldsgate 207, N-5500 Haugesund. Tel. 04/71-44-55. Fax 04/71-44-55. 58 rms (48 with bath). TV.

$ Rates (including breakfast): Mon–Fri, 650 kroner ($107.85) single, 850 kroner ($141) double; Sat–Sun 400 kroner ($66.35) single, 600 kroner ($99.55) double. Summer discounts available with Norway Fjord Pass: 360 kroner ($59.70) single; 540 kroner ($89.60) double. AE, DC, MC, V.

Located 5 minutes from the express boat terminal for Stavanger and Bergen in the commercial center of town at the end of the main street, this hotel does not have a bar or formal restaurant, but does offer an unlicensed cafeteria serving good-tasting Norwegian dishes. On the top floor is a terrace with a view of the harbor. Bedrooms are simply but comfortably furnished, and everything is well maintained.

WHERE TO DINE

LUTHES MAT & VINHUS, Skippergate 4. Tel. 71-22-01.
Cuisine: NORWEGIAN/FRENCH. **Reservations:** Required.
$ Prices: Appetizers 60–80 kroner ($9.95–$13.25); main dishes 150–190 kroner ($24.90–$31.50). AE, DC, MC, V.
Open: Restaurant, daily noon–midnight; pub, daily 6pm–1:30am.

This two-floor restaurant a 2-minute walk from the harbor is housed in a white clapboard-sided building constructed as a private home 150 years ago. The restaurant is on one side and a pub is on the other. To travel between the two sections, you need to go outside, "five steps down and five steps up." The decor of both places is old-fashioned and illuminated with a combination of oil lamps and candles. Service is polite and efficient in the restaurant, where you can order such specialties as lobster salad, poached filet of sole with butter sauce, and pepper steak. In the pub, a glass of wine costs 25 kroner ($4.15) and up.

CAPTAIN'S SALOON/CAPTAIN'S CABIN, Skjoldavn 1. Tel. 72-14-40.
Cuisine: NORWEGIAN. **Reservations:** Required on weekends.
$ Prices: Appetizers 58–78 kroner ($9.60–$12.95); main dishes 145–179 kroner ($24.05–$29.70). AE, DC, MC, V.
Open: Restaurant, Mon–Sat 6pm–midnight, Sun 2–11pm; pub, Mon–Sat noon–1am, Sun 1pm–1am.

The stone-sided building containing the best restaurant in Haugesund is owned by the Norwegian Seamen's Association. Its cellar, the Captain's Saloon, has an array of maritime artifacts salvaged from old ships. It offers a savory fish-inspired menu. You can sample freshly caught Norwegian fish prepared in many different ways. The bill of fare is likely to feature scampi, anglerfish, catfish, or shark. At street level is the pub, the Captain's Cabin, where a half liter of beer costs 28 kroner ($4.65). You can visit for lunch, ordering smørbrød, costing 25 to 55 kroner ($4.15 to $9.10), or a hot platter of food. It's located at the top of a flight of steps leading down to the harbor, a 1-minute walk from the town church.

CHAPTER 20

TRONDHEIM & MIDDLE NORWAY

Our exploration of middle Norway begins north of Bergen—often called the top of the fjord country. Ålesund, Geiranger, Åndalsnes, and Molde are four centers that make ideal headquarters, not only for their beauty and sights, but as starting points for excursions. The northward journey eventually continues to medieval Trondheim. Trondheim, the ancient capital of Norway, is the third most interesting city to visit in Norway, following Oslo and Bergen.

SEEING TRONDHEIM & MIDDLE NORWAY

GETTING THERE

Trondheim is in many ways the best gateway to middle Norway, because of its air connections with Bergen and Oslo and its rail link with Oslo. If you'd like to see the "top of the fjord country," consider flying to Ålesund from Bergen and using it as a base for exploring the area. A train from Oslo also runs to Åndalsnes, another good base for touring the northern sector of the western fjord district. If you're driving, plan to take a lot of car-ferries to get from one shore to another. Once you land at a gateway, frequent buses connect the major towns of interest.

A SUGGESTED ITINERARY

Days 1 & 2: From Oslo, take the E6 north to Trondheim. Spend the second day exploring the attractions in and around this historic city.
Day 3: Drive south or take public transport to Røros to explore this perfectly preserved copper-mining town.
Day 4: Head for the northern part of the western fjord country, flying from Trondheim to Ålesund for the night.
Day 5: Spend the morning seeing the sights of Ålesund, then take a bus to Åndalsnes for the night.
Day 6: Head south by bus to Geiranger to explore the most beautiful fjords.
Day 7: Return to Åndalsnes. Transfer by bus to Molde for the night.

---

1. ÅLESUND

79 miles west of Åndalsnes, 82 miles (and two ferry rides) of Kristiansund N, 37 miles (and one ferry ride) SW of Molde

GETTING THERE **By Plane** The easiest way to reach Ålesund is to fly from Bergen, arriving at Ålesund/Vigra airport (tel. 71/83-245 for flight information; 71/83-700 for airport), a 15-minute taxi or airport-bus ride from the town center. There are also daily flights from Bodø, Evenes, Haugesund, Kristiansand S, Oslo,

WHAT'S SPECIAL ABOUT MIDDLE NORWAY

Great Towns/Villages

☐ Trondheim, ancient capital of Norway and its third-largest city, filled with monuments.

☐ Røros, a national treasure, an old mining town so well preserved it's on the World Heritage List.

☐ Ålesund, "top of the fjord country," spread over three islands against a backdrop of the Sunnmøre Alps.

Ancient Monuments

☐ Nidaros Cathedral, at Trondheim, from the 11th century, once the burial place of medieval Norwegian kings.

Museums

☐ Trøndelag Folk Museum, outside Trondheim, Norway's main folk museum—there's even a tiny stave church.

☐ Sunnmøre Museum, outside Ålesund, depicting rural life from the Middle Ages to around 1900.

Scenic Wonders

☐ Geirangerfjord, considered by many Norwegians their most majestic fjord.

☐ Seven Sisters Waterfall, one of the most spectacular in Norway, with masses of water plunging downhill over a sheer rock face.

☐ Trollstein (Troll Road), the route to Åndalsnes, a zigzagging road with hairpin bends through the mountains.

Special Events/Festivals

☐ Molde Jazz Festival, in midsummer, drawing jazz artists from around the world.

Røros, Stavanger, Tromsø, and Trondheim. Flights are on Braathens SAFE, Skateflua (tel. 25-800) in Ålesund.

By Train   Go to Åndalsnes and then take a bus from the railway station to Ålesund. A daily train arrives from Oslo.

By Bus   Most tourist buses start running June 15. Good connections are possible from Åndalsnes, the nearest rail terminal. One bus a day also runs from Bergen, taking 11 hours. One or two buses a day arrive from Trondheim, taking 8½ hours.

By Coastal Steamer   The coastal steamer departs Bergen daily at 10pm and arrives at Ålesund at noon the following day.

By Car   Take the A69 west from Åndalsnes all the way to Ålesund. At press time, this road was closed but a car-ferry operates between Åndalsnes and Ålesund. Check the road's status before starting out.

ESSENTIALS   Tourist information is provided by **Ålesund Reiselivslag,** Rådhuset (tel. 071/21-202). The **telephone area code** for Ålesund is 071.

Ålesund is at the top of the fjord country, spread over three islands in an archipelago, with the snow-capped Sunnmøre Alps in the background. The islanders once earned their living from fishing.

After a fire destroyed the town in 1904, Ålesund was rebuilt in the "in" style of the times, art nouveau. Towers, turrets, and medieval romantic facades are pure art nouveau, and the Ålesund version includes elements from Nordic mythology.

WHAT TO SEE & DO

There are many sights in Ålesund, most works of nature. The mountain guardian of the area is **Aksla** (600 feet), a scenic sanctuary with a terrace restaurant, offering a view of fjord landscape, ancient Viking islands, and the Sunnmøre mountains. In the harbor nestles the flat island of **Giske,** believed to have been the birthplace of Rollo, 10th-century founder of the Duchy of Normandy and father of William the Conqueror. The island today is inhabited by farmers and people who earn their living from the sea.

Inquire at the tourist bureau about tours, as well as daily excursions to the fjords of **Romsdal, Geiranger,** and **Hjorund.** The most popular excursion is to **Fjellstua** (see my mountaintop dining recommendation in "Where to Dine," below).

Birdwatchers head for **Runde,** Norway's southernmost bird rock, where some 170,000 pairs of seabirds breed every year. It is Norway's third-largest bird cliff. Strict regulations protect the four bird sanctuaries—the western cliffs and the northern slopes of Runde, Kløfjellet and Hellestien, and the Grasøyane Islands. You can visit Runde by boat between June and the August 1, with departures at 11am. The trip costs 200 kroner ($33.20) for adults and 50 kroner ($8.30) for children. Departures are daily aboard the *Lea Kristina,* sailing from Skansegata in Ålesund. For reservations, call 31-666.

Tunnels now connect Ålesund to the islands of **Ellingsøy, Valderøy, Vigra,** and **Giske.** On Giske, visit the 12th-century marble church. The island has white sandy beaches and a bird sanctuary at Makkevika. The toll for the tunnel-bridge system is 30 kroner ($5) per car and driver, 10 kroner ($1.65) for each passenger.

SUNNMØRE MUSEUM, Borgundgavlen. Tel. 34-024.

The Sunnmøre Museum, on the outskirts of Ålesund midway between Ålesund and Spjelkavik, 2 miles east of the town center, includes some 40 original houses in open-air displays that show rural life in the Sunnmøre district from the late Middle Ages to around 1900. Outbuildings include a sawmill, a boat-builder's shed, a fishermen's inn, and a small 1743 boarding school. One of Norway's most complete collections of fishing boats is in the boat halls. Near the museum are the remains of a medieval town.

Admission: 20 kroner ($3.30) adults, 10 kroner ($1.65) children.

Open: May 20–June 19, Mon–Fri 11am–3pm, Sat–Sun noon–3pm; June 20–Aug 31, Mon–Fri 11am–4pm, Sat–Sun noon–5pm. **Bus:** 14, 16, 18.

ÅLESUND AQUARIUM, Nedre Strandgate 4. Tel. 24-123.

The aquarium, in the town center near the bus station, contains displays of a wide variety of fish and marine animals from the North Sea. Emphasis is given to presentation of a representative cross section of the rich marine life off Ålesund, extending from the wharves and shore to the open sea. You'll see spawning fish, hatching eggs, shell-changing crustaceans, and rare creatures of the deep.

Admission: 15 kroner ($2.50) adults, 10 kroner ($1.65) children.

Open: Mon–Fri 10am–5pm, Sat 10am–3pm, Sun noon–4pm.

ÅLESUND MUSEUM, Rasmus Rønnebergsgate 16. Tel. 23-170.

The development of hunting and fishing methods, shipbuilding, and life in Ålesund before and after the big fire of 1904 are the subjects of this museum off Korsegata near the harbor. Of special interest are a large-scale model of Ålesund and the boat *Uraed,* called *Brudeegget,* the prototype of today's covered rescue boats.

Admission: 10 kroner ($1.65) adults, 5 kroner (85¢) children.

Open: Daily 11am–5pm.

MITTELALTER-MUSEUM [Medieval Museum], Katevågen 2, Borgundkaupangen. Tel. 35-966.

Borgundkaupangen was the main center of Sunnmøre and the most important ecclesiastical center between Bergen and Trondheim from the end of the Viking period around 1000 to 1500. The Medieval Museum is built 2 miles east of Ålesund over the carefully excavated remnants of buildings from the 12th century. Artifacts from the excavations give an idea of the history of this small market town. Excavations uncovered the remains of dwelling houses, roads, jetties, and large warehouses. The finds reflect a versatile community, earning its living by fishing, hunting, trade, and different handcrafts.

Admission: 10 kroner ($1.65) adults, 5 kroner (85¢) children.

Open: Late May to Aug, Wed 5–7pm, Sat–Sun noon–3pm. **Closed:** Sept to mid-May. **Bus:** 14, 16, 18.

WHERE TO STAY

If you visit at midsummer or on a weekend year round, most hotels lower their prices.

VERY EXPENSIVE

RICA PARKEN, Storgata 16, N-6000 Ålesund. Tel. 071/25-050. Fax 071/22-164. 132 rms (all with bath), 6 suites. A/C MINIBAR TV TEL.

$ Rates (including breakfast): Weekdays (except summer), 1,025 kroner ($170.05) single; 1,320 kroner ($219) double. Summer and weekends in winter, 550 kroner ($91.25) single; 720 kroner ($119.45) double. Suites from 1,200 kroner ($199.10). AE, DC, MC, V.

Built in 1981, this hotel has a tasteful modern design, both inside and out. The bedrooms here are stylishly decorated and very comfortable. The hotel's Brasserie Normandie is one of the city's best dining places. A dancing bar, Queen's Park, is a popular disco, and the Galleri Flora is both a café and an art gallery. A health club with a sauna is also on the premises. The Rica Parken is a 5-minute walk north of the bus station.

EXPENSIVE

BRYGGEN HOME HOTEL, Apotekergata 1-3, N-6021 Ålesund. Tel. 071/26-400. Fax 071/21-180. 82 rms (all with bath), 1 suite, 3 mini-suites. A/C MINIBAR TV TEL **Bus:** Brunnholmen bus stops nearby.

$ Rates (including breakfast): Sun–Thurs, 820 kroner ($136.05) single, 950 kroner ($157.60) double; Fri–Sat, 450 kroner ($74.65) single, 580 kroner ($96.20) double. Suites 1,000–1,250 kroner ($165.90–$207.40). AE, DC, MC, V.

⭐ The steeply gabled, six-story building containing this hotel, originally constructed in 1906, was a fish-processing factory. Today it is a tasteful, well-run hotel, among the most luxurious in the area. It contains a library with a working fireplace and a glassed-in display of the tools used by the workmen who constructed the original building. The interior decor incorporates the trunklike original structure beams into an otherwise very modern design. Bedrooms are contemporary and comfortably and tastefully furnished. Many open onto views of the town's most famous canal, Brosundet. Use of the sauna and solarium is free to guests, and on weeknights the hotel sets out an evening buffet of waffles between 3 and 7pm.

RICA SKANSEN HOTEL, Kongensgata 27, N-6000 Ålesund. Tel. 071/22-938. Fax 071/26-660. 99 rms (all with bath). MINIBAR TV TEL.

$ Rates (including breakfast): Winter weekdays, 925 kroner ($153.45) single; 1,050 kroner ($174.20) double. Winter weekends, 525 kroner ($87.10) single; 625 kroner ($103.70) double. Summer, 420 kroner ($69.70) single; 620 kroner ($102.85) double. AE, DC, MC, V.

Originally built in 1954, most of what you see today is the result of a complete overhaul made in 1988 that turned this hotel into one of the most desirable in town. This conventional-looking hotel, at the edge of the historic center, a 2-minute walk north of the bus station, has bedrooms with comfortable and functional furniture. On the premises is an elegant restaurant, with an adjacent dance floor. There is also an informal brasserie and an indoor swimming pool with a sauna.

SCANDINAVIE, Løvenvoldgata 8, N-6002 Ålesund. Tel. 071/23-131. Fax 071/26-660. 75 rms (all with bath), 2 suites. MINIBAR TV TEL.

$ Rates (including breakfast): Winter weekdays, 800 kroner ($132.70) single; 900

kroner ($149.30) double. Summer and weekends in winter, 520 kroner ($86.25) single; 630 kroner ($104.50) double. Suites from 1,300 kroner ($215.65). AE, DC, MC, V.

Originally built in 1905, the Hotel Scandinavie boasts a pair of street-level restaurants that evoke the grand era of art nouveau. The glamorous restaurant is the Café Scandinavie at lobby level. Less expensive is the Kjelleren Pizza Pub set within the hotel cellar. The bedrooms' color schemes are cool pastels, and each has a color TV and radio, among other amenities. The Scandinavie is a 5-minute walk north of the bus station.

MODERATE

ATLANTICA, Rasmus Rønnebergsgata 4, N-6002 Ålesund. Tel. 071/29-100. Fax 071/26-252. 52 rms (all with bath). A/C MINIBAR TV TEL.

$ Rates (including breakfast): Winter weekdays, 620 kroner ($102.85) single; 720 kroner ($119.45) double. Summer and weekends year round, 420 kroner ($69.70) single; 550 kroner ($91.25) double. AE, DC, MC, V.

A modern and comfortable hotel beside the City Council building in the heart of town, this hotel was partly reconstructed in 1990. Today it is one of the best moderately priced establishments in town. From most of its tasteful, well-furnished bedrooms, in contemporary styling, there is a view of the Borgundfjord and the mountains beyond. Top-floor bedrooms have their own balconies. Transportation is convenient as the bus terminal is only 50 yards away, and there is also a taxi stand beside the hotel. The Café Brosundet serves both traditional Norwegian food and an international menu. The kitchen bakes its own bread and cakes.

WHERE TO DINE

SJØBUA FISKERESTAURANT, Brunholmgata 1. Tel. 27-100.
   Cuisine: SEAFOOD. **Reservations:** Recommended.
$ Prices: Appetizers 60–80 kroner ($9.95–$13.25); main dishes 180–220 kroner ($29.85–$36.50). AE, DC, MC, V.
   Open: Mon–Sat 2–11pm.

The rustic walls of a warehouse were retained in this restaurant, with part of the foundation on piers sunk into the harbor. The interior trusses and timbers were restored, making this restaurant as memorable architecturally as it is gastronomically. You can select a lobster from a holding tank near the entrance or have a drink in the marine-style bar, which has a blazing fireplace in winter. If you arrive in summer, you may prefer Flottman's Bar, next door under the same management—a floating barge skillfully converted into a bar with sun parasols.

Specialties include fresh fish from the Norwegian coast, some of which the owner buys directly from incoming boats. You might try the three-fish platter fried in butter, catfish with onion sauce, or whitefish with shrimp and mussels.

RESTAURANT FJELLSTUA, Fjellstua. Tel. 26-582.
   Cuisine: NORWEGIAN/CONTINENTAL. **Reservations:** Recommended. **Bus:** Brunnholmen.
$ Prices: Appetizers 49–65 kroner ($8.15–$10.80); main dishes 95–165 kroner ($15.75–$27.35). AE, DC, MC, V.
   Open: Upstairs restaurant, daily noon–midnight; outdoor terrace, summer, 11am–9pm. **Closed:** Jan–Feb.

You can drive to this restaurant's mountaintop location via a complicated system of roads, but some elect to climb the 418 rock-hewn steps from a park below. In warm weather you might sit on the outdoor terrace and order hamburgers, sandwiches, or beer from a charcoal grill. Full meals might include Ålesund fish soup, grilled lamb cutlets, pork medallions with béarnaise sauce, or steak in a red wine sauce

RESTAURANT GULLIX, Rådstugata 5B. Tel. 20-548.
   Cuisine: INTERNATIONAL. **Reservations:** Required.

$ Prices: Fixed-price menu 100 kroner ($16.60); appetizers 49–59 kroner ($8.15–$9.80); main dishes 109–169 kroner ($18.10–$28.05). AE, DC, MC, V.
Open: Daily 2–11pm.

Filled with decorative objects, this place, near the Town Hall, has the ambience of a charming Iberian *tasca*. Full meals include beef filet marinated in a red wine sauce, pepper steak, Scandinavian catfish, roast leg of pork, and when the ingredients are fresh, a Spanish paella.

EVENING ENTERTAINMENT

ENTERTAINMENT HOUSE, Keiser Wilhelmsgata 25. Tel. 27-014.

This is the major nightlife venue for Ålesund, consisting of a pub, disco, and piano bar. The **Musik Spielet Pub** serves Norwegian food, including smørbrød throughout the day, costing 30 to 35 kroner ($5 to $5.80), or daily hot platters priced at 65 kroner ($10.80) each. When it reopens it becomes a pub with live entertainment from local bands, most of them playing rockabilly music, blues, and jazz. The **Fregatten Disco** plays electronic dance music over a crowded floor, and the **Piano Bar** on the third floor has a live pianist and a more sedate ambience appreciated by conversationalists. The pub is open for lunch Tuesday through Sunday from 11am to 6pm, and the entire complex is open Tuesday through Saturday from 8:30pm to 3am. A beer costs 40 kroner ($6.65). Entertainment House is a 2-minute walk south of the bus station.

Admission: Disco, free Tues–Thurs, 50 kroner ($8.30) Fri–Sat.

---

2. GEIRANGER

307 miles NW of Oslo, 65 miles east of Ålesund,
50 miles south of Åndalsnes

GETTING THERE   By Plane   The nearest airport is Ålesund/Vigra airport (tel. 71/83-245 for flight information; 71/83-700 for airport). You go the rest of the way by bus.

By Train   The nearest railway station with direct bus connections is in Åndalsnes. The rest of the journey is by bus.

By Bus   Geiranger has bus connections with Åndalsnes, Ålesund, Otta, Stryn, and Nordfjordeid.

By Car   You have a choice of some of the most exciting roads and awe-inspiring scenery in Norway. Geiranger may be reached by Trollstigveien and Ørneveien from the north; by Geirangerveien, across the Grotli mountain moors, from the east; by the coast road from the south via Hellesylt, and then by ferry down the fjord; or from Ålesund via Linge.

By Boat   The *Bergen-Nordfjordeid* has express boat connections (with direct bus hookups). Call 071/630-99 at the Geiranger dock for schedule information.

ESSENTIALS   The **Geiranger og Stranda Reiselivslag,** Rådhuset (tel. 071/60-044), supplies information. The **telephone area code** for Geiranger is 071.

Most Norwegians consider the Geiranger their most majestic fjord. The village at the top of this narrow fjord is one of the most famous resorts in the fjord country.

WHAT TO SEE & DO

Perched on rocky ledges, high above the fjord, are a number of small farmsteads. Waterfalls, such as the celebrated **Seven Sisters (Syv Søstre),** the **Wooer,** and the **Bridal Veil,** cascade down the rock face.

Most hotels will arrange excursions by bus, boat, and car, or fishing trips on the fjord. Rowboats and fishing tackle are also available for rent at many hotels.

You can take a 3-hour boat cruise. En route to Valldal, on this tour yo already-mentioned Seven Sisters, a waterfall plunging down over a sheer w which change from season to season, are available from the tourist office Obviously, the most routes and the most tour options are available i summer visiting season, usually July to mid-August.

From Valldal, also connected by car-ferry to the village of Geiranger, you can continue on a 2-hour bus trip on **Trollstig Road** (Giant's Path) over the mountains, zigzagging down to the village of Åndalsnes, our next stopover.

Or you can return to Geiranger by bus on the **Eagle's Road.** This route allows you to visit a waterfall, then takes you down 3,280 feet with 11 hairpin turns. At the top, a toll road, open around mid-July, allows you to climb to the summit of **Dalsnibba** (4,757 feet) for a breathtaking panorama.

WHERE TO STAY & DINE

UNION TURISTHOTELL, N-6216 Geiranger. Tel. 071/63-000. 162 rms (all with bath). MINIBAR TV TEL.
$ Rates (including breakfast): 740 kroner ($122.75) single; 1,100 kroner ($182.50) double. AE, DC, MC, V.

An old family hotel going back to 1891, the Union has been updated. The public rooms, especially one done in the old style, are comfortable and pleasantly furnished. The Union is fully licensed, and in the peak season folk dancing is presented 2 or 3 nights a week. Dinners cost from 175 kroner ($29.05). The staff can arrange for you to go out in a rowing boat with or without outboard motors, and cars, owned by the hotel, can be rented for excursions. Outside, the hotel has a large garden with a heated swimming pool, and inside is another swimming pool, plus saunas and a Turkish steam bath. The hotel is in the town center overlooking the fjord.

GEIRANGER HOTEL, N-6216 Geiranger. Tel. 071/63-005. Fax 071/63-170. 129 rms (32 with bath). TEL.
$ Rates (including breakfast): 620 kroner ($102.85) single; 720–820 kroner ($119.45–$136.05) double. AE, DC, MC, V.

The traditional favorite, the Geiranger Hotel has been around in the middle of the village since 1973. The better units, facing the fjord, have balconies with great views. Each room is comfortably and tastefully furnished in modern styling. The hotel is licensed, with a cafeteria and a pizza bar, and is known for its good food, with a meal costing from 175 kroner ($29.05). One public room has dancing and an open fireplace (nights can be chilly here, even in summer).

Rowing boats are rented, and licenses can be easily obtained for fishing on the fjord. The hotel staff will book you on excursions to the waterfalls, glaciers, and mountain farms.

3. ÅNDALSNES

79 miles east of Ålesund, 658 miles west of Oslo

GETTING THERE By Train Trains run daily from Oslo to Åndalsnes, taking 6 to 8 hours.

By Bus Åndalsnes is linked by daily buses to Geiranger (in June and July only), taking 3 to 4 hours. Three to four daily buses connect to Ålesund, taking 2 hours 20 minutes.

By Car Take the E6 northwest from Oslo toward Lillehammer. At Dombås, head west on the E69 to Åndalsnes.

ESSENTIALS You can arrange lodgings with private families or obtain information at the tourist office, **Turistkontoret,** N-6301 Åndalsnes (tel. 072/21-622). The **telephone area code** for Åndalsnes is 072.

A summer resort at the foot of the mountains and at the head of the **Romsdal Fjord,** Åndalsnes attracts rock climbers and fishing enthusiasts (there are trout and salmon in the Rauma River).

One of the most exciting approaches to the village—and worth a day's excursion—is the zigzagging **Trollstien** (Troll Road), with hairpin bends through the mountains. Excursions are arranged in July to the **Geiranger Fjord** (past the Seven Sisters waterfall), to **Romsdal Valley,** and to **Eikesdal,** as well as to **Mardal Foss,** the highest falling water in northern Europe, a drop of 1,000 feet.

WHERE TO STAY & DINE

GRAND HOTEL BELLEVUE, Åndalsgate 5, N-6300 Åndalsnes. Tel. 072/ 21-011. 46 rms (all with bath). MINIBAR TEL.
$ Rates (including breakfast): 580–702 kroner ($96.20–$116.45) single, 800–900 kroner ($132.70–$149.30) double. MC, V.
Each bedroom in the Grand Hotel has a mountain view, and about half of them have views of the Romsdals fjord as well. The better accommodations are on the recently renovated third floor, where TV sets and improved accessories make this the most comfortable hotel in Åndalsnes. The hotel has a large dining room, the Fun Pub, and a disco. The Grand Hotel Bellevue is a quarter mile from the train station.

RAUMA PENSJONAT, Vollan 16, N-6300 Åndalsnes. Tel. 072/21-233. Fax 072/21-233. 15 rms (9 with bath). TEL.
$ Rates (including breakfast): 525 kroner ($87.10) single; 720 kroner ($119.45) double. AE, DC, MC, V.

Ⓢ A short walk from the train station, the Rauma Pensjonat is perfect for those who want a moderately priced place. Reopened in 1989 after a total overhaul, the hotel offers functionally furnished and tasteful bedrooms in light Nordic pastels. There are views of the mountaintops from the bedroom windows, all doubles. Nine contain TVs. The hotel's café offers a varied menu and a view of fjords and mountains.

NEARBY ACCOMMODATIONS

GJERSET PENSJONAT, Torvik, N-6320 Isfjorden. Tel. 072/25-966. 8 rms (none with bath). **Directions:** From Åndalsnes, take the bus marked MOLDE and ask the driver to let you off at the pension.
$ Rates: 190 kroner ($31.50) single; 302 kroner ($50.10) double. Breakfast costs 50 kroner ($8.30) extra. V.

Ⓢ This pension, at the head of the lake in this small Norwegian village, is a little guesthouse in idyllic surroundings. Rooms are pleasant, the food is good, and you can even catch your dinner in the lake, taking it back to the guesthouse to be prepared for you. Dinner costs 80 kroner ($13.25) and Gjerset is licensed for beer and wine. The pension is on Route 64 between Åndalsnes and Molde, 12 miles outside Åndalsnes.

---

4. MOLDE

31 miles NW of Åndalsnes, 43 miles NE of Ålesund

GETTING THERE   By Plane   Åro Airport is a 10-minute drive from the town center, 2 miles to the east. There are daily flights to Oslo, Bergen, and Trondheim.

By Train   You can go from Oslo as far as Åndalsnes by train. From there, you must take a connecting bus to Molde.

By Bus   Buses run from Åndalsnes to Molde, taking 1½ hours. In the same time, you can also take daily buses to Ålesund or Kristiansund N.

By Car   Driving should take about 1½ hours from Åndalsnes or Ålesund, 3 hours from Dombås, or 4 hours from Trondheim. From Trondheim, take the E6 south to Dombås and then connect with the E69 west. From Ålesund, take the E69 east. From Molde, board the ferry to Vikebukt and then go east on the E69.

By Ferry   Coming from either Ålesund or Åndalsnes, board the frequent car-ferries at Vikebut or at Vestnes for the crossing north to Molde.

By Coastal Steamer/Express Boat   The coastal steamer *Hurtigruten* visits Molde on its way between Bergen and Hammerfest (both directions). There is also a daily express boat going between Molde and Ålesund.

ESSENTIALS   The **Molde Travel Association,** Storgata 1, N-6401 Molde (tel. 072/57-133), will provide tourist information and assist in arranging excursions. It's open in summer Monday through Saturday from 9am to 6pm and on Sunday from 10am to 6pm; in winter, Monday through Saturday from 9am to 1pm.
   The **telephone area code** for Molde is 072.

Norway's "city of jazz and roses" is famed for its view of 87 white-capped Romsdal Alps. When the Nazis attacked Norway during World War II, Molde briefly became, in effect, the country's capital, since the king and the gold reserves were here. King Haakon VII hid in a forest outside the town until he and his son, King Olav V, could board a boat for England. Three hundred houses were destroyed during the German bombings in 1940.
   The name of Molde, from the Molde farm that occupied much of the area, has appeared in records since the Middle Ages. It was officially recognized as a trading place in 1614, and King Christian IV signed a royal decree declaring that Molde was a trading city in 1742. Plans are under way to celebrate the city's 250th anniversary in 1992.

WHAT TO SEE & DO

In addition to the sights below, guides will point out **Moldegård,** which was the main house of the old Molde farm, built in 1710 by Hans Nobel. Henrik Ibsen lived here in 1885. Bjørnstjerne Bjørnson, who wrote Norway's national anthem, among other poems, also visited often, as late as 1907.
   Don't miss the view of the 87 peaks of the Romsdal Alps. Best known are the Romsdalshorn (5,115 feet) and the Troll Tinder (6,250 feet). You can also see the island-studded fjord from the **Belvedere Varden,** 1,300 feet high. Visitors can take a taxi up and get the driver to wait for 20 minutes, or enjoy a 1-hour walk to the top.

MOLDE DOMKIRKE, Kirkebaken 2. Tel. 51-419.
   In the heart of town, Molde Cathedral, the largest postwar cathedral in Norway, was erected in 1957—the third church built on this site. Its simplicity and purity of line are enhanced by white-brick walls, deeply recessed mullion windows, a blue-and-beige ceiling, and a rose window behind a pipe organ. It's located near Torget.
   Admission: Free.
   Open: Daily 10am–3:30pm.

RÅDHUSET (Town Hall), Rådhusplassen. Tel. 53-233.

The modern Town Hall, near Torget, is probably one of the best-conceived municipal buildings in the world. Its executive offices on the upper level open onto a winter garden with hanging baskets. Marble floors and stone walls blend harmoniously, and domes and skylights capture the northern lights. The roof terrace has a garden with 2,000 roses.

Admission: Free.
Open: Mon–Fri 9am–5pm.

ROMSDALMUSEET (Romsdal Museum), Romsdal Park. Tel. 52-534.

The Romsdal Museum, a 10-minute walk from the town center, comprises some 45 wooden houses that have been carefully reassembled on the outskirts of Molde. In summer, children in regional costumes perform folk dances here. The buildings range from a 15th-century *aarestue* (log cabin) to a medieval-style chapel. Coffee, cakes, ice cream, and soft drinks are available.

Admission: 20 kroner ($3.30).
Open: Mid-June to mid-Aug, daily 10am–6pm; mid-Aug to mid-June, daily 10am–2pm.

NEARBY ATTRACTIONS

In **Bjorset,** about 1½ miles from Molde, are three rock carvings dating from prehistoric times. Admission is free.

The so-called **Troll Church,** near Eide, is a natural wonder, with several underground caves and grottos, many of them unexplored. There's also a 45-foot waterfall. To get there by car, take road no. 67 toward Eide, stopping at the TROLKYRKJA sign. From there, walk for 1½ hours over a steep path. You can catch a bus heading for Eide at the Molde terminal.

The **Vey Stone Church** on **Vey Island** dates from the 11th century. The little village of Kaupangen was the center of Romsdal until the 14th century. If you'd like to visit, make your request through the tourist office (see above), which will give a key to the church to a boatman who is hired on a chartered basis. Transit time is 30 minutes, and the cost is 50 kroner ($8.30) per person, providing four or five visitors agree to make the trip.

The **Fisheries Museum** (tel. 52-534) on the island of Hjertøya is part of the Romsdal Museum in Molde. Its collections consist of about 25 old buildings from the western coast of Romsdal, including dwellings, boathouses, a mechanics' workshop, and other maritime buildings. There are a number of authentic old fishing boats and fishing gear, and you can see how the Norwegian coastal fishermen, sealers, and whalers lived. The water taxi leaves from the marketplace, Torget, in the center of Molde during the museum's open hours, from mid-June to mid-August, Monday through Saturday from 10am to 3:30pm and on Sunday from noon to 3:30pm. Round-trip boat fare is 5 kroner (85¢) for adults, 10 kroner ($1.65) for children. Trip time is 10 minutes. The museum costs adults 30 kroner ($5); children, 15 kroner ($2.50).

WHERE TO STAY

Many of the hotels offer summer reductions to holders of the Norway Fjord Pass or the Scandinavian Bonus Pass (see "Getting Around," in Chapter 12).

ALEXANDRA HOTEL, Storgata 1-7, N-4601 Molde. Tel. 072/51-133. Fax 072/16-635. 151 rms (all with bath), 11 suites. MINIBAR TV TEL.

$ Rates (including breakfast): Weekends year round, 560 kroner ($92.90) single; 800 kroner ($132.70) double. Summer weekdays, 756 kroner ($126.90) single; 920 kroner ($152.65) double. Winter weekdays, 1,020 kroner ($169.20) single; 1,190 kroner ($197.40) double. Suites from 1,450 kroner ($240.55). AE, DC, MC, V.

This hotel on the main street of town overlooks the public garden and the nearby fjord. A streamlined, tasteful lobby leads to comfortable bedrooms, with leather-upholstered couches, carpeting, and large baths. On the premises are an indoor swimming pool, a sauna, several restaurants (one of which, Gamle Molde, is recommended separately; see "Where to Dine," below), and a popular bar.

HOTEL NOBEL, Amtm. Kroghsgaten 5, N-6400 Molde. Tel. 072/51-555.
Fax 072/15-954. 42 rms (all with bath). MINIBAR TV TEL.

$ **Rates** (including breakfast): Summer and Fri–Sat year round, 450 kroner ($74.65) single; 650 kroner ($107.85) double. Sun–Thurs (except summer), 620 kroner ($102.85) single; 880 kroner ($146) double. AE, DC, MC, V.

A few minutes' walk from the wharf, the main street, and the bus station, the Nobel is well decorated in light colors and rattan furniture. Owned by the nearby Alexandra, all the facilities of the larger hotel (see above) are available to guests at this bed-and-breakfast hotel. Rooms are simply but comfortably furnished.

HOTELL MOLDE, Storgata 19, N-6400 Molde. Tel. 072/15-888. Fax 072/15-890. 36 rms (all with bath). TEL.

$ **Rates** (including breakfast): 500 kroner ($82.95) single; 650 kroner ($107.85) double. AE, DC, MC, V.

This hotel is in the commercial center of town near Torget. All the comfortably functional rooms have private showers and toilets. The hotel also has a reasonably priced cafeteria (see "Where to Dine," below).

NEARBY ACCOMMODATIONS

KNAUSEN MOLDE, Hytter N-6400 Molde. Tel. 072/51-577. Fax 072/15-287. 50 rms (all with bath). TV TEL.

$ **Rates** (including breakfast): Summer and weekends year round, 420 kroner ($69.70) single; 560 kroner ($92.90) double. Winter weekdays, 600 kroner ($99.55) single; 680 kroner ($112.80) double. AE, DC, MC, V.

Lying close to the local airport 2 miles east of the town center, this hotel, which commands views over the Romsdals Mountains and the Fanne Fjord, caters to convention groups and nature lovers. About half the bedrooms have balconies overlooking the faraway fjord. Additional accommodations in 18 outlying cottages are known for their peace and quiet. A Missionhotel, it serves no alcohol, but well-prepared meals are offered in the dining room.

WHERE TO DINE
MODERATE

GAMLE MOLDE, in the Alexandra Hotel, Storgata 1. Tel. 51-133.
Cuisine: NORWEGIAN. **Reservations:** Recommended.

$ **Prices:** Appetizers 13–40 kroner ($2.15–$6.65); main dishes 150–168 kroner ($24.90–$27.85); daily platters (until 6pm) 65 kroner ($10.80). AE, DC, MC, V.
Open: Mon–Sat 11am–11pm, Sun noon–11pm.

Large portions of well-prepared food at reasonable prices are offered in the Gamle Molde, which is decorated like a Norwegian tavern, with antiques and massive ceiling timbers. At lunch, there is a well-stocked salad bar, and dinner main dishes are likely to include three kinds of grilled steak, marinated house salmon, and fresh fish. Filet of reindeer and chateaubriand are specialties. It's a short walk from the Town Hall in the center.

NAUST-GRYTA, Havnegata 47. Tel. 51-030.
Cuisine: SEAFOOD. **Reservations:** Recommended.

$ **Prices:** Appetizers 29–45 kroner ($4.80–$7.45); main dishes 75–130 kroner ($12.45–$21.55). V.
Open: Mon–Thurs 10am–11pm, Fri–Sat 10am–3am, Sun noon–11pm.

Naust-Gryta is the best fish restaurant in town, with a large dining terrace in summer and a nautical decor—even the tables are shaped like fish. Menu selections include "sea wolf," scallops, and the chef's special fish soup. Meat eaters can choose pepper steak or spareribs. At night many young people come here to order pizza and beer. It's on the waterfront near the bus station.

TOSCANA, Romsdalsgate 20. Tel. 56-411.
   Cuisine: ITALIAN. **Reservations:** Required.
$ **Prices:** Appetizers 45–65 kroner ($7.45–$10.80); main dishes 66–155 kroner ($10.95–$25.70). AE, DC, MC, V.
   Open: Sun–Thurs 2pm–midnight, Fri–Sat 1pm–midnight.

In a building constructed in 1910 as a private home, a 5-minute walk north of the bus station, this is the best Italian restaurant in the area. Its staff includes a combination of Italian and Norwegian cooks. Specialties include beef with gorgonzola, filet à la crème, pampas steak (with onions and spices, grilled), six kinds of pasta, and six preparations of fish. Naturally, the larder is filled with Italian wines.

INEXPENSIVE

KAFFISTOVA, in the Hotell Molde, Storgata 19. Tel. 51-711.
   Cuisine: NORWEGIAN. **Reservations:** Not required.
$ **Prices:** Soups 15 kroner ($2.50); salads 25 kroner ($4.15); smørbrød 25 kroner ($4.15). No credit cards.
   Open: Mon–Fri 11am–6pm, Sat 9am–3pm.

Kaffistova, in the Hotell Molde (see "Where to Stay," above), in the center near Town Hall, is one of the cheapest dining rooms in town. Pleasantly decorated, this cafeteria offers daily luncheon plates for 64 kroner ($10.60). Fish casseroles and wienerschnitzel are often featured. You can also enjoy open-face sandwiches throughout the day for the same price or even less, plus soups and salads.

KROVERTEN, Sandveien 14. Tel. 57-777.
   Cuisine: STEAKS/PIZZAS. **Reservations:** Not required.
$ **Prices:** Pizzas 82–98 kroner ($13.60–$16.25); grilled steaks 85–95 kroner ($14.10–$15.75); fixed-price daily platter (served 11am–6pm) 68 kroner ($11.30). MC, V.
   Open: Sun–Thurs 11am–1:30am, Fri–Sat 11am–2:30pm.

Many of the town's younger residents gravitate to this pizza and pasta emporium that also serves reasonably priced grilled steaks. At night, live musical groups occasionally appear upstairs. The place is very informal, as is the dress. It's on a side street midway between the cathedral and the Alexandra Hotel.

---

5. KRISTIANSUND N

42 miles north of Molde, 658 miles NW of Oslo, 405 miles north of Bergen

GETTING THERE By Plane Kvernberget Airport lies close to the town center. Three arrivals a day wing in from each of Norway's biggest cities: Trondheim, Oslo, and Bergen. The bus trip from the airport to the center takes 15 minutes, and the bus will stop at individual hotels.

By Train The nearest railway stations are in Oppdal and Åndalsnes, with bus connections meeting the trains.

By Bus There are daily bus connections to Trondheim, Molde, Oppdal, and Åndalsnes.

By Car From Molde in the south, drive north along Route 67 (two ferry crossings).

By Coastal Steamer The coastal steamer **Hurtigruten** arrives at Kristiansund twice a day—once southbound, the other headed for the North Cape.

ESSENTIALS The **Kristiansund Travel Association,** Kaptein Bødtkersgata, N-6501 Kristiansund N (tel. 073/77-211), offers tourist information and assistance. The **telephone area code** for Kristiansund N is 073.

SPECIAL EVENTS   Kristiansund has a special **Opera Week** in early February in the Festiviteten culture center. Ballets, concerts, and theater productions are staged, and sometimes jazz concerts.

Almost entirely destroyed in World War II, this coastal town spread over three islands has been rebuilt into a modern city. It is the main service base for oil activities on the mid-Norwegian continental shelf.

WHAT TO SEE & DO

With a fan-shaped ground plan and side walls that slope in toward the choir, the **Kirkelander Church** is a fine example of nontraditional ecclesiastical architecture.

At the **Nordmøre Museum,** Knudtzondalen (tel. 71-578), by the Atlanten Stadium, archeological exhibits show how people have lived in the Nordmøre district for 9,000 years, where codfish was perhaps the most sought-after product of the North Sea before the discovery of oil. In the museum, you can see how fish were treated and dried on rocks to produce "klippfish," a major export. All buses going to the center pass the museum; the bus stop is Idrettshall/Svømmehall. It's open Tuesday through Friday from 10am to 2pm and on Sunday from noon to 3pm. Admission is 15 kroner ($2.50) for adults and 10 kroner ($1.65) for children.

In the **Wolbrygga** section of the museum, at the Vågen (harbor), you can see a complete barrel-making operation, rope-making equipment, and some old boats from the area. Woldbrygga can be reached by taking the ferry *Sundbåten* to Gomalandet and walking from there.

At the same harbor is another part of the museum, **Mellomvaerftet,** where you can park your car and walk along the seaside to watch the restoration of old boats in the shipyard (*vareftet*). The museum branch lies on the west side of the bay and is a short walk from the center.

NEARBY ATTRACTIONS

Often likened to Scotland's St. Kilda, ✪ **Grip,** near Kristiansund, is one of the most fascinating of Norway's offshore islands and, until about 20 years ago, the only one permanently occupied. Today it has only summer residents, with regular boat service from Kristiansund, costing 90 kroner ($14.95) for adults and 45 kroner ($7.45) for children round-trip.

Of special interest on this flat, rocky piece of land is the 14th-century stave church. The walls of the choir were repainted and decorated in 1621 with motifs from the Old and New Testaments. The beautiful little altar chalice from 1520 is one of only two such cups in the country.

You can also visit the island of **Smøla** by taking the ferry from Kristiansund to Straumen, through the straits of Tustna. Pass Edøy with its stone church that dates from about 1250 and catch the bus from Straumen. The cost is 94 kroner ($15.60) for adults and 48 kroner ($7.95) for children.

WHERE TO STAY

If you arrive on a weekend or in summer, the following hotels are exceptional bargains.

BARON HOTEL, Hauggata 16, N-6500 Kristiansund N. Tel. 073/74-011.
 Fax 073/77-659. 45 rms (all with bath). 5 mini-suites. MINIBAR TV TEL.
$ Rates (including breakfast): Sun–Thurs, 900 kroner ($149.30) single, 1,150 kroner ($190.80) double; Fri–Sat, 450 kroner ($74.65) single, 550 kroner ($91.25) double. AE, DC, MC, V.
Originally built in the 1970s, this hotel was radically reconstructed in 1988 and is now one of the most alluring properties in the region. Bedrooms are modern and tastefully

and comfortably furnished. Mini-suites rent for the same prices as regular doubles and are distributed to favorite clients of the hotel. Each bedroom has individual character. The most elegant meeting place in town is the Piano Bar of this hotel. Everything is bright and inviting. The care and attention are exceptional. For example, special bed linen is provided for guests suffering from allergies. Its restaurant Baron is recommended separately (see "Where to Dine," below). The Baron is on the harborfront in the town center, a 2-minute walk west of the bus station.

GRAND HOTEL, Bernstorffstredet 1, N-6500 Kristiansund N. Tel. 073/ 73-011. Fax 073/72-370. 115 rms (all with bath), 2 suites. MINIBAR TV TEL.

$ Rates: Winter weekdays, 975 kroner ($161.75) single; 1,100 kroner ($182.50) double; from 1,200 kroner ($199.10) suite. Summer and weekends year round, 480 kroner ($79.65) single; 585 kroner ($97.05) double. AE, DC, MC, V.

Originally built in the 1890s as the grandest hotel in the region, the Grand was remodeled and doubled in size during two renovations in the 1980s. Rooms are modern, well furnished, and accessorized. The hotel's Restaurant Consulen and its Grippsalen Night Club are recommended separately (see "Where to Dine" and "Evening Entertainment," below). It's a 5-minute walk south of the bus station.

WHERE TO DINE

BARON RESTAURANT, in the Baron Hotel, Hauggata 16. Tel. 74-011.
Cuisine: NORWEGIAN/FRENCH. **Reservations:** Recommended.
$ Prices: Fixed-price menu 130 kroner ($21.55); appetizers 36–52 kroner ($5.95–$8.65); main dishes 158–195 kroner ($26.20–$32.35). AE, DC, MC, V.
Open: Dinner only, Mon–Sat 5–11pm, Sun 2–9pm.

A formal English-inspired bar, laden with dark colors and leather upholstered sofas, lies adjacent to this sophisticated restaurant that many consider the best in town. In an elegant setting, you can select from such house specialties as grilled meats. Try, if featured, such innovative dishes as catfish flambéed with cognac and served with a mango purée. For dessert, poached pears served with a house confectionary surprise is a delight. It's on the harborfront in the town center, a 2-minute walk west of the bus station.

CONSULEN, in the Grand Hotel, Bernstorffstredet 1. Tel. 73-011.
Cuisine: NORWEGIAN/FRENCH. **Reservations:** Recommended.
$ Prices: Appetizers 68–75 kroner ($11.30–$12.45); main dishes 146–169 kroner ($24.25–$28.05); one-plate lunch special 75 kroner ($12.45); three-course menu 145 kroner ($24.05). AE, DC, MC, V.
Open: Daily 1–11pm.

One of the most popular restaurants in town, a 5-minute walk south of the bus station, the Consulen is housed on the lobby level of the Grand Hotel (see "Where to Stay," above). The decor includes comfortable banquettes and lots of wood trim. Its fixed-price menu at both lunch and dinner is the most favored item on the menu. It changes daily and is usually most satisfying. Menu items include a combination plate of both smoked and marinated salmon for an appetizer, and such main courses as pepper steak, filet of anglerfish with mango sauce, and filet of blue halibut poached in red wine. A separate bar is attached where guests often arrive early for an apéritif.

EVENING ENTERTAINMENT

GRIPPSALEN NIGHT CLUB, in the Grand Hotel, Bernstorffstredet 1. Tel. 73-011.

The leading nightlife venue of town, the Grippsalen is a supper club where people come to drink and dance. You can also order full meals for 175 to 200 kroner ($29.05 to $33.20). A conservative crowd of well-dressed local residents patronizes this establishment, enjoying the sounds of a dance band. It's open Monday through Saturday from 9pm to 3am, but is most popular on Friday and Saturday nights. Beer costs 36 kroner ($5.95). The place is a 5-minute walk south of the bus station.
Admission: 45 kroner ($7.45).

6. TRONDHEIM

425 miles north of Bergen, 345 miles NW of Oslo

GETTING THERE By Plane Vaernes Airport is 20 miles from town. Bus service to the city center costs 40 kroner ($6.65) and takes about 30 minutes. Several flights arrive daily from Bergen and Oslo.

By Train Two trains a day connect Stockholm and Trondheim taking 12 hours. Three trains arrive daily on the 7-hour trip from Oslo.

By Bus Buses run between Trondheim and Bergen once a day, taking 15 hours. One or two buses also leave for Molde and Ålesund, taking 6 to 8 hours, respectively.

By Coastal Steamer The coastal express steamer on the northbound route from Bergen to Kirkenes calls daily at Trondheim.

By Car Take the E6 north of Oslo via Lillehammer all the way to Trondheim.

ESSENTIALS The **Trondheim Tourist Office,** Kongensgate 7 (tel. 52-72-01), with its entrance on the marketplace, is open in summer, Monday through Saturday from 9am to 8pm and on Sunday from 10am to 6pm; off-season, Monday through Friday from 9am to 4pm and on Saturday from 9am to 1pm. The tourist office will help with hotel accommodations or private home stays, for 180 kroner ($29.85) in a single and 240 kroner ($33.80) in a double.

The **telephone area code** for Trondheim is 07.

DEPARTURES Buses leave from the bus terminal, Erling Skakkes Gate 40, 75 minutes before departures of SAS and Braathens SAFE flights, driving via the SAFE terminal at the Royal Garden Hotel, Kjøpmannsgate 73.

Founded by the Viking king Olav Tryggvason in the 10th century, Trondheim is Norway's third-largest city, scenic, pleasant, and an active university center. The city lies on the south bay of the Trondheim Fjord, and at the mouth of the Nid River.

Noted for its timbered architecture, Trondheim retains much of its medieval past, most notably the Gothic-style Nidaros Cathedral. Until the early 1200s Trondheim was the medieval capital of Norway. Pilgrims came from all over Europe to worship at the shrine of Olav, who was canonized in 1031. But with the coming of the Reformation, the fortunes of the city declined.

GETTING AROUND

You can travel all over Trondheim and to outlying areas on Trondheim city buses, operated by **Trondheim Trafikkselskap (TT),** Prinsens Gate 32 (tel. 54-71-00). Several types of tickets are available, according to how much you intend to travel. Tickets for **single rides** are sold on buses for exact change (if you don't have the right amount and have to pay too much, you'll get a credit slip from the driver, which can be redeemed at the TT office or on a later trip). Tickets for a single ride cost 12 kroner ($2) for adults, 6 kroner ($1) for children 4 to 16, and 20 kroner ($3.30) for a family. **Multijourney Cards,** good for 10 trips, cost 132 kroner ($20.70) for adults, 60 kroner ($9.95) for children, and are sold at the TT office, at the bus station, post offices, kiosks, and at some shops. **Day Cards,** allowing unlimited travel within 24 hours, sell for 35 kroner ($5.80) per person, 50 kroner ($8.30) for a family.

WHAT TO SEE & DO

NIDAROS CATHEDRAL, Bispegaten. Tel. 50-12-12.
Dating from the 11th century, this cathedral is one of the major ecclesiastical buildings in Scandinavia. Once the burial place of the medieval Norwegian kings, it was also the site of the coronation of King Haakon VII in 1906, an event that marked the beginning of modern Norway.

A classical European cathedral representing different architectural styles, including Gothic and Romanesque, it features a stunningly intricate rose window on the west front. Gustav Vigeland carved the gargoyles and grotesques for the head tower and northern transept. The 12th-century **Archbishop's Palace,** Erkebispegården, is behind the cathedral. It's located in the town center near the Rådhus.

Admission: Cathedral and palace, 10 kroner ($1.65) adults, 5 kroner (85¢) children.

Open: Cathedral, May 1–14 and Sept 1–14, Mon–Fri 10am–2:30pm, Sat 10am–2pm, Sun 1:30–3pm; May 15–June 14, Mon–Fri 9:30am–3pm, Sat 9:30am–2pm, Sun 1:30–4pm; June 15–Aug, Mon–Fri 9:30am–5:30pm, Sat 9:30am–2pm, Sun 1:30–4pm; Sept 15–Apr, Mon–Fri noon–2:30pm, Sat 11:30am–2pm, Sun 1:30–3pm. Palace, mid-June to mid-Aug, Mon–Fri 9am–3pm, Sat 9am–2pm, Sun noon–3pm. **Bus:** 2, 5, 6, 7, 9.

STIFTSGÅRDEN, Munkegaten 23. Tel. 52-24-73.

This buttercup-yellow royal palace near the marketplace was built as a private home by a rich merchant's widow in the 1770s, when Trondheim began to regain its prosperity. It is the largest wooden building in Scandinavia, perhaps in all of northern Europe. The furnishings are unpretentious, an amalgam of various design styles.

Admission: 10 kroner ($1.65) adults, 5 kroner (85¢) children.

Open: June–Aug, Mon–Sat 11am–2pm. **Closed:** Sept–May. **Bus:** 2, 5, 6, 7, 9.

MUSEUM OF MUSIC HISTORY, 2 miles from the center of town at Ringve Manor. Tel. 92-24-11.

This museum can be viewed only on guided tours. At specified times musical presentations are performed on the carefully preserved antique instruments, including an impressive collection of spinets, harpsichords, clavichords, pianofortes, and string and wind instruments. Also on the premises is an old *kro* (inn), where visitors can have waffles, light refreshments, and coffee. The mansion was the birthplace of Admiral Tordenskiold, the Norwegian sea hero.

Admission: 30 kroner ($5) adults, 10 kroner ($1.65) children; family ticket, 70 kroner ($11.60).

Open: Guided tours, May 20–June, daily at noon, 1:30pm, and 3pm; July–Aug 10, daily at 11am and 12:30, 2:30, and 4:30pm; Aug 11–31, daily at 11am, 12:30pm, and 2:30pm; Sept, daily at noon and 2pm; Oct–May 19, Sun at 1:30pm. **Bus:** 1 to Lade Church.

TYHOLTTÅRNET, Blussuvoll. Tel. 51-31-66.

A 400-foot concrete tower, originally constructed for communications purposes, houses a revolving restaurant (see "Where to Dine," below) on top. You can visit the viewing gallery even if you don't patronize the restaurant for a panoramic view of Trondheim with the fjord and the mountains in the background.

Admission: 20 kroner ($3.30) adults, 10 kroner ($1.65) children.

Open: Viewing gallery, Mon–Sat 11:30am–midnight, Sun and hols. noon–7pm. **Bus:** 20, 60 (ask the driver to tell you when to get off).

TRØNDELAG FOLK MUSEUM, Sverresborg Allé. Tel. 52-21-28.

At Norway's main folk-culture museum, farmhouses, cottages, Samic huts, and city buildings depict scenes of everyday life and festivities for a 300-year period. There is even a tiny stave church. A special attraction is the ski museum with a lively introduction to this region's long skiing tradition. Every Sunday in July and August, demonstrations of old handcrafts are given. Tours are available in English.

Admission: 20 kroner ($3.30) adults, 10 kroner ($1.65) children.

Open: May 20–Aug, daily 10am–6pm. **Closed:** Sept–May 19. **Bus:** 8 or 9 from Dronningensgate to Wullumsgaarden.

MUSEUM OF NATURAL HISTORY AND ARCHEOLOGY, Erling Skakkesgate 47. Tel. 59-21-45.

Located at the University of Trondheim, this museum offers a fine exhibition of zoological art, including a bird diorama with recorded commentary. Of great interest are the artifacts and relics of the area, dating back to prehistoric times. There are also Lapp arts and crafts.

Open: May 2–May 31, daily noon–3pm; June–Aug, Mon–Sat 11am–3pm and Sun noon–3pm; Sept, daily noon–3pm; Oct–May 1, Sun noon–3pm.

Admission: 5 kroner (85¢) adults, 2 kroner (35¢) children.

ORGANIZED TOURS

June through August, a **bus tour** departs daily at noon from the marketplace, lasting 1½ hours and costing 70 kroner ($11.60). Its main attraction is a guided tour through the cathedral (admission not included in the price). During the last 3 weeks of July, an additional tour leaves at 2:30pm.

There are also daily boat trips, leaving Ravnkloa for **Munkholmen Island** at 10am and every hour thereafter until 5pm. Munks Island (its English name) was used in ancient times as an execution site. In the 11th century, Benedictine monks constructed a monastery here, probably one of the first two monasteries in Scandinavia. In 1658 it was turned into a prison fort. You're given a guided tour of the island's historical fortress. Lunch, not included in the fare, is available at Munkholmen. The boat fare is 20 kroner ($3.30) for adults, 12 kroner ($2) for children.

WHERE TO STAY

Remember that many hotels offer special summer prices from the end of June to the end of August. The rest of the year, hotels offer 2-night weekend reductions.

VERY EXPENSIVE

PRINSEN, Kongensgate 30, N-7000 Trondheim. Tel. 07/53-06-50. Fax 07/55-324. 85 rms (all with bath). MINIBAR TV TEL **Bus:** 2, 5, 6, 7, 9.

$ Rates: Summer (with a Scandinavian Bonus Pass), 485 kroner ($80.45) single; 620 kroner ($102.85) double. Winter, 775–920 kroner ($128.55–$152.65) single; 1,000–1,350 kroner ($165.90–$223.95) double. AE, DC, MC, V.

One of my longtime favorites, this prestigious hotel was built in 1959 and renovated in 1990. Bedrooms are well furnished. It has a number of facilities, including its Theatregrill and Wine Lounge (see "Where to Dine," below), a popular pub in a separate building across the courtyard in back. There's another cozy bar near the ground-floor reception area. The hotel serves the best breakfast and lunchtime buffets in Trondheim. Room service and laundry services are available.

ROYAL GARDEN HOTEL, Kjøpmannsgate 73, N-7001 Trondheim. Tel. 07/52-11-00. Fax 07/53-17-66. 300 rms (all with bath), 9 suites. MINIBAR TV TEL **Bus:** 54.

$ Rates (including breakfast): Summer and weekends year round, 640 kroner ($106.20) single; 830 kroner ($137.70) double. Winter weekdays 1,290 kroner ($214.00) single; 1,350 kroner ($223.95) double; from 2,200 kroner ($365) suites. AE, DC, MC, V.

This architecturally innovative hotel lies at the northwestern edge of the Old Town, a 10-minute walk southwest of the rail station. It opened in 1984, with a soaring lobby atrium and lavishly furnished and plant-filled public rooms. The comfortable bedrooms have color TVs with video, plus many other comforts. Each was designed as a double. On one of its indoor terraces, evening piano music is played at the bar. There are two elegant restaurants, Cicignon, with live dance music, and the more formal and expensive Prins Olav Grill, both with views of the harbor.

EXPENSIVE

HOTEL AUGUSTIN, Kongensgate 26, N-7011 Trondheim. Tel. 07/52-83-48. Fax 07/51-55-01. 75 rms (all with bath). TV TEL **Bus:** 2, 5, 6, 7, 9.

$ Rates: Summer and weekends year round, 475 kroner ($78.80) single; 600

kroner ($99.55) double. Winter weekends, 800 kroner ($132.70) single; 900 kroner ($149.30) double. AE, DC, MC, V.

In the center of Trondheim, only a short walk from the marketplace, the Augustin offers spacious and comfortable rooms with wide beds, trouser presses, and hairdryers. Some rooms are reserved for nonsmokers. Each room contains a small refrigerator well stocked with fruit juices and mineral water. Liquor can be purchased downstairs at the reception desk. The hotel serves only breakfast, but sandwiches and hot drinks are available 24 hours a day.

BRITANNIA HOTEL, Dronningens Gate 5, N-7001 Trondheim. Tel. 07/53-00-40. Fax 07/51-29-00. 177 rms (all with bath), 3 suites. MINIBAR TV TEL **Bus:** 2, 5, 6, 7, 9.

$ **Rates** (including breakfast): Summer and weekends year round, 525 kroner ($87.10) single; 800 kroner ($132.70) double. Winter weekdays, 825–1,150 kroner ($136.85–$190.80) single; 1,150 kroner ($190.80) double. Suites, from 1,750 kroner ($290.35) double. AE, DC, MC, V.

Originally built at the turn of the century, this is Trondheim's greatest hotel, with many of its original details intact. The columned, marble lobby is imposing, and the ornate Palm Garden (Palmehave) with its art nouveau winter garden, fountain, and violinist captures the grand spirit of the place. Each of the bedrooms has been renovated with soft carpets and pastel-colored upholsteries. There's also a stylish and intimate modern piano bar.

HOTEL RESIDENCE, Munkegaten 26, N-7000 Trondheim. Tel. 07/52-83-80. Fax 07/52-64-60. 66 rms (all with bath), 6 suites. MINIBAR TV TEL **Bus:** 2, 5, 6, 7, 9.

$ **Rates** (including breakfast): Summer and weekends year round, 520 kroner ($86.25) single; 620 kroner ($102.85) double and suite. Winter weekdays, 925 kroner ($153.45) single; 1,050 kroner ($174.20) double and suite. AE, DC, MC, V.

Located on the market square across the street from the Royal Palace, the Hotel Residence, built in 1915 in the Jugend style, has recently been renovated and there are extra amenities including color TVs, videos, radios, and safes. Suites cost the same as regular doubles. The American Bar is the popular watering hole in the evening; outside is the Wintergarden, a café where both refreshments and food are served. Next to the bar, you'll find an excellent dining room, known as "The Restaurant" with an exceptional wine cellar. A dinner here costs from 200 kroner ($33.20).

MODERATE

GILDEVAGEN HOTELL, Söndre Gate 22B, N-7010 Trondheim. Tel. 07/52-83-40. Fax 07/52-38-98. 74 rms (all with bath). MINIBAR TV TEL.

$ **Rates** (including breakfast): Mid-June to mid-Aug and weekends year round, 435 kroner ($72.15) single; 540 kroner ($89.60) double. Winter weekdays, 640–720 kroner ($106.20–$119.45) single; 640–835 kroner ($106.20–$138.55) double. AE, DC, MC, V.

Locals often cite this hotel as offering good value. It lies a short walk uphill from the harbor, near the Old Town's famous bridge and the train station. The best (most modern) rooms lie on the second and third floors, as they were the most recently renovated.

The bedrooms, for the most part, are quite large, most with phones, TVs, and videos. Meals, including the big Norwegian cold-table breakfast, are served in the old-fashioned dining room, but there is also a cheaper cafeteria.

LARSSENS HOTELL, Thomas Angells Gate 10, N-7000 Trondheim. Tel. 07/52-88-51. Fax 07/52-45-15. 30 rms (all with bath). MINIBAR TV TEL **Bus:** 2, 5, 6, 7, 9.

$ **Rates** (including breakfast): Summer and weekends year round, 420 kroner ($69.70) single; 520 kroner ($86.25) double. Winter weekdays, 660 kroner ($109.50) single; 760 kroner ($126.10) double. AE, DC, MC, V.

On a quiet street near the Trondheim Concert Hall, a 15-minute walk south of the cathedral, this hotel is intimate and personal. Its Jugendstil facade dates from around the turn of the century, and the interior has been tastefully modernized, as have the well-furnished bedrooms. Each bedroom has at least one original painting by a local artist. The hotel also serves good food (dinners between 5 and 8pm), and is licensed to sell beer and wine.

TRONDHEIM HOTELL, Kongensgate 15, N-7013 Trondheim. Tel. 07/52-70-30. Fax 07/51-60-58. 140 rms (all with bath). A/C MINIBAR TV TEL **Bus:** 2, 5, 6, 7, 9.

$ Rates (including breakfast): Summer and weekends year round, 350 kroner ($58.05) single; 450–500 kroner ($74.65–$82.95) double. Winter weekdays, 750 kroner ($124.45) single; 800 kroner ($132.70) double. AE, DC, MC, V.

The Trondheim Hotell, near the market square, offers spacious bedrooms filled with comfortably upholstered furniture in pastel shades, many with an extra foldaway bed. Some rooms are suitable for the handicapped and others are reserved for nonsmokers. Constructed in 1913, it was renovated and expanded in 1990. Its Pub Adrian serves light international meals, and its Sola Bar is a popular rendezvous. Guests of the hotel have free entrance to the hotel's nightclub and disco. Parking facilities are available, as is a self-service laundry.

BUDGET

SINGSAKER STUDENTERHJEM, Rogertsgate 1, N-7016 Trondheim. Tel. 07/52-00-92. 106 rms (16 with bath). TEL **Bus:** 63.

$ Rates (including breakfast): 285 kroner ($47.30) single without bath, 360 kroner ($59.70) single with bath; 435 kroner ($72.15) double without bath, 550 kroner ($91.25) double with bath. AE, DC, MC, V. **Closed:** Aug 20–June 15.

This student residential hall is also a choice bargain hotel in summer. It's about a 10-minute walk from the center of Trondheim. Bedrooms are comfortably cozy—and all have water basins. The dining room is plainly decorated but serves good, wholesome breakfasts. In the evening, young people gather around the open fireplace, watch television, and play billiards or other games. The hotel is licensed to sell beer and wine.

WHERE TO DINE

Try a local specialty **vafler med øst** (waffle and cheese), sold at most cafeterias and restaurants.

EXPENSIVE

BRYGGEN, Bakklandet 66. Tel. 52-02-30.
  Cuisine: NORWEGIAN/FRENCH. **Reservations:** Recommended.
$ Prices: Fixed-price menus 295–375 kroner ($48.95–$62.20); appetizers 45–75 kroner ($7.45–$12.45); main dishes 90–230 kroner ($14.95–$38.15). MC, V.
  Open: Mon–Sat 11am–10pm. **Closed:** Last 3 weeks of July.

This special atmospheric restaurant is a 15-minute walk from the town center at Gamle Bybro, the Old Town Bridge. The menu depends on ingredients in season. Before 3pm you can enjoy pancakes and light meals that are much cheaper than the dinner fare. You might begin with fish-and-shellfish soup, for which all the ingredients come from the area. For a main course, try Norwegian duck suprême, medallions of reindeer in a juniper-berry cream sauce, or the fresh fish of the day poached in wine and served with a sauce made of cream and herbs.

JONATHAN'S, in the Brittania Hotel, Dronningens Gate 5. Tel. 53-00-40.
  Cuisine: NORWEGIAN/FRENCH. **Reservations:** Required. **Bus:** 2, 5, 6, 7, 9.
$ Prices: Appetizers 45–95 kroner ($7.45–$15.75); main dishes 160–230 kroner ($26.55–$38.15). AE, DC, MC, V.

Open: Lunch Mon–Sat 11am–3pm; dinner Mon–Sat 6–11pm.

Rich with atmosphere, Jonathan's is designed like a Mediterranean wine cellar, with antiques, a big open fireplace, and waiters colorfully dressed as troubadours. Dinner might include canapés of shrimp, smoked salmon, and local caviar, followed by grilled salmon garnished with shellfish and fresh vegetables or several kinds of grilled steaks, perhaps a veal schnitzel.

TÅRNRESTAURANTEN GALAKSEN, Blussuvoll. Tel. 51-31-66.
Cuisine: INTERNATIONAL/NORWEGIAN. **Reservations:** Required. **Bus:** 20, 60.
$ Prices: Appetizers 65–75 kroner ($10.80–$12.45); main dishes 135–195 kroner ($22.40–$32.35). AE, DC, MC, V.
Open: Mon–Sat 11:30am–midnight, Sun noon–7pm.

This is the only revolving restaurant in Norway, located in the Tyholttårnet tower. The Galaksen is found just up the stairs from the view gallery. The floor makes one rotation an hour to give diners a panoramic look at Trondheim. Specialties include veal Cordon Bleu, a house composition of fish, the chef's special filet of beef, or a roulade of salmon. There is also a good wine list. Lunch costs from 175 kroner ($29.05).

MODERATE

HAVFRUEN FISKERESTAURANT, Kjøpmannsgata 7. Tel. 53-26-26.
Cuisine: SEAFOOD. **Reservations:** Required. **Bus:** 2, 5, 6, 7, 9.
$ Prices: Appetizers 55–65 kroner ($9.10–$10.80); main dishes 95–155 kroner ($15.75–$25.70). MC, V.
Open: Lunch Mon–Sat noon–3pm; dinner Mon–Sat 3–11pm.

Known as Trondheim's "one and only fish restaurant," Havfruen (in English, "mermaid") is located in a 19th-century warehouse near the Nide Iven River and decorated, naturally, in a nautical style. Only the freshest fish and produce are used. You might begin with a delectable fish soup or the fowl and fish pâté. Main dishes include a salmon schnitzel, oven-glazed halibut, and grilled angler fish in a curry-cream sauce.

TAVERN PÅ SVERRESBORG, Sverresborg Allé. Tel. 52-09-32.
Cuisine: NORWEGIAN. **Reservations:** Required. **Bus:** 8, 9.
$ Prices: Appetizers 36–45 kroner ($5.95–$7.45); main dishes 95–135 kroner ($15.75–$22.40). MC, V.
Open: Mon–Fri 4pm–midnight, Sat 2pm–midnight, Sun noon–midnight.

This 1739 wood-framed tavern, once a merchant's house, is now a national shrine. Trønder specialties at reasonable prices are served here. Try the blandet spekemat, served with flatbrød; it consists of thinly sliced smoked ham, diced meat, slices of salami, smoked mutton, and little garnishes of lettuce and tomato. Lots of other comparably priced items are offered to those who consider this fare too simple. You can order rømmegrøt (sour-cream porridge), *Finnbiff* (reindeer meat), omelets, and various preparations of herring.

THEATREGRILL & VINSTUA, in the Prinsen Hotel, Kongensgate 30. Tel. 53-06-50.
Cuisine: INTERNATIONAL. **Reservations:** Not required. **Bus:** 2, 5, 6, 7, 9.
$ Prices: Appetizers 45–55 kroner ($7.45–$9.10); main dishes 85–145 kroner ($14.10–$24.05). AE, DC, MC, V.
Open: Mon–Sat 3pm–midnight.

Close to the Trøndelag Theatre, this restaurant in the Prinsen Hotel serves a special theater platter on show nights. The restaurant has the traditional and intimate atmosphere of a Norwegian farmhouse. Specialties include roast monkfish, lamb kebab, roast filet of reindeer, and French onion soup with cheese, followed by a homemade caramel soufflé.

INEXPENSIVE

DICKENS, Kjøpmannsgaten 57. Tel. 51-57-50.
   Cuisine: INTERNATIONAL. **Reservations:** Not required. **Bus:** 2, 5, 6, 7, 9.
$ Prices: Appetizers 48–66 kroner ($7.95–$10.95); main dishes 65–155 kroner ($10.80–$25.70); pizzas 58–100 kroner ($9.60–$16.60). AE, DC, MC, V.
   Open: Mon–Fri 4pm–midnight, Sat noon–1am, Sun 2pm–1am.
Housed in a restored 18th-century warehouse, this old inn along the river, near the Royal Garden Hotel, is a 10-minute walk north of the bus station. The food is well prepared and tasty. Try such dishes as Mexican tacos, onion soup, steak tartare, prawn cocktail, filet of fried plaice, or the chef's pepper steak. Most diners come here for pizza and beer. In one large, drafty room, you'll find an array of tables, and against one wall is a large pub where people come to drink half liters of beer at 36 kroner ($5.95).

EVENING ENTERTAINMENT

STUDIO HJORTEN, in the Royal Garden Hotel, Kjøpmannsgate 73. Tel. 52-11-00.
   This hotel nightclub has a fun and relaxing ambience. You can dance into the wee hours of the morning to disco music, with live music on Sunday. Tuned to younger nightclubbers, it's open daily from 9am to 3pm. A beer will set you back 38 kroner ($6.30); a scotch and soda, 50 kroner ($8.30). Bus: 54.
   Admission: 40 kroner ($6.65) Tues–Thurs, 60 kroner ($9.95) Fri–Sat.

SOMMER'N, in the Prinsen Hotel, Kongensgaten 30. Tel. 53-06-50.
   A place popular with locals during the summer, Sommer'n offers live music as well as disco, and is a good place to go if you want to get away from the mobs of teenagers at other nightspots. It's open Monday through Saturday from 8pm to 2am; closed September to May. Beer costs 37 kroner ($6.15).
   Admission: 50 kroner ($8.30); free for hotel guests.

EASY EXCURSIONS

The islands of **Hitra** (Ansnes) and **Frøya** (Sistranda) can be reached by fast steamer operating from Trondheim daily except Sunday. For more information, ask at the tourist information office in Trondheim.
   Hitra is one of Norway's largest islands, with a weatherbeaten and varied scenery of forests, wooded hills, well-stocked lakes, weathered rocks, and small fjords. It is also known for the large herds of red deer that roam here. The **Dolm Church,** and **Dolmen town,** a miniature community designed and built by a Dolmoy crofter and fisherman, are other attractions. When you have reached Hitra, you should make the hop across to neighboring Frøya by ferry.

---

7. RØROS

99 miles SE of Trondheim, 248 miles north of Oslo

GETTING THERE   By Plane   The airport is near the town center. Flights wing in daily from Trondheim and Oslo.

By Train   Røros has rail links with Oslo and Trondheim. One or two daily trains arrive from Trondheim, taking 3 hours, and from Oslo, taking 5½ hours.

By Bus   One or two buses a day connect Trondheim with Røros, taking 3¼ hours.

By Car   From Trondheim, take the E6 south to the junction of Route 30, where you should head east for Røros.

ESSENTIALS   The tourist office, **Røros Reiselivslag,** Bergmannsplassen, N-7460 Røros (tel. 074/11-165), offers assistance in sightseeing and arranging accommodations. The **telephone area code** for Røros is 074.

Røros is perhaps the most characteristic of Norway's mining towns. More than 300 years old, with some 80 preserved houses still in use, Røros was the home of Johan Falkberget, the author who lived at Ratvollen and died in 1967.

WHAT TO SEE & DO

The best way to see Røros in summer is to take a **guided walk through the Old Town,** starting at the Røros tourist office and ending with a guided tour of the Røros Church built in 1650. From June 1 to June 22, tours leave Monday through Saturday at 11am; June 23 to August 19, Monday through Saturday at noon and 3pm and on Sunday at 3pm; and August 20 to September 9, Monday through Friday at 11am. Adults pay 20 kroner ($3.30); children, 10 kroner ($1.65).

At the tourist office (see above) you can also arrange a guided tour of **Olav's Mine,** which consists of two mines, Nyberget and Kronprins Olavsgruva. All other copper mines in the area have been closed; only these have been kept open to show people what they are like. Daily guided tours are conducted throughout the summer. Olavsgruva, site of the mine, is 6 miles east of Røros and buses run daily from the town center. The tourist office will give you a timetable.

Guided tours are conducted from June 1 to June 22, Monday through Saturday at 1pm and 3pm and on Sunday at noon; June 23 to August 10, daily at 10:30am, noon, and 1:30, 3, 4:30, and 6pm; August 20 to September 9, Monday through Saturday at 1pm and 3pm and on Sunday at noon. The admission is 32 kroner ($5.30) for adults and 16 kroner ($2.65) for children. Bus fares to reach the site are 50 kroner ($8.30) for adults and 10 kroner ($1.65) for children.

You'll find easy mountain rambling, excursions and boat trips on Lake Femunden, visits to Funäsdalen in Sweden, fishing in rivers and lakes, and good shopping and walking in the town center.

WHERE TO STAY & DINE

HOTEL RØROS, An-Bagrittsvei, N-7460 Røros. Tel. 074/11-011. Fax 074/10-022. 115 rms (all with bath), 1 suite, 3 mini-suites. MINIBAR TV TEL.
$ Rates (including breakfast): Summer, 525 kroner ($87.10) single; 680 kroner ($112.80) double. Winter, 780 kroner ($129.40) single, 1,020 kroner ($169.20) double. Suites from 1,080 kroner ($195.75). AE, DC, MC, V.
This hotel enjoys a good view from its high-altitude position over the town, a quarter mile north of the rail station. It was built in the mid-1950s but enlarged many times since. Bedrooms are comfortable and decorated in light pastels such as yellow, pink, or blue, each opening onto either a view of the town below or the mountains. An orchestra plays for dancing 6 nights a week, and the hotel has a disco, nightclub, swimming pool, and sauna. For outdoor sports, there is a tennis court and minigolf. A special feature of the hotel is its offering of a *mattorg* (a smörgåsbord to which barbecued foods have been added). A lunchtime visit to this table costs 135 kroner ($22.40), rising to 165 kroner ($27.35) in the evening. You can stay here in summer on a 2-night arrangement costing 1,250 kroner ($207.40) for one person with full board or 995 kroner ($165.05) per person based on double occupancy with full board.

BERGSTADENS TURISTHOTEL, Osloveien 2, N-7460 Røros. Tel. 074/11-111. Fax 074/10-155. 70 rms (all with bath). MINIBAR TV TEL.
$ Rates (including breakfast): Sun–Thurs year round, 760 kroner ($126.10) single; 875 kroner ($145.15) double. Summer, 600 kroner ($99.55) single; 800 kroner ($132.70) double. Certain weekend reductions granted. AE, DC, MC, V.
In the center of the resort, 200 yards from the rail station, this hotel was built before World War II. It is the most central and visible in town, blending in with the other buildings because of its exterior sheathing of brown wood. Each of the comfortably furnished bedrooms, many painted in pale pinks or blues, opens onto views of the

mountains. Most of the rooms were recently restored. It also contains more drinking and dining facilities than its competitors, including a pub, a disco, a cafeteria, and two different restaurants.

On weekends, there is a price reduction only if you agree to take full board, including dinner on Friday and continuing through lunch on Sunday. The whole weekend in summer would cost 800 to 1,000 kroner ($132.70 to $165.90) per person on that plan, or 900 to 1,450 kroner ($149.30 to $240.55) on a winter weekend. Singles pay a 120-krone ($19.90) supplement.

CHAPTER 21

BODØ, TROMSØ & NORTHERN NORWAY

The great stretch along the coast—beyond the Arctic Circle to the North Cape and Norwegian Lapland (Finnmark)—is a memorable journey. The first county in the land of sunlit nights is Nordland, beyond the Arctic Circle, with Bodø as its capital. Nordland is the second-largest county of Norway, and together with Troms and Finnmark comprise what is geographically known as northern Norway.

Nordland stretches northward along the border of Sweden, a full 310 miles to the mountains of Troms where the Vesterålen archipelago blends with the long arm of the Lofoten Islands. Nordland links southern and northern Norway, tenuously at one point, since it is only 4 miles wide between the sea and the Swedish border.

Its natural phenomena have figured into world literature. Edgar Allan Poe's maelstrom in the book *Tales of the Grotesque and Arabesque* is based on the Moskenesstraumen of Nordland, and Jules Verne wrote about the same maelstrom in his book *20,000 Leagues Under the Sea.*

The region of northern Norway is steeped in history and legend. At the end of the last Ice Age, Norse people arrived to make a precarious living between the glaciers and the water's edge. Their presence is immortalized in rock carvings. The original inhabitants, however, were the Lapps, who roamed the heaths and mountains with their reindeer herds. Where the E6 highway crosses the Arctic Circle, in the Saltfjell mountains, the Lapps erected their sacrificial stones in pagan times.

The weather is always unpredictable in the region. July, every now and then, brings snow.

Troms and Finnmark are northern Norway's northernmost provinces, and Tromsø is often called the "capital of the north." Viking lords once operated a trading empire from Troms. Today it is estimated that some half of the local citizens live offshore.

In Finnmark, everything is virtually new. The land was devastated by the fleeing Nazi army in World War II, and with the advance of the Soviet army and their bombs, Hitler ordered a "scorched earth" policy for Finnmark.

Most foreign visitors come to the north of Norway to see the **Nordkapp** (North Cape) and the **Midnight Sun,** which is visible from the middle of May until the end of July (see below). Kirkenes is the last town before you face the Soviet border.

WHAT'S SPECIAL ABOUT NORTHERN NORWAY

Great Towns/Villages

☐ Bodø, north of the Arctic Circle, the capital of Nordland, a county of scenic wonders.

☐ Tromsø, the capital of northern Norway, a bustling, thriving city of summer Midnight Suns and Arctic winters.

Scenic Wonders

☐ The Arctic Circle—crossing it is a major goal of world travelers.

☐ The Midnight Sun, north of the circle—sunny nights and bright days in midsummer.

☐ North Cape, the goal of the long trek north, a polar coastline, bleak and harsh—Europe's northernmost point.

☐ The aurora borealis, the flaming spectacle of the Arctic winter sky.

☐ Svartisen Glacier, an ice plateau covering 150 square miles of high mountains and narrow fjords.

Ace Attractions

☐ The Planetarium at Tromsø, the world's northernmost such site, best for viewing the mysterious Arctic sky.

Island Excursions

☐ The offshore polar islands of Lofoten-Vesterålen, a beautiful region, filled with bird life.

Special Events

☐ Two midsummer events—the North Norway Festival and the International Sea Fishing Festival at Harstad.

THE NORTHERN LIGHTS

The **Arctic Circle** marks the bounds of the ✪ **Midnight Sun** of the Arctic summer and the sunless winters of the north. Nevertheless, scientists have calculated that in spite of up to 2 months of twilight winter days in the north, the sunny nights and the bright days for the rest of the year, the moonlight, starlight, and northern lights together give more light in the course of a year than you can experience at the Equator.

Crossing the Arctic Circle is perhaps one of the primary reasons visitors choose to come to Scandinavia. To a tourist it is a major event in world exploration.

Then there are the northern lights, the ✪ **aurora borealis,** the flaming spectacle of the Arctic winter sky, with its flickering and undulating movement in yellow-green, green, red, and violet. During the hours of the magnetic midnight, between 6 and 10pm, the light can be so strong that you can read a newspaper outdoors. So mysterious, powerful, and alarming is the aurora that when it was observed in the more southerly skies, people took it as an omen of impending disaster. The lights are actually caused by electrically charged particles entering the atmosphere and controlled by the active magnetic fields of the earth itself.

SEEING NORTHERN NORWAY

GETTING THERE

The easiest way to explore the region is to take a Bergen coastal steamer that stops off at the North Cape, the northernmost extension of Europe, lit by the Midnight Sun. Bodø is the best center for exploring Nordland, and it can be reached by plane from Oslo. The county of Troms is best explored with Tromsø as your gateway. It, too, has

MIDNIGHT SUN

The sun is visible 24 hours a day as follows:

Spitsbergen, Norway	April 20–August 21
Hammerfest, Norway	May 12–August 1
Tromsø, Norway	May 14–July 30
Harstad, Norway	May 23–July 22
Svolvaer (Lofoten), Norway	May 23–July 22
Bodø, Norway	June 1–July 13

good plane connections with Oslo. Flying to Bodø and Tromsø is the fastest way of reaching this vast expanse of land.

The Nordland rail line ends in Bodø, but it's possible to travel from Stockholm to remote Narvik, north of Bodø, by train. There are airports at Alta, Lakselv, Vadsø, and Kirkenes, near the Soviet border, for those wishing to see Finnmark, the northernmost province of Norway. If you're traveling independently, exploring Finnmark by bus, Honningsvåg is the best center for viewing the North Cape. If you are going by car, the E6 and other roads will take you to many places, and ferries and bridges link the northern locales.

In the far north there are no rail lines. Visitors who prefer not to fly or drive can take the bus, which goes from village to village even in the worst weather.

A SUGGESTED ITINERARY

If you have time, northern Norway is a rewarding target in Europe. The problem is, it takes time.

Day 1: Go to Bodø for the night.
Day 2 & 3: From Bodø, take an excursion to the Lofoten and Vesterålen Islands, reached by boat or plane.
Day 4: Return to Bodø and fly to Tromsø to see its attractions.
Day 5: Transfer to Alta for the night.
Day 6: From a base either in Honningsvåg or Hammerfest, journey by boat and bus to the North Cape.

---

1. BODØ

889 miles north of Bergen, 466 miles north of Trondheim, 811 miles north of Oslo

GETTING THERE By Plane Bodø is connected to Oslo by daily flights, taking 1½ hours, and to Trondheim, taking 1 hour.

By Train Bodø can be reached from Oslo by rail, as it lies at the termination of the Nordland train. Two trains a day leave Trondheim for Bodø, taking 10 hours 20 minutes.

By Bus Fauske is a terminus transport hub along the E6 highway to the north and Route 80 west to Bodø. It has bus links to Bodø at the rate of two daily, taking 1 hour 10 minutes. If you take the train from Stockholm to Narvik, north of Bodø, you can make bus connections to Fauske and Bodø, taking 5 hours.

By Coastal Steamer Bodø is a stopover on the coastal express steamer (*Hurtigrute*) from Bergen in the south to Kirkenes in the north.

By Car Take the E6 highway north from Trondheim until you reach Fauske at the junction of Route 80 west to Bodø.

ESSENTIALS The **Bodø Tourist Office,** Sjøgaten 21, N-8000 Bodø (tel. 081/21-240), is in the town center. In summer, it's open Monday through Friday from 9am to 4:30pm and on Saturday from 9am to 2pm. The **telephone area code** for Bodø is 081.

This seaport, the terminus of the Nordland railway, lies just north of the Arctic Circle. Visitors flock to Bodø, the capital of Nordland, for a glimpse of the Midnight Sun, which shines brightly from June 1 to July 13. But don't always expect to have a clear view of it at this time, as many nights are rainy or hazy. Bodø citizens eventually pay for this extra daylight: The sun completely disappears from December 19 to January 9.

Excursions are possible in many directions—to both glaciers and bird islands, but most important, to the Lofoten Islands (see below).

WHAT TO SEE & DO

BODØ DOMKIRKE, Torv Gate 12. Tel. 31-735.

Completed in 1956, this is the most notable postwar building built since German bombers leveled Bodø on May 27, 1940. Inside, tufted rugs depicting ecclesiastial themes, wall hangings, and a stained-glass window that captures the northern lights. A memorial outside honors those killed in the war: "No one mentioned, no one forgotten." There's also an outstanding spire that stands separate from the main building.

Admission: Free.

Open: May–Sept, daily noon–3pm. **Closed:** Oct–Apr.

BODIN KIRKE, Gamle Riks Vei 74. Tel. 22-470.

Dating from 1242, this church is 2 miles east of the town center. Inside, you can see a baroque altarpiece.

Admission: Free.

Open: May–Sept, daily 10am–8pm. **Closed:** Oct–Apr. **Bus:** 12 from the station.

NORDLANDMUSEET (Nordland Museum), Prinsengate 116. Tel. 21-640.

Located in the city center, exhibits depict the history of the town and the lives of the Lapps. You can also see and appreciate the elegant lines of the Nordland boat.

Admission: 10 kroner ($1.65) adults, 2 kroner (35¢) children.

Open: Mon–Fri 9am–3pm, Sat 10am–3pm, Sun noon–3pm.

A NEARBY ATTRACTION

Panorama Senteret is the world's northernmost recreation park, with activities for children and adults. The park has domestic animals, a gold-mining camp replica, shooting gallery, grill area, disco, pub, and cafeteria in addition to its restaurant (see "Where to Dine," below). There's a panoramic view of Ronvikfjell. The park is 4 miles north of the town center, a 60-krone ($9.95) taxi ride. Admission is 30 kroner ($5) for adults, 20 kroner ($3.30) for children; 70 kroner ($11.60) for a family ticket.

SPORTS/RECREATION

If you feel like riding horseback into the Midnight Sun, **Bodø Hestecenter,** Soloya Gård (tel. 14-148), a little more than 9 miles from Bodø, rents horses. Buses go there Monday through Friday morning and evening and Saturday morning. For more information, call the Bodø Tourist Office. The cost is 60 kroner ($9.95) per hour.

Svommehallen, Sivert Nielsens Gate 63 (tel. 35-480), is an indoor swimming pool open Monday through Friday from 8:30am to 8pm, on Saturday from 12:30 to

8pm, and on Sunday from noon to 4pm. Price per hour is 20 kroner ($3.30) for adults and 10 kroner ($1.65) for children.

WHERE TO STAY

The Bodø Tourist Office will help you arrange for a room in a private home or hotel.

EXPENSIVE

DIPLOMAT HOTEL, Storgaten 23, N-8001 Bodø. Tel. 081/27-000. Fax 081/22-460. 104 rms (all with bath), 3 suites. MINIBAR TV TEL.

$ Rates (including breakfast): Summer, 520 kroner ($86.25) single; 600 kroner ($99.55) double. Winter weekdays, 1,000 kroner ($165.90) single; 1,250 kroner ($207.40) double. Winter weekends, 600 kroner ($99.55) single; 750 kroner ($124.45) double. Suites from 2,000 kroner ($331.80). AE, DC, MC, V. **Parking:** Available.

Opening onto a view of Vestfjorden, this is one of Bodø's best hotels, built in 1986 with another enlargement in 1990. All the well-furnished bedrooms have TVs with video, hairdryers, and large writing desks. The hotel's popular restaurants are recommended separately (see "Where to Dine," below). There is a covered car-parking area. The hotel is located at the harbor.

SAS ROYAL HOTEL, Storgaten 2, N-8000 Bodø. Tel. 081/24-100. Fax 081/27-493. 184 rms (all with bath), 6 suites. MINIBAR TV TEL.

$ Rates (including breakfast): May–Aug, 530 kroner ($87.95) single; 680–760 kroner ($112.60–$126.10) double. Winter Sun–Thurs, 1,050 kroner single; 1,300 kroner ($215.65) double. Winter Fri–Sat, 575 kroner ($95.40) single; 740 kroner ($122.75) double. Suites from 1,700 kroner ($282.05). AE, DC, MC, V.

By far the finest hotel in the area, this is a glistening modern hotel, with several bars and dining facilities. Bedrooms are furnished in sleek contemporary style, and rooms have such extra amenities as trouser presses and hairdryers. The Royal is on the main street directly on the harborfront.

Dining/Entertainment: Guests drink at the Marlene Bar or go dancing at Marlene Dancing, later enjoying a drink at the Top 13 Panorama Bar. Less formal facilities include the Pizzakjeller'n and the Baquette'n and Balustraden coffee shops.

Services: "Office-for-a-day," express laundry service, 16-hour room service, SAS airline check-in at lobby.

Facilities: Sauna, solarium.

MODERATE

BODØ HOTEL, Professor Schyttesgate 5, N-8001 Bodø. Tel. 081/26-900. Fax 081/25-778. 33 rms (all with bath). MINIBAR TV TEL.

$ Rates (including breakfast): Winter weekends and summer, 450 kroner ($74.65) single; 600 kroner ($99.55) double. Winter weekdays, 710 kroner ($117.80) single; 870 kroner ($144.35) double. AE, DC, MC, V.

Opening in 1987, this hotel quickly became known for its good value. In the town center 2½ blocks from the harbor, it has a helpful staff and comfortably furnished, modern rooms, each with satellite TV with 10 channels. It also offers no-smoking rooms and is equipped for the handicapped. A different color scheme is found on each of the hotel's five floors. The hotel is fully licensed, and operates the Skagen Café and Bistro on the premises, open daily until 11pm.

NORRØNA, Storgaten 4, N-8000 Bodø. Tel. 081/24-118. 101 rms (58 with bath). TV TEL.

$ Rates (including breakfast): 300 kroner ($49.75) single without bath, 540 kroner ($89.60) single with bath; 400 kroner ($66.35) double without bath, 730 kroner ($121.10) double with bath. AE, DC.

The Nørrona is run by the SAS Royal Hotel, which uses it primarily as a bed-and-breakfast. A functional, modern building, it stands in the center of Bodø, offering clean, comfortable, although simply furnished bedrooms. As a guest, you can enjoy the same privileges as patrons of the more expensive SAS Royal Hotel, which lies only 50 yards down the harbor. The hotel operates a coffee shop as well as a British-style pub, Piccadilly.

INEXPENSIVE

CENTRUM HOTEL, Storgaten 39, N-8001, Bodø. Tel. 081/24-888. Fax 081/25-890. 18 rms (none with bath). TV TEL.
$ Rates (including breakfast): Winter weekends and summer, 300 kroner ($49.75) single; 420 kroner ($69.70) double. Winter weekdays, 400 kroner ($66.35) single; 500 kroner ($82.95) double. AE, DC, V. **Parking:** Available.

Rooms in this boardinghouse near the harbor are adequately furnished, clean, and respectable. The upstairs restaurant serves beer and wine. Parking is available. It is located 20 yards from the railway terminal, 150 yards from the boat and bus terminals, and 5 minutes by taxi from the airport.

MIDNATTSOL GUESTHOUSE, Storgaten 65, N-8000 Bodø. Tel. 081/21-926. 16 rms (none with bath).
$ Rates (including breakfast): 325 kroner ($53.90) single; 430 kroner ($71.35) double. No credit cards. **Parking:** Available.

Particularly popular with motorists since it lies on the main street at the junction with Route 80, this hotel rents out adequately but sparsely furnished rooms. Once a private home, the guesthouse is 100 yards from the railway terminal, 300 yards from both the bus and boat terminals, and 10 minutes by taxi from the airport. The guesthouse is licensed to serve beer and wine. Parking facilities are available.

WHERE TO DINE

EXPENSIVE

MARLENE, in the SAS Royal Hotel, Storgaten 2. Tel. 24-100.
Cuisine: SEAFOOD/INTERNATIONAL/NORWEGIAN. **Reservations:** Recommended.
$ Prices: Summer seafood buffet 165 kroner ($27.35); appetizers 48–90 kroner ($7.95–$14.95); main dishes 146–198 kroner ($24.25–$32.85). AE, DC, MC, V.
Open: Daily noon–11:30pm.

Marlene has the best summer seafood buffet in town. From late June to late August you can enjoy various local seafood dishes, including fried squid, smoked halibut, fresh shrimp, coalfish, and cod. You have a selection of various sauces to go with the fish, as well as fish soup, prepared in the style of northern Norway, and finish with a selection of desserts. At any time of the year you can order such good-tasting dishes as cream of wild-mushroom soup, or a seafood appetizer that includes an entire fjord crab garnished with shrimp. Specialties are grilled filet of reindeer and grilled monkfish. It's located on the waterfront.

OASEN, in the Diplomat Hotel, Storgaten 23. Tel. 27-000.
Cuisine: SEAFOOD. **Reservations:** Required.
$ Prices: Appetizers 40–60 kroner ($6.65–$9.95); main dishes 65–175 kroner ($10.80–$29.05); daily lunch plate 76 kroner ($12.60). AE, DC, MC, V.
Open: Mon–Sat noon–11:30pm.

This is the most upscale restaurant in the Hotel Diplomat and one of the best dining rooms in the area. It is very modern in decor, with a theme based on autumnal colors, opening onto a view of the harbor. Fish is the specialty, beginning with fish soup, and followed by angler fish, salmon, or whatever the fishermen caught that day.

MODERATE

BLIX, in the Diplomat Hotel, Storgaten 23. Tel. 27-000.

Cuisine: NORWEGIAN. **Reservations:** Not required.

$ **Prices:** Appetizers 22–45 kroner ($3.65–$7.45); main dishes 64–138 kroner ($10.60–$22.90); daily lunch plate 76 kroner ($12.60). AE, DC, MC, V.

Open: Mon–Sat 3pm–midnight, Sun 2pm–midnight.

Not as expensive as the Oasen (see above) in the same hotel, this restaurant is preferred by the working locals. The decor has an old-fashioned allure with a scattering of antiques. On the lobby level, the restaurant has a separate entrance opening directly onto the street. Try lasagne, steaks, filet of reindeer, or other wholesome and ribsticking—and flavorful—fare. It's located on the harbor.

PANORAMA SENTERET TURISTHYTTA. Tel. 21-131.

Cuisine: NORWEGIAN. **Reservations:** Not required.

$ **Prices:** Appetizers 35–65 kroner ($5.80–$10.80); main dishes 85–135 kroner ($14.10–$22.40). AE, V.

Open: Summer only, daily noon–10pm. **Closed:** Winter.

On the top of a mountain with a magnificent view, this is the most popular excursion point for those who want to dine while watching the Midnight Sun. If you're on a budget, choose carefully from the à la carte menu. Many come just for drinks and snacks (there is a wide selection of open-face sandwiches), since the view is the big treat. Coalfish, a popular Norwegian dish, is always featured. The restaurant is located 4 miles north of the center, best reached by taxi.

INEXPENSIVE

NORMANDIE, Havnegata 1. Tel. 21-832.

Cuisine: PIZZAS. **Reservations:** Not required.

$ **Prices:** Pizzas 58–129 kroner ($9.60–$21.40); main dishes 49–79 kroner ($8.15–$13.10); salads 51 kroner ($8.45). AE, DC, MC, V.

Open: Daily 3pm–midnight.

A noted cheese-and-wine house (called *Vinhus* locally), the Normandie is a favorite with young people who come mainly in the evening to order from 10 different kinds of pizzas. Salads are good and fresh. The place is also a pub and wine bar, but all pretense at being a restaurant is rejected on Friday and Saturday after 7pm when only pizzas, beer, liquor, and wine are served. Beer costs 29 kroner ($4.80) per bottle, and wine goes for 22 kroner ($3.65) per glass. The wine is mostly Italian and French. The Normandie is on a main street 3 blocks inland from the harbor.

EVENING ENTERTAINMENT

TOP 13, in the SAS Royal Hotel, Storgaten 2. Tel. 24-100.

For a grand view of Bodø and the harbor, go to this "hut" perched like a top hat on the roof of the SAS Royal hotel. Take the elevator to the 12th floor and walk up one flight. There is bar service Monday through Saturday from 11am to 2am. Beer costs 38 kroner ($6.30).

MARLENE DANCING, in the SAS Royal Hotel, Storgaten 2. Tel. 24-100.

At Marlene Dancing, the preferred spot for dancing in Bodø, the surroundings are elegant and the latest in recorded music is played. Even though it opens earlier, most people don't show up until 9:30pm. The Marlene Cabinett, with a fireplace, is a little offshoot drinking area of the disco. The place is open Monday through Thursday from 6pm to 2am and on Friday and Saturday from 6pm to 3am. Beer runs 38 kroner ($6.30).

Admission: 40 kroner ($6.65).

VANHULLET NIGHTCLUB, in the Diplomat Hotel, Storgaten 23. Tel. 27-000.

Crowded and fun, the music is always recorded disco, and every Wednesday night is golden oldies. This club is on the lobby level of the Diplomat Hotel (see "Where to Stay," above). Dress is very casual. It's open Monday through Thursday from 8pm to

2am and on Friday and Saturday from 8pm to 3am. A bottle of beer costs 34 kroner ($5.65).

Admission: 40 kroner ($6.65).

EASY EXCURSIONS

THE MAELSTROM From Bodø, you can take a bus to the mighty maelstrom, the ✪ **Saltstraumen Eddy,** some 20 miles away. The variation between high- and low-tide levels pushes immense volumes of water through narrow fjords, creating huge whirlpools. When these whirling "kettles," as the eddies are called, and the surrounding vibrate, they produce an odd yelling sound. Saltstraumen is nearly 2 miles long and only about 500 feet wide, with billions of gallons of water pressed through at speeds of about 10 knots. The bus trip takes 40 minutes each way and leaves daily from the Bodø bus station five times a day, costing 35 kroner ($5.80) for adults, half price for children. It's best to go in the morning. A taxi excursion costs 300 kroner ($49.75).

A GLACIER EXCURSION One of Norway's major tourist attractions, **Svartisen** is second in size only to the Jostedal Glacier. This ice plateau 65 feet above sea level covers 150 square miles of high mountains and narrow fjords. About 100 miles from Bodø, the glacier can be reached by car, although a boat crossing over the Svartisenfjord is more exciting. Tours to the glacier on the Helgeland Express are offered from Bodø several times in summer on Saturday. The charge is 250 kroner ($41.50) for adults, 125 kroner ($20.75) for children under 16. The tours leave Bodø at 1pm and return at 8pm. You can go ashore to examine the Engaglacier and visit the inn there. For reservations and details, call **Saltens Dampskipsselskap** (tel. 21-020).

2. LOFOTEN & VESTERÅLEN ISLANDS

Svolvaer is 174 miles west of Narvik, 174
miles north of Bodø, 298 miles south of Tromsø

GETTING THERE By Plane Svolvaer is served by Widerøe Airline. Planes leave Bodø five times a day.

By Bus There are bus connections to Vesterålen and to Fauske/Bodø to coincide with train service. There are also connections to Narvik to link with the Swedish railway. You can take a bus to Ulvsvåg on the main E6, then catch a connecting bus to Skutvik, where you can board a ferry to Svolvaer.

By Car The quickest way to drive to the Lofoten Islands is to take the Skutvik–Svolvaer ferry, a 2-hour trip, with eight crossings daily in summer. There is also ferry service to the bird islands, Røst and Vaerky. For information and reservations, call **Ofotens og Vesterålens Dampskibsselskab** a/s, Box 57, N-8501 Narvik (tel. 082/47-252).

By Coastal Steamer Coastal steamers leaving from Bergen and other places along the coast call daily at Stamsund and Svolvaer. The steamer leaves Bodø at 3pm daily.

ESSENTIALS Tourist information is available from the **Lofoten Tourist Board,** Box 210, N-8301 Svolvaer (tel. 088/71-053). The **Vesterålen Travel Association,** Box 243, N-8401 Sortland (tel. 088/21-555), will help you figure out where to stay and what to do in the islands.

The **telephone area code** for Lofoten and Vesterålen is 088.

The island kingdom of Lofoten/Vesterålen, considered one of the most beautiful regions of Norway, lies 123 miles north of the Arctic Circle and has a population of

35,000 spread out among both the large and small islands. Many travelers come just to fish, but the area offers a rich bird life and abundant flora. The summer brings the Midnight Sun from mid-May to the end of July.

THE LOFOTEN ISLANDS

The Lofoten Islands start in the east at Vågan and stretch seaward toward the southwest to Røst and Skomvaer. The steep Lofoten mountain peaks—often called the Lofotwall—shelter a stretch of farmland and deep fjords, and offer natural protection from the elements resulting in stable weather.

The North Atlantic drift of the Gulf Stream contributes to the seasonal Lofoten fishing, Lofotfisket. Beyond Lofoten, and especially in the Vestfjord, are spawned the Arctic Sea codfish, with huge harvesting operations carried on between January and April.

The first inhabitants of the Lofoten were nomads who survived by hunting and fishing, but excavations show that agriculture was practiced here at least 4,000 years ago. Farming, fishing, and trading were Viking pursuits and examples of Viking housing sites can be seen on Vestbågøya, where more than 1,000 burial mounds from the period have been registered in the area.

Harsh treatment by the Nazis during World War II played a major part in the creation of the famous Norwegian resistance movement. Allied forces that landed here to harass the German iron-ore boats sailing from Narvik withdrew in June 1940. They took as many of the island civilians as they could with them to Scotland for the duration of the war.

Today the Lofotens and their neighbors to the north, the Vesterålen Islands (see below), have modern towns with shops, hotels, restaurants, and public transport.

WHAT TO SEE & DO

Outdoor activities range from mountain climbing to diving, canoeing, rambling through the countryside, birdwatching (see "Røst & Vaerøy," below), whale watching, sailing, riding, downhill and cross-country skiing, and ice fishing.

There are handcraft shops at Svolvaer, Leknes, Sørvågen, and Vaerøy.

Examples of a special old-fashioned method of knitting, needle binding, used as far back as Viking times, can also be found here. The **Glass Cabin** at Vikten, near Napp, is northern Norway's only such studio. Open to the public, it offers products of top-quality and original design. The craftsperson Hans Gjertsen, a smith at Sund, is known for his well-made cormorants cast in steel.

The Lofoten Islands are visited by many artists, and there are galleries at Svolvaer, Oersnes, Stamsund, and Leknes, with local and international artists represented. The North Norway Artists' Center is also in Svolvaer.

The fishing village of **Nusfjord** has been cited by UNESCO for its beautiful, well-preserved historic buildings, especially traditional *rorbuer* (see "Where to Stay," below), fishermen's cabins.

VESTVÅGØY MUSEUM, Fygleveien 109. Tel. 80-043.

At Fygle, near Leknes, this museum has exhibits depicting the life-style of the Lofoten fisherman-farmer. It's on the main road at Fygle, 1 mile from Leknes and 9 miles from Stamsund.

Admission: 10 kroner ($1.65) adults, 5 kroner (85¢) children.
Open: June–Aug, Mon–Fri 11am–4pm, Sat noon–3pm. **Closed:** Sept–May.

LOFOTEN MUSEUM, Kabelvåg. (No phone.)

The islands' regional museum, it depicts past life in the Lofoten Islands. Excavations are underway at the site of an old northern Norwegian trading post, Vagar, Europe's northernmost town in the Middle Ages. The museum is located on the outskirts of Kabelvåg, 3 miles from Svolvaer.

Admission: 10 kroner ($1.65) adults, 5 kroner (85¢) children.

Open: June–Aug, Mon–Fri 9am–3pm, Sat–Sun 11am–3pm. **Closed:** Sept–May.

Røst & Vaerøy

Mountains speckled with birds range from Andoy in the north all the way to the southern tip of Lofoten. Many different seabirds can be seen during nesting season, but the most famous nesting cliffs are at Røst and Vaerøy, remote Lofoten islands that can be reached by steamer, plane, or helicopter.

On the flat island of **Røstlandet,** the main attraction is the bird sanctuary, made up of approximately 1,000 little offshore islands comprising the mini-archipelago of Røst. Here, the highly prized eider duck can be found. Locals provide small nesting shelters for the ducks and collect the eiderdown after the ducklings are hatched. Cormorants and seagulls nest on the steep cliffs. Puffins nest at the end of narrow tunnels in the grassy hills, while the auk and the sea eagle nest high up on ledges.

Vaerky's **Mount Mostadfjell** is the nesting place for more than 1½ million seabirds, including sea eagles, auks, puffins, guillemots, kittiwakes, cormorants, and others that breed from May through August.

The **North Vaeroy Church,** with its onion-shaped dome, was brought here from Vagån in 1799. The altarpiece, from around 1400, is a late-medieval English alabaster relief depicting the Annunciation, the Three Magi, the Resurrection, and the Ascension.

For information about these islands, get in touch with the Lofoten Tourist Office or the ferry company, **Ofotens og Vesterålens Dampskibsselskab** a/s, Box 57, N-8501 Narvik (tel. 082/47-252).

WHERE TO STAY & DINE

In addition to hotels, guesthouses, and campsites, the Lofoten and Vesterålen Islands offer temporary (holiday) lodging in old traditional fishermen's cottages known as *rorbuer,* and a larger, usually more modern, version (often two stories), a *sjøhus* (sea house). The traditional *rorbu* was built on the edge of the water, often on piles, with enough room for 10 bunks, a kitchen, and an entrance hall used as a work and storage room. Many *rorbu* today are still simple and unpretentious, but some have electricity, a wood stove, a kitchenette with a sink, and running water. Others have been equipped with such modern amenities as separate bedrooms, with private showers and toilets.

The Lofoten Tourist Board publishes an accommodations guide to the Lofoten Islands, and information about lodging on the Vesterålen Islands is available from their tourist board (see "Essentials," above).

In Stamsunden

STAMSUND LOFOTEN, N-8340 Stamsunden. Tel. 088/89-300. Fax 088/89-655. 28 rms (all with bath). TV TEL.

$ Rates (including breakfast): Summer, 375 kroner ($62.20) single; 600 kroner ($99.55) double. Winter, 700 kroner ($116.15) single; 830 kroner ($137.70) double. AE, DC, MC.

This hotel is in the heart of town, with a view of the harbor. Bedrooms are simply furnished, but comfortable and well maintained. Many have TVs. On the premises is a licensed bar and restaurant. The luncheon buffet costs 150 kroner ($24.90).

In Svolvaer

LOFOTEN NORTON HOTEL, Sivert Nelsen Gate, N-8300 Svolvaer. Tel. 088/71-200. Fax 088/70-850. 48 rms (all with bath). MINIBAR TEL.

$ Rates (including breakfast): Weekdays, 835 kroner ($138.55) single; 980 kroner ($162.60) double. Weekends, 600 kroner ($99.55) single; 750 kroner ($124.45) double. AE, DC, MC, V.

About half the bedrooms at this 1978 hotel in the town center, 400 yards from the express steamer quay, overlook the sea. Bedrooms are well furnished and comfortably modern. On the premises is a fully licensed bar, a pleasant restaurant, and a lively disco. Meals range from 125 to 160 kroner ($20.75 to $26.55).

VESTFJORD HOTEL, Box 386, N-8301 Svolvaer. Tel. 088/70-870. Fax 088/70-854. 57 rms (all with bath). TV TEL.

$ Rates (including breakfast): 560–650 kroner ($92.90–$107.85) single; 680–950 kroner ($112.80–$157.60) double. AE, DC, MC, V.

This hotel, 100 yards from the quay and bus station, is the first thing yachtsmen see when they enter the harbor. Bedrooms are comfortable and functional; 20 contain a minibar, and many overlook the sea. On the premises is a wood-paneled restaurant specializing in fresh fish, and a fully licensed bar. Facilities include a lobby bar, sauna, solarium, and winter garden.

THE VESTERÅLEN ISLANDS

Farther north, but with a gentler landscape and richer farmlands than the Lofotens, the Vesterålen Islands, known for their fishing, have a landscape ranging from marshlands to farms to craggy mountains and white beaches.

The islands are linked with the E6 by six bridges. In addition there are three ports of call for the coastal steamer *Hurtigruten,* as well as two airports. On these islands, you can see the Troll Fjord, fishing villages, bird rocks, museums, old trading centers, and in summer, the Andenes Sea Fishing Festival and an arts festival, Sommer-Melbu, are held.

Like Lofoten, Vesterålen offers accommodations in both the *rorbu* and the *sjøhus* categories.

The **Vesterålen Travel Association,** Box 243, N-8401 Sortland (tel. 088/21-555), will help you figure out where to stay and what to do in the islands.

WHERE TO STAY IN SORTLAND

SORTLAND NORDIC HOTEL, 59 Vesterålsgaten, Langøy Island, N-8401 Sortland. Tel. 088/21-833. Fax 088/22-202. 82 rms (60 with bath). TV TEL.

$ Rates (including breakfast): Summer (with Scandinavian Bonus Pass), 480 kroner ($79.65) single; 560 kroner ($92.90) double. Winter weekdays, 860 kroner ($142.65) single; 1,250 kroner ($207.40) double. Winter weekends, 500 kroner ($82.95) single; 600 kroner ($99.55) double. AE, DC, MC, V.

The only hotel in town, a few hundred feet from the water, has comfortable, modern bedrooms. There's a restaurant, licensed bar, and the island's most popular disco. The hotel has its own activity room, a sauna, and a solarium. There is a boathouse and a pier where boats can be rented and fishing trips arranged.

3. NARVIK

982 miles west of Stockholm, 187 miles NE of Bodø, 919 miles north of Oslo

GETTING THERE   By Train   Two to three trains a day run from Stockholm, taking 21 to 24 hours.

By Bus   Two buses a day go from Fauske/Bodø, taking 5 hours.

By Car   The E6 highway that begins at Oslo continues north, passing through Narvik.

ESSENTIALS   The **tourist office** is located at Kongensgate 66 (tel. 082/43-309). The **telephone area code** for Narvik is 082.

This ice-free seaport on the Ofot Fjord is in Nordland fylke, 250 miles north of the Arctic Circle. Narvik boasts Europe's most modern shipping harbor for iron ore, founded in 1903 when the Ofoten railway line was completed to transport iron ore around the world. It's a magnificent scenic route (the northernmost electrified railway line in the world) through precipitous mountain terrain, tunnels, ridges, and across tall stone embankments.

Only 6½ miles from Narvik, Straumsnes station is the last permanent habitation as you go east. The last Norwegian station, Bjørnfjell, is well above the timber line and about 3 hours from Kiruna, Sweden, some 87 miles north of the Arctic Circle. You can catch a train there to Stockholm. In 1984 a road was opened between Kiruna and Narvik.

WHAT TO SEE & DO

To get a good look at Narvik, take the cable car, **Gondolbanen,** in back of the bus station. The car operates from March to October, charging 70 kroner ($11.60) round-trip. In just 13 minutes it takes you to an altitude of 2,100 feet, at the top of Fagernesfjell where you can admire the impressive panorama of the town and its surroundings. The last cable car returns at midnight.

The **Midnight Sun** shines from May 27 to July 19, and August is noted for its "mysterious lighting."

In the gardens at the railway station, you can see what may be the only remaining train engine constructed in Trollhattan, Sweden, in 1882.

NORDLAND RØDE KORS KRIGSMINNEMUSEUM (War Museum). Tel. 44-426.

Near Torghallene in the town center, this is one of the most important sights in town. Most of Narvik was destroyed by the Germans, who occupied it until the end of World War II. Following Hitler's attack on Denmark and Norway, a bitter battle raged for 2 months for Narvik and its iron ore. German forces fought troops from France, Poland, and Norway, and a considerable British flotilla at sea. The battle meant the destruction of the iron-ore-shipping installations and of the town. Depicted are events of that era as well as experiences of the civilian population and foreign POWs.

Admission: 20 kroner ($3.30) adults, 10 kroner ($1.65) children.
Open: Mon–Sat 10am–8pm, Sun 1–8pm.

OFOTEN MUSEUM, Parkhallen. Tel. 44-732.

In the town center, this museum preserves the cultural history of the area.
Admission: 15 kroner ($2.50) adults, 5 kroner (85¢) children.
Open: June 25–Aug 8, daily 10am–4pm; Aug 9–June 24, Mon–Fri 11am–4pm.

WHERE TO STAY

Narvik's hotels tend to be expensive, so your best bet is to book a room in a private home through the tourist office (see above). The average cost is from 180 kroner ($29.85) double nightly.

GRAND ROYAL, Kongensgate 64, N-8500 Narvik. Tel. 082/41-500. Fax 082/45-531. 110 rms (all with bath), 5 suites. MINIBAR TV TEL **Bus:** 14, 15, 16, 17.

$ Rates (including breakfast): Weekdays, 985 kroner ($163.40) single; 1,050 kroner ($174.20) double. Weekends, 535 kroner ($88.75) single; 680 kroner ($112.80) double. Suites from 1,500 kroner ($248.85). AE, DC, MC, V.

In the town center, this hotel, the largest and best equipped in Narvik, opens onto the main street midway between the rail station and the harborfront. Originally built in the 1920s, it has seen many enlargements since. It is one of the few buildings in Narvik to escape total destruction in World War II, and is called the Grand Royal because King Olav was a frequent visitor (his portraits adorn some of the public rooms). Bedrooms are traditionally furnished, among the most comfortable and tasteful in the area. The finest restaurant in town is also here (see "Where to Dine," below).

NORDST JERNEN HOTEL, Kongensgate 26, N-8500 Narvik. Tel. 082/ 44-120. 30 rms (all with bath). TV TEL **Bus:** 14, 16.

$ **Rates** (including breakfast): Weekdays, 480 kroner ($79.65) single; 580 kroner ($97.05) double. Weekends, 430 kroner ($71.35) single; 555 kroner ($92.05) double. No credit cards.

In the town center, a 15-minute walk south of the bus station, this is one of Narvik's few buildings to escape the burnings of World War II. It has long been known as one of the best hotels for value in the area offering comfortable, simply furnished bedrooms, short on style but clean and respectable. Rooms vary in size. Facilities include a fully licensed restaurant, a lounge, and a TV room.

BREIDABLIKK GJESTGIVERI, Tore Hundsgaten 41, N-8500 Narvik. Tel. 082/41-418. 20 rms (none with bath). **Bus:** 17.

$ **Rates:** 200 kroner ($33.20) single; 250 kroner ($41.50) double. Breakfast costs 45 kroner ($7.45) extra. No credit cards.

A 15-minute or six-block walk uphill from the station, this 1950s hotel has simply furnished rooms, with views overlooking the town and distant mountains. It stands on the eastern outskirts. Plenty of hot water and towels are provided. There is also a TV lounge.

WHERE TO DINE

ROYAL BLUE, in the Grand Royal, Kongensgate 64. Tel. 41-500.
   Cuisine: NORWEGIAN. **Reservations:** Required. **Bus:** 14, 15, 16, 17.
$ **Prices:** Appetizers 39–45 kroner ($6.45–$7.45); main dishes 149–199 kroner ($24.70–$33). AE, DC, MC, V.
   Open: Daily noon–11:15pm.

The best restaurant in the region is decorated with appropriate colors of strong royal blues. It is the preferred choice of all visiting dignitaries, including the King of Norway. Service is polite and the food delectable. Specialties include thinly sliced, sauna-smoked ham with asparagus, cured salmon with crème fraîche, reindeer curry with brussels sprouts and apricots, and large beefsteaks. It's located on the lobby level of the Grand Royal (see "Where to Stay," above).

---

4. TROMSØ

1,084 miles north of Oslo, 352 miles north of Bodø

GETTING THERE   By Plane   At Langnes Airport, there are eight daily flights from Oslo, nine from Bergen, five from Trondheim, and one from Svalbard. Flights from Oslo take 1 hour 40 minutes; flights from Bergen take 3 hours 10 minutes. You can easily fly here from Bodø.

By Train   No rail line runs to Tromsø. The nearest rail connection is through Narvik (see above). From there, you must go the rest of the way by bus.

By Bus   Two or three bus connections can be made from Narvik, taking 5½ hours.

By Car   Take the E6 from Oslo all the way north.

By Coastal Steamer   *Hurtigrute* steamer connections can be made from either Narvik or Bodø. There is also a daily year-round service of coastal express liners from Bergen to Tromsø. Northbound ships arrive at 2:15pm, and southbound ships leave at 11:45pm.

ESSENTIALS   The **Tromsø Arrangement** (Department Tourist Office) is located at Bankgata 1 (tel. 083/84-133). **Local transportation** in Tromsø is provided by a network of bus and fast ferry service. The **telephone area code** for Tromsø is 083.

Tromsø, the gateway to the Arctic, is a North Sea boom town, a trade and financial center. The surrounding snow-topped mountain peaks reach 6,000 feet, and mountain plateaus have good fishing lakes and birch forests.

With 50,000 inhabitants, Tromsø is the administrative center of the county of Troms, a trade center, and the site of one of Norway's four universities. It serves as the capital of northern Norway, and it's the country's fourth finance center.

Lying some 250 miles north of the Arctic Circle, Tromsø gets the Midnight Sun from May 19 to July 26—but not one ray comes through from November 25 to January 21. The climate has a heat record of 86° Fahrenheit and a low of −4°.

WHAT TO SEE & DO

In addition to the sights below, don't miss taking the **Tromsdalen funicular** (tel. 35-121), which leaves from Fjellheisen, the entry station to a cable car that takes passengers on a lofty ride to 1,400 feet above sea level, where you'll have an unparalleled view of Tromsø and its environs. A round-trip ticket is 40 kroner ($6.65) for adults and 20 kroner ($3.30) for children, and the funicular runs March to September, daily from 10am to 5pm. From June to August it also operates from 11:30pm to 12:30am if it's midnight sunny.

TROMSDALEN KIRKE (Arctic Church), along the E78. Tel. 37-611.

Across the longest (approximately 1,100 yards) suspension bridge in Scandinavia is the Arctic Church, a stunning example of modern architecture. It was built in the shape of an iceberg, with aluminum on the outside that glistens in the Midnight Sun. Organ recitals are given twice a week in summer.

Admission: 5 kroner (85¢).

Open: June to mid-Aug, Mon–Sat 10am–5pm, Sun 1–5pm. **Closed:** Mid-Aug to May. **Bus:** 30, 36.

TROMSØ CATHEDRAL, Kirkegata. Tel. 82-548.

· One of Norway's largest wooden churches, the 1861 Tromsø cathedral is the world's northernmost Protestant cathedral. Sunday services are at 11am. It's 200 yards from the harbor.

Admission: Free.

Open: June 15–Aug 15, Tues–Fri 11am–4pm. **Closed:** Aug 16–June 14. **Bus:** 27, 37, 38.

TROMSØ MUSEUM, Folkeparken. Tel. 45-000.

A 20-minute walk from the town center, the Tromsø Museum traces the life—both animal and human—inhabiting the wilderness north of the Arctic Circle. Of special interest is an extensive exhibition on Lapp culture. In addition, a good assortment of medieval church art and furnishings is displayed, plus botanical, zoological (Arctic birds and mammals), and geological displays.

Admission: 10 kroner ($1.65) adults, 5 kroner (85¢) children.

Open: June–Aug, daily 9am–6pm; Sept–May, Mon–Fri 8:30am–3:30pm, Sat noon–3pm, Sun 11am–4pm. **Bus** 21, 27.

POLARMUSEET, Søndre Tollbugate 11B. Tel. 84-373.

Founded in 1976 in an 1830s Customs warehouse, the Polar Museum contains exhibits depicting hunting and research activities in polar regions, especially in the Arctic. It stands opposite the Tromsø Museum, north of Stortorget.

Admission: 15 kroner ($2.50) adults; 5 kroner (85¢) children.

Open: May 15–Sept 15, daily 10am–5pm; Sept 16–May 14, daily 11am–3pm. **Bus:** 21.

NORDLYSPLANETARIET (Northern Lights Planetarium), Breivika. Tel. 76-000.

Here you can enjoy the northern lights, the Midnight Sun, and the starry sky in Norway's first planetarium open to the public, and the northernmost in the world. Experience the city in the film *Arctic Light* and the multimedia show

Tromsø, Tromsø, or travel into space with the space-shuttle film. It is especially recommended to those who arrive in Tromsø too late to view some of the wonders of the northern sky.

Admission: 40 kroner ($6.65) adults, 15 kroner (85¢) children.

Open: Variable schedule; call 10-000 for information on show times. **Bus:** 37.

WHERE TO STAY

You can arrange for a room in a private home through the **Tromsø Arrangement** (Department Tourist Office), Storgata 63 (tel. 10-000). Count on spending from 150 kroner ($24.90) for a single, from 200 kroner ($33.20) for a double in a private home, plus a 15-krone ($2.50) booking fee.

VERY EXPENSIVE

GRAND NORDIC HOTEL, Storgata 44, N-9001 Tromsø. Tel. 083/85-500. Fax 083/85-500. 102 rms (all with bath), 12 junior suites. MINIBAR TV TEL **Bus:** 21.

$ Rates (including breakfast): Winter weekends and summer, 525 kroner ($87.10) single; 600 kroner ($99.55) double. Winter weekdays, 1,000 kroner ($165.90) single; 1,225 kroner ($203.25) double. Suites from 1,300 kroner ($215.65). AE, DC, MC, V.

Located in the heart of the city's business and shopping area, the Grand Nordic is conveniently near public transportation and attractions. The hotel's bedrooms, including junior suites, have extra features like radios, trouser presses, and hairdryers. Twenty rooms are set aside for nonsmokers. The hotel has a restaurant, a rôtisserie, two bars, a nightclub, a pub, and a Winter Garden.

SAS ROYAL HOTEL, Storgata 7, N-9001 Tromsø. Tel. 083/56-000. Fax 083/56-110. 193 rms (all with bath), 7 suites. MINIBAR TV TEL **Bus:** 21.

$ Rates (including breakfast): Winter weekends and mid-June to mid-Aug, 585 kroner ($97.05) single; 720 kroner ($119.45) double. Winter weekdays, 1,230 kroner ($204.05) single; 1,450 kroner ($240.55) double. Suites for 1,500 kroner ($248.85). AE, DC, MC, V.

This handsome hotel, centrally located near the harbor, offers stunning views from the top floor. Built in the 1960s, the hotel is the most visible and prominent—and also the best—in Tromsø, with the most varied assortment of drinking, dining, and dancing facilities. Bedrooms are tastefully furnished and equipped with trouser presses and hairdryers. The Café Royal serves sandwiches, cakes, and coffee, as well as dinner. Charley's Bar & Grill, the Rorbua Pub, and Jonas, the pizza and beer emporium, are recommended separately (see "Where to Dine," below).

EXPENSIVE

SAGA HOTELL, Richard Withs Plass 2, N-9000 Tromsø. Tel. 083/81-180. Fax 083/82-380. 54 rms (all with bath). TV TEL **Bus:** 27, 37.

$ Rates (including breakfast): Winter weekends and midsummer, 450 kroner ($74.65) single; 550 kroner ($91.25) double. Winter weekdays, 845 kroner ($140.20) single; 1,000 kroner ($165.90) double. AE, DC, MC, V. **Parking:** 25 kroner ($4.15).

The accommodations at this 1970s hotel are cozy, and each has its own TV (including satellite TV with in-house video), coffee percolator, hairdryer, trouser press, and alcohol-free minibar. The restaurant serves good Norwegian food. There's a heated garage.

HOTEL WITH, Sjøgata 35-37, N-9000 Tromsø. Tel. 083/87-000. Fax 083/89-616. 76 rms (all with bath). MINIBAR TV TEL **Bus:** 28, 30, 36.

$ Rates (including breakfast): Midsummer and winter weekends, 580 kroner ($96.20) single; 720 kroner ($119.45) double. Winter weekdays, 900 kroner ($149.30) single; 1,040 kroner ($172.55) double. AE, DC, MC, V.

Directly on the harborfront a 10-minute walk north of the bus station, this hotel opened in 1989 and immediately became known as one of the best in town. The original building burned in 1972, but has been rebuilt faithfully in the same style. It has memorabilia in the lobby of its original owners, the local steamship company, Troms Fylkes dampskipsselskap. Each bedroom is decorated in a warm, earth-toned colored scheme. Most are carpeted, and often they open onto views of the port. The hotel has a sauna and a top-floor Jacuzzi.

BUDGET

HAVBLLIKK KAFE & PENSJONAT, Iver Walnumsvei 10, N-9020 Tromsdalen. Tel. 083/35-257. 11 rms (none with bath). **Bus:** 28, 30, 31.
$ Rates (including breakfast): 310 kroner ($51.45) single, 410 kroner ($68) double. No credit cards.

Ⓢ Lying 150 yards south of the cathedral, this place was built in 1917 as a private home, but in 1969 it was transformed into a cost-conscious boardinghouse. Its year-round prices are so low that no weekend or summer discounts are granted. It offers clean, comfortable, no-frills bedrooms. Adjacent to the hotel is a small cafeteria serving sandwiches for 15 kroner ($2.50) and up, and main dishes costing from 65 kroner ($10.80).

TROMSDAL GJESTGIVERI, Tyttebaerveien 11, N-9020 Tromsdalen. Tel. 083/35-944. 25 rms (18 with bath). TEL **Bus:** 30, 36.
$ Rates (including breakfast): Weekdays, 320 kroner ($53.10) single without bath, 415 kroner ($68.85) single with bath; 465 kroner ($77.15) double without bath, 600 kroner ($99.55) double with bath. Weekends, 280 kroner ($46.45) single without bath, 350 kroner ($58.05) single with bath; 420 kroner ($69.70) double without bath, 480 kroner ($79.65) double with bath. AE, DC, MC, V. **Parking:** Available.

Ⓢ Lying half a mile north of the Tromsø cathedral in a residential neighborhood, this little guesthouse is painted yellow, with a big parking lot. Originally constructed in the 1950s but enlarged 20 years later, it is surrounded by nature. Bedrooms are simple, functional, comfortable, and clean. The establishment's unpretentious restaurant is open daily, serving hot sandwiches, pizzas, and omelets, with main dishes costing 65 to 120 kroner ($10.80 to $19.90).

A NEARBY ACCOMMODATION

FAGERNES HOTELL, Hwy. E78, N-9027 Ramfjordbotn-Tromsø. Tel. 083/92-100. Fax 083/92-339. 19 rms (all with bath). MINIBAR TV TEL **Bus:** 14.
$ Rates (including breakfast): Midsummer and winter weekends, 400 kroner ($66.35) single; 550 kroner ($91.25) double. Winter weekdays, 460 kroner ($76.30) single; 650 kroner ($107.85) double. AE, DC, MC, V.
This hotel, 14 miles south of Tromsø, beside the main route leading south, originated as a simple roadside diner in 1982, but over the years it has prospered and expanded. An all-timber building, it has a prominent view of the fjord from many of its windows. Bedrooms are well furnished, completely sheathed in wood. Its restaurant is recommended separately (see "Where to Dine").

WHERE TO DINE
EXPENSIVE

CHARLEY'S BAR & GRILL, in the SAS Royal Hotel, Storgata 7. Tel. 56-000.
Cuisine: INTERNATIONAL. **Reservations:** Required. **Bus:** 21.
$ Prices: Appetizers 62–76 kroner ($10.30–$12.60); main dishes 159–204 kroner ($26.35–$33.85). AE, DC, MC, V.
Open: Daily 11am–11:30pm.
One floor above street level in the SAS Royal Hotel (see "Where to Stay," above), this

restaurant is elegant and formal, with a conservatively modern decor. The kitchen turns out a number of good-tasting specialties, including filet of reindeer, pan-fried, with blackcurrant sauce and mushrooms. A special entrecôte is served with corn on the cob and baked potatoes, or you may prefer a "symphony" of fish and shellfish. Adjacent to the restaurant is Charley's Bar (see below).

PEPPERMØLLEN MAT & VINHUS, Storgata 42. Tel. 86-260.
   Cuisine: NORWEGIAN. **Reservations:** Not required. **Bus:** 28, 30.
$ **Prices:** Fixed-price menus 260–300 kroner ($43.15–$49.75); appetizers 44–72 kroner ($7.30–$11.95); main dishes 156–210 kroner ($25.90–$34.85). AE, DC, MC, V.
   Open: Mon–Thurs 4–11pm, Fri–Sat 3–11:30pm.

⭐ A 5-minute walk south of the bus station, the oldest restaurant in town, originally built as a private home for a pharmacist, was a favorite stopover for famed explorer Roald Amundsen on his way to and from the Arctic Circle. The dining room, one flight up, has a sort of Gay '90s atmosphere and is decorated with photos of famous explorers. Dishes include smoked trout (cured), reindeer tongue in a white wine sauce, Peppermill steak, and a skewer of fish, as well as vegetarian dishes. Besides beverages, the low-key Apoteke Bar offers snacks and light meals. The bar is open Monday through Saturday from 3pm to midnight, charging 32 kroner ($5.30) for a bottle of beer.

MODERATE

BRANKOS MAT-OG VINHUS, Storgata 57. Tel. 82-673.
   Cuisine: YUGOSLAVIAN. **Reservations:** Recommended. **Bus:** 28, 30.
$ **Prices:** Appetizers 35–75 kroner ($5.80–$12.45); main dishes 85–215 kroner ($14.10–$35.65). AE, DC, MC, V.
   Open: Daily 4pm–midnight.
This genuine Yugoslav restaurant has an intimate, cozy atmosphere and attentive service. Specialties include two types of goulash, a gypsy sword (that is, shish kebab flambé), Serbian bean soup, rack of lamb, snails with garlic butter, and frogs' legs. Many Yugoslav wines are stocked. It's right across the street from the Grand Nordic Hotel.

VERTSHUSET SKARVEN, Strandtorget 1. Tel. 82-020.
   Cuisine: NORWEGIAN. **Reservations:** Recommended.
$ **Prices:** Appetizers 37–58 kroner ($6.15–$9.60); main dishes 70–185 kroner ($11.60–$30.70). AE, DC, MC, V.
   Open: Pub, Mon–Thurs noon–3am, Fri–Sat noon–1:30am, Sun 3pm–12:30am; restaurant, daily 4pm–midnight.
Originally built as a butter factory, this building in the center of Tromsø now houses the Strandtorgets Vertshus pub on the ground level, where a half pint of beer is 37 kroner ($6.15), and snacks or meals are available. One floor above street level is Restaurant Arctandria, serving an Arctic cuisine—dishes like reindeer casserole, the Arctandria special (a large plate of different types of fish and shellfish), marinated and grilled lamb, Arctic catfish, trout, porbeagle shark, seaweed-and-shellfish soup, codfish, and salmon. For dessert, a good choice is the marinated raspberries and cloudberries.

NEARBY DINING

FAGERNES RESTAURANT, in the Fagernes Hotell, Ramfjordbotn. Tel. 92-100.
   Cuisine: NORWEGIAN. **Reservations:** Recommended. **Bus:** 14.
$ **Prices:** Fixed-price menu 65 kroner ($10.80); appetizers 20–32 kroner ($3.30–$5.30); main dishes 65–110 kroner ($10.80–$18.25). AE, DC, MC, V.
   Open: Daily 7:30am–9pm.
Popular with motorists and sports people, this is a good Norwegian restaurant that grew from humble beginnings as a roadside diner. It offers simple and wholesome

food served by a helpful staff. Sunday is the busiest day, when many families drive down from Tromsø to dine here. Try salted lamb served with "swedes" (that's rutabagas), or rock cod from the nearby fjord. It is either stewed in a cream sauce or fried and served with cole slaw. There is also an array of steaks, and roast pork is invariably featured. It's 14 miles south of Tromsø, beside the main road leading south.

EVENING ENTERTAINMENT

CHARLEY'S BAR, in the SAS Royal Hotel, Storgata 7. Tel. 56-000.

This bar sits one floor above street level adjacent to Charley's Bar & Grill (see "Where to Dine," above). There is no dress code, and the minimum age is 25. The music is disco, and the atmosphere is elegant and sophisticated. It's open Monday through Thursday from 6pm to 1:30am and on Friday and Saturday from 6pm to 3:30am. Beer costs 38 kroner ($6.30). Bus: 21.

JONAS, in the SAS Royal Hotel, Storgata 7. Tel. 56-000.

This place sells only pizza and beer, and has a "color shock" decor with amusingly garish shades of yellows and reds. Pizzas come in small, medium, large, and the really humongous "maxi pizza"—the biggest in northern Norway—and cost 60 to 110 kroner ($9.95 to $18.25). Beer runs 38 kroner ($6.30). It's open Sunday through Thursday from noon to 1:30am and on Friday and Saturday from noon to 3:30am. Bus: 21.

RORBUA PUB, in the SAS Royal Hotel, Storgata 7. Tel. 56-600.

Beamed and rustic, and not very large, this is nevertheless the most famous pub in Tromsø. It's usually very crowded throughout the day, and sometimes live music is played on Friday and Saturday nights. Large mugs of beer are served—at 38 kroner ($6.30)—but the only food offered is a bowl of steamy and rich beef-and-potato soup, enough to stave off starvation; it costs 35 kroner ($5.80). Many people show up early in the day and order it as lunch. The pub is open daily from noon to midnight, and there's never a cover charge. Bus: 21.

5. ALTA

503 miles north of Bodø, 205 miles north of Tromsø,
1,236 miles north of Oslo

GETTING THERE **By Plane**   Daily flights leave Oslo for Alta, taking 3 hours.

By Bus   There are two daily buses from Fauske to Nordkjosbota, with one daily bus continuing to Alta for an overnight stopover; total trip time is 11 hours. One bus leaves Tromsø daily, taking 7 hours.

ESSENTIALS   The **tourist office** (tel. 35-041) is open in summer Monday through Friday from 9am to 7pm, on Saturday from 9am to 4pm, and on Sunday from noon to 7pm. The **telephone area code** for Alta is 084.

Alta is famous for attracting the world's millionaire fishermen to the Altafjord, said to have the best salmon waters in the world. But most visitors come to Alta because it is a major traffic hub for those going on to the North Cape; public transport stops in Alta for the night so travelers can take the connecting bus to Honningsvåg the following morning. Buses also depart from Alta along the great northern highway, the E6, heading south to Kautokeino or north to the final stop at Kirkenes.

For years, Alta belonged to Finland and was inhabited almost solely by Lapps, who until the end of World War II held a famous fair here. Because of fires and wars, everything in Alta is relatively new.

Alta is the administrative capital of Finnmark county. It is also home of the Alta Bataljon, which covered the retreat of the French and British forces from the Nazis at Narvik in the infamous battle of World War II.

WHAT TO SEE & DO

Alta has a limited number of accommodations, although it makes a good base for offbeat excursions to the Lapp village of **Masi,** 44 miles from town on the main road to Finland. In the village, which has a Lapp school, the locals usually wear colorful costumes.

From the Lapp village, you can take a **riverboat excursion** on a long, flat-bottom boat with an outboard motor, driven by costumed Lapps. You have to negotiate the price, which will be based on your skills and the number in your party. The excursion usually lasts 4 hours.

Guests usually take a packed lunch from their hotel, then stop along the way—preferably in a secluded spot by the riverbank—for a picnic. While in northern Norway, try Lappbiff (a reindeer-meat sandwich) or furstekake (almond cake).

From Alta, it's possible to take a riverboat excursion along the Alta River up to the Alta Canyon at Sausto, the biggest canyon in northern Europe. It has been dammed. For details, get in touch with **Alta Riverboat Service** (tel. 33-378).

Take time to visit the rock carvings in **Hjemmeluft,** dating from 2,000 to 5,000 years ago. Considered the largest area of prehistoric rock carvings in the north of Europe, the site is open mid-June to mid-August, daily from 8am to 8pm. Admission is 10 kroner ($1.65).

WHERE TO STAY

SAS ALTA HOTEL, Rte. 6, N-9501 Alta. Tel. 084/35-000. Fax 084/35-825. 154 rms (all with bath). TV TEL.
$ **Rates** (including breakfast): Weekdays, 1,050 kroner ($174.20) single; 1,230 kroner ($204.05) double. Weekends, 500 kroner ($82.95) single; 625 kroner ($103.70) double. AE, DC, MC, V.

A 10-minute walk from the harborfront, this is the best hotel in the area. Dating from 1987, it is completely modern, with the largest number of drinking, dining, and dancing facilities. Bedrooms are well furnished and comfortable. The finest restaurant in town, Henrik's, has an interconnected dance bar, Pernille's. The Fritz Disco, in the basement of the hotel, is open on Friday and Saturday nights from 8pm to 1am charging a 40-krone ($6.65) cover, with beer costing from 36 kroner ($5.95). The Café Eden is suitable for single-plate lunches, sandwiches, drinks, and coffee. The Alten Pizza Pub is also in the hotel.

FROKOSTHOTELLET, Rte. 6, N-9501 Alta. Tel. 084/36-211. Fax 084/36-380. 10 rms (all with bath). TV TEL.
$ **Rates** (including breakfast): Summer, 620 kroner ($102.85) single; 680 kroner ($112.80) double. Winter weekdays, 705 kroner ($116.95) single; 820 kroner ($136.05) double. Winter weekends, 420 kroner ($69.70) single; 520 kroner ($86.25) double. AE, DC, MC, V.

Built in 1987, this is a cozy alternative to the vastly larger and more expensive SAS Alta Hotel 100 yards to the north. Just off the "North Cape Road," it offers modern comfortable rooms. Other than breakfast, no meals are served, but many walk over to the SAS Hotel for that.

WHERE TO DINE

HENRIK'S, in the SAS Alta Hotel, Rte. 6. Tel. 35-000.
Cuisine: NORWEGIAN. **Reservations:** Recommended.
$ **Prices:** Appetizers 45–69 kroner ($7.45–$11.45); main dishes 120–198 kroner ($19.90–$32.85). AE, DC, MC, V.
Open: Daily 11am–10pm.
A 1-minute walk from the bus station, this is the finest restaurant in town, with a very

modern, mostly pink decor. It has a smattering of big-city style in this remote northern outpost. Specialties include filet of reindeer, salmon, trout, and game dishes from northern Norway. Immediately adjacent is the Pernille Dance Bar.

6. HAMMERFEST

1,326 miles north of Oslo, 593 miles north of Bodø

GETTING THERE **By Bus** April to September, three buses a week arrive here on the 3½-hour trip from Alta. In the same season you can take a thrice-weekly bus from Oslo if you can sit for the 29 hours it takes.

By Coastal Steamer A northbound steamer leaves daily from Harstad going to Kirkenes, with stopovers at Hammerfest.

By Car A long trek—take the E6 north from Oslo until you reach the junction of Route 94 west. Hammerfest lies at the end of that route.

ESSENTIALS For information, go to the **Hammerfest Tourist Office,** Sjøgata (tel. 12-185), in the town center a short walk from the dock. The **telephone area code** for Hammerfest is 084.

The Hammerfest area stretches from Måsøy, near the North Cape, to the municipality of Loppa in the south, embracing a wide area of geography, the most notable of which is the wild, rugged coasts ravaged by the Arctic Sea. The regional capital is Hammerfest, which many use as a center for exploring the North Cape.

Hammerfest is a major traffic hub for the area, and in summer there's a wide selection of regular excursions by boat and bus. The tourist office (see above) will have details of what's available at the time of your visit.

For an overview, take a zigzag walk up the 80-yard **Salen** "mountain" for a good view of the town. The old landmark on top of Salen was torn down during the war, but restored in 1984.

WHAT TO SEE & DO

This is the most northerly town in the world of any major size and a port of call for North Cape steamers. Destroyed in World War II by the retreating Germans, it has long since been rebuilt. Lapps from surrounding camps often come into town to shop. Count yourself lucky if they bring their reindeer with them.

The port is ice-free year round, and shipping and exporting fish is a major industry. The sun doesn't set from May 17 to July 28. On the other hand, it doesn't rise from November 21 to January 23.

Why not take time to do as 70,000 others have done and join the **Royal and Ancient Polar Bear Society** here? Apply in person and get a membership while you're in Hammerfest. The club is filled with stuffed specimens of Arctic animals. It has a small museum devoted to the hunting heyday of Hammerfest, when eagles, Arctic foxes, and polar bears were trapped. It's in the basement of the Town Hall, Rådhuspladssen, and is open Monday through Friday from 8am to 6pm and on Saturday and Sunday from 10am to 3pm. Admission is free.

CRUISES TO THE NORTH CAPE

The first tour ships arrived in 1879, and they've been coming ever since. **FFR** (tel. 084/14-344) operates cruises from Hammerfest to the North Cape, including meals, bus ashore, and guide. The cost is 465 kroner ($77.15) per person round-trip; children pay 261 kroner ($43.30). An additional bus ride to the North Cape costs another 85 kroner ($14.10). Tours run from June 11 to September 2, leaving Hammerfest daily at 5:30pm, arriving at Honningsvåg (see Section 7, below) where a bus takes you the final lap of the journey. A stop is made at **Hjelmsøystauren,** one of northern Europe's largest bird sanctuaries. Buses return from the North Cape sometime after midnight. Midnight is hardly the word—it's still daylight at departure time.

WHERE TO STAY

Accommodations are very expensive in Hammerfest.

RICA HOTEL HAMMERFEST, Sørøygata 15, N-9601 Hammerfest. Tel. 084/11-333. Fax 084/11-311. 95 rms (all with bath). TV TEL **Bus:** 1, 2.

$ Rates (including breakfast): Winter weekends and summer, 560 kroner ($92.90) single; 680 kroner ($112.80) double. Winter weekdays, 940 kroner ($155.95) single; 1,050 kroner ($174.20) double. AE, DC, MC, V.

In the town center, opening directly onto the waterfront, this is the preferred place to stay in the area. Built in the mid-1970s the hotel also has the best restaurant in Hammerfest. A member of a chain, it is the largest hotel in town and was completely redecorated in 1989. Bedrooms are modernized with a decor of Nordic-inspired pastels.

HAMMERFEST HOTEL, Strandgate 24, N-9600 Hammerfest. Tel. 084/ 11-622. Fax 084/12-127. 28 rms (all with bath). MINIBAR TV TEL **Bus:** 1, 2.

$ Rates (including breakfast): Winter weekends and summer, 375 kroner ($62.20) single; 550 kroner ($91.25) double. Winter weekdays, 750 kroner ($124.45) single; 950 kroner ($157.60) double. AE, DC, MC, V.

Right on Rådhusplassen, the Town Hall Square, this hotel dates from the 1950s but was restored in the mid-1980s. Bedrooms are comfortable and well furnished, many opening onto views of the harbor. Its restaurant, Bennoni, is recommended separately (see "Where to Dine," below).

WHERE TO DINE

RICA HOTEL RESTAURANT, in the Rica Hotel Hammerfest, Sørøygata 15. Tel. 11-333.
  Cuisine: NORWEGIAN. **Reservations:** Not required. **Bus:** 1, 2.

$ Prices: Appetizers 55–80 kroner ($9.10–$13.25); main dishes 139–208 kroner ($23.05–$34.50). AE, DC, MC, V.
  Open: Daily 11am–11pm.

Considered the best restaurant in town, this dining room in the cellar of the Rica Hotel Hammerfest (see "Where to Stay," above) opens directly onto the harborfront. Specialties are pepper steak and filet of reindeer. It also serves good-tasting fish dishes based on the day's catch from the fjord. After dinner, you can patronize the Rica Bar and Disco, also in the cellar of the hotel, which is open Sunday through Thursday from 5pm to 1am and on Friday and Saturday from 5pm to 3:30am. Admission is 50 kroner ($8.30), but only on Friday and Saturday night; other nights it's free. The minimum age is 20, and beer costs 38 kroner ($6.30) per half liter.

BENNONI, in the Hammerfest Hotel, Strandgate 24. Tel. 11-622.
  Cuisine: NORWEGIAN. **Reservations:** Not required. **Bus:** 1, 2.

$ Prices: Appetizers 40–65 kroner ($6.65–$10.80); main dishes 12–158 kroner ($2–$26.20); one-course fixed-price menu 60–80 kroner ($9.95–$13.27). AE, DC, MC, V.
  Open: Daily 11am–11pm.

Set one floor above street level in the Hammerfest Hotel (see "Where to Stay," above), this restaurant has a modern, all-pink decor. Locals consider it their favorite place in Hammerfest. Typical dishes include pepper steak, grilled filet of reindeer, or halibut in a white wine sauce.

KOKKEN'S GRILL, Strandgate 43. Tel. 11-550.

Cuisine: FISH/PIZZA. **Reservations:** Not required. **Bus:** 1, 2.
$ Prices: Pizzas 62–64 kroner ($10.30–$10.60); fish plates 60–90 kroner ($9.95–$14.95). AE, MC, V.
Open: Mon–Sat 9am–9pm, Sun noon–9pm.

Lying 200 yards from the bus station in the town center, this is a simple, clean place decorated with plants. It looks more like a café than a restaurant. Local artists hang the walls with paintings that are for sale. In summer, they offer a special fish plate of the day, which varies with the catch. Pizzas are the most favored bill of fare, however. Service is generally fast.

---

7. HONNINGSVÅG

74 miles north of Lakselv, 111 miles NE of Alta, 81 miles NE of Hammerfest

GETTING THERE   By Bus   Buses arrive daily from Alta, Lakselv, Hammerfest, Kautokeino, Karasjok, and Kirkenes.

By Coastal Steamer   These *Hurtigruten* arrive daily, with northbound arrivals reaching Honningsvåg daily at 5:30pm, and southbound departures at 6:45am.

By Car   Take the E6 north to the junction with Route 95 north. That route leads to Honningsvåg with one ferry crossing.

ESSENTIALS   The **Tourist Office** in Nord Kapphuset (tel. 084/72-894) can give you information on sightseeing boat trips, museums, walks, and deep-sea fishing. The **telephone area code** for Honningsvåg is 084.

SPECIAL EVENTS   The **North Cape Festival** is held for 1 week in the middle of June each year, with a wide display of local culture. During the festival, the **North Cape March** travels from Honningsvåg to the North Cape and back, a total of around 44 miles. For further information concerning the festival or the march, contact the tourist office (see above).

The world's northernmost village, the gateway to the North Cape, is a completely modern fishing harbor (only the chapel withstood the German destruction of 1944). It is some 50 miles nearer to the North Pole than Hammerfest, on the Alta–Hammerfest bus route.

Honningsvåg is on the southern side of the island of Magerøy, but is connected to the North Cape by a 22-mile-long road.

WHAT TO SEE & DO

NORDKAPPMUSEET, Nordkapphuset. Tel. 84/72-833.
This museum has exhibits relating to the cultural history of the area and fishery artifacts.

Admission: 10 kroner ($1.65) adults, 5 kroner (85¢) children.
Open: June 15–Aug 15, Mon–Sat 11am–3pm and 6–8pm; Sun 6–8pm; Aug 16–June 14, Mon–Fri 11am–3pm.

NORTH CAPE HALL, Nordkapp. Tel. 72-091.
This visitors' center has a video presentation and museum exhibits. Downstairs you'll find a supervideograph and a cave with a panorama window facing the Arctic Ocean. On the way to the cave you'll see several scenes from the history of the North Cape. A monument honors the visit of King Oscar (ruler of Norway and Sweden) to the cape in 1873, and another monument honors the exiled "citizen king" of France,

Louis Philippe of Orléans, who visited in 1855. There is also a monument marking the terminus of the "Midnight Sun Road."

Admission: 90 kroner ($14.95) adults, 35 kroner ($5.80) children.

Open: June–Aug, daily 9am–2am (it stays open so late because many people prefer to visit the cape at the peak period of the Midnight Sun); Sept and May, daily 9am–6pm. **Closed:** Oct–Apr.

A TRIP TO THE NORTH CAPE

The ✪ **North Cape** symbolizes the "top of Europe." (Actually, Knivskjellodden stretches about 1,500 yards farther north but is inaccessible.) In prehistoric times the North Cape Horn was a Sami place of sacrifice. Earlier, the name of the North Cape used to be Knyskanes, but in 1553 it was named "North Cape" by the English Lord Richard Chancellor, who was searching for a sea passage to China. The road to the North Cape is open to traffic from May 1 to October 20.

The first tour ships arrived in 1879. These anchored in Hornvika Bay, and the tourists had to climb 307 yards up to the plateau. After the road from Honningsvåg was opened in 1956, the flow of tourists turned into a flood. In summer four buses to the North Cape leave daily from the central marketplace at Honningsvåg, making a brief stop at the ferryboat terminal across from the Sifi Sommerhotell, then continuing to the visitors' center at the North Cape. The round-trip passage from any entry point along the route is 75 kroner ($12.45).

On the road to the cape is a Lapp encampment—a bit contrived perhaps, but visitors do get to go inside one of the tents, and they come away with an idea of how nomadic Lapps used to live.

WHERE TO STAY

ARCTIC BRYGGEN HOTEL, Vågen 1, N-9751 Honningsvåg. Tel. 084/73-777. Fax 084/73-678. 42 rms (all with bath). MINIBAR TV TEL.

$ Rates (including breakfast): 900 kroner ($149.30) single; 1,000 kroner ($165.90) double. AE, DC, MC, V.

Opened in 1990, this is a unique hotel in the north of Norway near the bus station off Storgata. Part of a harborfront headquarters the hotel is filled with facilities and accommodations for the fishing industry. In summer, some of the beds in the fishermen's cottages called *rorbuer* become available. The hotel itself offers well-furnished and comfortable bedrooms, all modernized with many amenities.

Dining/Entertainment: The hotel has a summer restaurant on the pier, seating 250 guests. It also has a pleasant bar, a Tavern/Pub, and a regular indoor restaurant. A dance bar, Tørrfeskloftet, is also available.

Services: Booking service for Arctic Adventures, boat rentals, water sports.

Facilities: Sauna, Jacuzzi, a sauna lounge for 20 people, shops.

SAS HOTEL NORDKAPP, Nordkappgata 2-4, N-9750 Honningsvåg. Tel. 084/72-333. Fax 084/73-379. 174 rms (all with bath), 3 suites. TEL.

$ Rates (including breakfast): Weekdays, 855–900 kroner ($141.85–$149.30) single; 1,080 kroner ($179.15) double. Weekends, 500 kroner ($82.95) single; 625 kroner ($103.70) double; from 1,150 kroner ($190.80) suites. AE, DC, MC, V.

The world's northernmost hotel, 2 miles from the airport and 21 miles from the North Cape, is located in the downtown area a few minutes' walk from the quay. Early reservations are strongly advised. This five-story, white-fronted building has been enlarged and considerably upgraded since it was first established in 1956. Bedrooms are carpeted and many of them open onto views of the harbor. They are furnished with modern pieces and decorated in neutral tones; most have TVs. The restaurant is recommended separately (see "Where to Dine," below). The hotel's bar is open to 3am, and in the cellar is a disco, open nightly from 8pm to 1 or 2am. Admission ranges from 30 to 45 kroner ($5 to $7.45).

SIFI SOMMERHOTELL, N-9750 Honningsvåg. Tel. 084/72-817. 40 rms (15 with bath). TEL.

$ **Rates** (including breakfast): 485 kroner ($80.45) single without bath; 525 kroner ($87.10) single with bath; 680 kroner ($112.80) double without bath, 800 kroner ($132.70) double with bath. MC, V. **Closed:** Oct–Apr.

Located near the ferry terminal only 22 miles from the North Cape, this simple place is known for its hospitality. Rooms are equipped with basins for hot and cold running water; toilets and showers are in the corridor, although some units have private plumbing. The hotel has a sauna and a fitness room. The restaurant serves typical Norwegian food, as well as beer and wine.

WHERE TO DINE

RESTAURANT CAROLINA, in the SAS Nordkapp Hotell, Nordkappgata 2-4. Tel. 72-333.

Cuisine: NORWEGIAN. **Reservations:** Recommended.

$ **Prices:** Appetizers 45–65 kroner ($7.45–$10.80); main dishes 120–190 kroner ($19.90–$31.50); summer buffet smörgåsbord 140 kroner ($23.25) per person. AE, DC, MC, V.

Open: Summer, daily noon–12:30am; winter, daily 7pm–12:30am.

In the cellar of the SAS Nordkapp Hotell (see "Where to Stay," above), this place is at its most elegant in winter (during the summer it is often filled with tour groups). In the evening music begins at 8pm, and the place is very popular with locals. It is decorated with old-fashioned photographs of Honningsvåg. In summer its smörgåsbord is one of the most attended events in town.

8. VADSØ

275 miles NE of Alta, 255 miles east of Honningsvåg,
107 miles west of Kirkenes

GETTING THERE By Plane Wilderøe Airlines has daily flights to Kirkenes and Alta.

By Bus Vadsø and Kirkenes have a bus link—one to two buses daily on the 3½-hour trip. Buses also go between Vadsø and Vardø (see below)—one to three daily, taking 1½ hours.

By Coastal Steamer Northbound and southbound coastal steamers between Harstad and Kirkenes call daily at Vadsø.

By Car Continue along the E6 from the south of Norway until you reach the faraway junction with Route 98; then go east to Vadsø.

ESSENTIALS For information, go to **Vadsø Byutvikling,** Vadsø Kommune (tel. 53-880), in the town center. The **telephone area code** for Vadsø is 085.

Vadsø, the capital of Finnmark, is on the southern coast of the Varanger Peninsula, on the Varangerfjord. Vadsø used to be a Finnish-speaking town, and nearly half the population of Vadsø, it is estimated, have Finnish origins. Norway's largest herring-oil factory is here, but public administration is the largest employer of Vadsø's some 6,000 inhabitants.

WHAT TO SEE & DO

In spring, summer, and autumn, Vadsø offers unforgettable experiences for nature lovers, anglers, and birdwatchesr. Ask at the tourist office (see above) about excursions and activities possible in the area. The only **birdrock** in Finnmark, at Ekkerøy, can be reached by car. It is a protected nature reserve but has trails for visitors. **Deep-sea fishing** can also be arranged at the SAS Vadsø Hotel (see "Where to Stay & Dine," below), as can excursions by boat on the Varangerfjord. One day's notice is necessary.

A guided sightseeing bus tour is arranged by **Lailas Gjestehus** (tel. 53-335). Tours go through the wilderness between Vardø and Hammingberg. Remnants from World War II can be seen.

The Vadsø area is also excellent for **hiking and skiing,** while numerous marked trails take you into the mountain plateau. You can also find small lakes and rivers where you can have a picnic (make arrangements with your hotel to have a lunch packed).

VADSØ MUSEUM, Hvistendahlsgata 31. Tel. 52-955.

The only remaining patrician buildings left in Finnmark, this museum includes the 19th-century Tuomainengården estate and Esbensengården estates. The museum also owns the airship mast to which Arctic explorer Roald Amundsen's *Norge* was moored in 1926. It was one of the few things to escape Nazi-set fires and Russian bombardments in World War II. This mast was also used on the famous North Pole expedition in 1928 of explorer Umberto Nobile.

Also part of the museum is Kjeldsen-bruket on Ekkerøy, a completely restored fish-processing complex with a quay that was built at the end of the 19th century.
Admission: 10 kroner ($1.65).
Open: Mon–Sat noon–5pm.

VADSØ KIRKE AND KONGENSTEINEN, Vadsø Kommune. Tel. 51-132.

Architect Magnus Paulsson called this church, built in 1958, an Arctic church. Outside the front door he placed two towers resembling two tall ice blocks to shelter people from the wind. The "king stone" from 1977 is placed right outside the church, bearing the signature of King Olav.
Admission: Free.
Open: June–Aug, daily 9am–2pm.

WHERE TO STAY & DINE

SAS VADSØ HOTEL, Oscars Gata 4, N-9800 Vadsø. Tel. 085/51-681. Fax 085/51-002. 67 rms (all with bath). TV TEL.
$ Rates (including breakfast): Weekdays, 950 kroner ($157.60) single; 1,130 kroner ($187.45) double. Weekends, 500 kroner ($82.95) single; 600 kroner ($99.55) double. AE, DC, MC, V.

Rising atop a rolling hillside in the town center, 3 miles from the airport, this long and stylishly modern hotel is the best in this accommodation-scarce area. It also has the most drinking and dining establishments around, attracting locals as well as visitors. Rooms are comfortably furnished, and more than half were renovated in 1989. The hotel has a restaurant seating 80 guests, serving northern Norway specialties such as reindeer and salmon. There's a dance bar for 110 guests and an even-bigger disco, for 150 patrons. It also has a well-patronized pizzeria.

9. VARDØ

44 miles east of Vadsø, 151 miles west of Kirkenes

GETTING THERE By Plane Vardø's Svartnes Airport is 2 miles from the town center. Several daily arrivals and departures connect Vardø with Kirkenes and the fishing village of Båtsfjord.

By Bus One or two buses a day run between Kirkenes and Vadsø, taking 3½ hours. Vardø is connected by bus to Vadsø (see above)—one to three daily, taking 1½ hours.

By Coastal Steamer Vardø lies on the coastal-steamer route. Northbound boats arrive from Harstad and southbound boats arrive from Kirkenes.

By Car Take the E6 north from the south of Norway, turning east onto Route 98, going via Vadsø to Vardø. To reach the island town, you must take the 2-mile-long underwater tunnel that connects the town to the mainland, the first of its kind in Norway. Its deepest point is 96 yards below sea level.

ESSENTIALS   For information, contact **Vardø Kommune,** Tiltakskonsulenten (tel. 085/87-171). The **telephone area code** for Vardø is 085.

Vardø, founded in 1789, is the only town in Norway situated in the Arctic climate zone. On most July days you can see your breath. Norway's lowest mean average temperature and its greatest number of stormy days are recorded here. Vardø is also the easternmost town in the country and claims the easternmost point in Norway, the island of Hornøya. It has 3,200 inhabitants and an area of 363 square miles, and is often called the gate to the Barents Sea. Most people are in the fishing industry.

Ancient geographers called this part of the habitable world Ultima Thule. In the Middle Ages the area was also called the "empire of the devil." In 1564 a cardinal, considered a mathematical genius, estimated that 2,655,866,746,664 little devils came into the world through Ultima Thule.

The worst prosecution against witches in Norway took place in the Vardø area from 1621 to 1692, making it "the Salem of Norway." Eighty women were found guilty and burned to death here for witchcraft. According to prosecution records of the time, the alleged witches were supposed to have had secret meetings with the devil on Domen mountain.

WHAT TO SEE & DO

The **Vardøhus fortification** is the most northernmost fortification in the world, built between 1734 and 1738. This was the third fortification erected in Vardø, the first dating from 1300 and the second from 1420. Guides are available to show you around the fortification from June 10 to August 31. Call 87-171 for information.

Vardøhus Museum, Pers Larssens Gate 32 (tel. 88-075), is housed in Lushaugen, and lies half a mile northeast of the town center, reached by taxi. Its main building dating from 1920, the museum has a *kongestokken* where you'll find the signatures of several kings. The museum also has artifacts of the area. It is open in summer daily from 10am to 3pm; in winter, only on Saturday and Sunday from 10am to 3pm. Admission is 15 kroner for adults ($2.50) and 5 kroner (85¢) for children.

At the **Vardø Post Office,** you can have your mail stamped, proving you have visited Norway's easternmost town. It's open Monday through Saturday from 9am to 3:30pm.

The little road that goes west from Vardø to the hamlet of **Hamningberg** has scenery that has been compared to a landscape on the moon.

WHERE TO STAY & DINE

HOTEL BARENTS, Keigate 8, N-9950 Vardø. Tel. 085/87-761. Fax 085/88-397. 42 rms (all with bath). TEL.
$ Rates (including breakfast): 550 kroner ($91.25) single; 700 kroner ($96.15) double. DC, MC, V.
In the center of town, 200 yards from the Vardøhus fortification and close to the steamer quay, this modern establishment is the best place in Vardø for rooms or food. Accommodations are modern and comfortable. Twenty rooms have TVs and some are equipped for the handicapped. The pleasant, quiet dining room becomes a place for dinner dances on occasion. The hotel also has a bar, a lounge with an open fireplace, a sauna, a small gym, a solarium, and a disco.

VARDØ GJESTEGÅRDEN, Strandgaten 72, N-9950 Vardø. Tel. 085/87-529. 7 rms (none with bath). TV.
$ Rates (including breakfast): 300 kroner ($49.75) single; 400 kroner ($66.35) double. No credit cards. **Closed:** Sept–Apr.
This little hotel—really a guesthouse—is clean and spartan. It is a wood-sided

building constructed as the town's police station in the 1920s. Each of its simple bedrooms is different. Visitors are welcome in summer, but in winter the place is occupied by students. Only breakfast is served, and guests are accepted between May and late August.

10. KIRKENES

327 miles north of Alta, 532 miles north of Tromsø, 1,521 miles north of Oslo

GETTING THERE   By Plane   The Kirkenes Airport lies 9 miles from the town center. Several planes land daily from various parts of Norway, including Trondheim and Tromsø. Four flights a day come in from Oslo, taking 3 hours.

By Bus   Buses from various parts of Finnmark arrive at Krikenes. Buses are connected with routes to Oslo, Tromsø, Alta, and Hammerfest, even northern Finland. Tickets can be purchased on board, and it's not necessary to reserve the ticket in advance. The bus from Alta to Kirkenes takes 12 hours.

By Coastal Steamer   Kirkenes is the end of the line for the coastal-steamer routes that begin in Bergen, with many stopovers along the way as outlined in previously previewed towns and cities.

By Car   The E6 begins its long and tortuous run in Oslo, finally ending in Kirkenes near the Soviet frontier.

ESSENTIALS   The **Kirkenes Tourist Office** (tel. 085/92-544) is behind the Rica Hotel on Passvikveien in a little wooden hut, lying off the E6. The **telephone area code** for Kirkenes is 085.

This iron-ore-mining town is the end of the line for travelers in Norway, 170 miles north of the Arctic Circle. The Midnight Sun shines on Kirkenes from May 20 to July 25, but from November to January people live in darkness.

Kirkenes was bombed repeatedly during World War II—307 raids in all, until nearly the whole town was destroyed by 1944. During the infamous German retreat from Finnmark that year, surviving areas were razed by evacuating Nazis who didn't want to leave anything behind for the Russians.

Kirkenes lies in a section of eastern Finnmark called Sør-Varanger. It is the only Norwegian region with a common border with the USSR—and 121 miles of it at that. It's also the only place in the world where everybody can take a look at the Soviet Union from a NATO country. Today's inhabitants of Kirkenes are descendants of Samic, Norwegian, Finnish, Russian, and other peoples.

Kirkenes opens onto the famous **Barents Sea,** where adventurers tried for centuries to trade furs, find the North Pole, or discover a passage to China. The enormous sea is named after a Dutchman, Willem Barents. After a shipwreck at Novaja Semlja in 1596, he had to spend the winter on the ice. It was his last expedition, and he died there. In the 18th century Russians from Arkhangelsk began sailing to Finnmark to trade with the Norwegians. This trading lasted until the Russian revolution of 1917.

It was not until 1878 that the Finnish-Swedish Arctic researcher, Nordenskiøld, succeeded in pushing forth through the North East Passage, looking for a northerly seaway to China. Later polar explorer Roald Amundsen followed this route with the ship *Maud.*

Large naval forces traveled through here in World War II, the ocean below becoming the graveyard of many soldiers on both sides of the conflict.

WHAT TO SEE & DO

The **Sør-Varanger Museum,** Strand, Pasvik (tel. 95-113), is decentralized and includes the Bygdetunet Bjorklund farm at Svanvik, Noatun at Vaffetem, and St.

Georg's Chapel in Neiden. You can also see King Oskar's Chapel at Grense-Jakobselv, a stone church built in 1869, as well as the wooden Neiden Chapel at Neiden. Admission is 10 kroner ($1.65) for adults, free for children. The main building of the museum at Strand, Pasvik, is 25 miles from Kirkenes on Route 885. There is no public transportation available. It's open June to August, daily from noon to 7pm; September to May, Monday through Friday from 9am to 2pm.

There's a **Monument to the Red Army,** a statue of a Russian soldier, erected in memory of the liberation of Finnmark by the Russians in 1944. There are also several memorials to Finnish and Norwegian soldiers killed in the war.

WHERE TO STAY

KIRKENES RICA HOTEL, Passvikveien 63, N-9900 Kirkenes. Tel. 085/ 91-491. Fax 085/91-159. 68 rms (all with bath). MINIBAR TV TEL.
$ Rates (including breakfast): Weekdays, 975 kroner ($161.75) single with bath; 1,130 kroner ($187.45) double with bath. Weekends, 500 kroner ($82.95) single; 700 kroner ($116.15) double. AE, DC, MC, V.
Located on top of a hill overlooking the town, half a mile from the quay, this hotel looks like a midwestern country club. Built in 1956 and totally renovated after a fire in 1987, its interior is colorful, with stained-glass accents and tapestries. Guests sometimes dance at night to the sounds of a combo. This licensed hotel also has a tennis and badminton court. Reindeer meat is a specialty of the Brasseriet. The hotel has a large parking place, and facilities are provided for laundry. It also offers room service. The airport bus stops by six times a day.

RICA ARCTIC HOTEL, Kongensgata 1-3, N-9901 Kirkenes. Tel. 085/92- 929. Fax 085/91-159. 80 rms (all with bath). MINIBAR TV TEL.
$ Rates (including breakfast): Summer, 645 kroner ($107) single; 840 kroner ($139.35) double. Winter weekdays, 1,000 kroner ($165.90) single; 1,130 kroner ($187.45) double. Winter weekends, 700 kroner ($116.15) single; 980 kroner ($162.60) double. AE, DC, MC, V.
This hotel, built in 1988, is the biggest and best in the area. Each of its bedrooms is attractive and comfortable. The decor includes a winter-inspired color scheme. In the center of Kirkenes, the hotel is 7 miles from the Kirkenes Airport, 2 miles from the coastal-steamer quay, and 100 yards from a taxi stand. Its restaurant is considered the best in town (see "Where to Dine," below).

SOLLIA GJESTGIVERI, Storskog, N-9900 Kirkenes. Tel. 085/90-820. 9 rms (none with bath). **Bus:** Grenfjell Jakobsel from the town center.
$ Rates (including breakfast): 300 kroner ($49.75) single; 450 kroner ($74.65) double. No credit cards.

About 10 miles east of Kirkenes, just 66 feet from the USSR border, this guesthouse is small, only 16 beds. The house is modestly furnished, and most guests reach it by renting a car in Kirkenes and driving here (the Kirkenes Tourist Office will give you a map). Reservations are needed, of course. The guesthouse is a white clapboard-sided structure originally constructed in 1935 as a children's orphanage, although it served briefly in World War II as a military hospital. Its family owners will prepare platters of food, costing 40 kroner ($6.65) at lunch and 70 kroner ($11.60) at dinner.

WHERE TO DINE

ARCTIC RESTAURANT, in the Rica Arctic Hotel, Kongensgate 1-3. Tel. 92-929.
   Cuisine: NORWEGIAN. **Reservations:** Not required.
$ Prices: Appetizers 45–75 kroner ($7.45–$12.45); main dishes 148–199 kroner ($24.55–$33); daily platters 45–75 kroner ($7.45–$12.45). AE, DC, MC, V
   Open: Daily 7am–11pm.
Generally considered the best restaurant in Kirkenes, this dining room is on the lobby level of the Rica Arctic Hotel (see "Where to Stay," above) a 5-minute walk south of

the bus station. The restaurant has a modern decor with dark colors. Daily platters are especially popular. Specialties include filet of reindeer and fresh Norwegian salmon.

GRILLSTUA, Dr. Wesselsgata 18. Tel. 91-287.
   Cuisine: NORWEGIAN. **Reservations:** Not required.
$ **Prices:** Pizzas 68–75 kroner ($11.30–$12.45); main dishes 60–85 kroner ($9.95–$14.10). No credit cards.
   Open: Daily 9am–10pm.

This is a simple café in a postwar building that once served as a makeshift movie theater. It's especially popular on weekends. Young people go here for pizzas, but hot food is also served. It's in the town center.

EASY EXCURSIONS

Some 75 miles south of the town is **Pasvik Valley,** known for its special flora and fauna. The trip takes you through the easternmost national park of Norway, where two different biological worlds, Asia and Europe, meet. The Pasvik River marks the boundary between Russia and Norway.

Along the way, you'll pass **Svanvik,** 25 miles from Kirkenes, where you can visit the beautiful Svanvik Chapel and see a government-owned experimental station.

ORGANIZED TOURS TO THE USSR

In summer, a bus departs at 12:30pm to explore the USSR border and the **Sør-Varanger open-pit mines,** near Lake Bjørnevatn. The cost is 100 kroner ($16.60) for adults and 50 kroner ($8.30) for children. The trip takes 2 hours. Confirm the departure time and the point of embarkation with the tourist office (see above).

In these *glasnost* days, it is now possible to penetrate the once-formidable Soviet border. Kirkenes is only 4½ miles from the Russian frontier. ✪ **Murmansk,** a large Russian seaport, the largest city in the world north of the Arctic Circle, is now open to visitors. In summer, a boat leaves Kirkenes daily at 8:30am, returning to Kirkenes at 12:30am. The boat trip is 4 hours one way, with a scheduled stopover in Murmansk of 7 hours. It is not necessary to have a visa, but the tour must be booked 14 days in advance. The cost is 990 kroner ($165.25). Reservations are made with **FFR** (Finnmark fylkesrederi og ruteselskap), N-9601 Hammerfest (tel. 084/11-655).

The journey in part is eerie, going at a speed of 43 m.p.h. You see Arctic nature, see animals, and birds up close through large panoramic windows. You are likely to be approached by a Soviet warship for control as this is one of the most heavily militarized areas in the world. You can see the Severomorsk naval base, with several hundred submarines, cruisers, and battleships. Sightseeing in Murmansk ends, after all your souvenir buying, at a soldier monument. The soldier looks toward the northeast, overseeing the "valley of the dead" of World War II.

On the way back over the Barents Sea, the Midnight Sun lights the way, and you can have a Russian midnight snack.

CHAPTER 22

GETTING TO KNOW SWEDEN

Sweden is one of the most paradoxical nations on earth. An essentially conservative country, it is nonetheless a leader in social welfare, prison reform, and equal opportunity for women. It has the highest wages and best standard of living in Europe.

The past and the future exist side by side in Sweden. In Stockholm and some of the cities along the west coast, you can enjoy stunning modern shopping complexes and dramatically up-to-date hotels. But a journey to Dalarna and Varmland or the historic walled city of Visby on the eastern coast transports you back to a more distant time.

Sweden was a poor backward nation at the dawn of the 20th century. Most of its citizens depended on farming for a living. But in one century it has transformed itself, becoming one of the examples of good living on the globe, a symbol of peace and prosperity.

The urbane and the untamed are said to live harmoniously in Sweden, where nearly everyone has room to live as they please. There are some 173,731 square miles for some 8.5 million residents.

Although Sweden has a long aristocratic history, it is a modern Western European democracy. It still has a king, who seems to be affectionately regarded by his people, but real power is in the hands of elected officials.

Within an hour's flying time of Stockholm, you can take in some of the climatic, cultural, and geographical variety of Sweden. That might include midsummer skiing on the northern snow fields, sunbathing on the tens of thousands of islands on both the east and west coasts, and thermal-spring bathing in the central forested plateau.

If you wander the Kungsleden (The King's Trail), past Sarek, you will be exploring the last wilderness of Europe. Collecting summer berries in one of the forested national parks is another national pastime. In winter, dog sledding in Lapland is all the rage.

Three huge lakes, Vättern, Vänern, and Mälaren, attract thousands of summer visitors, but there are some 100,000 other smaller lakes. Swedes in their 700,000 boats, ranging from dinghies to ocean racers, love to "take to the waters."

❔ DID YOU KNOW . . . ?

- Sweden, today's symbol of neutrality, was once a warmonger: It invaded Russia, conquered Britain, and grabbed Normandy.
- A survey showed that a large percentage of Americans think that Sweden is Switzerland.
- Half the couples living together in Sweden are unmarried.
- Sweden has added two words to international gastronomy: smörgåsbord and Absolut.
- The world's longest smörgåsbord was prepared in Sweden, stretching for 798 yards.
- James Joyce, F. Scott Fitzgerald, George Orwell, Marcel Proust, and Aldous Huxley *did not* win Sweden's Nobel Prize.
- Sweden is one of the five nations that established colonies in North America.

Among the cities, Stockholm is the political capital, with a population of 1,435,000; Gothenburg, the car center with 704,000; and Malmö, the port of trade with 458,000.

Many visitors come to explore "the Kingdom of Crystal" in Småland province, where dozens of so-called glass huts, such as Orrefors and Kosta-Boda, are tucked away in a landscape of lakes and forests.

In the 18th century King Gustavus III built theaters, palaces, museums, and even founded the Swedish Academy, which awards the Nobel Prize for literature. Many of these buildings can still be visited. But in spite of the midsummer celebrations in Dalarna or the Maypole dances on May 1, Sweden is no backward folkloric country.

Swedes are responsible for inventing much that has changed modern life, including the safety match, alternating current, the milk separator, the refrigerator, the vacuum cleaner, and the ball bearing, not to mention the zipper, which has led to all sorts of encounters between people all over the world.

1. GEOGRAPHY, HISTORY & POLITICS

GEOGRAPHY

Sweden is the fourth-largest nation in Europe—roughly the size of California—but it is sparsely inhabited. Forests cover more than half the land. From the manufacture of ball bearings to automatic beacons, Sweden is a heavily industrialized nation; less than 10% of the land is used for agriculture.

There is plenty of inland water, more than 100,000 lakes, including Vänern, the largest in Western Europe. The eastern half of the Scandinavian peninsula, Sweden shares more than 1,000 miles of frontier with Norway, but fewer than 350 with Finland.

Sweden is one of the countries on earth located farthest from the Equator. It extends from north to south at roughly the same latitude as Alaska or—in the Southern Hemisphere—the stretch of ocean between Cape Horn in South America and the Antarctic continent. In terms of area, it is similar to Spain or Iraq. In population, it is in the same league as New Jersey.

Ancient rock formations on both coasts created a huge number of bays and inlets. The northern coasts are still changing geologically, as new land areas continue to appear above the sea. Gotland and Öland, both in the Baltic, are the two biggest of Sweden's many islands.

Sweden is the largest country in Scandinavia, about twice the size of the United Kingdom. It has about 4% of the population of the United States, with a population density of 19 inhabitants per square kilometer. Nearly 80% of its people live in towns.

Sweden's sea coast is some 1,550 miles long. On the west it is bounded by the Kattegat and the Skagerrak, and on the east by the Gulf of Bothnia and the Baltic Sea. If all the inlets and islands were included, the coastline of Sweden would measure 4,650 miles.

Sweden is a long country, almost 992 miles from north to south. Much of it lies north of the Arctic Circle. The north, covered with ice and snow for some 8 months every year, is home to some 10,000 Lapps and approximately 50,000 Finns. Sweden's highest mountain, Kebnekaise, rising 6,946 feet, is in the far north. To reach the vast stretches of its land mass, Sweden maintains 7,440 miles of rail lines.

Its most important waterway is the Göta Canal, dating from the 19th century. It is 370 miles long, going from Gothenburg in the west to Stockholm in the east. Some 121 miles of canals were constructed to connect the various lakes and rivers that make up this waterway.

GÖTALAND Götaland forms the southern part of Sweden, taking its name from the Goths of ancient times who some historians believe settled in this region, which is similar in climate and architecture to parts of northern Europe, especially Germany. This is the most populated part of Sweden, taking in eight provinces, including Östergötland, Småland (the kingdom of glass), Västergötland, Skåne (the châteaux district), Dalsland, Bohuslän, Halland, and Blekinge, plus the islands of Öland and Gotland. The Göta Canal cuts through this district. **Gothenburg** is the most important port in the west, and **Stockholm,** the capital, the chief port in the east. Other than Stockholm, **Skåne** is the most heavily visited tourist zone, often compared to the countryside of Denmark. Many seaside resorts are found on both the west and east coasts, including the islands of Öland and Gotland.

SVEALAND Svealand is the name given the central region of Sweden, including the folkloric province of Dalarna (Dalecarlia in English) and Värmland (immortalized in the novels of Selma Lagerlöf). These are the districts most frequented by tourists. Other provinces include Västmanland, Uppland, Södermanland, and Närke. Ancient Svealand is often called the cultural heart of Sweden. Along its eastern coast are found some 20,000 islands.

NORRLAND Norrland is the north of Sweden, lying north of the 61st Parallel and taking in about 50% of the land mass, although it is populated by only about 15% of Sweden's citizens, including Lapps and Finns. Norrland consists of 24 provinces, of which **Lapland** is the most visited by tourists. It is a land of thick forests, fast-flowing (and cold) rivers, and towering mountain peaks. Lapland consists not of forests, but tundra, the home of the Lapp reindeer herds. **Kiruna** is one of Norrland's most important cities, because of its iron-ore deposits. Many of the bodies of water of Norrland are frozen for months every year.

DATELINE

- **44** Sweden is first mentioned in a book, *Germania* by Tacitus.
- **829** Christianity introduced by St. Anskar.

(continues)

HISTORY

The first mention of Sweden is found in *Germania,* by the Roman historian Tacitus (A.D. 77–117), who called the tribe Svear and described them as a "militant Germanic race." Later historians would describe them as "skiing hunters." The word *Sverige* (or the domain of the Svear) eventually became "Sweden."

IMPRESSIONS

Sweden appeared to me the country in the world most proper to form the botanist and natural historian; every object seemed to remind me of the creation of things, of the first efforts of sportive nature.
—MARY WOLLSTONECRAFT, *LETTERS WRITTEN DURING A SHORT RESIDENCE IN SWEDEN,* 1796

The early Swedes were Vikings who carried on a thriving slave trade. St. Anskar was a Frankish missionary who introduced Christianity in 829, hoping it would tame the ravaging Viking spirit. But it took at least 2 centuries for paganism to die out. By the second half of the 11th century, Christianity had a foothold.

Olaf Skottkonung, a ruler in northern Sweden, spread Christianity after he was converted, but in time a civil war ensued. Under King Eric IX, who ruled until 1160, Christianity became firmly entrenched. He took a crusade to Finland and later became the patron saint of Sweden.

Sweden's greatest medieval statesman was Birger Jarl, who ruled from 1248 to 1266, abolishing serfdom and founding Stockholm. His son, Magnus Ladulas, upon becoming king in 1275, gave great power to the Catholic church and founded a hereditary aristocracy.

AN INTRA-NORDIC UNION   Magnus VII of Norway (1316–74) was only 3 years old when he was elected to the Swedish throne, but his election represented a recognition of the benefits of increased cooperation within the Nordic World. Under his reign there developed a changing definition of Sweden's social classes. These included the aristocracy, the Catholic clergy (who owned more than 20% of the land), peasant farmers and laborers, and a commercial class of landowners, foresters, mineowners, and merchants. The fortunes and power of this last group were based on trade links with a well-organized handful of trading posts (the Hanseatic League) scattered within Germany and along the Baltic coastline. As trade increased, these cities (especially Visby on the island of Gotland) and their occupants thrived, and the power of the Hanseatic League grew.

The black death decimated the Swedes, beginning around 1350.

In 1389 the Swedish aristocracy, fearing the growing power of the Germans within the Hanseatic League, negotiated for an intra-Nordic union with Denmark and the remaining medieval fiefdoms in Norway and Finland. The birth process of this experimental union began in the Swedish city of Kalmar, which gave its name in 1397 to the brief but far-sighted Kalmar Union. A leading figure in its development was the Danish Queen Margaretha, who was already Queen of Denmark and Norway when the Swedish aristocracy offered the throne to her in 1389. Despite its good intentions, the union collapsed after about 40 years, a result of a revolt by merchants, miners, and peasants in defense of Sweden's trade links with the Hanseatic League, coupled with power struggles between Danish and Swedish noblemen.

Although the union was considered a failure, one of its most lasting benefits was the establishment—partly as a compromise between differing political factions—of a *Riksdag* (government) with representatives from different towns and regions. It included some limited representation for the peasant classes.

Queen Margaretha's heir (her nephew, Eric of Pomerania; 1382–1459) was the crowned head of three countries

DATELINE

- **1248** Birger Jarl abolishes serfdom and founds Stockholm.
- **1319** Magnus VII of Norway unites Sweden with Norway.
- **1389** Margaret rules Sweden, Norway, and Denmark by the Union of Kalmar.
- **1521** Gustavus Vasa founds the Vasa Dynasty.
- **1632** Gustavus II ensures the growth of Protestantism throughout Europe by winning the Battle of Lützen.
- **1648** Treaty of Westphalia grants Sweden the possessions of Stettin, Bremen, and West Pomerania.
- **1809** Napoleon names Jean Bernadotte as heir to the throne of Sweden.
- **1889** The Social Democratic party is formed.
- **1905** Sweden grants independence to Norway.
- **1909** Suffrage for men is granted.
- **1921** Suffrage for women and an 8-hour workday are granted.
- **1940** Sweden declares its neutrality in World War II.
- **1946** Sweden joins the United Nations.
- **1953** Dag Hammarskjöld becomes secretary-general of the United Nations.

(continues)

DATELINE

- **1973** King Karl XVI Gustaf ascends the throne.
- **1986** Olof Palme, prime minister and leader of the Social Democrats, is assassinated.

(Norway, Denmark, and Sweden). He spent most of his reign fighting with the Hanseatic League. Deposed in 1439, he was replaced by Christopher of Bavaria, whose early death in 1448 led to a major conflict, and eventual dissolution of the Kalmar Union. The Danish King Christian II invaded Stockholm in 1520, massacred the leaders who opposed him, and established an unpopular reign with much civil disobedience, until the rise of the Vasa Dynasty threw the Danes out.

THE VASA DYNASTY In May of 1520 a Swedish nobleman, Gustavus Vasa, returned from captivity in Denmark and immediately began to organize the military ejection of the Danes from Sweden. In 1523 he captured Stockholm from its Danish rulers, won official recognition for Swedish independence, and was elected King of Sweden. In a power struggle with the Catholic church, he confiscated most church-held lands (vastly increasing the power of the state overnight) and established Lutheranism as the national religion. He commissioned a complete translation of the Bible and important works of the Protestant Reformation into Swedish, and violently repressed local uprisings in the Swedish provinces. He also established the right of succession for his offspring and ruled that his son, Eric XIV, would succeed him as king (which he did in 1543).

Although at first Eric was a wise ruler, his eventual undoing stemmed partly from the growing conflicts with Swedish noblemen and his eventual marriage to his unpopular mistress, Karin Mansdotter. (Previously, he had unsuccessfully solicited a marriage with the English queen, Elizabeth I.) Eric eventually went insane before being replaced by Johan III and then (after a brief interlude) by Karl IX.

The next 50 years were defined by Danish schemes to regain control of Sweden, and Swedish schemes to conquer Poland, Estonia, and the Baltic trade routes leading into Russia. A dynastic link to the royal families of Poland led to the enthronement of Sigismund (son of the Swedish King Johan III) in Warsaw. When his father died, Sigismund became simultaneously king of both Sweden and Poland. His Catholicism, however, led to his violent ejection from Sweden, which led in turn to the ascension of Karl (Charles) IX and a lasting enmity and a dangerous and expensive series of wars with Denmark, Russia, and its former ally, Poland.

Sweden was fighting even to survive in 1611, at the time of the ascension to power of Gustavus II Adolfus (1594–1632). Viewed today as a brilliant politician and military leader, he was one of the era's most stalwart Protestants in a bloodthirsty century where political alliances were often formed along religious lines. Organizing an army composed mainly of farmers and fieldhands, financed from income from the copper mines at Falun, he secured Sweden's safety, and with his armies penetrated as far south as Bavaria. He died in battle in 1632 near the city of Lützen, fighting against the Habsburg emperor's Catholic army.

When he died, his heir and only child, Christina (1626–89), was 6 years old. Actual power was held by the respected Swedish statesman Axel Oxenstierna, who continued the Thirty Years' War in Germany for another 16 years. Through military and political maneuvering, the war ended with the Treaty of Westphalia in 1648. Christina, never at home with warmongering anyway, and having converted against the advice of her counsellors to an ardent faith in Catholicism, abdicated her throne in 1654 in favor of her cousin, Charles X Gustav (1622–60).

Ten years after his rise to power, Charles X (Karl) ejected the Danes from many of Sweden's southern provinces, establishing the borders of Sweden along lines that it has retained, more or less, to this day.

The long and fiscally traumatic reign of Charles XI (1655–97) followed. The endless series of wars with Denmark (and others with kingdoms in northern Germany) continued. Even more preoccupying was the growing power of the vastly wealthy Swedish nobles, who had amassed for themselves (usually through outright purchase from a cash-poor monarchy) an estimated 72% of Sweden's land. In a bitter and acrimonious process, Charles redistributed the land into approximately equal shares held by the monarchy, the nobles, and Sweden's independent farmers. The position of small landowners has remained secure in Sweden ever since, although power was funneled to an ever-increasing degree into the hands of an absolute monarch. With his new-found wealth, he greatly strengthened the Swedish military.

Charles XII (1682–1718) came to the throne at the age of 4, with his mother, the queen, ruling as his regent. Denmark, Poland, and Russia allied themselves against Sweden in the Great Northern War, which broke out in 1700. Charles invaded Russia but was defeated, and he was forced to escape to Turkey, where he remained as a prisoner for 4 years. In 1714 he returned to Sweden to continue fighting, but was killed in 1718. During his reign it can be said he presided over the collapse of the Swedish empire.

Under Frederick I (1676–1751), Sweden regained some of its old strength. Real power was in the hands of the chancellor, Count Arvid Horn (1664–1742). He formed an alliance against Russia with England, Prussia, and France. The Hattar (Hats) and Mossorna (Caps) were the two opposing parties in the Riksdag of the day, and the Hats started a war with Russia in 1741. The conflict continued through the reign of the next king, Adolphus Frederick (1710–71). Although he initiated many reforms, encouraged the arts, and transformed the architectural landscape of Stockholm, Gustavus III (1746–92) revived the absolute power of the monarchy, perhaps in reaction against the changes brought on by the revolution in France. He was assassinated by a group of fanatic noblemen at a ball in the Opera.

THE 19TH CENTURY Gustavus IV (1778–1837) followed on the throne. His hatred of Napoleon caused him to lead Sweden into the Third Coalition against France (1805–07). For his efforts, he lost Stralsund and Swedish Pomerania, and in 1808 Finland was lost in the wars against Russia and Denmark. In 1809 he was overthrown, following an uprising, and died in exile.

In 1808 a new constitution was written, giving an equal amount of power to the king and the Riksdag. Under these provisions, Charles XIII (1748–1818), the uncle of the deposed king, became the monarch.

Napoleon established his aide, Jean Bernadotte (1763–1844), as heir to the throne of Sweden. Bernadotte won a war with Denmark, forcing that country to cede Norway to Sweden. Upon the death of Charles, Bernadotte became king of Sweden and Norway, ruling as Charles XIV. During his reign Sweden began a policy of neutrality, and he established a royal line that is still on the throne today. He was followed by his son, Oscar I (1799–1859), who introduced many reforms, including freedom of worship and of the press.

The Industrial Revolution of the 19th century changed the face of Sweden. The Social Democratic party was launched in 1889, leading to a universal suffrage movement. All males were allowed to vote in 1909.

THE 20TH CENTURY Norway declared its independence in 1905, and Sweden accepted the secession. Sweden followed a policy of neutrality in World War I, although much of the country was sympathetic to the German cause. Many Swedish volunteers enlisted in the White Army during the Russian Revolution of 1917.

In 1921 women gained the right to vote, and an 8-hour work day was granted. The Social Democratic party continued to grow in power, and after 1932 a welfare state was established.

IMPRESSIONS

Sweden seems to me to be the most comfortable country in Europe—and the least cozy.
—KATHLEEN NOTT, *A CLEAN, WELL-LIGHTED PLACE*, 1961

Although Sweden offered weapons and volunteers to Finland in its Winter War against the Soviet Union in 1939, it declared its neutrality during World War II. It earned a long-lived resentment from its neighbor, Norway, whose cities were leveled by the Nazi troops who had been granted free passage across Swedish territories. Under heavy Allied threats against Sweden in 1943 and 1944, Nazi troop transports through the country were eventually halted. Throughout the war, Sweden accepted many impoverished and homeless refugees. The rescue attempts of Hungarian Jews led by Raoul Wallenburg have been recounted in books and films.

Sweden joined the United Nations in 1946, but refused to join NATO in 1949. Rather more disturbing was Sweden's decision to return to the Soviet Union many German and Baltic refugees who had battled against Russia in the war. They were presumably killed on Stalin's orders.

Dag Hammarskjöld, as secretary-general of the United Nations in 1953, did much to help Sweden regain the international respect that it had lost because of its wartime policies. He died in an air crash in 1961 toward the end of his second 5-year term.

Sweden continued to make reforms in the 1950s and '60s, launching a national health service.

Only 27 years old, King Karl XVI Gustaf became King of Sweden in 1973, following in the footsteps of his grandfather, Gustaf VI Adolf. The present king's father had died in an airplane crash when the king was still a child. In 1976 he married Silvia Sommerlath, who was born in Germany. King Karl XVI Gustaf and Queen Silvia have three children.

The Social Democrats ruled until 1976, when they were toppled by a Center/Liberal/Moderate coalition. The Social Democrats returned in 1982, but lost their majority in 1985 and had to rely on Communist support to get bills passed.

The leader of their party since 1969, Olof Palme, was prime minister until his assassination outside a movie theater in Stockholm in February 1986. A pacifist, he was a staunch critic of the United States, especially during the Vietnam War. In spite of an arrest, the murder has not been satisfactorily resolved.

Ingvar Carlsson was elected prime minister following Palme's death.

Sweden faces the 1990s with troubling problems, including an austerity program and slow economic growth. Inflation is rising rapidly. The Social Democrats, the Green party, and the Swedish Communist party continue their struggle for control.

POLITICS

Sweden is a constitutional monarchy. Since the days of Queen Christina (which have been long remembered both in Sweden and in Hollywood) there has been a law saying that only men could occupy the throne. However, the constitutional law was changed when the firstborn child of Queen Silvia and King Karl XVI Gustaf was a girl. The heir to the throne is now Crown Princess Victoria. A prime minister heads a cabinet appointed by the king, and the cabinet is in turn responsible to the single-chamber Riksdag, the Swedish parliament.

2. FAMOUS SWEDES

Carl Michael Bellman (1740–95) Sweden's historically most popular composer as well as a major poet. Among famous works are *Fredmans Epistlar och Sanguar* (1790) and *Fredmans Sangar* (1791).

Ingmar Bergman (1918–) Sweden's greatest film director made his debut in 1938 as an amateur director at a theater in Stockholm. His first feature film, *Crisis*, was released in 1945, but it wasn't until the 1950s that he became world famous. He made such highly acclaimed films as *The Seventh Seal, Wild Strawberries,* and *Cries and Whispers,* all hailed as classics. In three decades he directed more than 40 films, each dealing with a universal theme such as human isolation.

Ingrid Bergman (1916–82) One of the world's finest stage and screen actresses predicted that in spite of her impressive achievements, her obituaries would carry the headline—"Star of *Casablanca* Dies." And so they did. An unknown, she left Sweden for Hollywood to make *Intermezzo,* followed by such great films as *Gaslight* (her first Oscar), *For Whom the Bell Tolls, Notorious,* and *Anastasia.* She embodied virtue in such films as *The Bells of St. Mary's* and *Joan of Arc,* which perhaps led to a massive outcry against her when she left her Swedish husband and child to marry the Italian film director, Rossellini. Sixteen years later, *Murder on the Orient Express* brought her her third and final Oscar.

Baron Jons Jakob Berzelius (1779–1848) A father of modern chemistry, Berzelius was named a member of the Royal Academy of Sciences in 1808, becoming secretary-for-life there in 1818. His many books on chemistry included *Theory of Chemical Proportions and Chemical Action of Electricity* in 1844. He also created a system of chemical symbols and atomic weights of the elements.

Greta Garbo (1905–90) The screen goddess of *Anna Christie, Grand Hotel, Camille, Anna Karenina,* and *Ninotchka.* Born Greta Gustafsson in Stockholm. Among her early mentors was Mauritz Stiller, who directed her in the *Saga of Gosta Berling* (1922).

Dag Hammarskjöld (1905–61) In 1936, Dag Hammarskjöld became undersecretary in the Ministry of Finance and later president of the board controlling the Bank of Sweden. After serving as minister of state, he became secretary-general of the United Nations where he presided over bitter Cold War disputes. He was unanimously reelected for another 5 years in 1957. He met crisis after crisis, notably over the Suez Canal. His sending United Nations troops to the Belgian Congo was bitterly denounced by the Soviet Union, which demanded his resignation. He refused. He was posthumously awarded the Nobel Peace Prize.

John Hanson (1721–83) In 1781, when Maryland became the last of the 13 colonies to ratify the Articles of Confederation, the Continental Congress unanimously elected John Hanson the first president of the United States in a Congress assembled for a 12-month term—8 years before George Washington was elected. During his 1-year term (1781–82), he established the Departments of State, War, Navy, and Treasury, and set up a national judiciary, a national bank, and a post office. Virtually ignored or forgotten by most Americans, he is still remembered in Maryland on April 14, John Hanson Day.

Charles John (1763–1844) In 1810 Charles John was asked to become Prince of Sweden. He allied with Russia, Great Britain, and Prussia to take Norway from Denmark and to fight Napoleon. The Danes were defeated in 1813 in the Battle of Leipzig, and Charles John took control of Norway.

Selma Lagerlöf (1858–1940) The towering woman writer of her country. Her works, including *The Saga of Gösta Berling* and *The Wonderful Adventures of Nils,* have been translated into 40 languages. In 1909 she won the Nobel Prize for literature, and in 1914 was made the first woman member of the Swedish Academy. At 75 she published her last collection of short stories and was at work on a novel when she died at her beloved Marbâcka, outside Karlstad (open to the public).

Jenny Lind (1820–87) "The Swedish nightingale," Jenny Lind was launched in opera in 1837. She appeared in France and England before her 2-year triumphant tour of the United States. Settling in England, she appeared in oratorios and concerts, eventually becoming a professor of music. Her last public appearance was at Düsseldorf, Germany, on January 20, 1870, singing an oratorio composed by her husband, Otto Goldschmidt.

Karl Linnaeus (1707–78) Botanist responsible for developing the classification system for plants and animals currently used today.

Carl Milles (1875–1955) The most distinguished Swedish sculptor of the 20th century, he was greatly influenced by Rodin and sculpted in an impressionistic style, mainly in clay, wood, and stone. He worked in Sweden until 1930, but then lived in the United States where he became an American citizen and executed many notable commissions, including *Meeting of the Water* in St. Louis.

Alfred Nobel (1833–96) This 19th-century Swedish industrialist was the inventor of dynamite. He constructed and perfected detonators and amassed a great fortune, which he stipulated upon his death to go as prizes "to those who have conferred the greatest benefit on mankind."

Olof Palme (1927–86) A controversial leader, Palme was a leader of the so-called Socialist International, consisting of Social Democratic parties, and was particularly active in the Third World. His vehement attacks on the United States during the Vietnam War led to acrid exchanges with Washington.

Victor Sjostrom (1879–1960) Actor and director whose early masterpieces included *Ingeborg Holm* and *Terje Viega*. He went to Hollywood to make several films, the best known of which is *The Scarlet Letter* (1926). Most filmgoers know him for his role in *Wild Strawberries* by Ingmar Bergman.

August Strindberg (1849–1912) Sweden's greatest playwright, Strindberg exerted a profound influence on international drama. He tried many professions before publishing his widely acclaimed novel *The Red Room,* written in 1879. Between stormy marriages, he wrote many plays, including *The Father* (1887) and *Miss Julie* (1888).

Emanuel Swedenborg (1688–1772) Swedenborg, a scientist, philosopher, and theologian, influenced by Descartes, published many philsophical and pyschological works in the 1720s and 1730s, in which he saw the world as subject to mechanical laws. Concerned with the source and structure of matter, he concluded that the soul is material, as reported in his *Regnum Animale.* His theological insights had great influence on Dostoyevsky, Emerson, Balzac, Ezra Pound, and others; many congregations in the United States take Swedenborg's writings as their doctrinal basis. His *Journal of Dreams* is still widely read.

Anders Zorn (1860–1920) A member of the association of artists founded in the 19th century. Famous works include *Midsummer Nights' Dance* and *Young Girls Bathing.* His works can be seen in Dalarna, Stockholm, and Chicago.

3. SPORTS & RECREATION

CYCLING Much of Sweden is flat, lending itself to cycling tours. Places all over the country will rent bicycles, or sometimes country hotels will make them available, either free or for a small charge. Typical rentals cost 35 kronor ($6.10) a day. For more detailed information, write the **Swedish Cycling Association,** Box 6006, S-163 06 Spånga.

FISHING In Stockholm, within view of the king's palace, you can cast a line for what are considered some of the finest salmon in the world. Ever since a decree issued in 1636 by Queen Christina, Swedes have the right to fish in waters adjoining the palace. From the north to the south of Sweden, fishing is an everyday affair. It is estimated that one of every three citizens is an angler.

But to fish elsewhere than Stockholm, you'll need a license, the cost of which varies from region to region. Local tourist offices in any district will advise. Pike, pike-perch, eel, and perch are found in the heartland and the south of the country.

GOLF After Scotland, Sweden may contain more golf addicts than any country in Europe, with some 200 courses. Unlike the Caribbean or other parts of the world, the courses are rarely crowded. Visitors are often granted local membership cards, and

---

IMPRESSIONS

The Swede is, surely, the human blackbird, with his copious, rich and liquid voice, in a language that reaches the extreme of voluptuous volubility.
—EDMUND GOSSE, 1911

IMPRESSIONS

If ever there was a Yankeer than Yankee, he's a Swede.
—HENRY ADAMS, 1901

---

greens fees vary, depending on the club, but generally start at 150 kronor ($26.20) for a round. Many golfers fly from Stockholm to Lapland in summer just to play by the light of the Midnight Sun. For information on courses in Sweden, write **Svenska Golfförbundet,** Kevinge, S-182 31 Danderyd.

RAFTING White-water rafting and river rafting are the two major forms of this sport. For white-water rafting you go in a fast river boat, the trip made all the more exciting by a series of rapids. Both short trips and adventures lasting a week are organized in Lapland with a safety-conscious guide. For details, write **Jukkasjärvi,** Box 24, S-980 21 Jukkasjärvi.

River rafting is much tamer, as you gently go down a slow-moving river in Sweden's heartland. Many Swedes build their own log rafts. Adventurers sleep in tents and cook their food over campfires, but they should bring along plenty of mosquito repellent in summer. For details about trips along the Klarälven River in Värmland, write to **Vildmark i Värmland AB,** Sundbergsvagen 13, S-685 00 Torsby.

RIDING Sweden has many riding stables or even riding schools. Ask about them at local tourist offices. One of the most popular excursions in the country is a pony trek through the region of Sweden's highest mountain, Knebnekaise.

SAILING & CANOEING Canoes are for rent all over the country, from province to province, and details are available from local tourist offices. A day's rental costs about 65 kronor ($11.35). Often hotels situated near areas of water sports will rent you canoes. At places all over Sweden you can rent sailing boats as well. Again, most tourist offices have complete details.

SWIMMING If you don't mind your waters a bit on the cool side, Sweden has one of the world's longest coastlines, plus some 100,000 lakes, in which you can take the plunge. The best bathing beaches are on the west coast. Both the islands of Öland and Gotland contain popular summer seaside resorts. Beaches in Sweden are open to the public in general, and nude bathing is allowed on certain designated beaches. However, topless bathing for women is everywhere. If a Swedish lake is suitable for swimming, it is always signposted.

WALKING & JOGGING The almost-unlimited space of Sweden is ideal for either activity. Local tourist offices, depending on what part of Sweden you visit, generally will provide details and sometimes even free maps for the best trails or jogging paths. In Stockholm, hotel reception desks often tell you the best place to go jogging close to your hotel, as Stockholm has many "green lungs."

---

4. FOOD & DRINK

FOOD

The fame of the **smörgåsbord** is justly deserved. Utilizing a vast array of dishes—everything from Baltic herring to smoked reindeer—the smörgåsbord may either be eaten as hors d'oeuvres or as a meal in itself.

One cardinal rule of the smörgåsbord: Don't mix fish and meat dishes. It is customary to begin with sill (herring), prepared in many ways. Herring is usually followed by other treats from the sea (jellied eel, smoked fish, and raw pickled salmon); then diners proceed to the cold meat dishes, such as baked ham or liverpaste, which are accompanied by vegetable salads. Hot dishes, often Swedish meatballs, come next, and are backed up by cheese and crackers—perhaps a fresh-fruit salad.

The smörgåsbord is not served as often in Sweden as many visitors seem to believe, as it requires time-consuming preparation. Many Swedish families reserve it for special occasions. In lieu of the 40-dish smörgåsbord, some restaurants have taken to serving a plate of assietter (hors d'oeuvres). One of the tricks for enjoying smörgåsbord is timing. It's best to go early, when fish dishes are fresh. Late arrivals may be more fashionable, but the food is often stale.

The average times for meals in Sweden are generally from 8 to 11am for the standard continental breakfast, noon to 2:30pm for lunch, and as early as 5:30pm for dinner to around 8 or 8:30pm (many restaurants in Stockholm are open to midnight—but don't count on this in the small villages).

A Swedish breakfast at your hotel may consist of cheese, ham, sausage, egg, bread, and perhaps filmjölk, a kind of sour-milk yogurt. **Smörgas,** the famous Swedish open-face sandwich, like the Danish smørrebrød and Norwegian smørbrød, is a slice of buttered bread with something on top. It is eaten for breakfast or anytime during the day, and you'll find it at varying prices, depending on what you order and where you order it.

Unless you decide to have smörgåsbord (never served in the evening) at lunch, you'll find that the Swedes do not go in for lavish spreads in the middle of the day. The usual luncheon order consists of one course, as you'll observe on menus especially in larger towns. Dinner menus are for complete meals, with appetizer, main course and its side dishes, and dessert included.

Generally Swedish chefs tend to be far more exper with **fish dishes** (freshwater pike and salmon are star choices) than with meat courses. The Swedes go stark raving mad at the sight of kraftor (crayfish), in season from mid-August to mid-September. This succulent, dill-flavored delicacy is eaten with the fingers, and much of the fun is the elaborate ritual surrounding its consumption.

A platter of thin **pancakes,** served with lingonberries (comparable to cranberries), is the traditional Thursday-night dinner in Sweden. It is often preceded by yellow split-pea soup seasoned with pork. It's good any night of the week—but somehow better on Thursday.

The Swedish cuisine used to be deficient in fresh vegetables and fruits, relying heavily on the tin can, but this is no longer true. Potatoes are the staff of life, but fresh salad bars long ago peppered the landscape, especially in the big cities.

The calorie-laden Swedish pastry—the mainstay of the konditori—is tempting and fatal to weight-watchers.

FROMMER'S SMART TRAVELER: RESTAURANTS

1. Look for the daily special—reasonable in price and prepared fresh that day.
2. Order fixed-price menus, especially at lunch. Often you can dine in expensive restaurants in Sweden by patronizing them at lunch and ordering the set menu.
3. Do as many Swedes do and make one or two open-face sandwiches for lunch.
4. Watch the booze—it can add greatly to the cost of any meal.
5. Go ethnic—the country has some great inexpensive foreign dining. Swedish restaurants tend to be expensive.
6. Best bet for a quick and inexpensive meal is a self-service cafeteria.
7. Fill up at the traditional Swedish breakfast buffets, so you'll need only a light lunch.

DRINKS

Kaffe (coffee) is the universal drink in Sweden, although tea (taken straight) and milk are also popular. The water is perfectly safe to drink all over Sweden. Those who want a reprieve from alcohol might find the fruit-flavored **Pommac** a good soft-drink beverage, but Coca-Cola is ubiquitous.

The state monopoly, Systembolaget, controls the sale of alcoholic beverages. Licensed restaurants may sell alcohol after noon only (1pm on Sunday).

Snaps or aquavit—served icy cold—is a superb Swedish drink, often used to accompany smörgåsbord. The run-of-the-mill Swedish **beer** (pilsner) has only a small amount of alcohol. All restaurants serve *lättöl* (light beer) and *folköl,* a somewhat stronger brew. Swedish vodka, or **brännvin,** is made from corn and potatoes and flavored with different spices. All brännvin is served ice cold in snaps glasses. Keep in mind that aquavit is much stronger than it looks, and Sweden has strictly enforced rules about drinking and driving. Most Swedes seem to drink their liquor straight; mixed drinks are uncommon. Either way, the drink prices are sky-high.

5. RECOMMENDED BOOKS, FILMS & RECORDINGS

BOOKS

HISTORY & MYTHOLOGY *The Early Vasas: A History of Sweden, 1523–1611,* by Michael Roberts (CUP), covers one of the most dramatic and action-filled eras in Sweden's long history.

Scandinavian Folk & Fairy Tales, edited by Claire Booss (Avenel), is an extraordinary collection filled with elves, dwarfs, trolls, goblins, and other spirits of the house and barnyard.

BIOGRAPHY *Swedes in North America (1638–1988),* by Sten Carlsson (Streiffert & Co.), traces the lives of some of the 2% of the North American population that have some sort of Swedish background—from Greta Garbo to Charles Lindbergh.

Alfred Nobel and the Nobel Prizes, Nils K. Ståhle (Swedish Institute), traces the life of the 19th-century Swedish industrialist and creator of the coveted awards that bear his name.

Garbo: Her Story, by Antoni Gronowicz (Simon & Schuster), is a controversial, unauthorized memoir based on a long and intimate friendship, going behind the fabulous face, with many candid details of this most reluctant of movie legends.

LITERATURE & THEATER *A History of Swedish Literature,* by Ingemar Algulin (The Swedish Institute), is the best overview on the subject—from the runic inscriptions of the Viking age up to modern fiction.

The Story of Gösta Berling, by Selma Lagerlöf (in various international editions), is the acclaimed work that Garbo filmed, originally published in 1891.

The Wonderful Adventures of Nils, by Selma Lagerlöf (in many international editions). Originally a schoolbook for teaching Swedish children geography, this classic became a worldwide bestseller.

Three Plays: Father, Miss Julie, Easter, by August Strindberg (Penguin), provides an insight into the world of this strange Swedish genius who wrote a number of highly arresting dramas, of which these are some of the best known.

FILM *Ingmar Bergman: The Cinema as Mistress,* by Philip Mosley (Marion Boyars), is a critical study of Bergman's *oeuvre* dating from his earliest work as a writer/director in the late 1940s up to *Autumn Sonata.*

Swedish Cinema, from Ingeborg Holm to Fanny and Alexander, by Peter Cowie

(The Swedish Institute), covers the complete history of Swedish films, from the emergence of the silent era, to the rise of Ingmar Bergman, up to the most recent wave.

FILMS

The classics of Ingmar Bergman will perhaps be shown 100 years from now, including such works as *The Virgin Spring* (1959). *The Seventh Seal* opened new ground in the art of film upon its release in 1956. It concerned the fate of man in a world God has abandoned. *Wild Strawberries*, released in 1957, was viewed by some critics as his most formal and exquisite work. It dealt with a person's coming to self-knowledge by looking at the past.

Fanny and Alexander (1982) won worldwide recognition for Bergman, doing well in the United States. Set in 1907, it pays tribute to the director's recollection of his childhood, growing up in Uppsala.

The late 1980s and 1990 have found Ingmar Bergman retired, and Sweden's two great cinema actresses, Greta Garbo and Ingrid Bergman, dead.

A major talent has emerged in Carl Gustaf Nykvist whose *The Women on the Roof* achieved recognition at Cannes. It is set in a Stockholm rooming house on the verge of World War I.

RECORDINGS

BALLADS *Out in the Open* by Ulf Lundell (English lyrics by Roger Hinchliffe) continues the success of Lundell, who has achieved fame as both a novelist and a rock balladeer. His gravelly voice and lyrics evoke Bob Dylan. This song is often called "Sweden's second national anthem."

Fredman's Epistle No. 2 by Carl Michael Bellman (English lyrics by Paul Britten Austin) is a famed work by Sweden's most popular composer, who lived from 1740 to 1795 but is still widely performed today. It is said that Englishman Austin's command of "Bellmanese" is second to none.

Also available on records and cassette is *Fredman's Song No. 16* by Bellman, again with English lyrics by Austin. *Fredman's Epistle No. 45,* by Bellman, has English lyrics by Roger Hinchliffe.

Evert Taube (1890–1976) is honored in the re-release of *Calle Scheven's Waltz* (English lyrics by Helen Asbury and Roger Hinchliffe) as a "modern Bellman." Called a "living legend" in Sweden, Taube is still considered the most cosmopolitan of Scandinavian songwriters, even after his death. He often sings of the sea and the people who live there, as he does in this recording.

Swedish Ballads and Songs, performed by Håkan Hagegård with the Swedish Radio Symphony (Kjell Ingebretsen, conducting).

FOLK *The Lilac Years (Looking to America)* is a recently recorded Swedish traditional folk melody, with English lyrics by Kathy Green and Roger Hinchliffe. It tells of the mass immigration period to America in the mid-19th century.

CLASSICAL *Midsommarvaka,* performed by the New Philharmonic Orchestra, London (conducted by Paavo Berglund), is an orchestral work by 20th-century Swedish composer Hugo Alfven. Even more representative of his work (and conducted by him as well) is *Festspel Opus 25,* performed by the Royal Court Orchestra, Stockholm.

Pastoralsvit, Lyrisk fantasi for liten orkester, Opus 58, by Lars Erik Larsson, performed by the Stockholm Philharmonic Orchestra—lyrical and lighthearted music for small orchestras.

Drottningholmsmusiken/Sinfonia D Major, by Johan Helmich Roma, performed by the Drottningholm Chamber Orchestra. This recording gives a good idea of the small-scale orchestral performances popular among the Swedish aristocracy during the 18th century. This performance of the work of an 18th-century Swedish composer was recorded at Stockholm's perfectly preserved 18th century Drottningholm Theater, near the king's private residence.

FOLK MUSIC/JAZZ/POPULAR *Greatest Hits,* by ABBA, Volumes I and II. Rock and disco music from ABBA, the most profitable and internationally famous Swedish group of the 1970s and 1980s.

Jazz pa svenska, with Jan Johansson, piano, and George Riedel, guitar. Highly danceable supper-club music of the kind popular with conservative middle-aged Swedes on a night on the town.

Svenskt Festspel (Swedish Highlights). The Swedish Radio Symphony Orchestra plays patriotic songs, including the Swedish national anthem, and symphonic renderings of songs dear to the patriotic hearts of most Swedes.

CHAPTER 23

PLANNING A TRIP TO SWEDEN

This chapter is devoted to the nitty gritty of planning a trip to Sweden—costs, events, itineraries, and detailed practicalities like taxes, tipping, and emergencies. It should be read in conjunction with Chapter 1.

1. CURRENCY & COSTS

CURRENCY Sweden, too, has basic currency units of **kronor** and **öre,** but the Swedes spell kronor with an "o" instead of an "e" as in the kroner of Denmark and Norway. As of this writing, 1 krona is worth about 17¢ U.S. (about 5.72 kronor equal $1 U.S.) One krona is equal to 100 öre. Banknotes are issued in 10, 50, 100, 500, 1,000, and 10,000 kronor, and silver coins are issued in 10 and 50 öre, as well as 1, 3, and 5 kronor.

Warning: The Swedish krona (sometimes abbreviated SEK) differs in value from the Danish, Icelandic, and Norwegian krone, which cannot be used in Sweden.

WHAT THINGS COST IN STOCKHOLM	U.S. $
Taxi from the airport to the city center	48.00
Average taxi ride in the city center	10.50
T-bana from the train station to the suburbs	1.30
Local telephone call	.35
Double room at the Grand Hotel (deluxe)	245.00
Double room at the Eden Terrace Hotel (moderate)	157.00
Double room at the Hotel Örnsköld (budget)	87.00
Lunch for one at Eriks Bakfica (moderate)	25.00
Lunch for one at Orient Express (budget)	15.00
Dinner for one, without wine, at Operakällaren (deluxe)	90.00
Dinner for one, without wine, at Prinsens (moderate)	35.00
Dinner for one, without wine, at Slingerbulten (budget)	23.00
Pint of beer (draft pilsner) in a bar	7.50

WHAT THINGS COST IN STOCKHOLM	U.S. $
Coca-Cola in a café	3.50
Cup of coffee in a café	2.75
Roll of ASA 100 Kodacolor film, 36 exposures	7.50
Admission to Drottningholm Palace	3.25
Movie ticket	8.75
Theater ticket	3.50–13.70

WHAT THINGS COST IN KARLSTAD	U.S. $
Taxi from the airport to the city center	8.75
Bus from the airport to the city center	2.60
Local telephone call	.35
Double room at the Stadshotellet (first class)	210.00
Double room at the Gösta Berling (moderate)	110.00
Double room at the Hotell Drott (budget)	91.00
Lunch for one at Plaza Vivaldi (moderate)	30.00
Lunch for one at Värdshuset Alstern (budget)	22.00
Dinner for one, without wine, at Café Artist (first class)	52.00
Dinner for one, without wine, at Kalleren Munken (moderate)	38.00
Dinner for one, without wine, at Skogen Terrassen (budget)	28.00
Pint of beer (draft pilsner) in a pub	6.80
Coca-Cola in a restaurant	2.10
Cup of coffee	2.50
Roll of Kodacolor film, 24 exposures	4.70
Admission to a museum (usually free, except for exhibitions)	1.75
Movie ticket	7.50
Theater ticket	15.70

2. WHEN TO GO — CLIMATE, HOLIDAYS & EVENTS

CLIMATE Sweden's climate is hard to classify, since temperatures, aided by the Gulf Stream, vary considerably from the fields of Skåne to the wilderness of Lapland (the upper tenth of Sweden lies north of the Arctic Circle).

The country as a whole has many days of sun in summer, but it's not super-hot. July is the warmest month, with temperatures in both Stockholm and Gothenburg averaging around 64° Fahrenheit. February is the coldest, when the temperature in Stockholm averages around 26° Fahrenheit (Gothenburg is a few degrees warmer).

It's not always true that the farther north you go the cooler it becomes. During

THE KRONA & THE DOLLAR

At this writing $1 = 5.72 Swedish kronor (or 1 Swedish krona = 17.5¢), and this was the rate of exchange used to calculate the dollar values given in the Sweden chapters (rounded to the nearest nickel). This rate fluctuates from time to time and may not be the same when you travel to Sweden. Therefore the following table should be used only as a guide:

Kronor	U.S.	Kronor	U.S.
0.25	0.04	125	21.82
0.50	0.08	150	26.19
1	0.17	175	30.56
5	0.87	200	34.92
10	1.75	225	39.29
15	2.62	250	43.65
20	3.49	300	52.38
25	4.37	350	61.11
30	5.24	400	69.84
40	6.98	450	78.57
50	8.73	500	87.30
60	10.48	600	104.76
70	12.22	700	122.22
80	13.97	800	139.68
90	15.71	900	157.14
100	17.46	1,000	174.60

summer the northern parts of the country—from Halsingland to northern Lapland—may suddenly have the warmest weather and the bluest skies. Check the weather forecasts on television and in the newspapers, which are claimed by the Swedes to be 99% reliable.

Sweden's Average Daytime Temperatures (°F)

	Jan	Feb	Mar	Apr	May	June	July	Aug	Sept	Oct	Nov	Dec
Stockholm	27	26	31	40	50	59	64	62	54	45	37	32
Kalmar	36	34	31	40	53	60	63	60	55	44	33	33
Karesuando	6	5	12	23	39	54	59	51	44	31	9	5
Karlstad	33	30	28	37	53	63	62	59	54	41	29	26
Lund	38	36	34	43	57	63	64	61	57	47	37	37

A Note on the Midnight Sun: In summer the sun never fully sets in the northern part of the nation, and even in the south there is daylight as late as 11pm and the sun rises around 3am. Here are the best vantage points in Sweden and dates when you may see the thrilling spectacle of the Midnight Sun (all these locations are reached by public transportation): **Björkliden,** May 26 to July 19; **Abisko,** June 12 to July 4; **Kiruna,** May 31 to July 14; and **Gällivare,** June 2 to July 12.

Remember that although the sun may be shining brightly at midnight, it is not as strong as at midday. Bring along a warm jacket or sweater.

HOLIDAYS Sweden celebrates the following public holidays: January 1 (New Year's Day), January 6 (Epiphany), Good Friday, Easter Sunday, Easter Monday, May 1 (Labor Day), Ascension Day, Whitsunday, Whitmonday, Midsummer Day, All Saints' Day, and December 24, 25, and 26 (Christmas Eve, Christmas Day, and Boxing Day). Inquire at the tourist bureaus for the actual dates of most of these holidays, since some vary from year to year.

SWEDEN CALENDAR OF EVENTS

In what follows dates are merely general indications of time. Always check with the tourist office before planning to attend an actual event.

APRIL

☐ **Walpurgis Night.** Celebrations with bonfires, songs, and speeches welcoming the advent of spring. Particularly lively celebrations among the students of Uppsala, Lund, Stockholm, Gothenburg, and Umeå. April 30.

JUNE

☐ **Midsummer.** Swedes celebrate Midsummer Eve (June 22) all over the country. Maypole dances to the sound of the fiddle and accordion are the rule of the day. Dalarna has the most traditional celebrations. June 22 and 23.

☐ **Music on Lake Siljan.** Nine days of concerts, courses, seminars, morning walks, homestead evenings, and special children's programs. June 30 to July 8.

JULY

✪ *FALUN FOLK MUSIC FESTIVAL* *International folk musicians' meeting, with concerts, seminars, lectures, exhibitions, and films on folk music. International folkloric groups perform.*
   Where: Various venues in Falun. When: July 11–14. How: Contact Falun Folk Music Festival, S-791 71 Falun (tel. 023/19042).

☐ **John Ericsson/Sweden-America Festival.** Held in memory of one of Värmland's most famous sons, John Ericsson. The sea battle between the *Monitor* and *Merrimac* is reenacted on Daglosen Lake at Kyrkviken, Filipstad. July 29.

✪ *GOTLAND'S CHAMBER MUSIC FESTIVAL* *A major Swedish cultural event, this annual festival attracts world-class artists who perform in a medieval setting.*
   Where: Visby, Gotland. When: July 29 to Aug 5. How: Write the Tourist Office, Burmeisterska Huset, Strandgatan 9, S-621 58 Visby (Gotland).

AUGUST

☐ **Minnesota Day.** Swedish-American relations are celebrated at the Emigrants' Center, with speeches, music, singing, and dancing, climaxed by the election of the Swedish-American of the year. Utvandra Utvandrarnas Hus, Växjö (Småland).

STOCKHOLM
CALENDAR OF EVENTS

MAY

✪ **DROTTNINGHOLM COURT THEATRE** *Some 28 opera and ballet performances presented in a unique 18th-century theater, with original decorative paintings and stage mechanisms.*
Where: Drottningholm Court Theatre, Drottningholm. When: May 27 to September 26. How: Call 08/660-82-55 or 08/660-82-82 for tickets, costing 60 to 260 kronor ($10.50 to $45.40). Take the underground to Bromma and a bus from there.

JULY

☐ **Round Gotland Race.** The biggest and most exciting open-water sailing race of the Scandinavian season starts and finishes at Sandhamm in the Stockholm archipelago. About 450 boats, mainly from the Nordic countries, take part. July 1.

AUGUST

☐ **Stockholm Festival.** Opera, concerts, ballet, theater, exhibitions, and other cultural events at various venues in Stockholm. August 18 to September 9.

DECEMBER

☐ **Skansen Christmas Fair.** Sale of traditional handcraft articles, Christmas decorations, homemade candles, breads, and cakes. At Skansen open-air museum in Stockholm. Dec 2, 9, and 16.

✪ **NOBEL DAY** *The king and members of the royal family attend the Nobel Prize ceremony for literature, physics, chemistry, medicine, physiology, and economics. The ceremony is followed by a banquet at Town Hall.*
Where: Concert Hall, Stockholm. When: December 10. How: By invitation only.

3. GETTING AROUND

BY PLANE

The airports of Gothenburg and Stockholm are the major gateways to Sweden. **Scandinavian Airlines System (SAS)** and the Swedish domestic airlines, **LIN (Linjeflyg)** maintain connections to 38 domestic airports, including Kiruna in Swedish Lapland; Visby, on the island of Gotland; Malmö, capital of the château country; Karlstad, center for Värmland; and Kalmar, a good base for exploring the glassworks district. From around June 1 to mid-July, flights depart from Stockholm north to Swedish Lapland and the Midnight Sun.

Air travel in Sweden is moderately priced because during the summer SAS and LIN offer **mini-fares,** charging a one-way price for a round-trip ticket! An accompanying spouse and children (ages 12 to 26) pay only 200 kronor ($34.90) to travel to and from Stockholm to any place in the country, regardless of distance, with one exception explained below. Children 2 to 12 pay only 100 kronor ($17.45).

A minimum 2-night stay is required for these mini-fares, and you must depart and return between a Monday and a Friday. Always check with the airline or travel agency when buying your tickets about further restrictions.

The exception is between southern and northern Sweden (which includes Lapland, of course). For a change of aircraft in Stockholm and for nonstop travel between Gothenburg and Sundsvall, a surcharge of 100 kronor ($17.45) is assessed for each accompanying family member. Children under age 2 travel free.

Young people under 26 can take advantage of the SAS/LIN special **standby fares,** and senior citizens over 65 can apply for even more discounts, depending on their destination.

BY TRAIN

The Swedish word for train is *tåg,* and the national train system is Statens Järnvägar, the Swedish State Railways.

Swedish trains follow tight schedules. Trains leave Malmö/Helsingborg for Stockholm every hour throughout the day, Monday through Friday. The same applies to trains leaving Gothenburg for Stockholm. In fact, there are trains every hour, or every other hour, to most big Swedish towns.

On *expresståg* runs, seats must be reserved, at a cost of 15 kronor ($2.60).

On long journeys, couchette and sleeping-car facilities are provided. Sleeper charges are $18 per person in a three-bed compartment for second-class travel. Couchettes in second class are available on many routes for $12.50.

Ticket prices are based on the length of the journey, and the passenger never pays for more than 563 miles. The maximum price for a one-way second-class trip is 430 kronor ($75.10), rising to 688 kronor ($120.10) in first class.

Discount tickets, called **"red departures,"** are also available. On any day of the week, travelers can profit from one of these red departures, which provides a one-way second-class ticket valid for 36 hours at half price. No stopovers are allowed. These discounts are even better for senior citizens, who pay 56 kronor ($9.80), or to children and students, who are charged only 28 kronor ($4.90). Discount tickets can be bought on the train, but only if the ticket office is closed at the time of departure.

Children up to age 16 are given a 50% discount at all times in both first and second class. A maximum of two children under 12 can travel free with an adult, except when they occupy their own berths in a sleeping car, in which case they are charged half fare.

SENIOR CITIZEN DISCOUNTS   Sweden grants visitors over 65 years of age a 30% reduction on train tickets, good for both first- and second-class travel year round, plus a further 30% reduction for travel other than on a Friday or a Sunday. This discount is good on all transportation operated by the Swedish State Railways.

BY BUS

Where the train stops its run, especially in parts of the north, a bus takes over, linking remote, off-the-beaten-path villages. Buses are usually equipped with toilets, adjustable seats, reading lights, and telephone. Fares depend on the distance traveled.

Weekend buses operated on Friday and Sunday by the Swedish State Railways provide a cheap travel alternative to the train. A sample fare from Stockholm to Gothenburg, a bus route of 326 miles, is 140 kronor ($24.45) one way. Reservations are necessary; in Stockholm, call 08/22-50-60.

BY CAR-FERRY

For a country with some 100,000 lakes and one of the world's largest coastlines, ferries play a surprisingly tiny part in the overall transportation network.

After the car-ferry crossings from northern Germany and Denmark, the most popular car-ferry route is from the mainland to the island of Gotland (capital: Visby), in the Baltic. Services are available from Oskarshamn, Nynäshamn, and Västervik. The famous "white boats" of the Waxholm Steamship Company also travel to many destinations in the Stockholm archipelago.

BY CAR

Sweden has an adequate highway system, particularly in the southern provinces and the central lake district. Swedish Customs issues an insurance card for cars or motorcycles brought into the country. Current driver's licenses from Canada, Great Britain, New Zealand, and Australia and the United States are acceptable in Sweden.

RENTALS   All the major car-rental firms are represented in Sweden.

At **Budget Rent-a-Car**, weekly rates with unlimited mileage apply only if a reservation is made at least 2 business days before actual pickup of the car. Reservations should be made in advance in North America (tel. toll free 800/527-0700).

The least expensive car in Budget's Swedish fleet is a Ford Escort with manual transmission, capable of holding up to four passengers with their luggage. Budget provides a free child seat, luggage rack, and ski rack if you reserve them in advance. An Escort rents for around 1,750 kronor ($305.95), plus tax, per week, plus an additional 250 kronor ($43.70) for each additional day of rental.

Travelers who prefer a bigger car can opt for a larger and more powerful Swedish-made Volvo 440GL for an unlimited-mileage weekly rate of 2,364 kronor ($413.30); each additional day costs 338 kronor ($59.10).

During normal business hours Budget will deliver your car for no additional charge to most city hotels, although most clients arrange for pickups at railway stations or airports. Deliveries to remote or outlying locations require an additional fee.

Don't forget that the Swedish government adds a whopping 23.4% tax to the final bill.

All winter rentals are equipped with spiked snow tires. Also, unless you want to be financially responsible for the full value of any damages to your car in the event of an accident, you can purchase a collision-damage waiver for around 45 kronor ($7.85) per day.

Finally, if your rental-car itinerary begins, but does not necessarily end, in Stockholm, Budget will allow you to drop off your car at any other Budget location within Sweden for no additional charge. Dropoffs in Denmark or Norway are possible as well, for payment of an additional fee of 500 kronor ($87.40) for dropoffs in Oslo and 250 kronor ($43.70) for dropoffs in Copenhagen.

Price comparisons with the competition are complicated by the policy at **Hertz** (tel. toll free 800/654-3001) of automatically including the cost of a collision-damage waiver (and the government tax of 23.4%) in the price of a car rental. This policy eliminates a renter's choice of using (if it's available) the offer of a credit-card company to pick up the cost of a collision-damage waiver in the event of an accident. Many renters, however, appreciate the security that full insurance coverage (with few questions asked) can bring. Hertz offers smaller and cheaper cars than Budget, such as the Renault 5, as well as large and expensive cars with automatic transmission, including a Volvo 740. At press time, a midwinter special on Hertz's smallest car included all taxes, all insurance premiums, and unlimited mileage for $266 per week. For a client to qualify for this rate, Hertz required that a reservation be made 21 days *before a renter's departure from the U.S.*

The least expensive car at **Avis** (tel. toll free 800/331-2112) is a Ford Fiesta (smaller than a Ford Escort), costing $279 per week with collision-damage waiver included. The government taxes, however, are extra.

Midsized cars at Hertz and Avis are competitively priced with those at Budget. Cars with automatic transmission (the Volvo mentioned above) begin at $511 per week at Hertz, with tax, insurance, and unlimited mileage included. Cars with automatic transmission at Avis are usually top-of-the-line Mercedes, renting with unlimited mileage for more than $1,000 a week, plus tax.

Call for more information, as these offers may have changed by the time of your visit to Sweden.

AUTOMOBILE CLUBS   Motoring organizations in Sweden are the **Motormänns Riksforbund (National Association of Motorists)**, Sturegaten 32, S-102 48

Stockholm (tel. 08/782-38-00), and the **Kungl. Automobil Klubben (Royal Automobile Club),** Gyllenstiernsgatan 4, S-115 26 Stockholm (tel. 08/660-00-55).

GAS Nearly every village and certainly every town or city in Sweden has a filling station that sells "petrol" 24 hours a day. Gas is expensive. For a super-grade gasoline, you'll pay, as of this writing (but subject to change in these uncertain times), about 4.89 kronor (85¢) per liter, or about $3.22 a gallon. Gas is slightly cheaper in the self-service stations, but you'll need 10-krona ($1.75) or 100-krona ($17.45) notes to operate the pumps.

DRIVING RULES In Sweden, as in all of Scandinavia, traffic drives on the right. By law, you and your passengers must wear seatbelts. During the day you are required to have your headlights on dim. Speed limits on standard roadways are 70 kilometers per hour (watch it, that's less than 45 m.p.h.), slowing to 50kmph (under 31 m.p.h.) in built-up areas, and 30kmph (about 18 m.p.h.) in school zones. On the motorways, the limits are 90kmph (56 m.p.h.) to 110kmph (68 m.p.h.), depending on the width of the roadway and the density of traffic.

Be warned: Sweden has very strict drunk-driving laws, with heavy fines levied if you violate them. You can be prosecuted after imbibing the equivalent of two cans of a strong beer.

MAPS Ask for local road maps at local tourist offices, bookstores (for which you'll have to pay, of course), or at one of the Swedish automobile clubs (see above). The best commercial road maps, sold at most major bookstores in Sweden, are those published by **Hallweg.**

BREAKDOWNS In case of a breakdown, call the police or the local branch of **Larmtjänst,** an outfit operated by Swedish insurance companies with a 24-hour phone line. Look in a local Swedish telephone directory for the number of the branch nearest your breakdown. The Swedish national emergency number of 90-000 should be used only in case of a real emergency—that is, an accident or injury.

BY RV Mobile homes can be rented for 4,250 to 6,000 kronor ($772.05 to $1,047.60) per week. Two outfits that specialize in this type of rental include **Husbilspoien AB,** Box 2057, S-191 02 Sollentuna (tel. 08/35-83-00), and **Husvagnsuthyrning AB,** Kranvägen 6, S-194 54 Upplands-Våsby (tel. 0760/891-00).

SUGGESTED ITINERARIES

IF YOU HAVE 1 WEEK

Day 1: Settle into Stockholm, the capital city.

Days 2 & 3: Explore Stockholm's attractions, including the raised royal flagship *Wasa.* One afternoon should be reserved for a boat trip through the archipelago and another for exploring Drottningholm Palace on the island of Lake Mälaren.

Day 4: Take a day trip north to Sweden's oldest town, Sigtuna, on the shores of Lake Mälaren, and to the nearby 17th-century Skokloster Castle, which contains one of the most interesting baroque museums in Europe. Then it's on to the university city of Uppsala, and perhaps on to neighboring Gamla (Old) Uppsala to see Viking burial mounds.

Day 5: Begin a fast 4-day excursion through the most interesting folkloric provinces of Sweden, Dalarna and Värmland. Arrive first at the mining town of Falun to visit the Falun Copper Mine and the home of Carl Larsson, the famous Swedish painter. Spend the night here or in one of the smaller resort towns such as Tällberg, Rättvik, Mora, or Leksand.

Day 6: Visit the Lake Siljan towns just mentioned. This blue glacial lake, ringed by lush forests, is one of the most beautiful in Europe. Take a boat tour leaving from

Rättvik. On its outskirts you can visit Gammelgården, an old farmstead, for a glimpse of the past and stay overnight again in one of the lakeside villages or towns.

Day 7: From Falun, Route 60 heads south to Karlstad. You'll pass through the heart of Selma Lagerlöf country (Sweden's most famous novelist). Have lunch at Filipstad, the birthplace of John Ericsson, who designed the U.S. Civil War iron-clad ship *Monitor*. Spend the night in Karlstad.

IF YOU HAVE 2 WEEKS

Days 1–7: Spend the first week as described above. But instead of cutting short your trip in Karlstad, extend it another week, using the following itinerary.

Day 8: Spend another night in Karlstad, exploring its own attractions, and branching out into the environs, including Rotternos Manor.

Day 9: In the morning, head south along the eastern shore of Lake Vanern. After lunch in charming lakeside Lidköping, head for Gothenburg, the second-largest city of Sweden.

Day 10: Explore Gothenburg and branch out on short trips to such attractions as Kungalv or Marstrand, a once-royal resort.

Days 11–13: Take the Göta Canal ride, a distance of 350 miles. This trip begins at Gothenburg and heads east to Stockholm. You'll go through 58 locks and capture the "essence" of Sweden along the way.

Day 14: Arrive in Stockholm and prepare for your return flight to North America.

IF YOU HAVE 3 WEEKS

Days 1–14: In addition to the 2-week itinerary outline above, those with extra time may want to explore Sweden's southern region.

Days 15 & 16: Head south from Stockholm to the largest island of Sweden, Gotland, whose capital is Visby. Spend the next day exploring the island's attractions.

Day 17: Return to the mainland and head south to the old city of Kalmar, where you can explore Kalmar Castle and other attractions.

Day 18: Visit the Glassworks District, centering at Växjö. Within less than an hour's drive of Växjö are several glassworks, including Orrefors and Boda, which offer guided tours. You can purchase "seconds" in their workshops.

Days 19–21: Explore Skåne, the southernmost corner of Sweden, often called the country's château district. Malmö, the third-largest city of Sweden, is an ideal base because of its many hotels and attractions. The university city of Lund, northeast of Malmö, is also a good bet, and Ystad is a favorite stop along the southern coastline. From Helsingborg, north of Malmö, you can cross into Denmark and see Hamlet's Castle.

 SWEDEN

Business Hours   Banks are generally open Monday through Friday from 9:30am to 3pm. In some larger cities, banks extend their hours, usually on Thursday or Friday, until 5:30 or 6pm. Most **offices** are open Monday through Friday from 8:30 or 9am to 5pm (sometimes to 3 or 4pm in the summer); on Saturday, offices and factories are closed or open for only a half day. Most **stores and shops** are open Monday through Friday between 9:30am and 6pm, and on Saturday from 9:30am to somewhere between 1 and 4pm. Once a week, usually on Monday or Friday, some of the larger stores are open from 9:30am to 7pm (during July and August, to 6pm).

Camera/Film   Cameras (especially the famed Hasselblad), film, projectors, and enlarging equipment are very good values in Sweden. Practically all the world's brands are found here. Photographic shops give excellent service, often developing and printing in 1 day.

Currency   See "Currency & Costs," above.

Customs   The government allows you (unless you're under 15 years of age) to bring in—duty free—400 cigarettes or 100 cigars. If you're over 20, you are also allowed 1 liter of liquor, 1 liter of wine, gifts totaling 600 kronor ($104.75), and what the Swedes call a "reasonable" amount of perfume. There's no limit on the amount of currency you can bring in, but you can't take more than 6,000 kronor ($1,047.60) with you when you leave.

Dentists   For emergency dental services, ask your hotel or host for the location of the nearest dentist. Nearly all dentists in Sweden speak English.

Doctors   Hotel staffs can usually refer you to a local doctor, nearly all of whom speak English. If you need emergency treatment, your hotel should also be able to direct you to the nearest facility. In an accident or injury away from the hotel, call the nearest police station.

Driving Rules   See "Getting Around," in this chapter.

Drug Laws   There are severe penalties in Sweden for the possession, use, purchase, sale, or manufacturing of proscribed drugs. Penalties are often based on quantity, but all that can vary, of course. Possession of what is deemed a small amount of drugs, either hard or soft, can lead to a heavy fine and deportation. Possession of a "large" amount of drugs can elicit a prison term ranging from 3 months to 15 years, depending on the circumstances and the presiding judge.

Drugstores   Called an *apotek* in Sweden, drugstores are generally open Monday through Friday from 9am to 6pm and on Saturday from 9am to 1pm. In bigger cities one drugstore in every neighborhood stays open until 7pm. All pharmacies have a list of names and addresses of these *Nattapotek,* as they are called, in their windows.

Electricity   In Sweden, the electricity is 220 volts A.C. To operate North American hairdryers and other electrical appliances, you will need an electrical converter and plugs that fit the two-pin round continental electrical outlets that are standard in Sweden. Converters can be bought at hardware stores. Before using any American-made appliance, always ask at your hotel desk.

Embassies & Consulates   The **U.S. Embassy** is in Stockholm at Strandvägen 101, S-114 56 Stockholm (tel. 08/783-53-00). The **British Embassy** is at Skarpögatan 6-8, S-115 27 Stockholm (tel. 08/667-01-40); the **Canadian Embassy,** at Tegelbacken 4, S-101 23 Stockholm (tel. 08/23-79-20). The **Australian Embassy** is at Sergels Torg 12, S-103 27 Stockholm (tel. 08/24-46-60), and **New Zealand** does not maintain an embassy in Sweden.

Emergencies   Call **90-000** from anywhere in Sweden if you need an ambulance, the police, or the fire department (*brandlarm*).

Etiquette   Swedes generally dress up if invited to a private party or someone's home, unless the host specifically states blue jeans or casual wear. Always bring a gift—chocolates or flowers. When meeting a man or woman in Sweden, extend your hand. It is also customary in this rainy country to remove your shoes when entering a private home.

Hitchhiking   Although officially discouraged by the government, hitchhiking is not illegal in Sweden. The more presentably dressed you are, of course, the better your chances. There is always a certain risk involved. Drivers usually speak English. Because of weather conditions, hitchhiking is definitely not recommended in colder months, as you can get stranded in a wilderness somewhere when a driver lets you off.

Language   The national language is Swedish, a Germanic tongue, and there are many regional dialects. Some minority groups speak Norwegian and Finnish. But none of this need be a problem for you. English is required in school and is commonly spoken, even in the hinterlands, especially among young people. For the best phrase book, purchase a copy of ***Swedish for Travellers,*** published by Berlitz.

Liquor Laws   Most restaurants, pubs, and bars in Sweden are licensed to serve liquor, wine, and beer. Some places are licensed only for wine and beer. Purchases of wine, liquor, and export beer are available only through the government-controlled monopoly, **Systembolaget.** Branch stores, spread throughout the country, are usually open Monday through Friday from 9am to 6pm. The minimum age for buying alcoholic beverages in Sweden is 20.

Mail   Post offices in Sweden are usually open Monday through Friday from 9am to 6pm and on Saturday from 9am to 1pm. To mail a postcard to North America costs 3.10 kroner (55¢). Letters weighing not more than 20 grams are sent for 3.60 kroner (60¢). Post offices are easily recognizable by the sign of the yellow post horn on a blue background. You can also buy stamps in most tobacco shops and stationers.

Maps Many tourist offices supply routine maps of their districts free, and you can also contact one of the Swedish automobile clubs (see Section 8, "Getting Around," in this chapter). Bookstores throughout Sweden also sell detailed maps of the country and of such major cities as Gothenburg and Stockholm. The most reliable country maps are published by **Hallweg.** The best and most detailed city maps are those issued by **Falk,** which have a particularly good and properly indexed map to Stockholm.

Newspapers/Magazines In big cities, English-language newspapers, including the latest edition of the *International Herald-Tribune,* are usually for sale. English-language news magazines, such as *Time* and *Newsweek,* are also sold. American newspapers are not commonly available, but in Stockholm and Gothenburg you can purchase such London newspapers as *The Times.*

Pets My advice is to leave them at home. Sweden places nearly all animals, including cats and dogs, in quarantine before they're allowed inside the country.

Police In an emergency, dial **90-000** anywhere in the country.

Radio/TV In summer, Radio Stockholm broadcasts a special program for English-speaking tourists, "T-T-T-Tourist Time," on 103.3 MHz from 6 to 7pm daily. Swedish radio transmits P1 on 92.4 MHz (FM band) and P2 on 96.2 MHz in the Stockholm area. P3 is transmitted on 103.3 MHz (102.9 MHz in southern Stockholm), a wavelength shared by Radio Stockholm and local programs. Radio Stockholm also has a channel of its own on 98.3 MHz, Community Radio for special-interest organizations, transmitted on 88 MHz in the city district.

Rest Rooms The word for toilet in Sweden is *toalett,* and public facilities are found in department stores, rail and air terminals, and subway (T-bana) stations. They are also found along some of the major streets, parks, and squares. DAMER is for women and HERRAR is for men. Sometimes the sign is abbreviated to D or H, and often the toilet is marked WC. Most toilets are free, although a few have attendants to offer towels and soap. In an emergency you can also use the toilets in most hotels and restaurants, although in theory you're supposed to be a client.

Safety Whenever you're traveling in an unfamiliar city or country, stay alert. Be aware of your immediate surroundings. Wear a moneybelt and carry your camera or purse carefully. This will minimize the possibility of your becoming a victim of crime. Every society has its criminals. It is your responsibility to be aware and alert even in the most heavily touristed areas.

Shoe Repairs Shoe-repair shops rarely do their work while you wait. In summer, especially in July, many shops close, but the larger stores in the center of Stockholm have their own repair departments. If all you want is a new heel, look for something called *klackbar* in the stores or shoe departments of the department stores. They repair while you wait.

Taxes Sweden imposes a "Value-Added Tax," called **Moms,** of 23.4% on most goods and services, which makes an already-expensive country even more expensive. Visitors from the U.S. and Canada can beat the tax, however, by shopping in stores with the yellow-and-blue TAX-FREE SHOPPING sign. There are more than 13,000 such stores in Sweden. For purchases in one of these stores totaling more than 200 kronor ($34.90), you are entitled to a tax refund. You pay the tax along with the purchase price, but get a tax-refund voucher before you leave the shop. You'll get your Moms back, minus a small service charge, at your point of departure from the country (wherever you go through Customs). You can't use your purchase in Sweden, and it must be taken out of the country within 1 month. For tax-free shopping information in Sweden, phone 0410/19-560.

Telephone/Telex/Fax Information on these facilities in Stockholm will be found in "Fast Facts: Stockholm" in Chapter 24. The same rules apply to calling from public phones elsewhere in the country. Avoid placing long-distance calls from your hotel, where the charge may be doubled or tripled when you get your final bill.

Time   Sweden is on central European time, that is, Greenwich mean time + 1 hour or eastern standard time + 6 hours. The clocks are put forward 1 hour in summer.

Tipping   Hotels include a 15% service charge in your bill. **Restaurants,** depending on their class, add 13% to 15% to your tab. **Taxi drivers** are entitled to 8% of the fare, and **cloakroom attendants** usually expect 4 to 6 kronor (70¢ to $1.05).

Water   The water is perfectly safe to drink all over Sweden.

Yellow Pages   Sweden has *Yellow Pages,* but unless you speak the language, finding a service you need may be difficult. Swedish words are quite different in most cases from the English. If you didn't speak Swedish, how would you know to look up the nearest liquor store under "Systembolaget"? Also, the Swedish alphabet is different from English, using symbols English doesn't, including Ö and Å. The word *Åbogatan* doesn't appear after *Abborrvägen,* but follows *Zornvägen.*

INTRODUCING STOCKHOLM

Stockholm (pop. 1.4 million) is built on 14 islands on Lake Mälaren, marking the beginning of an archipelago of 24,000 islands, skerries, and islets that stretches all the way to the Baltic Sea. A city of bridges and islands, towers and steeples, cobblestone squares and broad boulevards, Renaissance splendor and steel-and-glass skyscrapers, Stockholm also has access to nature only a few minutes away. You can even go fishing in downtown waterways, thanks to a long-ago decree from Queen Christina.

Although the city was founded more than 7 centuries ago, it did not become the official capital of Sweden until the mid-17th century. Today it is the capital of a modern welfare state. The medieval walls of the Old Town (Gamla Stan) no longer remain, but the winding streets do, as they were spared the ravages of World War II.

1. ORIENTATION

ARRIVING

BY PLANE You'll arrive at **Arlanda International Airport,** about 25 miles north of Stockholm on the E4 highway. A long covered walkway connects the international and domestic terminals. For information on international flights, phone 08/780-39-10; for domestic flights, 08/780-33-51.

A bus outside the terminal building goes to the Central Railway Station, Vasagatan 6-14, about an 80-minute trip, for 40 kronor ($7). SAS has a limousine service from the airport, operated on a share-the-ride basis. It will take you from the limousine-service desk in the arrivals hall at Arlanda to central Stockholm for 235 kronor ($41.05). To arrange a return trip to the airport, call 08/15-12-10 well in advance of your flight.

A taxi to or from the airport is expensive, costing around 270 kronor ($47.15) on weekdays and 350 kronor ($61.10) on weekends.

BY TRAIN Trains arrive at Stockholm's **Central Station** at Vasagatan 6-14, where connections can be made to Stockholm's subway, the T-bana. Follow the sign marked TUNNELBANA.

Virtually every part of Sweden can be reached by rail from Stockholm's Centralstationen.

BY BUS Buses also arrive at the Centralstationen on Vasagatan, and from here you

WHAT'S SPECIAL ABOUT STOCKHOLM

Great Neighborhoods

☐ Gamla Stan, the Old Town, next to the Royal Palace, a warren of antique buildings and alleys dating from 1252.

☐ Skansen, the folklore center with more than 150 historic buildings, a summer rendezvous for Stockholm.

Monuments

☐ The Royal Palace, containing the Swedish crown jewels and the Royal Armory.

☐ Drottningholm Palace, home of the royal family, with one of the world's few surviving 18th-century theaters.

Parks/Gardens

☐ Millesgården, on Lidingö Island, the waterside residence of sculptor Carl Milles, containing his rich art collection.

☐ Djurgården (Deer Park), a former royal hunting ground; contains Skansen and the *Wasa*, but magnificent in its own right.

Events/Festivals

☐ The Nobel Prize awards in December. It's by invitation only, but you can attend speeches by the prize winners.

☐ Walpurgis Night, when Stockholm wakes up after a sleepy winter; bonfires in public places.

Ace Attractions

☐ *Vasa*, the world's oldest restored warship, which capsized on her maiden voyage in 1628.

Museums

☐ The Nordic Museum, on Djurgården, a repository of Swedish cultural life since the 16th century.

☐ National Museum of Art, the Swedish state collection of paintings and sculpture.

---

can catch the T-bana (subway) to your final Stockholm destination. For bus information or reservations, check with the bus system's ticket offices at the station (tel. 23-71-90). Offices within the station designated SJ RESEBYRÅ sell both rail and bus tickets.

BY CAR　Getting into Stockholm by car is relatively easy because the major national expressway highway from the south, the E4, joins with the national express highway E3 coming in from the west, and leads right into the heart of the city. Stay on the highway until you see the turnoff for Central Stockholm or Sentrum.

Parking in Stockholm is extremely difficult unless your hotel has a garage.

BY FERRY　Large ships, including the **Silja Line,** Kungsgatan 2 (tel. 22-21-40), and the **Viking Line,** Stureplan 8 (tel. 44-07-65), arrive at specially constructed berths jutting seaward from a point near the junction of Södermalm and Gamla Stan. This neighborhood is known as Stadsgården, and the avenue which runs along the adjacent waterfront is known as Stadsgårdshamnen. The nearest metro stop is Slussen, a 3-minute walk from the Old Town. Holders of the Eurailpass can ride the Silja ferries to Helsinki and Turku free with their passes if valid.

IMPRESSIONS

A Roman driver will stop his car to admire a beautiful girl. A Stockholm driver will stop his car to admire a beautiful salmon.
—ANONYMOUS

Other ferries arrive from Gotland (whose capital is Visby), but these boats dock at Nynäshamn, to the south of Stockholm. Take a Nynäshamn-bound bus from the Central Station in Stockholm or the SL commuter train to reach the ferry terminal at Nynäshamn.

TOURIST INFORMATION

The **Tourist Centre,** Sweden House, Hamngatan 27, off Kungsträdgården (Box 7542), S-103 93 Stockholm (tel. 08/789-20-00), is open mid-June to the end of August, Monday through Friday from 8:30am to 6pm and on Saturday and Sunday from 8am to 5pm; the remainder of the year, Monday through Friday from 9am to 5pm and on Saturday and Sunday from 9am to 2pm. Maps and other free material are available.

For more detailed information about study or cultural life, go to the **Swedish Institute Documentation Centre,** upstairs. Librarians will show you the many pamphlets available on anything you want to know. The center's automatic answering service (tel. 08/22-18-40) details the day's events.

In summer from 8am to 9pm, you can obtain information at **Hotell-centralen** (tel. 24-08-80), at the Central Railroad Station. Another tourist service offered in Stockholm is the English-language news broadcast daily in summer from 6 to 7pm on 103.3 MHz.

CITY LAYOUT

MAIN STREETS & ARTERIES

On the island of Norrmalm north of the Old Town are Stockholm's major streets, such as **Kungsgatan** (the main shopping street), **Birger Jarlsgatan,** and **Strandvågen** (leading to the Djurgården). **Stureplan,** which lies at the junction of the major avenues named Kungsgatan and Birger Jarlsgatan, is considered the commercial hub of the city.

About four blocks east of the Stureplan rises **Hötorget City,** a landmark of modern urban planning, that includes five 18-story skyscrapers. Its main, traffic-free artery is the Sergelgatan, a three-block shopper's promenade which eventually leads to the modern sculptures in the center of the Sergels Torg.

About nine blocks south of the Stureplan, at **Gustav Adolf's Torg,** lie both the Royal Dramatic Theater and the Royal Opera House.

A block east of the flaming torches of the Opera House is the verdant north-to-south stretch of **Kungstradgården,** part avenue, part public park, which serves as a popular gathering place for students and a resting perch for shoppers.

Three blocks to the southeast, on a famous promontory whose seafront also contains the landmark Grand Hotel lies the National Museum.

Most newcomers to Stockholm arrive either at the SAS Airport Bus Terminal, the Central Railway Station, or Stockholm's Central (Public) Bus Station. Each of these lie in the heart of the city, on the harborfront, about seven blocks due west of the Opera House.

Kungsholmen, King's Island, lies across a narrow canal from the rest of the city, a short walk west of the Central Railway Station. It is visited chiefly by those seeking a tour of Stockholm's elegant Stadtshuset (City Hall).

South of the island that contains Gamla Stan (Old Town), separated from it by a narrow but much-navigated stretch of water, is **Södermalm,** the southern district of Stockholm. Quieter and calmer than its northern counterpart, it is an important residential center with a distinctive flavor of its own.

To the east of Gamla Stan, on a large and forested island completely surrounded by the complicated waterways of Stockholm, is **Djurgården** (Deer Park). Considered the rustically unpopulated summer pleasure ground of Stockholm, and also the site of many of its most popular attractions, it contains the open-air museums of Skansen, the *Wasa* man-of-war, Gröna Lund's Tivoli, the Waldemarsudde estate of the "painting prince" Eugen, and the Nordic Museum.

FINDING AN ADDRESS All even numbers are on one side of the street, and all odd numbers on the opposite side. Buildings are listed in numerical order, but will often have an A, B, or C after the Arabic number.

NEIGHBORHOODS IN BRIEF

Any city spread across 14 major islands in an archipelago has many neighborhoods, but those that need concern the average visitor lie in Central Stockholm.

Gamla Stan (the Old Town) This is the very "cradle" of Stockholm, lying at the entrance of Lake Mälaren on the Baltic. Its oldest city walls date from the 13th century. The Old Town, along with the *Vasa*, is the biggest attraction of Stockholm. It has only a few hotels, but dozens of restaurants. Its major shopping mall is Västerlånggatan, but many little artisan galleries and antiques stores abound on its small lanes. Its main square, and the heart of the ancient city, is Stortorget.

Norrmalm North of Gamla Stan, this large island is the cultural and commercial heart of modern Stockholm. Once it was a city suburb, but now it virtually *is* the city. Your arrival will probably be at Norrmalm's Central Station on Vasagatan. Its major pedestrian shopping street is Drottninggatan, starting at the bridge to the Old Town.

The most famous park in Stockholm, Kungsträdgården (the King's Garden), is also in Norrmalm. In summer, this park is the major rendezvous point in the city. Norrmalm also embraces the important squares of Sergels Torg and Hötorget, the latter a modern shopping complex.

Vasastan As Norrmalm pushed ever northward, the new district of Vasastan was created. It is split by a trio of main arteries, including St. Eriksgatan, Sveavägen, and Odengatan. The area around St. Eriksplan is now called "the Off Broadway of Stockholm" because it has so many theater choices. Increasingly, this district is filled with fashionable restaurants and bars and has become a popular place to live for young Stockholmers on the rise in such fields as journalism, television, and advertising.

Kungsholmen Once known as "Grey Friars Farm," today Kungsholmen (King's Island) is an island to the west of Gamla Stan containing the City Hall. Established by King Charles XI in the 17th century as a zone for industry and artisans, it has now been gentrified. Its major arteries include Felmminggatan. Along Norrmälarstrand, old Baltic cutters tie up to the banks. Stockholm's newspapers' headquarters are at Marieberg on the southwestern tip of the island.

Södermalm South of Gamla Stan, Södermalm, where Greta Garbo was born, is the largest and most populated district of Stockholm. Once synonymous with poverty, today this working-class district is growing more fashionable, especially with artists, writers, and young people. If you don't come here to stay in one of the moderately priced hotels or to dine in one of its restaurants, you may want to take the Katarina elevator for a good view of Stockholm and its harbor.

Östermalm In central Stockholm, east of the main artery, Birger Jarlsgatan, is Östermalm. In the Middle Ages the royal family used to keep their horses, and even armies, here. Today it is the site of the Army Museum. There are wide, straight streets, and also one of the city's biggest parks, Humlegården, dating from the 17th century.

Djurgården To the east of Gamla Stan, the Old Town, is Djurgården (Deer Park), a lake-encircled forested island that is the summer pleasure ground of Stockholm. Here you can visit the open-air folk museums of Skansen, the *Wasa*

IMPRESSIONS

It [Stockholm] is not a city at all. It is ridiculous of it to think of itself as a city. It is simply a rather large village, set in the middle of some forests and some lakes. You wonder what it thinks it is doing there, looking so important.
—Ingmar Bergman

man-of-war, Gröna Lund's Tivoli (Stockholm's own version of the Tivoli), the Waldemarsudde estate and gardens of the "painting prince" Eugen, and the Nordic Museum. The fastest way there is over the bridge at Strandvägen/Narvavägen.

MAPS

Free maps of Stockholm are available at the tourist office, but if you want to explore the narrow old streets of Gamla Stan, you will need a more detailed map. The best is published by **Falk,** a pocket-size map with a street index that can be opened and folded like a wallet. It is sold at most newsstands in central Stockholm and at major bookstores including **Nya Akademibokhandeln,** Måster Samuelsgatan 32 (tel. 21-48-90).

2. GETTING AROUND

BY PUBLIC TRANSPORTATION

You can travel throughout all of Stockholm county by bus, local train, the underground (T-bana), and trams, going from Singo in the north to Nynashamn in the south. Routes are divided into zones, and one ticket is valid for all types of public transport in the same zone within 1 hour of when the ticket is stamped.

REGULAR FARES The basic fare for public transport (which in Stockholm means either underground, tram/streetcar, or bus) is with tickets purchased from the person in the toll booth on the subway platform, not from a vending machine. Each ticket costs 4.50 kronor (80¢), and to travel three stops requires one ticket. To travel within most of urban Stockholm, all the way to the borders of the inner city, requires only two tickets. The maximum ride, to the outermost suburbs, requires four tickets. You can transfer (or double back and return to your starting point) within 1 hour of your departure for free. Fares are doubled after midnight.

SPECIAL DISCOUNT TICKETS Senior citizens and young people under 18 are granted almost 50% reductions on all Stockholm public transportation.

Your best transportation bet is to purchase a **tourist season ticket.** A 1-day card, costing 24 kronor ($4.20), is valid for 24 hours of unlimited travel by T-bana, bus, and commuter train within Stockholm and the ferry to Djurgården. Most visitors will want the 3-day card for 76 kronor ($13.25), valid for 72 hours in both Stockholm and the county. It is also valid for admission to Skansen, Kaknåstornet, and Gröna Lund. Children under 16 pay half price, and two children up to 7 years of age can travel free.

Tickets are offered at tourist-information offices as well as in subway stations and at most news vendors.

The **Stockholmskortet (Stockholm Card)** is a personal discount card that allows unlimited free travel by bus, subway, and local trains throughout the city and county of Stockholm (except on airport buses). You can also take a free sightseeing tour with Turistlinjen, which allows you to get on and off as often as you want to, looking at the sights according to your own schedule. A free map and a guide booklet are given visitors who do not speak Swedish. These tours are available daily June to August; on Saturday and Sunday in April, May, and September to December; and on Sunday, January to March. The card also allows you to take a boat trip to the Royal Palace of Drottningholm for half price. Free admission to 50 attractions is included in the package.

You can purchase the card at several places in the city, including the Tourist Centre in the Sweden House, Hotellcentralen, the Central Railway Station, the tourist-information desk in City Hall (in summer), the Kaknäs TV tower, SL-Center Sergels Torg (subway entrance level), and Pressbyrån newsstands. The cards are stamped with the date and time at the first point of usage. A 24-hour card costs 75 kronor ($13.10) for adults. For a 48-hour card, the cost is 140 kroner ($24.45). For 3 days, it's 195 kronor ($34.05), and for 4 days, 260 kronor ($45.40).

BY T-BANA [SUBWAY] Before entering the subway, passengers tell the ticket seller the destination, then purchase tickets that they surrender when they get off at their station (any discrepancies will be ironed out by the ticket taker at the other end).

Subway entrances are marked with a blue "T" on a white background. For information about schedules, routes, and fares, phone 23-60-00.

BY BUS Where the subway leaves off, the bus begins. Therefore, if a subway connection doesn't conveniently cover a particular area of Stockholm, a bus will fill the need. The two systems have been coordinated to complement each other. Many visitors use a bus to reach Djurgården (although you can walk there), as the T-bana doesn't go there. For a list of bus routes, purchase the *SL Stockholmskartan,* which is sold at the tourist center at Sweden House, Hamngatan 27, off Kungsträdgården (tel. 789-20-00).

BY TAXI

Taxis are few in number and expensive—in fact, the most expensive in the world. Those that have the sign LEDIG may be hailed, or you can order one by phone (tel. 15-00-00; 15-04-00 for advance booking), but it will cost 25 kronor ($4.35) extra. If you're near a cab rank, it will be cheaper to take one there.

BY CAR

If you're driving around the Swedish capital, you will find several parking garages in the city center as well as on the outskirts. In general, you can park at marked spaces Monday through Friday from 8am to 6pm. Exceptions or rules for specific areas are posted at signs in the area. At Djurgården, parking is always prohibited, and from April to mid-September it's closed to traffic Friday through Sunday.

BY FERRY

Ferries from Skeppsbron in Gamla Stan (near the bridge to Södermalm) will take you to Djurgården if you don't want to go by bus or walk. They leave every 20 minutes Monday through Saturday, and about every 15 minutes on Sunday, from 9am to 6pm, charging 8 kronor ($1.40) for adults or 4 kronor (70¢) for senior citizens and young people 7 to 18 years old.

BY BICYCLE

Try **Cykel & Moped Uthyrningen,** Kajplats 24 (tel. 660-79-59), in a little hut on the river side of Strandvägen close to the Djurgårds bridge which is open from May 1 until late September daily from 9am to 10pm. It rents three- and six-speed bicycles for about 22 kronor ($3.85) for the first hour, plus 10 kronor ($1.75) for each additional hour. Mopeds cost around 55 kronor ($9.60) per hour or 275 kronor ($48) for a whole day, requiring a deposit of 300 kronor ($52.40).

 STOCKHOLM

American Express American Express is at Birger Jarlsgatan 1 (tel. 14-39-81), open in July and August, Monday through Friday from 9am to 5pm and on Saturday from 10am to 1pm; September to June, Monday through Friday from 9am to 5pm.

Area Code The telephone area code for Stockholm is 08.

Baby-Sitters Stockholm hotels maintain lists of competent women who baby-sit. Nearly all of them speak English. There is no official agency; it's rather a "word of mouth" thing. The average rate for one child is 70 kronor ($12.20) per hour; for two or three children, the charge goes up to 90 kronor ($15.70) per hour.

Bookstores For a good selection of English-language books, including maps and tour guides, try **Nya Akademibokhandeln,** Mäster Samuelsgatan 32 (tel. 21-48-90), open Monday through Friday from 9:30am to 6pm and on Saturday from 10am to 2pm.

Car Rentals See "Getting Around," in Chapter 23. In Stockholm, some of the big car-rental companies include **Avis,** Sveavägen 61 (tel. 34-99-10); **Hertz,** Mäster Samuelsgatan 67 (tel. 24-07-20); and **Europcar,** Birger Jarlsgatan 59 (tel. 23-10-70).

Currency Exchange There is a currency-exchange office, **Forex,** at the Central Station (tel. 11-67-34), open daily from 8am to 9pm. It's fully authorized by both the Bank of Sweden and the Swedish tourist authorities, gives some of the best exchange rates in town, and takes some of the lowest commissions for the cashing of traveler's checks. There's another branch, with less extended hours and no weekend hours, in the same building near the Arrivals Hall of the bus station.

Dentist Emergency dental treatment is offered at **Sct. Eriks Hospital,** Fleminggatan 22 (tel. 54-11-17), open daily from 8am to 7pm. Only urgent cases are dealt with after 7pm. After 9pm, consult the emergency dentist on duty (tel. 44-92-00).

Doctor If you need emergency medical care, check with **Medical Care Information** (tel. 84-04-00). There is also a private clinic, **City Skuten,** at Hollandargatan 3 (tel. 11-71-77).

Drugstore You'll find a pharmacy open 24 hours a day in Stockholm, **C. W. Scheele,** Klarabergsgatan 64 (tel. 24-82-80).

Embassies and Consulates The **U.S. Embassy** is at Strandvägen 101, (tel. 783-53-00); the **British Embassy,** at Skarpögatan 6-8 (tel. 667-01-40); the Canadian Embassy, at Tegelbacken 4 (tel. 23-79-20); and the **Australian Embassy** is at Sergels Torg 12 (tel. 24-46-60). **New Zealand** does not maintain an embassy in Sweden.

Emergencies Call 90-000 for the police, ambulance service, or the fire department. For car towing, call **Larmtjänst** (tel. 020/91-00-40).

Eyeglasses The **Nordikska Kompaniet,** Hamngatan 18-20 (tel. 762-80-00), one of the leading department stores of Stockholm, has a registered optician on duty at its ground-floor Service Center. The optician carries out sight tests, stocks a large selection of frames, and makes emergency repairs.

Hairdressers/Barbers For men or women, a reliable and stylish hairdresser is **Calle & Co.,** Östermalmstorg 4 (tel. 661-75-36). A man's haircut costs 210 kronor ($36.65); a woman's haircut, 230 kronor ($40.15).

Hospitals Dial 144-92-00 and an English-speaking operator will refer you to the hospital nearest your location.

Laundry **Hornsplans Skrädderi & Trättomat W&$,** Bergsunds Strand 48 (tel. 68-61-61), is a combination used-clothing store and laundry. Washers and dryer are in the back of the store.

Libraries The **Stockholms stadsbibliotek,** Sveavägen 73 (tel. 23-66-00), is the biggest municipal library in Sweden, with 2.4 million books (many in English) and audiovisual aids. It also subscribes to 1,500 newspapers and periodicals (many in English).

Lost Property If you've lost something on the train, go to the Lost and Found Office in the Central Station, lower concourse (tel. 762-20-00). The police also have such an office at the police station at Tjärhovsgatan 21 (tel. 41-04-32). The Stockholm Transit Company (SL) keeps its recovered articles at the Rådmansgatan T-bana station (tel. 736-07-08), and Waxholmsbolagat has one at Nybrokajen 2 (tel. 14-09-60, ext. 142).

Luggage Storage/Lockers Facilities are available at the Central Station on Vasagatan, lower concourse (tel. 762-25-50). Lockers can also be rented at the ferry stations at Värtan and Tegelvikshamnen, at the Viking Line's terminal, and at the Central Station.

Photographic Needs Stockholm abounds with photo shops. One of the most centrally located is **Hasselblads Foto Video,** Sveavägen 71 (tel. 31-97-99).

Police Call **90-000** in an emergency.

Post Office The main post office is at Vasagatan 28-34 (tel. 781-20-00), open Monday through Friday from 8am to 8pm and on Saturday from 9am to 3pm. General delivery (Post Restante) pickups can be made here.

Radio/TV The country has two TV channels and three national radio stations, plus a local station for Stockholm, broadcasting on 103.3 MHz (FM). Radio Stockholm broadcasts the news direct from the BBC, and in summer broadcasts a special program for English-speaking tourists, "T-T-T-Tourist Time," from 6 to 7pm daily. Many hotels are equipped to receive English-language TV programs broadcast from England, and many of the more expensive hotels have 24-hour CNN news broadcasts in English.

Religious Services There are some 160 Lutheran churches in the Swedish capital. Protestant services are held at **St. Peter and St. Sigfrid Anglican Church,** Strandvägen 76 (tel. 663-82-48), and at the **United Christian Congregation,** Santa Clara Church, Kyrkogata 8 (tel. 723-30-29). A Roman Catholic cathedral, **Domkyrkan,** is at Folkungagatan 46 (tel. 40-00-82), and **Santa Eugenia Church** is at Kungsträdgårdsgatan 12 (tel. 10-00-70). Jewish worshipers can attend the **Great Synagogue** (Conservative), Wahrendorffsgatan 3A (tel. 23-51-50), or **Adas Jisroel** (Orthodox), St. Paulsgatan 13 (tel. 44-19-95).

Rest Rooms Public facilities are found in the Central Station, all subway stations, and department stores, as well as along some of the major streets, parks, and squares. In an emergency you can also use the toilets in most hotels and restaurants, although in theory you're supposed to be a client.

Shoe Repair In the basement of **Nordiska Kompaniet,** Hamngatan 18-20 (tel. 762-80-00), one of the leading department stores of Stockholm, there is a shoe-repair place which also repairs, if possible, broken luggage.

Taxis See "Getting Around," in this chapter.

Telephone/Telex/Fax The **central telephone office,** open Monday through Saturday from 8am to midnight, is at Skeppsbron 2 (tel. 10-09-39), in the Old Town behind the Royal Palace. The office at the Central Station (tel. 10-64-39) is open Monday through Friday from 8am to 8pm and on Saturday from 9am to 10pm. For worldwide operator information, dial 24-28-00. Instructions in English are posted in public phone boxes, which you find on street corners. Pay phones are operated by 1-krona (17¢) coins. You can send a telegram by phoning 00-21 anytime, or from offices bearing the sign TELE or TELEBUTIK, as well as from some post offices. To send a Telex or fax, go to **Telecenter,** Skeppsbron 2 (tel. 780-78-90), in Gamla Stan, open in summer, daily from 8am to midnight; in winter, daily from 8am to 9pm.

Transit Information For information on all services, including buses and subways (Tunnelbana), even suburban trains (*pendeltåg*), call 23-60-00. Or else visit the **SL Center,** on the lower level of Sergels Torg. It provides information about transportation and also sells a map of the city's system, as well as tickets and special discount passes. Open in summer Monday through Thursday from 9am to 6pm, on Friday from 9am to 5:30pm, on Saturday from 9am to 4pm, and on Sunday from 10am to 3pm; the rest of the year, open only Monday through Friday.

3. NETWORKS & RESOURCES

FOR STUDENTS Near Sweden House, at Sergels Torg in Stockholm, is the **Kulturhuset** (Culture House) (tel. 700-01-00), a favorite gathering place for young people. You can sometimes enjoy live performances by local talent and international entertainers, view exhibitions (of art, craft and design, etc.), read books and newspapers in several languages, listen to records, watch TV, or eat at the snack bar.

Sweden has four major university centers—Stockholm, Gothenburg, Uppsala, and Lund, near Malmö—and each of these maintains a special **Student Reception Service** for visiting foreign students. Inquire about student accommodations, restaurants, a schedule of current events, discos, or whatever you need to know.

The student travel service, **SFS Resebyrå**, Kungsgatan 4 (tel. 23-45-15), books student flights and has information about low-cost youth fares on trains. It is open Monday through Friday from 10am to 5:30pm.

You can also visit the **Stockholms Universitets Studentkår** (Student Center), Universitetet (tel. 16-20-60), if you are in Stockholm between September and May (it's closed from June to August for summer vacation). The center is in the Allhuset, and is a beehive of activity, with a travel agent for students and places to dine, including the university restaurant, Lantis, where you can eat for about 40 kroner ($7). It is open Monday through Thursday from 11am to 6pm and on Friday from 11am to 2pm. T-bana: Universitetet.

FOR GAY MEN & LESBIANS   Sweden is not as stridently liberal as Denmark, where gay marriages are accorded the same rights as heterosexual marriages, but it has enacted an antidiscrimination law and there are many gay and lesbian organizations operating in Stockholm that welcome visitors from abroad.

Foremost among these is the **RFSL,** the Swedish Union for Sexual Equality, Sveavägen 57 (tel. 736-02-12), open Monday through Friday from 9am to 5pm. Established in 1950, it is located on the upper floors of the biggest gay nightlife center in Stockholm (see "Evening Entertainment," in Chapter 25). Two meetings are held weekly—a Wednesday 3pm meeting for gay men over 60 and a twice-monthly meeting of "Golden Ladies" (yes, they use the English expression) for lesbians over 50. They also operate a **Gay Switchboard** (tel. 24-74-65), staffed mostly with volunteers; call daily from 8 to 11pm for information. The center also runs the Rosa Rummet Bookstore, on the same premises, a nonprofit bookstore devoted to gay literature and information; open Monday through Friday from 6 to 7pm and on Saturday and Sunday from 3 to 8pm.

The RFSL distributes information on women's gay life, but a splinter group is known as **Lesbisk Nu!** (Lesbians Now), Götgatan 83 (tel. 41-86-16), which also dispenses information about lesbian-related activities.

The city also has a **Stockholm Gay Radio,** broadcasting at 88 MHz (FM) on Tuesday and Sunday at 7:30pm. Call 736-02-16 for information. The broadcast is in Swedish, but at least you can enjoy the music.

FOR WOMEN   Go to **Kvinnohuset,** Snickarbacken 10 (tel. 10-08-00), which is the major meeting place for feminists in Stockholm. Everybody speaks English, and foreign women are welcome. The women's center also operates a rape-crisis center.

FOR SENIORS   Go to **Sweden House,** center of tourist information, Hamngatan 27, off Kungsträdgården (tel. 789-20-00), and ask about special discounts for senior citizens in Stockholm. These could take the form of reduced transportation costs or discount admission to museums and certain attractions.

4. ACCOMMODATIONS

Reservations are advised in summer just to be on the safe side. In most cases a service charge, ranging from 10% to 15%, is added to the bill, plus the inevitable 23.4% Moms (Value-Added Tax).

Most of the medium-priced hotels are on the island of Norrmalm, north of the

Old Town. The least expensive lodgings are near the Central Station. There are comparably priced inexpensive accommodations within 10 to 20 minutes of the city, easily reached by subway, streetcar, or bus. I have a few selections in the Old Town, but these choices are limited and more expensive.

BOOKING SERVICES **Hotellcentralen** (tel. 24-08-80), on the lower level of the Central Station, is the city's official housing bureau, and arranges accommodations in hotels, pensions (boardinghouses), hospices, and youth hostels—but not in private homes. There is a 20-krona ($3.50) service fee. It's open from May to the end of September, daily from 8am to 9pm; from October to the end of April, Monday through Friday from 8:30am to 5pm.

Several private agencies help find a room for a fee, including **Hotelltjanst AB** (Hotel Service), at Vasagatan 15-17 (tel. 10-44-57). The English-speaking owner, Mats Elofs, will locate and book a room for you in a private home or hotel, for which you will be charged from 150 kronor ($26.20) in a single and from 175 kronor ($30.55) in a double. Mr. Elofs never charges a booking fee. He is confident he can find you a room, but because he is only a one-man operation, he cannot attempt to answer your request for a reservation. Just show up on his doorstep and hope for the best.

A NOTE ON PRICES By the standards of many cities in the United States or Canada, hotels in Stockholm are very expensive indeed, even the so-called moderate ones. In the listings that follow, hotels, such as the deluxe Grand, are labeled "Very Expensive" if they charge from $350 to $475 a night in a double; "Expensive" means doubles between $300 and $375; "Moderate," $200 to $250; and "Inexpensive," $125 to $180. "Budget" is a special category in Stockholm's case, youth hostels or private apartments or boardinghouses.

Before these high prices make you cancel your trip, read on. Dozens of hotels in Stockholm offer reduced rates on weekends all year and daily from June 18 to August 19. For further information, ask travel agencies or the tourist center (see above).

IN THE CENTER

VERY EXPENSIVE

GRAND HOTEL, Södra Blaisieholmshamnen 8, S-103 27 Stockholm. Tel. 08/22-10-20. Fax 08/21-86-88. 320 rms (all with bath), 19 suites. MINIBAR TV TEL **Tram:** 10, 11. **Bus:** 46, 55, 62, 76.

$ Rates (including breakfast): June 29–July 19 and Fri–Sun year round 700 kroner ($122.20) single; 950 kroner ($165.85) double. Mon–Thurs the rest of the year, 1,390–2,075 kroner ($242.70–$362.30) single; 1,960–2,700 kroner ($34.20–$471.40) double. From 4,000 kroner ($698.40) suites. AE, DC, MC, V. **Parking:** Valet.

Opposite the Royal Palace, this hotel is grand in name and deed, the finest in Sweden. It has been the choice of everybody from Sarah Bernhardt to Nobel Prize winners, a bastion of elite hospitality. Built in 1874, it has been continuously renovated, but its old-world style has always been maintained. Bedrooms come in all shapes and sizes, but each is elegantly appointed with traditional styling. Some contain air conditioning. Pale-blue fabrics and light woods predominate. The bathrooms are decorated with Italian marble and tiles and have heated floors. The hotel's ballroom is an exact copy of the Hall of Mirrors of Louis XIV at Versailles.

Dining/Entertainment: The Grand Veranda specializes in traditional food served from a buffet, and the Franska Matsalen is the gourmet restaurant of the hotel. The Cadierbar is one of the most sophisticated rendezvous spots in Stockholm.

Services: Shoeshine service, American Airlines check-in desk, valet parking, limousine service, 24-hour room service, business service center, same-day laundry and dry cleaning, ticket-securing concierge, house doctor.

Facilities: Beauty salon, sauna, hairstylist, drugstore, newsstand, florist, gift shop.

ROYAL VIKING HOTEL, Vasagatan 1, S-101 23 Stockholm. Tel. 08/22-

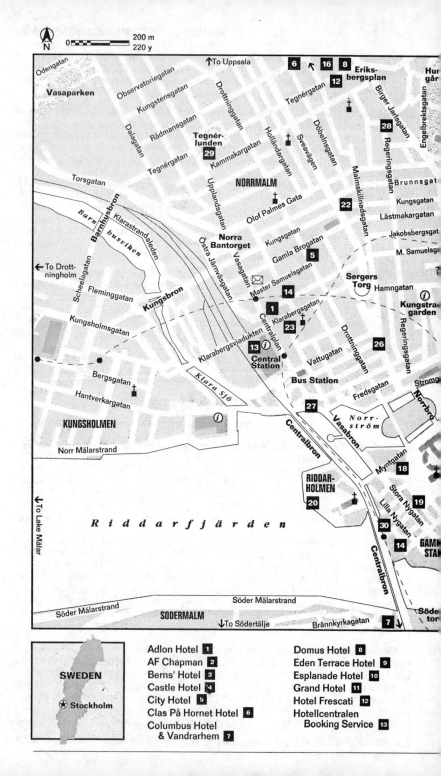

N

0 ⎯⎯⎯⎯⎯ 200 m
⎯⎯⎯⎯⎯ 220 y

↑To Uppsala

6 ↖ **16** **8** Eriksbergsplan

12 Hur
går

Tegnérgatan

28

Odengatan

Observatoriegatan

Kungstensgatan

Rådmansgatan

Drottninggatan

Tegnérgatan

Birger Jarlsgatan

Engelbrektsgatan

Vasaparken

Dalagatan

Tegnérlunden

29

Kammakargatan

Hollandergatan

Sveavägen

Döbelnsgatan

Regeringsgatan

Brunnsgat

Kungsgatan

Lästmakargatan

Jakobsbergsgat

Torsgatan

Tegnérgatan

NORRMALM

Olof Palmes Gata

Upplandsgatan

Malmskillnadsgatan

M. Samuelsga

Barn busviken

Klarastrandsleden

Norra Bantorget

Kungsgatan

Gamla Brogatan

5

22

Östra Järnvägsgatan

Sergers Torg

Hamngatan

←To Drottningholm

Fleminggatan

Kungsbron

Vasagatan

Master Samuelsgatan

14

1

Klarabergsgatan

23

Drottninggatan

(i) **Kungstra garden**

Regeringsgatan

Kungsholmsgatan

Klarabergsviadukten

13 (i)

Central Station

Vattugatan

26

Bergsgatan

Klara sjö

Bus Station

Fredsgatan

Strömo

Norrbro

Hantverkargatan

(i)

27

Norrström

Vasabron

KUNGSHOLMEN

Centralbron

Myntgatan

18

Norr Mälarstrand

RIDDARHOLMEN

Stora Nygatan

19

←To Lake Mälar

20

Lilla Nygatan

30

14

GAM STA

R i d d a r f j ä r d e n

Centralbron

Söder Mälarstrand

Söder Mälarstrand

SÖDERMALM

↓To Södertälje

Brännkyrkagatan

7 ↓

Söde
tor

SWEDEN

★ **Stockholm**

Adlon Hotel **1**
AF Chapman **2**
Berns' Hotel **3**
Castle Hotel **4**
City Hotel **5**
Clas På Hornet Hotel **6**
Columbus Hotel
 & Vandrarhem **7**

Domus Hotel **8**
Eden Terrace Hotel **9**
Esplanade Hotel **10**
Grand Hotel **11**
Hotel Frescati **12**
Hotellcentralen
 Booking Service **13**

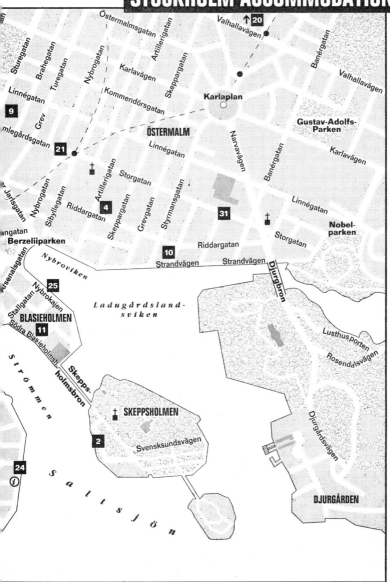

STOCKHOLM ACCOMMODATIONS

Subway – – –   Church ✝   Post Office ⊠   Information ⓘ

Hotelltjanst AB Booking Service	**14**
Jerum Hotel	**15**
Karelia Hotel	**16**
Kung Karl Hotel	**17**
Lady Hamilton Hotel	**18**
Lord Nelson Hotel	**19**

Mälardrottningen	**20**
Mornington Hotel	**21**
Residens Hotel	**22**
Royal Viking Hotel	**23**
Sara Hotel Reisen	**24**
SAS Strand Hotel	**25**
Sergel Plaza Hotel	**26**

Sheraton Stockholm & Towers	**27**
Stockholm Plaza Hotel	**28**
Tegnerlunden Hotel	**29**
Victory Hotel	**30**
Wellington Hotel	**31**

66-00. Fax 08/10-81-80. 336 rms (all with bath), 4 suites. A/C MINIBAR TV TEL **T-bana:** Central Station.

$ **Rates** (including breakfast): June 11–July 12 and Fri–Sat year round, 850 kroner ($148.40) single; 950 kronor ($165.85) double. Sun–Thurs the rest of the year, 1,150–1,950 kronor ($200.80–$340.45) single; 1,550–2,060 kronor ($270.65–$359.70) double. From 4,000 kroner ($698.40) suites. AE, DC, MC, V.

Near the Central Station, this airline-affiliated hotel stands next door to the Stockholm World Trade Center. Its Royal Atrium, the heart of the hotel, with its soaring ceiling, offers big buffets meals in light, airy surroundings. The bedrooms are superbly equipped and furnished in light pastels, with stylized modern furniture and such amenities as hairdryers and trouser presses. Some rooms are duplex suites with their own bar, stereo system, video, sauna with bathrobe and slippers, Jacuzzi, and terrace. The Royal Club is the executive "hotel within the hotel," where you are spoiled with your own check-in, safe deposits, and lots of extras.

Dining/Entertainment: The Royal Atrium offers breakfast and lunch, and the Piano Lounge serves draft beer and exotic drinks. The Délice is a bistro, offering fresh vegetable dishes and country fare. The Royal Room is the hotel's specialty restaurant, its food prepared, when possible, with Swedish-grown produce. It offers French flair and excellent wines. Take the glass elevator to the ninth floor for the hotel's skybar, with a panoramic view of the Old Town.

Services: Complimentary refreshments, SAS EuroClass check-ins, express laundry, office away from home, room service.

Facilities: Viking pool club, with saunas, Jacuzzi, and a temperature-controlled pool with underwater music.

EXPENSIVE

BERNS' HOTEL, Näckstromsgatan 8, S-111 47 Stockholm. Tel. 08/614-07-00. Fax 08/611-51-75. 63 rms (all with bath), 3 suites. A/C MINIBAR TV TEL **T-bana:** Östermalmstorg.

$ **Rates** (including breakfast): 1,375–1,875 kronor ($240.10–$327.40) single; 1,575–2,075 kronor ($275–$362.30) double; from 2,600 kronor ($453.95) suite. AE, DC, MC, V.

One of the gems of Stockholm, this newly restored hotel, part of a drinking-and-dining complex recommended separately, is near Nybroplan. The hotel has been beautifully furnished, with well-designed and amenity-filled bedrooms that include a video and CD player in every room, plus individually adjusted air conditioning. Bathrooms are all in Italian marble. There is a wide variety of rooms, the most spectacular of which is the tower suite, with the famous Berns clock, a 19th-century clock tower over Stockholm's most famous nightclub, as one of its windows. This suite has its own special sauna. Guests sit out in summer enjoying the view from the hotel's roof terrace. Breakfast is taken in the Red Room, once the haunt of dramatist August Strindberg.

SAS STRAND HOTEL, Nybrokajen 9, S-103 27 Stockholm. Tel. 08/22-29-00. Fax 08/20-44-36. 138 rms (all with bath), 18 suites. A/C MINIBAR TV TEL **T-bana:** Östermalmstorg.

$ **Rates** (including breakfast): July 1–Aug 15 and Fri–Sat year round, 750 kronor ($130.95) single; 1,050 kronor ($183.35) double. Mon–Thurs the rest of the year, 1,150–2,150 kronor ($200.80–$375.40) single; 1,750–2,150 kronor ($305.55–$375.40) double. From 3,000 kronor ($523.80) suite. AE, DC, MC, V.

In the center of Stockholm, near the Royal Palace and Gamla Stan, this hotel stands on the waterfront. It dates from 1912, but in the early 1980s was completely renovated and modernized. It still has tradition, but is filled with modern services and amenities. Bedrooms are furnished in light pastels and contain such appliances as hairdryers and trouser presses. Part of the hotel, the Royal Club, has more facilities, better rooms, and many extras such as your own electronic safe and your own ice bucket. Even your bathrobe and slippers are laid out for you.

Dining/Entertainment: Strand's Piazza is a glass-roofed wintergarden serving full meals, and the adjoining Strand's Bar is a popular meeting place. The specialty restaurant is Maritim, offering a buffet of fresh fish and shellfish. You can dance the night away in the hotel's disco.

Services: 24-hour room service, business service center, SAS airline check-in in lobby.

Facilities: Health club with swimming pool.

SERGEL PLAZA, Brunkebergstorg 9, S-103 27 Stockholm. Tel. 08/22-6600, or toll free 800/THE OMNI in the U.S. Fax 08/21-50-70. 406 rms (all with bath), 12 suites. A/C TV TEL **T-bana:** Central Station.

$ Rates (including breakfast): Fri–Sat, 780 kronor ($136.20) single; 1,040 kronor ($181.60) double. Sun–Thurs, 1,225–1,875 kroner ($213.90–$327.40) single; 1,710–2,025 kronor ($298.55–$353.55) double. From 2,200 kronor ($384.10) suite. AE, DC, MC, V.

Originally designed as living quarters for members of the Swedish parliament in Stockholm, this hotel, built in 1984 at the entrance to Drottninggatan, the main shopping street, has been improved to such an extent that today it is one of the city's leading hotels. The elegant decor includes 18th-century artwork and antiques. It is a bastion of comfort and good taste, as reflected by the beautifully decorated bedrooms, each furnished with modern but traditional styling in light pastels and "Nordic sky" colors. The hotel has a special executive floor.

Dining/Entertainment: The Anna Rella, the gourmet restaurant, offers both Swedish and international specialties. There is also a lobby and piano bar.

Services: Massage service, "office for a day," 24-hour room service, concierge.

Facilities: Hair- and beauty-care facilities, saunas, solariums, Jacuzzis.

SHERATON STOCKHOLM & TOWERS, Tegelbacken 6, S-101 23 Stockholm. Tel. 08/14-26-00. Fax 08/21-70-26. 445 rms (all with baths), 15 suites. A/C MINIBAR TV TEL **T-bana:** Central Station.

$ Rates (including breakfast): Jan–Aug 21 and Fri–Sat year round, 925 kronor ($161.50) single; 1,000 kronor ($174.60) double. Sun–Thurs Aug 22–Dec, 1,280–1,950 kronor ($223.50–$340.45) single; 1,480–2,150 kronor ($258.40–$375.40) double. From 3,250 kronor ($567.45) suite. AE, DC, MC, V.

Overlooking Gamla Stan, this hotel offers Stockholm's largest guest rooms, all of which have recently been renovated and are comfortably furnished and decorated in Scandinavian pastels. Seven rooms are equipped for the handicapped. The most luxurious accommodations are on the Towers floor.

Dining/Entertainment: The Sheraton Première Restaurant specializes in game, fish, meats, and fresh vegetables and fruits. Snacks or quick meals are served at Le Bistro. The hotel has a casino and the Lobby Lounge features live entertainment nightly. Die Ecke is a German Bierstube serving traditional Bavarian dishes.

Services: Laundry and valet service, secretarial assistance, same-day laundry and dry cleaning, 24-hour room service, wheelchairs upon request, physician on call.

Facilities: Sauna.

MODERATE

CASTLE HOTEL, Riddargatan 14, S-114 35 Stockholm. Tel. 08/24-19-00. Fax 08/21-20-22. 48 rms (all with bath). MINIBAR TV TEL **T-bana:** Östermalmstorg.

$ Rates (including breakfast): Early June to late Aug and Fri–Sun year round, 600 kronor ($104.75) single; 700 kronor ($122.20) double. Sun–Thurs the rest of the year, 1,150 kronor ($200.80) single; 1,300–1,500 kronor ($227–$261.90) double. AE, DC, MC, V.

A short walk east of the center in an expensive neighborhood, this house was originally built in 1920 as a private apartment house. In the late 1980s it was comfortably outfitted as a hotel. It has a gray marble floor in the lobby, and the bedrooms are decorated in Swedish colors of apple green and bitter blue, with gilded accents and art deco accessories to match the original construction of the building.

Several times a week they have jazz evenings in a room which serves as a simple lunch-only restaurant, serving meals daily from 11am to 2pm.

CLAS PÅ HORNET, Surbrunnsgatan 20, S-113 48 Stockholm. Tel. 08/16-51-30. Fax 08/612-53-15. 10 rms (all with bath), 1 suite. A/C MINIBAR TV TEL **Bus:** 46. **Tram:** 13.

$ Rates (including breakfast): Mon–Thurs, 1,165–1,550 kronor ($203.45–$270.65) single, 1,200–1,650 kronor ($209.50–$288.10) double; Fri–Sun, 850–1,200 kronor ($148.40–$209.50), 875–1,200 kronor ($152.80–$209.50) double. From 2,350 kronor ($410.30) suite. AE, DC, MC, V.

⭐ This 1731 aristocratic house with well-furnished and elegant rooms has an especially charming restaurant and bar, with wide floorboards, booths for intimate dining or drinking, lots of flickering candles, and waitresses wearing old-style dresses. "Clas on the Corner," its English name, has a distinct country-inn ambience. It doesn't have such amenities as Jacuzzis and panoramic bars, but it does offer intimacy and charm in the period style of Gustavus III.

EDEN TERRACE HOTEL, Sturegatan 10, S-114 36 Stockholm. Tel. 08/22-31-60. Fax 08/660-80-67. 70 rms (all with bath), 8 suites. MINIBAR TV TEL **T-bana:** Östermalmstorg.

$ Rates (including breakfast): June 23–Aug 7 and Fri–Sat year round, 720 kronor ($125.70) single; 920 kronor ($160.65) double. Sun–Thurs the rest of the year, 1,020–1,340 kronor ($178.10–$233.95) single; 1,490 kronor ($260.15) double. From 1,700 kronor ($296.80) suite. AE, DC, MC, V.

Located opposite the garden of the King's Library, in what looks like an office building, the Eden Terrace opened for the Stockholm Exhibition in 1930. It offers a large dining room and a rooftop terrace where guests enjoy drinks in the summer. The bedrooms are cozy and traditionally furnished, and come in many shapes and sizes. Also on the premises are a piano bar and a nightclub.

ESPLANADE HOTEL, Strandvägen 7A, S-114 56 Stockholm. Tel. 08/663-07-40. Fax 08/662-59-92. 33 rms (29 with bath). TV TEL **Bus:** 47.

$ Rates (including breakfast): 725 kronor ($126.60) single without bath, 1,225–1,325 kronor ($213.90–$231.35) single with bath; 1,425–1,850 kronor ($248.80–$323) double with bath. AE, DC, MC, V.

This informal hotel, next to the more expensive Diplomat, attracts diplomats from the nearby embassies and others who like its informal atmosphere. Originally constructed in 1910, it was transformed into a family-style hotel in 1954. Many of the rooms contain minibars, and each is comfortably furnished in an old-fashioned way. They're not super-stylish but are clean and respectable. Four of the rooms have a water view and the English lounge has a balcony with a view of Djurgården. Only breakfast is served.

KARELIA, Birger Jarlsgatan 35, S-111 83 Stockholm. Tel. 08/24-76-60. Fax 08/24-15-11. 103 rms (all with bath). TV TEL **T-bana:** Östermalmstorg.

$ Rates (including breakfast): Rooms: summer and Fri–Sun year round, 520 kronor ($90.80) single, 740 kronor ($129.20) double; Mon–Thurs the rest of the year, 1,020 kronor ($178.10) single, 1,300 kronor ($227) double. Cabins: summer and Fri–Sun year round, 375 kronor ($65.50) single, 525 kronor ($91.65) double; Mon–Thurs the rest of the year, 725 kronor ($126.60) single, 900 kronor ($157.15) double. AE, DC, MC, V.

Ⓢ The Karelia is an elegant old-world hostelry on a busy commercial street, with an impressive turn-of-the-century facade and copper-capped tower. You'll enter under a large Romanesque arch and climb a decorative double staircase. The bedrooms are clean and well designed. The basement-level "cabins," as they're called, are bargains and immensely popular. They are small and have no windows, but are comfortable, well ventilated, and well maintained. Many Swedish and Finnish visitors request them for their good value. The hotel has a small-stakes casino, a swimming pool, and three saunas, which have been used by everybody from the King of Sweden to the late prime minister, Olof Palme. There are two restaurants: one enlivened by Finnish dancing nearly every night and the other serving Russian cuisine (see "Stockholm Dining," in this chapter).

KUNG CARL, Birger Jarlsgatan 23, S-111 45 Stockholm. Tel. 08/611-31-10. Fax 08/24-79-83. 87 rms (all with bath). MINIBAR TV TEL **T-bana:** Östermalmstorg.

$ **Rates** (including breakfast): Midsummer and Fri–Sat year round, 700 kronor ($122.20) single; 760 kronor ($132.70) double. Sun–Thurs the rest of the year, 1,025 kronor ($178.95) single; 1,400 kronor ($244.45) double. AE, DC, MC, V.

The decor in this turn-of-the-century hostelry in the commercial center blends old-fashioned charm with examples of modern design. Some of the hallways, and many of the sitting areas, are richly detailed, with an occasional antique. The conservatively comfortable bedrooms are usually well furnished. There is a nearby parking area. The hotel was originally built in the 19th century as a shelter for women arriving from the countryside, and was run by a church. It was transformed into a conventional hotel in the 1870s, making it one of the longest continuously operated hotels in Stockholm.

MORNINGTON HOTEL, Nybrogatan 53, S-102 44 Stockholm. Tel. 08/663-12-40. Fax 08/662-21-79. 140 rms (all with bath). A/C TV TEL **T-bana:** Östermalmstorg.

$ **Rates** (including breakfast): June 21–Aug 4 and Fri–Sat year round, 700 kronor ($122.20) single; 850 kronor ($148.40) double. Sun–Thurs the rest of the year, 1,200 kronor ($209.50) single; 1,500 kronor ($261.90) double. AE, DC, MC, V.

Proud of its image as an English-inspired hotel, this efficiently modern establishment has a concrete exterior brightened with rows of flowerboxes. It was built in 1956 and renovated in 1959. About half the rooms have been completely modernized and upgraded into a stylish decor using exposed wood and blue, yellow, and brown color schemes. The lobby contains a small rock garden and modern versions of Chesterfield armchairs. The hotel offers laundry service, and also has no-smoking rooms and rooms for the disabled. It has a sauna and Turkish bath which are free to guests. Its Restaurant Eleonora serves both international and Swedish cuisine.

STOCKHOLM PLAZA, Birger Jarlsgatan 29, S-103 95 Stockholm. Tel. 08/14-51-20. Fax 08/10-34-92. 147 rms (all with bath), 8 suites. TV TEL **T-bana:** Hörtorget.

$ **Rates** (including breakfast): June 22–Aug 5 and Fri–Sat year round, 600 kronor ($104.75) single; 800 kronor ($139.70) double. Sun–Thurs the rest of the year, 1,195 kronor ($208.65) single; 1,300 kronor ($227) double. From 1,800 kronor ($314.30) suite. AE, DC, MC, V.

Looking almost like New York's Flatiron Building, this first-class hotel is a well-run and inviting choice in the city center. Bedrooms have light, fresh interiors, with many conveniences. Guests enjoy the food in the hotel's gourmet restaurant, the Cecil, which serves both French and Swedish specialties. In the cellar, the hotel also operates one of the city's most popular nightspots the Alexandra Charles, complete with caviar and champagne bar. King Carl Gustaf himself has been an honored guest here.

WELLINGTON, Storgatan 6, S-114 51 Stockholm. Tel. 08/667-09-10. Fax 08/667-12-54. 51 rms (all with bath). TV TEL **T-bana:** Östermalmstorg.

$ **Rates** (including breakfast): June 24–Aug 7 and winter weekends, 650 kronor ($113.50) single; 750 kronor ($130.95) double. Winter weekdays, 985 kronor ($172) single; 1,500 kronor ($261.90) double. AE, DC, MV, V.

This modern pleasant hotel filled with English decorative touches was built in the late 1950s in a quiet but convenient neighborhood near the Ármemuseum. The public rooms are filled with engravings of English hunting scenes and leather-covered Chesterfield chairs. Some of the small but stylish bedrooms overlook a flower-filled courtyard.

INEXPENSIVE

ADLON HOTEL, Vasagatan 42, S-111 20 Stockholm. Tel. 08/24-54-00. Fax 08/20-86-10. 72 rms (all with bath). TV TEL
$ Rates (including breakfast): Summer and Fri–Sat year round, 375–450 kronor ($65.50–$78.55) single; 500–700 kronor ($87.30–$122.20) double. Sun–Thurs the rest of the year, 550–750 kronor ($96.05–$130.95) single; 680–1,020 kronor ($118.75–$178.10) double. AE, DC, MC, V.

This 1890s building, only about 385 yards from the main train station and airport bus terminal, has gone through a total renovation on two of its floors. T-bana and bus stops are just outside. Bedrooms are equipped with radios, and the newly renovated units have hairdryers and controlled ventilation that eliminates tobacco smoke, among other amenities. There is 24-hour room service. A garage is one block away.

HOTEL CITY, Slöjdgatan at Hötorget 7, S-111 81 Stockholm. Tel. 08/22-22-40. Fax 08/20-82-24. 300 rms (all with bath). TV TEL **T-bana:** Hötorget.
$ Rates (including breakfast): Mid-June to Aug 7 and winter weekends, 680 kronor ($118.75) single; 800 kronor ($139.70) double. Winter weekdays, 930 kronor ($162.40) single; 1,050 kronor ($183.35) double. AE, DC, MC, V.

The City is run by the Salvation Army, which works hard to make this among the best hotels in its price bracket in Stockholm. It consists of two sections, one built as late as the 1980s. In a desirable location between two of Stockholm's biggest department stores, PUB and Åhléns, the hotel has small but comfortable bedrooms that have been elegantly redone using alluring combinations of mirror, hardwood trim, carpeting, and tilework. No alcohol is served in the restaurant off the lobby. Luxuriate in the hotel's sauna.

HOTEL RESIDENS, Kungsgatan 50, S-111 35 Stockholm. Tel. 08/23-35-40. 35 rms (22 with bath). TV TEL **T-bana:** Hötorget.
$ Rates (including breakfast): Fri–Sun, 300 kronor ($52.40) single without bath, 530 kronor ($92.55) single with shower; 530 kronor ($92.55) double without bath, 630 kronor ($110) double with bath. Mon–Thurs, 400 kronor ($69.85) single without bath, 680–740 kronor ($118.75–$129.20) single with bath; 630 kronor ($110) double without bath, 830–880 kronor ($144.90–$153.65) double with bath. AE, DC, MC, V.

This hotel is in the center of Stockholm at Hötorget, a few blocks from the Central Station and the airport bus terminal. An elevator takes you to the reception, breakfast, and TV rooms on the fifth floor. All rooms were renovated in 1985, and all are equipped with radios and video channels. Nine rooms have a toilet and sink but no shower, but all have hot and cold running water. There's a garage nearby.

HOTEL TEGNÉRLUNDEN, Tegnérlunden 6, S-113 59 Stockholm. Tel. 08/34-97-80. Fax 08/32-78-18. 104 rms (84 with bath). TV TEL **Bus:** 47 or 53 from the Central Station.
$ Rates (including breakfast): July and Fri–Sat year round, 545 kronor ($95.15) single; 600 kronor ($104.75) double. Sun–Thurs (except in July), 900 kronor ($157.15) single; 1,000 kronor ($174.60) double. AE, DC, MC, V.

In a 19th-century building at the edge of a favorite city park, this hotel has a few public rooms and a lobby, but no restaurant or bar. The hotel's best feature is its tasteful rooms, each blissfully quiet, especially those opening onto the rear. Twenty rooms are particularly comfortable for families, because they consist of two adjoining bedrooms sharing a bathroom. The rooms with shared bath cost 50 kronor ($8.75) less than the rates given above (no discount is granted on weekends). There's a sun terrace on one of the upper floors, a communal TV room, a sauna, and a nearby garage.

IN GAMLA STAN [OLD TOWN]

VERY EXPENSIVE

SARA HOTEL REISEN, Skeppsbron 12-14, S-111 30 Stockholm. Tel. 08/22-32-60, or toll free 800/223-5672 in the U.S. Fax 08/20-15-59. 114 rms (all with bath), 13 suites. MINIBAR TV TEL **Bus:** 46, 59.

$ Rates (including breakfast): June 15–Aug 9 and Fri–Sat year round, 900 kronor ($157.15) single; 980 kronor ($171.10) double. Sun–Thurs Aug 10–June 14, 1,350–2,090 kronor ($235.70–$364.90) single; 1,700–2,290 kronor ($296.80–$399.85) double. From 2,800 kronor ($488.90) suite. AE, DC, MC, V.

In the Old Town of Stockholm, facing the water, this hotel lies just three alleys from the Royal Palace. Dating from the 17th century, the three-building structure attractively combines the old and the new. A former coffee house that stood here was mentioned in the writings of national poet Carl Michael Bellman. Rooms are comfortably furnished in a stylish modern way, but inspired by traditional designs. Light florals and pastel colors are used.

Dining/Entertainment: The hotel's specialty restaurant, the Quarter Deck, serves a refined international and Scandinavian cuisine, and the Clipper Club specializes in grills. The Reisen also has the Library Bar and the Clipper Club Pianobar, with live entertainers Monday through Saturday.

Services: Laundry service, room service (7am to 11pm), guide services in summer, concierge.

Facilities: Indoor pool, sauna, Jacuzzis in some suites.

VICTORY HOTEL, Lilla Nygatan 5, S-111 28 Stockholm. Tel. 08/14-30-90. Fax 08/20-21-77. 44 rms (all with bath), 4 suites. A/C MINIBAR TV TEL **Bus:** 48, t3. **T-bana:** Gamla Stan.

$ Rates (including breakfast): Summer and Fri–Sat year round, 800 kronor ($139.70) single; 1,300 kronor ($227) double. Sun–Thurs the rest of the year, 1,700–2,000 kronor ($296.80–$349.20) single; 2,200 kronor ($384.10) double. From 3,200 kronor ($558.70) suite. AE, DC, MC, V.

 A small but stylish hotel, the Victory opened in 1980 on the foundations of a 1382 fortified tower. In the 1700s the owners of the house buried under the basement floor a massive treasure of silver, which is housed today in the Stockholm Museum.

(F) **FROMMER'S COOL FOR KIDS**
HOTELS

Sheraton Stockholm (see p. 425) This well-run chain has always pampered children. Spacious rooms are comfortably shared with parents.

Hotel Tegnérlunden (see p. 428) Twenty big, airy rooms are ideal for families on a budget.

Hotel Jerum (see p. 432) A student dorm in winter, but a family-oriented, good-value hotel in summer. Many triple rooms.

There's a shiny brass elevator, but if you take the stairs you'll see one of Sweden's biggest collections of 18th-century nautical needlepoints, many done by the sailors themselves during long sea voyages. The warm and inviting rooms, each named after a prominent sea captain, have a pleasing combination of exposed wood, carpeting, and antiques and 19th-century memorabilia.

Dining/Entertainment: The Restaurant Leijontornet specializes in fish, fowl, and game (see "Stockholm Dining," in this chapter). A bistro, Loherummet, named after the 18th-century family who lived in the building, serves Swedish home-cooking in a cozy, informal atmosphere.

Services: Room service, same-day laundry and dry cleaning, a complete travel and concierge desk.

Facilities: Safe-deposit boxes, heated bathroom floors and towel racks, saunas.

EXPENSIVE

LADY HAMILTON HOTEL, Storkyrkobrinken 5, S-111 28 Stockholm. Tel. 08/23-46-80. Fax 08/11-11-48. 34 rms (all with bath). MINIBAR TV TEL **T-bana:** Gamla Stan.

$ Rates (including breakfast): June 21–Aug 5 and Fri–Sat year round, 700 kronor ($122.20) single; 980 kronor ($171.10) double. Sun–Thurs Aug 6–June 20, 1,480 kronor ($258.40) single; 1,825 kronor ($318.65) double. AE, DC, MC, V.

This hotel, consisting of a trio of interconnected buildings, stands on a quiet street in the Old Town, surrounded by antiques shops and restaurants—a very desirable location indeed. Dozens of antiques are scattered among the well-furnished bedrooms. You'll get a sense of the 1470 origins of this hotel when you use the luxurious sauna, which contains the stone-rimmed well that used to supply the house's water. Extra touches include 18th-century paintings, an ivory ship model probably made by French prisoners in the 1700s, and several carved figureheads from old sailing vessels. The ornate staircase wraps around a large model of a clipper ship suspended from the ceiling. The Friday and Saturday special rates apply only if there isn't a convention in town and only if you agree to stay both nights.

MÄLARDROTTNINGEN, Riddarholmen, S-111 28 Stockholm. Tel. 08/24-36-00. Fax 08/24-36-76. 59 rms (all with bath). A/C TV TEL **T-bana:** Gamla Stan.

$ Rates (including breakfast): June 15–Aug 1 and Fri–Sat year round, 600 kronor ($104.75) single; 800 kronor ($139.70) double. Sun–Thurs Aug 2–June 14, 800–1,900 kronor ($139.70–$331.75) single; 1,250–1,950 kronor ($218.25–$340.45) double. AE, DC, MC, V.

This yacht is now permanently moored at a satellite island of the Old Town. Built in 1924 by millionaire C. K. G. Billings as the world's largest power yacht, it was subsequently owned by Woolworth heiress Barbara Hutton. In its heyday, its passengers' names and relationships would keep a gossip columnist busy for years.

The yacht's two dining rooms and seven suites have been stripped and divided into porthole-size cabins that rent as hotel rooms. The rooms are ranked as they were originally: Lowest in rank is seamen's cabins (suitable for only one occupant), followed by purser's cabins, first officer's cabin, captain's cabin, and owner's cabin. Only the owner's cabin has a double bed; the rest of the double units have twin beds. Space is definitely limited. There's a bar and a restaurant on the upper decks (see "Stockholm Dining," in this chapter). Each room has access to the ship's sauna, among other amenities.

MODERATE

LORD NELSON HOTEL, Västerlänggatan 22, S-111 29 Stockholm. Tel. 08/23-23-90. Fax 08/10-10-89. 31 rms (all with bath). TV TEL **T-bana:** Gamla Stan.

$ Rates (including breakfast): June 21–Aug 5 and Fri–Sat year round, 650 kronor ($113.50) single; 845 kronor ($147.55) double. Sun–Thurs Aug 6–June 20, 1,000–1,150 kronor ($174.60–$200.80) single; 1,330–1,485 kronor ($232.20–$259.30) double. AE, DC, MC, V.

In this gracefully designed glass and columned building, each floor is brightened by a full-length bay window filled with nautical memorabilia. Ships' helms, captains' chairs, military prints, navigational instruments, and a seaworthy reception desk crafted from teak and brass add to the decor's charm. The building dates from the late 16th century and was occupied by painter Ignatius Meuer from 1572 to 1589. Each comfortably efficient, although small, room is named after a type of ship and contains a private shower, not a tub. A sauna costs 70 kronor ($12.20).

NORTH OF THE CENTER

INEXPENSIVE

DOMUS HOTEL, Körsbarsvägen 1, S-114 89 Stockholm. Tel. 08/16-01-95. Fax 08/16-62-24. 82 rms (all with bath). T.V TEL **T-bana:** Tekniska Hogskolan. **Tram:** 23, 24, 25.

$ Rates (including breakfast): Summer and weekends year round, 575 kronor ($100.40) single; 675 kronor ($117.85) double. Winter weekdays, 800–915 kronor ($139.70–$159.75) single, 900–1,040 kronor ($157.15–$181.60) double. AE, DC, MC, V.

Just off a tree-lined boulevard, on a hillside with a good view, the Domus Hotel is within walking distance of the city air terminal and an open-air swimming pool. The hotel has a restaurant, Babylon, serving Swedish and international food, and there's an outdoor terrace. The hotel is just 5 minutes by subway from the Central Station. Its rooms are comfortable and well furnished to a good middle-class standard; 17 contain minibars. Services include baby-sitting, room service, and laundry service.

BUDGET

AF *CHAPMAN*, Vestra Brobänken, Skeppsholmen, S-111 49 Stockholm. Tel. 08/10-37-15. 40 cabins, 142 beds (none with bath). **Bus:** 65.

$ Rates: 84 kronor ($14.65) per person for members, 113 kronor ($19.75) for nonmembers. Bed linen costs 25 kronor ($4.35) extra; breakfast, 37 kronor ($6.45). Heating (mid-Sept to mid-May) costs 10 kronor ($1.75). No credit cards. **Closed:** Dec 16–Apr 1.

Moored off Skeppsholmen, near the Museum of Modern Art, this authentic three-masted schooner has been converted into a youth hostel. Its staterooms have two, four, six, or eight beds. One section is reserved for men, another for women. Each section has showers and washrooms, but there are no single cabins or family rooms. Personal lockers are available. The gangplank goes up at 1am, with no exceptions, and a 5-day stay is maximum. Rooms are closed from 10am to 4pm. No cigarette smoking or alcohol is allowed. A summer café operates on the ship's deck. Breakfast, at an extra charge, is available in the self-service coffee bar and dining room. International Youth Hostel association cards can be obtained at the af *Chapman*.

COLUMBUS HOTELL & VANDRARHEM, Tjärhovsgatan 11, S-116 21 Stockholm. Tel. 08/44-17-17. Fax 08/70-20-764. 40 rms (none with bath). **T-bana:** Medborgårplatsen.

$ Rates: Hostel, 275 kronor ($48) single; 350 kronor ($61.10) double; 105 kronor ($18.35) per person triple. Hotel, 420 kronor ($73.35) single; 530 kronor ($92.55) double. Breakfast costs 35 kronor ($6.10) extra. No credit cards.

This privately run hotel and hostel, originally built to house brewery workers, offers one of the lowest rates in central Stockholm for a bed. It's in a 1780 house in one of Stockholm's more interesting areas, Greta Garbo's childhood stomping ground. The staff speaks English. Breakfast is served for a supplemental charge, but you can use the kitchen, showers, and TV room for free. You can stay in the plain and simple hostel, which is functionally furnished and clean, or in one of the hotel rooms where you have more privacy and room, plus more comfortable furnishings. There is a café where you can get a cup of coffee in the evening. After you get off the subway, walk east about 325 yards. Open 24 hours a day year round. For a panoramic view, it's just a few minutes' climb up to the Mosebacke, so vividly described in Strindberg's novel *The Red Room.*

HOSTEL FRESCATI, Proffessorslingan 13-15, S-114 89 Stockholm. Tel. 08/15-94-34. 121 rms (all with bath). **T-bana:** Universitetet.
$ Rates: 225 kronor ($39.30) single; 280 kronor ($48.90) double. Breakfast costs 35 kronor ($6.10) extra. AE, MC, V. **Closed:** Sept–May.
Ten minutes from the city center by subway, in the northern part of Djurgården, this student-run hostel is open to all ages and both sexes. In fair weather you can sit out on the terrace. All accommodations contain private toilets and showers. There is a restaurant nearby serving primarily pizzas and spaghetti.

HOTEL JERUM, Studentbacken 21, S-114 89 Stockholm. Tel. 08/663-53-80. Fax 08/16-62-24. 120 rms (all with bath). **T-bana:** Gårdet. **Bus:** 62.
$ Rates (including breakfast): 325–400 kronor ($56.75–$69.85) single; 465–580 kronor ($81.20–$101.25) double. AE, DC, MC, V. **Closed:** Sept–May.
A good tourist hotel located in virtually its own park in northeastern Stockholm, the student-run Hotel Jerum is easily accessible from the city center. The hotel is part of three buildings joined by courtyards and glassed-in passageways. The streamlined Swedish-modern bedrooms have desks and armchairs. A complete breakfast is served in the cafeteria, including well-brewed coffee. The café also serves dinner at night.

5. DINING

Food is expensive in Stockholm, but those on a budget can stick to self-service cafeterias. At all restaurants other than cafeterias, a 12% to 15% service charge is added to the bill to cover tipping. Try ordering a *dagens ratt* (daily special).

One tip to save you a little inconvenience: Don't rush into a bar in Stockholm for your pick-me-up martini. "Bars" in Stockholm are self-service cafeterias, and the strongest drink that many of them offer is apple cider.

The category "Very Expensive" indicates restaurants where dinners generally cost $65 or more; "Expensive," around $45 to $50; "Moderate," around $25 to $35; and "Inexpensive," anything under that. Wine and beer can be lethal to your final bill, so proceed carefully.

IN THE CENTER
VERY EXPENSIVE

GOURMET, Tegnérgatan 10. Tel. 31-43-98.
   Cuisine: CONTINENTAL. **Reservations:** Required. **T-bana:** Rådmansgatan.
$ Prices: Appetizers 75–150 kronor ($13.10–$26.20); main dishes 185–285 kronor ($32.30–$49.75); gastronomic menu (four or five courses) 500 kronor ($87.30). AE, DC, MC, V.
   Open: Mon–Fri 11:30am–10:30pm, Sat 5–10:30pm. **Closed:** July.
This restaurant specializes in what it defines as modern Swedish cuisine, although with strong continental influences. The food is imaginative, and it's served in the cellar of a turn-of-the-century stone house. Two dining rooms are interconnected—one covered

with mirrors and mahogany paneling, the other painted in pale pastels. One of its classic dishes, served regardless of season, is crayfish flambéed in a mixture of Pernod and cognac and offered with a shellfish sauce. A lightly fried "tartare" of salmon is accompanied by an orange-and-green-peppercorn sauce, and fried breast of wild duck is prepared with sauce based on Italian balsamic vinegar. For dessert, the specialty is a Grand Marnier parfait with a strawberry salad.

MICHEL, Karlavägen 7. Tel. 662-22-62.

Cuisine: FRENCH. **Reservations:** Required. **T-bana:** Central Station.

$ Prices: Appetizers 165–265 kronor ($28.80–$46.25); main dishes 275–310 kronor ($48–$54.10). AE, DC, MC, V.

Open: Lunch Mon–Fri 11am–2pm; dinner Mon–Sat 6–10:30pm. **Closed:** July.

This upmarket restaurant is set in a turn-of-the-century house and is decorated like the private living room of the Swedish *grande bourgeoisie*. Pink velvet curtains, white tablecloths, and fresh flowers make it even more inviting. The food is among the most elegantly prepared and served in all of Sweden. Try slightly grilled duck liver with fresh beetroot and a caramelized port wine sauce, or marinated salmon in puff pastry with crème fraîche flavored with Swedish caviar and red onions. The main specialty is a *délices de la mer*, a mixture of sole, salmon, turbot, and flounder served with a chablis sauce mixed with trout roe. The dessert extravaganza is a white-chocolate mousse built up into a miniature pagoda set on a "lake" of raspberry sauce.

OPERAKÄLLAREN, Operahuset. Tel. 24-27-00.

Cuisine: FRENCH/SWEDISH. **Reservations:** Essential. **T-bana:** Kungsträdgården.

$ Prices: Smörgåsbord 190 kronor ($33.15); fixed-price menu 470 kronor ($82.05) for three courses, 610 kronor ($106.50) for the seven-course menu gastronomique; appetizers 100–230 kronor ($17.45–$40.15); main dishes 255–320 kronor ($44.50–$55.85); AE, DC, MC, V.

Open: Lunch Mon–Fri 11:30–2pm; dinner Mon–Fri 5–11:30pm; Sat 11:30am–11:30pm, Sun 5–11:30pm. AE, DC, MC, V.

Opposite the Royal Palace, this is the most famous and unashamedly luxurious restaurant in all of Sweden. Its elegant classic decor and style are reminiscent of a royal court banquet at the turn of the century. Its Paris equivalent would be Le Grand Véfour. Dress formally to enjoy its impeccable service and house specialties. Many come here for the elaborate smörgåsbord; others prefer the classic Swedish dishes or the modern French ones. A house specialty is the platter of northern delicacies, which includes everything from smoked eel to smoked reindeer along with Swedish red caviar. Salmon and game, including grouse from the northern forests, are both prepared in various ways.

PAUL AND NORBERT, Strandvägen 9. Tel. 663-81-83.

Cuisine: CONTINENTAL. **Reservations:** Required. **T-bana:** Östermalmstorg.

$ Prices: Appetizers 100–250 kronor ($17.45–$43.65); main dishes 180–340 kronor ($31.45–$59.35); eight-course *grand menu de frivolité* 935 kronor ($163.25). AE, DC, MC, V.

Open: Lunch Mon–Fri noon–3pm; dinner Mon–Fri 5:30–10:30pm. **Closed:** Most of July.

Right next to the Hotel Diplomat, this is the finest restaurant in Stockholm. In a patrician residence dating from 1873, and seating only 30, it has a vaguely art deco decor, a winter-inspired pastel color scheme, beamed ceiling, and dark paneling. German-born owners Paul Beck and Norbert Lang both worked in many of the top restaurants of Europe before opening this place. For appetizers, they prepare tantalizing tartares, including roe deer and salmon. It sounds banal, but their gooseliver terrine is the finest in town. Their fish platter, worthy of three stars, combines grilled filets of turbot, salmon, sole, and saltwater crayfish, served on a "mirror" of three different sauces (champagne, lobster, and truffle), although you might prefer their breast of pheasant and partridge.

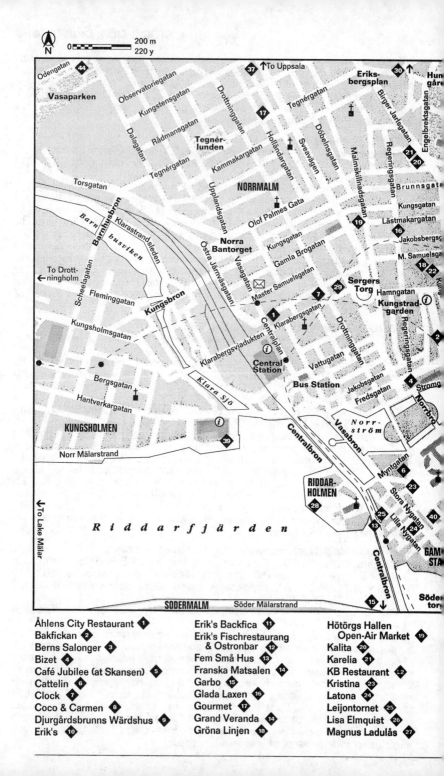

Åhlens City Restaurant ❶	Erik's Backfica ⓫	Hötorgs Hallen
Bakfickan ❷	Erik's Fischrestaurang	Open-Air Market ⑲
Berns Salonger ❸	& Ostronbar ⑫	Kalita ⑳
Bizet ❹	Fem Små Hus ⑬	Karelia ㉑
Café Jubilee (at Skansen) ❺	Franska Matsalen ⑭	KB Restaurant ㉒
Cattelin ❻	Garbo ⑮	Kristina ㉓
Clock ❼	Glada Laxen ⑯	Latona ㉔
Coco & Carmen ❽	Gourmet ⑰	Leijontornet ㉕
Djurgårdsbrunns Wärdshus ❾	Grand Veranda ⑭	Lisa Elmquist ㉖
Erik's ❿	Gröna Linjen ⑱	Magnus Ladulås ㉗

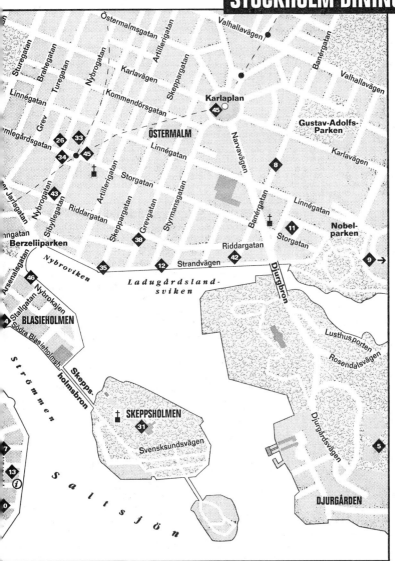

STOCKHOLM DINING

Subway – – – Church ♱ Post Office ⊠ Information ⊙

Mälardrottningen **28**
McDonald's **29**
Michel **30**
Moderna Museet
  Cafeteria **31**
Operakällaren **32**
Örtagarten **33**
Östermalms Hallen
  Open-Air Market **34**
Paul & Norbert **35**

Prinsens **36**
Räkan **37**
Smörgåsbord **38**
Solliden Cafeteria **5**
  (at Skansen)
Solliden Restaurant **5**
  (at Skansen)
Stadhuskällaren **39**
Stortorgskällaren **40**
Sturehof **41**

Tea House
  (Diplomat Hotel) **42**
Teatergrillen **43**
Tennstopet **44**
Tysta Mari **45**
Wedholm's Fisk **46**

EXPENSIVE

ERIK'S FISHRESTAURANG & OSTRONBAR, Kajplats 17, Strandvägen. Tel. 660-60-60.

Cuisine: SEAFOOD. **Reservations:** Required. **T-bana:** Östermalmstorg.

$ **Prices:** Appetizers 130–300 kronor ($22.70–$52.40); main dishes 165–300 kronor ($28.80–$52.40); four-course dinner 535 kronor ($93.40); two-course business lunch 155 kronor ($27.05). AE, DC, MC, V.

Open: Lunch Mon–Sat 11:30am–2:30pm; dinner Mon–Sat 6–11pm.

This is one of the city's most elegant restaurants, installed in a blue-and-white barge originally intended to haul sand from dredging channels to landfills. In summer, meals are served on the open deck, but in winter the dining room moves below deck. The chef prepares three different preparations of shellfish, or a savarin of lobster with other shellfish. The chef also offers a filet of sole daily, serving it with various sauces, perhaps champagne and crayfish. A whole sautéed turbot might be offered with a sweet lime sauce and cucumbers. A dessert specialty is the warm rose-hip soup with a floating "island" of homemade vanilla ice cream.

KALITA, in the Hotell Karelia, Birger Jarlsgatan 35. Tel. 24-76-60.

Cuisine: RUSSIAN. **Reservations:** Not required. **T-bana:** Östermalmstorg.

$ **Prices:** Appetizers 58–220 kronor ($10.15–$38.40); main dishes 105–308 kronor ($18.35–$53.75). AE, DC, MC, V.

Open: Dinner only, Mon–Sat 6pm–midnight.

Long considered the leading dining venue in Stockholm for Russian delicacies, and one of the few Russian restaurants in Sweden, this restaurant is on the second floor of this previously recommended good-value hotel (see "Stockholm Accommodations," in this chapter). Naturally, the most expensive item among the appetizers is Russian caviar. Main dishes are likely to include some rare delicacies, including brown bear. It doesn't come from Russia, but from Canada. Of course, others may prefer to begin with a bowl of borscht, then follow with blinis with roe, fresh grilled salmon, or pike-perch braised with a tomato and sour-cream sauce.

RÄKAN, Sveavägen 90. Tel. 32-63-50.

Cuisine: SEAFOOD. **Reservations:** Recommended. **T-bana:** Rådmansgatan.

$ **Prices:** Fixed-price menus 195–320 kronor ($34.05–$55.85); appetizers 62–101 kronor ($10.85–$17.65); main dishes 138–225 kronor ($24.10–$39.30). AE, DC, MC, V.

Open: Mon–Fri 11:30am–2pm, 6pm–midnight; Sun 5–11pm.

This restaurant has an artificial lagoon, and if you're seated next to it, you'll have platters of seafood sent to you on a miniature battery-powered boat. The rest of restaurant's decor is dark and rustic, with roughly textured beams and nautical accents.

The menu features shellfish from the western coast of Sweden. Three kinds of combination menus are offered, all starting with shrimp, then a hot fish plate, and ending with homemade desserts. A la carte, you might order fish ragoût served with rice, grilled salmon with dill-stewed potatoes, or grilled turbot with red wine and butter served with potatoes. Appetizers include sea crayfish gratin with herbs and garlic, and Swedish caviar with onion and sour cream.

WEDHOLMS FISK, Nybrokajen 17. Tel. 10-48-74.

Cuisine: SWEDISH/FRENCH. **Reservations:** Required. **T-bana:** Östermalmstorg.

$ **Prices:** Appetizers 60–165 kronor ($10.50–$28.80); main dishes 110–330 kronor ($19.20–$57.60). AE, DC, MC, V.

Open: Mon–Fri 11:30am–11pm, Sat 2–11pm. **Closed:** July 7–Aug 6.

This is one of the classic—and one of the best—restaurants of Stockholm. Housed in an old Swedish building whose decor has been stripped down to its rustic simplicity, it has no curtains at the windows and no carpets, but displays a collection of modern paintings by Swedish artists that is riveting. You might begin with marinated herring with garlic and bleak roe, or tartare of salmon with salmon roe. The chef has reason to be proud of such dishes as oysters with fresh spinach; sweet pickled herring with red onion, dill, and melted butter; or grilled filet of sole with a Dijon-flavored hollandaise. For dessert, try the homemade vanilla ice cream with cloudberries.

MODERATE

BERNS SALONGER, Näckströmsgatan 8. Tel. 22-06-00.

Cuisine: SWEDISH. **Reservations:** Recommended. **T-bana:** Östermalmstorg.

$ Prices: Appetizers 48–65 kronor ($8.40–$11.35); main dishes 93–149 kronor ($16.25–$26). AE, DC, MC, V.

Open: Daily 11am–midnight.

Built in 1860, this "pleasure palace" was one of the most famous restaurants and nighttime venues of Stockholm. It was dramatically renovated in 1989 and is now one of the most atmospheric choices for dining in the capital, with a main hall adorned with galleries, mirrors, and wooden paneling, and lit by a trio of monumental chandeliers. The Nya Röda Rummet (New Red Room) upstairs is ideal for a drink. The real Red Room was frequented by August Strindberg, who described it in his novel of the same name. It's still there, plush furniture and all, and available for private parties. Each day a different Swedish specialty is featured, including fried filet of suckling pig with fresh asparagus. You might also try calves' liver with garlic and bacon, or grilled tournedos. A disco, open from midnight to 3am, is on the premises, charging a 50-krona ($8.75) entrance fee. Frequent shows are staged in an adjoining theater.

ERIKS BAKFICA, Fredrikhovsgatan 4. Tel. 660-15-99.

Cuisine: SWEDISH. **Reservations:** Recommended. **Bus:** 47.

$ Prices: Dinner platters 75–85 kronor ($13.10–$14.85); luncheon platters 75–85 kronor ($13.10–$14.85); appetizers 55–120 kronor ($9.60–$20.95); main dishes 89–190 kronor ($15.55–$33.15). AE, DC, MC, V.

Open: Mon–Fri 11:30am–11pm, Sat 1–11pm.

Another Erik's, but this one is reasonably priced and excellent value. It offers several traditional Swedish dishes called *husmanskost* (home-cooking). The establishment contains both a bistro and a more formal dining room, although the menu choices are the same in both. A favorite opener is toast Skagen, with shrimp, dill-flavored mayonnaise, spices, and bleak roe. There is also a daily choice of herring appetizers. Try the "archipelago stew," a ragoût of fish flavored with tomatoes and served with garlic mayonnaise. Marinated salmon is served with hollandaise sauce, and you might also try Erik's cheeseburger with a special secret sauce.

KARELIA, in the Hotell Karelia, Birger Jarlsgatan 35. Tel. 24-76-60.

Cuisine: FINNISH. **Reservations:** Not required. **T-bana:** Östermalmstorg.

$ Prices: Appetizers 66–96 kronor ($11.50–$16.75); main dishes 136–198 kronor ($23.75–$34.55). AE, DC, MC, V.

Open: Dinner only, Mon and Wed 5pm–1am, Tues and Thurs 6pm–1am, Fri–Sat 6pm–3am.

The city's leading Finnish restaurant is on the second floor of a moderately priced hotel (see "Stockholm Accommodations," in this chapter) in the center of the city. Begin with the classic Finnish salmon soup served with rye bread, or a wild-mushroom soup made with tiny mushrooms. For your main course, consider grilled filet of salmon stuffed with pike-perch, a chef's specialty. For dessert, try cloudberries (from north of the Arctic Circle), served with a caramel sauce. There is live music and dancing 6 nights a week. There is a casino and cocktail bar in the restaurant.

PRINSENS, Mäster Samuelsgatan 4. Tel. 10-13-31.

Cuisine: SWEDISH. **Reservations:** Not accepted. **T-bana:** Östermalmstorg.

$ Prices: Appetizers 46–89 kronor ($8.05–$15.55); main dishes 93–159 kronor ($16.25–$27.75). AE, DC, MC, V.

Open: Mon–Thurs 11am–12:30am, Fri 11am–1:30am, Sat 1pm–1:30am, Sun 5–11:30pm.

A 2-minute walk from Stureplan, this is a favorite haunt of artists and has become increasingly popular with foreign travelers. Diners are seated on one of two levels. The cuisine is tasty, notably such Swedish dishes as veal patty with homemade lingonberry preserves, sautéed fjord salmon, and roulades of beef. For dessert, try the homemade vanilla ice cream. Later in the evening the restaurant takes on some of the quality of a drinking club.

STUREHOF, Stureplan 2. Tel. 14-27-50.
   Cuisine: SEAFOOD/SWEDISH. **Reservations:** Not required. **T-bana:** Hötorget.
   $ Prices: Appetizers 40–100 kronor ($7–$17.45); main dishes 80–170 kronor ($13.95–$29.70). AE, DC, MC, V.
   Open: Mon–Tues 11:30am–11pm, Wed–Sun 11:30am–midnight.
This seafood restaurant in the center of Stockholm was founded in 1897, and has a Scottish-style pub in front. Specialties include Swedish or Canadian lobsters and oysters, fried plaice, boiled salmon with hollandaise, and fresh shrimp. Appetizers might be assorted herring or mussel soup. A daily menu of genuine Swedish *husmanskost* (home-cooking) is a bargain. You might order the famous sotare, grilled small herring served with boiled potatoes.

TEATERGRILLEN, Nybrogatan 3. Tel. 10-70-44.
   Cuisine: SWEDISH/FRENCH. **Reservations:** Recommended. **T-bana:** Östermalmstorg. **Bus:** 46.
   $ Prices: Appetizers 75–179 kronor ($13.10–$31.25); main dishes 101–225 kronor ($17.63–$39.30). AE, DC, MC, V.
   Open: Lunch Mon–Sat 11:30am–2:30pm; dinner Mon–Sat 5–11:30pm. **Closed:** July–Aug 6.
For the theater buff, this restaurant decorated with theatrical memorabilia is near the Royal Dramatic Theater on Nybroplan, where Ingmar Bergman was once arrested on a tax investigation. Many typical Swedish dishes are offered at lunch, cooked grandmother's style, including fried herring with onion and potatoes, scrambled eggs with salmon, and pea soup with sausages. For dinner, try one of the roasts from the trolley, which are as good as Simpson's in the Strand in London. You can also order such elegant fare as snails braised in white wine with tarragon butter, partridge in casserole with goose liver, and roe deer noisettes with a juniperberry sauce. Elaborate desserts include crêpes Suzette or an ice-cream tart with a layer of almond crust and hot-chocolate sauce.

INEXPENSIVE

GLADA LAXEN, Gallerian, Regeringsgatan 23. Tel. 21-12-90.
   Cuisine: SEAFOOD. **Reservations:** Recommended. **T-bana:** Kungsträdgården.
   $ Prices: Appetizers 54–68 kronor ($9.45–$11.85); main dishes 56–179 kronor ($9.80–$31.25). AE, DC, MC, V.
   Open: Mon 11am–7pm, Tues–Fri 11am–7:30pm, Sat 11am–4pm, Sun noon–4pm.
Very popular because it offers some of the finest seafood in town, this gardenlike restaurant serves a wide range of soups (the shellfish bisque is superb) and many preparations of salmon: with orange sauce, with shrimp and mushrooms in cream sauce, in dill-flavored casseroles, or lightly fried with creamed chanterelles and roe of bleak (a freshwater fish). Guests can help themselves from the extensive seafood buffet or order a salmon cake with lobster sauce (a Scandinavian specialty). Glada Laxen is in the biggest shopping center in downtown.

BUDGET

GRÖNA LINJEN, Mäster Samuelsgatan 10. Tel. 11-27-90.
   Cuisine: VEGETARIAN. **Reservations:** Not required. **T-bana:** Östermalmstorg.
   $ Prices: Buffet 65 kronor ($11.35). No credit cards.

Open: Mon–Sat 10:30am–8pm.

Located in what appears to have been a very large private apartment, this self-service vegetarian place offers both raw and cooked selections. You help yourself from a large vegetarian buffet enjoying one of the best all-you-can-eat restaurant bargains of Stockholm. In the evening a fresh-fruit salad is added to the buffet, for which you pay an additional 10 kronor ($1.75).

IN GAMLA STAN [OLD TOWN]

VERY EXPENSIVE

ERIK'S, Österlanggatan 17. Tel. 23-85-00.
   Cuisine: FRENCH. **Reservations:** Required. **T-bana:** Gamla Stan.
$ **Prices:** Appetizers 95–212 kronor ($16.60–$37); main dishes 183–350 kronor ($31.95–$61.10); luncheon plates 85 kronor ($14.85). AE, DC, MC, V.
   Open: Mon–Fri 11:30am–11pm, Sat 1–11pm.

This restaurant occupying two floors of a building from the 1600s in the Old town has a warmly autumnal color scheme and English country-house decor. Some food critics in Stockholm regard it as the best restaurant in the Old Town. Dishes include grilled scallops with a sauce of peppered ginger and deep-fried leeks, and grilled duck liver with a sauce of port wine and shallots, but the chef's specialty is duckling, served in two courses—first the breast in cider sauce, followed by the leg in a green-pepper sauce.

LEIJONTORNET, in the Victory Hotel, Lilla Nygatan 3-5. Tel. 14-23-55.
   Cuisine: SWEDISH/INTERNATIONAL. **Reservations:** Required. **T-bana:** Gamla Stan.
$ **Prices:** Fixed-price meals 470 kronor ($82.05) at dinner, 200 kronor ($34.90) at lunch; appetizers 90–140 kronor ($15.70–$24.45); main dishes 200–300 kronor ($34.90–$52.40). AE, DC, MC, V.
   Open: Mon–Sat noon–midnight. **Closed:** July.

This is one of the Old Town's most stylish and fashionable restaurants, noted for its food and the quality of its service. From the small street-level bar where you can order a before-dinner drink, guests descend into the intimately lit cellar (the restaurant was built around a medieval defense tower). Typical dishes include poached filet of beef with vegetables, potato cake, and herb sauce; noisettes of lamb with zucchini gratinée; and marinated breast of pigeon with fried shiitake mushrooms

---

 FROMMER'S COOL FOR KIDS
RESTAURANTS

Räkan (see p. 436) Kids love this fish restaurant, especially the miniature battery-powered boat that delivers dinner.

Mälardrottningen (see p. 440) For your big night out on the town, this is the place to go with older children, who will relish dining on this ocean-going yacht.

The Skansen Dining Cluster (see p. 442) After a day spent watching the animals and enjoying the rides, kids like to patronize any of these places for their good, healthy food.

Dining at the Produce Market (see p. 444) This place is as busy as a circus, but it's a lot of fun for parents with children to eat right in the center of all the activity. Small and big appetites are catered to at this food fair.

and port wine sauce. To reach this restaurant, you need to negotiate a labyrinth of brick passageways through the Victory Hotel.

EXPENSIVE

FEM SMÅ HUS, Nygränd 10. Tel. 10-87-75.
Cuisine: SWEDISH/FRENCH. **Reservations:** Required. **T-bana:** Gamla Stan.
$ Prices: Three-course fixed-price dinner 325 kronor ($56.75); appetizers 62–118 kronor ($10.85–$20.60); main dishes 169–205 kronor ($29.50–$35.80). AE, DC, MC, V.
Open: Mon–Fri 11:30am–11:30pm, Sat–Sun 1–11:30pm.

This sophisticated historic restaurant is furnished like the interior of a private castle, with European antiques and paintings. After being shown to a candlelit table somewhere in the nine rooms of the labyrinthine interior, you can order assorted herring, slices of fresh salmon in chablis, braised scallops with saffron sauce, terrine of duckling with goose liver and truffles, filet of beef with herb sauce, and sorbets with seasonal fruits and berries.

MÄLARDROTTNINGEN, Riddarholmen. Tel. 24-36-00.
Cuisine: FRENCH. **Reservations:** Required. **T-bana:** Gamla Stan.
$ Prices: Fixed-price dinners 390 kronor ($68.10) for three courses, 460 kronor ($80.30) for five courses; appetizers 70–125 kronor ($12.20–$21.85); main dishes 150–225 kronor ($26.20–$39.30); business lunch 175 kronor ($30.55); lunch platters 75 kronor ($13.10); sandwiches 38–93 kronor ($6.65–$16.25). AE, DC, MC, V.
Open: Mon–Fri 11:30–2pm, Sat 5–11pm, Sun 5–10pm.

The yacht housing this restaurant was donated by Barbara Hutton, heiress to the Woolworth fortune, to the British navy in the early days of World War II. Today the yacht is permanently moored at a pier of a satellite island off the Old Town, Gamla Stan. There is also a hotel in this yacht (see "Stockholm Accommodations," in this chapter).

Platters of food at lunch are called "a boat lunch," but you can also order sandwiches, some of them quite elegant, especially the one with marinated salmon and mustard sauce. Bouillabaisse is a specialty, as is roast saddle of reindeer. Three different kinds of red Swedish caviar are offered as appetizers, followed by such selections as poached filet of lemon sole with savoy cabbage and a saffron sauce.

STORTORGSKÄLLAREN, Stortorget 7. Tel. 10-55-33.
Cuisine: SWEDISH. **Reservations:** Required. **T-bana:** Gamla Stan.
$ Prices: Three-course fixed-price dinner 225 kronor ($39.30); appetizers 70–98 kronor ($12.20–$17.10); main dishes 130–255 kronor ($22.70–$44.50). AE, DC, MC, V.
Open: Daily 11:30am–11:30pm.

Off a charming square opposite the Stock Exchange in the Old Town, this restaurant was created in the cellars whose vaulted ceilings date from the 15th century. The old walls and chandeliers are combined with plush carpeting and subtle lighting to create a sophisticated effect. In summer, diners can choose an outdoor table with a view of the square.

The menu changes often here. You might begin with three kinds of herring or the house specialty, cured salmon and white bleak roe served with crème fraîche and onions. Typical dishes are likely to include filet of sole cooked several different ways, salmon stuffed with saffron, and marinated lamb.

MODERATE

CATTELIN RESTAURANT, Storkyrkobrinken 9. Tel. 20-18-18.
Cuisine: SEAFOOD. **Reservations:** Recommended. **T-bana:** Gamla Stan.
$ Prices: Appetizers 29–92 kronor ($5.05–$16.05); main dishes 59–185 kronor ($10.30–$32.30); fixed-price lunch 45 kronor ($7.85). AE, DC, MC, V.
Open: Mon–Fri 11:30am–11pm, Sat noon–11pm, Sun 1–10pm.

Opened in 1897, this fish restaurant in Gamla Stan serves some of the finest food in the Old Town. Look for the *plat du jour,* including, on my most recent visit, grilled filet Oscar. You might also try the broiled fresh salmon with hollandaise, always a delight.

KRISTINA, Västerlanggatan 68. Tel. 20-05-29.
   Cuisine: SWEDISH. **Reservations:** Recommended. **T-bana:** Gamla Stan.
$ Prices: Appetizers 45–145 kronor ($7.85–$25.30); main dishes 69–145 kronor ($12.05–$25.30).
   Open: Daily 11am–11pm.

This restaurant, established in 1960 on an important pedestrian street, is located in a building that is decorated with carved helmeted heads and two cannons. Inside it's atmospherically lit by stained-glass windows rococo wall sconces set into paneled walls. Menu items include marinated salmon with mustard sauce, tournedos with gorgonzola sauce, and roast lamb with a creamy garlic sauce. For dessert, try, if featured, a cloudberry parfait with bilberry sauce.

MAGNUS LADULÅS, Österlånggatan 26. Tel. 21-19-57.
   Cuisine: SWEDISH. **Reservations:** Recommended. **T-bana:** Gamla Stan.
$ Prices: Three-course fixed-price menus 185–300 kronor ($32.30–$52.40); appetizers 40–80 kronor ($7–$13.95); main dishes 80–180 kronor ($13.95–$31.45). AE, DC, MC, V.
   Open: Dinner only, Mon–Sat 5–11pm.

This is a pleasant restaurant converted from a vaulted inner room of a 12th-century weaving factory. You can have a drink at the bar before your meal. A meal could include a mixed seafood plate with lobster sauce, fresh salmon from Lapland, filet of beef in puff pastry with a deviled sauce, good lamb stew, and a different sorbet made fresh every day.

AT KUNGSHOLMEN

STADHUSKÄLLAREN, Stadhuset. Tel. 50-54-54.
   Cuisine: SWEDISH/INTERNATIONAL. **Reservations:** Not required. **T-bana:** Rådhuset.
$ Prices: Three-course fixed-price dinner 260 kronor ($45.40); appetizers 65–95 kronor ($11.35–$16.60); main dishes 130–180 kronor ($22.70–$31.45); lunch plate 50 kronor ($8.75). AE, DC, MC, V.
   Open: Skänken, lunch only, Mon–Fri 11am–2pm; Stora Matsalen, Mon–Fri 11:30am–11:30pm, Sat 2–11:30pm.

Two dignified restaurants are located in the basement of the Town Hall, near the harbor (the entranceway is recognizable by its beautiful carved wooden doorway). The chefs here also prepare the banquet for the annual Nobel Prize winners. They'll even arrange a banquet with a Nobel menu for you. The interior is divided into two sections, the Skänken, which serves only at lunchtime, and the Stora Matsalen.

   Meat dishes might include filet of elk or saddle of young reindeer. Fresh Swedish salmon is invariably featured, as are other fresh fish dishes, depending on the catch of the day.

AT DJURGÅRDEN & SÖDERMALM

DJURGÅRDSBRUNNS WÄRDSHUS, Djurgårdsbrunnsvägen 68. Tel. 667-90-95.
   Cuisine: SWEDISH. **Reservations:** Not required. **Bus:** 69.
$ Prices: Appetizers 25–65 kronor ($4.35–$11.35); main dishes 65–150 kronor ($11.35–$26.20). AE, DC, MC, V.
   Open: Summer, daily 11am–8:30pm; winter, daily 11am–4pm.

This inn in the Royal Deer Park dates from 1740 and caters to all tastes, whether in the elegant main dining room, the English-style pub, or the outdoor Pavilion, which includes a garden grill in summer. Enjoy an inexpensive, Swedish home-style lunch in the self-service café, or maybe have just a drink and snack in the pub. The restaurant serves grilled salmon with morel-butter sauce or noisettes of deer with fresh vegetables. Frikadeller (meatballs) and plates of roast beef are also featured. Lunch in the café runs from 80 kronor ($13.95).

GARBO, Blekingegatan 32. Tel. 41-06-08.
   Cuisine: SWEDISH/INTERNATIONAL. **Reservations:** Suggested. **T-bana:** Skanstull.
$ **Prices:** Appetizers 75–95 kronor ($13.10–$16.60); main dishes 100–160 kronor ($17.45–$27.95). AE, DC, MC, V.
   Open: Mon–Sat 10:30am–11pm.

Movie lovers will appreciate this slickly decorated restaurant inside the ground floor of Greta Gustaffson's (Greta Garbo's) birthplace. Popular and filled with businesspeople at lunch, the restaurant is lined with her photographs and even the plates bear her famous silhouette.

The menu changes every month and is likely to include tagliatelle à la Garbo (pasta with smoked salmon), blackfish ragoût, shrimp with red sauce, and veal stuffed with exotic mushrooms (duxelles). Desserts include ice-cream concoctions that are named after the reclusive star's most famous roles.

SPECIALTY DINING
DEPARTMENT STORE DINING

With three restaurants, a bar, and (in summer) a cafeteria beside the main entrance, **Åhlens City,** Klarabergsgatan 50 (tel. 24-60-00), between the Central Station and Hötorget, is a popular place to eat and drink. A mezzanine café serves business lunches, pastries, and drinks Monday through Friday from 11am to 7pm, on Saturday from 11am to 5:30pm and on Sunday from noon to 4:30pm. Meals cost from 45 kronor ($7.85).

On Level 2, a self-service restaurant in elegant surroundings is the only such eating place in Sweden that is permitted to serve alcoholic drinks. Fixed-price menus and à la carte dishes are served, with meals starting at 39 kronor ($6.80). It's open Monday through Friday from 9:30am to 6:30pm, on Saturday from 9:30am to 5:30pm, and on Sunday from noon to 3:30pm.

Also on Level 2, the Caffino Bar offers coffee and drinks with or without alcohol. Irish coffee costs 50 kronor ($8.75). The bar is open from noon daily, closing at 6:30pm Monday through Friday, at 5:30pm on Saturday, and at 3:30pm on Sunday.

A tea room on Level 3, open Monday through Friday from 11am to 6:15pm and on Saturday from 10am to 3:45pm (closed Sunday), serves Danish open-face sandwiches, pastries, and tea and coffee by the pot. Expect to pay 45 kronor ($7.85). T-bana: Central Station.

SKANSEN DINING CLUSTER

Near the top of the Skansen compound, a Williamsburg-type park from 1891, **Cafeteria Solliden** (tel. 662-93-03) is actually a cluster of restaurants set in a sprawling building. This all-purpose dining emporium has an array of drinking, dancing, and dining facilities.

The least pretentious dining area is the ground-floor **cafeteria** featuring wood paneling, big windows, and budget prices. It serves open-face sandwiches and warm platters beginning at 45 kronor ($7.85). It's open Monday through Saturday from noon to 11pm and on Sunday from noon to 5pm. The ground-floor restaurant and an adjacent wood-sheathed pub are open all year.

Café Jubilee, on one of the upper floors, is one of the most idyllic tea and coffee houses in Stockholm. In a pink-and-red decor with art nouveau laminated chairs, flowers, and old photographs, you can enjoy coffee, sandwiches, and pastries. Open mid-May to late August, Tuesday through Sunday from 11am to 5pm.

Scattered among these dining rooms are elegantly antique conference chambers and private dining salons where everyone of importance in Sweden, from the king to the prime minister, has dined.

Restaurant Solliden (tel. 662-93-03) is the best of the lot, offering both Swedish and French cooking. It serves a Swedish smörgåsbord at 210 kronor ($36.65) and a (Monday through Friday) tourist menu at 155 kronor ($27.05). You can also order à la carte, with main dishes priced from 148 to 205 kronor ($25.85 to $35.80). Reservations aren't necessary but are recommended in summer. This upstairs dining room with ice-blue and crystal decor offers a panoramic view of Stockholm and attentive service. There's dance music nightly from 9pm to midnight. Main dishes include tournedos with morels and madeira sauce, roast breast of duck with cherry sauce, and saddle of lamb garni.

Also in the Skansen compound, **Stora Gungan** (tel. 660-66-01) is located an escalator flight up from the main entranceway. It retains a 19th-century rustic ambience with wood-plank floors and rough-hewn tables. Traditional Swedish meals might include a salmon platter, selections from a herring buffet, and meatballs. Regardless of what you order, at least part of your meal will be self-served from a buffet near the bar. You can enjoy a beer on the front porch.

To reach all these restaurants, take bus no. 44 or 47, or the Djurgården ferry lines.

A SELF-SERVICE CAFETERIA

MODERNA MUSEET CAFETERIA, Skeppsholmen. Tel. 666-42-50.
Cuisine: SWEDISH. **Reservations:** Not required. **Bus:** 65.
$ Prices: Appetizers 25–45 kronor ($4.35–$7.85); main dishes 45–85 kronor ($7.85–$14.85); daily special 45 kronor ($7.85). No credit cards.
Open: Tues–Fri noon–9pm, Sat–Sun 11am–5pm.
On the tiny island of Skeppsholmen, this is a luncheon-and-tea café in one corner of the main gallery. Weather permitting, the best way to dine here is to load up a tray at the counter, then take it out to the garden. The daily specials are the least expensive fare, and beer and wine are available.

LATE-NIGHT DINING

BIZET, Gustav Adolfs Torg 20. Tel. 10-42-22.
Cuisine: ITALIAN. **Reservations:** Recommended. **T-bana:** Kungsträdgården.
$ Prices: Fixed-price menus 195 kronor ($34.05) for two courses, 220 kronor ($38.40) for three courses; appetizers 52–98 kronor ($9.10–$17.10); main dishes 65–165 kronor ($11.35–$28.80). AE, DC, MC, V.
Open: Mon–Sat 11:30am–3am, Sun 1pm–3am.
Charmingly located at the corner of this landmark square at the opera, this restaurant overlooks the Royal Palace. It has a rustic old-fashioned charm, and satisfies a number of different tastes and pocketbooks. Veal and pasta dishes are featured, but most diners prefer the pizzas.

LATONA, Västerlånggatan 79. Tel. 11-32-60.
Cuisine: SWEDISH. **Reservations:** Recommended. **T-bana:** Gamla Stan.
$ Prices: Appetizers 45–210 kronor ($7.85–$36.65); main dishes 87–205 kronor ($15.20–$35.80). AE, DC, MC, V.
Open: Mon–Fri 11:30am–1am, Sat noon–1am, Sun 1–10pm.
In this medieval setting on the main pedestrian street of Gamla Stan, you can order some of the most delectable Swedish dishes from the north. Everything seems to come from a cold field or stream, including filet of reindeer, snow grouse, marinated salmon, fried Baltic herring. A bowl of salmon soup is the classic opener.

LIGHT MEALS

COCO & CARMEN, Banérgatan 7. Tel. 660-99-54.
Cuisine: CONTINENTAL. **Reservations:** Recommended. **T-bana:** Karlaplan.
$ Prices: Platters 58–95 kronor ($10.15–$16.60). AE, DC, MC, V.
Open: Mon–Fri 11am–3pm. **Closed:** July.

S Coca & Carmen is a stylish, appealing lunchtime restaurant with a minimalist decor heightened by art deco effects and turn-of-the-century curved glass. Meals here might include avocado with bacon salad, club sandwiches, cheese pie with parmesan, an assortment of frequently changing casserole dishes, and beer or wine. No distinction is made between appetizers and main dishes.

DINING AT THE PRODUCE MARKET

LISA ELMQUIST, Östermalms Saluhall, Nybrogatan 31. Tel. 60-92-32.
Cuisine: SEAFOOD. **Reservations:** Recommended. **T-bana:** Östermalm-storg.
$ Prices: Appetizers 50–89 kronor ($8.75–$15.55); main dishes 89–140 kronor ($15.55–$24.45). AE, DC, MC, V.
Open: Daily 11am–5:30pm.

In the Östermalms Saluhall, the produce market of Stockholm, one of the city's largest fish distributors runs this little café and oyster bar. The menu varies according to the catch but often begins with oysters at 25 kronor ($4.35) each. Some come here to order a portion of shrimp with bread and butter for 75 to 100 kronor ($13.10 to $17.45), depending on the size. Typical dishes include fish soup, salmon cutlets, sautéed filet of lemon sole, and filet of pike-perch. The establishment looks like a pleasant bistro under a tent at some country fair. The day's specials are written on a blackboard.

ÖRTAGÅRDEN, Östermalms Saluhall, Nybrogatan 31. Tel. 662-17-28.
Cuisine: VEGETARIAN. **Reservations:** Recommended. **T-bana:** Östermalm-storg.
$ Prices: Buffet 60–80 kronor ($10.50–$13.95). No credit cards.
Open: Mon–Fri 10:30am–9:30pm, Sat 11am–7:30pm, Sun noon–7:30pm.

S Because of its location above the indoor market Östermalms Saluhall, you are assured of fresh produce and ingredients in the dishes served here. The vegetarian buffet includes soup, hot dishes, 20 to 30 mixed salads, all sorts of different beans, natural salads, homemade bread fresh every day, butter, and cheese.

TYSTA MARI, Östermalms Saluhall, Nybrogatan 31. Tel. 662-60-36.
Cuisine: SWEDISH. **Reservations:** Recommended. **T-bana:** Östermalmstorg.
$ Prices: Sandwiches 30–70 kronor ($5.25–$12.20); hot plates 59–70 kronor ($10.30–$12.20). MC, V.
Open: Mon–Fri 9am–6pm, Sat 9am–3pm.

You select what you want from a glass counter and eat it under a canopy set out in one corner of the bustling marketplace. A meal might include a range of open-face sandwiches, lobster soup, and salmon pudding. Meals consist of platters of food which come with bread, butter, a salad, and either a light beer or coffee. Hot food is served during market hours on Saturday, but only from 11am to 4pm weekdays. After that, it's pastries along with coffee and tea. Typical dishes include Swedish herring, fish soup, Italian pasta, chicken, and a shrimp or chef's salad.

HOTEL DINING

FRANSKA MATSALEN, in the Grand Hotel, Södra Blasieholmshamnen 8. Tel. 24-52-14.
Cuisine: FRENCH. **Reservations:** Required. **T-bana:** Kungsträdgården.
$ Prices: Five-course fixed-price menu 695 kronor ($121.35); appetizers 115–245 kronor ($20.10–$42.80); main dishes 175–275 kronor ($30.55–$48). AE, DC, MC, V.
Open: Lunch Mon–Fri noon–2pm; dinner Mon–Sat 6–11pm.

✪ Widely acclaimed as one of the greatest restaurants of Stockholm, this elegant restaurant is on the ground level of Stockholm's most deluxe hotel. The dining room is one of the most imperial in Sweden, featuring an ensemble of polished mahogany, ormolu, and gilt accents—all placed under a richly ornate plaster ceiling. Tables on the enclosed veranda have a view of the Royal Palace and the Old Town.

Try such dishes as smoked breast of partridge with pears and celery, a millefeuille of marinated salmon with coriander and shellfish, or filet of roebuck with savoy cabbage in cream, served with a potato and truffle galette. Dessert might be what the chef calls "variations of lemon" or deep-fried coconut and pistachio ice cream.

DINING WITH A VIEW

GRAND VERANDA, in the Grand Hotel, Södra Blasieholmshamnen 8. Tel. 22-10-20.
  Cuisine: SWEDISH. **Reservations:** Required. **T-bana:** Kungsträdgården.
  $ Prices: Appetizers 75–110 kronor ($13.10–$19.20); main dishes 85–172 kronor ($14.85–$30.05); two-course fixed-price lunch 145 kronor ($25.30); three-dish *middag* 290 kronor ($50.65); Swedish buffet 180 kronor ($31.45). AE, DC, MC, V.
  Open: Lunch daily 11am–3pm; dinner daily 6–9:30pm.
On the ground floor of Stockholm's most prestigious hotel, this picture-window restaurant opens onto a stunning view of the harbor and the Royal Palace. The Veranda is famous for its daily buffets, which occasionally is a shellfish buffet that includes all the shrimp and lobster you want, costing 285 kronor ($49.75) at lunch and 395 kronor ($68.95) at dinner. Try such à la carte dishes as filet of reindeer marinated in red wine or braised wild duck and deep-fried root vegetables served with an apple-cider sauce.

SMÖRGÅSBORD

ULRIKSDALS WÄRDSHUS, 171 71 Solna. Tel. 85-08-15.
  Cuisine: SWEDISH. **Reservations:** Required. **Directions:** Take Sveavägen to Solna (Exit E18), 3 miles from Stockholm.
  $ Prices: Smörgåsbord 275–400 kronor ($48–$69.85); appetizers 115–245 kronor ($20.10–$42.80); main dishes 175–275 kronor ($30.55–$48). AE, DC, MC, V.
  Open: Mon–Fri 11:30am–10pm, Sat 12:30–10pm, Sun 12:30–6:30pm.
⭐ This out-of-town establishment is said to serve the best smörgåsbord in Sweden. On the grounds of Ulriksdal's Royal Palace on Edviken Bay, you can dine in the all-glass Queen Silvia Pavilion opening onto gardens still owned by the king and queen. The smörgåsbord, featuring 86 delicacies (both shellfish and meat), is usually accompanied by beer or aquavit. Most people eat the smörgåsbord in five courses, beginning with herring (20 varieties), following first with salmon and then meat dishes, including frikadeller (meatballs) or perhaps reindeer, then a selection of cheese, and finally dessert. Some dishes are based on old farm-style recipes, including Jansson's temptation, which melds anchovies, heavy-cream potatoes, and onion.
  A very Swedish experience. As the flag is lowered outside, diners stand and sing the national anthem.

THE BEST IN THE COUNTRYSIDE

EDSBACKA KROG, Sollentunavägen 220, Sollentuna. Tel. 96-33-00.
  Cuisine: SWEDISH. **Reservations:** Required. **Directions:** Take a taxi from the center, a 100- to 150-krona ($17.45–$26.20) ride.
  $ Prices: Appetizers 90–140 kronor ($15.70–$24.45); main dishes 200–300 kronor ($34.90–$52.40). AE, DC, MC, V.
  Open: Lunch Mon–Fri 11:30am–2:30pm; dinner Mon–Sat 5:30–10pm.
  Closed: July 15–Aug 15.
⭐ Lying 2½ miles north of the center of Stockholm, this restaurant occupies a white stucco building which was originally constructed in the park surrounding Edsberga Castle as an inn for passengers commuting between Stockholm and Uppsala in 1626. Today, amid a consciously simple country-inspired decor, Christer Lingstrom's Edsbacka Krog is considered by some food critics as the best restaurant in Sweden. Cooking, he told the press, "is a greater challenge when you create an elegant and tasty dish based on an inexpensive chicken than it is to create a dish based

on costly truffles." Innkeeper's chicken, his house specialty, won him the Chef of the Year award. It combines chicken with Jerusalem artichokes which used to grow on the property around the restaurant. Another specialty is a bacon-filled gâteau served as a main course and derived from an old recipe.

LOCAL FAVORITES

BAKFICKAN, Jakobs Torg 12. Tel. 24-27-00.

Cuisine: SWEDISH. **Reservations:** Not accepted. **T-bana:** Kungsträdgården.

$ Prices: Appetizers 53–67 kronor ($9.25–$11.70); main dishes 98–121 kronor ($17.10–$21.10). AE, DC, MC, V.

Open: Summer, dinner only, Mon–Sat 5–11:30pm; winter, Mon–Sat 11:30am–11:30pm.

Tucked away in the back of the Operakällaren, this is perhaps Stockholm's poshest restaurant, but a chic place to eat for a moderate price. Its food is from the same kitchen as the Operakällaren, but its prices are more bearable. Main dishes are likely to include salmon schnitzel, beef tartare, Backfickan's famous Lovbeef, or beef Ryberg (sliced thin tenderloin).

KB RESTAURANT, Smålandsgatan 7. Tel. 679-60-32.

Cuisine: SWEDISH/CONTINENTAL. **Reservations:** Recommended. **T-bana:** Östermalmstorg.

$ Prices: Fixed-price dinner 145 kronor ($25.30); appetizers 58–125 kronor ($10.15–$21.85); main dishes 110–210 kronor ($19.20–$36.65). AE, DC, MC, V.

Open: Mon–Fri 11:30am–11:30pm, Sat 5–11:30pm. **Closed:** July.

A traditional artists' hangout in the center of town, the KB Restaurant features good Swedish cookery as well as continental dishes. Fish dishes are recommended, and this place has wonderful sourdough bread. You might begin with salmon trout roe and Russian caviar, and follow with such dishes as boiled turbot or lamb roast with stuffed zucchini in a thyme-flavored bouillon. Desserts include sorbets with fresh fruits and berries, and a lime soufflé with orange-flower honey. A *middag* costs from 92 kronor ($16.05). There is also a relaxed and informal bar.

TENNSTOPET, Dalagatan 50. Tel. 32-25-18.

Cuisine: SWEDISH. **Reservations:** Not required. **T-bana:** Odenplan.

$ Prices: Appetizers 42–105 kronor ($7.35–$18.35); main dishes 60–168 kronor ($10.50–$29.35); two-course fixed-price lunch 168 kronor ($29.35). AE, DC, MC, V.

Open: Mon–Fri 11:30am–1am, Sat 2pm–1am, Sun 4pm–1am.

An English pub and restaurant, the Pewter Tankard is in the northern quarter of town, just two blocks from the Hotel Oden. Main dishes might include a ragoût of fish and shellfish, salmon schnitzel, plank steak, and the inevitable hamburger special. For lunch, you can have pork chops, vegetable, bread, butter, and coffee for 50 kronor ($8.75)—or just order a draft beer, toss some darts, and admire the setting. The place prides itself on serving genuine English pints, with two kinds of draft and 18 different bottled beers from Europe. A pint of lager costs 42 kronor ($7.35).

A TEA ROOM

TEA HOUSE, in the Hotel Diplomat. Strandvägen 7C. Tel. 663-58-00.

Cuisine: SWEDISH. **Reservations:** Not required. **Bus:** 69.

$ Prices: Afternoon tea 57 kronor ($9.95); fixed-price lunch 65 kronor ($11.35).

Open: Meals, Mon–Fri 11:30am–9pm, Sat noon–5pm; afternoon tea, Mon–Sat 2–5pm.

It is generally agreed that this attractively decorated tea room is the finest in Stockholm, and its well-attended afternoon tea is often a social event. It is also fashionable at lunch, offering such daily specials as wild duck with Calvados or poached filet of cod with horseradish.

PICNIC FARE & WHERE TO EAT IT

Fast-food eateries and fresh food markets abound in Stockholm, especially in the center of the city, around the Hötorget. There you can visit **Hötorgs Hallen,** a fresh food market where you can obtain the makings of an elegant picnic. Many Turkish food products are sold here by recently arrived immigrants, including stuffed pita bread.

For the most elegant fare of all, however, go to **Östermalms Hallen** at the corner of Humlegårdsgatan and Nybrogatan, east of the center. Here, stall after stall sells picnic fare, including fresh shrimp and precooked items which will be wrapped carefully for you.

Smörgas, Riddargatan 14 (tel. 10-64-87), in the center of town, two blocks from Stureplan, prepares a large choice of appetizing open-face sandwiches which they will wrap for you to take out. You can order delicious pâtés, cheese, ham, and shrimp. They also prepare tasty quiches. Open daily from 10am to 4pm. Closed: July.

With your picnic fixings in hand, head for **Skansen** or the wooded peninsula of **Djurgården.** If you like to picnic with lots of people around, go to **Kungsträdgården,** "the summer living room of Stockholm" in the center of town.

FAST-FOOD CHAINS

Stockholm has several branches of **McDonald's,** the biggest and most central of which is at Sergelgatan 4 (tel. 21-50-00), a few steps from the Central Station. It's open Sunday through Thursday from 10am to midnight and on Friday and Saturday from 10am to 3am. A Big Mac costs 27 kronor ($4.70).

For families with children, the branch at Hornsgatan 88 (tel. 84-12-18) is especially recommended (take the subway to Mariatorget). Near the toy museum, it has a miniature fairground inside for children, and they can eat while sitting in a toy train.

If you'd prefer to try the local fast food, head for the **Clock,** Sergelgatan 22 (tel. 21-40-44), for a "big clock" hamburger at 27 kronor ($4.70). The place sells eight kinds of hamburgers. This most central branch is open Monday through Friday from 9am to 9pm, on Saturday from 9am to 7pm, and on Sunday from 11am to 9pm. There are many other branches of this chain throughout the city.

CHAPTER 25

WHAT TO SEE & DO IN STOCKHOLM

1. SUGGESTED ITINERARIES
2. THE TOP ATTRACTIONS
- FROMMER'S FAVORITE STOCKHOLM EXPERIENCES
3. MORE ATTRACTIONS
4. COOL FOR KIDS
5. SPECIAL-INTEREST SIGHTSEEING
- WALKING TOURS
6. ORGANIZED TOURS
7. SPECIAL/FREE EVENTS
8. SPORTS/RECREATION
9. SAVVY SHOPPING
10. EVENING ENTERTAINMENT
11. EASY EXCURSIONS

Stockholm is loaded with things to do for people of all different ages no matter what time of year you visit. Everything from the *Wasa* Ship Museum to the changing of the guard at the Royal Palace to the Gröna Tivoli amusement park will keep your interest peaked. Even just window shopping for beautiful Swedish crafts can be an enjoyable way to spend an afternoon.

1. SUGGESTED ITINERARIES

IF YOU HAVE 1 DAY

Far too short, but take a ferry to Djurgården to visit the *Wasa* Ship Museum, Stockholm's most famous attraction, and to explore the open-air Skansen folk museum. In the afternoon, take Walking Tour 1 of Gamla Stan (Old Town) (see below) and have dinner at one of its restaurants.

IF YOU HAVE 2 DAYS

Day 1: See "If You Have 1 Day," above.
Day 2: Get up early and visit the Kaknästornet Television Tower for a panoramic view of Stockholm, its many islands, and the archipelago. Go to the Museum of Nordic History for insight into 5 centuries of life in Sweden. After lunch, visit the Millesgården of Lidingö, the sculpture garden and former home of Carl Milles.

IF YOU HAVE 3 DAYS

Days 1 & 2: See "If You Have 2 Days," above.
Day 3: Spend the morning taking Walking Tour 2 (see below). At noon (1pm on Sunday), return to Gamla Stan to see the changing of the guard at the Royal Palace. View this French-inspired building that has been the residence of Swedish kings for more than 700 years. In the afternoon, see the Nationalmuseum.

IF YOU HAVE 5 DAYS

Days 1–3: See "If You Have 3 Days," above.
Day 4: Take one of the many tours offered of the Stockholm archipelago. Return to Stockholm and spend the evening at the Gröna Tivoli amusement park on Djurgården.

Day 5: Visit Drottningholm Palace and its 18th-century theater. In the afternoon, explore the university of the city of Uppsala, north of Stockholm, easily reached by public transportation (see "Easy Excursions," in this chapter).

2. THE TOP ATTRACTIONS

Even the most hurried traveler will want to see the **changing of the Royal Guard.** In summer, you can watch the parade of the military guard daily, on Wednesday and Sunday in winter (on all other days you can see only the changing of the guard). The parade route on weekdays begins at Sergels Torg and proceeds along Hamngatan, Kungsträdgårdsgatan, Stromgatan, Gustav Adolfs Torg, Norrbro, Skeppsbron, and Slottsbacken. On Sunday the guard departs from the Army Museum, going along Riddargatan, Artillerigaten, Strandvagen, Hamngatan, Kungsträdgårdsgatan, Stromgatan, Gustav Adolfs Torg, Norrbro, Skeppsbron, and Slottsbacken. For information on the time of the march, ask at the Tourist Center in Sweden House. The actual changing of the guard takes place at noon Monday through Saturday (at 1pm on Sunday) in front of the Royal Palace in Gamla Stan.

KAKNÄSTORNET (Kaknäs Television Tower), Djurgårdsbrunnsvägen. Tel. 667-80-30.
The tallest artificial structure in Scandinavia is in the northern district of Djurgården, a radio and television tower that stands 508 feet high. Two elevators take visitors to an observation platform, where you can see everything from the cobblestone streets of the Gamla Stan to the city's new concrete-and-glass structures, and the archipelago beyond.
Admission: 12 kronor ($2.10) adults, 6 kronor ($1.05) children.
Open: Summer, daily 9am–midnight; winter, daily 9am–6pm. **Bus:** 69 from Nybroplan.

ROYAL FLAGSHIP *WASA*, Galärvarvet, Djurgården. Tel. 666-48-00.
This 17th-century man-of-war is the no. 1 sight in Scandinavia—and for good reason. Housed in a museum specially constructed for it at Djurgården near Skansen, the *Wasa* is considered the world's oldest identified salvaged Scandinavian ship.
In 1628, on her maiden voyage and in front of thousands of horrified onlookers, the Royal Flagship *Wasa* capsized and sank almost instantly to the bottom of Stockholm harbor. In a feat that was considered an engineering triumph, it was salvaged in 1961. On board were found more than 4,000 coins, carpenter's tools, sailor's pants (in a color known as Lübeck gray), fishbones, and other items of archeological interest. Perhaps best of all, 97% of the 700 original sculptures were found. Carefully restored and impregnated with preservatives, they are now back aboard the ship, which looks stunning now that it once again carries grotesque faces, lion masks, fish-shaped bodies, and other carvings, some still with the original paint and gilt.
There is an exhibition showing the results of ongoing research: 3,000 fragments of textile show how coarse woolen cloth was sewn into Spanish-inspired sailors' clothing, while a bottle of rum, a clay pipe, and a backgammon board indicate how the seafarers spent their spare time.
The great cabin of the ship has been rebuilt with the original oak panels decorated with elegant wood carvings and ingenious fold-out beds. Visitors can walk right through the cabin. Also, a 16-foot-long interior cut-through model has been built, with 90 dolls representing soldiers and crew.
Admission: 30 kronor ($5.25) adults, 10 kronor ($1.75) children.

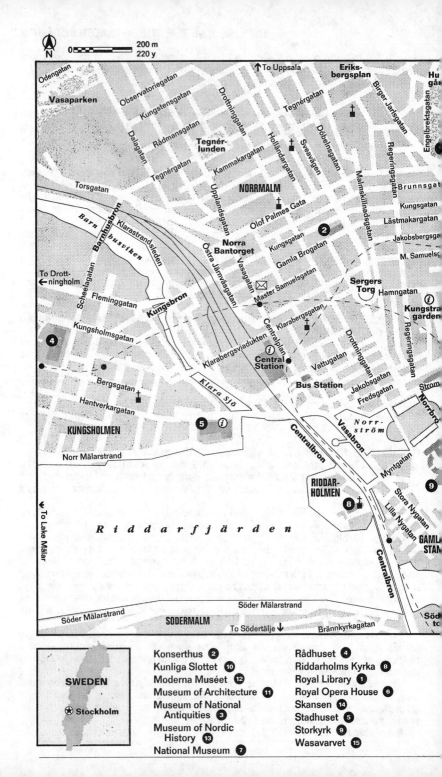

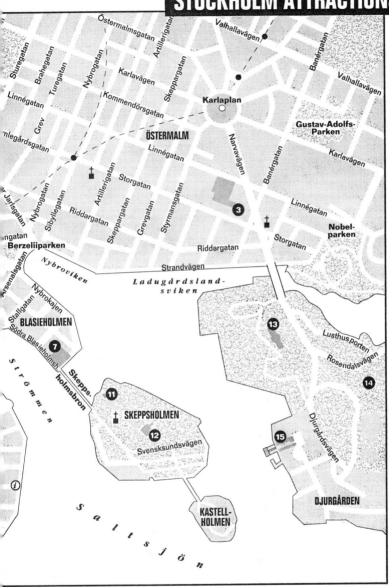

STOCKHOLM ATTRACTIONS

Östermalmsgatan

Valhallavägen

Banérgatan

Sturegatan

Brahegatan

Turegatan

Nybrogatan

Artillerigatan

Skeppargatan

Karlavägen

Valhallavägen

Linnégatan

Grev

Kommendörsgatan

Karlaplan

Gustav-Adolfs-
Parken

nlegårdsgatan

ÖSTERMALM

Narvavägen

Karlavägen

Linnégatan

Linnégatan

Banérgatan

Storgatan

Artillerigatan

**Nobel-
parken**

Jerisgatan

Nybrogatan

Sibyllegatan

Riddargatan

Skeppargatan

Grevgatan

Styrmansgatan

3

Linnégatan

Riddargatan

Storgatan

ngatan

Berzeliiparken

Nybroviken

Strandvägen

*Ladugårdsland-
sviken*

Arsenalsgatan

Nybrokajen

Stallgatan

BLASIEHOLMEN

Södra Blasieholmsh

7

13

Lusthusporten

Rosendalsvägen

S t r ö m m e n

Skepps-holmsbron

11

14

SKEPPSHOLMEN

Djurgårdsvägen

12

Svensksundsvägen

15

S a l t s j ö n

**KASTELL-
HOLMEN**

DJURGÅRDEN

Subway – – –   Church ✝   Post Office ⊠   Information ⓘ

Open: June–Aug, daily 9:30am–7pm; Jan–May and Sept–Nov, Thurs–Tues 10am–5pm, Wed 10am–8pm; Dec, daily 10am–5pm. **Bus:** 44, 47, 68, 69, 76. **Ferry:** From Slussen all year, from Nybroplan in summer only.

SKANSEN, Djurgården. Tel. 663-05-00.

⭐ Often called "Old Sweden in a Nutshell," this open-air museum is on Djurgården, near Gröna Lund's Tivoli. More than 150 dwellings from Lapland to Skåne, most from the 18th and 19th centuries, have been reassembled on some 75 acres of parkland.

The exhibits range from a windmill to a manor house to a complete town quarter. Browsers can explore the old workshops and see where the early book publishers, silversmiths, and druggists plied their trade. Many handcrafts for which Swedes later became noted (glassblowing, for example) are demonstrated here, along with such traditional peasant crafts as weaving and churning. For a tour of the buildings, arrive no later than 5pm (3pm off-season). Chamber-music recitals are given on Monday in July at the Skogaholm manor house. Folk dancing and open-air symphonic concerts are also featured. In summer, international stars perform at Skansen. Check the information office for these special events. There's much to do at night here (see "Evening Entertainment," in this chapter), and many places to eat.

Admission: 25 kronor ($4.35) adults, 10 kronor ($1.75) children.

Open: Historic buildings, May–Aug, daily 11am–5pm; Sept–Apr, daily 11am–3pm. Grounds, May, daily 9am–10pm; Sept–Apr, daily 9am–5pm. **Bus:** 47 from Nybroplan. **Ferry:** From Slussen to Gröna Lund.

MILLESGÅRDEN, Carl Milles Väg 2, Lidingö. Tel. 731-50-60.

⭐ On the island of Lidingö, northeast of Stockholm, is Carl Milles's former villa and sculpture garden beside the sea, now a museum. Many of his best-known works are displayed here (some are copies), as are works of other artists. Milles (1875–1955), who relied heavily on mythological themes, was Sweden's most famous sculptor.

Admission: 20 kronor ($3.50) adults, free for children under 12.

Open: May, daily 10am–5pm; June to mid-Aug, daily 10am–7pm; Oct–Apr, Tues–Sun 11am–3pm. **T-bana:** 13 or 14 to Ropsten; then transfer to a connecting tram and get off at Torsvik, just across Lidingö Bridge. **Steamer:** *Angantyr*, June to mid-Aug, departs from Nybroplan daily at 11:30am and 1:30 and 3:30pm; the trip to Torsvik about 50 minutes.

STADSHUSET (Stockholm City Hall), Hantverkargatan 1. Tel. 785-90-00.

Built in what is called the National Romantic Style, the Stockholm City Hall or Stadshuset, on the island of Kungsholmen, is one of the finest examples of modern architecture in Europe. Designed by Ragnar Ostberg, it was completed in 1923. The red-brick structure is dominated by a lofty square tower 348 feet high, topped by three gilt crowns, the symbol of Sweden, and the national coat-of-arms. There are two courts: the open civic court and the interior covered court. The Blue Hall is used for banquets and other occasions, including the Nobel Prize banquet. About 18 million pieces of gold and colored mosaics made of special glass cover the walls, and the southern gallery contains murals by Prince Eugen, the painter prince. The 101 City Council members meet in the council chamber.

Guided tours of the City Hall are held daily at 10am and noon.

Admission: 10 kronor ($1.75) adults, free for children under 12.

Open: May–Sept, daily 10am–3pm. **Closed:** Oct–Apr. **T-bana:** Central Station. **Bus:** 48, 53, 62.

KUNGLIGA SLOTTET (Royal Palace), Kungliga Husgerådskammaren. Tel. 789-85-00.

⭐ Kungliga Slottet is one of the few official residences of a European monarch that is open to the public. The king and his queen prefer to live and bring up their children at Drottningholm, although Kungliga Slottet remains the official address. Even the most hurried visitor may want to see the changing of the guard, Monday through Saturday at noon and on Sunday at 1pm. Built principally in the Italian baroque style between 1691 and 1754, the palace contains 608 rooms.

Visitors may walk through the Council Chamber where the king and his ministers meet several times a year. The **State Apartments,** with three magnificent baroque ceilings and fine tapestries, the **Bernadotte Apartment,** and the **Guest Apartment** are on view. They are beautifully furnished in Swedish rococo, Louis XVI, and Empire style.

In the cellar, the **Skattkammaren** (Treasury) (tel. 21-47-81) is worth a visit, exhibiting one of the most celebrated collections of crown jewels in Europe. You will see a dozen crowns, scepters, and orbs, along with stunningly beautiful pieces of antique jewelry. Nearly all visitors want to head for the **Royal Armoury,** Slottsbacken 3 (tel. 666-45-75), also housed in the cellars of the palace. Kings used to ride in these elegant gilded coaches. You will also see coronation costumes from the 16th century, weapons, and armor. Guided tours are conducted Monday through Friday at 2pm (there is also a Sunday tour for adults at 3pm, and a special tour for children at 2pm).

Remains of the old Three Crowns Castle, built in 1187 and symbolizing the union of Sweden, Denmark, and Norway, can be viewed in the **Palace Museum.**

Gustav III's collection of sculpture from the days of the Roman Empire can be viewed in the **Antikmuseum (Museum of Antiquities)** (tel. 789-85-00).

Finally, the **Rikssalen (Hall of State)** (tel. 789-85-00), where the present king makes his "State of the Nation" addresses, is also open to the public.

Admission: Apartments, 15 kronor ($2.60) adults, 5 kronor (85¢) children; treasury, 15 kronor ($2.60) adults, 5 kronor (85¢) children; Royal Armoury, 15 kronor ($2.60) adults, 5 kronor (85¢) children; Palace Museum, 5 kronor (85¢) adults, 2 kronor (35¢) children; Museum of Antiquities, 5 kronor (85¢) adults, 2 kronor (35¢) children; Hall of State, 5 kronor (85¢) adults, 1 krona (15¢) children.

Open: Apartments, May–Aug, Tues–Sat 10am–3pm, Sun noon–3pm; Sept–Apr, Tues–Sun noon–3pm. Treasury, May–Aug, Mon–Sat 10am–4pm, Sun noon–4pm; Sept–Apr, Mon–Sat 11am–3pm, Sun noon–4pm. Royal Armoury, May–Aug, Mon–Fri 10am–4pm, Sat–Sun 11am–4pm; Sept–Apr, Tues–Fri 10am–4pm, Sat–Sun 11am–4pm. Palace Museum, June–Aug, daily noon–3pm (closed Sept–May). Museum of Antiquities, June–Aug, daily noon–3pm (closed Sept–May). Hall of State, May–Sept, daily noon–3pm; Oct, Sat–Mon noon–3pm (closed Nov–Apr). **T-bana:** Gamla Stan.

RIDDARHOLM CHURCH, Riddarholmen. Tel. 789-85-00.

The second-oldest church in Stockholm is located on the tiny island of Riddarholmen, next to Gamla Stan. It was founded in the 13th century as a Franciscan monastery. Almost all the royal heads of state are entombed here, except for Christina, who is buried in Rome.

There are three principal royal chapels, including one—the Bernadotte wing—that belongs to the present ruling family. Queen Desideria, the first queen of the Bernadotte Dynasty, is buried here in a green marble sarcophagus.

Admission: Free.

Open: May 2–Aug, Mon–Sat 10am–3pm, Sun 1–3pm. **Closed:** Sept–May 1. **T-bana:** Gamla Stan. **Bus:** 48, 53.

NATIONALMUSEUM (National Museum of Art), Södra Blasieholmskajen. Tel. 666-42-50.

At the tip of a peninsula on Södra Blasieholmshamnen, a short walk from the Royal Opera House and the Grand Hotel, is the Swedish state's treasure house of paintings and sculpture. It includes a wide assortment of masterpieces by such artists as Rembrandt and Rubens (*Sacrifices to Venus*).

The first floor is devoted to applied arts (silverware, handcrafts, porcelain, Empire

FROMMER'S FAVORITE
STOCKHOLM EXPERIENCES

Ballooning Over Stockholm   In the early evening or early morning, pile into a wicker basket and ascend to a flight over Stockholm and the archipelago at 12 miles per hour. The pilot will head straight into a forest of old birch trees, only to pull free in a few seconds. Two hours of bird's-eye viewing ends in a champagne picnic and a diploma. Call Äventursresor (tel. 54-03-75) for reservations. Count on spending 1,125 kronor ($196.45) per person.

Experiencing Skansen   Butter churning or folk dancing, there's always something to excite and amuse people of all ages here. Wander at will through the world's oldest open-air museum, getting a preview of Swedish life in the long-ago countryside on some 75 acres of parkland.

Strolling Through Gamla Stan at Night   To walk the narrow cobblestoned alleys of the Old Town on foot at night, with special light effects, is like turning the clock and going back in time. It takes little imagination to envision what everyday life must have been like in this "city between the bridges."

Spending a Night on Barbara Hutton's Yacht   Even if you weren't around in the days of Cary Grant, and didn't get personally invited, you can either stay in Hutton's former cabin suite or dine at her former table, and if either of the above doesn't fit your budget, you can always go aboard the yacht *Mälardrottningen* for a beer. (See "Stockholm Accommodations," or "Stockholm Dining," in Chapter 24.)

Taking the Baths   Swedes, both men and women, are fond of roasting themselves on wooden platforms like chickens on a grill, then plunging into a shower of Arctic-chilled water. After this experience, bathers emerge lighthearted and light-headed into the northern fresh air fortified for an evening of revelry.

Watching the Summer Dawn   In midsummer at 3am, you can get out of bed, as many Swedes do, and sit out on balconies to watch the eerie blue sky—pure, crystal, exquisite. Gradually it's bathed in peach as the early dawn of a too-short summer day approaches. Swedes don't like to miss a minute of their summer, even if they have to get up early to enjoy it.

furnishings, and the like), but first-time visitors, if pushed for time, may want to head directly to the second floor.

Among the paintings from northern Europe is Lucas Cranach's most amusing *Venus and Cupid.* Also displayed is a rare collection of Russian icons, most of them—such as *St. George and the Dragon*—from the Moscow School of the mid-16th century.

On view is an exceptional number of excellent paintings by such masters as Perugino (*St. Sebastian*), Ribera (his oft-rendered *Martyrdom of Bartolomé*), El Greco (*Peter and Paul*), Giovanni Bellini (*Portrait of Christ*), Lotto (*Portrait of a Man*), and Poussin (*Bacchus*). The gallery contains some outstanding Flemish works, notably Pieter Brueghel II's *Winter Landscape,* Pieter de Hooch's *Interior with Mother at Cradle,* and Jan Brueghel's *Jesus Preaching from the Boat.*

Perhaps the most important room in the entire gallery has one whole wall featuring the works of Rembrandt (*Portrait of an Old Man* and *Portrait of an Old Woman*), along with his impressions of a maid (one of the more famous works in Stockholm). Here also is *The Oath of the Batavians.*

In yet another room is Watteau's *Lesson in Love,* and another salon is noted for its Venetian works by Guardi and Canaletto, as well as English portraits by Gainsborough and Reynolds.

Modern works include Manet's *Parisienne;* Degas's dancers; Rodin's nude male (*Copper Age*) and his bust of Victor Hugo; van Gogh's *Light Movements in Green;* landscapes by Cézanne, Gauguin, and Pissarro; paintings by Renoir, notably *La Grenouillère.*

Admission: 30 kronor ($5.25) adults, free for children.

Open: July–Aug, Tues–Sun 10am–5pm; Sept–June, Tues 10am–9pm, Wed–Sun 10am–5pm. **Bus:** 62, 65.

NORDISKA MUSEET [Nordic Museum], Djurgårdsvägen 6-16, Djurgården. Tel. 666-46-00.

On the island of Djurgården, this museum contains an impressive collection of implements, costumes, and furnishings of Swedish life from the 1500s to the present. The most outstanding museum of national life in Scandinavia houses more than a million objects. Highlights include dining tables, period costumes ranging from matching garters and ties for men to purple flowerpot hats from the 1890s. In the basement is an extensive exhibit of the tools of the Swedish fishing trade, plus relics from nomadic Lapps.

Admission: 20 kronor ($3.50) adults, free for children.

Open: June–Aug, Mon–Fri 10am–4pm, Sat–Sun noon–5pm; Sept–May, Tues–Wed and Fri 10am–4pm, Thurs 10am–8pm, Sat–Sun noon–5pm. **Bus:** 44, 47, 69.

DROTTNINGHOLM PALACE AND THEATER, Drottningholm. Tel. 759-03-10.

On an island in Lake Mälaren, **Drottningholm** (Queen's Island)—dubbed the Versailles of Sweden—lies about 7 miles from Stockholm and is easily reached by boat, escorted motorcoach tour, bus, and subway. Reflecting 18th-century French baroque trends, Drottningholm, with its courtly art, royal furnishings, and Gobelin tapestries, is surrounded by fountains and parks. The palace is inhabited by the royal family.

Nearby is the **Drottningholm Court Theater** (tel. 759-04-06), considered the best-preserved 18th-century theater in the world, with the original stage machinery and settings still in use. Performances are staged here each summer, between May and September (see "Evening Entertainment," in this chapter). There is also a museum that charts the development of the theater between the 1500s and 1700s.

The **Chinese Pavilion** (Kina Slott) (tel. 759-02-07) reflects Europe's fascination with the Orient at the turn of the century.

Nearby is a place for refreshments (Swedish waffles). Guided tours of the palace and theater are conducted every hour on the hour.

Admission: Palace, 20 kronor ($3.50) adults, 15 kronor ($2.60) children; Theater Museum, 22 kronor ($3.85) adults, 10 kronor ($1.75) children; Chinese Pavilion, 10 kronor ($1.75) adults, 5 kronor (85¢) children.

Open: Palace, May–Aug, Mon–Sat 11am–4:30pm, Sun 11am–4:30pm; Sept, Mon–Fri 1–3:30pm. Theater, May–Aug, Mon–Sat 11:30am–4:30pm, Sun 12:30–4:30pm; Sept, daily 12:30–3pm. Chinese pavilion, Apr and Sept, daily, 1–3:30pm; May–Aug, daily 11am–6:30pm (closed Oct–Mar). **T-bana:** Brommaplan; then transfer to the Mälarobuss bus to Drottningholm. **Ferry:** Leaves from the dock near the Stadshuset.

3. MORE ATTRACTIONS

PRINS EUGENS WALDEMARSUDDE, Prins Eugens Väg 6. Tel. 662-18-33.

This once-royal residence of the painting prince is an art gallery, surrounded by a sculpture garden on Djurgården overlooking the water. The prince, who died in 1947, was considered one of Sweden's major landscape painters; he created the murals at the Stadshuset. His large private collection, including works by Edvard Munch, is rewarding. The gallery and house are furnished as the prince left it. While at Waldemarsudde, see the Old Mill, built in 1784 and open only in the summer.

Admission: 20 kronor ($3.50) adults, free for children.

Open: June–Aug, Tues 11am–5pm and 7–9pm, Wed 11am–5pm, Thurs 11am–5pm and 7–9pm, Fri–Sun 11am–5pm; Sept–May, Tues–Sun 11am–4pm. **Bus:** 47 to end of the line.

MODERNA MUSEET [Museum of Modern Art], Skeppsholmen. Tel. 666-42-50.

On the tiny island of Skeppsholmen, a short walk from af *Chapman,* this museum shows contemporary works by Swedish and international artists, including kinetic sculptures. Highlights include a small but good collection of cubist art by Picasso, Braque, and Léger, Matisse's *Apollo* découpage, the famous *Enigma of William Tell* by Salvador Dalí, and works by Brancusi, Max Ernst, Giacometti, and Arp, among others. There is as well a collection of pop art—from Rauschenberg's *Monogram,* via Oldenburg, to Andy Warhol. Among 1960s works by prominent New York artists are the 12-foot-high *Geometric Mouse* by Claes Oldenburg; *Fox Trot,* an early Warhol; and *Total Totality All,* a large sculpture by Louise Nevelson. Outdoors, in front of the museum, is *The Four Elements* by Alexander Calder, and behind and around the house a number of works by Nordic artists have been installed. Farther away, near the Skeppsholmen bridge, is *The Paradise,* a sculpture group by Niki de Saint Phalle and Jean Tinguely.

The museum's activities include a children's workshop, concerts, films, discussions, and theater. There is a bookshop with posters, cards, books, and reproductions, plus a restaurant with fresh salads and wine that you can enjoy outdoors in the garden.

Admission: 30 kronor ($5.25) adults, free for children under 16; free for everyone Thurs.

Open: Tues–Fri 11am–9pm, Sat–Sun 11am–5pm. **Bus:** 65.

THIELSKA GALLERIET [Thiel Gallery], Sjotullsbacken 6-8, Djurgården. Tel. 662-58-84.

At the tip of Djurgården, this collection is one of Sweden's major art collections, surpassing, many feel, that of Waldemarsudde. The sculptures and canvases here were amassed by Thiel, a financier and banker who eventually went bankrupt. The collection was acquired by the Swedish state in 1924.

Some of the big names in Scandinavian art are here, including Norway's Edvard Munch and Sweden's Anders Zorn (see his nude, *In Dreams*). Gustav Fjaestad's furniture is also displayed. You'll also see a portrait of Nietzsche, whom Thiel greatly

---

IN THEIR FOOTSTEPS

John Ericsson (1803–89) Sweden's most famous inventor played a decisive role in the Civil War in the United States.

● **Birthplace:** He was born in Långbanshyttan, Sweden, on July 31, 1801.

● **Accomplishments:** Ericsson's marine propeller by 1843 had shown itself superior to the paddle wheel. His warship, *Monitor,* on May 9, 1862, defeated the Confederacy's *Merrimac,* saving the Yankee fleet.

● **Resting Place:** Ericsson died in the United States on March 8, 1889, and his body was transported to Sweden on the American armored cruiser *Baltimore,* with full honors. The John Ericsson Mausoleum in Filipstad was consecrated on July 31, 1895.

admired. Works by Manet, Rodin, and Toulouse-Lautrec, among others, round out the collection. Thiel is buried on the grounds beneath a statue of Rodin's *Shadow.*

Admission: 20 kronor ($3.50) adults, free for children.

Open: Mon–Sat noon–4pm, Sun 1–4pm. **Bus:** 69.

STADSMUSEET [Stockholm City Museum], Peter Myndes Backe 6. Tel. 700-05-00.

At Slussen, beside the Katarina Elevator, is the Stadsmuseet. It's best-known exhibit is the rich Lohe treasure, but it also shows 17th-century trades and crafts and life in the industrial city of the late 19th century.

Admission: 15 kronor ($2.60) adults, free for children.

Open: Mid-May to mid-Sept, Tues–Thurs 11am–7pm, Fri–Mon 11am–5pm; late Sept to early May, Tues–Thurs 11am–9pm, Fri–Mon 11am–5pm. **T-bana:** Slussen.

MUSEUM OF MEDIEVAL STOCKHOLM, Strömparterren, Norrbro. Tel. 700-05-00.

Built around archeological excavations, including parts of the old city wall dating back to 1530 (discovered in 1978–80), this museum traces the city's founding and development during the Middle Ages. The museum also contains the Riddarsholmsship, leather goods, ceramics, and metal articles.

Admission: 20 kronor ($3.50) adults, 5 kronor (85¢) children.

Open: June–Aug, Tues–Thurs 11am–7pm, Fri–Sun 11am–5pm; Sept–May, Tues and Thurs–Sun 11am–5pm, Wed 11am–9pm. **Tram:** 43.

MEDELHAVSMUSEET [Mediterranean Museum], Fredsgatan 2. Tel. 783-94-00.

Displayed here are 2,500-year-old terra-cotta sculptures from Cyprus that once stood in a temple dedicated to the god of fertility. Besides the museum's world-famous Cyprus collection, there are other Greek-Roman displays and a large Egyptian exhibition complete with mummies.

Admission: 20 kronor ($3.50) adults, 15 kronor ($2.60) children.

Open: Tues 11am–9pm, Wed–Sun 11am–4pm. **T-bana:** Kungsträdgården.

ÖSTASIATISKAMUSEET [Museum of Far Eastern Antiquities], Skeppsholmen. Tel. 666-42-50.

This small, intimate museum was opened in 1963 in an old building erected in 1699–1700 as stables for Karl XII's bodyguard. It's about a 7-minute walk from Karl XII Torg and very near the Museum of Modern Art. The permanent exhibition consists of archeological objects, fine arts, and handcrafts from China, Japan, Korea, and India. The collection is considered one of the finest and most important of its kind outside Asia. Among the outstanding displays are Chinese neolithic painted pottery, ritual bronze vessels, archaic jades, wood carvings, ivory, lacquerwork, enamelware, Chinese glass, Buddhist sculpture, Chinese painting and calligraphy, T'ang tomb pottery figurines, Sung classical stoneware such as celadon and temmoku, Ming blue-and-white wares, and Ch'ing porcelain made for both the Chinese and the European market.

Admission: 15 kronor ($2.60) adults, free for children under 16.

Open: Tues 11am–9pm, Wed–Sun noon–5pm. **Bus:** 46, 62, 65, or 76 to Karl XII Torg.

THE SUBWAY ART OF STOCKHOLM

In 1950 two women came up with the idea of commissioning artists to decorate the subway stations of Stockholm. Some of the country's finest artists were asked to decorate the subway stations, and their work is now in some 100 stations, all the way from the center of Stockholm to the suburbs, a 173-mile-long art exhibition, "the longest and deepest art gallery in the world." Some 70 artists contributed their work.

4. COOL FOR KIDS

The open-air park, Skansen (see "The Top Attractions," in this chapter), on Djurgården, offers **Lill-Skansen,** the children's own "Little Skansen," containing lots of small animals. Children can also enjoy pony rides, a car track, and a miniature train. Lill-Skansen is open daily in summer from 10am to 4pm.

Kids can spend a day or several at Skansen and not get bored. Before going to Skansen, stop off at the *Wasa* **Museum,** which many youngsters find an epic adventure. The evening can be capped by a visit to **Gröna Lund's Tivoli** (see "Evening Entertainment," in this chapter), which is also on Djurgården.

Some other activities that will amuse children include the following:

STOCKHOLMS LEKSAKSMUSEUM (Stockholm Toy Museum), Mariatorget 1. Tel. 41-61-00.
More than 10,000 items have been collected, including games, books, mechanical toys, and dolls and dollhouses. In the attic, tin soldiers, optical toys, and musical toys are displayed, as well as the interior of a nursery and the museum's theater. The museum's shop features books, souvenirs, and coffee.
Admission: 20 kronor ($3.50) adults, 5 kronor (85¢) children.
Open: Tues–Fri 10am–4pm, Sat–Sun noon–4pm. **T-bana:** Mariatorget. **Bus:** 55.

STADSTEATERN, in the Kulturhuset, Sergels Torg. Tel. 700-04-00.
The Stadsteatern performs a theatrical gem for children called *Unga Klara* (Young Klara), which has enough action, amusement, and fun to amuse kids in any language.
Admission: 65–75 kronor ($11.35–$13.10).
Open: Various times (call the box office). **Closed:** July. **T-bana:** Central Station.

5. SPECIAL-INTEREST SIGHTSEEING

FOR THE LITERARY ENTHUSIAST

STRINDBERGSMUSEET (Strindberg Museum), Drottninggatan 85. Tel. 11-37-89.
This building popularly known as "The Blue Tower" is where August Strindberg, dramatist and novelist, spent the last 4 years of his life (1908–12). It contains the library where he worked and where books, articles, and letters representing the last 20 years of his life can be seen. The library is a typical working author's library, with fiction and nonfiction works, including encyclopedias in Swedish, German, English, and French. Many of the volumes are full of pen and pencil markings—comments on the contents, heavily marked deletions of points he did not approve of, and underlinings indicating his diligent research into matters about which he wrote.

Of special interest to those familiar with Strindberg's plays is the fact that he furnished his rooms like stage sets from his plays, with color schemes as he visualized them. The dining room contains sculptures, casts of busts, and masks evoking for the writer people and events that were important to him. The museum also has a stage where Strindberg's plays are frequently presented.

Admission: 15 kronor ($2.60) adults, free for children.
Open: Tues–Fri 10am–4pm, Sat–Sun noon–5pm. **T-bana:** Rådmansgatan.

FOR THE ARCHITECTURE LOVER

In Stockholm, architects or those interested in the subject are captivated by the past, as reflected by such grand buildings as Drottningholm Palace and Riddarholm. But many of the expanding suburb "cities" of Stockholm are also worth seeing for their urban planning and architecture, which in Stockholm is considered among the most advanced in the world.

One of these model developments is **Farsta,** completed in 1960, although much altered since then. It lies 6 miles from the heart of Stockholm, and can be reached by the Farsta train departing from the Central Station, or by taking bus no. 18 to the end of the line. With its traffic-free shopping mall, its bright and airy modern apartment houses, its contemporary stores and restaurants, it makes for a good afternoon's tour.

Also pay a call at the:

ARKITEKTUR MUSEET [Museum of Architecture], Skeppsholmen. Tel. 11-75-10.

Near the Modern Art Museum, this museum has exhibits on the architecture of Stockholm, extensive archives, and a shop with books on architecture, past and present. Special exhibitions are also staged here.

Admission: 15 kronor ($2.60) adults, free for children.
Open: Tues 11am–9pm, Wed–Sun 11am–5pm. **Bus:** 65.

WALKING TOUR 1 — Gamla Stan [Old Town]

Start: Gustav Adolfs Torg.
Finish: Slussplan.
Time: 3 hours.
Best Time: Any day it's not raining.

Begin at:
1. **Gustav Adolfs Torg,** facing the Royal Palace, with the Royal Opera on your left. King Gustavus III, patron of the arts, was assassinated here at a masked ball in 1792.
     Walk across Norrbro Bridge heading toward the Royal Palace, passing on your right the:
2. **Swedish Parliament.** At Helgeandsholmen, the Parliament dates from 1897 when its foundation stone was laid. It can be visited only on guided tours. Along the bridge on your left are stairs leading to the:
3. **Medeltidsmuseet** (Museum of Medieval Stockholm), Stromparterren, with objects and settings from medieval Stockholm, including the Riddarholmship and parts of the old city wall.

REFUELING STOP   One of the hidden cafés of Stockholm, **4. Café Stromparterren** is also one of the most scenically located, lying next door to the Medeltidsmuseet. Many Stockholmers come here for a morning cup of coffee and a stunning view of the waterfront. Later they can fish for salmon—everybody can—right in front of the Royal Palace, a right that has existed since Queen Christina's day. In summer, tables are placed outside, and the interior of the café is built into the walls under Norrbro Bridge.

After leaving the museum, turn to the right and walk back to the bridge until you come to Slottskagen. Here, directly in front of the Royal Palace, make a right turn and head to Mynttorget, site of Kanslihuset, a government office building erected in the 1930s. The neoclassical columned facade remains from the Royal Mint of 1790.

Continue straight along Myntgatan until you reach Riddarhustorget. On your right is the:

5. Riddarhuset, the 17th-century House of Nobles, where the Swedish aristocracy met during the Parliament of the Four Estates (1668–65).

Continue straight across Riddarholmsbron (the bridge) until you come to the little island of:

6. Riddarholmen, called "the island of the knights." It is closely linked to the Old Town and its chief landmark, which you'll see immediately, is Riddarholmskyrkan with its cast-iron spire. Founded as an abbey in the 13th century, it has been the burial place of Swedish kings for 4 centuries.

Walk along the right side of the church until you reach Birger Jarls Torg. From there, take the one-block-long Wrangelska Backen to the water. Then go left and walk along Södra Riddarholmshammen until you come to a:

REFUELING STOP The **7. Mäladrottningen** was the yacht of the mink-swathed Woolworth heiress Barbara Hutton, who owned this vessel, built in 1924—at the time, the largest power-driven pleasure craft in the world. It was originally called *Vanadis,* and was donated by Miss Hutton to the British navy in the early days of World War II. During her brief ownership, the heiress and her guests, including Cary Grant (the press called them "Cash and Cary"), along with a crew of 50, visited some of the world's most celebrated ports. Today it's a hotel and a restaurant. You can stop for drinks in the Captain's Bar or order a fixed-price lunch Monday through Friday costing 175 kronor ($30.55).

After leaving the yacht, continue right along Södra Riddarholmshammen. Veer left by the railroad tracks, climb steps, and go along Hebbes Trappor until you return to Riddarholmskyrkan. From here, cross over Riddarholmsbron and return to Riddarhustorget.

Cross Störa Nygatan and take the next right onto Storkyrkobrinken, passing the landmark Cattelin Restaurant on your right. Continue along this street, past the Lady Hamilton Hotel, turning right onto Trångsund, which leads to:

8. Stortorget, where you'll find park benches for resting. Meaning "Great Square" in English, this plaza was the site of the Stockholm Blood Bath of 1520 when King Christian II of Denmark beheaded 80 Swedish noblemen and displayed a "pyramid" of their heads in the square. The Börsen on this square is the Swedish Stock Exchange, a building dating from 1776. Every year the Swedish Academy meets here to elect the Nobel Prize winners in literature.

At the northeast corner of the square, take Källargränd north to view the entrance to the:

9. Royal Palace, opening onto Slottsbacken. The present palace dates mainly from 1760 after a previous one was destroyed by fire. The changing of the guard takes place here on this square, which is also the site of the:

10. Storkyrkan, on your right. This church was founded in the mid-1200s but it has been rebuilt many times since. It is the site for coronations and royal weddings. Kings are also christened here. The most celebrated piece of sculpture is *St. George and the Dragon,* a huge piece of artwork dating from 1489. The royal pews have been used for 3 centuries, and the altar, mainly in ebony and silver, is stunning, dating from 1652. This is still a functioning church, and you should visit when no services are being conducted. It's open Monday through Saturday from 9am to 7pm and on Sunday from 9am to 5:30pm; admission is free.

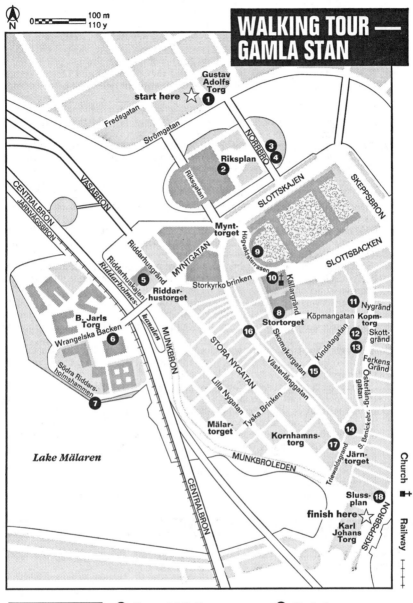

WALKING TOUR — GAMLA STAN

0 — 100 m / 110 y

N

start here ☆ **Gustav Adolfs Torg** ①

Fredsgatan

Strömgatan

NORRBRO

Riksplan ②

③
④

Riksgatan

VASABRON

CENTRALBRON

JÄRNVÄGSBRON

SLOTTSKAJEN

SKEPPSBRON

Mynt-torget

Riddarhusgränd

Högvaktsterrasen

⑨

SLOTTSBACKEN

Riddarhuskajen

Riddarholmen

MYNTGATAN

Storkyrko brinken

⑤ **Riddar-hustorget**

Kållargränd

⑩

⑪ Nygränd

B. Jarls Torg

Wrangelska Backen ⑥

Kanalen

MUNKBRON

⑧ **Stortorget**

⑯

STORA NYGATAN

Köpmangatan **Kopm-torg**

Skomakargatan

Kindstagatan

⑫ Skott-gränd

⑬

Ferkens Gränd

Österläng-gatan

Södra Riddars-holmshammen

⑦

Lilla Nygatan

Västerlånggatan

⑮

Mälar-torget

Tyska Brinken

Kornhamns-torg

⑭

S. Benickebr.

⑰ **Järn-torget**

Triewaldsgränd

Lake Mälaren

MUNKBROLEDEN

CENTRALBRON

Church ✠

Railway

Sluss-plan ⑱

finish here ☆

Karl Johans Torg

SKEPPSBRON

① Gustav Adolfs Torg
② Swedish Parliament
③ Medeltidsmuseet
④ Café Stromparterren
⑤ Riddarhuset
⑥ Riddarholmen
⑦ Mäladrottningen
⑧ Stortorget
⑨ Royal Palace

⑩ Storkyrkan
⑪ Köpmantorget
⑫ Österlånggatan
⑬ Stora Hoparegränd
⑭ Mårten Trotzigs Gränd
⑮ Tyska Kyrkan
⑯ Västerlånggatan
⑰ Järntorget
⑱ Slussplan

Continue right along Slottsbacken, either visiting the palace now or saving it for later. Go right as you reach Bollshusgränd, a cobblestone street of old houses leading to one of the most charming squares of the Old Town—

11. Köpmantorget, with its famous copy of the St. George and Dragon statue. From the square, take Köpmanbrinken, which runs for one block before turning into:

12. Österlånggatan, once the Old Town's harbor street, site of many restaurants and antiques shops. Continue along Österlånggatan, but take the first left under an arch, leading into:

13. Stora Hoparegränd, one of the darkest and narrowest of Gamla Stan streets. Some buildings along this dank street date from the mid-1600s. Walk down the alley toward the water, emerging at Skeppsbron. Turn right for two blocks until you reach Ferkens Gränd. Go right again up Ferkens Gränd, until you return to Österlånggatan. Go left on Österlånggatan until you come to Tullgränd. Take the street on your right, Prästgatan, named after the priests who lived on this street. As you climb this street, note on your left:

14. Mårten Trotzigs Gränd, a street of steps that is the narrowest in Gamla Stan. Continue along Prästgatan, passing a playground on your right. Turn right onto Tyska Brinken until you come to the church:

15. Tyska Kyrkan, on your right. Since the beginning of the 17th century, this has been the German church of Stockholm. The church has a baroque interior and is exquisitely decorated.

After leaving the church, the street in front of you will be Skomakargatan. Head up this street until you come to Stortorget once again. From Stortorget, take a little street, Kakbrinken, at the southwest corner of the square, until you reach:

16. Västerlånggatan, where you should turn left. This pedestrian street is the main shopping artery of Gamla Stan, and the best place to purchase gifts and souvenirs of Sweden. The street leads to:

17. Järntorget, which used to be known as Korntorget when it was the center of the copper and iron trade in the 16th and 17th centuries. At times in its long history it has been the place of punishment for "wrongdoers." The most unusual statue in Stockholm stands here. The statue is of Evert Taube, the troubadour and Swedish national poet of the early 1900s. He is carrying a newspaper under his arm, his coat draped nonchalantly, his sunglasses pushed up high on his forehead.

From the square, take Järntorgsgatan to:

18. Slussplan and the water. Here you can catch a bus to return to the central city or you can board a ferry to Djurgården and its many museums.

WALKING TOUR 2 — Along the Harbor

Start: Stadhuset.
Finish: Modern Art Museum.
Time: 3 hours.
Best Time: Any day it's not raining.

Start at the:

1. Stadshuset, Hantverkargatan 2, the town hall of Stockholm, on the island of Kungsholmen in the western part of the city. Kungsholmen has some of the loveliest and most varied waterfront walks in the city. It took 12 years, 8 million bricks, and 19 million gilded mosaic tiles to erect this town hall, which can be visited on a guided tour.

Go inside the courtyard on your own and admire the architecture. After exploring the building, exit and turn right, walking across Stadhusbron (Town Hall Bridge) to the island of Norrmalm. You'll see the Sheraton Hotel coming up on your left, and on your right is the Stadhuscafeet, where sightseeing boats

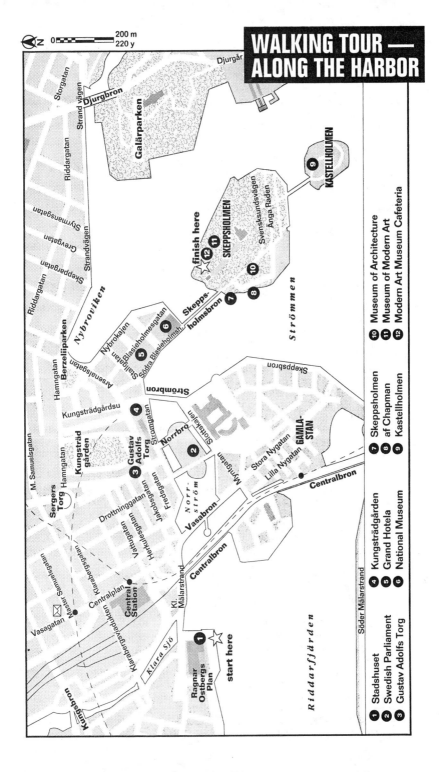

WALKING TOUR — ALONG THE HARBOR

0 200 m / 220 y

① Stadshuset
② Swedish Parliament
③ Gustav Adolfs Torg

④ Kungsträdgården
⑤ Grand Hotela
⑥ National Museum

⑦ Skeppsholmen
⑧ af Chapman
⑨ Kastellholmen

⑩ Museum of Architecture
⑪ Museum of Modern Art
⑫ Modern Art Museum Cafeteria

start here

finish here

SKEPPSHOLMEN

KASTELLHOLMEN

GALÄRPARKEN

Strömmen

Nybroviken

Berzeliiparken

GAMLA-STAN

Riddarfjärden

Ragnar Ostbergs Plan

Central Station

Sergers Torg

Kungsträd gården

Gustav Adolfs Torg

Norrbro

Vasabron

Centralbron

Kungsbron

Djurgbron

Skeppsholmsbron

Strömbron

Svensksundsvägen

Änga Raden

Söder Mälarstrand

depart on canal cruises in summer. Walk along past the boats and go under an underpass (watch out for fast-riding bicyclists).

Continue right along the canal until you reach Tegelbacken, a waterfront square. At the entrance to the Vasabron (bridge), cross the street and continue along Fredsgatan. Veer right at the intersection, hugging the canal. This will take you to Rosenbad, a little triangular park.

At the canal-bordering Strömgatan, the building on your right will be the:

2. Swedish Parliament, which can be visited on a guided tour.

Upon your arrival at:

3. Gustav Adolfs Torg, you'll have a panoramic view of the Royal Palace across the canal and of the Royal Opera straight ahead. This is one of the most famous landmark squares of Stockholm, and perhaps the most scenically located.

Strömgatan resumes at the corner of the Opera House, site of the Operakällaren, for many years considered the finest restaurant in Stockholm. Continue along until you reach the southern tier of the:

4. Kungsträdgården, which is the summer living room of Stockholm. These royal gardens reach from Hamngatan in the north down to the waters. Established in the 1500s as a pleasure garden for the court, they are now open to all, with their cafés, open-air restaurants, and refreshment kiosks.

Continue along the waterfront, past Strombron, a bridge leading to Gamla Stan, and emerge onto Södra Blasieholmshammen, site of the:

5. Grand Hotel, at no. 8. For decades this has been the prestige address of Stockholm, attracting Nobel Prize winners and most visiting dignitaries and movie stars. On your right, any number of sightseeing boats depart in summer for tours of the Stockholm archipelago. From this vantage point, you'll have a good view of the Royal Palace and Gamla Stan.

Continue along this street until you reach (on your right) the:

6. National Museum, Södra Blasieholmen, which is the repository of the state's art treasures, everything from Renoir to Rembrandt.

Cross the Skeppsholmsbron (bridge) leading to the little island of:

7. Skeppsholmen, which has a number of attractions, including the Modern Art Museum. After crossing the bridge, turn right along Västra Brobänken. On your right, you'll pass:

8. af *Chapman,* a "tall ship" with fully rigged masts that once sailed the seas under three different flags before going to permanent anchor here in 1949 as a youth hostel. Turn left onto Flaggmansvägen. The sculptures you see on your left belong to the Modern Art Museum. Continue along Holmamiralens Torg, passing the Nordiska Institute on your right. Cut right toward the water at Södra Brobänken. Take a right turn and cross the bridge leading to the mini-island of:

9. Kastellholmen, one of the most charming, but also the most undiscovered, in Stockholm. Head right along the water, going around Kastelholmskajen. Circle around and turn left at the end of Kastelleton. Walk back along Örlogsvägen, which runs through the center of the small island.

Cross the bridge, Kastellholmsbron, and return to the larger island of Skeppsholmen. This time go straight along Amiralsvagen, turning left onto Långaraden. Cut right and continue to walk along Långaraden, bypassing sculpture on your right. The first building on your left is the:

10. Museum of Architecture, which has slides and 500,000 architectural drawings and sketches from the last 100 years.

Bypass the museum and make a sharp right onto Svensksundsvägen. You'll approach the:

11. Museum of Modern Art, with a superb collection of both Swedish and international 20th-century art. It is also a venue for many temporary exhibitions of paintings, sculptures, and photographs.

REFUELING STOP   After such a long walk, the: **12. Modern Art Museum Cafeteria** is an ideal luncheon and tea café. When the weather permits, you can load up a tray and take it out into the sculpture garden to an umbrella-shaded table. You can order a selection of salads, sandwiches, vegetable plates, and daily specials, washed down with wine or juices, and finished off with an espresso.

6. ORGANIZED TOURS

CITY TOURS The quickest and most convenient way to see the highlights of Stockholm is to take one of the motorcoach tours that leave from Karl XII Torg, near the Kungsträdgården. **Stockholm Sightseeing,** Skeppsbron 22 (tel. 24-04-70), offers two "Grand City Tours," each lasting 2½ hours and costing 145 kronor ($25.30). The first (10am daily) is highlighted by a visit to the Royal Palace and a trip through Gamla Stan (Old Town), with a stop at the cathedral. The second tour, leaving at 2pm, goes to the *Wasa* Museum and visits the city hall.

Other tours operated by Stockholm Sightseeing include a guided afternoon tour of Drottningholm Palace and the Royal Court Theater, costing 150 kronor ($26.20). You can also do this on your own.

Also, a 2-hour **canal tour** leaves from May to October nine times daily from Stromkajen, in front of the Grand Hotel, passing under the bridges of Stockholm, through locks and canals. It costs 70 kronor ($12.20).

Stockholm Sightseeing offers daily ✪ **tours of the archipelago** that leads to the Baltic Sea. They leave Stromkajen from May to October at 8:30am, noon, 3:30pm, and 6:30pm, and cost 85 kronor ($14.85).

The company offers a 50% reduction to hostelers who can prove that they are residing in the af *Chapman*. This reduction is on all boat tours, including that of the archipelago.

Tickets and reservations for all tours may be obtained at all authorized travel agencies and tourist information centers.

OLD TOWN STROLLS Authorized guides lead 2-hour walking tours of the medieval lanes of Stockholm's Old Town. Called "Evening Walk in the Old Town," these walks are conducted from the end of May until mid-September, daily at 6:30pm, starting at the Obelisk on Palace Hill (Slottsbacken in Swedish). The fee is 30 kronor ($5.25) for adults (free for children under 16 who are accompanied by their parents). Reservations are not necessary.

In pricey Scandinavia, this tour is a remarkable bargain. Very often the evening ends with a cup of coffee and some sandwiches in an Old Town café.

THE GÖTA CANAL TRIP The most important boat trip in summer—and one of Sweden's major attractions—is the 4-day ✪ **Göta Canal** ride, which travels 350 miles from Gothenburg (Göteborg) in the west to Stockholm in the east, or vice versa. The trip takes you through 58 locks (the highest more than 300 feet above sea level), and includes four or five stops, varying according to the direction. Day trips and 5-day cruises with 11 to 15 stops are also offered.

The canal is a lovely waterway that passes the medieval Bohus Castle and goes through the narrow "Rock Canal" and into a lake district that includes Lake Vättern, the second-largest, and the most beautiful, lake in Sweden.

Arrangements for this trip can be made through the **Göta Canal Steamship Company,** Hotellsplatsen 2 (Bos 272), S-401 24 Göteborg (tel. 031/80-63-15), or through any travel agent. Tours operate between the middle of May and the beginning of September. The cheapest way to take this trip is to rent a shared cabin on the main deck. On the 4-day cruise, the cost ranges from $695 to $920 per person in a double, rising to $940 to $1,275 in a single. To extend it to 5 days, the supplement is $250 per person regardless of deck category. Food and admission to sightseeing attractions are included in the prices on cruises for 2, 4, and 5 days.

MOTORCOACH TOURS In summer the **Swedish State Railways,** St. Eriksgatan 113 (tel. 728-86-50), which also operates buses, arranges a number of motorcoach tours. A 2-day tour, for example, takes passengers from Stockholm to Copenhagen (or vice versa). The tour covers such areas as the glassworks district, the lake section, and the château country.

7. SPECIAL/FREE EVENTS

For major annual events, see the "Stockholm Calendar of Events" in Chapter 23. For other local events, *Stockholm This Week,* available at the tourist information center, is the best source for what's happening. Its "yellow pages" highlight everything from activities for children and auctions to special exhibitions, church music recitals, and other concerts. There's always a lot happening, regardless of the time of your visit.

On a summer night, head for the **Kungsträdgården,** the once-royal park in Norrmalm, adjacent to Sweden House. Concerts are presented here every evening—sometimes classical, often rock, even open-air theatrical performances. But perhaps best of all are the street musicians who entertain you, then pass around the hat. In winter an outdoor ice rink opens here.

In summer, the **Park Theater** performs in different open-air theaters throughout Stockholm. Thousands of people attend its productions, with a repertoire that is often classic. For information, call 61-79-45.

Thousands of international marathon runners participate in the **Stockholm Marathon,** which is usually in early June.

The June **Midsummer Celebration** is an excuse for the town to go wild. Special events are staged in the various parks, but the revelry doesn't need much organization as it has its own life.

During the last Friday and Saturday in June and the first weekend of July, a **Stockholm Jazz/Blues Festival** is presented. See *Stockholm This Week* for the venues.

In July and August, summer-night concerts—called **Sommarnättskonserterna**—are presented on the steps of the National Museum, Södra Blasieholmskajen (tel. 666-42-50).

Bellman Week, in mid-July, honors the national poet of Sweden, Carl Michael Bellman. Poetry and music are presented at Skansen.

In August, the Skansen open-air museum on Djurgården is the site of the **Augustimusiken** (August Music) presentation, with various folkloric and classical events. Admission to most of these events is covered by your park entrance ticket.

The finest sailing vessels in the Stockholm archipelago appear on **Sailboat Day,** the first weekend in September.

8. SPORTS/RECREATION

SPORTS

Soccer and **ice hockey** dominate spectator sports, and Stockholm offers world-class teams in both. Soccer is divided into a spring and fall season, and various stadiums host these matches. During the winter season (November through March) the top ice-hockey teams often appear at Globen, Johnneshov (tel. 600-34-00). **Basketball** is also played at this arena.

For schedules and ticket information, consult the tourist information office or pick up a copy of *Stockholm This Week,* which lists the times and places of the events.

One of the most popular sports, with gambling permitted, is trotting races, held at **Solvalla Stadium** (tel. 28-93-60 for information, directions, and ticket prices). Regular meets are held most of the year.

RECREATION

HORSEBACK RIDING, VIKING STYLE Iceland horses—gentle and small enough for children—can be ridden at the **Haninge Iceland Horse Center** at Hemfosa, 23 miles south of Stockholm, at a cost of 275 kronor ($48) per person for 2 days. Besides walking, galloping, trotting, and cantering, the horses also have another gait, the *tölt*, a kind of equine speedwalk which has no English translation. For more information, contact Sweden House, Hamngatan 27, off the Kungsträdgården (tel. 789-20-00).

ICE SKATING From October 20 to mid-March, the **Kungsträdgården,** the park outside Sweden House, is turned into an outdoor ice-skating rink, open Monday through Friday from 9am to 4:30pm and on Saturday and Sunday from 11am to 4:30pm. You can rent skates for 10 kronor ($1.75) per day.

JOGGING The best jogging tracks are found in **Djurgården Park,** a 10-minute walk from the city center.

SAUNA & SWIMMING There is a combination sauna, outdoor heated pool, and children's paddling pool, **Vanadisbadet,** at Vanadislunden, near Sveavägen (tel. 30-12-11), within easy walking distance of the Oden Hotel. Admission to the pool is 20 kronor ($3.50); the sauna is free. Bring your own towel. It's open Monday through Friday from 6:30am to 6pm and on Saturday and Sunday from 8am to 6pm.

If you want a more elegant sauna—one that has even attracted the King of Sweden—go to the **Hotell Karelia,** Birger Jarlsgatan 35 (tel. 24-76-60), which has strong Finnish connections. It costs 60 kronor ($10.50) if you're not a resident of the hotel. Open Monday through Friday from 3 to 10pm and on Saturday from 3 to 8pm. Massages are also available.

TENNIS, SQUASH & WEIGHTLIFTING Besides tennis at the **Royal Tennis Hall,** Lidingövägen 75 (tel. 667-03-50 for bookings), you can also use weights and enjoy a sauna and solarium. The center has 15 indoor Plexipave courts, 4 outdoor clay courts, and also 8 squash courts.

9. SAVVY SHOPPING

THE SHOPPING SCENE

Stockholm is filled with shop after shop of dazzling merchandise—often at dazzling prices. In the land of super-taxes and super-welfare, Swedish craftspeople are noted—and well paid—for their skill and efficiency, as reflected in the high prices.

Bargain shoppers should proceed with caution. There are some good buys, but it takes a lot of searching. If you're a casual shopper, you may want to confine your purchases to handsome souvenirs and gifts.

Swedish glass, of course, is world famous. Swedish wooden items are outstanding, and many prefer Sweden's functional furniture in blond pine or birch. Other items to look for include playsuits for children, silver necklaces, reindeer gloves, stainless-steel utensils, hand-woven neckties and skirts, sweaters and mittens in Nordic patterns, Swedish clogs, and colorful handcrafts from the provinces. The most famous souvenir to buy is the Dala horse from Dalarna.

TAXES & REFUNDS The Value-Added Tax in Sweden is called "Moms," and it is imposed on all products and services. When buying larger and more expensive items, you can avoid Moms if you spend over 200 kronor ($34.90). Just give the firm your name, address, and passport number and ask for a "Tax-Free Check." Leave the purchase sealed until you've left Sweden. The Customs official will want to see both the Tax-Free Check and your purchase. Cash refunds—minus a small commission— are granted on the spot. Hold onto your luggage until after you've received your refund, and then you can check your bag or carry the purchase on board if it's not too big. At the tourist information office (see above), you can pick up a pamphlet about tax-free shopping in Sweden.

SHOPPING STREETS & DISTRICTS Everybody's favorite shopping area in Stockholm is **Gamla Stan** (Old Town). Site of the Royal Palace, it even attracts such shoppers as the queen. The main street for browsing is called **Västerlånggatan.** Many antiques stores are found here; don't expect low prices.

In summer, **Skansen** is an interesting area to explore for the craftpeople who display their wares here. Many gift shops are found here (some selling "Skansen glass") as well as individuals who display their wares on temporary stands.

In the **Sergels Torg** area, the main shopping street is **Hamngatan,** site of the famous shopping center Gallerian, at the corner of Hamngatan and Sergels Torg, and crossing the northern rim of Kungsträdgården at Sweden House. Big department stores, such as NK and Åhléns, are located nearby.

The **Kungsgatan** area is another major district for shopping, stretching from Hötorget to the intersection of Kungsgatan with Vasagatan. **Drottninggatan** is one long pedestrian mall, flanked with shops. Many side streets branching off from it are also filled with shops. Hötorget, home to PUB Department store, is another major shopping district.

SHOPPING HOURS Stockholm **shops** are open Monday through Friday from 9am to 6pm and on Saturday from 9am to 2pm (usually later in winter). **Department stores** are generally open until 7pm on Monday and until 4pm on Saturday. Some Sundays they are open from noon to 4pm.

SHOPPING A TO Z
ART GALLERIES

ARONOWITSCH GALLERY, Sturegatan 24. Tel. 663-80-89.

One of the best-known galleries in Stockholm, this store was established in 1966. It is a showplace for nonobjective art, both Swedish and international. Some American artists are represented in the gallery's seasonal shows. It is closed from mid-June to September 1. T-bana: Östermalmstorg.

STRANDGALLERIET, Strandvägen 5B. Tel. 663-83-25.

This prestigious gallery accumulates only modern Swedish paintings, displayed in a single stark-white room near many embassies. It can always be counted on for having a startling array of modern art. Its owners keep up-to-date with changing trends in the art market. T-bana: Östermalmstorg.

AUCTIONS

AUKTIONSVERKET (The Stockholm Auction Chambers), Gallerian. Tel. 14-24-40.

One of the oldest auction companies in the world, dating from 1674, this auction house is now centrally located in the Gallerian mall, just up Hamngatan from Sweden House. Auctions are held 5 days a week from 9am to "whenever," and you are allowed two viewings, on Wednesday and Saturday from 8:30am to 3pm. It is estimated that some 150,000 lots a year are auctioned off here with the pound of a gavel—everything from ceramics to Picasso. T-bana: Kungsträdgården.

BOOKS & MAPS

AKADEMIBOKHANDELN, Mäster Samuelsgatan 28. Tel. 21-87-20.

One of the best-stocked bookstores in Stockholm, and one of the most centrally located, this store carries a wide range of English-language books including many travel-related materials, especially maps. T-bana: Hötorget.

SVERIGE BOKHANDELN, Hamngatan 27. Tel. 789-23-01.
Whatever's available in English about Sweden can be found at this bookstore off Kungsträdgården, in Sweden House above the information center. It has many rare items for sale, including records of Swedish music. T-bana: Kungsträdgården.

CERAMICS

BLÅS & KNÅDA, Hörnsgatan 26. Tel. 42-77-67.
This store sells the best merchandise of a cooperative of 35 Swedish ceramic artists and glassmakers. Prices begin at 50 kronor ($8.75) for single teacup, but rise to 50,000 kronor ($8,730) for exquisite, museum-quality pieces. T-bana: Slussen.

GUSTAVSBERG CERAMICS CENTER, Vardmö Island. Tel. 0766/356-50.
Bone china, stoneware dinner services, and other fine table and decorative ware are made at Gustavsberg Ceramics Center, on Varmdö Island, about 13 miles east of Stockholm. A museum at the center displays historic pieces such as Parian (a kind of plaster of paris or porcelain) statues based on the work of famous Danish sculptor Torvaldsen and other artists, hand-painted vases, Toby jugs, majolica, and willow-ware. There are also examples of Pyro, the first ovenware produced, of dinner services made for royalty, and sculptures by modern artists.

In summer, visitors to the center can watch potters at work and see artists hand-painting designs. You can even decorate a mug or plate yourself if you wish. There is also a shop at the center where you can purchase Gustavsberg ware, including seconds.

The ceramics center is open to the public Monday through Friday from 10am to 5pm, on Saturday from 10am to 3pm, and on Sunday from 11am to 3pm. You can get there on the steamer *Gustafsberg-VII* leaving from Hybroplan in Stockholm at 11:30am daily except Monday and Friday; or by bus no. 424 or 440 leaving from Slussen every 20 minutes.

CHILDREN'S CLOTHING

KAJS BARNKLADER, Humlegårdsgatan 13-15. Tel. 663-68-74.
Specializing in clothing for children ages 1 to 12, this store has a wide array of sweatsuits, dresses, sports clothes, and more. Each is suitably sturdy for the Swedish winter. Many are whimsical. T-bana: Östermalmstorg.

DEPARTMENT STORES

ÅHLÉNS CITY, Klarabergsgatan 50. Tel. 24-60-00.
In the center of Stockholm, this department store has a giftshop and a restaurant, and a food department that's famous. Also seek out the fine collection of home textiles and both Orrefors and Kosta crystal ware. The pewter with genuine Swedish ornaments makes a fine gift item. T-bana: Hötorget.

NORDISKA KOMPANIENT, Hamngatan 18. Tel. 762-80-00.
NK for short, this is the largest department store in Scandinavia. Most of the big names in Swedish glass are displayed at NK, including Orrefors (see the Nordic Light collection) and Kosta, the two most famous houses. Look also for Hackmanx stemware in original, unusual designs. Thousands of Swedish handcrafted items are found in the basement. Stainless steel, also a good buy in Sweden, is profusely displayed. T-bana: Kungsträdgården.

PUB, Hötorget. Tel. 791-60-00.
Greta Garbo got her start here in the millinery department. In general, the store offers less expensive merchandise than NK, but has many fine, high-quality items. There's a restaurant, too. T-bana: Hötorget.

DESIGN CENTER

DESIGNER CENTER STOCKHOLM, Norrlandsgatan 18. Tel. 10-03-77.
Come here if you're interested in contemporary Swedish industrial design. It also has a café and shop selling books and design magazines. There is also an information service. T-bana: Hötorget.

FLEA MARKETS

SKÄRHOLMEN SHOPPING CENTER, Skärholmen. Tel. 710-00-60.
Much of the stuff at this huge market is junk but you might find some pleasing gift item discarded from an attic in Värmland. Try to go on Saturday or Sunday (the earlier the better) when the market is at its peak. Admission is 5 kronor (85¢) for adults, free for children. It's open Monday through Friday from 11am to 6pm, on Saturday from 9am to 3pm, and on Sunday from 10am to 3pm. T-bana: Line 13 to Skärholmen, a 20-minute ride.

FURS

SOPHIE ERICSONS, Mäster Samuelsgatan 4. Tel. 20-27-64.
One of the largest and finest fur outlets in Scandinavia, with a century-old reputation. It also sells leather items from both Scandinavia and Turkey, and fur coats from Scandinavia and Germany for both men and women (the "wolf's coats" for men are especially popular). For women there are fox, muskrat, raccoon, and many different minks. T-bana: Östermalmstorg.

GEMS & MINERALS

GEOART, Tysta Marigången 5, Tegélbacken. Tel. 11-11-40.
Geoart has mineral crystals, minerals, jewelry, Scandinavian gems, Baltic amber, and lapidary equipment. T-bana: Hötorget.

GIFTS & SOUVENIRS

SLOTTSBODARNA (Royal Gift Shop), south wing of the Royal Palace, Slottsbanken. Tel. 789-86-30.
This unusual outlet sells products related or copied from the collections in the Royal Palace. Items are re-created in silver, gold, brass, pewter, textiles, and glass. T-bana: Gamla Stan.

GLASS & CRYSTAL

ROSENTHAL STUDIO-HAUS, Birger Jarlsgatan 6. Tel. 21-66-01.
This store has one of the biggest selections of modern crystal, porcelain, silverplate, and cookware in Stockholm. T-bana: Hötorget.

SVENSKT GLAS, Birger Jarlsgatan 8. Tel. 679-79-09.
Royal families patronize this establishment, but glass at every price level is featured. Orrefors, Kosta, and Boda glass are displayed here in stemware, candlesticks, flower-shaped bowls in full lead crystal, bar sets, vases, wine glasses, pitchers, and perfume bottles. A selection of beautiful crystal animals is sold here exclusively by Svenskt Glas. Worldwide shipping available. T-bana: Hötorget.

HANDCRAFTS & GIFTS

BRINKEN KONSTHANTVERK, Storkyrkobrinken 1. Tel. 11-59-54.

On the lower floor of a building near the Royal Palace in the Old Town, this mail-order business will send handcrafted brass, pewter, wrought-iron, or crystal anywhere in the world. About 95% of the articles sold are made in Scandinavia. T-bana: Gamla Stan.

DUKA, Kungsgatan 41. Tel. 20-60-41.

A large selection of crystal, porcelain, and gifts is available in this shop near the Konserthuset (Concert Hall). It offers tax-free shopping and shipping. T-bana: Hötorget.

GUNNARSSONS TRÄFIGURER, Drottninggatan 77. Tel. 21-67-17.

One of the city's most interesting collections of Swedish carved wooden figures includes such World War II figures as Winston Churchill and Franklin D. Roosevelt. Many are crafted from pieces of sweet-smelling juniper or shiny beech. T-bana: Rådmansgatan.

KONSTHANTVERKARNA, Mäster Samuelsgaten 2. Tel. 611-03-60.

Created by a group of artisans, this store has an unusual selection of some of the best Swedish handcrafts, all of which have passed a strict jury test before they are offered for sale. Choose from glass, sculpture, ceramics, wall textiles, clothes, jewelry, silver, brass, and wood and leather work. Each item is handmade and original. Ask about the tax-free service. T-bana: Hötorget.

SVENSK HEMSLOJD (Society for Swedish Handcrafts), Sveavägen 44. Tel. 23-21-15.

Svensk Hemslojd has a wide selection of glass, pottery, gifts, and wooden and metal handcrafts, the work of some of Sweden's best artisans. You'll also be shown a display of hand-woven carpets, upholstery fabrics, hand-painted materials, tapestries, lace, and embroidered items. You can also find beautiful yarns for weaving and embroidery. T-bana: Hötorget.

HOME FURNISHINGS

NORDISKA GALLERIET, Nybrogatan 11. Tel. 667-05-55.

This store features the finest in European furniture design, including the best from Scandinavian countries. Scattered over two floors are the latest designs in contemporary furniture. The store can arrange shipment. T-bana: Östermalmstorg.

SVENSKT TENN, Strandvägen 5. Tel. 63-52-10.

Along "embassy row," Swedish Pewter (its English name) has since 1924 been the most prominent store in Sweden for home furnishings. In spite of its name, pewter is no longer king and the shop now sells the best selection of home furnishings in Scandinavia—furniture, printed textiles, lamps, glassware, china, and gifts. No bargains here—just style. T-bana: Östermalmstorg.

HOUSEWARES

SVENSKT TENN, Strandvägen 5. Tel. 663-52-10.

For interior decoration and gifts, this is one of the most exclusive shops in Scandinavia. For your convenience, they will pack, insure, and forward your purchase anywhere in the world. The showroom features furniture, lamps, textiles, cutlery, plated ware, crystal, china, and gifts, often in stunning, sophisticated designs. They carry an exclusive collection of Josef Frank's hand-printed designs on linen and cotton. Closed on Saturday in July. T-bana: Östermalmstorg.

KITCHENWARE

CORDON BLEU, Vasagatan 48. Tel. 11-00-81.

A complete line of cookware, much of it imported from France, is sold here. If you're looking for the oddly shaped saucepan you've needed since your last gourmet dinner party, this place probably has it. They also carry a line of small wood-burning stoves which, for a price, they'll ship back to America. T-bana: Central Station.

MARKETS

ÖSTERMALMS SALUHALL, Hybrogatan 31.
One of the most colorful indoor markets anywhere in Scandinavia featuring cheese, meat, vegetable, and fish merchants who supply food for much of the area. You may want a snack or a meal at one of the restaurants here (see "Stockholm Dining," in Chapter 24). T-bana: Östermalmstorg.

PRINTS & LITHOGRAPHS

KONST-BIBIOFILEN, Västerlånggatan 6. Tel. 21-27-68.
One of the best collections of prints and lithographs, including limited editions, in Sweden. Closed Saturday and in July. T-bana: Gamla Stan.

SHOPPING MALLS

GALERIAN ARCADE, Hamngatan.
A short walk from Sweden House at Kungsträdgården, this modern two-story shopping complex is, to many, the best place in all of Sweden to go shopping. Merchandise in most of the stores is designed to appeal to local shoppers, not the tourist market, although in summer that changes a bit as more souvenir and gift items appear. T-bana: Kungsträdgården.

STUREGALLERIAN, Stureplan.
In the center of Stockholm, this mall opened in 1989 and was immediately acclaimed as "Shopping Center of the Year in Europe" by the International Council of Shopping Centers. It has a dazzling array of merchandise, both foreign and domestic, in store after store. The merchandise changes with the season. Summer brings out more displays of souvenirs and gift items from Sweden. T-bana: Östermalmstorg.

TEXTILES

HANDARBETETS VÄNNER, Djurgårdsslatten 82-84. Tel. 667-10-26.
One of the oldest and most prestigious textile houses in Stockholm, with art weaving and embroidery items sold here as well. Closed during July. Bus: 47.

TEXTILGRUPPEN, Hörnsgatan 6. Tel. 43-30-72.
This store was established in 1973 as a sales outlet for 44 of the best textile weavers in Sweden who weave in homes and workshops across the country. The outlet offers unique tapestries, prints, wall hangings, and unusual examples of what is called "fiber art," which are wall hangings. T-bana: Slussen.

TOYS

BULLERIBOCK, Sveavägen 104. Tel. 31-61-21.
You'll find a staggering selection of handmade and mass-produced wooden toys here, all made of natural materials. Many items were made in Sweden. T-bana: Rådmansgatan.

MJUKA DJUR, Hamngatan 11. Tel. 20-26-92.
This small one-room shop near Sweden House has one of the biggest selections in Scandinavia of stuffed animals—teddy bears, stuffed versions of cloth alligators, monkeys, whatever. The merchandise comes from all over the world—from New Zealand to Italy to Korea. T-bana: Kungsträdgården.

10. EVENING ENTERTAINMENT

Djurgården remains the favored spot for both indoor and outdoor spectacles on a summer evening. Although the more sophisticated may find it corny, it's the best bet in the early evening. Then you can make the jazz den and disco circuit—some of the clubs don't close until 3 or 4 in the morning.

THE ENTERTAINMENT SCENE

Pick up a copy of *Stockholm This Week,* distributed at the tourist information center (see above) at Sweden House to see what's on.

All the major opera, theater, and concert performances begin in autumn, except for special summer festival performances (see "Special/Free Events," in this chapter). Fortunately, most of the major opera and theatrical performances are funded by the state, which keeps the price of tickets reasonable.

THE PERFORMING ARTS

THE MAJOR CONCERT & PERFORMANCE HALLS

Berwaldhallen (Berwald Concert Hall), Strandvägen 69. Tel. 784-63-00.
Drottningholms Slottsteater, Drottningholm. Tel. 60-82-25.
Filharmonikerna i Konserthuset (Concert Hall), Hötorget 8. Tel. 22-18-00.
Kungliga Dramatiska Teatern (Royal Dramatic Theater), Nybroplan. Tel. 665-61-00.
Operan (Opera House), Gustav Adolfs Torg. Tel. 20-35-15.
Oscars 5D, Kungsgatan 63. Tel. 20-50-00.
Regina (The English Theatre), Drottninggatan 71A. Tel. 20-70-00.
Skansen, Djurgården. Tel. 663-05-00.

CONCERT HALLS

BERWALDHALLEN (Berwald Concert Hall), Strandvägen 69. Tel. 784-63-00.
This hexagonal concert hall is the National Radio's big music studio. The Radio Symphonic Orchestra plays here, but other musical events are also held in the hall, such as lieder and chamber-music recitals. The hall has excellent acoustics. The box office is open only for a very limited period, Monday through Friday from 9 to 11am. T-bana: Karaplan.
Prices: Tickets, 45–125 kronor ($7.85–$21.85).

FILHARMONIKERNA I KONSERTHUSET (Concert Hall), Hötorget 8. Tel. 22-18-00.
Home of the Stockholm Philharmonic Orchestra, this is the principal place to hear classical music in Sweden. The Nobel Prizes are awarded here. Originally constructed in 1920, the building contains two concert halls—one, seating 1,600, better suited for major orchestras; the other, seating 450, suitable for chamber-music groups. Besides local orchestras, the hall also features visiting ensembles, such as the Chicago Symphony Orchestra. Some series are entirely sold out in advance to subscription-ticket holders; others are less attended and visitors can obtain seats (phone 10-21-10 or 24-41-30 to order tickets). Sales begin 2 weeks before a concert and last up until the concert begins. Concerts are scheduled Tuesday through Thursday and on Saturday and Sunday, usually at 7:30pm. The box office is open Monday through Friday from 10am to 6pm and on Saturday from 10am to 1pm (closed in July). T-bana: Hötorget.
Prices: Tickets, 45–125 kronor ($7.85–$21.85).

OPERA & BALLET

DROTTNINGHOLMS SLOTTSTEATER, Drottningholm. Tel. 759-04-06.
Founded by King Gustavus III in 1766, this theater, unique in the world, stands on an island in Lake Mälaren, 7 miles from Stockholm. It stages operas and ballets with full 18th-century regalia, complete with period costumes and wigs. Its machinery and some 30 or more complete theater sets are still intact and are in use today. The theater, a short walk from the royal residence, seats only 450 patrons,

which makes tickets hard to get. Mozart is its perennial favorite. The season is May to September, and most performances begin at 8pm, lasting for 2½ to 4 hours. To order tickets in advance, phone 759-04-06 and give your American Express card number (only American Express is accepted).

To get to the theater, take the subway to Brommaplan and transfer there to the bus marked MÄLÄROBUS. Or you can take the special bus departing 45 minutes before each performance from in front of the Grand Hotel, Södra Blasieholmshamnen 8; a one-way ticket costs 25 kronor ($4.35).

Prices: Tickets, 75–400 kronor ($13.10–$69.85).

OPERAN (Opera House), Gustav Adolfs Torg. Tel. 20-35-15.

Founded by King Gustavus III, who was assassinated here at a masked ball, the Operan is the home of the Royal Swedish Opera and the Royal Swedish Ballet. The present building dates from the 1890s. Performances are traditionally given Monday through Saturday at 7:30pm (closed June 20 to August 20). The box office is open Monday through Friday from 11am to 7:30pm (closes at 6pm if no performance is scheduled) and on Saturday from 11am to 3pm. T-bana: Kungsträdgården.

Prices: Tickets, 50–200 kronor ($8.75–$34.90). Many tickets are discounted by 30% for seniors and students.

THEATER

The theater season begins in mid-August and lasts until mid-June.

KUNGLIGA DRAMATISKA TEATERN (Royal Dramatic Theater), Nybroplan. Tel. 665-61-00.

This is where Greta Garbo got her start (Ingmar Bergman used to be the director). The theater presents the latest experimental plays and the classics—but in Swedish only. Occasionally Shakespearean and other English-language plays are performed by visiting overseas troupes. Sometimes ballet performances are presented. The theater is open all year (with a slight slowdown in July), and performances are given Monday through Saturday at 7pm and on Sunday at 4pm. The box office is open Monday through Saturday from 10am to 7pm and on Sunday from noon to 4pm. Tram: 13, 14, 15.

Prices: Tickets, 70–135 kronor ($12.20–$23.55). Student discounts granted; Sunday tickets reduced for seniors.

OSCARS 5D, Kungsgatan 63. Tel. 20-50-00.

Oscars is the flagship of Stockholm's musical entertainment world, the home of classic operetta and musical theater since the turn of the century. It is known for its extravagant staging of traditional operettas, and was among the first theaters in Europe to produce such hits as *A Chorus Line,* in Swedish. The box office is open Monday through Saturday from 9am to 5pm. T-bana: Hötorget.

Prices: Tickets, 300–500 kronor ($52.40–$96.05).

REGINA (The English Theatre), Drottninggatan 71A. Tel. 20-70-00.

The English Theatre is the only permanent English-language theater in Sweden. It also stages some productions in Swedish, although most of its repertoire is in English. Originally built in 1911 as a cinema, the building was converted for drama in 1960. The Regina Theater Company was established in 1980, and presents everything from Victorian thrillers to Dickensian Christmas musicals. Its London-style theater pub, where beer goes for 15 kronor ($2.60) a glass, is unique in Sweden. Performances are given Tuesday through Saturday at 7:30pm. The box office is open Tuesday through Saturday from 10am to 5pm. American Express cardholders can reserve by phone. T-bana: Hötorget.

Prices: Tickets, 125 kronor ($21.85), regardless of location.

LOCAL CULTURAL ENTERTAINMENTS

SKANSEN, Djurgården. Tel. 663-05-00.

This open-air museum also functions as an outdoor dancing pavilion. Costumed musicians play, and the dances range from folk to *vals*. Weather permitting, couples over the age of 30 flock here every night—except Monday and Tuesday.

Tired dancers can also stroll over to the Solliden Restaurant, where there's a large bandstand with weekend performances—mostly vaudeville, operatic, and symphonic concerts, plus the Skansen Folk Dancers. Beer costs 42 kronor ($7.35). Open Wednesday through Sunday from 8:30 to 11:30pm.

Admission: 25 kronor ($4.35).

AN AMUSEMENT PARK

GRÖNA LUNDS TIVOLI, Djurgården. Tel. 665-70-00.
Unlike its Copenhagen namesake, this is an amusement park—not a fantasy land. For those who like Coney Island–type amusements, it can be a nighttime adventure. One of the big thrills of Tivoli is to go up on the revolving tower for its after-dark view of Stockholm; it costs 10 kronor ($1.75).

The park is open April 25 to June 5, Tuesday through Thursday from 6 to 11pm, on Friday from 6pm to midnight, on Saturday from 1pm to midnight, and on Sunday from 1 to 9pm; June 6 to July 27, Tuesday through Thursday from 1 to 11pm, on Friday and Saturday from 1pm to midnight, and on Sunday from 1 to 9pm; July 28 to August 16, Monday through Saturday from 1pm to midnight and on Sunday from 1 to 10pm; August 17 to mid-September, Monday through Thursday from 6 to 11pm, on Friday from 6pm to midnight, on Saturday from 1pm to midnight, and on Sunday from 1 to 9pm. Closed mid-September to April 24. Bus: 44, 47. Ferry: Djurgården ferry from Nybroplan.

Admission: 25 kronor ($4.35) adults, 15 kronor ($2.60) children 7–15, free for children under 7.

THE CLUB & MUSIC SCENE

NIGHTCLUBS/CABARET

BACCHI WAPEN, Järntorgsgatan 5. Tel. 11-66-71.
There's enough going on here to make an entire evening's entertainment. You can have dinner at tables set around the upper-level disco floor between 8pm and 1am, for 200 kronor ($34.90) and up. In winter only, they present strip shows, which are popular, safe, tongue-in-cheek, and among the funniest in Stockholm. Men strip on Wednesday, women on Thursday. Drag shows are also presented on Friday night. Beer costs 50 kronor ($8.75). Open Wednesday through Sunday from 8pm to 3am. T-bana: Gamla Stan.

Admission: 80 kronor ($13.95); before 9pm, one fee covers two people.

CAFÉ OPERA, Operahuset, Karl's Torg. Tel. 24-27-07.
Café Opera—Swedish beaux arts at its best—functions as a bistro, brasserie, and tea room during the day and one of the most crowded nightclubs in Stockholm in the evening. Visitors have the best chance of getting in around noon when a *dagens* lunch is offered for 72 kronor ($12.55). This establishment is not to be confused with the opera's main, and far more expensive, dining room, the Operakällaren, whose entrance is through a different door. Near the entrance to the café is a stairway leading to one of the Opera House's most beautiful corners, the clublike Operabären (Opera Bar), which is likely to be as crowded as the café. It is a monumental but historically charming place to have a drink; beer costs 43 kronor ($7.50). Disco action begins after 10pm. Open Monday through Saturday from 11:30am to 3am and on Sunday from 12:30pm to 3am. The lines are long at night. T-bana: Kungsträdgården.

Admission: 50 kronor ($8.75) after midnight.

VALENTINO, Birger Jarlsgatan 24. Tel. 14-27-80.
This chic supper club with an elegant soft-music disco is perhaps the most

fashionable in Stockholm, drawing a well-dressed crowd of Swedish VIPs. Go Gucci, Pucci, but not in jeans. Sometimes the disco is loud and raucous, and most often packed. The restaurant is far more subdued, decorated Italian style and graced with a music duo, usually a guitarist and an electronic pianist. Meals start at 300 kronor ($52.40). Food service ends at midnight, and the party continues to boogie until closing. It's open Monday through Saturday from 6pm to 3am. T-bana: Östermalmstorg.

DANCE CLUBS/DISCOS

THE DAILY NEWS/BACKSTAGE DISCO/MELODY THEATRE, Sverige-huset, at Kungsträdgården. Tel. 21-56-55.

Once past the coat-check area, you can go either upstairs into the spacious, angular bar or downstairs into one of the most popular and attractive discos in town, called Backstage. A restaurant section serves meals in a separate upstairs dining area where full dinners begin at 220 kronor ($38.40), although the upstairs café is the real reason most people go to the upper floor. The downstairs disco has a big dance floor. Beer costs 48 kronor ($8.40). The disco is open daily from 9pm to 3am; the upstairs café, daily from noon to 11:30pm.

The complex was enlarged in 1989 when management transformed a run-down theater next door into a home for a revolving series of concerts. The Melody Theatre presents concerts, most rock, jazz, or blues, more or less randomly. You can order tickets by calling 20-11-21. T-bana: Kungsträdgården.

Admission: Downstairs disco, 50–60 kronor ($8.75–$10.50) after 11:30pm Sun–Thurs and after 10pm Fri–Sat; Melody Theatre concerts, 100–150 kronor ($17.45–$26.20).

EMBASSY, Sturegatan 10. Tel. 61-60-07.

In this exclusive nightclub, restaurant, and piano bar, most of the well-dressed guests are over 25. The restaurant has good food, service, and an attractive ambience, and the piano bar always has good entertainment. Dance music is frequently performed by live bands. Dinners cost from 225 kronor ($39.30); beer costs 49 kronor ($8.55). Open daily from 8pm to 3am. T-bana: Östermalmstorg.

Admission: 70 kronor ($12.20), after midnight.

NIGHTCLUB KOLINGEN, Kornhamnstorg 59. Tel. 10-07-22.

A cellar club connected to the Pub Engelen (see "Jazz Clubs," below). Disco music is played. You can dance, or dine at one of the restaurants. A large beer will set you back 44 kronor ($7.70). Open daily from 7pm to 3am; dancing begins at 11pm. T-bana: Gamla Stan.

Admission: 35–60 kronor ($6.10–$10.50).

ROCK CLUBS

HARD ROCK CAFE, Sveavägen 75. Tel. 16-03-50.

The Swedish branch of the chain is fun and gregarious. Sometimes an American, British, or Scandinavian rock 'n' roll band presents a live concert; otherwise it's a rock blast on the sound track. Club sandwiches, hamburgers, T-bone steak, and barbecued spareribs available. Beer costs 46 kronor ($8.05), meals begin at 175 kronor ($30.55), and hamburgers run 83 to 119 kronor ($14.50 to $20.80). The café is open daily from 11am to 2am. T-bana: Rådmansgatan. **Admission:** Concerts, 120 kronor ($20.95).

JAZZ CLUBS

PUB ENGELEN, Kornhamnstorg 59B. Tel. 10-07-22.

Located in Gamla Stan, this bar has live performances, including jazz bands and singers, on Sunday from 9pm to midnight. The pub is connected to the Restaurant Engelen, which offers some of the best steaks in town. Meals cost from 190 kronor ($33.15); beer, 44 kronor ($7.70). Open daily from 4 to 11:30pm. T-bana: Gamla Stan.

STAMPEN, Stora Nygatan 5. Tel. 20-57-93.

This fun-loving pub attracts a crowd of jazz lovers in their 30s and 40s. Guests crowd in to enjoy live Dixieland, New Orleans, mainstream, and swing music from the 1920s, 1930s, and 1940s. From the high ceiling, a menagerie of stuffed animals and lots of old, whimsical antiques are suspended. Downstairs is a slightly less hysterical drinking bar, where a pint of beer costs 54 kronor ($9.45). Open Monday through Saturday from 8pm to 1am. T-bana: Gamla Stan.

Admission: 70 kronor ($12.20).

STUREHOF, Stureplan 2. Tel. 14-27-50.

At this previously recommended pub and restaurant, live jazz, soul, and blues— some of the best in Stockholm—are performed 4 nights a week. It also makes a good place for drinking and dining. There's a quieter room one floor above street level which is separated from the hubub. Beer costs 44 kronor ($7.70). Performances are on Wednesday, Thursday, Friday, and Saturday nights, beginning at 9pm until closing. The pub is open on Monday and Tuesday from 11:30am to 11pm and Wednesday through Sunday from 11:30am to midnight. T-bana: Östermalmstorg.

Admission: 40–50 kronor ($7–$8.75).

THE BAR SCENE

CADIER BAR, in the Grand Hotel, Södra Blasieholmshamnen 8. Tel. 22-10-20.

Named after the original builder of this deluxe hotel—one of the most famous in Europe—the bar enjoys a view of the harbor and the Royal Palace. It's one of the most sophisticated places for a rendezvous in Stockholm. You can also enjoy light meals—open-face sandwiches, smoked salmon, etc.—at any time of day in the extension overlooking the waterfront. Drinks run 94 to 196 kronor ($16.40 to $34.20); export beer, 50 kronor ($8.75). Open daily from noon to 2am, with a piano player performing Monday through Saturday from 6:30 to 7:30pm and 9:30pm to 1:30am. T-bana: Kungsträdgården.

CLIPPER CLUB, in the Hotel Reisen, Skeppsbron 12-14. Tel. 22-32-60.

The brass tables, mirrors, soft lighting, and live piano music make this one of Stockholm's favorite bars. The service is courteous. Drinks run 59 to 90 kronor ($10.30 to $15.70). Open Monday through Saturday from 4pm to 2am. T-bana: Gamla Stan.

VICTORIA CAFE MATSALAR, Kungsträdgården. Tel. 10-10-85.

This place, the most central café in Stockholm, gets crowded after 9pm, attracting a diverse crowd of patrons, including many gay people. You can have lunch or dinner in an inner section past the bar. Meals begin at 160 kronor ($27.95) and might include reindeer or fried salmon trout with almonds. There is a large bar, suitable for cruising and conversation. A pint of lager will set you back 42 kronor ($7.35). Open Monday through Friday from 11am to 3am and on Saturday and Sunday from noon to 3am. T-bana: Kungsträdgården.

GAY DRINKING & DINING

ALICE B., Sveavägen 57. Tel. 31-55-33.

The biggest gay nightlife center in Stockholm is Alice B., with its adjacent Café Timmy and Pride Disco, all interconnected. The restaurant serves a bistro-style menu with continental flair, including such dishes as sole Waleska, lamb chops provençal, and entrecôte Café de Paris. You might finish with a chocolate-mousse cake. Dinners begin at 140 kronor ($24.45). You should make reservations for Friday and Saturday nights. Alice B. is open on Monday, Tuesday, and Thursday from 6pm to midnight, and on Wednesday, Friday, and Saturday from 6pm to 1am.

The adjoining **Café Timmy** (tel. 736-02-14) is a pleasant spot from which to survey the scene with its marble floors, skylight, and fountain. Sometimes live music is presented. A beer will set you back 48 kronor ($8.40). The café is open on Monday, Tuesday, and Thursday from 11am to midnight, on Wednesday and Friday from 11am to 3am, and on Saturday from 3pm to 3am.

The **Pride Disco** (tel. 31-55-33), which attracts quite a lot of young men in drag on Saturday night, is in the back. The later you go here, the better. Beer costs the same as at the Café Timmy. Tuesday is lesbian night. The disco is open on Tuesday, Friday, and Saturday from 10pm to 3am, and on Thursday from 10pm to 1am. T-bana: Radsmangatan.

Admission: Disco, 60 kronor ($10.50) Fri–Sat, free Tues and Thurs.

11. EASY EXCURSIONS

Some of Sweden's best-known attractions are clustered around Lake Mälaren— centuries-old villages and castles (Uppsala and Gripsholm) that revive the pomp and glory of the 16th-century Vasa Dynasty.

A very busy day can be spent exploring Sigtuna, Skokloster Castle, Uppsala, and Gamla Uppsala, staying overnight in Sigtuna or Uppsala where there are good hotels. Another easy day trip is to Gripsholm Castle in Mariefred or Tullgarn Palace.

A popular route is to take the boat from Klara Stand in Stockholm at 9:45am, going along the beautiful waterway, Mälaren, and the Fyris River to Sigtuna for a 2-hour stop before arriving at Uppsala at 5 pm. There you can visit the magnificent cathedral and other interesting sights, dine, and return via train, a 45-minute trip. Trains run every hour until 11pm.

SIGTUNA

Founded at the beginning of the 11th century, Sigtuna, on the shores of Lake Mälaren, northwest of Stockholm, is Sweden's oldest town. Its **High Street (Stora Gatan)**, with its low timbered buildings, is thought to be the oldest street in Sweden that still follows its original route. Traces of Sigtuna's Viking and early Christian heritage can be seen throughout the town.

It abounds in church ruins, mostly from the 12th century. Chief among them is **St. Per's,** Sweden's first cathedral. The 13th-century **Monastery of St. Maria** is open to the public daily. The well-preserved **Town Hall** dates from the 18th century.

Wander the narrow streets, and if you have time, visit the **Sigtuna Fornhem,** the archeological museum, where artifacts that were found in and around Sigtuna, dating back to the early medieval period, can be viewed.

Founded near the turn of the century, the **Sigtuna Foundation** is a Lutheran retreat and cultural center, often frequented by writers and one of the reasons for Sigtuna's resurgence. It is open to the public daily from 1 to 3pm.

Daily buses and trains connect Stockholm to Sigtuna and Uppsala. From Stockholm take a train to Marsta, then a bus for the 10-minute ride to Sigtuna. In summer boats run from Klara Strand in Stockholm and from Uppsala to Sigtuna.

WHERE TO STAY & DINE

SIGTUNA STADSHOTELL, Stora Nygatan 3, S-193 00 Sigtuna. Tel. 0760/50-100. 27 rms (all with bath). TV TEL.

$ Rates (including breakfast): Sun–Thurs, 660 kronor ($115.25) single; 825 kronor ($144.05) double. Fri–Sat, 525 kronor ($91.65) single; 560 kronor ($97.80) double. MC, V.

This Victorian-style hotel in the town center is a traditional choice, with the most comfortable accommodations in town. Rooms have an old-fashioned style, but are well kept, clean, and inviting.

Full meals are served daily, with dinners going for 250 kronor ($43.65) à la carte. These might include Gorgonzola-flavored cream of morel soup, scallop of salmon with vermouth sauce, medallions of reindeer with juniper berries, and braised snow grouse in cream sauce with apples and Calvados—all topped off by warm cloudberry jam with strawberry ice cream. The restaurant is open from 11:30am to 10pm daily, with a fixed-price menu at 55 kronor ($9.60) offered Monday through Saturday from 11:30am to 3pm.

SIGTUNA FOUNDATION, Manfred Bjorkquists Allé 2-4, S-193 00 Sigtuna. Tel. 0760/51-610. 45 rms (none with bath).

$ Rates (including full board): 480 kronor ($83.80) for one, 720 kronor ($125.70) for two. No credit cards.

This can be one of your most memorable stopovers in Sweden—it's more a way of life than a hotel. The foundation was built to serve as a center where various sociological and philosophical viewpoints could be aired. Over the years, guest lecturers have included the Dalai Lama and an assortment of Indian gurus. The establishment fulfills a threefold function as a conference center, a school, and a guesthouse. If you show up, there will be no proselytizing. There are secluded courtyards, lush rose and herb gardens, fountains, and soundproof rooms built high in a tower. Some units are streamlined and modern; others, comfortably old-fashioned. Management prefers visitors to phone or write in advance so that a room can be guaranteed. The foundation is about a mile from the town center.

SKOKLOSTER CASTLE

Skokloster, Skokloster, S-198 00 Bålsta (tel. 018/38-60-77), is a splendid 17th-century castle and one of the most interesting baroque museums in Europe. It is located next to Lake Mälaren, 40 miles from Stockholm and 31 miles from Uppsala. With original interiors, the castle is noted for its rich collections of paintings, furniture, applied art, tapestries, arms, and books. Admission is 30 kronor ($5.25) for adults, 15 kronor ($2.60) for children, and it's open daily from May to September. You must view the castle on a guided tour, offered every hour from noon to 4pm.

The **Skokloster Motor Museum** (tel. 018/38-61-00) is on the palace grounds and contains the largest collection of vintage automobiles and motorcycles in the country. One of the most notable cars is a 1905 eight-horsepower De Dion Bouton. Unlike the castle, the museum is open all year. It costs 20 kronor ($3.50) for adults, 15 kronor ($2.60) for children. Open May to September, daily from 10am to 5pm; October to April, daily from 11am to 4pm.

UPPSALA

The major university city of Sweden, Uppsala, 42 miles northwest of Stockholm, is the most popular destination of day-trippers from Stockholm, and for good reason. Uppsala not only has a great university, but a celebrated 15th-century cathedral and a 16th-century castle. Even in the time of the Vikings, Uppsala was a religious center, the scene of animal and human sacrifices in honor of the old Norse gods and was once the center of royalty as well. Queen Christina occasionally held court here. The church is still the seat of the archbishop, and the first Swedish university was founded here in 1477.

The best time to be in Uppsala is on April 30, Walpurgis Eve, when academics celebrate the rebirth of spring with a torchlight parade and rollicking festivities lasting until dawn throughout the 13 student "nations" (residential halls).

The town is easily reached by train, in about 45 minutes from Stockholm's Central

Station. Trains leave about every hour during the peak daylight hours. Boats from Stockholm to Uppsala (or vice versa) also stop at Skokloster and Sigtuna. For details, check with the tourist office in any of these towns. Some visitors prefer to stay in Uppsala and take the commuter train back to Stockholm at the end of the day. If you have a Eurailpass, you ride free.

The **Tourist Information Center,** S:t Persgatan 4, Gamla Roget (tel. 018/11-75-00), is open daily year round (except Sunday in winter). From June to the end of August it closes at 7pm Monday through Saturday and at noon on Sunday; other months, at 6pm Monday through Friday and 2pm on Saturday.

The **Uppsala Student Reception Service** schedules frequent mixers and dances in the summer. Check with the tourist office for details.

Bus no. 700 follows **"the tourist trail,"** in Uppsala, leaving from the Central Station daily from June 25 to August 19 at 11am and 1pm. It is equipped with a recorded commentary in English, describing the places of interest en route. Trip time is 2 hours.

WHAT TO SEE & DO

UPPSALA DOMKYRKA, Domkyrkoplan 5. Tel. 018/18-72-01.

⭐ The largest cathedral in Scandinavia, this twin-spired Gothic structure, nearly 400 feet tall, was founded in the 13th century. It was severely damaged in 1702 in a disastrous fire that swept over Uppsala, then was restored near the turn of this century. Among the regal figures buried in the crypt is Gustavus Vasa. The remains of St. Erik, patron saint of Sweden, are entombed in a silver shrine. Botanist Linnaeus and philosopher-theologian Swedenborg are also buried here. A small museum displays ecclesiastical relics of Uppsala.

Admission: Cathedral, free; museum, 5 kronor (85¢) adults, 2 kronor (35¢) children.

Open: June–Aug, daily 8am–8pm; Sept–May, daily 8am–6pm. **Bus:** 1.

UPPSALA CASTLE, Nedre Slottsgatan. Tel. 018/14-48-10.

This 16th-century castle—founded by Gustavus Vasa in 1540—was the setting for one of the most memorable moments in Scandinavian history: the abdication of Queen Christina in 1654. It was badly damaged in the fire of 1702 and was partially restored in 1752 and 1816, but it never regained its original grandeur.

Admission: 10 kronor ($1.75).

Open: Late Apr to Sept, daily 11am–4pm. **Closed:** Oct to mid-Apr. **Directions:** Walk straight from the rail station along Bangårdsgatan and Slottsgränd.

LINNAEUS GARDEN AND MUSEUM, Svartbäcksgatan 27. Tel. 018/13-65-40.

The garden and former home of Swedish botanist Carolus Linneaus (sometimes known as Carl von Linné), who developed a classification system for the world's plants and flowers, is located on the spot where Uppsala University's first garden was laid out by Linnaeus, resembling a miniature baroque garden. Linnaeus, who arranged the plants according to his so-called sexual classification system, left detailed sketches and descriptions of the garden, which have been faithfully followed.

Linnaeus was professor of medicine and botany at Uppsala University. His house has been restored to its original design and may be visited. A summer art gallery exhibits contemporary local artists.

Admission: 10 kronor ($1.75).

Open: Gardens, May–Sept, daily 9am–9pm; townhouse museum, Tues–Sun 1–4pm. **Closed:** Oct.–Apr. **Directions:** Walk straight from the rail station to Kungsgatan, turn right, and walk for about 10 minutes to Svartbäcksgatan.

CAROLINA REDIVIVA (University Library), Drottninggatan. Tel. 018/18-39-00.

At the end of Drottninggatan is the Carolina Rediviva, with its more than three million volumes and 30,000 manuscripts, among them many rare works from the Middle Ages. But the one manuscript that draws the visitors is in the exhibition room of the library—the *Codex Argenteus* (Silver Bible), translated into the Old Gothic language in the middle of the 4th century in about A.D. 525. It is the only book extant in the Old Gothic script. Also worth seeing is *Carta Marina,* the earliest map (1539), a fairly accurate map of Sweden and its neighboring countries.

Admission: Free.

Open: Exhibition Room, June 16–Aug 15, Mon–Fri 9am–7:30pm, Sat 9am–5:30pm, Sun 1–3:30pm. **Closed:** Aug 16–June 15. **Bus:** 1.

An Excursion to Gamla Uppsala

About 15 centuries ago ☺ **Gamla Uppsala** was the capital of the Svea kingdom. In its midst was a sacrificial grove where both human and animal sacrifices were made. Viking burial mounds dating from the 6th century are believed to have contained the pyres of three kings.

Nearby, on the site of the old pagan temple, is a 12th-century parish church, once badly damaged by fire and never properly restored. Indeed, some people describe it as a stave church that has been turned into stone. Before Uppsala Cathedral was erected, Swedish kings were crowned here.

Across from the church is **Disagården,** an open-air museum with reassembled buildings depicting peasant life in Uppland. It's open from mid-May until the end of August, daily from 9am to 5pm. Tours are conducted Monday through Friday at 1 and 2pm and on Saturday and Sunday every hour on the hour from noon to 4pm. Admission is 20 kronor ($3.50).

Gamla Uppsala, about 2 miles north of Uppsala, is easily reached by bus no. 24, which leaves frequently from the Central Station.

WHERE TO STAY

To give Uppsala and its environs the attention they deserve, you'll have to spend the night. The hotels are adequate and much improved in recent years, but hotel prices are often lower in summer.

MODERATE

HOTEL LINNÉ, Skolgatan 45, S-750 02 Uppsala. Tel. 018/10-20-00. 117 rms (all with bath). MINIBAR TV TEL.

$ Rates (including breakfast): Aug 12–June 20, Sun–Thurs, 1,075 kronor ($187.70) single, 1,440 kronor ($251.45) double; Fri–Sat 720 kronor ($125.70) single, 920 kronor ($160.65) double. June 21–Aug 11, 560 kronor ($97.80) single; 820 kronor ($143.15) double. AE, DC, MC, V. **Parking:** Free.

This is one of the best-managed and most comfortable hotels in town. Rooms feature modern furniture and plumbing, and each unit contains a refrigerator. It's a good-value hotel, the only drawback being that the less expensive doubles are a bit cramped. The hotel has a bar and restaurant serving typically Scandinavian food. Free outdoor parking is available, and services include laundry facilities and room service. There is also a sauna. The hotel is at the edge of the Linnaeus Gardens.

HOTEL UPLANDIA, Dragarbrunnsgatan 32, S-751 40 Uppsala. Tel. 018/10-21-60. 133 rms (all with bath). MINIBAR TV TEL **Bus:** 801.

$ Rates (including breakfast): Winter weekdays, 1,210 kronor ($211.25) single; 1,500 kronor ($261.90) double. Summer and weekends year round, 570 kronor ($99.50) single; 790 kronor ($137.95) double. AE, DC, MC, V.

The best hotel in town offers clean and comfortably furnished bedrooms with such extras as a trouser press. A whirlpool and sauna are on the premises. On the lobby level is an elegant cocktail lounge, plus a spacious restaurant. Full meals, priced from 175 kronor ($30.55), are likely to include a mousse of shrimp and salmon, noisettes of veal with creamed leeks and red wine sauce, Alsatian sauerkraut, grilled meats, and a selection of all-vegetarian platters. The hotel is adjacent to the city's bus terminal.

SARA HOTEL GILLET, Dragarbrunnsgatan 23, S-751 42 Uppsala. Tel. 018/15-53-60. 169 rms (all with bath). A/C TV TEL **Bus:** 801.

$ Rates (including breakfast): Weekdays, 1,100 kronor ($192.05) single; 1,450 kronor ($253.15) double. Weekends, 520 kronor ($90.80) single; 820 kronor ($143.15) double. AE, DC, MC, V.

This attractively designed, first-class hotel has well-furnished, comfortable rooms, a breakfast room, and a cozy cocktail bar and lounge. Other facilities include a swimming pool and sauna. The Season is a top-rated restaurant serving fine meals, everything from international dishes to Swedish country food. It's open on Monday and Tuesday from 11:30am to 11pm, Wednesday through Saturday from 11:30am to 1am, and on Sunday from 12:30 to 9pm.

BUDGET

DIAKONISTIFTELSEN SAMARITERHEMMET, Hamnesplanaden 16, S-751 25 Uppsala. Tel. 018/17-71-80. 35 rms (12 with bath). **Bus:** 14, 22, 54.

$ Rates (including breakfast): 250 kronor ($43.65) single without bath, 300 kronor ($52.40) single with bath; 380 kronor ($66.35) double without bath, 480 kronor ($83.80) double with bath. No credit cards.

One of the best bargains in town, this large guesthouse has spotlessly maintained rooms, and you are allowed to use a kitchenette with a refrigerator. It is run by a Christian charity which is supported by gifts and donations. The house has a TV lounge. A good lunch is offered for just 42 kronor ($7.35).

WHERE TO DINE

RESTAURANT HALLEN, Saluhallen, Sankt Eriks Torg. Tel. 018/15-01-50.

Cuisine: SWEDISH/FRENCH. **Reservations:** Recommended.

$ Prices: Appetizers 66–116 kronor ($11.50–$20.25); main dishes 129–248 kronor ($22.55–$43.30). AE, DC, MC, V.

Open: Lunch Mon–Fri 11:30am–3pm; dinner Mon–Fri 6–11pm.

A walk through the city food market will prepare your palate for the specialties served here up a flight of stairs. Specialties include halibut with chantarelles and a truffle dressing, fried filet of reindeer with Roquefort sauce, and grilled entrecôte with a red wine sauce. Dessert might be pistachio ice cream with roasted pears or any of the tempting pastries.

DOMTRAPPKÄLLAREN, Sankt Eriksgränd 15. Tel. 018/32-11-32.

Cuisine: SWEDISH. **Reservations:** Recommended.

$ Prices: Appetizers 60–80 kronor ($10.50–$13.95); main dishes 120–200 kronor ($20.95–$34.90). AE, DC, MC, V.

Open: Lunch Mon–Fri 11am–3pm; dinner Mon–Sat 5–11pm.

There isn't another restaurant in Uppsala that can compete with this one for charm and atmosphere—it was built in the town center on the ruins of 12th-century cathedral buildings. The vaulted ceilings and copies of Jacobean paintings in the main dining room are complemented by the low-ceilinged, sun-flooded intimacy of the upper floors. If you request it, you can dine in a narrow room that imprisoned unruly students in the Middle Ages or in another that served as a classroom in the 17th century. The restaurant serves delectable salmon and reindeer and specializes in game. Salads are often exotic, including breast of pigeon with roasted nuts. For dessert, try the homemade chocolate cake. You might begin with fresh Scottish oysters served with lemon.

SLOTTSKÄLLEN, Svandammen. Tel. 018/11-15-10.

Cuisine: SWEDISH. **Reservations:** Recommended. **Bus:** 24.

$ Prices: Appetizers 53–100 kronor ($9.25–$17.45); main dishes 100–200 kronor ($17.45–$34.90). AE, DC, MC, V.

Open: Mon–Fri 11:30am–10pm, Sat–Sun 1–10pm.

Located on what used to be the king's bathhouse grounds in 1880, this restaurant is a trio of dining rooms lit by crystal chandeliers and lined with antique oil portraits.

Specialties include Swedish salmon with a cucumber sauce and grilled filet of beef. In autumn, game dishes appear on the menu. The salads are always well made and freshly prepared, and the dessert list is tempting.

RESTAURANT FLUSTRET, Svandammen. Tel. 018/13-01-14.
   Cuisine: FRENCH. **Reservations:** Recommended. **Bus:** 24.
$ Prices: Fixed-price menus 93–160 kronor ($16.25–$27.95); appetizers 50–80 kronor ($8.75–$13.95); main dishes 100–150 kronor ($17.45–$26.20). AE, DC, MC, V.
   Open: Dinner only, Tues–Sat 6–10pm.
In a riverside setting near the castle, this whimsical restaurant is an exact replica of the Victorian building that once stood here. Its spacious ground-floor dining room serves tasty meals, which might include salmon "boathouse style," fried scampi, veal steak Oscar, pepper steak, pheasant Véronique, lobster soup, and bananas flambé. Upstairs is a disco that charges 50 to 60 kronor ($8.75 to $10.50) admission and is open on weekends from 9:30pm to 2am.

EVENING ENTERTAINMENT

BAROWIAK TRÄDGÅRD & VERANDA, Svandammen. Tel. 018/12-40-30.
   One of the most popular youth-oriented nightspots in Uppsala, presenting some kind of live music at least three times a week. Food is served, and beer costs 39 to 50 kronor ($6.80 to $8.75). Open Wednesday through Saturday from 6 to 9pm and on Sunday from 6pm to midnight. Bus: 24.
   Admission: 50 kronor ($8.75) for live performance.

GRIPSHOLM CASTLE

On an island in Lake Mälaren, Gripsholm Castle, (tel. 0159/101-94)—the fortress built by Gustavus Vasa in the late 1530s—is one of the best-preserved castles in Sweden, near Mariefred, an idyllic small town known for its vintage narrow-gauge railroad. The castle is 38 miles from Stockholm, easily reached by driving along the E3 south or taking the subway from central Stockholm to Liljeholmen, and boarding bus no. 40 which leaves every hour for Mariefred. In Stockholm, boats also leave mid-May to September at 10am from Stadhuset, the Klara Malarstrand Pier. The castle is a 5-minute walk from the center of Mariefred.
   During the reign of the 18th-century actor-king Gustavus III a theater was built at Gripsholm, but the outstanding feature of the castle is its large collection of portrait paintings.
   Even though Gripsholm was last occupied by royalty in 1864 (Charles XV), it is still considered a royal castle. It's open May to the end of August, daily from 10am to 4pm; in March, April, September, and October, Tuesday through Friday from 10am to 3pm and on Saturday and Sunday from noon to 3pm; November to February, only on Saturday and Sunday from noon to 3pm. Admission is 25 kronor ($4.35) for adults, 10 kronor ($1.75) for children.

WHERE TO STAY

GRIPSHOLMS VÄRDHUS & HOTEL, Kyrkogatan 1, S-647 00 Mariefred. Tel. 0159/130-20. 30 rms (all with bath), 15 suites. A/C MINIBAR TV TEL.
$ Rates (including breakfast): Winter Mon–Thurs and summer, 1,250 kronor ($218.25) single; 1,650 kronor ($288.10) double. Fri–Sun year round, 920 kronor ($160.65) single; 1,260 kronor ($220) double. Suites from 2,000 kronor ($349.20). AE, DC, MC, V.
   Originally built as an inn in 1609, making it among the oldest in Sweden, this building was restored and reopened in 1989, becoming the most stylish and charming hotel in the region. It's a few steps from the village church, in the center of Mariefred, a 10-minute walk from the castle. Each bedroom is individually decorated and furnished with a mixture of antiques and contemporary pieces. Walls

and ceiling decors are painted in the old style. Amenities include sucn thoughtful extras as a bathrobe, hairdryer, and a bathroom with heated floors and towel racks.

Dining/Entertainment: The hotel has the best restaurant in the region (see "Where to Dine," below) as well as a pub for less formal meals. It keeps the same hours as the restaurant and serves platters of homemade Swedish cooking for 80 to 120 kronor ($13.95 to $20.95).

Services: Room service.

Facilities: Solarium, massage room, recreation center, sauna, copper tub for ice baths, public bar.

WHERE TO DINE

GRIPSHOLMS VÄRDHUS RESTAURANT, Kyrkogatan 1. Tel. 0159/ 130-20.

Cuisine: FRENCH/SWEDISH. **Reservations:** Recommended. in the center, a few steps from the village church, a 10-minute walk from the castle.

$ **Prices:** Fixed-price menu 365 kronor ($63.75); appetizers 86–148 kronor ($15–$25.85); main dishes 165–240 kronor ($28.80–$41.90). AE, DC, MC, V.

Open: Lunch Mon–Fri 11:30am–3pm; dinner Mon–Fri 6–10pm, Sat 1–11pm, Sun 1–6pm.

⭐ Traditional Swedish food and local game dishes are served along with an international cuisine at this elegantly appointed restaurant. The main dining room has an adjoining veranda opening onto Gripsholm Bay. Tastings can be arranged in the wine cellar. The menu changes according to the season, but is likely to include such dishes as mousse of wild grouse with port wine jelly and lingonberries, marinated salmon with a mild mustard sauce, or breast of wood pigeon braised in port (served with a sauce of wild berries and apple chutney).

TULLGARN PALACE

The royal castle (tel. 0755/720-11), begun in 1719 in a beautiful setting on a bay of the Baltic Sea, was the favorite of Gustavus V (1858–1950), the great-grandfather of Sweden's present king. The well-kept interiors are from the late 19th century. Admission is 25 kronor ($4.35) for adults, 10 kronor ($1.75) for children. The palace is open to the public from May 15 to September 15. Guided tours leave the main entrance every hour from 11am to 4pm.

It lies 37 miles south of Stockholm. If you are driving, take the E4 south about 37 miles and follow the sign to the right directing you to Tullgarns Slott, near Vagnhärad. It's another quarter of a mile to the palace. Or take the Blue Train from the Central Station in Stockholm to Södertälje Södra, (about 20 minutes), and catch a bus to Trosa.

For lunch or dinner, the **Tullgarns Värdhus,** in Vagnhärad (tel. 0755/720-26), offers Swedish/French meals for 215 kronor ($37.55). It's open May 15 to September 15, Monday through Friday from noon to 2pm and 5 to 7pm and on Saturday and Sunday from noon to 7pm. Located in a wing of Tullgarn Palace, this inn offers three-course lunches or dinners. You can sample such dishes as salted salmon with creamed potatoes, an old Swedish specialty, or perhaps pâté of wild boar. You can also order breast of wild duck with a mousse of chicken liver or poached filet of salmon with a chive-flavored butter sauce.

You can also order a picnic lunch and eat in the royal park. Picnics of cold chicken or roast beef, with beer or coffee, in a take-away basket or a cup of coffee with a sandwich, can be ordered at the inn daily from 11am to 5pm. MC, V.

SANDHAMN & VAXÖN & THE ARCHIPELAGO OF STOCKHOLM

Stockholm is in what the Swedes call a garden of skerries, more than 24,000 islands (including some rocks jutting out of the water). The islands nearest to Stockholm have become part of the suburbs, thickly populated and connected to the mainland by car-ferries or bridges, but many are still wild and largely deserted, attracting those who can boat out to them for picnics and swimming. Summer homes dot some of the islands. July is the peak vacation month, when yachts crowd the waters.

You can see the islands by taking a boat trip from Stockholm harbor. For a stopover at one of the resorts, consider **Sandhamn,** where you will find shops, restaurants, and a hotel. The entire island takes about an hour to explore on foot. The beaches at the eastern tip are the best in the archipelago. **Vaxholm,** a bathing resort on the island of Vaxön, sometimes called "the gateway to the northern archipelago," with full tourist facilities also makes a good stopover. Many artists and writers have traditionally been drawn to Vaxholm, and some hold exhibitions during the summer when the population quadruples as tourists throng into town. The west harbor and the main sea route north are filled with pleasure craft.

Throughout the year (but much more frequently in summer), boats operated by several different companies depart from in front of the Grand Hotel at Södra Blasieholmshamnen. Most of them are labeled Vaxholm, although boats often continue to Sandhamn after a stopover in Vaxholm. Be sure to ask before boarding.

The trip to Sandhamn takes 3 hours one way and costs 65 kronor ($11.35), while going to Vaxholm takes only 35 minutes one way and costs 25 kronor ($4.35). Vaxholm-bound boats depart every hour in summer and about five times a day in winter. For information, call the Vaxholm steamship company, **Vaxholmes Bolaget** (tel. 08/14-08-30).

Buses to Vaxholm (nos. 670, 671, 672, and 673) often (but not always) go on to Sandhamn. They depart from the East Railway Station every 30 minutes beginning at 6am. The last bus from Vaxholm leaves at 1am. A one-way ticket costs 20 kronor ($3.50).

WHERE TO STAY

In Vaxholm

VAXHOLM HOTEL, S-185 00 Vaxholm. Tel. 0764/301-50. 32 rms (all with bath). TV TEL.

$ Rates: Sun–Thurs (including breakfast), 900 kronor ($157.15) single; 1,150 kronor ($200.80) double. Fri–Sat (including half board), 725 kronor ($126.60) single; 1,250 kronor ($218.25) double. AE, DC, MC, V.

Built in 1900, this stone hotel, painted a bright yellow, offers comfortably furnished bedrooms with modern furnishings. Its summer disco is open on Wednesday, Friday, and Saturday from 9pm to 2am, charging a cover of 60 kronor ($10.50). An informal pub, Kabyssen, is at street level. One floor above is the Vaxholm Hotel Restaurant (see "Where to Dine," below). It's directly at the pier where the ferryboats from Stockholm dock.

In Sandhamn

HOTEL SANDHAMN, S-130 39 Sandhamn. Tel. 0766/530-03. 20 rms (none with bath).

$ Rates (including breakfast): 460 kronor ($80.30) single; 600 kronor ($104.75) double. AE, DC, MC, V.

The hotel has been enlarged over the years, expanding from its original 1880 single-story core into the larger, several-story building you see today in the center, a 1-minute walk south of the ferryboat dock. Entire families used to come down from Stockholm to spend several weeks here in summer in the comfortably old-fashioned bedrooms. The hotel serves breakfast only on an outdoor terrace, but light snacks can be ordered later.

WHERE TO DINE

In Vaxholm

VAXHOLM HOTEL RESTAURANT, Vaxholm. Tel. 0764/301-50.
Cuisine: SEAFOOD. **Reservations:** Required in summer.

$ Prices: Appetizers 38–85 kronor ($6.65–$14.85); main dishes 65–200 kronor ($11.35–$34.90). AE, DC, MC, V.

Open: Summer, Mon–Sat 11:30am–10:30pm, Sun noon–9pm; winter, daily 11:30am–9pm.

This restaurant, opening onto a view of the water directly at the pier where the ferryboats from Stockholm dock, is the best place to dine in Vaxholm. When queried, the chef said his specialties are "fish, fish, fish." The uncompromising house specialty is a platter of pan-fried Swedish herring served with mashed potatoes. It is also the best buy in the restaurant.

In Sandhamn

SANDHAMNS VÄRDHUS, Sandhamn. Tel. 0766/530-51.

Cuisine: SWEDISH. **Reservations:** Not required.

$ Prices: Appetizers 35–85 kronor ($6.10–$14.85); main dishes 85–155 kronor ($14.85–$27.05). AE, DC, MC, V.

Open: Sun–Thurs noon–10pm, Fri–Sat noon–11pm.

The favorite restaurant of the island locals, established in 1672. It opens onto a view of the moored boats on the harborfront. You can always get a good and reasonably priced meal here by selecting one of the fish dishes or the local choice, steak with red onions. Dinners are cozy affairs.

DALARNA, VÄRMLAND & CENTRAL SWEDEN .

T wo provinces in the heart of Sweden's southern region represent the soul of this Scandinavian nation. In the province of Dalarna lies Lake Siljan, and in Värmland, farther south, is Lake Vänern, the third-largest inland sea in Europe.

Dalarna is the most traditional of all the provinces—replete with everything from maypole dancing and fiddlers' music, to folk costumes and handcrafts, including the Dala horse. Dalarna means valleys, and you'll sometimes see it referred to as Dalecarlia, the Anglicized form of the name.

Lake Siljan, maybe the most beautiful lake in Europe, is ringed with resort villages and towns. Leksand, Tällberg, and Rättvik attract visitors during summer with sports, folklore, and a week of music. In winter, people come here for skiing.

Karlstad, on the shores of Lake Vänern, makes an ideal stopover for exploring the province of Värmland. Lake Vänern is 87 miles long and 46 miles across at its widest point. Among its chief waterways are the Göta River and the Göta Canal. A smaller body of water, Lake Vättern, lies to the east of Vänern.

Anytime is ripe for a visit to Dalarna, but during midsummer, June 23 to June 26, the Dalecarlians celebrate the custom of maypole dancing. At that time they race through the forest gathering birch bows and nosegays of wildflowers with which they cover the maypole. Then the pole is raised and they dance around it—under the midsummer-lit sky—until dawn, a good old respectable pagan custom.

The quickest and easiest way to reach this province is by train from the Central Station in Stockholm, a 4½-hour trip. All the towns below have good rail connections with each other. Motorists from Oslo can stop over in Dalarna before venturing on to the Swedish capital. Similarly, visitors to Gothenburg can head north to both Värmland and Dalarna before seeing Stockholm. Our first stopover could also be a day's excursion from Stockholm.

SEEING DALARNA, VÄRMLAND & CENTRAL SWEDEN

GETTING THERE

By car is the best way, as you can see more of the scenery, including a drive along the road between Vadstena and Jönköping, which is spectacular as it winds along the eastern shore of Lake Vättern. If you want to see the area in a hurry, and are dependent on public transportation, you can fly to Mora and use it as a center for exploring Dalarna, or fly from Stockholm to Karlstad and use that city as a base for exploring the Värmland district. Both Karlstad and Mora also have good rail

WHAT'S SPECIAL ABOUT DALARNA, VÄRMLAND & CENTRAL SWEDEN

Great Towns/Villages

☐ Tällberg, the most genuine tourist village in Dalarna, overlooking Lake Siljan.

☐ Karlstad, capital of Värmland, lying at the point where the Klaralven River enters Lake Vänern.

☐ Vadstena, an important town from the Middle Ages with a beautiful Renaissance castle.

Castles

☐ Vadstena Castle, founded by Gustavus Vasa, king of Sweden in 1545, one of the most splendid of the Renaissance Vasa castles.

☐ Läckö Castle, founded in the 13th century, containing 250 rooms; stands on an island in Lake Vänern.

Abbeys/Churches

☐ Habo Church, near Lake Vättern, an old barn-red frame church from 1721.

☐ Vadstena Abbey Church, built between the mid-14th century and the 15th, launched by Saint Bridget of Sweden and rich in medieval art.

Literary Shrines

☐ Marbacka, the former home of Selma Lagerlöf, 1909 Nobel Prize winner, known for her *The Saga of Gösta Berling*.

☐ Rottneros Manor, the Ekeby in the saga of Lagerlöf, outside Sunne.

Special Events/Festivals

☐ Music at Lake Siljan, the first week of July, Sweden's biggest music festival; lots of fiddling.

☐ The 50-mile Vasa Race, a major ski event of Sweden in March at Mora in Upper Dalarna.

---

connections from Stockholm. Many visitors see a "nutshell" preview of central Sweden by taking the Göta Canal trip (see "Organized Tours," in Chapter 25).

A SUGGESTED ITINERARY

Day 1: From Stockholm, head to Leksand for your first night, the best "gateway" to Dalarna.

Day 2: Visit Tällberg and Rättvik en route to Mora for another night.

Day 3–4: From Mora, drive south along Route 234 to Karlstad. Spend the following day exploring sights in the environs, including the manors associated with Selma Lagerlöf.

Day 5: From Karlstad, head southwest along Route 45, cutting east again on Route 44 for Lidköping. This takes you along the western shore of Lake Vänern. Overnight in Lidköping and, depending on your time, explore Läckö Castle then or see it the following morning.

Day 6: Connect with the E3 east, but turn south at the junction of Route 50 to Vadstena for an overnight stopover. From Vadstena, the nearby E4 express highway returns you to Stockholm, after you've traversed the historic "tourist trail" through central Sweden.

---

1. FALUN

303 miles east of Gothenburg, 142 miles west of Stockholm

GETTING THERE   By Train   Direct trains from Stockholm take 3 hours, and trains in the west from Gothenburg take 6 hours. Several trains run daily in both directions.

By Bus Buses from Stockholm service Falun once a day Friday through Sunday. For information in Stockholm, call **Varsatrafik** at 08/771-10-80. Buses from Gothenburg, although the distance is greater, arrive three times daily but make frequent stops along the way. These buses, run by **Swebus,** can be called in Gothenburg at 031/71-80-90.

By Car From Stockholm, take the E18 expressway northwest to the junction with Route 70. From there, continue to the junction with Route 60, where you head northeast.

ESSENTIALS For information, go to the **Tourist Office,** Storatorget (tel. 023/83-314). The **telephone area code** for Falun is 023.

The old capital of Dalarna, Falun lies on both sides of the Falu River. This town is noted for its copper mines, the income from which supported many a Swedish king. Just 6½ miles northeast, you can visit the home of the famed Swedish painter Carl Larsson (1853–1919).

WHAT TO SEE & DO

You might go first to the market square, Stora Torget, and view the **Kristine Church,** a copper-roofed structure dating from the mid-17th century (the tower dates from 1865).

Falun is the site of one of the country's largest sports complexes, **Lugnet.** Here you can find Falun's famous ski jump and the largest sports hall in Scandinavia. Alpine skiers can enjoy the slopes at the Bjursberget ski resort, only 12½ miles from Falun.

FALUN COPPER MINE, Gruvplatsen. Tel. 158-25.

This copper mine, now in the town center, was the world's largest producer of copper during the 17th century, and supplied the raw material for the roof of Versailles. The mine tour begins with an elevator trip 180 feet below the surface. Guides take you through old chambers and winding passages dating from the Middle Ages. In one section of the mine you'll see a shaft divided by a timber wall more than 650 feet high, possibly the world's highest wooden structure.

Admission: 40 kronor ($7) adults, 15 kronor ($2.60) children under 18.

Open: May–Aug, daily 10am–4:30pm; Sept–Nov 15 and Mar–Apr, Sat–Sun 12:30–4:30pm. **Closed:** Nov 16–Feb.

CARL LARSSON-GÅRDEN, Carl Larssons Väg 12, Sundborn. Tel. 600-53.

A short 20-minute trip from Falun will take you to Sundborn, a small village whose main claim to fame is Lilla Hyttnas, Carl Larsson's home, now known as Carl Larsson-gården. Larsson became Sweden's most admired artist during his lifetime. Through his watercolors, this house has become known throughout Sweden. There are guided tours throughout the day, and English-language tours are sometimes available.

Public buses leave from the Falun bus station several times a day, dropping visitors in Sundborn, 5 minutes away from Carl Larsson-gården. Sundborn is a 4-hour train ride from Stockholm.

Admission: 35 kronor ($6.10) adults, 10 kronor ($1.75) children.

Open: May–Sept, Mon–Sat 10am–5pm, Sun and hols. 1–5pm. **Closed:** Oct–Apr. **Bus:** 64 from Falun.

WHERE TO STAY & DINE

SARA GRAND HOTEL, Trotzgatan 9-11, S-791 71 Falun. Tel. 023/187-00. Fax 023/141-43. 183 rms (all with bath), 1 suite. TV TEL.

$ Rates (including breakfast): July and Fri–Sat year round, 420 kronor ($73.35) single; 580 kronor ($101.25) double. June and Aug, 580 kronor ($101.25) single or double. Sun–Thurs Sept–May, 1,000–1,240 kronor ($174.60–$215.60) single; 1,395 kronor ($243.55) double; from 1,400 kronor ($244.45) suite. AE, DC, MC, V.

This buff-colored hotel 100 yards south of the landmark Falun Church was built in the late 19th century, and a modern addition was constructed in 1974. The whole complex was renovated in the 1980s so that the bedrooms, featuring a tasteful modern or Chippendale-inspired decor, are among the best decorated and most comfortable in town. Ask about summer reductions, which tend to be substantial. About 23 of the bedrooms have a minibar. On the premises are a small indoor pool, a piano bar, a sauna, and a restaurant, where there's dance music twice a week.

HOTEL BERGMÄSTAREN, Bergskolegränd S-791 26 Falun. Tel. 023/ 636-00. 89 rms (all with bath). TV TEL.

$ Rates (including breakfast): Summer and Fri–Sat year round, 360 kronor ($62.85) single; 480 kronor ($83.80) double. Sun–Thurs in winter, 760 kronor ($132.70); 940 kronor ($164.10) double. AE, DC, MC, V.

Sweden's first government-owned liquor store was in this building, and the hotel isn't allowed to remove the sign SYSTEMBOLAG (liquor store in English), set in stone. The hotel, refurbished in 1985, is small and cozy, and its rooms, for the most part, are decorated in a typical Dalarna style with antique furnishings and traditional trappings. In summer, it is a breakfast-only hotel, but in winter, a smörgåsbord is served nightly for 95 kronor ($16.60), including both hot and cold dishes, a selection of cheese and desserts, including bread and beverage. It is extremely good value. Facilities include a sauna and solarium. It's in the town center.

2. LEKSAND

166 miles NW of Stockholm, 322 miles NE of Gothenburg

GETTING THERE By Plane The nearest airport is **Dala-Airport,** in Börlange, 36 miles away, from which there is frequent bus and train service to Leksand. Car rentals are available at the airport.

By Train There is a direct line from Stockholm to Mora that stops in Leksand; travel time is 3½ hours. For reservations and information, call 0247/101-15.

By Bus Express buses run from Gothenburg to Gävle and Falun, stopping at Börlange, where bus and rail connections can be made to Leksand; total travel time is 8 hours. To reserve a ticket, call 0243/270-50.

By Boat One major boat, *Gustaf Wasa,* runs regularly on short tours and cruises, making one long trip from Mora to Leksand at 10am on Friday, going via Rättvik. One-way fare is 90 kronor ($15.70) per passenger, and tickets are sold on board. Call 010/52-32-92 for information and reservations.

By Car From Stockholm, take the E18 express highway northwest to the junction of Route 70, which continues northwest all the way to Leksand.

ESSENTIALS For more information, contact the **Leksands Turistbyrå Norsgatan** (tel. 0247/803-00). The **telephone area code** for Leksand is 0247.

SPECIAL EVENTS Sweden's biggest music festival, **Music at Lake Siljan,** takes place during the first week of July. It consists of some 100 concerts covering a wide range of music at venues in both Leksand and Rättvik. Much of it is folk music, "the meeting of the fiddlers." For information, write Music at Lake Siljan, Box 28, S-795 00 Rättvik (tel. 0248/102-90).

Leksands Noret, as it is called, is a doorway to Lake Siljan, and no less an authority than Hans Christian Andersen found the setting idyllic. Leksand—in its present form—dates back to around the turn of the century, when it was reconstructed after a fire had razed the settlement. But a settlement of some sort has been on this site since pagan times.

Many of the old traditions of the province still flourish here. Women still don traditional dress for church on Sunday and in June and July the long "church boats" from Viking times may cross the lake carrying parish residents to church. These same boats compete in a church-boat race on the first Sunday in July. Since World War II a miracle play, *The Road to Heaven*, has been presented in open-air performances, providing an insight into the customs and folklore of Dalarna. The play runs for 10 days at the end of July.

WHAT TO SEE & DO

The **parish church** with its onion-shaped dome was founded in the 13th century. Near the lakeside church is an open-air **museum** with several buildings dating from the 18th and 19th centuries. Examples of peasant art can be seen at the museum, where 18th- and 19th-century artists depict Christ and his Apostles in Dalarna dress. You can also visit a glass-blowing factory and several handcraft shops.

Sports is a major pursuit in Leksand, and several tracks for walking and skiing start from here. Downhill skiing facilities are located at Karingberget and Asleden, less than 4 miles away. Other skiing facilities include electrically lit cross-country tracks. A sports center has a swimming pool, sauna, skating rink, and curling hall, and tennis and miniature golf are available when the weather is right for them.

Visitors who want to hook up with one of the **boat trips** around Lake Siljan or go on a tour of the province should stop at the tourist bureau for information.

WHERE TO STAY

During the summer, you might find it fun to rent a *stuga* (log cabin) with four beds for 250 kronor ($43.65) per night. The **Leksands Turistbyrå** office, Box 52, S-793 01 Leksand (tel. 0247/803-00), will book you into one. You can also inquire about renting a room in a private home.

MOSKOGEN MOTEL, S-793 00 Leksand. Tel. 0247/146-00. Fax 0247/ 144-30. 60 rms (all with bath). TV TEL.

$ Rates (including breakfast): 480 kronor ($83.80) single; 720 kronor ($125.70) double. MC, V.

Termed "a self-service holiday village," this motel of red-painted wood-sided huts makes a good base for excursions into the Lake Siljan environs. Bedrooms are well furnished and comfortable. Accommodations contain a tiny kitchen, TV, shower, toilet, and phone. A restaurant on the premises sells simple lunches and dinners. Facilities include a Jacuzzi, sauna, solarium, and gym room. The Moskogen is a mile west from the railway station.

HOTEL KORSTÄPPAN, Hjörtnasvagen 33, S-793 00 Leksand. Tel. 0247/100-37. Fax 0247/141-78. 32 rms (all with bath). TV.

$ Rates (including breakfast): June 15–Aug 15, 285 kronor ($49.75) single; 375 kronor ($65.50) double. Aug 16–June 14, 385–435 kronor ($67.20–$75.95) single; 700 kronor ($122.20) double. AE, DC, MC, V.

This yellow building beside the lake, half a mile east of the railway station, was originally constructed in 1906. The Blomgren family, the owners, live in one of the two annexes on the property; the other contains seven of the hotel's bedrooms. Each room is pleasantly old-fashioned, with serviceable furnishings. The owner's three sons take turns at cooking in the hotel restaurant, which is open daily from noon to 10:30pm. The house specialty is fresh fried herring served with mashed potatoes. At lunch a daily platter costs 85 kronor ($14.85), and at dinner a three-course fixed-price menu goes for 110 kronor ($19.20).

WHERE TO DINE

BOSPOREN, Torget 1. Tel. 132-80.
   Cuisine: SWEDISH. **Reservations:** Not required.
$ **Prices:** Appetizers 45–65 kronor ($7.85–$11.35); main dishes 85–140 kronor ($14.85–$24.45); lunch specials 48–68 kronor ($8.40–$11.85). AE, DC, MC, V.
   Open: Daily 11am–11pm.
This restaurant, 600 yards west of the railroad station, was given its Istanbul-derived name by its Turkish-born owners, who maintain longer and more reliable hours than any other place in town. In spite of the name, the cuisine is traditionally Swedish. The food is good and is enjoyed by more locals than visitors. Dishes include many types of fresh fish, wienerschnitzel, and fish Waleska. You might begin in summer with a fresh tomato salad or liver pâté on toast.

OLD CURTIS INN, Norsagatan 21. Tel. 105-70.
   Cuisine: SWEDISH. **Reservations:** Not required.
$ **Prices:** Appetizers 49–55 kronor ($8.55–$9.60); main dishes 59–119 kronor ($10.30–$20.80).
   Open: Tues 5–8pm, Wed–Thurs 5pm–midnight, Fri 3pm–1am, Sat noon–1am, Sun 1pm–midnight.
One floor above street level, this restaurant in the center, across the street from the town's only liquor store, is over its companion establishment, the town's most popular pub, where a large glass of Swedish beer costs 35 kronor ($6.10). The house containing these places dates from the 1920s, and the atmosphere is decidedly casual, perhaps too much so for some tastes. The fare is simple, including fish and chips, steak, and roast chicken.

3. TÄLLBERG

8 miles north of Leksand, 174 miles west of Stockholm,
322 miles NE of Gothenburg

GETTING THERE   By Train   Trains from Gothenburg require about 7 hours, with a change in Börlange. There are direct trains daily from Stockholm, but with many stopovers (trip time is 3½ hours). Trains also make the 10-minute run between Leksand and Tällberg.

By Bus   There is no direct bus service from Stockholm or Gothenburg. Bus passengers get off at either Leksand or Rättvik, where local bus connections can be made.

By Car   Take the E18 expressway northwest from Stockholm, then turn onto Route 70 toward Börlange and drive all the way to Tällberg, a 3-hour drive.

ESSENTIALS   For **information,** the Leksand Tourist Office handles queries (see above). The **telephone area code** for Tällberg is 0247.

This lakeside village, charmingly in tune with the spirit and tradition of Dalarna, is my favorite spot in the whole province, and the area of choice for nature lovers in both summer and winter. Skiing, curling, skating, and sleigh rides are popular sports, and swimming and boating lure summer visitors.
   Tällberg's beauty was discovered after artists and other cultural celebrities built summer houses in the village. One of the artists created **Holens Gammelgård** (farmstead), which later became the center of the Dalarna folklore movement. The old farmhouse of **Ankarcrona** is now a summer museum, located at the highest point of Tällberg, with a superb view over Lake Siljan.

WHERE TO STAY & DINE
EXPENSIVE

ÅKERBLADS I TÄLLBERG, S-793 03 Tällberg. Tel. 0247/508-00. Fax
0247/506-52. 36 rms (all with bath), 15 mini-suites. TV TEL.
$ Rates (including breakfast): 640 kronor ($111.75) single; 920 kronor ($160.65)
double; from 1,290 kronor ($225.25) mini-suite. Special weekend discounts
Sept–May. AE, DC, MC, V.

An old-fashioned family hotel since 1910, this establishment is 1¼ miles from
Tällberg station at the crossroads leading down to Lake Siljan. The core of the house is
still the wooden storehouse in the courtyard, but there has been much rebuilding over
the years, including a recent addition of 15 mini-suites with complete baths, TVs, and
minibars. All the rooms at the hotel are done in an attractive Dala style. A massage
pool, sauna, solarium, and tennis court are some of the features. During the winter,
sleigh rides are arranged and guests return to a log fire and hot mulled and spiced
wine. Bicycles are also available for free.

The hotel restaurant is known for its "grandmother's good cooking," buffets, and
homemade bread. There is also a replica of an old pub where you can get a drink or a
cheap pub lunch.

MODERATE

GREEN HOTEL, S-793 03 Tällberg. Tel. 0247/502-50. Fax 0247/501-30.
101 rms (all with bath). TEL.
$ Rates (including full board): 660–1,975 kronor ($115.25–$344.85) single;
1,120–2,300 kronor ($195.55–$401.60) double. MC, V.

This hotel, whose wide array of rooms ranges from budget to VIP, is located on a
lawn sloping down toward the lake half a mile west of the railway station. The staff
wear regional costumes, and the lounge has a notable art collection. On the premises
are five saunas and a swimming pool whose surface is covered every Saturday night
with a glass top and converted to a dance floor. Open all year, the hotel offers an array
of summer and winter sports. A few of the more luxurious bedrooms have their own
fireplaces and private saunas, and some contain a TV. The hotel has a restaurant and
bar.

HOTEL KLOCKAREGÅRDEN, S-793 03 Tällberg. Tel. 0247/502-60. Fax
0247/502-16. 36 rms (all with bath). TV TEL.
$ Rates (including breakfast): 650 kronor ($113.50) single; 1,100 kronor ($192.05)
double. AE, DC, MC, V.

Off Route 70 in the center of town, most of the accommodations of this 1959 hotel
are in 20 old timber cottages. Most units contain radio, TV, and phone. Each room is
individually styled with traditional motifs, and many of the accommodations are
virtual suites, with balcony, open fireplace, private sauna, a Jacuzzi, and other
amenities. Music, folk dancing, and theme evenings are presented, as well as art and
handcraft exhibitions. An excellent Swedish cuisine is served.

INEXPENSIVE

LÅNGBERG, Toppen i Tällberg, S-793 03 Tällberg. Tel. 0247/502-90. Fax
0247/505-60. 52 rms (all with bath). TEL.
$ Rates (including breakfast): 360 kronor ($62.85) single; 690 kronor ($120.45)
double. AE, DC, MC, V.

At 1,000 feet above sea level, on a hillside overlooking the town half a mile west
of the railroad station, this hotel offers a fine view of Lake Siljan and its
surroundings. Rooms are equally divided between the original hotel, built
around 1930, and a newer annex erected in 1980 in basically the same architectural
style. The buildings are set about 25 yards apart, and each has a view. The better and
more charming rooms are the older ones because of their larger size, higher ceilings,

and old-fashioned charm. The newer rooms are still very comfortable, furnished in a Nordic modern. There is a sauna on the premises, plus a restaurant offering fixed-price lunches for 100 kronor ($17.45) and dinners for 260 kronor ($45.40).

BUDGET

SILJANSGÅRDEN, S-793 03 Tällberg. Tel. 0247/500-40. 28 rms (16 with bath), 10 cottages. TEL.

$ Rates (including breakfast): Hotel, 280 kronor ($48.90) single without bath; 350–425 kronor ($61.30–$74.20) double without bath; 560–720 kronor ($97.80–$125.70) double with bath. Cottages, 240 kronor ($41.90) per person. DC, MC, V.

Originally built in 1915, this charming, rustic, timber-sided hotel stands on 12 acres on the shores of the lake 1 mile west of the railroad station. On the grounds is a bathing beach, a tennis court, a rowboat, a minigolf course, and a sauna. The hotel bedrooms are simply furnished but comfortable and, in addition, some rustic cottages are rented, suitable for up to four occupants, which make them a family favorite. A restaurant in the main building is licensed for beer and wine only, serving a one-course lunch for 65 kronor ($11.35) and a three-course dinner for 120 kronor ($20.95). In spite of the winter snows, the hotel is open all year, although the cottages are available only in summer. Private phones are available only in the hotel rooms. Cottage renters bring their own sheets and sleeping bags, although sheets can be rented from management.

---

4. RÄTTVIK

13 miles from Leksand, 31 miles east of Mora, 171 miles NW of Stockholm

GETTING THERE   By Train   Three to five trains a day make the 30-minute run between Mora and Rättvik. Rättvik also has rail lines to Leksand; trip time is also 30 minutes.

By Bus   Daily buses run between Mora and Rättvik and Leksand and Rättvik, taking 40 minutes.

By Car   From Stockholm, take the E18 express highway northwest, reaching the junction with Route 70 where you should continue northwest all the way to Rättvik.

ESSENTIALS   For **information,** contact Leksand Turistbyrå (see above). The **telephone area code** for Rättvik is 0248.

Rättvik is one of the most popular resorts bordering Lake Siljan, which has some of the best hotels in the district. In summer there are conducted tours around Lake Siljan from here. Culture and tradition are always associated with Rättvik—peasant costumes, folk dancing, Dalarna paintings, arts and crafts, "church boats," and fiddle music. There's an expression: "If you meet two men from Rättvik, three of them will be fiddlers." The old style of architecture is still alive, and you will find many timber houses. Carpenters and painters from Rättvik are known for their craftsmanship.

WHAT TO SEE & DO

For a view over the area, go to the top of the old wooden tower at **Vidablick** (tel. 100-13), about 3 miles out of town on the road to Falun.

One mile from the village is **Gammelgården** (tel. 114-45), an old Dalarna farmstead. It is open mid-June to mid-August, Monday through Saturday from 11am to 6pm and on Sunday from 2:30 to 6pm. Guided tours are conducted at 1 and 3pm. Admission is 10 kronor ($1.75).

If you're interested in art, you can visit the artists' village at **Rättviks Hantverksby,** Gårdebyn (tel. 302-50), established by the Swedish artist Sören Erikson. Children can take a ride on a miniature train.

WHERE TO STAY

SCANDIC ACTIVE HOTEL, S-795 00 Rättvik. Tel. 0248/111-50. Fax
0248/111-77. 95 rms (all with bath), 1 suite. TV TEL **Bus:** 58, 70.

$ Rates (including breakfast): Midsummer, 625 kronor ($109.15) single; 740 kronor
($129.20) double. Winter Fri–Sat 440 kronor ($76.80) single; 540 kronor ($94.30)
double. Winter Sun–Thurs, 800 kronor ($139.70) single; 945 kronor ($165)
double. AE, DC, MC, V.

Near the top of a hill overlooking Rättvik, a 10-minute walk north from the lake, this
hotel is a 1988 stylish rebirth of a turn-of-the-century hotel that had fallen onto bad
days. The only remaining part of the original is the Lerdalshöjden Restaurant, which
retains the original walls and feeling of the old place (see "Where to Dine," below).
Bedrooms are well furnished and maintained, and decorated with modern accessories
and amenities. The hotel has a sauna with a view over the lake, plus an exercise room.

HOTEL GÄRDEBYGARDEN, S-795 00 Rättvik. Tel. 0248/100-07. Fax
0248/11-02-57. 50 rms (26 with bath). **Bus:** 58, 70.

$ Rates (including breakfast): 385–475 kronor ($67.20–$82.95) single; 700–800
kronor ($122.20–$139.70) double. MC, V.

This very good value hotel, located off Storgaten in the town center, was started
in 1906 and is today owned by the Swedish Mission Church. A big breakfast is
served every day—almost like a Swedish smörgåsbord—and almost every
night there's some form of entertainment, often Dalarna fiddlers. Some nights are
devoted to communal sing-alongs. Within a short walk of the lake, the hotel has
expanded into a pair of outlying buildings. The bedrooms are comfortably and
sedately furnished with conservative furniture. Some have a view of the lake.
Cross-country ski trails and jogging paths are a short distance away.

WHERE TO DINE

LERDALSJÖJDEN, in the Scandic Active Hotel, Rättvik. Tel. 111-50.
Cuisine: SWEDISH. **Reservations:** Recommended.

$ Prices: Appetizers 50–105 kronor ($8.75–$18.35); main dishes 100–190 kronor
($17.45–$33.15); fixed-price lunch 50 kronor ($8.75). AE, DC, MC, V.
Open: Lunch Mon–Fri 11:30am–2:30pm; dinner Mon–Fri 6–10:30pm, Sat–Sun
5–9pm.

Near the top of a hill overlooking Rättvik, a 10-minute walk north from the lake, this
restaurant is the only original remaining section left from the 1988 remodeling of a
turn-of-the-century hotel. It has long been a favorite with locals from the nearby lake
district. They like its traditional Swedish home-style cookery, including fresh fish and
beef dishes. Try, for example, steak tartare with bleak roe or fried ptarmigan with red
currant sauce. In winter, the region's most popular dinner-dance is staged here every
Saturday.

5. MORA

327 miles NE of Gothenburg, 204 miles NW of Stockholm

GETTING THERE By Plane Mora is connected by daily air service from
Stockholm, taking 40 minutes. The airport lies about 4 miles from the center. Taxis
meet arriving flights.

By Train There is direct service daily from Stockholm to Mora; trip time is 4
hours.

By Bus Certain weekend buses leave from Stockholm's Central Station on the
4¼-hour trip to Mora.

By Car   Take the E18 express highway northeast from Stockholm until you connect with Route 70 heading northeast all the way to Mora.

By Boat   The *Gustaf Wasa* cruises between Mora and Leksand. Departures from Leksand are in the afternoon. Departures from Mora are at 10am on Friday, costing 90 kronor ($15.70) one way. Call 010/52-32-92 for information and reservations.

ESSENTIALS   For information, contact the tourist bureau, **Mora Turistbyrå,** Angbåtskajen (tel. 0250/265-50). The **telephone area code** for Mora is 0250.

_____

In Upper Dalarna, between Lake Orsa and Lake Siljan, the provincial town of Mora is our final stopover in the province. Summer travelers find this business and residential center a good base for exploring the district.

Mora was the village where Gustavus Vasa—after an initial unsuccessful attempt—finally rallied the peasants in Sweden's 16th-century war against Danish rule. In March of every year, this event is commemorated by a 50-mile Vasa Race, one of the major ski events.

WHAT TO SEE & DO

Mora has opened a **Santa complex,** inaugurated for the Christmas of 1984, featuring Santa's house and his factory. Visitors can meet "Santa," and see his favorite helpers making and gift-wrapping presents for children all over the world.

Mora was also the hometown of Anders Zorn (1860–1920), perhaps Sweden's most famous painter, and the town's three top sights are all associated with him. The first, **Lisselby,** is an area near the Zorn Museum made up of old houses that are now used as arts and crafts studios and boutiques. At **Balder-Lisselby,** a craft center, you can watch handcrafts being made Monday through Saturday between 9am and 6pm, except at lunchtime.

ZORNMUSEET [Zorn Museum], Vasagatan 36. Tel. 165-60.

This museum contains not only a wide collection of the artist's own works (among them, *Midnight*), but paintings from his private collection—including works by Prinz Eugen and Carl Larsson, also of Dalarna. Major foreign artists (sculpture by Kai Nielsen of Denmark and drawings by Auguste Rodin) are also presented, along with rural art and handcrafts of Dalarna.

Admission: 15 kronor ($2.60) adults, 2 kronor (35¢) children.

Open: Summer, Mon–Sat 9am–5pm, Sun 11am–5pm; winter, Mon–Sat 10am–5pm, Sun 1–5pm.

ZORNSGÅRDEN, Vasagatan 36. Tel. 165-60.

The artist's former home, adjoining the museum, has been left just as it was when Mrs. Zorn died in 1942. Its chief attraction, aside from the paintings displayed, is Zorn's personally designed studio on the top floor.

Admission: 20 kronor ($3.50) adults, 2 kronor (35¢) children.

Open: Summer, Mon–Sat 10am–5pm, Sun 11am–5pm; winter, Mon–Sat 12:30–5pm, Sun 1–5pm.

WHERE TO STAY

MORA HOTEL, Strandgatan 12, S-792 00 Mora. Tel. 0250/117-50. Fax 0250/189-81. 145 rms (all with bath), 2 suites. MINIBAR TV TEL.

$ Rates (including breakfast): Midsummer and Fri–Sat year round, 435 kronor ($75.95) single; 590 kronor ($103) double. Sun–Thurs in winter, 740 kronor ($129.20); 880 kronor ($153.65) double; from 1,150 kronor ($200.80) suites. AE, DC, MC, V.

A modern hotel, in the center of town across from the lakefront a minute's walk from the tourist bureau, the Mora Hotel has been renovated over the years to include sun terraces and glassed-in verandas. The interior is tasteful with bright colors. All accommodations have comfortable furniture, nonalcoholic minibars, and radios, as well as other amenities. On the premises is an indoor pool, along with several dining facilities. The best of them is the Terrassen, (see "Where to Dine," below). The hotel has a disco on Friday and Saturday charging a 50- to 65-krona ($8.75 to $11.35) admission.

HOTEL MORAPARKEN, Parkvagen 1, S-792 00 Mora. Tel. 0250/178-00. Fax 0250/185-83. 75 rms (all with bath). TV TEL.

$ Rates: Mid-June to Aug (including breakfast), 550 kronor ($96.05) single or double. Sept to early June, Sun–Thurs (including breakfast), 600 kronor ($104.75) single; 780 kronor ($136.20) double. Sept to early June, Fri–Sat (including half board and a dance), 880 kronor ($153.65) per person. AE, DC, MC, V.

With a wooden facade, this spacious, rambling hotel is beside the Osterdal River in the vacation resort of Moraparken a quarter mile from Mora. Sports include swimming, sailing, tennis, minigolf, and a wide array of winter sports. Rooms are comfortably modern. The hotel has a sauna, solarium, and outdoor swimming pool.

SILJAN HOTEL, Moragatan 6, S-792 00 Mora. Tel. 0250/130-00. Fax 0250/130-98. 44 rms (40 with bath). TEL.

$ Rates (including breakfast): June 24–Aug 5, 350 kronor ($61.10) single without bath; 400 kronor ($69.85) double without bath, 550 kronor ($96.05) double with bath; Aug 6–June 23, 375 kronor ($65.50) single without bath, 675 kronor ($117.85) single with bath; 530 kronor ($92.55) double without bath, 850 kronor ($148.40) double with bath. AE, DC, MC, V. **Parking:** Available.

In the center of the resort a block from the tourist office, the hotel dates from 1965 and was renovated in 1990. Bedrooms are modernized and tastefully and comfortably furnished. Within walking distance of the hotel are tennis courts, a swimming pool, a health club, and car-rental services. The hotel also has a restaurant and bar, serving international food. On the same street is a Chinese restaurant. Parking is provided.

WHERE TO DINE

TERRASSEN, in the Hotel Mora, Strandgatan 12. Tel. 117-50.
   Cuisine: SWEDISH. **Reservations:** Recommended but not required.
$ Prices: Appetizers 45–100 kronor ($7.85–$17.45); main dishes 110–205 kronor ($19.20–$35.80). AE, DC, MC, V.
   Open: Lunch daily 11am–3pm; dinner daily 3–11pm.

This is one of the finest dining rooms in the area, and it's a good bet for a meal even if you aren't a guest of the Mora Hotel (see "Where to Stay," above). Fresh produce is used whenever possible, and fresh fish and Swedish beef dishes are a feature. You might begin with herring or enjoy a freshly made salad. Service is both polite and efficient.

NEARBY EXCURSIONS

NUSNÄS   In Nusnäs, about 6 miles southeast of Mora, are two places where you can watch the Dalarna horses being made. You are free to walk around the workshops watching the craftspeople at work, and the finished products can be purchased at shops on the premises. They also sell wooden shoes and other craft items. **Nils Olssons Hemslojd** is open Monday through Friday from 8am to 3pm, and **Grannas A. Olssons Hemslojd** can be visited from 8am to 4pm, also on weekdays. To find Nusnäs, take the main road east out of Mora, turning off to the right at Farnas.

VÄRMLAND   Sometimes described as Sweden in miniature, Värmland is picturesque: mountains, rolling hill country, islands, and rivers. Värmland is also a province of festivals, music, art, literature, and handcrafts. Tourists can enjoy boating, fishing, skiing, hiking, folklore, and historic sights.

   Forests still cover a large part of Värmland, and the 170-mile-long Klaralven River carries logs to the industrial areas around Lake Vanern. In one of her most famous works, *The Saga of Gösta Berling,* Nobel Prize winner and native Swede Selma Lagerlöf lyrically described Värmland life in the early 19th century. Today the province remains much as she saw it.

---

6. KARLSTAD

154 miles NE of Gothenburg, 186 miles east of Stockholm

GETTING THERE   By Plane   Nine flights on Linjeflyg connect Stockholm and Karlstad daily, the "jump" taking 45 minutes.

By Train   Six trains a day run between Gothenburg and Karlstad, taking 3 hours; 10 trains a day arrive from Stockholm, taking 3 hours; and 3 trains a day from Oslo on the 3-hour trip.

By Bus   Three buses a day arrive from Gothenburg, taking 4 hours; four weekly from Stockholm, taking 4½ hours; and two weekly from Oslo, taking 4½ hours. Check locally for bus schedules, which change from month to month.

By Car   From Stockholm, take the E18 west all the way, and from Gothenburg head north along the E6 expressway, turning northeast at the junction of Route 45, which runs all the way to Karlstad.

ESSENTIALS   Contact the **Karlstad Tourist Bureau,** Tingvallagatan 1D, S-651 84 Karlstad (tel. 054/19-59-02). The **telephone area code** for Karlstad is 054.

The capital of Värmland, this port city is at the mouth of the Klarälven River. Karlstad has many attractions for visitors, plus many moderately priced restaurants and comfortable hotels. Because of its location, it has long been a center for administration, trade, and transport, and is a good starting point for many of the tourist routes of Värmland.

WHAT TO SEE & DO

A trading center called Thingwalla first stood on the site of the city, but in 1584, Duke Charles—later Sweden's King Charles IX—founded Karlstad. Here you can see Sweden's longest stone bridge, East Bridge, built in the 18th century. The oldest quarter, **Almen,** on Älvgatan, was saved from a disastrous fire in 1865 and can be visited, along with the old grammar school and the Bishop's House.

One of the best ways to acquire a quick orientation of Karlstad is to take a guided tour on a **Sola sightseeing boat,** leaving from the Residens Park (from the inner harbor at low water) at 1, 3, 5, and 7pm daily from mid-June to late August, with an additional 8:30pm trip in July, provided you reserve before 7pm (tel. 19-59-01). Passage costs 35 kronor ($6.10) for adults, 15 kronor ($2.60) for children.

VÄRMLANDS MUSEUM, Sandsgrundsudden. Tel. 11-14-19.
    This museum traces the prehistory of the area and the culture of its residents. You can see collections of coins, textiles, arts, and crafts. The museum, in a park on the northern edge of town, is a 5-minute walk from the city center.
    Admission: Free.
    Open: June–Aug, Mon–Fri 11am–7pm, Sat–Sun noon–4pm; Sept–May, Tues and Thurs–Sun noon–4pm, Wed noon–8pm.

MARIEBERGSSKOGEN, Mariebergs Park. Tel. 15-92-00.
    Mariebergsskogen is one of Sweden's top pleasure parks, with a fair, dancing, a theater, and an open-air museum, as well as an animal park and a restaurant. It's on the southern outskirts, a 10-minute walk from the town center.
    Admission: Free.
    Open: Lillskogen children's zoo, daily 11am–6pm; fun fair, Mon–Fri 11am–6pm, Sat–Sun noon–6pm.

ALSTERS HERRGÅRD, on the E18 Hwy. Tel. 83-40-81.

Alster Manor is maintained in the memory of Gustaf Fröding, one of Sweden's leading poets, who was born here in 1860. There is also a museum on the history of the provincial ironworking industry. In one of the wings is a small exhibition on emigration from Värmland to America. There is a café on the premises, and you can stroll through the Fröding Grove. The manor is 5 miles east of Karlstad on the Stockholm road.

Admission: 15 kronor ($2.60) adults, free for children.

Open: Mid-May to mid-Sept, daily 11am–6pm. **Closed:** Late Sept to early May. **Bus:** 15.

A NEARBY ATTRACTION

ALFRED NOBEL'S BJÖRKBORN, Karlskoga. Tel. 0586/818-94.

Some 30 miles east of Karlstad, near Karlskoga on Lake Möckeln, is the home of the manufacturer, inventor, and philanthropist who established the Nobel Prizes. You can visit the home (now a museum) and view the libraries, the study with Nobel's personal belongings, his bedroom, and the elegant salon. There is a café where you can enjoy food and drinks.

Admission: 20 kronor ($3.50) adults, free for children.

Open: June–Aug, daily 1–5pm. **Closed:** Sept–May. **Directions:** Take the E18 east from Karlstad; turn off at the road sign for the Björkborn, 2 miles away.

WHERE TO STAY

The Karlstad Tourist Bureau (see above) arranges accommodations in hotels and private homes.

EXPENSIVE

PLAZA HOTEL KARLSTAD, Västra Torggatan 2, S-652 25 Karlstad. Tel. 054/10-02-00. Fax 054/10-02-24. 101 rms (all with bath). TV TEL.

$ Rates (including breakfast): Summer and Fri–Sat year round, 435 kronor ($75.95) single; 600 kronor ($104.75) double. Sun–Thurs in winter, 920–1,020 kronor ($160.65–$178.20) single, 1,190–1,290 kronor ($207.80–$225.10) double. AE, DC, MC, V.

This hotel in the town center, a minute's walk from the bus station, has been considerably upgraded and improved since it was built in 1984. Upstairs, each of the comfortable rooms contains built-in furniture. Rooms on the fourth and fifth floors are especially luxurious. If a guest asks for something extra, every effort is made to comply. The hotel has a garden and a greenhouse-style roof off the lobby containing the Plaza Garden Restaurant, actually a brasserie in the French style. For information about its restaurant Plaza Vivaldi, one of the best in town, see "Where to Dine," below.

SARA HOTEL WINN, Norra Strandgatan 9-11, S-652 24 Karlstad. Tel. 054/10-22-50. Fax 054/11-12-65. 199 rms (all with bath). TV TEL.

$ Rates (including breakfast): 950 kronor ($165.85) single; 1,150 kronor ($200.80) double. 50% discounts during summer and on weekends. AE, DC, MC, V.

The most up-to-date and stylish hotel in town, in the center by the Klarälven, the Sara Hotel Winn has an alluring lobby-level piano bar and an in-house restaurant, the Café Artist (see "Where to Dine," below). Each of the bedrooms contains carpeting, video movies, radio, trouser press, and stylish brass-accented furniture. Some 28 rooms have a minibar. Laundry facilities and room service are available.

STADSHOTELLET, Kungsgatan 22, S-651 05 Karlstad. Tel. 054/11-52-20. Fax 054/18-82-11. 139 rms (all with bath). TV TEL.

$ Rates (including breakfast): Sun–Thurs in winter, 985 kronor ($172) single; 1,200 kronor ($209.50) double. Summer and Fri–Sat year round, 450 kronor ($78.55) single; 600 kronor ($104.75) double. AE, DC, MC, V. **Parking:** Available.

⭐ One of the most impressive Stads hotels in all of Scandinavia, this hotel with its yellow-and-white imperial neobaroque facade was built as a guesthouse by the Swedish government in 1873. A treaty signed here in 1905 gave Norway its independence. Bedrooms range from sedately modern to the more old-fashioned, but all rooms were renovated in 1985. Twenty rooms contain minibars. Same-day laundry service is provided. The hotel is a 5-minute walk north from the rail station.

The gourmet restaurant Matsalon serves first-class food. The Cafeet Statt, open from 7am and continuing with lunch, afternoon beverages, and early or late dinner, offers dancing in the evening. You can dine amid elaborately carved turn-of-the-century walls beneath a ceiling embellished with sea serpents. On Friday and Saturday there is a 50-krona ($8.75) cover charge. Also featured is the Olle Ferms Bar. Separate male and female saunas and solariums, and a garage and parking lot are provided.

MODERATE

GÖSTA BERLING, Drottninggatan 1, S-652 24 Karlstad. Tel. 054/15-01-90. 75 rms (all with bath). TV TEL.
$ **Rates** (including breakfast): Late Aug to early June, 500–575 kronor ($87.30–$100.40) single; 625–725 kronor ($109.15–$126.60) double. Mid-June to mid-Aug, 325 kronor ($56.75) single; 425 kronor ($74.20) double. AE, DC, MC, V.
Located at the beginning of the biggest shopping street in Karlstad, this relatively bland hotel has no real public rooms to speak of beyond a small lobby and unpretentious breakfast room. The heart and soul of the establishment are the comfortable, cozy, and plushly carpeted rooms, recently renovated. The hotel has a sauna.

GRAND HOTEL, Västra Torggatan, S-652 25 Karlstad. Tel. 054/11-52-40. Fax 054/11-79-57. 69 rms (all with bath), 1 suite. TV TEL.
$ **Rates** (including breakfast): Summer and Fri–Sat year round, 450 kronor ($78.55) single; 550 kronor ($96.05) double. Sun–Thurs in winter, 700–850 kronor ($122.20–$148.40) single; 800–1,000 kronor ($139.70–$174.60) double; from 1,300 kronor ($227) suites. AE, DC, MC, V.
No longer the grandest hotel in town, it still has an old-fashioned charm. Dating from the late 19th century, it is the oldest hotel in Karlstad. It has a reddish brown semi-ornate facade and is located in the center of town 200 yards north of the railroad station. Each of the spacious high-ceilinged bedrooms has, among other amenities, a trouser press and radio. Meals are served in a dark-walled Victorian dining room.

WHERE TO DINE
MODERATE

CAFE ARTIST, in the Sara Hotel Winn, Norra Strandgatan 9-11. Tel. 10-22-50.
Cuisine: SWEDISH/FRENCH. **Reservations:** Recommended.
$ **Prices:** Appetizers 64–118 kronor ($11.15–$20.60); main dishes 146–236 kronor ($25.50–$41.20). AE, DC, MC, V.
Open: Mon–Fri 11:30am–midnight, Sat–Sun 6pm–midnight.
The hand-rubbed glow of its paneling and its 19th-century pinewood antiques make this one of the most interesting restaurants in town, occupying the ground floor of the Sara Hotel Winn (see "Where to Stay," above), 200 yards from the market square. The plush comfort of the Piano Bar is a good place for an apéritif. Dishes served in the main dining room include raw pickled salmon with herb sauce, filet of pork with Calvados and cream, a collage of shellfish and fish from nearby lakes and seas, scampi in either a lobster sauce or with Pernod, filet of venison with green-pepper sauce and ginger, whisky-flambéed filet of beef with Gorgonzola sauce, and a dessert favorite of homemade vanilla ice cream with warm cloudberries.

KÄLLAREN MUNKEN, Västra Torggatan 17. Tel. 11-02-16.
Cuisine: CONTINENTAL. **Reservations:** Recommended.

$ Prices: Appetizers 59–75 kronor ($10.30–$13.10); main dishes 124–185 kronor ($21.65–$32.30). AE, DC, MC, V.
Open: Dinner only, Mon–Sat 6pm–midnight.
Located off a central-city pedestrian walkway a third of a mile north of the railroad station in a 17th-century crypt and cellar, this restaurant has vaulted ceilings and pinewood paneling dating from 1653. The restaurant has two different seating areas. If you want to drink and have a snack, turn left inside the vestibule for the Hollandia Pub. There you can order roast beef, potato or tuna salad, along with portions of cheese. Platters of food cost around 100 kronor ($17.45) here.

The more formal, and more interesting, dining area lies to the right of the vestibule. Flickering candles and stained-glass windows create the ambience. Dishes include filet of sole Walewska, filet of veal Oscar, succulent beef dishes (some smothered in mushroom gravy), and platters of fresh fish. Don't overlook a flavorful dessert of deep-fried Camembert with cloudberries.

PLAZA VIVALDI, in the Plaza Hotel Karlstad, Västra Torggatan 2. Tel. 10-02-00.
Cuisine: SWEDISH. **Reservations:** Recommended.
$ Prices: Appetizers 60–100 kronor ($10.50–$17.45); main dishes 140–210 kronor ($24.45–$36.65). AE, DC, MC, V.
Open: Lunch daily noon–2pm; dinner daily 6–11pm.
One of the best and most elegant restaurants in Karlstad is on the lobby level of the Plaza Hotel (see "Where to Stay," above). Its decor combines modern with antique and traditional. Specialties of the chef are likely to include lime- and ginger-marinated salmon flavored with coriander, noisettes of reindeer with chanterelles, filet of veal in a creamy morel sauce, breast of pheasant with white wine sauce and grapes, and filet of monkfish.

VÄRDSHUSET ALSTERN, Morgonvagen 4. Tel. 83-49-00.
Cuisine: FRENCH/SWEDISH. **Reservations:** Recommended.
$ Prices: Appetizers 50–120 kronor ($8.75–$20.95); main dishes 215–245 kronor ($37.55–$42.80); one-course lunch 125 kronor ($21.85). AE, DC, MC, V.
Open: Lunch only, daily 1–7pm. **Closed:** 2 weeks in Jan.
Two miles north of Karlstad near Route 63 on a hillside above Lake Alstern, this place makes a fine luncheon excursion. It occupies a 1920s Dutch-gabled building. Depending on the season, you can enjoy game specialties such as elk with hand-picked berries and wild mushrooms, along with nouvelle-inspired fish dishes, meats, and vegetables prepared just right.

INEXPENSIVE

SKOGEN TERRASSEN, Mariebergsskogen. Tel. 15-92-03.
Cuisine: SWEDISH. **Reservations:** Recommended.
$ Prices: Smörgåsbord 165 kronor ($28.80). AE, MC, V.
Open: Summer, Mon–Sat 11:30am–2pm; winter, Mon–Sat 11am–6pm.
The allure here is the copious smörgåsbord buffet. You can eat either on a rustic terrace with a view of the spruces ringing the lake and the nearby amusement park, a 15-minute walk east of the center, or choose the veranda, or the spacious dining hall with its high wooden ceilings and antiques. You are presented with a lavish array of Swedish delicacies, including herring, shrimp, fish, salads, and meat, topped by a homemade dessert table.

---

7. SUNNE

236 miles west of Stockholm, 179 miles east of Gothenburg

GETTING THERE   By Train   Four or five trains arrive daily on the 4½-hour trip from Stockholm, and from Gothenburg, another four or five trains a day, taking 3 hours 40 minutes. You always have to change trains in Kil, and sometimes in Hallsberg, depending on the train. From Oslo there are two trains a day, requiring a change in Kil; trip time is 3 to 4 hours.

By Bus From Stockholm, it's too complicated with too many transfers—take the train. From Gothenburg, one bus a day arrives Monday through Friday on the 7¼-hour trip; transfer in Karlstad.

By Car Drive north along Route 234 from Karlstad.

ESSENTIALS For information, go to **Sunne Turistbyrå**, Mejerigatan 2 (tel. 0565/135-30). The **telephone area code** for Sunne is 0565.

Lying on Lake Fryken, Sunne is the center for tourism in Fryksdalen (Fryken Valley). Known as the "Land of Legend," Fryksdalen is associated with the writings of Selma Lagerlöf. In fact, Sunne was the prototype for the village of Bro in *The Saga of Gösta Berling*. From Sunne, you can take boat trips on Lake Fryken, or play golf on a nine-hole course.

WHAT TO SEE & DO

SUNDSBERGS GÅRD, Ekebyvägen. Tel. 103-63.

This museum shows three centuries of life in a Varmland manor house, from the kitchen to the drawing room. It's south of the town center, close to the landmark Hotel Selma Lagerlöf.

Admission: 15 kronor ($2.60) adults, free for children.

Open: Mid-June to mid-Aug, Tues–Sun 1–6pm. **Closed:** Late Aug to early June.

ROTTNEROS MANOR, Rottneros. Tel. 0565/602-95.

⭐ The Ekeby in the saga of Selma Lagerlöf, Rottneros Manor, on the western shore of the lake, is one of Sweden's major attractions. You can only visit the park and sculpture garden, which has more than 100 pieces of sculpture, including works by Carl Milles. The foremost sculptors of each of the neighboring Scandinavian countries are also represented: Kai Nielsen of Denmark, Gustav Vigeland of Norway, and Waino Aaltonen of Finland. On the grounds is a cafeteria and a licensed restaurant.

Admission: 40 kronor ($7) adults, 15 kronor ($2.60) children.

Open: Mid-May to Aug, daily 9am–6pm. **Closed:** Sept–mid-May.

MÅRBACKA MINNESGÅRD, Mårbacka. Tel. 0565/310-27.

⭐ On the other side of the water, 6 miles from Sunne and 36 miles north of Karlstad, Mårbacka is the former home of Selma Lagerlöf, who won the Nobel Prize for literature. The pillared building is kept much as she left it at the time of her death in 1940 (she was born here in 1858). The estate is filled with her furnishings and mementos. It was Lövdala in *The Saga of Gösta Berling*.

Admission: 25 kronor ($4.35) adults, 15 kronor ($2.60) children.

Open: May–Aug, daily 9am–6pm; Sept, Sat–Sun 10am–6pm. **Closed:** Oct–Apr.

WHERE TO STAY & DINE

HOTEL SELMA LAGERLÖF, Ekebyvägen, S-686 00 Sunne. Tel. 0565/130-80. Fax 0565/123-66. 156 rms (all with bath). TV TEL.

$ Rates (including breakfast): 685 kronor ($119.60) single; 880 kronor ($153.65) double. Weekend and July discounts. AE, DC, MC, V.

⭐ With its mansard roof and stately dimensions, it's difficult to believe that this hotel, one of the best in Sweden, was built only a few years ago in a consciously old-fashioned manor-house style. Its sweeping lawn overlooks Lake Fryken 5 minutes south from the center where the hotel has warm-weather sports facilities. Winter enthusiasts find easy access to the nearby Sunne Ski Center. Each room is comfortable and well decorated. An indoor pool, saunas, bars, and high-quality restaurants are on its premises.

Food is served from 11:30am to 2:30pm and 6 to 10pm Monday through Friday, on Saturday from noon to 3pm and 6 to 10pm and on Sunday from noon to 8pm.

LÅNSMANSGÅRDEN, Ulfsby Herrgård, S-686 00 Sunne. Tel. 0565/ 103-01. Fax 0565/118-05. 28 rms (all with bath). TV TEL.

$ Rates (including breakfast): 550 kronor ($96.05) single; 720 kronor ($125.70) double. AE, DC, MC, V.

The original stately white-walled manor house 2½ miles north of Sunne built in 1810 was supplemented a few years ago with a modern extension stretching into a pleasant garden. Each bedroom has a radio, and about a dozen open onto private gardens. Each of the rooms is named after a character in the Selma Lagerlöf novel *The Saga of Gösta Berling*. Known for its food, the hotel serves generous meals in charming old-fashioned dining rooms daily from noon to 3pm and at 6 or 7pm. Rowboats can be rented.

8. FILIPSTAD

167 miles west of Stockholm, 192 miles east of Gothenburg

GETTING THERE   By Train   It's not possible to go by train to Filipstad anymore. The nearest station is at Kristinehamn, from which you can make bus connections to Filipstad.

By Bus   Daily connections are possible from Karlstad.

By Car   Follow Route 61 via Arvika to Kil. Drive via Forshaga to Route 63 to Malkam and Filipstad.

ESSENTIALS   The **Långban Information Center,** S-682 00 Filipstad (tel. 054/221-15), is open, early June to the end of August, daily from 9:30am to 6pm. The **telephone area code** for Filipstad is 054.

The tourist center for the Bergslag (mining) area of Värmland, Filipstad was founded in 1611. It is almost certain that iron ore was mined in this region even before the Black Death of the 13th century, and documentary evidence establishes it as being a thriving business in 1413. The main mine products were iron and manganese ore, but silver, copper, lead, and zinc ore were also found. Even gold has occasionally been unearthed.

Today the Filipstad Bergslag smelting houses have vanished and only two mines remain in operation, but visitors can see the old open mine shafts, ruins of ironworks, and grand manor houses where the ironmasters once lived. Other industries here include the making of Wasa Crispbread (knäckebröd) and tourism. Canoeing and hunting for minerals are favorite summer activities, while downhill and cross-country skiing lure winter visitors.

Filipstad's main claim to fame for Americans is that inventor John Ericsson (who was born in nearby Långban) was brought back from his adopted home in the United States and buried here. When Ericsson immigrated to the United States, he was already a successful inventor, but gained further renown with his invention of the marine propeller. But it was for his warship *Monitor* that he earned a place in history. The ship he built fought the *Merrimack* of the Confederacy to a draw on May 9, 1862, saving the Union fleet and helping to win the Civil War at sea.

Other Ericsson successes include two heavy steel-drilled guns which he gave to the Swedish Navy, the steam fire engine, the hot-air engine or caloric engine, and improvements on steam boilers. Ericsson's brother was Baron Nils Ericsson, a noted construction engineer in Sweden.

Another well-known Filipstad figure is poet Nils Ferlin, whose realistic statue sits on a park bench in the center of town.

WHAT TO SEE & DO

On the peninsula of Lake Hyttsjon is **Tibergs Udde** (Tibergs Point), a beautiful nature reserve.

STORBROHYTTAN, Hembygådsgården, Munkeberg. Tel. 140-28.

Half a mile from the town center, this restored blast furnace and ironworks has been made into a mining museum with a wealth of mining artifacts.

Admission: 20 kronor ($3.50) adults, 10 kronor ($1.75) children.
Open: June 5–Aug 19, daily 10am–6pm **Closed:** Aug 20–June 4.

LÅNGBANS GRUVBY, Hyttbacken. Tel. 221-81.

A visit to Filipstad wouldn't be complete without an excursion to this little settlement 12 miles northeast of town. The Långbans mines were known in the 19th century for producing manganese, and during the last decades of activity they were primarily sources of dolomite. More than 300 different kinds of minerals have been found here. Långban today is a well-preserved mining village with mine holes, shaft towers, and Långban Manor.

Admission: 20 kronor ($3.50) adults, 10 kronor ($1.75) children.
Open: June 5–Aug 19, daily 10am–6pm. **Closed:** Aug 20–June 4.

WHERE TO STAY & DINE

HENNICKEHAMMARS HERRGÅRD, S-682 00 Filipstad. Tel. 054/125-65. Fax 0590/11-717. 55 rms (all with bath). TV TEL.

$ Rates (including breakfast): 600–650 kronor ($104.75–$113.50) single; 800–950 kronor ($139.70–$165.85) double. AE, DC, MC, V.

Built in 1725 as the home of a wealthy landowner, this hotel, with its elegant detailing and symmetrical facade, is a comfortable country spot loaded with personality and charm. On lawns close to the edge of Lake Hemtjarn, 2½ miles west of Filipstad, rooms here are either in one of several outbuildings or in the main manor house itself. Guests can swim in the lake, rent horses at a nearby riding school, play tennis, or enjoy golf at a course about 9 miles away. Each unit is stylishly comfortable, thanks to a renovation. The hotel restaurant is open daily from noon to 2pm and 6 to 8pm, charging 280 kronor ($48.90) for a fixed-price dinner. Many outside guests visit for the daily luncheon smörgåsbord at 180 kronor ($31.45).

---

9. GRÄNNA

174 miles SW of Stockholm, 143 miles east of Gothenburg

GETTING THERE By Train The town of Tranås, 25 miles from Gränna, is on the main rail route between Stockholm and Malmö. From there a bus connects with Gränna (see below).

By Bus Gränna is connected by several buses a day from Tranås, the nearest rail link.

By Car Take the E4 west from Stockholm.

ESSENTIALS The **Tourist Information Bureau,** Torget (tel. 0390/110-10), lies in the town center and is open only in summer. The **telephone area code** for Gränna is 0390.

An idyllic little town founded in 1652, Gränna was built on the slopes of Grännaberget (hill) in a series of steps leading down to a centuries-old church and village on Lake Vättern. A bus from Jonköping makes the 25-mile run to Gränna.

Many wooden buildings have been preserved since the town's origin, and the original town plan is still followed.

WHAT TO SEE & DO

Grännaberget can be reached either by car from the road between Gränna and Tranås or by climbing the steps that are found in a couple of places in town up to the top. Here, you'll find a splendid view and a fine area for walking, plus a few buildings from the 17th century. If you're energetic, you can walk along a trail to **Skogstornet** (the Forest Tower), from which the view of the area around Lake Vättern is breathtaking. The Gränna area is a rich repository of Iron Age weapons, tools, menhirs, and burial grounds, some 4,000 years old.

Gränna was the birthplace of the North Pole balloonist-explorer Salomon August Andrée, who made an ill-fated attempt in 1897 to cross the pole in the balloon *Ornen* (Eagle). The remains of the expedition were found in 1930 and may be seen in the **Andrée Museum,** Brahegatan 38 (tel. 110-15). Museigården, a part of the museum, houses exhibits illustrating the history of the area. The museum is open mid-May to late August, daily from 10am to 5pm; late August to mid-May, from noon to 4pm.

NEARBY VISINGSÖ ISLAND

A 20-minute ferry trip will take you from Gränna to the island Visingsö for 30 kronor ($5.25) round-trip. The distance is 4 miles across the water. Ferryboats leave every hour during the day in summer, and at the rate of eight per day in winter. Boats depart from the central harbor at Gränna. For information, call the harbormaster (tel. 110-25) or the ferryboat office (tel. 36-29-90). There is a tourist office (summer information) near the point where the ferryboat docks (tel. 410-93 for information).

The island can be traversed by car in 5 minutes, as it is long but very narrow. There are no road names or street numbers. In summer, some of the island residents meet arriving ferries with saddled horses for a 30-minute excursion past the architectural highlights of the island (see below). The cost is about 30 kronor ($5.25) per ride. There is no phone to call for information—it's all very casual. This has been an important site since humans first set foot here, some 6,000 years ago, and large gravefields from the Viking era indicate how busy this area once was. On the southern part of the island are the remains of Sweden's oldest secular building, **Näs Castle,** built around 1150. According to the Icelandic sagas, it had a large treasury and was an important target in the fighting between the eastern and western parts of southern Sweden in the Middle Ages. The castle burned down in 1319.

The remains of another castle, **Visingsborg,** are by the harbor. This was the seat of the Brahe family whose progenitor, Per Brahe, Count of Visingsö, was a power in the Middle Ages in Sweden and Finland. Per Brahe also built the island's **parish church** in the 1680s, using the walls of the Stroja medieval church as the foundations. The tower and the door of the sacristy are from the old church, the door having old runic writing signifying that it was made in the 11th century. The church is baroque, unusual by Swedish standards. Also to be seen on Visingsö are herbaceous gardens in Count Brahe's reconstructed 17th-century garden.

Kumlaby Church, whose oldest parts date from the 12th century, has well-preserved 15th-century murals. Visitors can climb the tower to a small roof balcony where they have a panoramic view of the island.

WHERE TO STAY & DINE

SCANDIC HOTEL GYLLENE UTTERN, S-563 00 Gränna. Tel. 0390/108-00. Fax 0390/118-80. 53 rms (all with bath), 2 suites. TV TEL.
$ Rates (including breakfast): 785–1,020 kronor ($137.05–$178.20) single; 925–1,220 kronor ($161.50–$213) double; from 1,450 kronor ($253.15) suite. AE, DC, MC, V.

"The Golden Otter," its English name, is the honeymoon Shangri-La of Sweden, complete with a baroque wedding chapel in the basement. A step-gabled imitation castle (built in 1937), overlooking Lake Vättern a mile outside Gränna on the road to Stockholm, Gyllene Uttern offers the best in food and lodgings. The inn also offers 10 multilevel cottages and two annexes on its grounds. The main dining room, its deeply set windows with views of the lake, is highlighted by gilt-framed paintings, copies of great masters, medieval suits of armor, and a bas-relief fireplace. Food is served from noon to 10:15pm and fish from the lake is a specialty.

Although the dining room and public rooms are in the main building, it contains only nine accommodations; the rest of the rooms are spread across the grounds in the annexes or cottages that were constructed in the 1960s. Room prices are complicated, but guests in the cottages pay about 200 kronor ($34.90) less than occupants of the regular single and double rooms. On Friday and Saturday, rooms in the annex are discounted, but rooms in the main building are not. Because of the wide range of prices, when checking in always determine the type of accommodation and the price.

10. VADSTENA

159 miles west of Stockholm, 161 miles east of Gothenburg

GETTING THERE By Bus   On Saturday and Sunday bus no. 855 departs from the Central Station in Stockholm. Bus no. 650 runs daily from Linköping.

By Car   By far the best way to go. Take the E4 southwest from Stockholm; at the junction of Route 206, head northwest.

ESSENTIALS   The tourist bureau, **Vadstena Turistbyrå,** is located at Rådhustorget, S-592 00 Vadstena (tel. 0143/151-25). The **telephone area code** for Vadstena is 0143.

The most important stopover on the Göta Canal trip is this medieval town full of narrow streets and old frame buildings on the eastern shores of Lake Vättern. It is known all over Sweden for its handmade lace—to see samples of this delicate product, walk along High Street.

WHAT TO SEE & DO

VADSTENA CASTLE, Slottsvägen. Tel. 102-20.

Founded by Gustavus Vasa, king of Sweden, in 1545, but not completed until 1620, this is one of the most splendid Renaissance Vasa castles, erected during a period of national expansion. It dominates the town from its moated position on the lake, just behind the old courthouse in the southern part of town. Vadstena was last inhabited by royalty in 1715, and was restored in the 19th century. Since 1899 the greater part of the castle has been used for provincial archives.

Admission: May–Sept, weekday tours, 20 kronor ($3.50) adults, 7 kronor ($1.20) children.

Open: Hours are different yearly; check with the tourist office (see above).

KLOSTERKYRKAN (Abbey Church), Lasarettsgatan. Tel. 109-43.

Built between the mid-14th and the 15th century to specifications outlined by its founder, Saint Birgitta (Bridget) of Sweden, this Gothic church is rich in medieval art. Parts of the abbey date from 1250. The abbey housed the nuns of Saint Birgitta's order until their expulsion in 1595.

The New Monastery and Church, built in 1973, show the same traditional simplicity of style Saint Birgitta prescribed for her order. The view through the huge windows is the only decoration in this otherwise stark church. The nuns, who returned to Sweden in 1963, will show the church and their guesthouse to interested visitors at times convenient to their own schedule. It's a 3-minute walk from Stora Torget.

Admission: 7 kronor ($1.20).
Open: Daily 10am–5pm.

WHERE TO STAY & DINE

The tourist bureau, **Vadstena Turistbyrå,** at Rådhustorget, (tel. 151-25), dispenses information about private homes that accept paying guests. It's an excellent way to economize while experiencing life in a Vadstena home.

KUNGS STARBY HOTELL & RESTAURANG, Ödeshögsvägen, S-592 00
Vadstena. Tel. 0143/114-20. Fax 0143/102-63. 45 rms (all with bath). TV TEL **Bus:** 610 from Motala.

$ Rates (including breakfast): Fri–Sat, 600 kronor ($104.75) single; 700 kronor ($122.20) double. Sun–Thurs, 650 kronor ($113.50) single; 820 kronor ($143.15) double. AE, DC, MC, V.

On the southern outskirts of the town, this licensed restaurant and inn was an old manor house. The hotel portion dates from 1984. As an estate, Starby dates back to the 13th century and was owned by the Vasa Dynasty. Bedrooms are furnished in bright modern designs with pastel colors and sleek functional styling. The inn is known for its buffets. Facilities include a swimming pool and a health club.

VADSTENA KLOSTERHOTELL, Klosterområdet, S-592 00 Vadstena. Tel.
0143/115-30. Fax 0143/136-48. 25 rms (all with bath). TV TEL.

$ Rates (including breakfast): 550 kronor ($96.05) single; 650 kronor ($113.50) double. AE, DC, MC, V.

This hotel is a former convent and royal summer castle dating from the 12th century. Completely modernized, it offers well-appointed rooms. You can see the nuns' refectory, adapted for a conference room, and the nuns' dormitory, its 59 cells opening onto the longest triple barrel vault (more than 190 feet long) in the north. On the lake, northeast of the castle, the hotel adjoins the historic abbey church. There are three lounges, all fresh and light. Breakfast is served in the 13th-century Kings' Hall.

CHAPTER 27

KALMAR & THE BALTIC ISLANDS

Kalmar, while a good base for exploring the district, is well worth exploration itself. It was here that the Agreement of Kalmar was signed in 1397, uniting Denmark, Norway, and Sweden in an ill-fated union. Across the water from Kalmar is the Baltic island of Öland, settled in prehistoric times.

Before journeying on to Kalmar or Öland, we'll hop over to Sweden's most popular tourist island, Gotland, nestled in the Baltic. In the forest-rich province of Småland, you'll find some of the most famous glass factories in the world, like Orrefors.

SEEING KALMAR & THE BALTIC ISLANDS

GETTING THERE

Gotland, with Visby as its capital, is the summer playground of Stockholm, the beach life taking on a real *joie de vivre*. It can be reached on a 30-minute flight from Stockholm, and the airport is just 2 miles from the city. If you'd like to take a car or the train, the point of embarkation is Nynäshamn, south of Stockholm.

Kalmar, an interesting city in its own right, is the gateway to the glassworks district and an easy city to reach from Stockholm by plane, train, and bus. From Kalmar, a bridge leads to the island of Öland, best explored by private car because of inadequate bus transportation.

A SUGGESTED ITINERARY

Days 1 & 2: Fly or take the car-ferry to Visby. Spend 1 day exploring the town and another seeing the attractions on the island of Gotland.
Day 3: Go to see the historic city of Kalmar.
Day 4: Drive across the bridge and explore the island of Öland, which can be done while still based in Kalmar.
Day 5: You can still use Kalmar as a base, or check into a hotel in Växjö and explore the major factories of the glassworks district.

1. GOTLAND (VISBY)

136 miles south of Stockholm, 93 miles south of Nynäshamn,
55 miles east of the Swedish mainland

GETTING THERE   By Plane   Daily flights from Stockholm take 30 minutes. Bus service between Visby and the airport is 20 kronor ($3.50) each way.

By Train   There is no rail service on Gotland.

By Bus & Car-Ferry   From Stockholm, take a bus south to the port of Nynäshamn, a 1-hour ride. From there, take the car-ferry to Visby; it leaves at midnight, taking about 5 hours. In summer there are also day connections. You can

WHAT'S SPECIAL ABOUT KALMAR & THE BALTIC ISLANDS

Great Towns/Villages

☐ Visby, once a great medieval European city, capital of the island of Gotland, former Viking stronghold.

☐ Kalmar, one of Sweden's oldest towns, fortified in the 11th century as a stronghold against Denmark.

☐ Växjö, a former Iron Age trading station that's now the center for exploring Sweden's glassworks district.

Castles

☐ Kalmar Slott, once "the key to Sweden," a moated medieval fortress transformed into a Renaissance palace.

Ancient Monuments

☐ Eketorp Ring-Fort, on Öland, an excavated prehistoric fortified village.

☐ Dominican Monastery of St. Nicholas, from the early 13th century, now in ruins.

Ace Attractions

☐ Lummellunda Caves, north of Visby, with fossil remains, subterranean waters, and stalactite and stalagmite formations.

☐ The House of Emigrants, Växjö, which documents the 1.3 million Swedes who developed "America Fever" and emigrated.

Glassworks

☐ Orrefors Glasbruk, a famous name in Swedish glass, where you can watch glassblowers work.

☐ Kosta Boda Glassworks, founded in 1742, another big name in Swedish glass.

Special Events

☐ Medieval Week in Visby, in August, when the old Hanseatic city reverts to its "golden age."

---

make reservations through your travel agent or directly with the ferry service for cabin and/or car space. It's wise to book deck space if you plan to go on a weekend. The ferry service is **Gotlandslinjen Bokningscentral** (tel. 08/23-61-70 in Stockholm).

By Car   Take Route 71 south to Nynäshamn and the car-ferry from there (see above).

ESSENTIALS   The tourist bureau **Turistbyrån,** Strandgaten 9 (tel. 0498/109-82), is open Monday through Friday from 9am to 5pm. The **telephone area code** for Gotland is 0498.

SPECIAL EVENTS   For 8 days in August during **Medieval Week,** Visby becomes a Hanseatic town again. At the harbor, Strandgatan swarms with people in medieval dress, many of them tending market stalls. You meet the blacksmith, barber, cobbler, and trader. Musicians play the hurdy-gurdy, the fiddle, and the flute, while jesters play the fool. Toward nightfall a kingly procession comes into the square. The program has more than 100 such events during the festival, along with medieval mystery plays, masses, choral and instrumental music, tournaments, and displays of horses as well as archery competitions, fire-eaters, belly dancers, and walking tours of the medieval town.

In the middle of the Baltic sits the ancient home of the Goths, the island of Gotland, about 75 miles long and 35 miles wide. The Swedes go to Gotland for sunny holidays by the sea; North Americans are more interested in the old walled city of Visby. But an investment of a little extra time will reveal that Gotland, with its cliffs, odd rock formations, bathing beaches, and rolling countryside, is rich territory. Buses traverse the island, as do organized tours out of Visby.

At the end of the 12th century and during the 13th, the walled city of Visby rose to its zenith of power as the seat of the powerful Hanseatic merchants and as the trade center of northern Europe. Seventeen churches sprouted up during its heyday. Step-gabled houses were built of stone, and the townspeople lived in splendor. It was soon ransacked by the Danes, however, and the city subsequently declined. It has only recently become a tourist center, after it was recognized as a treasure house of medieval art, becoming the No. 1 spot in all of Scandinavia for those seeking the charm of the Middle Ages.

WHAT TO SEE & DO

Visby is a town meant for walkers. It can easily be explored on foot, but you may want to take one of the three organized tours that are offered in season. Since so many of the sights, particularly the ruins of the 13th- and 14th-century churches, are better appreciated with some background, I recommend the tour.

The 2-hour combined bus and walking tour leaves daily from the 17th-century Lübeck merchant's house, **Burmeister,** Strandgaten 9, near the tourist bureau. It operates from mid-June to mid-September, departing at 11am. The cost is 50 kronor ($8.75) for adults and 25 kronor ($4.35) for children, including entrance fees.

The tour takes guests to the old **Hanseatic harbor** (not the same harbor used today) and includes a walk through the beautiful **Botanical Gardens** (you'll know why Visby is called "the city of roses"), and passes two of the most famous towers in the old wall—the **Maiden's Tower** (a peasant girl was buried alive here for helping a Danish king) and the **Powder Tower** (the oldest fortification in Visby). Later the bus passes Gallow Hill, a medieval hanging station in use until the mid-19th century.

You'll have a chance to leave the bus and take a walk to the old ruins of the former **Dominican Monastery of St. Nicholas,** once part of a Dominican monastery. The church has a rose window cut from a single big stone—its diameter is more than 10 feet. Work began on the monastery in 1230 but it was destroyed by Lübeck forces in 1525.

Finally, the tour goes to the 13th-century Gothic and Romanesque **Cathedral of St. Mary.**

Another sightseeing recommendation—to be done on your own—is the **Gotlands Historical Museum,** Strandgatan 12-14 (tel. 173-60), opposite the Burmeister House on a medieval street noted for its step-gabled houses. The museum contains some of the most interesting artifacts discovered on Gotland, including carved stones dating back to A.D. 400, art from medieval and later periods, plus furniture and household items. It is open daily from 11am to 5pm, costing 20 kronor ($3.50) (children under 16 free).

A tour of the island—different every day—leaves from the tourist bureau. The price may be as low as 55 kronor ($9.60) or as high as 160 kronor ($27.95). But each day the tour visits the **Lummellunda Caves,** north of Visby, with their stalactite

---

IN THEIR FOOTSTEPS

Carolus Linnaeus (Carl von Linné) (1707–78) The great Swedish botanist compiled *Species Plantarum* (Plant Species) in 1753, which is a definitive catalog of plants. Nicknamed "the little botanist" at the age of 8, he began the modern system of botanical nomenclature.
   • **Birthplace:** South Rashult, Sweden, on May 23, 1707.
   • **Favorite Haunts:** Uppsala University, where he was given a chair of botany in 1742; Gotland and Öland, which he wrote of in his travels.
   • **Residences:** 27 Svartbacksgatan, the Linnaeus Garden and Museum at Uppsala (open to the public). Here he received a "patent of Nobility" and the new name Carl von Linné.
   • **Resting Place:** After suffering an apoplectic attack, he died on January 20, 1778, and was buried in the University of Uppsala Cathedral.

and stalagmite formations, fossil remains, and subterranean waters. Visits on your own cost 25 kronor ($4.35) for adults, 15 kronor ($2.60) for children.

ISLAND TOURS Ask at the **Turistbyrån,** Strandgatan 9 (tel. 109-82), in Visby about what island tours are featured during your visit. These tours are the best way to get a quick preview of Gotland.

Northern Gotland and **Fårö** are explored on one tour, costing 150 kronor ($26.20) for adults and 90 kronor ($15.70) for children. A coach runs to the ferry port of Fårösund, with a 10-minute trip over the strait followed by a tour around Fårö (Sheep Island) exploring dwarf forest and moor.

Returning to Gotland, the tour visits the open-air cultural history museum at **Bunge,** documenting the old peasant culture. That is followed by a tour of the **Blase limestone museum** in Fleringe, with two limekilns from the turn of the century that have been restored. Tours are conducted on Tuesday and Thursday in summer at 8:30am, ending at 5:30pm.

Another tour, on Wednesday from 9am to 5:30pm, costing 150 kronor ($26.20) for adults and 90 kronor ($15.70) for children, goes to the south point and the legendary "old man of **Hoburgen,**" a rock formation known as a chalk stack. The Iron Age village at **Gervide** is also explored, as are two farms from the 17th century. The journey goes along the west coast, with its windswept shoreline.

WHERE TO STAY

For all its attractions, Visby doesn't have enough hotels. Accommodations are packed in summer—so reserve in advance.

But if you haven't, head for the Accommodation Center of the tourist bureau (see above). The English-speaking personnel will arrange rooms in hotels or private homes in or near Visby. The average rate for an accommodation in a private home is 160 kronor ($27.95) per person per night in a single or 285 kronor ($49.75) in a double. It's better to telephone for reservations from Stockholm.

VERY EXPENSIVE

SARA HOTEL SNÄCK, S-621 21 Visby. Tel. 0498/600-00. Fax 0498/78431. 213 rms (all with bath). TV TEL.

$ Rates (including breakfast): 905 kronor ($158) single; 1,430 kronor ($249.70) double. Children up to 15 stay free in their parents' room. AE, DC, MC, V.

The most luxurious hotel on the island, this chain establishment lies on the beach, 2 miles outside Visby and a half a mile from the airport. After a 30-minute flight from Stockholm it's convenient for speedy check-ins, as your luggage is transported here directly from the airport. You even get a boarding card when checking out.

Rooms are attractively decorated with modern furnishings, and all have a balcony opening onto a view of the Baltic. The hotel restaurant, The Gourmet, offers some of the best food on the island, both regional and international dishes. There is also a coffee shop and a piano bar for entertainment. There is dancing several nights a week. Guests can also enjoy the sports activities, including an indoor pool, sauna, solarium, outdoor pool, tennis courts, jogging tracks, and a private beach.

MODERATE

HOTEL S:T CLEMENS, Smedjegatan 3, S-621 55 Visby. Tel. 0498/795-75. Fax 0498/79443. 50 rms (all with bath). TV TEL.

$ Rates (including breakfast): Fri–Sun, 550 kronor ($96.05) single; 650 kronor ($113.50) double. Mon–Thurs, 685 kronor ($119.60) single; 820 kronor ($143.15) double. DC, MC, V.

This 18th-century building in the town center has been successfully transformed into a well-run little hotel. It is decorated tastefully in a modern style, with light pastels used effectively. It's open all year, and the staff is helpful and efficient. Only breakfast is served. The hotel is equipped for handicapped guests. A sauna is provided.

HOTEL SOLHEM-PALISSAD, Solhemsgatan 3, S-621 58 Visby. Tel. 0498/790-70. Fax 0498/790-70. 112 rms (35 with bath). TEL.
$ **Rates** (including breakfast): 365 kronor ($63.75) single without bath, 860 kronor ($150.15) single with bath; 640 kronor ($111.75) double without bath, 1,035 kronor ($180.70) double with bath. AE, DC, MC, V.

On a hilly slope overlooking the harbor, just outside the wall, a 5-minute walk from the center, this is one of the best hotels in Visby. Rooms are clean and comfortable and furnished in a simple Nordic modern. Thirty-four of the rooms contain minibars and TVs. The hotel has a restaurant, a bar, and a sauna.

STRAND HOTEL, Strandgatan 34, S-621 02 Visby. Tel. 0498/126-00. Fax 0498/78111. 120 rms (all with bath). TV TEL.
$ **Rates** (including breakfast): 660–720 kronor ($115.25–$125.70) single; 730–920 kronor ($127.45–$160.65) double. Reductions of 25% Fri–Sat year round and Aug 10–June 10. AE, DC, MC, V.

One of the town's most inviting hotels, the Strand offers excellent bedrooms, furnished in a tasteful modern style. Many are for nonsmokers, and some are reserved for the handicapped. The hotel offers breakfast only, which is served in a modern courtyard. Facilities include a sauna and an indoor swimming pool.

A NEARBY ACCOMMODATION

TOFTA STRANDPENSIONAT, Tofta S-621 98 Visby. Tel. 0498/650-09. Fax 0498/654-37. 80 rms (all with bath). **Bus:** 31 from Visby.
$ **Rates** (including half board): 555 kronor ($96.90) single; 890 kronor ($155.40) double. Discounts available for children. AE, MC, V.

Eleven miles south of Visby, this hotel, dating from 1930, has a series of bungalows in a beach setting, with pines as a backdrop. There are also self-catering cottages with kitchen facilities. Several comfortable lounges, a sauna, and a fully licensed restaurant are on the premises. Scandinavian and international food are served. The guesthouse is near golf, tennis, and windsurfing facilities. English is spoken. Clients can rent bikes from the hotel.

WHERE TO DINE
MODERATE

BURMEISTER GARDEN, Strandgatan 6. Tel. 103-73.
   Cuisine: INTERNATIONAL. **Reservations:** Not required.
$ **Prices:** Appetizers 45–75 kronor ($7.85–$13.10); main dishes 100–155 kronor ($17.45–$27.05); pizzas 30–40 kronor ($5.25–$7). AE, DC, MC, V.
   Open: Summer, restaurant and disco, daily noon–2am; winter, nightclub only, Fri–Sat 10pm–2am.

This large restaurant in the town center at the tourist office offers dining indoors or under shady fruit trees in the garden of a 16th-century house originally built for the wealthiest citizen of Visby. From many of the tables, diners can look out on the surrounding medieval buildings. The well-prepared menu is Swedish, with choices of salmon, pork, and veal. A sizzling outdoor barbecue offers such dishes as Texas-size steaks and lamb chops. At night, pizza is the most popular item. After 10pm it becomes a disco, with no cover charge. In winter, Burmeister operates only as a nightclub, open on Friday and Saturday from 10pm to 2am. No cover is charged, but a large draft beer costs 33 kronor ($5.75).

GUTEKÄLLAREN, Stortorget 3. Tel. 100-43.
   Cuisine: SWEDISH. **Reservations:** Not required.
$ **Prices:** Appetizers 67–85 kronor ($11.70–$14.85); main dishes 79–185 kronor ($13.80–$32.30). AE, DC, MC, V.
   Open: Lunch Mon–Sat 11:30am–2pm; dinner Mon–Sat 6:30–10pm.

This restaurant and bar in the town center has been installed in one of the city's oldest buildings, a stone-sided inn dating back to the 11th century. It offers fresh fish and meat dishes, including some vegetarian specialties. You might begin with a fish soup made with lobster and shrimp, then follow with filet of sole Waleska or roast lamb chops. The dessert specialty in summer is a parfait made of local berries.

MUNKKÄLLAREN, Lilla Torggrand 2. Tel. 714-00.

Cuisine: SWEDISH. **Reservations:** Required in summer.

$ Prices: Appetizers 58–78 kronor ($10.15–$13.60); main dishes 116–148 kronor ($20.25–$25.85). AE, DC, MC, V.

Open: Mon–Tues 5pm–midnight, Wed–Sun 5pm–2am. **Closed:** Sun in winter.

You'll recognize this place in the center of Visby by its brown wooden facade. The dining room is only a few steps from the street, and it is sheathed in white stone, parts of it dating from 1150. The restaurant, while not necessarily the most expensive in town, is considered one of the best. In summer, management opens the doors to another three or four pubs within the compound. Glasses of beer cost 36 kronor ($6.30). The main pub, Munken, offers platters of husmanskost (Swedish home-cooking), including frikadeller (meatballs). In the restaurant you might begin with escargots in creamy garlic sauce or toast with Swedish caviar. Specialties include shellfish stew, salmon-stuffed sole with spinach and a saffron sauce, and venison in port wine sauce.

VÄRDSHUSET LINDGÅRDEN, Strandgatan 26. Tel. 187-00.

Cuisine: SWEDISH. **Reservations:** Not required.

$ Prices: Appetizers 25–98 kronor ($4.35–$17.10); main dishes 110–180 kronor ($19.20–$31.45); business lunch 125 kronor ($21.85). AE, DC, MC, V.

Open: Summer, Mon–Fri 11am–11pm, Sat noon–11pm, Sun 1–11pm; winter, Mon–Fri 11am–11pm, Sat 3–11pm.

A 10-minute walk from the ferryboat terminal in the center of Visby, this restaurant offers pleasant garden dining and decent prices. Especially good dishes include boiled and mustard-fried lamb with pearl onions, Brussels sprouts, and creamy potatoes, a specialty of Gotland. You can also order filet of reindeer and breast of hazel grouse served with morels in a Calvados sauce with potato croquettes. Another delight is the fried sole stuffed with shellfish and served with a hollandaise sauce. A daily special is offered for 44 kronor ($7.70).

UNO'S, Hastgatan 20. Tel. 716-17.

Cuisine: INTERNATIONAL. **Reservations:** Not required.

$ Prices: Appetizers 45–52 kronor ($7.85–$9.10); main dishes 92–117 kronor ($16.05–$20.45). AE, DC, MC, V.

Open: Sun–Thurs 5pm–midnight, Fri–Sat 5pm–2am.

A solid middle-bracket eatery with tasty food, this restaurant is in the heart of Visby near Osterportgate on the street level of a building originally constructed 80 years ago. Swedish dishes are featured, but the chef wanders down to France, Italy, and elsewhere for his repertoire. Try the carpaccio of beef, beef filet with peanut sauce and rice, and filet of sole with white wine and lobster sauce. Fifteen kinds of pizza are offered, priced from 55 to 65 kronor ($9.60 to $11.35).

2. KALMAR

254 miles south of Stockholm, 211 miles east of Gothenburg

GETTING THERE **By Plane** Kalmar Airport receives daily flights, from Stockholm, taking 50 minutes.

By Train Seven trains a day make the 6½-hour run between Stockholm and Kalmar. Eight daily trains arrive from Malmö, taking 3 hours 40 minutes.

By Bus Three to seven buses a day come from Stockholm on the 7-hour trip. From Gothenburg, there is one bus on Friday and Saturday, taking 6 hours.

By Car From Stockholm, take the E66 south.

ESSENTIALS The Kalmar tourist office, **Turism i Kalmarbygåden,** is located at Larmagatan 6, S-391 20 Kalmar (tel. 0480/153-50), near the railway station, right in the town center. The office is open in summer, Monday through Friday from 9am to 9pm, on Saturday from 9am to 6pm, and on Sunday from noon to 7pm; shorter hours in winter.

The **telephone area code** for Kalmar is 0480.

Today a thriving commercial center, this gateway city still retains many of its 17th-century buildings and sea captain's homes, clustered particularly around Stortorget. The first Swedish immigration to America, more than 3 centuries ago, originated from Kalmar, ending in Wilmington, Delaware.

WHAT TO SEE & DO

Kalmar boasts good **swimming** right in town, and a big **outdoor market** is held in front of the cathedral every Saturday from 8am to 3pm.

The largest and oldest handcrafts shop in Sweden, **Hemslöjden,** Larmgatan 26 (tel. 209-01), invites browsers and shoppers, and it has an export department.

KALMAR SLOTT, Slottsvägen. Tel. 563-51.

Founded in the 12th century, this strategically situated castle was once called the key to Sweden, and it's the principal sight in town. In the 16th century, under orders of King Gustavus Vasa and two of his sons, Erik XIV and Johan III, this moated medieval fortress was transformed into a Renaissance palace. Be sure to see the prison for women from the 18th and 19th centuries and the restored castle chapel. Tours are conducted mid-June to mid-August, daily every hour. To get there, from the train station turn left on Tullbron.

Admission: 20 kronor ($3.50) adults, 10 kronor ($1.75) children 7–15.

Open: Apr, daily 1–3pm; May to mid-June and mid-Aug to Sept, Mon–Sat 10am–4pm, Sun 1–4pm; mid-June to mid-Aug, Mon–Sat 10am–6pm, Sun 1–5pm; Oct, daily 1–3pm; Nov–Mar, Sun 1–3pm.

DOMKYRKAN (Kalmar Cathedral), Stortorget.

From the marketplace, you can wander over to Stortorget to visit the town's 17th-century cathedral.

Admission: Free.

Open: Mon–Fri 8am–7pm, Sat 8am–6pm, Sun 8:30am–6pm.

KALMAR LANS MUSEUM (Kalmar County Museum), in Kalmar Slott on Slottsvägen and at Skeppsbrogatan 51. Tel. 563-00.

This county museum is partly housed in Kalmar Slott, where you can see royal furnishings, military artifacts, and maritime objects. The majority of the museum's exhibits, however, are in an old industrial house on the harbor. An interesting exhibit concerns the royal ship *Kronan,* which sank in the Baltic Sea off the island of Öland during a sea battle against the Danes in 1676 (only 42 of the 840 people on board survived). The museum is responsible for excavations at the wreck site, and the objects found by the marine archeologists—glass bottles, tin plates, nautical instruments, a seaman's chest, and many gold coins—are on display.

Admission: 20 kronor ($3.50) adults, 10 kronor ($1.75) children.

Open: June 15–Aug 15, Mon–Sat 10am–6pm, Sun 1–5pm; Aug 16–June 14, Tues–Fri 10am–4pm, Sat–Sun 1–4pm.

WHERE TO STAY

Kalmar offers an adequate range of accommodations, although many choose to stay on the island of Öland.

The Kalmar tourist office (see above) can help you rent rooms in private homes at 90 kronor ($15.70) for a single and 120 kronor ($20.95) for a double, plus a booking fee starting at 25 kronor ($4.35).

EXPENSIVE

HOTEL WITT, Södra Långgatan 42, S-391 22 Kalmar. Tel. 0480/152-50. Fax 0480/15265. 112 rms (all with bath). TV TEL.

$ **Rates** (including breakfast): 660–860 kronor ($115.25–$150.15) single; 940–1,400 kronor ($164.10–$244.45) double. Summer discounts granted. AE, DC, MC, V.

In the town center overlooking Kalmarsund, this establishment, part of the Sara Hotel chain, is one of Kalmar's leading hotels, with a high standard of comfort. Bedrooms are pleasant, large, and well furnished, with luxurious baths. All units have radios, color TVs, and automatic alarm clocks. The hotel has a restaurant with a steakhouse, a cocktail bar, a casino, an inn, and a pub. There is also a large swimming pool, a sauna, and an exercise room.

KALMAR STADSHOTELL, Stortorget 14, S-392 32 Kalmar. Tel. 0480/151-80. Fax 0480/15847. 140 rms (all with bath). MINIBAR TV TEL.

$ **Rates** (including breakfast): Summer, 580 kronor ($101.25) single; 740 kronor ($129.20) double. Winter, 825 kronor ($144.05) single; 1,050 kronor ($183.35) double. AE, DC, MC, V.

Located on the main square in the heart of the city, this hotel was built in 1906. The recently renovated bedrooms feature hairdryers, radios, and trouser presses, among other amenities. Lunch, served in the cafeteria, costs from 75 kronor ($13.10). The hotel has four restaurants, a cocktail bar, a nightclub, a Jacuzzi, a sauna, and a solarium.

PACKHUSET HOTEL, Skeppsbrogatan 26, S-392 31 Kalmar. Tel. 0480/570-00. Fax 0480/86642. 68 rms (all with bath). MINIBAR TV TEL **Bus:** 1, 2, 3, 7, 8.

$ **Rates** (including breakfast): Summer (June 28–Aug 3) and weekends year round, 590–730 kronor ($103–$127.45) single; 760–890 kronor ($132.70–$155.40) double. Winter weekdays, 1,060–1,090 kronor ($185.10–$190.30) single; 1,140–1,180 kronor ($199.05–$206.05) double. AE, DC, MC, V. **Parking:** Free.

This elegant hotel, opened in 1986, is housed in an 18th-century warehouse on the shore of Kalmarsund. It is a living part of Kalmar's seafaring, shipbuilding, and ship-owning past, and old exposed beams and wooden braces are a key decorative motif inside. Facilities include an outdoor terrace used during the day as a café, plus a clubroom. The recreation area has a sauna and dressing room.

SLOTTSHOTELLET (Castle Hotel), Slottsvägen 7, S-392 33 Kalmar. Tel. 0480/882-60. Fax 0480/11993. 36 rms (all with bath). TV TEL.

$ **Rates** (including breakfast): 910–1,190 kronor ($158.90–$207.80) single; 1,060–1,450 kronor ($185.10–$253.15) double. AE, DC, MC, V. **Parking:** Available.

Offering modern comfort in a 19th-century environment, this 1864 hotel close to the castle is surrounded by 17th- and 18th-century buildings. It has one main building, two annexes, a pavilion, and its own parking lot. Bedrooms are individually decorated. Breakfast and evening coffee are served in the pavilion. In winter, an open fire adds to the cozy atmosphere, and the doors are opened onto the garden in summer. The hotel has a sauna and a solarium.

BUDGET

HOTEL VILLA ÄNGÖ, Baggensgatan 20, S-392 30 Kalmar. Tel. 0480/854-15. 9 rms (all with bath). TEL.

$ **Rates:** 220–275 kronor ($38.40–$48) single; 380 kronor ($66.35) double. Breakfast costs 30 kronor ($5.25) extra. AE, MC, V.

This stately Swedish house, almost like a manor house, is a good possibility for motorists who prefer a location 10 minutes from the town center, near Ölandsbridge. Rooms are immaculately kept and come in many sizes. Some of the more spacious rooms are ideal for families, accommodating three to five guests.

Breakfast is the only meal served, although you can order sandwiches in the evening. Facilities include a TV room, a sauna, a solarium, and billiards.

WHERE TO DINE
VERY EXPENSIVE

KALMAR HAMN KROG, Skeppsbrogatan 30. Tel. 110-20.
Cuisine: INTERNATIONAL. **Reservations:** Required.
$ Prices: Appetizers 60–90 kronor ($10.50–$15.70); main dishes 180–228 kronor ($31.45–$39.80); five-course gourmet menu 430 kronor ($75.10). AE, DC, MC, V.
Open: Lunch daily 12:30–2pm; dinner daily 6pm–midnight. AE, DC, MC, V.

✪ This restaurant, established in 1988, quickly became the most stylish and gastronomically sophisticated in Kalmar. It was built from scratch on an old pier where steamships used to deposit passengers from Öland. The interior is all blue and white. You might begin with a tomato-and-mozzarella salad or gooseliver pâté, following with filet of roe deer with chanterelles, fresh baked lobster with two cold sauces, filet of saddle of lamb with cream sauce, or poached filet of sole with a saffron-flavored lime sauce. Wines from Austria, the United States, Italy, and France are featured.

WITTEN'S DANCE RESTAURANT, in the Hotel Witt, Södra Långgatan 42. Tel. 152-50.
Cuisine: CONTINENTAL. **Reservations:** Recommended.
$ Prices: Appetizers 89–159 kronor ($15.55–$27.75); main dishes 142–240 kronor ($24.80–$41.90). AE, DC, MC, V.
Open: Dinner only, Tues–Sat 7pm–2am.

The clientele tends to be 35 years of age or older, and the dance music is traditional. This is the best-known supper club in the area. The Saturday-night dinner-dance is so popular that the hotel features a package offering a room (double occupancy), parking, the sauna, the dinner/dance, and breakfast for 480 kronor ($83.80) per person. Menu items include a symphony of seafood, with mussels, lobster, crab, and shrimp, or perhaps peppersteak and filet of breast of wild duck in a cream sauce. It's located on the lower level of the Hotel Witt (see "Where to Stay," above).

MODERATE

"BYTTAN" RESTAURANT, Slottsvägen 1. Tel. 100-85.
Cuisine: SWEDISH. **Reservations:** Recommended in summer.
$ Prices: Appetizers 35–88 kronor ($6.10–$15.35); main dishes 60–185 kronor ($10.50–$32.30); lunch platters 48 kronor ($8.40). AE, DC, MC, V.
Open: Summer, daily 11am–midnight; winter, daily 11am–3pm.

In the City Park a 10-minute walk south of the town center near the base of the castle, this terraced pavilion, an institution for 50 years, overlooks the water and is one of the best spots for dining in Kalmar. Main courses range from omelets to filet of beef with red wine sauce and forest mushrooms. For an appetizer you can order everything from a bowl of freshly made soup to Swedish caviar. Guests may dine in the pavilion or in the vine-covered courtyard. The food is attractively prepared, and even if you don't come for a meal, the restaurant is a good place to have afternoon tea.

COSTA KROG, Larmgatan 6. Tel. 115-70.
Cuisine: SWEDISH/FRENCH. **Reservations:** Recommended.
$ Prices: Appetizers 32–108 kronor ($5.60–$18.85); main dishes 88–178 kronor ($15.35–$31.10). AE, DC, MC, V.
Open: Mon–Sat 5pm–midnight, Sun noon–10pm.

Behind a brick facade on one of Kalmar's main streets midway between the rail station and the harbor, the interior of this restaurant has big crystal chandeliers and small bistrolike tables. It is informal and often a delight. The kitchen cooks with a certain flair. You might begin with the house platter of herring and shellfish or a

French tomato salad, then follow with chateaubriand à la Costa, filet of reindeer, a very good fricassée of halibut and shellfish in a cream-based wine sauce, or perhaps souvlaki.

MS CAPTAIN LINDSTRÖM, in the Hotel Witt, Södra Långgatan 42. Tel. 152-50.
   Cuisine: SWEDISH. **Reservations:** Recommended.
$ Prices: Appetizers 40–80 kronor ($7–$13.95); main dishes 105–150 kronor ($18.35–$26.20); luncheon platters 49–55 kronor ($8.55–$9.60); two-course business lunch 120 kronor ($20.95). AE, DC, MC, V.
   Open: Lunch Mon–Tues 11:30am–2pm; dinner Mon–Tues and Thurs 5pm–midnight, Wed and Fri–Sat 7pm–1am.

Within a 5-minute walk of the Kalmar waterfront, this restaurant on the lower level of the Hotel Witt (see "Where to Stay," above) offers good value and an appealing cuisine prepared with fresh ingredients. A dish invented in this dining room in the 19th century, a favorite of a regular client, Captain Lindström, was suggested to the chef. Today it is one of the most famous dishes of Sweden, beef Lindström, combining chopped beef with capers and pickled beetroot formed into a patty and fried. Many of the main courses are displayed raw for clients in glass-fronted cabinets. You indicate to the chef what you want and how you want it. You might, for example, prefer two small beef filets with your choice of sauces. For the price of a main course you have access to a help-yourself salad bar.

3. VÄXJÖ

67 miles west of Kalmar, 275 miles south of Stockholm

GETTING THERE   By Plane   Daily flights wing in from Stockholm to Växjö, taking 50 minutes.

By Train   Train connections are possible from Gothenburg, leaving at 8am daily and arriving in Växjö at 11:16am; from Malmö, leaving at 9am and arriving in Växjö at 11:16am; and from Stockholm, leaving at 10:06am and arriving in Växjö at 3:16pm.

By Bus   Bus connections are possible from Stockholm, leaving on Friday and Sunday (take SJ Buss) at 2pm and arriving in Växjö at 8:55pm.

By Car   From Stockholm, take the E4 south to Norrköping, then continue south along the E66 to Kalmar. At Kalmar, head west on Route 25.

ESSENTIALS   The **Växjö Tourist Information Office** is located at Kronobergsgatan 8 (tel. 0470/414-10). The **telephone area code** for Växjö is 0470.

Sweden's "Kingdom of Crystal" starts in Växjö, the central community for all of Småland. Some 16 factories here produce world-renowned Swedish glass. The name Växjö comes from *Vägsjön,* the "lake where the roads meet." Aside from glassworks, this 14th-century city is filled with lakes and forest, and traditional red-timbered cottages.

WHAT TO SEE & DO

In Växjö, there are numerous sports facilities, including one of Europe's most modern indoor swimming halls.

In summer, tours on Helgåsjön are arranged on the century-old steamer *Thor.* It costs 50 kronor ($8.75 for adults) and 25 kronor ($4.35) for children under 12. For information on this and other activities, contact the tourist office.

SMÅLANDS MUSEUM, Södra Järnvägsgatan 2. Tel. 451-45.
   Sweden's oldest provincial museum, located near the rail station, will give you a

better sense of the area as well as a look at the history of Swedish glass. You'll see tools and archives from the early days of this craft, with a special collection of more than 25,000 pieces. In a separate exhibit are displays of the finest artistic examples of Swedish glass produced over the centuries.

In other areas of the museum you can see one of Sweden's largest coin collections, art exhibits, religious objects, weapons, and a special room housing an ethnological collection. Forestry and agriculture exhibits are also included.

Admission: 10 kronor ($1.75) adults, free for children.

Open: Mon–Fri 9am–4pm, Sat 11am–3pm, Sun 1–5pm.

SVENSKA EMIGRANTINSTITUTET MUSEIPARKEN (The House of Emigrants), Strandvägen 4. Tel. 201-20.

This institution, founded in 1968, documents the 1.3 million Swedish people who left their homeland during the "American Fever" years, the 1850s to the 1920s, and moved to America. The house contains exhibits on emigrant history as well as archives and a research library. A permanent exhibition, the *Dream of America*, presents insights into the background and consequences of the emigration. Minnesota Day is a folk festival held the second Sunday in August each year, drawing thousands of Swedes and Swedish-Americans. The museum is near the Växjö railroad station.

Admission: 10 kronor ($1.75) adults, 5 kronor (85¢) children.

Open: Mon–Fri 9am–4pm, Sat 11am–3pm, Sun 1–5pm.

VÄXJÖ CATHEDRAL, Linnégatan. Tel. 181-89.

Legend says that this cathedral stands on the spot where St. Sigfrid (Småland's missionary from York, England, in the 11th century) erected his little wooden church. The cathedral has copper-clad towers and a bright interior and its chimes are heard three times a day. Summer concerts are held in the cathedral on Thursday at 8pm.

Adjacent to the cathedral is **Linnéparken** (Linné Park), named for Carl von Linné (Carolus Linnaeus), the Swedish botanist who developed the scientific categories of plants. In the park an arboretum displays all 24 such categories of perennials. There are also other flower gardens throughout and a playground for children. The cathedral is in the town center, by Linnéparken.

Admission: Free.

Open: May–Sept, daily 8am–9pm; Oct–Apr, daily 8am–4pm. The museum in one of the turrets is open during summer, at times listed at the entrance.

TELEBORG SLOTT, Teleborgatan. Tel. 410-00.

An impressive edifice in local granite, this castle was built in 1896 to 1900. It was the residence of Count Fredrik Bonde and lies in a public park a 5-minute bus ride from the town center. It can only be visited on a public guided tour in a group.

Admission: 10 kronor ($1.75).

Open: Bus departures are from the tourist office (see above), which will inform you of time and departure of group tours.

NEARBY ATTRACTIONS

Between Kalmar and Växjö, within an hour's drive, are several glassworks, including Orrefors, Boda, and Kosta, where you can see the master glassblowers at work.

ORREFORS GLASBRUK, Rte. 31, S-380 40 Orrefors. Tel. 0481/340-00.

Orrefors, between Nybro and Lenhovda, 25 miles west of Kalmar, is one of the most famous names in Swedish glass. Guided tours are conducted Monday through Friday at fixed hours during the tourist season and on request during the rest of the year. The factory shuts down for annual vacations in July, but glassblowers demonstrate their work during this period. It is possible to purchase seconds (in most cases hardly distinguishable from perfect pieces), and gift shipments can be arranged. Tax-free shopping can also be arranged in the factory's shop.

Admission: Free.

Open: Museum and shop, Mon–Fri 9am–6pm, Sat 9am–3pm, Sun noon–4pm.

STROMBERGSHYTTAN, Hovmantorp. Tel. 0478/117-70.

This is part of the Orrefors group. You can watch glass being hand-painted. You can even have a go at painting some glass yourself and shop around in the factory outlet while you wait for your masterpiece to dry. It's 15 miles from Växjö, just after Lessebo on Route 25.
Admission: Free.
Open: Mon–Fri 8am–4pm.

KOSTA BODA GLASSWORKS, Hwy. 28. Tel. 0748/503-00.
Founded in 1742 and expanded since then, this is the main headquarters of the Kosta complex. Here you can see the Old Kosta Museum, with articles from the 18th and 19th centuries as well as exhibitions of contemporary glass. It's located between Eriksmala and the junction with Route 31, 12 miles east of Orrefors.
Admission: Free.
Open: Mon–Sat 9am–4pm. **Closed:** July, but one workshop remains open all summer.

KOSTA BODA GLASSWORKS, Storgatan, Hwy. 25. Tel. 0481/240-00.
Boda Glassworks was founded in 1864, but long ago merged with Kosta. It is in an old work environment with a number of craft shops. It's 12 miles west of Nybro.
Admission: Free.
Open: Tourist shops and exhibition rooms, Mon–Fri 9am–6pm, Sat 9am–3pm, Sun noon–4pm; glassworks, Mon–Fri 10am–3pm. **Closed:** July, but one workshop remains open all summer. **Bus:** 135 from Emmaboda.

LESSEBO PAPERMILL, Hwy. 25. Tel. 0478/106-00.
In the heart of the glassworks district, the small town of Lessebo, on Route 25, 22 miles west of Orrefors, has as its great attraction the famous Lessebo Papermill, the world's oldest working producer of handmade paper. In existence since 1693, the mill is open to the public so you can watch as paper passes through the various stages, from cotton pulp to individual sheets that are pressed and hung to dry. There is a gift shop where you can purchase the handmade products, and tours are available in English.
Admission: Free
Open: Tours, daily at 9:30 and 10:45am and 1 and 2:15pm.

WHERE TO STAY & DINE

SARA HOTEL STATT, Kungsgatan 6, S-351 06 Växjö. Tel. 0470/134-00.
Fax 0470/44837. 130 rms (all with bath). TV TEL.
$ Rates (including breakfast): Summer (June 10 to mid-Aug) and weekends year round, 480 kronor ($83.80) single; 680 kronor ($118.75) double. Winter weekdays, 1,020–1,090 kronor ($178.10–$190.35) single; 1,370–1,530 kronor ($239.20–$267.15) double. AE, DC, MC, V.
This venerable old hostelry has, after several restorations, become a choice place to stay, successfully combining the old and the new. This landmark hotel, conveniently located in the center of town near the railroad station, has welcomed guests since 1840. The hotel's four restaurants serve excellent meals of Scandinavian, American, French, and Italian food. In summer, one of the restaurants serves outdoors. If you're looking for relaxation, try the Golden Grace and the Gyllene Oxen pub. The hotel also has a health club, sauna, and swimming pool, with a whirlpool bath and solarium, a cocktail bar.

HOTEL ROYAL CORNER, Liedbergsgatan 11, S-352 32 Växjö. Tel. 0470/100-00.
Fax 0470/126-44. 158 rms (all with bath). TV TEL.
$ Rates (including breakfast): June 29–Aug 5 and weekends year round, 450 kronor ($78.55) single; 600 kronor ($104.75) double. Weekdays Aug 6–June 28, 875–975 kronor ($152.80–$170.25) single; 1,050–1,150 kronor ($183.35–$200.80) double. AE, DC, MC, V.
This first-class hotel in the town center offers spacious bedrooms with refrigerators

and hairdryers. Well-prepared meals are served in the restaurant, or you might choose to have lighter meals in the café. A piano bar is a popular rendezvous. Guests are free to use the workout gym, with a swimming pool, whirlpool, solarium, and sauna.

SCANDIC HOTEL, Hejareg 15, S-352 46 Växjö. Tel. 0470/220-70. 106 rms (all with bath). TV TEL **Tram:** 4 from the center.

$ Rates (including breakfast): Summer and Fri–Sat year round, 440 kronor ($76.80) single; 530 kronor ($92.55) double. Sun–Thurs in winter, 800 kronor ($139.70) single; 1,020 kronor ($178.10) double. AE, DC, MC, V.

One of the best-value hotels in Växjö, built in 1979, the Scandic offers furnished bedrooms, including some large enough for families. Each room is the same size, fitted in bright shades of blue, green, or pink and yellow. There's a restaurant and a self-service cafeteria, along with a small indoor swimming pool and a sauna. The hotel lies 2 miles west of the center of town on the road going to the airport.

A NEARBY ACCOMMODATION

HOTEL ORREFORS, Kantavägen 29, S-380 46 Orrefors. Tel. 0470/300-35 or 301-12. 10 rms (all with bath).

$ Rates (including breakfast): 425 kronor ($74.20) single; 545 kronor ($95.15) double; 645 kronor ($112.60) triple. DC, MC, V.

⑤ This simple hotel in the center of the village near the Orrefors factory, is in a turn-of-the-century building last renovated in 1988. Rooms are furnished in a modern functional style, and although they have private baths, they lack TVs or phones. A family-run place, it serves breakfast only.

---

4. ÖLAND

25 miles east of Kalmar, 291 miles south of Stockholm

GETTING THERE   By Train   The island has no train service.

By Bus   Buses run from the Kalmar terminal to Borgholm on Öland in less than an hour; take no. 101 or 106.

By Car   From Kalmar, take the bridge over the sound, then turn left onto Route 136 to reach Borgholm.

ESSENTIALS   For information, contact the **Öland Tourist Association,** Box 115, S-387 00 Borgholm (tel. 0485/123-40). The **telephone area code** for Öland is 0485.

More Swedes emigrated from Öland to the United States during the 19th century than from any other province in Sweden. The Baltic island lost a quarter of its population. Many emigrées, however, returned to retire on this island.

Little wonder, considering how beautiful it is, with its sandy beaches, its treeless steppe (*Alvaret*) covered with wildflowers, its birdlife, and its profusion of windmills silhouetted against the summer sky.

Europe's longest bridge, nearly 4 miles long, connects Kalmar with Öland, a popular summer beach resort. The island is 87½ miles long and 10 miles wide. Beaches run along both coasts, and there is only one town, **Borgholm,** a quiet summer retreat. The royal summer residence is **Solliden.** To rent a summer house on the beach, get in touch with the **Öland Tourist Association** (see above).

WHAT TO SEE & DO

One of the more interesting attractions on Öland is **Eketorp Ring-Fort,** a prehistoric fortified village that has been excavated and reconstructed so that visitors can see how people lived in this area many centuries ago. Eketorp is one of 15 known prehistoric forts on the island. Excavations have shown three phases of settlement here, from A.D. 300 to 1300. Today a large section of the massive wall that encircled this ring-fort has been reconstructed, along with Iron Age houses within the walls. You can see dwellings, cattle byres, and storehouses reconstructed using ancient crafts and materials, as well as species of livestock. Objects found in the excavations include simple tools, skillfully crafted jewelry, and weapons. The best of these finds are exhibited in a museum inside the fort wall. Unless you have a car, getting there is tricky, although four buses a day (no. 112) go there from the Mörbylånga bus station. Two buses make the run on Saturday and only one on Sunday. Check with the tourist office for bus timetables.

Eketorp can be visited from May to the first week in June, daily from 9am to 5pm daily, with guided tours weekdays at 2 and 4pm and on Saturday and Sunday at 10am, noon, and 2 and 4pm; from the first week in June to mid-August, daily from 9am to 6pm, with guided tours in English at 1pm, and other tours on the hour from 10am to 7pm; from mid-August to the end of the month, daily from 9am to 5pm, with tours at 10am, noon, and 2 and 4pm; during September, daily from 9am to 5pm, with guided tours on weekdays at 11am and 4pm and on Saturday and Sunday at 11am, 1pm, and 3pm. Admission is 15 kronor ($2.60) for adults, 5 kronor (85¢) for children.

WHERE TO STAY
EXPENSIVE

HALLTORPS GÄSTGIVERI, S-387 00 Borgholm. Tel. 0485/850-00. 35 rms (all with bath). TV TEL.

$ Rates (including breakfast): 650 kronor ($113.50) single; 900 kronor ($157.15) double. AE, DC, MC, V.

This hotel, launched in 1975, is in one of the oldest manors of Öland, dating from the 17th century. A charming oasis, it is in a tranquil setting, 6 miles south of Borgholm, with a view across the Kalmarsund and the Halltorp Wood. Once it was a royal farming estate, and later a home for the elderly before it was transformed into an inn. Rooms are cozy and intimate, often with beamed ceilings; six of them have a lounge and loft. Laundry facilities and room service are provided.

The inn prides itself on its food, some of the best in the area. Ingredients are fresh, and the inn's home-spiced schnapps are flavored with herbs picked in nearby meadows. Lunch is 65 kronor ($11.35); a three-course menu of the week is 225 kronor ($39.30). There is an à la carte menu as well. Food is served May to September, daily from noon to midnight.

STRAND HOTELL, Villagatan 4, S-380 70 Bornholm. Tel. 0485/110-20. 100 rms (all with bath) TV TEL.

$ Rates: Summer (including breakfast), 800 kronor ($139.70) single; 940 kronor ($164.10) double. Winter Fri–Sat (including half board), 650 kronor ($113.50) per person. Winter Sun–Thurs (including breakfast), 1,025 kronor ($178.95) single; 1,250 kronor ($218.25) double. AE, DC, MC, V.

With a view over Kalmarsund, the Strand is right in the center of the island's entertainment. Some of its six restaurants and bars are open 24 hours a day in summer. Self-catering apartments are offered on a weekly basis. Twenty of the hotel bedrooms are privately owned and used as vacation homes by urbanites; these are rented to the public as regular hotel rooms when the residents aren't there. About half of the rooms contain a minibar. The hotel has a swimming pool, sauna, solarium, fitness room, restaurant, and tavern. Disco dancing is offered every night during the season. There are tennis courts and a marina in the hotel complex. The hotel also has its own yacht basin, which once won an award as the best privately owned yacht harbor in Sweden. It also has its own beach.

MODERATE

GUNTORPS HERRGÅRD, Guntorpsgatan, S-387 00 Borgholm. Tel. 0485/130-00. Fax 0485/13319. 20 rms (all with bath). TV TEL.

$ Rates (including breakfast): 580–685 kronor ($101.25–$119.60) single; 685–785 kronor ($119.60–$137.05) double. AE, DC, MC, V.

This is a clean, comfortable place to stay, about half a mile from the town center. Built in 1919, with new wings added in 1986, it offers rooms in its main building and some kitchen units in an adjacent building. Fourteen of the rooms have a minibar. The hotel has a pleasant dining room, and a riding stable and beaches are nearby. It can arrange for baby-sitting and it also provides room and laundry service. It has even been known to help Swedish-American guests find their long-lost relatives. The hotel has a heated outdoor swimming pool.

HOTELL BORGHOLM, Trädgårdsgatan 15, S-387 00 Borgholm. Tel. 0485/110-60. Fax 0485/12466. 29 rms (24 with bath). TV TEL.

$ Rates (including breakfast): 420 kronor ($73.35) single without bath, 650 kronor ($113.50) single with bath; 500 kronor ($87.30) double without bath, 775 kronor ($135.30) double with bath. AE, DC, MC, V.

Built in 1880 and redecorated in 1984, this hotel in the town center east of the main street, Storgatan, is known mainly for its restaurant, Bakfickan (see "Where to Dine," below), but it also rents clean, comfortable, although simply furnished bedrooms. The hotel, open all year, also has a bar. In the center of Borgholm, it is near tennis courts, swimming pools, health clubs, and car-rental agencies. There's a disco in summer.

WHERE TO DINE

RESTAURANT BAKFICKAN, in the Hotel Borgholm, Trädgårdsgatan 15. Tel. 110-60.

Cuisine: SWEDISH/FRENCH. **Reservations:** Required in summer.

$ Prices: Three-course fixed-price dinner 250 kronor ($43.65); appetizers 50–110 kronor ($8.75–$19.20); main dishes 165–205 kronor ($28.80–$35.80). AE, DC, MC, V.

Open: Late Apr to mid-Sept, daily 6pm–midnight. **Closed:** Late Sept to mid-Apr.

The best restaurant on the island, Bacfickan ("hip pocket" in English) takes pride in its fish, especially delectable Swedish salmon, and in its lamb dishes. If your table isn't ready, order an apéritif at the bar. Food items are well chosen and are based on market-fresh ingredients. The place becomes quite festive in summer, and deserves its widely acclaimed reputation. It's east of the main street, Storgatan.

CHAPTER 28

MALMÖ, HELSINGBORG & SKÅNE

- **WHAT'S SPECIAL ABOUT SKÅNE**
1. **BÅSTAD**
2. **HELSINGBORG**
3. **MALMÖ**
4. **LUND**
5. **YSTAD**
6. **SIMRISHAMN**

In Sweden's southernmost corner, the province of Skåne offers varied scenery, large forests, and many waterways. The sea is always within easy reach, with ample, uncrowded beaches. Many of the larger towns discussed have a continental air, because of the nearness of Denmark and the rest of Europe.

Skåne's major urban cities are Malmö, Helsingborg, and the university and cathedral city of Lund, but many visit the little villages and undiscovered coastal towns in the summer months.

The topography of the area encapsulates almost every type of Nordic scenery, except fjords and snow-capped Lapp mountains. For decades, poets, authors, and painters have found it inspirational. On the tip of the Scandinavian peninsula was where the Selma Lagerlöf's *The Wonderful Adventures of Nils* began. The hero of this story, who travels on the back of a wild goose, has been translated into all major languages.

The first settlers were deer hunters and fishermen who moved from the south of Europe as the ice melted. Over thousands of years their ancestors left many traces—from the Stone Age right to the Viking Age and the early beginnings of Christianity. There are no fewer than 300 small medieval parish churches in the province—all still in use. Castles and mansions, many founded 400 or 500 years ago, dot the landscape.

Once Skåne belonged to Denmark, but since 1658 it has firmly been part of the Swedish kingdom. The famous Swedish smörgåsbord is a Skåne tradition, and it is said that the most authentic smörgåsbords are served in the province. Skåne is known as the Swedish Riviera. For swimming and sunbathing, there are many beaches along its coast.

Skåne might be associated with the wild goose of young Nils, but actually this web-footed, flat-billed, and large-bodied bird is tame, never traveling far from home. That is, until November 10 when Scanians celebrate their almost sacred bird with a gargantuan dinner, enjoyed by all but the bird.

SEEING MALMÖ, HELSINGBORG & SKÅNE

GETTING THERE Skåne is easy to reach. You have a wide choice of flights, either to Malmö's Sturup Airport or to the Copenhagen Airport from which there are frequent hovercraft connections directly to the center of Malmö. Hovercraft also run between downtown Copenhagen and Malmö; and every 15 or 20 minutes—day or night—connections are possible by car-ferry from Helsingør, Denmark, to Helsingborg, Sweden.

If you're traveling by car, there are ferry routes from Denmark, Germany, and Poland.

✓ WHAT'S SPECIAL ABOUT SKÅNE

Great Towns/Villages

☐ Malmö, Sweden's third-largest city and an important seaport.

☐ Lund, a great university city and the site of a major cathedral.

☐ Helsingborg, a major port with many attractions in its historic core and in the environs.

Castles

☐ Castle of Bösjokloster, site of a 1080 Benedictine convent, today filled with thousands of flowers and exotic shrubs.

☐ Christinehof Castle, on the Ystad–Kristianstad road, a fully furnished château with a wildlife sanctuary.

☐ Bäckaskog, the former country palace of King Charles XV, set in a 40-acre park.

Ancient Monuments

☐ Glimmingehus, between Ystad and Simrishamn, the best-preserved medieval keep in Scandinavia.

☐ The Kivik Tomb, one of the most remarkable monuments of the Bronze Age, discovered in 1748.

Churches

☐ The Cathedral of Lund, where romanesque architecture in Scandinavia reached its zenith.

☐ Dalby Church, outside Lund, an 11th-century former bishop's church, the oldest in Scandinavia.

A SUGGESTED ITINERARY

Day 1: Most arrivals are from Denmark, landing at Helsingborg, where a night's stopover is suggested to see the attractions of the town.

Day 2: Head south to Malmö for a day of sightseeing and stay the night.

Day 3: While still in Malmö, take the short train ride to Lund for a day's excursion to this old university town.

Day 4: Head for Ystad for the night and schedule a visit to the Castle of Bosjökloster, northeast of Lund. If time remains, visit Backaskog, the country palace of King Charles XV.

Day 5: From a base in Simrishamn, spend a day sightseeing in the area, visiting Backakra, the farm of Dag Hammarskjöld, and the Kivik Tomb, a prehistoric find.

1. BÅSTAD

125 miles south of Gothenburg, 65 miles north of Malmö,
341 miles west of Stockholm

GETTING THERE **By Train** Båstad is accessible by train on the run from Gothenburg to Malmö. Trains run frequently throughout the day.

By Bus Six buses a day run from Helsingborg to Båstad, taking 1 hour.

By Car From Malmö, take the E6 north to the Båstad turnoff. Båstad lies 4 miles off the main road. From Gothenburg, head south on the E6.

ESSENTIALS For tourist information, contact **Båstads Turistbyrå**, Stortorget, S-269 01 Båstad (tel. 0431/750-45). The **telephone area code** for Båstad is 0431.

Jutting out on a peninsula, surrounded by hills and a beautiful landscape, Båstad is the most fashionable international seaside resort in Sweden.

All the famous international tennis stars have played on the courts at Båstad. Swedish players of today have had much of their training here, inspired by the feats of Björn Borg. There are more than 50 courts in the district, in addition to the renowned Centre Court. Tennis was played here as early as the 1880s, and became firmly established in the 1920s. King Gustaf V took part in these championships for 15 years from 1930 onward under the pseudonym of "Mr. G," and Ludvig Nobel guaranteed financial backing for international tournaments.

Golf has established itself almost as much as tennis, and the Bjäre peninsula offers a choice of five courses. In 1929 Nobel purchased land at Boarp for Båstad's first golf course. The bay provides opportunities for regattas and different kinds of boating. Windsurfing is popular, as is skin-diving. In summer, seabathing is also popular along the coast.

The Bjäre peninsula, a traditional farming area, is known for its early potatoes, which are in demand all over Sweden for the midsummer table with a selection of pickled herring.

WHAT TO SEE & DO

The scene of international tennis matches in summer, Båstad is also noted for one of the principal attractions of southern Sweden—the ✪ **Norrvikens Trädgårdar (Norrviken Gardens)**, Kattvik, S-269 00 Båstad (tel. 710-70), 1½ miles from the resort's center. Founded in 1906 by Rudolf Abelin, these gardens have been expanded and maintained according to his plans, embracing a number of styles, with exotic birds throughout. One garden is in Italian baroque style, with a pond framed with pyramid-shaped boxwood hedges and tall cypresses. A Renaissance Garden is reminiscent of the tapestry art of 15th-century Italy, with its boxwood patterns, and the flower garden, with bulb flowers competing with annuals. There are also a Japanese Garden, Oriental Terrace, Rhododendron Dell, a Romantic Garden, and a Water Garden.

At Villa Abelin, designed by the gardens' founder, wisteria climbs on the wall and is in bloom twice a year. The villa houses shops, exhibits, and information facilities. There is also a restaurant in the grounds.

The gardens may be viewed from May 1 until September 10, daily from 10am to 6pm. Admission is 35 kronor ($6.10) for adults, 30 kronor ($5.25) for children.

WHERE TO STAY & DINE

HOTEL RIVIERA, Rivieravägen, S-269 00 Båstad. Tel. 0431/708-70. Fax 0431/76100. 50 rms (all with bath). TV TEL.
$ **Rates** (including breakfast): 750 kronor ($130.95) single; 1,130 kronor ($197.30) double. MC, V. **Closed:** Oct–Apr.
Often a favorite venue for conferences, this is one of the better hotels in the area, taking on a somewhat festive air in summer. Located by the sea, half a mile from the railroad station, it offers views from many of its bedrooms, as well as its 300-seat restaurant. Bedrooms are comfortably furnished and modernized. Many guests sit out in the gardens or on the terrace, while others prefer to play on the tennis courts. There is a large, cozy bar, plus a summer café on a sun-filled loggia. The à la carte meals are excellent, a combination of Scandinavian and international food, and dinners with dancing to a live band are often presented in season.

GRAND HOTEL SKANSEN, Kyrkogatan 2, S-269 01 Båstad. Tel. 0431/720-50. Fax 0431/700-85. 52 rms (all with bath). TV TEL.
$ **Rates** (including breakfast): 575 kronor ($100.40) single; 800 kronor ($139.70) double. AE, DC, MC, V.
This former grain warehouse a few minutes' walk from the marina and beach has been transformed into a handsome and comfortable hotel. Its main building dates back to 1877, a beautiful old Swedish building listed as a cultural monument. The interior has a beamed roof, pillars, and views over the sea. Guests can relax on the

terrace or have lunch or drinks at the little tables in the courtyard. Bedrooms, contained in five buildings constructed around tennis courts, have recently been modernized and are decorated to a high standard. The hotel also has a nightclub, Grand Slam.

HOTEL-PENSION ENEHALL, Stationsterrassen 10, S-269 00 Båstad. **Tel. 0431/750-15.** 60 rms (all with bath). TV TEL.
$ Rates (including half board): 350–440 kronor ($61.10–$76.80) per person daily. AE, DC, MC, V.

On a slope of Hallandsåsen mountain only a few minutes' walk from the sea, this cozy, intimate place caters mainly to Swedish families, and some occasional Danes and Germans. There are many personal touches here and the rooms, although small, are adequately equipped. The food is tasty, the service polite and efficient.

---

2. HELSINGBORG

143 miles south of Gothenburg, 347 miles
SW of Stockholm, 39 miles north of Malmö

GETTING THERE By Train Trains run hourly during the day between Helsingborg and Malmö, taking 50 minutes. Trains also arrive daily on the 7-hour trip from Stockholm.

By Bus Three buses a day run between Malmö and Helsingborg, but only Friday through Sunday; the trip takes 1 hour 10 minutes. Two daily buses leave Gothenburg for Helsingborg on Friday and again on Sunday, taking 3½ hours.

By Ferry Ferries from Helsingør, Denmark, leave the Danish harbor every 15 to 20 minutes, day or night; trip time is 25 minutes.

By Car From Malmö, head north on the E6; from Gothenburg, drive south on the E6.

ESSENTIALS The tourist bureau, **Turistforeningen i Helsingborg,** S-251 11 Helsingborg (tel. 042/12-03-10), is open in June and August, Monday through Friday from 9am to 7pm, on Saturday from 9am to 5pm, and on Sunday from 3 to 6pm; in July, Monday through Friday from 9am to 8pm, on Saturday from 9am to 7pm, and on Sunday from 3 to 8pm; September to May, Monday through Friday from 9am to 5pm and on Saturday from 9am to noon (closed Sunday).

The **telephone area code** for Helsingborg is 042.

At the narrowest point of the Øresund, 3 miles across the water that separates Sweden and Denmark, is this industrial city and major port. Many people from Copenhagen who visit Kronborg Castle at Helsingør take a 25-minute ferry ride across the sound (leaving every 15 to 20 minutes) for a look at Sweden. You can take a medium-size car with two passengers across the sound from Sweden to Denmark for 240 kronor ($41.90). A one-way passenger fare is 25 kronor ($4.35).

Of course, what they see isn't "Sweden," but a modern city with an ancient history. Helsingborg jointly controlled shipping along the sound with Helsingør in the Middle Ages. It is mentioned in the 10th-century *Nial-Saga*, and documents show that there was a town here in 1085. The city now has more than 100,000 inhabitants, with the second-busiest harbor in the country. It is the city that introduced pedestrian streets to Sweden, and it has long shore promenades along the sound.

WHAT TO SEE & DO

Built in 1897, the **Town Hall (Rådhuset),** Drottninggatan 7 (tel. 10-50-00), has handsome stained-glass windows depicting scenes from the town's history. Two memorial stones outside were presented by the Danes and the Norwegians to the Swedes for their assistance during World War II. There is also a sculpture relief representing the arrival of Danish refugees.

In the main town square, the **Stortorget,** is a monument commemorating General Stenbock's victory at the Battle of Helsingborg in 1710 between Sweden and Denmark.

KÄRNAN, off the Stortorget.

For a quick view of Helsingborg, go to the *terrassen* (terrace) of the Stortorget, which has steps leading up to the 12th-century thick-walled medieval keep, the Kärnan. From the tower there's an excellent panorama of the sound and the Swedish and Danish coasts. The tower, one of the most important medieval monuments in Sweden, represents the remains of Helsingborg Castle, torn down in the 17th century.

Admission: Elevator to the top, 10 kronor ($1.75).
Open: Daily 10am–8pm.

HELSINGBORGS MUSEUM, Södra Storgatan 31. Tel. 10-59-50.

Exploring this museum is like wandering in the city's attic. Anything the city didn't know what to do with they placed it here: bottled fish, still life paintings, baby carriages, stuffed sharks, stuffed birds, antique dolls and clothing.

Admission: 10 kronor ($1.75) adults, free for children. The same ticket will admit you to the Kärnan (see above), the Vikingsbergs Konstmuseum (Vikingsberg Art Museum), on Vikingsgatan, and the Fredriksdals Open-Air Museum (see below).
Open: May–Aug, Mon–Sat 11am–6pm, Sun noon–6pm; Sept–Apr, Tues–Sun 11am–4pm, Sun noon–5:30pm. The Vikingsbergs Konstmuseum is open the same hours.

SOFIERO, Sofierovägen. Tel. 14-52-59.

At this summer residence of the late King Gustav Adolf VI, the Helsingborgs Museum also maintains historical and art exhibitions. Built in 1864–65, the palace is a 5-minute drive north of Helsingborg in a large park. It has a café and restaurant, and there are also playhouses for children.

Admission: 20 kronor ($3.50) adults, 10 kronor ($1.75) children.
Open: May–June and Aug to mid-Sept, daily 10am–6pm; July, daily 10am–8pm.
Closed: Late Sept to Apr. **Bus:** 250, 252.

MARIAKYRKAN (Church of St. Mary), Södra Storgatan. Tel. 18-02-35.

A short walk east from the harbor at the intersection of Norra Storgatan, this church was built in the 13th century but substantially rebuilt in the 15th century. It is noted for its medieval altarpiece and its intricately carved Renaissance pulpit.

Admission: Free.
Open: Mon–Sat 8am–6pm, Sun 9am–6pm.

FREDRIKSDAL OPEN-AIR MUSEUM AND BOTANICAL GARDEN, Oscar Trapps Väg. Tel. 11-06-78.

This museum features farmhouses, a windmill, barns, even a malt drier that have been reassembled and the grounds of an 18th-century mansion donated to the Helsingborgs Museum. The botanical gardens contain chiefly the vegetation of Skåne.

Admission: Free.
Open: Daily 10am–6pm. **Bus:** 202, 204, 232, 506, 520.

WHERE TO STAY

Although listed as expensive, many of these hotels are moderate in price in summer and on Friday or Saturday nights.

EXPENSIVE

GRAND HOTEL, Stortorget 8-12, S-251 11 Helsingborg. Tel. 042/12-01-70. Fax 042/11-88-33. 130 rms (all with bath). MINIBAR TV TEL **Bus:** 1, 6.

$ Rates (including breakfast): Summer, 650 kronor ($113.50) single; 800 kronor

($139.70) double. Winter, 875 kronor ($152.80) single; 1,050 kronor ($183.35) double. AE, DC, MC, V.

In the town center a 2-minute walk from the Rådhuset, this renovated but still comfortably old-fashioned 1920s establishment has retained its grand manner. Antiques, old paintings, numerous chandeliers, and bowls of fresh flowers are everywhere. The first-class bedrooms feature color TVs, video, hairdryers, and trouser presses, among other amenities. Use of the sauna and solarium are included in the prices. The Grand has an elegant dining room. From the hotel you can take a bus to Angelholm Airport.

HOTEL HORISONT, Gustav Adolfs Gate 47, S-252 27 Helsingborg. Tel. 042/14-92-60. 170 rms (all with bath). TV TEL **Bus:** 1, 6.

$ **Rates** (including breakfast): Summer and Fri–Sat year round, 500 kronor ($87.30) single; 600 kronor ($104.75) double. Sun–Thurs in winter, 920 kronor ($160.65) single; 1,050 kronor ($183.35) double. AE, DC, MC, V.

Set in a park at the edge of the commercial center of town, the angular and futuristic facade of this hotel was erected in 1985. It is considered the most alluring palace in town. The bedrooms are comfortably conservative, with plush upholstery and soundproof windows. On the premises is a warmly attractive piano bar lined with brick and touches of brass, and a high-ceilinged formal restaurant with potted palms. Relaxation facilities include a center with saunas, whirlpools, and solariums. The hotel is about a mile south of the ferryboat terminal.

HOTEL MOLLBERG, Stortorget 18, S-251 10 Helsingborg. Tel. 042/12-02-70. Fax 042/14-96-18. 115 rms (all with bath). MINIBAR TV TEL **Bus:** 1, 6.

$ **Rates** (including breakfast): Summer and Fri–Sat year round 475 kronor ($82.95) single; 700 kronor ($122.20) double. Sun–Thurs in winter, 1,175 kronor ($205.15) single; 1,280 kronor ($223.50) double. AE, DC, MC, V.

Sweden's oldest continuously operating hotel and restaurant, the Mollberg dates back to the 14th century. Its elaborate wedding-cake exterior and high-ceilinged interior were most recently restored in 1986. Its first-class rooms all are equipped with color TVs, videos, trouser presses, and hairdryers, among other amenities. Use of the solarium and sauna are included in the rates. The Mollberg has a dining room, piano bar, and a cocktail lounge, decorated with dark paneling and opulent gilded-era accessories. The Café Mollberg is open Monday through Saturday from 11am to 11pm, offering a light cuisine and beverages.

MODERATE

HOTEL HELSINGBORG, Stortorget 1, S-252 23 Helsingborg. Tel. 042/12-09-45. Fax 042/11-54-61. 48 rms (all with bath). TV TEL **Bus:** 1, 6.

$ **Rates** (including breakfast): June 21–Aug 8, 390 kronor ($68.10) single; 520 kronor ($90.80) double. Aug 9–June 20, 600–780 kronor ($104.75–$136.20) single; 840–900 kronor ($146.65–$157.15) double. AE, DC, MC, V.

Of the three hotels that lie along this grand avenue, this one is closest to the city's medieval tourist attraction, the Karnan. It has a heroic neoclassical frieze and three copper-sheathed towers, and occupies four floors of what used to be a bank headquarters. Bedrooms are pleasantly modernized, very comfortable, and flooded with sunlight from the large windows.

HOTELL MAGNUS STENBOCK, Lilla Strandgatan 5, S-252 23 Helsingborg. Tel. 042/12-62-50. Fax 042/24-15-93. 28 rms (all with bath). TV TEL **Bus:** 1, 6.

$ **Rates** (including breakfast): 785 kronor ($137.05) single; 925 kronor ($161.50) double. 30% midsummer discounts. AE, DC, MC, V.

Rebuilt in 1989, this hotel in the town center has a 19th-century brick facade. In summer sunlight filters through rows of flower boxes near the arched windows of the breakfast room. Bedrooms are modern and very clean, with streamlined furniture. Five are reserved for nonsmokers.

WHERE TO DINE

ELINOR, Kullagatan 53. Tel. 12-23-30.
Cuisine: SEAFOOD. **Reservations:** Required. **Bus:** 1, 6.
$ Prices: Fixed-price meals 210 kronor ($36.65) at dinner; 165 kronor ($28.80) at lunch; appetizers 50–130 kronor ($8.75–$22.70); main dishes 125–250 kronor ($21.85–$43.65). AE, DC, MC, V.
Open: Lunch Mon–Sat noon–2:30pm; dinner Mon–Sat 6–11:30pm.

One of the best restaurants in town, Elinor is located on a pleasant pedestrian walkway in the town center, surrounded by boutiques and antiques shops. This is Helsingborg's answer to the sophisticated demands of nouvelle cuisine. There's a bar in back, along with a well-upholstered dining room.

The small but select menu changes frequently depending on seasonal ingredients and the chef's imagination. Dishes might include a ragoût of shrimp with chanterelles and combinations of crayfish, lobster, turbot, salmon, trout, and seasonal game.

RESTAURANT OSCÁR, Sundstorget 7. Tel. 11-25-21.
Cuisine: SEAFOOD. **Reservations:** Recommended. **Bus:** 1, 6.
$ Prices: Appetizers 45–130 kronor ($7.85–$22.70); main dishes 125–225 kronor ($21.85–$39.30); fixed-price lunch 125 kronor ($21.85). AE, DC, MC, V.
Open: Lunch Mon–Fri 11:30am–2:30pm; dinner Mon–Sat 6–11pm.

For a really first-class meal, this is one of the best fish restaurants in town. Decorated in a tavern style, it overlooks a large parking lot near the ferryboats. The seafood is always fresh, whether it's included in the fish soup or served as grilled fish or bouillabaisse. Fresh vegetables and salads are also well prepared. Specialties include poached filet of sole with a chablis sauce and whitebait roe and crab filled with lemon sole and served with a saffron sauce, rice pilaf, and shrimp.

LA PLAGE, Strandvägen. Tel. 14-97-20.
Cuisine: SEAFOOD. **Reservations:** Required. **Bus:** 4.
$ Prices: Appetizers 50–90 kronor ($8.75–$15.70); main dishes 75–200 kronor ($13.10–$34.90). AE, DC, MC, V.
Open: Lunch Mon–Fri 11:30am–2pm; dinner Mon–Fri 6–11pm, Sat–Sun 1–11pm. **Closed:** Oct–Apr.

La Plage is so small that unless you knew better you'd think it was a kiosk. It's about 2½ miles north of the city center, in an isolated spot between the road and the seawall. Its walls are painted in a kaleidoscopic design of stripes, but inside is a formal dining room with Queen Anne chairs. Reservations are needed for a table inside, but you can usually get an outdoor table in warm weather without an advance call. Full meals include meat dishes and a fresh selection of well-prepared seafood. Specialties include several preparations of salmon, trout, shrimp, and herring, along with gratin of lobster, curried filet of sole, and crab stuffed in its own shell.

3. MALMÖ

177 miles south of Gothenburg, 384 miles SW of Stockholm

GETTING THERE By Plane Malmö's airport is at Sturup, outside the city, which receives international flights from London, plus flights from cities within Sweden, including Gothenburg (50 minutes) and Stockholm (1 hour). However, its major international link with the world is Kastrup Airport at Copenhagen, to which Malmö is connected by hovercraft service.

By Train The Stockholm–Copenhagen express train going via Helsingborg has a branch service through to Malmö. Service is frequent between Gothenburg and Malmö. From Helsingborg to Malmö, trains leave hourly on the 50-minute trip.

By Bus Two buses each on Friday and Sunday make the 4½-hour run from Gothenburg to Malmö. Buses from Helsingborg to Malmö run on Friday and Sunday, taking 1 hour 10 minutes.

By Hydrofoil Malmö and Copenhagen are linked by *Flygbåtana* (hydrofoil), with hourly service year round from 5am to midnight, taking 45 minutes. Should the Øresund freeze over, service is suspended. SAS runs a hovercraft from Kastrup Airport outside Copenhagen to Malmö from 8am to 8pm, taking 45 minutes.

ESSENTIALS The **Malmö Tourist Office** is at Hamngatan 1, S-211 22 Malmö (tel. 040/34-12-70), usually open Monday through Friday from 9am to 5pm and on Saturday from 9am to 1pm. The **telephone area code** for Malmö is 040.

Sweden's third-largest city, a busy port across the Øresund sound from Copenhagen, is the capital of Skåne. A good base for exploring the ancient castles and manors nearby, it's an old city, dating from the 13th century.

From early days, Malmö prospered because of its location on a sheltered bay. In the 16th century when it was the second-largest city in Denmark, it vied with Copenhagen for economic and cultural leadership. Reminders of that age are Malmöhus Castle (see below), the Town Hall, and the Stortorget, plus several homes of rich burghers. Malmö has been a Swedish city since the end of a bloody war in 1658, when the Treaty of Roskilde incorporated the province of Skåne into Sweden.

WHAT TO SEE & DO

The **Malmökortet Card** entitles visitors to discounts and free admission to most of the city's attractions, free travel in Malmö's local buses, half-price fare on local trains, and substantial discounts on other excursions. A card good for 1 day (24 hours) costs 50 kronor ($8.75) for adults, 25 kronor ($4.35) for children. For 2 days the price is 60 kronor ($10.50) for adults, 30 kronor ($5.25) for children; 3 days, 70 kronor ($12.20) for adults, 35 kronor ($6.10) for children; and for 1 week, 100 kronor ($17.45) for adults, 50 kronor ($8.75) for children. The Malmökortet is available at a number of outlets, including the Malmö Tourist Office (see above).

The Renaissance-era square surrounding the fountain on Stortorget is important architecturally, but the fountain itself is one of the most charming and imaginative in Scandinavia, including a nightingale, the symbol of Malmö. Built in 1964, it commemorates the most major dates in the city's history. Nearby is the 16th-century **Town Hall,** which still retains its look of Renaissance splendor. The **City Theater** at Fersens Väg, completed near the end of World War II, is considered one of the best equipped in Europe.

Four major attractions are under the direction of Malmö Museums, Box 406, S-210 24 Malmö (tel. 34-10-00). Heading the list is **Malmöhus Castle,** Malmöhusvågen founded in the 15th century by Eric of Pomerania and rebuilt by Christian III in the 16th century. Once a prison (the Earl of Bothwell, third husband of Mary Queen of Scots, was incarcerated here from 1568 to 1573), the castle now houses the **City Museum,** the **Natural History Museum,** the **Aquarium,** and the **Art Museum.** The last contains a collection of old Scandinavian masters, especially those from southern Sweden, such as Carl Fredrik Hill (1849–1911), now considered one of Sweden's best landscape painters and a forerunner of European modernism. Most interesting is the large collection of Russian oil paintings from around 1900—the largest collection outside the Soviet Union. It also houses some modern art, and good samples of Swedish furniture and textiles. The lyrical sketches in the foyer are by Carl Larsson, one of Sweden's best-known artists. West of Stortorget, the castle can easily be reached on foot.

Also in the group, across the street from the castle is **Kommendanthuset Malmöhusvägen,** a military museum and a piece of history in its own right, displaying military artifacts and equipment. **Tekniska Museet och Sjöfarts- museet** (the Museums of Technology and Shipping), Malmöhusvägen, is near the Kommendanthuset. Ancient means of communication are exhibited, as well as the submarine *U-3.* Technical history can be followed from the steam engine to the jet. The children's department even has a pirate ship, and in summer an old-fashioned tramway is in operation. **Vagnmuseet** (the Carriage Museum), housed in the former military horse stable at Drottningtorget, displays carriages since the 18th century, coaches, and cycles.

A ticket costing 20 kronor ($3.50) for adults, 5 kronor (85¢) for children 15 and under, admits you to all these sites if visited on the same day. The museums are open Tuesday through Saturday from noon to 4pm and on Sunday from noon to 4:30pm.

Limhamn's Museum, Limhamnsvägen 102 (tel. 15-78-10), is an old soldier's cottage furnished like an ancient fisherman's home. Admission is 3 kronor (50¢) for adults, 2 kronor (35¢) for children. It's open on Wednesday from 6 to 8pm and on Sunday from 1 to 4pm.

Malmö's S:t Petri (St. Peter's Church) (tel. 35-90-40) is another major sight, a copper-roofed brick church dating from the 14th century. Off Stortorget, it is noted for its Renaissance altar, baptismal font, and elegantly carved pulpit. It's open daily from 8am to 4pm.

One of the town centers for handcrafts is the painstakingly restored **Lilla Torg,** where half-timbered 16th-century houses surround cobblestones, fountains, and cafés. The Sparbanken Skåne, at one of the corners, is the most antique bank in town—some furnishings are at least 100 years old.

Nearby Attractions

Svaneholm, between Malmö and Ystad, was founded in 1530 as a fortress, and was later partially converted into an Italian-style palace. Today it houses a museum of paintings, furnishings, and tools dating primarily from the 18th and 19th centuries. The establishment is owned by the Svaneholm Castle Co-operative Society Ltd., and you can buy share certificates to help with the maintenance. For information, write Jordberga, S-230 00 Klagstorp (tel. 0411/42-090).

Admission to the castle is 15 kronor ($2.60) for adults, 5 kronor (85¢) for children. It's open March, April, and September to December, Wednesday through Sunday from 11am to 4pm; May to August, Tuesday through Sunday from 11am to 5pm; closed in January and February.

WHERE TO STAY

The **Malmö Tourist Office** (see above) will help you book a hotel room. On weekends and in summer, special rates provide good accommodation at moderate prices.

VERY EXPENSIVE

SAVOY HOTEL, Norra Vallgatan 62, S-201 80 Malmö. Tel. 040/702-30.
Fax 040/97-85-51. 100 rms (all with bath), 8 suites. MINIBAR TV TEL **Bus:** 14, 17.
$ Rates (including breakfast): June 26–Aug 3 and Fri–Sat year round, 550 kronor ($96.05) single; 650 kronor ($113.50) double. Aug 4–June 25 Sun–Thurs, 1,200–1,400 kronor ($209.50–$244.45) single; 1,300–1,600 kronor ($227–$270.65) double; from 1,800 kronor ($314.30) suites. AE, DC, MC, V.

This hotel has figured prominently in Malmö history; famous guests have included Dag Hammarskjöld, Liv Ullman, Alan Alda, and Johnny (Tarzan) Weissmuller. Upstairs you'll find some of the most plushly decorated accommodations in Sweden. Each bedroom contains champagne-colored upholstery, cabriole-legged or Chippendale-style furniture, and all the sophisticated extras of a deluxe hotel. For the various dining and drinking facilities of this prestigious hotel, see "Where to Dine," below.

SHERATON MALMÖ HOTEL & TOWERS, Triangeln 2, S-200 10 Malmö. Tel. 040/74-000, or toll free 800/325-3535 in the U.S. Fax 040/23-20-20. 214 rms (all with bath), 14 suites. A/C MINIBAR TV TEL **Bus:** 10C, 15C.

$ **Rates** (including breakfast): June 22–Aug 19 and Fri–Sat year round, 640 kronor ($111.75) single; 740 kronor ($129.20) double. Sun–Thurs Aug 20–June 21, 1,190–1,600 kronor ($207.80–$279.35) single; 1,290–1,700 kronor ($225.25–$296.80) double; from 2,200 kronor ($384.10) suite. AE, DC, MC, V. **Parking:** 100 kronor ($17.45).

Malmö's first international luxury hotel lies in the city center, close to the Triangeln shopping center, the theater, the art hall, and the congress hall. It has a lobby bar in a glass-roofed garden, and a roof garden. The most expensive rooms are in the Sheraton Towers, three top floors with a separate check-in desk and its own lounge on the 20th floor. All bedrooms are tastefully and often luxuriously appointed, with many amenities.

Dining/Entertainment: "Upstairs" is the prestige restaurant of the hotel, with beautifully laid tables and attentive service. Meals are created from fresh products. International dishes are combined with Swedish home-cooking and Scandinavian specialties. Piano entertainment is presented in the lobby. Adjacent is a casino offering roulette and blackjack.

Services: Room service, laundry and valet service.
Facilities: World-class fitness center, parking area.

EXPENSIVE

HOTEL KRAMER, Stortorget 7, S-201 21 Malmö. Tel. 040/701-20. Fax 040/23-09-37. 115 rms (all with bath). TV TEL **Bus:** 14, 17.

$ **Rates** (including breakfast): Summer and Fri–Sat year round, 500 kronor ($87.30) single; 650 kronor ($113.50) double. Sun–Thurs in winter, 1,050 kronor ($183.35) single; 1,250 kronor ($218.25) double. AE, DC, MC, V.

⭐ Set at the side of the town's main square, this châteaulike twin-towered building is one of the two landmark hotels in town. Built in 1875, it was renovated at the height of the art deco era, and half the rooms were redecorated in the mid-1980s. Rooms are among the most alluring in town, many designed like the largest staterooms of a 1930s ocean liner. You'll enjoy marble bathrooms, dark-grained paneling, curved walls, and beds where Mae West might have felt at home.

HOTEL NOBLE HOUSE, Gustav Adolfs Torg 47, S-211 39 Malmö. Tel. 040/10-15-00. Fax 040/11-68-37. 128 rms (all with bath), 4 suites. MINIBAR TV TEL **Bus:** 14, 17.

$ **Rates** (including breakfast): June 15–Aug 12 and Fri–Sat year round, 600 kronor ($104.75) single; 700 kronor ($122.20) double. Sun–Thurs Aug 13–June 14, 1,110 kronor ($193.80) single; 1,320 kronor ($230.50) double; from 1,420 kronor ($348) suite. AE, DC, MC, V.

⭐ Named after the bestselling novel by James Clavell, this is one of the most modern and up-to-date hotels in town, and certainly the most glamorous. The comfortable pastel-colored rooms are decorated with copies of early 20th-century paintings. Because of the hotel's convenient location in the town center, its quietest rooms face the interior courtyard.

SAS ROYAL HOTEL, Östergatan 10, S-211 25 Malmö. Tel. 040/23-92-00. Fax 040/11-28-40. 221 rms (all with bath). MINIBAR TV TEL **Bus:** 14, 17.

$ **Rates** (including breakfast): Fri–Sat, 600 kronor ($104.75) single; 690 kronor ($120.45) double. Sun–Thurs, 1,160 kronor ($202.55) single; 1,260 kronor ($220). **Parking:** 60 kronor ($10.50). AE, DC, MC, V.

One of the best-equipped and run hotels in the south of Sweden, it is filled with tastefully decorated rooms, each with elegant bathrooms and such amenities as video, hairdryer, trouser press, and radio. Built in 1988, the hotel is seven floors high and was designed to accommodate the disabled.

Dining/Entertainment: An exceptionally good restaurant, Thott's serves an elegant Scandinavian and continental cuisine in a half-timbered house from the mid-16th century. For fast meals, try the cafeteria. There is also a bar.

Services: Room service, baby-sitting, SAS EuroClass check-in on hovercraft to Copenhagen, express laundry, business service center.

Facilities: Heated garage with direct access from the hotel.

MODERATE

HOTEL ANGLAIS, Stortorget 15, S-211 22 Malmö. Tel. 040/714-50. Fax 040/23-09-37. 82 rms (all with bath). TV TEL **Bus:** 14, 17.

$ **Rates** (including breakfast): Summer and Fri–Sat year round, 550 kronor ($96.05) single; 650 kronor ($113.50) double. Sun–Thurs in winter, 850 kronor ($148.40) single; 1,000 kronor ($174.60) double. AE, DC, MC, V.

This efficiently run 1912 hotel has few frills but plenty of comfort. Located on the main square facing the town hall, it's one of the Salvation Army's best old-world showcases. Rooms are cavernous enough to offer bed-sitting areas and all is very clean. All units have showers or complete baths. The hotel has a tea room and a restaurant, open Monday through Friday from 6:30am to 5:30pm, with two daily *dagens* menus priced from 48 to 53 kronor ($8.40 to $9.25).

SARA HOTEL WINN, Jörgen Kocksgatan 3, S-201 20 Malmö. Tel. 040/10-18-00. Fax 040/11-44-33. 101 rms (all with bath). TV TEL **Bus:** 14, 17.

$ **Rates** (including breakfast): Summer and Fri–Sat year round, 445 kronor ($77.70) single; 660 kronor ($115.25) double. Sun–Thurs in winter, 840 kronor ($146.65) single; 1,020 kronor ($178.10) double. AE, DC, MC, V.

The Sara Hotel Winn is a quiet and calm place to stay, despite its location in the heart of Malmö, only a couple of minutes from the hydrofoils to Denmark and a short distance from the railway station and airport buses. Bedrooms are large, with comfortable chairs and beds and generously sized shower/bathrooms. Each has a radio and automatic alarm clock, and 20 contain a minibar. The hotel has a sauna and a recreation room.

WHERE TO DINE

Malmö has more restaurants than almost any other Swedish city, and most of them are in the central part of town. **Saluhallen,** by Lilla Torg, is an indoor food market with several small restaurants.

All the following selections are in the moderate category.

CASA MIA, Södergatan 12. Tel. 23-05-00.
 Cuisine: ITALIAN. **Reservations:** Recommended. **Bus:** 14, 17.
$ **Prices:** Appetizers 55–85 kronor ($9.60–$14.85); main dishes 110–185 kronor ($19.20–$32.30). AE, DC, MC, V.
 Open: Mon–Fri 11am–midnight, Sat–Sun noon–midnight.

Suggestions of the gondola moorings of Venice ornament the front terrace of this Nordic version of a neighborhood trattoria. Troubadours stroll from table to crowded table singing Neapolitan ballads, and your waiter is likely to address you in Italian. You can begin with a steaming bowl of stracciatella alla romana or the fish soup of the house, then penne with shrimp, basil, cream, and tomatoes, or spaghetti with seafood. Later you can dig into saltimbocca alla romana, a portion of grilled scampi, escalope of veal stuffed with goose liver, or an array of grilled meats with aromatic herbs. There are 15 types of pizza on the menu and pastries are offered for dessert.

GRILLEN, in the Savoy Hotel, Norra Vallgata 62. Tel. 702-30.
 Cuisine: SWEDISH. **Reservations:** Recommended. **Bus:** 14, 17.
$ **Prices:** Appetizers 65–125 kronor ($11.35–$21.85); main dishes 110–280 kronor ($19.20–$48.90). AE, DC, MC, V.

Open: Mon–Fri 11:30am–midnight, Sat 5pm–midnight, Sun 1pm–midnight.
A cozy and intimate dining spot, Grillen has 17th-century Windsor chairs, touches of gleaming copper, and candlelight. Full dinners include an array of grilled specialties that you can watch being prepared. Your meal might include grilled salmon tartare with salmon roe, three kinds of pickled herring, smoked reindeer, filet of pork flambéed with tequila, chateaubriand with cognac and Gorgonzola, and a Swedish classic dish of ice-cellar salted salmon with creamed dill-flavored potatoes. Lunch costs from 55 kronor ($9.60).

KOCKSKA KROGEN, Frans Suellsgatan 3. Tel. 703-20.
Cuisine: SWEDISH/FRENCH. **Reservations:** Recommended. **Bus:** 14, 17.
$ Prices: Appetizers 65–110 kronor ($11.35–$19.20); main dishes 99–270 kronor ($17.30–$47.15). AE, DC, MC, V.
Open: Mon–Fri 11:30am–midnight, Sat 6pm–midnight.
Kockska Krogen is named after a 16th-century Danish mayor who lived in the thick brick vaults of this building in the Old Town. To reach it, pass beneath an ornate fortified entrance used during the Renaissance as the city mint. Stop for a beer in the pub near the entrance or proceed into the labyrinth or plaster-covered vaults that make up the many dining rooms. Each of the well-prepared specialties is named after a legendary person important in the history of Malmö. You can order a concoction of Dover sole with lobster and chestnuts, flambéed beef filet, honey-fried breast of duck, followed by one of 10 succulent desserts, perhaps rum-raisin ice cream in flambéed crêpes.

OLGA'S RESTAURANT, Pildammsparken, Pildammsvägen. Tel. 12-55-26.
Cuisine: SWEDISH. **Reservations:** Recommended. **Bus:** 36.
$ Prices: Appetizers 40–95 kronor ($7–$16.60); main dishes 105–200 kronor ($18.35–$34.90); one-course lunch 55 kronor ($9.60). AE, DC, MC, V.
Open: Mon–Fri 11:30am–11:30pm, Sat 1–11pm, Sun 1–8pm.
Originally built for the 1914 Baltic Exposition, this building is about half a mile south of the city center at the edge of a freshwater reservoir in a city park. The view from the terrace overlooks willows, ducks, and boxes of geraniums. Dinners might include Swedish scampi, pepper steak, veal filet garnished with shrimp, and succulent preparations of salmon. You might enjoy a before- or after-dinner drink in the modern cellar bar.

O'YES, Skeppsbron 2. Tel. 10-43-70.
Cuisine: INTERNATIONAL. **Reservations:** Recommended. **Bus:** 14, 17.
$ Prices: Appetizers 55–120 kronor ($9.60–$20.95); main dishes 80–160 kronor ($13.95–$27.95); one-course lunch and access to salad bar 57 kronor ($9.95). AE, DC, MC, V.
Open: Mon–Fri 11:30am–1am, Sat 5:30pm–2am.
Built on a 19th-century foundation next door to the Central Station, this restaurant has glass walls that give it a greenhouselike look. Views are of the harbor and wood tables are deliberately without tablecloths. On some nights there are live concerts by leading jazz artists of Sweden. In 1987 O'Yes was voted "restaurant of the year" in Sweden. Try such dishes as jambalaya or gumbos inspired by New Orleans, perhaps Texas chili, "tiger chicken," or a pasta with mussels and garlic. There is also an array of Swedish *husmanskost* (home-cooked) dishes.

RÅDHUSKÄLLEREN, Kyrkogatan 6. Tel. 790-20.
Cuisine: SWEDISH. **Reservations:** Recommended. **Bus:** 14, 17.
$ Prices: Appetizers 45–101 kronor ($7.85–$17.65); main dishes 90–240 kronor ($15.70–$41.90); one-course lunch 55 kronor ($9.60). AE, DC, MC, V.
Open: Mon–Sat 11:30am–11pm, Sun 1–6pm.
Even if your schedule doesn't allow you to dine here, you should at least drop in for a drink at the most atmospheric place in Malmö, the cellar of the Town Hall. Its severe exterior and labyrinth of underground vaults were built in 1546. Have a drink in the rustic pub or in the more formal crescent-shaped cocktail lounge before heading into

the dark-vaulted dining room that for centuries stored gold, wine, furniture, and foodstuffs. Full à la carte meals include a changing array of daily specials and such staples as filet of sole Washington, stuffed sole, filet of veal, pepper steak, and roast duck.

RESTAURANT GOURMET, Låndbygatan 4. Tel. 12-08-35.
   Cuisine: SWEDISH/FRENCH. **Reservations:** Recommended. **Bus:** 14, 17.
$ **Prices:** Appetizers 63–79 kronor ($11–$13.80); main dishes 135–240 kronor ($23.55–$41.90); three-course dinner 310 kronor ($54.15); one-course lunch 49 kronor ($8.55). AE, DC, MC, V.
   Open: Lunch Mon–Fri 11:30am–2:30pm; dinner Mon–Fri 5:30–11pm, Sat 1–11pm.
Near Lilla Torg, this elegant restaurant is in an 18th-century brick-vaulted cellar. To reach it, pass through a small garden where tables are placed in summer. The true elegance of the place comes out at night with the three-course fixed-price menu, and an à la carte selection costs about the same. Specialties include Canadian lobster, scallops poached with white wine and served with Swedish caviar, and filet of lemon sole stuffed with blue mussels and crab. The chef's special pride is his house duckling.

RESTAURANT SAVOY, in the Savoy Hotel, Norra Vallgatan 62. Tel. 702-30.
   Cuisine: SWEDISH. **Reservations:** Not required. **Bus:** 14, 17.
$ **Price:** Appetizers 65–110 kronor ($11.35–$19.20); main dishes 99–290 kronor ($17.30–$50.65). AE, DC, MC, V.
   Open: Mon–Fri noon–midnight, Sat–Sun 1pm–midnight.
The main appeal of this restaurant is the crowds of city residents who show up for lunch, afternoon tea, dinner, and the late-night disco. Originally designed as a ballroom, it's on the lobby level of the Savoy Hotel (see "Where to Stay," above). The black marble dance floor and octagonal mirror hanging from the ceiling during disco hours add a high-tech allure. A fixed-price lunch costs 55 kronor ($9.60).

SAVVY SHOPPING

MATTSSONS PÄLS, Norra Vallgatan 98. Tel. 12-55-33.
   One of Sweden's leading furriers. Saga mink coats and jackets are the best buy, but Mattssons has a full range of fine furs at prices lower than in the United States. In the boutique are fur-lined poplins and accessories, all tax free for tourists. Bus: 92, 93, 94.

NK [NORDISKA KOMPANIET], Stora Nygatan 50. Tel. 770-00.
   At this branch of Sweden's largest department store, you'll find "A Very Special Swedish Shop," with glass, goods, handcrafts, and souvenirs of Sweden. Bus: 11, 19, 21.

SILVERBERGS MOBLER, Baltzarsgatan 31. Tel. 740-80.
   For glassware and crystal, this famous store competently and reliably ships its stunning collection of glassware, crystal, furniture, and gifts all over the world. Bus: 14, 17.

EVENING ENTERTAINMENT

Since Copenhagen is nearby, Malmö does not have much nightlife, but there are a few spots where you might find fun.

FOLKETS PARK (People's Park), Amiralsgatan 35. Tel. 709-90.
   From May to September, locals head for these sprawling amusement grounds and pleasure gardens, with dancing pavilions, vaudeville performances, open-air concerts, and restaurants. There is also a reptile center. Children will find a playhouse, plus a small zoo and a puppet theater. Bus: 32, 36, 37, or 38 from Gustav Adolfs Torg.
   Admission: Sat–Sun, 25 kronor ($4.35) adults, free for children under 12; Mon–Fri, free for all.

NIGHTCLUB ETAGE, Stortorget 6. Tel. 23-20-60.

Probably the most innovative and creatively designed nightspot in the region, Etage is reached by climbing a circular staircase from an enclosed courtyard next to the main town square. There's a piano bar on the second floor, but the heart of the place is the third-floor restaurant, bar, and disco. There, amid a glittering decor of midnight-blue, black, and sparkling chrome, you'll find a futuristic-looking dance floor. The continental menu features a meal for 200 kronor ($34.90); drinks run 55 kronor ($9.60). Open Wednesday through Saturday from 8pm to 3am. Bus: 14, 17.

Admission: Disco, 70 kronor ($12.20) after 10pm, including first drink.

GOLDEN DAYS, Stora Nygatan 59. Tel. 785-85.

English through and through, this place is decorated in the Ye Olde English Music Hall motif, with playbills on the walls and old records played continuously. You can get such main dishes as marinated salmon and stewed potatoes with dill, a special on Monday night. There's no dancing but there is entertainment nightly. A lunch costs 45 kronor ($7.85) to 75 kronor ($13.10). Beer costs 38 kronor ($6.65). Open Monday through Saturday from 11:30am to 1am and on Sunday from 1pm to 1am. Bus: 14, 17.

O'YES, Skeppsborn 2. Tel. 10-43-70.

A fun and whimsical place for food and drink in Malmö, popular with a young clientele, O'Yes occasionally offers jazz nights with some leading Malmö musicians. It is known primarily as a restaurant (see "Where to Dine," above), but many of its clients come here just to drink, especially enjoying the exotic cocktails at about 65 kronor ($11.36); beer costs 36 kronor ($6.30). It's open Monday through Friday from 11:30am to 1am and on Saturday from 5:30pm to 2am. Bus: 14, 17.

4. LUND

11 miles NE of Malmö, 187 miles south of Gothenburg, 374 miles SW of Stockholm

GETTING THERE   By Train   Trains run hourly from Malmö, a 15-minute ride.

By Bus   Hourly buses run from Malmö, taking 30 minutes.

By Car   From Gothenburg, head south along the E6; Malmö and Lund are linked by express highway (head in toward Route 15), a 20-minute drive.

ESSENTIALS   The tourist information office, **Lunds Turistbyrå,** is at Kattesund 6, S-221 00 Lund (tel. 046/15-50-40), open in June, Monday through Friday from 9am to 6pm and on Saturday from 9am to 1pm; in July and August, Monday through Friday from 9am to 6pm, on Saturday from 9am to 1pm, and on Sunday from 11am to 1pm; and September to May, Monday through Friday from 9am to 6pm.

The **telephone area code** for Lund is 046.

Lund was probably founded in 1020 by Canute the Great, ruler of the united kingdoms of England and Denmark, when this part of Sweden was a Danish possession. But the city really made its mark when its cathedral was consecrated in 1145. The city's 1,000-year anniversary was celebrated in 1990, since archeological excavations show that a stave church was built here in 990. Lund quickly became a center of religion, politics, culture, and commerce for all of Scandinavia.

The town has winding passageways, centuries-old buildings, and the richness of a university town—Lund University, founded in 1666, continues to play an active role in town life.

The most exciting time to be in Lund, as in Uppsala, is on Walpurgis Eve, April 30, when student revelries signal the advent of spring—but a visit to Lund at any time is a pleasure.

WHAT TO SEE & DO

DOMKYRKAN (Cathedral of Lund), Sandgatan.

★ With this ancient cathedral, Romanesque architecture in Scandinavia reached its height, and the eastern exterior of the church is one of the finest expressions of Romanesque architecture in northern Europe. The sandstone interior has sculptural details similar to those in Lombardy and other parts of Italy in quality and character. There is also a crypt with a high altar dedicated in 1123, and intricately carved choir stalls from about 1375.

A partly reconstructed 14th-century **astronomical clock** not only tells the time and the date, but stages a splashy tournament from the Middle Ages—complete with clashing knights and the blare of trumpets. That's not all: The three Wise Men come out to pay homage to the Virgin and Child. To see all this, time your visit to the cathedral for when the clock strikes noon (1pm on Sunday) and 3pm.

Admission: Free.
Open: Mon–Fri 8am–6pm, Sat 9am–6pm, Sun 9:30am–6pm. **Bus:** 1, 137.

KULTUREN (Museum of Cultural History), Tegnérsplatsen. Tel. 15-04-80.

After leaving the cathedral, walk across the university grounds to Adelgatan, which the local citizens consider their most charming street. Here you'll find Kulturen, another open-air museum of Sweden—this one containing reassembled, sod-roofed farms and manor houses, a carriage museum, ceramics, peasant costumes, Viking artifacts, and old handcrafts, even a wooden church moved to this site from the glassworks district.

Admission: 20 kronor ($3.50) adults, free for children.
Open: May–Sept, daily 11am–5pm; Oct–Apr, daily noon–4pm. **Bus:** 1, 137.

HISTORISKA MUSEET, Kraftstorg 1. Tel. 10-70-00.

Founded in 1805, this is the second-largest museum of archeology in Sweden. Collections trace the development of the people of Skåne from antiquity to the Middle Ages. One of the skeletons found during an excavation is that of a young man, one of the oldest finds of a human body in northern Europe, dating around 7000 B.C. Most collections from the Bronze Age came from tombs. During excavations in eastern Skåne, a large gravefield was unearthed with jewelry and weapons which are on display. The medieval exhibition is dominated by church art.

Admission: 5 kronor (85¢) adults, free for children.
Open: Tues–Fri 11am–1pm. **Bus:** 1, 137.

WHERE TO STAY

The tourist office (see above) can help you obtain housing in private homes for as little as 110 kronor ($19.20) per person. There is a booking fee of 25 kronor ($4.35).

EXPENSIVE

GRAND HOTEL, Bantorget 1, S-221 04 Lund. Tel. 046/11-70-10. Fax 046/14-73-01. 83 rms (all with bath), 4 suites. MINIBAR TV TEL **Bus:** 1, 137.

$ **Rates** (including breakfast): Summer, 420 kronor ($73.35) single; 620 kronor ($108.25) double. Fri–Sat in winter, 640 kronor ($111.75) single; 820 kronor ($143.15) double. Sun–Thurs in winter, 1,050 kronor ($183.35) single; 1,280 kronor ($223.50) double; from 1,450 kronor ($253.15) suite. AE, DC, MC, V.

★ This château-style hotel, the most prestigious in town, overlooks the fountains and flowers of a city park. The marble lobby is grand. Upstairs, each room has an old-fashioned decor and a few modern touches including a radio. The rooms in the hotel's conical corner tower are the most desirable. The elegant restaurant offers fixed-price meals beginning at 155 kronor ($27.05).

HOTEL LUNDIA, Knut den stores gata 2, S-221 04 Lund. Tel. 046/12-41-40. Fax 046/14-19-95. 97 rms (all with bath). TV TEL **Bus:** 1, 137.

$ **Rates** (including breakfast): Summer and Fri–Sat year round, 600 kronor ($104.75) single; 720 kronor ($125.70) double. Sun–Thurs in winter, 1,015 kronor ($177.20) single; 1,200 kronor ($209.50) double. AE, DC, MC, V.

Operated by the same management as the Grand Hotel (see above), this is perhaps the most pleasantly situated and most modern hotel in town, located in a quiet section of the old town. The interior has modern winding staircases, white marble sheathing, and big windows. Each bedroom has its own tile bath, clothes press, and refrigerator, and is designed with Scandinavian fabrics and unusual lithographs. Guests interested in a formal meal usually head for the dining room at the Grand, about a block away. Those interested in a less formal meal can patronize the in-house brasserie (see "Where to Dine," below). On the premises is a stylish nightclub, often one of the liveliest spots in town (see "Evening Entertainment," below).

MODERATE

HOTEL CONCORDIA, Stalbrogatan 1, S-222 24 Lund. Tel. 046/13-50-50. Fax 046/13-74-22. 49 rms (all with bath). TV TEL **Bus:** 1, 137.

$ Rates (including breakfast): June 24–Aug 12 and Fri–Sat year round, 585 kronor ($102.15) single; 640 kronor ($111.75) double. Sun–Thurs Aug 13–June 23, 800 kronor ($139.70) single; 940 kronor ($164.10) double. AE, DC, MC, V.

Next door to the brick house where August Strindberg lived in 1897, this charming ornate building was renovated a few years ago into a pleasant hotel. The modern rooms are sedate, and a few are reserved for nonsmokers. On the premises is a sauna. It's a 5-minute walk south of the rail station.

INEXPENSIVE

HOTEL AHLSTRÖM, Skomakaregatan 3, S-223 50 Lund. Tel. 046/11-01-74. 15 rms (1 with bath). TEL **Bus:** 1, 137.

$ Rates (including breakfast): 285 kronor ($49.75) single without bath; 375 kronor ($65.50) double without bath, 475 kronor ($82.95) double with bath. No credit cards.

The Ahlström is a small hotel on a cobblestone commercial street in the town center. Inside, everything is comfortable and clean. Rooms are simply furnished but well maintained.

WHERE TO DINE

CARLSSONS TRADGÅRD, Märtenstorget 6. Tel. 13-81-20.
Cuisine: SWEDISH. **Reservations:** Not required. **Bus:** 1, 137.
$ Prices: Appetizers 35–55 kronor ($6.10–$9.60); main dishes 85–110 kronor ($14.85–$19.20). MC, V.
Open: Mon–Thurs 11am–1am, Fri–Sat noon–2am, Sun noon–midnight.

A British pub-style place, Carlssons Tradgård is set back from the market square on a cobblestone courtyard and built in the half-timbered style. The food is fairly good: Try fried filet of beef with Gorgonzola, pepper steak, salmon and prawns, or whisky-poached salmon. During the day it's strictly self-service, but in the evening there is table service. The pub offers evening entertainment.

STAKET, Stora Sodergatan 6. Tel. 11-93-67.
Cuisine: SWEDISH. **Reservations:** Recommended. **Bus:** 1, 137.
$ Prices: Appetizers 35–50 kronor ($6.10–$8.75); main dishes 80–130 kronor ($13.95–$22.70). AE, DC, MC, V.
Open: Mon–Fri 11am–11pm, Sat–Sun noon–11pm.

An old tavern that serves good food in an unspoiled atmosphere, this 15th-century cellar in a narrow, step-gabled, brick building is one of the city's finest restaurants. It caters to hearty appetites, and dishes are likely to include fish soup, wienerschnitzel, mussel salad, entrecôte, and tournedos flavored with cognac. Fondues are a specialty.

GRIFO, Knut dens stores 1. Tel. 14-51-00.
Cuisine: INTERNATIONAL/STEAKS. **Reservations:** Recommended. **Bus:** 1, 137.

$ Prices: Appetizers 30–50 kronor ($5.25–$8.75); main dishes 80–125 kronor ($13.95–$21.85). AE, DC, MC, V.
Open: Mon–Sat noon–10pm.

A favorite with students, this modern tavern with outdoor summer tables is located near the train station and opens onto a tree-shaded pedestrian mall. Meals are likely to include beef steak, spaghetti, fried Camembert, fried scampi, beef Stroganoff, lamb cutlet, and tournedos Rossini.

BRASSERIE LUNDIA, in the Hotel Lundia, Knut den stores gata 2. Tel. 12-41-40.
Cuisine: SWEDISH. **Reservations:** Required on weekends only. **Bus:** 1, 137.
$ Prices: Appetizers 30–50 kronor ($5.25–$8.75); main dishes 80–120 kronor ($13.95–$20.95); *dagens* menu 49 kronor ($8.55). AE, DC, MC, V.
Open: Mon–Sat 11:30am–11:30pm.

S One of the most popular cafeterias in town, and the only restaurant in Lund with its own in-house bakery. You'll find crisp salads, open-face sandwiches, and hot dishes as part of the full cafeteria meals. At night, the place becomes an à la carte restaurant with waitress service, serving brasserie steak tartare, fettuccine with salmon, tagliatelle bolognese, grilled filet mignon, grilled pork cutlet with pepper sauce, deep-fried Camembert, and seven kinds of alcohol-rich after-dinner coffees. It has a sophisticated decor with wood and russet-colored marble tables.

EVENING ENTERTAINMENT

In addition to the following, **Carlssons Tradgård** (see "Where to Dine," above) offers nighttime entertainment in the pub.

LUNDIA NIGHTCAFÉ, Knut den stores gata 2. Tel. 12-41-40.
In the cellar of the Hotel Lundia (see "Where to Stay," above), there is a small-stakes casino (blackjack and roulette), two different bars, a dance floor, and a modern cellar-style decor popular with students. Residents of the Hotel Lundia and clients of the Brasserie Lundia enter free, but everyone else pays a cover charge. Draft beer costs 47 kronor ($8.20). It's open Wednesday through Saturday from 9pm to 2am. Bus: 1, 137.
Admission: 60 kronor ($10.50); free for hotel guests.

EASY EXCURSIONS

From Lund, you may want to make a side trip to **Dalby Church,** in Dalby, 8 miles east of Lund. This starkly beautiful and well-preserved 11th-century former bishop's church is the oldest in Scandinavia; be sure to visit its crypt. Open daily from 9am to 5pm. Several buses a day run between Lund center and Dalby.

About a 30-minute drive northeast of Lund (off Route 23) is the **Castle of Bosjökloster,** S-243 00 Hoor (tel. 0413/250-48), once a Benedictine convent founded around 1080. It was closed during the Reformation in the 16th century. The Great Courtyard is spectacular, with its thousands of flowers and exotic shrubs, terraces, and a park with animals and birds. Indoors is the vaulted refectory and the Stone Hall where native arts and crafts, jewelry, and other Swedish goods are displayed. You can picnic on the grounds or enjoy a lunch at the self-service cafeteria in the garden, costing around 60 kronor ($10.50).

The park and gardens are open daily from 8am to 8pm; the restaurant and exhibition rooms are open May to October, daily from 9am to 6pm. Admission is 25 kronor ($4.35) for adults and 10 kronor ($1.75) for children. Don't miss the 1,000-year-old oak tree in the park. The castle is reached by taxi or private car.

5. YSTAD

34 miles east of Malmö, 28 miles west of Simrishamn

GETTING THERE **By Train** Monday through Friday, trains run roughly on the hour between Malmö and Ystad, taking 1 hour. On Saturday there are four daily trains, and on Sunday, six trains.

By Bus   There are three daily buses Monday through Saturday from Malmö to Ystad taking 1 hour. On Saturday and Sunday, there is only one bus.

By Car   From Malmö, take the E14 east.

ESSENTIALS   The tourist bureau, **Ystads Turistbyrå,** S:t Knuts Torg, S-271 00 Ystad (tel. 0411/772-98), is located at the bus station in the same building as the art museum (Kunstmuseum). It is open mid-June to mid-August, Monday through Friday from 9am to 7pm and on Saturday from 9am to 6pm; late August to early June, Monday through Friday from 9am to 5pm.
   The **telephone area code** for Ystad is 0411.

Ystad makes a good base for exploring the castles and manors of Skåne. An important port during the Middle Ages, Ystad retains its ancient look, with about 300 half-timbered houses, mazes of narrow lanes—even a watchman who sounds the hours of the night in the tower of St. Mary's Church.

WHAT TO SEE & DO

For a glimpse of medieval Sweden, head for **Per Häisas Gård** in the town center, a courtyard encircled by brick-and-timbered houses.
   Don't overlook **St. Mary's Church** at Stortorget, dating back to the early 1200s, noted for its white-and-gilt baroque interior. It's open mid-May to mid-September, daily from 9am to 6pm, charging no admission.
   The **Town Hall,** also at Stortorget, was built on the site of a burned medieval municipal center. It still has the original vaulted cellar.
   The **Museum of Modern Art** is on S:t Knuts Torg (tel. 77-285) in central Ystad, and includes a small military museum. Permanent exhibits feature mainly Scandian and Danish art from the last 100 years. The museum is open Monday through Friday from noon to 5pm and on Sunday from 1 to 5pm. In summer, it is also open on Saturday from 11am to 3pm. Admission is free. The Ystad Tourist Office is in the same building as the museum.
   The **Charlotte Berlin Museum,** Dammgatan 23 (tel. 18-866), is right behind the Museum of Modern Art in central Ystad and keeps the same hours. The mid-19th-century house has been preserved in its original state and gives a good idea of late 19th-century bourgeois taste in interiors.
   The only museum in Sweden in a medieval monastic house is the **City Museum in the Greyfriars Monastery,** S:t Petr Kyrkoplan (tel. 77-286). Built in 1267, the building is a monument from the Danish era in the town of Ystad. Various antiquities in the museum trace the history of the area. The admission-free museum is open Monday through Friday from noon to 5pm and on Sunday from 1 to 5pm; in summer also on Saturday from 11am to 3pm.

NEARBY ATTRACTIONS

CHRISTINEHOF, Ystad-Kristianstad. Tel. 0417/261-10.
   Built in the 18th century, this fully furnished château, northwest of Eljarod, is preserved essentially as it was when it was first built and features hunting museum exhibitions. Safaris, costing 5 kronor (85¢), are held in the castle's wildlife sanctuary, full of wild boar and deer.
   Admission: 15 kronor ($2.60) adults, 8 kronor ($1.40) children.
   Open: May–June, Sat–Sun and hols. 11am–5pm; July to mid-Aug, Tues–Sun 11am–5pm; mid-Aug to Sept, Sat–Sun 11am–5pm. **Closed:** Oct–Apr.

BÄCKASKOG, S-290 34 Fjälkinge. Tel. 044/53-250.

Nine miles north of Kristianstad, this country palace of King Charles XV stands in a 40-acre park, managed by the Swedish Forest Service. The castle, a National Trust building, was originally a monastery founded in the early 13th century. The chapel dates from 1230 and the tower of the house of worship is from 1640. There's a lot to see at Bäckaskog, including a biblical garden, featuring trees, bushes, and herbs mentioned in the Bible or having some other religious connection. There is a restaurant, and some hotel rooms are available at the castle.

Exhibitions and sales of art and country furniture can be attended even when the castle is not open to visitors. Barn dances are held on Saturday during the summer. The palace can be reached by taxi from Kristianstad.

Admission: 15 kronor ($2.60).

Open: Mid-May to mid-Aug, daily 10am–5pm. **Closed:** Late Aug to early May.

WHERE TO STAY

YSTADS SALTSJÖBAD, Saltsjöbadsvagen 6, S-271 00 Ystad. Tel. **0411/136-30.** Fax 0411/11835. 108 rms (all with bath). MINIBAR TV TEL.

$ Rates (including breakfast): 900 kronor ($157.15) single; 940 kronor ($164.10) double. AE, DC, MC, V.

Beautifully located almost at the tip of Sweden near the sea, this hotel, opened in 1897, overlooks an expansive stretch of beach. The rooms are well-furnished. The surrounding area offers excellent opportunities for sports and exercise, including tennis courts and an 18-hole golf course. The hotel also has an outdoor swimming pool with a waterslide and a sauna.

The hotel's Apotheket gourmet restaurant serves good international cuisine and features dancing several nights a week. There's a relaxing cocktail bar and two summer outdoor cafés.

HOTEL CONTINENTAL DU SUD, Hamngatan 13, S-271 00 Ystad. Tel. **0411/137-00.** Fax 0411/125-70. 52 rms (all with bath). A/C MINIBAR TV TEL.

$ Rates (including breakfast): Sun–Thurs, 800 kronor ($139.70) single; 950 kronor ($165.85) double. Fri–Sat, 540 kronor ($94.30) single; 640 kronor ($111.75) double. AE, DC, MC, V.

In spite of modern appointments, this may be Sweden's oldest hotel, dating from 1829. The hotel is attractively decorated. Bedrooms are furnished with tasteful Italian-inspired decor and a number of modern amenities. A restoration added a marble sheathing to the lobby and a glint of crystal chandeliers. The dining room is classically decorated, offering efficient and courteous service. The hotel owners take a personal interest in the welfare of their guests. It is located opposite the ferry terminal.

WHERE TO DINE

RÅDHUSKÄLLAREN YSTAD, Stortorget. Tel. **185-10.**

Cuisine: SWEDISH. **Reservations:** Not required.

$ Prices: Appetizers 45–70 kronor ($7.85–$12.20); main dishes 85–155 kronor ($14.85–$27.05). AE, DC, MC, V.

Open: Mon–Sat 11:30am–11pm, Sun 1–10pm.

In a vaulted 16th-century stone cellar with small tables and a romantic candlelight atmosphere, this restaurant in the town center offers meals that include gratin of sole and beef filet stuffed with lobster. Lunch costs from 55 kronor ($9.60).

SANDSKOGENS VÄRDSHUS, Sandskogen. Tel. **147-60.**

Cuisine: SWEDISH/HUNGARIAN. **Reservations:** Recommended.

$ Prices: Appetizers 40–65 kronor ($7–$11.35); main dishes 85–155 kronor ($14.85–$27.05). MC, V.

Open: Daily noon–10pm. **Closed:** Christmas–March.

A late 19th-century villa just outside Ystad a 5-minute ride east of the town center, this is a good place to get an excellent meal, and it's popular with local families. The service is polite, and English is spoken. A special Sunday lunch is offered for 150 kronor ($26.20) and a two-course lunch costs 130 kronor ($22.70).

6. SIMRISHAMN

391 miles south of Stockholm, 59 miles east of Malmö,
25 miles east of Ystad

GETTING THERE   By Train   Four trains a day (three on weekends) make the
45-minute trip between Malmö and Simrishamn.

By Bus   Nine buses a day arrive from Kristianstad (four a day on weekends), and **10**
buses a day from Ystad (three on weekends). From Lund, there are eight daily buses.
Tickets can be purchased on board the bus.

By Car   From Ystad, take Route 10 northeast.

ESSENTIALS   For information about hotels, boardinghouses, summer cottages,
and apartments, check with the tourist bureau, **Simrishamns Kommun
Turistbyrå,** Tullhusgatan 2, S-272 00 Simrishamn (tel. 0414/106-66). The **telephone area code** for Simrishamn is 0414.

One of the most idyllic towns along the Skåne coastline, Simrishamn features old
half-timbered buildings, courtyards, and gardens. This seaport is the jumping-off
point to the Danish island of Bornholm.

WHAT TO SEE & DO

Be sure to see the 12th-century, step-gabled **St. Nicholai Church** (open daily from
10am to 6pm), built of sandstone and containing a baroque altar. Ship models are
suspended from the ceiling. A visit to the park, **Bergengrenska Trädgården,** off
Stortorget, reveals one of the most charming aspects of the town.

NEARBY ATTRACTIONS

BACKAKRA, S-270 20 Loderup. Tel. 0411/260-10.

Located off the coastal road between Ystad and Simrishamn is the farm that
Dag Hammarskjöld, the late United Nations secretary-general, purchased in
1957 and intended to make his home. Although he died in a plane crash before
he could live there, the old farm has been restored according to his instructions. The
rooms are filled with gifts to Mr. Hammarskjöld—everything from a Nepalese
dagger to a lithograph by Picasso.
   The site is 19 miles southwest of Simrishamn, and can be reached by the bus from
Simrishamn marked Ystad. Likewise, a bus from Ystad, marked SIMRISHAMN, also
goes by the site. Scheduling your return might be difficult because of infrequent
service—check in advance.
   Admission: 10 kronor ($1.75) adults, 5 kronor (85¢) children.
   Open: May 12–June 10 and Aug 20–Sept 16, Sat–Sun noon–5pm; June 11–Aug
19, daily noon–5pm. **Closed:** Sept 17–May 11.

GLIMMINGEHUS, Hammenhög. Tel. 0414/320-39.

Located 6 miles southwest of Simrishamn, this bleak castle was built between
1499 and 1505. It is the best-preserved medieval keep in Scandinavia, but the
somewhat Gothic, step-gabled building is unfurnished. Visitors can order
snacks or afternoon tea at a café on the premises.
   Admission: 10 kronor ($1.75) adults, 5 kronor (85¢) children.
   Open: Apr–Sept, Tues–Sun 9am–5pm. **Closed:** Oct–Mar.

KIVIK TOMB, Bredaror.

Discovered in 1748, this remarkable find is north of Simrishamn along the coast
of Kivik. In a 1931 excavation, tomb furniture, bronze fragments, and some
grave carvings were uncovered. Kivik has been recognized as one of the most
amazing monuments of the Bronze Age. You can reach the site by car.

Admission: 3 kronor (50¢).
Open: May–Aug, daily 9am–5pm. **Closed:** Sept–Apr.

WHERE TO STAY & DINE

HOTEL SVEA, Strandvägen 3, S-270 00 Simrishamn. Tel. 0414/117-20.
Fax 0414/14314. 61 rms (all with bath). TV TEL.
$ Rates: Summer, 450 kronor ($78.55) single; 620 kronor ($108.25) double.
Winter, 790 kronor ($137.95) single; 950 kronor ($165.85) double. AE, DC, MC,
V.

Built in 1986, this waterfront hotel in the town center is the best in town. Many of its
well-appointed and comfortably furnished bedrooms overlook the yacht harbor. Its
lobby-level restaurant, the Svea, serves excellent food Monday through Saturday from
11am to 2pm and 3 to 10pm, and on Sunday from 11am to 5pm. Set with a view of
the harbor, the restaurant makes a good luncheon stopover if you partake in the
reasonably priced *dagens* menu, a one-course lunch for 50 kronor ($8.75).

HOTEL KOCKSKA GÅRDEN, Storgatan 25, S-272 99 Simrishamn. Tel.
0414/117-55. 18 rms (all with bath). TV TEL.
$ Rates (including breakfast): 480 kronor ($83.80) single; 600 kronor ($104.75)
double. MC, V.

Like an unspoiled black-and-white half-timbered coaching inn, this hotel is built
around a large medieval courtyard in the town center. Its lounge combines the old and
new, with a stone fireplace contrasting with balloon lamps. Bedrooms have been
modernized, and the furnishings are up-to-date with tastefully coordinated colors.
The only meal served is breakfast.

GOTHENBURG

Called the gateway to northern Europe, Gothenburg (Göteborg in Swedish) is the country's chief port and second-largest city. Swedes say that Gothenburg is a friendlier town than Stockholm. Canals, parks, and flower gardens enhance its appeal.

The city has a large number of museums and the largest amusement park in northern Europe. It is a convenient center for excursions to the fishing villages and holiday resorts north of the city.

A walk down "The Avenue" is a Gothenburg tradition. This is Kungsportavenyn, called Avenyn (The Avenue) with its many outdoor cafés to watch the passing parade. Start at Parkgatan, at the foot of the Avenue. Gothenburg's pedestrian street is heated by underground pipes in the winter so that the snow melts quickly.

Gothenburg received its city charter from King Gustavus Adolphus II in 1621. The port contains a shipyard, Cityvarvet, and a manufacturer of platforms for oil rigs, Götaverken/Arendal. The city is also the home of the Volvo car manufacturer (the plant is about 15 minutes by car from the heart of the city), and of the Hasselblad space camera. Spanning the Göta River, Alvsborgs Bridge (the longest suspension bridge in Sweden) is almost 3,000 feet long and built high enough to allow ocean liners to pass underneath.

SEEING GOTHENBURG

GETTING THERE

Gothenburg is one of the most easily reached ports in Scandinavia, with frequent flights from Copenhagen and Stockholm. It also maintains ferry links with Denmark and England. Train connections are good from all the major Swedish cities, including Helsingborg, Malmö, and Stockholm.

A SUGGESTED ITINERARY

Days 1&2: Gothenburg deserves at least this much of your attention, as it has a number of attractions and is, in summer at least, one of the most festive cities of Scandinavia.

Day 3: Take an excursion north to visit the sights and attractions at Kungälv and on the island of Marstrand.

1. ORIENTATION

ARRIVING

BY PLANE The premier airline of Scandinavia, **SAS** operates eight daily flights from Copenhagen to Gothenburg, most of them nonstop. Flights from the Danish

WHAT'S SPECIAL ABOUT GOTHENBURG

Great Towns/Villages

☐ Gothenburg, the focal point of the west coast of Sweden, principal seaport of Scandinavia.

☐ Kungälv, a merchant town occupied since the 10th century, a fortress border town between Sweden and Norway.

☐ Marstrand, 16th-century herring center, now an island for summer fun.

Castles

☐ Bohus Fortress, at Kungälv, dating from the 14th century, which played a role in Nordic kingdom wars.

☐ Carlstens Fortress, built in 1658 by King Charles X Gustaf to protect the west coast fleet, towers over the island of Marstrand.

Ace Attractions

☐ The Göteborg Maritime Center, with displays of ship models from Viking times to the present day; rich west-coast seafaring traditions live on here.

☐ Lisepark Park, the largest amusement park in Scandinavia and, in terms of visitors, the biggest tourist attraction of Sweden.

Special Events

☐ The international regatta days in July or August on the island of Marstrand.

---

capital are scheduled between 7:30am and 10:30pm. (Many Swedes living on the west coast of Sweden view Copenhagen as a more convenient airport for them than the one at Stockholm.) SAS also operates 10 to 15 daily flights between Stockholm and Gothenburg, departing from as early as 7:05am and continuing until early evening. There are no flights from Malmö to Gothenburg, although a hovercraft crosses the sound from Malmö to Copenhagen where there are connecting flights to Gothenburg.

Arrivals are at **Landvetter Airport,** 16 miles east of Gothenburg. Airport buses run about every 20 minutes into the center. Catch the Flygbuss daily from 6am to 11:30pm; a one-way passage costs 40 kronor ($7). The bus takes 30 minutes to get to Drottningtoret, outside the Central Station. On Friday and Saturday, a night bus (no. 691 or 692) runs from the airport to the heart of the city at 1:30am and again at 3am.

BY TRAIN The Oslo–Copenhagen express train runs via Gothenburg and Helsingborg connecting two Scandinavian capitals. Trains run frequently on a north/south route between Gothenburg and Helsingborg/Malmö in the south. The most traveled rail route is between Gothenburg and Stockholm, with trains leaving hourly in both directions; trips take 4 hours 40 minutes.

Trains arrive at the **Central Station,** on one side of Drottningtorget. Inside the station is a currency-exchange bureau and an SJ office selling bus tickets for connections to the environs.

BY BUS Buses run from Gothenburg to Helsingborg/Malmö (and vice versa) on Friday and Sunday at the rate of two each day. Trip time from Gothenburg to Helsingborg is 3½ hours; Gothenburg to Malmo, 4½ hours. On Friday, three daily buses connect Stockholm and Gothenburg, and two buses run on Sunday. Trip time is 7 to 8 hours. If you're going by public land transportation on other days of the week, including Saturday, take the train.

BY FERRY Stena Line (tel. 42-09-40) has six crossings a day in summer from North Jutland. The ferries take about 3 hours to cross. For information about specific times of crossing (which vary seasonally), telephone 031/42-09-40. The vessels have excellent dining rooms.

In summer there is a daily ferry service between Harwick (England) and Gothenburg, taking 24 hours. During the rest of the year, service is curtailed to three times a week. From June to mid-August, there is also twice-weekly service from Newcastle-upon-Tyne (England) to Gothenburg, also taking 24 hours. This service is operated by **DFDS/Scandinavian Seaways** (tel. 031/675-06-00) for information. There is no railpass discount on the England–Sweden crossings.

BY CAR From either Malmö or Helsingborg, the two major "gateways" to Sweden on the west coast, take the E6 north. Gothenburg is 173 miles north of Malmö and 141 miles north of Helsingborg. From Stockholm, take the E4 west to Jonköping and continue west the rest of the way via Borås to Gothenburg, a distance of 292 miles.

TOURIST INFORMATION

The **Gothenburg Tourist Office** is located at Basarsgatan 2 (tel. 10-07-40). For tourist information, "What Is on Today," call **Miss Tourist** (tel. 11-74-50). At the tourist bureau, visitors to Gothenburg can apply to meet a local family ("of similar background and interests"). Sometimes it takes at least 2 days to arrange a visit, so make sure you'll be in Gothenburg that long. There is no charge for this service.

CITY LAYOUT

The layout of Gothenburg, with its network of streets separated by canals, is reminiscent of Amsterdam—not surprisingly, since it was designed by Dutch architects in the 17th century. And its wealth of parks and open spaces have given it a reputation as Sweden's greenest city.

Some of the old canals have now been filled in, but you can explore the major remaining waterway and the busy harbor—the most important in Sweden—by taking one of the city's famous Paddan sightseeing boats. *Paddan* is the Swedish word for "toad," and the allusion is to the squat shape of the boats which enables them to navigate under the many low bridges. A Paddan service takes you from the point of embarkation, Drottningtorget, near the main railway station, direct to the Liseberg amusement park. The park is the most popular visitor attraction in the area, luring some three million visitors annually.

The best place to start sightseeing by foot is Kungsportsavenyen, called the **Avenyn,** a wide tree-lined boulevard with many sidewalk cafés. Avenyn leads to the **Götaplatsen,** a square whose centerpiece is a huge bronze fountain with a statue of the sea god Poseidon. The statue is by Carl Milles, and the square is the city's artistic and historical center.

The old and commercial section of the city lies on either side of the central canal. At the central canal is **Gustav Adolfs Torg,** dominated by a statue of Gustav himself. Facing the canal is the **Börshuset** (Stock Exchange building). On the western side is the **Rådhuset** (Town Hall), originally constructed in 1672. Around the corner, moving toward the river, the **Kronhuset,** off Kronhusgatan, is a 17th-century Dutch-designed building, the oldest in Gothenburg, from 1643.

Gothenburg is dominated by its **harbor,** which is best viewed from one of the Padden boats. The major attraction here is the **Maritime Center** (see below). The shipyards, whose spidery forms look like they were made from an erector set, are dominated by the IBM building and other industries. Part of the harbor is connected by an overhead walkway to the shopping mall of **Nordstan.**

2. GETTING AROUND

Visitors to the city can buy a **Göteborgskortet (Gothenburg Card)** through Swedish travel agents that is good daily from mid-June to mid-August and on weekends year round. It offers accommodation in top-class hotels at discounted prices. The Göteborgskortet, a discount card, also entitles the holder to unlimited free travel on local trams and buses, free sightseeing tours, and free admission to the city's leading museums, and other attractions.

The discount card also can be obtained from the Tourist Information Office (see Section 1, "Orientation," above). A ticket valid for 24 hours costs 75 kronor ($13.10) for adults, 40 kronor ($7) for children. One for 2 days costs 140 kronor ($24.45) for adults, 75 kronor ($13.10) for children; 3-day tickets go for 195 kronor ($34.05) for adults, 100 kronor ($17.45) for children, and those for 4 days are 245 kronor ($42.80) for adults, 125 kronor ($21.85) for children.

For seniors, if you're planning to make excursions in the environs of Gothenburg, inquire at the Central Station before booking a train ticket. Sweden grants visitors 65 and older a 30% reduction on train tickets, good for both first- and second-class travel year round, plus a further 30% reduction for travel other than on Friday and Sunday. This discount is good on all transportation operated by the Swedish State Railways.

BY PUBLIC TRANSPORTATION

BY TRAM   A single tram ticket costs 9 kronor ($1.55); a 24-hour travel pass costs 22 kronor ($3.85). If you don't have an advance ticket, board the first car of the tram and buy one from the driver. When you finally have purchased the 9-krona ($1.55) ticket, you have to get the time of entry stamped by inserting it into an automatic machine.

BY TAXI   Taxis are not as plentiful as you'd want them to be when you really need one. However, you can always find one by going to the Central Station. To call a taxi, dial 65-00-00. An average taxi ride within the city costs about 130 to 150 kronor ($22.70 to $26.20).

BY CAR   Because of parking problems, a car is not a practical means to tour Gothenburg. To compensate for its lack of parking, the city has good public transportation. A car is needed to tour the environs. **Avis** (tel. 17-04-10) has a rental office at the Central Station and another at the airport (tel. 94-60-30). **Hertz** has an office in the center of town at Stampgatan 16 (tel. 94-62-10) and one at the airport (tel. 94-60-20). Compare rates and make sure you understand the insurance coverage before you sign the contract.

FAST FACTS   GOTHENBURG

American Express   This agency is represented in Gothenburg by **Nyman & Schultz,** Norra Hamngatan 18 (tel. 80-58-40).

Area Code   The telephone area code for Gothenburg is 031.

Bookstores   The biggest and most central is **Akademi Bokhandeln,** Norra Hamngatan 32 (tel. 80-58-30).

Business Hours   **Shops** are generally open Monday through Friday from 9am to 6pm, Saturday 9am to 1pm; **banks,** Monday through Friday from 9:30am to 3pm; **offices,** Monday through Friday from 9am to 5pm.

Currency Exchange   Currency can be exchanged at **Forex,** in the Central Station (tel. 15-65-16). There is also a currency-exchange desk at Landvetter Airport, open daily from 8am to 8pm.

Dentist   Call the referral agency **Akuttandkliniken** (tel. 80-31-40) daily from 8am to 9pm.

Doctor   If it's not an emergency, your hotel can call a local doctor and arrange an appointment. If it is an emergency, go to **City Akuten,** Drottninggatan 45 (tel. 10-10-10).

Drugstores A 24-hour pharmacy is **Apoteket Vasen,** Götagatan 12, Nordstan (tel. 80-44-10).

Embassies/Consulates There is no U.S. consulate at Gothenburg; Americans must go to Stockholm, along with those from Australia, Ireland, and New Zealand. The **British Consulate** is at Norra Hamngatan 32 (tel. 80-07-78), and it's open Monday through Friday from 9:30am to 4pm.

Emergencies The number to call for nearly all emergencies (fire, police, medical) is **90-000.**

Eyeglasses Go to **Wasa Optik,** Vasaplatsen 7A (tel. 11-05-35).

Hairdressers/Barbers A good one is **Salong Noblesse,** Södra Lårmgatan 6 (tel. 11-71-30).

Laundry/Dry Cleaning Laundries are hard to find. There's one at **Kärralund Camping,** Olbersgatan (tel. 25-27-61). For dry cleaning, go to **City Kem,** Drottninggatan 61 (tel. 11-22-22).

Libraries The main library is **Göteborgs Stadsbibliotek,** located at Götaplatsen (tel. 81-04-80), open Monday through Friday from 11am to 7pm and on Saturday and Sunday from 11am to 4pm.

Liquor Laws You must be 18 to drink. No alcohol can be served before noon (before 1pm on Sunday). Most pubs quit serving drinks at midnight, except special nightclubs with licenses to stay open until 2 or 3am. Liquor can be purchased at state-owned liquor shops, known as Systembolag.

Lost Property Go to the police station (see "Police," below).

Luggage Storage/Lockers It is possible to store luggage and rent lockers at the **Central Station** (tel. 80-50-00).

Photographic Needs An excellent store is **Hasselblad AB,** Östra Hamngatan 3 (tel. 10-24-00).

Police The main police station is a **Polismyndigheten,** Skånegatan 5 (tel. 61-80-00).

Post Office The main post office is at **Posten Nordstan,** at the Nordstan Shopping Center (tel. 62-30-00), next to the railway station.

Radio/TV Gothenburg has Swedish-language TV broadcasts on TV1, TV2, TV3, and receives such foreign channels as Super Sky and BBC broadcasts from London. National radio stations include P1, P2, and P3; Radio Gothenburg broadcasts on 101.9 MHz (FM).

Religious Services The **Catholic church** is at Parkgatan 14 (tel. 11-92-65). The Swedish Reformed church has services at **Domkyrkan,** Kungsgatan. The **Gothenburg Synagogue** is at Östra Lårmgatan 12 (tel. 88-12-15).

Shoe Repair Try **Service-Hörnan,** Postgatan 26-32 (tel. 15-58-08). Repairs are made while you wait.

Taxes Gothenburg imposes no special city taxes other than the Value-Added Tax ("Moms"), which is nationwide.

Taxis Call **Taxi Göteborg** at 65-00-00.

Telegrams/Telex/Fax Go to **Telebutiken,** Hvitfeldtsplatsen 9 (tel. 90-

200), open Monday through Friday from 9:30am to 6pm and on Saturday from 10am to 2pm.

Transit Information   For tram and bus information, call 80-12-35; for train information, call 80-50-00.

3. ACCOMMODATIONS

Reservations are important, but if you need a place to stay on the spur of the moment, you can try the **Gothenburg Tourist Office** at Basarsgatan 2 (tel. 10-07-40), which lists the city's hotels and boardinghouses and reserves rooms in private homes. Reservations can be made in advance, by letter or phone. The tourist board charges a booking fee of 35 kronor ($6.10). Single rooms in private homes start at 150 kronor ($26.20) and doubles begin at 200 kronor ($34.90).

The hotels listed as expensive actually become moderate in price on Friday and Saturday and during midsummer.

VERY EXPENSIVE

SAS PARK AVENUE HOTEL, Kungsportsavenyn 36-38, S-400 16 Göteborg. Tel. 031/17-65-20. Fax 031/16-95-68. 320 rms (all with bath), 11 suites. MINIBAR TV TEL **Tram:** 1, 4, 5, 6. **Bus:** 40.

$ Rates (including breakfast): June 23–Aug 8 and Fri–Sat year round, 680 kronor ($118.75) single; 780 kronor ($136.20) double. Sun–Thurs Aug 9–June 22, 1,195 kronor ($208.65) single; 1,310 kronor ($228.75); from 1,800 kronor ($314.30) suite. AE, DC, MC, V. **Parking:** 100 kronor ($17.45).

Constructed in 1950 and renovated in 1985, this modern hotel, part of the prestigious SAS chain, stands on Gothenburg's major boulevard. Everyone from Henry Kissinger to the Beatles, from David Rockefeller to the Rolling Stones, has stayed here. The hotel has 10 floors, with attractively designed bedrooms. Those on the top enjoy excellent views of the city. Rooms contain a work desk, cable TV, hairdryer, and trouser press.

Dining/Entertainment: The Harlequin Restaurant and Music Bar has a charcoal grill, providing tender steaks, succulent grilled spareribs, giant hamburgers, and other fare such as fresh garden salads. The hotel's gourmet dining room, Belle Avenue, is one of the best known in Gothenburg, specializing in game or fresh fish from the Atlantic. The hotel's famous nightclub, Lorsenberg, is recommended separately (see "Evening Entertainment," in this chapter).

Services: SAS Airline check-in, "office-for-a-day," valet parking, house doctor, same-day laundry and dry cleaning, 24-hour room service.

Facilities: Garage, beauty salon, sauna, solarium, newsstand.

SHERATON GÖTEBORG HOTEL & TOWERS, Södra Hamngatan 59-65, S-401 24 Göteborg. Tel. 80-60-00. Fax 031/15-98-88. 300 rms (all with bath), 40 suites. A/C MINIBAR TV TEL **Tram:** 1, 4, 5, 6. **Bus:** 40.

$ Rates (including breakfast): June 23–Aug 19 and Fri–Sat year round, 825 kronor ($144.05) single; 890 kronor ($155.40) double; Sun–Thurs Aug 20–June 22, 1,175–1,565 kronor ($205.15–$273.25) single; 1,340–1,750 kronor ($234–$305.55) double; from 2,500 kronor ($436.50) suite. AE, DC, MC, V. **Parking:** 100 kronor ($17.45).

★ This unusual deluxe hotel was built around a large atrium, which seems like a tree-lined city square right inside the hotel. Opposite the rail station, it is one of the best-run and equipped hotels in Sweden. Rooms are large and luxuriously appointed (some suitable for the handicapped), and they're decorated in pastel shades. Opened in 1986, the hotel offers the finest bedrooms in town. Each room is stylishly decorated, with a high standard of comfort. The uppermost floor of the hotel is reserved for the Sheraton Towers, with the most exclusive accommodations. Guests who have stayed in the Royal Suite include everyone from Liza Minnelli to Michael Jackson, from Luciano Pavarotti to the royal family of Sweden.

Dining/Entertainment: In the atrium lobby are three restaurants: an Italian restaurant called Frascati, the Frascati Café, and a gourmet restaurant, Madeleine. There is also a piano bar and casino in the lobby. Finally, there's a nightclub, Mirage.

Services: 24-hour room service.

Facilities: Health club, large swimming pool, Jacuzzi, saunas, solariums, indoor garage.

EXPENSIVE

HOTEL EKOXEN, Norra Hamngatan 38, S-411 06 Göteborg. Tel. 031/ 80-50-80. Fax 031/11-33-76. 75 rms (all with bath). TV TEL **Tram:** 1, 4, 5, 6. **Bus:** 40.

$ Rates (including breakfast): June 29–Aug 5 and Fri–Sat year round, 600 kronor ($104.75); 725 kronor ($126.60) double. Sun–Thurs Aug 6–June 28, 945 kronor ($165) single; 1,145 kronor ($199.90) double. AE, DC, MC, V.

One of the SAS-associated hotels, Ekoxen is an up-to-date and well-run hotel that often attracts business travelers, although summer visitors will gravitate to it as well. All rooms are individually designed and tastefully furnished. Other amenities such as a trouser press are also included. Most of the single bedrooms contain a studio-size bed. Included in the room price is a free sauna and Jacuzzi.

HOTELL ROYAL, Drottninggatan 67, S-411 07 Göteborg. Tel 031/80-61- 00. Fax 031/15-62-46. 80 rms (all with bath). TV TEL **Tram:** 1, 4, 5, 6. **Bus:** 60.

$ Rates (including breakfast): June 15–Aug 15 and Fri–Sat year round, 500–600 kronor ($87.30–$104.75) single; 700–900 kronor ($122.20–$157.15) double. Sun–Thurs Aug 16–June 14, 745–900 kronor ($130.10–$157.15) single; 1,000– 1,300 kronor ($174.60–$227) double. AE, DC, MC, V.

Founded in 1852, the oldest hotel in Gothenburg still in use, is next to the Sheraton Hotel about a quarter mile from the rail station (all major bus and tram lines pass by within a two-block radius). It is decorated in a typical 19th-century style, with wrought-iron banisters and heavy cast-bronze lamps at the stairs. At the reception is a unique hand-painted glass ceiling. The hotel was carefully renovated in 1989. Rooms are individually designed and modernized, offering much comfort. The breakfast buffet included in the price is generous. Although the hotel serves breakfast only, many restaurants are nearby.

NOVOTEL GÖTEBORG, Klippan 1, S-414 51 Göteborg. Tel. 031/14-90- 00. Fax 031/42-22-32. 150 rms (all with bath). A/C MINIBAR TV TEL **Tram:** 3.

Directions: From Gothenburg, follow signs on the E3 to Frederickshavn, then the signs to Kiel; exit at Klippan, where signs direct you to hotel.

$ Rates (including breakfast): Summer (mid-June to mid-Aug) and most weekends, 645 kronor ($112.60) single; 725 kronor ($126.60) double. Winter weekdays, 950–1,025 kronor ($165.85–$178.95) single; 1,140–1,185 kronor ($181.60– $206.90) double. AE, DC, MC, V. **Parking:** Free.

This recently converted harborfront brewery 2½ miles west of the center is now a stylish hotel run by the French hotel conglomerate, Accor. Each plushly carpeted room has panoramic views of the industrial landscape. When it was completed in the 1980s, it was considered one of the most unusual restorations of a 19th-century building in Sweden. Two free in-house movies are shown daily. Within the hotel is a well-accessorized sauna. Laundry facilities are available.

You can enjoy a drink at La Rochelle Bar, or order a full meal at Le Restaurant where the menu features both Gallic and Swedish specialties. Fixed-price lunches cost 125 kronor ($21.85); à la carte dinners, 190 kronor ($33.15).

PANORAMA HOTEL, Eklandagatan 51-53, S-400 22 Göteborg. Tel. 031/81-08-80. Fax 031/81-42-37. 341 rms (all with bath). TV TEL **Bus:** 40.

$ Rates (including breakfast): Summer (June 29–Aug 5), 445 kronor ($77.70) single; 620 kronor ($108.25) double. Winter, 845–985 kronor ($147.55–$172) single; 1,050 kronor ($183.35) double. AE, DC, MC, V. **Parking:** Free.

Spacious and dramatic, the soaring tower of this hotel is a 10-minute walk from the center of town. It has a plant-filled lobby with a skylight, a piano bar, and a balcony-level restaurant. The bedrooms have stylish furnishings and soft lighting. On the premises is a whirlpool, along with a sauna and solarium.

RAMADA HOTELL, Gamla Tingstadsgatan 1, S-402 76 Göteborg. Tel. 031/22-24-20. Fax 031/51-21-00. 120 rms (all with bath). TEL **Bus:** 40, 45.

$ Rates (including breakfast): June 15–Aug 12 and Fri–Sat year round, 550 kronor ($96.05) single or double; Sun–Thurs in winter, 1,000 kronor ($174.60) single; 1,220 kronor ($213) double. AE, DC, MC, V.

This hotel built in 1975 lies 2 miles from the ferry terminal and 17 miles from Landvetter Airport; it takes about 5 minutes by bus into the city center. This is a modern and well-run hotel, with large, tastefully decorated bedrooms in light pastels and many amenities. The lobby bar is a favorite meeting place, and the Restaurant Royal serves regional and continental specialties. Facilities include a swimming pool, hot sauna, and solarium.

SARA HOTEL SCANDINAVIA, Kustgatan 10, S-401 02 Göteborg. Tel. 031/42-70-00. Fax 031/12-29-65. 323 rms (all with bath). TV TEL **Tram:** 1, 4, 5, 6. **Bus:** 40.

$ Rates: June 23–Aug 14 and Fri–Sat year round, 380 kronor ($66.35) single; 600 kronor ($104.75) double. Sun–Thurs Aug 15–June 22, 825–1,025 kronor ($144.05–$178.95) single; 1,025–1,150 kronor ($178.95–$200.80) double. AE, DC, MC, V. **Parking:** Free.

This hotel in the center of the port area offers rooms with a sweeping view of the harbor, magnificent Alvsborgs Bridge, and the islands beyond. Six rooms accommodate disabled persons. Guests have the use of two saunas, a pool with a bar, a solarium, and an English billiard room. There is also a VIP sauna in Finnish style.

The hotel's well-known restaurant, Kusten, seats 300 guests and its piano and cocktail bar, Musslan, is an inviting place to relax over a drink, play roulette, or order a simple platter from the bar.

MODERATE

HOTEL EGGERS, Drottningtorget, S-401 25 Göteborg. Tel. 031/17-15-70. Fax 031/15-42-43. 77 rms (all with bath). TV TEL **Tram:** 1, 4, 5, 6. **Bus:** 40.

$ Rates (including breakfast): June 15–Aug 15 and Fri–Sat year round, 460 kronor ($80.30) single; 610 kronor ($106.50) double. Sun–Thurs Aug 16–June 14, 845 kronor ($147.55) single; 945 kronor ($165) double. AE, DC, MC, V.

The second-oldest hotel in Gothenburg was built in 1859, predating the Swedish use of the word to describe a building with rooms for travelers. Many emigrants to the New World spent their last night in the old country at the Hotel Eggers, and in World War II Germans and the Allies met here for secret negotiations. Today it is just as good or better than ever, with stained-glass windows, ornate staircases, and wood paneling. All rooms are individually furnished, and beautifully appointed, often with luxurious bathrooms. Room sizes vary. The gilt leather tapestry and polished mahogany evoke the 19th century in the hotel dining room.

HOTEL ÖRGRYTE, Danska Vägen 68-70, S-416 59 Göteborg. Tel. 031/19-76-20. Fax 031/84-94-65. 70 rms (all with bath), 6 suites. TEL **Tram:** 1, 3, 6.

$ Rates (including breakfast): Summer (late July to early Aug) and Fri–Sat year round, 525 kronor ($91.65) single; 750 kronor ($130.95) double. Sun–Thurs in winter, 780 kronor ($136.20) single; 900 kronor ($157.15) double; from 1,250 kronor ($218.25) suite. AE, DC, MC, V.

Polished and well managed, this is an appealing choice in spite of an impersonal exterior, lying east of the center. The modern interior is a blend of light-wood paneling and deep carpeting, with lots of lounging room. Rooms are furnished with built-in furniture in contemporary style. During the day sandwiches, coffee, tea, cakes, beer, lemonade, and wine are offered, but not hot meals.

TIDBLOMS, Olskroksgatan 23, S-416 66 Göteborg. Tel. 031/19-20-70. Fax 031/19-78-35. 43 rms (all with bath). TV TEL **Tram:** 1, 4, 5, 6. **Bus:** 40.

$ Rates (including breakfast): June 18–Aug 13 and Fri–Sat year round, 400 kronor ($69.85) single; 540 kronor ($94.30) double. Sun–Thurs Aug 14–June 17, 790 kronor ($137.95) single; 945 kronor ($165) double. AE, DC, MC, V.

A stylish, modernized hotel in an 1897 tower-capped building, Tidbloms is just outside the town center, near the Riddargatan exit on the highway to Stockholm. There is a sophisticated restaurant and a stone-trimmed cocktail bar on the premises, and each of the bedrooms is conservatively designed and comfortable, with such extras as radios and hairdryers.

BUDGET

OSTKUPAN, Mejerigatan 2, S-412 77 Göteburg. Tel. 031/40-10-50. 230 beds. **Bus:** 64 from Brunnsparken to Gräddgatan.

$ Rates: 65 kronor ($11.35) per person for members, 90 kronor ($15.70) for nonmembers. Breakfast costs 40 kronor ($7) extra. No credit cards. **Closed:** Sept–May.

This youth hostel in the southern sector of the city is well run, but the accommodations are basic. Rooms contain two or three beds, and there's a communal kitchen for members. Guests are given their own keys. The reception desk is open from 7:30am to 10:30pm.

4. DINING

VERY EXPENSIVE

RESTAURANG RÄKAN, Lorensbergsgatan 16. Tel. 16-98-39.
Cuisine: SEAFOOD. **Reservations:** Recommended. **Tram:** 1, 4, 5, 6. **Bus:** 40.
$ Prices: Appetizers 56–142 kronor ($9.80–$24.80); main dishes 220–395 kronor ($38.40–$68.95). AE, DC, MC, V.
Open: Mon–Thurs noon–1am, Fri noon–2am, Sat 5pm–2am, Sun 5pm–1am.

One of the best seafood restaurants in Gothenburg, it naturally has a nautical decor with buoy lamps, wooden-plank tables typical of the Swedish west coast, and a shallow-bottomed re-creation of a Swedish lake. Your seafood platter will arrive on a battery-powered boat with you directing the controls. You can order various combinations of crayfish (in season), along with prawns, poached sole, mussels, lobster, oysters, filet of gray sole, and fresh crabs. A full wine list is available.

EXPENSIVE

BRASSERIE LIPP, Kungsportsavenyn 8. Tel. 11-50-58.

Cuisine: SWEDISH/FRENCH. **Reservations:** Recommended. **Tram:** 1, 4, 5, 6. **Bus:** 40.

$ **Prices:** Appetizers 65–89 kronor ($11.35–$15.55); main dishes 98–198 kronor ($17.10–$34.55); daily platters 56 kronor ($9.80). AE, DC, MC, V.

Open: Mon–Sat 11:30am–11:30pm.

On the main avenue of town, this brasserie is modeled after the legendary Left Bank bistro of Paris, with palate adjustments for Swedish tastes. Its food is a tantalizing combination of French and Swedish, as reflected by such dishes as escargots, sauerkraut (which is the most famous dish served at the Paris namesake), and pepper steak, along with many different kinds of fish, most of them caught in waters near Gothenburg. The salmon is delectable. The bar with a limited snack menu remains open until 1am on Monday, Tuesday, and Wednesday and until 2am on Thursday, Friday, and Saturday.

FISKEKROGEN, Lillatorget 1. Tel. 11-21-84.

Cuisine: SWEDISH. **Reservations:** Recommended. **Tram:** 1, 2, 3, 4, 5, 7.

$ **Prices:** Appetizers 50–100 kronor ($8.75–$17.45); main dishes 80–250 kronor ($13.95–$43.65); one-course *dagens* lunch menu 79 kronor ($13.80); two-course shopper's menu 179 kronor ($31.25). AE, DC, MC, V.

Open: Mon–Sat 11:30am–11pm.

Established in 1929, this restaurant stands on the site of what was once the town's central fish market. It's about 200 yards from the main tramline junction of Gothenburg, beside one of the city's oldest Dutch-built canals. An appetizer might include a platter of pickled Baltic herring or an elaborately arranged platter of local shellfish. For a main course, you can order grilled Baltic herring if you didn't select it as an appetizer. Swedes call this home-style cooking *husmanskost*. A favorite dish of Napoleon's Polish-born mistress, Marie Walewska, is sole Walewska (poached in white wine, gratinéed in the oven, and served with a lobster- and mushroom-studded mornay sauce). It's usually closed sometime around July, but the actual dates change from year to year.

LILLA LONDON, Avenyn/Vasagatan 41. Tel. 18-40-62.

Cuisine: SWEDISH/FRENCH. **Reservations:** Recommended. **Tram:** 1, 4, 5, 6. **Bus:** 40.

$ **Prices:** Appetizers 33–98 kronor ($5.75–$17.10); main dishes 90–215 kronor ($15.70–$37.55); daily lunch specials 50 kronor ($8.75). AE, DC, MC, V.

Open: Mon–Thurs 11:30am–1am, Fri–Sat 11:20am–2am, Sun 3pm–1am.

With a quiet publike atmosphere, the bar here is a local favorite. The restaurant, down a flight of steps, is dark and attractively designed, with illuminated paintings of clipper ships and nautical accents. Full meals might include grilled chicken with morels, beef and lamb filet in a mustard-flavored cream sauce, filet mignon, and broiled salmon with fresh asparagus. Light, less expensive meals are also available. The pub sells 10 different kinds of beer.

THE PLACE, Archivgatan 7. Tel. 16-03-33.

Cuisine: CONTINENTAL. **Reservations:** Required. **Tram:** 1, 4, 5, 6. **Bus:** 40.

$ **Prices:** Appetizers 85–145 kronor ($14.85–$25.30); main dishes 90–245 kronor ($15.70–$42.80). AE, DC, MC, V.

Open: Dinner only, Mon–Thurs 6–11:30pm, Fri–Sat 5–11:30pm.

This restaurant and brasserie is located outside the ground floor of a turn-of-the-century apartment building, dividing its floor space between a less formal bistro and a grand *luxe* gourmet restaurant. You enter a marble-floored reception area, then turn right for the bistro or go through glass doors to enter the restaurant. The restaurant is one of the most acclaimed in the city, although the bar is popular in its own right, as many people come here just to drink. Modern paintings decorate the walls. Food is likely to include such dishes as beef tartare à la Anton Wagner (with Russian caviar), smoked breast of pigeon with lukewarm salad and beetroot, suprême of chicken with goose liver wrapped in savoy cabbage and served with a lemon sauce, or warm fresh lobster with carrot tagliatelle and lobster sauce.

Desserts are often spectacular, including fresh figs in baklava pastry with a cognac sauce.

RESTAURANT STALLGÅRDEN, Kyrkogatan 33. Tel. 13-03-16.

Cuisine: SWEDISH. **Reservations:** Required. **Tram:** 1, 4, 5, 6. **Bus:** 40.

$ Prices: Appetizers 69–169 kronor ($12.05–$29.50); main dishes 145–229 kronor ($25.30–$40); three-course lunch 179 kronor ($31.25). AE, DC, MC, MV.

Open: Mon–Fri 11:30am–10:30pm, Sat 1–10pm, Sun 1–9pm.

A table in this restaurant's enclosed courtyard is one of the most sought-after things in town. The black-and-white half-timbered walls were built in 1789 as a stable and dormitory, and the building has been declared a historic monument.

Enjoy an apéritif in the art deco–inspired cocktail lounge before dinner in one of the candlelit dining rooms. Dishes include curried lobster, veal steak, good terrines, baked hake, grilled scallops, lamb, broiled turbot with Norwegian lobster butter, saddle of reindeer with cloudberry-cream sauce, and a handful of vegetarian dishes. A daily buffet—the best in town—costs 80 kronor ($13.95).

RESTAURANT TIDBLOMS, in the Hotel Tidbloms, Olskroksgatan 23. Tel. 19-20-70.

Cuisine: SWEDISH. **Reservations:** Recommended. **Tram:** 1, 4, 5, 6. **Bus:** 40.

$ Prices: Appetizers 48–56 kronor ($8.40–$9.80); main dishes 152–169 kronor ($26.55–$29.50); *dagens* menu 68 kronor ($11.85). AE, DC, MC, V.

Open: Lunch Mon–Fri 11am–2pm; dinner Mon–Fri 6–10pm, Sat 5–11:30pm.

This restaurant will give you a taste of Sweden. The chef specializes in fresh fish and, in season, game dishes. The reindeer steak here is excellent. The *dagens* menu comes with free access to a particularly elaborate salad bar. A much more elaborate three-course business lunch costs 196 kronor ($34.20). The menu changes every week, and you always get a choice of two appetizers and four main courses. The food is very fresh, tuned to the season and correctly assembled flavors. The decor is inspired by something you might have found in southern Europe, vaguely Spanish or Italian.

SJÖMAGASINET, Klippans Kulturreservat. Tel. 24-65-10.

Cuisine: SEAFOOD. **Reservations:** Required. **Tram:** 4. **Directions:** From the town center, head west on the E3, following signs to Frederickshavn and then to Kiel; exit at Klippan and then follow the signs for the Novotel.

$ Prices: Appetizers 69–170 kronor ($12.05–$29.70); main dishes 145–229 kronor ($25.30–$40). AE, DC, MC, V.

Open: Lunch Mon–Fri 11:30am–2:30pm; dinner Mon–Fri 6–10:30pm, Sat 2–10:30pm, Sun 2–7pm.

By far the most interesting and intriguing restaurant in town, Sjömagasinet is located near the Novotel in the western suburb of Klippan, about 2½ miles from the center. You can have a drink in the cozy English colonial bar, or in the other bar in the eyrie, before dinner.

Very fresh seafood is served here: shrimp-stuffed crêpes with dill, shellfish with curry sauce, baked filet of beef and lobster, poached filets of sole with crayfish, and turbot béarnaise. Veal Oscar with asparagus, and deep-fried Camembert with cloudberry jam and a dessert soufflé flavored with Swedish punch are also available.

MODERATE

ATTA GLAS RESTAURANT, Göta Canal at Kungsportsbron. Tel. 13-60-15.

Cuisine: SWEDISH. **Reservations:** Recommended. **Tram:** 1, 5, 6. **Bus:** 40, 60.

$ Prices: Appetizers 60–93 kronor ($10.50–$16.25); main dishes 59–170 kronor ($10.30–$29.70). AE, DC, MC, V.

Open: Mon–Thurs 11:30am–midnight, Fri–Sat 11:30am–1:30am, Sun 1–10pm.

This stationary old ship from the Sessan line serves good food with fast service in an elegant atmosphere. Each day fresh fish plates are offered, and the meat dishes, including the pepper steak, are also good. For an appetizer, you might try the fish soup or marinated salmon. Daily platters are offered, including, for example, filet of beef with a béarnaise sauce and potatoes. Fresh fish is always featured. The barge dates from 1937, but has spent most of its life wining and dining the residents of Gothenburg, as it never left the confines of the Göta Canal.

LA GONDOLA, Kungsportsavenyn 4. Tel. 11-68-28.
   Cuisine: ITALIAN. **Reservations:** Recommended. **Tram:** 1, 4, 5, 6. **Bus:** 40.
$ Prices: Fixed-price menu 120 kronor ($20.95); appetizers 34–70 kronor ($5.95–$12.20); main dishes 59–171 kronor ($10.30–$29.85). AE, DC, MC, V.
   Open: Sun–Thurs 11am–midnight, Fri–Sat 11am–1am.
This restaurant evokes Venice with its striped poles, sidewalk awnings, and summer outdoor café. It does a lively pizza trade, and I recently enjoyed the pizza Margherita, but it offers an elaborate menu as well, with many classic Italian dishes. The spaghetti Gondola is very good, and the saltimbocca ("jump in your mouth") alla romana is tasty. You might also try one of the grilled specialties, or fried scampi or plank steak. The minestrone is good and filling, and some velvet-smooth ice cream is served. There is a different lunch specialty every day, and an à la carte dinner is served daily.

INEXPENSIVE

GONDOLIERE, Kungsportsavenyn 2. Tel. 11-16-93.
   Cuisine: ITALIAN. **Reservations:** Not required. **Tram:** 1, 4, 5, 6. **Bus:** 40.
$ Prices: Appetizers 55–75 kronor ($9.60–$13.10); main dishes 65–155 kronor ($9.60–$27.05); pizzas 60–80 kronor ($10.50–$13.95). AE, DC, MC, V.
   Open: Sun–Fri 11am–midnight, Sat noon–1am.
A favorite of young locals, this restaurant/pizzeria is in an ornately elegant 19th-century building of neoclassical bay windows and carved pilasters. A black-and-white awning stretches over the sidewalk tables, and a side row of glass windows looks out over the nearby chestnut trees. A different lunch specialty is served every day, and lunch costs 59 kronor ($10.30). You can also enjoy a lunch pizza—from capricciosa to cacciatora—or expensive dinners beginning with spaghetti bolognese. More expensive main dishes such as Tuscan-style chicken and grilled meats are also served, as are desserts including fresh-fruit sorbets.

SPECIALTY DINING

DINING CLUSTER/COMPLEXES

Two dining areas, each distinctly different, are at Vasagatan 43B. The **White Corner Steakhouse** (tel. 81-28-10), in the cellar, has a dark and intimate ambience where thousands of empty wine and whisky bottles hang from the ceiling and country/western and theater posters line the walls. Here you can order nine kinds of steak, lamb cutlets, or grilled sole, with full meals costing from 165 kronor ($28.80). A two-course menu costs 125 kronor ($21.85). Open Monday through Saturday from 6pm to 1am and on Sunday from 3 to 9:30pm.

   The **Mikado Restaurant,** also at Vasagatan 43B (tel. 81-48-05), serves Japanese dinners for a fixed price of 120 kronor ($20.95). It's open Monday through Friday from 11:30am to 2:30pm and 6pm to 1am, on Saturday from 6pm to 1am, and on Sunday from 3 to 11pm. They are found one floor above street level.

LISEBERG PARK   At Liseberg Park, there are many places to eat and drink, including **Wärdshuset,** Liseberg Park (tel. 83-62-83), which is a pocket-size manor decorated with antiques and chandeliers, with verandas opening onto the main square. There are several hot main dishes offered daily. The food is Swedish, with many fresh fish and meat dishes. Meals start at 165 kronor ($20.80), and dinner is served Monday through Friday from 5 to 11pm and on Saturday and Sunday from 3pm to midnight.

Rondo, also at Liseberg Park (tel. 40-07-16), is a large, splendidly modish dance place in the middle of the park. There's dancing and food service nightly from 9pm to midnight. Meals cost from 175 kronor ($30.55), and the food is typically Swedish. Fresh ingredients are used, and the fish dishes are the most reliable choices.

VEGETARIAN

ANNORLUND, Haga Nygata 17. Tel. 11-00-84.
Cuisine: VEGETARIAN. **Reservations:** Not required. **Tram:** 1, 3, 4.
$ **Prices:** Appetizers 30–50 kronor ($5.25–$8.75); main dishes 70–100 kronor ($12.20–$17.45); three-course fixed-price lunch or dinner 100 kronor ($17.45); *dagens* menu lunch 45 kronor ($7.85). No credit cards.
Open: Daily 9am–8pm.

Near the harborfront, this restaurant was originally all vegetarian, but because of popular demand, they added a limited selection of fish and meat dishes, such as salmon and entrecôte. They are the oldest (established 1982) and best vegetarian restaurant in town. At lunch, the system is cafeteria style, but at night there is table service. Salads are fresh and taste homemade, as do the hearty soups.

LOCAL FAVORITES

FROKEN OLSSONS CAFE, Östra Larmgatan 14. Tel. 13-81-93.
Cuisine: SWEDISH. **Reservations:** Not required. **Tram:** 1, 4, 5, 6. **Bus:** 40.
$ **Prices:** Coffee 15 kronor ($2.60); *dagens* menu 50 kronor ($8.75); hot pies with salad 49 kronor ($8.55); sandwiches 28–48 kronor ($4.90–$8.40). MC, V.
Open: Mon 8am–7pm, Tues–Thurs 8am–10pm, Fri 8am–1am, Sat 10am–5pm and 9pm–4am.

Less than two blocks from the Avenyn, this traditional favorite with Gothenburgers is one of the preferred rendezvous spots of town. It is popular, crowded, and noisy at lunchtime. Even though it has a large interior, the scene overflows onto an outdoor terrace in summer. At night hot pies with a salad are featured, as is an array of baguette sandwiches containing such ingredients as shrimp or ham and cheese. They also serve a light beer, but no wine or liquor. Basically, it's light café dining, with homemade soups and such main courses as entrecôte.

A GAY RESTAURANT

BACCHUS, Bellmansgatan 7-9. Tel. 13-20-43.
Cuisine: SWEDISH/FRENCH. **Reservations:** Recommended. **Bus:** 40.
Tram: 1, 4, 5, 6.
$ **Prices:** Three-course dinner 170 kronor ($29.70); appetizers 40–50 kronor ($7–$8.75); main dishes 90–120 kronor ($15.70–$20.95); two-course Sunday special 90 kronor ($15.70). AE, DC, MC, V.
Open: Fri–Mon 9pm–2am.

This, the leading gay bar, disco, and restaurant of Gothenburg, is in a building constructed 115 years ago as a restaurant. The decor is pseudo-Italian with Mediterranean accents, and the disco and restaurant both share the street level. Specialties include smoked salmon with a mousseline sauce, coeur de filet provençal, giant shrimp, and a "melon surprise."

PICNIC FARE & WHERE TO EAT IT

Go to **Saluhallen,** Kungstorget, for the makings of an elegant picnic. Built in 1888, this is the colorful indoor market of Gothenburg. Shops sell meat, fruit, vegetables, and delicatessen products. Much of the food is already cooked and will be packaged for you to take out. The hall is open Monday through Thursday from 9am to 6pm, on Friday from 8am to 6pm, and on Saturday from 8am to 1pm. Take tram no. 1, 4, 5, or 6 to Kungsportsplatsen.

Take your picnic basket to any of Stockholm's major parks (see "Parks and Gardens" below). **Slottsskogen,** because of its size and secluded places, is the most ideal park for a picnic. It also has an outdoor café where you can purchase drinks and perhaps ice cream at the end of your picnic.

5. ATTRACTIONS

SUGGESTED ITINERARIES

IF YOU HAVE 1 DAY

Day 1: Have a cup of coffee at one of the cafés along the Avenyn in the center of Gothenburg; then take the classical *Padden* boatride, traveling through the moat and canal out to the harbor and the giant docks. Return for a stroll along the Avenyn; then take one of the summertime vintage trams for a look at the part of the city ashore. Go to Liseberg amusement park in the evening.

IF YOU HAVE 2 DAYS

Day 1: See "If You Have 1 Day," above.
Day 2: Take a boat trip to Elfsborg Fortress, leaving from the Stenpiren in the Gothenburg harbor and continuing under the Älvsborg Bridge to Elfsborg. In the afternoon visit the Göteborgs Konstmuseum and the Botanical Gardens.

IF YOU HAVE 3 DAYS

Days 1 & 2: See "If You Have 2 Days," above.
Day 3: Get up early to take in the fish auction at the harbor (begins at 7am); then visit the Feskekörka (the Fish Church) nearby. Take tram no. 6 to Guldhedens Vättentorn (water tower) for an overview of Gothenburg. Go to Götaplatsen to see the famed *Poseidon* fountain by Carl Milles. In the afternoon visit the Röhsska Museum of Arts and Crafts and stroll through the rose-filled Trädgardsforeningen across from the Central Station.

IF YOU HAVE 5 DAYS

Days 1–3: See "If You Have 3 Days," above.
Day 4: Take an excursion to Marstrand and Kungälv, north of the city.
Day 5: Visit Nordstan, the biggest shopping center in Scandinavia. Spend the remaining part of the day exploring the southern archipelago, which you can do free with your Gothenburg Card (see "Getting Around," in this chapter). The M/S *Styrsö* and the steamboat *Bohuslän* depart from Skeppsbron/Stenpiren on trips around the archipelago.

THE TOP ATTRACTIONS

For a quick orientation to Gothenburg, visit the **Guldhedens Vättentorn** (Water Tower), 400 feet high. Take tram no. 6 from the center of the city, about a 10-minute ride. The elevator ride up the tower is free, and there's a cafeteria-snack bar on top.

Early risers can take in the daily **fish auction** at the harbor, the largest fishing port in Scandinavia. The amusing auction begins at 7am sharp. You can also visit **Feskekörka** (the Fish Church), on Rosenlundsgatan, which is in the fish market. It's open Tuesday through Friday from 9am to 5pm and on Saturday from 9am to 1pm.

For a look at Gothenburg, the traditional starting point is the cultural center, **Götaplatsen,** with its **Poseidon Fountain,** the work of Carl Milles, Sweden's most important sculptor. The big triumvirate of buildings here is the **Concert Hall,** the municipally owned **theater,** and the **Göteborgs Konstmuseum.**

GÖTEBORGS KONSTMUSEUM, Götaplatsen. Tel. 61-10-00.

Götesborgs Konstmuseum is the leading art museum of Gothenburg, with a good collection of modern art, notably from French impressionists. Bonnard, Cézanne, van Gogh—even Picasso—are represented, along with sculptures by Milles and Rodin. The gallery is noted for its collection of the works of 19th- and 20th-century Scandinavian artists (Zorn and Larsson of Dalarna, Edvard Munch and Christian Krohg of Norway). Old masters are also represented, including Rembrandt and Rubens. The modern section includes work by Francis Bacon and Henry Moore.

Admission: 20 kronor ($3.50), free for children.

Open: May–Aug, Mon–Sat noon–4pm, Sun 11am–5pm; Sept–Apr, Tues and Thurs–Sat noon–4pm, Wed noon–4pm and 6–9pm, Sun 11am–5pm. **Tram:** 4, 5. **Bus:** 40.

RÖHSSKA MUSEUM OF ARTS AND CRAFTS, Vasagatan 37-39. Tel. 20-06-05.

This museum houses a large collection of European furnishings, china, glass, pottery, and Asian artifacts plus permanent and temporary exhibitions of modern handcraft and industrial design. Among the exhibits are books, silver, and Chinese and Japanese art. Lecture series and guided tours are part of the museum's program.

Admission: 10 kronor ($1.75), free for children under 16.

Open: May–Aug, Mon–Sat noon–4pm, Sun 11am–5pm; Sept–Apr, Tues and Thurs–Sat noon–4pm, Wed noon–4pm and 6–9pm, Sun 11am–5pm. **Tram:** 3, 4.

GÖTEBORG MARITIME CENTER, Lilla Bommen Quay. Tel. 10-12-90.

Located on the harbor, this museum is partly aboard the destroyer *Småland,* equipped with guns and torpedoes, and the *Fryken.* In authentic settings, you can see stockboats from the Stone Age, lightships, steamships, and tugboats, among other water craft. There are also opportunities to see Gothenburg either by one of the museum boats or by helicopter. There are cafés at the center and on the quay. Call for information on the boat or air trips and prices.

Admission: 30 kronor ($5.25) adults, 15 kronor ($2.60) children.

Open: Mar 31–June 28 and Aug 18–Nov 11, Sat–Sun 11am–5pm; June 29–Aug 17, daily 11am–5pm. **Closed:** Nov 12–Mar 30. **Tram:** 5 to Lilla Bommen.

MORE ATTRACTIONS

STADSBIBLIOTEKET, Kungsportavenyn. Tel. 81-04-80.

Toward the end of the Avenyn is the public library, on the left at Götaplatsen. This is the main library of Gothenburg, the home of some 400,000 volumes in 40 languages—and a café. The library also contains a listening room with recorded music, as well as a reading room with more than 100 foreign daily newspapers. In one hall exhibitions continuously change.

Admission: Free.

Open: Mon–Thurs 10am–8pm, Fri 10am–6pm. **Tram:** 1, 4, 5, 6. **Bus:** 40.

LISEBERG PARK, Korsvägen. Tel. 40-01-00.

In terms of numbers of visitors, Liseberg Park is the No. 1 tourist attraction in Sweden, and the largest amusement park in Scandinavia. For dining, nightlife, and entertainment in general, Gothenburgers head for this pleasure garden of fountains, pavilions, and flowers. The festively lit park comes alive with music, artists, dances, 21 rides, and open-air vaudeville shows on seven stages.

Admission: 30 kronor ($5.25) adults, free for children under 7.

Open: Mid-Apr to the end of Apr and Sept 1–23, Sat–Sun 10am–11pm; May–Aug, daily 10am–11pm. **Closed:** Late Sept to mid-Apr. **Tram:** 4 or 5 from the city.

EASTINDIA HOUSE, Norra Hamngatan 12. Tel. 71-27-70.

This is a museum of archeology, ethnography, and history—all in the same house. In the archeological museum you'll find prehistoric artifacts excavated in western Sweden from the end of the Ice Age to the time of the Vikings. Walks to ancient sites in the region can be arranged every spring and autumn (tel. 61-25-80 for more information). In the ethnographical museum are collections from all over the world, with a particular emphasis on Latin America. Unique artifacts, including the more than 2,000-year-old Paracas textiles from Peru, are displayed. In the historical museum you'll find collections illustrating western Swedish culture and history.

Admission: 10 kronor ($1.75).

Open: May–Aug, Mon–Sat noon–4pm, Sun 11am–5pm; Sept–Apr, Tues–Sat noon–4pm, Sun 11am–5pm (also Wed 6 to 9pm). **Tram:** 2, 3, 4, or 7 to Lilla Torget.

COOL FOR KIDS

At **Liseberg amusement park** (see above), every day is children's day. The Liseberg Cirkus is a fun fair, and there are always comic characters to play with children. The pony merry-go-round, children's boats, and a fun-on-wheels merry-go-round are all free for tots.

Your children may like Scandinavia's most visited attraction so much they'll want to live there. That, too, is possible. From June 23 to August you can stay at the **Hotel Liseberg Heden** (tel. 031/20-02-80) at a special summer rate—a two-bedroom unit costs 245 kronor ($42.80) per person per night, including breakfast, admission to Liseberg for the whole family, and one ticket book (for the rides) per person. Call the hotel to work out arrangements for one of the family rooms.

Children delight in trips on the *Paddan* boats for a look at Gothenburg from the water (see "Organized Tours," below).

The **Natural History Museum,** Slottskogen (tel. 14-56-09), contains stuffed animals from all over the world, including the only stuffed blue whale. Ecological displays are presented, along with an impressive collection of fauna from all over the world. It is open May to August, Monday through Saturday from noon to 4pm and on Sunday from 11am to 5pm; January to April and September to December, on Tuesday and Thursday through Saturday from noon to 4pm, on Wednesday from noon to 4pm and 6 to 9pm, and on Sunday 11am to 5pm. Admission is 10 kronor ($1.75) for adults, free for children. Tram: 1, 2, 6. Bus: 51 to Linnéplatsen.

You can also visit a **Children's Zoo** at Slottsskogen from May to August (see "Parks & Gardens," below).

SPECIAL-INTEREST SIGHTSEEING

FOR THE ARCHITECTURE ENTHUSIAST

QUEEN CHRISTINA'S HUNTING LODGE, Ötterhallegatan 16. Tel. 13-34-26.

One of the oldest dwellings in Gothenburg, the hunting lodge was saved from demolition in 1971 by the Ötterhallen Historical Preservation Society and the Historical Museum. Today you can visit the 17th-century house for an inspection and enjoy coffee and waffles in its old-world atmosphere. Waffles cost 18 kronor ($3.15).

Admission: Free.

Open: Daily 11am–4pm. **Tram:** 2, 3, 4, 7 to Lilla Torget.

PARKS & GARDENS

TRADGÅRDSFÖRENINGEN, Slussgatan, across from the Central Station.

On a fair day, another oasis in the city center is this park across the canal from the Central Station. In the center are a large rosarium containing some 10,000 roses of 4,000 different species and the Palm House, a large hothouse. Now and then there are various activities in the park, such as exhibitions, children's theater, and lunchtime music.

Admission: Park, free; Palm House, 10 kronor ($1.75) adults, 5 kronor (85¢) children.

Open: May–Aug daily 7–7pm. **Closed:** Sept–Apr. **Tram:** 1, 4, 5, 6.

BOTANISKA TRADGÅRDEM, Carl Skottsbergsgata 22. Tel. 41-37-50.

In southern Gothenburg, the botanical garden, located opposite Slottsskogen Park, contains trees and shrubs from Asia, rock gardens, orchid plants, and greenhouses. The rhododendrons bloom in May and June.

Admission: Garden, free; greenhouses, 5 kronor (85¢).

Open: Garden, daily 9am–sunset. Greenhouses, May–Aug, daily 10am–6pm; Sept–Apr, Mon–Fri 10am–3pm, Sat–Sun 11am–3pm. **Tram:** 1, 2, or 7 to Botaniska Tradgården.

SLOTTSSKOGEN, near Linnéplatsen.

This is the largest park in Gothenburg, with some 274 acres. It was first laid out in 1874 in a naturally wooded area, and today contains beautiful walks, animal enclosures, a saltwater pool, bird ponds, and an aviary, as well as a children's zoo open May to August. A variety of events and entertainment is planned in the park in summer. There's an outdoor café at the zoo, plus restaurants at Villa Bel Park and Björngardsvillan.

Admission: Free.

Open: Daily 24 hours. **Tram:** 1 or 2 to Linnéplatsen.

ORGANIZED TOURS

A sightseeing boat trip along the canals and out into the harbor will show you the old parts of central Gothenburg from the canals, and take you under 20 bridges and out into the harbor. ✪ **Paddan Sightseeing Boats** (tel. 13-30-00) offer 55-minute tours May to September, daily from 10am to 4pm. They leave from the terminal at Kungsportsplatsen in the city center. Adults pay 40 kronor ($7); children, 27 kronor ($4.70); and families (two adults and two children), 105 kronor ($18.35).

The *Nya Elfsborg* is docked in the 17th-century fortress at the harbor's mouth. The boat takes you from Stenpiren on a 20-minute tour through the harbor to **Elfsborg Fortress.** The fortress was built in the 17th century to protect the Göta Älv estuary and the western entrance to Sweden during the 18th century. It still bears traces of hard-fought sea battles against the Danes. Carvings on the prison walls tell tales of threats and hopes of the 19th-century lifetime prisoners. A guide will be waiting for you at the cafeteria, museum, and souvenir shop. Departures are seven times a day from mid-May to the end of August. Adults pay 40 kronor ($7); children, 27 kronor ($4.70); and families, 105 kronor ($18.35). It is also possible to visit the fortress by public land transportation. Take tram no. 2, 3, 4, or 7 or bus no. 85 or 86 to Lilla Torget.

You can travel free in the southern archipelago with the Gothenburg Card (see Section 2, "Getting There," in this chapter). M/S *Styrsö* and the steamboat *Bohuslän* depart from Skeppsbron/Stenpiren on **trips around the Gothenburg archipelago** and Marstrand island. The M/S *Poseidon* takes you for an evening cruise of the archipelago. For information about tours possible at the time of your visit, check with the tourist bureau (see Section 1, "Orientation," in this chapter) which provides excursion packages, brochures, tickets, and time tables.

If you'd like to participate in a guided **bus tour of Gothenburg,** go to the tourist office or call 10-07-40 for details. City tours are offered April to September daily, costing 60 kronor ($30.50) for adults and 33 kronor ($5.75) for children.

6. SPECIAL/FREE EVENTS

Dates cited are subject to change from year to year. Check with the tourist board for exact dates.

Walpurgis Night, on April 30, is celebrated throughout Gothenburg, with bonfires, songs, and speeches in praise of the advent of spring.

The **Göteborg Music Festival,** June 24–30, is an international music festival for choirs, brass bands, big bands, and other groups. In one year alone, 30 brass bands, 10 choirs, and 10 big bands from eight nations participated. Much of the music is played on the streets and squares of the city. Exact locations are announced in the newspapers.

The **International Regatta Days** (check with the tourist office for annual dates) at Marstrand are the dream goal for the yachting set in July or August, depending on the year. Tall-masted yachts swarm the quayside and suntanned visitors stroll the waterfront, taking in all the nautical plush.

September is the time for the **International Consumer Goods Fairs** at Gothenburg, featuring "Household of Today" exhibits.

7. SAVVY SHOPPING

THE SHOPPING SCENE

Many Danes from Copenhagen to Helsingør come to Gothenburg just for the day to buy Swedish merchandise. You can too, but you should shop at stores bearing the yellow-and-blue TAX FREE SHOPPING sign. These stores are scattered throughout Gothenburg. For purchases in one of these stores totaling more than 200 kronor ($34.90), you are entitled to a tax refund. You pay the tax along with the purchase price, but ask for a tax-refund voucher before leaving the shop. You will get the tax refunded, minus a small service charge, at your point of departure from the country when you clear Customs. You can't use such a purchase in Sweden, and it must be taken out of the country within 1 month of purchase.

MAJOR SHOPPING DISTRICTS **Nordstan,** with its 150 shops and stores, restaurants, hotel, pâtisseries, coffee shops, banks, travel agencies, and the post office is the largest shopping mall in Scandinavia. Here you can find almost anything, ranging from exclusive clothing boutiques to outlets for the major confectionary chains to bookshops. There is also a tourist information center. Most shops here are open Monday through Friday from 9:30am to 7pm and on Saturday from 9:30am to 4pm.

Kungsgatan/Fredsgatan is Sweden's longest pedestrian mall, stretching 2 miles in length. The selection of shops is big and varied. Near these two streets you will also find a number of smaller shopping centers, including Arkaden, Citypassagen, and Kompassen.

At **Grönsakstorget/Kungstorget** little trolleys are put up daily with flowers, fruits, handcrafts, and jewelry, among other items. It's right in the city center, a throwback perhaps to the Middle Ages.

The often-mentioned **Avenyn,** with its many restaurants and cafés, also contain a number of stores selling merchandise of interest to the visitor.

Kronhusbodarna, Kronhusgatan, was originally a series of workshops of the Gothenburg Artillery. But now they contain shops in turn-of-the-century style, specializing in such crafts as goldsmithing, glass blowing, watchmaking, pottery making, and coppersmithing. It is open Monday through Friday from 11am to 4pm and on Saturday from 11am to 2pm. Tram: 1 or 7 to Brunnsparken.

GOTHENBURG SHOPPING A TO Z

DEPARTMENT STORES

BOHUSSLÖJDS, Kungsportsavenyn 25. Tel. 16-00-72.
This store has one of the best collections of Swedish handcrafts in Gothenburg. Amid a light-grained birchwood decor, you'll find wrought-iron chandeliers, carved wooden furniture, unusual wallpaper, fabric by the yard, and such other items as hand-woven rugs, pine and birchwood bowls, and assorted knickknacks, ideal as gifts or souvenirs. Bus: 40.

C. J. JOSEPHSSONS GLAS PORSLIN, Korsgatan 12 and Kyrkogatan 34. Tel. 17-56-15.

For Swedish glass, I recommend this store, which has been doing business since 1866 and has established an enviable reputation. The selection of Orrefors crystal and porcelain is stunning. Even more intriguing are the "ice blocks" of Vicke Lindstrand of Kosta. The well-known designers Bertil Vallien and Goran Warff are represented with signed original pieces. There is a tourist tax-free shopping service plus full shipping service. The staff speaks English. Tram: 1, 2, 3, 4, 5, 7. Bus: 60.

NORDISKA KOMPANIET [NK], Östra Hamngatan 42. Tel. 17-33-00.

Most shoppers head first for this leading department store, recommended previously in Chapter 25, the Stockholm shopping section. The store's packing specialists take care to send your merchandise safely home. Typically Swedish and Scandinavian articles are offered—more than 200,000 items, ranging from Kosta "sculpture" crystal, Orrefors crystal in all types and shapes, Rorstrand high-fired earthenware and fine porcelain, stainless steel, pewter items, dolls in national costume, leather purses, Dalarna horses, Finnish carpeting, books about Sweden, Swedish records, and much, much more. Bus: 40.

HANDCRAFTS

Aside from some of the markets or streets already mentioned, the following establishments are centers for handcrafts as well:

KONSTHANTVERKSHUSET, Trädgårdsföreningen, Slussgatan 1.

This handcrafts center is housed in the Botanical Garden's former seed store. It presents exhibition and sales of handcrafts from 40 different Swedish artists. It's open Tuesday through Friday from noon to 6pm and on Saturday and Sunday from 11am to 4pm. Tram: 1, 2, 3, 6, 7, or 8 to Central Station.

LERVERK, Chalmersgatan 27. Tel. 18-22-66.

This is a permanent exhibition center for 30 potters and glass-making craftspeople. It is open Monday through Friday from 11am to 6pm, on Saturday from 11am to 4pm, and on Sunday from noon to 4pm. It is closed in July. Tram: 1, 4, 5, or 6 to Valund.

8. EVENING ENTERTAINMENT

To the Gothenburger in summer, there is nothing more exciting than sitting out at a café along the Avenyn enjoying their short-lived summer. The townspeople are also fond of taking the whole family to the Liseberg amusement park (see "Attractions," above). Although clubs function in midsummer, they are not well patronized until cool weather sets in.

You must consult the newspapers or inquire at the tourist office for a listing of entertainment events staged at the time of your visit.

THE PERFORMING ARTS

THE MAJOR CONCERT & PERFORMANCE HALLS

Folkteatern, Olof Palmes Plats, by Järntorget. Tel. 11-74-11.
Konserthuset, Götaplatsen. Tel. 16-70-00.
Stadsteatern, Götaplatsen. Tel. 16-44-00.
Stora Teatern, Kungsparken. Tel. 13-13-00.

THEATER

The Gothenburg Card (see "Getting Around," in this chapter) allows two tickets for the price of one. Call the theater in question or the tourist office for program information. Presentations are also announced in the newspapers.

FOLKTEATERN, Olof Palmes Plats, by Järntorget. Tel. 11-74-11.
This theater also stages productions of Swedish plays or foreign plays translated into Swedish. The season is from September to May, and performances are Tuesday through Friday at 7pm and on Saturday at 6pm. Tram: 1, 3, 4.
Admission: Tickets, 85 kronor ($14.85).

STADSTEATERN, Götaplatsen. Tel. 16-44-00.
This is the major theater center of Gothenburg, but without exception the plays are performed in Swedish. Ibsen translated into Swedish might be a bit hard to take without a knowledge of the language, but a musical might be understandable. The season runs from September to May. Performances are usually Tuesday through Friday at 7pm, on Saturday at 6pm, and on Sunday at 3pm. Bus: 40.
Admission: Tickets, 90 kronor ($15.70).

OPERA & BALLET

STORA TEATERN, Kungsparken. Tel. 13-13-00.
The opera season lasts from mid-August to June 1. If you're in Gothenburg during that period, by all means attend a performance at this 19th-century opera house where Eleonora Duse and Sarah Bernhardt appeared in front of the footlights. The theater presents not only operas, but operettas and ballets as well. Tram: 4, 5.
Admission: Tickets, 75–175 kronor ($13.10–$30.55).

CLASSICAL MUSIC

KONSERTHUSET, Götaplatsen. Tel. 16-70-00.
In the very center of Gothenburg, this is the major performance hall for classical music. In season, top world-class performers appear. The season is September to June. Bus: 40.
Admission: Tickets, 75–175 kronor ($13.10–$30.55), but could range lower or higher, depending on the performance.

THE CLUB & MUSIC SCENE

NIGHTCLUBS

GAMLE PORT, Östra Larmgatan 18. Tel. 11-07-02.
This restaurant, part of an evening entertainment complex, has a turn-of-the-century atmosphere. The oldest restaurant and nightclub in Gothenburg, this place is called a pleasure palace. One flight up is Gamle Port's nightclub, one of the leading ones in the city, and one flight below is an English pub if you'd like to have a beer. And the three floors also contain a winter garden, piano bar, and casino. The restaurant is open daily from 11:30am to 11pm or midnight; dinners cost from 175 kronor ($30.55). The pub is open daily from 11am to 1am, and a beer will set you back 42 kronor ($7.35). The nightclub is open daily from 9pm to 3am; minimum age for entry is 23 for men, 21 for women. Bus: 40.
Admission: Free Sun–Thurs, 50 kronor ($8.75) Fri–Sat; free entry for anyone with the Gothenburg Card.

LORENSBERG, in the SAS Park Avenue Hotel, Kungsportsavenyn 36–38. Tel. 17-65-20.
The leading nightclub along the west coast of Sweden, the dinner-dance room here features international stars. In days gone by, they might have been Marlene Dietrich or Eartha Kitt or a name orchestra. The dance floor is usually well packed. The food—an international menu—is among the finest in Gothenburg. You can dine lightly, feeding on crab salad or toasted sandwiches, or you can order a banquet, including chateaubriand. Dinners begin at 275 kronor ($48); beer costs 48 kronor

($8.40). The club is open Tuesday through Saturday from 9pm to 2am. Tram: 1, 4, 5, 6. Bus: 40.

Admission: 60 kronor ($10.50); hotel guests enter free.

MIRAGE NIGHT CLUB AND CASINO, in the Sheraton Göteborg Hotel & Towers, Södra Hamngatan 59-65. Tel. 80-60-00.

You can begin your evening early here in the Lobby Bar, which features piano entertainment every evening, before retiring to the casino to try your luck. At the adjoining Mirage, international flair and disco music are provided by the famous Juliana's of London. The nightclub has a professional sound-and-light installation, and has been known to hold as many as 250 patrons. It also offers a well-stocked record library, with a professional DJ. A beer will set you back 48 kronor ($8.40). The nightclub is open daily from 9pm to 2am. Tram: 1, 4, 5, 6. Bus: 40.

Admission: 60 kronor ($10.50).

DANCE CLUBS

HEARTBREAK HOTEL, Östra Nordstan. Tel. 80-66-70.

This is a combination restaurant and disco, whose most vivacious night is Thursday. It's in a cellar in the middle of a shopping center a short walk from the Avenyn, and it turns to America for its decor inspiration. Minimum age is 23 for men, 21 for women. Meals start at 125 kronor ($21.85), and a beer costs 40 kronor ($7). It's open daily from 9pm to 2am. Tram: 1, 4, 5, 6. Bus: 40.

Admission: 50 kronor ($8.75).

VALAND, Vasagatan 41. Tel. 18-30-93.

This combination restaurant and disco, one floor above street level in the center of town, is the biggest and most famous in Gothenburg. You enter to face a restaurant on your left and a large bar and dance floor on your right. There is also a small-stakes casino offering blackjack. Minimum age for entry is 25 for men, 22 for women. The restaurant, open Monday through Saturday from 7:30pm to 3am, offers only 10 menu choices; for more memorable food, head for Lilla London, one floor below (see "Dining," in this chapter). Meals begin at 125 kronor ($21.85); a beer costs 45 kronor ($7.85). The disco, open daily from 7:30pm to 3am, becomes the most crowded after 9:30pm, the most fashionable after 11pm. Tram: 1, 4, 5, 6. Bus: 40.

Admission: 60 kronor ($10.50).

THE BAR SCENE

HUNTERS PUB, Östra Hamngatan 30-34. Tel. 15-07-30.

This time-tested pub and dance club opens onto Gustav Adolfs Torg in the center of the city. Music is featured in the evening, but most patrons come here just to drink; a beer costs 40 kronor ($7). Pizzas, costing 60 to 80 kronor ($10.50 to $13.95), and some other Italian dishes are available. It's open daily from 11am to 2am. Tram: 1, 4, 5, 6. Bus: 40.

WAGTANN PUB & DISCO, Vasagatan 43B. Tel. 81-28-11.

Although this place serves food, it is more popular as a disco and pub, much frequented Thursday through Sunday. There is a small-stakes casino on the premises, but a lot of space is devoted to the bar; a beer runs 45 kronor ($7.85). Every Thursday at 8:30pm a 1-hour show is devoted to male striptease, with lots of women crowding in. It's open daily from 7pm to 3am. Tram: 1, 4, 5, 6. Bus: 40.

Admission: 50 kronor ($8.75).

GAY GOTHENBURG

BACCHUS, Bellmansgatan 7-9. Tel. 13-20-43.

This is the leading gay bar and disco of Gothenburg, although it's also a restaurant (see "Dining," in this chapter). Technically, Swedes must have an annual membership card to patronize this establishment, but foreign visitors are allowed in for the price of the cover charge. The disco and restaurant both share the street level, and upstairs is a

small room with an additional bar and a small-stakes casino and roulette table. The atmosphere is cruisy. Beer costs 42 kronor ($7.35). It's open Friday through Monday from 9pm to 2am. Tram: 1, 4, 5, 6. Bus: 40.
Admission: 60 kronor ($10.50) Fri–Sat and Mon, 15 kronor ($2.60) Sun.

9. NETWORKS & RESOURCES

FOR STUDENTS The **Kärralund Camping Site** is a great center for meeting and sharing a life with an international crowd of young people in summer. It's also a popular site with families.

Public showers are available at the Central Station in Gothenburg, costing 10 kronor ($1.75), and luggage can be stored there at the rate of 5 to 10 kronor (85¢ to $1.75) per 24 hours.

Other centers for young people include a youth hostel, **Ostkupan (IYHF)** at Mejerigatan 2 (tel. 40-10-50), near Liseberg Park. Take tram no. 1, 3, or 6 to Redberg, then transfer by bus no. 62 to Gråddgatan. It is open June to August only.

Many young people gather in summer at **Leonis,** Kungsportsavenyn 32, which offers some of the cheapest food in town. Freshly made salads with a generous serving of bread cost only 35 kronor ($6.10). It is open Monday through Saturday from 10:30am to 8pm and on Sunday from noon to 7pm.

FOR GAY MEN & LESBIANS **Touch,** Esperantoplatsen 7 (tel. 11-61-51), is run by the Gothenburg chapter of the Swedish Gay Union. It's small and doesn't always keep regular hours, but if you can get someone here on the phone you will be informed of any gay-related activities taking place in the city. The best times to call are Sunday through Friday from 9pm to 1am and on Saturday from 9:30pm to 2am. A bookstore that stocks gay-related literature, **Rosa Rummet,** operates out of the same address.

The **Gay Radio Station** broadcasts locally on Sunday from 7:45 to 9pm and Monday from 7 to 7:30pm, but in Swedish only.

The gay liberation center in Stockholm is **RFSL-Centre-Göteborg 2,** Pusterviksgatan 9 (tel. 11-61-51), which is open on Friday and Saturday only from 9pm to 4am.

10. EASY EXCURSIONS

Several days could be spent exploring towns and fishing villages along the west coast north of Gothenburg, such as **Lysekil, Smögen,** and **Stromstad** near the Norwegian border. Bathers can lie on the rocks along this shore, lounging in the sun against a backdrop of yachts and fishing craft. There are several day trips and evening cruises from Gothenburg to the archipelago. For tickets and information, consult the tourist office.

KUNGÄLV

If you're pressed for time, at least see Kungälv, 11 miles north of Gothenburg and reached by bus no. 301 or 330 from the Central Station. For information, contact **Kungälv Kommun,** Fästningsholmen S-442 81 Kungälv (tel. 0303/12-35). Kungälv, known by the Vikings as Kongahalla, has 1,000-year-old traditions.

On the E6 highway lie the ruins of the 14th-century **Bohus Fortress** (tel. 0303/992-00). This bastion played a leading role in the battles among Sweden, Norway, and Denmark to establish supremacy. Bohus Castle and Fortress (Bohus Fastning) was built by order of Norway's King Haakon on Norwegian territory. It was later used as a prison, after it was ceded to Sweden in 1658. Climb the tower— "Father's Hat"—for a splendid view. Bohus is open May 1 to August 15, daily from 10am to 8pm, and August 16 to September 15, daily from noon to 6pm, charging 10 kronor ($1.75) for adults, 7 kronor ($1.20) for children.

WHERE TO STAY & DINE

HOTEL FARS HATT, Torget, S-442 00 Kungälv. Tel. 0303/109-70. Fax 0303/196-37. 130 rms (all with bath). MINIBAR TV TEL.

$ Rates (including breakfast): Summer (mid-June to mid-Aug), 600 kronor ($104.75) single; 700 kronor ($122.20) double. Winter, 910 kronor ($158.90) single; 1,100 kronor ($192.05) double. AE, DC, MC, V.

Established in the 17th century in the town center, the site was used to refresh travelers with fish, game, and ale, and today the tradition continues. An outdoor swimming pool, lakeside pier, a sauna, a solarium, conference rooms, a nearby golf course, jogging tracks, tennis courts, and airy dining rooms are some features. Bedrooms are well-furnished, each modern and recently renovated, painted in pastels.

LÖKEBERGS KURSGÅRD PENSIONAT, Lökeberg, S-442 00 Kungälv. Tel. 0303/271-90. Fax 0303/27205. 100 rms (all with bath). TV TEL **Bus:** 303 or 312 from Kungälv.

$ Rates (including breakfast): 450 kronor ($78.55) single; 630 kronor ($110) double. AE, DC, MC, V. **Closed:** July.

Flat-roofed and modern, the cluster of buildings that make up this vacation hotel are on a meadow that slopes down to a lake 22 miles north of Gothenburg and 6 miles north of Kungälv. The public rooms are paneled with light-grained wood and on the premises is a modern restaurant, as well as a sauna. Each bedroom is furnished in a modern style and comfortably equipped. The decor is in light pastels or earth tones.

MARSTRAND

This once-royal resort, frequented by the former Swedish king, Oscar II, is on a secluded island. Its little shops, art galleries, and pleasant walks are reminiscent of Nantucket, Massachusetts. Part of the fun of Marstrand is the trip to it.

To reach the island, motorists can head north along the E6 from Gothenburg and turn at the exit to Ytterby. From there they can drive along a little secondary road to Tjuvkll where they must park their car in the lot and take the ferry the rest of the way to Marstrand. The ferry departs every 15 minutes in summer, somewhat less frequently in winter, depending on weather conditions. The one-way fare is 10 kronor ($1.75). No cars are allowed to cross over, except service vehicles.

A bus, the *Marstrand Express,* also departs from the Central Station in Gothenburg. The one-way fare is 40 kronor ($7). Departures are hourly in summer, every 2 hours off-season. No reservations are necessary. The bus drops passengers off at the ferryboat landing at Tjuvkll.

Young people from Gothenburg and the surrounding district flock to Marstrand on weekends, filling up the clapboard-sided hotels. The resort, quiet all week, comes alive with the sounds of folk singers and the twang of guitars. But the big event on Marstrand's calendar is the **international regatta,** held annually—usually the first 2 weeks in July.

Don't miss the 17th-century **Carlstens Fortress,** S-440 30 Marstrand (tel. 0303/602-65), towering over the island. After a climb up the hill, pay a visit to the chapel, then walk through the secret tunnel to the fortress, charging admission of 14 kronor ($2.45) for adults, 8 kronor ($1.40) for children. In 1658 King Charles X Gustaf arrived at Marstrand and decided that a fortress should be built to protect the Swedish west-coast fleet. The bastions around the lower castle courtyard were constructed in 1689–1705, and were completed during the first half of the 19th century.

Street addresses aren't used on the island, but since it's so small, buildings are easy to find.

WHERE TO STAY & DINE

VILLA MARITIME, S-440 30 Marstrand. Tel. 0303/610-25. 70 apts.
$ Rates: 4,500–7,000 kronor ($785.70–$1,221.20) per week for apt. MC, V.
Villa Maritime is next to the marina midway between the water and the stone fortress.
Its red-tile roof, big windows, and glassed-in veranda are reminiscent of an updated
Edwardian villa. The apartments, housing two, four, or six guests, are well furnished
and color-coordinated, with sitting rooms, one or two bedrooms, and kitchens. Most
of them also have private balconies. The villa has a gym, sauna, solarium, and laundry
room. On the premises are pleasant cocktail lounge and a dining room.

BÅTELLET, S-440 30 Marstrand. Tel. 0303/600-10. 98 beds.
$ Rates: Summer, 110 kronor ($19.20) per person; winter, 80 kronor ($13.95) per
person. Breakfast costs 35 kronor ($6.10) extra. No credit cards.
This is a former bathing house in the town center that has been converted into a youth
hostel with four to five beds per room. It attracts an international crowd. Highest
prices are charged from June to August. Breakfast is served only in season; at other
times of the year, you can make your own in the communal kitchen. Guests make their
own beds.

EVENING ENTERTAINMENT

OSKAR'S, S-440 30 Marstrand. Tel. 0303/615-54.
Set at street level in the town center, this is a combination restaurant and disco
whose cozy interior is sheathed in wood. There's a large and convivial bar that is
crowded in summer with gregarious Swedes. Music begins at 9:30pm for the dance
floor. You can also order meals for 125 kronor ($21.85) and up, including sandwiches,
pepper steak, veal steak, and hamburgers. Beer costs 45 kronor ($7.85). Oskar's is
open daily from noon to 3am (closed September to April).
   Admission: Disco, 50 kronor ($8.75).

TROLLHÄTTAN

Trollhättan is an important river town on the Göta Canal, with one of the largest
power stations in Europe. The canal and lock area is an imposing sight set against a
backdrop of rocks and islands. To see the river rush forth into the old riverbed is a
dramatic experience you can enjoy at 2pm on Saturday and Sunday in May and June
and on Wednesday and Sunday in July and August.

WHERE TO STAY & DINE

**STRÖMSBERGS TURISTATION, S-461 57 Trollhättan. Tel. 0520/129-
60.** Fax 0250/15600. 27 rms (all with bath), 19 dormitory beds. TV TEL
$ Rates: Hotel (including breakfast): Midsummer and Fri–Sat year round, 420
kronor ($73.35) single; 520 kronor ($90.80) double. Sun–Thurs in winter, 550
kronor ($96.05) single; 680 kronor ($118.75) double. Dormitory, 85 kronor
($14.85) per person for members, 117 kronor ($20.45) for nonmembers. Breakfast
costs 45 kronor ($7.85) extra. AE, DC, MC, V.
   This establishment on a hill on the western bank of the Göta Canal, a
15-minute walk from the town's market square, has two different sections—
the first with 19 beds divided among four dormitories, each room with hot and
cold running water; showers are in the corridor. The dormitory is in the original
wood-sided building from 1867. The modern annex, built in 1974 but renovated in
1990, lies a few steps away. Rooms here are modern and comfortably furnished. The
hotel offers a small cafeteria and a restaurant all in one room. Lunches begin at 85
kronor ($14.85), with dinners priced at 120 kronor ($20.95).

SWEDISH LAPLAND

Swedish Lapland—or Norrland, as the Swedes call it—is the last wilderness of Europe. This vast northern land of the Midnight Sun has crystal-blue lakes and majestic mountains, glaciers, waterfalls, rushing rivers, and forests. Norrland covers roughly half of the area of Sweden, and one-quarter of the country lies north of the Arctic Circle.

The sun doesn't set for 6 weeks in June and July and the sky is illuminated with brilliant colors. In spring and autumn many visitors come here to see the northern lights.

Swedish Lapland is a paradise for hikers and campers—if you don't mind the mosquitoes in summer. You should get in touch with the **Svenska Turistföreningen (Swedish Touring Club)** before you go. This outfit maintains mountain hotels, and it has built bridges and marked hiking routes. It has even introduced regular boat services on some lakes.

There are hundreds of miles of marked hiking and skiing tracks. (March, April, and even May are recommended for skiing.) Some 90 mountain hotels or Lapp-type huts (called *fjällstugor* and *kåtor*) are offered, with beds and bedding, cooking utensils, and firewood. Huts can be used for 1 or 2 nights only. The club also sponsors mountain stations *(fjällstationer)*.

You must be in good physical condition and have suitable equipment before setting out, as most of the area is uninhabited. Neophytes should join one of the hiking or conducted tours offered by the STF. For more details, contact the Swedish Touring Club, Box 25, S-101 20 Stockholm (tel. 08/790-31-00).

THE LAPPS (SAMI) IN SWEDEN The Lapps, or Sami, of whom 15,000 to 17,000 live in Sweden, have inhabited the country since ancient times. Some 2,500 still lead the nomadic life of their ancestors, herding reindeer in their multicolored costumes. The area of Lapp settlement *(Sapmi)* extends over the entire Scandinavian Arctic region and stretches along the mountain districts on both sides of the Swedish-Norwegian border down to the northernmost part of Dalarna.

Many Lapps maintain links to their ancient culture; others have completely assimilated.

The language of the Lapps belongs to the Finno-Ugric group. A large part of Lapp literature has been published in northern Sami, which is spoken by approximately 75% of Lapps. Like all arctic peoples, oral literature—not written—has played the most prominent role. Among Lapps, this oral tradition takes the form of *yoiking,* a sort of singing. Once governments tried to suppress this, but now yoiking is enjoying a renaissance. One of the classic works of Lapp literature is Johan Turi's *Tale of the Lapps,* first published in 1910.

WHAT'S SPECIAL ABOUT SWEDISH LAPLAND

Great Towns/Villages

☐ Kiruna, the most northerly town in Sweden, at the same latitude as central Greenland.

☐ Luleå, the gateway to Lapland, founded by Gustavus Adolphus in 1621.

☐ Kvikkjokk, one of the most beautiful resorts of Lapland, on the doorstep of the largest wilderness in Europe.

Ace Attractions

☐ The Midnight Sun, which can be viewed from many vantage points at midsummer.

☐ The Sami or Lapps, a mysterious Arctic people with ancient traditions.

☐ The Kungsleden (Royal Trail), covering a distance of 210 miles—trail blazing through the last wilderness of Europe.

National Parks

☐ Sarek National Park, the largest wilderness area in Europe, filled with fascinating flora and fauna—for the adventurous only.

☐ Abisko National Park, called "ocean forest" by the Lapps, rich in flora, including orchids.

Museums

☐ Ajtte Museum at Jokkmokk, a rich repository of the culture of the Sami people.

Special Events/Festivals

☐ The great winter market of the Lapps at Jokkmokk, a tradition going back 400 years.

Handcrafts play an important role in the Lapp economy. Several homecraft designers have developed new forms of decorative art, bringing about a revival in Lapp handcraft tradition.

Lapp is not a native term and is gradually being replaced by the indigenous minority's own name for itself, *sábme,* or other dialect variations. Many members of the Sami community feel that the term "Lapp" has negative overtones. In English, a translation might be Saami or Sami. Sami seems to be the most favored English translation of Lapp, and the word is being introduced in English translations by local institutions and organizations.

SEEING SWEDISH LAPPLAND

GETTING THERE

There are airports at Umeå, Luleå, Kiruna, and Gällivare. From Stockholm to Kiruna, flying time is 95 minutes, for example. You can take the train from Stockholm to Narvik in Norway, but before going to Norway, you can explore Swedish Lapland. There are three major rail junctions—Boden, Östersund, and Gällivare—from which rail traffic is funneled all over the rest of Lapland.

The express train *Nordpilen* takes 1 day and a night to travel from Stockholm to far north of the Arctic Circle. Once there you'll find mail-coach buses connecting the other villages and settlements.

A SUGGESTED ITINERARY

Day 1: Begin your exploration in the Luleå district.
Day 2: Transfer to Arvidsjaur for the night.
Day 3: Go to Jokkmokk for a day of exploration.
Day 4: Head west for an overnight stay at Kvikkjokk.
Day 5: Spend this day and night in the Gällivare region.

Day 6: Explore the district around Kiruna.
Day 7: Head for the wilderness, overnighting in either Abisko or Björkliden.

SOUTHERN LAPLAND

The best centers of southern Lapland are Luleå, Kittelfjall, and Tärnaby, previewed below. South of the Arctic Circle, Lapland is less forbidding. The mountains are easier to scale. If you hike to Rissjoen, you'll find one of the most attractive mountain lakes in Scandinavia.

---

1. LULEÅ

578 miles north of Stockholm, 213 miles east of Kiruna

GETTING THERE   By Plane   There are 12 flights between Stockholm and Luleå each weekday (10 on Saturday and Sunday), taking 1 hour 15 minutes. There are 11 flights each weekday between Gothenburg and Luleå (7 on Saturday and Sunday), taking 2 hours 15 minutes. And 10 flights arrive weekdays from Malmö (6 on Saturday and Sunday) on the 3-hour trip.

By Train   Six trains arrive daily on the 15-hour trip from Stockholm, 6 trains daily from Gothenburg, taking 19 hours, and 4 trains daily make the 22-hour run from Malmö. Trains from Stockholm to Kiruna deposit passengers bound for Luleå at the railway junction at Boden, 6 miles from Luleå. There they board one of three connecting trains a day going between Boden and Luleå. Train traffic from Gothenburg to Luleå also requires a transfer in Boden.

By Bus   A bus runs between Stockholm and Luleå on Friday and Sunday, taking 14 hours. There is also bus service on Friday from Oslo, taking 17 hours.

By Car   From Stockholm, take the E4 all the way. It's best to break up the trip with an overnight stopover.

ESSENTIALS   For tourist information, go to the **Luleå Turistbyrå,** Rådstugatan 9 (tel. 0920/937-46). The **telephone area code** for Luleå is 0920.

Often called the gateway to Lapland, Luleå is on the east coast of Sweden 70 miles south of the Arctic Circle. Founded by Gustavus Adolphus in 1621, this port city stands at the northern end of the Gulf of Bothnia. It is the biggest town in Norrbotten, and from its quay boats leave to visit some 300 offshore islets and skerries, known for their flora and fauna.

Luleå has a surprisingly mild climate—its average annual temperature is only 3° to 5° lower than Malmö's, on the southern tip of Sweden.

A port for shipping iron ore in summer, its harbor is frozen over until May. Fire has destroyed most of the Old Town. The location here of a state-owned ironworks has led to a dramatic growth in population.

The settlement has had an interesting history. Once it was ravaged by Russian Cossacks. Getting a city established this far north was laden with difficulties until development really took hold after 1940. Today, as the seat of the University of Luleå, the town has a population of 70,000 and is livelier when the students are there in winter, although most foreigners—other than businesspeople—see it only in summer.

WHAT TO SEE & DO

Gammelstad is 6 miles north of the city center. Gathered around its 15th-century church, the largest of its kind in Norrland, are 30 old houses and the largest "church village" in Sweden, consisting of more than 450 small church cottages. These cottages are still used today the way they used to be—that is, for overnight lodgings for faithful parishioners during important religious festivals.

Gammelstad Bay was part of a navigable channel into Luleå, but sailing ceased there when the city moved in 1649. Since then the bay has become shallow and is now a wetland area. In this area, just 3 miles north of the city center, ornithologists have counted 285 different species of birds during the spring migration. The area is classified as a nature reserve, but the public has access to it. Signposted tracks lead to the birdwatching tower and barbecue fireplaces.

The **Norbottens Museum,** close to the city center at Hermelin Park, presents a comprehensive look at Norrbotten's history over the centuries, showing how people lived in these northern regions in olden times. The museum possesses what is perhaps the most complete collection of Lapp artifacts. It is open on Monday from 1 to 5pm, Tuesday through Friday from 9am to 4pm, and on Saturday and Sunday from noon to 4pm. Admission is free.

WHERE TO STAY & DINE

Although rated expensive, the following hotels are actually moderate in price if you visit in midsummer—the peak of the tourist invasion—or on a Friday or Saturday night. These hotels also provide the best food available in town.

STADSHOTELLET LULEÅ, Storgatan 15, S-951 31 Luleå. Tel. 0920/104-10. Fax 0920/670-92. 135 rms (all with bath), 3 suites. TV TEL.

$ Rates (including breakfast): Fri–Sat June 29–Aug 5, 790 kronor ($137.95) single; 990 kronor ($172.85) double; from 2,400 kronor ($419.05) suite. Sun–Thurs Aug 6–June 28, 1,190 kronor ($207.80) single; 1,390 kronor ($242.70) double. AE, DC, MC, V.

The oldest, grandest, and most traditional hotel in town is located in a stately and ornate brick-and-stone building in the center of town adjacent to the waterfront. Inside, the sedately modernized public area retains a few old-fashioned details from the original building. On the premises is a lounge with an open fireplace, a bar, and a restaurant. The bedrooms are comfortable and well furnished.

SAS LULEÅ HOTEL, Storgatan 17, S-951 24 Luleå. Tel. 0920/940-00. Fax 0920/94-000. 208 rms (all with bath). TV TEL.

$ Rates (including breakfast): Summer and weekends year round, 425 kronor ($74.20) per person. Winter weekdays, 1,020–1,250 kronor ($178.10–$218.25) single; 1,190–1,500 kronor ($207.90–$261.90) double. AE, DC, MC, V.

Redecorated in 1987, this hotel is located on the main street, less than 6 miles from the airport. Each bedroom contains a radio and trouser press, among other amenities; half of them offer minibars. The most expensive accommodations are in the Royal Club. For dining you can choose between the gourmet French restaurant Amphion, and the cozy Cook's Inn, with charcoal-grilled meat as a specialty. The Chapman Bar, connected to the Amphion, is a popular rendezvous spot, and the Cleo nightclub, open 4 nights a week, is known throughout northern Sweden. There is also a unique dining room called the Northbothnia Room, designed with a decor like that of a 19th-century coastal farm, with a rôtisserie and baker's oven built into the room. If you need to relax, there is the pool club, with an indoor swimming pool, gym, solarium, saunas, and billiards. Express laundry service is available.

MAX HOTEL, Storgatan 59, S-951 31 Luleå. Tel. 0920/202-20. Fax 0920/947-90. 83 rms (all with bath). MINIBAR TV TEL.

$ Rates: July, 500 kronor ($87.30) single or double. Aug–June, 725–925 kronor ($126.60–$161.50) single; 1,175 kronor ($205.15) double. Breakfast costs 25 kronor ($4.35) extra. AE, DC, MC, V.

If you're taking the bus from the airport, it will stop in front of the Max, on the main commercial street of town. Designed tastefully with clean lines and simple furniture, the hotel offers comfortable bedrooms, each with its own radio and color TV with seven-channel video, among other amenities. Free coffee, tea, and hot chocolate are offered day and night in the lobby. There's an in-house sauna, a garage, a very pleasant bistro, and dozens of thoughtful extras that appeal to the hotel's loyal cadre of business travelers. The hotel has a gym with board tennis and a solarium.

2. TÄRNABY & HEMAVAN

223 miles NE of Umea, 273 miles north of Östersund,
626 miles north of Stockholm

GETTING THERE By Plane There is no airport. The nearest airport is at Umeå, in the east. Bus connections are possible from Umeå to Tärnaby.

By Train Two trains depart daily from Stockholm to the far northern rail junction of Storuman. Trains from Gothenburg headed for Storuman also are routed through Stockholm. From Storuman, it is necessary to go the rest of the way by bus.

By Bus From the rail junction at Storuman, there are three or four buses a day making the 78-mile run to Tärnaby. From the airport at Umeå, there are three or four buses a day going to Tärnaby, but it takes 5 hours.

By Car Take the E4 north to Stockholm, transferring onto Route E75 at the junction to Östersund. From there, take Route 88 north to Storuman, then head northwest on the E37 to Tärnaby.

ESSENTIALS For information, go to **Turistinformation,** in the town center (tel. 0954/104-50). The **telephone area code** for Tärnaby is 0954.

Tärnaby is considered the center of Sweden's most accessible alpine region, offering beautiful mountains and a chain of lakes. Hikers can strike out for Artfjället, Norra Storfjället, Mortsfjället, and Atoklinton, perhaps with hired guides. And Laxfjället, with its fine ski hills and gentle slopes, is nearby on the Blå Vägen (European Road 79).

Hemavan is the largest tourist resort in the area. Many paths lead toward Norra Storfjället. A delta formed by the River Ume is particularly rich in birdlife.

The greatest trail is the **Kungsleden** (Royal Trail), running from Hemaven to Abisko for a distance of 210 miles. This is considered one of the most fascinating trails in Europe. For more information, see "Abisko," in this chapter.

WHERE TO STAY & DINE

TÄRNABY FJÄLLHOTELL, Östra Strandvagen 16, S-920 64 Tärnaby. Tel. 0954/104-20. Fax 0954/106-27. 36 rms (all with bath). TEL.

$ Rates (including breakfast): Summer, 445 kronor ($77.70) single; 575 kronor ($100.40) double. Winter, 565 kronor ($98.65) single; 780 kronor ($136.20) double. AE, DC, MC, V.

This is the larger of the two hotels in the town center. Its rooms are comfortably furnished and well maintained. The hotel offers a sauna, table tennis, a ski room, a "drying off" room, and several lounges. In addition to the regular rooms, the hotel rents 30 different apartments, each with private bath, TV, and phone. However, these apartments—suitable for six to eight people—rent by the week, costing 4,110 to 6,400 kronor ($717.60 to $1,117.45).

LAISALIDENS FJÄLLHOTELL, S-920 64 Tärnaby. Tel. 0954/210-63. Fax 0954/211-63. 18 rms (none with bath).

$ Rates (including breakfast): 410 kronor ($71.60) single; 580 kronor ($101.25) double. No credit cards. **Open:** Feb 16–May 6 and June 15–Sept 2.

With windows opening onto views of the lakes, this traditionally decorated mountain hotel offers pleasant but undistinguished rooms that are kept immaculate. The hotel will arrange fishing trips as well as motorboat excursions to the nearby lakes.

SÅNNINGGÅRDEN, Klippen, S-920 66 Hemavan. Tel. 0954/330-38. Fax 0954/303-04. 17 rms (none with bath).

$ Rates (including breakfast): 250 kronor ($43.65) per person single or double. AE, DC, MC, V. **Closed:** Mid-May to mid-June and Oct to mid-Feb.

A warm, inviting country house, originally an 1850 farmhouse, set against the backdrop of wilderness 16 miles northwest of Tärnaby this is a fishing camp along the River Ume, which has challenging rapids. It attracts anglers and hunters. The rooms are pleasantly furnished. The food is good here, and the portions generous, with lunches or dinners costing 49 to 145 kronor ($8.55 to $25.30). The nearby Björnberget is a so-called south mountain with a profusion of flowers on its lower slopes.

3. AMMARNÄS

590 miles north of Stockholm

GETTING THERE   By Train   Take the train from Stockholm to Östersund, where you must change trains for a continuation of the northern route to Sorsele. From there, it's necessary to go to Ammarnäs by bus.

By Bus   From the south of Sweden, beginning at Stockholm, you should use the train as far as it runs. At Sorsele, buses meet arriving trains, and it's only a short run to Ammarnäs, depending on weather conditions.

By Car   Take the E4 north from Stockholm all the way to Umeå, where you connect with Route 363 heading toward the Norwegian frontier and going via Sorsele to Ammarnäs.

ESSENTIALS   The **telephone area code** for Ammarnäs is 0952.

A holiday paradise, Ammarnäs is in the Swedish highlands in the center of one of Europe's largest nature reserves, the Vindel Mountains. Leisure activities abound—you can fish, ski, or hike, depending on the time of year. The area is rich in varieties of birdlife.

WHAT TO SEE & DO

Local craftspeople specialize in the traditional handcrafts of the Sami, a seminomadic tribe of reindeer herders. If you visit here at the summer solstice, around June 21, you can take part in the **Sami Festival.** The best time to be here for an unforgettable experience, however, is in September, when you can watch the yearly **reindeer roundup.**

Don't miss seeing the **Potato Hill.** It's one of nature's mysteries—a place where tasty Mandel potatoes grow in abundance, often defying the laws of nature.

Ammarnäs has air taxis in summer and snow-scooter taxis in winter, to take you to the mountain and rivers. The village has such facilities as a filling station, post office, library, church, and store, and a skiing and leisure center at **Näsberget** (Näs mountain) nearby. Slalom skiing, ski lifts, and ski schools are all provided.

The famous **Kungsleden** (Royal Trail) hiking trail goes near here, leading down to Hemavan, visited above.

WHERE TO STAY & DINE

AMMARNASGÅRDEN HOTEL, S-902 75 Ammarnäs. Tel. 0952/600-03. 30 rms (none with bath).

$ Rates (including breakfast): Summer (May 11–Aug 10), 310–380 kronor ($54.15–$66.35) single; 460 kronor ($80.30) double. Winter, 360–410 kronor ($62.85–$71.60) single; 520 kronor ($90.80) double. Half board costs 380–480 kronor ($66.35–$83.80) per person per day. No credit cards. **Closed:** Nov to late Dec.

In the licensed restaurant, you can sample freshly caught fish or reindeer. Once or twice a week there are dances in the Gobbakallar, a disco. A swimming pool, with a children's pool, and two saunas are on the premises. Rooms are furnished in a basic Swedish mountain-chalet style.

NORTHERN LAPLAND

This is true Lapp country, and if you have a limited amount of time, you will want to explore it instead of the southern sector. A wide range of centers, from Lapp settlements to mining towns to lakeside Arctic Circle resorts, are previewed below.

---

4. JOKKMOKK

740 miles north of Stockholm, 38 miles south of Gällivare

GETTING THERE By Plane   The nearest airport is in Luleå, 123 miles away. From there you must take a bus.

By Train   There is one daily train from Stockholm to Jokkmokk, requiring a change of trains at Östersund.

By Bus   There is a single bus, which is deliberately timed to meet the plane's arrival, running daily from Luleå to Jokkmokk.

By Car   The E4 runs all the way from Stockholm north to Luleå, from which Route 97 then heads northwest to Jokkmokk.

ESSENTIALS   For information, the **Jokkmokk Turistbyrå** is at Porjusvägen 4 (tel. 0971/121-40). The **telephone area code** for Jokkmokk is 0971.

This community on the Luleå River, just north of the Arctic Circle, has been a Lapp trading and cultural center since the 17th century. With its population of 3,400 hearty souls, Jokkmokk (which means "bend in the river") is the largest population center in the *kommun*. Bus routes link Jokkmokk with the other villages in the area.

WHAT TO SEE & DO

The Lapps have an **۞ annual market** here in early February, when they sell their local handcrafts. Called the Great Winter Market, it's a tradition dating back 400 years. It is held on the first Thursday, Friday, and Saturday of each February, attracting some 30,000 buyers to the area. Actually people come to the market not so much to buy and sell, but more for the special experience of the place. If you're planning a sub-zero visit, you'll need to make hotel reservations a year in advance.

   Salmon fishing is possible in the town's central lake, and locals jump in the river in summer to take a dip, but I suggest that you watch from the sidelines because of the temperature of the water. Jokkmokk is one of the coldest places in Sweden in winter, with temperatures plunging below-30°F for days at a time.

   At the command of King Karl IX, the winter meeting place of the Jokkmokk Sami was chosen as the site of a market and church. The first church was built in 1607. Known as the **Lapp Church,** it was forced because of cold weather to have corpses interred in wall vaults until the spring thaw came and burial in the ground was possible.

   You can visit a hill known as **Storknabben,** which has a café from which, given clear weather, the Midnight Sun is visible for around 20 days at midsummer.

   Jokkmokk is the center of Sami culture in the area. Visit the local museum, **۞ Ajtte Museum,** Storgatan (tel. 170-70), in the center of town on the main street. This museum is the headquarters of Sami culture, and the many artifacts illustrate the lives of these once-nomadic people. It is one of the biggest museums of its type in the world, and wealthy in ethnographical detail. Entrance is free. The museum is open in summer daily from 9am to 6pm.

WHERE TO STAY & DINE

HOTELL GÄSTIS, Herrevägen 1, S-960 40 Jokkmokk. Tel. 0971/100-12. 20 rms (all with bath). TV TEL.

$ Rates (including breakfast): 550 kronor ($96.05) single; 650 kronor ($113.50) double. AE, MC, V.

Dating from 1932, this hotel in the exact center of the town, about 200 yards from the rail station, is a landmark in the area. In some respects it has the qualities of a frontier-country hotel. Despite that, its restaurant has won many awards and offers well-prepared dishes, including what the Swedes call *husmanskost* (good home-cooking), as well as continental dishes. In addition to this distinguished main restaurant, winner of several gastronomic awards, there is also a pizzeria and pub, Åkkjan. Entertainment and dancing are presented once a week. Run by the Åkerlund family, the hotel offers well-maintained bedrooms with modern furnishings. The sauna is free.

5. KVIKKJOKK

689 miles north of Stockholm, 60 miles west of Gällivare, 107 miles west of Luleå

GETTING THERE   By Train   Take the train to Jokkmokk (see Section 6, above), from which you must change to a bus to Kvikkjokk.

By Bus   There are two buses a day running between Jokkmokk and Kvikkjokk, a distance of 74 miles. Unfortunately, the buses do not always connect with train arrivals from Stockholm.

By Car   Take the E4 north from Stockholm to Luleå, then head northwest along Route 97 via Boden to Jokkmokk. From there, take Route 805 to the end of the line.

ESSENTIALS   The **telephone area code** for Kvikkjokk is 0971.

One of the most beautiful resorts of Lapland, this mountain village is the gateway to **Sarek National Park,** the largest wilderness area in Europe, and one of the most representative of the highland regions. It's virtually inaccessible, almost entirely without tracks, huts, or bridges. Nevertheless, the most adventurous tackle it, as it contains fascinating flora and fauna.

The national park, between the Stora and Lilla Luleälv, covers a distance of 750 square miles. It contains some 100 glaciers along with 87 peaks rising more than 5,900 feet. Eight peaks tower more than 6,500 feet. The most visited valley, **✪ Rapadel,** opens onto Lake Laidaure. In winter sled dogs pull people through this valley. The park contains remains of silver mines dating from the 17th century.

Sweden established this nature reserve in the wilderness in 1909 so that it could be preserved for future generations. Of course, to take a mountain walk through the entire park would take at least a week, and most visitors settle for a visit of only a day or two. The park should only be explored if accompanied by an experienced guide. Hotels in the area will put interested parties in touch with these guides.

Kvikkjokk, at the end of Route 805, is the starting or finishing point for many hikers using the **Kungsleden** (Royal Trail), already mentioned. One-day or 2-day outings can be made in various directions, as can an interesting boat trip accompanied by a local guide (inquire at the hotel recommended below). The boat explores a fascinating delta where the Tarra River and Karnajokk River meet. The area also good for canoeing.

Kvikkjokk was a silver-ore center in the 17th century, and there are many historical relics from that period to be seen in the area today.

WHERE TO STAY

KVIKKJOKK FJÄLLSTATION, S-960 45 Kvikkjokk. Tel. 0971/210-22.
18 rms (none with bath).
$ Rates: 420 kronor ($73.35) double. Half board costs 300 kronor ($52.40) per person. AE, MC, V. **Closed:** Sept 9–June 20.

Ⓢ Run by the Swedish Touring Club, this mountain chalet offers views over the rivers, lakes, and peaks of Sarek National Park. Fishing and hiking trails fan out in all directions. Canoes can be rented, and a guide conducts half-day hikes. Furnishings are traditional—in all, a no-nonsense atmosphere. On the premises is a sauna.

---

6. KIRUNA

818 miles north of Stockholm, 78 miles north of Gällivare

GETTING THERE   By Plane   Flights, which take 95 minutes, arrive from Stockholm daily.

By Train   Two daily trains run between Gällivare (one of the major rail junctions from Stockholm) and Kiruna, taking 1½ hours. Two to three trains a day make the 16-hour trip from Stockholm to Gällivare.

By Bus   There is daily bus service between Kiruna and Gällivare.

By Car   Take the E4 north from Stockholm to the junction of Route 98, at which point you head northwest to Kiruna.

ESSENTIALS   For information, go to the **Kiruna Turistbyrå**, Hjalmar Lundbomsvägen 42 (tel. 0980/188-80). The **telephone area code** for Kiruna is 0980.

Ⅽovering more than 3,000 square miles, Kiruna is the largest (in terms of geography) city in the world. This town has such extensive boundaries that it incorporates both Kebnekaise Mountain and Lake Torneträsk within its borders.

The most northerly town in Sweden, Kiruna lies at about the same latitude as Greenland. The Midnight Sun can be viewed from mid-May to mid-July.

WHAT TO SEE & DO

Kebnekaise Mountain, 50 miles away from the commercial center of town, rises 6,965 feet above sea level, the highest mountain in Sweden. Take a bus to **Aroksjokk** village, where you can get a motorboat to the Lapp village of **Nikkaluokta.** From here, it's 13 miles by foot, including a short boat trip, to Kebnekaise, where Lapp families can put you up overnight and arrange hikes or boating trips for you. The Swedish Touring Club has a mountain station at Kebnekaise, and the station guide there arranges mountaineering parties to the summit. It takes about 4 hours to reach the peak.

The town, which developed at the turn of the century, owes its location to the nearby deposits of the iron ore. **Guided tours of the mines** are offered in summer for 35 kronor ($6.10). Details and bookings are available at the tourist office (see above); children under 10 aren't permitted to go on the tour. The tours go through an underground network of tunnels and chambers.

Southeast of the railroad station, the tower of the **Rådhus** dominates Kiruna. It is open in summer, Monday through Saturday from 10am to 5pm and on Sunday from 11am to 5pm; in winter, daily from 9am to 5pm. Inside there's an art collection and some Sami handcraft exhibitions.

A short walk up the road leads to the **Kiruna Kyrka,** which is open in summer daily from 10am to 6pm. This church was constructed like a stylized Sami hut, an origami design of rafters and wood beams. You can also visit the nearby **Hjalmar Lundbohmsgården,** which is open June to August, daily from 10am to 8pm. Admission is free. This manor house contains displays of the town and some Sami artifacts.

The **Kiruna Samegård,** Brytaregatan 14, is open mid-June to September, daily from 10am to 6pm, charging an admission of 5 kronor (85¢). It contains an exhibition of Sami artifacts.

WHERE TO STAY & DINE

HOTEL KEBNE, Mangigatan 4, S-981 34 Kiruna. Tel. 0980/123-80. Fax 0980/821-11. 54 rms (all with bath). TV TEL
$ Rates (including breakfast): Fri–Sun, 500 kronor ($87.20) single; 710 kronor ($123.95) double. Mon–Thurs, 845 kronor ($147.55) single; 1,050 kronor ($183.35) double. AE, DC, MC, V. **Parking:** Free.

Next to the police station on the main road through Kiruna (the airport bus stop at its door), this hotel consists of two buildings, both of which were renovated in the 1980s. Bedrooms are modernized and comfortably furnished, and room service is available until 11pm. The hotel also operates one of the best restaurants in Kiruna, serving both Scandinavian and international food. Facilities include a sauna and a solarium.

HOTELL FERRUM, Lars Janssongatan 15, S-981 21 Kiruna. Tel. 0980/ 186-00. Fax 0980/145-05. 170 rms (all with bath). TV TEL.
$ Rates (including breakfast): June 9–Aug 20 and Fri–Sat year round, 580 kronor ($101.25) single; 910 kronor ($158.90) double. Sun–Thurs Aug 21–June 8, 900 kronor ($157.15) single; 1,100 kronor ($192.05) double. AE, DC, MC, V. **Parking:** 50 kronor ($8.75).

This hotel, run by the Reso chain, is functional and uniform in design. It is one of your best bets for lodging and also for food in Kiruna, as it offers a good restaurant, plus a cocktail bar and casino. Bedrooms are modern and well furnished, with a number of amenities. Rooms for the allergic are available, and some accommodations are suitable for the handicapped. A garage is on the premises. The hotel also has a sauna.

7. KARESUANDO

114 miles NE of Kiruna, 967 miles north of Stockholm

GETTING THERE By Train Take the train from Stockholm via Boden to Kiruna. Three trains run daily. Some have transfers; others offer direct service. At Kiruna, continue on by bus.

By Bus There are several buses a day linking Kiruna, the nearest rail junction, with Karesuando.

By Car Head north from Stockholm along the E4, continuing north after Luleå along Route 392 and Route 400 until you reach Karesuando.

ESSENTIALS For information, go to the **Karesuando Turistbyrå** (tel. 0981/ 202-05), in the town center, open in summer only. The **telephone area code** for Karesuando is 0981.

From Kiruna, a bus goes to the most atmospheric Lapp center at Karesuando, Sweden's most northerly village, near the Finnish border. This excursion, and certainly Karesuando, is decidedly offbeat.

Some adventurous motorists drive to Karesuando, 120 miles north of the Arctic Circle. For 7 midwinter weeks the sun disappears. To compensate, it never sets at all between May 26 and July 17.

Once at Karesuando, you can make car-ferry connections to Finland, where the road continues north through tundra regions to the most northerly part of Scandinavia. The Finnish tourist resort of Kilpisjarvi lies 72 miles northwest of Karesuando.

WHERE TO STAY

GRAPES HOTELL, Fack 34, S-980 16 Karesuando. Tel. 0981/200-22. Fax 0981/202-65. 39 rms (35 with bath). TV TEL.

$ Rates (including breakfast): Summer, 375 kronor ($65.50) single without bath, 475 kronor ($82.95) single with bath; 600 kronor ($104.75) double with bath. Winter, 375 kronor ($65.50) single without bath, 445 kronor ($77.70) single with bath; 495 kronor ($86.45) double with bath. AE, DC, MC, V.

This hotel was originally built in the 1930s by a German family. However, most of the present building dates from 1980s. It is owned today by a family from Israel. They offer comfortably furnished and well-kept bedrooms in this remote part of the world. The hotel has a sauna.

---

8. ABISKO

911 miles north of Stockholm

GETTING THERE By Train Go first to Kiruna (see Section 9, above). From there, take the bus.

By Bus Several buses service Abisko from Kiruna, with continuing service to Narvik.

By Car Take the E4 north from Stockholm, going northwest beyond Luleå onto Route 98, which runs to Kiruna and Abisko and beyond.

ESSENTIALS For **information,** make inquiries at the Turistbyrå at Kiruna (see above). The **telephone area code** for Abisko is 0980.

A resort north of the Artic Circle is a curiosity: Abisko, a resort on the southern shore of Lake Torneträsk, includes a scenic valley, a lake, and an island. A lift takes passengers to Mount Nuolja. Nearby is the protected Abisko National Park, containing remarkable flora, including orchids.

WHAT TO SEE & DO

Abisko National Park, established in 1903, is situated around the Abiskojokk River, including its mouth where it flows into Lake Torneträsk. It is a typical alpine valley with a rich variety of flora and fauna whose highest mountain is Slåttatjåkka, 3,900 feet above sea level. There is also the mountain of Njulla, rising 3,800 feet, which has a cable-transport line. The name Abisko is a Lapp word meaning "ocean forest." The park's proximity to the Atlantic gives it a maritime character, with milder winters and cooler summers than the more continentally influenced areas east of the Scandes or Caledonian mountains.

Another park in the area, **Vadvetjåkka National Park,** is smaller. Established in 1920, it lies northwest of Lake Torneträsk, with its northern limits set by the Norwegian frontier. It is comprised of mountain precipices and large tracts of bog and delta. It also has rich flora, along with impressive brook ravines. Its highest mountain is Vadvetjåkka, with a southern peak at 3,650 feet above sea level. Abisko is more easily accessible than Vadvetjåkka. Three sides of Vadvetjåkka Park are bounded by water which is difficult to wade through, and the fourth side is rough terrain with treacherously slippery slope bogs and steep precipices complete with rock slides. This park was once inhabited by settlers who eventually abandoned the land.

Abisko is one of the best centers for watching the **Midnight Sun,** visible from

June 13 to July 4. It's also the start of the longest marked trail in the world, the Kungsleden. You'll also see a reconstruction of a Lapp encampment at the resort.

THE ROYAL TRAIL The ✪ **Kungsleden** or Royal Trail runs from Abisko to Hemaven—about 210 miles. It's marked, of course, and mountain huts are spaced a day's hike apart if you can maintain the pace. Most of the stops are at what Swedes call *kåtors*. Here you cook your own food and clean up before leaving. At points the trail crosses lakes and rivers, where boats will be found for that purpose. The trail actually follows the old nomadic paths of the Lapps. Those with less time or energy will find the trail broken up into several smaller routings.

WHERE TO STAY & DINE

ABISKO TURISTATION, S-980 24 Abisko. Tel. 0980/400-00. Fax 0980/401-40. 109 rms, 52 cottages (none with bath).
$ Rates: 240 kronor ($41.90) single; 385 kronor ($67.20) double. Full board costs 310–450 kronor ($54.15–$78.55) per person. No credit cards. **Closed:** Sept 30–Feb 24.

Owned by the Swedish Touring Club, this big, modern hotel about 500 yards from the train station offers accommodations in the main building, the annex, and in bungalows. From the hotel you look out onto the lake and backdrop of mountains. The staff is helpful about providing information about excursions. Rooms are comfortable, and some have exceptional views.

HOTEL GÄSTGÅRDEN, Abisko Östra, S-980 24 Abisko. Tel. 0980/401-00. Fax 0980/401-00. 45 rms (3 with bath).
$ Rates: 260 kronor ($45.40) single without bath, 340 kronor ($59.35) single with bath; 280 kronor ($48.90) double without bath, 350 kronor ($61.10) double with bath. Half board costs 200–300 kronor ($34.90–$52.40) per person. No credit cards.

This simple hotel 50 yards from the railroad station is a welcome oasis in this part of the world. Twelve of the rooms are strictly self-catered. An additional 13 bedrooms, a shop, and a small restaurant are found in the main building, and others are in annexes. Boats and canoes are available for rent, and a small swimming pool is 50 yards from the hotel. You can ski, fish, take walks in the mountains, look at the Midnight Sun in summer or the northern lights in winter in a fantastically clean and natural atmosphere.

CHAPTER 31

GETTING TO KNOW FINLAND

One of the world's northernmost countries, Finland is the last frontier of Western Europe. Lapland, which occupies nearly a third of its surface, is north of the Arctic Circle.

Technically Finland is not part of Scandinavia, but in spirit it is, as reflected in its modern architecture; its high standard of living; its avant-garde designs in textiles, furniture, and ceramics; and its advances in education (it claims almost 100% literacy).

Geographically remote (although easily accessible), Finland does not attract the visitors that Denmark, Norway, and Sweden do—and that's a shame, for Finland has much to offer the visitor in both summer and winter.

1. GEOGRAPHY, HISTORY & POLITICS

GEOGRAPHY

Suomi (its Finnish name) is one of the largest countries of Europe, stretching 718 miles in length, with a maximum breadth of 335 miles. It has a coastline of approximately 682 miles. It is also among the least populated countries of Europe, with some 4.9 million, for a population density of 15.7 inhabitants per square kilometer.

Finland shares its western border with Sweden, a land frontier of 363 miles, and with Norway, a border stretching 444 miles. But its longest frontier—a distance of 787 miles—is shared with the Soviet Union to the east.

Most of the country is lowland, its highest point being Halti, at 4,344 feet above sea level. Some 8% of the land is cultivated, while 65% is forested. Finland has more lakes than any other country, some 187,888 of them—10% of the country's surface is covered with water. The largest, Lake Saimaa, with its adjoining waters, is the fourth in size in Europe. However, many of the lakes are quite shallow, with an average depth of 24 feet.

In the south and west the country is bounded by the Gulf of Bothnia, the Gulf of Finland, and the Baltic Sea. Its largest archipelago is Saaristomeri, with some

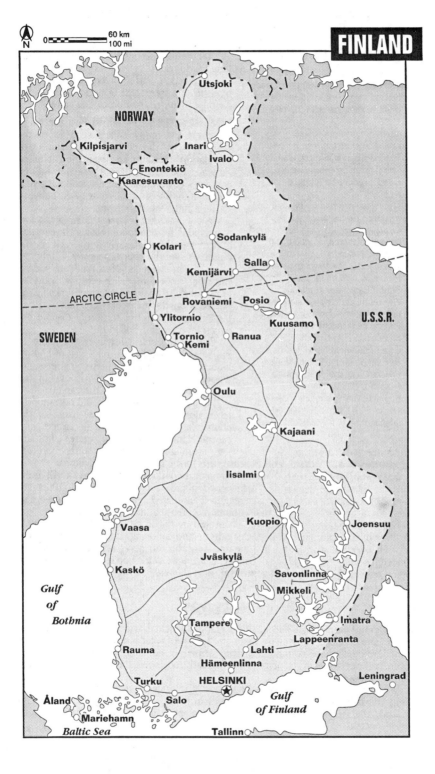

❓ DID YOU KNOW . . . ?

- Finland is a country of some 188,000 lakes and 180,000 islands.
- Finland was the first country to grant women the right to vote, in 1906.
- That vote was put to use: Today, one-quarter of the members of Finland's parliament are women.
- Two Finnish brothers hold the world's record for sitting on an anthill.
- The legendary bird of fairytale and mythology—the whooper swan, *Cygnus musicus*—has been saved from extinction and once again nests in Finland.
- The world's northernmost film festival is held under the Midnight Sun of Lapland at Sodankylä.
- Finland has its own version of the tango, a far cry from Argentina's.
- Finland has launched news broadcasts in Latin.
- One of the most heavily forested regions on earth, Finland makes baseball bats out of fiberglass.
- Finland is the leading book-publishing country in the world—17.1 titles per 10,000 inhabitants.

17,000 islands and skerries. To the west is the large archipelago of the Åland Islands, between Sweden and Finland. Finnish rivers tend to be short; the longest river is the Kemijoki-Kitinen, stretching 342 miles.

THE REGIONS **Helsinki** and the south are the most industrialized sections of the country, with the densest concentration of population. Helsinki has been the capital of Finland since 1812. It is the center of the country's government, culture, and entertainment, standing at the crossroads between Eastern and Western Europe.

In the southwest, **Turku** is Finland's former capital, founded more than 750 years ago at the mouth of the Aura river. It is the country's southwestern gateway. Only 10 miles to its west is **Naantali,** a seaside summer resort of 18th-century wooden houses, brightly painted. West of Turku lie the **Åland Islands,** an archipelago that was long the subject of a bitter territorial dispute between Sweden and Finland.

One of the oldest towns in the south of Finland, **Porvoo** lies 31 miles east of Helsinki, a town of narrow cobblestone streets and wooden buildings that make it one of the most popular outings from the capital.

Finland's **lake region** would take months to explore, maybe a lifetime. Most of the country's 188,000 lakes lie in eastern and central Finland. Many of these lakes are interconnected, and in summer lake steamers cruise the waters around **Lappeenranta, Kuopio,** and **Savonlinna** in the lake district of Saimaa.

Lake Päijänne in central Finland connects two modern cities, **Jväsklylä** in the north and **Lahti** in the south. **Tampere,** Finland's second-largest city, 100 miles north of Helsinki, is part of the lake region. It is situated in the middle of the western lake district and is one of the main points of embarkation for lake cruises.

Nearly three-quarters of Finland is covered by forest, an exotic Lapp wilderness ideal for hiking, camping, white-water rafting, and canoeing. **Lapland** lures visitors from all over the world, and in June and July the sun never sets. Lapland is also reindeer country and the home of Santa Claus, whose workshop is there. The modern capital of Finnish Lapland is **Rovaniemi,** near the Arctic Circle at the confluence of the Kemijoki River and the Ounasjoki River.

HISTORY

Ten thousand years ago, as the ice sheets gradually melted, widely scattered Stone Age settlements developed among the lakes and forests of what is now Finland. The tribes who developed these communities were probably nomadic Lapps of Mongolian origin, although the mists of time have greatly obscured the exact nature of the communities.

With the arrival of new tribes of Finno-Ugric origin (starting in the 1st century A.D.) and other unrelated Germanic tribes from the southern edge of the Gulf of Finland, the original Lapps retreated farther and farther north. Today genetic research into the distribution of blood groups points to evidence that about two-thirds of the modern Finnish population is of Western (that is, European) origin. (Nonetheless, philologists stress the uniqueness of the Finnish language, Suomia, whose only close relative is Hungarian. Both tongues are members of the Finno-Ugric subdivision of the Uralic subfamily of the Ural-Altaic family, unrelated to the Indo-European family to which almost all Western European languages belong.)

The Viking incursions, for which written records begin in about A.D. 800, established cultural and trade routes as far east as Byzantium and Constantinople. Residents of the region now known as Finland early in their recorded history probably had multiple contacts with the Russian empire, and others with the maritime kingdoms of Estonia and Latvia. More important, they also established north-south trade links with the shores of the southern Baltic, to what is now Poland and the eastern regions of modern Germany. Many different cultures and bloodlines met and mingled in Finland, often with bloody wars between the various Finnish tribes, until the Swedes—fearing for the stability of their eastern neighbor—launched a series of attacks into territory within the old eastbound trade routes.

SWEDISH INTRUSIONS Eric IX, assisted by the English-born bishop of Uppsala, St. Henry, in A.D. 1155, launched a crusade for the political and religious conversion of the Finnish tribes. Their major opposition broke out in eastern Finland (Karelia) from the Novgorodians (at the time a powerful Russian kingdom) who were grabbing land and spreading the Russian Orthodox faith from the east. Their most famous battle occurred in 1240 at the River Neva, when Alexander Nevski, one of the most famous heroes of Russian literature, defeated the Swedes. Later, a treaty between the Swedes and the Novgorodians in 1323 divided Finland's easternmost province of Karelia between Novgorod and Sweden. Eastern Finland, from that moment on, became part of the Russian-Byzantine world, and although it shared a common language with its western brothers, would not be completely united to the rest of Finland again until a brief period early in the 20th century.

Meanwhile, with the largest section of Finland under Swedish rule, most of the population in the centuries to come enjoyed considerable autonomy, and (usually) mercantile prosperity, and the Swedish language became the medium of culture. Under Gustavus I, Helsinki became one of the Swedish Empire's most important trading bases in the Baltic. Lutheranism was introduced into Finland by Michael Agricola (1506–57) who, because of his translation into Finnish of the New Testament and his compilation of a Finnish grammar, is called "the father of Finnish literature."

King John III (1537–92) granted Finland the status of a grand duchy in 1581. Unfortunately, Finland became a battleground in the continuing wars with Russia, Sweden,

DATELINE

- **100** Finland is inhabited by people from the southern Gulf of Finland and by Finno-Ugrians.
- **1155** Eric IX, king of Sweden, brings the crusades to Finland.
- **1581** John III of Sweden makes Finland a grand duchy.
- **1713–21** Russia invades and occupies Finland.
- **1721** Sweden regains control of western Finland, but loses much Finnish territory in the east to Russia.
- **1809** Finland becomes a grand duchy of Russia under Tsar Alexander I.
- **1821** The capital is moved from Turku to Helsinki.
- **1878** Under Alexander II, Finland gains its own conscript army, and Finnish replaces Swedish as the official language.
- **1905** Finns launch a national strike to oppose the oppressive policies of Nicholas II, who had revoked Finnish autonomy in 1899.
- **1906** Finland is allowed a single-chamber Diet with 200 elected deputies.
- **1917** Russia restores Finnish autonomy, as Finland declares its independence.

(continues)

DATELINE

- **1918** Mannerheim succeeds in driving Russian forces from Finland.
- **1919** Finland establishes a constitution.
- **1920** Finland joins the League of Nations.
- **1939–40** The first Russo-Finnish War launched.
- **1941–44** Russo-Finnish Continuation War rages, with Finland allied to Germany.
- **1955** Helsinki hosts the Olympic Games, as Finland pursues a policy of neutrality.
- **1956** Urho Kekkonen becomes president of Finland and presides over the long and tense Cold War era.
- **1982** Kekkonen resigns, as Mauno Koivisto is elected president.
- **1988** Koivisto reelected to a second 6-year term, as Communists decline in power.

Denmark, and Poland. The year 1671 established new boundaries, as Moscow was forced to yield certain lands in Karelia.

Finland entered the Thirty Years' War on Sweden's side, to which it was subjugated, its own language and culture suppressed in favor of Sweden's. The great famine of 1676 killed one-third of the population.

During the reign of Charles XII (1682–1718), Russia invaded and occupied Finland from 1713 to 1721. At the end of the war Sweden still ruled Finland, although some eastern territories, including southern Karelia, passed back to Russia. Russia gained new territories in another Swedish-Russian war, which raged from 1741 to 1743.

In 1808 Russia finally seized all of Finland at the peak of the Napoleonic wars. Finland was granted the status of grand duchy under Tsar Alexander I (1777–1825), and enjoyed broad autonomy throughout the 19th century, developing a democratic system relatively unimpeded by St. Petersburg.

LIFE UNDER THE RUSSIANS Turku was the capital of Finland until 1821 when the tsar moved it to Helsinki. In 1878 under Alexander II (1818–81) Finland gained its own independent conscript army, and the Finnish language was adopted as the official language of the land in 1863, replacing Swedish.

Although Alexander III (1845–94) tried to follow a liberal policy regarding Finland, most of his advisors opposed him, preferring to keep Finland as a buffer zone between the then Russian capital of St. Petersburg and the rest of Europe. Alexander's conservative and reactionary son, Nicholas II (1868–1918), revoked Finnish autonomy in 1899 and began an intensive campaign of Russification. Russian became the official language in 1900, and in the following year the separate Finnish army was abolished. Mass arrests followed. Finns in 1905 called a national strike to protest these conditions, forcing Nicholas to ease some of his edicts. In 1906 Finland was allowed to have a unicameral parliament (the Diet) composed of 200 elected deputies, but it had little real power.

At the outbreak of World War I, Russia totally dominated Finland, and Finnish autonomy became a memory. The grand duchy status was removed and the country became a dominion of its more powerful neighbor to the east.

AN INDEPENDENT FINLAND Finland was saved by the outbreak of the Russian Revolution and the collapse of tsarist rule. The Russian provincial government restored Finnish autonomy on March 20, 1917. Nevertheless, Finns called a general strike, seeking total independence. A civil war followed, in which the leftist, pro-Russian Red Guard, supporting Russian troops in Finland, was opposed by the conservative-nationalist civil guard, the Whites.

On November 15, 1917, a proclamation placed control of the country's affairs in the hands of a Finnish government, and on December 6, President Svinhufvrud (1861–1944) declared the independence of Finland. Russia recognized Finnish independence on January 5, 1918, yet 40,000 Russian troops remained stationed in Finland supporting the Red Guard.

Baron Carl Gustaf Emil von Mannerheim (1867–1951) assumed control of the

IMPRESSIONS

A race of men very different in character and morals from the Swedes, namely the Finlanders; and as this race prevails among the inhabitants, a greater vivacity of spirit, a more irascible disposition, and a propensity to criminal actions begins to be manifested.
—E. D. CLARK, TRAVELS IN VARIOUS COUNTRIES, 1824

Whites and was determined to drive the Russians from Finland. With the help of a German expeditionary force, he managed to win the civil war, which ended on May 16, 1918. At the end of the war, Finland faced starvation.

Mannerheim was named regent of Finland on December 12, 1918, and in June of the following year a constitution was established, by which Finland became a republic. The new constitution called for the election of a president every 6 years. Mannerheim would wield supreme executive power, as did K. J. Stahlberg (1865–1952), the first president.

At Tartu in October of 1920, a peace treaty was signed between Russia and Finland. Russia got East Karelia. Finland joined the League of Nations on December 16, 1920, and in the following year the League ruled that Finland—not Sweden—was entitled to the Åland Islands.

The 1920s saw continuing struggles between the government and Finnish communists. In 1923 the Communist party was declared illegal, but it came back reincarnated as the Democratic League. During the 1930s many social and economic reforms were made.

WARS WITH RUSSIA A Soviet-Finnish nonagression pact was signed on January 12, 1932, but Russia continued to make demands upon Finland, including the annexation of the Hanko peninsula for use as a Soviet naval base. When Finland refused, Russian troops invaded on November 30, 1939.

The Winter War of 1939 and 1940 was one of the harshest ever fought in Finland, but the Finns, greatly outnumbered, resisted with bravery and courage. In March 1940 they accepted Russian terms, ceding territories in the north, the province of Viipuri, and the naval base at Hanko. The inhabitants of those districts left their homeland and moved within the new borders of Finland.

Resentment against the Russians led to a treaty with Germany. Hitler's request for transit rights across Finland was granted. Finland tried to remain neutral when the Nazis invaded Russia on June 22, 1941, but Russia bombed towns in southern Finland, and Mannerheim launched the Russo-Finnish Continuation War. Territories lost to the Russians were regained. But in 1944 Russia launched a big attack and Finland was forced to sue for peace. Russia regained the territory it had taken from Finland, and imposed severe war reparations. Matters were complicated since German troops stationed in northern Finland refused to withdraw. Thus Finland had to launch a war against the Nazis in Lapland in 1945.

Mannerheim was made president in 1944 but was forced to withdraw in 1946 because of ill health. In Paris in 1947 Finland and Russia signed an armistice.

MODERN FINLAND J. K. Paasikivi assumed the presidency of Finland in 1946, and concluded a mutual assistance treaty with the Soviet Union in 1948. In 1952

IMPRESSIONS

O to be in finland
now that russia's here.
—E. E. CUMMINGS, FROM "O TO BE IN FINLAND," 1950

Helsinki became the site of the Olympic Games, focusing world attention on Finland, which in 1955 joined the United Nations.

In 1956 Urho Kekkonen became president of Finland, and he was to preside over the long Cold War era, resigning in 1982 because of ill health. During most of the Cold War Finland pursued a cliffhanging and neurosis-inducing policy of neutrality, earning for itself a reputation as a skillful diplomatic force. In 25 years in office he successfully walked the line between East and West, owing to his many-sided and dynamic personality. At the end of his regime, in the early 1980s, he saw the decline of the Communist party in Finland. In 1975 he had been host to the Conference on Security and Cooperation in Europe. He received the heads of state and the heads of government of 35 countries who signed the Helsinki Agreement in 1975.

Upon his resignation in 1982, Mauno Koivisto was elected president. Nearing the end of the long Cold War, Koivisto was reelected to a second 6-year term in 1988.

POLITICS

Under the amended 1919 constitution, the head of state of the Finnish republic is the president, elected to a 6-year term by a 300-member electoral college, which is selected by direct popular vote. The president plays a leading role in foreign policy and can influence legislation considerably. The 200 members of the unicameral parliament (the Eduskunta) are elected to 4-year terms by proportional representation. The chief executive body is the cabinet, headed by a prime minister, and responsible to parliament. Since World War II, most Finnish administrations have had to rely on coalitions between the major parties; today these are the leftish Social Democrats, the conservative National Coalition, and the Center Party, whose strongest support is in the rural north and east. Farthest to the left are the People's Democratic League and the Democratic Alternative (DEVA), neither with many seats in parliament.

Since 1988 the country has been divided into a dozen *lääni* or provinces, one of which, Åland, has enjoyed considerable autonomy since 1920.

2. FAMOUS FINNS

Alvar Aalto (1898–1976) Architect, furniture designer, and sculptor. Famous for his functionalist approach. He designed public buildings, apartment houses, factories, and whole communities like Rovaniemi.

Waino Aaltonen (1894–1966) Sculptor. See the Aleksis Kivi monument in Railway Square in Helsinki and the statue of athlete Paavo Nurmi.

Erik Bryggman (1891–1955) Architect. Among his best works are the Abo Akademie Library and the Turku's Cemetery Resurrection Chapel, the last example of the Finnish desire to integrate architecture and landscape.

Aksell Gallen-Kallela (1865–1931) Finland's most versatile artist, Gallen-Kallela painted portraits and landscapes in both watercolor and oil. His reputation

IMPRESSIONS

From the beginning of your history onward, men and women of Finnish blood have played important roles in the development of our country. Their industry, stability, and resourcefulness have made them an important element in American nationality.
—FRANKLIN D. ROOSEVELT

rests mainly on his paintings, especially those based on the national epic, the *Kalevala*. He also designed furniture, textiles, and buildings. In the Finnish national romanticism movement, he remains a towering figure. His home, Tarvaspää, outside Helsinki, can be visited.

Urho Kekkonen (1900–86) Kekkonen was the longtime president of Finland (1956–82), presiding over some of the tensest years of the Cold War, as he walked a tightrope between East and West. For three decades he served in various cabinet posts and was once prime minister. Only 17 when Finland became independent, he fought to keep it that way.

Aleksis Kivi (1834–72) First great master of Finnish language. His *Seven Brothers* has been translated into 20 languages.

Mauno Henrik Koivisto (1923–) The president of the republic became a member of the cabinet in 1966 as minister of finance. Author of five books on economics and politics, he was elected president in 1982 and was reelected to a second term in 1988.

Eino Leino (1878–1926) Finland's most original lyric poet. His major work, *Helkavirsiä* (Songs of the Festival of Spring) was originally published in 1903 and 1916 in two different collections. In his work, he attempted to express the aspirations and spirit of modern 20th-century people. Many of his poems were accompanied by the Finnish national instrument, the *kantele*, a kind of zither.

Elias Lonnrot (1802–84) A philologist who collected Finland's ancient songs and legends and published them as the *Kalevala* (1835), the national epic.

Eliel Saarinen (1873–1950) Architect who, with his partner, Lindgren, created buildings of bold sculptural masses with rough-hewn textures, including the National Museum and the railway station in Helsinki. In America he designed many of the performance halls at the Berkshire Music Center as well as the Sports Stadium at Yale.

Esa-Pekka Salonen (1958–) This gifted young Finnish conductor has been named music director of the Los Angeles Philharmonic, a post he will take in September 1992. One of the world's most sought after-artists, he became a guest conductor at the Finnish National Opera in the 1981–82 season and in the 1984–85 season he made his triumphant American debut. In 1985 he signed with CBS Masterworks to record Nielsen's Symphony No. 1 and Symphony No. 4 with the Swedish Radio Symphony Orchestra, as part of a complete Nielsen cycle.

Jean Sibelius (1865–1957) Composer. Wrote music for violin and piano as well as chamber and orchestral music. His *Finlandia* (1900) conjures up the savage beauty of the Finnish countryside. Considered by his contemporaries to be one of the great composers of the time.

Mika Waltari (1908–79) Achieved international fame with such novels as *The Egyptian* (1945), *The Adventurer* (1948), and *The Dark Angel* (1952).

IMPRESSIONS

Other composers offer their public a cocktail. I offer mine pure spring water.
—JEAN SIBELIUS, COMPOSER OF FINLANDIA

3. SPORTS & RECREATION

THE SAUNA—A NATIONAL INSTITUTION Regardless of where you've bathed, you really haven't been cleaned to the core until you've participated in the local ritual—a Finnish sauna. Whether for giving birth to babies or entertaining Russian ambassadors, the Finns regard the sauna as a national institution. It is estimated that there is one sauna in Finland for about every six citizens. The most authentic ones are log cabins beside a lake. Families and friends strip and head inside the chamber to take their places on slats. Later, someone throws water on heated rocks that give off hissing sounds. As is the custom, well-meaning friends pick up water-soaked birch boughs and switch the backs of fellow saunatics—great for the circulation, Finns claim. When the heat becomes unbearable—usually after 10 or 15 minutes for neophytes unaccustomed to 140° Fahrenheit temperatures—the bathers sprint out of the sauna and run to the icy-cold blue waters of a Finnish lake. In winter, rolling in the snow serves the same purpose.

Public saunas—contrary to popular foreign belief—are not mixed, and there are very few left. Attending a mixed sauna would invariably be a private affair, requiring an invitation. To be invited to a sauna by a Finn is the epitome of hospitality. To turn down the offer would be as gauche as burning the Stars and Stripes at an American Legion meeting.

Today in Finland, as in North America, most hotel saunas are heated by electricity. But unlike a Turkish bath, the air in a sauna is dry (until the water-on-the-rocks maneuver, anyway). Some saunas have attendants who soap, scrub, scour, and rinse you, but you can also go to a do-it-yourself one.

SKIING Skiing conditions in Finland are among the best in the world. The season is long and the trails are good. The best skiing season in northern Finland is March to April, when there can be up to 16 hours of sunshine daily. But the early winter—*kaamos,* the season when the sun doesn't rise at all—has its own attractions for visitors after something different.

Finland is 620 miles long, so there are two extremities in the country. The south consists of gently rolling hills, with elevations not exceeding 3 feet, but the farther north one goes, the more deeply forested and mountainous the country becomes. The highest fells are in Lapland.

The slopes of Finnish ski resorts are known for the excellent condition in which they are kept. Skiing instruction—both cross country and downhill—is arranged at most resorts, and equipment can be rented on the spot.

Long-distance ski races are becoming increasingly popular, and the long trails, ranging from 25 to 55 miles, attract more and more participants from all over the world every year. As many as 15,000 skiers take part in the biggest event—the Finlandia Ski Race. A fair number of resorts organize guided ski treks. These take a few days, and overnight accommodation is arranged along in the trail in farmhouses or, in Lapland, in wilderness huts or shelters.

FISHING In Finland there are more than 6,000 professional fishermen and about 1.5 million people fishing for recreation. For foreign visitors who fish for recreation, the usual fishing methods permitted are summer and winter angling, and fishing with lure and fly.

In Finland most fishing waters are privately owned, and cities and private companies also own fishing waters. The National Board of Forestry administers state fishing waters, mainly in northern and eastern Finland.

Foreign visitors must purchase a general fishing license for recreational fishing, and these are obtainable at most offices, costing 27 markkaa ($7.36) per person.

GOLF   There are 49 golf clubs in Finland, the best courses being in Helsinki. These include Tali Manor, 4 miles from the center, and the Espo Golf Course. Information about golf course and entry requirements and greens fees are available from the **Finnish Golf Union,** Radiokatu 20 in Helsinki (tel. 90/1581).

4. FOOD & DRINK

Many restaurants bring variety to their menus with typically Finnish dishes, particularly those that serve the Scandinavian smörgåsbord. There are restaurants to suit every purse and taste in Finland, and also an increasing number of ethnic restaurants in the bigger towns.

Breakfast is usually served between 7 and 10am, lunch between 11am and 2pm, and dinner any time from 4pm onward. Some restaurants in big cities stay open as late as 1am, and often nightclubs and discos—some of which serve food—are open until 3am.

Restaurants are called *ravintola* and many serve the smörgåsbord (called *voileipäpöytä* in Finnish). It includes a variety of fish and meat delicacies and hot dishes to choose from at a fixed price.

Inexpensive lunches are served at places called *kahvila* and *baari*. Baari is a place serving food and perhaps a mild beer, although coffee is the more usual drink consumed. All internationally known beverages are served throughout Finland in fully licensed restaurants and bars.

Potatoes, meat, fish, milk, butter, and rye bread are the mainstays of the Finnish diet. Soups are popular, especially pea soup and rich meat soups in which potatoes and vegetables are cooked together with chunks of beef.

FOOD   Every Finn looks forward to the crayfish season between July 20 and September, when some 225,000 pounds of this delicacy are caught in inland waters. Finns approach the eating of crayfish like an art, sucking out every morsel of flavor. After devouring half a dozen, they down a glass of schnapps. Called **rapu,** the crayfish is usually boiled in salt water and seasoned with dill. Of course, with all this slurping and shelling, you'll need a bib. Unless you're accustomed to schnapps, I suggest that you break with local custom and order a beer or glass of white wine instead.

The icy-cold waters of Finland produce some very fine fish, some of which are

---

 FROMMER'S SMART TRAVELER:
RESTAURANTS

1. Look for the daily special, reasonable in price and prepared fresh that day.
2. Order fixed-price menus, especially at lunch. Often you can dine in expensive restaurants in Helsinki by patronizing them at lunch and ordering the set menu.
3. Do as many Finns do and make one or two open-face sandwiches for lunch.
4. Watch the booze—it can add greatly to the cost of any meal.
5. Eat at fast-food emporiums, shopping complexes, cafés, and self-service cafeterias. Food costs are sometimes one-third the price of more formal restaurants.
6. Fill up at the traditional Finnish breakfast buffets, so you'll need only a light lunch.

IMPRESSIONS

It is important to remember that in Finland the lavatory for men is called Miehille, *and for women* Naiselle. *For a gentleman to say* Viekää minut Naiselle *("Guide me to women") is to court disaster, and in any case the beds are very lumpy.*
—KARL BAEDEKER, 1914

---

unknown elsewhere in the world. A cousin to the salmon, the 2-inch-long **muikku fritti** is found in inland waters of Finland. The fish is highly praised by gastronomes, and its roe is considered a delicacy. The most common fish, however, is **silakka** (Baltic herring), which is consumed in vast quantities. Rarely larger than sardines, the herring is not only pickled, but fried and grilled as well. Sometimes it's baked between layers of potato, the sauce made with milk, cheese, and egg. The fish is usually spiced with dill; in fact, dill seems to be the most popular herb in the country.

Finland has its own version of the Swedish smörgåsbord. It's called **voileipäpöytä,** which means "bread and butter table." That definition is too literal. Expect not only bread and butter, but an array of dishes, including many varieties of fish—such as pickled salt herring and fresh salted salmon—along with several cold meat dishes, including smoked reindeer.

Along with elk, bear, or reindeer tongue, Finns like the sharp taste of **puolukka,** a lingonberry. I hope you'll also have a chance to enjoy the Arctic cloudberry.

With any array of dishes, you can expect the two most popular salads of Finland: beet and cucumber. Bread is invariably served as well, including brown, white, black, and rye versions. The most typical is called **ruisleipa,** a dark, sour rye. Those open-face sandwiches, so familiar in all Scandinavian countries, are called **voileivat** here.

Fresh vegetables are plentiful in the summer, appearing less frequently during the long winter months. Boiled new potatoes are the most common vegetable and are served with sprays of fresh dill. Only in the most elegant places will you be served a convoluted morel known as "the black truffle of the north." It's the prize of all the mushrooms that grow in the vast forests of Finland.

Some Finnish hors d'oeuvres are especially good, especially **vorschmack.** Herring is ground finely, then mixed with garlic, onions, and lamb, which is then cooked in butter over a low flame for a long time, often several hours. This dish may have been introduced by Russian officers from St. Petersburg in the mid-19th century. The Russians have introduced a lot of dishes to Finland, and beef Stroganoff appears on many menus, especially in Helsinki. Borscht, a beet soup with sour cream, is another ubiquitous item.

One of the best-known regional specialties is from the province of Savo. **Kalakukko** is a mixture of a whitefish (known only in Finland) and pork baked in rye dough.

Another typical dish—this one from Karelia—is **karjalanpaisti,** a hotpot made with a combination of different meats. Another entry from Karelia is **karjalan piirakka,** oval-shaped rye pasties made with either rice or potatoes.

Boiled or broiled **pike-perch** and **smoked whitefish** are some of my favorite Finnish dishes, and perhaps you'll like them too.

The Finns are hearty eaters, so portions are usually generous.

DRINK The national drink of Finland is **milk** (sometimes curdled), and it can be drunk safely by North Americans. Similarly, water throughout Finland is safe to drink. Two famous Finnish liqueurs should be tasted: **lakka,** made from the saffron-colored wild cloudberry, and **mesimarja,** made from the Arctic brambleberry.

The Finns are heavy drinkers (**schnapps** is their favorite for an all-around tipple). A federal monopoly regulates the sale of alcohol, as Finland's well-intentioned attempt at prohibition didn't work out. But hard liquor, often imported, is expensive—and anyone on a budget had better stick to a domestic **beer** (Lahti is a good local brand).

5. RECOMMENDED BOOKS, FILMS & RECORDINGS

BOOKS

BIOGRAPHY *Sibelius,* by Erik Tawaststjerna (Faber & Faber), is a splendid panoramic look at Finland's most renowned composer. Much of the research of this five-volume work was based on private papers made available by the composer's descendants. The title above is only the first volume published, covering the period from the composer's birth in 1865 up to 1904.

Axel, by Bo Carpelan (Manchester, England; Carcanet Press) is an easier read as it is a fictionalized but accurate portrait of the relationship of Sibelius with his patron, Axel Carpelan, great-uncle of the author. Carpelan had a tremendous influence on the life of Sibelius, even suggesting the name for his masterpiece *Finlandia*.

FICTION *The Unknown Soldier,* by Väinö Linna (Panther). Presented on both stage and screen, this masterpiece depicts soldiers in the Winter War with Russia. Most portraits of that period portrayed Finnish soldiers as larger than life—"heroes in white"—but this was a more realistic "warts and all" depiction.

Kalevala (Harvard University Press). This is the greatest cultural masterpiece of the Finnish folkloric repertoire. It was gathered by Lönnrot, a regional doctor, and it is the embodiment of the oral traditions of ancient Finland and has been translated into many languages.

FILMS

Available on video cassette, *Ihmiselon ihanuus ja kurjuus* (The Glory and the Misery of Life) was a Grand Prix winner at the Festival of Nordic Cinema in Rouen in 1989. It was acclaimed as Matti Kassila's best film in years. The biggest name in Finnish cinema in the 1950s, Kassila returned to the screen with this adaptation of Sillanpää's autobiographical novel about a famous author coming to terms with his egoism.

The all-enduring Finnish cinema classic *The Unknown Soldier* is frequently revived and is available on cassette. Edwin Laine adapted the war novel of Väinö Linna, and it was first released in 1955, a powerful presentation of the intense physical experience of war. Its realistic setting is the Winter War of 1939–40 between Finland and Russia.

RECORDINGS

CLASSICAL A superb recording of Symphony no. 6, one of the less-performed works of Jean Sibelius, is on the RCA label, no. 60157. It contains the memorable *Scènes Historiques,* Suites 1 and 2, depicting various regional legends. The music is interpreted by Jukka-Pekka Saraste conducting the Finnish Radio Symphony Orchestra.

Ondine 730-2 was chosen as "record of the year" in 1989 by the Finnish Broadcasting Company. It is music so timeless that it can be performed any year. Timo Korhonen, a Finnish-born classical guitarist, interprets works by contemporary composers, including Koskelin, Donatini, and Ginastera. The record, incidentally, does not please all critics, as some found it "untraditional in sound."

Ondine 745-2 was called by one Finnish music critic "avant-garde classical music at its most hip and pleasurable best." Jarmo Sermila's "Contours," "Quatro Rilievi," "Love Charm Songs," and "A Prague Thoroughfare" are presented on this recording.

Finlandia 021 Oskar Merikanto: The Most Beautiful Song presents the music of

Jorma Hynninen, the Finnish baritone and soloist who has appeared at the New York Metropolitan Opera. Hynninen, accompanied on this recording by pianist Ralf Gothoni, is the classic songwriter of Finland, and, as one critic put it, the sound is "appropriately nostalgic."

FOLK *The Old and the New Kantele,* SFLP 8578 (LP); SFMK 8578 (MC), introduces the national Finnish musical instrument, the *kantele,* in all the forms in which it has ever existed. Performing on the kantele in this recording are Martti Pokela, Eeva-Leenn Pokela-Sariola, and Matti Kontio, all experts. Folkmusic tunes for the kantele were gathered from all over Finland.

Suvitunnelma, OMLP (LP), OMK 5 (MC), is a good introduction to Finnish folk music, as played on the violin, viola, double-bass, and harmonium. The music covers all of central, southern, and western Finland, including the Swedish-speaking regions. The performing group is the Kankaan Pelimannit, based at Kaustinen, site of an annual folk festival.

Musta Lindu, OMLP 22 (LP), OMK 22 (MC), is performed by the Varttina masters of Karelia from eastern Finland. This music had been much neglected since the 1940s because of its perceived similarity to the music of Finland's oppressor, Russia. As antagonism against the Russians has subsided, this music is coming in for renewed appreciation. The tunes are traditional—some of them arranged in a modern style, and instruments include the violin, kantele, taljanka (a two-row accordion), and double-bass.

JAZZ *Downtown Dixie Tigers: 30th Anniversary Concert* (LP and MC) is the most famous traditional band in Finland, playing jazz. Their appearances in the country draw packed houses.

Pekka Poyry: Happy Peter (LP). This artist was the most talented alto sax and flute player in Finland until his death in 1980. This collection includes recordings made in the 1960s and 1970s, with leading Finnish bands.

Edward Vesala: Ode to the Death of Jazz (LP/CD) is an internationally known drummer, who in this recording leads a 10-piece orchestra with original modern compositions.

CHAPTER 32

PLANNING A TRIP TO FINLAND

This chapter is devoted to the nitty gritty of planning a trip to Finland—costs, events, itineraries, and detailed practicalities like taxes, tipping, and emergencies. It should be read in conjunction with Chapter 1.

1. CURRENCY & COSTS

CURRENCY The Finnish unit of currency is the mark—**markka** (plural markkaa) in Finnish—which is divided into 100 **pennia** (abbreviated "p"). At press time, 1 Finnish markka is equal to about 27¢ in U.S. coinage. It takes about 3.67 markkaa to make $1 U.S. Coins are issued in denominations of 5p, 10p, 20p, and 50p, and 1 and 5 markkaa. Notes are issued in 5, 10, 50, 100, and 500 markkaa.

THE MARKKA & THE DOLLAR

At press time $1 = 3.67 Finnish markkaa (or 1 markka = 27¢), and this was the rate of exchange used to calculate the dollar values given in the Finland chapters (rounded to the nearest nickel). This rate fluctuates from time to time and may not be the same when you travel to Finland. Therefore the following table should be used only as a guide:

Markkaa	U.S. $	Markkaa	U.S. $
0.25	0.07	125	34.09
0.50	0.14	150	40.91
1	0.27	175	47.72
5	1.36	200	54.54
10	2.73	225	61.36
15	4.09	250	68.18
20	5.45	300	81.81
25	6.82	350	95.45
30	8.18	400	109.08
40	10.91	450	122.72
50	13.65	500	136.35
75	20.45	600	163.72
100	27.27	700	190.89

WHAT THINGS COST IN HELSINKI   U.S. $

Taxi from the airport to the city center	29.00
Single ticket on a tram or bus	2.00
Local telephone call	.55
Double room at the Hotel Hesperia (deluxe)	278.00
Double room at the Hoelli Anna (moderate)	142.00
Double room at the Hotel Finn (budget)	104.00
Lunch for one, without wine, at Karl König (moderate)	22.00
Lunch for one, without wine, at Happy Day (budget)	10.00
Dinner for one, without wine, at George (deluxe)	82.00
Dinner for one, without wine, at Kosmos (moderate)	41.00
Dinner for one, without wine, at Barbecue (budget)	29.00
Pint of beer (draft pilsner) in a bar	4.50
Coca-Cola in a café	3.00
Cup of coffee in a café	2.60
Roll of ASA 100 color film, 36 exposures	11.00
Admission to a museum	1.35–4.00
Movie ticket	8.50
Theater ticket	15.00–44.00

WHAT THINGS COST IN TURKU   U.S. $

Taxi from the airport to the city center	16.00
Taxi within the city center	7.00
Local telephone call	.55
Double room at Hamburger Börs (deluxe)	213.00
Double room at the Cumulus (moderate)	164.00
Double room at the Turun Keskushotelli (budget)	108.00
Continental breakfast in a hotel	7.00
Lunch for one, without wine, at Brahenkellari (moderate)	18.00
Lunch for one, without wine, at Pinella (budget)	10.00
Dinner for one, without wine, at Le Pirate (deluxe)	33.00
Dinner for one, without wine, at Café/Restaurant Lyra (moderate)	19.00
Dinner for one, without wine, at Verso (budget)	15.00
Pint of beer (draft pilsner) in a pub	2.40
Coca-Cola at a café	2.00–3.00
Cup of coffee at a café	1.50–3.00
Roll of ASA 100 color film, 36 exposures	7.00
Admission to a museum	1.35–3.00
Movie ticket	8.00
Theater ticket	16.00–27.00

2. WHEN TO GO — CLIMATE, HOLIDAYS & EVENTS

CLIMATE   The joke is that summer in Helsinki lasts from Tuesday through Thursday. In Lapland the **Midnight Sun** and the mosquitoes offer the visitor an unforgettable experience. The Midnight Sun is continuously above the horizon in the far north in Utsjoki from May 17 to July 28, in Ivalo from May 23 to July 22, in Sodankylä from May 30 to July 5, on the Arctic Circle and in Rovaniemi from June 6 to July 7, in Kuusamo from June 13 to July 1, and in Kemi from June 19 to June 25. There are almost 20 hours of daylight in Helsinki in the summer months.

Spring arrives in May, and the summers are short. July is the warmest month, with temperatures averaging around 59° F. The coldest months are January and February, when the Finnish climate has been compared to that of New England. The snow arrives in southern Finland in December, in northern Finland in October. It lasts until late April in Lapland.

Finland's Average Daytime Temperatures [°F]

	Jan	Feb	Mar	Apr	May	June	July	Aug	Sept	Oct	Nov	Dec
Helsinki	26	25	32	44	56	66	71	68	59	47	37	31
Turku	26	26	33	45	58	66	72	69	59	47	28	31
Tampere	24	24	32	44	57	66	72	68	58	45	36	29
Jyväskylä	21	21	31	43	56	66	71	67	55	42	33	26
Ivalo	17	17	26	27	47	60	67	62	50	37	28	21

HOLIDAYS   The following holidays are observed in Finland: January 1 (New Year's Day), Epiphany, Good Friday, Easter Monday, May 1 (Labor Day), Ascension Day, Whitmonday, Midsummer Eve, Midsummer Day (a Saturday), All Saints' Day, December 6 (Independence Day), and December 24–25 (Christmas and Boxing Days).

FINLAND CALENDAR OF EVENTS

FEBRUARY

☐ **Finlandia Ski Race,** Hämeenlinna-Lahti. Almost 50 miles of cross-country skiing, a mass event that is part of the Euroloppet and Worldloppet competitions. February 24–25.

MARCH

☐ **Tar Skiing Race,** Oulu. This cross-country ski race has been repeated every year without a break since first established more than a century ago. Following a course that stretches over 47 miles, with participation by hundreds of contestants, it is the oldest long-distance cross-country ski race in the world. March 11.

☐ **Ounasvaara Winter Games,** Rovaniemi. International skiing and ski-jumping events, including skiing World Cup finals. March 31 and April 1.

JUNE

☐ **Kuopio Dance and Music Festival,** Kuopio. International dancing event that takes a different theme every year, such as "Dance in the Mediterranean Countries." June 3–10.

☐ **Joensuu Song Festival,** Joensuu. An international event with concerts of symphonic and popular music, solo concerts, exhibitions, dance and theater performances. June 19–23.

✪ *SAVONLINNA OPERA FESTIVAL   One of Europe's most important and best-known music festivals it's part of a cultural tradition established in 1912. Dozens of performances are traditionally held in the island fortress of Olavinlinna Castle in July. The performers include artists of international repute from around the world, and in addition to the dozens of other offerings, at least one Finnish opera is presented.*

*   **Where:** Savonlinna. **When:** June 30 to July 29. **How:** For details and complete information, contact the Savonlinna Opera Festival, Olavinkatu 35, 57130 Savonlinna (tel. 957/514-700).*

JULY

☐ **Pori Jazz Festival,** Pori. Big open-air concerts and jam sessions attract top jazz players from all over the world, including Finland's own big names. July 12–15.

☐ **Turku Music Festival,** Turku. Programs stretch from the Renaissance and the baroque—played on the original instruments—to modern, light music. August 10–19.

AUGUST

☐ **Arctic Canoe Race,** Kilpisjärvi-Tornio. An international race for canoes and kayaks along a demanding route of 334 miles. August 4–11.

NOVEMBER

☐ **All Saints Ice Regatta,** Rovaniemi. The opening of the world's ice sailing season. November 3–4.

HELSINKI
CALENDAR OF EVENTS

FEBRUARY

☐ **Helsinki International Boat Show,** Helsinki. Boat show featuring the industry's latest models, developments, and sales pitches. Staged at the Fair Centre. February 9–18.

APRIL

☐ **International Vermo Cup,** Helsinki-Vermo. One of the main trotting events in Finland. April 29.

MAY

☐ **Women's 10km,** Helsinki. A 6-mile-long running event for women. May 27.

JUNE

☐ **Finland Sports Festival,** Helsinki. An international sports event that draws athletes mainly from Scandinavia, but also from around the world. Some events are staged at Espoo and Vantaa. June 6–10.

AUGUST

✪ *HELSINKI FESTIVAL   A major music event of Scandinavia, the Helsinki Festival presents orchestral concerts by outstanding soloists and ensembles, chamber music and recitals, exhibitions, ballet, theater, and opera performances, along with jazz pop, and rock concerts.*
  ***Where:** Helsinki. **When:** August 23 to September 9. **How:** For complete information about the program or whatever, contact the Helsinki Festival, Unioninkatu 28, 00100 Helsinki (tel. 90/659-688).*

NOVEMBER

☐ **Children's Festival,** Helsinki. Concerts, theater performances, and other events for children. Dates vary.

3. GETTING AROUND

BY PLANE

Finnair offers the lowest domestic airfares in Europe and has one of the densest routings, covering towns and cities with about 100 inland flights daily.

It also offers an unlimited-mileage **holiday ticket** that entitles a passenger to travel on all Finnair (also Karair and Finnaviation) domestic routes for a 15-day period. Total cost is around $250 (U.S.); those ages 12 to 23 pay $200 for the same ticket and conditions. This special ticket is sold through travel agents and major airlines in North America. The ticket can also be purchased in Finland, provided it is paid for in dollars and you can prove that you're not a permanent resident of Scandinavia. You can also purchase it in other Scandinavian countries with proof of non-Scandinavian residency. It cannot be transferred. This bargain gives North Americans a chance to see Lapland and the Finnish lake district and to travel north of the Arctic Circle. Regular flights to such points would cost far more.

BY TRAIN

Finland has its own **Finnrail Pass** for use on the country's elaborate network of railroads. The pass entitles a person to unlimited travel on all passenger trains of the Finnish State Railways. An 8-day ticket costs $90 (U.S.) in second class or $135 in first class, a 15-day costs $145 in second class and $218 in first class, and a 22-day costs $181 in second class and $272 in first class. Second-class trains in Finland are equivalent in quality to first-class trains in many other countries. The Finnrail Pass can be purchased in both Finland and the United States.

As trains tend to be crowded, it's recommended that you book a seat in advance; the reservation fee is 12 markkaa ($3.25) on ordinary express trains, 15 markkaa ($4.10) on all express trains marked EP on the timetable.

For more information, contact the **Finnish State Railways,** Vilhonkatu 13, SF-00101 Helsinki (tel. 90/7071). In the United States, contact **Holiday Tours of America,** 40 E. 49th St., Suite 1602, New York, NY (tel. 212/832-9072, or toll free 800/223-0567).

For other railway information, telephone 90/659-411 (in Helsinki) Monday through Friday from 7am to 9pm, on Saturday from 7am to 6pm, and on Sunday from 9am to 6pm. Train tickets are sold at the main railway station in Helsinki Monday through Saturday from 6:30am to 10:10pm.

Senior Citizen Discounts   Visitors over age 65 may buy a special card for 50 markkaa ($13.65) at any railway station in Finland, which entitles the holder to a 50% discount on any trip covering at least 76km (47 miles) one way. The card is not valid Christmas Eve, Good Friday, Midsummer Eve, or 3 days before any of those holidays (a surcharge is added).

BY BUS

Finland has an extensive network of private bus companies. If you'd like to find out about bus travel, call 90/602-122 (in Helsinki) Monday through Friday from 7:30am to 7pm, on Saturday from 7:30am to 3:30pm, and on Sunday from 9:30am to 5pm. Tickets can be purchased on board or at the bus station Monday through Friday from 7:30am to 7pm, and on Saturday and Sunday from 7:30am to 6pm.

For Seniors   "65 Tickets" are sold at bus stations, at travel agencies, and on buses to those who have a special **65 Card,** available to those age 65 or over. The price of the card is 20 markkaa ($5.45), and it entitles the holder to a reduction of 30% for a ride of at least 75km (46 miles). A photograph and passport are necessary when the card is bought.

BY TAXI

Most public transportation stops after midnight, and a taxi *(taksi)* is used for getting around. If you're not near a taxi stand, cabs can be called. Look up "Taksiasemat" in the local *Yellow Pages*. Taxis are very expensive in Helsinki, but much cheaper in provincial towns. After a base charge of 10 markkaa ($2.75) or more, you generally pay 5 markkaa ($1.35) per kilometer. Surcharges are added on weekends and at night. If people share, of course, the cost is greatly reduced.

BY CAR

Because of the far-flung locations of Finland's attractions, and the relative infrequency of its trains and buses outside the cities, touring the country by car is the best way to savor its sights and charms. If you bring your own car into the country, you need to show proof of ownership and some insurance documentation, but if you rent a car in Finland, a valid U.S., Canadian, or other driver's license, plus the presentation of a cash deposit or major credit card and a passport, is the only paperwork you'll need.

Roads are surprisingly good, even in the north, but once you leave the main highways, roads can be confusing. Sometimes the road markings point to villages known only to local residents, and distances are sometimes vast. Because of this, a good map is essential. Spiked snow tires are required by highway authorities during winter. All car-rental companies will provide them during the appropriate seasons as standard equipment.

CAR RENTALS   All of the "Big Three" American car-rental companies are represented in Finland: **Hertz** (tel. toll free 800/654-3001), **Avis** (tel. toll free 800/331-2112), and **Budget** (tel. toll free 800/527-0700). Each company maintains between 22 and 32 locations throughout Finland, usually in town centers or at airports, but sometimes in obscure locations. For those who want to begin and end their Finnish odysseys in different cities, all three companies allow free dropoffs at other Finnish locations if a rental lasts for at least 2 weeks. Hertz and Avis (not Budget) allows dropoffs at several other of their offices in Scandinavia, provided that the customer pays a service charge and the cost of ferry transit from one of three or four Swedish or Danish ports back to Helsinki.

Most of the companies will give you free child seats and rooftop racks, and charge only a nominal fee for a ski rack if you request in advance.

Charges for rentals of luxury cars with automatic transmission are so high (more than $1,000 U.S. per week, sometimes with extra charges for mileage) that most people quickly adapt to the manual transmissions that are considered standard equipment in Finland.

If you plan to do a lot of touring, you'll probably find that a weekly rental (which most companies define as between 5 and 7 days) with unlimited mileage is your most economical rental option.

At both Hertz and Avis the cheapest cars (a Ford Fiesta or Opel Corsa) rent for $539 and $529 per week, respectively, each with unlimited mileage, all insurance coverage, and all taxes included. (With Finnish VAT on car rentals set at a staggering 20.48%, this inclusion of the taxes makes an enormous difference in the final bill.) To qualify for this rate, Hertz requires a 21-day reservation and imposes a $50 cancellation fee for any changes or alteration in the prearranged rental dates. Avis is much more lenient, requiring no advance payment, no cancellation fees, and only a 2-day advance notification between the reservation and the actual pickup of the car.

Budget calculates its prices differently from its competitors. Budget requires only a 2-day advance notification before pickup of a car, and prices its cars without including insurance and taxes. Its cheapest cars, the same Ford Fiesta offered at Hertz and Avis, rents for $483 per week, with unlimited mileage, plus VAT. In addition, without paying an additional 40 markkaa ($10.90) per day for extra insurance (Budget calls it a collision-damage waiver), a renter would be fully liable for up to the first $1,360 worth of damage in the event of an accident.

These prices and policies can—and probably will—change by the time of your arrival in Finland. Therefore, the information above should be used as a guideline and so you'll know what questions to ask in making a car-rental agreement.

DRIVING RULES   Finland observes right-hand traffic, and speed limits of 60, 80, 100, or 120kmph are strictly enforced. Many streets in Helsinki are one way. It is illegal to drive a motor vehicle under the influence of alcohol, and the penalties for doing so are severe; the alcoholic content of one's blood may not exceed 0.5%.

BY RV

Recreational touring is called caravanning in Europe. Before you go, write for a free guide to RV driver safety: Stock – D13149 from **AARP Fulfillment**, 1909 K St. NW, Washington, DC 20049. The **Recreational Vehicle Industry Association** is at 1896 Preston White Dr. (P.O. Box 2999), Reston, VA 22090 (tel. 703/620-6003).

In Finland, RV rentals can be arranged by **Aartai Ky Motorhome Hire,** Kasperinkuja 10C, 00840 Helsinki (tel. 90/698-5397). Vehicles are rented year round, but high season is from June to August 31. Most of this company's vehicles offer five beds.

FLY & DRIVE

Finnair, Avis, Budget, and **Hertz** offer tours combining flight and car rentals. Prices are in three different categories. When flying on the much-frequented "Blue Flights," the package price consists of a normal-tariff airfare and the car-rental rate. There are no discounts. When using the domestic less-traveled "Black Flights," a 25%

discount on the normal airfare is offered in conjunction with the car rental. On even less frequented domestic "Red Flights," a 50% discount is granted on the airfare. Car-rental rates range from 360 to 840 markkaa ($98.15 to $229.05) a day (but prices will rise by the time of your visit). Rates include unlimited mileage, full insurance, tax, and car delivery to the airport.

All travel agencies can make these arrangements, or you can call the **Finnair Tour Desk** in Helsinki at 90/818-7900. You can also request a copy of a "Finland Fly & Drive" brochure at Finnair offices around the world.

BY FERRY

Using ferries to cross the lakes of Finland often avoids the more circuitous road network. However, be warned that ferry prices tend to be high considering the mileage covered, and the progress is slow. But, to compensate, you get to see the Finnish lakeland. The routes are multifarious, and conditions and schedules change based on the season. Therefore, it's best to go to the local tourist office in the area in which you're visiting for information on schedules, fares, and connections. A sample fare, for the 11-hour ferry run between Lahti and Jyväskylä, is 250 markkaa ($68.20).

SUGGESTED ITINERARIES

IF YOU HAVE 1 WEEK

Unlike the rest of Europe, in Finland it's not customary to drive around the country. Most people rely on trains and airplanes more frequently than they might in other places. However, I have outlined a week-long driving tour through Finland's "southern triangle." If you take the entire tour, the distance will be a total of 317 miles.

Days 1–3: The first day is spent flying to Helsinki and recovering from a transatlantic flight. Day 2 can be spent seeing the sights. The third day is devoted to exploring the nearby islands of the Baltic, such as Suomenlinna, or taking a steamer to Porvoo, the second-oldest town in Finland.

Day 4: Drive from Helsinki to Hämeenlinna, a distance of 61 miles. Take the E79 past forest-covered hills and meadows which eventually give way to open country dotted with lakes. About 20 miles south of Hämeenlinna you can visit Riihimaki, which has a Glass Museum (Suomen Lasimuseo) and a glass shop. By afternoon you'll be in Hämeenlinna, Finland's oldest inland town, founded in 1639, and the birthplace of Jean Sibelius. You can also explore a castle on the shores of Lake Vanajavesi. Hämeenlinna is the starting point of many Silver Line cruise boats which run to Tampere. However, those on a rushed schedule will want only to overnight in Hämeenlinna and continue our tour.

Day 5: Leave Hämeenlinna and drive along the E79 for 50 miles to Tampere. Folk dances and open-air concerts are performed in Hameenpuisto Park in summer, and the city boasts one of the most famous summer theaters in the world. Many lake tours start from here. Spend the night in Tampere.

Day 6: Head for Turku on the west coast. Leaving Tampere, it's only 10 miles to Nokia, famous for its rapids in the Nokia River. Continue southwest on Route 41 for 33 miles until you reach Vammala. The road continues to Huittinen, only 56 miles from Turku. Plan to spend the night in Turku, Finland's oldest city, taking in its many attractions.

Day 7: From Turku you may return straight to Helsinki on the E3. This 103-mile run may be broken by a stop at Salo, a lively town 33 miles from Turku. About 6 miles past Salo you can stop at the Muurla Glass Factory. Spend the night in Helsinki.

IF YOU HAVE 2 WEEKS

Days 1–7: Spend the first week as suggested in "If You Have 1 Week," above.
Day 8: Spend a full day in Helsinki getting to know the city better.

Day 9: After Helsinki, head northeast to Lappeenranta, one of Finland's most charming provincial towns, 137 miles from Helsinki and only 10 miles from the Soviet border, for a full day of sightseeing in Finland's glorious lake district.

Day 10: After Lapeenranta, continue northeast to the historic city of Imatra, favored by the tsars and site of the famous Imatra rapids.

Days 11 & 12: From Lappeenranta, go to Savonlinna for 2 nights. On the first day explore the land attractions, and on the next tour by lake steamer.

Day 13: Go to Kuopio, in the north lake district, for a day of sightseeing.

Day 14: Journey to Joensuu, the major municipality of northern Karelia, for a day's sightseeing in this richly folkloric province, half of which Finland was forced to cede to the Soviet Union in World War II.

IF YOU HAVE 3 WEEKS

Days 1–14: See "If You Have 2 Weeks," above.

Days 15 & 16: Fly to Rovaniemi, capital of Lapland, for an exploration of the area at the Arctic Circle. On the second day, take a tour to the Arctic Circle and go shopping at Santa's Village, 5 miles north of Rovaniemi.

Day 17: Visit Ranua, 45 miles south of Rovaniemi, seeing its main attractions, the Ranua Wildlife Park. You can either overnight in Ranua or use Rovaniemi as your base.

Day 18: Visit the towns of Kemi and Tornio on the west coast of Finland, opening onto the Gulf of Bothnia. Tornio is only 5½ miles from Kemi.

Day 19: Go to Sodankylä, which many claim is the place where the real Lapland begins. Rovaniemi lies 81 miles to the south. Try your hand at "gold washing" in the environs.

Days 20 & 21: Fly to Ivalo and visit Inari. A good part of the day will be absorbed in making transportation to Ivalo, and the remaining time can be spent exploring the attractions of Inari, which is the name of a small village some 25 miles north of Ivalo but also the name of the largest county in Finland.

 FAST FACTS **FINLAND**

American Express   This company is represented in Finland by **Travek Travel Bureau,** Katajanokan Pohjoisranta (tel. 90/66-16-31). Ask about possible affiliated travel agencies that might be tied in with American Express when you're visiting provincial towns. Sometimes there's an affiliate travel agency that can handle American Express clients.

Business Hours   Most **banks** are open Monday through Friday from 9:15am to 4:15pm. You can also exchange money at the railway station in Helsinki Monday through Saturday from 8:30am to 8pm and on Sunday from 12:30 to 7pm, and at the airport daily from 6:30am to 11pm.

The hours for **stores and shops** can vary. Most are open Monday through Friday from 9am to 5pm and on Saturday from 9am to 2pm. Nearly everything is closed on Sunday. There are **R-kiosks,** selling confectionery, tobacco, toiletries, cosmetics, and souvenirs, all over Helsinki and in other towns, which are open Monday through Saturday from 8am to 9pm and on Sunday from either 9 or 10am until 9pm.

Camera/Film   Most international brands of film are available in camera shops, but often at higher prices than in the U.S. It's better to bring in film duty free for your stay in Finland.

Cigarettes   American and British brands are available in all Finnish cities and towns—but they're expensive. In Finland smokers buy their tobacco at one of the R-kiosks, which are all over the major towns.

Climate   See "When to Go," above.

Crime   See "Safety," below.

Currency   See "Currency & Costs," above.

Customs   All personal effects, including cameras and a reasonable amount of film, bedding, and other such personal articles are duty free. Gifts to the value of 1,500 markkaa ($409.05) may be brought in duty free. You can bring in 400 cigarettes or 1 pound of other manufactured tobacco. You can also bring in either 2 liters of beer, 1 liter of wine, and 1 liter of spirits or 2 liters of beer and 2 liters of wine. You need to be over 20 to bring in spirits and over 18 to bring in beer and wine. There are no restrictions on the amount of Finnish or foreign currency you can bring in, but you can only take it out if you can prove that you brought it in with you.

Driving Rules   See "Getting Around," above, in this chapter.

Drug Laws   Drug offenses are divided into two categories: normal drug offenses and aggravated drug offenses. Normal drug offenses include the possession of a small amount of marijuana carrying a maximum penalty of 2 years in prison and a minimum penalty of a fine for Finns and possible deportation for non-Finns. Aggravated drug offenses mean anything to do with ownership, sale, or dealing in drugs considered extremely dangerous, such as cocaine and heroin. This offense always carries a prison term ranging from 1 to 10 years. Penalties for smuggling across Finnish frontiers are even more severe.

Drugstores   Medicines are sold at pharmacies (*apteekki* in Finnish). Chemists (*kemikaalipauppa* in Finnish) sell cosmetics only. Some pharmacies are open 24 hours, and all display notices in their windows giving the address of the nearest one on night duty.

Electricity   Finland operates on 220 volts A.C. Plugs are usually the continental size with rounded pins. Always ask at your hotel desk before plugging in any electrical appliance. Without the appropriate converter or adapter, you'll probably destroy the internal mechanics of your appliance and/or blow out one of the hotel's fuses and upset the management.

Embassies & Consulates   The **U.S. Embassy** is at Itäinen Puistotie 14A, SF-00140 Helsinki (tel. 90/171-931); the **British Embassy** is at Uudenmaankatu 16–20, SF-00120 Helsinki (tel. 90/647-922); and the **Canadian Embassy** is at Phjoisesplanadi 25B, SF-00100 Helsinki (tel. 90/171-141). Travelers from **Australia** and **New Zealand** should contact the British Embassy.

If you're going to the Soviet Union from Finland, you should have arranged for your visa in your home country; there could be considerable delays if you apply in Finland, and you might lose the chance. Sometimes it takes 8 weekdays to get a visa, maybe more. Take your problems to the **Embassy of the Union of Soviet Socialist Republics,** Tehtaankatu 1B, SF-00140 Helsinki (tel. 90/661-876).

Emergencies   In Helsinki, dial 000 or 181-000 for medical. All hospitals have doctors on duty around the clock. Municipal central and regional hospitals charge about 60 markkaa ($16.35) for a visit to an outpatient clinic and 75 markkaa ($20.45) a day in a ward in local and central hospitals. This includes treatment, the doctor's fee, and medicine. Private hospitals are considerably more expensive.

Etiquette   Both women and men shake hands when introduced. If invited for dinner, bring wine, flowers, or candy. In a sauna there is no loud joking or laughing. It's even considered impolite to whistle.

Gasoline   See "Getting Around," above, in this chapter.

Hitchhiking   See "Getting Around," above, in this chapter.

Holidays   See "When to Go," above, in this chapter.

Language   The Finns speak a language that, from a point of view of grammar and linguistics, is radically different from Swedish and Danish. Finnish is as difficult to learn as Chinese, and a source of endless frustration to newcomers. More than 90% of Finland speaks Finnish, while the remaining citizens usually speak Swedish. Finland is officially a bilingual country, as you'll quickly see from maps and street signs in Helsinki, which usually list street names in both languages.

The use of English, however, is amazingly common throughout Finland, especially among young people. In all major hotels, restaurants, and nightclubs, English is spoken almost without exception. The best phrase book is the *Berlitz Finnish for*

Travellers, with 1,200 phrases and 2,000 useful words, with pronunciation shown throughout.

Laundry   For listings of self-service laundries, see the individual city chapters.

Liquor Laws   Alcohol is retailed only from **Alko,** the state liquor-monopoly shops. These are open Monday through Thursday from 10am to 5pm, on Friday from 10am to 6pm, and on Saturday from 9am to 2pm; they're closed on Sunday and on May 1 and September 30. Drinks can also be purchased in hotels, restaurants, and nightclubs. Some establishments, incidentally, are licensed only for beer or for beer and wine. Only beer can be served from 9 to 11am. In Helsinki most licensed establishments stay open until midnight or 1am (until 11pm in some of the other cities).

A person age 20 can buy any kind of alcoholic drink from the Alko shops; those who are 18 and 19 years of age can purchase only the weaker alcoholic drinks containing less than 17% alcohol, such as wine and beer.

Mail   Airmail letters take about 7 to 10 days to reach North America, and surface letters—sent by boat—take 1 to 2 months. Parcels are weighed and registered at the post office, which may require you to make declaration on a preprinted form as to the value and contents of a package. Stamps are sold at post offices in all towns and cities, at most hotels, sometimes at news kiosks, and often by shopkeepers who provide service not for profit but for convenience. In Finland, mailboxes are painted bright yellow, and they have a trumpet embossed upon them. Postal rates for airmail letters and postcards to the United States are 3 markkaa (80¢) for letters and 2.50 markkaa (70¢) for postcards.

Maps   The following maps are published by the National Board of Survey: *Road map of Finland* (GT 1:200,000), an accurate, detailed road and touring map, and *Motoring Road Map* (1:800,000), a new edition of the *Motoring Road Map of Finland,* appearing annually, and the only map with complete information on road surfacing. These maps are the most important ones, although the board also publishes numerous touring maps. They are for sale at major bookstores in Helsinki (see "Fast Facts: Helsinki" in Chapter 33) or may be obtained from the **Map Center of the National Board of Survey,** Karttakeskus Espa, Eteläesplanadi 4 (PB 209), 00131 Helsinki (tel. 90/154-3168).

Newspapers/Magazines   English-language newspapers, including the *International Herald-Tribune,* are available at the larger bookstores, the railway station, and many kiosks in central Helsinki and other cities.

Pets   Live animals may be imported only with a permit from the Veterinary Department of the Ministry of Agriculture and Forestry. Dogs and cats, however, can be brought in provided they are accompanied by a certificate issued by a competent veterinary surgeon in the country of origin. The animal must have been vaccinated against rabies at least 30 days and not more than 12 months prior to importation. Travelers should remember that animals imported to Finland cannot be taken to Sweden or Norway without a quarantine period of 4 months in either country.

Police   Dial 002 in Helsinki. In smaller towns, ask the operator to connect you with the nearest police station.

Radio/TV   "Northern Report," a program in English, is broadcast at 558 kHz on the AM dial in Helsinki daily at 9:30am, 9:35pm, and at midnight. There's also a special Saturday-morning program from 10:30 to 11:30am. A news summary in English is given on the domestic FM networks 1 and 4 daily at 10:55pm. Radio Finland international programs on 100.8 MHz (FM) in Helsinki are presented daily at 5:30, 7:35, 9:30, 11, and 11:30am, at 1:30, 2, 3, 4, 5:05, and 9:35pm, and at midnight, as well as on 94.0 MHz (FM) in Helsinki at 10:30pm. For information and a free publication, *Radio Finland,* about radio programs in foreign languages, telephone 90/401-3733 in Helsinki.

Rest Rooms   Most public rest rooms are located in terminals (air, bus, and rail). Hotels usually have very clean toilets, as do the better restaurants and clubs. Most toilets are designated by appropriate symbols to distinguish between facilities for men or women. Otherwise, *naisille* is for women and *miehille* is for men.

Safety Whenever you're traveling in an unfamiliar city or country, stay alert. Be aware of your immediate surroundings. Wear a moneybelt and don't sling your camera or purse over your shoulder; wear the strap diagonally across your body. Every society has its criminals. It's your responsibility to be aware and alert, even in the most heavily touristed areas.

Taxes A tax is added to most retail purchases in Finland. However, anyone residing outside the country can shop tax-free in Finland, saving about 11% on purchases over 200 markkaa ($54.55). Look for the TAX-FREE FOR TOURISTS sticker which will guide you to shops participating in the program. Such shops will give the customer a check covering the tax, which can be cashed when leaving the country—even if the goods were bought on a credit card. The check and goods purchased must be presented at the point of departure from the country, and the amount of the check will be given to you. Tax-free purchases must be taken out of Finland, not used within the country. The refunds can be collected at airports, ferry ports, or highway border points.

Telephone, Telex & Fax Finland has such a complicated system of telephone networks that it's best for you to inquire about making a call in the area where you're stopping. For information and number inquiries, phone 92020, and for price inquiries, 92023. Direct dialing is possible to most countries from Finland, and to order such a call, dial 92022.

To call to Finland from abroad, dial the international prefix, the country code to Finland, 358, the trunk code (without the prefix 9 otherwise given in the trunk code for in-Finland calls), and the number you are trying to reach.

It is customary in Finland to send faxes and the increasingly outmoded Telex messages from your hotel. If your hotel is too small to own a fax, go to one of the larger hotels in whatever town you're staying in. Usually the staff will send a Telex or fax for you—sometimes at cost, at other times for a small charge.

Time Finland has "summer time" from March 28 (3am) to September 26 (4am). In summer, it is 3 hours ahead of Greenwich mean time (GMT); in winter, 2 hours ahead of GMT. The time difference between U.S. eastern standard time and Finnish standard time is 7 hours. When it is midnight in New York, it is 7am in Finland. The time difference between eastern daylight time in the United States and Finnish daylight time is still 7 hours.

Tipping **Hotels and restaurants** add a service charge of 15%, and usually no further tipping is necessary. In restaurants, it's customary to leave just the small change. **Taxi drivers** do not expect a tip. However, it's proper to offer from 4 markkaa ($1.10) to **cloakroom personnel and doormen. Bellhops** usually get 5 markkaa ($1.35) per bag, but most often in Finnish hotels you carry your own luggage up. At railway stations, **porters** get 4 markkaa ($1.10) a bag, a fixed charge. But I dare you to find one when you need him. **Hairdressers and barbers** do not expect to be tipped.

Water Water in Finland is generally safe to drink.

Yellow Pages Forget them! To a foreigner, the yellow pages in Finnish phone books are a disaster. You can't find anything unless you know the Finnish language. Better ask someone at your hotel the phone number or address of a service you are seeking.

INTRODUCING HELSINKI

Helsinki may stand on the doorway to the Soviet Union, but its cultural links are firmly in Scandinavia. It was originally founded in 1550 on orders of the Swedish king Gustavus Vasa, halfway between Stockholm and Leningrad, and is still known to the Swedes as Helsingfors.

Surrounded by water on three sides and fringed by islands, Helsinki grew up around a natural harbor overlooking the Gulf of Finland. A city of wide streets, squares, and parks, adorned with sculpture, Helsinki was one of the world's first planned municipalities, and is noted for its 19th-century neoclassical architecture. As it is relatively compact, most of the city can be reached on foot.

From the capital of an autonomous grand duchy of Russia, Helsinki was transformed in 1917, the year of the Russian Revolution, into the capital of the newly independent Finland. Today it is not only a center of government but the nation's intellectual capital, with a major university and many cultural and scientific institutions. Although also a business and industrial center (most major Finnish firms have their headquarters here), and the hub of Finland's air, rail, and road networks, Helsinki is relatively pollution free.

With a population of about half a million, Helsinki today is a city of urban sophistication—although locals still speak of it as "a big village." And its people are some of the most educated, best clothed, best fed, and best housed on earth.

1. ORIENTATION

ARRIVING

BY PLANE **Helsinki-Vantaa Airport** (tel. 8251) lies 12½ miles from the center of Helsinki, about a 30-minute bus ride. Buses to the airport leave from the Air Terminal at Asema-aukio 3 and the Hotel Inter-Continental in Helsinki, Töölön 21, two to four times an hour between 5:45am and 10:15pm; tickets cost 13 markkaa ($3.55). The coach also departs from the Hotel Ramada Presidentti, Eteläinen Rautatiekatu 4, hourly Monday through Friday from 6:05am to 8:20pm, on Saturday from 8:20am to 5:20pm, and on Sunday from 10:55am to 7:20pm; a ticket costs 10 markkaa ($2.75). From the Railway Square (Platform 26), bus no. 615 leaves one to three times an hour from 5:25am to 11:50pm, also costing 10 markkaa ($2.75). A taxi ride into the center costs 105 markkaa ($28.65).

WHAT'S SPECIAL ABOUT HELSINKI

Monuments
- ☐ Suomenlinna Fortress, the "Gibraltar of the North," in the archipelago guarding the approach to Helsinki.
- ☐ Sibelius Monument, created by Eila Hiltunen to honor Finland's most famous composer.

Buildings
- ☐ The Finnish Parliament, a red granite structure from 1931, famous for its "gallery of nudes."
- ☐ The Cathedral, Senate Square, the 19th-century Evangelical-Lutheran cathedral designed by Engel and commissioned by the Russian tsar.

Museums
- ☐ Mannerheim Museum, the former residence of Baron Mannerheim, considered the 20th century's military saviour of Finland.
- ☐ National Museum of Finland, repository of many of the country's historical and artistic treasures.

Parks/Gardens
- ☐ Seurasaari Open-Air Park, set in a national park on an island, a miniature preview of Old Finland.
- ☐ Botanical Gardens of the University of Helsinki, filled with exotic plants, including palms and orchids.

Events/Festivals
- ☐ Helsinki Festival, highlight of the Finnish summer, attracting international artists for a 3-week-long program.

For the Kids
- ☐ The Helsinki Zoo, on Korkeasaari Island, with its collection of northern European animals, including wild forest reindeer.
- ☐ Linnanmäki, a fun fair run by the Children's Foundation of Finland.

You must check in 20 minutes early for a domestic flight, 30 minutes for a European flight, 40 minutes for a flight to the Soviet Union, and 45 minutes for a flight to the United States.

BY TRAIN Helsinki Railway Station at Kaivokatu (tel. 65-94-11) has luggage storage lockers costing 10 markkaa ($2.75). The lost luggage department is open daily from 6:30am to 10:30pm.

BY BUS Helsinki Bus Station does not have a street address but it is located between Salomonkatu and Simonkatu in the city center (tel. 180-44-55). Using Stockholm as your embarkation point for Finland, take a ferry to Turku on the west coast. At Turku, you can board one of 21 daily buses that make the 2½-hour run to Helsinki.

BY CAR Helsinki is connected by road to all Finnish cities. If you arrive in the west at the port of Turku on a car-ferry from Sweden, you can take the E3 express highway east to Helsinki.

BY FERRY Ferries arrive at Viking Line Terminal, Etelasatama (tel. 123-51) or at Silja Line Terminal on Laivasillankatu (tel. 180-44-55).

TOURIST INFORMATION

The **Helsinki City Tourist Office,** Pohjoisesplanadi 19, SF-00100 Helsinki (tel. 90/169-3757), is open May 16 to September 15, Monday through Friday from 8:30am to 6pm and on Saturday from 8:30am to 1pm; September 16 to May 15, on Monday from 8:30am to 4:30pm and Tuesday through Friday from 8:30am to 4pm.

The **Helsinki Tourist Association** is at Lönnrotinkatu 7 (tel. 645-225). For **recorded information** on what's happening in Helsinki, call 058.

CITY LAYOUT
MAIN ARTERIES & STREETS

Helsinki (Helsingfors in Swedish) is a peninsula city, skirted by islands and skerries. The main artery is the wide and handsome **Mannerheimintie,** named in honor of the former field marshal. East of Mannerheimintie, opening onto Kaivokatu, is the **Central Station.** Toward the harbor is **Senaatintori,** crowned by the landmark cathedral. This Senate Square, designed by Engel, also includes the government and university buildings.

Continuing east is a bridge crossing over a tiny island—**Katajanokka**—dominated by the Eastern Orthodox cathedral. Back across the bridge, sticking close to the harbor, past the President's Palace, is the most colorful square in Helsinki, the **Kauppatori (Marketplace)** (see it early in the morning when it's the most animated). From the pier there, it's possible to catch boats for **Suomenlinna,** fortified islands that guard the sea lanes to Helsinki.

The great promenade street of Helsinki—**Esplanadi** (the Esplanade)—begins west of the Marketplace. Directly north of the esplanade and running parallel to it is **Aleksanterinkatu,** the principal shopping street.

FINDING AN ADDRESS

Street numbers always begin on the south side of streets running on a north-south axis, and on the eastern end of streets running east-west. All odd numbers are on one side of the street and all even numbers on the opposite side. In some cases, where a large building contains several establishments, there might be an A or B attached to the number.

NEIGHBORHOODS IN BRIEF

Helsinki divides roughly into distinct districts.

Downtown The monumental heartland stretches from **Senaatintori (Senate Square)** to **Esplanadi.** Senate Square is dominated by a Lutheran cathedral in its center, and Esplanadi itself is an avenue lined with trees. At one end of Esplanadi, the monumental **Mannerheimintie,** stretching for 3 miles, is the main road from the city center to the expanding suburbs. The section south of Esplanadi is one of the wealthiest in the capital, lined with embassies and elaborate houses, rising into **Kaivopuisto Park.**

Kruununhaka & Hakaniemi The district of **Kruununhaka** is one of the oldest. Helsinki was founded in 1550 at the mouth of the Vantaa River, but was resited in 1640 on the peninsula of Vironniemi in the place that is today known as Kruununhaka. This section, along with neighboring **Hakaniemi,** contain what buildings remain of Helsinki of the 17th century. The waters of Kaisaniemenlahti divide the districts of Hakaniemi and Kruununhaka.

The Islands Helsinki also contains several islands, some of which are known as "tourist islands," including **Korkeasaari,** site of the Helsinki Zoo. The main islands are linked by convenient ferries and water taxis.

Called "fortress of Finland" and the "Gibraltar of the north," **Suomenlinna** consists of five main islands, all interconnected, and is the site of many museums. You can spend a day here, exploring the old fortifications. **Seurasaari,** another island, contains a bathing beach and recreation area, and is also the site of a national park and the largest open-air museum in Finland.

Espoo In the environs, many workers in Helsinki treat Espoo as a bedroom suburb. Actually, since 1972, when it achieved its charter, it is the fourth-largest city of Finland, with a population of 150,000 people.

Tapiola Another "suburb city," Tapiola was founded in 1951, providing homes for some 16,000 residents. This "model city" greatly influenced housing developments around the world, with its wide variety of housing which ranges from multistory condo units to more luxurious one-family villas. The greatest Finnish architect, Alvar Aalto, was one of its planners.

MAPS

The best city map of Helsinki is called *Falk plan*. Containing a highly detailed and alphabetized street index, it can easily be carried in your pocket. *Falk plan* maps are sold at nearly all bookstores and many news kiosks in the central city, including the major bookstore of Helsinki, **Academic,** Keskuskatu 1 (tel. 121-41).

2. GETTING AROUND

Helsinki has an efficient transportation network, which includes buses, trams, subway (metro), ferries, and taxis.

BY PUBLIC TRANSPORTATION

DISCOUNT PASSES Visitors to Helsinki can purchase the **Helsinki Card,** offering unlimited travel on the city's public buses, trams, subway, and ferries, and a free guided sightseeing tour by bus (in summer daily, in winter on Saturday), as well as free entry to about 40 museums and other sights in Helsinki. It also includes attractive hotel packages in several hotels in the capital. The Helsinki Card is available for 1-, 2-, or 3-day periods. The price of the card for adults is 70 markkaa ($19.10) for 1 day, 100 markkaa ($27.25) for 2 days, and 120 markkaa ($32.70) for 3 days. A card for children costs 40 markkaa ($10.90) for 1 day, 50 markkaa ($13.65) for 2 days, and 60 markkaa ($16.35) for 3 days. The cards can be bought at 35 sales points in the Helsinki area, including the Helsinki City Tourist Office, the Hotel Booking Center (see Section 1, "Helsinki Accommodations," in Chapter 33), travel agencies, and hotels. For further information, check with the Finnish Tourist Board, 655 Third Ave., New York, NY 10017 (tel. 212/949-2333), or the Helsinki Tourist Association, Lönnrotinkatu 7 (tel. 645-225).

You can also purchase a **tourist ticket,** at 48 markkaa ($13.10) for adults and 24 markkaa ($6.55) for children, allowing unlimited travel on city transport lines within 24 hours. This ticket is sold in the City Transport Office, the city tourist office, and the hotel-booking center.

BY METRO/BUS/TRAM The **City Transport Office** is at the Rautatientori metro station (tel. 472-2252), open Monday through Friday from 7am to 7pm and on Saturday and Sunday from 9am to 5pm. The transport system operates daily from 6am to 11pm. A single ticket costs 6.50 markkaa ($1.80) for adults, 2.50 markkaa (70¢) for children. It's cheaper to purchase a multitrip ticket, allowing 10 individual journeys for 58 markkaa ($15.80) for adults, 14 markkaa ($3.80) for children. Transfers are allowed for single and multi-trip tickets within 1 hour of the time stamped on the ticket.

BY FERRY Ferries depart from the end of Eteläesplanadi (no terminal) heading for the offshore islands of Suomenlinna and Korkeasaari (Zoo).

BY TAXI

There are a number of taxi stations around Helsinki, but cabs can also be hailed in the street or ordered by phone. A taxi is available if the yellow *taksi* dome is lit. Taxis are metered, and a basic fare costs 12 markkaa ($3.25) in Helsinki; an extra charge of 5 markkaa ($1.35) is imposed at night and on weekends from 2pm on Saturday until 6am on Monday. To arrange for a taxi a day in advance, call 1824.

Tipping has become fairly common, although taxi drivers do not expect it.

BY CAR

Driving around Helsinki by car is not recommended, because of limited parking. Either walk or take public transportation. However, touring the environs by car is ideal.

CAR RENTALS The major car-rental companies maintain offices in Helsinki. These include **Avis Rent a Car,** Fredrikinkatu 67 (tel. 441-114); **Budget Rent a Car,** Fredrikinkatu 61A (tel. 694-5300); and **Hertz,** Mannherheimintie 44 (tel. 446-910).

PARKING There are two parking garages in the center of Helsinki. They are **Forum-parkkihalli,** Mannerheimintie 20 (tel. 694-7500), and **City Paikoitus Oy,** Kaivokatu 8 (tel. 177-077). It's usually very difficult to find a place to park on the street.

BY BICYCLE

Bicycles can be rented at the **Youth Hostel Stadionin Maja,** Pohjoinen Stadionintie 3V, at the Olympic Stadium (tel. 496-071). The fee is 35 markkaa ($9.55) a day, plus a deposit of 100 markkaa ($27.25). No deposit required if you have an international youth hostel card.

 HELSINKI

American Express The representative of American Express in Helsinki is **Travek Travel Bureau,** Katajanokan Pohjoisranta 9–13 (tel. 661-631).

Area Code The telephone area code for Helsinki is 90.

Baby-Sitters Every hotel in Finland has a list of employees, such as maids, who with advance notification will agree to baby-sit for your child. Most speak English. The rate in Helsinki is about 50 markkaa ($13.65) per hour (slightly less in provincial towns).

Bookstores The most famous bookstore in Finland—and the best stocked, with thousands of English titles—is **Academic Bookstore,** Keskuskatu 1 (tel. 121-41).

Business Hours Most **banks** are open Monday through Friday from 9:15am to 4:15pm. You can also exchange money at the railway station Monday through Saturday from 8:30am to 8pm and on Sunday from 12:30 to 7pm, and at the airport daily from 6:30am to 11pm.

Most **businesses and shops** are open Monday through Friday from 9am to 5pm and on Saturday from 9am to 2pm. Nearly everything is closed on Sunday. Many shops in the center of Helsinki are open until 8pm on certain nights, particularly on Monday and Friday. Shops in the Station Tunnel are generally open Monday through Saturday from 10am to 10pm and on Sunday from noon to 10pm. Gift and souvenir shops on the fourth floor of the Finnjet terminal in Katajanokka are open on days of arrival and departure of Finnjet.

There are **R-kiosks,** selling confectionery, tobacco, toiletries, cosmetics, and souvenirs, all over Helsinki and in other towns, which are open Monday through Saturday from 8am to 9pm and on Sunday from 9 or 10am until 9pm.

Currency Exchange You can exchange dollars for markkaa at most banks and often in your hotel, if it's big enough. However, hotels are more for convenience as their exchange rates are not as favorable as the banks'. There is a currency-exchange kiosk at the Central Station, open daily from 11:30am to 6pm; after 4pm it imposes a 4-markka ($1.10) surcharge.

Dentist There are English-speaking dentists on duty around the clock in Helsinki; call 736-166.

Doctor To summon a physician for **emergency calls,** call 008. For private medical service, contact the **Aleksi Medical Station** in the City Passage, Aleksanterinkatu 21S, fifth floor (tel. 176-199 for an appointment), open Monday through Friday from 8am to 6pm. Most doctors speak English.

Drugstores Pharmacies dispensing medicines are known as *apteeki.* The **Yliopiston apteekki,** Mannerheimintie 96 (tel. 415-778), is open 24 hours daily, and service from 7am to midnight is available at Mannerheimintie 5 (tel. 79-092).

Embassies & Consulates The **United States Embassy** is at Itäinen Puistotie 14B (tel. 171-931); the **Canadian Embassy,** at Pohjoiesplanadi 25B (tel. 171-141); and the **Embassy of the United Kingdom,** at Uudenmaankatu 16–20 (tel. 647-922). Citizens of **Australia** and **New Zealand** should go to the British Embassy.

Emergencies Dial **000 or 181-000** for medical help, police, or a fire alarm. To call for an **ambulance,** dial 006. An emergency hospital for foreigners is the **Helsinki University Central Hospital,** Meilahti Hospital (for both medical and surgical care), at Haart-maninkatur 4 (tel. 4711).

Eyeglasses Finland offers dozens of high-quality opticians who can make new glasses in about a day. One well-recommended company is **Nissen,** Keskuskatu 3 (tel. 659-499), open Monday through Friday from 9am to 6pm and on Saturday from 9am to 2pm.

Gas Station Open 24 hours a day is **Esso,** Pohjoinen Rautatiekatu 27 (tel. 440-611).

Hairdressers/Barbers **Salon Tittihaapala,** Eerikinkatu 12 (tel. 611-110), is a large, modern, and hip hair emporium that cuts and styles hair for both sexes. Another good hairdresser to try (both men and women) is **Elhair,** Bulevardi 1A (tel. 612-1585).

Hospitals An emergency hospital for foreigners is the **Helsinki University Central Hospital,** Meilahti Hospital (for both medical and surgical care), at Haart-maninkatur 4 (tel. 4711).

Laundry/Dry Cleaning Doing 1-day dry cleaning on the premises, **Lindström Ltd.** has shops in the City Passage (City-käytävä) opposite the railway station (tel. 657-251) in Helsinki and in the shopping center in Tapiola (tel. 463-633). At the laundry **Exprès Pikapesula,** Laivurininne 2 (tel. 639-524), clothes brought in early in the morning can be ready by the 5:30pm closing time.

Libraries The **Helsinki City Library** has a main branch close to the Pasili Railway Station (the second most important rail station in town) at Rautatielaisenkatu 8 (tel. 159-7501). A more centrally located, but secondary, branch of the Helsinki Public Library is at Rikhardinkatu 3 (tel. 166-2820).

Liquor Laws The legal age to consume beer and hard liquor in Helsinki is 18. Many nightclubs, however, with every legal right, admit only "well-dressed clients," who in some cases are 24 or older. Laws against drunken driving are rigidly enforced in Helsinki, much to the delight of taxi drivers who take home drunken club patrons.

Lost Property The Lost Property Office is at Päijänteentie 12A (tel. 189-3180), open September to May, Monday through Friday from 8am to 4:15pm; June to August, Monday through Friday from 8am to 3:15pm.

Luggage Storage/Lockers These facilities are found at the Central Station on Kaivokatu. The staff offers both a system of lockers with take-away keys and an employee-staffed area where you get a ticket for your luggage. The charge is 10 markkaa ($2.75) per bag. The service operates daily from 6am to 10:30pm.

Photographic Needs One of the best-stocked camera stores in town— and the most centrally located—is **Helios,** Mannerheimintie 14 (tel. 680-1400), open Monday through Friday from 9am to 5pm and on Saturday from 9am to 2pm (closes at 1pm in summer). It takes only 1 hour to develop prints.

Police In an emergency, dial **002.** Otherwise, go to the **police headquarters** at Pieni Robertinkatu 1–3 (tel. 1891).

Post Office   For post office **information,** call 195-5117. The **main post office** in Helsinki is at Mannerheimintie 11, open Monday through Friday from 9am to 5pm. If you don't know your address in Helsinki, have your mail sent 00 100 *Poste Restante* (general delivery) in care of the main post office in Helsinki. At this Poste Restante, you can pick up mail (upon presentation of your passport) Monday through Saturday from 8am to 10pm and on Sunday from 11am to 10pm. You can purchase stamps at the railway station post office Monday through Friday from 7:15am to 8pm and on Saturday and Sunday from 10am to 8pm. Yellow stamp machines outside post offices function with 5-markka coins.

Radio/TV   **Radio Finland** broadcasts news in English every day on the national YLE-3 network at 9:55pm. The external service of the **Finnish Broadcasting Company** has daily programs in English which can be heard on 103.7 MHz (FM) Monday through Friday at 7:30, 9:30, 11, and 11:30am, and 1:50, 3, 4, 5, and 9:30pm, midnight, and 2am. **Radio One** features a BBC World Service News daily at noon (in winter, broadcasts are at 11am). Helsinki has two TV channels. Programs from abroad, such as those from the United States and Britain, are broadcast in their original languages, with Finnish subtitles.

Religious Services   Lutheranism is the major religion of the population. Smaller groups—Catholics, Jews, Greek Orthodox—are also represented, and there is religious freedom for all. For Protestants, the Temppeliaukio Church, Lutherinkatu 3 (tel. 494-698), conducts an English-language service every Sunday at 3pm. **Roman Catholic** services are conducted at St. Henrik's Church, Puistokatu 1 (tel. 637-853). The **Anglican** church, Cathedral Chapel, Senate Square (tel. 563-4829), has services in English on Sunday at 10:30am. There's a **synagogue** at Malminkatu 26 (tel. 694-1302 for information).

Rest Rooms   There's a centrally located public toilet at Sofiankatu 2. Otherwise, many locals use café toilets (it's polite to at least order a cup of coffee or a soft drink), or they make use of the facilities at transit terminals.

Shoe Repairs   A centrally located shop providing this service is **Presidentin Suutari,** Olavinkatu 2 (tel. 694-3631), open Monday through Friday from 8am to 5:30pm and on Saturday from 9am to 2pm.

Taxes   Helsinki, like the rest of Finland, imposes a Value-Added Tax of 20.48% on goods and services.

Taxis   See "Getting Around," in this chapter.

Telephones/Telegrams/Telex/Fax   For information and number inquiries, call 92-020 in Helsinki. If you're thinking about calling home (providing you're not calling collect) and want to know how much it'll cost, dial 92-023.

Automatic intercity (long-distance) calls can be made from call boxes, located throughout the city, that take 1-markka (25¢) and 5-markka ($1.35) coins; the routing numbers and rates are listed in the phone directory. Automatic calls to other countries can be made from these call boxes, or from the **Tele-Service** office, Mannerheimintie 11B. The Tele-Service office also handles other long-distance calls, telegrams, and Telex; it is open daily from 7am to 11pm, but it offers 24-hour service by phone (tel. 021).

If you call from your hotel, the bill might be doubled or tripled.

For local calls inside the city limits of Helsinki, you do not need to dial 90.

It is customary to send faxes from hotels. If your hotel is too small to have a fax, go to one of the larger hotels and request that the staff there send a fax. You'll be billed not only for the fax, but perhaps a surcharge as well.

Transit Information   The City Transport Office is at the Rautatientori metro station (tel. 472-2252). For railway information, call 010-115, and for information about city buses, trams, and metro, dial 010-111 or 765-966.

Weather   Summers in Helsinki tend to be long and sun-filled, but temperatures rarely are so high as to be uncomfortable. (see "When to Go," in Chapter 32). The best weather is in July, which experiences the highest temperature, a comfortable 63°F on the average. Nights are greatly extended in midsummer in Helsinki when Lapland is bathed in the Midnight Sun. In winter, temperatures hover between 21°

and 27°F, but it's not true that polar bears roam the streets.

3. NETWORKS & RESOURCES

FOR STUDENTS For travel arrangements, go to **Travela,** Mannerheimintie 5 (tel. 624-101), right near the train station. For students with proper IDs, it offers discount travel opportunities, and is familiar with making arrangements to tour not only Finland, but the Soviet Union and Eastern Europe as well. It's open Monday through Friday from 9am to 5pm.

The **Finnish Youth Hostel Association,** Yrjönkatu 38B (tel. 694-0377), south of the bus station, is another good source of information. It's especially helpful to young people planning to go hiking in Finland, including Lapland. The headquarters will provide information about all youth hostels in Finland. It's open Monday through Friday from 9am to 4pm.

Socially, the best place to meet fellow university students is **KY-Exit** (see "Evening Entertainment," in Chapter 35), which is owned and run by the Student Union of the Helsinki School of Economics.

Summer courses in Finnish for foreign university students are arranged by the Finnish Ministry of Education. Further information is available from the Council for Instruction of Finnish for Foreigners, Pohjoisranta 4A, 00170 Helsinki. A helpful booklet, "Courses in Finnish Language and Culture," is available from Finnish embassies and consulates, from university teachers of Finnish or Finno-Ugric languages abroad, or by writing to the Council for Instruction of Finnish for Foreigners (see above).

FOR GAY MEN & LESBIANS The gay scene for both men and women is dominated by a blanket organization called SETA, actually a loose confederation of "sexual minority groups." Each summer they stage Gay Pride Days, and foreign visitors are welcome to participate in these. Both men and women can find out what's happening in Helsinki by visiting the **SETA** headquarters at Mäkelänkatu 36A (tel. 769-642), open Monday through Friday from 11am to noon and 2 to 6pm. There's someone at the SETA switchboard dispensing information on Wednesday, Thursday, Friday, and Sunday from 6 to 9pm.

SETA sponsors a gay disco on Monday night, called "Triangle," at **Berlin,** Töölönkatu 3 (tel. 499-002), a club usually devoted to heavy rock or the latest "acid" sounds.

The major gay bar of Helsinki is **Gambrini** (see "Evening Entertainment," in Chapter 35). "Every other Saturday" at this club is reserved for women.

Many gay men and lesbians also patronize **Vanhan Kellari** (see previous recommendation), although this cellar is predominantly straight.

FOR WOMEN The headquarters of the **Finnish Feminists' Union (Naisasialiitto Unioni)** is at Bulevardi 11A (tel. 642-277), in the center of Helsinki. This is a friendly, helpful center, especially for women traveling alone in Helsinki. On the premises is **Naistenhuone,** a women's café and bookshop, open Monday through Friday from 4 to 9pm, on Saturday from noon to 6pm, and on Sunday from 2 to 6pm.

Women find Helsinki a safe destination, although the usual discreet precautions one follows anywhere should be observed here. Violent crimes such as rape against women are extremely rare. In such an unlikely emergency, women are advised to call the police at 002.

CHAPTER 34

HELSINKI ACCOMMODATIONS & DINING

1. HELSINKI ACCOMMODATIONS

- **FROMMER'S COOL FOR KIDS: HOTELS**

2. HELSINKI DINING

- **FROMMER'S COOL FOR KIDS: RESTAURANTS**

There's a big selection of accommodations and dining establishments in Helsinki. The trick is finding something that suits your budget. As is the rest of Scandinavia, Finland is not cheap. Your best bet with hotels is to plan in as far advance as possible and to take advantage of any discounts that might be offered. To make the most of dining in Finland, eat lunch at the more expensive places when prices will be greatly reduced and eat lightly or cheaply for dinner. Always watch the bar bill—drinking can make any meal expensive.

1. HELSINKI ACCOMMODATIONS

Hotels are classified as "Very Expensive," "Expensive," "Moderate," and "Inexpensive," with a few "Budget" suggestions. These categories are based on individual peak-season winter rates in a double room with private bath. It can be assumed that accommodations in the two pricier categories have baths in every room.

Price categories are as follows: "Very Expensive," $260 to $330; "Expensive," $215 to $235; "Moderate," $110 to $180; and "Inexpensive," $82 to $105. However, if you stay Friday to Sunday night (Friday or Saturday in some hotels) or in midsummer, you get substantial discounts. Discounted prices are provided for comparison.

In Helsinki, peak rates are charged in winter, because most of the major hotels depend on winter business travelers—not summer tourists—to fill their rooms. The tourists still do not make up for the disappearing Finns who leave Helsinki for other summer pleasures.

A ROOM IN A HURRY The **Hotellikeskus (Hotel Booking Center),** Asema-aukio 3 (tel. 171-133), located in the heart of the city between the railroad station and the main post office, is open May 16 to September 15, Monday through Friday from 9am to 9pm, on Saturday from 9am to 7pm, and on Sunday from 10am to 6pm; September 16 to May 15, Monday through Friday from 9am to 6pm only. You state the price you're willing to pay and the English-speaking attendant will phone a hotel and provide you with a map and instructions for reaching your lodgings. The secretary at the Hotellikeskus charges a booking fee of 10 markkaa ($2.75) for a single or double room. Ask for special "Helsinki Card" hotel rates, which do not have a booking fee (see "Getting Around," in Chapter 32).

FINLAND

Helsinki

Academica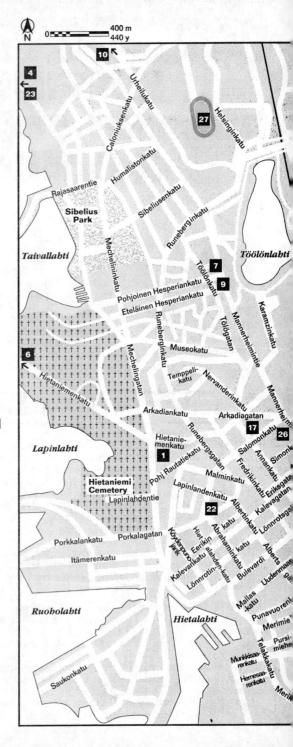
Anna **2**
Arctia Hotel Marski **3**
Dipoli **4**
Finn **5**
Haaga **6**
Hesperia **7**
Hospiz **8**
Inter-Continental **9**
Kalastajatorppa **10**
Klaus Kurki **11**
Martta **12**
MetroCity **13**
Olympia **14**
Palace **15**
Park Hotel Käpylä **16**
Ramada Presidentti **17**
Rivoli Jardin **18**
Seurahuone-Socis **19**
Sokos Helsinki **20**
Strand Inter-Continental **21**
Summerhotel
  Satakuntatalo **22**
Tapiola Garden **23**
Torni **24**
Ursula **25**
Vaakuna **26**
Youth Hostel
  Stadoinin Maja **27**

HELSINKI ACCOMMODATIONS

16 ↗

Sturenkatu

14

Aleksis Kivisgata

Lautatarhank

Helsinginkatu

Helsingegatan

Sörnasstrandväg

Agricolankatu

Castréninkatu

Siltasaarenkatu

Porthaninkatu

Hämeentie

Sörnäistenrantatie

Kolmaslinja

Eläintar-banlahti

Säästöpank

25

Hakanranta

Pitkansillanranta

21

Siltavuoren-salmi

Kaisan-iemen-lahti

Siltavuorenranta

Kaisaniemenranta

Nora Kajan

Maurinkatu

rain Station

8

Unioninkatu

Snellmaninkatu

Elisabetsgatan

Mariankatu

Mertullinkatu

Pohjoissatama

Fabianinkatu

Unionsgatan

Snellmansgatan

Kirkkokatu

Mariegatan

Kaisaniemenkatu

13

Hallituskatu

Pohjoisranta

20

19

Aleksanterinkatu

3

Pohjois esplanadi

Nesplanaden

Laivas tokatu

Katajan

Luotsikatu

Kanavakatu

Kronbergsgatan

11

Hogbergsgatan

Kasarmikatu

Fabianinkatu

Kaserngatan

Kanalgatan

Iso Roobertinkatu

Laivasillankatu

15

Eteläsatama

To Suomenlinna & Helsinki Zoo

Tähtitornik Observgatan

18

Jääkärinkatu

Bergmansgatan

Valksaari

Vuorimiehenkatu

Fabriksgatan

Itainen Puistotie

Ehrenströmintie

Luoto

Ryssasaari

Tehtaankatu

Puistokatu

Iso Puistotie

Osta Allen

Pietarinkatu

Stora Allen

Puolimatkansaari

uhani hontie

Kaivopuisto

Havsgatan

Merisatamaranta

Ehrenströmintie

IN THE CITY CENTER

VERY EXPENSIVE

HOTEL HESPERIA, Mannerheimintie 50, SE-00260 Helsinki. Tel. 90/43-101. Fax 90/431-0995. 372 rms, 4 suites. A/C MINIBAR TV TEL **Tram:** 3B, 3T.

$ Rates: 780–880 markkaa ($212.70–$240) single; 1,020–1,140 markkaa ($278.15–$310.90) double; from 1,800 markkaa ($490.85) suite. Breakfast costs 32 markkaa ($8.75) extra. AE, DC, MC, V. **Parking:** Available.

A leading Finland hotel, near Hesperia Park and the Finnair Terminal, the elegant Hesperia is a favorite of the business traveler. Built of Carrara marble, it has a color scheme of warm browns and light tints. Rooms are elegantly furnished, and the suites are named and decorated after Finland's other Nordic neighbors. The bedrooms have extra-wide beds and a number of amenities, such as trouser presses and radios. Each room contains a sofa.

Dining/Entertainment: The Fransmanni is a French-style restaurant, specializing in juicy steaks from a lava grill, and the Pub Fransmanni is open until 1am. The Lobby bar offers coffee, sandwiches, and salads. The hotel's specialty restaurant is the Russian Room, offering the late 19th-century cuisine of Imperial Russia. A nightclub features dancing to live music.

Services: Laundry, baby-sitting, room service, masseur.

Facilities: Four saunas, swimming pool, gym, barbershop, hairdresser, solarium, parking in hotel yard and a garage, gift shop, bank, travel agency.

INTER-CONTINENTAL, Mannerheimintie 46, SF-00260 Helsinki. Tel. 90/40-551. Fax 90/405-5255. 543 rms, 12 suites. **Tram:** 3B, 3T.

$ Rates (including breakfast): 820–890 markkaa ($223.60–$242.70) single; 930–990 markkaa ($253.60–$269.95) double; from 2,000 markkaa ($545.40) suite. AE, DC, MC, V. **Parking:** Available.

Built in 1971 as one of the largest hotels in Finland, this is the northernmost European link in this famous chain. It's affiliated with another smaller Inter-Continental, also in Helsinki. Quality, comfort, and dependability are its motto. Behind a modern concrete facade and a small ornamental garden, it has a host of facilities and bedrooms. Within walking distance of the business center, it stands near the Finlandia Congress and Concert Hall. Bedrooms are tasteful and well furnished. The air terminal is in the same complex as the hotel.

Dining/Entertainment: The premier seafood restaurant of Helsinki, Galateia merits a separate recommendation (see Section 2, "Helsinki Dining," in this chapter). The Brasserie is an all-day restaurant featuring local specialties. The Baltic Bar is a cozy rendezvous point.

Services: 24-hour room service, laundry and valet service, travel-service desks, masseur.

Facilities: Parking, beauty parlor, hairdresser, car-rental desk, Finnair check-in service, shopping gallery, three Finnish saunas, indoor swimming pool, no-smoking rooms.

PALACE, Eteläranta 10, SF-00130 Helsinki. Tel. 90/171-114. Fax 90/654-786. 59 rms, 6 suites. A/C MINIBAR TV TEL **Tram:** 3B. **Bus:** 16.

$ Rates (including breakfast): 780–1,300 markkaa ($190.90–$354.50) single; 920–1,560 markkaa ($250.90–$425.50) double; from 2,300 markkaa ($627.20) suite. AE, DC, MC, V.

A gem of a hotel overlooking the Presidential Palace, a few steps down from the Market Square, the Palace is a favorite among more discriminating travelers. It's part of a chain that includes some of the best restaurants in Helsinki, including the Havis Amanda for seafood and Alexander Nevski for Russian cuisine. The hotel offers bedrooms overlooking the harbor. Rooms are decorated with an elegant but restrained taste, and the most expensive ones have balconies. For a five-star hotel it's small, but that ensures more personal service.

Dining/Entertainment: The specialty restaurant of this hotel, Palace Gourmet (see "Helsinki Dining," in this chapter), is considered the best in Finland, offering a stunning view from the 10th floor. The Ristorante La Vista is a second-floor restaurant, serving some of the best and freshest Italian food in the capital (see "Helsinki Dining," in this chapter). The American Bar enjoys an 11th-floor perch (see "Evening Entertainment," in Chapter 35). There is also a cafeteria on the second floor.

Services: Pressing and valet service, 4-hour laundry service, dry cleaning, 24-hour news service, 24-hour room service, complimentary 5 o'clock tea, Telex and fax service.

Facilities: TV lounge with terrace, garage, three saunas on the 11th floor with open-air terrace and one heated with logs, safety deposit boxes, currency exchange, tour and car-rental desks, four guest elevators, barbershop.

RAMADA PRESIDENTTI HOTEL, Eteläinen Rautatiekatu 4, SF-00100

Helsinki. Tel. 90/69-11. Fax 90/694-7886. A/C MINIBAR TV TEL 500 rms. **Tram:** 3B, 3T.

$ Rates: 820–960 markkaa ($223.60–$261.80) single; 940–960 markkaa ($256.35–$261.80) double. Breakfast costs 32 markkaa ($8.75) extra. AE, DC, MC, V.

Built in 1980 and recently renovated, this hotel stands in the commercial center of Helsinki, close to Finlandia Hall, Parliament House, and the railway station. Rated five stars, it's an imposing granite-and-copper structure with lots of drinking and dining facilities. Rooms are warm, comfortable, modern, and filled with such conveniences as hairdryers and trouser presses. Windows are triple glazed. Bus no. 614 departs from here directly to the airport.

Dining/Entertainment: The main restaurant, Four Seasons, the first carvery in Finland, features all you can eat carved from various joints of meat. The Evergreen Lounge is a piano bar, also serving light meals, and Le Club Pressa features international bands. Inexpensive lunches are served at the late-night Café Maria, and fresh-baked croissants direct from Paris are a feature in Café de Paris.

Services: Room service (7am to midnight), laundry service.

Facilities: Swimming pool, three saunas.

SEURAHUONE-SOCIS, Kaivokatu 12, 00100 Helsinki. Tel. 90/170-441.

Fax 90/664-170. 118 rms, 5 suites. A/C TV TEL **Tram:** 3T.

$ Rates: June 15–Aug 5 and weekends year round, 350 markkaa ($95.45) single; 440 markkaa ($120) double. Weekdays Aug 6–June 14, 650–760 markkaa ($177.25–$207.25) single; 850–920 markkaa ($231.85–$250.90) double; from 1,200 markkaa ($327.25) suite. Breakfast costs 35 markkaa ($9.55) extra. AE, DC, MC, V.

In the center of Helsinki, opposite the railway station, this hotel actually dates from 1833 and was moved to its present location in 1914. An old and traditional favorite, it's the nostalgic choice for many. Guests are housed either in the charming original building or in the modern wing. Rooms are either in a functional modern style or traditionally furnished. All are comfortable.

Dining/Entertainment: The art nouveau Café Socis is the traditional rendezvous point in the early hours of the morning in Helsinki, as it's open daily until 5am. The Socis Pub is open until 1am, and the Discothèque Rose dances until 2am. There is no major restaurant, although lunches are served in the café.

Services: Laundry service, car-rental service, sightseeing tickets available, room service until 10pm.

Facilities: Two saunas.

STRAND INTER-CONTINENTAL, John Stenbergin Ranta 4, 00530 Helsinki. Tel. 90/39-351. Fax 90/761-362. 190 rms, 10 suites. **Trams:** 3T, 7.

$ Rates: July and weekends year round, 445 markkaa ($121.35) single; 520 markkaa ($141.80) double. Weekdays (except July), 900–980 markkaa ($245.45–$267.25) single; 1,050–1,080 markkaa ($286.35–$294.50) double; from 2,100 markkaa ($572.65) suite. Breakfast costs 30 markkaa ($8.20) extra. AE, DC, MC, V.

Set at the edge of the water behind a bay-windowed facade of beige and brown brick, this is a great new addition to Helsinki's hotels. Opened in 1988, it has the most dramatic atrium in the capital, festooned with plants and containing glass elevators rising to the top. The octagonal shape is repeated throughout the hotel's design. Rooms were designed by some of Finland's best talent, and decorated with local designs, including weaving and Finnish parquet floors. Marble from Lapland was used extensively. Half the well-furnished bedrooms open onto views of the harbor. Some bedrooms have facilities for the handicapped and others are for nonsmokers.

Dining/Entertainment: The Pamir Restaurant is one of the best fish and game restaurants in Helsinki (see "Helsinki Dining," in this chapter). Guests enjoy breakfast or late-night salad buffets in the Atrium Plaza Restaurant, or drinks in the Atrium Lounge and Bar.

Services: Key-card door lock, 24-hour room service, laundry and valet, tour and guest-relations desk.

Facilities: Four saunas, swimming pool, business center, movie channels, gift shop.

EXPENSIVE

ARCTIA HOTEL MARSKI, Mannerheimintie 10, SF-00100 Helsinki. Tel. 90/68-061. Fax 90/642-377. 228 rms, 6 suites. MINIBAR TV TEL **Trams:** 3B, 3T, 6.

$ Rates: Winter weekdays, 760 markkaa ($207.25) single; 880 markkaa ($240) double; from 1,800 markkaa ($490.85) suite. Summer and weekends in winter, 450 markkaa ($122.70) single; 550 markkaa ($150) double. Breakfast costs 30 markkaa ($8.20) extra. AE, DC, MC, V.

Although it looks like an office building from the outside, this is the finest hotel in the town center. The comfortable bedrooms are furnished with plush upholstery in warmly neutral colors, and every room has a hairdryer and trouser press, among other amenities.

Dining/Entertainment: Its breakfast buffet was voted the best in Helsinki. The basement-level Marskin Kellari is a favorite, serving reasonably priced meals in a tavern atmosphere. The Fizz Bar and Night Club is recommended separately (see "Evening Entertainment," in Chapter 35).

Services: Laundry service, room service, message service.

Facilities: Warm garage, two saunas, no-smoking floor, 13 rooms for allergic persons.

HOTEL KLAUS KURKI, Bulevardi 2, SF-00120 Helsinki. Tel. 90/618-911. Fax 90/608-538. 135 rms. MINIBAR TV TEL. **Tram:** 3B, 3T, 6.

$ Rates (including breakfast): 680 markkaa ($185.45) single; 840 markkaa ($229.05) double. AE, DC, MC, V.

Opposite the Swedish Theater and a short walk from the Stockmann Department Store, this 1912 brick building was originally a lodging for hardware buyers. Constructed in the Romantic Jugend style, it was renovated in 1985 and turned into a stylish and up-to-date hotel with elegant public rooms. Bedrooms are comfortably and traditionally designed, with such extra amenities as hairdryers and radios.

Dining/Entertainment: Even if you don't stay at the hotel, don't overlook the Neo-Victorian cellar wine bar where exposed brick, ceiling beams, and ornate brass floor lamps offer an after-work rendezvous. There's also a richly paneled English bar, and a well-designed restaurant a few steps above the lobby.

Services: Same-day laundry service.

Facilities: Sauna with two lounges, two bedrooms for allergy sufferers.

RIVOLI JARDIN, Kasarmikatu 40, SF-00130 Helsinki. Tel. 90/177-880. Fax 90/656-988. 54 rms, 1 suite. MINIBAR TV TEL **Tram:** 3, 10.

$ Rates (including breakfast): Sun–Thurs, 690 markkaa ($188.15) single; 790 markkaa ($215.45) double; from 1,700 markkaa ($463.60) suite. Fri–Sat, 400 markkaa ($109.10) single; 500 markkaa ($136.35) double. AE, DC, MC, V.

This sophisticated hotel opened in 1984 in the business center, with a slickly designed format of thick carpets, pink-and-black Finnish marble, murals, and shiny lacquer. You reach the hotel, a Best Western affiliate, by walking under a covered passage that leads to an open courtyard. The attractively designed rooms feature built-in furniture and wall-to-wall carpeting, and each room has extra amenities, such as hairdryers. Sixteen of the rooms are doubles with queen-size beds. Every window in the hotel is triple insulated. The suite has a private sauna.

Dining/Entertainment: Guests enjoy the garden-style bar and the skylighted and plant-filled winter garden breakfast room, as well as the lobby bar.

Services: Room service, laundry.

Facilities: Sauna, Jacuzzi; special rooms for the allergic, nonsmokers, and the disabled.

TORNI HOTEL, Yrjönkatu 26, SF-00100 Helsinki. Tel. 90/131-131. Fax 90/131-1361. 147 rms, 8 suites. MINIBAR TV TEL **Tram:** 3, 4, 8.

$ Rates: June 22–Aug 5 and weekends year round, 335 markkaa ($91.35) single; 450 markkaa ($122.70) double. Weekdays Aug 6–June 21, 660 markkaa ($180) single; 790 markkaa ($215.45) double; from 1,050 markkaa ($286.35) suite. Breakfast costs 35 markkaa ($9.55) extra. AE, DC, MC, V.

The Torni was the first "skyscraper" built in Helsinki, and many irate locals demanded that it be torn down. But instead it prospered, and became the No. 1 choice for such visiting foreign stars as Josephine Baker and Zarah Leander, and a meeting place for such Finnish artists as composers Jean Sibelius and Mika Waltari. Even the illegal Communist party used to meet here. During the Winter War it had to use paper sheets, and in the postwar era it became the headquarters of the Soviet Control Commission. Once a meeting place of diplomats and spies in World War II, this refurbished 1931 hotel has an entrance lobby and paneled dining room that retain its old look, with recently renovated bedrooms that are comfortably contemporary. Each has big windows and carpeting.

Dining/Entertainment: There's an American Bar (named after the longtime resident American ambassador), plus another bar on the 13th floor, Atelier, opened in 1951 with changing art exhibits. The Irish pub, O'Malley's, is in the hotel, as is the foremost Spanish restaurant of Helsinki, Parilla Torni. The gourmet restaurant of the hotel is Ritarisali (Knight's Table).

Services: Room service, laundry service.

Facilities: Four saunas, summer terrace, rooms for nonsmokers.

MODERATE

HOTELLI ANNA, Annankatu 1, SF-00120 Helsinki. Tel. 90/648-011. Fax 90/602-664. 60 rms (all with bath). MINIBAR TV TEL **Tram:** 3.

$ Rates (including breakfast): Weekdays Aug 5–June 14, 380 markkaa ($103.65) single; 520 markkaa ($141.80) double. June 15–Aug 4 and weekends year round, 330 markkaa ($90) single; 450 markkaa ($122.70) double. AE, MC, V.

A cozy and intimate brick building from 1925, this hotel is in a desirable downtown neighborhood that is a 3-minute walk from one of Helsinki's major intersections—the corner of Mannerheimintie and Esplanadi near the cathedral. Rooms are comfortably—even plushly—furnished with carpets and chintz curtains. One floor is reserved for nonsmokers. There's a sauna on the premises, as well as a restaurant, where freshly baked breads and pastries are served in the evening. Laundry services are provided.

HOTEL HOSPIZ, Vuorikatu 17, SF-00100 Helsinki. Tel. 90/170-481. Fax 90/626-880. 170 rms (145 with bath). TV TEL **Tram:** 3, 6.

$ Rates (including breakfast): July to mid-Aug and weekends year round, 290 markkaa ($79.10) single without shower, 320 markkaa ($87.25) single with shower; 450 markkaa ($122.70) double with shower. Weekdays mid-Aug to June, 290 markkaa ($79.10) single without shower, 480 markkaa ($130.90) single with shower; 630 markkaa ($171.80) double with shower. AE, DC, MC, V.

A large and well-maintained establishment, this is owned and operated by the YMCA and accepts both men and women. It was built at the turn of the century with a newer wing added in 1950. The neighborhood is quiet, even though it's only a 4-minute walk from the main train station. Only a handful of the impressively clean and comfortable bedrooms don't have private baths, and the better rooms contain minibars. Those without bath are singles, which are rented for the same price year round. There's an inexpensive restaurant on the premises that serves a luncheon buffet for around 65 markkaa ($17.75) and a full dinner for 95 markkaa ($25.90).

MARTTA HOTELLI, Uudenmaankatu 24, SF—00120 Helsinki. Tel. 90/ 646-211. Fax 90/680-1266. 45 rms (all with shower). TV TEL **Tram:** 3T.

$ **Rates** (including breakfast): Midsummer and weekends year round, 280 markkaa ($76.35) single; 360–410 markkaa ($98.15–$111.80) double. Weekdays in winter, 370 markkaa ($100.90) single; 460–510 markkaa ($125.45–$139.10) double. AE, DC, MC, V. **Parking:** Free.

Half a mile north of main rail station, in a quiet residential part of town, this cozy little hotel is owned by a women's organization that was originally founded in 1899 as a radical feminist group committed to the educational advancement of Finland and at first suppressed by the tsarist government. No longer radical, having achieved all their goals, they now run a home economics educational program. Their hotel was built in the late 1950s on land bequeathed by a wealthy donor. It is clean, comfortable, and inexpensive. Men and women are accepted. Bedrooms are in a streamlined Finnish design. The restaurant on the upper floor serves breakfast and lunch. At night, room service is available. Facilities include a sauna and a free covered parking area.

PARK HOTEL KÄPYLÄ, Pohjolankatu 38, 00600 Helsinki. Tel. 90/799- 755. Fax 90/792-781. 40 rms (all with bath). MINIBAR TV TEL **Tram:** 1.

$ **Rates:** June 14–Aug 12 and weekends year round, 330 markkaa ($90) single; 420 markkaa ($114.55) double. Weekdays Aug 13–June 13, 450 markkaa ($122.70) single; 580 markkaa ($158.15) double. AE, DC, MC, V.

Rather undiscovered, known mainly to Finns, this hotel is set in a district of wooden houses, many inhabited by artists. Bedrooms are attractively decorated and are fully soundproof, each with several amenities such as radios. Baths are tiled and fully modern. A terrace and an inner courtyard are summer favorites, and there is also a well-stocked bar. Guests enjoy such recreation possibilities as a swimming pool and three saunas. The hotel has an excellent restaurant with many Finnish specialties.

URSULA, Paasivuorenkatu 1, SF—00530 Helsinki. Tel. 90/750-311. Fax 90/701-4527. 39 rms (29 with bath). MINIBAR TV TEL **Tram:** 3B, 7, 10.

$ **Rates** (including breakfast): Midsummer and weekends year round, 200–265 markkaa ($54.55–$72.25) single; 300–350 markkaa ($81.80–$95.45) double. Weekdays in winter, 300 markkaa ($81.80) single without bath, 420 markkaa ($114.55) single with shower; 400 markkaa ($109.10) double without bath, 520 markkaa ($141.80) double with shower. AE, DC, MC, V.

Built in 1956, this hotel is across the water from the Botanical Gardens, near a small park and off a busy boulevard. The emphasis here is on properly furnished bedrooms, and not on a fancy lobby or an impressive interior. Rooms have wall-to-wall desks, sofa beds, and large picture windows. It's one of the finest of the small bargain hotels of Helsinki, if you don't mind its lack of such facilities as a restaurant or sauna.

INEXPENSIVE

HOTEL FINN, Kalevankatu 3B, SF—00100 Helsinki. Tel. 90/640-904. 28 rms (14 with bath). TV TEL **Tram:** 3, 4, 7, 10.

$ Rates: 250 markkaa ($68.20) single without bath, 290 markkaa ($79.10) single with shower; 300 markkaa ($81.80) double without bath, 380 markkaa ($103.65) double with shower. Breakfast costs 25 markkaa ($6.80) extra. MC, V.

The guests staying in this clean and functional hotel are likely to include a scattering of tourists, dockworkers from western and northern Finland, and a handful of Moscow diplomats on business. There is no bar, no restaurant, and no sauna; the hotel's only real public room is a large, starkly furnished lobby. It prides itself on being among the least expensive hotels in Helsinki.

AT THE OLYMPIC STADIUM

HOTEL OLYMPIA, Läntinen Brahenkatu 2, SF–00510 Helsinki. Tel. 90/750-801. Fax 90/750-801. 99 rms (all with bath). TV TEL **Tram:** 3B.

$ Rates (including breakfast): Mon–Thurs, 460 markkaa ($125.45) single; 560 markkaa ($152.70) double. Fri–Sun, 280 markkaa ($76.35) single; 380 markkaa ($103.65) double. AE, DC, MC, V.

Built in 1962, this hotel is more famous for its dining and drinking establishments than it is for its accommodations—although few overnight guests are disappointed with the comfortably modern units. It's near the main Sports Hall of Helsinki, slightly more than a mile north from the central train station. The hotel has a famous Russian restaurant, Kazbek. Room service and laundry are available, as is a sauna; a swimming pool and tennis courts are at the Sports Stadium next door. The tennis courts and an outdoor pool freeze over in winter and become hockey rinks. A bowling alley is nearby.

WEST OF THE CENTER

HOTEL KALASTAJATORPPA, Kalastajatorpantie 1, SF–00330 Helsinki. Tel. 90/488-011. Fax 90/458-1668. 236 rms (all with bath). A/C MINIBAR TV TEL **Tram:** 4.

$ Rates: Midsummer, 250 markkaa ($68.20) single; 350 markkaa ($95.45) double. Winter Fri–Sat, 350 markkaa ($95.45) single; 450 markkaa ($122.70) double. Winter Sun–Thurs, 710 markkaa ($193.60) single; 850 markkaa ($231.80) double. AE, DC, MC, V. **Parking:** Available indoors.

Translated from the Finnish, the tongue-twisting name of this hotel means "cottage of the fisherman." However, all that this place has in common with a cottage is its proximity to the water 2 miles northwest of the city center. Located on a ridge of land between two arms of the sea, this pair of marble- and granite-faced buildings were designed to meld as closely as possible with the surrounding landscape of birch and pines. The core of the hotel dates from 1937, and the newer sections contain some of the most modern convention facilities in Finland. Rooms are either in the main building or the hotel's seashore annex. On the premises

---

 FROMMER'S COOL FOR KIDS

Hotels

Martta Hotelli *(see page 620)* Good, safe haven—comfortable rooms, moderate prices.

Hotel Olympia *(see page 621)* Great for children because of its location near the Sports Stadium.

Academica Hotel *(see page 622)* A family favorite in summer with swimming pool and moderately priced restaurant.

is the state guesthouse where former president Ronald Reagan rested en route to Moscow.

The Round Room is a restaurant for dining and dancing, and the Fiskis Bar & Café is an informal place for light meals and drinks. The Red Room is a leading Helsinki nightclub (see "Evening Entertainment," in Chapter 35). The Terrace summer restaurant offers grills and opens onto a sea view. Laundry service, room service, and a message service are provided, and guided walks can be arranged. The hotel has a business center, hairdresser, gift shop, bank, a car-rental desk, and two heated parking garages. To keep you in shape there's a gym, five saunas (sometimes overheated guests dive directly into the sea), two indoor swimming pools, and a private beach.

SUMMER HOTELS

ACADEMICA HOTEL, Hietaniemenkatu 14, SF–00100 Helsinki. Tel. 90/402-0206. 217 rms (115 with bath). TEL **Tram:** 3T from the Central Station.

$ Rates: 195 markkaa ($53.20) single without bath, 245 markkaa ($66.80) single with bath; 240 markkaa ($65.45) double without bath, 320 markkaa ($87.25) double with bath. Breakfast costs 25 markkaa ($6.80) extra. AE, MC, V. **Closed:** Sept–May

This hotel features a dining room, an authentic sauna set by the edge of the water, a swimming pool, and a souvenir shop. In the 1968 addition, each room has a private toilet and bath, as well as a refrigerator. In the 1952 wing, rooms have hot and cold running water. The furnishings are compact. You can order your main meals in the fully licensed restaurant, where dinner costs 80 to 100 markkaa ($21.80 to $27.25). To return to the station, take tram no. 3B.

HOTEL DIPOLI, Jämeräntäival 1, SF–02150 Espoo. Tel. 90/435-811. 240 rms (all with shower). TEL **Bus:** 102 from platform 52 at the Helsinki bus station.

$ Rates (including breakfast): 275 markkaa ($75) single with shower; 380 markkaa ($103.65) double with shower. AE, DC, MC, V. **Closed:** Sept–May.

Six miles from downtown Helsinki, this student-run hotel is on the seashore surrounded by pine forests. The Dipoli offers about 600 beds in neat, college-dorm-type rooms at reasonable rates. There is a beer tavern, and two restaurants service the hotel—one outdoors.

SUMMERHOTEL SATAKUNTATALO, Lapinrinne 1A, SF–00180 Helsinki. Tel. 90/694-0311. Fax 90/694-2226. 65 rms (none with bath). TEL **Bus:** 55 from the railway station.

$ Rates: 170 markkaa ($46.35) single without bath; 220 markkaa ($60) double without bath. Breakfast costs 25 markkaa ($6.80) extra. AE, DC, MC, V. **Closed:** Sept–May.

On a tiny street a short walk from the bus station, this hotel accepts tourists of all ages. There is only one shower on each floor, but there are two saunas and a laundry room with a washing machine. Also on the premises is a licensed restaurant where lunch and dinner cost 75 markkaa ($20.45); a self-service lunch costs from 50 markkaa ($13.65).

2. HELSINKI DINING

Food can be expensive in Helsinki, with many fat-cat tabs resembling the war indemnity slapped on Finland by Russia. But don't retreat. Because the cost of living is so high, consumers have banded together, as in Sweden, to form cooperative movements. These co-ops virtually dominate the distribution of food—and they've gone into the restaurant business too, specializing in reasonably priced meals. Eating at the chain restaurants and self-service cafeterias is another way to save some money.

Even though I've classified restaurants by price category, the cost of dining in a Helsinki restaurant depends in large part on what you order. Dishes that have to be imported always carry higher tabs. Yet on the same menu you'll find a number of reasonably priced Finnish dishes, such as Baltic herring and whitefish. In a restaurant rated "Very Expensive," expect to spend $65 and up per person for dinner; "Expensive," $50 to $60; and "Moderate," $25 to $45. Anything under $25 is considered "Inexpensive" by Finnish standards.

IN THE TOWN CENTER
VERY EXPENSIVE

GEORGE, Kalevankatu 17. Tel. 647-662.
Cuisine: FINNISH. **Reservations:** Required. **Tram:** 3B, 3T.
$ Prices: Appetizers 58–102 markkaa ($15.80–$27.85); main dishes 148–184 markkaa ($40.35–$50.20). AE, DC, MC, V.
Open: Aug–June, Mon–Fri 11am–midnight, Sat 4pm–midnight. **Closed:** July.
One of the most expensive and elegant restaurants in Helsinki, this place—established in 1986—has an enduring charm and popularity. Its owner, George Saarela, modeled it a bit after the Georges V in Paris. One floor above street level, it has a decor that might be called 19th-century Nordic bourgeois. If you order caviar or lobster (which is seasonal), the prices will be much higher than those indicated above, depending on market fluctuations. Likewise, exotic seafood, also seasonal, can mean a much higher tab. For an appetizer, try a warm timbale of beetroot with flap mushrooms or a tartare of slightly salted perch with a mosaic of fresh vegetables served with rye bread. A main-dish specialty is salmon which he cooks "glow-fried" (his secret). You might also prefer a gratineé filet of lamb or noisettes of reindeer. Dessert might be one of his homemade ice creams, including whisky with a passionfruit sauce.

HAVIS AMANDA, Unioninkatu 23. Tel. 666-882.
Cuisine: SEAFOOD. **Reservations:** Required. **Tram:** 1, 2, 3T, 4. **Bus:** 14.
$ Prices: Fixed-price meals 275 markkaa ($75) at dinner, 115–175 markkaa ($31.36–$47.70) at lunch; appetizers 60–115 markkaa ($16.35–$31.35); main dishes 75–163 markkaa ($20.45–$44.45). AE, DC, MC, V.
Open: Mon–Sat 11am–1am.
The finest seafood place in Helsinki, this cellar restaurant is decorated in a luxurious tavern style. In the peak of the summer you will see signs proclaiming that crayfish season has begun (it usually starts the last week of July). The crayfish is boiled Louisiana style and often is consumed with ice-cold beer or an even icier koskenkorva. At any time of the year you can enjoy such good-tasting specialties, as fish soup of the house or assorted roes served as hors d'oeuvres, turbot braised in sour cream, and grilled salmon with those creamy morels. For dessert, it's most traditional to order Lapland cheese with cloudberry jam.

PALACE GOURMET, in the Palace Hotel, Eteläranta 10. Tel. 171-114.
Cuisine: FINNISH/FRENCH. **Reservations:** Required. **Tram:** 3B. **Bus:** 16.
$ Prices: Fixed-price meals 350 markkaa ($95.45) for a four-course *menu finlandaise*, 420 markkaa ($114.55) for a six-course *menu dégustation*, 120–250 markkaa ($32.70–$68.20) for lunch; appetizers 75–175 markkaa ($20.45–$47.70); main dishes 115–190 markkaa ($31.35–$51.80). AE, DC, MC, V.
Open: Aug–June, Mon–Fri 11am–1am. **Closed:** July.
Offering exquisite cuisine since 1952, this place, on the 10th floor of the Palace Hotel (see "Helsinki Accommodations," in this chapter), is the most acclaimed restaurant in Helsinki. It offers excellent service and a unique ambience, with a stunning view of the harbor. It relies on the excellence of its cuisine and the beauty and fame of its decor to sell itself. The design hasn't been changed since Uiljo Rewell created it in 1952 (Rewell was the second most famous architect in Finland in the

FINLAND

Helsinki

Alexander Nevski **1**
Ateljé **2**
Aurinkotuuli **3**
Barbecue **4**
Bellevue **5**
Bellman **6**
Bulevardin Kahvisalonki **7**
Café Ekberg **8**
Café-Brasserie Kapelli **9**
Carrols **10**
Chez Marius **11**
El Greco **12**
Elite **13**
Fanny's **14**
Fazer Café **15**
Four Seasons **16**
Galateia **17**
George **18**
Happy Days **19**
Havis Amanda **20**
Hollywood Restaurants **21**
Karl König **22**
Kasvisravintola **23**
Kazbek **24**
Kellarikrouvi **25**
Kosmos **26**
La Vista **27**
McDonald's **28**
Mechelin **29**
Mestarikrouvi **30**
Mikado **31**
Ostrobotnia **32**
Palace Gourmet **33**
Pamir **34**
Pampan **35**
Parilla Torni **36**
Picnic Sandwich & Salad Bar **37**
Pizza Hut **38**
Pizzeria Rivoli **39**
Rivoli Restaurant **39**
Savoy **40**
Solna **41**
Svenska Klubben **42**
Vanhan Kellari **43**
Walhalla **44**
Wellamo **45**

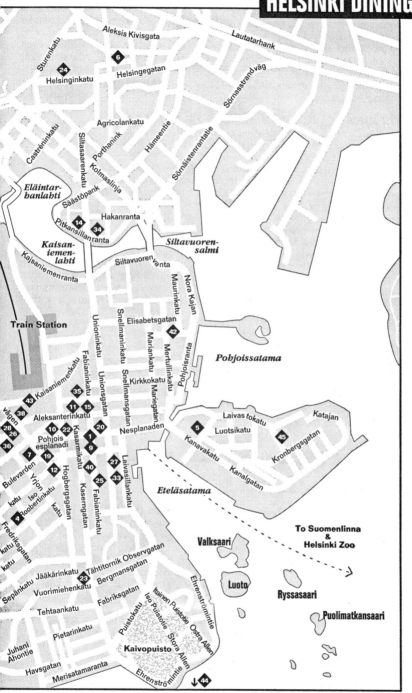

1950s, competing with Aalto). It has wood paneling, a live pianist, large panoramic windows and—to a trained eye—the clue that its decor is among the finest examples of postwar Finnish design in the world. Its wine cellar is one of the best in the country, having won many awards. Fixed-price menus at lunch supplant à la carte meals. Even a two-course uncomplicated traditional lunch is featured. But, mainly, the restaurant is known for its superb à la carte dishes, including a timbale of Jerusalem artichokes with cold smoked salmon and roe of vendace, a soup of oxtail with beetroot, tongue of reindeer with cranberry sauce, and for dessert, a cake of Arctic brambleberries.

RESTAURANT SAVOY, Eteläesplanadi 14. Tel. 176-571.
   Cuisine: FINNISH. **Reservations:** Required. **Tram:** 3B.
   $ Prices: Appetizers 65–76 markkaa ($17.75–$20.75); main dishes 105–145 markkaa ($28.65–$39.55). AE, DC, MC, V.
   Open: Lunch Mon–Fri 11am–3pm; dinner Mon–Fri 3pm–1am.

In an office building near the harbor, this restaurant has a decor that represents the quintessence of Finnish modernism. In 1937 Finland's greatest architect, Alvar Aalto, designed every detail of the place, even the lighting fixtures. The restaurant, a national monument, has been kept almost exactly as he designed it. Its most famous customer was Finland's most celebrated military hero, Marshal Mannerheim, who came here for his favorite schnapps, Marskin Ryyppy, made with vodka, aquavit, dry vermouth, and dry gin, stirred together and served icy cold. The food has changed with the times. You might begin with blinis stuffed with duck and duck liver, or smoked reindeer with salmon jelly. Main dishes are likely to include filet of wild boar, breast of ptarmigan with a Lapp cheese sauce, or filets of perch with cabbage in a sweet-and-sour sauce. Desserts are often imaginative, including, for example, a fruit ratatouille with a blackcurrant sauce.

EXPENSIVE

ALEXANDER NEVSKI, Pohjoisesplanadi 17. Tel. 639-610.
   Cuisine: RUSSIAN. **Reservations:** Required. **Tram:** 3.
   $ Prices: Appetizers 38–148 markkaa ($10.35–$40.35); fixed-price menus 170–270 markkaa ($46.35–$73.65). AE, DC, MC, V.
   Open: Aug–June, Mon–Fri 11am–1am, Sat noon–1am; July, dinner only, daily 6pm–1am.

IN THEIR FOOTSTEPS

Baron Carl Gustaf Emil von Mannerheim (1867–1951) The most distinguished Finnish soldier and statesman, Mannerheim is virtually "the father of his country" to Finnish people. He fought in the Russo-Japanese War of 1904, became regent of Finland, and later, as field marshal, directed operations in the Winter War (1939–40) and the Continuation War (1941–44) against Russia. As president of the republic (1944–46), he presided over a peace treaty with Russia in which Finland had to surrender vast territories, including East Karelia.

   • **Birthplace:** Villnäs, near Turku, on June 4, 1867.
   • **Favorite Haunts:** Restaurant Savoy (still serving his favorite schnapps, Marskin Ryyppy) and Karl König (where the marshal and his generals ate his favorite dish, Vorschmack).
   • **Residences:** 14 Kallionlinnantie, Helsinki, now a museum containing memorabilia of an illustrious career.
   • **Resting Place:** He died at Lausanne, Switzerland, on January 27, 1951, and is buried in Hietaniemi Cemetery in Helsinki.

At the southern corner of the Market Square, this is the finest Russian restaurant in Helsinki. Set in a 200-year-old building, the restaurant is named for the 12th-century Russian military hero. It has large beveled mirror panels in pastel frames, Lapland marble floors, stained-glass windows emblazoned with Romanov double-headed eagles and *faux-marbre* columns. The cuisine is a mixture of the best of the imperial tsarist cuisine with the best of Russian regional (peasant) dishes. A specialty is roast bear meat prepared in a clay pot. You might begin with Russian fish soup or a selection of appetizers called zakuska. Cabbage rolls arrive in a clay pot stuffed with filet strips of veal. The shashliks here are famous. The perfect apéritif is a mixture of Russian vodka with a Finnish liqueur made from brambleberries and raspberries, and for dessert you can sample iced berries with a caramel-fudge sauce.

BELLEVUE, Rahapajankatu 3. Tel. 179-560.

Cuisine: RUSSIAN. **Reservations:** Required. **Tram:** 4.
$ **Prices:** Appetizers 29–165 markkaa ($7.90–$45); main dishes 65–138 markkaa ($17.75–$37.65); fixed-price lunch 95 markkaa ($25.90). AE, DC, MC, V.
Open: Lunch Mon–Fri 11am–2pm; dinner Mon–Sat 5pm–midnight. **Closed:** July.

In the heart of Helsinki, next to the Uspenski Orthodox church, the Bellevue has since 1922 been an enduring favorite because of its good cuisine and moderate prices. You can dine in a long corridorlike main dining room or select one of the cozier and tinier side rooms. Herring, still served Russian style, is always a good beginning, or perhaps blinis and caviar. The chicken Kiev is a recommended main dish. For dessert, a flaming baba cake is carried through the main dining room, the presentation of which one long-time patron likened to "a wake for Tsar Nicholas II." Real Russian wine is offered.

PARILLA TORNI, in the Hotel Torni, Yrjönkatu 26. Tel. 131-131.

Cuisine: SPANISH. **Reservations:** Recommended. **Tram:** 3, 4, 8.
$ **Prices:** Appetizers 39–74 markkaa ($10.65–$20.20); main dishes 74–140 markkaa ($20.20–$38.20). AE, DC, MC, V.
Open: Tues–Fri 11am–midnight, Sat 4pm–midnight, Sun noon–midnight.

Its decor is *faux española,* and the stuffed bull's head and the crossed Spanish sabers against the roughly textured plaster evoke Iberian kitsch. In spite of that, the food is excellent and well prepared. The tascalike restaurant is on the street level of the famous Hotel Torni, once the rendezvous place of such artists as Jean Sibelius or the site of secret meetings of the illegal Communist party. Begin with smoked turkey and lentils soup; then follow with chicken and olives, perhaps grilled chicken with chocolate sauce, even herb-fried red snapper with garlic mayonnaise. The paella Valenciana requires a minimum order of two. For dessert, you can settle for a typical flan (caramel custard) or order something more elaborate such as almond flambé bananas with cinnamon ice cream.

MODERATE

KARL KÖNIG, Mikonkatutel 4. Tel. 171-271.

Cuisine: SCANDINAVIAN. **Reservations:** Required. **Tram:** 3B, 3T.
$ **Prices:** Appetizers 25–45 markkaa ($6.80–$12.25); main dishes 40–98 markkaa ($10.90–$26.70). AE, DC, MC, V.
Open: Daily 11am–midnight.

Established in 1892, this restaurant is perhaps the most traditional in Helsinki, lying in the cellars beneath one of the four largest banks of Finland, the SKOP bank. The great architect Saarinen redesigned the restaurant long after its founding into a precursor of the internationally modern style that later would sweep the world. Here, in what was at the time a private dining room, Marshal Mannerheim and his generals would gather for food and strategy talks during the darkest days of World War II. The place has hosted all of Finland's presidents and many of its greatest artists and composers, including Jean Sibelius. Dishes might include pike-perch Waleska, smoked whitefish à la König, blinis with seasonal roe, filet de boeuf à la patronne, and a seasonal variety of fish.

KELLARIKROUVI, Pohjoinen Makasiinikatu 6. Tel. 179-021.
   Cuisine: INTERNATIONAL. **Reservations:** Recommended. **Tram:** 3B, 3T.
$ **Prices:** Appetizers 35–59 markkaa ($9.55–$16.10); main dishes 54–135 markkaa ($14.75–$36.80). AE, DC, MC, V.
   Open: Mon–Sat 11am–midnight, Sun noon–midnight.
This 1901 cellar, near the marketplace in the town center, has a long series of interconnected underground vaults. It has attracted large crowds of devoted followers ever since it opened in the 1960s, when it was the first restaurant in the country to serve beer on tap. The decor is eclectic and old-fashioned—religious statues in niches, stained glass, Windsor chairs, a beamed ceiling, and filled bookshelves. Many differently decorated rooms for dining and drinking are offered, including the Rebecca Room, the English study with a fireplace, and (upstairs) the Fabian Music Bar, a meeting place for young adults. Each day different specialties are offered. The menu features such game dishes as game pâté, a salad of smoked reindeer tongue, braised salmon, creamed morels, and pickled Baltic herring. In season, snow grouse is on the menu. There's a small open-air terrace in summer.

KOSMOS RESTAURANT, Kalevankatu 3. Tel. 647-255.
   Cuisine: FINNISH. **Reservations:** Recommended. **Tram:** 3B, 3T. **Bus:** 15, 17.
$ **Prices:** Appetizers 42–74 markkaa ($11.45–$20.20); main dishes 42–106 markkaa ($11.45–$28.90); fixed-price lunch 75 markkaa ($20.45). AE, DC, MC, V.
   Open: Mon–Fri 11:30am–midnight.
Near the center of Helsinki's main street, the Mannerheimintie, this restaurant is known throughout Finland as a gathering place for artists, writers, and television personalities. The decor is decent and simple, and the menu specialties include terrine of cold smoked rainbow trout with herb sauce, sweetbreads gourmet, stuffed mutton chops, and fried Baltic herring. Light meals, such as open tartare sandwiches, vorschmack with duchesse potatoes, and borscht, are also available. (Vorschmack is made with chopped mutton, herring, and anchovies, and it's served with baked potatoes, salted cucumbers, and beets.) In the summertime you can order "deep-fried" strawberries for dessert; pears drenched with a chocolate-cream sauce are also delicious. The special lunch is served until 3pm.

OSTROBOTNIA, Dagmarinkatu 2. Tel. 446-940.
   Cuisine: FINNISH. **Reservations:** Recommended. **Tram:** 4, 7, 10.

IN THEIR FOOTSTEPS

Jean Sibelius (1865–1957) Finland's greatest composer was often inspired by legend and national romanticism. His *Finlandia*, published in 1900, established his reputation, a tone poem conjuring up the wildness of the Finnish countryside. Awarded a life grant from the state, he produced seven symphonies, each filled with an emotional intensity. *Tapiola* was one of his great symphonic poems.
   • **Birthplace:** He was born at Tavastehus on December 8, 1865.
   • **Favorite Haunts:** Karl König restaurant in Helsinki; Kapelli in Helsinki, where he had a favorite table.
   • **Residences:** Ainola, in Jarvenpää, outside Helsinki.
   • **Resting Place:** Sibelius died on September 20, 1957, at Traeskaenda, near Helsinki, and was buried with his wife, Aino, on their property at Ainola.

$ Prices: Appetizers 30–57 markkaa ($8.20–$15.55); main courses 57–105 markkaa ($15.55–$28.65). AE, MC, V.
Open: Mon–Sat 11am–midnight.

Set in a residential neighborhood several blocks west of the Inter-Continental Hotel and the Finnair Bus Terminal, this restaurant prides itself on both its cuisine and its collection of 19th-century Finnish paintings lining the walls. There's a popular and interesting bar with an outdoor terrace which you'll see as you enter. You can enjoy such specialties as fresh fish, grilled noisettes of beef, sautéed reindeer, breast of chicken stuffed with sweetbreads, and wild berry pie.

PAMPAN, Hallituskatu 15. Tel. 653-936.

Cuisine: FRENCH. **Reservations:** Recommended. **Tram:** 3T.
$ Prices: Appetizers 17–35 markkaa ($4.65–$9.55); main dishes 56–105 markkaa ($15.25–$28.65). AE, DC, MC, V.
Open: Mon–Sat 11am–midnight, Sun 2–11pm.

Across from the Helsinki Hotel, this place looks a lot like a French bistro. It features an array of "light dishes," costing 49 to 63 markkaa ($13.35 to $17.20) for those watching their waistlines. The kitchen always offers at least two different vegetarian main dishes. Specialties include fish soup à la Marseillaise, grilled salmon with stewed wild mushrooms, chateaubriand with butter sauce, and chicken breast in garlic sauce with rice. Italian espresso is featured, along with several coffee drinks made from liqueur—one is a café banana with rum from Martinique. In summer you can dine outside. Sometimes diners come as early as 3:30 in the afternoon to order dinner.

RAVINTOLA RIVOLI, Albertinkatu 38. Tel. 643-455.

Cuisine: FRENCH/FINNISH. **Reservations:** Recommended. **Tram:** 3B.
$ Prices: Appetizers 39–75 markkaa ($10.65–$20.45); main dishes 45–135 markkaa ($12.25–$36.80); fixed-price lunch 68 markkaa ($18.55). AE, DC, MC, V.
Open: Mon–Fri 11am–midnight, Sat 5pm–midnight.

The dining room is a florid and recently installed art nouveau fantasy set within a labyrinthine dining room, with upholstered banquettes. One of its subdivisions is named "Fish Rivoli," and from its separate menu you can order some of the finest seafood dishes in the city. In both dining rooms, you can enjoy such fare as filet of perch with herb butter, grilled salmon with mustard sauce, chicken with garlic and sour cream, and pepper steak with potato croquettes. At lunchtime, special *husmanskost* cookery is offered, a reference to "grandmother's style," featuring such dishes as onion soup and grilled rainbow trout. The establishment also operates an adjoining pizzeria.

INEXPENSIVE

BARBECUE, Annankatu 6. Tel. 680-1701.

Cuisine: BARBECUE. **Reservations:** Required for four or more. **Tram:** 3B.
$ Prices: Barbecue 105 markkaa ($28.65). AE, DC, MC, V.
Open: Mon–Fri 11am–midnight, Sat–Sun 1pm–midnight.

A great dining bargain, this pick-and-choose format offers flavorful meals and a welcome culinary theatricality. After being seated at a bare table, you serve yourself from a soup or salad buffet. A second visit to the counter allows you to select your choice of fresh thinly sliced cuts of pork, beef, chicken, or reindeer, along with a garnish of fresh vegetables. A uniformed chef will ask which of four sauces or cooking oils you prefer. Then as you watch, the ingredients are sautéed into a yummy stir-fry feast. One price covers all the food you want, but drinks cost extra.

CAFE BRASSERIE KAPELLI, Eteläesplanadi 1. Tel. 179-242.

Cuisine: INTERNATIONAL. **Reservations:** None. **Tram:** 3B. **Bus:** 16.

$ **Prices:** Appetizers 23–25 markkaa ($6.25–$6.80); main dishes 54–68 markkaa ($14.75–$18.55); sandwiches 27–35 markkaa ($7.35–$9.55); pizzas 39–42 markkaa ($10.65–$11.45); pastas 32–36 markkaa ($8.75–$9.80). AE, DC, MC, V.

Open: Mon–Sat 8am–2am, Sun 9am–2am.

Ⓢ This famous restaurant and drinking complex is a Victorian Gothic fantasy set like an oversize gazebo in the middle of Esplanade Park, near the harborfront. Originally built in 1837 as a rendezvous for artists and "high-society gentlemen" (Sibelius had a favorite table), it was closed for many years until its restoration in 1976. You'll find a variety of different seating areas, even a cellar pub where pizza and pasta are served. In the oldest section, the café, most guests order sandwiches, pastries, or coffee. The centermost section is the main restaurant, Runeberg, where white linen tablecloths, increased elbow room, and formal service are the hallmarks. Main dishes, remarkably inexpensive by Finnish standards, include chateaubriand, pepper steak, entrecôte, fried salmon with red wine and pepper sauce, or whitefish.

CHEZ MARIUS, Mikonkatu 1. Tel. 669-697.
Cuisine: FRENCH. **Reservations:** Recommended. **Tram:** 3, 4.
$ **Prices:** Appetizers 30–40 markkaa ($8.20–$10.90); main dishes 60–70 markkaa ($16.35–$19.10); luncheon specials 35–40 markkaa ($9.55–$10.90). No credit cards.

Open: Mon–Fri 11am–6pm.

The French ambience helps to make this a charming bistro. The walls are covered with hand-painted murals of Paris life, as well as a picture of the owner greeting former French president Giscard d'Estaing; the tables have red-checked cloths. Usually crowded with neighborhood office workers, the restaurant offers a daily special, which, with a drink, is all many clients seem to need at lunchtime. When I was last here, the special was cannelloni Marius served every Wednesday, and (I was told) a favorite dish of many regular clients. The à la carte items include onion soup, snails, medallions of veal house style, steak au poivre, and veal Oscar. If you're alone, you can dine at the bar.

HAPPY DAYS, Pohjoisesplanadi 2. Tel. 624-023.
Cuisine: INTERNATIONAL. **Reservations:** Not required. **Tram:** 3B, 3T.
$ **Prices:** Appetizers 25–35 markkaa ($6.80–$9.55); main dishes 50–125 markkaa ($13.65–$34.10). AE, DC, MC, V.

Open: Mon–Sat 10am–midnight, Sun 11am–11pm.

Overlooking a flower-filled central park near the marketplace, this dining-and-drinking emporium contains four different eating and drinking spots. The least expensive is a self-service lunch restaurant. You'll find more upscale food—and higher prices—at the adjoining Café Royale, where a full array of salads, meat, and fish dishes is offered. Also on the premises is the Sitting Bull steakhouse where you can have Hereford steaks. Finally, there's a drinking pub called the Trattoria, which can become rowdy. It's sometimes possible to get the specialties of one area served in another. In summer the operation expands onto several outdoor terraces, each of which offer views of some of Helsinki's most famous promenades.

VANHAN KELLARI, Kaivokatu 3. Tel. 174-321.
Cuisine: FINNISH. **Reservations:** Not required. **Tram:** 3B, 3T.
$ **Prices:** Appetizers 37–51 markkaa ($10.10–$13.90); main dishes 49–94 markkaa ($13.35–$25.65). MC, V.

Open: Restaurant, daily 11am–1am; beer cellar, daily 9am–1am.

Opposite Stockmann's Department Store in the center of Helsinki, this is a popular lunch spot. In the evening it becomes a dimly lit, atmospheric, and very sudsy beer cellar, perhaps the most frequented in town. To enter this famous beer cellar, you descend a set of modern steps wide enough to accommodate a pair of Cadillacs. During the day you can settle for a sandwich, ranging from 45 to 55 markkaa ($12.25 to $15), but in the evening you can order a full range of hearty fare, including pepper steak with rice and tomato salad, grilled liver, salmon soup, or marinated herring. If you come just to drink, a half pint of lager costs 16.50 markkaa ($4.50).

NORTH OF THE CENTER
VERY EXPENSIVE

GALATEIA, in the Hotel Inter-Continental, Mannerheimintie 46. Tel. 40-551.
Cuisine: SEAFOOD. **Reservations:** Required. **Tram:** 3B, 3T.
$ Prices: Appetizers 49–110 markkaa ($13.35–$30); main dishes 92–124 markkaa ($25.10–$33.80). AE, DC, MC, V.
Open: Dinner only, Mon–Fri 6:30pm–midnight.

⭐ The most elegant seafood restaurant in Helsinki, this establishment is on the ninth floor of a deluxe hotel, offering a panoramic view of the city. Only fresh fish (not frozen) flown in from Europe and the Caribbean is served. The favorite appetizers are two platters of cold marinated fish—"the catch from the Finnish archipelago," with salted salmon, marinated lamprey eels, marinated herring, and shrimp, and a cold Caribbean fish plate with marinated raw and cooked fish from the West Indies, including spiny Caribbean red snapper or perhaps even a reptile, alligator. Sashimi is available in many different variations. The least imaginative day is Monday when (because of delivery schedules) only Finnish fish is available. The most exotic catch appears Wednesday through Friday nights.

SVENSKA KLUBBEN, Maurinkatu 6. Tel. 135-4706.
Cuisine: FINNISH. **Reservations:** Required. **Bus:** 18.
$ Prices: Appetizers 55–100 markkaa ($15–$27.25); main dishes 85–145 markkaa ($23.20–$39.55); fixed-price lunch 100–140 markkaa ($27.25–$38.20). AE, DC, MC, V.
Open: Mon–Sat 11am–1am.

This place was originally conceived as a private club, and over the years its membership has included some of the city's most important businessmen, many of whom adorned its interior with their portraits and memorabilia. Today it accepts nonmembers into its dining rooms, and functions as both a private and a desirable public restaurant. Constructed in 1900 as a private home by a Finnish businessman for his Scottish-born wife, it has English Edwardian styling, from its 12-foot ceiling to the paneling used for decoration. The street level is open to the public, along with its adjoining pub, Patrick's. You can enjoy an apéritif in the bar, whose wintertime

---

 FROMMER'S COOL FOR KIDS
Restaurants

Kellarikrouvi (*see page 628*) Here there is a special children's menu for only 25 markkaa ($6.80). Children can enjoy the activity of the marketplace before coming here for lunch.

Ravintola Rivoli (*see page 629*) This excellent restaurant offers a special children's menu for 30 markkaa ($8.20), which might include a "fantasy pizza," a pasta, or a main dish with salad. Children delight in the special dessert menu, including everything from lingonberry ice cream to blackcurrant pie.

Barbecue (*see page 629*) Children delight in being taken here where they get to select their choice of meats for barbecuing: chicken, beef, pork, or reindeer ("No, I won't eat Prancer!"). It's one of the best family-dining values in Helsinki.

fireplace is charming. A fish-and-salad buffet is featured at lunch, although not considered a full meal—rather, a first course. The place is known for its game dishes, which the chef prepares without frills or fussy adornments, macho style. Wild duck with a cognac-flavored cream sauce is a great favorite, as is smoked roast elk or juniper-smoked salmon.

MODERATE

BELLMAN RESTAURANT, Fleminginkatu 21. Tel. 753-4300.
   Cuisine: FINNISH. **Reservations:** Required. **Tram:** 3. **Bus:** 17.
$ **Prices:** Appetizers 25–35 markkaa ($6.80–$9.55); main courses 70–110 markkaa ($19.10–$30). AE, DC, MC, V.
   Open: Mon–Fri 11am–2pm and 5pm–midnight, Sat 3pm–midnight.
In Kallio district on a street once known for bootlegging, the Bellman adds a touch of class. There's live music here several nights a week, and sometimes admirers of the 18th-century Swedish poet Carl Mikael Bellman sing some of his ballads. Lunch menus change daily, but might include game soup, mussels with julienne vegetables, or pike-perch quenelles with crayfish sauce. A la carte dinner offerings are frequently changed, but two popular constants are herring ice cream with gravlax and roast mutton and reindeer combined on a single platter.
   You can reach the Bellman by taxi, by bus, by tram, or from the railroad station. Walk along Vaasankatu to the right after you come up the escalator.

FANNY'S RESTAURANT, Fanny & Alexander's, Siltasaarenkatu 2. Tel. 753-2332.
   Cuisine: FINNISH/CONTINENTAL. **Reservations:** Recommended. **Bus:** 17, 64, 72.
$ **Prices:** Appetizers 40–50 markkaa ($10.90–$13.65); main dishes 65–98 markkaa ($17.75–$26.70). AE, DC, MC, V.
   Open: Mon–Fri 11am–midnight, Sat 6pm–1am.
A charming second-floor establishment owned by the Arctia hotel chain, Fanny's Restaurant stands across from the Strand Inter-Continental. In spite of its stark exterior, its interior is lushly Edwardian, filled with turn-of-the-century bric-a-brac. A dimly lit and intimate corner bar, with chintz-patterned wallpaper, palms, and fringed and beaded hanging lamps, lies near the restaurant's entrance. Full meals might include the house-style risotto, a casserole of flap mushrooms, sole stuffed with salmon mousse, filet steak, lobster soup, or cheese raclette. See "Evening Entertainment," in Chapter 35 for Alexander's, a disco in the same building.

MECHELIN, Mechelininkatu 7. Tel. 493-481.
   Cuisine: FINNISH/CONTINENTAL. **Reservations:** None. **Tram:** 8.
$ **Prices:** Appetizers 15–50 markkaa ($4.10–$13.65); main dishes 29–81 markkaa ($7.90–$22.10); fixed-price lunch platter (with salad and coffee) 30 markkaa ($8.20); Finnish Sunday buffet 70 markkaa ($19.10). AE, DC, MC, V.
   Open: Mon–Fri 11am–midnight, Sat–Sun noon–11pm.
   Lying half a mile east of the Central Station, this restaurant is run by a foundation called the Helsinki Culinary School, and is staffed by its trainees. All the cooking, however, is professionally supervised, and served efficiently and politely in attractive modern surroundings. The food is prepared with enthusiasm and served with a certain flair. Specialties include "Finnish pasta," served with salmon and cold-smoked reindeer steak, or a vegetarian pasta made with tagliatelle, olives, and vegetables in a tomato sauce. Other dishes include lime-marinated salmon with stewed mushrooms and, the major bestseller, pepper steak flambéed at your table. The Sunday buffet is a real bargain.

MESTARIKROUVI, Töölöntorinkatu 7. Tel. 496-386.
   Cuisine: FINNISH. **Reservations:** Required. **Tram:** 3B, 3T.
$ **Prices:** Appetizers 35–50 markkaa ($9.55–$13.65); main dishes 65–95 markkaa ($17.75–$25.90). AE, DC, MC, V.
   Open: Mon–Fri 11am–11:30pm, Sat–Sun noon–11:30pm.

Although at first glance you'd think this was nothing more than a cozy **S** neighborhood restaurant, the service and the Finnish specialties give it an added dimension. Sometimes the place, whose name in English means "tavern of champions," serves as a pleasant oasis for guests from the nearby Inter-Continental Hotel, but locals also appreciate the paneled bar, framed pictures, and homelike checked curtains. Finnish cuisine, such as elk filet with juniper berries and a selection of fish dishes, are the featured items. Try the cold smoked rainbow trout with mustard sauce. Usually you can find a staff member to translate the menu into English. There's an upper level as well.

ON KUSTAANMIEKKA ISLAND

RESTAURANT WALHALLA, Kustaanmiekka Island, Suomenlinna. Tel. 668-552.

Cuisine: FINNISH. **Reservations:** Not required. **Bus:** Waterbus to Walhalla.
$ Prices: Appetizers 45–85 markkaa ($12.25–$23.20); main courses 95–165 markkaa ($25.90–$45); fixed-price lunch 100 markkaa ($27.25). AE, DC, MC, V. **Open:** May–Sept 15, Mon–Sat noon–midnight, Sun noon–6pm. **Closed:** Sept 16–Apr.

You can only get to this restaurant by boat, as it's on the fortress island of Kustaanmiekka. Many claim that the trip is half the fun. This collection of sandblasted brick-and-granite vaults is right in the center of the Viapori fortress, so dining here is like eating in a living museum. Several eating places are on the premises, including a self-service restaurant, a panoramic terrace with waiter service, and a café. Traditional Finnish dishes, such as salmon soup, are served, followed by filet of reindeer and fried snow grouse. You can make your selections from the Delwing table, a Scandinavian buffet. A compote of fresh Finnish berries makes a perfect summer dessert.

SPECIALTY DINING
LIGHT, CASUAL & FAST FOOD

CARROLS, Keskuskatu 3. Tel. 655-514.

Cuisine: AMERICAN. **Reservations:** Not required. **Tram:** 3B, 3T.
$ Prices: Clubburger 19.50 markkaa ($5.30); french fries 8.20 markkaa ($2.25). No credit cards.
Open: Mon–Thurs 10am–11pm, Fri–Sat 10am–midnight, Sun 11am–11pm.
Regardless of how good Finnish cuisine is, the craving for a hamburger can be satisfied by Carrols. The most central locations are near the railway station in City-käytävä (City Passage; tel. 611-632) and at Keskuskatu 3 (tel. 655-514). (The two restaurants are on different sides of the famed Stockmann Department Store.) Another location is at Mannerheimintie 19 (tel. 490-469).

Outside the center, Carrols has restaurants in Puotinharju, a suburb east of Helsinki (tel. 339-264), and in Tapiola district in the town of Espoo (tel. 462-508). In addition to the burgers, other fast food is also featured.

All branches are open the same hours.

McDONALD'S, Mannerheimintie 16. Tel. 604-506.

Cuisine: AMERICAN. **Reservations:** None. **Tram:** 4, 10.
$ Prices: Big Mac 19.90 markkaa ($5.60). No credit cards.
Open: Sun–Thurs 10am–midnight, Fri–Sat 10am–1am.
When you've had your fill of roast reindeer with juniper berries and the omnipresent Baltic herring, and when only a Big Mac will satisfy your appetite, head for this centrally located outlet. It's clean and rather cheerful, lying in the most congested part of the main town. If you don't want a Big Mac, you'll find other selections, along with the standard french fries and other accompaniments. Finns like this place a lot, although it's no longer as "exotic" as it used to be for them.

PIZZA HUT, City-käytävä. Tel. 627-490.

Cuisine: PIZZA. **Reservations:** None. **Tram:** 3B, 3T.
$ Prices: Pizzas 32–125 markkaa ($8.75–$34.10). AE, DC, MC, V.
Open: Mon–Thurs 11am–11pm, Fri–Sat 11am–midnight, Sun noon–11pm.

At Pizza Hut you can help yourself at the salad bar or choose a thin and crispy Italian-type pizza. The Super Supreme deep-pan pizza is available in three sizes, the smallest big enough to share among three or four persons. The deep-pan pizza is freshly made, light and fluffy on the inside, crispy and crunchy on the outside. Pizza Hut restaurants also serve wine.

There's another branch in the Tapiola district in Espoo (tel. 465-452) some 10 miles outside Helsinki.

PIZZERIA RIVOLI, Albertinkatu 38. Tel. 607-455.

Cuisine: PIZZA/PASTA. **Reservations:** Not required. **Tram:** 3B.
$ Prices: Pizzas 52–58 markkaa ($14.20–$15.80); pastas 50–52 markkaa ($13.65–$14.20). AE, DC, MC, V.
Open: Mon–Fri 10am–midnight, Sat noon–midnight, Sun 2–11pm.

Amid a pleasantly uncluttered decor evocative of southern Europe, you can enjoy some of the best pizzas in Helsinki. You have a choice of 20 different kinds of pies, or you can order one of the pasta dishes, a filling meal in itself. This is the least expensive of the restaurants run by Rivoli, which also operates a more expensive restaurant next door, specializing in a French/Finnish cuisine.

LOCAL FAVORITES

ELITE, Etläinen Hesperiankatu 22. Tel. 495-542.

Cuisine: FRENCH. **Reservations:** Recommended. **Tram:** 3.
$ Prices: Appetizers 38–55 markkaa ($10.35–$15); main dishes 49–102 markkaa ($13.35–$27.80). AE, DC, MC, V.
Open: Mon–Fri 11am–1am, Sat–Sun 1pm–1am.

A short walk west of Finlandia Hall, this pub-café was once the haunt of Helsinki artists. It now draws a wide range of clients. Established in 1938, it offers inexpensive food and good house wines. Begin with a soup or Baltic herring, perhaps a selection from the salad bar; then go on to such main courses as filet of beef with morels and smoked salmon, or a double filet of fried herring. In summer you can order drinks on the patio.

RAVINTOLA ATELJÉ, Arkadiankatu 14. Tel. 493-110.

Cuisine: FINNISH. **Reservations:** Not required. **Tram:** 3.
$ Prices: Appetizers 28–40 markkaa ($7.65–$10.90); main dishes 50–100 markkaa ($13.65–$27.25). MC, V.
Open: Mon–Fri 11am–1am, Sat 5pm–1am.

Near the Ramada Presidentti Hotel, this restaurant occupies three levels of a building which served for many years as the atelier of Gunnar Finne, the famous Finnish sculptor (1886–1952). Although in his will he bequeathed most of his work to his son, he requested that his sculpture be displayed in a restaurant on the premises of his former atelier. The result is an aesthetically pleasing gathering place for Helsinki artists. Placed around the three levels are some 30 sculptures, some of them plaster models for pieces that were eventually cast in bronze. You can begin with such classic Finnish dishes as salmon soup or slightly marinated Baltic herring, then follow with fried whitefish with forest mushrooms, perhaps grilled filet of beef with garlic potatoes and a chanterelle sauce. For dessert, a homemade cake is baked fresh daily.

WELLAMO, Vyokatu 9. Tel. 663-139.

Cuisine: FINNISH. **Reservations:** Not required. **Tram:** 4.
$ Prices: Appetizers 30–35 markkaa ($8.20–$9.55); main dishes 60–90 markkaa ($16.35–$24.55). AE, MC, V.
Open: Tues–Fri 11am–11pm, Sat 4–11pm, Sun 1–8pm.

Not for everyone, this place is a local hangout with a bit of workaday charm. It's in a century-old house on the island of Katajanokka, abutting the northeastern edge of the south harbor. The classic Finnish meat patty, vorschmack, is a specialty, as is slightly salted marinated salmon. Lamb is prepared in many different ways, including roasted and served with either a garlic or mint sauce. Another specialty is balmaani, a Russian dish similar to Italian ravioli; the patty is stuffed with minced and seasoned lamb and served with a sour-cream sauce. Hearty regional soups precede most meals. The decor is warm, unpretentious, and cozy, and the service is overburdened, but hard-working.

HOTEL DINING

FOUR SEASONS RESTAURANT, in the Ramada Presidentti Hotel, Etäläinen Rautatiekatu 4. Tel. 69-11.
Cuisine: FINNISH. **Reservations:** Recommended. **Tram:** 3B, 3T.
$ Prices: Buffet 212 markkaa ($57.80) at dinner, 150 markkaa ($40.90) at lunch; appetizers 55–79 markkaa ($15–$21.55), main dishes 101–129 markkaa ($27.50–$35.20). AE, DC, MC, V.
Open: Lunch daily 11:30am–2:30pm; dinner daily 7–11pm.

Set on the third floor of one of Helsinki's most prominent hotels, this is a favorite luncheon stopover of Finnish president Mauno Koivisto, whose favorite dish is gutted and fried Baltic herring, silakka, prominently displayed on the buffet table. Designed in an elegant motif of dark paneling, big windows, and abstractly intriguing Finnish paintings, the restaurant features the most attractive spread of buffet foods in Helsinki. It is, in fact, the only carvery in Finland, and it's based on English models, but with a decidedly Baltic touch. Guests might begin with canapés of salmon tartare and follow with a second course from the self-service buffet table laden with fish, meats, salads, and vegetables. The same system, with such upgraded appetizers as braised lobster rolls with spinach or forest-mushrooms soup, is offered at night. There is also an à la carte menu, featuring such dishes as wild duckling with fresh lingonberries.

PAMIR, in the Strand Inter-Continental, John Stenbergin Ranta 4. Tel. 39-351.
Cuisine: GAME. **Reservations:** Required. **Tram:** 3T, 7.
$ Prices: Appetizers 60–110 markkaa ($16.35–$30); main dishes 90–180 markkaa ($24.55–$49.10). AE, DC, MC, V.
Open: Lunch Mon–Fri 11:30am–3pm; dinner Mon–Fri 6pm–midnight.
Recently designed by one of Finland's top interior architects, this restaurant is sheathed in Karelian birch and upholstered in cool colors inspired by a Finnish stream. It contains rack upon refrigerated rack of fine European and American wines. Service is impeccable. Pamir is the premier game restaurant of Helsinki, although it also offers some of the best fish dishes as well. The menu changes with the season. For an appetizer, choices might include whitefish roe with blinis or tartare of smoked Baltic herring with endive. For a main course, a parade of dishes await you, including filet of hare in rosemary sauce, entrecôte of elk with pumpkin-ginger loaf, filet of turbot braised in sour cream, or braised pike-perch with ginger sauce.

DINING WITH A VIEW

LA VISTA, in the Palace Hotel, Eteläranta 10. Tel. 171-114.
Cuisine: ITALIAN. **Reservations:** Recommended. **Tram:** 3B. **Bus:** 16.
$ Prices: Fixed-price meal 235 markkaa ($64.10); appetizers 37–58 markkaa ($10.10–$15.80); pastas 39–56 markkaa ($10.65–$15.27); main dishes 78–96 markkaa ($21.25–$26.20). AE, DC, MC, V.
Open: Mon–Fri 11am–1am, Sat 1pm–1am, Sun 1–11pm.
This isn't the most expensive restaurant or the most prestigious in the harborfront Palace Hotel, but many visitors prefer it because of its market-fresh Italian food prepared with flair and served with a view overlooking the water. Many of the menu choices are displayed behind a glass counter, representing the best of an abundant Italian harvest of foodstuffs. For appetizers, choices include polenta with snails or stuffed squid with a saffron sauce. Many visit just for the pastas, including lasagne or

tagliatelle with a seafood sauce. Daily specials are likely to include noisettes of wild boar with a rosemary sauce or noisettes of pork with a fig sauce. The seafood casserole with garlic bread is recommended. Dessert selections are made from a trolley.

FOR BREAKFAST

CAFE EKBERG, Bulevardi 9. Tel. 605-269.
    Cuisine: BAKED GOODS/PASTRIES. **Reservations:** Not required. **Tram:** 3B, 3T, or 6.
$ **Prices:** Buffet breakfast 35 markkaa ($9.55); sandwiches 25–45 markkaa ($6.80–$12.25); soups 32–45 markkaa ($8.75–$12.25). No credit cards.
    Open: Mon–Fri 7:45am–5pm, Sat 9am–3:30pm, Sun 11am–4pm.

With its fin-de-siècle atmosphere and 19th-century fixtures, this is one of the finest choices for breakfast in the Finnish capital. It is also suitable for afternoon tea, when open-face sandwiches are served at the little green marble tables. The baked goods are made fresh daily in the back. A buffet breakfast is one of the most popular in town, served daily except Monday until 11am. On the buffet table are eggs, porridge, Finnish cheese, ham, fruit, and an array of baked breads. After 11am a lunch menu is offered. In summer tables are placed out on the sidewalk platform.

LATE-NIGHT DINING

MIKADO, Mannerheimintie 6. Tel. 607-463.
    Cuisine: FINNISH/INTERNATIONAL. **Reservations:** Recommended. **Tram:** 4.
$ **Prices:** Appetizers 38–120 markkaa ($10.35–$32.70); main dishes 55–139 markkaa ($15–$37.90). DC, MC, V.
    Open: Mon–Fri 11am–2am, Sat–Sun noon–2am.

Don't let the name fool you. This restaurant, next door to the Marski Hotel, isn't Japanese. The name was established by a former owner who was an opera lover. The food, some of which is international, is basically Finnish—so Finnish it even offers Marshal Mannerheim's favorite dish, vorschmack, a fried-meat patty served with baked potatoes, salted cucumbers, and beet root. As an appetizer, try a blini with seasonally changing fish roe, ranging from salmon roe to whitefish roe, and the most prized of all, vendace roe. You can also sample Finnish salmon soup with rye toast, fried Baltic herring with mashed potatoes, and chicken breast with garlic stuffing. Food orders are accepted to 1:30am.

CAFES

FAZER CAFE, Kluuvikatu 3. Tel. 666-597.
    Cuisine: FINNISH. **Reservations:** Not required. **Tram:** 3, 4.
$ **Prices:** Appetizers 35–50 markkaa ($9.55–$13.65); main dishes 70–89 markkaa ($19.10–$24.25); lunch 43–50 markkaa ($11.75–$13.65). AE, DC, MC, V.
    Open: Mon–Fri 11am–9pm, Sat 11am–6pm.

Fazer began as a pastry and chocolate shop in 1891, and today, many incarnations later, the pastries are still delicious, but the place is considerably more modern and the cuisine more comprehensive. There is a conservatively decorated dining room on the left as you enter, and lunches can include salmon soup, veal with morels, fried pork filet, and tournedos Rossini. The spacious café on the right, however, is the really popular section of this place. It contains a bistro-style, summery decor of ice-cream wagons, red-and-white tablecloths, framed artworks, a deli case loaded with salads and cakes, and dozens upon dozens of pastries and chocolates. You can also select from the racks of deli and *konditorei* shelves in another part of the store.

VEGETARIAN

AURINKOTUULI, Lapinlahdenkatu 25. Tel. 694-2563.
    Cuisine: VEGETARIAN. **Reservations:** Not required. **Bus:** 65A.

$ Prices: Soup 24 markkaa ($6.55); food platters 32–37 markkaa ($8.75–$10.10). MC, V.

Open: Mon–Fri 11am–6pm.

Everything here is self-service at this large vegetarian buffet. The price of your meal is based on if you take a small plate or a large plate to the buffet. Soups cost extra. This establishment is on the street level, with a simple decor, attracting budget-conscious young people.

KASVISRAVINTOLA, Korkeavuorenkatu 3. Tel. 179-212.

Cuisine: VEGETARIAN. **Reservations:** Not required. **Tram:** 10.

$ Prices: Large buffet dinner plate 45–50 markkaa ($12.25–$13.65); luncheon specials 28–36 markkaa ($7.65–$9.80). AE, DC, MC, V.

Open: June 15–Aug 15, Mon–Fri 11am–5pm, Sat–Sun noon–5pm; Aug 16–June 14, Mon–Fri 11am–6pm, Sat noon–6pm, Sun 1–5pm.

Southeast of the railroad station in the Eira district of Helsinki, this place has a simple interior, with neutrally finished wood planking, handmade weavings, and a changing exhibition of original artworks. A uniformed staff works at the cafeteria counter which features salads, soups, whole-wheat grains, and many of the standard vegetarian specialties, including macrobiotic dishes. Guests are allowed to fill a large dinner plate from the buffet, and the cost of the plate also includes a cup of soup. Certain low-cost luncheon specials, however, are available only from 11am to 2pm.

PICNIC FARE & WHERE TO EAT IT

PICNIC SANDWICH AND SALAD BAR, Mannerheimintie 20. Tel. 693-1378.

Cuisine: SANDWICHES. **Reservations:** Not required. **Tram:** 3B, 3T.

$ Prices: Sandwiches 15–25 markkaa ($4.10–$6.80); salads 28–32 markkaa ($7.65–$8.75). No credit cards.

Open: Mon–Fri 7:30am–9pm, Sat 10am–4pm.

From its cramped but immaculate premises on the main commercial thoroughfare of Helsinki, this little shop dispenses health-conscious fast-food-to-go items, many of which would be ideal for take-away picnics. On request (and at no extra cost), the plastic-wrapped take-away food will include plastic knives, forks, spoons, and disposable napkins.

With your little picnic basket, you can head for the national park on the island of Seurasaari, the most ideal spot in all of Helsinki for a family outing.

CHAPTER 35

WHAT TO SEE & DO IN HELSINKI

Helsinki is loaded with all types of things to do from exploring museums, to enjoying a Finnish sauna, to taking a summer cruise through the archipelago, or even just testing out a Finnish smörgåsbord. If your time is limited though, be sure not to miss the Mannerheim Museum, the Home of Sibelius, the Seurasaari Open-Air Museum, or the Suomenlinna Fortress. For those with more time, and money to burn, Helsinki also offers a number of specialty shops. For an overview, stop in at Stockmann, Helsinki's largest department store.

---

1. SUGGESTED ITINERARIES

IF YOU HAVE 1 DAY

Day 1: Start the morning with a visit to Market Square, and, following in the footsteps of Lyndon Johnson, have coffee and a Karelian meat pie. The market opens at 7am. See the Presidential Palace and Uspenski Cathedral, and visit Senate Square and Eliel Saarinen's Railway Station. Before it's too late, call at the Stockmann Department Store or walk along Pohjois Esplanadi for a look at modern Finnish design in the store windows.

IF YOU HAVE 2 DAYS

Day 1: See "If You Have 1 Day," above.
Day 2: Visit the home of Baron Carl Gustaf Mannerheim, Finland's former field marshal and president, now a museum. Go to the Olympic Stadium to see the controversial statue of the famous runner Paavo Nurmi, and call on Finlandia Hall, Helsinki's main concert hall, designed by Alvar Aalto. Visit the National Museum and stroll through Sibelius Park, with its monument to the famous composer.

? DID YOU KNOW . . . ?

- Helsinki is famed for its architects, but it was a German, Carl Ludvig Engel, who designed the layout of the present inner city.
- Two brothers designed Temppeliauko Church out of a solid rock; it takes up most of a block, but from the street only the dome is visible.
- The Havis Amanda fountain, scandalized the city when it was placed in the Market Square in 1908, but now it's the symbol of Helsinki.
- The major boulevard, Esplanadi, was once a political dividing line—Finns walked on the south side and Swedes on the north.
- Wäinö Aaltonen caused an uproar in 1952 when his statue of Paavo Nurmi, the champion runner of the 1920s, was unveiled—he had depicted Nurmi fully nude.

IF YOU HAVE 3 DAYS

Days 1 & 2: See "If You Have 2 Days," above.

Day 3: Visit some of the attractions in the archipelago, including the Seurasaari Open Air Museum and Suomenlinna Fortress.

IF YOU HAVE 5 DAYS

Days 1–3: See "If You Have 3 Days," above.

Day 4: Head north on an excursion to visit the home of Jean Sibelius at Ainola in Järvenpää. Explore the nearby town of Hämeenlinna and see the birthplace of Sibelius.

Day 5: Take a 1-day excursion to Porvoo, the second-oldest town in Finland, 30 miles northeast of Helsinki.

2. THE TOP ATTRACTIONS

MANNERHEIM MUSEUM, Kallionlinnantie 14. Tel. 635-443.

This is the home of Baron Carl Gustaf Mannerheim, Finland's former field marshal and president—a sort of George Washington in this country, considered one of the most effective military strategists of his era. Now a museum, his former residence houses his collection of European furniture, Asian art and rugs, and personal items (uniforms, swords, decorations, gifts from admirers) that he acquired during his long career as a military man and statesman. The house remains the same as it was when he died in 1951.

Admission (including guided tour): 15 markkaa ($4.10) adults, 5 markkaa ($1.35) children over 12.

Open: Fri–Sat 11am–3pm, Sun 11am–4pm. **Tram:** 3B, 3T.

AINOLA, in Järvenpää. Tel. 287-322.

Few countries seem as proud of one of their native composers as the Finns are of Jean Sibelius, who lived here for more than half a century. He named the house after his wife, Aino (sister of artist Eero Järnefelt), and lived here from 1904 until he died in 1957; he and his wife are buried on the property. Considered avant-garde at the time of its construction, the house was designed by Lars Sonck, who also designed the summer residence of the president of Finland. The wooden interior of Ainola is lined with books and some surprisingly modern-looking furniture. Järvenpää is not quite 24 miles from Helsinki; there are no street names, but there are signs to Ainola.

Admission: 10 markkaa ($2.75).

Open: May–Sept, Tues and Thurs–Sun 10am–6pm, Wed noon–8pm. **Bus:** From Platform 1 of the Helsinki bus station, following the Helsinki–Hyryla–Järvenpää route, to point where the road forks at sign saying AINOLA, a 4-minute walk from the home. **Train:** Järvenpää station.

FINLAND

Helsinki

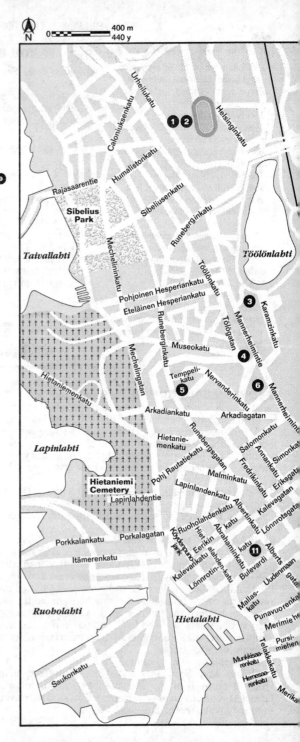

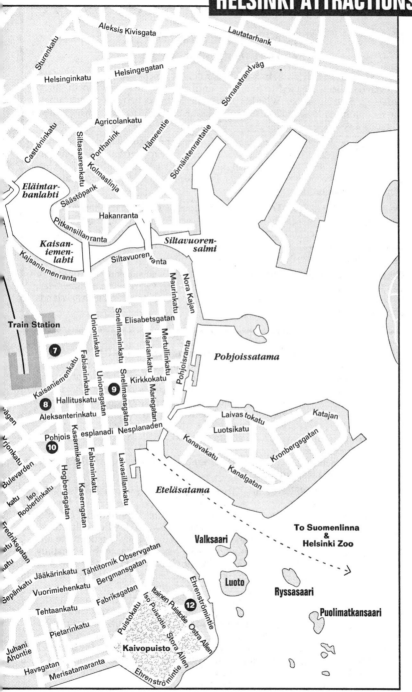

HELSINKI ATTRACTIONS

FROMMER'S FAVORITE
HELSINKI EXPERIENCES

Enjoying a Finnish Sauna   Regardless of where you've bathed before, you haven't been cleaned to the core until you've participated in the local ritual—a Finnish sauna. Whether for giving birth to babies or entertaining Russian ambassadors, the saunatics of Helsinki regard the sauna with almost religious awe.

Hearing a Sibelius Concert   To experience the work of Finland's greatest composer, Jean Sibelius, is a moving experience. This sensitive, vulnerable artist achieved a universal melodic language. In his lifetime, Sibelius and his music became the symbol of Finland, a nation striving for independence and recognition.

Partaking of a Finnish Smörgåsbord   Feast on the harvest of the sea, Baltic herring in a tangy marinade, followed by lightly salted fish and roe, smoked and other cold fish dishes. Then smoked reindeer meat for a touch of Lapland (flavored with lingonberries), and for a finale, a selection of Finnish desserts, including fresh Arctic berries.

Cruising the Archipelago   Since Helsinki is the capital of a country of 188,000 lakes, it, too, is best seen from the water. On a warm summer day, strike out on a cruise through the archipelago, passing innumerable little islands and navigating around peninsulas.

SEURASAARI OPEN-AIR MUSEUM, Seurasaari. Tel. 484-712.
Located on the island of Seurasaari, a national park, this museum is a cluster of about 100 authentically furnished buildings, including a 17th-century church and an 18th-century gentleman's manor. In addition, visitors can see an "aboriginal" sauna, which resembles a smokehouse. A restaurant operates in summer, and on most evenings from June to August (usually on Monday, Tuesday, Thursday, and Sunday nights), there's folk dancing to the tunes of a fiddler.
   Admission: 10 markkaa ($2.75) adults, 5 markkaa ($1.35) children; 25 markkaa ($6.80) for folk dancing.
   Open: May–Sept, daily 11am–5pm. **Bus:** 24 from Erottaja to the island; the 3-mile ride takes about 15 minutes.

GALLEN-KALLELA MUSEUM, Tarvaspää, Gallen-Kallelantie 27, in Espoo. Tel. 513-388.
Located on a wooded peninsula in a suburb of Helsinki, this museum is dedicated to the great Finnish artist Akseli Gallen-Kallela (1865–1931), who built the studio between 1911 and 1913 to his own specifications, calling it his "castle in the air." A restless, fanciful personality, Gallen-Kallela today has a reputation based mainly on his paintings, especially those from the *Kalevala* ("Land of Heroes"). This Finnish national epic, first published in 1835, and often compared to Homer's *Iliad* and *Odyssey*, was illustrated by the artist. He wanted to illustrate all the cantos, but only managed a small part, which rank among the greatest masterpieces of Finnish art. The museum contains a large collection of his paintings, graphics, posters, and industrial design products. A café is beside the museum, in a wooden villa from the 1850s.
   Admission: 20 markkaa ($5.45) adults, 5 markkaa ($1.35) children.
   Open: May 15–Aug, Mon–Thurs 10am–8pm, Fri–Sun 10am–5pm; Sept–May 14, Tues–Sat 10am–4pm, Sun 10am–5pm. **Tram:** 4 to Munkkiniemi; then from Munkkiniemi, take bus no. 33 to Tarvo or walk about 1½ miles along the seaside (bus no. 33 runs Mon–Sat 9:20–11am and 1–3pm).

SUOMENLINNA FORTRESS

⭐ Known as the Gibraltar of the North, this 18th-century fortress (tel. 668-154) lies in the Baltic's archipelago on five interconnected islands guarding the maritime approaches to Helsinki. With their walks and gardens, cafés, restaurants, and old frame buildings, the islands make for one of the most interesting outings from Helsinki. Originally built in the mid-18th century when Finland was a part of Sweden, the fortress was named Sveaborg by the Swedes, and later became known by the Finns and Russians (who took it over in 1808) as Viapori. After Finland gained independence in 1917, it was given its present name, Suomenlinna, which means "the fortress of Finland." It served as a working part of the nation's defenses until 1973.

Today the main attraction is the part of the fortress sited on **Susisaari** and **Kustaanmiekka** islands, which are now joined together as one land body. Specifically, the sights include a small, well-preserved bastioned fort on Kustaanmiekka, with defense walls and tunnels, and another, larger, fortress on Susisaari, which includes a number of parks, squares, and gardens.

You can take a **ferry** from the Market Square to Suomenlinna year round beginning at 6:20am. The boats run at intervals of about an hour, and the last one returns from the island at 1:45am. The round-trip ferry ride costs 15 markkaa ($4.10) for adults, 7 markkaa ($1.90) for children.

The island has no "streets," but individual attractions are signposted.

An **information kiosk** by Tykistolahti Bay is the starting point for **guided tours**—offered in English—of the fortress; you can also buy maps and souvenirs at the kiosk. The tours are offered June through August, daily at 12:30pm and at 2:30pm, and they cost 15 markkaa ($4.10) for adults and 8 markkaa ($2.20) for children.

In addition to the following museums, other sights of Suomenlinna are the **Ryhmateatteri (summer theater),** where plays are performed (in Finnish) at the Good Conscience Bastion (tel. 718-622 for information).

THE MUSEUMS OF SUOMENLINNA

A number of minor museums are found on either Susisaari or the connected island of Kustaanmiekka. These can be explored if you have the time.

COASTAL ARTILLERY MUSEUM, Kustaanmiekka. Tel. 161-5295.

In a vaulted 1776 powder room, this museum contains displays mainly from World Wars I and II. Opened in 1948, the museum is comprehensive, tracing the stages in the defense of Finnish shores from prehistoric times up until today. The weapons for defending the coastline today include missiles, motorized artillery, and turret guns. Also on display are equipment for directing fire, range-finders, and a marine surveillance camera. The newer technology is represented by close-range missiles and a laser range-finder.

Admission: 5 markkaa ($1.35) adults, 2.50 markkaa (70¢) children.
Open: Mid-May to Aug, daily 11am–5pm. **Closed:** Sept to mid-May.

EHRENSVÄRD MUSEUM, Susisaari. Tel. 668-154.

At this historical museum that includes a model ship collection and officers' quarters from the 18th century, there are also displays based on Suomenlinna's military history. The museum bears the name of Augustin Ehrensvärd, who directed construction of the fortress and whose tomb is on Susisaari.

Admission: 6 markkaa ($1.65) adults, 3 markkaa (80¢) children.
Open: May, daily 10am–4pm; June–Sept, daily 10am–5pm. **Closed:** Oct–Apr.

VESIKKO, Susisaari. Tel. 161-15-295.

The submarine *Vesikko* was built in Turku and launched in 1933. Germany had ordered the submarine built for experimental purposes, but Finland bought it in 1936. The submarine fought actively during World War II, and it torpedoed the 4,100-ton Russian ship *Vyborg.* In the Paris peace treaty of 1947, Finland was forbidden to have submarines, and all of them except the *Vesikko* were scrapped. It was opened as a museum in 1973.

Admission: 6 markkaa ($1.65) adults, 3 markkaa (80¢) children.
Open: May, daily 10am–4pm; June–Sept, daily 10am–5pm. **Closed:** Oct–Apr.

ARMFELT MUSEUM, Kustaanmiekka. Tel. 668-131.

A reconstruction of a 19th-century upper-class home in a former barracks. The setting is ideal for its assemblage of porcelain and furniture, much of it dating from the 18th century. The objects exhibited were from a manor house owned by the Armfelts, a distinguished local family.

Admission: 6 markkaa ($1.65) adults, 3 markkaa (80¢) children.
Open: Mid-May to Aug, daily 11am–5:30pm; Sept, Sat–Sun 11am–5:30pm.
Closed: Oct to mid-May.

JETTY BARRACKS GALLERY, Nordic Arts Centre, Susisaari. Tel. 668-143.

This gallery features changing exhibits of Finnish and Scandinavian art, some watercolors, others oil-based. Some of the painters were inspired by scenes in the archipelago.

Admission: Free.
Open: Early Apr to mid-Sept, Tues–Sun 11am–5pm. **Closed:** Mid-Sept to early Apr.

3. MORE ATTRACTIONS

EDUSKUNTATALO (Finnish Parliament), Mannerheimintie 30. Tel. 4321.

A short distance from the post office, this building of red Finnish granite, built in 1931, shelters the 200 members of the one-chamber parliament, one quarter of whose members are women. The building is austere on the outside, but warms up considerably inside—especially in the gallery of nudes. Members meet in a domed cathedral, decorated with sculpture by Wäinö Aaltonen. The architect was J. S. Sirén, whose aim was to celebrate the new republic. He built it in a modernized neoclassic style that some critics found uncomfortably similar to that of Nazi Germany and oddly out of place in a democratic country like Finland. The parliament is open to visitors only when it is not in session.

Admission: Free.
Open: Summer, Mon–Fri at 2pm, Sat at 11am and noon, Sun at noon and 1pm.
Closed: Winter. **Bus:** 69.

LUTHERAN CATHEDRAL, Senaatintori. Tel. 656-365.

Dominating the city's skyline on Senate Square is this green-domed, 19th-century Evangelical-Lutheran cathedral. It was designed by the German-born architect Carl Ludvig Engel when he was planning all the city's public buildings in the neoclassic style during the reconstruction of Helsinki (a fire had destroyed most of the town after the Russian tsar annexed the country in the early 19th century). Considered one of the city's most visible symbols, it was built between 1830 and 1852.

Admission: Free.
Open: May–Sept, Mon–Sat 9am–7pm, Sun noon–7pm; Oct–Apr, Mon–Sat 9am–5pm, Sun noon–5pm. **Tram:** 1, 2.

OLYMPIC STADIUM, Olympiastadion. Tel. 440-363.

Helsinki was host to the Olympic Games in 1952, and leftover from its impressive sports stadium is a tower in which an elevator whisks passengers up for an exciting view of the city as well as the archipelago. The stadium was originally constructed in 1940, but those games were cancelled when war broke out. Outside the stadium is a statue by Wäinö Aaltonen of the great athlete Paavo Nurmi, "the Flying Finn." The runner is depicted in full stride and also completely nude, which caused a lot of controversy when it was unveiled in 1952.

Admission: 5 markkaa ($1.35) adults, 2 markkaa (55¢) children.
Open: Sun–Fri 9am–6pm, Sat 9am–8pm. **Tram:** 3B, 3T, 4, 10. **Closed:** During athletic competitions.

SIBELIUS MONUMENT, Sibelius Park, on Mechelininkatu.

This is a magnificent monument created by sculptor Eila Hiltunen in 1967 in honor of the celebrated Finnish composer Jean Sibelius (1865–1957). The monument is welded into an impressive and rhythmical whole out of hundreds of steel pipes.

Admission: Free.
Open: Daily 24 hours. **Bus:** 18 from railroad station, leaving every 10 minutes.

TEMPPELIAUKIO CHURCH, Lutherinkatu 3. Tel. 494-698.

Built into solid rock and consecrated in 1969, this church, called the "rock church," is about two blocks west of the National Museum in the Töölö residential district west of Mannerheimintie. Only the roof is visible from outside. Two brothers, Tuomo and Timo Suomalainen, were the architects. They selected a rocky outcrop rising some 40 feet above street level. Interior walls were blasted from bedrock. Because of its superb acoustics, the church is often used as a concert hall.

Admission: Free.
Open: Mon–Sat 10am–8pm, Sun noon–2pm and 5–9pm. **Tram:** 3B, 3T.

HELSINKI CITY MUSEUM, at Villa Hakasalmi, Karamizininkatu 2. Tel. 169-3444.

The history of Helsinki from its founding up to modern times is presented. A small-scale model of the town in the 1870s is on display, and there are exhibits of home decorations from the 18th and 19th centuries, glass, porcelain, and toys.

Admission: 5 markkaa ($1.35) adults, 2 markkaa (55¢) children.
Open: Sun–Wed and Fri noon–4pm, Thurs noon–8pm. **Bus:** 69, 69A.

NATIONAL MUSEUM OF FINLAND, Mannerheimintie 34. Tel. 405-01.

Designed in the National Romantic style, this museum opened in 1916 and contains three major sections—prehistoric, historic, and ethnographic. Archeological finds on display reveal that from the earliest days of the Stone Age humans made their homes in Finland. Church art of the medieval and Lutheran periods, folk-culture artifacts, folk costumes and textiles, furniture, and an important coin collection are exhibited, and of particular interest are the Finno-Ugric collections.

Admission: 10 markkaa ($2.75) adults; 5 markkaa ($1.35) children.
Open: Mon and Wed–Sat 11am–3pm, Tues 11am–3pm and 6–9pm, Sun 11am–4pm. **Tram:** 4, 7A, 7B, 10.

HELSINKI ZOO, Korkeasaari Island. Tel. 199-81.

An interesting collection of northern European animals, including a herd of wild forest reindeer, wolverines, northern owl species, and a large number of other mammals and birds from Europe and Asia, can be found here. The Helsinki Card (see "Getting Around," in Chapter 33) covers admission to the zoo and includes free rides on the ferry and the waterbus.

IMPRESSIONS

I became aware at once of the translucent, transparent, pure, elusive, clean, and clinical quality of Helsinki. I began to hate the almost paralyzing perfection of modern buildings, equipment, accommodation, accessories, service.
—James Kirkup, One Man's Russia, 1968

Admission: 26 markkaa ($7.10) adults, 12 markkaa ($3.25) children.
Open: May–Sept, daily 10am–8pm; Oct–Feb, daily 10am–4pm; Mar–Apr, daily 10am–6pm. **Ferry:** From Market Square. **Waterbus:** Leaves from Hakaniem-enranta in front of Merihotelli. **Bus:** 16 (in winter).

KRIEGSMUSEUM (Military Museum), Maurinkatu 1. Tel. 161-6387.

Founded in 1929, this museum records, preserves, and displays material and traditions associated with the Finnish defense forces and with general military history. The museum possesses more than 60,000 items, only some of which can be displayed. Highlights include objects from the days of Swedish rule, as well as collections from the era between the two world wars. An exhibition of particularly gripping photographs from the war years 1939 to 1945 is displayed in the north corridor.

Admission: 3 markkaa (80¢) adults; 1.50 markkaa (40¢) children.
Open: Sun–Fri 11am–3pm. **Bus:** 16, 18.

URHO KEKKONEN MUSEUM, Tamminiemi Seurasaarentie 15. Tel. 480-684.

Urho Kekkonen, the Finnish president who held the longest term in office of any other, from 1956 until 1982, lived at Tamminiemi from the first year he took office until he died of ill health in 1986. Finns are especially fond of visiting this former seat of Scandinavian power, but foreign visitors will find it interesting too, as the house remains just as Kekkonen left it.

Admission: 10 markkaa ($2.75) adults, 5 markkaa ($1.35) children.
Open: May 2–Sept 15, daily 11am–4pm; Sept 16–Apr 30, Mon–Sat 11am–3pm, Sun 11am–4pm. **Bus:** 24 from Erottaja.

PARKS & GARDENS

BOTANICAL GARDENS, University of Helsinki, Unioninkatu 44. Tel. 708-55.

These gardens, a 5-minute walk from the Central Station, feature a large collection of palms, orchids, cacti, and other exotic plants. Outdoors are shrubs and flowers, herbs, ornamentals, Finnish wildflowers, and indigenous trees and bushes.

Admission: Greenhouses, 10 markkaa ($2.75) adults, 5 markkaa ($1.35) children; gardens, free.
Open: Greenhouses, May–Aug, Sat–Wed noon–3pm; Sept–Apr, Sat–Sun noon–3pm. Gardens, daily 7am–9pm.

PIHLAJASAARI RECREATIONAL PARK. Tel. 630-065.

A popular attraction, this park is made up of two small neighboring islands filled with sandy beaches—it's a summer playground for the city. A restaurant and a café are in the park.

Admission: Free.
Open: Daily 24 hours. **Transportation:** Motorboat leaves from the end of Laivurinkatu daily at 9am, 9:30am, and then at hourly intervals until 8:30pm, May to mid-October, depending on weather.

SIBELIUS PARK, Mechelininkatu.

Called Sibeliuksen puisto in Finnish, this park was laid out to honor Jean Sibelius, Finland's most famous composer. The grounds are not particularly manicured, but are instead kept in a somewhat natural state. Old birch trees shade park benches and rocky outcrops divide the landscapes. The park was meant to evoke the rugged natural beauty of Finland itself, as inspired by Sibelius's work *Finlandia*. At one side of the park rises the monumental sculpture, Eila Hiltunen's monument to Sibelius, which was dedicated to the genius whose music was considered to give form to the soul of Finland. The monument was unveiled in 1967, a decade after the composer's death. It is said that it took 6 years to complete. Sibelius is depicted at the peak of his powers and his career.

Admission: Free.
Open: Daily 24 hours. **Tram:** 3B.

4. COOL FOR KIDS

There are a lot of activities of interest to children in Helsinki, not the least of which involves traveling on the **ferryboats and waterbuses** that link the city's various islands and attractions. The Helsinki Card (see "Getting Around," in Chapter 33) entitles them to free admittance or reduced rates at a number of the places visited elsewhere in this chapter. Among these, I have noted that children like the "Helsinki by the Sea" **boat tours** (see "Organized Tours"), the **Helsinki Zoo** (see "More Attractions"), the **Linnanmäki Amusement Park** (see "Evening Entertainment"), the **Pihlajasaari Recreational Park** (see "More Attractions"), **Suomenlinna Fortress** and the model-ship collection in the Ehrensvärd Museum and the submarine *Vesikko* on **Susisaari Island** (see "The Top Attractions"), the outdoor **Swimming Stadium** (see "Recreation"), and many other sights and excursions.

5. SPECIAL-INTEREST SIGHTSEEING

FOR THE ARCHITECTURE LOVER

Hvittrask, in Luoma, Kirrkkonummi (tel. 297-5779), the studio home of architects Eliel Saarinen, Armas Lindgren, and Herman Gesellius, was built of logs and natural stone and ranks among the most remarkable architectural creations of its time. The artistic unity of the house with its forest surroundings was considered a highly influential achievement. Today it is used as a center for exhibits of Finnish art and handcrafts. A first-rate restaurant, Hvittrask (tel. 297-6033) is open on Monday from noon to 8pm, Tuesday through Thursday from noon to 11pm, on Friday from noon to 8pm, and on Saturday and Sunday from noon to 8pm.

Admission is 10 markkaa ($2.75) for adults, 5 markkaa ($1.35) for students. It's open May to August, Monday through Friday from 10am to 7pm and on Saturday and Sunday from 11am to 6pm. To get there, take bus no. 166 from the central bus station, Platform 62, then walk about 1¼ miles. Or take the train to Luoma, then walk about 1¼ miles. By car, follow the Jorvas motorway about 12¼ miles, turn off at the Kivenlahti exit, drive 3 miles in the direction of Kauklahti, and then follow the Hvittrask signs.

Perhaps the most model of the model communities of Scandinavia is **Tapiola,** a self-contained city-within-a-city 6 miles west of Helsinki in the capital's neighbor, Espoo. This garden city is filled with parks, splashing fountains, handsomely designed homes and apartments, shopping centers, playgrounds, schools, and churches. In the center of Tapiola is a large office building with a self-service cafeteria on top (a good choice for lunch). To get here, take bus no. 52 or 53 marked TAPIOLA; the buses from the bus station leave about every 10 minutes.

WALKING TOUR — Downtown Helsinki

Start: Senate Square.
Finish: Helsinki Railway Station.
Time: Allow 3 hours, not including museum and shopping stops.
Best Times: Any day it's not raining.

Worst Times: Between 8 and 9:30am and 5 and 6:30pm, because of the heavy traffic.

The tour begins at:

1. **Senate Square,** at the base of the monument to Russian Tsar Alexander II, erected in his honor shortly after the annexation of Finland. Helsinki's most historic and beautiful square was designed in the early 1800s at the height of the Russian Empire's fascination with the architectural glories of ancient Greece and Rome. The designer was Berlin-born Carl Ludvig Engel, who had created other public buildings in St. Petersburg (now Leningrad). The:

2. **Lutheran Cathedral,** Senate Square, stands on the north side of the square. Capped with triplicate statues of saints, it has four small cupolas ringing its central dome.

As you face the cathedral, the Senate, capped by a low dome, and graced by six Corinthian columns, is on your right. Opposite the cathedral, on the south side of the square, stands the yellow ocher facade and Ionic columns of a house from 1762 which was redesigned by Engel.

Leaving the square, ascend the steeply inclined Unioninkatu, skirting the right-hand (western) edge of the square. The street was dedicated to the tsar in 1819 and, because of its difficult terrain, considered extremely expensive at the time of its construction. The elegantly graceful building opposite the western facade of the cathedral is the:

3. **Library of the University of Helsinki.** Some critics consider this the most beautiful of the many buildings created by Engel. Admire its rhythmically repetitive Corinthian pilasters and columns before continuing uphill. At the northwestern corner of the cathedral's rear side rises the spire of the:

4. **Russian Orthodox Church of the Holy Trinity,** with an ocher-colored facade. Designed by Engel in 1827, it has an artfully skewed Orthodox double cross placed above its doorway.

After passing Kirkkokatu, turn right (east) onto Rauhankatu. The statue of the young girl, set onto a porphyry base near the corner, is named *Dawn* and the gray-fronted modern building serving as the statue's backdrop contains the printing presses and engravers' shops for banknotes issued by the Bank of Finland. Continue east on the same street, passing an ornately neoclassical building with a trio of wise women set on its pediment. This is the storage space for the:

5. **Finnish State Archives,** originally designed in 1890. As they grew, they were greatly expanded with annexes and underground vaults.

At the corner of Snellmaninkatu, turn right. The russet-fronted temple with four Corinthian columns and a single acanthus leaf at the pinnacle of its pediment is the:

6. **House of Scientific Studies,** erected in 1891. Just below its heraldic plaques is a heroic frieze cast in solid bronze, paying homage to the generosity of Tsar Alexander II, who promised to retain the internal laws and religion of Finland after its 1809 annexation. For many years the frieze was the largest bronze casting in Finland. Across the Snellmaninkatu is a somber gray building set above a steep embankment—the central headquarters of the:

7. **Bank of Finland,** designed by a Russian-German architect, Bohnsted, in 1892. In front of the bank stands a statue of the Finnish statesman J. V. Snellman, the patriot whose life was devoted to placing Finnish legally on the same linguistic footing with Swedish. Snellman was also responsible for replacing Russian rubles with Finnish markkaa as the official currency of the country.

Continue to walk downhill along Snellmaninkatu, skirting the eastern edge of the cathedral's outbuildings. Shortly you'll reenter Senate Square. Proceed to the bottom of the square and turn left onto Aleksanterinkatu. At no. 14 on that street, behind a russet-colored 1823 facade, is the:

8. **Official residence of the Lord Mayor of Helsinki,** standing next door to the Theater Museum at Aleksanterinkatu 12.

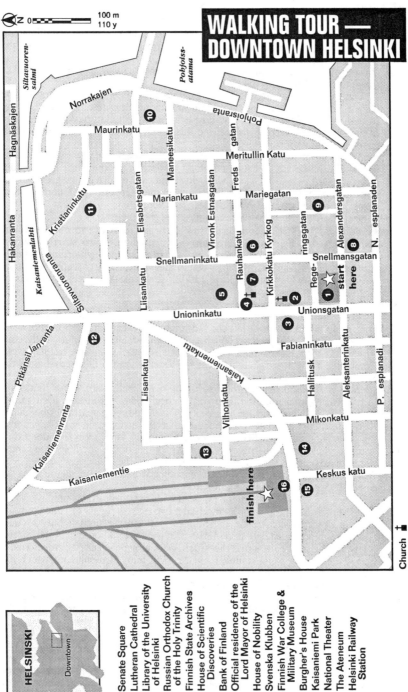

WALKING TOUR —
DOWNTOWN HELSINKI

100 m
110 y

Siltavuoren-salmi
Pohjoissatama
Norrakajen
Maurinkatu
Meritullin Katu
Pohjoisranta
Maneesikatu
Elisabetsgatan
Mariankatu
Mariegatan
Freds gatan
Vironk Estnasgatan
Snellmaninkatu
Rauhankatu
Kirkkokatu Kyrkog
Rege-ringsgatan
Alexandersgatan
N. esplanaden
Snellmansgatan
Kristianinkatu
Hakanranta
Hagnäskajen
Kaisaniemenlahti
Siltavuorenranta
Liisankatu
Unioninkatu
Unionsgatan
Fabianinkatu
Kaisaniemenkatu
Aleksanterinkatu
Hallitusk
P. esplanadi
Mikonkatu
Keskus katu
Kaisaniemenranta
Pitkänsillanranta
Liisankatu
Vilhonkatu
Kaisaniementie
start here
finish here
Church

Continue walking east along Aleksanterinkatu. In a short time you'll enter a small gate dotted with a handful of birch trees. Behind the trees rises the Neo-Venetian facade of the:

9. House of Nobility, completed in 1861 as a private club and the reunion hall of the Finnish and Russian aristrocracy.

Walk along Aleksanterinkatu, crossing Marinakatu, and continue toward the harbor. Some of the buildings along here are among the oldest in Helsinki, dating from the 1760s. At the waterfront, turn left onto Meritullintori, skirting the edge of the harbor. A sweeping vista of the Russian Orthodox Uspenski Kathedralen (cathedral) comes into view.

At this point the street changes its name to Pohjoisranta, and continues to follow the harborfront. Continue along this street to the third intersection, Maneeskikatu, where the quay will widen into a formal park, ringed with art nouveau buildings, some of the finest in Helsinki. On the park's northwestern corner, behind a stately Edwardian facade is your:

REFUELING STOP Until just a few years ago, entrance to the prestigious social club, **10. Svenska Klubben,** at Maurinkatu 6, was strictly reserved only for members. Today, in more egalitarian times, its high-ceilinged dining room and Edwardian elegance are open to the public, many of whom revel in its enviable history. Originally built in 1900, it serves meals, coffee, and drinks to visitors.

After your refreshment, exit from the club's front door and, facing the park once again, notice on your left the red-brick Neo-Victorian mass of the:

11. Finnish War College and Military Museum, Liisankatu, originally constructed as a barracks in the 1880s. Turn left onto Liisankatu, heading west. Completed in 1813, the street honored the Russian Tsarina Elisabeth (Liisa is the Finnish version of Elisabeth).

Take the second right, turning uphill onto Meritullinkatu. Cross (but don't turn onto) Kulmakatu. At this point, Meritullinkatu transforms itself into a pedestrians-only walkway for residents of the surrounding apartment buildings. At the dead end, turn left and negotiate a narrow, elevated sidewalk high above the street running below (Kristianinkatu). One block later, cross (but don't turn onto) Kulmakatu. A few paces later, at Kristininkatu 12, you'll see the simple stone foundation and ocher-colored clapboards of the:

12. Burger's House, Helsinki's oldest remaining wooden house, dating from the early 1800s and now housing a minor museum.

A few steps later, Kristianinkatu dead-ends at a pedestrians-only sidewalk, Oikokatu. Go right (downhill), descending two narrow flights of concrete stairs heading toward the lake. At the bottom, you emerge onto a busy avenue, Siltavuorenranta; turn left and notice the stylish bulk of the Hotel Strand Inter-Continental rising across the water. Walk along the curving embankment for a while, coming to the tramway and car traffic hub of Unioninkatu, which you should cross. You'll then enter:

13. Kaisaniemi Park ("The Company Keeping Park"), beloved by residents of Helsinki. Until the 1830s this tract of waterfront land was only a marshy bogland until it was drained and opened as Helsinki's first park. The park contains the Botanical Gardens of the University of Helsinki, which date from 1833.

Walk through the park, flanking the water on your right, and then follow the natural left-bending southward curve of the park's main path. Don't cross any of the railway tracks. After exiting from the park, your path will become Lantinen Teatterikuja, in a neighborhood of art nouveau apartment buildings. Follow the street for a block through the theatrical headquarters of Finland. On your left stands the:

14. National Theater, vaguely reminiscent of the Opera House in Vienna. Note the decorative sculptures on its facade, especially the representation of bears. The theater was designed by the architect Tarjanne, in 1902. Across the square, immediately opposite the National Theater, is:

15. The Ateneum, designed by Hoijer and completed in 1887. Its interior contains the best art museum in Finland (closed for restoration as of this writing). The western side of the square (to your right as you face the Ateneum) is one of the most famous public buildings in Europe, the:

16. Helsinki Railway Station, designed by Eliel Saarinen in 1916. The sculptures are evocative of the monumental works of Pharaonaic Egypt. It has been copied endlessly ever since by avant-garde set designers of plays and films, including *Batman.*

At the end of this tour you will have walked 2 miles.

6. ORGANIZED TOURS

CITY TOURS   A city tour lasting 1½ hours is offered by **Suomen Turistianto Oy,** at Mannerheimintie 97 (tel. 588-5166); it departs at 11am and 1pm and costs 50 markkaa ($13.65) for adults and 25 markkaa ($6.80) for children 12 or under. The tour takes in the most important city sights, including the Sibelius Monument. Tickets can be purchased on the bus 15 minutes before departure.

For an **orientation sightseeing trip** without a guide, catch tram no. 3T which takes you by 35 major buildings and monuments of the city. The 45-minute trip is conducted only in summer. Tram no. 3T may be boarded in front of the railway station or at the Market Square Monday through Saturday from 6am to 1am and on Sunday from 7:30am to 1am. It leaves regularly every 5 to 15 minutes, costing 6.50 markkaa ($1.80) for adults, 2.50 markkaa (70¢) for children 12 or under.

HARBOR TOUR   Try to schedule your time to take the **Helsinki by the Sea,** a guided boat tour from the South Harbor, around the islands of Suomenlinna, Kulosaari, and Seurasaari. The tour operates from June to August, daily at 11am, noon, and 1, 2, 3, and 4pm, taking 1½ hours. Departures are from Market Square. **Royal Line,** Jokipolku 2 (tel. 358-228), operates the tour. It costs 47 markkaa ($12.80) for adults; children pay half price.

7. SPECIAL/FREE EVENTS

The **Helsinki Festival** is a highlight of the Finnish summer and a prelude to the capital city's generous autumn arts program. Attracting international artists, the festival is held at the end of August and the beginning of September. The nearly 3-week-long program offers concerts, opera, ballet, theater, films, exhibitions, jazz, and pop music. The main stage is the Finlandia Hall, Helsinki's concert and convention center opened in 1971. The Helsinki Festival, a member of the European Association of Music Festivals, is preceded by the **Helsinki Summer Concerts** in July. Further details may be obtained from Helsinki Festival, Unioninkatu 28, SF-00100 Helsinki (tel. 90/659-688). The hotel situation is rather difficult in Helsinki during the festival season, so travelers should make their reservations well in advance.

A free event popular with all visitors—is the **Changing of the Guard** at the Main Guard Post, behind the President's Palace every day at 1pm. It doesn't match the changing of the guard at Buckingham Palace, but it's a well-attended and much-photographed event, nevertheless.

8. RECREATION

Major sports events take place at the **Olympic Stadium,** Etälainen Stadionintie 3 (tel. 440-363), with its 236-foot tower which was designed by Yrjö Lindegren and Toivo Jäntti. In front is a nude statue of gold-medal runner Paavo Nurmi, called "The Flying Finn." In summer, soccer games between Finland and other countries of Europe are scheduled. *Helsinki This Week* publishes a program of events taking place at the stadium at the time of your visit. Tram: 3T.

HORSEBACK RIDING There are some strictly private riding stables close to Helsinki, but most of these clubs require references and membership. The best bet for riding devotees lies 37 miles west of Helsinki in the town of Vihti. **Vihdinratsastuskeskus,** Pääkslahti, SF-03400 Vihti (tel. 90/224-4676), is a privately owned stable enjoying a good reputation with the Finnish Equestrian Foundation. At the stable you can rent one of about a dozen horses for between 80 and 100 markkaa ($21.80 and $27.25) per hour. You can ride within a covered rink or—weather permitting—go for a trail ride through the surrounding forests. Telephone in advance for more details and reservations.

JOGGING To keep fit, Finns are just as fond of jogging as Americans or Canadians. The best paths are close to **Olympic Stadium** (see above) and in **Kaivopuisto Park** in the southern part of Helsinki. There are also some good jogging trails around **Hesperia Park,** which is the most convenient if you're staying at a hotel in the city center.

SAUNAS & SWIMMING POOLS Most of the hotels recommended have public saunas, which guests rent individually or with others to share the expense. If your hotel doesn't have a sauna, go to the outdoor **Swimming Stadium,** Hammarsk-jöldintie (tel. 402-9383), which is open only July through September, daily from 9am to 8pm. The charge is 10 markkaa ($2.75) for adults and 2 markkaa (55¢) for children.

Another sauna more centrally located is in the cellar level of the **Ramada Presidentti Hotel,** Eteläinen Rautatiekatu 4 (tel. 69-11). Nonresidents at Ramada can rent the entire sauna—suitable for a group of friends—for 1½ hours at a cost of 100 markkaa ($27.25), plus a 35-markka ($9.55) charge for each participant.

Far more interesting would be to go 5 miles north of Helsinki to a point on the windswept, often fog-bound Gulf of Finland. There you can visit the ✪ **Suomen Sauna Seura (Finnish Sauna Association),** at the end of Vaskenimemetie in the district of Vaskiniemi Lauttasaari (tel. 678-677), which, though it's technically a private club, welcomes foreign visitors. Established in 1937, it is the oldest (and perhaps only) sauna society in Finland. The society maintains four saunas, each of them authentically wood-burning, and each requiring a 5- to 6-hour warmup daily. Two of the four saunas are old-fashioned "smoke saunas." A wharf is built into the gulf for swimming. In winter, a hole is chopped into the ice to allow year-round bathing. No one wears bathing suits at this ritual. The association is open for men on Tuesday, Wednesday, and Friday from 2 to 8pm for men, and on Saturday from noon to 6pm. On Thursday, it is reserved for women and open from 1 to 8pm. It is closed Sunday and Monday, and the month of July. Entrance for nonmembers is 65 markkaa ($17.75). To reach it from the Svenska Theater off Mannerheimintie, take bus no. 20.

For year-round swimming, try **Keskusta Pool,** Yrjönkatu 21 (tel. 60-981), in the city center near the Forum Shopping Center. It divides its time among men and women; usually men swim in the morning and women in the afternoon, but call for the schedule before going. The cost for a swim, a sauna, and a towel is 20 markkaa ($5.45). Tram: 3B.

SKIING From January to March, cross-country skiing is popular in the Helsinki area. You can rent equipment—usually around 100 markkaa ($27.25) per day for skis, boots, and poles—at **Stadion Retkeilymaja,** Pohjois Stadionintie 3B (tel. 496-071).

TENNIS   The best bet for playing tennis in Helsinki is to travel 6 miles west of the center to the Pitäjämäki district. There the **Tali SportsCenter,** Kutonokuja 3, Pitäjämäki (tel. 556-271), welcomes foreign visitors. The center maintains 10 indoor tennis courts and 6 outdoor courts. In winter, 5 of the 6 outdoor courts are covered with a plastic "bubble." A reserved court ranges from 46 to 84 markkaa ($12.55 to $22.90) per hour. You can rent a tennis racquet for 10 markkaa ($2.75) and buy tennis balls once you're there. Take bus no. 14 or 39 from the center of the city. It's open daily from 6am to 10:30pm, but call first to see if courts are free before going there.

9. SAVVY SHOPPING

Finland has taken a bold, creative lead in the highly competitive world of interior design. Search out ceramics and glassware (Arabia is famous), hand-woven articles, hand-carved wood, jaunty fashions, and rugs (don't walk on a *ryijy*—hang it on the wall).

Textiles and jewelry also bear the distinctive stamp of Finland, and toy stores brim with educational toys for each stage of a child's development. Among souvenirs, the range includes decorations made from reindeer skin, costume dolls, baskets, and pungently unusual berry liqueurs made from the yellow cloudberry, the cranberry, and the Arctic brambleberry. Of course, you'll find all your sauna needs here as well.

THE SHOPPING SCENE

Most stores are open Monday through Friday from 9am to 5pm and on Saturday from 9am to 2pm. Sometimes stores stay open until 4pm on Saturday, especially in the summer months.

SHOPPING AREAS   The most important shopping neighborhoods are in the center of the city. These include **Esplanadi,** for those seeking the finest of Finnish design (but at high prices). Even if you don't buy anything, it's a delightful street for promenading in summer. Airline offices, banks, and travel agencies share the street with shops filled with the best of Finnish crafts, as well as a number of art galleries.

Esplanadi leads from the commercial heart of town all the way to the waterfront. At the bottom of the street, bordering the water, is **Market Square (Kauppatori),** a fresh open-air market open Monday through Saturday. In summer, peddlers set up trolleys and tables to display their wares. Most of the items for sale are produce (some of them ideal for picnic makings), but some souvenir and gift items also appear.

The other main shopping section is called simply **Central,** beginning at Esplanadi and stretching to the famous Helsinki Railway Station. Many of the big names in Finnish shopping are here, none more notable than the Stockmann Department Store. Many shopping complexes are also in this district, including Forum. One of the main streets for shopping in the district is **Aleksanterinkatu,** running parallel to Esplanadi, stretching from the harborfront to Mannerheimintie.

Other shopping streets, all in the center, include **Iso-Roobertinkatu** and **Bulevardi,** lying off Esplanadi. Bulevardi, starting at the Klaus Kurki Hotel, winds its way to the water.

Nearly all stores arrange shipment of large purchases.

RECOVERING TAX   Tax-free shopping is available at stores which display FINLAND TAX-FREE SHOPPING signs in their windows. This tax-free shopping is available to all visitors who reside outside the Nordic countries. The purchase tax on articles bought in these shops is refunded to you when you leave Finland. The tax-free minimum purchase is 200 markkaa ($54.55).

Most main department stores and shops will send your purchases directly to your home address. That way you avoid having to file a claim at Customs. If you take the merchandise with you, ask for a check for the tax amount. This check can be cashed at the airport or harbor from which you depart. The savings works out at about 11% and applies to both cash and credit-card purchases. However, should you use the goods before leaving Finland, you will forfeit the tax refund. Most international credit cards, such as American Express or VISA, are accepted at major shops, but always ask beforehand.

If you have any questions about the tax-free shopping scheme, contact **Finland Tax-Free Shopping,** Yrjönkatu 29C (tel. 693-2433).

A PREVIEW OF FINNISH DESIGN Before you begin to shop, you might want to have an overview of Finnish design in this century. Go to the **Museum of Applied Crafts,** Korkeavuorenkatu 23 (tel. 174-455), which is open daily except Monday from 11am to 5pm, charging 10 markkaa ($2.75) for adults and 5 markkaa ($1.35) for children. In what used to be a schoolhouse, the museum has on permanent display the best of Finnish design in wood, textiles, ceramics, glass, and other materials.

SHOPPING A TO Z
ART GALLERIES

BRONDA GALLERY, Kasarmikatu 44. Tel. 626-494.

This is a well-established gallery, with an always-interesting range of paintings for sale. Sculpture is also exhibited, but rarely. Paintings come from different countries. Sometimes one country, such as Spain, is highlighted as part of a temporary exhibition. The gallery is on the street level of a modern building. Tram: 3B.

GALLERY STRINDBERG, Pohjoisesplanadi 33. Tel. 628-404.

Originally established in 1898, this is the oldest art gallery in all of Scandinavia. It sells mostly paintings—both antique and modern—as well as a smattering of sculpture. This is the doyen of Finnish art galleries, and one with the most prestigious collection. Tram: 3B.

BOOKS

ACADEMIC BOOKSTORE, Keskuskatu 1. Tel. 121-41.

Sprawling over two floors crammed with books in many different languages, this store, from the number of titles in stock, is the largest bookstore in Europe. It offers many English-language books, along with a number of travel aids. It also carries the finest stationery department in Finland and sells greeting cards as well as high-quality gift and hobby articles. If you're here on a Friday, you can attend a literary get-together which assembles writers and members of the reading public, held in the store. All of Finland's major authors and leading politicians, as well as many foreign writers, including Kurt Vonnegut and Liv Ullman, have attended these meetings. The building, with large skylit windows and Carrara marble slabs, was designed by Alvar Aalto. Tram: 3B.

DEPARTMENT STORES

STOCKMANN, Aleksanterinkatu 52. Tel. 176-181.

Helsinki's largest department store is also Finland's finest and oldest. Its main entrance is on Aleksanterinkatu, with other entrances on Keskuskatu and Mannerheimintie. Stockmann has a little bit of everything, the most diversified sampling of Finnish and imported merchandise of any store—the glassware, stoneware, ceramics, lamps, furniture, furs, contemporary jewelry, clothes and textiles, handmade candles, reindeer hides—everything. Purchases made through the store's Export Service grant you a full and immediate 16% deduction, and you don't have to carry your purchases home yourself. It maintains small shops at the airport, the Hotel Kalastajatorppa, and the Hotel Inter-Continental. In 1981 it also opened a store in Tapiola at Länsituulentie 5. Tram: 3B.

FASHION

ANNIKKI KARVINEN, Pohjoisesplanadi 33. Tel. 633-837.

Ms. Karvinen became famous for elevating *poppana*, Finnish cotton, into the stellar peaks of fashion. All poppana fabrics are hand-woven, and she has adapted the same style to velvet, silk, and wool for more formal and more expensive fashion. She designs jackets for both indoors and outdoors. In addition, her outlet offers a number of household items for sale, including tablecloths and bedspreads. Tram: 3B.

LENA REWELL TEXTILE SHOP, Yrjönkatu 14B. Tel. 649-070.

Each of the richly textured woolens in this shop was designed by one of Finland's best-known textile designers. Since 1960 Lena Rewell's softly colored coats, hats, scarves, gloves, and sweaters have been exported throughout Europe and America. Two of her most popular items are the hand-woven mohair blankets and wrap-around stoles. You must call before going and arrange an appointment, at which time you will be shown around her studio. Tram: 3B.

MARIMEKKO, Pohjoisesplanadi 31. Tel. 177-944.

Ever since Jacqueline Kennedy in the early 1960s was photographed in Marimekko clothing, the name has been a familiar one to Americans. Meaning "Mary's frock," Marimekko offers large-scale prints in vivid colors splashed against the gray Finnish landscape of winter. The company was founded in 1951 by Armi Ratia, and now includes a collection of unusually textured fabrics sold by the yard for decorating homes and offices. Equally important are the knitted sportswear, placemats, and many other goods that are sold here, including Marimekko's famous knitted T-shirts and dresses. The inventory of shirts and colors changes with the season. Tram: 3B.

PENTIK, Pohjoisesplanadi 27. Tel. 625-558.

This outlet sells clothes, usually for women, made of leather and suede products from Finland. Other garments, especially the silks and cottons, come from Italy. They offer a few items of clothing, including some jackets, for men, but their main specialty is catering to style-conscious women. Tram: 3B.

FURNITURE

ARTEK, Keskuskatu 3. Tel. 177-533.

Established in 1935, Artek offers furniture based on designs of the late, great architect Alvar Aalto. His first models were avant-garde pieces designed in the late '20s and early '30s. Today they are considered classics, representing the best of their era. Aalto's works include the Paimio chair, with a laminated birch frame and his famous three-legged birch stool. Seats of the latter are often traditionally covered in black leather, but you can also get them in veneered ash. Designs by his wife, Aino, are also for sale, including pressed-glass tumblers and pitchers she made in the Bolgeblick pattern for the Karhula glassworks in 1932. In addition to furnishings, the store sells lamps, ceramics, glassware, tableware, and textiles. Tram: 3B.

SOKEAIN MYYMALA, Annankatu 16. Tel. 604-893.

The work of blind people, this is an impressive collection of unusual and well-designed furniture in rattan. The furnishings have style and flair, and are suited to both indoor and outdoor living. Tram: 3B.

GLASS, PORCELAIN & CERAMICS

ARABIA, Pohjoisesplanadi 25. Tel. 170-055.

This shop gathers together under one roof the products of some of the world's most prestigious manufacturers of household porcelain and art ceramics. Most of the products are made by Arabia, although some glass and art glass by Nuutajarvi is also offered. Located in the center of Helsinki's most prestigious shopping district, it inventories first-rate household goods designed by Finland's leading designers. The multilingual staff can arrange for any of your purchases to be mailed overseas.

Arabia was established in a suburb of Helsinki (Arabia) in 1873. Today its ceramic factories are among the most modern in the world. Arabia's artists create their own works of art, sometimes in highly collectible limited editions.

Although most visitors purchase their goods at the company's main store (see above), Arabia maintains a small museum and a spacious discount sales area at its factory in the environs of Helsinki at Hameentie 135 (tel. 39-391). Take tram no. 6 to the end of the line to reach it. Here, discontinued styles as well as slightly imperfect seconds are sold—always at a serious reduction off the regular prices. Tram: 3B.

I-SHOP, Pohjoisesplanadi 27A. Tel. 663-305.

i-Shop is the local representative of a glassworks that has been in business for a century. The factory is Iittala, founded in 1881. In 1936 it produced, for example, Alvar Aalto's famed Savoy vase, which has now become the company's signature. You can purchase reproductions of the vase in four colors, including cobalt blue or opal white, in many different sizes. In 1981 Iittala merged with the equally famous Nuutajarvi glassworks, which was founded in 1793. i-Shop also carries that firm's best offerings.

Aalto's organic vases are classic standards within the repertoires of Finnish design, but this retail outlet also keeps abreast of changing styles and fashions, occasionally introducing the works of new designers. Many shoppers prefer the Kolibri series of unadorned wineglasses by Timo Sarpaneva. If you have the time, you can ask the shop to direct you to their factory outside town. There you can often find slightly flawed "seconds" at about 30% off the regular retail price. You can also go on a guided tour of the factory, although it's a good idea to arrange the details with the shop before you go. Tram: 3B.

HANDCRAFTS

AARIKKA, Pohjoisesplanadi 27. Tel. 652-277.

One of Finland's best selections of wooden toys for children is found here. Many different and unusual household utensils, each fashioned from wood, are also sold. The shop also sells gifts made in Finland, along with a selection of jewelry. Tram: 3B.

ARTISAANI, Unioninkatu 28. Tel. 665-225.

Near the Market Place, Artisaani is a cooperative of artisans who sell their own arts and crafts fresh from their country workshops. Ceramic sculptures, pottery, glassware, gold, silver, and bronze jewelry, leather goods, printed fabrics, and other textiles are displayed. Tram: 3B.

KALEVALA KORU [LAHJAVAKKA], Unioninkatu 25. Tel. 171-520.

Although this store is best known for its collection of jewelry, it sells a fine collection of handcrafts and gifts as well. Its most visible offering is knitwear, which usually comes in both traditional and modern designs. In inventory are knit dresses, coats, pullovers, caps, and mittens for both men and women. Designs from Lapland are usually dyed in subtle colors with naturally produced vegetable and mineral dyes, while the traditional garments from the folkloric regions of Finland's farmland are usually accented with more colorful stripes and patterns. Also for sale are a collection of handmade ceramic ornaments (usually designed to be hung from the top of a window), wood carvings, rugs, and unusual textiles sold by the yard. Tram: 3B.

RYIJYPALVELU, Kasarmikatu 34, Esplanadia. Tel. 660-615.

A crowded and well-stocked second-floor shop specializing in Finnish weavings called *ryas,* it is operated as a charitable foundation by the Women's Organization of the Disabled War Veteran's Association, as an assistance program for the many veterans disabled in Finland's bloody wars. The traditional and modern Finnish rugs that are sold here range in size from about 3 by 5 feet to 5 by 7 feet or larger. The rugs can be bought ready-woven for about $800 to $1,450, or you can buy them as kits to produce the same rugs at home. The kits cost about a third as much as the finished products. Tram: 3B.

SUOMEN KÄSITYÖN YSTÄVÄT (Friends of Finnish Handcraft), Tamminiementie 3. Tel. 482-010.

Suomen Käsityön Ystävät was founded in 1879 to maintain and develop the traditions of Finnish handcrafts. The center of activity is in an old villa about 3 miles from the city center. Here you can see a permanent exhibition of museum-quality *ryijy* tapestries. Textiles, table linens, towels, and gift items, such as shawls and embroidered work, including early 20th-century Jugendstil patterns, can be purchased here. Export service is available. Bus: 24 from the Swedish Theater at Erottaja, the terminus.

JEWELRY

GALERIE BJÖRN WECKSTRÖM, Unioninkatu 30. Tel. 655-529.

Specializing in Lapponia jewelry, as well as in sculpture and glass, this store has won Grand Prix prizes in international jewelry competitions. Björn Weckström has earned a reputation for making shapes inspired by nature, and the jewelry sold here has been called miniature sculpture. The glass collection of bowls, bottles, and dishes sometimes comes in lovely, mysterious colors whose exact ingredients remain a secret of the manufacturer. Tram: 3B.

KALEVALA KORU, Unioninkatu 25. Tel. 171-520.

Founded in 1937, this store is owned by the Association of Kalevala Women in Finland, whose aim is to preserve the best cultural traditions of a long-ago Finland. They accomplish this through educational programs and through sales of the most authentic reproductions of traditional designs and styles they can find. (See "Handcrafts," above, for some of their offerings.) The name of their organization is derived from the *Kalevala,* the Finnish national epic.

The store sells both traditional and modern jewelry in bronze, silver, and gold. Many of these pieces are based on originals uncovered in archeological excavations that date from the 10th and 11th centuries. Each is produced by some of Finland's foremost artisans. Copies of Lapp jewelry are also sold. The store works in close cooperation with the Finnish National Museum. Tram: 3B.

MUSIC

DIGELIUS MUSIC SHOP, Laivurinrinne 2. Tel. 666-375.

Offering a complete selection of both Finnish jazz and Finnish folk music, this shop is not the biggest music store in Helsinki, but it has one of the most knowledgeable and helpful English-speaking staffs. They are familiar with their stock, and are well informed about Finland's musical history. Tram: 3B.

FUGA, Unioninkatu 28. Tel. 631-181.

One of the best record stores in Helsinki, it has a good collection of classical records from all over Europe, as well as folk music recordings and a smattering of jazz. One of the two Nuotio brothers will advise. Tram: 3B.

SAUNA

SAUNA SOPPI-SHOP, Aleksan-terinkatu 28. Tel. 634-733.

Two Finnish women established this shop in 1974 because they believe in the therapeutic and emotional benefits of sauna rituals. Everything they sell is functionally important to the sauna. They offer buckets, ladles, thermometers, linen seatcovers, washing mitts, door labels saying SAUNA, loincloths, and even a sauna-related "visitors' book." This is perhaps the most complete selection of sauna-related articles in the world. Tram: 3B.

SCULPTURE

SCULPTORA, Yrjönkatu 11. Tel. 646-903.

The organization that maintains this store, the Association of Finnish Sculptors, was originally established in 1910. Today it's the oldest association of artists in Finland, comprising 200 carefully screened members. This gallery exhibits only works by members, each of whom is Finnish. Only the work of living artists, or the work of artists deceased in the past 2 years, is exhibited. Sculptures are crafted from wood, bronze, stone, plastic, aluminum, steel, or ceramics. The range is from small medallions to monumental pieces. Tram: 3B.

SHOPPING COMPLEXES

FORUM, Mannerheimintie 20.

Stretching for one block, Forum shelters 120 shops, restaurants, and service enterprises—making it the No. 1 shopping center in Finland. An atrium rises seven stories high. You'll find a wide array of merchandise for sale here—art, gold, jewelry, food, decorating items, clothing, yarns, leather, records, glasses, rugs, watches, and sporting goods, to cite only some of the items. Shops are open Monday through Friday from 9am to 8pm and on Saturday from 9am to 5pm. Cafés and restaurants are also open on Sunday to 5pm. Tram: 3B, 3T, 7A, 7B.

SPECIALTY SHOPS

SENAATTI CENTER, Aleksanterinkatu 22-28.

This recently renovated shopping quarter in the old center of Helsinki, located between the cathedral and Market Square, contains a group of small, specialized shops selling lots of unique gifts. The complex has another entrance on Unioninkatu and Sofiankatu and is open Monday through Friday from 10am to 6pm, on Saturday from 10am to 3pm, and on Sunday from noon to 4pm. Tram: 3B.

STAMPS

SUOMEN POSTIMERKKEILY OY, Ludviginkatu 5. Tel. 642-501.

This shop's owner, Ilppo Ylismaa, is considered Finland's leading authority on his country's postage stamps. His shop stocks and specializes in Finnish stamps "from the beginning"—in this case, from 1856. Those first stamps were issued with a portrait of the Russian tsar. This shop, established in 1943 during the darkest days of World War II, is the headquarters for many stamp auctions and sales. Tram: 3B.

YARD GOODS

VERHO SELLGREN, Frederikinkatu 33. Tel. 645-979.

This outlet sells an attractive assortment of yard goods for interior designs, most of it for curtains and upholstery. Most fabrics are woven—not always by hand—in Finland and are sold by the meter. Tram: 3B.

10. EVENING ENTERTAINMENT

Nightlife is not the reason to visit Suomi, although there are the usual restaurants with three- or four-piece bands. Finland has few nightclubs with shows.

THE ENTERTAINMENT SCENE

Nightlife in Finland is primarily the domain of the young, who flock to what they call "nightclubs," but which people in other parts of the world call "discos." Friday and Saturday nights are impossibly overcrowded, and if you're going out at all, you should show up early at a club—or risk not getting in. The older crowd sticks mainly to bars in the more popular hotels, such as the Strand Inter-Continental. Gambling is strictly small stakes, not for the serious devotee, but useful to beginners for learning the rules and rituals of the gambling process.

Theater is confined almost exclusively to the Finnish or Swedish languages. However, music is universal, and the Helsinki cultural landscape is always rich in music, either winter or summer. The major orchestral or concert performances take place in Finlandia Hall (see below). Operas at the Finnish National Opera are sung in their own languages.

The main agency for concert and opera tickets is **Musiikki-Fazer,** Aleksanterinkatu (tel. 560-11). Another agency for tickets to the opera, concerts, theater, and cinema is **Lippupalvelu,** Mannerheimintie 5 (tel. 643-043), in the Forum Shopping Complex.

Your best source of information—virtually your only source other than Finnish newspapers—is a little magazine called *Helsinki This Week,* distributed free at most hotels and at the tourist office. It has complete listings, not only of cultural events, but virtually anything that's happening in the Finnish capital—from the Baltic herring market to body-building contests.

THE PERFORMING ARTS
THE MAJOR PERFORMANCE/CONCERT HALLS

Finnish National Opera, Bulvardi 23-27 (tel. 129-255).
Finlandia Hall, Karamzininkatu 4 (tel. 40-241).
Suomen Kansallisteatteri (Finnish National Theater), Läntinen Teatterikuja 1B (tel. 1733-1331).
Svenska Teatern (Swedish Theater), Norra Esplanaden 2 (tel. 171-244).

THEATER

SUOMEN KANSALLISTEATTERI (Finnish National Theater), Läntinen Teatterikuja 1B. Tel. 1733-1331.

The Finnish National Theater enjoys international fame, but its performances are all in Finnish. The theater itself, considered one of the architectural gems of 19th-century Helsinki, was established in 1872 and stages about 850 performances a year, including some 10 premières. Tram: 3B.

Prices: Tickets, 40–65 markkaa ($10.90–$17.75).

SVENSKA TEATERN (Swedish Theater), Norra Esplanaden 2. Tel. 171-244.

You might want to visit the horseshoe-shaped Swedish Theater if you speak Swedish. It has been presenting plays since 1866. The theater is in the absolute center of Helsinki, opposite the Stockmann Department Store. The theater is closed from June until August 1, resuming performances at the beginning of September. The box office is open on Monday from 10am to 6pm, Tuesday through Friday from 10am to 7pm, and on Saturday from noon to 7pm. The theater is closed on Sunday. Tram: 3B.

Prices: Tickets, 70–90 markkaa ($19.10–$24.55).

OPERA & BALLET

FINNISH NATIONAL OPERA, Bulevardi 23-27. Tel. 129-255.

The ballet and opera presentations by this company enjoy international fame. Operas are sung in their original languages and, of course, the language of ballet is universal. The Finnish National Opera was built in the 1870s as a Russian garrison theater. A new, larger opera house, currently under construction, is slated for completion in 1991. The season runs from August to May, and the box office, at Albertinkatu 34B, is open Monday through Friday from 10:30am to 5pm and on Saturday from 10am to 1pm; it opens 1½ hours before opera performances begin. Tram: 3B.

Prices: Tickets, 40–150 markkaa ($10.90–$40.90).

CLASSICAL MUSIC & CONCERTS

HELSINGIN KAUPUNGINORKESTERI (Helsinki Philharmonic Orchestra), Finlandia Hall, Karamzininkatu 4. Tel. 40-241.

The oldest symphony orchestra in the Scandinavian countries performs from September to May in the gracefully modern Finlandia Hall, designed by Alvar Aalto of white Carrara marble. Located a short walk north of the town center, it's considered the musical nerve center of Finland. Its box office opens 1 hour before the beginnings of concerts. For information and reservations, call Lippupalvelu (tel. 643-043). Concerts begin at 7:30pm. Tram: 3B.

Prices: Tickets, 40–65 markkaa ($10.90–$17.75).

LOCAL CULTURAL ENTERTAINMENTS

See Section 7, "Special/Free Events," in this chapter, for information on the **Helsinki Summer Concerts,** held in July, and the **Helsinki Festival,** held during the late summer.

THE CLUB & MUSIC SCENE
NIGHTCLUBS/CABARET

FIZZ BAR AND NIGHTCLUB, in the Arctia Hotel Marski, Manner-heimintie 10. Tel. 68-061.

This club attracts some of the capital's most stylish visitors and residents. Decorated in exotic hardwood paneling from floor to ceiling, it has a stand-up bar and a collection of plushly comfortable high-backed chairs. At the small-stakes casino, roulette chips sell for only 5 markkaa ($1.35) each. The entrance on the street level of the Arctia Hotel Marski (see "Helsinki Accommodations," in Chapter 34). Beer costs 20 markkaa ($5.45). The club is open daily from 8pm to 3am. Tram: 3B.

Admission: 30 markkaa ($10.90) Mon–Sat, free Sun; free to hotel guests.

NIGHTCLUB PRESSA, in the Ramada Hotel Presidentti, Etaläinen Rautatiekatu 4. Tel. 69-11.

Deep in the cellars of one of Helsinki's biggest hotels (see "Helsinki Accommodations," in Chapter 34), this club offers a large and crowded bar and welcomes hundreds of nonresidents to its dramatically shadowy interior. From a raised stage at one end of the dance floor a rotating series of musical groups performs eminently danceable music. They might be from anywhere, often the Philippines or the United States. Many guests wear jacket and tie, and there's a small-stakes casino in the club. Beer costs 20 markkaa ($5.45). It's open daily from 9pm to 3am. Tram: 3B.

Admission: 50 markkaa ($13.65); free for hotel residents Sun–Thurs.

THE OLD BAKER'S, Mannerheimintie 12. Tel. 605-607.

In many ways, the Old Baker's offers Helsinki's most complete nightclub entertainment. The upper floor contains a restaurant, two bars, a small-stakes casino, a disco, and lots of space for milling around with the energetic crowd. The Scottish-red-and-black carpeted Restaurant Sakkipilli, Kalevankatu 2, is in the pub's complex. Dinner is served in one of three or four different rooms, some of them more intimately secluded than others, and is available either à la carte or by ordering a fixed-price dinner costing 160 to 240 markkaa ($43.65 to $65.45). Menu specialties include fish salad, Teno River salmon, consommé of smoked meat, many beef dishes, several kinds of fresh fish, and potatoes prepared seven different ways. Although the place caters to a crowd aged roughly between 25 and 35, no blue jeans are permitted. A beer will set you back 15.50 to 25 markkaa ($4.25 to $6.80). The club is open Monday through Saturday from 11am to 1am. Tram: 3B.

Admission: Free Mon–Thurs, 30 markkaa ($8.20) Fri–Sat.

THE RED ROOM, in the Hotel Kalastajatorppa, Kalastajatorpantie 1. Tel. 488-011.

On the outskirts of Helsinki, the Red Room is among the most frequented nightclubs in town. Everything about the place—everything, that is, except the clients—is red, making a dramatic visual impact. It's customary for men to wear a jacket and tie. Many of the guests are staying at the hotel, but a lot of young professional people from Helsinki are also attracted to the place. Beer costs 20 markkaa ($5.45), and it's open Tuesday through Saturday from 9pm to 3am. Tram: 4 to its terminus.

Admission: Free Tues–Thurs, 50 markkaa ($13.65) Fri–Sat.

ROCK

BERLIN, Töölönkatu 3. Tel. 499-002.
The leading heavy-metal and acid-rock club in all of Finland, Berlin is off Mannerheimintie, near Finlandia Hall, three floors above street level in a 19th-century building. Monday is gay night, Wednesday is reggae night, Thursday is heavy metal, and Friday is "black beat" or soul music. On Saturday the house plays just about any kind of music it wants to, and on Sunday night the venue is "whatever we think we can get away with," a staff member claims. Enter into an all-black decor. A beer will set you back 23 markkaa ($6.25). Berlin is open Wednesday through Monday from 8pm to 1am. Tram: 3B.
Admission: 25–30 markkaa ($6.80–$8.20).

RIVERBOAT MUSIC BAR, Ruoholahdenkatu 4. Tel. 694-5118.
Although it's decorated like one of those Mississippi steamboats from the grand old days, here you can drink, chatter, and listen to recorded music of the greatest names of rock 'n' roll or new wave. Lunch is served from 10am to 2pm for a reasonable 35 to 49 markkaa ($9.55 to $13.35), a light dinner begins at 75 markkaa ($20.45), and a beer costs 21 markkaa ($5.75). It's open Monday through Friday from 10am to 1am, on Saturday from noon to 1am, and on Sunday from noon to midnight. Tram: 3B.
Admission: Free.

DANCE CLUBS/DISCOS

ALEXANDER'S DISCO, in Fanny & Alexander's, Siltasaarenkatu 2. Tel. 753-2332.
Fanny and Alexander's is a two-in-one dining-and-drinking complex that is a popular nighttime venue in the city, especially among young people (see "Helsinki Dining," in Chapter 34). The disco section is two flights above street level. It has a good sound-and-light system, and the DJ plays all the latest recordings from Britain, the United States, and the continent. A beer costs 15.50 markkaa ($5.25). It's open Monday through Saturday from 7pm to 1:30am. Bus: 17, 64, 72.
Admission: Free Mon–Thurs, 35 markkaa ($9.55) Fri–Sat.

COME BACK, Eerikinkatu 14. Tel. 680-6295.
Near the Forum shopping complex, off Mannerheimintie in the city center, this music bar prides itself on its computer-controlled sound system which penetrates into every nook and cranny of this two-level watering hole. All kinds of people come here, especially office workers after a long day. Happy hour, with heavily discounted drinks, is Monday through Friday from 4 to 8pm and all day on Saturday. The upstairs is more animated than the street level. Beer costs 22 markkaa ($6). The place is open daily 2pm to 2am. Tram: 3B.
Admission: Free.

HELSINKI CLUB, in the Sokos Hotel Helsinki, Hallituskatu 12. Tel. 171-401.
The Helsinki Club is one of the most sophisticated discos in town. Although the establishment is inside the Sokos Hotel Helsinki most guests enter through a separate sidewalk entrance. Inside there's a circular series of glass or mirrored bars, a collection of small tables, a dance floor with a centerpiece of potted palms, and lots of peach-colored and black glass. The sound here is designed so that you're able to engage in conversation. The minimum age is 23, but many patrons are a few years older than that. Drinks cost 32 markkaa ($8.75); beer, 21 markkaa ($5.75). It's open daily from 8pm to 2am. Tram: 3T, 4.
Admission: Free Sun–Tues, 20 markkaa ($5.45) Wed–Thurs, 35 markkaa ($9.55) Fri–Sat; free for hotel guests.

KY-EXIT, Phojoinen Rautatiekatu 21. Tel. 407-238.

Lying 500 yards west of the Helsinki Railroad Station, this place is owned by the Student Union of the Helsinki School of Economics. There has been some kind of social club here since the place was built in the 1940s, and today it's a disco with three levels and a different drinking area on each floor. The quietest is the Rock Dog Bar at street level, but the top floor is the one with the panoramic balcony opening onto a view of the dance floor. Management requests that clients wear clothing "other than jeans." Every night offers a different type of music. Beer runs 14 to 16 markkaa ($3.80 to $4.35). It's open daily from 8pm to 2am. Tram: 3B.

Admission: 15 markkaa ($4.10) Sun–Thurs, 40 markkaa ($10.90) Fri–Sat.

PAR 4, Unioninkatu 30. Tel. 607-092.

The sound system projects its recorded music to every corner of this bar, where the clientele is likely to wear jeans and leather jackets and be in their 20s. Lots of mingling and meeting takes place on a green marble floor. At lunch, a fixed-price meal costs 38 markkaa ($10.35), including a main platter of such dishes as fried salmon, vegetarian specialties, or macaroni and cheese, with access to a salad bar, soup, and either coffee or dessert. At night no one is interested in anything but the music, the beer, and the possible contacts, although pizza is available, at 18 markkaa ($4.90); beer costs 23 markkaa ($6.25). Par 4 is open Monday through Saturday from 10:30am to 2pm and 4pm to 1am. Tram: 3B, 3T.

Admission: Free.

THE BAR SCENE
PUBS

O'MALLEY'S PUB, in the Torni Hotel, Yrjönkatu 26. Tel. 131-131.

This is a cramped, convivial, and gregarious pub, which evokes Ireland in spite of its Finnish doorman and Finnish clientele. Bar snacks are served, but as the evening progresses, drinking and more drinking—and lots of animated conversation—rule the night. Beer costs 20 markkaa ($5.45). O'Malley's is open Monday through Saturday from 9am to 1am and on Sunday from noon to midnight. Tram: 3B.

PATRICK'S PUB, Lisenkatu 2. Tel. 135-1070.

This pub, next door to Svenska Klubben (see "Helsinki Dining," in Chapter 34), was named for the son of a Finnish businessman and a Scottish woman who moved to England in 1935 and later worked hard for the war effort. The pub, which has never acquiesced to the dictates of fashion, is authentically English, and offers a flavorful fixed-price lunch for 36 markkaa ($9.80), which includes a platter of whatever food is available that day, along with salad, bread, and coffee. Of course, many Helsinki residents consider it their favorite "local" for a dropping in for a drink. Beer costs 20 markkaa ($5.45). It's open Monday through Saturday from 11am to 1am. Bus: 18.

RICHARD'S PUB, Rikhardinkatu 4. Tel. 179-281.

Established in 1968, this is the oldest English-inspired pub in Helsinki, and is immensely popular. It's an old-fashioned-looking establishment, with high ceilings and red velvet wall coverings. In the spacious dining room you can enjoy such dishes as entrecôte Richard, Caucasian shashlik, fish and chips, Russian herring, and salmon sandwiches; main dishes run 38 to 78 markkaa ($10.35 to $21.25). Many people, however, come here just to drink, either at a table or at the stand-up bar; beer costs 16.50 to 23.50 markkaa ($4.60 to $6.40). Richard's is open Monday through Friday from 9am to 11:45pm and on Saturday and Sunday from 10am to 11:45pm. Tram: 3, 6, 10.

WINE BARS

BEER & WINE CELLAR, in the Hotel Klaus Kurki, Bulevardi 2. Tel. 618-911.

To reach this wine bar, pass through the lobby of the Hotel Klaus Kurki (see "Helsinki Accommodations," in Chapter 34). In a cozy cellar you'll find a large bar and a warren of semiprivate banquettes. You can buy wine by the glass, for about 13 markkaa ($3.55), or by the bottle, from as far away as California, Spain, France, and Italy. The wine cellar, which has a woodsy Victorian-style decor, also offers food. The bill of fare includes such items as Finnish salmon soup, hamburgers *weinkeller* style, entrecôte in butter sauce, and for dessert, fresh-fruit profiteroles stuffed with blueberries and raspberries. Main dishes cost 41 to 91 markkaa ($11.20 to $24.80). It's open Monday through Saturday from 11am to 12:30am and on Sunday from noon to 12:30am. Tram: 3B, 3T, 6.

PINOT NOIR, Annankatu 6. Tel. 680-1701.

This is an underground wine bar—one of the best in Helsinki—part of the previously recommended dining-and-drinking complex Barbecue (see Section 2, "Helsinki Dining," in Chapter 33). Established in 1990, it is mostly white with bare wooden tables and high-tech accessories. The bar sells about 150 different wines from all parts of the world; a glass will set you back 15 to 50 markkaa ($4.10 to $13.65). Coupled with this is an array of highly digestible food designed to go with the wine. Soups and salads are available for 30 to 40 markkaa ($8.20 to $10.90), as are cheese and fruit platters. You can also order such main dishes as filet steak; main dishes cost 45 to 98 markkaa ($12.25 to $26.70). Pinot Noir is open Monday through Friday from 11am to 1am, on Saturday from 1pm to 1am, and on Sunday from 1 to 11pm. Tram: 3B.

THE BARS

AMERICAN BAR, in the Palace Hotel, Eterläranta 10. Tel. 134-561.

It has been suggested that if Betty Grable and Marilyn Monroe were trying to find *How to Marry a Millionaire* today, they would show up at this lofty retreat. Now a fashionable bar in a fashionable hotel, this 11th-floor room actually dates from the 1960s when it was originally designed as a men's toilet. Those memories are all but forgotten today in this charming little bar with glowing paneling and nautical accessories. In summer, tables are placed on an outdoor terrace overlooking the harbor. Special cocktails include Singapore Slings. Drinks cost 33 markkaa ($9); beer runs 22 markkaa ($6). The bar is open Monday through Friday from 11am to 1am. Tram: 3B.

ATELIER BAR, in the Hotel Torni, Yrjönkatu 26. Tel. 131-131.

Its tables are cramped, and the eagle's-nest position it occupies requires the ascent of an impossibly narrow iron staircase. On the uppermost floor of the famous old Hotel Torni (see "Helsinki Accommodations," in Chapter 34), site of many well-documented episodes of espionage during World War II, this is one of the most famous bars of Helsinki, yet many foreign visitors never find it. It welcomes some of the artists and writers of Helsinki, who don't seem to mind the lack of elbow room. Walls are decorated with original paintings, some of them by regular patrons. Take the elevator as far up as it will go and then navigate the rest of the way on foot. Drinks cost 33 markkaa ($9), and beer runs 21 to 31.50 markkaa ($5.75 to $8.60). It's open daily from 3pm to midnight. Tram: 3, 4, 8.

CAFE MARGUERITA, Annankatu 6. Tel. 680-1701.

This bar has a high-tech, minimalist decor attracting young people who enjoy its gossip and the exotic cocktails and coffees. You can order various forms of margaritas, including those made with strawberries and such Mexican temptations as a tequila sunrise. Mexicana coffee is also offered, as is Finlandia coffee, the latter flavored with vodka and cloudberry liqueur. Cocktails begin at 33 markkaa ($9); coffees, 34 markkaa ($9.25). It adjoins the Barbecue restaurant complex (see "Helsinki Dining," in Chapter 34), and is open Monday through Friday from 8am to 1am and on Saturday and Sunday from 1pm to 1am. Tram: 3B.

KARL KÖNIG BAR, Mikonkatutel 4. Tel. 171-271.

Visiting diplomats and the haute bourgeoisie are attracted to this landmark restaurant and bar (see "Helsinki Dining," in Chapter 34). Established in 1892, it has a bar designed by Saarinen, one of Finland's greatest architects. The bar is paneled with wood and sheathed in a carefully restored leather wallpaper. Portraits of the most famous clients of the 1930s hang on the walls (a kind of historical gallery of Finland's famous) and the food is relatively inexpensive, considering the poshness of the place. It's possible, however, to come here just to drink, although a bar menu contains such items as club sandwiches and salads. Sandwiches cost 30 markkaa ($8.20) and salads run 24 to 34 markkaa ($6.55 to $9.25). Drinks go for 22 markkaa ($6); beer, 15.50 markkaa ($4.25). It's open daily from 4pm to 2am. Tram: 3B, 3T.

THE LOBBY BAR, in the Hotel Klaus Kurki, Bulevardi 2. Tel. 618-911.
On the street level of the Hotel Klaus Kurki (see "Helsinki Accommodations," in Chapter 34), this fashionable bar is vividly scarlet, with formal architectural detailings and a hanging collection of 19th-century engravings. Find yourself a cubbyhole within the labyrinth of seating arrangements, and perhaps order yourself the bartender's special, a "Finnish Marguerita" (Finnish vodka, Cointreau, and lemon juice). Drinks run 24 to 43 markkaa ($6.55 to $11.75). The bar is open Monday through Saturday from 11am to 12:30am and on Sunday from noon to 12:30am. Tram: 3B, 3T, 6.

MORE ENTERTAINMENT

AN AMUSEMENT PARK

LINNANMÄKI AMUSEMENT PARK, Linnanmäki.
Linnanmäki, 2 miles north of Helsinki, is a fun fair of splashing fountains, merry-go-rounds, ferris wheels, restaurants, cafés, theaters, and discos. Founded in 1950 by the Children's Foundation to raise funds to care for the thousands of war orphans, Linnanmäki continues today to raise money to aid a new generation of children. The amusement park has a total of 25 different rides, including Europe's highest "big dipper," a fun house, and a railway for kids.
   Admission: 10 markkaa ($2.75) adults, 5 markkaa ($1.35) children.
   Open: June–Aug, Tues–Fri 4–10pm, Sat–Sun 1–9 or 10pm. **Closed:** Sept–May. **Tram:** 3B, 3T.

MOVIES

There are about 50 cinemas in Helsinki. Films are shown in their original language, with Finnish and Swedish subtitles. Showings are usually daily at 6pm and 9pm. Details of what's on and exact times of showings are given in the daily newspapers and a weekly publication available at the City Tourist Office.
   Generally, the most interesting cinema is **Nordia,** Yrjönkatu 36 (tel. 131-19-250), which has three screens. It usually offers a fine program, screening both new "art" films as well as golden oldies and cult favorites.

GAMBLING CASINOS

In addition to the listing below, there are also small-stakes casinos in the **Old Baker's,** Mannerheimintie 12 (tel. 605-607), and the **Fizz Bar & Nightclub,** in the Arctia Hotel Marski, Mannerheimintie 10 (tel. 68-061), both discussed above.

NIGHTCLUB PRESSA, in the Ramada Hotel Presidentti, Etaläinen Rautatiekatu 4. Tel. 69-11.
In this nightclub (see above) is a small-stakes casino, with bets mandated at between 10 and 30 markkaa ($2.75 and $8.20) each. You can, with the help of the friendly croupiers, brush up on your skills at roulette and blackjack. Between bouts of trying your luck, you can enjoy the live dance music and/or drink. Beer costs 20 markkaa ($5.45). It's open daily from 9pm to 3am. Tram: 3B.

Admission: 50 markkaa ($13.65); free for hotel guests Sun–Thurs.

GAY NIGHTLIFE

GAMBRINI, Iso Roobertinkatu 3. Tel. 644-391.
It has only been in the last few years that gay people in Finland began to be allowed to congregate in public enclaves, and Gambrini is the result of that changing sociology. Today it's the premier gay bar of Finland. There's disco dancing in a small room to the side, but most of the guests gather near the leather/levi bar. Women's nights are staged every other Saturday. The entire staff speaks English. Beer costs 16.50 markkaa ($4.50) before 9pm, 21.50 markkaa ($5.85) after 9pm. Gambrini is open daily from 6pm to 1am. Tram: 3B.
    Admission: Free Sun–Thurs, 25 markkaa ($6.80) Fri–Sat.

11. EASY EXCURSIONS

PORVOO (BORGÅ)

This colorful little town, 30 miles northeast of Helsinki, gives visitors a look at what a small town in this area was like a century or so ago; it's the second-oldest town in Finland. Simply strolling the Old Quarter with its narrow winding streets is a fun way to spend an afternoon.
    Founded as a Swedish town in 1346 at the mouth of a river, Porvoo was already an important trading center in the Middle Ages, and even before the town was given its charter, the Swedes had a wooden fortress on a hill that helped to control river and sea trade for several centuries. After Sweden finally relinquished Finland to the Russians, Porvoo was the scene of the first Finnish Diet in the early 19th century, when Tsar Alexander I made the little country a grand duchy.
    Many of the citizens of Porvoo still consider themselves Swedes, and almost half the town's residents speak Swedish and cling to the old Swedish name of this town, Borgå.
    The town's most important industry today is the publishing firm of Werner Soderstrom, established in 1853, one of the largest in Scandinavia.

GETTING THERE

The most interesting way to come to Porvoo is by M/S *J. L. Runeberg,* which sails in summer from the Market Square in Helsinki on Wednesday, Friday, Saturday, and Sunday. A one-way ticket costs 85 markkaa ($23.20) for adults, 30 markkaa ($8.20) for children. A round-trip ticket costs 120 markkaa ($32.70) for adults. For bookings and inquiries, contact the **Ageba Travel Agency,** Olympia Terminal (tel. 669-193).
    The **City Tourist Office** is at Rauhankatu 20, SF-06100 Provoo (tel. 915/170-145).

WHAT TO SEE & DO

If you come to Porvoo via boat, you will get a good view of the old merchants' houses and warehouses along the water—most from the 18th century.

DOM VON PORVOO, Kirkkotori. Tel. 915/147-002.
This stone 15th-century cathedral, where the first Diet of the grand duchy met, has been much restored. The belfry is a mixture of materials, part of it dating from medieval times; what you see today was built in the 18th century.
    Admission: Free.
    Open: May–Sept, Mon–Sat 10am–6pm, Sun 2–5pm; Oct–Apr, Tues–Sat noon–4pm, Sun 2–4pm.

PORVOON MUSEUM, Valikatu 11. Tel. 915/170-589.

This museum's collections are housed in two buildings, the **Historical Museum** in the Old Town Hall and the art collection in the **Edelfelt-Vallgren Museum**, originally a merchant's house. The stone buildings stand on the Museum Square (also known as the Old Town Hall Square) of the Old Town, and both buildings contain artifacts from the 1700s that survived the last big fire in 1762 and the 1800s. The art museum also has collections of Finnish art nouveau furniture and ceramics.

Admission: 10 markkaa ($2.75) adults, free for children under 16.

Open: May–Aug, daily 11am–4pm; Sept–Apr, Wed–Sun noon–4pm.

JOHN LUDVIG RUNEBERG HOUSE, Aleksanterinkatu 3. Tel. 915/171-330.

Porvoo is particularly proud of its association with the Finnish national poet John Ludvig Runeberg, who spent the last 25 years of his life here. His home is now a museum. Works of the poet's son, sculptor Walter Runeberg, can be seen here, including an interesting statue of his father. Runeberg's tomb is also in Porvoo, in the old cemetery west of the river.

Admission: 6 markkaa ($1.65) adults, 3 markkaa (80¢) children.

Open: May–Aug, Mon–Sat 9:30am–4pm, Sun 10:30am–5pm; Sept–Apr, Mon–Sat 11am–3pm, Sun noon–4pm.

WHERE TO DINE

WANHA LAAMANNI, Vuorikatu 17. Tel. 915/130-455.

Cuisine: FINNISH. **Reservations:** Recommended.

$ Prices: Appetizers 50–150 markkaa ($13.65–$40.90); main courses 70–160 markkaa ($19.20–$43.65); fixed-price lunch 80 markkaa ($21.80) Mon–Thurs, 125 markkaa ($34.10) Sat–Sun. AE, DC, MC, V.

Open: Summer, daily 11am–midnight; winter, Mon–Sat 11am–11pm, Sun noon–8pm.

Originally constructed as a private house near the medieval cathedral, not quite in the center, this late Gustavian-style restaurant whose name translates as "The Old Judge's Chambers," has an 18th-century decor. The chef turns out many Finnish specialties, such as smoked whitefish with creamed spinach or roasted filet of reindeer with game sauce.

HYVINKÄÄ

This young town, which was granted its charter as recently as 1960, has long been linked to Finland's railway network and is visited today chiefly because of its National Railway Museum (see below). Located 35 miles north of Helsinki, Hyvinkää can be reached by "H train," which leaves twice an hour from Helsinki, and by car, which takes an hour on Route 3. Buses labeled Hyvinkää also run here from the Helsinki bus station.

This rapidly growing industrial and commercial center is set in a part of Finland with beautiful scenery. Visitors can walk through **Hyvinkää Sveitsi,** the "Switzerland" of Hyvinkää a park within walking distance of the center of town, which has marked and lit walking paths and skiing tracks of various lengths. It also has a jogging track and ski slopes and jumps.

Hyvinkää's connection with the railway dates from 1850, when the link was added between Hämeenlinna and Helsinki. This railway culture is preserved in the **National Railway Museum,** in the center of town, at Hyvinkäänkatu 9 (tel. 914/18-351). The museum is housed in the original railway buildings dating from the 1870s. Exhibits include the oldest steam engine preserved in Finland, *Passi,* from 1868; Finland's oldest rail car, a Fiat from 1914; and a model railway, the largest of its kind in the country. But my favorite exhibit is a three-coach imperial train dating from the 1870s. Built for the tsar of Russia, the imperial coach train originally consisted of five coaches; the coaches of the tsar and tsarina, a saloon, a dining room, and a kitchen coach. The Railway Museum was founded in 1898 in Helsinki but was transferred to Hyvinkää in 1974. It is open May to August, Tuesday through Sunday from 11am to

4pm (in July, also on Monday); September to April, Tuesday through Friday from noon to 3pm and on Saturday and Sunday from noon to 4pm. Admission is 10 markkaa ($2.75) for adults and 5 markkaa ($1.35) for children.

HÄMEENLINNA

Finland's oldest town, located 61 miles north of Helsinki, Hämeenlinna was founded in 1639. It is one of the starting points for cruises on the Silver Line vessels (*Suomen Hopealinja*), which run to Tampere or along the scenic route to the ridge of Kangasala. Hämeenlinna is also the starting point for a series of 1-day cruises, the most popular of which goes to the Aulanko Tourist Center and to sculptor Emil Wikström's studio museum, Visavuori. If you go on one of these cruises, your car can be driven by the car-pilot service to await your arrival.

WHAT TO SEE & DO

The large park at **Aulanko,** about 2½ miles from the center of Hämeenlinna, is one of the best-known tourist centers of Finland. Here you'll find a hotel (see below), a panoramic tower, tennis courts, a golf course, and a bathing beach.

Further information about the town is available at the **City Tourist Office,** Palokunnankatu 11 (tel. 917/202-388).

SIBELIUKSEN SYNTYNÄKOTI, Hallituskatu 11. Tel. 917/25-698.

The great composer Jean Sibelius was born at Hämeenlinna on December 8, 1865, in this wooden house. Today it's not only a tourist attraction, but is also the setting for small chamber concerts. It stands in the center of town, about 50 yards from the Marketplace. The Sibelius archives are housed here, and the museum sells tapes of Sibelius's music.

Admission: 3 markkaa (80¢) adults, 2 markkaa (55¢) children.

Open: May–Aug, daily 10am–4pm; Sept–Apr, Sun–Fri noon–4pm.

HÄME CASTLE. Tel. 917/26-820.

Häme Castle dominates the town. Construction here has been going on for 700 years. The oldest sections date from the 1260s and are known as the fortified camp, including a square gray-stone wall with defensive towers at three corners. Once the residence of mighty nobles, the castle later became a strictly supervised outpost of the Swedish Crown. As the years went by, it served as both a granary and a prison. It now houses changing exhibits, and there is a café and restaurant on the grounds.

Admission: 14 markkaa ($3.80) adults, 7 markkaa ($1.90) children.

Open: May–Aug, daily 10am–6pm; Sept–Apr, daily 10am–4pm. **Bus:** 5 or 12 from the Marketplace.

WHERE TO STAY

RANTASIPI AULANKO, SF-13230 Aulanko. Tel. 917/295-21. Fax 917/21-922. 250 rms (all with bath). MINIBAR TV TEL.

$ Rates (including breakfast): 585 markkaa ($159.55) single; 720 markkaa ($196.35) double. AE, DC, MC, V.

Its name is instantly recognizable throughout Finland because of its location in one of the country's best-known nature preserves. It sits at the edge of Vanajavesi Lake near a sweep of open grassland surrounded by forested hillsides. Each room has an open-air balcony. On weekends through the year the dining room is likely to be overflowing. On the premises are tennis courts, a golf course, a labyrinth of walking paths, three saunas, a lakeside bathing beach, an indoor pool, riding stables, and a masseuse. In winter, cross-country skiing is a popular activity here. The hotel, a venue for important congresses, lies at the end of a series of prominent signs in Aulanko Park, 3 miles north of the rail station at Hämeenlinna.

HOTEL CUMULUS, Raatihuoneenkatu 16-18, SF-13230 Aulanko. Tel. 917/52-811. Fax 917/733-7299. 100 rms (all with bath). MINIBAR TV TEL.

$ Rates (including breakfast): Weekdays Aug 6–June 20, 475 markkaa ($129.55) single; 620 markkaa ($169.05) double. June 21–Aug 5 and weekends year round, 260 markkaa ($70.90) single; 360 markkaa ($98.15) double. AE, DC, MC, V.

Located next to the main commercial street of town, within walking distance of Kauppatori Market Square, this modern concrete-and-glass hotel has comfortable bedrooms and three attractive restaurants: Mama Leone, Prince Albert, and Tiffany. Two saunas are on the premises, plus a swimming pool. It's possible to book a no-smoking room, but you must specifically request it when making your reservations. Children under 14 are accommodated free with existing beds; otherwise, an extra bed costs 100 markkaa ($27.25) a day. The all-you-want breakfast includes fruit juice, eggs, cheese, cold cuts, salads, vegetables, and porridge.

WHERE TO DINE

VALENTINO'S, Sibeliuksenkatu 3. Tel. 28-777.
   Cuisine: FINNISH. **Reservations:** Recommended.
$ Prices: Appetizers 30–45 markkaa ($8.20–$12.25); main dishes 60–94 markkaa ($16.35–$25.65). AE, DC, MC, V.
   Open: Dinner only, Mon–Sat 7pm–2am.

This is not only considered the best restaurant in town, but also the leading entertainment complex, offering not only a restaurant, but two different bars and the town's most popular disco. Specialties include pepper steak, salmon with a cream-and-mushroom sauce, and filet of reindeer with juniper berries. Service is polite and efficient. Dancing to disco music begins at 9pm, with beer costing 20 markkaa ($5.45); admission to the disco ranges from 20 to 40 markkaa ($5.45 to $10.90). Music is recorded except on Monday, Wednesday, and Thursday when it's live.

KOTKA

Lying 83 miles east of Helsinki at Kotka, ✪ **Langinkoski** (tel. 952/210-50) was the imperial fishing lodge of the Russian tsar's family, the summer retreat for Alexander III from 1889 to 1894. A log house, it stands on the River Kymi, and provides an insight into how the Romanovs lived long before the family met violent deaths in the Russian Revolution. Near the Langinkoski Rapids for which it is named, the lodge is open May to September, daily from 10am to 7pm, charging an admission of 5 markkaa ($1.35).

Information is available from the **Kotka Tourist Office,** Keskuskatu 17 (tel. 952/274-424). Kotka is a 2-hour drive from Helsinki if you have a car. Otherwise Kotka-bound buses depart frequently from the bus station in Helsinki. For example, if you take the 9:30am bus from Helsinki, you arrive at Kotka at 11:40am. Once there, you must take a 10-minute taxi ride to the tsar's former lodge. Otherwise, take bus no. 20.

The mysterious Anastasia used to run wild along the turbulent rapids. Her girlish "A" can still be seen in the guestbook. The tsar choose a spot in Finland's premier salmon-fishing area to build the lodge.

The lodge was constructed in 1889 on property consisting of half a dozen small islands interconnected by bridges. Its deliberately unpretentious architecture was in the Finnish style of hand-hewn pine logs, far removed from the grandeur of the family's 900-room palace outside St. Petersburg (now Leningrad).

The tsarina often prepared the family meals herself, and the copper pots she used can still be seen. Alexander III died in 1894, and the lodge held little appeal for his more formal son, Nicholas II, last of the Romanovs.

Ask at the Finnish Tourist Board, 655 Third Ave., New York, NY 10017 (tel. 212/949-2333), about dates of theatrical performances in July of *One Day in the Life of the Tsar.* Tour packages are sold for overnight stays in the area.

CHAPTER 36

TURKU & THE ÅLAND ISLANDS

1. TURKU
- **WHAT'S SPECIAL ABOUT TURKU & THE ÅLAND ISLANDS**
2. THE ÅLAND ISLANDS

Almost as interesting as Helsinki itself, Finland's former capital, Turku, is an ancient town with close links to Sweden. Swedes affectionately call it Åbo, and perhaps regret its loss. It is a town with proud traditions, and was the former center of the spiritual, secular, and commercial life of Finland before the capital was moved by the Russians to Helsinki.

Turku is Finland's oldest town. Records don't indicate the exact date, but it's estimated that Turku was founded around 1229.

In the Middle Ages, trade and seafaring were the main means of livelihood for the people of Turku. A university was founded in 1640, adding to its prestige. Tragedy struck on September 4, 1827, when Turku suffered the biggest fire ever to ravage a Scandinavian town. Following the fire, the Academy of Turku, the first university in Finland, was transferred to Helsinki. But following the independence of Finland, a Swedish-language university, Åbo Akademi, was founded, and Turku regained some of its lost prestige.

Turku, a city of 160,000 inhabitants, makes the ideal gateway for visiting the Åland Islands, an archipelago in the Baltic midway between Sweden and Finland. Many Swedes use the Ålands as a summer playground.

The islands are relatively autonomous, with 23,000 inhabitants, who have their own parliament and government, their own flag and culture, even their own postage stamps.

During the time of its world-famous shipowner Gustaf Erikson, Åland was able to boast the biggest fleet of sailing ships in the world. Its traditions as a maritime "nation" are ancient.

SEEING TURKU & THE ÅLAND ISLANDS
GETTING THERE

Turku is often used as a gateway to Finland, and it has rail and air links with Helsinki, and air and sea links to Stockholm. From Turku, you can go by boat to Mariehamn, capital of the Åland Islands, or you can fly there directly, often from Stockholm, but with more frequent flights from Helsinki.

A SUGGESTED ITINERARY

Days 1 & 2: Allow this amount of time to get to Turku and see the city's attractions.
Day 3: Take excursions to Naantali and Rauma.
Days 4 & 5: Settle into Mariehamn and spend any time left over exploring some of the attractions of the archipelago.

1. TURKU
102 miles west of Helsinki, 96 miles east of Tampere

GETTING THERE **By Plane** Turku Airport is 4 miles from the center of town. It receives international flights from Stockholm as well as domestic connections,

WHAT'S SPECIAL ABOUT TURKU & THE ÅLAND ISLANDS

Great Towns/Villages
- ☐ Turku, the oldest town in Finland, its former capital.
- ☐ Naantali, 12 miles north of Turku, an excellent example of a Finnish town of the Middle Ages.
- ☐ Rauma, 60 miles north of Turku, third-oldest town in Finland.
- ☐ Mariehamn, the capital of the Åland Islands archipelago—a favorite with the summer yachting crowd.

Cathedrals
- ☐ Turku Cathedral, dating from the 13th century, one of the most important medieval monuments of Finland.

Museums
- ☐ City Historical Museum, Turku, housed in Finland's largest medieval castle from the 13th century.

- ☐ Wäinö Aaltosen Museum, Turku, containing many of the paintings and sculptures of one of Finland's greatest artists.
- ☐ Åland Maritime Museum, superb collections from the great sailing-ship era of the Åland Islands.

Special Events/Festivals
- ☐ Turku Music Festival in August, music from the Renaissance and baroque eras played on the original instruments.
- ☐ Åland Music Festival in July, offering various kinds of music, from jazz to blues to heavy metal.

---

mainly from Helsinki, from within Finland. For information about flights to Turku, call 921/513-600 in Turku or 90/89-881 in Helsinki.

By Train   Trains make the 2¼-hour run from Helsinki and Turku (and vice versa) at the rate of seven daily. Six trains a day leave in each direction between Turku and Tampere, taking 2½ hours.

By Bus   Twenty buses make the 2½-hour run back and forth between Helsinki and Turku daily, and 16 buses travel each way between Turku and Tampere, taking 3 hours.

By Car   From Helsinki, head west along the E3 all the way. From Tampere, go southwest on the E80 all the way.

By Ferry   Two ferries a day depart from Stockholm's harbor heading for Turku, taking 12 hours for the trip. There is a connection between Stockholm and Turku every morning and every evening. For information, call the **Silja Line** in Turku at 652/233.

ESSENTIALS   For information, go to the **City Tourist Office,** Käsityöläiskatu 3, SF-20100 Turku (tel. 921/336-366), or to the **Tourist Information Booth** at Aurakatu 4.

A **Turku Tourist Ticket** entitles you to unlimited travel on the city's buses within a 24-hour period. It costs 15 markkaa ($4.10) and can be purchased at the City Tourist Office.

The **telephone area code** for Turku is 921.

On the western coast, at the confluence of three rivers, the seaport of Turku (Åbo in Swedish) is the oldest city in Finland and was once the most important city in the country; it was both an ecclesiastical center and a trade center. In addition to the cathedral, the city acquired a citadel in the late 13th century—thereby achieving a position of power by the standards of the Middle Ages. Turku's cultural and financial power was solidified when the King of Sweden, who then controlled Finland, made Turku the seat of government directed by his representative.

In the 17th century an academy was established in Turku, and in 1808 Russia conquered Finland and moved its capital to Helsinki, which was closer to St. Petersburg (now Leningrad) and theoretically easier to administer. In 1827 a fire demolished much of Turku's old wooden city.

But Turku bounced back, developing into not only an important port and industrial city, but also a university town, with both a Swedish and a Finnish Academy. It was rebuilt by Carl Ludvig Engel, who designed Helsinki, with stone and brick buildings, a grid plan, and wide streets.

The legendary long-distance runner, Paavo Nurmi (1897–1973), known as "the Flying Finn," was the most famous son of Turku. He won a total of nine gold and three silver medals in three different Olympics.

WHAT TO SEE & DO

CITY HISTORICAL MUSEUM, Turun linna. Tel. 303-300.

Finland's largest medieval castle was constructed in the 13th century, but its main building was renovated after World War II. The outer castle houses the City Historical Museum whose collections include 17th- to 19th-century furniture, porcelain, tapestries, silver, pewter, glass, local history, ethnography, and costumes. Refreshments and light snacks are offered in the self-service cafeteria in the south wing.

Admission: 5 markkaa ($1.35).

Open: May–Sept, daily 10am–6pm; Oct–Apr, daily 10am–3pm. **Bus:** 1.

TURKU CATHEDRAL, Cathedral Square. Tel. 510-651.

The foundation of this brick cathedral also dates back to the 13th century, but it represents the architectural styles of many centuries. One of the most important medieval monuments in Finland, the cathedral, regarded as a national shrine, contains the tombs of many famous Scandinavians, including bishops, military heroes, and one queen, Karin Mansdotter, the wife of Erik XIV of Sweden. The cathedral museum houses a collection of relics and liturgical artifacts dating from the Middle Ages.

Admission: Cathedral, free; museum, 5 markkaa ($1.35) adults, 2 markkaa (55¢) children.

Open (cathedral and museum): June–Aug, Mon–Fri 9am–7pm, Sat 9am–3pm, Sun 2:30–4:30pm; Sept–May, Mon–Fri 10am–4pm, Sat 10am–3pm, Sun 2:30–4:30pm. **Bus:** 25.

LUOSTARINMÄKI HANDCRAFTS MUSEUM, on Luostarinmäki (Cloister Hill). Tel. 337-150.

The outdoor compound housing this handcraft museum is a collection of little 18th-century cottages on a hillside, about a 5-minute walk from the city center, south of Vartiovuori hill near the Open-Air Theater. This is the only part of Turku that escaped the fire of 1827, and the 18 original structures now make up the working museum. You can watch a potter, goldsmith, bookbinder, and makers of wigs, gloves, and combs as they ply their trades. Displays of Finnish arts and crafts of all types can be seen.

Admission: 5 markkaa ($1.35).

Open: May–Sept, daily 10am–6pm; Oct–Apr, daily 10am–3pm.

SIBELIUS MUSEUM, Piispankatu 17. Tel. 654-494.

Although Finland's beloved composer neither lived nor worked in Turku, there is a fine collection of Sibeliana here, along with collections of instruments. Music lovers can sit in a small concert hall and listen to the works of the master once a day or at free concerts held on Wednesday evenings in spring and summer from 6 to 8pm. The Wednesday concerts sell out early so stop by in the morning to buy your ticket.

Admission: 15 markkaa ($4.10) adults, 5 markkaa ($1.35) children.

Open: Tues–Sun 11am–3pm. **Bus:** 25.

TURUN TAIDEMUSEO, in Puolalapuisto Park, Aurakatu 26. Tel. 330-954.

The Finnish art collection of the Turku Art Society, from the beginning of the 19th century to the present, is the second-largest and most important collection in Finland. Artworks from other Nordic countries and international graphics are also exhibited. The museum is near the Market Square.

Admission: 15 markkaa ($4.10) adults, 10 markkaa ($2.75) children.

Open: Mon–Wed and Fri–Sat 10am–4pm, Thurs 10am–4pm and 6–8pm, Sun 10am–6pm.

WÄINÖ AALTOSEN MUSEUM, Itäinen Rantakatu 38. Tel. 355-690.

One of the best-known Finnish artists, Wäinö Aaltosen began his career on Hirvensalo, the big island owned by the city. The museum on the eastern bank of the Aurajoki River contains many of Aaltosen's own paintings and sculptures, as well as a permanent collection of contemporary Finnish pictures, sculptures, and other artwork. Changing short-term exhibitions are also featured.

Admission: 5 markkaa ($1.35) adults, 2 markkaa (55¢) children under 12.

Open: Mon–Fri 10am–4pm and 6–8pm, Sat 10am–4pm, Sun 10am–6pm. **Bus:** 7, 15, 17 from the Market Place.

MARITIME MUSEUM/ASTRONOMICAL COLLECTION, at Vartiovuori. Tel. 337-410.

Local maritime history and the astronomical collections of academician Yrjö Väisälä are the subject of this museum in an observatory built for the Academy of Turku in 1819. It's near the Open-Air Theater southeast of Hämeenkatu.

Together with the City Historical Museum, the Handcraft Museum, Qwensel House and the Pharmacy Museum, and the Biological Museum, all described above, the maritime and astronomical museum is a part of the Turku Provincial Museum, Kalastajankatu 4 (tel. 303-300).

Admission: 5 markkaa ($1.35).

Open: May–Sept, daily 10am–6pm; Oct–Apr, daily 10am–3pm.

MARKET HALL, Eerikinkatu 16 and Linnankatu 15. Tel. 314-912.

A visit to Turku's cobblestone marketplace and the market hall, southeast of the train station, is the best way to experience the rhythms of the city at no cost. At the market hall, stalls in long corridors are filled with fresh vegetables, the best of Finnish cheeses, meat, fish, bread, cakes, health foods, and souvenirs. There's a café and a bank handy if you want to sip coffee or change traveler's checks. Other stalls in the market square offer lingonberries, cloudberries, salmon, and other typical Scandinavian foods.

Admission: Free.

Open: Open-air markets, mid-May to mid-Sept, Mon–Fri 8am–1pm and 4–8pm, Sat 8am–1pm; mid-Sept to mid-May, Mon–Sat 8am–1pm. Covered market hall, Mon–Fri 8am–5pm, Sat 8am–1pm.

ORGANIZED TOURS

June 16 to August 31, a 2-hour **guided bus tour** (in English) leaves daily at 1pm from in front of the Tourist Information Booth at Aurakatu 4; it includes a visit to the cathedral, among other sights. Tickets cost 45 markkaa ($12.25) for adults and 15 markkaa ($4.10) for children.

IMPRESSIONS

Turku is a wretched capital of a barbarous province.
—SIR N. W. WRAXALL, IN A *TOUR ROUND THE BALTIC*, 1775

Boat tours to the Turku archipelago depart from the Tourist Information Booth, from near the Auransilta bridge, and from the Martinsilta bridge, and are offered daily from June 1 to August 31. For information about islands and sights in the archipelago, see "Excursions," below.

WHERE TO STAY
EXPENSIVE

ARCTIA MARINA PALACE, Linnankatu 32, SF-20100 Turku. Tel. 921/ 336-300. Fax 921/516-750. 183 rms (all with bath). MINIBAR TV TEL.
$ Rates (including breakfast): 680 markkaa ($185.45) single; 900 markkaa ($245.45) double. AE, DC, MC, V. **Parking:** 52 markkaa ($14.20).

An international hotel of a high standard, the Marina Palace, in the center of Turku by the Aurajoki River, is a modern chain-run hotel offering much comfort and good facilities. Its bedrooms are generally spacious, inviting, and comfortable, containing a number of amenities such as trouser press and hairdryer. The room price always includes a good breakfast, a sauna, and a dip in the hotel's indoor pool.

Dining/Entertainment: The eighth-floor Riverside Gourmet Restaurant opens onto a panoramic view of the city. Other dining and entertainment choices include the Dancing Marina Restaurant; the Calamare, a restaurant specializing in seafood; and a summer restaurant, Sunmarina. The Pub Nelson is a popular drinking spot.

Services: Room service, baby-sitting.

Facilities: Four saunas, a swimming pool, solarium, and sauna bar.

HAMBURGER BÖRS, Kauppiaskatu 6, SF-20100 Turku. Tel. 921/511-211. Fax 921/511-211. 160 rms (all with bath). MINIBAR TV TEL.
$ Rates (including breakfast): June 16–Aug 15, 350 markkaa ($95.45) single; 420 markkaa ($114.55) double. Aug 16–June 15, 620 markkaa ($169.05) single; 780 markkaa ($212.70) double. AE, DC, MC, V.

The leading hotel of Turku, this five-star choice near Kauppatori, the Market Square, in the city center, has long been a favorite with discriminating visitors. Guests enjoy the maximum luxury and comfort that Turku offers, from a morning sauna and swim to a breakfast buffet, with food and drink services all through the day, ending with a nightcap in the hotel's nightclub. Bedrooms are furnished in a traditional but modern styling, each with a number of amenities such as trouser press and satellite programs on TV.

Dining/Entertainment: In the lobby, the Café de Paris is a French-style café, ideal for snacks or drinks, and Le Bar also has a French ambience. The Brasserie Valtin offers both modern and traditional French cuisine, and is named for the founder of the hotel, Wallina Valtin. YläBörs on the second floor is a first-class gourmet restaurant, offering elaborate Finnish buffets. Hearty food and beer are served in the Hamburger Hof, and the most popular nightclub in town is the Börs Club, attracting artists from all over Europe.

Services: Room service, baby-sitting.

Facilities: Finnish sauna, swimming pool.

PARK HOTEL, Fredsgatan 1, SF-2001 Turku. Tel. 921/617-000. Fax 921/617-722. 20 rms (all with bath). A/C MINIBAR TV TEL.
$ Rates (including breakfast): Mon–Fri, 650 markkaa ($177.25) single; 900 markkaa ($245.45) double. Sat–Sun, 480 markkaa ($130.90) single; 575 markkaa ($156.80) double. AE, DC, MC, V.

This charming small hotel in the center near the station and Puolalaparken, originally a private home in 1904, has been skillfully converted into a well-run private hotel under the supervision of the dynamic Eva Dziedzic, who also directs the well-recommended Hansa Hotel. Bedrooms are furnished in great taste, using subtle pastels for the most part, and every room is made homelike and comfortable. Bathrooms are tiled and well maintained, and each room is different. A dining room and bar are available for guests only, and the hotel has a sauna.

MODERATE

CUMULUS HOTEL, Eerikinkatu 28, SF-20100 Turku. Tel. 921/638-211.
Fax 921/638-2299. 214 rms (all with bath). MINIBAR TV TEL.
$ Rates (including breakfast): June 21–Aug 5 and weekends year round, 280 markkaa ($76.35) single; 380 markkaa ($103.65) double. Weekdays Aug 6–June 20, 460 markkaa ($125.45) single; 600 markkaa ($163.60) double. AE, DC, MC, V.

Near Town Hall, three blocks from Market Square and one block from the main post office, this is one of the most modern hotels in the commercial center of town and caters to Scandinavian businesspeople. The bedrooms are tastefully contemporary, and some are equipped for the disabled or the allergic. The single rooms overlook a central courtyard, and doubles have views of the city. The Kirjava Satama Restaurant, adjacent to the reception area, serves well-prepared food in an ambience of abbreviated lattices and ornamental palms. There's an outdoor terrace lined with geraniums for summer drinks, plus a Harry's Bar. Room service and laundry facilities are offered, and four saunas, a swimming pool, a children's playroom, and a solarium are available to guests.

HANSA HOTEL, Kristinegatan 9, SF-20100 Turku. Tel. 921/617-000.
Fax 921/617-722. 66 rms (all with bath). A/C MINIBAR TV TEL.
$ Rates (including breakfast): Mon–Fri, 480 markkaa ($130.90) single; 640 markkaa ($174.55) double. Sat–Sun, 350 markkaa ($95.45) single; 450 markkaa ($122.70) double. AE, DC, MC, V.

Built on the third and fourth floor of the Hansa Shopping Center, the major shopping center of Turku, this small hotel is one of the finest in western Finland. It is directed by Eva Dziedzic, a woman of considerable charm who does much to provide for the comfort of her international guests. Bedrooms are tastefully designed and furnished, sometimes with pastel colors, and the atmosphere in each is homelike and inviting. Each of the accommodations is well maintained, and the baths are modern. The hotel has an attractive lobby bar and an excellent restaurant, providing an international and Finnish cuisine. Specialties include reindeer and salmon, and lunch is offered daily from 11am to 3pm and dinner from 5 to 8pm, with meals costing from 120 markkaa ($32.70).

HOTEL HENRIK, Yliopistonkatu 29A, SF-20100 Turku. Tel. 921/320-921. Fax 921/518-870. 94 rms (all with bath). A/C MINIBAR TV TEL.
$ Rates (including breakfast): June–Aug 15 and weekends year round, 270 markkaa ($73.65) single; 380 markkaa ($103.65) double. Weekdays Aug 16–May, 380 markkaa ($103.65) single; 540 markkaa ($147.25) double. No credit cards.
Parking: Available.

Located near the Market Square, 50 yards from the bus station, on the most important commercial street in town, Hotel Henrik is one of the best hotels in the moderate-price range. Each room is smallish but stylishly furnished and clean and comfortable. The hotel's restaurant, Henrikin Krouri, has a good reputation, and there is also the Café Henrik in the hotel, open 24 hours. Guests are invited to use the hotel's sauna at no additional charge. There is a place for parking.

HOTEL JULIA, Eerikinkatu 4, SF-20110 Turku. Tel. 921/503-300. Fax 921/511-750. 118 rms (all with bath). MINIBAR TV TEL.
$ Rates (including breakfast): June 15–Aug 15 and weekends year round, 280 markkaa ($76.35) single; 380 markkaa ($103.65) double. Weekdays Aug 16–June 14, 495 markkaa ($135) single; 640 markkaa ($174.55) double. AE DC, MC, V.
Parking: Available.

An attractive hotel in the center of town near the Market Square, the Julia has comfortably furnished bedrooms, with 36 of them reserved for nonsmokers. In addition to parquet floors and crisp colors, each room has a trouser press, hairdryer, and hair curler. The hotel's French-style restaurant offers good food, and the Hunter's Pub offers music; room service is available. In addition, there's a modern shopping center, banks, a cinema, a car-rental firm, a Finnair office, a sauna department with two saunas for 5 people and one for 20 plus an attractive sauna bar, a lounge with a fireplace, and a roof terrace.

HOTEL SCANDI, Matkustajasatama, SF-20100 Turku. Tel. 921/302-600. 78 rms (all with bath). MINIBAR TV TEL. **Bus:** 1.
$ Rates (including breakfast): June–Aug, 300 markkaa ($81.80) single; 400 markkaa ($109.10) double. Sept–May, 360 markkaa ($98.15) single; 480 markkaa ($130.90) double. AE, DC, MC, V.

A renovated harborfront warehouse decorated in a Neo-Gothic red-brick style, the Hotel Scandi is about 2 miles from the center of town, easily reached by bus. A team of architects left the hand-hewn beams, the basilica-shaped interior, and the massive iron trusses as part of the interior decoration, and added carpeting, clusters of rustic armchairs, and plantings. The bedrooms are attractive, comfortable, and well furnished; four are equipped for the disabled. A cocktail bar and a restaurant serving Finnish and international dishes are on the premises, and room service is offered. Two saunas with whirlpool bath and postsauna sitting and conference rooms, a solarium, and a gym are available.

RITZ HOTEL, Humalistonkatu 7, SF-20100 Turku. Tel. 921/651-111. Fax 921/336-699. 166 rms (all with bath). A/C MINIBAR TV TEL.
$ Rates (including breakfast): June 15–Aug 15 and weekends year round, 270 markkaa ($73.65) single; 360 markkaa ($98.15) double. Weekdays Aug 16–June 14, 490 markkaa ($133.60) single; 670 markkaa ($182.70) double. AE, DC, MC, V. **Parking:** Available.

In the center of town near the train station, half a mile from the bus station, the Ritz has been a tradition and a landmark in Turku since 1928. It is a comfortable, modernized hotel. Each of its bedrooms has been tastefully renovated, with a number of amenities, and some rooms are designed for nonsmokers and the allergic. The Ritz's primary claim to distinction is its unusual dance restaurant, the Maritza, which is located in a former movie palace designed by the great Finnish architect, Alvar Aalto. There is a dance area and a free-standing bar shaped like a double horseshoe. Scandinavian and international dishes are served. The hotel's other restaurants seem to have names that rhyme, including the Fritz and the Restaurant Gourmet Ritz. A music bar, the Pub Beeritz, is also on the premises. Baby-sitting, laundry facilities, room service, and translation and guide services are offered, as well as three saunas, parking places, and a garage.

INEXPENSIVE

TURUN KESKUSHOTELLI, Yliopistonkatu 12A, SF-20100 Turku. Tel. 921/337-333. Fax 921/337-333. 62 rms (all with bath). TV TEL.
$ Rates (including breakfast and morning sauna): June 22–July 29 and weekends year round, 215–290 markkaa ($58.65–$79.10) single, 310–370 markkaa ($84.55–$100.90) double. Weekdays July 30–June 21, 315–410 markkaa ($85.90–$111.80) single; 395–470 markkaa ($107.70–$128.15) double. AE, DC, MC, V.

The interior of this modern three-star hotel makes full use of such Finnish materials as marble and birch. Established in 1974, and massively renovated in 1987, it is built around a graceful inner courtyard and lies in the heart of the city near the bus station. Extra facilities in the bedrooms include trouser presses and hairdryers. Some of the rooms are studios—one part bedroom, one part living room. A free morning sauna is included in the rates. The hotel serves evening coffee and snacks, but many restaurants are nearby.

SUMMER HOTELS

DOMUS ABOENSIS, Piispankatu 10, SF-20500 Turku. Tel. 921/329-470. 76 rms (all with bath). TEL.
$ Rates (including breakfast): 190 markkaa ($51.80) single; 250 markkaa ($68.20) double. MC, V. **Closed:** Sept–May.

Owned and operated by the Åbo Academy, this is the best and most centrally located of the student hotels in Turku; it's near the cathedral. The spacious bedrooms are the most winning feature here: many are decorated like Mondrian paintings, with large rectangular blocks of color. The summer hotel also operates an unlicensed cafeteria.

SUMMERHOTEL IKITUURI, Pispalantie 7, SF-20510 Turku. Tel. 921/376-111. 144 rms (all with bath). TEL **Bus:** 50.

$ Rates (including breakfast): 215 markkaa ($58.65) single; 280 markkaa ($76.35) double. AE, DC, MC, V. **Closed:** Sept–May.

About 1½ miles from the marketplace, this hotel offers a swimming pool, games, bicycles, saunas, a gym, and a solarium. A bus goes to the marketplace four times an hour, and there's a taxi station in front of the hotel. In a separate building you'll find a disco and pub. Meals are served in the hotel's restaurant until 12:30am. Rooms are furnished modestly in a college-dormitory style.

WHERE TO DINE
EXPENSIVE

LE PIRATE, Boren Puisto. Tel. 511-443.
   Cuisine: FRENCH. **Reservations:** Not required.
$ Prices: Appetizers 29–45 markkaa ($7.90–$12.25); main courses 55–85 markkaa ($15–$23.20). AE, DC, MC, V.
   Open: Restaurant, mid-Apr to Sept, Mon–Fri 11am–11pm, Sat 1–11:30pm, Sun 1–10pm; Oct to mid-Apr, Mon–Fri 11am–11pm, Sat 1–11:30pm. Deck, 9am on, weather permitting.

Originally launched in 1907, this broad-beamed and stocky steamboat carried tar and timber through the inland waterways of eastern Finland. Today, though it's permanently moored in the river in the town center, you can enjoy café snacks and drinks on its upper deck, where the polite waiters speak English, or you can head for the restaurant below deck, which is warmly decorated in a nautical style. The French-inspired meals include half a dozen snails, scallops sautéed in snail-flavored butter, scampi flambé, fish of the day, hors d'oeuvres maison, fish terrine made with crayfish, and tempting desserts. In summer, from 10am to closing, weather permitting, tables from this establishment spill over onto a parklike terrace on the nearby riverbank.

SAMPALINNA, Sampalinna Park. Tel. 311-165.
   Cuisine: FINNISH. **Reservations:** Recommended.
$ Prices: Appetizers 29–45 markkaa ($7.90–$12.25); main courses 59–85 markkaa ($16.10–$23.20). MC, V.
   Open: Sun–Thurs 11am–1am, Fri–Sat 11am–2am.

Every taxi driver in town knows about this richly ornate Victorian building, which still retains its original complicated gingerbread from a century ago. It's near the river in the center of Turku, near the Myuysilta bridge. An outdoor café terrace ringed with trees near a bandshell features recorded jazz during the summer; nightly dance music begins here at 8pm. The food includes beef à la Sampalinna with Roquefort cheese and a red wine sauce, roast mutton with garlic-flavored potatoes, morel soup, salmon soup with rye bread, sizzling beefsteak on a plank, vegetarian platters, and a summer dessert of fresh cloudberries with a brandy-flavored cream sauce. Late at night you can order Scandinavian hash.

SEAPORT MATKUSTAJASATAMA, Matkustajasatama. Tel. 35-821.
   Cuisine: FINNISH/FRENCH. **Reservations:** Not required. **Bus:** 1.
$ Prices: Fixed-price menus 80 markkaa ($21.80); appetizers 60–120 markkaa ($16.35–$32.70); main courses 50–100 markkaa ($13.65–$27.25). AE, MC, V.
   Open: Daily 9am–2am.

A few steps from the harbor, this former warehouse contains the biggest dance floor in Turku, with dance band music beginning at 8pm nightly. Full meals might include platters of herring, pepper steak, reindeer chops in cream sauce, chili con carne, shrimp salad, Finnish salmon soup, or fresh fish dishes. There is also a cozy nautical-style bar, which sometimes attracts many of the sailors who happen to be in port for the night.

MODERATE

BRAHENKELLARI, Puolalankatu 1. Tel. 325-400.
Cuisine: FINNISH. **Reservations:** Recommended. **Bus:** 1.
$ **Prices:** Appetizers 29–39 markkaa ($7.90–$10.65); main courses 35–80 markkaa ($9.55–$21.80). AE, DC, MC, V.
Open: Nov–May, Mon–Sat 11am–1am, Sun noon–11pm; June–July, Mon–Fri 11am–4pm; Aug–Oct, Mon–Fri 11am–5pm.

Turku's best-known wine restaurant is set within ancient stone walls. Diners can enjoy not only the atmosphere but also some of the best dishes—both meat and fish—in town. The service is polite and attentive, and the wine list is excellent, but expensive. Several routine dishes are served, but the menu also contains more exotic specialties such as reindeer.

CAFE/RESTAURANT LYRA, Humalistonkatu 4. Tel. 323-255.
Cuisine: FINNISH. **Reservations:** Not required.
$ **Prices:** Appetizers 39–59 markkaa ($10.65–$16.10); main dishes 35–80 markkaa ($9.55–$21.80). MC, V.
Open: Summer, daily noon–7pm; winter, Sat–Sun noon–6pm.

This old timbered building along this colorful street in the town center has been likened to a doll's house. The most expensive dining is on the ground floor, where there is a restaurant serving good food. Specialties include Baltic herring, salmon, and reindeer. Upstairs is a café where you can enjoy coffee and cake, or light snacks.

RESTAURANT PINELLA, Porthaninpuisto. Tel. 500-074.
Cuisine: ITALIAN. **Reservations:** Not required.
$ **Prices:** Appetizers 29–45 markkaa ($7.90–$12.25); main courses 45–85 markkaa ($12.25–$15.55); lunch 35 markkaa ($9.55). MC, V.
Open: Restaurant, daily 11am–midnight; Pub Jajazzo, daily 4pm–midnight.

Located on the banks of the Jokiranta River between a city park and two of the busiest bridges in town, this restaurant has been a focal point for artists and philosophers since it was established by an Italian immigrant to Turku in 1848. The entrance to Pub Jajazzo, where snacks are served, is beneath a neoclassical arcade facing the river. The main dining area, Puu-Pinella (Wooden Pinella), faces the park, and you can dine on the veranda leading into it. You can select from a Finnish buffet or order such specialties as veal in aspic, several preparations of herring, Miss Emmy's meatballs (named after the owner who made herself famous cooking here from 1936 to 1946), and an array of pizzas, including "Mamma Mia." Fresh fish from the Baltic and Finland's lakes and rivers is also served.

BUDGET

RESTAURANT VERSO, Linnankatu 3. Tel. 510-956.
Cuisine: VEGETARIAN. **Reservations:** Not required.
$ **Prices:** Appetizers 16–30 markkaa ($4.35–$8.20); main courses 28–39 markkaa ($7.65–$10.65). AE, V.
Open: Sept–May, Mon–Fri 11am–5pm, Sat 11am–4pm; June–Aug, Mon–Fri 11am–5pm.

The only vegetarian restaurant in town, this is located in an art nouveau villa near the Italian consulate and the Town Hall. The high-ceilinged second-floor dining rooms have roughly textured tables in a consciously simple decor. You order the vegetarian specialties at a cafeteria counter. The restaurant steers away from eggs, fish, and (obviously) meat, and no smoking is permitted inside.

SHOPPING

AARIKKA, Yliopistonkatu 27. Tel. 313-562.

Everything sold in this imaginative and well-stocked shop was made and designed in Finland. It's one of the best addresses in town for buying imaginative children's toys, Finnish crystal, textiles, wooden jewelry, and a full menagerie of carved wooden animals in several sizes.

MARIMEKKO, Hansa/Thalia, Aurakatu 10. Tel. 514-333.

This shop represents the world-famous Marimekko design and offers clothes for men, women, and children, including dresses, blouses, and shirts of printed cotton. It is in the big Hansa Shopping Center, which has 117 shops selling clothes, furs, leather, shoes, jewelry, books, records, cameras, furniture, and giftware. You can take a break from your shopping spree in one of Hansa's cafés and restaurants, and under the same roof are banks with currency-exchange and other services.

NEOVISKA, Rajakivenkatu 31-32. Tel. 421-262.

This is the place to see and purchase unique hand-woven wall carpets by textile designer Pia Neovius; they're tax-free when they are sold by the artist. There are no set hours for display, but Pia Neovius will be glad to show her textiles by appointment—call her at home at the above telephone number.

PENTIK, Yliopistonkatu 25. Tel. 335-005.

Carefully arranged within this shop's many carved armoires are some of the most beautiful ceramic table settings in town, all in a vivid range of northern colors. The shop also sells smooth-sanded wooden cups from Lapland and representations of Arctic birds in polychrome-covered wood.

STOCKMANN DEPARTMENT STORE, Yliopistonkatu 22. Tel. 337-344.

At the "Harrods of Turku," you can find Finnish and international fashions, textiles, jewelry, and cosmetics. Finnish goods, such as Arabia pottery and china, Marimekko fabrics, and Iittala crystal are also sold, and Stockmann will ship your purchases home for you. When you need a break from shopping, you can have coffee and cake in the Stockmann cafeteria.

SYLVI SALONENOY, Yliopistonkatu 25. Tel. 334-100.

This shop features hand-sewn screens, linen towels, and tablecloths, and many other kinds of handcrafts. Poppana cotton from Karelia province and *ryijy* rugs in bold designs are available here; the rug selection is reputedly the largest in the country. The store also offers both decorative and everyday handmade articles from natural materials.

EXCURSIONS FROM TURKU
RUISSALO

This little island, 6 miles from Turku, has a number of privately owned, elegant summer villas built during Ruissalo's heyday as a fashionable resort early in the 19th century. Today the island is owned by the city of Turku and is a national park. Finland's largest oak woods and a sandy beach make this a popular spot for walking, sunning, and swimming. At the busy marina, you can rent a boat for the day or book passage for a sailboat excursion among the islands.

NAANTALI

The people of this town resisted change so successfully in the 17th century that today Naantali remains a fine example of a medieval Finnish town. Naantali, 12 miles north of Turku, takes its name from a convent and monastery of Saint Birgitta, called "the Valley of Grace," which moved to the coast in 1443. The convent was rich, and the little town prospered until the Reformation brought an end to the religious house.

Today you can stroll through little narrow lanes, called "cat tails," from medieval days, lined with wooden houses still on their original sites. In medieval times each house had its own name on a plaque over the door. Some of these plaques have survived, and the houses are known by their original names. The present buildings of the Old Town date from the late 18th and early 19th centuries.

After the Reformation, Naantali declined until the town became a popular health resort after a spa was established in 1863. The town enjoyed its heyday around the turn of the century. It was particularly popular with the Russians, who considered it a better health resort than St. Petersburg. This tradition has been revived recently and a new spa hotel has opened at Lalevanniemi.

The **Musiikkijuhlat,** an international music festival, is held at Naantali in June, and the main concerts are heard in the 15th-century Convent Church, with vesper hymns sung at 8pm. The **Tourist Office of Naantali** is located at Kaivotori 2, SF-21000 Naantali (tel. 921/850-850).

Getting There

The easiest way to get to Naantali is to take a bus from Turku; buses run every 15 minutes and the trip takes 25 minutes. Car-ferries take passengers between Naantali and Kapellskär (Sweden), with two departures a day; the voyage takes 10 hours.

What to See & Do

The convent was demolished, but you can still see the **Convent Church,** completed in 1462 and renovated a number of times, including the addition of a tower in 1797. Exhibits in the church's collection include relics from the former convent, such as the crown worn by nuns when they took their vows and a Gothic tabernacle for the Reserved Sacrament. The church is open from May to the middle of August, daily from noon to 7pm; from the middle of August through April, daily from noon to 3pm.

At the **Naantali Musuem,** Katinhanta 1 (tel. 921/755-321), you can visit three old wooden houses with outbuildings in the heart of the Old Town. Admission is 5 markkaa ($1.35) for adults, 3 markkaa (80¢) for children. The museum is open June through August, daily noon to 6pm. The remainder of the year it can be seen by prior arrangement.

Kulturanta, a massive granite house on Luonnomaa Island, across the bay from the Convent Church, is the summer home of the president of the Finnish Republic. Visitors aren't allowed inside the house, but you can see the rose garden, which has more than 3,500 rosebushes. Admission is free, and the garden is open May to September, daily from 6 to 8pm.

Where to Stay & Dine

NAANTALI SPA, Kalevanniemi, SF-21100 Naantali. Tel. 921/857-711.
Fax 921/857-790. 93 rms (all with bath). A/C TV TEL
$ Rates (including breakfast): Summer, 600 markkaa ($163.60) single; 770 markkaa ($210) double. Winter, 550 markkaa ($150) single; 700 markkaa ($191) double. AE, DC, MC, V.

This spa, built in 1984, accommodates both holiday visitors and those seeking rehabilitation through its spa facilities. Bedrooms are furnished in a simple but comfortable modern style. Some have balconies, and there are specially equipped rooms for the disabled. The hotel has two fully licensed restaurants, a cafeteria, and an open-air restaurant operating in summer, plus two public lounges. Vegetarian and special diets are available.

Spa facilities include a Finnish sauna, Turkish bath, hot-water Roman pool with Jacuzzi, general swimming pool, and water and brush massage. Special courses are offered to cure stress, muscular maladies, insomnia, obesity, and tiredness, among other things. Beauty and fitness courses are also available.

RAUMA

At a harbor on the Gulf of Bothnia 60 miles north of Turku, the town of Rauma is the third oldest in Finland. The town was already a center of trade when it was chartered in 1442. Only ruins remain of the first house of worship, the Church of the Holy

Trinity, but a Franciscan monastery was also constructed here—before 1449—and its Church of the Holy Cross has survived.

What to See & Do

The most prominent structure is the **Town Hall,** which was built in 1776 and houses the **Rauma Museum,** Kauppakatu 13. The museum features demonstrations of lace-making on Sunday from 2 to 5pm, and contains a permanent exhibition of artifacts related to navigation, bobbin lace-making, and other old professions. Admission to the museum is 5 markkaa ($1.35) for adults, 3 markkaa (80¢) for children. It's open May 15 to August 15, daily from 10am to 6pm.

The network of narrow streets and the building plots date from the 16th and 17th centuries, although most buildings are from the 18th and 19th centuries. **Kirsti House,** a lace-maker's home from the 18th century, is open May 15 to August 15, daily from 10am to 6pm; and **Marela House,** a ship-owner's home and a well-preserved example of the affluence brought to Rauma by the maritime trade, is open May 15 to August 15, daily from 10am to 6pm.

Held at the end of July each year, **Rauma Lace Week** is a festive occasion, with exhibitions of folk art, folk-music concerts, and feasting on authentic local Finnish dishes. The highlight of the event is, of course, the making of lace. Demonstrations are given and various examples of the lace of Rauma are exhibited. For information on the festival, contact the **Rauma Tourist Office** at Eteläkatu 7, SF-26100 Rauma (tel. 938/224-555).

Where to Stay & Dine

CUMULUS RAUMA, Aittakarinkatu 9, SF-26100 Rauma. Tel. 938/37-821. Fax 938/378-2299. 104 rms (all with bath). MINIBAR TV TEL.

$ Rates (including breakfast): June 21–Aug 5 and weekends year round, 280 markkaa ($76.35) single; 380 markkaa ($103.65) double. Weekdays Aug 6–June 20, 410 markkaa ($111.80) single; 560 markkaa ($152.70) double. AE, DC, MC, V. **Parking:** Available.

This hotel, south of Laivuripolku, has comfortable accommodations, two saunas, two restaurants, a bar, a swimming pool, and a large parking area with an ingenious plug-in method of keeping a car engine warm during a frosty night. The hotel's restaurants are open daily from 10am to 1am.

2. THE ÅLAND ISLANDS

The Ålands, off the west coast of Finland, between Turku and Stockholm, form an archipelago of 6,500 islands, islets, and skerries. The land mass is made up of 510 square miles, with 500 miles of roads. Yet it is the water that you remember—the sea stretches in all directions. Most of the islands are not inhabited, and there are only some 23,000 residents throughout the archipelago, but an estimated one million tourists visit the Ålands each year.

Åland comes from a word in the Old Norse language that meant "water island," and the English word "island" is also derived from the same word. The archipelago was settled some 5,000 years ago by seal hunters; large burial cairns can still be seen. In the Viking Age the lands became the most densely populated part of Scandinavia.

From medieval times until 1809 Åland was part of Sweden, but in that year Sweden lost both Åland and Finland to Russia. After the fall of the tsar in 1917, Åland petitioned the king of Sweden to be allowed to rejoin his country, but Finland objected. The matter was settled by the League of Nations in 1921, which granted Finland sovereignty over the chain but protected Swedish culture and left Swedish as the official language. Today the residents of Åland are still more Swedish than Finnish, but technically Åland (pronounced oh-lant) still belongs to Finland. However, the Finnish government has given the people much autonomy, including the right to fly their own flag and, since 1982, to issue their own stamps—which are highly prized by collectors. Also, the young men of the islands are exempt from serving in the Finnish armed forces.

GETTING AROUND

Most of the inhabited islands are connected by a series of bridges, causeways, and ferry services. Except for the M/S *Kumlinge,* fares are not charged on the local car-ferries unless you travel the complete route from end to end. "Road ferries" are always free, as they are intended as a road extension between the islands.

The largest island, 30 miles long, is called **"mainland,"** and about 90% of the population lives here. The island has dark coniferous woodland, much farmland and pastureland, fishing ports, and rocky fjords. The mainland is also known for its old fortresses and 11 medieval churches—the oldest built from the 12th to the 15th centuries. The reddish-brown and gray masonry of this outstanding collection of ecclesiastical architecture has given them the appellation "speckled hens," and a car or bicycle tour can easily include a visit to all of them.

The second-largest settlement, **Eckerö,** is the westernmost municipality in Finland. It was once a station on the mail route between Sweden and Imperial Russia.

Other major island targets include **Kumlinge,** which has a 15th-century church and is served by a ferry line from Långnäs; the crossing takes 2 hours.

Vårdö: This is the closest settlement to the Åland mainland, only 5 minutes away. The lush part of the island is in the south.

Brändö: The ferryboat from Långnäs (the same one that serves Kumlinge) also goes to this island—a municipality of some 1,000 islands. The largest of these are connected by causeways and bridges.

Föglö: Some 600 residents live on these clusters of islands, some of which are linked by bridges and causeways. Föglö, the largest of the island municipalities, is about 30 minutes from the Åland mainland.

Sottunga: From Långnäs, there is a 1½-hour ferry trip to Sottunga. Once there, you'll find only 150 residents in what is considered the smallest municipality in the Ålands.

Kökar: A rather bleak landscape. The remains of a 2,500-year-old Bronze Age community have been found at Karlby. Kokar is reached on a 2½-hour ferry crossing from Långnäs.

MARIEHAMN

The capital of the Ålands, Mariehamn is the only real town in the archipelago and has a population of 10,000. Founded in 1861, Mariehamn was named after the empress of Russia, Marie Alexandrova, wife of Alexander II. It lies on an isthmus with harbor facilities, and thousands of linden trees line its streets. The people here have always looked to the sea for their livelihood—that is, before the days of tourism.

The town is small, so no buses are required to get from one place to the other. However, there is a bus that runs from the harbor to the center of town, a distance of 2 miles.

The **Tourist Information Office** is located at Storagatan 18, SF-22100 Mariehamn (tel. 928/16-575). The **telephone area code** for the Åland Islands is 928.

GETTING THERE

The **airport** at Mariehamn is 2 miles outside the center of town. There are two round-trip flights daily from Stockholm, and four or five daily from Turku. Each flight takes about 20 minutes.

There is **bus service** in summer from both Helsinki and Turku, traveling via the inter-island ferries.

The Viking Line runs **seagoing ferries** from Stockholm to Turku, with a stop en route at Mariehamn, and the Silja Line also makes the 6½-hour run from

Stockholm to Mariehamn. There is usually one ship per day on each line. For prices, tickets, and information, contact the Viking Line at Stureplan 8 in Stockholm (tel. 08/222-480), or the Silja Line on the Stureplan in Stockholm (tel. 08/222-140 in Stockholm, 921/652-244 in Turku).

WHAT TO SEE & DO

Because Mariehamn is the administrative and economic center of Åland, the **Åland Self-Government House** is here. Also inside the town limits is **Tullarns äng Park,** a nature reserve open to visitors.

In Town

ÅLANDS MUSEUM, Öhbergsvägen. Tel. 282-5000.

At the eastern harbor between the Town Hall and Parliament, this museum traces the history of the island beginning with the early settlers 5,000 years ago.

Admission: 7 markkaa ($1.90) adults, 4 markkaa ($1.10) children.

Open: Summer, Wed–Mon 10am–4pm, Tues 10am–8pm. **Closed:** Winter.

ÅLAND MARITIME MUSEUM, Storagatan. Tel. 11-930.

This museum has a superb collection of exhibits from the great sailing-ship era of Åland.

Nearby is the four-masted barque *Pommern.* Built in Glasgow in 1903, it's a 310-foot clipper ship that participated in the Great Grain Race to Australia in the 1930s. Here you can see what life was like on board one of the windjammers.

Admission: Museum, 10 markkaa ($2.75) adults, 5 markkaa ($1.35) children; *Pommern,* 10 markkaa ($2.75) adults, 5 markkaa ($1.35) children under 12.

Open: Museum, May–Aug, daily 10am–5pm; Sept–Apr, daily 10am–4pm. *Pommern,* mid-Apr to June and mid-Aug to Oct 20, daily 9am–7pm (closed July to mid-Aug and Oct 21 to mid-Apr).

MERCHANT'S HOUSE, Parkgatan.

This museum of crafts and commerce includes the interior of a shop from the turn of the century.

Admission: Free.

Open: Mid-June to mid-Aug, Mon–Fri 1–3pm. **Closed:** Mid-Aug to mid-June.

Around the Island

There are also many nearby places worth a trek, including the **Ramsholmen Nature Reserve** and the region around the Lemstrom Canal. You can also take a drive out to **Ytternäs** and along the road across Nato to Jarso. Another inviting spot, on the other side of Slemmern Bay, southeast of Mariehamn, is **Chapel Bay,** which has its Lembote Chapel on a hilltop, the ruin of a medieval seafarers' chapel.

The **Jomala Church,** one of the most interesting churches, is 4 miles north of Mariehamn; part of it is from the 12th century, and it still contains 13th-century murals. About 8 miles southeast is the 13th-century **Lemland Church,** which has a triumphal cross and Madonna from the 14th century and a reredos from the 15th century.

At **Bomarsund,** 22 miles northeast of Mariehamn, you can see the ruins of a fortress built by Imperial Russia. Also of interest, the 13th-century **Kastelholm Ruins,** 6 miles from Bomarsund, are from when the Swedes constructed a fortress to mark their sovereignty over the islands.

WHERE TO STAY

Expensive

HOTEL ARKIPELAG, Strandgatan 31, SF-22100 Mariehamn. Tel. 928/14-020. Fax 928/24-384. 86 rms (all with bath). A/C MINIBAR TV TEL.

$ Rates (including breakfast): 700 markkaa ($190.90) single; 900 markkaa ($245.45) double. AE, DC, MC, V.

This leading hotel in town is located between the commercial center and the marina. The rooms are well furnished and well maintained. Most of them open onto a view of the yachts in the harbor. This is the plushest place to stay in the islands.

Dining/Entertainment: The huge restaurant, Arkipelag, is open Monday through Friday from 10am to 2am, on Saturday from 11am to 2am and on Sunday from 11am to 1am. The pleasant bar is open Monday through Saturday from 6pm to 1:30am and on Sunday from noon to 6pm; the nightclub is open daily from 9pm to 3am.

Services: Room service.

Facilities: Two saunas with an indoor and outdoor swimming pool, a small-stakes casino, conference and convention facilities, sailboat rentals from the facilities at the water's edge just across the road.

Moderate

ESPLANAD HOTEL, Storagatan 5, SF-22100 Mariehamn. Tel. 928/16-333. 28 rms (all with bath). TV TEL.

$ Rates (including breakfast): 360 markkaa ($98.15) single; 480 markkaa ($130.90) double. AE, DC, MC, V. **Parking:** Free.

The limited number of bedrooms in the Esplanad, a comfortable and intimate hotel in the center of town, ensures a personalized touch. A lighthearted restaurant, La Cave, is in the basement and features vegetarian platters and Finnish specialties. Laundry facilities are available.

HOTEL ADLON, Hamngatan 7, SF-22100 Mariehamn. Tel. 928/15-300. Fax 928/281-507. 52 rms (all with bath). A/C MINIBAR TV TEL.

$ Rates (including breakfast): 480 markkaa ($130.90) single; 620 markkaa ($169.05) double. AE, DC, MC, V.

One of the most popular hotels in town, opened in 1973, this hotel has an ideal location—next to the western harbor where all the ferries and cruise ships berth. The restaurant is known for its good plain Scandinavian food and à la carte dishes. Rooms are comfortably and attractively furnished.

HOTEL CIKADA, Hamngatan 1, SF-22100 Mariehamn. Tel. 928/16-333. Fax 928/17-363. 84 rms (all with bath). A/C TV TEL.

$ Rates (including breakfast): 300–415 markkaa ($81.80–$113.15) single; 410–550 markkaa ($111.80–$150) double. AE, MC, V.

A cluster of trees helps conceal this hotel, about 300 yards from the boat terminal, from the industrial sections of the nearby harbor. Each comfortable bedroom has its own narrow loggia, and many of the rooms overlook the rectangular swimming pool. Thirty rooms contain balconies. There are three different saunas for unwinding, plus a warm-weather drink-and-snack service on the outdoor terrace. The hotel's restaurant is open daily from 10am to 10pm.

HOTEL POMMERN, Norragatan 8-10, SF-22100 Mariehamn. Tel. 928/15-555. Fax 928/150-77. 55 rms (all with bath). A/C TV TEL.

$ Rates (including breakfast): 450–460 markkaa ($122.70–$125.45) single; 575–610 markkaa ($156.80–$166.35) double. AE, DC, MC, V.

Right in the center of town, the Hotel Pommern has functional, modern bedrooms. Some contain minibars. The hotel's Restaurant Pommern, Mariehamn's fish restaurant, has gained a high reputation for its seafood dishes with a special local touch; it's open daily from 11am to 11:30pm. The hotel is linked by a tunnel to the Sabina nightclub and restaurant, open Monday through Saturday from 7pm to 3am and on Sunday from 7pm to 1am.

PARK ÅLANDIA HOTEL, Norra Esplanadgatan 3, SF-22100 Mariehamn. Tel. 928/14-130. 79 rms (all with bath). TV TEL.

$ Rates (including breakfast): 450 markkaa ($122.70) single; 600 markkaa ($163.60) double. AE, DC, MC, V.

Each of the accommodations in this hotel 1 mile from the ferry harbor contains big windows and comfortable modern furniture. Both its in-house bar, Brittany, open from 11am to 2am, and its comfortable restaurant, open daily from 11am to midnight, extend onto the flag-draped boulevard. Facilities include a sauna and a swimming pool. Room service and laundry facilities are available.

WHERE TO DINE

RESTAURANT NAUTICAL, Hamngatan 2. Tel. 11-931.
   Cuisine: FRENCH/FINNISH. **Reservations:** Required.
$ Prices: Fixed-price meals 35–90 markkaa ($9.55–$24.55); appetizers 52–78 markkaa ($14.15–$21.25); main dishes 94–135 markkaa ($25.65–$36.80). AE, DC, MC, V.
   Open: Mon–Sat 10am–1am.
This pleasant restaurant has the look of a ship about to steam out to sea. It's in the same building as the land Maritime Museum, at the western harbor overlooking the museum ship *Pommern*, and as you'd expect, fresh seafood is one of the kitchen's specialties, including herring and fresh shellfish, with occasional lobster. Local ingredients are used whenever possible. As an appetizer, you might begin with slightly salted salmon with horseradish sauce or perch pâté with a spinach-and-scampi sauce. For a main dish, try the fried filet of perch stuffed with salmon in a fish-roe sauce or chateaubriand flavored with garlic. At least one vegetarian main dish always appears on the menu.

CHAPTER 37

THE LAKE REGION

- **WHAT'S SPECIAL ABOUT THE LAKE REGION**
1. **TAMPERE**
2. **LAHTI**
3. **JYVÄSKYLÄ**
4. **LAPPEENRANTA**
5. **IMATRA**
6. **SAVONLINNA**
7. **JOENSUU**
8. **KUOPIO**

Saimaa, an extensive lake district in eastern Finland, has thousands of islands and straits and lots of blue water. It's a land of sunshine, small villages, holiday centers, and pleasant people, wrapped in the peace and quiet of the wilderness.

From Lappeenranta, the center of Finnish lake tourism, you can book cruises lasting 2 hours or 2 days in the southern part of Lake Saimaa, or you can take a cruise to the Saimaa Canal and see the Russian border. In this region, you can swim in clean, clear water, fish with a seine, eat your catch cooked on a campfire, sail, windsurf, paddle a boat, dance, and enjoy saunas.

Tampere, Finland's second-largest city, is also set in a geographic area of myriad lakes. Tampere is a center for culture, tourism, and commerce, and its surrounding Pirkanmaa region is known for its vast waterways and forests.

Jyväskylä is often called the "capital" of central Finland. The hometown of Alvar Aalto, the great architect, Jyväskylä is the setting for the Thousand Lakes rally, a major boat competition in August.

Lahti, a busy commercial center, is also a sports center, site of many world skiing championships. It's a good base for exploring Lake Päijänne.

SEEING THE LAKE REGION

GETTING THERE

You can drive around the lake district, although the ideal way to go is by lake steamer, using Savonlinna as a gateway. For a preview of the lakes, the most popular steamer routes are the Kuopio–Savonlinna–Kuopio run, taking 12 hours, or the Savonlinna–Lappeenranta–Savonlinna run, taking 9 hours. But much shorter tours are also possible.

You can fly to many of the major "gateways," such as Tampere, Savonlinna, Jyväskylä, or Mikkeli. Trains and buses also service all the tourist centers we recommend, with daily departures from Helsinki. The entire area, in fact, can be explored by bus. You can take an express bus to a main center, then explore the remotest corners by bus.

A SUGGESTED ITINERARY

Day 1: Leave Helsinki and overnight in Lappeenranta.
Day 2: Drive or take public transportation to Imatra in the northeast for another day's sightseeing; spend the night.
Days 3&4: Transfer to Savonlinna and spend 2 nights exploring not only its own attractions but those in the environs. Allow a day for traveling on the lakes.

WHAT'S SPECIAL ABOUT THE LAKE REGION

Great Towns/Villages

☐ Savonlinna, in the middle of the Saimma lake system, site of the famous opera festival in summer.

☐ Tampere, Finland's "second city," a leading industrial town and filled with attractions.

☐ Lappeenranta, the southerly port-of-call of the boats on Lake Saimma and one of the best centers for exploring the eastern province of Karelia.

Museums

☐ Alvar Aalto Museum, Jyväskylä, honoring Finland's greatest architect in a town filled with buildings he designed.

☐ Old Kuopio Museum, in Kuopio, taking up a city block and offering a look back at the Finland of yesteryear.

Ancient Monuments

☐ Linnoitus, the fortress of Lappeenranta, defensive fortification begun by the Swedes as protection against Russian invasions.

☐ Olavinlinna Castle, at Savonlinna, a medieval fortress from 1475.

Ace Attractions

☐ Imatra Rapids, at Imatra, a mighty torrent that even drew the tourist interest of Catherine the Great.

Special Events/Festivals

☐ The Jyväskylä Arts Festival, oldest regular art festival in Finland.

☐ Savonlinna Opera Festival, in July, the major opera festival of Scandinavia.

Day 5: Head west cross country for an overnight stay in Jyväskylä.

Day 6: Go to Tampere in the southwest for a day of sightseeing and spend the night. Tampere is a good point to head back to Helsinki and your next destination.

---

1. TAMPERE

107 miles north of Helsinki, 96 miles NE of Turku

GETTING THERE   By Plane   Tampere-Pirkkala airport, 9 miles from the city center, has air links with some towns in Finland. But Tampere's air link to the world is via Helsinki, from which there are frequent flights.

By Train   There are trains almost every hour making the 2¼-hour trip to and from Helsinki. Seven trains a day also connect Tampere with Turku, taking 2¼ hours.

By Bus   Five buses a day, taking 2 hours, run back and forth between Helsinki and Tampere, and five buses a day, taking 2½ hours, link Tampere with Turku.

By Boat   From June 4 to August 11, boats run between Tampere and Hämeenlinna in the south. This makes an interesting tour, as Hämeenlinna was the birthplace of Jean Sibelius. The one-way fare is 170 markkaa ($46.35).

By Car   Both Helsinki and Turku are a 2-hour drive from Tampere. From Helsinki, take Route 3 north, and from Turku head northeast on Route 41.

ESSENTIALS   The **City Tourist Office,** Verkatehtaankatu 2 (P.O. Box 87), SF-33211 Tampere (tel. 931/126-652), helps arrange for guides, sightseeing tours, and maps, and provides miscellaneous information. The office is open June through August, Monday through Friday from 8:30am to 8pm, on Saturday from 8:30am to 6pm, and on Sunday from noon to 6pm; September through May, Monday through Friday from 8:30am to 4pm.

The **telephone area code** for Tampere is 931.

SPECIAL EVENTS Beginning in 1975 the **Tampere International Choir Festival** has taken place every other year (1991, 1993). The concert series consists of performances by the best choirs in Finland, with foreign choirs invited as well.

The **Tampere International Theater Festival** since 1969 has been Finland's only festival of professional theater, taking place in mid-August. Foreign companies also are invited to perform.

The **Tampere Jazz Happening** is considered the best jazz festival in Finland. Ever since 1982 it has been a festival of modern jazz, organized in October or November.

Located on a narrow isthmus between two lakes, Lake Näsijärvi and Lake Phyäjärvi, Tampere is Finland's second-largest city (pop. 170,000) and is primarily an industrial center; however, it remains one of the cleanest, brightest cities in Scandinavia and is filled with parks, water, museums, art galleries, theaters, and statues including some works by Wäinö Aaltosen. One statue he sculpted depicted a tax collector in the nude.

A vibrant young city with a university life, Tampere is host to one of Scandinavia's major attractions: the outdoor theater on Pyynikki with a revolving auditorium. Tampere's Swedish name is Tammerfors.

WHAT TO SEE & DO

The **Tampere Service Card** is available for tourists June through August, costing 50 markkaa ($13.65) for adults and 25 markkaa ($6.80) for children. It is valid for 24 hours, and grants free rides in the city buses (TAKL), a daily sightseeing tour of the city, and entrance to several museums. It is available at the City Tourist Office and at various hotels.

ORGANIZED TOURS

From June 1 to August 31, a daily guided tour of the city leaves at 2pm from in front of the City Tourist and Congress Service, Verkatehtaankatu 2 (tel. 126-652), costing 25 markkaa ($6.80) for adults, 10 markkaa ($2.75) for children under 16. The trip lasts 1 hour and 25 minutes, and the commentary is given in English.

From mid-June to mid-August, Tampere is the meeting point of two popular lake cruises, **Finnish Silverline** and **Poet's Way**, which both have good restaurants. Route descriptions are available from Laivayhtioiden Tilauskeskus (Boatlines Booking Center), Verkatehtaankatu 2 (tel. 124-803). Boats run from June 4 to August 11.

THE SÄRKÄNNIEMI LEISURE CENTER

About a mile from the center of Tampere is the 25-acre Särkänniemi Leisure Center at Särkänniemi (tel. 231-333). A joint ticket, the Särkänniemi-passport, includes entrance to the dolphinarium and any five of the following: observation tower, aquarium, planetarium, children's zoo, amusement park, and Sara Hildén Art Museum. The passport, valid from the end of April to September 4, costs 60 markkaa ($16.35) for adults and 40 markkaa ($10.90) for children 12 or under. You can get to Särkänniemi by city bus no. Y4.

NÄSINNEULA, in the Särkänniemi Leisure Center.
Towering over the grounds is the 560-foot-tall Näsinneula, the tallest observation

tower in Finland, with a café, a revolving restaurant, and an open observation platform.

Admission: 10 markkaa ($2.75) adults, 5 markkaa ($1.35) children 12 or under; free with the Särkänniemi-passport.

Open: Daily 10am–8pm.

AQUARIUM, in the Särkänniemi Leisure Center.

The Aquarium has on display 2,000 specimens representing nearly 200 different species. It also has a seal pool with feeding times at 11am and 4pm.

Admission: 20 markkaa ($5.45) adults, 10 markkaa ($2.75) children 12 or under; free with the Särkänniemi-passport.

Open: Daily 10am–8pm.

PLANETARIUM, in the Särkänniemi Leisure Center.

Here you can lean back in an armchair and follow the movements of the firmament, accompanied by expert commentary. During the show you can see the movements of 6,000 stars through the skies.

Admission: 30 markkaa ($8.20) adults, 15 markkaa ($4.10) children 12 or under; free with the Särkänniemi-passport.

Open: May–Aug, daily on the hour 11am–7pm; Sept–Apr, daily on the hour noon–4pm.

FUNFAIR, in the Särkänniemi Leisure Center.

In summer only, the Funfair provides such entertainment as ferris wheels and merry-go-rounds.

Admission: 5 markkaa ($1.35); free with the Särkänniemi-passport.

Open: Apr 30 to mid-May and Aug 15–31, Sat–Sun noon–8pm; mid-May to Aug 14, daily noon–8pm. **Closed:** Sept–Apr 29.

CHILDREN'S ZOO, in the Särkänniemi Leisure Center.

Just west of the Näsinneula observation tower, the Children's Zoo provides a common playground for children and domestic animals, most of which are familiar to children. Pony rides and rides in donkey-pulled carriages are available.

Admission: 20 markkaa ($5.45) adults, 10 markkaa ($2.75) children 12 or under; free with the Särkänniemi-passport.

Open: May 12–Aug 15, daily 10am–7pm. **Closed:** Aug 16–May 11.

DOLPHINARIUM, in the Särkänniemi Leisure Center.

At this Dolphinarium, the only one in Finland, there are five dolphins giving five performances daily.

Admission: 30 markkaa ($8.20) adults, 15 markkaa ($4.10) children 12 or under; free with the Särkänniemi-passport.

Open: May 30–Sept 2, performances daily at 11:30am and 1, 2:30, 4, and 5:30pm. **Closed:** Sept 3–May 29.

SARA HILDÉN ART MUSEUM, in the Särkänniemi Leisure Center.

At the foot of the Näsinneula observation tower, this museum presents changing exhibitions of modern art. The Sara Hildén Foundation was founded in 1962 by Sara Hildén, who donated the works of art in her possession. Since then the collection has been greatly expanded, concentrating mainly on postwar art, including sculpture by Henry Moore and a painting by Francis Bacon. The museum is in beautiful lakeside surroundings, and some of the sculpture is displayed on the shores of Lake Näsijärvi, next to the museum.

Admission: 10 markkaa ($2.75) adults, 3 markkaa (80¢) students and children 12 or under; free with the Särkänniemi-passport.

Open: Daily 11am–6pm. **Bus:** 16 from the railroad station (in summer, also the Y4).

IMPRESSIONS

*In Tampere it was a natural to approve of the factories as in Mecca one would
the mosques.*
—JOHN SYKES

MUSEUMS

TAMPERE ART MUSEUM [District Art Museum of Pirkanmaa], Puutarhakatu 34. Tel. 121-244.

Collections here include paintings, sculpture, drawings, graphics, regional art since
the early 19th century, and the Tampere art collection. The museum also has
changing art exhibits.
Admission: 10 markkaa ($2.75) adults, 3 markkaa (80¢) children 12 or under.
Open: Daily 11am–7pm. **Bus:** 1, 2, 3, 16, 25.

HAIHARA DOLL MUSEUM, Haihara Manor, Kaukajärvi. Tel. 630-350.

About 5 miles outside Tampere, this is one of the most unusual museums in the
world—it has a collection of nearly 2,500 dolls of every material, age, and type
imaginable. Of special note are the talisman dolls, of which the oldest and most
mysterious is a Peruvian rag doll from the grave of an Inca child. There are also
Christmas dolls, theater dolls, toys, dollhouses, and costume dolls from more than 80
countries. The museum also organizes various displays of the history of costume and
culture.
   If you drive here by car, go east from Tampere on Route 12, then turn right at the
traffic light crossing at Lake Kaukajarvi and continue to the site.
Admission: 15 markkaa ($4.10) adults, 5 markkaa ($1.35) children 12 or under.
Open: Apr 15–Sept, daily noon–6pm. **Closed:** Oct–Apr 14. **Bus:** 24 from
Tampere.

LENIN MUSEUM, Hämeenpuisto. Tel. 127-313.

Material dealing with Lenin and the history of the Russian Revolution is presented
here, as well as material illustrating Lenin's connection with Finland.
Admission: 6 markkaa ($1.65) adults, 2 markkaa (55¢) children 12 or under.
Open: Tues–Sat 11am–3pm, Sun 11am–4pm. **Bus:** 1, 2, 3.

WHERE TO STAY

Tampere has more hotels than any other city in Finland except Helsinki. I've included
several four- and five-star hotels, but the prices quoted below are high-season tariffs,
which means winter rates. In summer, which is considered the *low season,* these
prices will be reduced. These hotels also have lower weekend rates, although getting
them often involves some negotiation at the desk. Nearly every hotel in Tampere has a
sauna.

EXPENSIVE

ARCTIA HOTEL ROSENDAHL, Pyynikintie 13, SF-33200 Tampere. Tel. 931/112-233. Fax 931/233-375. 207 rms (all with bath). TV TEL **Bus:** 12.

$ Rates (including breakfast): July and weekends year round, 360 markkaa ($98.15)
single; 460 markkaa ($196.35) double. Weekdays Aug–June, 600 markkaa
($163.60) single; 720 markkaa ($196.35) double. AE, DC, MC, V.
Located about 1½ miles from the center of town, this hotel has a dramatic design
enhanced by its position in a quiet forest at the edge of Lake Phyhäjärvi. The hotel

was built in 1977 in a softly angled design of mirrored walls, polished stone, and lacquered ceilings—it's one of the most avant-garde hotels in the region. The elegant bedrooms are quiet, each with a trouser press, among other amenities. Most of them offer minibars. The Silver Line ships stop at the hotel's pier, and there's a lakeside bathing beach. The world-famous outdoor theater, Pyynikki, is nearby.

Dining/Entertainment: Many travelers stop for a meal in one of the hotel's several sun-flooded restaurants, including both a main dining room and a cozy little restaurant La Rose. The hotel also has a pub, a small-stakes casino, and a many-tiered basement-level nightclub (Joselin's) where live bands provide dance music.

Services: Massage, room service.

Facilities: Tennis courts, miles of cross-country ski and hiking trails, swimming pool, children's pool, squash, minigolf, golf simulator, six saunas, solarium.

HOTEL ILVES, Hatanpäänvaltatie 1, SF-33100 Tampere. Tel. 931/121-212. Fax 931/132-565. 334 rms (all with bath). A/C MINIBAR TV TEL **Bus:** 1, 2, 3.

$ Rates (including breakfast): June 14–Aug 3 and Fri–Sun year round, 500 markkaa ($136.35) single or double. Mon–Thurs Aug 4–June 13, 600 markkaa ($163.60) single; 800 markkaa ($218.15) double. AE, DC, MC, V. **Parking:** 50 markkaa ($13.65).

Architecturally the most dramatic hotel in town (built in 1986), the Ilves is a member of Finland's well-respected Sokos hotel chain. Each of the bedrooms is handsomely outfitted in five-star comfort, with modern Finnish furniture, plus textiles, and climate control.

Dining/Entertainment: Four different restaurants are on the premises (the Fransmanni Restaurant is recommended separately; see "Where to Dine," below). In the morning, a popular and airy café and lobby bar doubles as a busy breakfast room, with copious buffets presented. A nightclub and disco have a glittering ambience of colored lights, plants, and mirrors.

Facilities: Hairdresser, three saunas, sauna bar, swimming pool, parking area.

MODERATE

GRAND HOTEL TAMMER, Satakunnankatu 13, SF-33100 Tampere. Tel. 931/125-380. Fax 931/307-57. 90 rms (all with bath). MINIBAR TV TEL **Bus:** 1, 2, 3.

$ Rates (including breakfast): June 14–Aug, 350 markkaa ($95.45) single; 400 markkaa ($109.10) double. Sept–June 13, 485 markkaa ($132.25) single; 650 markkaa ($177.25) double. AE, DC, MC, V. **Parking:** 50 markkaa ($13.65).

When this hotel was built (between rolling hills near a city park), by the well-known Finnish architect Bertal Strommer in 1929, it was considered the most glamorous hotel in town. Today its old-fashioned glamour offers the best perspective in town for an insight into Finnish art deco. To enter the dimly lit reception area, you pass beneath a five-story archway that soars to the roofline. The high-ceilinged, well-scrubbed bedrooms are comfortably furnished and have radios and trouser presses. Don't overlook the outdoor terrace, which offers pleasant views of the water. The hotel is a well-respected member of the nationwide Sokos hotel chain.

Dining/Entertainment: The high-ceilinged dining room with Renaissance detail serves buffet lunches for 110 markkaa ($30). At night both Finnish and international food is served. The hotel's nightclub, Club Grandy, is open daily from 8pm to 3am.

Services: Laundry service, room service.

Facilities: Garage, swimming pool, car-rental desk.

HOTEL CUMULUS, Koskikatu 5, SF-33100 Tampere. Tel. 931/242-4111. Fax 931/242-4111. 230 rms (all with bath). A/C MINIBAR TV TEL **Bus:** 1, 2, 3.

$ Rates (including breakfast): June 24–Aug 7 and weekends year round, 250 markkaa ($68.20) single; 370 markkaa ($100.90) double. Weekdays Aug 8–June 23, 455 markkaa ($124.10) single; 600 markkaa ($163.60) double. **Parking:** 50 markkaa ($13.65). AE, DC, MC, V.

The popularity of its wining and dining facilities, plus its dramatic exterior, make this one of the most exciting hotels in town. Built in 1979, it sits at the edge of the graceful Koskipuisto Park near the river in the center of town, and the Finnair City Bus Terminal is immediately adjacent to the hotel. Each of the bedrooms is stylishly decorated with contemporary furniture. Some rooms are suitable for nonsmokers. The Mona Lisa Wine Bar and the Tiffany Bar are on the lobby level. Room service is offered, and two saunas, a swimming pool, garage, children's playroom, fitness room, and solarium are available.

HOTEL TAMPERE, Hämeenkatu 1, SF-33100 Tampere. Tel. 931/121-980. Fax 931/221-910. 260 rms (all with bath). TV TEL **Bus:** 1, 2, 3.

$ Rates (including breakfast): July and Fri–Sat year round, 300 markkaa ($81.80) single; 380 markkaa ($103.65) double. Sun–Thurs Aug–June, 460 markkaa ($125.45) single; 580 markkaa ($158.15) double. AE, DC, MC, V.

A long-enduring traditional favorite opposite the railway station, this is still one of the biggest and most popular hotels in town. It offers clean and comfortable accommodations in a wide variety of styles. The newest rooms overlook a glass-capped atrium whose fountains and plants lend natural accents to the boutiques and cafés. There is a series of bars, cafeterias, and restaurants on the premises, including the Restaurant Emma, and room service is offered. Six saunas (a few of which are reserved for official occasions), an indoor swimming pool, fitness gymnasium, and solarium are available to guests.

INEXPENSIVE

HÄRMÄLÄ HOTEL, Niolialantie 48, SF-33900 Tampere. Tel. 931/650-400. Fax 931/650-400. 85 rms (all with shower). **Bus:** 1.

$ Rates: 210 markkaa ($57.25) single; 345 markkaa ($94.10) double. AE, DC, MC, V. **Closed:** Sept to mid-May.

About 3 miles from the center of Tampere, this motel is located in the woodland beside Lake Phyäjärvi, where you can swim, boat, or take waterbus trips. Each bedroom is tastefully furnished in contemporary style and is equipped with simple cooking facilities and refrigerators, among other amenities. The restaurant, which serves lunch and dinner, has a lake view. There are living-room lounges on each floor, plus separate rooms for washing and ironing. Best of all is a pine-paneled Finnish sauna. The staff speaks English.

HOTEL MARTINA, Hämeenkatu 11, SF-33100 Tampere. Tel. 931/221-380. 64 rms (all with bath). TV TEL **Bus:** 1, 2, 3.

$ Rates (including breakfast): 350 markkaa ($95.45) single; 480 markkaa ($130.90) double. AE, MC, V.

Renovated in 1984, this centrally located hotel is bright, airy, and modern. The rooms are designed for comfort. Furnishings are functional and everything is well maintained. An attractive bar and restaurant are on the premises. The hotel has a sauna.

HOTELLI VICTORIA, Itsenäisyydenkatu 1, SF-33100 Tampere. Tel. 931/30-640. Fax 931/242-5100. 100 rms (all with bath). TV TEL **Bus:** 1, 2, 3.

$ Rates (including breakfast): June 18–Aug 19, 230 markkaa ($62.70) single; 330 markkaa ($90) double. Aug 20–June 17, 320 markkaa ($87.25) single; 480 markkaa ($130.90) double. AE, DC, MC, V. **Parking:** Available.

On the outskirts of the main commercial center behind a forecourt clustered with fruit trees, this hotel contains one of the most likable bars and informal restaurants in town, the Tunneli, where exposed brick and 19th-century mannequins create an ambience you'd expect to find near Piccadilly Circus in London. Most of the bedrooms contain a color scheme of pink or blue, lots of exposed wood, and a hairdryer, among other amenities. There's a Chinese restaurant adjacent to the hotel entrance, plus a garage, a parking area, a sauna, and an indoor swimming pool.

BUDGET

DOMUS, Pellervonkatu 9, SF-33540 Tampere. Tel. 931/550-000. Fax 931/225-409. 200 rms (90 with shower). **Bus:** 25.

$ Rates: 150 markkaa ($40.90) single without bath; 220 markkaa ($60) single with shower; 200 markkaa ($54.55) double without bath; 280 markkaa ($76.35) double with shower. Breakfast costs 25 markkaa ($6.80) extra. MC, V.

⑤ One of Finland's finest student-run hotels, this is a compound of modern buildings with grassy courtyards located in the Kaleva district less than a mile from the center. The compact bedrooms are decorated in Finnish-modern style and have wall-to-wall desks, birch armchairs, wall shelves, built-in wardrobes, sofa beds, and brightly colored fabrics. Each room also has a small refrigerator and stove. The sauna and swimming pool can be used free in the morning. On the premises is the Fun Pub Rocky.

WHERE TO DINE

MODERATE

FINLAYSONIN PALATSI, Kuninkaankatu 1. Tel. 125-905.
   Cuisine: FINNISH/INTERNATIONAL. **Reservations:** Recommended. **Bus:** 1, 2, 3.
$ Prices: Appetizers 26–55 markkaa ($7.10–$15); main dishes 75–110 markkaa ($20.45–$30). AE, DC, MC, V.
   Open: Daily 11am–1am.

A palace built in 1899, this is an elegant eating place with a number of dining rooms and cozy private rooms. On the first floor are the Winter Garden, the Palace Hall, the Venetian Hall, and Alexander's Private Room. In summer, an outdoor restaurant is open in the park surrounding the palace. Although many international dishes are offered, the chef concentrates on using local products wherever possible. The Finnish fish dishes, such as salmon and whitefish, are outstanding. You can also order herring—prepared in various ways—as an appetizer, perhaps reindeer as a main dish.

FRANSMANNI RESTAURANT, in the Hotel Ilves, Hatanpäänvaltatie 1. Tel. 121-213.
   Cuisine: INTERNATIONAL. **Reservations:** Recommended. **Bus:** 1, 2, 3.
$ Prices: Appetizers 20–70 markkaa ($5.45–$19.10); main dishes 60–120 markkaa ($16.35–$32.70). AE, DC, MC, V.
   Open: Daily 11am–1pm.

To reach this restaurant, you have to cross through the lobby of the Hotel Ilves (see "Where to Stay," above). The restaurant is elegantly decorated in a regional style, with candles on the tables, a fireplace, and a beamed ceiling. The hotel calls the Fransmanni their "leisurely food restaurant," and it's ideal for a summer meal. Specialties come from "the fishermen's net" or a steak grilled to your specifications. Lamb is a special dish, and dishes for children are also prepared. The dessert specialty is cheesecake with strawberry sauce.

MONA LISA WINE BAR, in the Hotel Cumulus, Koskikatu 5. Tel. 35-500.
   Cuisine: INTERNATIONAL. **Reservations:** Not required. **Bus:** 1, 2, 3.
$ Prices: Appetizers 28–54 markkaa ($7.65–$14.75); main dishes 52–105 markkaa ($14.20–$28.65). AE, DC, MC, V.
   Open: Daily 10am–1am.

The designers of this hotel decided that a newcomer's best introduction to their hotel was a supremely popular wine bar and restaurant. Consequently, even while guests register in the lobby, the sound of conversation and laughter from the restaurant filters in. Amid a warmly rustic decor of exposed brick, heavy beams, and softly burnished pine, you can order Indonesian nasi goreng, Sri Lankan chicken with curry and mango, Mexican veal, an array of salads and game dishes, seafood—such as trout or bouillabaisse—quiche Lorraine, baked potatoes with garlic and shrimp, feta cheese filled with paprika, chicken au gratin, seafood salad, and for dessert, a kiwi tart with mint sauce.

RESTAURANT NÄSINNEULA, Särkänniemi. Tel. 124-697.

Cuisine: FINNISH. **Reservations:** Recommended. **Bus:** Y4.

$ Prices: Appetizers 28–55 markkaa ($7.65–$15); main dishes 65–120 markkaa ($17.75–$32.70). DC, MC, V.

Open: Mon–Sat 10am–midnight, Sun 10am–8pm.

Near the city's recreational headquarters, Särkänniemi, this revolving circular restaurant has a panoramic view of two lakes, acres of heavily forested woodland, and an amusement park. You take a high-speed elevator to reach the restaurant. Full meals include salmon soup, morel-cream soup, pepper steak, noisettes of veal, chicken with fruit, smoked reindeer salad, sea trout braised with cream, and for two diners, a combination of flank steak and braised salmon.

RUSTHOLLI, Rusthollinkatu 16, Aitolahti. Tel. 620-111.

Cuisine: FINNISH. **Reservations:** Recommended. **Directions:** Best to drive, since it is 5 miles from the center toward Aitolahti.

$ Prices: Appetizers 28–55 markkaa ($7.65–$15); main dishes 59–95 ($16.10–$25.90). AE, DC, MC, V.

Open: Daily 9am–1am.

A fun restaurant near the lake, this has been an unmatched eating place for more than 30 years. Not only can you dine in the midst of nature, but you can also swim and then have a sauna before dinner. All dishes on the menu are à la carte. The restaurant is fully licensed. Specialties include fresh salmon, whitefish, Baltic herring, and reindeer.

TIILIHOLVI, Kauppakatu 10. Tel. 121-220.

Cuisine: INTERNATIONAL. **Reservations:** Essential for dinner. **Bus:** 1, 2, 3.

$ Prices: Appetizers 26–47 markkaa ($7.10–$12.80); main dishes 42–135 markkaa ($11.45–$36.80). AE, DC, MC, V.

Open: Mon–Fri 11am–midnight, Sat noon–midnight, Sun noon–7pm.

In the center of Tampere in an intimate atmosphere of red-brick walls, wooden tables, and candlelight, this restaurant features the specialties of the Finnish cuisine and good charcoal-grilled dishes. Much of the food is influenced by France, although made, whenever possible, with Finnish products. The chef respects the natural taste of his produce. Specialties include morel soup à la Lapone, roast sea trout with black sesame seeds, and snow grouse à la Paris, and for dessert, cardamom ice cream. At a wine cellar, a new part of the restaurant, light meals are offered for 35 markkaa ($9.55), with small dishes and wine served by the glass.

SHOPPING

KEHRÄSÄÄRI BOUTIQUE CENTRE. Tel. 28-080.

More than 40 boutiques here sell the best of Finnish art, handcrafts, glasswork, children's toys, ceramics, and an array of woven textiles in alluring shades of earth and sky. Even if you don't make a purchase, you might order a drink in the courtyard café.

PIRKANMAAN KOTITYÖ OY, Verkatehtaankatu 2. Tel. 37-161.

This well-stocked shop is owned and managed by a quasi-governmental association for the promotion of the region's handcrafts. You'll find a changing exhibition and sale of handcrafted textiles, toys, and knitware. Many crafts are inspired by Finnish design.

EVENING ENTERTAINMENT

PYYNIKKI SUMMER THEATER, Postilokero 246. Tel. 126-792 for reservations.

About a mile from the center of Tampere, this is the first outdoor theater in the world built with a revolving auditorium, and it seats 800. The plays are in Finnish, and a free synopsis of the action is outlined in English; but for most of these action-packed plays you don't need to know the subtleties of dialogue. Reserving tickets in advance is imperative. Summer plays are presented from mid-June to mid-Aug, Tuesday through Sunday at 7pm; two performances are given each weekends night. **Bus:** 12.

Prices: Tickets, 80 markkaa ($21.80) adults, 55 markkaa ($15) children 12 or under.

2. LAHTI

64 miles north of Helsinki; 78 miles east of Tampere

GETTING THERE By Train Direct trains run several times daily between Helsinki and Lahti, taking 1½ hours.

By Bus From the Helsinki bus station, Lahti-bound buses leave almost every hour, taking 1½ hours.

By Car From Helsinki, take the E4 express highway north for 64 miles.

ESSENTIALS For information, go to the **Lahti City Tourist and Congress Bureau,** Torikatu 3B (tel. 918/818-2580). The **telephone area code** for Lahti is 918.

Best known for its winter sports attractions, Lahti has been called "the most American city" in Finland because it is industrial and modern. Founded in 1905, this former market crossroads lies in the center of southern Finland at the junction of major traffic routes. On the southern shore of Lake Vesijärvi, it was built between the two ridges of Salpausselka and marks the beginning of some of the most scenic lake districts of Finland. Lahti is considered the "gateway to central Finland." It lies at the southern end of one of the country's largest lake systems.

WHAT TO SEE & DO

With a population of 100,000, the seventh-largest city of Finland, Lahti has a rich cultural life, as reflected by its recurring festivals ranging from poetry marathons to organ-player festivals. But, as mentioned before, it is mainly known as a winter sports center. Skiers follow ridges formed during the Ice Age. Its **Ski Stadium,** said to be the best in the world, was host to the 1989 World Ski Championships. Even if you're a summer visitor you can visit the stadium, where from the top of the highest ski jump there are beautiful views over the forest and Lake Päijänne and Lake Vesijärvi. Near the bottom of the ski jumps is a swimming pool. The sightseeing platform at nearly 300 feet is open June through August, Monday through Friday from 11am to 6pm and on Saturday and Sunday from 10am to 5pm.

Even though Lahti is a modern city, it has some notable buildings, including the **City Hall,** Harjukatu (tel. 814-11), which was designed by Eliel Saarinen and completed in 1912, although restored in 1985. (Saarinen is best known for his design of the Helsinki Railway Station.) Alvar Aalto designed the parish church of Lahti, the **Church of the Cross,** Kirkkokatu 4 (tel. 891-290), which was completed in 1978 in the city center near the marketplace. Services, sometimes in English, are held on Sunday at 10am. One of the most visited places is the **Mukkula Tourist Center** on the shores of Lake Vesijärvi (tel. 305-553), 3 miles north of the city center. It was under the ancient oaks in the park that writers and people who specialized in reciting verses met in years gone by. Facilities range from a romantic manor hotel to a camping ground. Open year round, daily from 10am to 5pm, the center has tennis courts, miniature golf, rowboats, bicycles, and surfboards for rent.

You can also visit the 30-mile-long **Saimaa Canal,** dating from the mid-1850s, which connects Lake Saimaa to the Gulf of Finland through Russia. The Finnish territory can be visited on a cruise. For details about these and other matters, contact the City Tourist Office (see above).

WHERE TO STAY

ASCOT HOTEL, Rauhankatu 14, SF-15110 Lahti. Tel. 918/897-11. Fax 918/897-1224. 232 rms (all with bath). MINIBAR TV TEL

$ Rates (including breakfast): June 14–Aug 6, 400 markkaa ($109.10) single or double; Aug 7–June 13, 250 markkaa ($141.80) single; 650 markkaa ($177.25) double. AE, DC, MC, V. **Parking:** 30 markkaa ($8.20).

Close to the bus station and the marketplace in the center of town, and not far from the sports center, this is one of the best hotels of Lahti. The bedrooms have a cozy, homelike decor, and are decorated in soft pastel hues, with cane furniture. Each offers continental-width beds. The hotel has seven different restaurants and drinking establishments patronized by the local community. Laundry facilities, baby-sitting, and room service are offered, and six saunas, a swimming pool, gym, and solarium are available for guest use.

LAHDEN SEURAHUONE, Aleksanterinkatu 14, SF-15110 Lahti. Tel. 918/25-161. Fax 918/523-164. 121 rms (all with bath). MINIBAR TV TEL

$ Rates (including breakfast): June 22–July 31, 320 markkaa ($87.25) single; 420 markkaa ($114.55) double. Aug–June 21, 575 markkaa ($156.80) single; 660 markkaa ($180) double. AE, MC, V.

One of the best hotels in town, on a central, tree-lined street near Tori, the marketplace, this place has comfortable bedrooms with well-designed, modern decors. Special rooms are available for guests suffering from allergies and for nonsmokers. There are also two saunas, a swimming pool, and an Arctic dip pool. This establishment has had many distinguished guests, including King Carl XVI Gustav of Sweden, Crown Prince Harald of Norway, Khrushchev, Bulganin, and Marshal Mannerheim. The hotel offers five restaurants and drinking establishments.

WHERE TO DINE

IN THE ASCOT HOTEL The Ascot Hotel, Rauhankatu 14 (tel. 897-11), has a total of seven places to eat and drink, the most in town. This is also the best place to go for evening entertainment. The **Café Bistro** is inspired by a farmhouse in Provence, offering herb-flavored French meals in a cozy atmosphere of wood floors, sofas, and an open fire. Wine is sold by the glass. The dining action overflows onto the Bistro Terrace in summer. The **Café Catalina Ristorante** is strictly Italian, with red-striped awnings, tile roofs, an open kitchen, and a salad trolley set up on the "square." Pizzas and pastas are the main fare here, although you can also order such main-dish specialties as steak. Finish off with an espresso after having the house ice cream. The festive **Emmanuel** is the No. 1 dance spot in town, with a big bar, and the **Bar Cabaña** is an ideal place for an exotic cocktail. In summer you can dine at the **Terrazza** under a giant parasol, and later check out the action in either the **Pub Nelson,** with its dark-paneled walls and long bar, or in **Music Bar Wendy's,** where the music is nonstop.

Food service is from 11am to 1pm, and meals cost 85 to 175 markkaa ($23.20 to $47.70), depending on what you order. These restaurants lie close to the town marketplace in the center.

IN THE LAHDEN SEURAHUONE HOTEL The Lahden Seurahuone Hotel, Aleksanterinkatu 14 (tel. 25-161), offers a choice of five places to eat, each one different. The **Marco Polo** is a rendezvous point in town for younger people, a good place for snacks and drinks in the early evening. For an à la carte meal of Finnish and international specialties, sample **Hämesali** or the **Eden,** the latter specializing in spicy peppered delicacies such as steak. The **Amoroso** nightclub is a major place in Lahti for evening entertainment. In summer, the **Pihatto** outdoor restaurant serves drinks and light meals.

Wednesday night is grand buffet night at the hotel. Meals range in price from 75 to 185 markkaa ($20.45 to $50.45), depending on what you order. Food service is daily from 11am to 1pm.

---

3. JYVÄSKYLÄ

106 miles north of Lahti, 168 miles north of Helsinki

GETTING THERE By Plane Finnair flies nonstop between Helsinki and Jyväskylä. Frequency of flights depends on the time of year, usually taking 80 minutes. The airport is 10 miles north of Jyväskylä in Tikkakoski. Buses connect with arriving planes and takes passengers to the city center.

By Train Jyväskylä lies on the rail route from Tampere, from which connections can be made to Helsinki. Seven trains a day run back and forth between the two cities, taking 1¾ hours.

By Bus From Helsinki 10 buses daily go all the way to Jyväskylä, going via Lahti and Jämsä. You can, for example, take an 8am bus from Helsinki, arriving in Jyväskylä at 1:05pm. From Turku there are five daily buses, and from Tampere, six to eight buses.

By Car From Helsinki, head north to Lahti on the E4. Pass through the city and continue on the E4 via Jämsä to Jyväskylä.

By Boat In summer, you can tour Lake Päijänne, the longest and deepest lake in Finland. The big white ships sailing the lake—S/S *Suomi,* M/S *Suometar,* and M/S *Suomen Neito*—begin their journey in Jyväskylä, Lahti, or Heinola. You can step on board at one of the intermediate landing stages on any day of the week. Pick up a cruise schedule from the tourist office (see below), or purchase a ticket at any travel agent. For more details, contact **Päijänne Risteilyt,** Pellonpää, SF-40820 Haapaniemi (tel. 941/618-885).

ESSENTIALS The **City Tourist Office** is at Vapaudenkatu 38 (tel. 941/624-903). The **telephone area code** for Jyväskylä is 941.

SPECIAL EVENTS The **Jyväskylä Arts Festival** in June is the oldest regular art festival in Finland, offering a wide variety of exhibitions, cultural events, and seminars on sociology, politics, economics, and the arts. For more information, you can call 615-624 if you'd like to attend. Dates vary from year to year.

In 1834, Tsar Nicholas II of Russia founded Jyväskylä on the site of an ancient marketplace at the northern end of Lake Päijänne, and today it's one of the most popular tourist cities of Finland. An old university city, it has long been a cultural center, with activities reaching their peak at the annual Jyväskylä Arts Festival in summer. The first Finnish-language secondary school in the country was founded here, and Jyväskylä today remains "a town of schools."

WHAT TO SEE & DO

ALVAR AALTO MUSEUM, Alvar Aalton Katu 7. Tel. 624-809.
Jyväskylä was the home of the famous Finnish architect Alvar Aalto. He designed the modern buildings of the university and the City Theater, and his other works can be studied here in another building he designed. The museum has a permanent

collection of Aalto memorabilia, including the architect's central design concepts and buildings. The design collection contains some 900 objects, such as classicist Aalto furniture from the 1920s. It also produces special exhibitions of Aalto's work.

Admission: 5 markkaa ($1.35) adults, 1 markka (25¢) children.
Open: Tues–Sun noon–6pm.

FINNISH HANDCRAFT MUSEUM, Seminaarinkatu 32. Tel. 941-624.

Established in 1982, this institution functions as a national museum of handcrafts. The collection includes both domestic and foreign handcrafts, and most of it dates from 1910 to 1930. In addition to the permanent displays illustrating various artisanal skills, short-term exhibitions of handcrafts are also staged here.

Admission: 5 markkaa ($1.35) adults, 1 markka (25¢) children.
Open: Tues–Sun noon–7pm.

KESKI-SUOMEN ILMAILUMUSEO [Air Museum of Central Finland], Kuikantie 1, Tikkakoski. Tel. 752-125.

Near the E4 express highway about 12 miles north of Jyväskylä, this museum has displays of aircraft from World War I to the present day.

Admission: 15 markkaa ($4.10) adults, 5 markkaa ($1.35) children.
Open: June–Aug 20, daily 10am–8pm; Aug 21–May, daily noon–7pm. **Bus:** 23, 23, 24 leaving hourly from the Jyväskylä bus station.

VIHERLANDIA, Kuokkalanti 6. Tel. 261-255.

This is the largest garden center in the country. Here you can wander through large areas containing a massive variety of exotic plants. You can also visit special exhibitions and have snacks and drinks at the Café Eden.

Admission: Free.
Open: May–Aug, Mon–Fri 9am–8pm, Sat 9am–6pm, Sun 10am–6pm; Sept–Apr, Mon–Fri 9am–8pm, Sat 9am–4pm, Sun 11am–6pm.

VESILINNA WATER TOWER, Harju Ridge. Tel. 626-701.

This tower is the most prominent landmark in town. A series of 143 stone steps built in 1925 lead up the ridge to the summit where the tower is located. The observation terrace of the tower offers a panoramic view of the city and the lakes beyond. On the ridge is a jogging track and summer theater.

Admission: 3 markkaa (80¢) adults, 1 markka (25¢) children.
Open: June–Aug, daily 10am–8pm. **Closed:** Sept–May.

WHERE TO STAY

EXPENSIVE

ALEXANDRA, Hannikaisenkatu 35, SF-40100 Jyväskylä. Tel. 941/212-611. Fax 941/212-611. 133 rms (all with bath). MINIBAR TV TEL

$ Rates (including breakfast): July, 300 markkaa ($81.80) single; 400 markkaa ($109.10) double. Aug–June, 510 markkaa ($139.10) single; 650 markkaa ($177.25) double. AE, DC, MC, V.

A first-class hotel in the heart of town near the City Tourist Office, this place has elegant rooms featuring modern amenities. The Alexandra Restaurant is open Monday through Saturday from 10am to midnight and on Sunday from 10am to 10pm. Facilities include a special sauna section with sauna bar, whirlpool baths, solarium, and Acu-massage.

RANTASIPI LAAJAVUORI, Laajavuori, SF-40101 Jyväskylä. Tel. 941/628-211. Fax 941/628-500. 205 rms (all with bath). MINIBAR TV TEL

$ Rates (including breakfast): June 25–Aug 5, 300 markkaa ($81.80) single; 400 markkaa ($109.10) double. Aug 6–June 24, 520 markkaa ($41.80) single; 700 markkaa ($190.90) double. AE, DC, MC, V.

Located in a forest of spruces 2½ miles from the town center, this hotel is near a lake, which is visible through many of its large windows. The comfortable bedrooms have stylishly modern Finnish furniture. Each is well maintained and inviting.

Dining/Entertainment: The Salitintti restaurant is known throughout the region. You can dine on pork in an aquavit-flavored fruit sauce, reindeer tongue with morels, or several different preparations of fresh salmon before heading into the hotel's nightclub. Dining facilities are open on Monday from 7am to 1am, Tuesday through Saturday from 7am to 3am, and on Sunday from 7am to midnight. The hotel also has a nightclub.

Services: Room service.
Facilities: Sauna, swimming pool, outdoor sports.

MODERATE

**CUMULUS JYVÄSKYLÄ, Väinönkatu 3-5, SF-40100 Jyväskylä. Tel.
941/215-211.** Fax 941/653-299. 203 rms (all with bath). MINIBAR TV TEL
$ **Rates** (including breakfast): June 21–Aug 5, 280 markkaa ($76.55) single; 380 markkaa ($103.65) double. Aug 6–June 20, 480 markkaa ($130.90) single; 600 markkaa ($163.60) double. AE, DC, MC, V.
A member of one of Finland's major hotel chains, the Cumulus is in the center of town a block from the rail station; the Finnair depot for airport buses is adjacent to the hotel. The hotel, built in 1976 and added onto in 1983, has comfortable bedrooms. A café and a pleasant restaurant, which serves from 10am to 2am, are on the premises. Facilities include two saunas and a swimming pool.

INEXPENSIVE

HOTEL MILTON, Asema-aukio, SF-40100 Jyväskylä. Tel. 941/213-411.
34 rms (all with bath). TV TEL
$ **Rates** (including breakfast): July, 230 markkaa ($62.70) single; 330 markkaa ($90) double. Aug–May, 320 markkaa ($87.25) single; 420 markkaa ($114.55) double. AE, DC, MC, V.

⑤ A good bargain, this small hotel is in the center of town, near the railway station, in a tall, white commercial building. Doubles have showers or baths. The hotel is clean with functionally furnished but comfortable bedrooms. The hotel has a sauna.

SUMMER HOTELS

**SUMMER HOTEL RENTUKKA, Tationiekantie 9, SF-40740 Jyväskylä.
Tel. 941/252-211.** Fax 941/251-174. 140 rms (all with bath). **Bus:** 25.
$ **Rates** (including breakfast): 220 markkaa ($60) single; 300 markkaa ($81.80) double. MC, V. **Closed:** Sept–Apr.

⑤ Nine minutes by foot from the main downtown square, this hotel is in a university housing complex of apartments and dormitories, near such conveniences as a bank, filling stations, a post office, and two supermarkets. There is a good restaurant in the hotel, charging moderate prices by Finnish standards, where nightly dancing is offered. The bedrooms contain contemporary blond-wood student furnishings, and there are complete cooking facilities (bring your own utensils) and refrigerators.

WHERE TO DINE

KATINHÄNTÄ, Asemakatu 7. Tel. 618-115.
Cuisine: FINNISH. **Reservations:** Recommended.
$ **Prices:** Appetizers 25–49 markkaa ($6.80–$13.35); main dishes 75–118 markkaa ($20.45–$32.20); Fixed-price lunch 75 markkaa ($20.45). AE, DC, MC, V.
Open: Daily 10am–10pm.
The best and most charming restaurant in town is a 3-minute walk north of the railroad station, in a modern building one floor above street level. This "Tail of the Cat" (its English translation) is known for its good food and efficient service, at reasonable prices. Try such dishes as blinis with roe, onions, and sour cream to begin with, or perhaps one of the good-tasting soups such as mushroom or borscht. You

might also prefer the slightly salted marinated salmon, followed by noisettes of pork. A specialty is sautéed salmon in a morel cream sauce.

---

4. LAPPEENRANTA

138 miles NE of Helsinki, 10 miles west of the Soviet border

GETTING THERE   By Plane   In summer 30-minute flights between Helsinki and Lappeenranta operate 12 times a week (twice a day Monday through Friday and once a day on weekends). In winter, four flights a day operate Monday through Friday.

By Train   Seven trains a day run between Helsinki and Lappeenranta, taking 4 hours. There are also good train connections to the neighboring towns of Imatra, Savonlinna, and Mikkeli.

By Bus   Five to seven express buses a day make the 4-hour run between Helsinki and Lappeenranta. Buses also run every hour between Lappeenranta and Imatra, taking 30 minutes to 1 hour, depending on the bus.

By Car   Take the E4 north from Helsinki to Lahti, where you connect with Route 12 east until you reach the junction of Route 6 for the final approach to Lappeenranta.

ESSENTIALS   The **Lappeenranta Tourist Service,** Matkailutoimisto (tel. 953/560-860), will provide you with information, arrange guides, and help you with sightseeing tours. The **telephone area code** for Lappeenranta is 953.

This historic town, a border town between two different cultures, was founded in 1649 by Queen Christina of Sweden. It was fortified first by the Swedes who governed Finland as a province, then by the Russians. Lappeenranta has assumed increasing importance since World War II, following the loss of large parts of Karelia. For more than a century and a half the town has been a spa, and today Lappeenranta is one of the most important summer resort and excursion centers in eastern Finland. A bright, modern town, it nestles at the southern edge of the large Lake Saimaa.

WHAT TO SEE & DO
IN THE FORTRESS

Linnoitus, the fortress of Lappeenranta, on Kristiinankatu, was begun by the Swedes and continued by the Russians as a link in their chain of defenses. The entire chain fell into disuse after the Peace of Turku in 1812, when the part of the country known as Old Finland, including Lappeenranta, was reunited with other Finnish territory. The fortress was turned over to the town in 1835 and the defenses slowly deteriorated, but restoration has been ongoing since 1976. There are potteries and other handcraft shops in the fortress area.

The following three attractions—the Orthodox Church, the South Karelian Museum, and the Cavalry Museum—are all located within the fortress precincts.

The old **Orthodox Church** was completed in 1785, but only the high and narrow nave belong to the original building. One of the most valuable icons here is the *Communion of the Holy,* which is more than 200 years old. The Orthodox Church of Finland owes allegiance to the Ecumenical Patriarch of Constantinople.

The **Etela-Karjalan Museo (South Karelian Museum)** (tel. 518-514) is located at the northern end of the fortress in the 19th-century military storehouse. Museum displays include a model of the former Finnish town of Viipuri (Vyborg). The textile department of this museum is worth looking at, as there are examples of traditional Karelian clothing here. An **art museum** is now established in the soldiers barracks next to the Orthodox Church.

Admission to both museums is 10 markkaa ($2.75). However, by buying one ticket you can visit three museums, including the Cavalry Museum, described below. The two museums are open in summer, Monday through Friday from 10am to 6pm and on Saturday and Sunday from 11am to 5pm; in winter, Tuesday, Wednesday, and Friday through Sunday from 11am to 5pm, on Thursday from 11am to 8pm.

The **Cavalry Museum** (tel. 518-514) is in the oldest building in Lappeenranta, the former guardhouse of Linnoitus by the town gates, built in 1772. The history of the Finnish cavalry from the *hakkapeliitat* (the cavalry in the 1618–48 war) until modern times is depicted through uniforms, guns, and objects related to horse care. Admission is 10 markkaa ($2.75). The museum is open in summer, Monday through Friday from 10am to 6pm and on Saturday and Sunday from 11am to 5pm; in winter, Tuesday, Wednesday, and Friday through Sunday from 11am to 5pm, on Thursday from 11am to 8pm.

AROUND TOWN

As noted, Lappeenranta is a lake town, the heart of Lake Saimaa and the eastern lake district. Both passenger ships and private boats sail from the harbor of Lappeenranta to the lake and down the Saimaa Canal to the Gulf of Finland. For a good view of the town, the lake, and the surrounding islands, take the elevator to the top of the pillar-supported **Vesitorni Observation Tower,** Pohjolankatu, open in June and July, daily from 10am to 8pm; in May and August, daily from 11am to 6pm. Admission is 5 markkaa ($1.35) for adults, 2 markkaa (55¢) for children.

This is also a cultural town, with **summer concerts** held in the parks and **summer theater** on the fortified walls. Cavalrymen dressed in traditional skeleton tunics and red trousers, the uniform worn in 1922, ride in the fortress and harbor area in summer. **Guard parades and evening tattoos** are held several times during the summer months.

The **Marketplace** (see it in the morning), in the center of town, is the place to meet the local Karelian people and eat boat-shaped Karelian pies.

Near the Sports Stadium, the **Laura Korpikaivo-Tamminen's Museum for Textile Handicrafts,** Kantokatu 1 (tel. 518-506), has a collection of 2,000 handmade objects, including wall hangings, tablecloths, woven designs, and lace. Admission costs 5 markkaa ($1.35), and it's open Tuesday through Sunday from 11am to 5pm.

A VISIT TO THE SOVIET UNION

A popular side trip from Lappeenranta is a visit to the Soviet Union; write to the tourist office (above) for information. From May to September, the M/S *Carelia* carries 300 passengers on day trips to Vyborg, the old capital of Karelia before Finland was forced to cede it to the Soviet Union in World War II. The 1-day trips can be made by passengers from all countries having diplomatic relations with the Soviet Union, and no visa is required. Reservations and identification information must be cleared with the **Matka-Lappee Travel Agency,** Valtakatu 46, SF-53100 Lappeenranta (tel. 953/53-430), at least 2 weeks before you wish to travel. The 1-day journeys include lunch and a sightseeing tour.

Two-day trips to Vyborg, either by boat both ways or one way by boat and one by bus, are also offered. This trip includes first-class accommodations at the Hotel Druzhba in Vyborg in double rooms with full board and a sightseeing tour. A passport and visa are obligatory for all passengers for this 2-day trip, regardless of nationality. Bookings and visa applications with three photographs and a copy of the ID pages of your passport must be submitted to a Finnish travel agency at least 2 weeks before you wish to travel.

WHERE TO STAY
EXPENSIVE

HOTEL CUMULUS, Valtakatu 31, SF-53100 Lappeenranta. Tel. 953/50-870. Fax 953/578-299. 94 rms (all with bath). MINIBAR TV TEL
$ **Rates** (including breakfast): June 21–Aug 5, 280 markkaa ($76.35) single; 380

markkaa ($103.65) double. Aug 6–June 20, 430 markkaa ($117.25) single; 560 markkaa ($152.70) double. AE, DC, MC, V.

In the heart of the city on the main shopping street near the City Theater, this hotel, opened in 1982, is a member of Finland's Cumulus hotel chain. The hotel has units for those with allergies. Bedrooms are modern, comfortable, and attractively furnished.

Dining/Entertainment: Three hotel dining and drinking establishments—one called Hullu Hanhi or "Crazy Goose," the Ferrari Pub, and the Tiffany Pub—are the most popular in town.

Services: Room service.

Facilities: Fitness room for exercise, two saunas, swimming pool.

HOTEL LAPPEE, Barhenkatu 1, SF-53100 Lappeenranta. Tel. 953/ 5861. Fax 953/693-1349. 206 rms (all with bath). TV TEL Directions:

$ Rates (including breakfast): 520 markkaa ($111.80) single; 620 markkaa ($169.05) double. AE, DC, MC, V.

A member of Finland's Sokos chain, this three-story white hotel, in the center next to the Town Hall, is one of the best in town. Each of the comfortable bedrooms features wheat-colored Finnish textiles and built-in birchwood furniture. From the windows of the chrome and red-velvet bar, you can see the sculpture and well-maintained buildings, which give Lappeenranta much of its charm.

Dining/Entertainment: On the premises are five restaurants and a popular nightclub that features live bands.

Services: Room service.

Facilities: Swimming pool, five saunas.

MODERATE

CARELIA CONGRESS HOTEL, Marssitie 3, SF-53600 Lappeenranta. Tel. 953/52-210. 36 rms (all with bath). TV TEL **Bus:** 26.

$ Rates (including breakfast): 380 markkaa ($103.65) single; 480 markkaa ($130.90) double. AE, DC, MC, V.

About a mile from the town center on the shore of Lake Saimaa, this is a high-standard conference and training hotel, but in summer it's more of a pleasant tourist accommodation. Bedrooms are comfortably and attractively furnished, and rooms are available for individuals with allergies. The hotel has a good restaurant serving Scandinavian and international food. Facilities include jogging paths, skiing tracks, tennis and squash courts, a swimming pool, and two saunas on the beach.

MAISEMAHOTELLI KASTELLI, Route 6, SF-54530 Luumaki. Tel. 953/ 73-311. Fax 953/735-20. 35 rms (all with bath). TV TEL

$ Rates (including breakfast): Summer, 280 markkaa ($76.35) single; 360 markkaa ($98.15) double. Winter, 340 markkaa ($92.70) single; 430 markkaa ($117.25) double. AE, DC, MC, V. **Parking:** Free.

Located about 16 miles from Lappeenranta by Route 6, on the Kuovola–Lappeenranta bus run, this hotel, renovated in 1986, has comfortable, attractively furnished, and quiet bedrooms with balconies. Special rooms are available for persons with allergies. In winter there are several sports-related events taking place on the ice covering the lake, including car races. The record of building the biggest snow house in the world was made here. In summer, however, the lake is given over to water sports, such as jet skiing. Rowboats can also be rented. The hotel also has a large parking area (free). A restaurant, cafeteria, and bar are on the premises, and live entertainment is organized weekly; room service is offered. Guests can use a solarium, an outdoor tennis court, three saunas (two of which are on the shore of Lake Kivijärvi), and a swimming pool.

INEXPENSIVE

KARELIA PARK, Korpraalinkuja 1, SF-53810 Lappeenranta. Tel. 953/ 10-405. Fax 953/28-454. 90 rms (all with bath). TEL **Bus:** 26.

$ Rates (including breakfast): 180 markkaa ($49.10) single; 230 markkaa ($62.70) double. MC, V. **Closed:** Sept–May.

A mile west of the town center near Lake Saimaa, this hotel has modern, well-equipped rooms. The restaurant is decorated with Finnish dragon symbols, and half and full board are available. The hotel has two saunas. Good swimming beaches and walking paths are in the neighborhood.

WHERE TO DINE

Lappeenranta is known for its excellent restaurants, which range from quiet dining spots to those where you can dance. Traditional South Karelian dishes or international cuisine will be found in most restaurants.

MODERATE

ADRIANO BAR, Kauppakatu 27. Tel. 13-454.
   Cuisine: ITALIAN. **Reservations:** Recommended.
$ Prices: Appetizers 35–45 markkaa ($9.55–$12.55); main dishes 65–85 markkaa ($17.75–$23.20). DC, MC, V.
   Open: Mon–Tues and Thurs 10am–midnight, Wed and Fri–Sun 10am–1am.
This restaurant in the center near the Marketplace has three sections: a dining room, a disco, and a self-service section. You might try a large order of veal steak with french fries and a salad, or a plate-size pizza with lots of cheese. Disco nights are Friday and Saturday.

KASINO, Ainonkatu 10. Tel. 10-200.
   Cuisine: FINNISH. **Reservations:** Recommended. Directions:
$ Prices: Appetizers 45–50 markkaa ($12.25–$15); main dishes 85–105 markkaa ($23.20–$28.65). AE, MC, V.
   Open: May–Sept, Mon–Sat 11am–2am. **Closed:** Oct–Apr.
While wining and dining here, you can enjoy a splendid view of Lake Saimaa. Kasino has an excellent menu of fish and meat dishes—salmon done different ways, whitefish, Baltic herring, pork, veal, and prime beef. Special lunches are offered, and there is dancing to a live orchestra.

KIPPURASARVI, Rantatie in Lemi. Tel. 46-470.
   Cuisine: FINNISH. **Reservations:** Required.
$ Prices: Appetizers 28–55 markkaa ($7.65–$15); main dishes 65–85 markkaa ($17.75–$23.20). MC, V.
   Open: Daily 11am–8pm.
About 15 miles from Lappeenranta (go by private car or taxi), this restaurant specializes in traditional meals and is famous for its traditional sara, a mutton dish baked in a wooden trough, served with potatoes, homemade rieska bread, and home brew. Kippurasarvi has four different sections, plus a terrace in summer.

RANTAPUISTO, Kipparinkatu 7. Tel. 15-747.
   Cuisine: FINNISH. **Reservations:** Recommended.
$ Prices: Appetizers 25–45 markkaa ($6.80–$12.25); main dishes 65–85 markkaa ($17.75–$23.20). MC, V.
   Open: Mon–Fri 8:30am–11pm, Sat–Sun 11am–11pm.
Furnished in the Russian style, this is a cozy wine tavern and dining room is in the town center in the harbor area. Many visitors patronize it only at lunch for its good food at moderate prices, but it's cozier and more festive in the evening. The chef uses local products when available, and you get the best of Finnish cuisine from the lakes, rivers, and fields. Begin with Baltic herring or try the Finnish salmon or reindeer.

ROSSO E NERO, Raatimiehenkatu 13. Tel. 13-446.
   Cuisine: ITALIAN. **Reservations:** Not required.
$ Prices: Appetizers 12–14 markkaa ($3.25–$3.80); pizzas 40–59 markkaa ($10.90–$16.10); pastas 36–42 markkaa ($9.80–$11.45); main dishes 68–98 markkaa ($18.55–$26.70). MC, V.

Open: Daily 10am–midnight.

The main pizza parlor of town, in the center a short walk south of the harborfront, this reasonably priced place also serves pastas and grilled steaks. It is also fully licensed. Popular with the young people of town, it is decorated entirely *à l'italienne* in shades of red and black. It keeps some of the longest serving hours of any establishment in town. Many people drop in after the movies let out.

TASSOS, Valtakatu 41. Tel. 12-965.
   Cuisine: GREEK. **Reservations:** Usually not required.
$ Prices: Appetizers 20–50 markkaa ($5.45–$13.65); main dishes 50–100 markkaa ($13.65–$27.25). AE, DC, MC, V.
   Open: Daily 11am–1am.

One of the few Greek restaurants outside Helsinki, this tavern is decorated with lots of Greek accessories. It lies half a mile north of the rail station, in the center of town 600 yards from the harborfront. Bringing an exotic cuisine to Karelia, its chef offers dishes from various regions of Greece. Locals come here for an evening of fun. All the lamb and kebab dishes are featured, along with Greek salads and wine.

A NEARBY CAFE

MAJURSKA, Kristiinankatu 1. Tel. 10-554.
   Cuisine: FINNISH. **Reservations:** Recommended.
$ Prices: Cakes 15 markkaa ($4.10). No credit cards.
   Open: Summer, daily 10am–8pm; winter, daily 10am–6pm.

The most famous café in Lappeenranta, Majurska is located at the fortress 500 yards from the town center, and is known for its homemade cakes made from different berries, which are considered to be the best in town. You might also try their tempting onion pie, which many visitors prefer as a light lunch. An adjacent shop has many interesting Finnish items, including wool blankets and animal skins. The decor is in the style of the late 1800s.

5. IMATRA

159 miles east of Helsinki, 22 miles east of Lappeenranta

GETTING THERE   By Plane   You can fly from Helsinki to Lappeenranta in 30 minutes, then take a bus to Imatra.

By Train   There is frequent service daily between Helsinki and Imatra, taking 3 hours.

By Bus   Imatra has good bus links with Helsinki, taking 3½ hours, and with many neighboring cities, including Savonlinna and Lappeenranta (call 954/23-555 for schedules, which change seasonally).

By Car   Head east from Helsinki toward the Soviet frontier all the way to Imatra.

ESSENTIALS   The **City Tourist Office,** Keskusasema, SF-55121 Imatra (tel. 954/201-511), will provide you with information, arrange guides, and help you with sightseeing tours. The **telephone area code** for Imatra is 954.

Already an attraction in the days of the Russian tsars, Imatra is today a lively industrial and tourist city. Cooperation between Finland and the Soviet Union strongly influences Imatra's economy; this city is, after all, on Finland's southeastern edge and shares a 12-mile border with Russia.

WHAT TO SEE & DO

The   ✪ **Imatra Rapids,** a mighty torrent rushing through a cleft in the rock cut by the Vuoksi River, became Finland's most celebrated tourist attraction in the 18th century when Catherine the Great ruled Russia and came to see them. The fall of the rapids, one of the most forceful in Europe, is 75 feet, stretching almost 1,000 feet. They are surrounded by the Crown Park, established by Tsar Nicholas I, which contains a handsome art nouveau building, Valtionhotelli (see below). The largest hydraulic power station in Finland stands on the river. The rapids were harnessed at Imatrankoski, the power being used for a hydroelectric plant, but they are released as a tourist attraction daily in summer.

Besides the rapids, the **Church of the Three Crosses,** designed by Alvar Aalto, is worth seeing; it was the architect's first "multipurpose church." The **Industrial Workers House Museum,** Imatra Ritikanrant (tel. 22-584), shows how living conditions have changed for Finnish workers since the turn of the century. The museum is open May 2 through August, Tuesday through Sunday from 10am to 6pm. Admission is 5 markkaa ($1.35) for adults, 2 markkaa (55¢) for children. Also, in **Niskalampi** you can see restored turn-of-the-century houses in the working-class quarter.

The **Karelian Farmhouse Open-Air Museum,** in the Pässiniemi section (tel. 646-77), takes you back to a 19th-century South Karelian farm setting and comprises 11 different buildings. It's open May 2 to August 1, Tuesday through Sunday from 10am to 6pm. Admission is 5 markkaa ($1.35) for adults, 2 markkaa (55¢) for children 12 or under.

Imatra's beautiful natural surroundings provide excellent opportunities for sports and recreation in both summer and winter. The **Imatra Leisure Center** at Ukonniemi on Lake Saimaa offers a wide range of activities all year. An 18-hole golf course of international standard is in a lovely setting in the meadows and woodland on the shores of Lake Immalanjärvi; it has a clubhouse and a winter practice course, and equipment can be rented.

Imatra's **summer markets** offer special South Karelian delights, and you'll also find interesting items for souvenirs and gifts in the city's cottage-industry shops.

WHERE TO STAY

IMATRAN VALTIONHOTELLI (Imatra State Hotel), Torkkelinkatu 2, SF-55100 Imatra. Tel. 954/605-111. Fax 954/672-68. 150 rms (all with bath). MINIBAR TV TEL.

$ Rates (including breakfast): Congress section, 460 markkaa ($125.45) single; 550 markkaa ($150) double. Castle section, 550 markkaa ($150) single; 720 markkaa ($196.35) double. AE, DC, MC, V.

One of the most unusual hotels in Scandinavia, standing on parklike grounds in the city center, this hostelry was built in 1903 as an art deco vacation hideaway for the grandest titles of the Russian Empire and was designed in semifortified art nouveau grandeur, complete with a series of conical towers and romantically ornate carvings. In 1988 it was almost completely rebuilt, and today the castlelike hotel has bedrooms that are undeniably stylish, each with a color scheme that decorators re-created from faded photographs, carpeting woven by a Dutch factory to the original abstract patterns, and all the modern electronic conveniences. Additional bedrooms were added in a glass-and-steel annex, the Congress Hotel, which features saunas and a greenhouse-style bar. A total of 96 rooms in the Congress section have a minibar. Room service is provided.

IMATRAN KYLPYLÄ (Imatra Spa Hotel), Vapaa-Aikakeskus, SF-55420 Imatra. Tel. 954/954-2051. Fax 954/205-339. 94 rms (all with bath). MINIBAR TV TEL.

$ Rates (including breakfast): 425 markkaa ($115.90) single; 580 markkaa ($158.15) double. AE, DC, MC, V.

On a forested piece of lakeside land 3½ miles west of the town center, this hostelry is considered the most modern and health-conscious hotel in eastern Finland. Owned by one of Finland's largest industrial conglomerates, it exists for the pursuit of relaxation and better health. Most clients stay here for a week or more, enjoying the array of hydrotherapy, physical therapy, and beauty treatments. Each of the bedrooms is furnished in a comfortable style and has a refrigerator. On the premises is a small library, reading room, and a free washing machine for use by guests.

KESAHOTELLI MANSIKKALA (Summer Hotel Mansikkala), Rastaan-katu 3A, SF-55120 Imatra. Tel. 954/221-33. 52 rms (none with bath). **Bus:** 1, 3.

$ **Rates:** 200 markkaa ($54.55) single; 260 markkaa ($70.90) double. Breakfast costs 25 markkaa ($6.80) extra. DC, MC, V.

Closed: Aug 13–May. **Parking:** Available.

⑤ This hotel 2 miles from the center has double rooms that can be used as singles or turned into triples with the addition of an extra bed. Groups of four units share a shower, toilet, and kitchenette. The hotel offers hostel accommodations, although guests must bring their own bed linen. The hotel has two saunas, an unlicensed café, and ample parking space.

WHERE TO DINE
EXPENSIVE

CASTLE ROOM, in the Imatran Valtionhotelli, Torkkelinkatu 2. Tel. 632-44.

Cuisine: INTERNATIONAL. **Reservations:** Recommended.

$ **Prices:** Appetizers 45–65 markkaa ($12.25–$17.75); main dishes 85–105 markkaa ($23.20–$28.65). AE, DC, MC, V.

Open: Lunch Mon–Fri 11am–2pm, Sat–Sun noon–3pm; dinner daily 6–10pm.

A turn-of-the-century dining room, this place has walls stenciled with art nouveau impressions of Karelian designs and Gothic-inspired arches. The menu here might include several preparations of salmon, a three-pepper beefsteak, noisettes of veal with bacon, and roast chicken with kiwi-and-apple stuffing.

KEISARISALI, in the Imatran Valtionhotelli, Torkkelinkatu 2. Tel. 632-44.

Cuisine: RUSSIAN. **Reservations:** Required.

$ **Prices:** Appetizers 45–85 markkaa ($12.25–$23.20); main dishes 85–120 markkaa ($23.20–$32.70). AE, DC, MC, V.

Open: Dinner only, daily 6–10pm.

Steeped in the Russian style, this downtown restaurant occupies the ground-floor premises that were once reserved for the exclusive use of the Russian tsar. Smaller and more intimate than the hotel dining room next door, it has as its centerpiece a large 1987 impressionist painting of the nearby rapids and also features a stenciled ceiling and antique chairs. Full meals might include shashlik of chicken (inspired by a late 19th-century recipe), chicken cutlet Kiev, fried whitefish, and Russian-style poached salmon.

MODERATE

BUTTENHOFF CAFE-RESTAURANT, Lappeentie 4. Tel. 613-16.

Cuisine: INTERNATIONAL. **Reservations:** Recommended.

$ **Prices:** Appetizers 25–45 markkaa ($6.80–$12.25); main dishes 45–80 markkaa ($12.25–$21.80). No credit cards.

Open: Mon–Tues 8:30am–11:30pm, Wed–Thurs 8:30am–10:30pm, Fri 8:30am–1am, Sat 9am–11:30pm, Sun 11:30am–7:30pm.

⑤ In the center of town one floor above street level, this restaurant is decorated in traditional Karelian style. It's a cozy place to have lunch, and the menu offers such dishes as borscht made according to grandmother's own recipe, reindeer pot roast, specialties from the Russian kitchen—including chicken Kiev—and such international fare as tournedos with morels or pepper steak. The kitchen also turns out pizzas and a number of Karelian dishes. Certain nights are devoted to Russian food, others to French cuisine.

INEXPENSIVE

KARJALAN PORTTI (Gate of Karelia), Asematie 1, Rauha. Tel. 288-80.
  Cuisine: KARELIAN. **Reservations:** Recommended.
$ Prices: Appetizers 10–25 markkaa ($2.75–$6.80); main dishes 30–60 markkaa ($8.20–$16.35). MC, V.
  Open: Summer, daily 10am–8pm. **Closed:** Winter.

Its country Victorian gingerbread and paneled walls re-create the elaborate and ornate carpentry that once helped make Karelia so famous. The restaurant is in the village of Rauha, about 2½ miles southwest of Imatra, and combines an antique store (the only one around) with a pleasant restaurant. In winter it offers a Karelian buffet lavishly set out on trestle tables. Main dishes are likely to include filet of roast reindeer with juniper berries, Karelian steak in a pot, and pepper steak, plus an array of sandwiches and daily platters.

---

6. SAVONLINNA

209 miles north of Helsinki, 143 miles NE of Lappeenranta

GETTING THERE   By Plane   Two to four Finnair flights travel here daily from Helsinki, taking 50 minutes.

By Train   Trains run daily between Helsinki and Savonlinna, taking 5 hours.

By Bus   Daily buses connect Helsinki with Savonlinna. If you leave Helsinki on the 11:30am bus, arrival time in Savonlinna is 5pm.

By Car   From Helsinki, take the E4 to Lahti, then connect with Route 5 northeast. Take Route 5 to the junction of Route 14 going east to Savonlinna.

ESSENTIALS   The **Savonlinna Tourist Service** is at Puistokatu 1, SF-57100 Savonlinna (tel. 957/13-492). A **tourist information office** at the central railway station is open daily from 8am to 10pm; the staff is helpful in finding accommodations for tourists. In summer, a second office is open on the Marketplace during the same hours.

The **telephone area code** for Savonlinna is 957.

SPECIAL EVENTS   The ✪ **Savonlinna Opera Festival,** traditionally held in July in Olavinlinna Castle, is an international event. For information, contact the Savonlinna Opera Festival Office, Olavinkatu 35, SF-57130 Savonlinna (tel. 957/22-684). Tickets range from 100 to 570 markkaa ($27.25 to $155.45).

Founded in 1639, Savonlinna is the oldest town in eastern Finland. Its major attraction, the Castle of Olavinlinna (see below), dates back to 1475, built to protect what was then the eastern border of Sweden. The town slowly grew up on the islands around the castle.

The area around the town, forming part of the Saimaa waterway, has more lakes than any other area in Finland. Because of its strategic location, Savonlinna has been the scene of many battles. In fact, it belonged to Russia for 70 years until Savonlinna was returned to the Grand Duchy of Finland in 1812. In its heyday, wealthy families from what was then St. Petersburg used Savonlinna as a holiday and health resort.

The old spa familiar to tsarist Russia burned in 1964, and only a few tsarist villas and the Wanha Kasino summer restaurant were spared. However, the Kylpylä Hotelli Casino, Kasinonsaari (tel. 22-864) (see below), attracts spa enthusiasts to the area.

WHAT TO SEE & DO

The **Olavinlinna Castle** (Castle of St. Olof) (tel. 211-64), a three-towered medieval fortress founded in 1475, is the major attraction. It's on a small island in the middle of Kyronsalmi Straits and is reached by a rotating bridge. Some medieval features remain in the rooms of the castle. There have been several stages in the construction of Olavinlinna, one undertaken at the end of the 18th century, when the Russians replaced a badly damaged tower with a massive three-story structure called the Thick Bastion. Admission is 14 markkaa ($3.80) for adults, 7 markkaa ($1.90) for children 12 or under. The castle is open June to August 21, daily from 10am to 5pm; the rest of the year, daily from 10am to 3pm. Held in the castle since 1912, the opera festival (mentioned above) features performers of international repute, and a Finnish opera is always presented.

Suruton Villa, previously the summer residence of Aino Ackte, Mika Waltari, and Eino Leino, is in Savonlinna on Kasinonsaari island. Since its restoration, an exhibition presenting the history of the opera festivals is displayed here.

Other sites include the **S/S *Salama* museum ship,** built in Vyborg in 1874; it's the only steam schooner in Finland—perhaps in the world. The ship is docked in Riihisaari and is open only from May 18 to September 15, Tuesday through Sunday from 11am to 5pm. Adults pay 10 markkaa ($2.75) for admission; 2 markkaa (55¢) for children 12 or under.

The **Marketplace** in Savonlinna is one of the most interesting in Scandinavia and is the town's focal point in summer. In addition to local concerts that are arranged in conjunction with the festivals, numerous other musical events take place here. Ask at the tourist office about any events.

As in Venice, sightseeing in Savonlinna is done by boat. Many around-the-town **cruises** depart from the harbor every day. In addition to the local tours, there are cruises to Punkaharju, Puumala, Rantasalmi, Kuopo, Mikkeli, and Lappeenranta.

Retretti, in Punkaharju (tel. 314-253), is an art center opened in 1982 in a grotto about 14 miles south of Savonlinna. It includes a concert hall, and during the opera festival in Savonlinna, chamber-music concerts are presented here. The major attraction is an exhibition of sculptures displayed on various levels of the cave with extraordinary lighting effects. It can be reached by boat from the Marketplace in Savonlinna; the trip costs 40 markkaa ($10.90) for adults, 20 markkaa ($5.45) for children 12 or under. It can also be reached by bus from the Savonlinna bus station, a round-trip costing 20 markkaa ($5.45). Entrance to the art center costs 50 markkaa ($13.65) for adults, 20 markkaa ($5.45) for children 12 or under. It's open from the middle of May to the middle of September, daily 10am to 7pm, and in July until 8pm.

WHERE TO STAY
MODERATE

HOTEL RAUHALINNA, Lehtiniemi, SF-57310 Savonlinna. Tel. 957/523-119. 5 rms (none with bath). TV TEL.
$ Rates (including breakfast): 260–420 markkaa ($70.90–$114.55) single; 380–520 markkaa ($103.65–$141.80) double. **Closed:** Aug 22 to mid-June.
This hotel, an old wooden villa and sightseeing attraction 10 miles west of Savonlinna, can be reached by road, and sightseeing boats also make the 40-minute trip here. It was built as the holiday castle villa of a tsar's general in 1897, and its tower commands a view over its own park grounds to the waters of Lake Haapavesi and beyond toward Savonlinna. An avenue of linden trees leads down to the shore. There are only five double bedrooms here, but they are handsomely furnished. There is a first-class restaurant, which is open Tuesday through Saturday from 10am to 8pm and on Sunday and Monday from 11am to 6pm, and serves an excellent cuisine, with an emphasis on Finnish and Russian dishes. In season, game is featured.

HOTEL TOTT, Satamakatu 1, SF-57130 Savonlinna. Tel. 957/514-500. Fax 957/514-504. 56 rms (all with bath). MINIBAR TV TEL **Bus:** 1, 2, 3, 4.
$ Rates (including breakfast): 420 markkaa ($114.55) single; 580 markkaa ($158.15) double. AE, DC, MC, V.
One of the most impressive hotels at the resort, this used to be the town's most historic hotel; however, it had to be rebuilt after a fire. Renovated in 1988, it is now better than ever. The hotel has a sauna and an indoor pool. Its rooftop bar is sheltered

from the wind by glass walls, with a sweeping view of the lake. There's also a ground-floor disco. Bedrooms are comfortably and attractively furnished, all in a sleek modern style.

KYLPYLÄ HOTELLI CASINO, Kasinonsaari, SF-57101 Savonlinna. Tel. 957/228-64. Fax 957/125-24. 79 rms (all with bath). MINIBAR TV TEL.

$ Rates (including breakfast): 500 markkaa ($136.35) single; 640 markkaa ($174.55) double. AE, DC, MC, V.

Accessible by walking across a bridge from the central railway station or driving just over half a mile, the hotel has a first-class restaurant and a spa department. Its modern facilities include not only the baths but clay treatment, massage, a swimming pool, and saunas. Bedrooms are well maintained and comfortably furnished, each with a balcony. Rooms are large enough to allow space for an extra bed. The "islands of the Casino" form a quiet, relaxing natural park—yet they're right in the center of Savonlinna. In good weather you can jog along the tracks; in winter, ski across frozen Lake Haapavesi.

PUNKAHARJUN VALTIONHOTELLI, SF-58450 Punkaharju. Tel. 957/311-761. Fax 957/311-784. 28 rms (15 with bath), 15 cottages. TV TEL

$ Rates (including breakfast): 360 markkaa ($98.15) single without bath, 395–510 markkaa ($107.70–$139.10) single with bath; 445 markkaa ($121.35) double without bath, 545–605 markkaa ($148.60–$165) double with bath. MC, V. **Closed:** Sept–Apr.

This hotel, surrounded by park land, evolved from a forester's house erected on the top of Punkaharju ridge 17 miles from Savonlinna in 1845 by order of Tsar Nicholas I, and the building became the center of Finland's first tourist business. In addition to the 28 rooms, there are 15 cottages rented in summer. Bedrooms are furnished in a comfortably old-fashioned way. The hotel has a restaurant and summer dining on the sun terrace where Finnish specialties are served. Sports facilities are on the premises, including tennis, badminton, volleyball, and minigolf. There are warm coves with sandy beaches, and in winter this is ideal skiing country.

SUMMER HOTELS

SUMMERHOTEL MALAKIAS, Pihlajavedenkuja 6, SF-57170 Savonlinna. Tel. 957/23-283. Fax 957/12-524. 220 rms (all with bath). TEL.

$ Rates (including breakfast): 190 markkaa ($51.80) single; 260–310 markkaa ($70.90–$84.55) double. AE, DC, MC, V. **Closed:** Mid-Aug to May.

On Route 14 a mile outside town, this hotel is perfectly suitable for a Finnish holiday. The rooms are comfortably furnished and contain small kitchenettes. The hotel has a breakfast room, and guests often take their meals at the far more luxurious Spa Hotel Casino, which is run by the same management.

SUMMERHOTEL VUORILINNA, Kasinonsaari, SF-57130 Savonlinna. Tel. 957/24-908. Fax 957/12-524. 150 rms (all with bath). TV TEL.

$ Rates (including breakfast): 220–280 markkaa ($60–$76.35) single; 300–580 markkaa ($81.80–$158.15) double. AE, DC, MC, V. **Closed:** Sept–May.

In the courtyard square of the Spa Hotel Casino, you can stay right on Casino Island, within walking distance over a footbridge to the center of town, enjoying all the facilities of the larger hotel. All the simply furnished units are equipped with shower, kitchenette, and wall-to-wall carpeting. There is no elevator. The Wahna Kasino, next to the hotel, is a favored rendezvous on a summer evening. The island is in the midst of beautiful lakeland scenery.

WHERE TO DINE
MODERATE

RESTAURANT SHIP *HOPEASALMI*, Kauppatori. Tel. 21-701 in summer, 21-092 in winter.

Cuisine: FINNISH. **Reservations:** Recommended. **Bus:** 1, 2, 3, 4.
$ Prices: Appetizers 22–33 markkaa ($6–$9); main dishes 69–120 markkaa ($18.80–$32.70). AE, MC, V.
Open: Summer, daily 9am–1 or 2am; winter, Fri–Sat 5pm–1am.
In front of the Marketplace, this restaurant complex consists of a wharfside terrace for summertime drinks and dining, and a pierbound passenger steamer originally built in 1903 and now permanently in dock. There is also a smaller boat for food service, which in 1927 was built as a lake-district cargo ship. The house specialty is a small Lake Saimaa freshwater fish, called *muikka*. Several are fried and served on the same plate with a green sauce and small new boiled potatoes. The fish soup is a good beginning, and you can also order pepper steak and filet of reindeer.

SNELLMAN'S, Olavinkatu 31. Tel. 13-104.
Cuisine: FINNISH. **Reservations:** Required in summer. **Bus:** 1, 2, 3, 4.
$ Prices: Appetizers 40–50 markkaa ($10.90–$13.65); main dishes 64–108 markkaa ($17.45–$29.45); fixed-price lunch 60 markkaa ($16.35). AE, DC, MC, V.
Open: Daily 10:30am–10pm.
Lying only 100 yards east of the Marketplace, this centrally located restaurant is in a century-old building originally constructed as a bank. Reservations are absolutely vital during the music festival, but less important at other times. One of its features is its three-course lunch, which includes generous helpings from a fish and salad buffet, plus a main dish and a "cocktail" of smoked reindeer, fried rainbow trout, roast pepper steak, spicy shashlik with rice, and noisettes of veal with slightly salted salmon. Many of the loyal patrons come here for the roast lamb with a sour-cream sauce. Adjacent is an English-style pub open daily from 2pm to 1am.

WANHA KASINO, Kylpylaitoksentie Kasinosaari. Tel. 22-572.
Cuisine: FINNISH. **Reservations:** Recommended.
$ Prices: Appetizers 35–50 markkaa ($9.55–$13.65); main dishes 55–105 markkaa ($15–$28.65). DC.
Open: Late May to late Aug, Tues–Sat 8pm–1:30am.
Adjacent to the spa hotel, the Kylpylä Hotelli Casino (see "Where to Stay," above), 220 yards from the railroad station, this is the preferred spot for dining. The pink-clapboard Wanha preserves the old atmosphere so beloved by vacationing members of the Russian Imperial court. Meals are likely to include "gentleman's hash," fried rainbow trout, and salad of cold smoked salmon. Guests can dance to live band music.

INEXPENSIVE

MUSTA PÄSSI, BELLA RISTORANTE, Tulliportinkatu 2. Tel. 22-228.
Cuisine: ITALIAN. **Reservations:** Recommended. **Bus:** 1, 2, 3, 4.
$ Prices: Appetizers 25–40 markkaa ($6.80–$10.90); main dishes 36–70 markkaa ($9.80–$19.10); fixed-price menu 50 markkaa ($13.65). AE, DC, MC, V.
Open: Daily 10am–midnight.
Near the bus station, this is two restaurants in one, a popular gathering place in town, especially for young people. An array of pizzas and pastas is the lure. A specialty is pepper steak provençal. The restaurant offers reasonable prices and polite service.

EXCURSIONS

The boats for 1½-hour **cruises around the Savonlinna isles** via Rauhalinna leave twice within 2 hours from 10am to 4pm daily in summer. The cruise rates are 30 to 40 markkaa ($8.20 to $10.90) for adults, 10 to 20 markkaa ($2.75 to $5.45) for children 12 or under.
There is regular boat traffic to **Punkaharju** by the S/S *Heinävesi* and local cruises in Punkaharju on the M/S *Princess* every day. At Punkaharju you can take a bus for local sightseeing, which includes a visit to a summer art exhibit, a look at a

typical holiday village, and a leisurely lunch at a restaurant in the holiday village or at Valtionhotelli, an old and historic hotel.

At Punkaharju, 15½ miles from Savonlinna, Lake Puruvesi is divided by a long Ice Age ridge stretching for 4½ miles and forming a causeway between the Puruvesi and Pihlajavesi Lakes. This "thread" has been turned into a national park, one of the most famous and photographed beauty spots of Finland. You can also reach Punkaharju by bus or by train, but the preferred method is by boat.

Kerimäki, 14½ miles from Savonlinna and connected by frequent bus service, has the biggest wooden church in the world. Built more than a century ago and large enough to accommodate 3,300 parishioners, the admission-free church is open May to September, Monday through Friday from 9am to 8pm, on Saturday from 9am to 6pm, and on Sunday from 11am to 8pm. To climb the adjacent bell tower, adults pay 5 markkaa ($1.35); children 12 or under, 2 markkaa (55¢).

In addition, by boat you can visit the **Hytermä nature reserve and museum islands,** where you'll see a large folkloric collection. Nearby is **Putkinotko,** the setting for Joel Lehtonen's novel of the same name. A little museum, with mementos of the author, is open June 19 to June 25, Tuesday through Sunday; daily from June 26 to August 6, daily; and August 7 to 19, Tuesday through Sunday. When it's open, visiting hours are always noon to 6pm, and admission is 10 markkaa ($2.75).

If you want to spend a leisurely day on a boat while viewing the beautiful archipelago, take a cruise to Kuopio on the M/S *Heino* or M/S *Kuopio,* or to Lappeenranta aboard the M/S *Kristina Brahe.*

---

7. JOENSUU

273 miles NE of Helsinki, 84 miles east of Kuopio

GETTING THERE   By Plane   Joensuu has air links with Helsinki and any number of small towns in Finland. Flight frequency depends on the time of year. You can take an 11am plane from Helsinki and be in Joensuu 45 minutes later. The airport lies 7 miles outside Joensuu.

By Train   Seven trains a day run between Helsinki and Lappeenranta, with continuing service to Joensuu.

By Bus   Buses run north to Joensuu via Lappeenranta, and there are also bus connections through Savonlinna in the west. A 9:30am bus leaving Lappeenranta will arrive in Joensuu by 1:30pm.

By Car   Take Route 6 all the way from Helsinki, going via Lappeenranta.

ESSENTIALS   The **North Karelian Tourist Office** is at Koskikatu 1 (tel. 973/201-362), open June 15 to August 15, Monday through Friday from 9am to 6pm and on Saturday from 9am to 2pm; the rest of the year, on Monday from 8am to 5pm and Tuesday through Friday from 9am to 4pm.

The **telephone area code** for Joensuu is 973.

J oensuu, founded in the mid-19th century at the mouth of the Pieliskjoki River, is the major municipality of northern Karelia. A busy little city with a population of 47,000, it's the administrative and commercial center of the district. It is also a university town and has a flourishing local cultural life.

WHAT TO SEE & DO

The **Town Hall,** at Rantakatu 4, was designed in 1914 by Eliel Saarinen, who was the architect responsible for the famous railway station in Helsinki. Nearby at Rantakatu 2 you may want to purchase local handcrafts, for which the district is so well known. These include hand-woven linen cloth, hand-knitted goods, shoes or knapsacks of birch bark, and soft leather slippers, among other items.

Both the Karelian and Orthodox traditions are still cherished by many people in the area, especially by those who live in the country. For a glimpse of that life, you can visit **Pohjois-Karjalan Museo,** Siltakato 1 (tel. 201-634), on the island of Ilosaari in Karjalantalo. The museum displays prehistoric articles, an Orthodox ecclesiastical art collection, and other memorabilia from northern Karelia, including textiles, crafts, and folk art. It is open on Tuesday, Thursday, and Friday from noon to 4pm, on Wednesday from noon to 8pm, on Saturday from 10am to 4pm, and on Sunday from 10am to 6pm. Admission is 3 markkaa (80¢) for adults and 2 markkaa (55¢) for children 12 or under. A restaurant on the premises serves traditional food and drink Tuesday through Friday from noon to 4pm (to 8pm on Wednesday), on Saturday from 10am to 4pm, and on Sunday from 10am to 6pm.

The surrounding area still carries out many of the traditions of the Orthodox church, and several religious processions, known as *praasniekka,* occur in summer.

On the western shore of Lake Pielinen, on which you can take boat excursions in summer, the **Koli Hills** rise to 1,070 feet, the highest point in northern Karelia. They are about 40 miles due north of the city and offer some of the most dramatic lake and river views in Finland.

If you're driving, you can continue north to **Nurmes,** which lies on an inlet of the northern part of Lake Pielinen. Here the chief attraction is the **Bomba Karelian Village** at Ritoniemi, which is a log manor house, beautifully decorated in a regional style. Accommodations are provided in holiday cottages, and Karelian food is served.

You can explore the eastern side of the lake going through **Lieksa,** where you can visit the **Pielinen Outdoor Museum,** Pappilantie 2 (tel. 204-90), which has 60 buildings containing authentic Karelian furnishings. Located along Route 73 less than a mile from the town center of Lieska, the museum is open mid-May to mid-August, daily from 9am to 6pm; mid-August to mid-September, daily from 10am to 6pm; and mid-September to mid-May, Tuesday through Friday from 10am to 3pm and on Saturday and Sunday from 11am to 3pm. Admission is 10 markkaa ($2.75) for adults and 2 markkaa (55¢) for children 12 or under. Some 16 miles from the town on the eastern border, the **Ruunaa wilderness rapids** thunder down. At **Ilomantsi** village, 45 miles east of Joensuu, is an authentic center of Karelian culture, with a viewing platform at the top of the Ilomantsi water tower.

In this once war-torn area of eastern Finland, especially in **Petkeljarvi National Park,** you'll find many reminders of lost wars with the Russians, including trenches, machine-gun nests, and graveyards of fallen soldiers.

WHERE TO STAY

HOTEL KIMMEL, Itäranta 1, SF-80100 Joensuu. Tel. 973/73-1771. Fax 973/177-2112. 229 rms (all with bath). MINIBAR TV TEL.
$ Rates (including breakfast): 460 markkaa ($125.45) single; 560 markkaa ($152.70) double. AE, DC, MC, V.
On a peninsula of flat land in the city's center curving into the city's river, this modern hotel serves as one of the town's social centers. Bedrooms are cozily and efficiently furnished with Finnish textiles and built-in birchwood furniture. There's a large main restaurant where dance music is featured on certain nights. The hotel also has a more intimate steakhouse, an illuminated swimming pool, a disco, and a sauna with an adjacent snack bar.

POHJOIS-KARJALA, Torikatu 20, SF-80100 Joensuu. Tel. 973/27-311. Fax 973/27-323. 77 rms (all with bath). TV TEL.
$ Rates (including breakfast): 420 markkaa ($114.55) single; 520 markkaa ($141.80) double. AE, DC, MC, V.
Its proximity to the town's Market Square makes this hotel's pleasant pub and dance restaurant popular with commercial travelers. In three upper stories are the rooms, including seven for nonsmokers. Rooms are furnished comfortably and attractively in a modern style. In the hotel's restaurant you can have dinner Monday through Friday from 4 to 8pm for 85 markkaa ($23.20), and on Saturday and Sunday from 6 to 8pm for 65 markkaa ($17.75).

WHERE TO DINE

TEATTERI-RAVINTOLA, Rantakatu 4. Tel. 293-06.
   Cuisine: FINNISH. **Reservations:** Recommended.
$ Prices: Appetizers 45–55 markkaa ($12.25–$15); main dishes 56–100 markkaa ($15.25–$27.25); four-course lunch 45 markkaa ($12.25). AE, MC, V.
   Open: Daily 11am–1am.
Considered the best restaurant in town, it is like a Finnish version of a Ratskeller, set into the basement of the town's most famous monument, the Town Hall dating from 1914. The restaurant has an antique and charming decor. Its fixed-price lunch includes access to the salad table. At night, you can enjoy such tempting dishes as fried pike-perch flavored with herbs, salmon sautéed and served with a caper sauce, and filet of beef with either a mustard or a cream sauce.

---

8. KUOPIO

244 miles NE of Helsinki, 89 miles NE of Jyväskylä

GETTING THERE **By Plane** Frequent 35-minute flights connect Helsinki with Kuopia. The airport lies 11 miles from the center.

By Train Frequent trains make the 5-hour run between Helsinki and Kuopio, and six trains a day go between Kuopio and Jyväskylä, taking 3¾ hours. Five trains a day take 1¾ hours to run between Mikkeli and Kuopio.

By Bus Daily buses make the 5-hour run between Kuopio and Helsinki, and three buses a day run from Jyväskylä to Kuopio, taking 2¼ hours.

By Car From Helsinki, head north on the E4 to Lahti, which will join the E80 at Jämsä. From there, continue northeast along the E80 until you reach Kuopio.

By Steamer Traveling by steamer takes 12 hours from Savonlinna. Kuopio is the northernmost point served by the Saimaa lake steamers.

ESSENTIALS The **City Tourist Office** is at Haapaniemenkatu 17 (tel. 971/182-584), open June 4 to August 19, Monday through Friday from 8am to 6pm and on Saturday from 8am to 2pm; the rest of the year, Monday through Friday from 9:30am to 4pm. The **telephone area code** for Kuopio is 971.

The tourist capital of the eastern lake district of central Finland, Kuopio is the cultural and economic center of Savo province and is located in one of Finland's most beautiful areas. Visitors flock to this old lakeside garrison town in summer to take cruises on the Saimaa steamers, some of which are rather antiquated. Overlooking beautiful Lake Kallavesi, the town is a good starting point for excursions to Savonlinna. There is daily service on a Saimaa steamer, and the trip takes about 12 hours.

WHAT TO SEE & DO

Dominating Kuopio is the 770-foot **Puijo Hill**, a wooded area about 1½ miles northwest of the town. In summer it is reached by a good road, and in winter it's covered with ski trails. At the top of this hill is a tower and a restaurant, both discussed below.
   The town center is the lively **Market Square**, called Kauppatori in Finnish, which contains fruit and vegetable displays. The **town hall** here dates from 1882. If you're visiting in summer, you can explore the narrow peninsula of **Vainolanniemi**, which has a bathing beach, a summer restaurant, and playgrounds.

PUIJON TORNI, at the top of Puijo Hill. Tel. 114-841.

This tower, with a revolving restaurant (see "Where to Dine," below), is at the site of the international Puijo Winter Games on the top of Puijo Hill immediately north of the city. This wooded hillside is a major recreational area in both summer and winter for the residents of Kuopio. The tower was constructed in 1963 at a height of 245 feet. It offers two panoramic viewing platforms, with a revolving floor moving at 360° per hour.

Admission: 10 markkaa ($2.75) adults, 8 markkaa ($2.20) children; free if you dine at the restaurant.

Open: June–Aug, daily 8am–11pm; May and Sept, daily 10am–6pm; Oct–Apr, Sat–Sun 10am–6pm.

ORTHODOX CHURCH MUSEUM, Karjalankatu 1. Tel. 118-818.

In the southeastern sector of town, this church has collections from old Karelian churches and monasteries, unique in the West. It is considered a major cultural statement. Its rich and beautiful exhibits mirror the history of the Orthodox church and include collections from such ancient monasteries as Valamo, Konevista, and Petsamo.

Admission: 10 markkaa ($2.75) adults, 4 markkaa ($1.10) children 12 or under.

Open: May–Aug, Tues–Sun 10am–4pm; Sept–Apr, Mon–Fri 10am–2pm, Sat–Sun noon–5pm. **Bus:** 7.

KUOPION KORTTELIMUSEO (Old Kuopio Museum), Kirkkokatu 22. Tel. 182-625.

Occupying an entire block of the town in the town center 200 yards south of Kuopio Church, this museum contains a representative section of the town's old, low wooden buildings, some on their original sites and others moved here and restored. The museum shows how people lived in Kuopio from the late 18th century to the 1930s, with residences, warehouses, an old hall of assizes, and other buildings. Guided tours are offered.

Admission: Free.

Open: Mid-May to mid-Sept, Tues and Thurs–Sun 10am–5pm, Wed 10am–7pm; mid-Sept to mid-May, Tues–Sun 10am–3pm.

WHERE TO STAY

EXPENSIVE

RIVOLI KUOPIO, Satamakatu 1, SF-70100 Kuopio. Tel. 971/195-111.

Fax 971/195-170. 141 rms (all with bath). A/C MINIBAR TV TEL.

$ Rates (including breakfast): June–July and Fri–Sat year round, 480 markkaa ($130.90) single; 600 markkaa ($163.60) double. Sun–Thurs Aug–May, 580 markkaa ($158.15) single; 700 markkaa ($190.90) double. AE, DC, MC, V.

The best place to stay in town, this stylish hotel is set on manicured lawns at the edge of a lake near the city center. The bedrooms are attractively furnished and decorated; the most desirable ones have windows opening onto the lake. One of the most popular sections of the hotel is the terrace, overlooking the lake and lit by flaming torches at night.

Dining/Entertainment: The Rivoli has the most sophisticated dining and drinking facilities in town, including a gourmet restaurant.

Services: Room service.

Facilities: Three saunas, indoor swimming pool, solarium, massage room.

MODERATE

HOTEL CUMULUS, Puijonkatu 32, SF-70100 Kuopio. Tel. 971/154-111.

Fax 971/154-299. 143 rms (all with bath). MINIBAR TV TEL.

$ Rates: June 21–Aug 5 and Fri–Sat year round, 280 markkaa ($76.35) single; 380 markkaa ($103.65) double. Sun–Thurs Aug 5–June 20, 420 markkaa ($114.55) single; 580 markkaa ($158.15) double. AE, DC, MC, V. **Parking:** 35 markkaa ($9.55).

A handsome modern building in the town center, this chain-run hotel has a concrete facade, metallic windows, and a terrazzo-floored lobby. Bedrooms are well furnished and comfortable. Built in the 1970s, the hotel has some of the best facilities in town, including three different restaurants, three saunas, a swimming pool, and a sauna bar. Its traditional Citybar is one of the most frequented in town, open from noon to 1am daily. There is a 22-car garage on the hotel premises.

HOTEL ISO-VALKEINEN, Päiväranta, SF-70420 Kuopio. Tel. 971/341-444. Fax 971/341-344. 98 rms (all with bath). TV TEL.

$ **Rates** (including breakfast): June 9–Aug 13, 300 markkaa ($81.80) single; 380 markkaa ($103.65) double. Aug 14–June 8, 410 markkaa ($111.80) single; 520 markkaa ($141.80) double. AE, MC, V. **Parking:** Available.

At the edge of a lake 3 miles from the town center, this hotel overlooks a rolling lawn and surrounding trees, an unspoiled natural setting. Motorists can park near their bedrooms, which are in wings near the driveways and all have radios. The staff can recommend the best walking trails. Bedrooms are furnished in a modern, functional style. There are two modern restaurants and a bar, and room service is offered. Facilities include three saunas and a swimming pool.

HOTELLI RAUHALAHTI, Katiskaniementie 8, SF-70700 Kuopio. Tel. 971/311-700. Fax 971/311-843. 106 rms (all with bath). MINIBAR TV TEL **Bus:** 20, 23.

$ **Rates** (including breakfast): 420 markkaa ($114.55) single; 520 markkaa ($141.80) double. AE, DC, MC, V.

In a secluded part of the forest, 3 miles south of the town center on the shore of Lake Kallavesi, this hotel—built in 1981—offers rooms that are furnished in a comfortable modern style. Some of the units have private balconies overlooking the lake. Nearby is a smoke sauna, in the old log Jatkankamppa Cabin, where you bask in the gentle heat and then swim in the lake water (via a hole in the ice in winter, if you're hardy enough). There are five restaurants (one with live music) and the biggest dance floor in the region. Room service and massage are offered, and there's a beauty parlor, squash courts, two saunas, outdoor tennis, small gym, and solariums.

PUIJONSARVI GRAND HOTEL, Minna Canthinkatu 18, SF-70100 Kuopio. Tel. 971/123-333. Fax 971/170-117. 231 rms (all with bath). MINIBAR TV TEL.

$ **Rates** (including breakfast): 430–480 markkaa ($117.25–$130.90) single; 550–600 markkaa ($150–$163.60) double. AE, DC, MC, V.

This centrally located brick hotel with bay windows is above a row of shops that were built into its street level. Each room has a radio, hairdryer, and trouser press. Furnishings are in an attractive modern style. Half a mile from the railroad station, the hotel has two restaurants, one with cabaret shows, and a lobby-level bar with its own summer outdoor terrace. Room service is available, and four saunas, a Turkish bath, and a Jacuzzi are on the premises.

SAVONIA, Sammakkolammentie 2, SF-70200. Tel. 971/225-333. Fax 971/358-71. 50 rms (all with bath). MINIBAR TV TEL.

$ **Rates** (including breakfast): June 26–Aug 10, 280 markkaa ($76.35) single; 340 markkaa ($92.70) double. Aug 11–June 25, 400 markkaa ($109.10) single; 480 markkaa ($130.90) double. Summerhotel Savonia (June–Aug 10): 190 markkaa ($51.80) single; 240 markkaa ($65.45) double. AE, MC, V.

⑤ A student-run red-brick and concrete hotel near Puijo Tower a mile north of the center, this hotel offers one of the best bargains around. The rooms are furnished in a modern, functional style. In addition to the 50 rooms listed above, an additional 26 rooms are offered in a nearby annex, Summerhotel Savonia. The hotel also operates a fine restaurant run by students who are learning the hotel trade; for dinner, expect to pay around 85 markkaa ($23.20). The staff is polite and helpful and will give you good advice about touring the area. Your morning swim is free.

INEXPENSIVE

MARTINA, Tulliportinkatu 23, SF-70100 Kuopio. Tel. 971/123-522. 41 rms (all with bath). TV TEL.

$ Rates (including breakfast): 270–310 markkaa ($73.65–$84.55) single; 370–410 markkaa ($100.90–$111.80) double. No credit cards.

Right in the center of town off the principal shopping street of Kuopio, Martina, owned by a cooperative chain, is more suited for overnight stopovers than for long stays. Its rooms were recently renovated. A sauna is on the premises.

SPORTHOTEL PUIJO, by Puijo Tower, SF-70330 Puijo. Tel. 971/114-841. 20 rms (all with bath). TV TEL.

$ Rates (including breakfast and sauna): June–Aug, 250 markkaa ($68.20) single; 300 markkaa ($81.80) double. Sept–May, 310 markkaa ($84.55) single; 400 markkaa ($109.10) double. AE, DC, MC, V.

⑤ Outside the center of Kuopio on a hill, this hotel mainly functions as a winter ski hotel. The bedrooms have simple birch furnishings, and the hotel has three saunas. In the older section, you can dine in a rustic restaurant.

WHERE TO DINE

MUSTA LAMMAS, Satamakatu 4. Tel. 123-494.
Cuisine: SEAFOOD/CONTINENTAL. **Reservations:** Recommended.
$ Prices: Appetizers 45–80 markkaa ($12.25–$21.80); main dishes 85–120 markkaa ($23.20–$32.70). AE, DC, MC, V.◻**Open:** Mon–Fri 11am–midnight, Sat 2pm–midnight.

In a windowless cellar that was formerly a brewery, this is the gourmet restaurant of the city. The menu is not extensive, but it is well chosen, and whenever possible, fresh ingredients are used—including fish from the lakes of eastern Finland. There are also many continental dishes. Try whitefish in foil, lobster cardinal, or paupiettes of sole in lobster sauce.

PUIJON TORNI, by the Puijo Tower. Tel. 114-841.
Cuisine: FINNISH. **Reservations:** Recommended.
$ Prices: Appetizers 35–45 markkaa ($9.55–$12.25); main dishes 65–105 markkaa ($17.75–$28.65). AE, MC, V.
Open: Daily 11am–1am.

If you want to enjoy good food and an excellent view from the highest tower in eastern Finland, come to this revolving restaurant in the Puijo Tower (see "What to See & Do," above). The restaurant makes one revolution per hour, and the panoramic view of the woodlands and lakeland scenery is extraordinary. The highest platform is almost 750 feet above Lake Kallavesi. If you dine here, you don't have to pay admission charges to go up in the tower. Meals might include reindeer steak, rainbow trout, or fried flounder.

TAVERNA, Kauppakatu 40-42. Tel. 127-646.
Cuisine: FINNISH. **Reservations:** Recommended. **Bus:** 3, 21.
$ Prices: Appetizers 33–45 markkaa ($9–$12.25); main dishes 40–116 markkaa ($10.90–$31.65). AE, DC, MC, V.
Open: Mon–Sat 11am–7pm.

This restaurant is in the mall, a block west of the marketplace. If available, request an order of kalakukko, Kuopio's local food dish. From the province of Savo, this is a pie made from pork and a small whitefish native to Finland. When you order, keep in mind that the helpings are large. Other main dishes include chateaubriand, coeur de filet à la maison, and grilled rainbow trout. For lunch, you might prefer the tuna salad.

CHAPTER 38
FINNISH LAPLAND

- **WHAT'S SPECIAL ABOUT FINNISH LAPLAND**
1. **ROVANIEMI**
2. **RANUA**
3. **KEMI**
4. **SODANKYLÄ**
5. **INARI/IVALO**

Above the Arctic Circle, Lapland comprises one-third of Finland, the country's northernmost as well as its largest and most sparsely populated province. It is often called "The Last Wilderness in Europe," and you will experience a spacious land of unspoiled nature and scenic grandeur.

Lapland has four seasons, but the people sometimes talk about eight seasons a year. In the summer, the vegetation sprouts, flowers, and bears fruit all within 3 months, because the sun doesn't set for weeks on end. In Utsjoki, in the northernmost part of Lapland, starting in the middle of May, the sun does not set for nearly 70 days. If summer with its "Midnight Sun" is an extraordinary experience for the traveler, then so is the polar night, the twilight time of the year, when darkness is never really total, the sun glowing softly on the horizon.

The period of time in October and November, when there is no sun, is called *Kaamos*. Winter is the longest time of the year, but it includes the night light show of the northern lights. After the polar night come the dazzling spring snows, great for skiing until May when the sun gives twice as much light as it did in the dead of winter.

Lapland is a country of great forests, making their management and agriculture the most important sources of income. Finland's longest river, the Kemijoki, runs through the area, and its lower reaches are terraced with seven hydroelectric plants. Lapland also has Western Europe's largest artificial lakes—Lokka and Porttipahta.

Despite human intrusion, this is still a land of bears, wolves, eagles, and wolverines; however, the animal that symbolizes this land is the reindeer, and there are more than 300,000 here. The true natural wilderness has been preserved untouched in many nature reserves.

It is easy to travel to the far reaches of Lapland. Regular flights go to the province's capital, Rovaniemi, and beyond the Arctic Circle to Ivalo. By bus, one can travel comfortably to every corner of the province. Lapland also offers the traveler an array of events including the midsummer celebrations on Ounasvaara, Aavasaksa fells, and in Posio; the Midnight Sun Film Festival in Sodankylä; the Goldpanning Competition in Tankavaara; the Whitefish Festival in Kukkolankoski; the Cloudberry Fair and Market in Ranua; Hetta's music festival; and the increasingly popular Arctic Canoe Race from Kilpisjärvi to Tornio.

ARCTIC ACCOMMODATIONS   There is a great variety of hotels, summer hotels, motels, hostels, and cabins in Lapland, the cheapest being the youth hostels. There are 30 hostels in the province, with prices from 30 to 75 markkaa ($8.20 to $20.45) per night if you have an International Youth Hostel membership card. Otherwise the prices are 45 to 68 markkaa ($12.25 to $18.55) a night if you have your own sheets. You can also buy or rent sheets here. Many youth hostels have family rooms and even single rooms. For further information, contact the **Finnish Youth Hostel Association,** Yrjonkatu 38B, SF-00100 Helsinki (tel. 90/649-0377).

The summer hotels have higher standards, and the lodging houses (*matkustajakoti*) also have moderate prices—125 to 200 markkaa ($34.10 to $54.55)

WHAT'S SPECIAL ABOUT FINNISH LAPLAND

Great Towns/Villages

☐ Rovaniemi, the capital of Lapland, a modern town designed by Alvar Aa'-to, the great architect, in the wilderness.

☐ Sodankylä, where the Lapps say the *real* Lapland begins—the gateway to the majestic fell country.

☐ Kemi, the seaport on the Gulf of Bothnia, one of the oldest areas of habitation in Finland.

Ace Attractions

☐ The Arctic Road, one of the world's great engineering feats, stretching for 620 miles to the very edge of Europe.

☐ The 50-mile-long Lake Inarijärvi, in Inari country, containing more than 3,000 islands.

Cool for Kids

☐ Santa Claus Village at the Arctic Circle, outside Rovaniemi, where a child can meet Prancer.

☐ Ranua Wildlife Park, at Ranua, where you can introduce your kids to a large zoo of exotic Lappish animals.

Sporting Activities

☐ Panning for gold at Tankavaara Gold Village, 143 miles north of the Arctic Circle.

Special Events/Festivals

☐ The International Midnight Sun Film Festival in June at Sodankylä, with screenings of the latest films under the Midnight Sun.

---

per person. There are many varieties of cabins, from high-level ones with their own saunas and kitchens to cheaper ones with just beds.

Note that the Arctic hotels have high- and low-season prices; high season is March and April. Breakfast is normally included in the prices, and nearly all hotels and motels have saunas.

ARCTIC DINING There is a wide range of restaurants too, from first class to small cozy coffee bars. From 11am to 1pm on weekdays, many restaurants offer solid lunches at low prices. Priced from 45 markkaa ($12.25), they are usually from a buffet that consists of salads, soups, and main courses, plus desserts. In the evening you can order from an à la carte list or ask for a fixed-price dinner. In the north, don't forget the "Lapland à la carte menu," which includes all the delicacies of the province, such as grouse, reindeer, salmon, and berries.

THE ARCTIC ROAD North of the Arctic Circle, the Arctic Road lies as far north as the roadless tundras of Alaska, Greenland, and Siberia. The ✪ **Arctic Road,** however, provides easy access to the diverse scenery of the north.

As early as the 1930s, tourists from all over Europe traveled north in their cars, heading for Petsamo, the end point of the Arctic Road at that time. Today the Arctic Road is an adventure, stretching for more than 620 miles. It starts near the Arctic Circle at Rovaniemi and passes through central and northern Lapland, as it heads toward the Arctic Ocean and eastern Finnmark, on the very edge of Europe.

The views along the Arctic Road reveal the respect people have for their environment. Extensive areas have been protected and preserved for future generations to admire.

Modern transportation brings you to the start of your adventure. Rovaniemi, the point of departure, can be reached by car, train, or plane.

SEEING FINNISH LAPLAND
GETTING THERE

Since the whole of northern Finland is a vast wilderness, regular air flights are the fastest way to see the area. Many Americans settle for a quick Midnight Sun flight from Helsinki in midsummer, a fast overnight stay, and a return the next morning. But the region merits more attention than that. You can travel by train to Rovaniemi, and from there take one of the buses that spread like a fan across the region. Finnair flies as far north as Ivalo.

A SUGGESTED ITINERARY

Day 1: Drive north to Kemi for the night and explore this seaport opening onto the Gulf of Bothnia.

Days 2&3: Continue northeast to Rovaniemi where you can see the attractions of the area. The next day you can make journeys to the Arctic Circle and take a side trip to Ranua in the southeast.

Day 4: Continue north deep into the fell country for an overnight stopover in Sodankylä.

Days 5&6: Continue north for the final look at the "top of Finland." While still based in either Ivalo or Inari, spend your last day taking in the sights of the environs.

1. ROVANIEMI

518 miles north of Helsinki, 178 miles south of Ivalo

GETTING THERE By Plane There are frequent daily flights between Rovaniemi and Helsinki, taking 1½ hours. The airport lies 6 miles from the center of Rovaniemi.

By Train Four trains a day leave from Helsinki for Rovaniemi. If you take the 7am departure from Helsinki, arrival time in Rovaniemi is 5pm.

By Bus Rovaniemi is the bus terminal for the north of Finland. If you're in Helsinki, it's best to fly or take the train. But once you arrive in Rovaniemi, the bus becomes the all-important link for exploring Lapland. There are daily bus connections between Rovaniemi and Oulu, Kemi, Kemijärvi, Kuusamo, Ranua, Kittilä, Sodankylä, Ivalo, Inari, and farther north—even all the way to the North Cape in Norway.

By Car The E4 goes all the way from Helsinki to Rovaniemi in the north.

ESSENTIALS The **City Tourist Office** is at Aalonkatu 1 (tel. 960/16-270), open June to August, Monday through Friday from 8am to 7pm and on Saturday and Sunday from 10am to 7pm; September to May, Monday through Friday from 8am to 4pm.
The **telephone area code** for Rovaniemi is 960.

When the Nazis began their infamous retreat from Lapland in 1944, they burned Rovaniemi, the gateway to Lapland and a prime rail and communications center, to the ground. But with characteristic Finnish *sisu* (suggesting courage and bravery against overwhelming odds) Rovaniemi bounced back, becoming a completely modern town, designed largely by Finland's greatest architect, Alvar Aalto, who created roads shaped like reindeer antlers.

Five miles south of the Arctic Circle, Rovaniemi is at the confluence of two great Finnish rivers, the Kemijoki and the Ounasjoki. This capital of Finnish Lapland goes back some 8,000 years, and the settlement at Rovaniemi was mentioned in documents in the 1400s. As a tourist and travel center, Rovaniemi has excellent road, rail, and air connections. Highway 4, which passes through the city, stretches from southern Finland to Inari in Lapland. You can drive to northern Norway on the Great Arctic Highway and to Kiruna, Sweden, and Narvik, Norway, by following the North Calotte Highway.

If you arrive by air, chances are you'll take a bus into Rovaniemi, although a reindeer-drawn *pulkka* would be a more colorful vehicle. Lumberjacks and an occasional Lapp may be seen, but they are not typical of the thousands of progressive Finns who inhabit Rovaniemi.

Regardless of the time of your arrival, you'll surely escape the heat. In July, the "hot" month, the temperature remains coolly under the 60° Fahrenheit mark; however, you won't escape the mosquitoes from the swampy wastelands.

WHAT TO SEE & DO

ROVANLEMEN KIRKKO, Kirkkotie 1.

This church, the Evangelical Lutheran parish church of Rovaniemi, was built in 1950 to replace the church destroyed during the war. Architect Bertel Liljequist designed it, and it stands on the same spot where three other churches were erected. The interior is quite beautiful, noted for its wall and ceiling decorations by Antti Salmenlinna, wood carvings by Gunnar Uotila, and the best yet, the altar fresco *Fountain of Life* by Lennart Segerstrale, which features everyday Lapp motifs.

Admission: Free.

Open: June to mid-Sept, daily 9am–8pm. **Closed:** Mid-Sept to May.

LAURI-TUOTTET OY, Pohjolankatu 25. Tel. 225-01.

This log cabin in the center of town is built in the typical architectural style of the Perapohjola region. Inside are workshops where craftspeople turn out both modern and traditional decorative articles, using such items as reindeer antlers or the gnarled roots of pussy willows as raw materials. In the café is a permanent sales exhibition, featuring curly birch products, wool and leather goods, jewelry, and Puukko knives.

Admission: Free.

Open: Mon–Fri 9am–6pm, Sat–Sun 10am–3pm.

LIBRARY HOUSE, Hallituskatu 9. Tel. 960-3221.

Library House, designed by Alvar Aalto, has a valuable Lapland collection.

Admission: Free.

Open: June to mid-Aug, Mon–Fri 11am–7pm, Sat 10am–4pm; mid-Aug to May, Mon–Fri 11am–8pm, Sat 10am–4pm.

LAPPIA HOUSE, Hallituskatu 11. Tel. 322-2497.

Also designed by Alvar Aalto, Lappia House is the theater, convention, and concert hall building of Rovaniemi.

Admission: Tours, free.

Open: Tours given June–Aug 15, Mon–Fri at 10am, 1pm, and 4pm.

LAPLAND PROVINCIAL MUSEUM, Hallituskatu 11. Tel. 322-2483.

This museum, in the same building as Lappia House, features some Lapland exhibits.

Admission: 5 markkaa ($1.35) adults, 2 markkaa (55¢) children 12 or under.

Open: May–Aug, Tues–Sun 10am–6pm; Sept–Apr, Tues–Sun noon–4pm.

WHERE TO STAY

Houses that take in paying guests are the best bargains in expensive Rovaniemi. For the most part these are simple places sprinkled throughout the town, and although they aren't bleak, they lack luxuries and frills. Generally they are run by a small staff (usually a family), and the rooms are neat and modern (at least post–World War II).

But don't expect a private bath; most of the accommodations have sinks with hot and cold running water.

Regardless of the type of accommodations you want, I strongly recommend making advance reservations during the summer.

EXPENSIVE

RANTASIPI POHJANHOVI, Pohjanpuistikko 2, SF-96200 Rovaniemi. Tel. 960/313-731. 216 rms (all with bath). MINIBAR TV TEL.

$ Rates (including breakfast): 595 markkaa ($162.25) single; 740 markkaa ($201.80) double. AE, DC, MC, V.

The oldest and most flamboyant hotel in town and the biggest in northern Scandinavia, this hostelry in the center off Koskenranta caters to European tourists. Originally built in 1936, it was reconstructed in 1947. From the sweeping windows of many of the sprawling public rooms, you can watch thousands of logs floating downriver to cutting mills. The bedrooms are comfortable and stylish, outfitted with shades of warm colors and well-chosen Finnish fabrics.

Dining/Entertainment: There is a well-frequented disco, a small-stakes casino, and a nightclub with live entertainment. Dance music usually accompanies meals in the large main restaurant. A second, more elegant restaurant, Valkoinen Peura, is recommended separately (see "Where to Dine," below).

Services: Room service.

Facilities: Saunas, swimming pool with liquor service in an adjacent blue-tile alcove.

MODERATE

CITY HOTEL, Pekankatu 9, SF-96200 Rovaniemi. Tel. 960/314-501. Fax 960/311-304. 97 rms (all with bath). TV TEL.

$ Rates (including breakfast and sauna): 430 markkaa ($117.25) single; 540 markkaa ($147.26) double. AE, MC, V.

The management maintains a handful of wilderness cottages for rent outside the city limits, but the original section of this most serviceable hotel is in the center of Rovaniemi north of Ruokasenkatu. The hotel has a pair of saunas with a communal lounge with a fireplace, a ground-floor bar, and a restaurant. The tastefully modern, carpeted bedrooms feature in-house movies, recorded music, and built-in birchwood furniture. Don't forget to ask the friendly receptionist about the hotel's Arctic Safaris, which offer a view of natural life north of the Arctic Circle.

HOTEL POLAR, Valtakatu 23, SF-96200 Rovaniemi. Tel. 960/23-751. Fax 960/23-751. 64 rms (all with bath). A/C MINIBAR TV TEL.

$ Rates (including breakfast): 480 markkaa ($130.90) single; 620 markkaa ($169.05) double. AE, DC, MC, V.

This establishment in the center, on a street running parallel to Korkalonkatu, is probably the best hotel in town, and the attention to food and decor is unmatched by any other property in the region. You might be tempted to have a drink in the richly upholstered English-style bar before heading to your spacious paneled room, outfitted with a pleasing color scheme of warm earth tones and conservatively modern furnishings. There are private saunas in four rooms, as well as special rooms for nonsmokers and the allergic persons. The elegant restaurant here is the Lapponia (see "Where to Dine," below). There is an English-style bar. Pisto, a popular beer house, is also in the building. Room service is available, and there are two saunas and a swimming pool.

The hotel owns a luxurious country lodge a 19-mile drive from Rovaniemi. Guests go there to take part in a wide range of sporting and outdoor activities, including "ice golf" and motor-sledge safaris, slalom skiing, and hunting and fishing.

HOTELLI OPPIKPOIKA, Korkalonkatu 33, SF-96200 Rovaniemi. Tel. 960/20-321. Fax 960/16-969. 40 rms (all with bath). MINIBAR TV TEL.

$ Rates (including breakfast): 400 markkaa ($109.08) single; 480 markkaa ($130.90) double. AE, DC, MC, V.

Built in 1975 and completely remodeled in 1986, the rooms here are comfortably furnished, large, and tastefully decorated with parquet floors and original art. The entire third floor is reserved for nonsmokers, and there is a special room for invalids. Each floor has a sitting room, and there are two saunas, a swimming pool, a workout gym, and a first-class restaurant specializing in continental and Lapland cuisine. In addition to the regular staff, students are involved in running the hotel. It's in the town center near the library.

SKY HOTEL OUNASVAARA, Ounasvaara, SF-96400 Rovaniemi. Tel. 960/23-371. Fax 960/313-997. 69 rms, 7 apartments (all with bath). MINIBAR TV TEL.

$ Rates (including breakfast): June–Aug 15, 360 markkaa ($98.15) single; 450 markkaa ($122.70) double. Aug 15–May, 470 markkaa ($128.15) single; 580 markkaa ($158.15) double; 650 markkaa ($177.25) apartments. AE, DC, MC, V.

This is probably the region's premier hotel, and it's devoted almost entirely to skiing and hiking. It is on a hilltop 1½ miles west of the town center amid more than 9 miles of illuminated cross-country ski trails and five downhill slopes with a chair lift and two T-bars. There's tobagganing down a stainless-steel chute from May to September. All but 20 of the rooms, which are comfortable and furnished in an attractive modern style, have their own saunas, TVs with video movies and satellite reception, and radios. Apartments for two have their own kitchenettes and sauna. Laundry facilities are provided.

BUDGET

ROVANIEMEN AMMATTIKOULUN KESAHOTELLI, Kairatie 73-75, SF-96100 Rovaniemi. Tel. 960/192-651. 36 rms (all with bath).

$ Rates (including breakfast): 200 markkaa ($54.55) double. No credit cards. **Closed:** Aug 8–June 15.

This establishment 1½ miles from the railroad station becomes a summer hotel after its students leave on vacation. The bedrooms, all doubles, are simple but comfortable.

WHERE TO DINE

Most hotels have a lunchtime buffet from 11am to 1pm, which normally includes salad or soup, three main courses, dessert, bread and butter, plus milk, buttermilk, or homemade malt drinks. The prices begin at 55 markkaa ($15) in smaller hotels and restaurants. You can eat as much as you wish.

RESTAURANT LAPPONIA, in the Hotel Polar, Valtakatu 23. Tel. 23-751.
Cuisine: FINNISH. **Reservations:** Recommended.
$ Prices: Appetizers 45–55 markkaa ($12.25–$15); main dishes 60–135 markkaa ($16.35–$36.80). AE, DC, MC, V.
Open: Daily 10am–midnight.

You might enjoy a drink or two at one of the bars at the entrance before entering the intimate English-style dining room decorated with 19th-century portraits and shelves of leather-bound books. The well-prepared specialties include salmon tartare, raw pickled beef with a salad of forest mushrooms, chanterelle soup, fried salmon with tartar sauce, reindeer chops, salmon in white wine, snow grouse (ptarmigan) with a salad, tournedos Rossini, and temptingly caloric desserts.

RESTAURANT OUNASVAARA, in the Sky Hotel Ounasvaara, Ounasvaara. Tel. 23-371.
Cuisine: LAPPISH. **Reservations:** Recommended.
$ Prices: Appetizers 43–54 markkaa ($11.75–$14.75); main dishes 67–145 markkaa ($18.25–$39.55). AE, DC, MC, V.
Open: Lunch daily 11am–4pm; dinner daily 4–10pm.

This restaurant is on the second floor of a previously recommended hotel (see "Where to Stay," above) and offers panoramic views. Its consciously simple furniture was designed as a foil for the grand vistas of lake and forest outside. Well known for its Lapp specialties, the establishment serves meals that include sautéed reindeer with red whortleberries, salmon soup, a herring tray, fried Camembert with cloudberry sauce, and several preparations of fresh trout and salmon. Dance music is featured 3 nights a week.

RESTAURANT VALKOINEN PEURA, in the Hotel Rantasipi Pohjanhovi, Pohjanpuistikko 2. Tel. 313-731.
Cuisine: FINNISH. **Reservations:** Required.
$ Prices: Appetizers 45–55 markkaa ($12.25–$15); main dishes 65–140 markkaa ($17.75–$38.20). AE, DC, MC, V.
Open: Daily 7pm–1am.

To reach the White Reindeer, the specialty restaurant in the Pohjanhovi Hotel, you have to pass through the hotel's main lobby and restaurant. From the rooms with modern decor of marbelized ceilings and stained-glass windows imprinted with reindeer heads, you can watch thousands of logs floating down the nearby river. The menu features Finnish Lapland specialties including salmon from the River Teno, reindeer tongue braised in a red wine sauce, chateaubriand with a cream-and-morel sauce, grilled or sautéed rainbow trout, wild duck with cream sauce, and whitefish baked in foil. Summer desserts are made from local berries.

SHOPPING

One popular item for sale up here is a certificate that proves a traveler has actually visited the Arctic Circle.

THE TRADING POST [SANTA'S VILLAGE], Arctic Circle, Hwy. 4. Tel. 620-96.
Five miles north of Rovaniemi right on the Arctic Circle (*Napapiiri*), this is one of the most unusual collections of boutiques in northern Europe. On the two floors of elegant shops, you'll find cloudberry jam, engraved horn-handled knives, birch and pinewood children's toys, beautifully detailed hand-knit sweaters, and the best of hand-woven Finnish tablecloths and textiles. Also sold are pieces of regional jewelry fashioned from silver and a unique semiprecious form of feldspar called spectrolite (found only in parts of Russia, Canada, and Finland, it was first quarried in the 1950s).

One store sells Saga mink coats for, the owner claims, less than half of what a similar coat would go for in a large city in North America, not counting Customs duty. Another boutique is in a log cabin, which was built in 6 days for the postwar visit of Eleanor Roosevelt to the devastated Rovaniemi. A few steps away, a family of reindeer grazes behind a wooden barricade.

You can buy a certificate to prove that you've been north of the Arctic Circle, and if you mail your postcards from here, they'll receive a special Arctic Circle postmark. There's also an outdoor café for summertime Midnight Sun watching and a guestbook where, if you inscribe the names of your favorite small-fry, they'll receive a special Christmas postcard anywhere in the world "from Santa." In summer, the complex is open daily from 9am to 8pm; in winter, it's open daily from 9am to 5pm.

If you're traveling with youngsters, don't overlook the **Hundred Elves' House** (tel. 61-242), at the trading post, where for 10 markkaa ($2.75) for adults and 5 markkaa ($1.35) for children under 16 you can see the greatest elves' house in Scandinavia.

MIESSI KY, Korkalonkatu 12. Tel. 313-370.
You won't want to miss this store, which sells unusual silver pendants, cups, rings, and brooches that you won't find anywhere else. Many of the semipagan, quasi-regional designs are inspired by ancient objects excavated from Viking ruins. Don't miss the array of Lappish gemstones. One of them, spectrolite, is a semiprecious form of dark-hued feldspar whose iridescence is similar to that of an opal. This unusual store also maintains a second branch at Napapiiri, on the E4 just north of the Arctic Circle.

AN EXCURSION TO THE ARCTIC CIRCLE

If you don't have a car, the easiest way to travel to the Arctic Circle is to take one of the **sightseeing buses** that depart from near the City Tourist Office, Aalonkatu 1 (tel. 16-270), mid-June to mid-August at 5pm on Tuesday and 3pm on Sunday. Tours last 3 hours and cost 50 markkaa ($13.65) for adults and 30 markkaa ($8.20) for children.

Also, the **Arctic Circle bus,** local bus no. 8, takes you to the Santa Claus Village, costing 8 markkaa ($2.20) each way. Trips begin Monday through Friday at 7:30am, and the last one returns at 8:30pm; Saturday runs begin at 8:45am, with a final return trip at 2:30pm.

The most noteworthy sites are the **Arctic Circle Lodge** and **Santa Claus Village,** where you can mail postcards with a special Arctic Circle postmark.

---

2. RANUA

45 miles south of Rovaniemi, 56 miles south of the Arctic Circle

GETTING THERE **By Train** Go to Rovaniemi (see Section 1, above), then take the bus south to Ranua.

By Bus Frequent buses run back and forth between Rovaniemi and Ranua, and there is also bus service from Helsinki.

By Car Take Route 4 north to Rovaniemi (see Section 1, above), then go south to Ranua on Route 78.

ESSENTIALS For **information,** ask at the Rovaniemi City Tourist Office (see Section 1, above). The **telephone area code** for Ranua is 960.

SPECIAL EVENTS In August, Ranua holdes the Cloudberry Fair and Market.

Ranua is a thriving county of agricultural and forest production and service industries, with many beautiful lakes and rivers, including the Simojoki River, stocked for salmon fishing.

WHAT TO SEE & DO

RANUA WILDLIFE PARK, Ranuan Eläinpuisto, Repoharju. Tel. 51-921.

This wildlife park is on Route 79, 2 miles north of the town center. It includes a zoo with large enclosures, public walkways, and viewing terraces. You can see bears, wolves, lynxes, wolverines, pine martens, stoats, wild forest reindeer, lemmings, voles, and many other animals native to the cold countries, as well as about 35 bird species. A geological exhibition features examples of most of the common minerals and rocks found in Finland. The park also offers horseback riding, minigolf, a mini–car track, a nature trail, and a forest trail, plus a children's zoo with domestic animals for the youngsters to wander among.

Admission: 40 markkaa ($10.90) adults, 30 markkaa ($8.20) children 12 or under.

Open: May and Sept, daily 9am–6pm; June–Aug, daily 9am–8pm; Oct–Apr, daily 10am–4pm. **Closed:** Dec 24–26.

FINNISH SUBMARINE TOURS LTD., Takatie 4. Tel. 52-088.

The newest attraction in Ranua is a trip on a miniature submarine in Lake Simojärvi. Inside the sub you can observe the pilots at work and watch the underwater panoramas unfold across the large cockpit window. An accompanying tape-recorded interpretation is available in English. Trips last approximately 1 hour, with a maximum diving depth of about 65 feet, although the vessel can dive to 300 feet safely.

Admission: 250 markkaa ($68.20) adults, 150 markkaa ($40.90) children 12 or under.

Open: June–Aug, daily 9am–9pm. **Closed:** Sept–May.

WHERE TO STAY & DINE

HOTEL ILVESLINNA, Keskustie 10, SF-9770 Ranua. Tel. 960/51-201.
37 rms (all with bath). A/C
$ Rates (including breakfast): 360 markkaa ($98.15) single; 420 markkaa ($114.55) double. AE, DC, MC, V.

The greenery, comfortable furnishings, soft lighting, and good service make this hotel, built in 1986 on the main road from Rovaniemi to Kajaani, a pleasant place to stay—whether for a night or for a week. The bedrooms range from singles to units accommodating four people, and several were designed for individuals with allergies. Most, but not all, rooms contain TV, minibar, and phone.

In the main restaurant, a ceiling of stars lends a touch of Christmas year round. Finnish and Scandinavian specialties, along with some Lappish regional dishes, are served. There is also a Finnish beer house and a cocktail bar. In summer, drinks are served on the terraces, and food is also offered in a Lapp tent restaurant. An orchestra plays three times a week in the main restaurant.

Laundry facilities, baby-sitting, room service, and guides are available, and facilities include tennis courts, a lakeside swimming beach, and transport rentals ranging from bicycles to canoes to snowmobiles.

---

3. KEMI

446 miles NW of Helsinki, 155 miles SW of Rovaniemi

GETTING THERE By Plane There are daily flights between Kemi and Helsinki. If you depart Helsinki on an 11:50am flight, you'll arrive in Kemi at 1:30pm.

By Train From Oulu in the south, which has rail links to Helsinki, four trains a day pass through Kemi heading for Tornio on the border with Sweden. It takes 2 hours from Oulu to Kemi.

By Bus From Helsinki you should fly or take the train. But from Oulu in the south, there are good bus connections to Kemi. There are also daily bus connections from Rovaniemi to Kemi.

By Car From Helsinki, take the E4 northwest all the way; from Rovaniemi, head southwest on the E4.

ESSENTIALS The **Kemi Tourist Office** is at Torikatu 4, SF-94100 Kemi (tel. 9698/199-465). The **telephone area code** for Kemi is 9698.

The mouth of the Kemijoki River is one of the oldest areas of habitation in Finland. Merchants have come to the area since the 1300s because of the great stock of fish. Kemi, with a population of about 27,000, is the center of the province's wood-processing industry. Its two harbors function as Lapland's ports to the rest of the world through the Gulf of Bothnia.

In Kemi, the sea becomes trapped under a barrier of ice in winter more than a yard thick. Nevertheless, ocean-going ships continue to ply routes to Kemi's northern harbor. Shipping lanes are kept open with the help of special ice-breaking vessels.

WHAT TO SEE & DO

The finest view of Kemi is from the roof of the **city hall,** on town square, open daily from 8am to 6pm. Near here, Finland's largest river was blocked off in 1947 by the Isohaara hydroelectric plant and the accumulation of floating logs above the power station toward the end of each summer is probably the most extensive in Europe.

KEMI ART MUSEUM, at the Cultural Center, Pohjoisrantakatu 9. Tel. 198-247.

This museum contains works by Finnish or Swedish-speaking Finnish artists who live mainly on the west coast of the country. Special exhibitions are staged. The museum is housed in an old fisherman's house, where you can see the original fish-smoking hut.

Admission: Free.

Open: Summer, Mon–Fri 10am–5pm, Sat–Sun 11am–5pm; winter, Tues–Fri 10am–7pm, Sat 10am–5pm, Sun noon–7pm.

GEMSTONE GALLERY, Kauppakatu 29. Tel. 20-300.

This is one of the best gemstone museums in Europe and shows how the products of Lapland jade (serpentine) are made. You can also purchase Lapland jade products in the mineral shop at about 20% below normal prices.

Admission: 30 markkaa ($8.20) adults, 15 markkaa ($4.10) children 12 or under.

Open: Daily 10am–8pm.

WHERE TO STAY

HOTEL MERIHOVI, Kesuspuistokatu 6-8, SF-94100 Kemi. Tel. 9698/23-431. Fax 9698/16-316. 71 rms (all with bath). TV TEL.

$ Rates (including breakfast): Mon–Fri 460 markkaa ($125.45) single; 600 markkaa ($163.60) double. Sat–Sun 335 markkaa ($91.35) single; 430 markkaa ($117.25) double. AE, DC, MC, V.

In the center of town near a fountain, on a street running south of the main artery, Valtakatu, this member of the Arctia hotel chain is warmly decorated in soft plywood and plush fabrics. The rooms are styled in a Finnish decor of exposed wood and tasteful colors. Each is comfortable and well maintained. Nine of the bedrooms are fitted with private saunas, and special rooms are reserved for nonsmokers and allergy sufferers. Another special floor is reserved exclusively for business guests.

The main dining room serves salted salmon and Riimi beef with a forest-mushroom salad, "hidden" salmon (that is, a casserole of charcoal-broiled salmon with creamed morels), and workman's reindeer delicacy (reindeer filet stew with a bacon-and-game pepper sauce). There is also a fireplace lounge. Many locals patronize the long Ankkuri Bar on the ground floor. In summer there is an open-air restaurant and summer terrace on the sixth floor. Room service is available. Facilities include two saunas, a squash court, indoor and outdoor tennis courts, hydrotherapy, and a hairdresser.

CUMULUS HOTEL, Hahtisaarenkatu 3, SF-94100 Kemi. Tel. 9698/22-831. Fax 9698/228-3299. 119 rms (all with bath). MINIBAR TV TEL.

$ Rates (including breakfast): June 21–Aug 5 and Sat–Sun year round, 280 markkaa ($76.35) single; 380 markkaa ($103.65) double. Aug 6–June 20, Mon–Fri 440 markkaa ($120) single; 590 markkaa ($160.90) double. AE, DC, MC, V.

This modern hotel in the center of town near the Marketplace, built in 1982, is designed in the same compact format that has made the Cumulus chain well respected in Finland. There is an array of conference facilities, and the bedrooms are comfortable, each furnished in an attractive tasteful modern style. Some are suitable for nonsmokers and allergy sufferers. There are two restaurants, one with evening dance music, and room service is offered. To keep you in shape, the hotel has three saunas, a swimming pool, and two squash courts.

WHERE TO DINE

KULTAKURA, Nahjurinkatu 6. Tel. 15-421.
Cuisine: FINNISH. **Reservations:** Not required.
$ **Prices:** Appetizers 25–45 markkaa ($6.80–$12.25); main dishes 50–130 markkaa ($13.65–$35.45). AE, MC, V.
Open: Sun–Fri 10am–midnight, Sat 10am–9pm.

This popular restaurant in the center near the town hall shares its premises with a pub that keeps the same hours. It is a reasonably priced choice for Finnish and Lapp dishes. Plank steak cooked on a hot stove is a specialty, as is "butler's beefsteak," along with fresh Finnish salmon. Reindeer is prepared in several different ways.

SAMAANI, Valtakatu 1. Tel. 15-192.
Cuisine: STEAKS. **Reservations:** Recommended.
$ **Prices:** Main dishes 50–85 markkaa ($13.65–$23.20). MC, V.
Open: Mon–Fri 10am–6pm, Sat–Sun 10am–9pm.

At this fully licensed restaurant on the main street you can enjoy a steakhouse allure, with lots of red (symbolizing blood) and wood paneling. Although many people come here to drink, it is more of a restaurant than a pub. Other than the salad bar, there are no appetizers, and the salad is included in the price of your main course. It is completely and exclusively a steakhouse for beef (not reindeer or elk). There are 18 different cuts of beef from which to choose, and you can specify how you want it cooked.

KONDITORIA MIORITA, Valtakatu 3. Tel. 16-811.
Cuisine: PASTRIES/SANDWICHES. **Reservations:** Not required.
$ **Prices:** Pastries 15 markkaa ($4.10); sandwiches 28–38 markkaa ($7.65–$10.35); hot plates 32–55 markkaa ($8.75–$15). MC, V.
Open: Mon–Fri 8am–6pm, Sat–Sun 9am–4pm.

On the main street near the town hall, this is a popular gathering place during the day, and it's ideal either for a light lunch or a cup of good coffee, perhaps a proper sit-down tea, as the English say. You can also order freshly made sandwiches.

---

4. SODANKYLÄ

81 miles NE of Rovaniemi, 598 miles north of Helsinki

GETTING THERE By Plane Fly to Rovaniemi, then take a connecting bus the rest of the way.

By Train Go to Rovaniemi; then continue the journey to Sodankylä by bus.

By Bus A 5:15pm bus leaving Rovaniemi will arrive in Sodankylä at 7:35pm.

By Car Drive to Rovaniemi (see Section 1, above) and then continue along Route 4 all the way to Sodankylä.

ESSENTIALS The **telephone area code** for Sodankylä is 9693.

SPECIAL EVENTS Several events are listed below, under "What to See & Do."

Many say that the *real* Lapland begins at Doankyla, and that Rovaniemi is only the gateway. The fell country begins here, on Route 4 going north. In the south rises the Luosto fell, and in the north is the well-known Saariselka area with its grand fell district.

WHAT TO SEE & DO

The best sights are the **Tankavaara gold washings and museum** (see below) and the **Finnish and World Goldpanning Championships** in summer. The **wooden church,** built in 1689, is the oldest in Lapland. Porttikoski's **logging games** are an important summer event, as are the **International Midnight Sun Film Festivals** in June and the **Jutajaiset-Lappish Folklore event.**

WHERE TO STAY & DINE

KANTAKIEVARI SODANKYLÄ, Unarintie 15, SF-9960 Sodankylä. Tel. 9693/21-926. Fax 9693/13-545. 53 rms (all with bath). MINIBAR TV TEL.

$ **Rates** (including breakfast): Summer, 300 markkaa ($81.80) single or double. Winter, 400 markkaa ($109.10) single; 530 markkaa ($144.55) double. AE, DC, MC, V.

In many ways, this hotel is the focal point of the surrounding community, and you'll recognize its prominent red-brick facade in the center of the village. On the premises is a sauna, a children's playroom, a swimming pool, an air-rifle range, a lounge with a fireplace, and table-tennis facilities. There's a warmly decorated tavern and a large restaurant, where you can order such dishes as whitefish rolls simmered in a dill-cream sauce or double reindeer chops with a morel sauce and mashed potatoes gratinée. For dessert, a selection of berries from Finland—blueberries, cloudberries, lingonberries, and cranberries—are served with whipped cream. Each of the comfortably modern bedrooms has a radio and video movies. Furnishings are simple and functional, and special rooms are available for the allergic.

KANTAKIEVARI LUOSTO, Luosto, SF-99601 Sodankylä. Tel. 9693/13-681. Fax 9693/13-688. 71 rms (all with bath). TEL

$ **Rates** (including breakfast): 330 markkaa ($90) single; 440 markkaa ($120) double. AE, DC, MC, V.

Set in a forest of soaring evergreens in the nearby Luostotunturi fell district, this hotel has a dining room and only six rooms in its single-story log headquarters, but 25 additional units are found in two other nearby log buildings and around 40 more in individual cabins. Additional space is devoted to motor caravans and camping vehicles. On the premises are a sauna, three ski lifts, downhill slopes of cross-country skiing facilities, a kiosk for ski rentals, a skating rink, year-round fishing, and a Lapp village of tents. In the woodsy dining room, a good local cuisine features such specialties as reindeer noisettes Luosto style (that is, fried and served with a cream sauce and rowanberry jelly).

AN EXCURSION TO TANKAVAARA

About 62 miles from the village of Sodankylä and 143 miles from Rovaniemi and the Arctic Circle, near Route 4, to the north, is the **Tankavaara Gold Village** (tel. 9693/46-158), where you can try your luck at finding the precious metal. For 100 markkaa ($27.25), you can wash gold for a whole day, getting an introduction to gold panning and a pan for your own use; the price includes a place for a tent at the camping site. Or you can rent a cabin: they cost 190 to 240 markkaa ($51.80 to $65.45) and can accommodate two to four people; cabins with private baths cost 280 to 380 markkaa ($76.35 to $103.65). If you just want to try gold washing for a little while, you can take a course and get a pan for 30 markkaa ($8.20).

Tankavaara is also a gateway to a large nature park named for President Urho Kekkonen, and the information center for the park is in this village.

The **Gold Museum** (tel. 9693/46-171) traces the history of gold prospecting in Finnish Lapland for more than a century—exhibits are both indoors and outdoors. Admission is 15 markkaa ($4.10), and it is open June to mid-August, daily from 9am to 6pm; mid-August through September, daily from 10am to 5pm; the rest of the year, daily from 10am to 4pm. See below for the Old Gold-Diggers Café in the Gold Village complex.

WHERE TO DINE

OLD GOLD-DIGGERS CAFE, in the Gold Village Complex. Tel. 9693/46-158.
  Cuisine: LAPPISH. **Reservations:** Not required.
$ **Prices:** Appetizers 12–48 markkaa ($3.25–$13.10); main dishes 39–93 markkaa ($10.65–$25.35). No credit cards.
  Open: Daily 8:30am–9pm.
This café in the center of the complex has an award-winning kitchen. Try the "Prospector's Steak," which is served from a gold pan and includes a giant reindeer steak, pea stew, and mashed potatoes, plus a salad.

---

5. INARI/IVALO

698 miles north of Helsinki, 180 miles north of Rovaniemi

GETTING THERE By Plane There are flights to Ivalo from many parts of Finland, including Joensuu, Jyväskylä, Kemi, Kuopio, and Lappeenranta. A 10:35am flight from Helsinki will arrive in Ivalo at 1:10pm.

By Train Go to Rovaniemi (see above) and continue the rest of the way by bus.

By Bus Three buses a day run between Rovaniemi and Ivalo, taking 5 hours. The village of Inari is also linked twice daily by bus to Rovaniemi, taking 6 hours.

By Car Drive to Rovaniemi (see above), then continue along Route 4 all the way to Ivalo and Inari. Route 4 runs across Inari through its largest settlements to the Arctic Ocean. There is a good road network from western Lapland, Kirkkoniemi, and Murmansk, USSR.

ESSENTIALS The **Tourist Information Office** is at Pisskuntie 5, SF-99800 Ivalo (tel. 9697/12-521), open daily from 8am to 8pm in summer, 8am to 3pm in winter. The **telephone area code** for Ivalo and Inari is 9697.

▌nari is Finland's largest county in area and its most remarkable feature is the 50-mile-long Lake Inarijärvi, containing more than 3,000 islands.

WHAT TO SEE & DO

IVALO/SAARISELKÄ The administrative center of the Inari area is the little town of Ivalo, which has daily connections with Helsinki. Some 6 miles north of Ivalo is a place along Route 4 where you can get a good view of the **scenery of Lake Inari,** with an **exhibition** depicting life in the area through the centuries. This and the scenic lookout are open from the beginning of June to mid-August from 8am to 1pm daily. For information, call the Hotel Riekonlinna at Saariselkä (see "Where to Stay & Dine," below) (tel. 9697/81-601).
    The **Saariselkä resort area,** Finland's largest, has 11 downhill ski runs, six lifts, marked ski trails, 20 miles of lit ski track, and marked hiking routes with wilderness huts. Activities include skido and reindeer safari, supper at a Lapp hut, and trips to Lapland's gold-panning area. Sights to see near the Saariselkä area are the **Ivalo River gold fields** with buildings and equipment (this was the site of Finland's first gold strike) and the heights of **Kaunispää,** where you can look out over the whole Saariselkä landscape and far into Russia.

INARI Inari is also the name of a small village some 25 miles north of Ivalo that opens onto the huge lake. In the village, you can take a waterbus to the ancient sacrificial island of **Ukko.** Trips can be arranged at 2pm in June and August and at 10am, 2pm, and 6pm in July. A trip costs 50 markkaa ($13.65) per person and takes about 2 hours.

An outdoor **Lapp Museum** in the village features a herdsmen's settlement, a fishing colony, and exhibits of wild-animal snares and Lapp costumes. The museum is open June to September 20, daily from 9am to 4pm.

In Inari, you can also see original Lapland handcrafts at **Samekki** (tel. 9697/51-086), open June to the end of September, daily from 10am to 8pm; in winter, on Friday, Saturday, and Monday from 10am to 4pm.

Owned by a Lappish family, the **Inari Reindeer Farm,** 8½ miles from the village of Inari toward Kittilä, specializes in reindeer ranching and also raises racing reindeer, which have done well in the **Inari Reindeer King Races** held in March. On the farm, you can drive reindeer, help feed the herd, taste coffee made over the tepee's open fire, and learn about reindeer care and the Lapp culture. The farm is open all year and advance reservations are required (tel. 9697/56-512).

OTHER AREA ATTRACTIONS   In the northern part of the country there are several interesting villages. For example, **Lemmenjoki** provides boat trips to the gold fields and **Sevettijarvi** is a place to study Lappish culture.

WHERE TO STAY & DINE

HOTEL IVALO, Ivalontie 34, SF-99801 Ivalo. Tel. 9697/21-911. Fax 9697/21-905. 62 rms (all with bath). TV TEL.
$ Rates (including breakfast): 420 markkaa ($114.55) single; 490 markkaa ($133.60) double. AE, DC, MC, V.
This hotel in the center of Ivalo offers much modern comfort in a wilderness tract about 30 miles south of Inari. You can rent a boat for the nearby river and swim in the hotel's pool after using a sauna. Bedrooms are furnished in a tasteful modern. Meals are noteworthy, especially the regional specialties, which include game soup which is made with thin slices of snow grouse, reindeer meat, reindeer tongue, and smoked reindeer in a clear broth (it's served with warm unleavened potato bread). For your main course, you might try the reindeer pie with creamed morels.

HOTEL RIEKONLINNA, SF-99830 Saariselkä. Tel. 9697/81-601. Fax 9697/81-602. 124 rms (all with bath). TV TEL.
$ Rates (including breakfast): 620 markkaa ($169.05) single; 780 markkaa ($212.70) double. AE, DC, MC, V.
In the town center, the Hotel Riekonlinna is a high-class conference and holiday hotel offering rooms with balconies, refrigerators, and drying cabinets for sportswear, among other amenities. Some rooms also have saunas. Special accommodations are available for families and persons suffering from allergies.

SAARISELÄN TUNTURIHOTELLIT, Saariseläntie 14, SF-99830 Saariselkä. Tel. 9697/81-11. Fax 9697/81-771. 97 rms, 30 apartments (all with bath). TV TEL **Bus:** From the Ivalo airport for 16 miles.
$ Rates (including breakfast): 370 markkaa ($100.90) single; 620 markkaa ($169.05) double; 850 markkaa ($231.80) apartment. AE, DC, MC, V.
This hotel complex offers cozy accommodations: either singles or doubles in the main building; or a holiday cottage apartment with one to three rooms, a well-equipped kitchen, an open fireplace, and a sauna. A total of 22 rooms contain a minibar. Each unit is comfortably furnished in a modern functional style. The hotel offers a dance and dinner restaurant, a bar, nightclub, and pub.

HOTEL INARIN KULTAHOVI, SF-99870 Inari. Tel. 9697/51-221. Fax 9697/51-250. 30 rms (all with bath). TV TEL.
$ Rates (including breakfast): 340 markkaa ($92.70) single; 380 markkaa ($103.65) double. AE, MC, V.
On the banks of the Juutuanjoki River in the town center, this comfortable and traditional hotel was recently remodeled. It has a good restaurant, the Kultarammo (Sluice Box) café, a TV and sitting lounge, a sauna on the banks of the river, and a garage.

INDEX

GENERAL INFORMATION

DENMARK

FINLAND

NORWAY

SWEDEN

DESTINATIONS

DENMARK

NOTE: An asterisk * indicates an author's favorite

FINLAND

NORWAY

NOW, SAVE MONEY ON ALL YOUR TRAVELS!
Join Frommer's™ Dollarwise® Travel Club

Saving money while traveling is never a simple matter, which is why the **Dollarwise Travel Club** was formed 31 years ago. Developed in response to requests from Frommer's Travel Guide readers, the Club provides cost-cutting travel strategies, up-to-date travel information, and a sense of community for value-conscious travelers from all over the world.

In keeping with the money-saving concept, the annual membership fee is low —$20 for U.S. residents or $25 for residents of Canada, Mexico, and other countries—and is immediately exceeded by the value of your benefits, which include:

1. Any TWO books listed on the following pages.
2. Plus any ONE Frommer's City Guide.
3. A subscription to our quarterly newspaper, *The Dollarwise Traveler.*
4. A membership card that entitles you to purchase through the Club all Frommer's publications for 33% to 40% off their retail price.

The eight-page **Dollarwise Traveler** tells you about the latest developments in good-value travel worldwide and includes the following columns: **Hospitality Exchange** (for those offering and seeking hospitality in cities all over the world); **Share-a-Trip** (for those looking for travel companions to share costs); and **Readers Ask . . . Readers Reply** (for those with travel questions that other members can answer).

Aside from the Frommer's Guides and the Gault Millau Guides, you can also choose from our Special Editions. These include such titles as **California with Kids** (a compendium of the best of California's accommodations, restaurants, and sightseeing attractions appropriate for those traveling with toddlers through teens); **Candy Apple: New York with Kids** (a spirited guide to the Big Apple by a savvy New York grandmother that's perfect for both visitors and residents); **Caribbean Hideaways** (the 100 most romantic places to stay in the Islands, all rated on ambience, food, sports opportunities, and price); **Honeymoon Destinations** (a guide to planning and choosing just the right destination from hundreds of possibilities in the U.S., Mexico, and the Caribbean); **Marilyn Wood's Wonderful Weekends** (a selection of the best mini-vacations within a 200-mile radius of New York City, including descriptions of country inns and other accommodations, restaurants, picnic spots, sights, and activities); and **Paris Rendez-Vous** (a delightful guide to the best places to meet in Paris whether for power breakfasts or dancing till dawn).

To join this Club, simply send the appropriate membership fee with your name and address to: Frommer's Dollarwise Travel Club, 15 Columbus Circle, New York, NY 10023. Remember to specify which single city guide and which two other guides you wish to receive in your initial package of member's benefits. Or tear out the next page, check off your choices, and send the page to us with your membership fee.

FROMMER BOOKS
PRENTICE HALL PRESS
15 COLUMBUS CIRCLE
NEW YORK, NY 10023
212/373-8125

Date_____

Friends: Please send me the books checked below.

FROMMER'S™ GUIDES

(Guides to sightseeing and tourist accommodations and facilities from budget to deluxe, with emphasis on the medium-priced.)

☐ Alaska	$14.95	☐ Germany	$14.95
☐ Australia	$14.95	☐ Italy	$14.95
☐ Austria & Hungary	$14.95	☐ Japan & Hong Kong	$14.95
☐ Belgium, Holland & Luxembourg	$14.95	☐ Mid-Atlantic States	$14.95
☐ Bermuda & The Bahamas	$14.95	☐ New England	$14.95
☐ Brazil	$14.95	☐ New Mexico	$13.95
☐ Canada	$14.95	☐ New York State	$14.95
☐ Caribbean	$14.95	☐ Northwest	$16.95
☐ Cruises (incl. Alaska, Carib, Mex, Hawaii,		☐ Portugal, Madeira & the Azores	$14.95
Panama, Canada & US)	$14.95	☐ Scandinavia	$18.95
☐ California & Las Vegas	$14.95	☐ South Pacific	$14.95
☐ Egypt	$14.95	☐ Southeast Asia	$14.95
☐ England & Scotland	$14.95	☐ Southern Atlantic States	$14.95
☐ Florida	$14.95	☐ Southwest	$14.95
☐ France	$14.95	☐ Switzerland & Liechtenstein	$14.95

☐ USA $16.95

FROMMER'S $-A-DAY® GUIDES

(In-depth guides to sightseeing and low-cost tourist accommodations and facilities.)

☐ Europe on $40 a Day	$15.95	☐ Israel on $40 a Day	$13.95
☐ Australia on $40 a Day	$13.95	☐ Mexico on $35 a Day	$14.95
☐ Costa Rica; Guatemala & Belize		☐ New York on $60 a Day	$13.95
on $35 a day	$15.95	☐ New Zealand on $45 a Day	$14.95
☐ Eastern Europe on $25 a Day	$16.95	☐ Scotland & Wales on $40 a Day	$13.95
☐ England on $50 a Day	$13.95	☐ South America on $40 a Day	$15.95
☐ Greece on $35 a Day	$14.95	☐ Spain on $50 a Day	$15.95
☐ Hawaii on $60 a Day	$14.95	☐ Turkey on $30 a Day	$13.95
☐ India on $25 a Day	$12.95	☐ Washington, D.C. & Historic Va. on	
☐ Ireland on $35 a Day	$13.95	$40 a Day	$13.95

FROMMER'S TOURING GUIDES

(Color illustrated guides that include walking tours, cultural and historic sites, and other vital travel information.)

☐ Amsterdam	$10.95	☐ New York	$10.95
☐ Australia	$10.95	☐ Paris	$8.95
☐ Brazil	$10.95	☐ Rome	$10.95
☐ Egypt	$8.95	☐ Scotland	$9.95
☐ Florence	$8.95	☐ Thailand	$10.95
☐ Hong Kong	$10.95	☐ Turkey	$10.95
☐ London	$10.95	☐ Venice	$8.95

(TURN PAGE FOR ADDITONAL BOOKS AND ORDER FORM)

0391

FROMMER'S CITY GUIDES

(Pocket-size guides to sightseeing and tourist accommodations and facilities in all price ranges.)

☐ Amsterdam/Holland	$8.95	☐ Minneapolis/St. Paul	$8.95
☐ Athens	$8.95	☐ Montréal/Québec City	$8.95
☐ Atlanta	$8.95	☐ New Orleans	$8.95
☐ Atlantic City/Cape May	$8.95	☐ New York	$8.95
☐ Barcelona	$7.95	☐ Orlando	$8.95
☐ Belgium	$7.95	☐ Paris	$8.95
☐ Berlin	$8.95	☐ Philadelphia	$8.95
☐ Boston	$8.95	☐ Rio	$8.95
☐ Cancún/Cozumel/Yucatán	$8.95	☐ Rome	$8.95
☐ Chicago	$9.95	☐ Salt Lake City	$8.95
☐ Denver/Boulder/Colorado Springs	$7.95	☐ San Diego	$8.95
☐ Dublin/Ireland	$8.95	☐ San Francisco	$8.95
☐ Hawaii	$8.95	☐ Santa Fe/Taos/Albuquerque	$10.95
☐ Hong Kong	$7.95	☐ Seattle/Portland	$7.95
☐ Las Vegas	$8.95	☐ St. Louis/Kansas City	$9.95
☐ Lisbon/Madrid/Costa del Sol	$8.95	☐ Sydney	$8.95
☐ London	$8.95	☐ Tampa/St. Petersburg	$8.95
☐ Los Angeles	$8.95	☐ Tokyo	$8.95
☐ Mexico City/Acapulco	$8.95	☐ Toronto	$8.95
☐ Miami	$8.95	☐ Vancouver/Victoria	$7.95

☐ Washington, D.C. $8.95

SPECIAL EDITIONS

☐ Beat the High Cost of Travel	$6.95	☐ Motorist's Phrase Book (Fr/Ger/Sp)	$4.95
☐ Bed & Breakfast—N. America	$14.95	☐ Paris Rendez-Vous	$10.95
☐ California with Kids	$16.95	☐ Swap and Go (Home Exchanging)	$10.95
☐ Caribbean Hideaways	$14.95	☐ The Candy Apple (NY with Kids)	$12.95
☐ Honeymoon Destinations (US, Mex &		☐ Travel Diary and Record Book	$5.95
Carib)	$14.95	☐ Where to Stay USA (From $3 to $30 a	
☐ Manhattan's Outdoor Sculpture	$15.95	night)	$13.95

☐ Marilyn Wood's Wonderful Weekends (CT, DE, MA, NH, NJ, NY, PA, RI, VT) $11.95
☐ The New World of Travel (Annual sourcebook by Arthur Frommer for savvy travelers) $16.95

GAULT MILLAU

(The only guides that distinguish the truly superlative from the merely overrated.)

☐ The Best of Chicago	$15.95	☐ The Best of Los Angeles	$16.95
☐ The Best of France	$16.95	☐ The Best of New England	$15.95
☐ The Best of Hawaii	$16.95	☐ The Best of New Orleans	$16.95
☐ The Best of Hong Kong	$16.95	☐ The Best of New York	$16.95
☐ The Best of Italy	$16.95	☐ The Best of Paris	$16.95
☐ The Best of London	$16.95	☐ The Best of San Francisco	$16.95

☐ The Best of Washington, D.C. $16.95

ORDER NOW!

In U.S. include $2 shipping UPS for 1st book; $1 ea. add'l book. Outside U.S. $3 and $1, respectively.
Allow four to six weeks for delivery in U.S., longer outside U.S.

Enclosed is my check or money order for $_____

NAME _____

ADDRESS _____

CITY _____ STATE _____ ZIP _____

0391